STUDIES AND TEXTS

36

THE MIRROR
OF THE NEW CHRISTIANS
(ESPELHO DE CHRISTÃOS NOVOS)
OF
FRANCISCO MACHADO

EDITED, TRANSLATED, AND WITH AN INTRODUCTION

BY

MILDRED EVELYN VIEIRA

AND

FRANK EPHRAIM TALMAGE

PONTIFICAL INSTITUTE OF MEDIAEVAL STUDIES
TORONTO 1977

ACKNOWLEDGEMENT

This book has been published with the help of a grant
from the Humanities Research Council of Canada,
using funds provided by the Canada Council

Canadian Cataloguing in Publication Data

Machado, Francisco, fl. 1550.
   The mirror of the new Christians (Espelho de Christãos novos) of Francisco
Machado

(Studies and texts - Pontifical Institute of Mediaeval Studies; 36 ISSN 0082-5328)

Text in Portuguese and English.
Bibliography: p.
Includes index.
ISBN 0-88844-036-7

1. Jesus Christ - Messiahship. 2. Jesus Christ - Jewish interpretations.
I. Vieira, Mildred Evelyn, 1927-1970. II. Talmage, Frank Ephraim, 1938-
III. Title. IV. Series: Pontifical Institute of Mediaeval Studies. Studies and Texts
- Pontifical Institute of Mediaeval Studies; 36.

BT230.M33 1977   232'.1   C77-001049-0

PRINTED BY UNIVERSA PRESS, WETTEREN (BELGIUM)

For

AARON BENJAMIN VIEIRA

TABLE OF CONTENTS

PREFACE

The present edition of the *Mirror of the New Christians* is based upon the doctoral dissertation of Professor Mildred Evelyn Dordick Vieira, which was completed at the University of Wisconsin in 1965 and entitled "An Edition of the Sixteenth Century Portuguese Manuscript *Espelho de Christãos Novos* by Frei Francisco Machado." Since I was teaching at the University of Wisconsin at that time, Professor Vieira and I had frequent opportunity to discuss her work which was akin to my own interests. As a result of these discussions, we planned to collaborate on the final publication of the edition. During the summer of 1967, we worked intensively at the Harvard College Library and the Harvard Divinity School on the materials for the source study of the text. She then prepared the first draft of the translation, while I worked on the first draft of the notes. Professor Vieira suffered from illness during this time but continued to work with vigor. In 1971, she tragically succumbed and our collaboration was brought to a close. I have, to the best of my ability, attempted to bring the project to a successful conclusion. Two visits to Lisbon, one brief in 1973 and one extended in 1974, enabled me to examine the original manuscript of the *Mirror* and make certain emendations in the original edition. These visits, as well as a period of study at the Jewish National and University Library in Jerusalem, allowed me to examine the historical and literary background of the *Mirror* more closely. Two papers based on this research, one in the *Proceedings of the Sixth World Congress of Jewish Studies, 1973* and one in the jubilee volume honoring Professor Alexander Altmann, are shortly to appear. The Introduction to this volume is based on those studies and on Professor Vieira's original introduction. The English translation is a revision of Professor Vieira's original draft.

I wish to express my gratitude to Professor Nelson Vieira of Brown University, Mrs. Vieira's husband, for making much material available to me, to Professor Benjamin Ravid of Brandeis University for his readiness, as always, to offer his judicious suggestions, and to Professor Daniel J. Lasker of Kirkland College for comments and bibliographic references relating to the philosophical arguments. Acknowledgement is expressed to the following libraries for their assistance: the Libraries of the University of Wisconsin, Harvard University, the University of

Toronto, the Pontifical Institute of Mediaeval Studies, the New York Public Library, the Lisbon National Library (B.N.L.), the National Archives of the Torre do Tombo (A.N.T.T.), the Faculty of Letters of the University of Lisbon, and the Jewish National and University Library, Jerusalem.

I am most indebted to the Canada Council for a generous grant and for their constant encouragement in this project. I pray that this volume be worthy of the energy, skill, and devotion invested in it by my collaborator.

Toronto   *Frank Talmage*
April, 1975
Yom Haatsmaut, 5735

LIST OF ABBREVIATIONS

ACPJ	*Ad convincendum perfidiam Judaeorum* (see Bibliography, Hieronymus de Sancta Fide)
AJ	*Adversus Judaeos* (see Bibliography, Williams)
Albeck, Bereshit Rabbah	Midrash Bereshit Rabbah, ed. J. Theodor and Ch. Albeck.[2] 3 vols. Jerusalem, 1965
Ant.	*Antiquities* (see Bibliography, Josephus)
A.N.T.T.	Arquivo Nacional da Torre do Tombo
A.Z.	'Avodah Zarah
BHN	*Biblioteca Hispana Nova* (see Bibliography, Antonio)
B.N.L.	Biblioteca Nacional de Lisboa
BRMD	Bereshit Rabbah of Moses the Preacher (Mosheh ha-Darshan) as preserved in *PF* (see text, chap. 9, n. 10)
B.T.	Babylonian Talmud
CC	*Corpus Christianorum Series Latina*
Chron.	*Chronicon* (see Bibliography, Isidore)
CSEL	*Corpus Scriptorum Ecclesiasticorum Latinorum*
DE	*Diálogo Evangélico* (see Bibliography, Barros)
Deuteronomy Rabbah	Midrash Devarim Rabbah, ed. Saul Lieberman.[2] Jerusalem, 1964-1965
DHP	*Dicionário de história de Portugal.* 4 vols. Lisbon, 1961-1971
DJC	*Disputatio Judei et Christiani* (see Bibliography, Crispin)
DPA	*Dialogus* (see Bibliography, Petrus Alfonsi)
DTC	*Dictionnaire de Théologie Catholique.* 15 vols. in 30. Paris, 1902-1950
Etym.	*Etymologiae* (see Bibliography, Isidore)
FF	*Fortalitium Fidei* (see Bibliography, Alphonsus de Spina)
Galatinus	Petrus Galatinus, *De arcanis catholicae veritatis*
GCS	*Griechischen Christlichen Schriftsteller*
GEPB	*Grande enciclopédia portuguesa brasileira.* 40 vols. Lisbon, n.d.
GO	*Glossa ordinaria*
HS	*Historia Scholastica* (see Bibliography, Petrus Comestor)
HUCA	*Hebrew Union College Annual*
JE	*Jewish Encyclopedia.* 12 vols. New York, 1901-1906
JSS	*Jewish Social Studies*
M.	Mishnah
Midrash Mishle	Midrash Mishle, ed. Solomon Buber. Vilna, 1893
Midrash Tehillim, ed. Braude	*The Midrash on Psalms,* ed. Wm. G. Braude. 2 vols. New Haven, 1959
Midrash Tehillim, ed. Buber	Midrash Tehillim, ed. Solomon Buber. Vilna, 1887
PF	*Pugio fidei* (see Bibliography, Martini)

PG	Patrologiae Cursus Completus, Series Graeca, ed. J. P. Migne. Paris 1857-1884
PL	Patrologiae Cursus Completus, Series Latina, ed. J. P. Migne. Paris, 1857-1866
Post.	*Postilla* (see Bibliography, Nicolas de Lyra)
P.T.	Palestinian Talmud
Rabbati	Midrash Bereshit Rabbati, ed. Ch. Albeck. Jerusalem, 1940
REJ	*Revue des Études Juives*
Rosenthal, *Milḥamot*	Jacob ben Reuben, *Milḥamot ha-Shem,* ed. Judah Rosenthal. Jerusalem, 1963
SBB	*Studies in Bibliography and Booklore*
Shorashim	David Kimhi, *Sefer ha-Shorashim,* ed. J. Biesenthal and F. Lebrecht. Berlin, 1847
Sifra	Sifra (Torat Kohanim), ed. I. H. Weiss. Vienna, 1862; photoreprint New York, 1947
Sifre	Sifre de-ve Rav, ed. Meir Friedmann. Vienna, 1864; photoreprint n.p., 1968
Sonc.	Soncino English translation of the Babylonian Talmud. 35 vols. London, 1935-1952. Soncino English translation of Midrash Rabbah. 13 vols. in 10. London, 1939
SRHJ	*A Social and Religious History of the Jews* (see Bibliography, Baron)
T.	Tosefta
Tanḥuma, Buber	Midrash Tanḥuma, ed. Solomon Buber. Vilna, 1885
TJ	Targum Jonathan, Standard Editions of the Rabbinic Bible
Yalquṭ Shimeoni	Yalquṭ Shimeoni. New York, 1925-1926; photoreprint Jerusalem, 1951-1952
ZDMG	*Zeitschrift der Deutschen Morgenländischen Gesellschaft*

INTRODUCTION

In the late summer of 1541, Brother Francisco Machado of the Order of Cîteaux sat in his "sibylline cave"[1] at the Monastery of Alcobaça writing the *Mirror of the New Christians*. From his own statement in the *Mirror*,[2] confirmed by the few biographical notices extant,[3] Machado had returned to Portugal some time previously from Paris where he had taken his doctorate. Of his early years we know nothing, except that he is reported to have been born in Soure in the diocese of Coimbra.[4] Diogo Barbosa Machado, who at times reads more like a hagiologist than a bibliographer, notes that John III himself, impressed by Machado's talents, was responsible for Machado's going to Paris where he is said to have excelled in his studies.[5] If so, Machado might well have expected some position of prominence upon his return to Portugal. It is true, of course, that in all modesty he advised his readers that "I do not seek dioceses or abbeys." Yet, he added, "I came close to this, but God was not served because man was not disposed to it. ..."[6]

Machado, however, was to gain eventual recognition. From the introduction to his *In septem psalmos penitentiales quaedam paraphrases*, it appears that he was abbot of the Cistercian Monastery of Santa Maria dos

---

[1] *Mirror*, fol. 1r.

[2] *Mirror*, fol. 1r.

[3] Bernardo de Brito, *Chrónica de Cister* (Lisbon, 1602), fols. 460v-462r; Karl de Visch, *Biblioteca scriptorum sacri ordinis cisterciensis*[2] (Cologne, 1656), n.p.; C. J. Imbonati, *Biblioteca latina hebraica* (Rome, 1694), 5, n. 176; Johann Christoph Wolf, *Biblioteca hebraea* (Hamburg, 1715-33), 2:1033; Diogo Barbosa Machado, *Bibliotheca lusitana* (Lisbon, 1747; photoreprint Coimbra, 1966), 2:178f.; Nicolás Antonio, *Biblioteca hispana nova* (Madrid, 1783), 1:422f.; António Ribeiro dos Santos, "Ensayo de huma Biblioteca anti-rabbinica, ou Memorial dos escritores portuguesses que escreverão de controversia anti-judaica," *Memórias de litteratura portugueza publicadas pela Academia Real das Sciencias de Lisboa*, 8 (1806) 324 (no mention made of the *Mirror*); Meyer Kayserling, *Biblioteca española-portugueza-judaica* (Strassburg, 1890; photoreprint New York, 1971), p. 116b; J. Lúcio de Azevedo, *História dos Cristãos Novos Portugueses* (Lisbon, 1921), p. 132 (no mention made of *Mirror*); Martin A. Cohen in introduction to Samuel Usque, *Consolation for the Tribulations of Israel* (Philadelphia, 1965), p. 9. The most extensive treatment has been that of I. S. Révah in *DE*, pp. lix-lxvi.

[4] Barbosa Machado, *Biblioteca lusitana*, 2:178f.

[5] Ibid.

[6] *Mirror*, fol. 1r.

Tamarães near Tomar in 1564.[7] Exactly when he was elevated to that position is not known. Bernardo de Brito in his *Chrónica de Cister* cites the most explicit data — some correspondence between Machado and Cardinal Henry written during Machado's tenure at Tamarães. Unfortunately, however, the year of writing was omitted.[8] Yet, if they do not help to determine the chronology of Machado's life, the letters do yield other biographical details.

A number of posthumous miracles had been attributed to the "blessed queens," Teresa and Sancha, daughters of King Sancho I (1185-1211), who were buried at the Convent of Lorvão. Henry commissioned Machado with the task of verifying the accounts of these miracles and concluded his request[9] with the following charge: "Since it is necessary for you to enter the convent for this task, I give you license this time to do so, trusting that because of your virtue and good example you will do all in a manner which will redound to the credit of your person and piety."[10] Machado did indeed undertake this mission with all seriousness, studying the affidavits and interrogating those who claimed to have personally experienced the intervention of the sainted ladies. If any doubt remained in his mind as to the veracity of these reports, he could assure the Cardinal: "I myself had a rather large cyst. They removed it from me at the very moment I went to rub it on their gravestones, so that on the very next day I had not a trace of it."[11]

Since the two sisters had not been beatified and could consequently not be appealed to in prayer, it was the custom of the religious to recite the seven penitential psalms at their tomb. Those who had done so testified that "every need for which they appealed" had been granted.[12] It was perhaps this experience which stimulated Machado's special interest in the penitential psalms. His commentary on them, apparently

---

[7] B.N.L. MS Alcobacense 81, fol. B1r.

[8] Brito, *Cister*, fol. 461r. These letters are probably the *Vitae et miracula dictarum beatarum, Teresae et Sanctiae reginarum, et sanctimonialium ordinis cisterciensis* mentioned by Barbosa Machado, *Bibliotheca lusitana*, 2:128f. De Visch refers to them as *Epistolas varias ad Henricum Lusitaniae Principem S. R. E. Cardinalem, Bibliotheca Scriptorum, s.v.* Franciscus Machado.

[9] De Visch indicates that Henry was acting on behalf of King Sebastian for whom he acted as regent from 1562 to 1568.

[10] Brito, *Cister*, fol. 461v: "E sendouos necessario pera esta diligencia entrar dentro do mosteiro, vos dou licença por esta vez, confiando de vossa virtude, & bom exemplo, que tudo fareis como conuem ao credito de vossa pessoa & religião."

[11] Brito, *Cister*, fol. 461r: "e a mim que tinha hum grande lobinho, mo tirarão na mesma hora, que cheguei a o esfregar pellas sepulturas d'ambas de duas, de feição, que ao outro dia eu não tinha nimigalha."

[12] Brito, *Cister*, fols. 460v-461r.

his sole work of exegesis, was completed on August 20, 1565 and dedicated to his former comrades, the monks of Alcobaça. [13]

Although Machado tried his hand at exegesis, he is chiefly remembered today for his polemical activity. The *Mirror of the New Christians* (*Espelho de Christãos Novos*)[14] was written rapidly. Begun in early August, 1541, it was completed on the twentieth day of September of that same year.[15] This feverish burst of activity clearly indicates a sense of urgency on Machado's part, which can only be understood in the context of the problematic history of the New Christians of Portugal.

THE NEW CHRISTIANS OF PORTUGAL

Following the expulsion of the Jews from Spain in 1492, many of the exiles settled among their coreligionists in the neighboring Kingdom of Portugal. Throughout the Middle Ages, the Jews in that country had led a comparatively irenic existence[16] and it appeared that Portugal might offer a safe place of refuge. Their hopes were short-lived. King Manuel, wishing to secure a political and dynastic alliance with Spain through his marriage with Isabel, daughter of the Catholic Monarchs, agreed to her demand that the Jews be expelled from his realm as well. Manuel, however, had no desire to follow the precedent of Spain and lose whatever material benefits the Jews provided. He therefore decided upon an alternative approach. Rather than expel the Jews, he would expel Judaism. On December 24, 1496, he enacted an Edict of Expulsion according to which all Jews were to vacate the kingdom by the end of October, 1497. Yet when the fateful day came, the entire Jewish community of Portugal — with literally only a handful of exceptions — were baptized by force. In this way, the class of the New Christians (Marranos, *conversos*) — Christians of Jewish origin — was created.

Manuel's policy toward the new converts was relatively moderate.

[13] B.N.L. MS Alcobacense 81, fol. 2r. On the manuscript, see *Inventário dos Códices Alcobacenses*, 5 vols. in 1, (Lisbon, 1930-32), pp. 75f.

[14] Machado himself apparently did not give a title to the work. On the basis of the word *espelho* in a marginal addition (fol. 12v), the bibliographer João Franco Barreto (1600-74) gave the work the title "Espelho de Christãos Novos e convertidos." (See *DE*, p. lxvi, n. 1). The "e convertidos" has here been omitted as redundant.

[15] *Mirror*, fol. 63r.

[16] On the Jews of medieval Portugal, see Meyer Kayserling, *Geschichte der Juden in Portugal* (Leipzig, 1867) = *História dos Judeus em Portugal* (São Paulo, 1971); José Amador de los Rios, *Historia social, política, y religiosa de los Judíos de España y Portugal*, 3 vols. (Madrid, 1875-76; latest edition, Madrid: Aguilar, 1973); Joaquim Mendes dos Remedios, *Os Judeus em Portugal*, 2 vols. (Coimbra, 1895-1928); M. J. Pimenta Ferro, *Os Judeus em Portugal no século XIV* (Lisbon, 1970). Additional bibliography in António H. de Oliveira Marques, *Guia do estudante de história medieval portuguesa* (Lisbon, 1964), pp. 89f.

They were left unmolested in order to allow them sufficient time to become assimilated to their new social and religious status. In 1497, he granted them a twenty year immunity from investigation and persecution and renewed this pledge in 1512. When Manuel's son, John III, ascended to the throne in 1521, he continued the policy established by his father. However, subjected as he was to various political and ecclesiastical pressures and inspired by religious zeal,[17] he initiated proceedings to establish an inquisition after the fashion of that in Spain. After five years of opposition and hindrance, the Inquisition was established in 1536, with John's brother, the youthful Prince Henry, assuming the office of Grand Inquisitor in 1537. On September 20, 1540, exactly one year to the day before the completion of the *Mirror of the New Christians,* the first *auto-da-fé* was held in Lisbon.[18] Thus began the long and intricate history of the Portuguese Inquisition and its efforts to purge the Lusitanian monarchy of its heresies — especially the alleged judaizing of the New Christians.

Current scholarship is sharply divided, if not polarized, concerning the true religious condition of these New Christians. One school, whose foremost advocate has been A. J. Saraiva,[19] maintains that the judaizing of the New Christians was a fabrication of the Inquisition: since the New Christians are to be largely identified with the well-to-do middle class, the Inquisition, supported by the State, wished to eliminate them and confiscate their wealth. The other point of view, advocated by the late I. S. Révah[20] and more recently reinforced by Y. H. Yerushalmi,[21] insists on the essential reality of the Judaism — or at least the judaizing — of most of the New Christians of Portugal.

---

[17] On alternate assessments of John III, see Elizabeth F. Hirch, *Damião de Gois* (Hague, 1967), pp. 160-90.

[18] See literature cited above and J. Lúcio de Azevedo, *História dos Christãos Novos Portugueses* (Lisbon, 1921); A. Herculano, *History of the Origin and Establishment of the Inquisition in Portugal* (Stanford, 1926; photoreprint New York, 1972 with valuable prolegomenon by Y. H. Yerushalmi); Nahum Slouschz, *Ha-'Anusim be-Portugal* (Tel Aviv, 1932); *SRHJ*, 13:44-54. For a description of the first *auto-da-fé* in Lisbon (translated from Oliveira-Martins), see Kingley G. Jayne, *Vasco da Gama and His Successors* (London, 1910), pp. 176-80.

[19] António J. Saraiva, *A Inquisição Portuguesa* (Lisbon, 1956); *História da cultura em Portugal* (Lisbon, 1962), 3:107; *Inquisição e Cristãos Novos* (Oporto, 1969). Saraiva's thinking resembles that of Benzion Netanyahu, *The Marranos of Spain from the Late XIVth to the Early XVIth Century according to the Hebrew Sources* (New York, 1966).

[20] Révah, "Les Marranes," *REJ*, 118 (1959), 27-77; "Les Marranes Portugais et l'Inquisition au xvie Siècle," Richard D. Barnett, *The Sephardi Heritage* (New York, 1971), pp. 479-526.

[21] Y. H. Yerushalmi, "Prolegomenon" to Herculano, *Origin*, pp. 34ff.; *From Spanish Court to Italian Ghetto* (New York and London, 1971), pp. 5ff. See also the interesting comments of H. P. Salomon in his review of Yerushalmi, revised and reprinted from *The Journal of the American Cultural Society*, 6 (1972), 59-65; 7 (1973), 69-75.

The debate over this issue has been prompted not only by historiographical considerations[22] but also by methodological concerns. While a wide variety of sources, both Jewish and Portuguese, have been used, a key problem has been the validity of the records of the inquisitorial archives. This point was the center of a debate between Révah and Saraiva.[23] The former had made extensive use of the protocols of the Inquisition in his investigation of Marranism. The latter, however, denied the admissibility of this material as evidence since he construed it as propagandistic.

A second important source of information relied upon by Révah in his analysis was the anti-Marrano polemical literature of the sixteenth century. For him, this literature, especially the writings of João de Barros and Francisco Machado, served as important corroboration for his point of view. On the basis of the *Mirror*, Révah maintained that "during this entire decisive period [of the establishment of the Inquisition], the New Christians judaized almost without exception. The simple believers held fast to ancestral practices; the learned, despite prohibitions, maintained contact with the texts in which their religious culture expressed itself."[24] This literature is to be seen then as confirmation of the records of the "trials of the new-born Inquisition [which] will show that the Jews, in most cases, remained faithful to their ancestral creed. If the atmosphere of hatred which surrounded them prevented this from coming to light, in the privacy of their homes, they maintained their own form of worship."[25]

Francisco Machado does indeed complain of judaizing throughout his work. In both thought and deed, the New Christians are portrayed as recalcitrant and inwardly unconverted.

> You, however, obstinate and incredulous, have no wish other than to die in your disbelief, unwilling to acknowledge the arrival of the Lord Messiah. Instead, you falsely gloss the prophecies that refer to the Messiah, attributing them to others as we shall prove, because you will not be persuaded to admit that the Messiah came. Nevertheless, I am convinced that were you willing to enter into a debate with us, you would surely fall upon the truth. However, you do not [do so] ... but prefer

[22] See the schematic survey of Marrano historiography in Anita Novinsky, *Cristãos Novos na Bahia* (São Paulo, 1972), Chap. 1; F. Talmage, "The New Portugal and the New Christians," *Association for Jewish Studies Newsletter*, February, 1975, pp. 13ff.

[23] Reviewed in Gerard Nahon, "Les Sephardim, les Marranes, les inquisitions peninsulaires et leurs archives dans les travaux récents de I.-S. Révah," *REJ*, 132 (1973), 38-44.

[24] Révah, *DE*, p. xxiii.

[25] Révah, *DE*, p. xxxvi.

rather to go from one corner to another forming synagogues[26] and assemblies of falsehood and error and to read Moses whom you understand
only according to the flesh and not according to the spirit (fol. 8*v*).

Moreover, the New Christians are

obstinate disbelievers of Christ's faith. You ... mock Christians and their
law while all the while feigning that you too now have this law and believe
in it. Yet, you continue to form a thousand synagogues and deceitful
gatherings (which have of late become well known to us) at which you
proceed to persuade and demonstrate to your simple, foolish, and uncouth people that the Messiah has still not come (fol. 6*r*).

For Machado, the New Christians are guilty of all the customary
charges: "You are so clever and wily that you do not want to marry
your daughters to Old Christians but always to New Christians" (fol.
15*r*). "Tell me, then, why do you judaize? Why do you keep the Sabbath and the feasts of the Law of Moses?" (fol. 42*v*). "Yet, you, gentlemen, walk with your Sabbath on your backs, not doing anything on it,
but calling in poor and doltish Christian women to prepare your food
— putting yourselves and those wretches in hell" (fol. 43*r*). In no uncertain terms, Machado believes that the Jewish ritual is very much

[26] By the time Francisco Machado wrote the *Mirror*, edifices used and designated as synagogues
were of course not to be found in Portugal. In the following verses, written by a malcontent after
1516, *ignogas* refers to the New Christian community:

> A terra esta
> de ignogas bem chea
> e fazem a cea
> dos asmos por caa,
> uereis enfeitados
> os sabados todos,
> uereis de mil modos
> capuzes frisados.

(*Excerptos de um Cancioneiro Quinhentista: Trovas que se fizeram nas terças em tempo de Elrei D. Manoel*
[Evora, 1883], p. 19). The fate of the synagogues in Portugal was described by the poet Garcia de
Resende (d. 1536) in his documentary poem published in 1545. Referring to the mass conversion in
Lisbon in 1497, he wrote:

> Hos judeus vij caa tornados
> todos nūo tempo christãos,
> hos mouros entã lançados
> fora do reyno passados,
> & ho reyno sem pagãos,
> vijmos synogas, mezquitas
> em q̃ sempre era dictas
> e pregadas heresias,
> tornados [*sic*] em nossos dias
> Igrejas sanctas benditas.

(Garcia de Resende, *Miscellanea*, ed. Mendes dos Remedios (Coimbra, 1917), stanza 142, p. 51.)

alive and that the rabbis still preach their deceits (fol. 12*v*). In short, the Jews are "an obstinate and incredulous people. Even though you have been baptized and live and converse with us, you are recalcitrant and walk backwards like the crab" (fol. 13*v*). If they *do* appear to be Christians, "they are only so because they cannot endure anymore or because they are afraid of fire or exile" (fol. 52*v*).

It is this state of affairs, described here by Machado, that prompted him to compose the work. He complained, as had others,[27] that the New Christians had been neglected by the clergy and that no serious attempts had been made to catechize them. He informs his readers that he "was aghast at the princes and bishops (not mine, surely) for being lax concerning this" (fol. 1*r*). Yet, despite his concern, Machado maintains that he would not have acted of his own accord. Rather, he was "implored" and "beseeched by devout and Christian persons, ecclesiastics as well as laymen," to prepare a work which might serve as a corrective to clerical laxity (fol. 1*r*). This, in brief, is the genesis of the *Mirror of the New Christians*.

Machado's testimony is striking in that it is the most unequivocal of all statements concerning the New Christians in sixteenth century Portuguese polemical literature. This literature, like earlier Portuguese anti-Jewish polemics,[28] is sparse. There are in fact only three or four works in addition to the *Mirror* which were written in the 1500's.[29] In an article especially devoted to the subject,[30] I have argued that this literature by and large cannot be used as evidence for active judaizing in metropolitan Portugal in this period. One of these texts, for exam-

---

[27] On the awareness of the need for more effective catechization of the New Christians, see *DE*, p. 1; Pereira, *Tratado*, fol. xvi*v*.

[28] Révah in his introduction to *DE*, pp. xxvf. ; António Ribeiro dos Santos, *Memórias de litteratura portugueza*, 8 (1806), 308-72 ; Mario Martins, "A polémica religiosa nalguns códices de Alcobaça," *Brotéria*, 42 (1946), 241-50 (= *Estudos de Literatura Medieval* (Braga, 1956), pp. 307-16) ; "Fr. João, Monge de Alcobaça e Controversista," *Brotéria*, 42 (1946), 412-21 (= *Estudos*, pp. 317-26); "A filosofia esotérica no "Speculum Hebreorum," *Estudos*, pp. 349-58; José M. da Cruz Pontes, *Estudo para uma Edição Crítica do Livro da Corte Enperial* (Coimbra, 1957).

[29] These works include João de Barros' *Ropica Pnefma* or *Spiritual Merchandise* (written 1531) and his *Diálogo evangélico sobre os artigos da fé contra o Talmud dos Judeus (Evangelical Dialogue concerning the Articles of the Faith against the Talmud of the Jews*, written 1541); Diogo de Sá's *Inquisiçam, e segredos da fee, contra a obstinada perfidia dos Iudeus (Inquisition and Mysteries of the Faith against the obstinate Jewish Perfidy*, A.N.T.T. MS da Livraria 360, written in 1550's); Dom Gaspar de Leão Pereira's translation (*Tratado*) of Hieronymus de S. F., *ACPJ* (1564). To these may be appended the 1534 copying of Master António's *Support of the Faith (Ajuda da fé)* (1486). On this literature, see "To Sabbatize in Peace" (below, n. 30).

[30] "To Sabbatize in Peace: Jews and New Christians in Sixteenth-Century Portuguese Polemics" to appear in the jubilee volume honoring Professor Alexander Altmann.

ple, Dom Gaspar de Leão Pereira's translation of Hieronymus de Sancta Fide's (né Joshua Lorki) *Ad Convincendum Perfidiam Judaeorum* (*Hebraeomastix*) (published Goa, 1564)[31] was intended for professing Jews residing in or passing through Goa. João de Barros' *Ropica Pnefma* (1531) and Diogo de Sá's *Inquisiçam* (written in the 1550's) use the Jew or the New Christian as a foil to present a social critique or an exposition of theological doctrines. Barros himself speaks of what he calls a potential Judaism; yet he does not voice much awareness of any *active* judaizing. To be sure, the dedicatory to Prince Henry of Barros' *Evangelical Dialogue* enumerates concrete instances of judaizing. Yet this list is virtually a stereotype of that found in a letter of Prince Henry himself to his representative at Rome, Pier Domenico, dated February 10, 1542. It is not certain, therefore, that Barros can be relied upon as an independent witness. It is Machado then who appears to provide the most explicit reactions to the phenomenon of judaizing. Here too, however, there are questions to be raised.

Machado was apparently not a worldly person. We know him only in his "sibylline cave" and as a traveler in ecclesiastical circles. Nor, if we compare him to such humanists as Barros or Damião de Góis, was he fully a man of the sixteenth century. True, in an appendix to the *Mirror*, he voices his hopes for a Christian conquest of all of Moorish Africa.[32] Yet unlike the other polemicists mentioned above, he had no direct involvements with the East. Nor does his style betray — over and above the few classical references — an affinity to the literary currents of the Renaissance.[33]

If Machado then does not seem to have been active in public life, where did he have the opportunity to see the judaizers he berates? Indeed, it may well be that he never did. He informs us only that when he returned to Portugal, he "*heard talk* of the establishment of many synagogues in many places together with numerous complaints and grievances" (fol. 1r). He laments "a thousand synagogues and false and deceitful gatherings (*which have of late become well known to us*) at which you proceed to persuade and demonstrate to your simple, foolish, and uncouth people that the Messiah has still not come" (fol. 6r). The rabbis of Portugal are for him none too discreet in concealing their activities: "You therefore go about organizing perfidious assemblies, con-

---

[31] Bibliographic information on the literature cited here is given in detail in the study cited in n. 30.

[32] See below, pp. 37-38.

[33] See below, p. 36.

venticles, and synagogues in order to deceive the simple people, sacrifice to Moses, judaize, and affirm that the Messiah has not yet come ..." (fol. 13v).

For this information, Machado never explicitly states his source but assures his readers only that "this judgment is not mine alone but is shared by many Old Christians who see it for themselves" (fol. 15r). It is not unlikely that some of these Old Christians, at least, were none other than those same "devout and Christian persons" who commissioned the work. Machado mentions some of these patrons by name. In admonishing the New Christians, he commends them to certain preachers whom he clearly esteems: "I heard of the questioning of the New Christians and the fine sermons delivered against them by such distinguished and learned preachers as Vila Franca, Soares, Frias, Hulmedo, and Padilha" (fol. 1r). Machado knows them as "learned men, well versed in the New as well as the Old Testament [who] call to you with their horns and trumpets to convert. They are at your disposal at Court every day: Vila Franca, Soares, Padilha, Frias, Hulmedo, Santiago, Álvaro Gomes and Romeiro, the latter doctors of Paris. Seek them out and confer with them," he advises; "they are great physicians. They will bleed you and remove the errors in which you are enveloped" (fol. 38v). Concerning Santiago, he adds, "You have very learned men to examine you, such as Brother Jorge de Santiago of the Order of Preachers. Follow his doctrine and teachings and you will not err" (fol. 8v).

Most of these preachers can be readily identified:

Francisco de Vila Franca was a Spanish Augustinian brought by John III to Portugal in 1535 to initiate the reform of Augustinian monasteries.[34]

João Soares (1507-1572) received his doctorate in theology at Salamanca in 1529. He preached for a time in Braga but he was not greatly appreciated because of his allegedly "obtuse Castilian." Yet in time he seems to have been received with better favor. He was brought to the Court where he served as almoner and preacher to the king and tutor to his sons. On July 16, 1539, two years before the composition of the Mirror, he was appointed to the Council of the Inquisition by Prince Henry. Of his abilities it was said: "He was most eminent in his pulpit ministry, so that the greatest preachers of the time saw him as their better and hailed him as a second Demosthenes."[35]

---

[34] Pedro de Mariz, Diálogos de vária história (Lisbon, 1647), pp. 485f.; Fortunato de Almeida, História da Igreja em Portugal (Oporto, 1967), 2:141; Herculano, Origin, pp. 431, 490.

[35] Nicolás Antonio, Bibliotheca hispana nova (= BHN) (Madrid, 1788), 1:783; Almeida, Igreja, 2:448,

Jerónimo de Padilha was a Spaniard who was appointed reformer of the Dominican Order by John III in 1538. The Monastery of S. Gonçalo de Amarante was founded through his initiative, and he was known as a "very learned preacher." Yet he was not esteemed in all quarters. It appears that "he had practiced violence and disobeyed apostolic orders, for which he was excommunicated; but he continued to exercise his ministry, showing contempt for censures." In 1542, he was serving as representative of the Inquisition at Rome.[36]

Frias is apparently to be identified with the Dominican preacher António Freire (1485-1575) who took orders at the Monastery of S. Domingos de Benfica and his doctorate in theology at Coimbra. He was confessor to John III and Prince John, father of King Sebastian. Freire was a prolific writer but his zeal as a preacher was stressed by Pedro Monteiro, chronicler of the Portuguese Dominicans: "He was fervent in the ministry of his pulpit which lasted sixty years, constantly seeking the salvation of souls."[37]

Little is known of João Hulmedo (Olmedo). He was a master of theology and a "clérigo de mesa" of the king.[38]

Jorge de Santiago (d. 1561), a Dominican, and, like Machado, a doctor of the Sorbonne, was appointed to the Council of the Inquisition on November 10, 1540 — less than a year before the composition of the *Mirror*. Because of his fame as a preacher, he played an important role at the Council of Trent and was appointed Bishop of Angra in 1552. He was an active participant in the intrigues of the Inquisition.[39]

Álvaro Gomes, another recipient of a Sorbonne doctorate, was a native of Evora. He lectured at various Iberian universities for twenty years and was appointed reader in theology at Coimbra in 1545 and confessor to the king and tutor to the Infante Dom Afonso, Archbishop of Lisbon. Gomes was one of the first censors of books and manuscripts

605f.; Barbosa Machado, *Bibliotheca lusitana*, 2:138; Herculano, *Origin*, pp. 429-31, 490f., 582; *Grande enciclopédia portuguesa brasileira* (= *GEPB*), 29:326-28; Révah, *La Censure inquisitoriale portugaise au XVIᵉ siècle* (Lisbon, 1960), pp. 51f.; *Dicionário de história de Portugal* (= *DHP*), 4 vols. (Lisbon, 1961-71), 4:209. João de Barros mentioned him as tutor to the prince in *Diálogo em louvor de nossa linguagem* (Coimbra, 1947), p. 7.

[36] Mariz, *Diálogos*, p. 486; Almeida, *Igreja*, 1:211, 457; Herculano, *Origin*, pp. 431, 491, 503; *GEPB*, 19:929.

[37] *BHN*, 1:119; Pedro Monteiro, *Claustro Dominicano*, 3:153-156; Barbosa Machado, *Bibliotheca*, 1:281f.; *GEPB*, 11:823.

[38] Almeida, *Igreja*, 2:99; Herculano, *Origin*, p. 431.

[39] *BHN*, 1:539; Monteiro, *Claustro Dominicano*, 1:29f., 169; 3:42f., 226; Barbosa Machado, *Bibliotheca lusitana*, 2:815; Almeida, *Igreja*, 2:434; Herculano, *Origin*, p. 613; *GEPB*, 28:285f.; A. Pimenta, *D. João III* (Oporto, 1936), p. 208; *DHP*, 4:209.

to be appointed by Dom Afonso. Two of his own writings, however, were — for reasons best known to the Inquisitors — denied the imprimatur in the period 1540-50.[40]

Like Gomes and Santiago, Marcos Romeiro (Romeu, d. 1511) received his doctorate at Paris. On October 31, 1545, he was appointed lecturer in Scripture at Coimbra by John III. Romeiro served as a censor of John III and as tutor to the Infante Dom Duarte at the Convent of Santa Marinha da Costa near Guimarães. On a visit to this convent, the eminent Dutch humanist, Nicholas Claenarts, claimed to have been favorably impressed by Romeiro's scholarship.[41]

In examining this roster of those individuals singled out by Machado as the best equipped to achieve the conversion of the Jews, we find then that they are none but the court theologians of John III himself. All actively involved in the Inquisition, they are portrayed by Alexandre Herculano as being none too moderate in their zeal.[42] If, then, Machado gained his information about judaizing in Portugal from such men as these, who were part and parcel of the inquisitorial establishment, his credibility is only as good as theirs. In other words, whether one espouses the point of view of Saraiva or that of Révah or any modification thereof, Machado does not appear to present any truly independent testimony.

Yet it is not only his testimony that is of relevance but his attitude and motivations. According to Révah, Machado had hoped to evangelize the New Christians in order that they might escape the fires of the Inquisition. In this, he links Machado and João de Barros with the humanist tradition of Nicholas Claenarts.[43] Claenarts, who ironically had been the tutor of Prince Henry, the Grand Inquisitor, had advocated a peaceful crusade without swords. The conversion of Jews and Muslims was to be accomplished through learning their languages and literatures and demonstrating to them the superiority of Christianity.[44]

[40] *BHN*, 1:58; Barbosa Machado, *Bibliotheca lusitana*, 1:104; *GEPB*, 12: 153; Révah, *Censure*, pp. 34-39. See below, n. 75.

[41] Mariz, *Diálogos*, p. 477; Almeida; *Igreja*, 2:598; Pimenta, *D. João III*, p. 283; M. G. Cerejeira, *Clenardo e a sociedade portuguesa do seu tempo* (Coimbra, 1949), p. 327; *GEPB*, 16:168; Révah, *Censure*, p. 23; *DHP*, 2:276; 4:151.

[42] See Herculano, *Origin*, pp. 431, 490.

[43] On Claenarts see the work of Cerejeira cited in n. 41.

[44] *DE*, pp. xxi, li *et seq*. On the advocating of adequate education for neophytes in fifteenth-century Spain, see Alonso de Cartagena, *Defensorium unitatis christianae*, ed. M. Alonso (Madrid, 1943), pp. 343-65.

Machado does indeed voice genuine concern for the salvation of the souls of the New Christians. He admonishes them: "Leave Moses. Abandon him because of what you owe God and virtue. I do not desire dioceses or abbeys ... but only your salvation and conversion" (fol. 14r). It grieves him that they refuse to believe (fols. 17v, 45v). He pleads with them not to give themselves "over to sin, but rather to go from virtue to virtue so that [they] may see the God of Zion and enjoy eternal life" (fol. 29r). All that is done now is done "so that you may attain eternal bliss. By your lives," he exhorts, "have no quarrel with me for I insist that I am not writing against you because I wish you harm or because I feel hostility toward you. Rather, it grieves me to see you stray in error without the eternal glory for which you were created" (fol. 8v). Repeatedly, he begs the New Christians not to think ill of him: "By your life, gentlemen, do not think ill of me if at times I speak more than I ought" (fol. 60r), for, he assures them, "I only desire your well-being and salvation. I would be happy to see you blessed and good Christians; friends of Christ and not of Moses who brings you not salvation but death ..." (fol. 58v). Indeed, the very closing remarks of the *Mirror* assure Machado's intended audience: "I beg you, for the love of our Lord, do not think ill of me because of this manual which I have composed in order to benefit and not to discredit you. For if you are in error, you will find in reading it some remedy with which to cure your wounds" (fol. 63v).

One must agree that in one sense at least Machado cannot be accused of espousing the more extreme aspects of Iberian antisemitism of this period. He does not speak at all of the concept of blood purity (*limpeza de sangue, limpieza de sangre*) — freedom from Jewish or Moorish blood or of the blood of one condemned by the Inquisition.[45] Unlike others,[46]

---

[45] Saraiva, *A Inquisição Portuguesa*, p. 105; A. Castro, *The Structure of Spanish History* (Princeton, 1954), pp. 521-44.

[46] As late as 1748, the New Christian António Nunes Ribeiro Sanches, urging (from Paris) the reform of the Inquisition, mentions the following among its counterproductive effects: "We have shown that all those who wish to enter ecclesiastical office or any state position must have their lineage examined. Hence it follows that not only are the New Christians to be deprived of these advantages, but they are also entirely separated from the Old Christians. The latter will never marry their daughters to them; so it follows that the New Christians and all their progeny are obliged to mix and marry among themselves. Since [their sons] cannot be clerics nor their daughters nuns, they all marry, multiplying themselves at the same time that the Old Christians diminish. It thus follows that if there are two of the Jewish blindness within fifty families of New Christians, in fifty years they will all tend to the same belief; for as they mix and multiply, they will necessarily come to fall into the error of those two families, with whom all their descendants are linked." From *Christãos Novos e Christãos Velhos em Portugal* (Oporto, 1973), p. 48. Because of the

Machado advocated that "if Old Christians married New Christians, the integrity of Christ's faith would be preserved: The New Christians would not dare to judaize [for St. Paul says] that an unfaithful man is sanctified by the faithful woman!" (fol. 15r).

Yet, despite this, the identification of New Christian and Jew remains intact.[47] In this way, at least, Machado's apparent benevolence becomes infused with traditional antisemitic thought patterns. Machado reviews Jewish obstinacy. He voices his astonishment that "you are such an obstinate and incredulous people. Even though you have been baptized and live and converse with us, you are recalcitrant and walk backwards like the crab" (fol. 13v). The New Christians, "obstinate and incredulous, have no wish other than to die in [their] disbelief" (fol. 8v). It is not that they do not know the truth; they do not *want* to know it (fols. 17r, 24v). They indeed are aware of the truths of Christianity but "refuse to disclose them for fear of cutting your throats with your own knife" (fol. 31v). For this, the only fate that awaits them is the torment of hell (fols. 13v, 36v).

This ambivalence of Machado is seen in yet another characteristic of his writing. In his original manuscript, he often uses vituperative language. Yet in the margins and between the lines, additions and emendations are often made which soften the impact. Thus, "gentlemen" may be substituted for "Jews" (fols. 6, 17v, 18v, 24v) or the word "Jew(s)" may be deleted (fols. 5, 6r, 35r). Elsewhere, "gentlemen" is added to the original phrasing (fols. 12r, 13v, 15v, 18v, 22v, 26v, 35v, 36v, 60r). In one passage, he deletes "wretches" (fol. 13r) and in another adds "dearly beloved brothers" (fol. 15v, cf. fol. 40r). "You gentlemen" is employed to replace "poor miserable wretches" (fols. 40r, cf. fol. 43r) or "your error is great" (fol. 19r). Whole sentences are rephrased: "You wretches still wait for him [Antichrist]" becomes "I do not know, gentlemen, how you still wait for him" (fol. 13r). "See how the devil leads you" is mitigated to "see how you go about" (fol. 15v) or "It is your blindness, malice, and wickedness" to "It is your blindness, I do not say malice or wickedness" (fol. 12v). Indeed, at times, the most incongruous additions are made. To "Yet you, gentlemen, blind, ob-

---

propagandistic nature of his pamphlet, the historicity of Ribeiro Sanches' remarks should be taken advisedly. See also Révah, "Marranes," pp. 490f.

[47] On the persistent identification of New Christians with Jews and their various cognomens (*homens da nação,* etc.) through the eighteenth century, see, e.g., Yerushalmi, "Prolegomenon" to Herculano, *Origin,* pp. 38f. and António N. Ribeiro Sanches, *Christãos Novos e Christãos Velhos em Portugal,* ed. Rego (Oporto, 1973).

stinate and incredulous" is appended "I am of the opinion, however, that you are very good Christians and better than the Old" (fol. 6or).

Even more striking are his occasional apologies. Where he says "Do you know the source of your simplemindedness?" he adds: "Pardon me if I call it simplemindedness" (fol. 6ov). He regrets his acerbity. "Pardon me," he pleads, "if I say that with some anger" (fol. 13v, cf. fols. 6v, 39r, 42v). Above all, he asks for indulgence, "if on occasion, I seem to be putting my foot in my mouth, slandering or insulting them ..." (fol. 2v).

This unevenness in tone was to become a characteristic of the style of Machado's successors, the inquisitorial preachers of the seventeenth and eighteenth centuries. In his analysis of the sermons preached at *autos-da-fé* in this period, Edward Glaser observes:

> A more perplexing problem, not to be solved by conventional devices of rhetoric, is the choice of the proper tone for the sermons. While the heretical depravity of the Marranos merits the severity of tongue lashings, one must not forget that conversion is above all a labor of love, and the listener can hardly be put into the proper frame of mind if he is exposed to a barrage of insults. ... [Yet] it is not unusual for the fathers to reveal right at the outset the intensity of their anti-Jewish feelings. Terms such as "you vile, wretched, groveling people" are by no means exceptionally violent, and the pejoratives "blasphemous, perfidious, ignorant and treacherous" enjoy a constant vogue.[48]

Yet Machado — even in the sixteenth century — was not altogether unique in his ambivalence to the New Christians. A writer far more distinguished than Machado, the playwright Gil Vicente, gave classic expression to it. In Vicente's "devotional works" (*obras de devoçam*) such as the *Auto da Barca do Inferno* and the *Diálogo sobre a Ressurreição*, the Jew is portrayed as a diabolical figure. On the other hand, in his social satires, such as *Inês Pereira* or *Juiz da Beira*, the Jew (=New Christian) is treated with a humor which is no more biting than that directed toward any other element of society. Still more favorable are Vicente's famous protest against the massacre of New Christians in Lisbon in 1506 and his letter to John III, defending the New Christians against the accusation that they caused the Santarem earthquake of January 26, 1531.[49]

---

[48] Edward Glaser, "Portuguese Sermons at Autos-da-Fé: Introduction and Bibliography," *SBB*, 2 (1955-56), p. 55.

[49] See my forthcoming study "To Sabbatize in Peace," cited above in n. 30.

I. S. Révah explained this apparent internal contradiction in Vicente's attitude in accord with his interpretation of Machado and João de Barros. He saw a basic hostility toward the Jew tempered with the conviction that the latter should be won over to Christianity by peaceful means rather than be made to suffer indignities and loss of life and limb. Here, Vicente — like Machado and Barros — is linked to the humanist tradition of Nicholas Claenarts.[50]

In his study of the Jew in the writings of Gil Vicente,[51] Celso Láfer has proposed another possibility. Láfer discerns the root of Vicente's ambivalence in the very neo-Platonic world-view shared by him and so many other sixteenth-century writers. This view is given expression in Vicente's letter to John III after the Santarem earthquake in 1531:

> ... Our most high and sovereign God has two worlds: the first has always been and will always be. It is that of His resplendent glory, of constant repose, of quiet peace, of calm without strife, of abounding pleasure, of prevailing harmony. [This is] the first world.
> Infinite wisdom has constructed this, the second [world], in which we live, in the opposite fashion — all without rest, without stability, without certain pleasure, without enduring splendor, all brief, all fragile, all false, fearful, weary, tired, imperfect — so that, by contrast, the perfections of joy of the first world will be known.[52]

This division of the universe into the sacred world and the world of men is, according to Láfer, the key to the understanding of Vicente's ambivalence toward the Jew. In the sacred world, which takes literary expression in the *obras de devoçam*, the Jew has no function except as a representative of the diabolical and perfidious. Yet in the world of men, which manifests itself in Vicente's satires and his intervention on behalf of the New Christians, the latter, the Jew, has his place.

This "mirroring" of the heavenly world in the earthly world is of course characteristic of much of sixteenth-century literature. To Camões, in *Babel e Sião*, the material world was only the reflection of an eternal perfect reality, the Divine Land. The title "Mirror" (*Speculum, Espelho, Espejo, Specchio*) was a common one in this century — as in previous centuries — for works of a doctrinal or didactic nature.[53] It is as a mirror, we recall, that Machado conceived his own work.

---

[50] *DE*, pp. xxi, li *et seq.*

[51] Celso Láfer, *O Judeu em Gil Vicente* (São Paulo, 1963).

[52] *Obras Completas*, ed. Braga, 6:252.

[53] The Alcobaça collection (now in the B.N.L.) contained a number of such works: Bernard of Clairvaux's *Speculum de honestate vite* and *Speculum monachorum* as well as Bernard Guy's *Speculum sanc-*

Of Vicente, it may be said that he lived in both worlds — the sacred and the secular. Machado — for all we can tell — lived primarily in the former. His image of the New Christians was derived from what he heard from the mouths of court clerics and inquisitorial preachers. Thus the veracity of his own perceptions is largely, if not exclusively, dependent on theirs. It would appear that Machado was ready to accept the existence of the judaizers whether they existed or not; and whether they existed or not, they remained — as did all Jews — in their obstinacy and disbelief.

THE *MIRROR OF THE NEW CHRISTIANS*

The *Mirror of the New Christians* is to all intents and purposes — in format, style, and method — a medieval polemical treatise. In twenty-three chapters, the author enumerates twenty "characteristics" (*propriedades*) of the Messiah and demonstrates that they were fulfilled in Jesus. The first two, relatively lengthy, chapters establish the chronology of the world in six ages in terms of the division established by Augustine.[54] It is at the beginning of the sixth that Christ came as predicted. From this it follows that Christ fulfilled all the Old Testament prophecies — either literally or spiritually as the occasion demanded — or that he demonstrated his Messianic mission through his life's work. Several chapters are devoted to doctrinal matters such as the Trinity, Incarnation, etc. As has been noted, the theme of Jewish incredulity is woven throughout.

To support his arguments, Machado used a variety of sources. Scripture, of course, is foremost. It is often cited paraphrastically and in forms at variance with the Vulgate. These departures have been

torale; the "Espelho dos Monges" (B.N.L. MS Alc. 200) based on John Climacus; a Portuguese translation of Dominic Cavalca's *Specchio di Croce* (B.N.L. MSS Alc. 89, 221); Cristina di Pisano's *Specchio* (Lisbon, 1518); Henricus de Herph's *Espelho de perfeyçam* (Lisbon, 1533), etc. Noteworthy among these works is the thirteenth-century John of Alcobaça's "Speculum disputationis" or "Speculum hebraeorum" (B.N.L. MSS Alc. 236, 270), of which the author wrote: "Ipsum autem intitulavi speculum Hebraeorum, ut sicut in speculo potest homo cernere maculas faciei, ita etiam in hoc libro Hebraei pariter et conversi possint errores veteres intueri." (José Maria da Cruz Pontes, *Estudo para uma edição crítica do livro da Corte Enperial* (Coimbra, 1957), p. 75). On these manuscripts, see the *Inventário dos códices alcobacenses* cited in n. 13 above and the literature cited in n. 28.

[54] On the intricacies of the division of world history into ages, see Jean Danielou, "La Typologie de la semaine au ive siècle," *Recherches des Sciences Religieuses,* 35 (1948), 382-441. On Jewish refutations of this chronological schematization, followed in Isidore's *Etymologies* and *Chronicon* and in the *Estoria* of Alfonso the Wise, see Y. F. Baer, *History of the Jews in Christian Spain* (Philadelphia, 1966), 1:59.

discussed in the notes to the text. With respect to later sources, Machado notes that "in many passages I followed the work of St. Isidore the Spaniard which was written against the Jews [i.e., *De Fide Catholica Contra Judaeos*]. I also followed the most reverend Petrus Alfonsi, a converted Jew, extremely learned and articulate. In many passages and places, I followed Nicholas de Lyra as well" (fol. 1r). Among other sources cited or used may be listed Jerome, Augustine, Peter Comestor, Gregory, Thomas Aquinas, the *Glossa Ordinaria*, Peter Lombard, Durand de Saint-Pourçain, as well as Aristotle, Josephus, and classical writers.

Yet Machado's most frequently cited source in the *Mirror* is not Christian but rabbinic literature. Machado liberally cites the Targumim, the early Aramaic translations of the Bible attributed to Onkelos (Pentateuch) and Jonathan ben Uzziel (Prophets) as well as the paraphrastic Jerusalem Targum (Targum Yerushalmi) to the Pentateuch. Many too are the various quotations from the Talmud as well as the various compilations of the midrash (rabbinic and medieval homiletico-exegetical literature). The latter include the early Sifra on Leviticus and the Sifre on Numbers and Deuteronomy; the Midrash Rabbah on the Pentateuch and Five Scrolls; the Midrash on Psalms (Midrash Tehillim); the Tanḥuma on the Pentateuch; the Midrash on Proverbs (Midrash Mishle); and the Genesis Rabbati of Rabbi Moses the Preacher (*Bereshit Rabbah le-Mosheh ha-Dareshan*) of Narbonne (11th century) — a work frequently cited in Christian anti-Jewish polemics from the thirteenth century on and one not without its problems.[55] Machado generally refers to the *Rabbati* as the *Grão Grande* (the "Great Great"), presumably on the basis of Raymundus Martini's appelations, "magna," "major," etc. (see below). Finally, among the medievals, Machado cites the classic exegetes Solomon ben Isaac (Rashi, 1040-1105) and Abraham Ibn Ezra (1088-1167) as well as the eminent jurist and philosopher Moses Maimonides (1135-1204).

In addition to these standard rabbinic sources, Machado, according to the fashion of the period,[56] quotes the kabbalah or Jewish mystical

---

[55] See text, chap. 9, n. 10.

[56] See Joseph L. Blau, *The Christian Interpretation of the Cabala in the Renaissance* (New York, 1949); François Secret, *Le Zôhar chez les Kabbalistes chrétiens de la Renaissance* (Paris, 1958); *SRHJ*, 13:172-81; Gershom Scholem, *Kabbalah* (New York, pp. 196-200. Christian use of kabbalistic literature and motifs was so widespread as early as the twelfth and thirteenth centuries that Profiat Duran wrote in his *Reproach of the Gentiles* (ca. 1397) that Jesus and his disciples were indeed kabbalists but that "their kabbalah was corrupt." (*Kelimat ha-Goyim*, ed. Adolf Posnanski, *Ha-Zofeh le-Ḥokhmat Yisrael*, 2:143). The frequent references to "cabalistas" in Portuguese polemics from the *Ajuda da Fé* of

literature. He cites the ancient Book of Creation (*Sefer Yezirah*), accepted by kabbalists as a proto-kabbalistic work, and the twelfth century *Book Bahir*.[57] He also acknowledges the divine inspiration of the kabbalah: "... These very obvious allusions which clearly demonstrate that the Messiah would be God and Man could not be known by these doctors [the rabbis] except through the art of the kabbalah. Fathers would transmit them to their sons but only with the utmost caution and care. Afterwards, when they saw that the Jews converted to the faith of Christ at the time of the early Church, they pronounced a ban against revealing those secrets" (fol. 29r, cf. fols. 38r, 40v).

In this statement can be seen the underlying rationale for the longstanding use of Jewish literature by Christian apologists in their polemics against the Jews.[58] The truth of Christianity, it was maintained, was known to the rabbinic leadership; yet in their obstinacy they refused to reveal it to the masses. Thus, once again, an ambivalence in attitudes is manifested. On the one hand, the rabbis, ancient and modern, are denounced as blasphemers and corrupters of Israel. On the other, their words — in passages considered Christological — are held to be authoritative. In the latter half of the thirteenth century, Christian use of rabbinics reached its greatest sophistication in the Iberian peninsula. It was evident in the 1263 Barcelona disputation and reached its classic expression in the *Pugio Fidei* (1273) of Raymundus Martini, a disciple of Raymundus de Penyafort, the founder of colleges for the teaching of Semitic languages for the purpose of training missionaries to Jews and Muslims. The *Pugio Fidei* was followed by a series of imitative works in southern Europe, not the least important of which was the *Hebraeomastix* (*Ad Convincendum Perfidiam Judaeorum*), writ-

---

Master António (1486) to Barros (see *DE*, p. 102 and the literature cited by Salomon in his review of Yerushalmi [see above, n. 21], p. 18, n. 26) and Machado (see my study "To Sabbatize in Peace") are probably due to more than just the general Renaissance interest in kabbalah. Fifteenth-century Lisbon served as a domicile for longer and shorter periods for a number of Hebrew writers oriented or sympathetic to kabbalah. These include Isaac Abravanel, Joseph Hayyun, the teacher of Joseph Jabez, Jabez himself, Judah Hayyat, who passed through briefly, and Abraham Saba. (Faithful to nineteenth-century German historiography, Kayserling notes that "Saba is still appreciated despite his mystical tendency" [*História*, p. 108].) It may be noted here that fifteenth-century Lisbon has been largely treated as a footnote to Iberian Jewish history in which it is seen primarily as a way station for Spanish refugees. The rich cultural life of its Jewish community, as evidenced by its scientists, exegetes, philologists, homilists, scribes, and illuminators, surely deserves more serious study.

[57] See Gershom Scholem, *Major Trends in Jewish Mysticism* (Jerusalem, 1941), *passim; Kabbalah* (Jerusalem, 1973), 23-30, 312-16, *et passim; SRHJ*, 9:105ff. and notes; *DE*, pp. lxxxiv ff.

[58] A major study is Chen Merchavia, *The Talmud as Viewed by Christianity* (Hebrew; Jerusalem, 1970).

ten sometime after 1412 by the convert Hieronymus de Sancta Fide
(Joshua Lorki). This work was itself divided into two parts: the first,
citing the alleged Christological passages in rabbinic literature; the
second, denouncing the Talmud's supposed blasphemies. The first half
of the *Hebraeomastix* was adapted and translated into Portuguese by
Master António, court physician to John II, in 1486 ; as noted above, it
was published in Portuguese in its entirety in Goa in 1565. Other works
of this nature include Alfonso de Spina's *Fortalitium Fidei* and the
writings of Petrus Galatinus and H. Fino which João de Barros used in
composing the *Evangelical Dialogue.*

Machado's attitude toward rabbinic literature shared the same
dialectic as the authors of these other cited works. On the one hand, he
speaks of "your stupid and simple doctors" (fol. 60r), the "cause of your
perdition" (fol. 6r), who utter sayings which "appear to be childish and
mere deceits to trap the simple. They are founded on texts which they
do not understand and which they interpret erroneously according to
the flesh rather than the spirit" (fol. 59v). On the other hand, "many
other parables to be found in the Talmud demonstrate that the Messiah
has come" (fol. 12v). Yet, in their obstinacy, "your rabbis, the priests in
the synagogues, keep silent about them and do not want to reveal this
to you, so that you will not convert" (fol. 12v). "If the rabbis were to
disclose these things, they would cut their throats with their own knife"
(fol. 31v; cf. fols. 6r, 13r).

Yet while Machado shared the attitudes and general methodology of
his predecessors, the presentation of the common material differs
markedly. It reminds one, strangely, of the trout stream that flowed
through the kitchen of the Monastery of Alcobaça. Whenever the friars
had a desire for fish, they had only to dip into the stream and draw
them out. It is in this random, almost capricious, fashion that Machado
seems to have angled in the sea of rabbinic literature. Most of the time,
passages are cited in a distorted or corrupted form — at times quite
beyond recognition. It is clear that Machado had no real knowledge or
Hebrew.[59] He thought, for example, that the three Hebrew letters *'alef,*

---

[59] Not all Christian writers who cited rabbinic material knew Hebrew of course; yet few distorted and misunderstood the texts as much as did Machado. On João de Barros' somewhat confused
conceptions of the Hebrew language, see Maria L. Carvalhão Buescu, ed., *Gramática da lingua por-*
tuguesa (Lisbon, 1971), p. xlix and cf. *DE*, p. 53. On Alfonso de Spina, who seems not to have had
much Hebrew learning either, see Benzion Netanyahu, "Alonso de Espina: was he a New
Christian?" *Proceedings of the American Academy for Jewish Research*, 43 (1976), 144-46. Diogo de Sá
frequently copies words in Hebrew script in the margins of his *Inquisiçam*, but his manner of doing
so shows that he had no conception of what he was writing; see my "To Sabbatize in Peace." An

mem, and *shin* were one single letter with the name of *com* and that the letter *mem* was the fifteenth (and not the thirteenth) letter of the Hebrew alphabet (fol. 21r). His transliterations of Hebrew words were often corrupt. At times, of course, this was due to his copying the errors of the printed editions. Thus he presents *vagitta* (properly: *va-yiqra*) as the Hebrew form of *vocabit*, and *victare* (correctly: *va-yiqqare*) as the Hebrew equivalent of *vocabitur* (fol. 22) — the same spellings found in printed editions of Nicholas de Lyra's *Postilla*.[60] Yet he is apparently responsible for a number of his own errors. Thus Behemoth or *behemod* is written as two separate words: *de herrod*.[61]

More revealing, however, is the fact that he cited his rabbinic sources without really understanding their true nature. While Machado did not share Barros' notion that the Talmud was sacred to Muslims,[62] he was under the impression that it was compiled in Cairo (fols. 8r, 11v, 29r). This may have stemmed from what he heard about Maimonides who spent most of his life in that city. He does indeed mention "Rabbi Moses of Egypt" (fol. 33r), although he wrongly ascribes material to him, since the Rabbi Moses in question in that particular passage is Moses the Preacher of Narbonne.[63] Machado did not personify the Talmud as had others who spoke of that which "dixit Rabbinus Talmud."[64] Yet other rabbinic writings are frequently given the title of "teacher," "doctor," etc. "Midrash Tehillim, your doctor"; "Midrash Tehillim in a book which he composed"; "Rabbi Midrash, another commentator says ..."; "Rabbi Midrash asked Rabbi Abba"; "Numidrash, your doctor"; "Rabbi Midrash Ruth"; "Rabbi Barezid" (*Bereshit* = Genesis); "Two of your doctors, the sons of Reuben and Gad, af-

---

example of a scholar who knew no Hebrew but had a reasonable conception of the rabbinic material which he copied from secondary sources is Marsilio Ficino in the *De religione christiana et fide* (1474), which cites, as does Machado, the *Book Bahir* (*Lucido*). See *Opera* (ed. Basel, 1576; photoreprint Turin, 1962), 1:1-77. See Umberto Cassuto, *Gli Ebrei a Firenze nell'età del rinascimento* (Florence, 1918; photoreprint Florence, 1965), pp. 277f. = *Ha-Yehudim be-Firenze bi-Tequfat ha-Renesans* (Jerusalem, 1967), pp. 218ff.

[60] *Mirror*, fol. 22; see text, Chap. 5 notes 36 and 37.

[61] Among others, *veara* for na'arah (fol. 20); *edid* for *yedid* (fol. 26r); *leuiathe* for *lemarbeh* (fol. 22r) — but cf. *leuathe* in Nicolas de Lyra, *De probatione*, p. 182; *heloy matem* for *'elohim atem* (fol. 53v); *Rabi Cateua* for Rabbi Kattina (fol. 13v); *Rabi Aquila* for Rabbi Akiba (fol. 15v [although it is cited correctly as *Aquiba* on fol. 19v]); *Rrabi Auiana* for Rabbi Hanina (fol. 25v). For some reason, R. Hoshaiah (Genesis Rabbah 78:12) appears as *Rrabi Cabet* (fol. 32r). The most frequent scribal confusions seem to be *n* for *u* or *v*, *ui* for *m*, *r* for *t*, *b* for *h*, *rr* for *m*.

[62] Barros, *DE*, p. lxxviii.

[63] Maimonides is cited as *Rrabi Moises* on fol. 19v.

[64] Henricus Synensis cited in A. L. Williams, *Talmudic Judaism and Christianity* (London, 1933), p. 30.

firm this"; "your doctor, Embresit Rraba"; "Rabbi Joshua Nave."[65]

Names of rabbinic works, or chapters in them, are often corrupted: "In your books *Canedim* and *Aboahara*" (Sanhedrin and Avodah Zarah); "in the book called *Sabat*" (Shabbat); "*Addobarim Arrabal*" (Devarim Rabbah); "in a book called *Barahot*" (the talmudic tractate Berakhot); "a book called *Serafim*"; "in a book called *Desir*" (*Yezirah*) or "*Cefer Abair*" (*Sefer ha-Bahir*).[66]

At times names of works or "chapters" appear in Portuguese translation: Torat Kohanim (Sifra) appears correctly as *Lei dos Sacerdotes* (*Law of the Priests*) (fol. 39*v*); "in the Talmud in the chapter on fasts" (Tractate Ta'anit) (fol. 30*v*); "in the chapter that begins 'one does not stand'" (*nom estarão*, Chap. 5 of Tractate Berakhot) (fol. 52*v*). The most remarkable is "in a chapter that begins 'before their downfall'" in which *lifene 'edehem* (the title of the first chapter of Tractate 'Avodah Zarah) is translated as if the word *'ed* were the biblical "calamity" rather than the etymologically different but orthographically identical rabbinic *'ed*, "Gentile festival" (fol. 12*v*).

Considering then the misunderstandings of rabbinic material, hardly any of which are to be found in the earlier polemical works,[67] it is in order to ask what the sources of Machado's citations were. Machado does refer to a work which "God occasioned for me — a book which was composed by a Jew, now a Christian, in which many of their errors are

[65] Midras Telim, vosso doutor (fols. 12*r*, 21*r*) ; Midras Telim ... numa sua grosa diz ... (fol. 23*v*); Midras Telim, num liuro que compos ... (fol. 27*r*); Rrabi Midras (fols. 46*v*, 47*r*); Rrabi Midras, outro grosador, diz ... (fol. 29*r*); Esto confirma Rrabi Midras ... (fol. 33*r*); Rrabi Midras perguntou a Rrabi Abba estando praticando sobre a vinda do Mexia, que nome auia d'auer ... Nom vos parece que auia de ser Deos, pois que, segundo estes vossos doutores, Midras [e] Abba, ... (fol. 26*r*); Midras, vosso doutor, grosador do psalteiro (fol. 32*v*); Midras, grosador do salteiro ... (fol. 54*v*); Rresponde Midras, dizendo ... (fol. 27*r*); A rezão de Midras ... (fol. 34*r*); A isto daa Midras autoridade ... (fol. 34*v*); Este confirma Midras, vosso doutor ... (fol. 35*r*); Numidras, hum vosso doutor ... segundo o dizer deste doutor ... (fol. 25*r*); Dimidras Rrabi, grosador do salteiro (fol. 25*v*); Rrabi Midras Rrut (fol. 26*v*); Midras de Rrut, hum vosso doutor ... (fol. 33*v*); Rrabi Ona e Rrabi Iacob, confirmando ho dizer de Midras Rrut ... (fol. 26*v*); Rraba Barezid, expondo aquel passo ... (fol. 46*r*); Helia Rabi (fol. 13*r*); Esto confirmarão dous teus doutores, filhos de Rroubem e de Guad ... (fol. 28*v*); Assi tambem isto afirma Embresit Rraba, vosso doutor ... (fol. 12*v*); Rrabi Josua Naue (fol. 23*r*). Cf., however, Em Midras Telim se escreue que ... (fol. 35*v*); Em Midras Telim se põe uma pergunta ... (fol. 12*v*).

[66] Em Canedim e Aboahara, liuros vossos assi chamados ... (fol. 12*v*); Cenadrim (fol. 28*v*); Canedrim (fol. 30*v*); Cenedrim (fol. 19*v*); Num liuro chamado Sabat (fol. 34*v*); Num liuro chamado Cifre (fol. 35*r*); No liuro Cifre (fol. 45*v*); Num liuro chamado Barahot (fol. 52*v*); Isto se confirma no liuro chamado Serafim (fol. 55*r*); Num liuro chamado Desir (fol. 27*r*); num liuro chamado Cefer Abair ... (fol. 27*v*); Num liuro chamado Adobarim Arrabal (fol. 51*r*).

[67] For the phrase "antes de seu quebranto" for "lifene 'edehen" in earlier literature, see below, chap. 4, n. 49.

manifested" (fol. 1r). Yet this helps little. Practically all Christian scholars who cited rabbinic material in this period — Lyra, Martini, Spina, or Galatinus — were considered converts to Christianity or sons of converts.[68] Yet none of the works of these authors — or of the genuine converts Hieronymus de Sancta Fide or Master António — appears to have served as Machado's source. While he cites basically the same material found in the others, the presentation differs considerably. First, the material rarely appears elsewhere in such a corrupt form. Second, no single one of these works contains all the material cited by Machado.[69] The references from the *Bahir* and the *Yeẓirah* (fol. 27) in particular are to be found in none of them.

It is conceivable, of course, that Machado used a book, now lost to us, written by a convert to Christianity, who himself had confused the material. There is, however, an additional possibility: that Machado — in addition to written material — might have used an oral informant.[70] To such an informant, Machado might allude indeed when he speaks on one occasion of what "a Jew[71] told me" (fol. 14r). If that is the case, Machado may simply not have taken sufficient time to comprehend, transcribe, and record the words of his interlocutor. Indeed, several errors in the *Mirror* may be more easily understood as auditive rather than visual errors.

Thus we find that Machado tells us: "Numidras hum vosso doutor, expondo aquel passo dos Canticos, diz ..." ("One of your doctors, Numidras, explains the passage from Song of Songs ...," fol. 25r). Without altering the pronunciation at all, one might reconstruct: "No midras, hum vosso doutor, expondo aquel passo dos Canticos, diz ..." ("In the midrash, a doctor of yours, explains the passage ..."). In another instance, Machado refers to a sage by the name of Embresit Rraba: "Assi tambem ... isto afirma Embresit Rraba, vosso doutor."

---

[68] *SRHJ*, 9: 105; Glaser, "Invitation", p. 38. Hieronymus de Sancta Fide and Master António were, of course, former Jews.

[69] For example, the citation from B. T. Shabbat 66a (fol. 16v) is found in *PF·*(p. 434) and not in Hieronymus, while the passage from Midrash Tehillim 4:2 (fol. 25v) is found in *ACPJ* (pp. 6of.) but not in *PF*. The following citations are found in neither source: Midrash Tehillim 10:2 (ed. Buber, p. 92) (fol. 12v); Midrash Mishle 22:20 (fol. 28v); the commentary of Abraham Ibn Ezra on Ps. 2:12 (fol. 29r); B. T. Shabbat 152b (fol. 34v); Targum Yerushalmi to Gen. 49:18 (fol. 55r).

[70] On the possibility that Raymundus Martini used informants, see *SRHJ*, 9:300, n. 9.

[71] While Machado may be referring to a New Christian, the possibility that he had contacts with professing Jews in France or even in Portugal is not to be excluded. On the existence of such Jews in the Iberian peninsula in the sixteenth century, see Y. H. Yerushalmi, "Professing Jews in Post-Expulsion Spain and Portugal", *Salo Wittmayer Baron Jubilee Volume* (New York and London, 1975), pp. 1023-58.

("This is also what your doctor, Embresit Rraba, affirms ...," fol. 12v).
Here too a minor revision yields: "Assi tambem ... isto afirma em
Bresit Rraba vosso doutor" ("This is also what your doctor affirms in
Bereshit Rabbah [Midrash Genesis Rabbah]"). The third of Machado's
rabbis is "Dimidrash Rrabi" — "Dimidras Rrabi, grosador do salteiro,
expondo ho p*salmo* diz ..." ("Rabbi Dimidras, commentator on the
Psalter, in expounding the psalm, says ...," fol. 25v). This may hark
back to a phrase such as "Isto é de Midras Rraba" ("This is from
Midrash Rabbah"). Again, the mysterious *liuro Desir* (fol. 27v) is, of
course, the *liuro d'esir[a]*, that is, the *Book of Yeẓirah*. The last and most
complex example is the passage: "Esto confirmarão dous teus doutores,
f*ilhos* de Rroubem e de Guad assi chamados, dizendo que tres pessoas —
Padre, Filho, Sp*iritu* Santo — criarão o mundo" ("Two doctors of
yours, called the sons of Reuben and Gad, confirmed this and said that
three persons — Father, Son, and Holy Spirit — created the world ...,"
fol. 28v). This passage is a corruption of the trinitarian interpretation
of Joshua 22:21ff.: "Then the children of Reuben and the children of
Gad and the half-tribe of Manasseh answered ... God, God, the Lord,
God, God, the Lord. He knows. ..." It is likely that Machado's source
had said: "Os filhos de Rroubem e de Guad confirmarão que tres
pessoas — Padre, Filho, e Spiritu Santo — criarão o mundo, dizendo,
El, Elohym, Adonay" ("The sons of Reuben and Gad confirmed that
three persons — Father, Son, Holy Spirit — created the world when
they said 'God, God, the Lord' ").

On the basis of such instances then, the thesis of an oral informant is
proposed as the most tenable solution to the problem of Machado's
sources, until such time as further information be revealed.[72]

THE FATE OF THE *MIRROR*

Machado had apparently hoped that the *Mirror* would have a wide
circulation. It was for this reason that he wrote his work in Portuguese

---

[72] On errors due to "auditive" as opposed to visual mistakes, see Ludwig Bieler, "The Grammarian's Craft: A Professional Talk," *Folia: Studies in the Christian Perpetuation of the Classics*, 10 (1958),
39, n. 55; H. J. Chaytor, "The Medieval Reader and Textual Criticism," *Bulletin of the John Rylands
Library*, 26 (1941-2), 49-56. Precisely the kind of confusion found in Machado was exhibited in an
undergraduate's examination paper: "Another important dogma or belief is the study of Torah. As
can be seen in 'The Fathers of the Ethics,' study is even more important than performing a [com-
mandment]." Among the several infelicities here are the confusion of the titles of "The Ethics of
the Fathers," a tractate of the Mishnah, and "The 'Fathers' of Rabbi Nathan," a midrashic com-
pilation based on the former.

even though — as he asserted — he did not feel comfortable with it as a literary language.[73] Yet despite the esteem in which Machado was held by Prince Henry, to whom the work was dedicated, its publication was not licensed by the Inquisition and it has remained unpublished in manuscript until the present day.[74] In this, of course, the *Mirror* was not unique. The establishment of the Inquisition in 1536 had a great restrictive effect on Portuguese publishing. I. S. Révah has noted that many manuscripts, although quite orthodox and often dedicated to the king, the queen, or to the Prince Cardinal, were rejected apparently only because they did not personally satisfy the tastes of the censors. Thus it was that the *Evangelical Dialogue* of João de Barros and the *Inquisiçam* of Diogo de Sá shared the same fate as that of the *Mirror*.[75] Yet in the case of Machado, there might have been other factors at work. With the prohibition against Hebrew and Jewish books,[76] Marranos would ironically use Christian anti-Jewish literature in order to learn about Judaism. Such material frequently tended to perpetuate rabbinic literature rather than contribute to its desuetude.[77]

Yet there is another factor which no doubt played a role in cooling the enthusiasm which the Inquisition might have felt toward the *Mirror*. Machado, as we recall, was no less critical of the ecclesiastical hierarchy than he was of the New Christians themselves. Machado's chief concern seemed to be that many complained of Judaism but few were prepared

---

[73] *Mirror*, fols. 1v, 63v. In contrast to this, his contemporaries João de Barros and Diogo de Sá stress the importance of Portuguese as an instrument for the propagation of culture. Cristóvão Roiz Acenheiro, the sixteenth-century copyist of Master António's *Ajuda da Fé*, praises the latter's "fine Portuguese." See my study "To Sabbatize in Peace."

For a striking similarity in attitude toward the use of the vernacular by a Jewish writer, cf. R. Moses Almosnino in his introduction to *Regimiento de la vida* (Salonica, 1564): "I aunke mas fasil fuera escrivirte en nuestra sanktisima y fekundisima lengua por ser a mi mas familiar, no me kero eskuzar del trabažo de escrivir en romance komo me ruegas lo aga. ..." Cited by Henry V. Besso, "Judaeo-Spanish — Its Growth and Decline," in Richard D. Barnett, *The Sephardi Heritage* (New York, 1971), p. 606.

[74] João Franco Barreto, "Bibliotheca lusitana," MS 803 da Casa Cadaval, fol. 463: "Espelho de Christãos Novos e convertidos, o qual se mandou recolher."

[75] Révah, *Censure,* pp. 32ff., *DE*, p. lxxxix.

[76] A. Ribeiro dos Santos, "Da Litteratura sagrada dos Judeus portugueses no Século XVI," *Memórias de litteratura portugueza,* 2 (1792), 355; "Memória sobre as origens da tipographia em Portugal no século XV", *Memórias,*[2] (Lisbon, 1856), 13:43; but see Yerushalmi, "Prolegomenon" to Herculano, p. 43.

[77] Y. H. Yerushalmi, *From Spanish Court to Italian Ghetto* (New York and London, 1971), p. 289. It is noteworthy that Prince Henry was unhappy about the dissemination of the distinguished humanist Damião de Góis' *Faith of the Ethiopians* in Portugal. It was felt in part that the Ethiopian rites were too close to Judaism and that the New Christians might learn to judaize from it. See Hirsch, *Damião de Gois,* p. 154.

to do anything about it. Not he, however. Taking his mission seriously, he devoted the last chapter of his treatise to a discussion of "how it behooves the shepherds and Inquisitors to look after the sheep who have been entrusted to them, and for whom they shall render a long account" (fol. 62r).[78] In expressing his consternation that the princes and bishops had allowed judaizing to continue (fol. 1r), he voiced his dismay that "the name of Jesus is shamed and humiliated in this kingdom because everyone is at loggerheads; all are not of the same faith or belief. Yet this does not surprise me very much, since where there are Moors, Negroes, Indians, and Jews, it is inevitable that each go his own way and follow his own sect. *What I do find astonishing is that no one has put a stop to this; no one has changed this"* (fol. 62v).

Machado here voices the complaints of those — such as the Inquisitors — who insisted on a tightening of the reins against the *conversos* in contradistinction to those — such as the first official Grand Inquisitor, Fr. Diogo da Silva, Dom Fernando Coutinho, Bishop of Algarve, Dom Diogo Pinheiro, Bishop of Funchal, and the Vatican itself[79] — who were against the use of strong-arm tactics with respect to the New Christians. For Machado, it is only the Inquisitors who stand in the breach: "Now, however, according to current report and what I have heard said, the name of Jesus has been exalted and dignified somewhat, because very Christian, Catholic Inquisitors, who are most learned and eloquent, have been appointed" (fol. 62v).

We note too though that Machado does not confine his strictures to the clergy alone. He couples princes with prelates and, in several outbursts, vents his spleen against the former: "If Christ is not venerated everywhere, the fault lies with the Christian kings who will have some tall explaining to do to God as to why they do not all band together to crush that great dog of a Turk who has the Promised Land under his control" (fol. 33r). More pointedly, and stressing the evangelical dimension of Portuguese expansionism,[80] he notes that although Africa possesses all the goods of the world, "the best, the name of Jesus, is lacking, even though it had been known and honored there, only to be lost through the fault of the Christian princes and kings. ... But our most serene, Catholic, and excellent king will make it great — as we

[78] On the image of good and bad shepherds, cf. *DE,* pp. 1f.

[79] Kayserling, *História*, p. 113; Yerushalmi, "Prolegomenon" to Herculano, *Origin,* pp. 24f. *et passim.*

[80] On João de Barros' view of the Portuguese conquest as an extension of the Crusades, see *DHP,* I, 307f.

hope — in our days and may the most high God preserve him for the exaltation of His faith that we may see (as I hope) Portugal and Africa one kingdom united in the faith of Christ" (fol. 64v). Yet royal responsibility is not limited to the East. He laments that "there is no shepherd who grieves over the loss or injury of the sheep who are wandering about lost throughout the Kingdom of Portugal" (fol. 63r). Without mincing words, he postulates that "perhaps it is due to the favors, connivings, and courting of the princes and others who fail to exercise their responsibilities that Jesus' name has been blasphemed in Portugal" (fol. 14r).

It is unlikely that John III or his Inquisitors were accustomed to such reproof and this no doubt served as a further hindrance to the *Mirror*'s receiving the imprimatur.

Confirmation of this may be seen in the fact that Machado had better success a quarter of a century later in a revised Latin version of his treatise, free of the vituperations against the clergy and the monarchy and, at the same time, disembarrassed of the rabbinic material.[81] This was the *Veritatis repertorium, per Fratrem Franciscum Securim* [Machado's Latin name] *Doctorem Parinsiensem [sic] omnium minimum editum in Hebraeos, quos vulgus novos vocitat Christianos,* published at Coimbra in 1567.[82]

The Manuscript

The unique manuscript of the *Mirror*, which is in the author's own hand,[83] is in the National Library of Lisbon, MS 6747 in the collection known as the Fundo Geral. The condition of the manuscript is good. Only one folio (6v) has a bad vertical stain toward the lower third of the folio which covers part of the last twelve lines. A wormhole at the

---

[81] For an example of the tempering of the earlier material, compare *Mirror*, fol. 7r with the Latin text: *"Ecce adsum.* Hoc dixerat, quia festinus erat futurus eius aduentus. Esset nimium temerarium Lusitaniae regem et ciuibus Vllissipponensibus dicere prope diem, Ecce adsum vobiscum, et suum adventum usque ad decennium differre" (fol. 2v). Also: "Nonne stolidum tibi videbitur, si Lusitaniae Rex nuntium Conimbricam ad praeparandas eius vias statim missum faceret, ipse autem non proficisceretur, nisi anno quadragesimo expleto? Idcirco, ad quod expectans o Israelita a [anno ?] tanto praeterito ipsum Messiam?" (fols. 3v-4r).

[82] According to Machado's statement in B.N.L. MS Alcobacense 81, fol. B1r, it was completed some time in December, 1564. It is this and the *Mirror* which de Visch probably means by Machado's "duo egregia volumina contra Iudaeos." There are two copies of the *Repertorium* at the B.N.L. See A. J. Anselmo, *Bibliografia das obras impressas em Portugal no século XVI* (Lisbon, 1926), p. 54.

[83] The hand is identical to that in B.N.L. MS Alcobacense 81. See above, n. 13.

upper inside corner penetrates the entire manuscript but does not affect the written area.

The work is written in cursive script in light brown ink. Bound in parchment are 79 folios, 68 of which are textual material, with 6 blank folios at the beginning and 5 at the end. Folios 1 through 63 comprise the *Mirror of the New Christians*, while folios 64 through 68r contain a chapter on the Moors and Islam which was added later as a supplement. It is written in a slightly lighter color ink than the *Mirror*. Dated 1542 (fol. 68r), it is entitled "Capitulo unico ou hum soo que demostra como hos mouros vivem errados obedecendo ao seu Alcoram no qual a seyta de Mafamede esta escrita." This chapter is not included in this edition of the *Mirror* but is being prepared for publication elsewhere.

The signatures run from A to H, beginning after the first six blank folios. Thus: A1 = fol. 1, B1 = fol. 9, C1 = fol. 17, D1 = fol. 25, E1 = fol. 33, F1 = fol. 41, G1 = fol. 49, H1 = fol. 57. Foliation is sporadically recorded in Arabic numerals. It is difficult to determine if the foliation that does occur is in the author's own hand since at times there are differences, though slight, from the numerals occurring within the body of the text. The numbers that do appear do not correspond to the numbering of the folios in this edition. The first folio which has a number written on it (20) is 19r in Professor Vieira's foliation. All numbers are written in the upper right hand corner of the folio, generally on the recto but occasionally on the verso.

Almost all the pages have writing in the margin which appears to be in the author's own hand and which is generally of two types: additions which are to be incorporated into the text and some source references. This writing is found in both the left- and right-hand margins with occasional additions in the lower margin as well.

Words or phrases are frequently expunged and replaced by others. Words that are not written clearly or that are considered by the author to be misspelled are expunged and written anew. There are also interlinear additions.

The manuscript measures 20.5 × 14.5 centimeters. The written material on folio 1r measures 16.5 × 10 centimeters. All pages save one (fol. 1v) have chapter headings with the chapter numbers written out. The number of lines to a page ranges from 34 to 41, not counting the marginalia.

Chapter thirteen precedes chapter twelve, but indications to this effect are in the manuscript, no doubt with the reade or future printer in mind. At the close of chapter eleven (fol. 37v) is written: "Aqui se

mete ho capitolo duodecimo que esta às tres folhas adiante neste '*b*'."
This letter '*b*' can be found in the left-hand margin of fol. 40*v* where
chapter twelve commences. At the bottom of folio 40*v* the author has
written: "Daqui torna atras no começo desta folha onde achares esta
letra '*A*'." This letter is found in the upper left-hand margin of folio
40*r*, opposite the first line of the text.

This Edition

Modern punctuation and division into paragraphs have generally
been followed. Modern Portuguese practice has generally been followed regarding capitalization and word division, except in the case
of archaic words such as *todoslos*, customarily written as one word. In
the case of the contraction of the preposition *de* with a word beginning
with a vowel, modern practice has been followed. Where a contraction
is not in accord with current usage, an apostrophe has been employed
rather than a restoration of the *e* in the preposition. Such occurrences,
frequent as they are (*d'outra, d'entender, d'antre, d'auer,* etc.), no doubt
represent current usage at Machado's time. For this reason, Professor
Vieira retained his spelling of such words as *nenhum*, viz., either *nhūm*
or *nhū*, with never any sign of suppression over the initial *n*; the tran-
scription is thus either "nhūm" or "nhum."

In general, the orthography of the original has not been altered. In
spite of the modernization of punctuation and the regularizing of
capitalization to facilitate reading and comprehension, an effort was
made to conserve the form of the written words as they appear in the
manuscript. No attempt has been made to hyphenate verbs and tense
forms and their occurrence with object pronouns; nor is *elrei* hyphen-
ated. The manuscript has been followed in this regard.

As in the original text, this edition bears no accentuation with the exception of the grave accent which has been used with the preposition *a*
contracted with the feminine article *a*. In some cases, it has been difficult to determine whether the author intended *à* or the article or
preposition alone. In these cases, however, the intended meaning is
generally not lost regardless of whether one reads *a* or *à*.

The *til* (˜) has been conserved only where nasalization is involved.
The otiose *til* has been eliminated over such words as *quaes, afirmaes, po-
siuees,* which ordinarily appear with a *til* in the manuscript.

The *ç* has been conserved only where pronunciation calls for the
sibilant rather than the velar stop. It has likewise been restored where
Machado, apparently through carelessness, has failed to use it. A purely
orthographic cedilla has been eliminated.

Footnotes to the Text and Translation

The following symbols are used in the notes to the Portuguese text:

+	manuscript adds
exp.	expunged
int.	interlinear addition
marg.	marginal addition
MS	manuscript reads

Passages from rabbinic literature cited by Machado are quoted in the notes to the translation from standard English translations (Soncino, Braude, etc.) where they exist. Elsewhere, I have used my own translations. If Machado's version of a rabbinic passage bears a particular resemblance to that found in a text such as *PF* or *ACPJ*, the latter has been cited in Latin.

Espelho de Christãos Novos

Mirror of the New Christians

[*fol. 1r*] Ao muito R*reuerendissi*mo *Sen*hor e clarissimo P*ri*ncipe Infante Dom Anrrique, Arcibispo da nobre cidade d'Eura, e Comendatario do real e reformatissimo mosteiro d'Alcobaça, frei Francisco Machado, doctor de P*ar*is, deseia muita saude e a benauenturança et*er*nal.

Duas cousas são as p*re*cipuas e pr*i*ncipaes que fazem hos homen[s] escreuer algu*m*a obra. A primeira he po*l'*aproueitar a rrepubrica ou pouo vniu*er*sal, como fez Tito Liuio escreuendo hos feitos dos rroma*n*os pera docume*n*to dos que auiam de soçeder e*m* Rroma. Assi ho confirma Sam Paulo escreuendo aos Rroma*n*os, no capitolo xv: "Todas as cousas que são escritas, pera nossa doutrina e e*n*sinança são escritas." A segunda he, que "muito mal parece a tocha estar debaixo da mesa, a qual auia de alomear a todos," e "muito desp*ra*zer traz a doutrina escondida e ho tesouro posto debaixo do chão." Assi ho dixe nosso Redentor (Mathei, quinto capite), e ho sabedor no Ecclesiastico, capite xx. Estas duas cousas, O Pr*i*ncipe muito alto, me constra*n*gerão a fa*ze*r esta obra, a qual fiz rroguado por algu*m*as pessoas deuotas, amiguas de D*eo*s, e zelantes à fee de Chr*is*to, a qual viam desp*re*zada e anichilada polos falsos christãos, hos quaes chamão nouos na fee.

Certame*n*te, depois que eu vim dos estudos de Paris, eu ouui falar em muitas sinaguoguas que se faziam em muitos luguares, ouuindo queixumes e querimonias, e eu mesmo me espantaua dos pr*i*ncipes e bispos (no*m* porem meo, ne*m* modo algu*m*) acerqua disto.

Aguora, vendo que D*eo*s inspirou en Ciro, e ouuindo hos exames que se fazem polos christãos nouos e has altas p*re*guações que se fazem contra elles por altos e doctos p*re*guadores como he Villafranca, Soaires, Frias, Hulmedo, Padilha, posto que a estas cousas não seia chamado, qua mitido nesta coua de Sibilla, determinei de lançar minhas setas desta pobre aliaua que D*eo*s me deu pera seu siruiço e louuor, e pera confusão daq*ue*les que no*m* cree*m* em Chr*is*to, afirmando que ho Mexia

---

[1] At the time the dedication was written, Prince Henry, brother of King John III, was the first archbishop of Evora, a post he assumed in 1540. He also held the position of Inquisitor General, appointed by the king in 1539 when he was only twenty-seven years of age, although he was not officially recognized as such by the Vatican until 1547. In 1546 he received the Cardinal's hat and in 1578 became Portugal's seventeenth king on the death of his nephew King Sebastian. Francisco Machado's Latin version of the *Mirror* was still dedicated to Henry, but the text of the dedication was altered as follows: "Ad Lusitaniae Cardinalem Dominum Henricum Illustrissimum Principem, omnium Portugalliae regnorum moderatorem, et fidei orthodoxae indagatorem a latere etiam legatum, et Vlyssiponensem Metropolitanum, insuper et totius ordinis apud Portugalliam Cisterciensium praesulem optimum" (title page).

[2] Livy, *Ab urbe condita*, pref., 9-10. Cf. the declaration of Alfonso X in the prologue to the *General estoria*: "... trabaiaron se los sabios omnes de meter en escripto los fechos que son passados para auer remembrança delos como si entonces fuessen e quelo sopiessen los que auien de uenir assi como ellos. ... Et esto fizieron, porque delos fechos delos buenos tomassen los omnes exemplo po-

[*fol. 1r*] For the Most Reverend Lord and Illustrious Prince, the Infante, Prince Henry, Archbishop of the noble city of Evora, and Commander of the royal and very reformed Monastery of Alcobaça, Brother Francisco Machado, doctor of Paris, desires well-being and eternal happiness.[1]

There are two basic and fundamental reasons which motivate men to write. The first is for the benefit of the republic or general polity. This is exemplified by Titus Livy, whose writings of the deeds of the Romans served as a testimony for later generations in Rome.[2] Saint Paul confirms this in his Epistle to the Romans, chapter 15: *All that has been written has been so for the purpose of instructing us.*[3] The second reason is that *the torch ought not to be under the table, for it is to illuminate all*[4] and *hidden learning as well as the treasure buried under the floor only leads to displeasure.*[5] Thus spoke our Redeemer (Matthew, chapter 5) and the sage in Ecclesiasticus, chapter twenty. These two reasons, most noble Prince, compelled me to write this work. I have been implored to do so by some devout persons, beloved of God and zealous in the faith of Christ, which they saw scorned and undermined by those false Christians who are called new in the faith.

To be sure, when I returned from my studies in Paris, I heard talk of the establishment of many synagogues[6] in many places together with numerous complaints and grievances. I myself was shocked at the princes and bishops (not mine, surely) for being lax concerning this.

Now, since God inspired Cyrus,[7] I heard of the questioning of the New Christians and the fine sermons delivered against them by such distinguished and learned preachers as Vila Franca, Soares, Frias, Hulmedo, and Padilha.[8] Since I am not called to these things, lodged here as I am in this sibylline cave,[9] I set my mind on sending forth my arrows from this humble quiver which God gave me that I might best serve and praise Him, confounding those who do not believe in Christ and who affirm that the Messiah has not yet come. This is the case with

---

ra fazer bien, et delos fechos delos malos que recibiessen castigo por se saber guardar delo non fazer" (*General estoria,* ed. A. Solalinde [Madrid, 1930], pt. 1, p. 3).

[3] Rom. 15:4.

[4] Matt. 5:15.

[5] Ecclus. 20:32.

[6] See Introduction.

[7] Cf. Ezra 1:1; 2 Chron, 36:22.

[8] On these names, see Introduction.

[9] The writer is comparing the *covas* in which the monks of Alcobaça lived to the cave of the Sibyl of Cumae. See A. J. Saraiva, *A Cultura em Portugal* (Lisbon, 1950), 1:213.

nom veo, como foi Montenegro, grande iudeu, ho qual neste tempo moderno muitos sequazes teem.

Assi que eu, rroguado por pessoas deuotas e christãas, assi ecclesiasticas como laicaes, determinei, O Rreuerendissimo Senhor, de satisfazer aos seus votos e pitição pia e deuota. E pera milhor seer, Deos me trouxe às mãos, começando eu esta obra, hum liuro composto por um iudeu, ia feito christão, em ho qual muitos erros seus se demostrão. Este liuro sigui em muitos passos, e sigui nesta obra Sam Isidoro Hispalensi, no liuro que fez contra hos iudeus. Sigui aquele reuerendissimo padre, de iudeu feito christão, chamado Pedr'Afonso, varão doutissimo e disertissimo. [fol. 1v] Sigui, tambem, Nicolão de Lira em muitos passos e luguares. Assi que nesta obra mais sigui as sentenças dos doutores que não a minha propria, a qual eu não quis preferir à opinão e sentença de tantos varões e tam doutos. "Et quia miserrimi ingenij est inuentis, nihil addere," e do meu, alguma cousa acrecentei.

Ho fim principal desta obra he, O clarissimo Senhor, persuadir e demostrar aos iudeus, polos seus doutores e rrabijs, e polos talmudistas, e polos profetas, e pola sua Lei, que ho Mexia ia he vindo; e são passados 1541 annos, e que todas as propriedades que erão escritas polos profetas e polos seus doutores do Mexia, todas forão communicadas e mais apropriadas a Christo, nosso Redentor e nosso Saluador, polo qual bem se demostrara andarem muito enganados e ceguos, vestidos com ho veeo de Moises, ho qual nom se ha de tirar senão conuertendosse elles à fee de Christo. Assi ho afirma Sam Paulo escreuendo aos Chorinthios na Segunda Epistola, capite 3º, onde diz que enquanto Moises se leer, sempre este veeo ha de estar sobre ho coração deles. Prazera a Deos que lendo elles esta obra, a qual composta foi por amor deles, este veeo e esta ciguidade se tirara d'ante seus olhos.

Diuidi esta obra per seus capitolos, como se uera polo processo do liuro, pera nom ser tanto fastio ao leedor. Escreui, Senhor Principe, esta obra em purtugues (e mais quisera em latim por que milhor me desenuoluera) pera que todos ha possão leer e entender, assi christãos velhos como nouos, "ob quos hec tempestas orta est."

Cuidando eu e pensando a quem dirigiria esta obrizinha, estas minhas primitias, vossa altissima pesoa e sublime alteza loguo sobreveo à memoria, sendo elle ho grande e zeloso inquisidor da fee orthodoxa,

---

[10] Montenegro, the "Jew of India," returned to Portugal in 1538 and was imprisoned. He apparently incriminated many in an effort to save himself but was nevertheless burned in 1540. See *DE*, p. lxi.

[11] See Introduction.

the well-known Jew, Montenegro,[10] who even in these modern times has many followers.

Thus, beseeched by devout and Christian persons, ecclesiastics as well as laymen, I decided, most reverend lord, to satisfy their requests and their pious and devout petition. Happily, as I began this work, God occasioned for me a book which was composed by a Jew, now a Christian, and in which many of their errors are manifested.[11] I followed this book in many passages as well as the work of Saint Isidore the Spaniard[12] which was written against the Jews. I also followed the most reverend father Petrus Alfonsus,[13] a converted Jew, extremely learned and articulate. [*fol. 1v*] In many passages and places in my text I followed Nicholas de Lyra[14] as well. Thus more often than not I followed the opinions of learned men rather than my own, not wishing to prefer the latter to the former. *Et quia miserrimi ingenij est inuentis, nihil addere,* I added something of my own.

The aim of this work, O most illustrious lord, is to persuade and to demonstrate to the Jews that the Messiah has already come. This I propose to do by citing their own rabbis and learned men; the talmudists and the prophets, and their Law. There have now passed 1541 years since all the characteristics of the Messiah that were foretold by the prophets and sages were found to be fulfilled in and appropriate to Christ, our Redeemer and Savior. For this reason it will be shown how the Jews walk in blindness and error, covered with the veil of Moses which will not be removed until they are converted to the faith of Christ. Saint Paul affirms this in his Second Epistle to the Corinthians, chapter three, where he says that this veil will cover their hearts so long as Moses is read. May it please God that this veil and this blindness be torn from their eyes as they read this book which was written for their sake.

I have divided this work into chapters, as will be seen in due course, so that the reader will not become weary. I have written, Prince, this work in Portuguese (although I would have much preferred Latin in which I can best develop my ideas) so that all Old Christians as well as New may read and understand what I have set forth here, *ob quos hec tempestas orta est.* While I pondered and considered to whom I might dedicate this little work, my first fruits, there came to mind your most distinguished excellency and exalted highness, the great and zealous

---

[12] Isidore of Seville (seventh century), author of the *Contra Judaeos*. See Introduction.

[13] Petrus Alphonsi (1062-1110), author of the *Dialogus Petri et Moysi Judaei*. See Introduction.

[14] The *Postilla* of the Franciscan exegete, Nicholas de Lyra (ca. 1270-1349).

debaixo do qual iaz toda a proteição e defendime*n*to da nossa sacratissima fee catholica, e nele esta exalçala, como faz, e veemos por experientia.

À Vossa Alteza, pois, enderenço, e mais, ofereço esta minha obrizinha, a qual sera defendida de toda enueia, odio, malquerença, se Vossa Alteza quis*er* ser defensor e proteitor dela, defendendoa debaixo das duas pias asas. Porem, pera que ella seia pura e limpa de todo ioio e erruillaca, deseio que passe pola ioeira da grande scientia e doutrina, e pola foria e lima de Vossa Alteza. Porque se ella passar polas suas mãos, sei que carecera de toda rrep*r*ehe*n*são, ho qual se fe*z*er, a maiores trabalhos me prouocara.

Vale et age ut annos nestorios deguas 1541. Ex cenobij tui Alcobatie Academia octauo idus Septembris.

[*fol. 2r*] Seguesse ho Prologuo

Olhando muitas vezes, magnificos e piadossos ledores, e pe*n*sa*n*do na memoria dos passados philosophos, vendo ho que fezerão e dixerão e aconselharão nos seus ditos e dizeres, assi naturaes como moraes; vendo sua vida, sua abstine*n*tia, castidade, qua nas minhas entradanhas concebo hu*m*a grande amiração, e esto, *c*ertame*n*te, no*m* sem algu*m*a pequena de paixão. Vendo, pois, seus ditos ta*m*bem polidos, ornados, alegrome; bendiguoos. Mas quando da outra pa*r*te veio seus errores, sua condenação p*er*petua, leuo grande desp*r*azer; grande noio e descontentamento.

Que*m* pensasse na santidade de Socrates, na continentia, contemplação e grande theologia de Platon diuino, do qual ates hos deoses auião enueia; na saguacidade, cientia de Aristoteles; na pobreza de Diogenes; no estudo de Empedocles que tanto amor teue à cientia, que po*r* amor dela tirou hos olhos. Mas assi como estes teuerão estas grandes *v*irtudes pera de todos sere*m* imitadas e seguidas, asi teuerão grandes errores por onde forão apa*r*tados da gloria celestrial senão guostarão da fee de Christo. Assi na nação judaica ouue home*n*s de grandes *v*irtudes e de manificas perfeições. Leede polo Testamento Velho q*ue* todo cheo he. Calo Habraa*m*, Isaac, Iacob, Moises, Aaron, Iosue, Dauid, Samuel, grandes zeladores da Lei. E todos estes conhecerão ho Mexia por fee; conhecerão ho tempo dete*r*minado pera vinda do Mexia.

---

[15] Machado was accustomed to using such expressions in writing dates. In his dedication to the commentary on the seven penitential psalms, he writes "et annos degas felices" (B.N.L. MS Alcobaça 81, fol. *2v*) and in his letter to Prince Henry "Nosso Senhor alargue a vida de V.A. & lhe pros-

Inquisitor of the orthodox faith, under whom lies all the protection and defense of our most sacred Catholic faith. For it is you who exalt it, as you do and as we can see through experience.

It is to your Highness, then, that I direct and offer this little work of mine. It will be guarded from all envy, hatred, and ill-will, if Your Highness protect and defend it under your two pious wings. However, so that it may be pure and free of all weeds and vetch, I desire that it pass through the sieve of great knowledge and learning, through the forge and file of Your Highness. For if it passes through your hands, I know it will be free of all reprehension, and if this be the case, I will be spurred on to greater works.

Vale et age ut annos nestorios deguas[15] *1541. Ex cenobij tui Alcobatie Academia octauo idus Septembris.*

[*fol. 2r*] Prologue

I have often reflected, most worthy and pious readers, on the philosophers of the past and their deeds, words and counsel, expressed in their judgments, natural and moral. When I consider their life, their abstinence, and their chastity, there wells up within me great admiration, not devoid of passion. Indeed, when I see their polished and florid utterances, I rejoice, I bless them. On the other hand, when I see their errors and their perpetual condemnation, I feel great displeasure, discontent and considerable disgust.

One might think of the sanctity of Socrates, of the continence, contemplation and noble theology of the divine Plato, whom even the gods envied; of the knowledge and wisdom of Aristotle; of the poverty of Diogenes; and of the eagerness of Empedocles who loved Knowledge so much that he tore out his eyes for her. Yet, just as these men were the possessors of these great virtues, worthy of being followed and imitated, they were also guilty of great errors which kept them from celestial glory in that they had not enjoyed the faith of Christ. Likewise, in the Jewish nation there were men of great virtues and glorious perfections. Read the Old Testament which is replete with them. I need not name Abraham, Isaac, Jacob, Moses, Aaron, Joshua, David, Samuel, all of whom were ardent zealots of the Law. All of them knew the Messiah and the time of His coming through faith.

pere o estado por muy compridos annos" (Brito, *Cister*, fol. 462r). The introduction to the *Veritatis repertorium* likewise concludes: "et annos ad fidei augmentum orthodoxae degas Nestorios. ..."

Hora, venhamos aos modernos: ceguos, obstinados, duros, asperos na sua saluação. Nom creem que veo ho Mexia, mas falsamente esperão por elle fazendo sinaguoguas, aiuntamentos, lendo Moises, ho qual nom entendem senão segundo a carne e nom segundo spiritu. Vendohos eu assi andar errados, rroguado por algumas pessoas virtuosas, determinei de compoor esta obrazinha pera veer se hos posso e amouer e tirar deste grande erro em ho qual andão, crendo que ho Mexia ha de vir, ho qual, ha 1541 annos que veo tomar carne humana. Ha minha, pois, entenção he neste liuro lhes persuadir e demostrar polos profetas e Lei velha, e polos seus doutores talmudistas, que ho Mexia ia he vindo, e que todas as cousas que estauão escritas do Mexia, todas forão communicadas a Christo e nisto nos nom temos debate, senão hos iudeus. Onde, pois, O leedor, achares cousas de teu gosto, da graças a Deos; e onde desgosto, argue humanamente.

Esta obra, porem, someto à Santa Madre Igreia cuio filho eu som, e espero de ser enquanto viuer e à sua correição protestando, que nom he a minha entenção dizer alguma cousa contra a Santa Madre Igreia, mas defendela ates por ela morrer. Nem he a minha vontade maldizer dos christãos nouos com odio ou malquerencia que eu lhes tenha. E se nesta obra passo ho pee alem da mão, às vezes malfalando ou iniuriandoos, perdoeme, que nom no diguo senão por ver alguns andar errados, e assi demando perdão.

[fol. 2v] Capitolo Primeiro fala de como desde tempo de Adam ates a vinda do Mexia, correrão cinco idades.

A primeira idade deste mundo se começou en nosso primeiro padre Adam, e durou ates ho diluuio, onde correrão mil e quinhentos e seis anos, segundo a suputação e conta dos Hebreus. Mas, segundo hos setenta enterpretadores e Sam Isidoro, durou dous mil duzentos e corenta e dous anos. Sam Ieronimo fiqua nos dous mil anos. Porem, Sam Augustinho, no quinto liuro da Cidade de Deos, no capitolo xx, diz que durou dous mil duzentos e sesenta e dous anos.

A segunda idade se começou em ho patriarcha Noe, e estendeose ates Habraam, a qual durou duzentos e nouenta e dous anos, segundo a

¹ On the division of history into ages, see Introduction.
² Ie., biblical chronology. The actual Hebrew chronology is 1656 years.
³ Translators of the Septuagint.
⁴ The above, including the reference to Jerome, is drawn from Petrus Comestor, HS, Gen. 30, PL, 198:1081. Cf. Isidore, Chron. 6, PL, 83:1022.

Now let us come to these Jews of today: blind, obstinate, hard, obdurate in their belief in their salvation. They do not believe that the Messiah has come, but rather wait for him, forming synagogues and gatherings and reading Moses whom they comprehend according to the flesh but not according to the spirit. Having seen them thus in error and having been implored by several virtuous men, I resolved to compose this little work to see if I could turn them from this gross error in which they find themselves: believing that the Messiah is yet to come, although 1541 years have passed since He took human form. My intention in this book is therefore to persuade them and to show them through the prophets and the Old Law, as well as through their own talmudists, that the Messiah has indeed come, and that all that has been written of the Messiah has been fulfilled in Christ. The Jews, not we, dispute this. Thus, O reader, where you find things in this work which please you, give thanks to God; and where I state things not to your liking, argue humanely.

This work I now submit to the Holy Mother Church whose son I am and hope to be as long as I live. I protest at any attempts to correct it that it is not my intention to say anything against Holy Mother Church but rather to defend her even unto death. Nor is it my wish to speak badly of the New Christians with such hatred or ill feeling I may bear towards them. So if on occasion, I seem to be putting my foot in my mouth, slandering or insulting them, I ask for pardon. I do this only because I see some in error.

[*fol. 2v*] Chapter One speaks of the five ages between the time of Adam and the coming of the Messiah.[1]

The first age began with our first father Adam and lasted until the flood. According to the computation of the Hebrews,[2] this period lasted one thousand five hundred and six years. However, according to the Seventy Interpreters[3] and Saint Isidore, it lasted for two thousand two hundred and forty-two years. Saint Jerome says two thousand years.[4] However, Saint Augustine, in the fifth book of the *City of God*, chapter twenty,[5] says that this first age lasted two thousand two hundred and sixty-two years.

The second age, which lasted two hundred and ninety-two years according to the computation of the Jews,[6] began with the patriarch Noah and continued until Abraham. However, according to the reckoning of

[5] The correct reference is *Civitas Dei* 15.20.
[6] *I.e.,* biblical chronology.

computação dos iudeus. Mas segundo a conta dos setenta enterpretadores e Sam Isidoro, durou nouecentos e corenta e dous anos.

A terceira idade se começou em ho grande patriarcha Habraam, e durou ates ho rreal profeta Dauid, na qual, segundo Santo Isidoro, correrão nouecentos e corenta e hum anos. Mas, porem, hos hebreus dizem que durou nouecentos e corenta anos. Deste Habraam descenderão hos iudeus, segundo a carne, e nos christãos, segundo a fee; polo qual veiamos aqui a causa e rrezão pola qual aos filhos de Isrrael hora chamamos hebreus hora iudeus. Alguns dizem que hos iudeus se chamão hebreus porquanto elles descendem de Habraam. Mas isto nom pode estar nem traz rezão porque Habraam começase per esta letra hebraica *aleph*, ho qual nome, porem, nom se começa senão por esta letra hebraica *aym*; por onde parece que de Heber descendem hos hebreus, e non de Habraam.

A linguoa primeira que ouue no mundo foi a hebraica, a qual se falou e durou ates que hos filhos de Noe começarão de edificar a Torre de Babel (Genesis, capitolo xi), a qual foi diuidida en setenta e duas linguoas, e ha linguoa hebraica fiquou en casa e familia de Heber do qual se faz menção no Genesis no capitolo xi°. E porquanto Habraam descendeo deste Heber e era da sua familia, se chamou hebreu, segundo se contem no Genesis, capitolo xiiij, onde se dizie: "Hum daqueles que escapou denunciou ha Habraam Hebreu que Loth era tomado e preso."

Assi que teens deste dizer que os iudeus sam chamados hebreus, não por descenderem de Habraam, mas emquanto descendam de Heber, no tempo do qual a linguoa foi diuidida en setenta [e] duas linguoas, mas ha hebrea sempre fiquou na sua familia de Heber.

[*fol. 3r*] Chamamse ainda hos iudeus isrraelitas por amor do nome de Isrrael, ho qual foi posto a Iacob quando lutou com ho anio, segundo se contem no Genesis, capitolo xxij, onde se escreue que lhe dixe ho anio: "Ia ho teu nome nom sera Iacob, mas Isrrael, porque se foste forte contra Deos, muito mais seras contra hos homens." Outro nome teem mais prezado, que se chamão iudeus, por amor do tribu de Iuda, ho qual foi rreal e guouernador e rregedor de todos os outros tribus.

---

[7] *Chron.* 12, *PL*, 83:1024.

[8] In *Chron.* 12, *PL*, 83:1029, the figure cited is 940 years.

[9] See Nicholas de Lyra, *Post.* to Gen. 17:6, 1, Fiv*v*. On the discussion of the derivation of the term *Hebrew* in patristic literature, see Bernhard Blumenkranz, *Die Judenpredigt Augustins* (Basel, 1946), p. 182, n. 5.

[10] The belief that Hebrew was the mother of all languages was commonly held in both the Jewish and Christian traditions and persisted well into the Renaissance. See esp. Isidore, *Etym.*, 9.1. *PL*, 82:325; Pico della Mirandola, *Opera*, 1:89, N° 80; Johann Reuchlin, *De verbo mirifico* (Lyon, 1556), 2:6, 8, 19, pp. 124f., 136, 196f. On the subject in general, see Arno Borst, *Der Turmbau von Babel* (Stuttgart, 1957-63). For the Jewish tradition, see A. S. Halkin, "The Medieval Attitude Towards Hebrew," in Alexander Altmann, *Biblical and Other Studies* (Cambridge, Mass., 1963), pp. 233-250.

the Seventy Interpreters and Saint Isidore, it lasted nine hundred and forty-two years.[7]

The third age, which lasted nine hundred and forty-one years,[8] according to Saint Isidore, started with the great patriarch Abraham and extended to the royal prophet David. The Jews, though, say that it lasted nine hundred and forty years. From Abraham are descended the Jews, according to the flesh, and we Christians, according to the faith. We may see here the reason why we call the children of Israel now Hebrews and now Jews. Some say that the Jews are called Hebrews because they are descended from Abraham. Yet this could not be the case because the name Abraham begins with the Hebrew letter *'alef*, whereas the word *Hebrew* commences with the letter *'ayin*. Therefore it would appear that it is from Eber that the Hebrews are descended and not from Abraham.[9]

The first language in the world was Hebrew,[10] which was spoken until the children of Noah began to build the tower of Babel (Genesis, chapter eleven). It was then divided into seventy-two languages[11] but Hebrew was still spoken in Eber's home and amongst the members of his family. Mention of this can be found in chapter eleven of Genesis. Since Abraham was descended from Eber and was of his family, he was called a Hebrew, according to Genesis, chapter fourteen, where it states: *One of those who escaped informed Abraham the Hebrew that Lot was taken prisoner.*[12]

Thus you have evidence here that the Jews were called Hebrews, not because they descended from Abraham, but rather from Eber, at a time when the language was divided into seventy-two tongues, though Hebrew remained in the family of Eber.

[*fol. 3r*] The Jews are also called Israelites after Israel, the name given to Jacob when he fought with the angel. Reference to this may be found in Genesis, chapter twenty-two, where it is written that the angel said to him: *Your name will no longer be Jacob, but Israel, for if you were strong against God, much more so will you be against men.*[13] Another name, more highly esteemed, is *Jews*, after the royal tribe of Judah which ruled and governed all the other tribes. Since it was the first tribe that passed through the Red Sea[14] when Moses made the twelve paths with his rod

---

[11] The number of nations or languages, as based upon the calculation of the number of descendants of Noah, is seventy in the Jewish tradition and seventy-two in the Christian. See Moritz Steinschneider, "Die kanonische Zahl der Muhammedanischen Secten und die Symbolik der Zahl 70-73," *ZDMG*, 4 (1850), 150ff.

[12] Gen. 14:13f.

[13] Gen. 32:28.

[14] See *HS*, Exod. 21, *PL*, 198:1157f.; *Post.*, 1, Nivr. On the Jewish source for this tradition, see L. Ginzberg, *Legends of the Jews* (Philadelphia, 1947), 3:21f.; 6:6f.; *Covenant*, p. 44.

Porquanto foi ho primeiro tribu que passou polo maar Vermelho
quando Moises fez as doze carreiras com sua vara pera passarem hos
doze tribus, e porquanto nhũm tribu foi ousado de passar senão ho
tribu de Iuda, do qual antão era guiador e duque Aminadab; por isso,
este tribu fiquou ho principal donde se chamarão iudeus, e com este
nome se prezam elles muito.

Assi que este Habraam foi ho primeiro que se apartou da idolatria,
apartandose de adorar ho foguo, ho qual adorauão hos caldeus con-
strangidos por aquele grande tirano Menbrot. Adorou Habraam a hum
deos, seruindoo e adorandoo, polo qual Deos lhe mandou que se saise de
Caldea e se fosse pera terra de Chanaam (Genesis, xijº). Deste sairão
duques e grandes senhores. Assi lho prometeo Deos, prometendolhe que
dele auia de descender ho Mexia que foi figurado por Isaac, ho qual
por mandado de Deos, elle quisera sacrificar no monte Moria onde ho
Mexia foi imolado e sacrificado.

De Isaac descendeo Iacob, eligido e predestinado à gloria eterna, do
qual procederão hos doze tribus, e Isau rreprouado e escolhido pera
damnação eterna. Estes doze tribus forão peregrinos e estrangeiros por
espaço de quatrocentos anos (Genesis xv); que cento e nouenta anos andarão perigrinando desde nacimento de Isaac, ates que Iacob descendeo
ao Egito con toda sua familia; e duzentos e dez esteuerão no Egito ates
que veo Moises e hos tirou do catiueiro delrrei Pharão e hos trouxe por
espaço de corenta anos polo deserto; e finalmente entrarão na Terra da
Promissão, a qual lhes foi diuidida por Iosue e Caleph, e todos hos
outros que sairão do Egito morrerão no deserto, tirando estes dous que
nom murmurarão contra Deos. Desde tempo de Iosue ates ho tempo
que Heli sacerdote guouernou ho pouo, regerão doze iuizes, dos quaes
Othoniel foi ho primeiro e Samsão ho derradeiro, por espaço de CCC
anos; e despois destes regerão dous sacerdotes: Heli XL anos, e Samuel
XL anos. Porem, no duodecimo ano Saul foi vngido por rei. Pidirão
rrei, ho qual foi Saul, mas por amor da sua desobedientia não rreinou

---

[15] *Post.*, 1, Nivv; Ginzberg, *Legends* 2:33; 6:6, n. 36.

[16] The tradition concerning Chaldean pyrolatry is based upon the fact that the name of
Abraham's birthplace, Ur, has the meaning of fire in Hebrew. See Ginzberg, *Legends*, 1:198ff.;
5:212ff.; Vulg. to Neh. 9:7 ("*de igne Chaldaeorum*"); Jerome, *Hebr. quaest. in Gen., CC*, 72:15 (*PL*,
23:1005); Isidore, *Chron.* 9, *PL*, 83:1023; *GO* to Gen. 11:31., *PL*, 113:115.

[17] Gen. 12:1.

[18] Gen. 17:6.

[19] Gen. 22:2.

[20] Gen. 15:3.

[21] The Bible records two traditions concerning the duration of the sojourn in Egypt, one of 400
years (Gen. 15:3) and one of 430 years (Exod. 12:40). The early commentators generally un-

in order that the twelve tribes could pass through,[15] and since no other tribe save that of Judah, of which Aminadab was the leader and guide, dared to pass, it stands to reason that this was the principal tribe and the one from which the Jews took their name on which they greatly pride themselves.

Abraham was thus the first to eschew idolatry. He stopped worshiping fire which the Chaldeans[16] were compelled to worship because of the tyrant Nimrod. Abraham worshiped and served one God, wherefore God commanded him to leave Chaldea and to go to the land of Canaan (Genesis 12).[17] From Abraham came forth leaders and great men.[18] God had promised him this saying that from him would be descended the Messiah, prefigured by Isaac whom Abraham had wished to sacrifice by God's command on Mount Moriah[19] where the Messiah was immolated and sacrificed.

Jacob, who was chosen and predestined for eternal glory, was descended from Isaac. From him the twelve tribes came forth. Esau was descended from Isaac as well but was condemned to and selected for eternal damnation. These twelve tribes were wanderers and aliens for a period of four hundred years (Genesis 15).[20] They traveled for a period of one hundred and ninety years, from the time of the birth of Isaac until Jacob arrived in Egypt with his entire family and remained in Egypt two hundred and ten years.[21] At the end of that time, Moses came and freed them from their captivity by the Pharaoh and led them through the desert for a period of forty years. Finally they entered the Promised Land which was divided for them by Joshua and Caleb. These were the only two among those who left Egypt who did not utter a word against God while the others had died in the desert. From the time of Joshua until Eli, the priest, governed the people, twelve judges ruled for a period of three hundred years.[22] Othoniel was the first and Samson the last. After these judges two priests ruled: Eli for forty years,[23] and Samuel for forty years.[24] However, in the twelfth year Saul was anoin-

---

derstood the latter to be the precise figure while the former was considered a round number. (Josephus, *Ant.*, 2.9.1; 2.15.2). The figure of 190 years from the birth of Isaac to the descent of Jacob accords with biblical reckoning while 210 is simply the difference. Josephus, following the Septuagint, was of the opinion that the actual sojourn in Egypt was 215 years to be counted from the arrival of Abraham in Canaan until the descent of Jacob into Egypt (*Ant.*, 2.15.2). Cf. *ACPJ*, 1,2, p. 32; Jerome's Eusebius, *Eusebii Pamphili Chronici Canones*, ed. F. K. Fotheringham (London, 1923), pp. 42, 62.

[22] *HS* (Jud. 19, *PL*, 198:1290) cites 299 years while Isidore (*Chron.*, 19-27, *PL*, 84:1027ff.) gives 289.

[23] 1 Sam. 4:18.

[24] The Bible itself gives no chronological information concerning this. Isidore gives the combined period of leadership of Samuel and Saul as forty years (*Chron.* 28, *PL*, 84:1029). Cf. Eusebius (*Chronica, PG*, 19:165) who lists the combined leadership of Eli and Samuel as forty years.

muito tempo, mas em seu luguar socedeo Dauid (Primeiro Regum, xvi), ho qual tanto aprouue a Deos que dixe: [fol. 3v] "Achei homem segundo ho meu coração." Bem parece que este Dauid muito aprouue a Deos, porque quanto desprouue Saul, tanto este Dauid, amiguo de Deos, lhe aprouue.

A quarta idade se começou neste bento e bendito rrei, a qual durou ates ho catiueiro feito por elrrei Nabuchodonosor, ho qual destruio a Santa Cidade com ho Templo, esbulhandoo dos vasos santos, catiuando ellrrei Sedechias con toda a frol de Isrrael, segundo se conta no Quarto Liuro dos Rreis, no capitolo xxv. Durou esta idade por espaço de quatrocentos e outenta e cinquo anos, segundo a sentença de Sam Isidoro. Nesta idade rreinarão muitos rreis, porque no tribu de Iuda, contando de Dauid ates Sedechias, reinarão XXIJ rreis por espaço de CCCCLXXXIIIIº anos e seis meses. Em Hisrrael reinarão rreis XVIIJ por espaço de CC e cinquoenta anos VII dias, assi da parte de Isrrael depois que hos tribus forão diuididos no tempo de Rroboam, como da parte de Iuda, dos quaes Saul foi ho primeiro e ho derradeiro Sedechias.

E posto que na primeira idade Adam profitizasse do Mexia quando dixe: "Aguora, este osso he dos meus ossos, e carne da minha carne. E por amor disto leixara ho homem a mãi e ho pai e se cheguara pera sua molher" (Genesis, capitolo ijº), isto sinificaua ho aiuntamento do Mexia com a Igreja, polo qual alguns doutores dizem que, posto que Adam nom pecara, ainda ho Mexia tomara carne humana, contra Sam Thomas.

Ainda outros muitos profitizarão da uinda do Mexia, como foi Balaam, que profitizou do Mexia na terceira idade, segundo se contem no Liuro dos Numeros, no capitolo xxiiii, onde se diz: "Nacera huma estrela de Iacob e aleuantarsea huma vara de Isrrael."

Mas, porem, nesta quarta idade, muito mais claramente do Mexia profitizarão os profetas como foi Dauid, ho qual falou de todos hos misterios do Mexia muito euidentemente. Depois dele, profitizarão aqueles grandes profetas como foi Isaias, Ieremias, Ezechiel. Daniel, polo numero das suas somanas, demostrou a uinda do Mexia onde se montarão quatrocentos e nouenta anos, ates que ho Mexia morreo. Do

[25] According to Josephus (Ant. 6.13.5). For further clarification, cf. H. St. J. Thackeray's note in his edition of the Antiquities (London, 1934), 313, note c.

[26] 1 Sam. 11:14f.

[27] 1 Sam. 13:13f.

[28] The correct reference is 1 Sam. 13:14.

[29] 2 Kings 25:1.

[30] Chron., 41, PL, 84:1033; Etym. 5.39, ed. W. M. Lindsay, 1, ad loc. (PL, 82:224).

ted king.[25] They requested a king, who was Saul,[26] but because of his disobedience he did not reign for long and David succeeded him (I Kings 16).[27] The latter so pleased God that He said: [*fol. 3v*] *I have found a man after my own heart.*[28] David did please God greatly; as greatly as Saul displeased Him, so did David, the beloved of God, please Him.

The fourth age commenced with this blessed and holy king and continued until the captivity imposed by King Nebuchadnezzar who destroyed the Holy City with its Temple and plundered the holy vessels. It was he who captured King Zedekiah and all the flower of Israel, as is stated in the Fourth Book of Kings, chapter 25.[29] This age lasted for a period of four hundred and eighty-five years, according to the judgment of Saint Isidore. Many kings reigned during this age, for twenty-two kings reigned in the tribe of Judah for a period of 484 years and six months, counting from David to Zedekiah.[30] In Israel there reigned eighteen kings over a period of two hundred and fifty years and seven days.[31] So it was in the Kingdom of Israel, after the tribes were divided in the time of Rehoboam, as it was in the Kingdom of Judah, of which Saul was the first king and Zedekiah the last.

Inasmuch as Adam had prophesied in the first age concerning the Messiah, when he said: *Now this is bone of my bones, and flesh of my flesh. For this reason a man will leave his mother and father and cleave to his wife* (Genesis, chapter 2).[32] This would signify the union of the Messiah with the Church.[33] For this reason some doctors,[34] disagreeing with St. Thomas, say that even though Adam were not to have sinned, the Messiah would still have assumed human form.[35]

There are yet many others who prophesied the coming of Christ, such as Balaam in the third age, according to the Book of Numbers, chapter 24, where it is said: *A star will be born out of Jacob and a staff will rise out of Israel.*[36]

However, it was in the fourth age that the predictions of the prophets concerning the Messiah were clearer. Especially so were those of David who spoke unequivocally of the mysteries of the Messiah. After David there followed the great prophets Isaiah, Jeremiah, and Ezekiel. Daniel, through the number of his weeks, also revealed the coming of the Messiah, computing four hundred and ninety years until His death.[37]

[31] Source unknown.
[32] Cf. Gen. 2:23f.
[33] Cf. Eph. 5:22f.
[34] Duns Scotus, *Reportata parisiensa*, 3, 7, 4.
[35] Thom. Aquinas, *Summa theologiae*, 3, 1, 3.
[36] Num. 24:17.
[37] Cf. Dan. 9:26f.

tempo que ho anio Guabriel falou com Daniel, profitizarão hos doze profetas e todos estes falarão do Mexia, huns na quarta idade antes do catiueiro, e outros depois do catiueiro, como Malachias e outros.

A quinta idade se começou na transmigração de Babilonia, quando hos iudeus forão catiuos por Nabuchodonosor e leuados a Babilonia onde esteuerão setenta anos en catiueiro, como Isaias lhes tinha profitizado no capitolo vinte e tres. Esta idade durou ates a uinda do Mexia, por espaço de quinhentos anos, comprehendo hos setenta que esteuerão no catiueiro.

[fol. 4r] Estes anos desta quinta idade, segundo alguns dizem, se começarão no vndecimo ano do rreinado delrrei Sedechias e se acabarão no segundo ano delrrei Dario; assi ho afirma Eusebio. Iosepho, no liuro das *Antiguidades*, e Sam Ieronimo sobre ho profeta Ezechiel, começão de contar estes anos do terciodecimo ano delrrei Iosias, ates ho terceiro ano de Ciro, rrei de Persia. Assi que as opiniões sam diuersas acerqua destes anos e desta idade quinta pera saber quando se começou, a qual durou ates a uinda do Mexia promitido na Lei de Moises. Como elle dixe ao pouo: "Hum profeta vos suscitara ho Senhor d'antre vos outros, e este ouuirees como a mim mesmo," no Deuteronomio, no capitolo xviijº.

Esta profeta foi concibido na fim da quinta idade e no tempo que elrrei Herodes rreinaua en Iudea, segundo a profetia de Iacob que tinha profitizado que ho Mexia nom auia de vir senão quando ho rregimento fosse tirado do tribo de Iuda (Genesis, xlix), por huma virgem, chamada Maria, como Isaias tinha predito e prenunciado (capitolo vijº). Esto se aconteceo numa sesta feira aos vinte e cinquo dias de Março, en Nazareth, cidade em Gualilea. E este concibimento foi denunciado polo anio Guabriel, mandado por Deos à Virgem, denunciandolhe que auia de conceber do Spiritu Santo, como loguo concebeo num dia de sesta feira em ho qual Adam foi criado no campo damaceno (que esta a paar de Hebrom), do limo da terra vermelha e loguo no mesmo dia sexto

---

[38] Dan. 8:15-26, 9:21-27.

[39] Isa. 23:15.

[40] Isidore cites 587 years (*Chron.* 65, *PL*, 84:1038).

[41] Cf. J. K. Fotheringham, ed., *Eusebii Pamphili Chronici canones* (London, 1923), pp. 176, 186.

[42] Both Josephus (*Ant.*, 10) and St. Jerome (*Comm. in Ezec.* 1:4, *CC*, 75:44ff. [*PL*, 25:44f.]) list the lengths of the reigns of the king but do not speak in terms of the ages as does Machado. See *HS, PL*, 198:1473.

[43] Cf. Deut. 18:15.

[44] Cf. Isa. 7:14.

[45] Cf. Gen. 49:10.

[46] Cf. Luke 1:26-35.

From the time the angel Gabriel spoke with Daniel,[38] the twelve prophets also made predictions regarding the Messiah, some in the fourth age before the captivity, and others afterwards, such as Malachi and others.

The fifth age commenced with the transmigration of the Jews from Babylonia where they were taken by Nebuchadnezzar and where they remained in captivity for seventy years, as Isaiah had prophesied in chapter twenty-three.[39] This age continued for a period of five hundred years including the seventy in captivity, until the coming of the Messiah.[40]

[fol. 4r] According to Eusebius and others, the years of the fifth age began in the eleventh year of the reign of King Zedekiah and ended in the second year of the reign of King Darius.[41] However, according to Josephus in the *Antiquities* and Saint Jerome on the prophet Ezekiel, this age is reckoned from the thirteenth year of the reign of Josiah until the third year of the reign of Cyrus, king of Persia.[42] Thus, as you can see, there are diverse opinions concerning these years and the beginning of the fifth age, which lasted until the coming of the Messiah. He was promised in the Law of Moses, as he said to the people in Deuteronomy, chapter 18: *The Lord will bring forth a prophet from among you, and you will listen to him as you would to Me.*[43]

This prophet was conceived by a virgin called Mary (as was predicted by Isaiah, chapter 7)[44] at the end of the fifth age when King Herod was reigning in Judea. This is in accord with the prophecy of Jacob who had foretold that the Messiah would not come until the dominion be taken from the tribe of Judah (Genesis 49).[45] This conception took place on a Friday, the twenty-fifth day of March, in Nazareth, a city of Galilee. Gabriel, sent by God to the Virgin, revealed to her that she was to conceive through the Holy Spirit,[46] as she did on a Friday. So, too, was Adam created on a Friday in the field of Damascus[47] (which is near Hebron)[48] from the clay of the red earth.[49] On that very same Friday, after creation, Adam was placed in a terrestrial paradise[50] where Eve was

---

[47] This tradition has its source in Jerome who cited a Jewish tradition that the name Damascus is derived from the Hebrew *dam shaqeh* ("drinking blood") and that it was the site of the fratricide of Abel. Later writers report that it was the very birthplace of Adam. See *HS*, Gen. 13, *PL*, 198:1067; *Post.* to Gen. 2:8, 1, Cxv.

[48] Machado appears to be confusing the account of Adam's birth with that of his burial in Hebron in the Cave of the Machpelah. See below, chap. 14, n. 8; *Pirqe de Rabbi Eliezer*, xxi; ed. Friedlander, p. 156.

[49] Cf. Gen. 2:7. The reference to "red" is based on a Hebrew play on words in which *'adam* (Adam, man), *'adamah* (earth), and *'adom* (red) are connected. See Josephus (*Ant.*, 1.1.2), who is cited in this connection in *HS*, Gen. 18, *PL*, 198:1071.

[50] Cf. Gen. 2:8, 15.

depois da criação, foi leuado ao paraiso terreal onde Eua, da sua propria costa foi formada, pecando no mesmo dia, no qual loguo forão lançados fora. Assi que neste dia de sesta feira ho Mexia foi concibido, que foi no fim da quinta idade, e na sesta feira, reuolutos trinta e tres anos, partio deste mundo ia na sesta idade, como prouaremos. E porquanto na sesta feira se acontecerão estas cousas tão grandes e excelentes, portanto, este dia he de muita veneração acerqua dos christãos. E segundo alguns dizem, na sesta feira, Abel iusto, primeiro martir e figura do Mexia, no qual, segundo Sam Gregorio, se começou a Igreia, foi morto por Cain; e Melchesedech, no mesmo dia, a Deos ofereceo pam e vinho; Isaac foi imolado e sacrificado no monte Moria; Sam Iohão Baptista deguolado; e Santiaguo Zebedeu, por mandado de Herodes, no mesmo dia morte e paixão padeceo, em ho qual Christo quis sofrer paixão.

Esta he a nossa fee, peçouos que esta seia tambem a uossa. Amen.

[*fol. 4v*] Capitolo Segundo fala de como a sexta idade se começou no Mexia, e dos seus misterios que elle obrou ates a morte.

A sexta idade se começou no nacimento de Christo, nosso Redentor e Saluador, Mexia promitido na Lei de Moises, como estaua prenunciado e declarado polos profetas, acabados desdo[a] começo do mundo ates ho nacimento do Mexia cinquo mil e cento e nouenta e oyto anos. Per espaço de tanto tempo quis ho Mexia prolonguar e difirir sua vinda pera que hos filhos de Adam esteuerem ia conuincidos polas leis da natureza e de Moises. Esta idade durou por espaço de mil e quinhentos e corenta e hum anos ates ho tempo presente. Nem sabemos quando fenecera nem quando se ella deue de acabar, porque esta certeza pera si Deos eterno rreseruou e guardou, polo qual nom sabemos ho dia nem ha hora. Porem, bem sabemos que esta idade deue de fenecer no tempo do antichristo, e durara ates ho dia do iuizo, do qual ninguem nom sabe por certeza quando sera depois da vinda do antichristo, nem quanto durara. Esta idade sera a seitima que se começara no antichristo, e a outaua idade se começara nos bemauenturados e durara pera todo sempre.

Tornando a nossa idade sexta, na qual estamos e viuemos, dizemos que se começou no nacimento do Mexia, ho qual naceo na cidade de

a　+*do*

51 Cf. Gen. 2:22.

formed from his own rib.[51] When they sinned on that very day, they were both hurled forth.[52] Thus was the Messiah conceived on a Friday at the end of the fifth age, departing from this world in the sixth age, after thirty-three years, as we shall prove. With so many great and wonderful things having occurred on Friday, it is no wonder that this day is greatly venerated among Christians. According to some, it was on Friday that Abel the Just, the first martyr and figure of Christ, and the one with whom — according to Saint Gregory — the Church began, was killed by Cain.[53] Further, on this same day Melchizedek offered God bread and wine; Isaac was immolated and sacrificed on Mount Moriah, Saint John the Baptist was beheaded, and Saint James Zebedee, by order of Herod, suffered and died on that very day on which Christ wished to suffer the passion.

This is our faith. I ask that it be yours as well. Amen.

[*fol. 4v*] Chapter Two speaks of how the sixth age began with the Messiah, and of the mysteries He worked until His death.

The sixth age commenced with the birth of Christ, our Redeemer and Savior, the Messiah promised in the Law of Moses, as predicted and declared by the prophets. Five thousand one hundred and ninety-eight years passed from the beginning of the world until He was born.[1] The Messiah wished to postpone His coming this long so that the children of Adam might become convinced by the laws of nature and of Moses. This age lasted for a period of one thousand five hundred and forty-one years, that is, until the present time. We know neither the hour nor the day when this age will terminate, for God eternal guards this knowledge for Himself. However, we do know that this age is to come to an end in the time of the Antichrist and is to continue until the Day of Judgment. No one knows for a certainty how long after the coming of the Antichrist this day will come nor how long it will last. The seventh age commences with the Antichrist; the eight age with the blessed, and this will endure forever.

Turning now to our sixth age in which we live, we say that it began with the birth of the Messiah who was born in the city of David, called Bethlehem. This was the prediction of the prophet Micah, chapter five,

---

[52] Cf. Gen. 3:6.
[53] *Hom. in Ezec.*, 2.3, *PL*, 76:966. Cf. *Mor. in Job*, 29, *PL*, 76:515.
[54] I have not been able to locate the source of these traditions.

[1] Comestor lists 5196 years in addition to an anonymous reckoning of 5199 years. *HS*, Evang. 5, *PL*, 198:1540.

Dauid, chamada Betlee*m*. Assi ho p*r*edixe ho profeta Micheas no
capitolo quinto, onde diz, falando do nacime*n*to do Mexia: "E tu,
Betleem, terra de Iudea, en nhu*m*a maneira es pequena antre hos p*r*incipes de Iuda, mas de ti saira hum duque, ho qual regera ho meu
pouo." Isto confirmarão hos doutores iudeus a Herodes quando lhes
pe*r*guntou onde auia de nacer ho Mexia, vindo hos reis maguos em
busqua dele (Mathei, 2º capitolo). Naceo este Mexia no ano qua-
dragesemo segundo do emperador Outauiano Cesar Augusto, ho qual
todos hos rroma*n*os adorauão como a D*e*os e lhe[b] atribuião ho louuor e
temor e honrra diuida a D*e*os ete*r*no porqua*n*to tinha ho rreino em
muita paz e concordia. Mas a sibila, por D*e*os inspirada no ceo, lhe
demostrou a V*ir*gem co*n*sagrada co*m* ho menino Mexia no colo, por
onde Outauiano conheceo que outro D*e*os auia no mu*n*do maior que
não elle, polo qual não quis consintir que aquela honrra deuida a D*e*os
lhe fosse mais co*m*municada. Assi que polos grandes misterios que se
acontecerão no nacimento deste minino, bem podemos concludir que
elle era ho Mexia prometido na Lei de Moises porque taes e tão nobres
cousas nu*n*qua se virão en nacimento algu*m*, e posto que hos co*n*-
cibime*n*tos e nacimentos de Isaac, Hismael, Sampsão fossem grandes e
dinos de muita amiração, no*m* como ho de Ch*r*i*s*to.

[*fol. 5r*] Estes são hos grandes misterios que acontecerão ao Mexia no
seu nacimento, que loguo hos anios naquela noytee que elle naceo em
Betleem parecerão e canta*n*do e alegra*n*do se derão graças e louuores a
D*e*os ete*r*no, ho q*ue* uos no*m* acharas[c] no vosso[d] Testamento *ser* communicado a algu*m*a pessoa. E hos pastores loguo ho forão adorar e lhe
leuarão dooe*n*s, e ho boy e ho asno lhe demostrarão veneração no
presepe e ma*n*iadoura onde iazia, como Isaias tinha profitizado (capitolo p*r*imei*r*o), porque "ho boi e ho asno conhecerão seu se*n*ho*r*; mas
Isrrael na*m* no conheceo." Hos rreis maguos aos treze dias ho vierão
adorar, trazendolhe ouro, ence*n*so, mirra. Assi ho tinhão profitizado
Dauid e Isaias, segundo se prouara qua*n*do falarmos das prop*r*iedades
co*m*municadas ao Mexia.

b MS *lhes*   c + *O iudeu* exp.   d + *teu* exp.

[2] The correct reference is to Matt. 2:6 which is based on Mic. 5:1 (5:2).
[3] Cf. Matt. 2:1-6.
[4] *HS*, Evang. 5, *PL*, 198:1540.
[5] Sibylline literature enjoyed popularity in Europe during the sixteenth century. Gil Vincente (d.
ca. 1536) dedicated one play to the sibyl, his *Auto da Sibila Cassandra*. In his *Auto chamado de Mofina
Mendes* there is a reference to the legend of the sibyl's appearance before Augustus Caesar:

where he says, speaking of the birth of Christ: *And you, Bethlehem, land of Judah, are in no way little among the princes of Judah, for from you a leader will come forth who will rule My people.*[2] This was confirmed to Herod by the Jewish doctors when he asked them where the Messiah was to be born, when the three Wise Men had come in search of Him (Matthew, chapter 2).[3] The Messiah was born in the forty-second year of the emperor Octavian Augustus Caesar,[4] whom all the Romans adored as if he were God. They bestowed on him the praise, awe, and honor due to God eternal, because there was peace and concord in the kingdom during his reign. But the Sibyl, inspired by God in heaven, showed him the Holy Virgin with the Christ Child in her arms and Octavian then knew that there was another God in the world greater than he. From that time on he no longer wished to receive honor in a way appropriate only to God.[5] Thus, because of these great mysteries attached to the birth of the child, we can well conclude that He was the Messiah promised in the Law of Moses. Never have such noble things occurred with any birth. Although the conceptions and births of Isaac, Ishmael, and Samson may have been great and worthy of much admiration, they in no way surpass that of Christ.

[*fol. 5r*] These are the great mysteries that surrounded the Messiah at his birth. On the night after He was born in Bethlehem, the angels appeared, singing and rejoicing, and giving such thanks and praises to God eternal, as you[6] will find ascribed to no one in your Testament. Then the shepherds went with gifts to adore him; the ox and the ass paid reverence to Him in the manger at the crib where He lay, as Isaiah had prophesied (chapter one), because *the ox and the ass knew their master; but Israel knew him not.*[7] Thirteen days later, the Three Kings came to adore Him, bringing Him gold, incense, and myrrh.[8] This had been prophesied by David and Isaiah, as will be demonstrated when we speak of the characteristics attributed to the Messiah.

> Cassandra del rey Priamo
> mostrou essa rosa frol [the Virgin]
> com hū menino a par do sol
> a Cesar Octoauiano
> que o adorou por Senhor (fol. 21*v*).

This popular legend refers to the sibyl of Tibur (and not Vicente's Cassandra) who was supposed to have prophesied the coming of the true Messiah to Octavius. (Réné Schneider, *Rome: Complexité et harmonie,* 10th ed., [Paris, 1908], p. 103). The *Legenda aurea sanctorum* of Jacobus de Voragine (d. 1298) relate briefly, but in more detail than does Machado, the account of Octavius' meeting with the sibyl. Two copies of Voragine's *Legenda sanctorum,* one or both of which Machado may have seen, are in the Alcobaça manuscript collection at the National Library in Lisbon, MSS 39 and 40.

[6] MS has "O Jew" expunged. See note *c*.

[7] Isa. 1:3.

[8] Matt. 2:11.

Acabados quorenta dias depois do seu nacimento, presentado foi no Templo a Simão, ho qual ho ofereceo a Deos, dando por elle dooens que estauão ordenados pola Lei no Leuitico, capitolo xij°. Neste comenos, querendo Herodes, que era rrei estrangeiro, rreinar no rreino, auendo porem medo que ho Mexia rreinasse, mandou matar todos hos mininos daquela comarca, acabados dous anos depois do nacimento, cuidando que podesse tambem matar ho minino Mexia. Mas ho anio loguo amoestou a Ioseth que se partisse com Maria e com ho menino pera ho Egito, onde esteuerão per espaço de sete anos, segundo diz a Grosa Ordinaria no segundo capitolo de Sam Matheus ᵉ(outros dizem que cinquo).ᵉ Aqui se comprio a profitia de Isaias no capitolo xix, onde se diz: "Olha que ho Senhor subira sobre huma nuuem muito leue," (que era a carne humana que tomou sem pecado), "e entrara no Egito e todolos idolos se comouerão." E assi foi que todolos idolos cairão quando ho menino entrou no Egito.

Isto se aconteceo no ano primeiro do nacimento do Mexia, e no tricesimo ano do rreinado de Herodes. E no trigesimo oytauo ano do seu rreinado feneceo e morreo maa morte, segundo se contem na *Hestoria Escolastica*. E loguo no oytauo ano do nacimento do Mexia mandou ho anio a Ioseph que se tornasse pera Iudea. Antão se comprio a profitia do profeta Osee, capitolo xi, onde se diz: "Do Egito chamei ho meu filho." E posto que esta profitia se entenda do pouo de Isrrael, ho qual Deos chamou do Egito pera Terra da Promissão, esto porem he impropriamente; mas propriamente se entende do Mexia, ho qual era filho natural de Deos, e ho pouo de Isrrael era adoutiuo. Assi como dizemos que aquilo que se escreue no Primeiro Liuro de Paralipemenom, capitolo xxij°: "Eu serei seu pai e elle sera meu filho," [*fol. 5v*] se entende de Salamão em alguma maneira, mas propriamente se entende do Mexia, como Sam Paulo proua no primeiro capitolo da Epistola dos Hebreus.

Morto Herodes, socedeo no reino seu filho Archelao, tão cruel e maluado como ele, e no seu primeiro ano do reinado se tornou Ioseph

---

e-e int.

⁹ Cf. Luke 2:25-28.
¹⁰ Cf. Lev. 12:6-8.
¹¹ Two years or younger according to Matt. 3:16.
¹² Matt. 2:13-16.
¹³ No source located. In the MS, this phrase is an interlinear addition. See note *e*.
¹⁴ *PL*, 114:76.
¹⁵ Isa. 19:1.

Forty days after His birth, He was presented to Simon in the Temple, who consecrated Him to God[9] and made offerings for Him as was ordered by the Law in Leviticus, chapter 12.[10] At that time, King Herod, who was a foreigner, feared that the Messiah would rule over his kingdom. He thus ordered that all the male children in that district who had reached the age of two[11] be killed, thinking that in that way he might also be able to kill the Christ child. But the angel warned Joseph and told him to depart with Mary and the child for Egypt,[12] where they remained for a period of seven years, (some say five),[13] according to the *Glossa Ordinaria*, Saint Matthew, second chapter.[14] Thus was fulfilled the prophecy of Isaiah in chapter 19, where it says: *Behold the Lord will mount upon a very swift cloud,* (which was the human flesh, free from sin, which He took), *and will enter Egypt and all the idols will be shaken.*[15] So it was that all the idols fell when the child entered Egypt.

This occurred in the first year of the birth of the Messiah and in the thirteenth year of the reign of Herod. According to the *Scholastic History*, Herod died a cruel death during the thirty-eighth year of his reign.[16] When the Messiah was eight years[17] old the angel ordered Joseph to return to Judea. Thus was fulfilled the prophecy of Hosea, chapter 11, where it is said: *I called my son out of Egypt.*[18] It is improper to refer this prophecy to the children of Israel whom God called forth from Egypt to go to the Promised Land. Rather this prophecy properly refers to the Messiah who was the natural son of God while the people of Israel was the adopted son.[19] In like manner we say that that which is written in the First Book of Chronicles, chapter 22: *I will be his father and he will be my son,*[20] [*fol. 5v*] is in some way to be interpreted as referring to Solomon. Yet it is properly to be understood as referring to the Messiah, as Saint Paul proves in his first chapter of the Epistle to the Hebrews.[21]

Joseph and Mary returned to Judea with the child, during the first year of the reign of the cruel and wicked King Archelaus who succeeded his father king Herod to the throne,[22] when the latter died.

---

[16] *HS*, Evang., 5, 18, *PL*, 198:1540, 1547, according to which Herod died in the thirty-seventh year of his reign rather than in the thirty-eighth.

[17] Cf. Matt. 2:19f. The age of eight years is based on the assumption of a seven year exile.

[18] Hos. 11:1.

[19] Cf. Matt. 2:15; Jerome, *Comm. in Matt., CC,* 77:14 (*PL* 26:27), A polemic against this christological interpretation of Hos. 11:1 is found in Jewish tradition. See the Targum *ad loc.* and the references in *CC*, 76:120f. (*PL*, 25:914f.) and *Post.,* 2, hhhr.

[20] 1 Chron. 22:10.

[21] Heb. 1:1-5.

[22] *HS*, Evang. 18, *PL*, 198:1547.

com Maria e com ho menino pera Iuda. Amoestados pelo anio, e auendo medo de Archelao que reinaua en Iuda, se forão pera Galilea e morarão en Nazareth, sendo ho Mexia de oyto anos, do qual hos euangelistas nom fazem menção senão depois que chegou aos trinta anos, tirando, porem, Sam Lucas que diz que, sendo elle de doze anos, se desputou com hos doutores da Lei no Templo (Luce, ij° capitolo).

Sendo ho Mexia de quinze anos, morreo Outauiano, segundo emperador de Roma (porque Iulio Cesar foi ho primeiro), depois que emperou e rreinou cinquoenta e sete anos e seis meses e dez dias, rreinando com elle quatorze anos Antonio. Outros dizem que rreinou cinquoenta e seis anos; outros affirmão cinqoenta e oyto anos e meo, e morreo de idade de setenta e sete anos.

Depois deste loguo socedeo ho terceiro emperador, chamado Tiberio Cesar. No ano quintodecimo deste fez ho Mexia trinta anos, andando Sam Iohão baptizando no rio de Iurdão (Luce, 3° capitolo), ao qual Christo foi pera tomar ho seu bautismo. E como foi bautizado, foise pera ho deserto que esta antre Ierusalem e Ierricho, onde ieiunou quorenta dias e corenta noites sem comer e sem beber (Mathei, 4° capitolo), hos quaes como fossem acabados, loguo escolheo doze discipolos principaes e setenta e dous menos principaes e hos mandou preguar por Iudea a sua vinda, dandolhes poder de fazerem milagres e sobre hos demonios (Mathei, x° capitolo).

Christo, porem, sabendo que Sam Iohão era deguolado, loguo pubricamente começou de preguar aos iudeus, demostrandose ser elle ho Mexia e profeta promitido na Lei, e Filho de Deos, isto fazendo por espaço de tres anos e meo, polo qual tanto odio conceberão Anas Caiphas, e escriuaes e phariseus, que falsamente ho acusarão a Pontio Pilato que antão em Iudea era presidente, ho qual deu a sentença contra Christo que morresse crucificado no monte Moria, chamado Caluario.

Morreo, pois, Christo aos vinte e cinquo dias de Março, luna quintadecima. Iouue no sepulcro por espaço de corenta horas, rresurgindo aos vinte e sete dias de Março, aparecendo aos seus discipolos per espaço de corenta dias, hos quaes acabados, subio aos ceos no monte

[23] *HS*, Evang. 23, *PL*, 198:1549.

[24] Luke 2:42-47.

[25] Cf. Eusebius, *Chron.* (ed. Fotheringham), pp. 188, 239; Isidore, *Etym.* 5.39.25, ed., W. M. Lindsay, 1, *ad loc.* (*PL*, 82:226).

[26] This paragraph follows *HS*, Evang. 26, *PL*, 198:1550.

[27] *HS*, Evang. 27, *PL*, 198:1551.

[28] *HS*, Evang. 30, *PL*, 198:1552.

[29] *HS*, Evang. 35, *PL,* 198:1556.

[30] Matt. 4:2.

However, since they were warned by the angel and feared Archelaus who was reigning in Judea, they went to Galilee and dwelled in Nazareth.[23] At that time the Messiah was eight years old. The Evangelists make no mention of His age until He is thirty, with the exception of Saint Luke who says that, when He was twelve, He disputed in the Temple with the doctors of the Law (Luke, chapter 2).[24]

When the Messiah was fifteen, Octavian, the second emperor of Rome (Julius Caesar was the first),[25] died after having reigned as emperor for fifty-seven years, six months and ten days. Anthony reigned along with him for fourteen years. There are those who claim that he reigned for fifty-six years and still others who affirm that it was for fifty-eight years and a half and that he died at the age of seventy-seven.[26]

Tiberius Caesar succeeded Octavian and became the third emperor.[27] In the fifteenth year of his reign, the Messiah attained the age of thirty years, and went to Saint John, who was baptizing in the River Jordan (Luke, chapter 3), to be baptized.[28] After He was baptized, Christ went to the desert that lies between Jerusalem and Jericho and there fasted for forty days and forty nights,[29] neither eating nor drinking (Matthew, chapter 4).[30] At the end of that time, He chose twelve principal disciples and seventy-two lesser ones[31] and sent them to preach His coming throughout Judea, granting them the power to perform miracles and power over devils (Matthew, chapter 10).[32]

When Christ knew that Saint John had been beheaded. He began to preach publicly to the Jews, proving to them that He was the Messiah promised in the Law: the Son of God. This he did for three and one-half years. During this time he was hated by Annas Caiaphas and the scribes and Pharisees, and they falsely denounced him to Pontius Pilate who was then procurator of Judea. Pilate passed sentence on Him, ordering His death by crucifixion on Mount Moriah, called Calvary.[33]

So Christ died on the twenty-fifth day of March,[34] the fifteenth day of the lunar month,[35] and lay in the sepulchre for forty hours. He arose on the twenty-seventh day of March, appearing before His disciples for a period of forty days.[36] He then ascended into heaven from the top of

---

[31] Luke 10:1. Cf. *HS*, Evang. 67, *PL*, 198:1572: "In coronis ecclesiarum sunt duodecim majores turres, quasi duodecim apostoli, et duodecim minores, quasi duodecim prophetae".

[32] Matt. 10:1.

[33] Matt. 27:2, 26; Mark 15:1, 15; Luke 23:1, 24, 33; John 18:12f., 28f.; 19:16.

[34] Ecclesiastical tradition, following Tertullian, places the crucifixion on March 25. The other dates mentioned here follow from this. See Tertullian, *Adversus Judaeos*, ch. 8; Louis Marie Duchesne, *Christian Worship: Its Origin and Development* (London, 1927), pp. 262ff.

[35] The fifteenth day of Nisan, the first month in the Jewish calendar.

[36] Matt. 28:1ff.; Mark 16:1ff.; Luke 24:1-6, 33; John 20:1ff.

Oliuete aos tres dias de Maio, e mandou ho Spiritu Santo sobre hos discipolos aos treze dias de Maio, polos quaes esta nossa Igreia foi fundada, sem a fee da qual ninguem nom se pode saluar.

Vees aqui[f], irmãos, a nossa fee que afirma que ia ho Mexia veo, segundo aqui vos prouaremos.

Esta he, pois, a nossa fee, peçouos que tambem seia a uossa. Amen.

[*fol. 6r*] Capitolo Terceiro fala de como a vinda do Mexia foi apresada depois que hos profetas dele começarão de profitizar.

Nos christãos, geeração nobre e rregual, cremos na Santa Madre Igreia, fora da qual nom ha hi saluação nem saude. Cremos que ninguem nom se pode saluar sem ha aguoa do bautismo. Cremos em Ihesu Christo, Filho de Deos eterno, Mexia promitido na Lei que ia veo tomar carne humana no ventre da sacratissima Virgem Maria, pera saluar a geeração humanal. Creemos que Christo ha de vir iulguar hos viuos e mortos e dara a cada hum segundo seu mericimento.

Vos outros, porem, senhores,[a] estaes obstinados na fee de Christo e encredolos, nom crendo nada dessas cousas, mas antes escarneces dos christiãos e da sua Lei, fingindo vos que ha tendes e que nela credes; mas, porem, nom leixaes de fazer mil sinaguoguas e aiuntamentos falsos, enguanosos — e aguora nestes dias passados forãonos veer manifestos — nos quaes persuades e demostraes ao vosso pouo simplez e idiota e boçal que ho Mexia ainda nom he vindo. Polo qual, neste liuro, vos prouaremos que ho Mexia he vindo, polos vossos profetas e polo vosso Talmud, ho qual foi causa da vossa perdição, e polos vossos talmudistas, e que todas as propriedades e cousas que erão escritas do Mexias, todas forão communicadas e achadas em Christo, nosso Saluador. E pera fundamento desta obra vos proponho esta conclusão e proposição chatolica e fiel e verdadeira, a qual quem nom creer, nom se pode saluar. Ha mil e quinhe[n]tos e corenta e hum anos que ho Mexia veo a este mundo tomar carne humana pera nos saluar, e ia nom vira senão iulguar hos viuos e mortos.

A primeira propriedade do Mexia foi que a sua vinda era apresada e que cedo avia de vir depois que hos profetas começarão de profitizar. Malachias ho profeta diz, pera proua disto, no terceiro capitolo: "Ex aqui eu vos mando ho meu anio, ho qual aparelhara ho caminho diante

---

f +*O iudeu* exp.   a marg. +*iudeus* exp.

[37] MS has "O Jew" expunged. See note *f*.

[1] Cf. John 14:6.
[2] Cf. John 3:5.

the Mount of Olives on the third day of May. On the thirteenth day of May, He imbued His disciples with the Holy Spirit. They founded the holy Church without whose faith no one can be saved.

Here,[37] brothers, is our faith which affirms that the Messiah has already come, as we shall prove to you.

This, then, is our faith, and I ask that it be yours as well. Amen.

[fol. 6r] Chapter Three speaks of how the coming of the Messiah was imminent after the prophets began their predictions of Him.

We Christians, a noble and regal race, believe in Holy Mother Church, outside of which there is neither salvation nor well-being.[1] We believe that no one can be saved without the water of baptism.[2] We believe in Jesus Christ, Son of God eternal, the Messiah promised in the Law, who had become incarnate in the womb of the Most Holy Virgin Mary to save mankind. We also believe that Christ will come to judge the quick and the dead[3] and that each will receive his due.[4]

You, gentlemen,[5] however, are obstinate disbelievers of Christ's faith. You believe in none of these things but rather mock Christians and their law while all the while feigning that you too now have this law and believe in it. Yet, you continue to form a thousand synagogues and false and deceitful gatherings (which have of late become well-known to us) at which you proceed to persuade and demonstrate to your simple, foolish and uncouth people that the Messiah has still not come. For this reason, we will prove to you in this book that the Messiah has come and that all the characteristics that were written of Him were found in Christ, our Savior. We shall do this by referring to your own prophets, and your talmudists, the cause of your perdition. As the foundation of this work I propose this true and faithful Catholic principle and proposition which must be believed if one is to be saved: one thousand five hundred and forty-one years ago, the Messiah came to this world and assumed human form in order to save us. He will now return only to judge the quick and the dead.

The first characteristic of the Messiah was that His coming was imminent and that He would come soon after the prophets began their prophecies. To prove this, the prophet Malachi says in the third chapter: *Behold My angel whom I send to you who will prepare the way before Me;*

---

[3] Cf. Acts 10:42; 2 Tim. 4:1, 1 Peter 4:5.
[4] Marginal addition. Original reading, "Jews," is expunged. See note *a*.
[5] The foregoing is based upon the Apostles' Creed.

da minha face, e loguo vira pera ho seu templo ho dominador e senhor que vos buscaes, e ho anio do testamento que vos queres." Hos nossos doutores dizem que esta profitia ia he comprida, a qual se entende do Mexia e do seu precursor Sam Iohão Baptista. Mas hos vossos[b] doutores grosadores[c] dizem que ainda nom he conprida, porque se entende do Mexia e de Helias, polo qual vos outros esperaes. Esta vossa sentença nom pode estar nem traz rrezão, porque diz Malachias que ho Mexia hauia de vir ao templo de Salamão. Hora, se este templo he ia destruido e nunqua mais sera rreedificado, por que esperaes por este Mexia, ho qual iamais entrara no templo de Salamão, pois que ia por muitas vezes nele entrou?

[fol. 6v] Se quiserdes dizer, que posto que aguora esteie destruido, que se podra outra vez edificar quando vier ho Mexia, mas dizei por vossa vida, e quem edificara este tempolo? Certamente elle nom sera polos christãos edificado, porque ho noso templo que he a nossa Santa Madre Igreia, excede e sobrepoia ho templo de Salamão; nem por vos outros, [d]meus senhores,[d] porque ates a fim do mundo seres soieitos e catiuos, e nunqua teres mando nem emperio tão alto pera ho poderes edificar; nem polo Mexia sera edificado, como vos credes, porque elle ia veo, e segundo ho dizer de Malachias, ho templo deuia de ser edificado antes que viesse ho Mexia.

E quanto he ao que dizees que esta profitia se entende de Helias Thesbites, ho qual deue de ser precursor do Senhor, entendes isto mal quanto he a uinda do Mexia en carne, [e]e perdoaime,[e] nem essa não foi ha entenção do profeta; mas quanto he a uinda pera iulguar hos viuos e mortos, certamente antão sera Helias precursor, segundo ho proua Malachias no capitolo quarto. E porquanto vos outros ignoraes e nom sabees as duas vindas do Mexia — a da carne e a de iulguar — portanto, nom entendes hos vossos profetas. Isto, porem, poderees creer comnosco, que Helias vira com Enoch, hos quaes estão no paraiso terreal, e virão conuerteruos quando a Lei toda ouuer de ser huma.

Creede que ia ho Mexia esteue no templo de Salamão e iamais la entrara, porque se elle loguo no ouuera de vir ao templo de Salamão, nom

---

b +teus exp.   c +iudeus exp.   d-d +iudeus exp.   e-e int.

6 Mal. 3:1.
7 See Jerome, ad loc., CC, 76A:927ff. (PL, 25:1564f).
8 MS reads "Jews" expunged. See note c.
9 This tradition is cited by Jerome, ibid. For a fuller discussion, see JE, 5:126f.
10 Cf. Jerome, ibid.; Hieronymus de Sancta Fide, ACPJ, 1,2, p. 24.
11 MS reads "Jews" expunged. See note d.
12 Interlinear addition. See note e.
13 Mal. 4:5.

then will the ruler and lord whom you seek come to His temple, and the Angel of the Testament Whom you love.[6] Our doctors say that this prophecy, which is understood to refer to the Messiah and his precursor Saint John the Baptist,[7] has already been fulfilled. But your learned[8] commentators say that it still has not been fulfilled for it is understood to refer to the Messiah and to Elijah, for whom you wait.[9] This opinion bears no truth and cannot be maintained for Malachi says that the Messiah would come to Solomon's Temple. Now, if this Temple has already been destroyed and will never again be rebuilt, why do you continue to wait for the Messiah who entered the Temple many times but will never again do so?[10]

[*fol. 6v*] You may wish to say that although the Temple is now destroyed, it can be rebuilt when the Messiah comes. But tell me, by your life, just who will build this Temple? Certainly not the Christians! For our Temple, which is the Holy Mother Church, excels and surpasses Solomon's Temple. Nor will you, gentlemen,[11] because until the end of time you will be held captive and enslaved and will never have the power or necessary authority to be able to undertake such a task. Nor will it be rebuilt by the Messiah, as you believe, because He has already come and, according to Malachi, the Temple was to be built before the Messiah had come.

Your interpreting this prophecy to refer to Elijah the Tishbite, who must be the precursor of the Lord, leads you to assume erroneously that it speaks of the coming of the Messiah in the flesh. However, excuse me if I say[12] that this was not the intention of the prophet either! For where it concerns the advent of the Messiah to judge the quick and the dead, Elijah will then certainly be the precursor, as Malachi proves in chapter four.[13] Since you are unaware of the two comings of the Messiah — the one in the flesh and the other to render judgment — it follows that you do not understand your own prophets. However, you may be able to believe this along with us: That Elijah will come with Enoch,[14] both of whom are now in the terrestrial paradise, and that they will come to convert you when the Law shall be one.

Believe that the Messiah has already been in the Temple of Solomon and that he will never again enter therein. Had He not come to

---

[14] According to patristic tradition, the "two witnesses" of Rev. 11:3 are Enoch and Elijah who are to appear at the advent of the Antichrist. See Tertullian, *De anima*, 50, *PL*, 2: 780; *Post.* (to Mal. 4:5), 3, PPP*r*.

dixera ho profeta: "Ex aqui; vem." Mas isto dixe porque via a vinda do
Mexia ser apresurada e festina, portanto poos "Ex aqui," que he
sinificada por esta dição latina *ecce*, a qual s[in]ifica tempo apresado e
muito festino. E pois que Sam Ieronimo de hebraico tresladando ho
Testamento Velho em latim neste pa[ss]o poos esta dição *ecce*, a qual
traz tempo apresurado e festino, parece que no hebraico ho mesmo
sinificaua como "veelo aqui," "eu[l]o aqui." Certamente isto dizia ho
profeta porque via ia quase ho Mexia presente porque elle foi ho que
derradeiro profitizou da vinda do Mexia.

E pera saberdes como Malachias falaua da vinda do Mexia apresada,
olhai ho que diz no capitolo primeiro: "Diz o Deos dos exercitos ou das
batalhas: 'Ia vos outros me aborrecestes e caistes da [von]tade, e portanto, sabee que ia nom ey de receber doom algum ou sacrifitio da [voss]a
mão. Mas sabee que desde oriente ates ho ponente, grande h[e] ho meu
nome antre hos gentios, [*fol. 7r*] e em todo luguar hum sacrifitio limpo e
puro me he ofericido, porque ho meu nome he grande antre hos gentios.'" Esta profitia bem demostra que hos vossos sacrifitios e vossas
cerimonias e modos de viuer ia a Deos auorrecião e nam hos queria
receber, como ia no tempo passado tinha recibido, onde se demostra
claramente que, pois, taes cousas como estas, dizia ho profeta que nom
erãoᶠ senão porquanto ia ho Mexia estaua de caminho, porque nos vemos esta profitia comprida, segundo isto que nela se contem. Diz ho
profeta que Deos nom auia de aceitar hos vossos sacrifitios, e vos bem
vedes que não são aceitos porque, segundo vossa Lei, ho luguar de sacrificar nom era senão na cidade de Ierusalem (Deuteronomio xvi°), pois
aguora nela nom se oferece vosso sacrifitio mas ho nosso, no Santo
Sepulcro, onde se celebra ho nome de Ihesus. Como dixe ho profeta
que ho seu nome auia de ser grande antre hos gentios, assi he aguora
que ho seu nome he grande en toda Europa, em Asia, e ia foi en Africa.
Assi que nom tenhaes debate nem duuida porque certamente esta profitia
ia he comprida.

Bem se parece que a vinda do Mexia foi apresada depois que este
profeta começou de profitizar a vinda do Mexia, ho qual se demostrou
por esta dição latina *ecce*, que quer dizer, assi em latim como em
hebraico, "Eulo aqui, eulo; vem." Palauras sam mais do tempo presente
que não do futuro. Ho profeta Zacharias disto daa testimunho quando
diz, no capitolo nono: "Alegrate asaz, filha de Sion; alegrate, filha de

f MS era

[15] For the notion that *ecce* in these verses implies immediacy, see *ACPJ*, 1, 2, pp. 24ff.; Alphonsus
de Spina, *FF*, fol. 35*v*.

Solomon's Temple, the prophet would not have said: *Behold, he comes.* He said this, however, because he saw that the coming of the Messiah was to be imminent and proximate. Consequently he wrote *Behold,* which represents the Latin *ecce,* which in turn signifies a time which is imminent and proximate. In translating the Old Testament from Hebrew into Latin, Saint Jerome also used this word *ecce,* which indicates an imminent and proximate event and it appears that in Hebrew it also signifies "see him," "behold him." It is obvious that this prophet said this because he felt the Messiah to be almost present, for Malachi was the last to prophesy the coming of the Messiah.[15]

So that you may know how the prophet spoke of the imminent advent of the Messiah, see what he says in the first chapter: *The God of hosts and of battles says: You have displeased Me and have fallen from My favor; thus, know that no more shall I receive any offering or sacrifice from your hand. Yet know that from East to West, great is My name amongst the nations, [fol. 7r] and that a clean and pure sacrifice has everywhere been offered to Me, for great is My name among the nations.*[16] This prophecy unquestionably shows that your sacrifices, ceremonies and way of life were displeasing to God and that He no longer wished to receive them as He had in days of old. It is clear then that such things as these were said by the prophet because the Messiah was already on His way; for this prophecy has been fulfilled, according to that which is contained therein. The prophet says that God would not accept your sacrifices, and you can well see that they are not accepted: According to your law, the sacrificial place was none other than the city of Jerusalem (Deuteronomy 16).[17] Now our sacrifice and not yours is offered there in the Holy Sepulchre where the name of Jesus is celebrated. As the prophet said that His name would be great among the nations, so is it now great in all of Europe and Asia and lately in Africa. Neither debate them nor doubt because this prophecy has certainly been fulfilled.[18]

It indeed appears that the advent of the Messiah was soon to take place after this prophet began to foretell His coming. This has been demonstrated by this Latin word *ecce,* which means in Latin, as in Hebrew, "Here he is, behold, he comes." These words pertain more to the present than to the future. The prophet Zechariah gives testimony

---

[16] Mal. 1:1of.

[17] Cf. Deut. 16:2. The Pentateuch does not specifically mention Jerusalem as the chosen site.

[18] The essence of this paragraph is found in Jerome, *ad loc., CC,* 76A: 911f. (*PL,* 25:1557f.). Cf. the Jewish refutation of this concept, according to which Mal. 3:11 refers not to the Gentiles themselves but to the Jews scattered among them. See David Kimhi, *Comm., ad loc.*

Ierusale*m*, ex aqui ho teu Rrei, vem a ti Iusto e Saluador, elle pobre en-
cima dũma asna e sobre ho filho da asna.''

Se Purtugual ouuese de ser limpo de herisias e de cerimonias
iudaicas, ᵍe de mouros e negros,ᵍ daqui a mil anos, mal soaria dize*r*se:
"Alegrate, Pu*r*tugual, que ex aqui ho teu bem.'' Mas aue*n*do isto de ser
cedo como esperamos, se D*eo*s quiser, antão caie bem diz*er*: "Alegrate,
Pu*r*tugal, por*que* ex aqui ho teu bem. Alegra*te*, Lixboa, que aguora
seras boa.''

Assi ta*m*bem dizemos que porquanto ho profeta sabia q*ue* cedo ho
Mexia auia de vir visitar ho mo*n*te de Sion e a cidade nobre de Ierusalem, portanto dizia: "Ex aqui ho teu Rrei, ve*m*,'' como se esteu*e*ra
ia presente, ho que causaua a claridade da profitia segu*n*do a qual
claramente ho profeta via a vinda do Mexia ap*r*esada. Isto confirma
Isaias, capitolo lxii, quando diz: "Ex aqui ho teu Saluador, vem; ex aqui
a m*e*rce dele co*m* elle, e a obra delle co*m* elle.'' Este profeta ta*m*bem
demostra q*ue* ho Mexia estaua dep*r*esa por esta dição *ecce*. [*fol. 7v*] Mais
claramente desta vinda ap*r*esada fala Isaias no capitolo ci*n*coenta e
dous, falando pola boca de D*eo*s aos vossos predecessores, hos quaes
blasfemauão ho nome de D*eo*s, quando diz: "Por amor disto sabera ho
meu pouo ho meu nome naquele dia, por*que* eu mesmo q*ue* falaua, (*Ecce
adsum*) 'Ex me aqui p*r*esente.''' Nu*n*qua ho profeta dixera "Ex me aqui
p*r*esente'' senão soubera q*ue* ia ho Mexia estaua dep*r*esa, por*que* elle que
falara ao vosso pouo no monte de Sinay e a Moises polo anio, aguora
estaua ia p*r*estes pera elle vir mesmo e falar elle p*er* si como falou co*m*
hos vossosʰ predecessores e no*m* p*er* outr*ar* pessoa, ne*m* per anio, ne*m* por
profeta.

Por vossa vida, que olhes bem estes dizeres destes profetas e to-
mailhe[s] bem ho tento, e especulai sua entença*m*, por*que* no*m*
demostrão outra cousa senão a vinda do Mexia ser ap*r*esada e
ap*r*esurada. E pera maior confirmação disto, olhai ho que diz ho
mesmo profeta no capitolo li, fala*n*do na vinda do Mexia: "Ia ho meu
iusto esta p*er*to, ia ho meu Saluador he saido.'' Que profitia queres mais
clara que esta pera conhec*er* que ho Mexia estaua dep*r*esa pera vir
quando ho profeta isto dixe?, que não dixe isto senão como home*m* que

---

g-g int.   h   +*teus* exp.

---

[19] Zech. 9:9.
[20] "Of Moors and Negroes" interlinear addition. See note *f*. It is estimated that at the time of
Machado's writing, fully ten per cent of the population of Portugal consisted of slaves. Nicholas
Claenarts wrote that "slaves pullulate everywhere. All services are performed by Negro and
Moorish captives," while Garcia de Resende expressed the somewhat exaggerated fear that slaves

to this when he says, in chapter nine: *Rejoice greatly, daughter of Zion; rejoice, daughter of Jerusalem, here is your King, He comes to you, the Just One and the Savior, humble upon an ass, and upon the son of the ass.*[19]

If Portugal were only to be cleansed of heresies and of Jewish ceremonies, as well as of Moors and Negroes,[20] one thousand years from now, one could hardly say: "Rejoice, Portugal, for your beloved is here." But, hoping this will happen soon, God willing, it is appropriate to say: "Rejoice, Portugal, for behold your beloved is here. Rejoice, Lisbon, for now you are well."

We say then that since the prophet knew that the Messiah would soon come to Mount Zion and to the noble city of Jerusalem, he therefore said: "Behold your King comes," as if He were already present. This makes explicit the intent of the prophecy according to which the prophet clearly saw the immediate coming of the Messiah. This is confirmed in Isaiah, chapter 62, when he says: *Behold your Savior comes. Behold his reward with him and his work with him.*[21] This prophet also shows that the Messiah's arrival was proximate through his use of the word *ecce.* [*fol. 7v*] Isaiah speaks more clearly of this in chapter fifty-two when he speaks through the mouth of God to your ancestors (who blasphemed the name of God) and says: *By reason of this My people will know My name on that day, because it was I who said, (ecce adsum) "Behold, I am here."*[22] The prophet never would have said "Behold, I am here" if he had not known that the Messiah was to arrive quickly, for He who had spoken to your people on Mount Sinai and to Moses through the angel[23] was now about to come and speak, not through an angel or through anyone else, but for Himself, as He spoke with your ancestors.[24]

By your lives! Look at the sayings of these prophets, paying close attention to them. Ponder their meaning, for they indicate nothing but that the coming of the Messiah is to be immediate and close. For a greater confirmation of this, look and see what the same prophet says in chapter 51, in speaking of the advent of the Messiah: *Now my Just One is near: now my Savior has gone forth.*[25] What clearer prophecy than this could you wish in order to know that the Messiah was about to come when the prophet said this. For truly he said this as a man who already

---

would soon outnumber free men. See *DHP*, 2:77ff. ; Joel Serrão, *A Emigração Portuguesa* (Lisbon, 1972), p. 68. According to Herculano, Moorish and Negro slaves in this period were baptized but given no religious instruction or real christianization. See *Origin*, pp. 369ff. [501 ff.]

[21] Isa. 62:11.

[22] Isa. 52:6.

[23] Cf. Exod. 19f., Acts 7:30f.

[24] See Gilbert Crispin, *Disputatio Judei et Christiani*, ed. B. Blumenkranz (Utrecht, 1956), p. 58.

[25] Isa. 51:5.

ia ho via à porta. Porque, se ho Mexia ouuera de difirir sua vinda ates este tempo presente, como vos credes falsamente, nom dixera, "Ia ho meu iusto esta perto," mas falara por outros termos que não forão tão declaratiuos da vinda sua apresada. Porque, desdo tempo que ho profeta dixe "Ho meu Saluador he saido," ates este tempo moderno no qual viuemos, correrão dous mil e tantos anos. Se ho antichristo nom ouuer de vir senão daqui a dous mil anos, pareceuos que sera bem dito isto: "Ia he saido, eulo aqui, ia esta presente"? Certamente, mal pareceria este modo de falar por amor da distancia do tempo. Assi, tambem, se ho profeta sintira grande distancia do tempo do Mexia, não dixera, "Ia he saido." Mas porque Deos eterno determinaua cedo de mandar ho Mexia, por isto assi falaua pola boca do profeta, dando a denotar que ia estaua prestes pera vir a este mundo.

Como quer que polos profetas falando da vinda do Mexia, muitas vezes se pooem estas dições em latim: *ecce, adsum, prope, cito,* certamente dão a entender que a entenção dos profetas he [de] demostrar que a uinda do Mexia era apresada depois que ho Templo foi rreedificado, ho qual fora destruido por mandado delrrey Nabuchodonosor. E dali por diante mui claramente começarão hos profetas a demostrar a vinda do Mexia ser muito apresada.

[*fol. 8r*] Bem vedes, senhores, como a uinda do Mexia por estes profetas acima aleguados foi declarada apresada, ho que elles não dixerão senão ia sintindo a vinda do Senhor muito cheguada. Portanto, estai comnosco; crede ho que cremos; nom duuidaes desta vinda; nom tenhaes mais debate nem duuida alguma. Vos bem sabees que emquanto hos filhos de Iacob andarão polo deserto, nom traerão profeta que profi[ti]zasse do Mexia, senão Moises que dixe que d'antre elles auia de sair hum profeta. E depois que entrarão na Terra da Promissão esteuerão muito tempo sem profeta, senão Dauid que profitizou do Mexia, nom preguando ao pouo, mas escreuendo, e isto causou a tardança do Mexia que ainda nom esteua prestes pera vir, nem ho tempo ainda nom era cheguado.

Mas como ho tempo se começou de cheguar, loguo começarão de profitizar tres[i] profetas iuntamente da vinda do Mexia, preguando ao pouo e demostrando que ho Mexia estaua ia perto, e nom auia muito de tardar. E necessario era que viesse pois que elle tinha tempo determinado pera sua vinda, a qual conhecendo, hos profetas começarão de dizer: "Eulo aqui; vem. Ia esta perto." Este tempo deter-

i + *dous*

saw Him at the door! For if the Messiah had postponed His arrival until the present time, as you falsely believe, he would not have said, *Now
my Just One is near,* but would have spoken in terms which did not stress
the immediate quality of His coming. For from the time the prophet
said *My Savior is come forth* up to the present time in which we live, some
two thousand years have passed. If the Antichrist is not to come for
another two thousand years, does it seem right to you to say "Now he is
come forth; behold him; now he is present"? This manner of speaking
would certainly not be justified were the time for the Messiah's coming
not imminent. It thus follows that if the prophet had not felt as he did,
he would not have said, *Now he is come forth.* But because God eternal
determined early to send the Messiah, He spoke this way through the
mouth of the prophet, indicating that He was about to come to this
world.

The prophets' frequent use of such words as *ecce, adsum, prope, cito,*
when speaking of the advent of the Messiah, would certainly imply that
the intention of these men was to indicate that the Messiah was to come
shortly after the rebuilding of the Temple which had been destroyed by
order of King Nebuchadnezzar.[26] From that time on the prophets began
very clearly to show that the coming of the Messiah was approaching.

[*fol. 8r*] You can well see, gentlemen, how these prophets announced
this coming. They would not have done so had they not felt the coming
of the Lord to be very near. Therefore, be with us; believe as we
believe; do not doubt His coming or have any doubts or reservations.
You know very well that while the sons of Jacob marched across the
desert, they had no prophet but Moses, who said that a prophet would
come forth from among them.[27] After they entered the Promised Land,
they were without prophets for a long time. Only David prophesied the
Messiah but he did not preach to the people but rather wrote down his
prophecies. This was due to the fact the Messiah was not ready to
come, for it was not yet time.

But when the time *was* approaching, three prophets began to foretell
His coming to the people, showing that the Messiah was near and
would not delay much longer. It was necessary, however, that He come,
for a time for His advent had already been determined. The prophets
had recognized this, saying *Here He is; He comes. He is already near.* The
time fixed for His coming was before the destruction of the second
Temple and of the Holy City by Titus. As Daniel had foretold in chapter

[26] Cf. 2 Kings 24:10ff., 25:8f.
[27] Cf. Deut. 18:15; *DJC,* p. 34.

minado estaua que antes da segunda destruição do Templo e da Santa
Cidade, a qual foi feita por Tito. Como Daniel tinha profitizado,
capitolo nono, ho Mexia auia de vir tomar carne humana, por onde
desde tempo da sua encarnação, ates a segunda destruição do Templo
correrão setenta e cinquo anos e meo.

Bem diziam loguo hos profetas que a uinda do Senhor era apresada e
festina, como certamente foi. Leede vos ho vosso Talmud e as grossas
sobre elle, e creo que achares alguns verdadeiros testimunhos desta
vinda apresada do Mexia. Ao menos bem sei que no Talmud se alegua
hum texto dos Prouerbios que diz: "Toda a cousa he muito boa no seu
tempo." Sobre este texto, diz ho Talmud: "Esta cousa boa he ho Mexia,
ho qual ia nom pode tardar muyto, mas depresa he a sua vinda." Posto
que isto seia falso do Talmud porque quando isto se escreueo no Cairo
do Egito, ia ho Mexia era vindo, mas dixerão isto hos vossos doutores
porquanto sabiam polos profetas que a vinda do Mexia era apresada.
Mas, por amor da sua obstinação e incredulidade, nom conhecerão ho
tempo determinado do Mexia. Veedes aqui como esta propriedade que
era escrita do Mexia foi communicada a Christo, que foi ho Mexia.

Esta he a nossa fee e crença, peçouos por merce que esta seia tambem
a uossa. Amen.

[fol. 8v] Capitolo Quarto fala de como ho Mexia veo no tempo determinado e ordenado segundo hos ditos dos profetas e dos talmudistas.

A segunda propriedade do Mexia que estaua dele escrita era que auia
de vir no tempo certo e determinado polos profetas e polo Talmud e
talmudistas, a qual foi comprida em Christo Mexia, segundo aqui neste
capitolo vos prouaremos.

Nos christãos por fee e crença temos que ho Mexia veo a este mundo.
E ia sam passados mil e quinhentos e corenta e hum anos, e isto temos
prouado e manifestado polos quatro euangelistas, por Sam Paulo, por

[28] Dan. 9:24f.; Jerome, ad loc., CC, 75A:917ff. (PL, 25:567).

[29] The figure of seventy-five and a half years from the birth of Jesus to the destruction of the
Temple is repeated in chapter five. In agreement with this, in chapter eighteen, a figure of forty-
two years is given for the period between the crucifixion and the arrival of Titus in the Holy Land,
which Machado apparently equates with the date of the destruction of the Temple. However, in
chapter four, Machado cites forty-three years for this period. Still another calculation, seventy-
three and a half years from the birth of Jesus to the destruction, is cited in chapter five. This is
based on an exegesis of Isa. 9:6, according to which forty years were to have passed from the
crucifixion to the destruction. Cf. Martini, PF, p. 763 and see below.

[30] Prov. 15:23.

[31] The source has not been located. Machado's passage may be a corruption of one in B.T.
Sanhedrin (98a) based upon Isa. 60:22 rather than Prov. 15:23 (cited by Martini, PF, p. 395): "It is
written, in its time [will the Messiah come], whilst it is also written, I (the Lord) will hasten it! — If they
are worthy, I will hasten it: if not, [he will come] at the due time" (Sonc., p. 663).

nine, the Messiah would take human form,[28] and from the time of his incarnation until the destruction of the second Temple seventy-five and one-half years would pass.[29]

Hence, the prophets spoke well when they foretold that the coming forth of the Lord was near and at hand as it indeed was. If you read your Talmud and its glosses, I am sure you will find genuine proof of this imminent coming of the Messiah. At least I know that in the Talmud there is the quotation from Proverbs which says: *Everything is good in its time.*[30] On this text the Talmud says: "The good refers to the Messiah who will not delay much longer, for his coming is at hand."[31] Now this interpretation of the Talmud is false because when it was written in the city of Cairo in Egypt,[32] the Messiah had already come. Yet your doctors nevertheless said this since they knew through the prophets of the approaching arrival of the Messiah. But because of their obstinacy and unbelief, they did not know the fixed time of the Messiah. You can see here how this characteristic written of the Messiah was true of Christ, who was He.

This is our faith and belief. I ask you as a favor that this also be yours. Amen.

[*fol. 8v*] Chapter Four speaks of how the Messiah appeared at the time determined and ordained for His coming as is found in the sayings of the prophets and talmudists.

The second characteristic written of the Messiah was that he would appear at the time fixed and determined by the prophets, the Talmud, and the talmudists. This was fulfilled in Christ the Messiah, as we will prove to you in this chapter.

We Christians, through faith and belief, hold it to be true that the Messiah came to this world. One thousand five hundred and forty-one years have now passed. We have proved and shown this through the four Evangelists, Saint Paul, Saint Peter, Saint James Alpheus,[1] Saint

---

[32] This notion is apparently peculiar to Machado and might be based on a misunderstanding of a passage such as that in Hieronymus de S.F., *ACPJ*, 2, 5, p. 181, in which the author, in discussing the development of the Talmud, cites "Rabbi Moyses de Aegypto" (Maimonides, d. 1204). Other Christian writers were better informed concerning the history of the Talmud. Cf. Machado's contemporary, João de Barros, *DE*, p. 60.

[1] On the problem of the authorship of the Epistle of St. James in Catholic tradition, see *DTC*, 8, pt. 1, 272ff.

Sam Pedro, por Santiaguo Alpheu, por Sam Iohão Euangelista, por Sam
Iudas, polos quatro concilios geeraes, polos doutores quatro da Santa
Madre Igreia, e por outros muitos doutores que composerão sobre as
cousas da fee.

Assi que, acerqua da uinda do Mexia, nom teemos duuida nem debate
algum. Vos outros, porem, obstinados e encredolos, nom queres senão
morrer na vossa profia, nom querendo confessar a uinda do Senhor
Mexia, mas falsamente grosaes as profitias que são do Mexia, atribuin-
doas a outras pessoas, como prouaremos, senão pera nom serdes
conuincidos confessar que ho Mexia veo. E eu tenho para mym que se
uos outros quiseseis entrar comnosco por modo de disputa, que cairies
na verdade. Mas vos nom querees comnosco communicar nem praticar
esta vinda do Mexia, senão polos cantinhos andaes fazendo sinaguoguas
e aiuntamentos falsos e erroneos, lendo Moises, ho qual nom entendees
senão segundo a carne, e nom segundo spiritu.

E proua era a Deos que mais cedo se começara esta Inquisição, per
que tantas almas das de vos outros nom se perderão. Portanto, não vos
pese de se fazer esta exequção, porque virees en conhicimento da verdade.

Homens doutissimos teendes que vos examinão, como he ho doutissimo padre e doutor frei Iorge de Santiaguo da ordem dos pre-
guadores; segui a sua doutrina [e] ensenança e nom errares. Rroguai
pola uida e rreal estado do inuictissimo e clarissimo rrei de Purtugual
dom Iohão, ho qual teue por bem de olhar por vossas almas e conscientias, as quaes andauão muito agrauadas e mitidas no iudaismo.
Nom rrogues mal a quem olha por vossas almas e por vossas vidas,
porque isto se faz pera que vos possaes alcançar a benauenturança. De
mim nom vos aqueixees, por vossa vida, porque protesto que não
escreuo contra vos por mal que vos queiro ou por odio que vos tenha,
senão pesame de vos ver assi andar errados e fora da gloria eterna pera
qual fostes criados.

[fol. 9r] Iacob ho patriarcha, estando pera morrer, mandou chamar
todos hos seus filhos pera lhes declarar as cousas vindoiras e que auião
de soceder depois da sua morte, e pera hos benzer segundo ho custume
da Lei. Cheguando ao quarto filho, que era Iudas, dixelhe: "Ho
rregimento e cetro nom sera tirado do tribu de Iuda, nem duque e
regedor da sua casa e coia, ates que nom venha aquele que ha de ser
enuiado, ho qual sera [a] esperança dos gentios" (Genesis, xlix capito-

---

[2] The Councils of Nicaea, Constantinople, Ephesus, and Chalcedon. Cf. St. Gregory the Great as
cited in M. J. Rouet de Journel, *Enchiridion Patristicum* (Brescia, 1922), p. 721.

John the Evangelist, Saint Jude, the four General Councils,[2] and the four doctors of the Holy Mother Church,[3] and through many other doctors who have written concerning matters of faith.

Thus there if neither doubt nor controversy among us concerning the Messiah's advent. You, however, obstinate and incredulous, have no wish other than to die in your disbelief, unwilling to acknowledge the arrival of the Lord Messiah. Instead, you falsely gloss the prophecies that refer to the Messiah, attributing them to others as we shall prove, because you will not be persuaded to admit that the Messiah came. Nevertheless, I am convinced that were you willing to enter into a debate with us, you would surely fall upon the truth. However, you do not wish to enter into such a discussion with us concerning this point, but prefer rather to go from one corner to another forming synagogues and assemblies of falsehood and error and to read Moses whom you understand only according to the flesh and not according to the spirit.

So did it become evident to God that the sooner the Inquisition[4] was established, the fewer of your souls would be lost. Therefore, do not be disturbed about its activities for through them you will come to know the truth.

You have very learned men to examine you, such as Brother Jorge de Santiago of the Order of Preachers.[5] Follow his doctrine and teachings and you will not err. Pray for the life and royal estate of the most invincible and noble King John of Portugal who thinks it well to look after your souls and consciences which are greatly afflicted with Judaism. Do not pray for the ill of him who concerns himself with your souls and lives for this is done so that you may attain bliss. By your lives! Have no quarrel with me for I insist that I am not writing against you because I wish you harm or because I feel hostility towards you. Rather, it grieves me to see you stray in error without the eternal glory for which you were created.

[fol. 9r] When Jacob the Patriarch was about to die, he called for all his sons in order to reveal to them the things that were to happen after his death and to bless them according to the custom of the Law. When he came to the fourth son, Judah, he said to him: *The rule and scepter will not be taken from the tribe of Judah nor a leader or ruler from his house or thigh until he who is to be sent comes who will be the hope of the nations* (Genesis, chapter 49).[6] All our doctors refer this prophecy to the Messiah, saying

[3] The four Doctors *par excellence* of the Roman Church, St. Ambrose, St. Jerome, St. Augustine, and St. Gregory the Great. It should be noted that in sixteenth-century Portuguese sculpture, St. Thomas often replaces St. Gregory. See C. Láfer, *O Judeu em Gil Vicente* (São Paulo, 1963), pp. 66f.

[4] See Introduction.

[5] See Introduction.

[6] Gen. 49:10.

lo). Esta profitia todos hos nossos doutores declarão do Mexia, dizendo
que quando no tribu de Iuda, que era ho real, faltasse duque ou rrei,
que loguo avia de vir ho Mexia, como veo, porque rreinando Herodes,
que nom era iudeu mas estrangeiro de Idumea, veo ho Mexia, que foi
Christo, que antão naceo em Betleem, ho qual vossos predecessores nom
conhecerão por seu mal, e portanto, vos outros, falso entendimento
daes a esta prof[it]ia. Dizees que esta profitia nom se deue de entender
do Mexia, mas dellrrei Saul, ho qual vngido foi por rrei en Silo, luguar
assi chamado, onde estaua ha arca do Testamento a qual tinha as
taboas onde estauão escritos hos Mandamentos — tres que pertencem a
Deos na primeira taboa, e hos sete que pertencem ao proximo na
segunda taboa. Estaua a vara que enfloreceo na mão de Aarom, e ha
vrna ou vaso onde estaua ho mana. E porquanto Saul nom era do tribu
de Iuda mas de Beniamim, dizees que antão foi esta profitia comprida,
dizendo que onde nos teemos no latim, "donec veniat qui mittendus
est" (ates que venha aquel que ha de ser enuiado), no hebraico esta,
"donec veniat Silo," dizendo que esta profitia se auia de comprir en
Silo. E porquanto Saul foi vngido por rrei en Silo, dizees que antão se
comprio ho que dixera Iacob, afirmando que este nome Silo he nome
comum e às vezes sinifiqua "enuiamento," e outras vezes "luguar
proprio," e que nesta profitia se põe por aquele luguar que estaua a par
de Ierusalem, chamado Silo.

Diguouos que estas vossas rrezões carecem de fundamento, porque
falso he ho que dizes, que quando ellrei Saul foi vngido por rrei que a
arca do Testamento estaua em Silo. Certamente se beem leerdes ho
capitolo septimo do Primeiro Liuro dos Rreis achares que a archa
naquele tempo estaua no luguar chamado Chariathiarim, e nom em
Silo, como vos dizees. [fol. 9v] E quanto he ao que dizees que Silo nesta
profitia de Iacob sinifiqua "luguar proprio" — aquele que estaa a paar
de Ierusalam onde ia esteuera a arca do Testamento — falso he, mas
sinifiqua na dita profitia "enuiamento" — aquele do Mexia ho qual foi
enuiado no tempo de Herodes — por onde concludimos que se este
nome Silo nom fora comum, mas nome proprio, nom errarie[a] vos como
errastes, dizendo que na dita profitia Silo se põe por nome proprio de
luguar, ho que nos neguamos, e nom por enuiamento, como nos afirmamos.

a MS erraires

[7] Cf. 1 Sam. 10:1.
[8] Cf. 1 Sam. 4:3.
[9] This division of the decalogue is Augustinian. See *Quaestiones in Heptateuchum*, 71, *PL,* **34**: 620ff.;
HS, Exod. 40, *PL,* 198:1164; *DTC,* 4:166.
[10] Heb. 9:4. Cf. also *Post.,* 1, Nviiiv; Alfonso el Sabio, *General estoria,* p. 398. The rabbinic source

that when there fails to be a duke or king in the royal tribe of Judah
then would the Messiah come, as He did. It was during the reign of
Herod, who was not a Jew but a foreigner from Idumea, that the
Messiah came, Who was Christ, born in Bethlehem. Your ancestors did
not know Him because of their wickedness and for this reason you interpret this prophecy erroneously. You say that it does not pertain to
the Messiah but rather to King Saul who was anointed as king in the
place called Shiloh.[7] In Shiloh stood the ark of the covenant[8] on which
were written the commandments — three which pertained to God on
the first tablet and seven which pertained to man on the second.[9] There
also were the rod that flowered in Aaron's hand and the urn or vessel
which contained the manna.[10] Since Saul was not of the tribe of Judah,
but rather of Benjamin, you therefore say that this prophecy was
fulfilled; for, you continue, where we in Latin have *donec veniat qui mittendus est (until he who is to be sent comes),* in Hebrew one reads *donec veniat
Ṣilo.* According to you, this would prove that this prophecy would be
fulfilled in Shiloh. Consequently, since Saul was anointed king in
Shiloh, you then say that Jacob's words were so fulfilled. In this way,
this very name "Shiloh" is a common noun which sometimes signifies
"sending" while at other times it refers to a particular place. In this
prophecy it refers to that place that was near Jerusalem called Shiloh.[11]

I say to you that this reasoning of yours has no basis, because what
you say is false: that when King Saul was anointed king, the ark of the
covenant was in Shiloh. Surely now, if you read chapter seven of the
First Book of Kings well, you will find that the ark at the time was in a
place called Kiriath-jearim and not in Shiloh, as you say.[12] [*fol. 9v*] False
also is your claim that "Shiloh" in this prophecy of Jacob refers to a
particular place which was near Jerusalem and where the ark of the
covenant had already been. Rather, in this prophecy, it signifies the
"sending" of the Messiah who was sent during the time of Herod. We
conclude therefore that if this name Shiloh had not been a common but
rather a proper noun, you would not have erred in your thinking as
you did. For you claim that in the aforementioned prophecy Shiloh is
used as a proper noun designating place, as we deny, rather than having
the meaning of "sending," as we affirm.

---

for this is B.T. Bava Batra 14a and T. Yoma 3:7. Cf. B.T. Yoma 52b and Gersonides and
Abravanel on 1 Kings 7:9.

[11] See Hieronymus de S.F. *ACPJ*, 1, 4, p. 54. On the interpretation of Gen. 49:10, see Adolf
Posnanski, *Schiloh; ein Beitrag zur Geschichte der Messiaslehre* (Leipzig, 1904), 2 vols. Cf. David Kimhi,
Shorashim, s.v. shly, ed. Biesenthal-Lebrecht, p. 388.

[12] Cf. 1 Sam. 7:1f.

Outros vossos doutores no*m* fartos nem contentos co*m* ha exposição acima posta, veem e danlhe outro entendimento mais ex*t*rauaga*n*te, dizendo que esta profitia de Iacob se entende de Ieroboam, ho qual foi co*n*stituido rrei sobre hos dez tribos que se apa*r*tarão de Rroboa*m* polo seu mao rregimento. Q*u*ando ho coroarão por rrei dos dez tribus em Silo, polo qual dão esta exposição à profitia, "donec veniat Silo," ex-poe*m*, dizendo: "Ieroboa*m* pera ser coroado em Silo."

Dig*u*ouos que ho dizer destes vossos doutores conteem dous errores. Ho p*r*imeiro he que falso he que hos dez tribus coroarão por rrei a Ieroboa*m* em Silo, mas em Sichem foi aleuantado por rrei e no*m* em Silo, e assi ho achares no T*er*ceiro Liuro dos Rreis, no capitolo xij°. Ho segundo erro he que ho dominio ne*m* ma*n*do foi tirado do tribu de Iuda, como diz a profitia, porque ho dominio e ma*n*do fiquou com Rroboa*m* ace*r*qua do tribu de Iuda e Beniamim.

Outros vossos doutores expoe*m* esta profitia delrrei Nabuchodo-nosor, ho qual veo a Ierusale*m* por mandado de D*eos* e catiuou ellrei Sedechias, por onde antão ho dominio e mando foi tirado aos vossos p*r*edecessores.

Todas estas exposições sam falsas e erroneas e contra ho sentido literal, e contra ha enteção do profeta, ho qual falou pola boca[b] do Spi*rit*u Santo dete*r*mina*n*do a vinda c*er*ta do Mexia, polo qual con-cludimos que esta profitia no*m* se pode declarar senão de vosso Mexia. E que assi seia, leede vos ho caldeu sobre este passo e acharees que onde no hebraico tendes Silo ("donec veniat Silo"), no caldeu esta, "donec veniat Messias" (ates q*ue* venha ho Mexia). Vos bem sabees que no*m* podes neguar a tresladação caldaica do hebraico feyta por Ionathas, chamado no hebraico Thargum, mas maior fee lhe daes que não à hebraica por o*n*de podees bem creer q*ue* esta profitia de Iacob no*m* se pode ente*n*d*er* senão do Mexia.

[*fol. 10r*] Porquanto ia entramos na proua da uinda do Mexia, a qual polos profetas foi p*r*enunciada que avia de s*er* en tempo c*er*to e deter-minado, portanto he necessario que leixemos hos rregnatos e q*ue* venhamos àquele grande rrei e profundo de Daniel, ho qual polas suas somanas nos demostra euidenteme*n*te e co*m* estilo mui claro, ho Mexia ser vindo a este mu*n*do.

b MS *poca*

[13] *Post.*, 1, Kiiiiv; *FF,* 1, 40*va*. On Jewish sources, such as Samuel ben Meir, see Posnanski, *Schiloh*, 1:127f.

[14] Correctly Rehoboam and not Jeroboam.

[15] Cf. 1 Kings 12:1.

[16] *Post.*, 1, Kiiiiv; *FF,* 1, 40*vb*. This interpretation was current in the geonic period and among the

Other doctors of yours, who are not satisfied with the above exposition, give it another, more extravagant meaning. They say that Jacob's prophecy refers to Jeroboam who was appointed king over the ten tribes of Israel who had seceded from the kingdom of Rehoboam because of his bad rule. Since he was crowned king of these same tribes, your doctors thus explain *donec veniat Silo* to mean "Jeroboam to be crowned in Shiloh."[13]

I tell you that this interpretation of your doctors contains two errors. The first is that Jeroboam[14] was crowned king in Shiloh, when actually it was in Shechem as you will find in the Third Book of Kings, chapter 12.[15] The second error is that the dominion and sovereignty were to be taken from the tribe of Judah, as the prophecy says, because they remained in the hands of Rehoboam and consequently with the tribe of Judah and Benjamin.

Then there are other doctors of yours who claim that this prophecy pertains to King Nebuchadnezzar who came to Jerusalem by God's command and captured King Zedekiah. At that time, dominion and sovereignty were taken from your ancestors.[16]

All these expositions are false and erroneous, against the literal sense, and contrary to the intention of the prophet who spoke through the mouth of the Holy Spirit and determined the true coming of the Messiah. For this reason, we conclude that this prophecy can only refer to your Messiah. To make that clear, read the Chaldean version of this passage and you will find that where you have "Shiloh" in the Hebrew (*donec veniat Silo*), the Chaldean reads *donec veniat Messias* (until the Messiah comes). You well know that you cannot deny the Chaldean translation made by Jonathan from the Hebrew and called in Hebrew the Targum.[17] You give greater credence to it than to the original. Consequently, then, you can believe that this prophecy refers not to Jacob but to the Messiah.

[*fol. 10r*] Since we have already entered into a discussion of the evidence pertaining to the coming of the Messiah, predicted by the prophets for a specifically determined time, it is thus necessary for us to leave our discussion of the reigns and to come to that of the great and profound king[18] of Daniel. The latter, in a very clear manner, shows us through his "weeks" that the Messiah has undoubtedly come to this world.

Karaites. See Posnanski, *Schiloh*, pp. 1:101, 252, 269, 271ff. On Hayyim Ibn Musa's (1390-1460) refutation of De Lyra, see Posnanski, *Schiloh*, 1:251f.

[17] The Targum or Aramaic translation of the prophets is attributed by tradition to Jonathan ben Uzziel. Cf. *PF*, p. 312; *Post.*, 1, Kiiiiv.

[18] *Ie.*, the Messiah.

En Daniel, no capitolo nono, se conta que estando elle em catiueiro
com hos filhos de Iacob, vendo a grande aflição e afronta que se fazia
aos do seu sangue por parte dos babilonios que hos afligião, por onde
hos iudeus leixauão as leis paternaes e cerimonias da Lei, e paguaizauão
seguindo hos rritos e custumes gentios, loguo se poos em ieiuns e en
aflições e começou a horar mui eficadamente. E perseuerando no seu
proposito e instituto, mereceo de ser doutrinado e ensinado polo anio
Guabriel, ho qual ho enformou das cousas que aviam de acontecer ao
seu pouo, afirmando a vinda certa e tempo certo do Mexia, dizendolhe:
"Daniel, porquanto deseias de saber as cousas vindeiras e que ham de
acontecer ao teu pouo, portanto soom vindo pera te enformar de tudo;
por iso, tu olha a visão e entende a minha palaura. Sabe que setenta
somanas são abreuiadas sobre ho teu pouo e sobre a tua Santa Cidade
pera que a preuaricação do pecado seia acabada e consumida, e pera
que ho pecado se acabe e tenha fim, e a maldade sera apaguada, e a
iustiça sempiterna sera trazida, e a visão e profitia se acabara, e ho
Santo dos santos sera vngido."
Nesta proficia em geeral comprendeo ho anio Guabriel todos hos
anos que correrão desde dia que isto foi dito a Daniel, ates que ho Templo com a cidade foi destruida por Tito, onde correrão quatrocentos e
nouenta anos. E estes anos diuidio ho anio en especial a Daniel, contando por cada somana sete anos, porque assi como às vezes por hum
dia se conta hum ano na Sagrada Escritura (Ezechielis, 4° capitolo), assi
por huma somana contamos sete anos, porque setenta vezes sete ou sete
vezes setenta fazem quatrocentos e nouenta. Isto noto he ao arismetico.
Hora veiamos como ho anio diuidio estes anos por partes e por tem-
pos diuisos, dizendo: "Portanto entende, Daniel, e olha, que deste dia
que esta profitia te he denunciada, ates que a cidade de Ierusalem seia
edificada, correrão sete somanas." Tantas somanas correrão ates ho
tempo que Ciro mandou ho pouo [fol. 10v] que se tornasse pera
Ierusalem, dandolhes licença que edificassem a praça de Ierusalem,
guiandoos Zorobabel, segundo se contem no primeiro capitolo do
Primeiro Liuro de Esdras, como Ieremias tinha profitizado, capitolo
xxv°, dizendo, que acabados hos setenta anos, Deos auia de visitar ho seu
pouo. E isto he ho que o anio Guabriel dixe, que auiam de correr sete
somanas desde tempo que isto denunciou a Daniel ates que a cidade de
Ierusalem fosse edificada, a qual fora destruida por mandado de
Nabuchodonosor, estando ella destruida por espaço de setenta anos.

[19] Dan. 9:23f.
[20] Cf. Ezek. 4:6.

In chapter nine of the Book of Daniel, it is told that when he was in captivity with the children of Jacob, he witnessed the great affliction and anxiety his people endured at the hands of their Babylonian tormentors. These caused them to abandon their ancestral laws and ceremonies and to perform pagan rites and customs instead. He then fasted and afflicted himself and began to pray very intently. Since he persevered in his aim and intention, he was worthy of being instructed by the angel Gabriel who informed him of things that would befall his people. He indicated the time determined for the true coming of the Messiah and said to him: *Daniel, because you want to know the future and that which is to befall your people, I have come to inform you of everything. Look then at the vision and understand my word. Know that seventy weeks are decreed upon your people and upon your holy city so that the transgression may be finished and done, and so that sin be brought to an end and iniquity extinguished; that everlasting justice take its place and the vision and prophecy be terminated, and the Holy of Holies be anointed.*[19]

The angel Gabriel included in this prophecy the sum total of the years from the day this was told to Daniel until the Temple and city were destroyed by Titus — a total of four hundred and ninety years. The angel then divided these weeks for Daniel, counting seven years for every week, since one day is sometimes equal to one year in the Holy Scriptures (Ezekiel, chapter 4).[20] We thus count one week as seven years, because seventy times seven or seven times seventy are four hundred and ninety. This is the way one calculates in arithmetic.

Now let us see how the angel divided these years. Continuing his revelations to Daniel, he said: *Therefore understand and hear this, Daniel, that from this day in which this prophecy is revealed to you, until the city of Jerusalem is destroyed, seven weeks will pass.*[21] This number of weeks passed until the time that Cyrus ordered the people [*fol. 10v*] to return to Jerusalem and permitted them to rebuild the square in that city, guided by Zerubbabel. This follows that written in the first chapter of the First Book of Ezra,[22] and that which Jeremiah had prophesied in chapter 25, saying that after a period of seventy years God would visit His people.[23] Thus did the angel Gabriel speak when he said that seven weeks would pass from the time that his prophecy was revealed to Daniel until the rebuilding of the city of Jerusalem, which had been destroyed by order of Nebuchadnezzar and had remained so for a period of seventy years.

[21] Dan. 9:25.
[22] Cf. Ezra 1:3.
[23] The reference is to Jer. 29:10 which Machado has apparently confused with 25:12.

Assi que desdo tempo que ho anio Guabriel falou com Daniel, ates que a cidade foi edificada com angustia de tempo, correrão sete somanas, que fazem anos corenta e noue.

Dixelhe mais ho anio: "E a praça de Ierusalem sera edificada com presa e com angustia de tempo; e depois de sesenta e duas somanas sera Christo morto." Aqui declara ho anio a Daniel quantos anos correrão do tempo que a cidade foi edificada ates ho tempo que hos vossos predecessores matarão a Christo, verdadeiro Mexia, onde correrão e passarão sesenta e duas somanas, has quaes fazem quatrocentos e trinta e quatro anos, hos quaes, se aiuntarmos com hos quorenta e noue anos que se passarão ates a cidade ser edificada, serão quatrocentos e oytenta e tres anos.

E tantos correrão desdo tempo que ho anio Guabriel falou com Daniel ates que Christo morreo, e fiquão sete anos pera se fazerem hos quatrocentos e nouenta anos compreendidos nas setenta somanas, hos quaes sete anos se entendem naquilo que dixe ho anio a Daniel. E ha derradeira somana quando faltar ho sacrifitio e oblação, confirmara estes anos. Isto dixe ho anio Guabriel por amor do tempo, que a cidade de Ierusalem estaua cerquada por Tito; que tanta era ha angustia antre ho[s] vossos predecessores naquele tempo que nhũm sacrificio se fazia (Iosephus, *De Bello Iudaico*). E portanto, dixe ho anio a Daniel: "E antão ho pouo neguara ho seu duque quando diziam: 'Nom habemus regem nisi cesarem,' e a cidade e ho santuario destruira ho pouo rromano com ho duque Tito, e a fim da cidade sera a sua destruição, e sera hum desemparo perpetuo e durara pera todo sempre, e faltara ha hostia e sacrifitio na cidade de Ierusalem."

En estas palauras acabou ho anio Guabriel, por onde vos bem vos enguanaes crendo que ho Templo ainda ha de ser edificada e que nele hahinda hão de sacrificar a Deos como d'antes. [*fol. 11r*] Afirmouos que se eu fora iudeu e leera esta profitia tão clara e manifesta da vinda do Mexia, que loguo, sem tardança, me ouuera de conuerter à fee de Christo, porque ella asaz demostra a vinda do Mexia ia ser comprida, e todas as cousas que nela se contem ia são passadas e aconteçerão a Christo nosso Redentor e ho vosso Mexia, e a cidade de Ierusalem foi destruida por Tito e esta desemparada de vos outros. Assi que nom sei pera que queres debate nem duuida alguma da vinda do Mexia pois que ho anio assi tão manifestamente declarou esta vinda do Mexia auer de ser comprida no tempo determinado.

---

[24] Dan. 9:25f.

Thus, from the time that the angel Gabriel spoke to Daniel until the city was rebuilt in troubled times, there passed seven weeks, which equal forty-nine years.

In addition, the angel told him: *And the square of Jerusalem will be rebuilt quickly in troublous times; and after sixty-two weeks Christ will be put to death*.[24] It is here that the angel Gabriel states the number of years that passed from the time that the city was rebuilt until the time that your ancestors killed Christ, the true Messiah. This would be sixty-two weeks or, in other words, four hundred and thirty-four years. If we add these to the forty-nine years that passed until the city was rebuilt, the total would be four hundred and eighty-three years.

This then is the number of the years that passed from the time that the angel Gabriel spoke with Daniel until Christ died. The seven years that remain bring the total to four hundred and ninety years which are included in the seventy weeks and are understood to signify the seven weeks about which the angel spoke to Daniel. This numeration will be confirmed by the last week when the sacrifice and the offering shall cease. The angel Gabriel said this with reference to the time that Jerusalem was besieged by Titus, for the distress was great among your predecessors at that time because no sacrifice was being made (Josephus, *De Bello Iudaico*).[25] Therefore the angel said to Daniel: "Then the people denied their leader when they said: '*Non habemus regem nisi cesarem*,' and the Roman people with their leader Titus will destroy the city and the sanctuary. The destruction will spell the end of the city and the destitution will be everlasting, and sacrifice and offering will cease in the city of Jerusalem."[26]

The angel Gabriel concluded with these words which show you how you deceive yourselves by believing that the Temple will still be rebuilt and that sacrifices will still be made in it to God as before. [*fol. 11r*] I tell you most assuredly that if I were a Jew and were to read this clear and manifest prophecy concerning the advent of the Messiah, I would immediately convert to the faith of Christ because it proves that His coming has already been fulfilled. It shows that all that is contained in it has come about and happened through Christ, our Redeemer and your Messiah, and that the City of Jerusalem was destroyed by Titus and abandoned by you. I thus do not know why you need debate or doubt the coming of the Messiah since the angel clearly declared His coming to have been fulfilled at the appointed time.

[25] *De Bello Judaico*, 6.2.1.
[26] Paraphrase of Dan. 9:26f.

Assi que teemos concludido polas somanas de Daniel que ho Mexia he vindo, porque setenta somanas forão abreuiadas ou rregistadas na vontade e mente diuina, que forão hos quatrocentos e nouenta anos que se passarão desta profitia pronunciada e dita polo anio Guabriel, ates que ho Templo foi destruido por Tito, segundo se conta na dita profitia, onde fala no duque que auia de vir com ho pouo rromano à cidade de Ierusalem, como foi, con grande frota e aparato de guerra.

Ho anio diuidio estas setenta somanas en tres partes. Primeiramente en sete somanas que fazem corenta e noue anos, hos quaes correrão ates que a cidade foi edificada. Segundariamente, forão diuididas en sesenta e duas somanas, que fazem quatrocentos e trinta e noue anos, hos quaes correrão desda edificação do Templo ates a morte de Christo. Terceiramente, forão diuididas em huma somana, a qual correo depois da paixão, onde se continhão sete anos. E nesta derradeira somana hos apostolos forão preguar a fee de Christo por todo ho vniuerso mundo.

E a cidade com ho Templo foi destruida por Tito, pera nunqua mais em Ierusalem auer sacrifitio, nem iudeu nunqua mais ali sacrificar, acabados corenta e tres anos depois da paixão, em ho qual tempo Tito destruio ho Templo e catiuou hos iudeus que antão forão derramados polo vniuerso mundo. Esta destruição, ates ho tempo presente, dura e durara ates a fim do mundo, porquanto ali iamais Iuda adorara nem morara pera a Deos sacrificar.

E asi ho concludio ho anio na fim da dita profiti[a], dizendo: "E depois da batalha acabada, sera desemparada pera todo sempre Ierusalem." Isto bem ho veedes e conhecees, posto que creaes que ainda Ierusalem se edificara.

[fol. 11v] A opinião dos vossos talmudistas he que a cidade de Ierusalem estara desolada e desemparada ates que ho Mexia vença a Got e Magot (Ezechielis, xxxviii) na batalha que ha de teer contra elles, e loguo antão se edificara ho Templo. Pera confirmação disto dizem que no hebraico na profitia, no fim dela, esta dũma maneira, e no latim, d'outra; e portanto no nosso latim soa a profitia que a cidade iamais sera edificada, e no hebraico soa no fim da batalha, nom estara pera todo sempre destruida senão ates ho fim da batalha, a qual cuidaes que ho Mexia ha de teer com Got e Magot. E nom sabees quam enguanados estaes, porque vos cuidaes que a batalha da qual falou ho anio Guabriel

[27] I.e., 587-538 B.C.
[28] Correctly: 434 years.
[29] See above, Chap. 3, n. 29.

We thus have concluded, through the weeks of Daniel, that the Messiah has come, because seventy weeks were noted or registered in the divine will and mind. These were the four hundred and ninety years from the time that the angel Gabriel foretold this prophecy until the time that the Temple was destroyed by Titus. This is told in the prophecy itself which speaks of the leader that would come with the Roman people to the city of Jerusalem with a great fleet and battle force, as actually happened.

The angel divided these seventy weeks into three parts. First there were the seven weeks that are forty-nine years, which ran to the time of the building of the city.[27] Second, there were the sixty-two weeks that amount to four hundred and thirty-nine years,[28] which ran from the time of the rebuilding of the Temple until the death of Christ. Third, there was the one week which came after the Passion and which contained seven years. In this last week, the apostles went out to preach the faith of Christ throughout the entire world.

Thus the city with the Temple was destroyed by Titus. Nevermore were there to be sacrifices made in Jerusalem nor were there to be offerings made there by a Jew; for forty-three years after the Passion,[29] Titus destroyed the Temple and captured the Jews who were then dispersed throughout the world. This destruction has lasted up to the present time and will endure until the end of the world inasmuch as Judah will never again worship there nor dwell there so as to be able to make offerings to God.

And thus the angel concluded his prophecy saying: *And after the battle has ended, Jerusalem will be desolate forevermore.*[30] It would be well for you to see and understand this since you believe that Jerusalem will still be rebuilt.

[*fol. 11v*] The opinion of your talmudists is that the city of Jerusalem will be desolate and abandoned until the Messiah conquers Gog and Magog (Ezekiel, 38) in the war he is to wage against them. It is then, they believe, that the Temple will be rebuilt. To confirm this they say that the end of the prophecy is written in Hebrew in one way and in Latin in another. Thus, in Latin it reads that the city will never be rebuilt whereas in Hebrew it does not say that the city will remain desolate for all time but only until the end of the war which you believe the Messiah is to wage against Gog and Magog. Yet you do not realize how wrong you are; for you think that the war about which the angel Gabriel spoke at the conclusion of the prophecy was to be with Gog

---

[30] Cf. Dan. 9:26. Although Machado's discussion of this passage has elements in common with those of other interpreters (cf. *Post.*, 2, EEEiiv; *ACPJ*, 1, 2, pp. 42ff.), his computations differ.

no fim da profitia que ha de ser com Got e Magot, e a sua entenção foi falar do fim da batalha que auia de ser feita por Tito.

E pera mais vosso enguano dizem estes vossos talmudistas que onde esta no nosso latim, "et post finem belli statuta desolatio" (que depois da batalha sera a cidade pera todo sempre desemparada), que esta no hebraico "et vsque ad finem belli statuta desolatio" (e ates a fim da batalha estara a cidade desemparada), concludindo que depois da batalha com Got e Magot, se emparara. Pera confirmarem seu maldito enguano, onde nesta profitia no hebraico estaua huma dição que tanto sinificaua como este nosso aduerbio "post," que quer dizer "depois," que he esta dição hebraica ayn, mudarãona e poserão esta out[r]a deleth, a qual en latim sinifiqua "vsque," que quer dizer "ates." Isto fezerão hos vossos doutores porquanto estas duas dições hebraicas se escreuem com as mesmas letras ayn, deleth, e como que hos puntinhos são aqueles que fazem voguar as letras, por isso poserão hos pontos que quiserão e mudarão as sentenças como quiserão, fazendo mil enguanos e corronpendo ho Testamento Velho com puntuações falsas e enguanosas. E pera maior enguano de vos outros, estes vossos doutores, vendo que no tempo do emperador Constantino muitos gentios se conuertião à fee de Christo e muitos iudeus, conuencidos por Dauid, ho qual muito claramente fala do conuertimento dos gentios, e por Daniel, se aiuntarão estes vossos doutores naquela grande cidade que esta no Egito, chamada Cairo, e ali composerão ho Talmud maldito e malauenturado (porque este he ho que vos assi traz enguanados), no qual corronperão muytos textos que falauão da vinda do Mexia ia passada e com seus pontinhos mudarão sentenças e corronperão sentenças, onde diuidirão ho Testamento Velho em lei e prophetas e agiographa, lançando fora [fol. 12r] a Dauid e Daniel do numero dos profetas pera que vos outros nom lhes deseis tanta autoridade, e hos poserão antre hos agiographas que são de menor autoridade.

Asi que tornando ao nosso instituto e primeiro proposito, diguouos que vos enguanaes crendo que ho Mexia ha de teer guerra ou batalha com Got e Magot e que depois ho Templo ha de ser edificado, e que nele ho Mexia ha de rreinar temporalmente, e que ha de suiuguar hos gentios, e que sera emperador de Rroma.

Todas estas cousas que credes são paruoices e meninices e simplicidades e falsos entendimentos que daes à Sagrada Escritura, nam na en-

---

[31] This entire discussion is found in *Post.* to Dan. 9:26, 2, EEEiiv. The Hebrew alphabet consists of consonants with vowels indicated by sub- and superlinear vowel signs known as points. In this instance, the Hebrew 'd can be vocalized 'ad (usque) as in the masoretic text or 'od, understood as *post* in the Vulgate.

and Magog, but his intention was to speak of the end of the war which Titus was to wage.

To deceive you further, your talmudists say that where we in Latin have "*et post finem belli statuta desolatio*" (after the battle the city will be abandoned forever), the Hebrew has "*et vsque ad finem belli statuta desolatio*" (and the city will be desolate until the end of the battle), concluding that after the war with Gog and Magog, the city will be refortified. Now in this prophecy there is a Hebrew word that is like our adverb *post*, which means "after." In Hebrew this word is *'ayin*. However, in order to substantiate their wicked deceit, your talmudists changed this word and added the letter *dalet* which in Latin signifies *vsque* which means "until." Your doctors were able to do this for these two words are written with the same consonants *'ayin* and *dalet*. Since it is the points which vocalize a letter, it follows that they therefore used them as they wished, changing the sentences as they so desired.[31] They thereby caused innumerable errors but also corrupted the Old Testament with false and erroneous pointings.[32] They went even further to deceive you. In time of the emperor Constantine, your doctors saw that many Gentiles and Jews were converting to the faith of Christ, when they became convinced by Daniel and by David who spoke very clearly of the conversion of the Gentiles. It was then that your doctors assembled together in that great city in Egypt called Cairo,[33] and there composed that wicked and wretched Talmud (for this is the cause of your deception). In it they corrupted many passages that spoke of the coming of the Messiah which had already taken place. With their points, they changed and corrupted sentences. They divided the Old Testament into the Law, Prophets, and Hagiographa, and expelled [*fol. 12r*] David and Daniel from among the group of prophets and placed them among the hagiographers which are of lesser authority.

Turning now to our first intent and proposition, I tell you that you deceive yourselves if you think that the Messiah will wage a war or battle against Gog and Magog, after which the Temple will be rebuilt, and that the Messiah will reign in it temporally subjugating the nations and becoming emperor of Rome.

All these things that you believe are idiocy, childishness, and simplemindedness and reflect the false interpretation that you give to the

---

[32] On the charges and counter-charges of the corruption of Scripture in the Middle Ages, see Marcel Simon, *Verus Israel* (Paris, 1948), pp. 184ff. Cf. Bernhard Blumenkranz, *Juifs et Chrétiens dans le monde occidentale* (Paris, 1960), p. 224; Frank Talmage, "R. David Kimhi as Polemicist," *Hebrew Union College Annual*, 38 (1967), pp. 216f. A. Marmorstein, *REJ*, 66 (1914), 256; B. Smalley, *Study of the Bible in the Middle Ages* (London, 1958), p. 162; Hailperin, *Rashi*, p. 169 et seq., p. 315. Cf. *DE*, pp. 16f.

[33] See above, Chap. 3, n. 32.

tendendo. Nem ho vosso Talmud entendes porque se ho vos enten-
deseis, vos nele achariaes muitos passos e muitas grosas dos vossos
doutores que afirmão ho Mexia ser vindo, como loguo polos seus ditos
vos prouaremos. E portanto, leixai essa opinião e sede, roguouos, da
nossa fee.

Midras Telim, vosso doutor, nom conhecendo ho Mexia e sabendo
que ho tempo ia era acabado da sua vinda, num liuro que compoos da
tardança do Mexia começou a dizer: "Senhor, por que estas longe? Por
que nom veens?" Rabi Ionas lendo este passo glosouho, dizendo: "Ia ho
Senhor esteue perto e aguora esta longe, porque tres anos e meo esteue
a influentia diuina no monte Oliuete preguando." Este vosso doutor
dixe verdada, porque tres anos e meo pregou ho Mexia, estando muito
perto dos vossos predecessores, falando com elles, praticando,
disputando, e finalmente se alonguo deles, sobindo aos ceos. E ainda
aguora esta longe de vos outros, senhores,[c] por amor da uossa incredulidade. Assi que este vosso doutor conclude, dizendo "Vos
bradastes por Deos e veo e vos nam no conhecestes, e aguora que por elle
bradaes, nom vira."

Verdade he que hos padres santos bradarão por elle e nom ho virão
en carne, posto que em spiritu ho conhecerão. E hos vossos predecessores ho virão e com elle falarão e nam ho conhecerão. Esto se confirma no Talmud, onde se diz: "Requerei a Deos emquanto se acha, e
chamai por elle emquanto ho tendes perto de vos." Sobre este passo se
põe no mesmo Talmud huma pergunta: "Que tal he que quer dizer
aquele ditado daquela profitia que diz assi: 'Quando chamei, nom
ouuirão. Chamarmeam, e nom ouuirei'?" (Esaie, xxv capitolo). E pera
responder a esta pergunta põe este exemplo pera demostrar como ho
Mexia vos[49] chamou e nom ho quisestes ouuir.

[fol. 12v] "Chegou hum almocreue à porta dum estalaiadeiro, sendo ia
noyte. Porem, nom quis entrar dentro na estalaiem nem quis pousar
dentro, senão leixousse fiquar fora. Mas como se fizesse mais noite veo
ho estalaiadeiro, dizendolhe: 'Senhor hospede, entrai pera dentro por-

---

c int.

[34] See Introduction.
[35] Ps. 10:1 (9B:1).
[36] Midrash Tehillim to Ps. 10:3, ed. Buber, p. 92; ed. Braude, 1:151. Machado and PF (p. 848)
are closer to ed. Warsaw, 1875, p. 30: "O Lord, why do you stand from afar? (Ps. 10:1). It is thus written, When He called, they did not hear (Zech. 7:13). R. Yohanan said: For three and a half years the
Presence stood on the Mount of Olives declaring: Seek the Lord where He may be found; call Him when
He is near." The passage is cited also in FF, fol. 48vb.
[37] Interlinear addition. See note b.

Holy Scriptures, since you do not understand them. You do not even understand your own Talmud. If you did, you would find many passages and commentaries therein made by your own doctors which affirm that the Messiah has come, as we will prove to you through their own words. For this reason, abandon these views of yours and be, I implore you, of our faith.

Your doctor, Midrash Tehillim,[34] did not know the Messiah, but he did know that the time for his coming had passed. In a book he composed, regarding the delay of the Messiah, he wrote: "*Lord, why are you so far away? Why do you not come!*"[35] Rabbi Ionas glossed this passage as follows: "The Lord was already near and now He is far, because for three and one-half years the divine influence was preaching on the Mount of Olives."[36] This doctor of yours spoke the truth, because the Messiah did preach for three and one-half years. He was very close at that time to your ancestors and spoke, conversed and disputed with them, whereafter He withdrew and ascended to heaven. Even now, however, He is still far from you, gentlemen,[37] because of your incredulity. This doctor of yours concluded by saying, "You cried out for God and He came, but you did not know Him, and now that you cry out to Him, He will not come."[38]

It is indeed true that the holy Patriarchs cried out for Him and did not see Him in the flesh for they knew Him in the spirit. Your ancestors however, saw Him and spoke with Him but did not know Him. This is confirmed in the Talmud, where it is said: *Seek God while He may be found, and summon Him while you have Him near you.*[39] A question is raised in the Talmud on this very passage: "What is meant by that part of the prophecy that says: 'When I called, they did not hear. They will call Me and I will not hear'" (Isaiah, chapter 25)?[40] To answer this question a parable is related to show how the Messiah called to you but you did not want to hear.

[*fol. 12v*] "One night a muleteer came to the door of an inn. In spite of the lateness of the hour, he did not care to go inside and spend the night but preferred to remain outside. But as it was getting even later the innkeeper came out and said to him: "Sir, come inside because

---

[38] Conclusion of above passage from Midrash Tehillim.

[39] Isa. 55:6. Machado is apparently unaware that this is a scriptural passage.

[40] This quotation from the "Talmud" and "Isaiah" seems actually to reflect the continuation of the above passage from Midrash Tehillim to Ps. 10:2, ed. Buber, pp. 92f.; ed. Braude, 1:152: "The Holy One, blessed be He, replied: 'When I sought you, you did not heed Me. Now that you seek Me, I will not hear you. Measure for measure!' Hence it is said, *It came to pass that, as He called, and they would not hear; so they shall call, and I will not hear, said the Lord of hosts*" (Zech. 7:13).

quanto por aqui andão lobos de noyte e ladrões e aconteceruosha algum dano e perda.' Ho almocreue começou de zombar e nom querendo entrar, fechou o estalaiadeiro suas portas e lançouse na sua cama.

"Sendo ia muito tarde começarão hos lobos e ladrões de trautar mal ho almocreue,[d] ho qual se foi à porta rrogando ao estalaiadeiro que ho quisese recolher na pousada. Mas elle, nom lhe querendo abrir, lhe dixe: 'E te chamei e nom quiseste entrar, aguora tu chamasme, e eu nom te quero abrir.'" Assi fez ho Mexia que vos chamou quando veo tomar carne humana, e vos nam no quisestes siguir nem ouuir, e aguora esperaes por elle e nunqua vira senão iulguar hos viuos e hos mortos.

Houtros muitos enxemplos se põem no Talmud, hos quaes demostrão ho Mexia ser vindo, mas hos vossos rrabinos, sacerdotes nas sinaguoguas, calamnos e nom nos querem descubrir ao pouo pera que se nom conuerta. Esta he a uosa ciguidade ([e]nom diguo[e] malitia e maldade) por onde andaes errados e fora de todo caminho da verdade e mitidos nas profundezas do inferno, do qual iamais saires pera todo sempre senão se vos conuerterdes, como espero, lendo uos este *Espelho*.

Assi tambem isto afirma Embresit Rraba, vosso doutor, dizendo no liuro chamado Grão Grande, que quando hos irmãos de Iosehth esteuerão con elle no Egito (Genesis, capitolo xlvij°), que se chegou Iudas a Ioseph, dizendo: "Alegrarnosemos." Veem a grosa sobre isto e diz: "Que quer dizer 'Alegrarnosemos e letificarnosemos en ti'? E quando nos deuemos de alegrar en Deos?" Responde, dizendo: "Isto sera quando a enfluentia de Deos esteuer no monte de Oliuete." Assi ho diz Zacharias profeta, capitolo xiiij°.

Certamente que vos deuees de creer que todas estas cousas ia são passadas e compridas, porque tres anos e meo pregou ho Mexia na Terra da Promissão.

Em *Canedim* e em *Aboahara*, liuros vossos assi chamados, num capitolo que se começa, "Antes do seu quebranto," se diz assi: "Leemos que He-

---

d int. + *hospede*   e-e int. + *e* exp.

---

[41] Based in a continuation of the passage cited in n. 40: "R. Ḥanina told a parable of a traveler journeying on the highway. As it grew dark, he came to a military post. The commander said to him: 'Come into the post away from wild beasts and away from robbers!' But the traveler replied: 'It is not my custom to go into a military post.' As he went on his way, midnight and thick darkness overtook him, and he returned to the post and cried and prayed to the commander that he open up for him. The commander answered: 'It is not customary for a military post to be opened at

wolves and thieves roam around here at night and some harm may come to you." The mule-driver began to laugh at him and did not want to go inside, so the innkeeper closed his doors and went to bed.

"It was now very late and the wolves and thieves began to molest the muleteer. For this reason he went to the door of the inn and begged the keeper to take him in. But the latter refused to open the door for him and said: 'I called to you but you did not want to enter, but now you call to me and I do not wish to open.'"[41] So it was with the Messiah who called to you when He came and took human form; yet you did not want to follow Him or listen to Him. Now you wait for Him but He will never come except to judge the quick and the dead.

Many other parables to be found in the Talmud demonstrate that the Messiah has come. But your rabbis, the priests in the synagogues, keep silent about them and do not want to reveal this to you, so that you will not convert. It is your blindness (I do not say[42] malice and wickedness) that causes you to be in error and leads you from the path of truth; that places you in the very depths of hell whence you will never emerge except through converting, as I hope you will do, by reading this *Mirror*.

This is also what your doctor *Embresit Rraba*[43] affirms in his book *Grão Grande*,[44] saying that when Joseph's brothers were with him in Egypt (Genesis, chapter 47), Judah came to Joseph and said, "Let us rejoice." The gloss of this passage says, "What does *'we shall rejoice and be happy in you'*[45] mean? And when shall we be happy in God?" He answers by saying: "This will occur when God's influence is on the Mount of Olives." So Zechariah the prophet says in chapter 14.[46]

You certainly must believe that all these things have already come to pass because the Messiah was in the Promised Land preaching for three years and a half.

In your books *Canedim*[47] and *Aboahara*,[48] there is a chapter that begins

---

night, nor is it the commander's custom to receive at such an hour. When I asked you in, you were unwilling; now I cannot open up for you.'" (Braude, *Midrash*, pp. 151f.) This parable is found neither in *PF* nor in *ACPJ*.

[42] "I do not say" interlinear addition. See note *d*.

[43] See Introduction.

[44] See Introduction.

[45] Song of Songs 1:4.

[46] Zech. 14:3f. This passage from the *BRMD* is no longer extant in a Hebrew source but is found in *PF*, p. 848; *ACPJ*, 1,2, p. 30, and *FF*, fol. 36*vb*. The Hebrew as translated from *PF* reads: "*We will exult and rejoice in you.* When are we to be joyful? When the feet of the Presence stand on the Mount of Olives."

[47] *Sanhedrin*. Talmudic tractate dealing with aspects of the Sanhedrin or High Court.

[48] *'Avodah Zarah*. Talmudic tractate dealing with relations between Jews and pagans.

lias dixe que seis mil anos auia de durar ho mundo e no seitimo auia de ser destruido, rrepartindoos desta maneira: de vaam gloria, dous mil anos; e dous mil da Lei; e de miséria, dous mil." [*fol. 13r*] Rabi Cateua sobre estes anos diz: "E enfortelecersea ho S*enh*or naquele dia mil, que era ho ano sexto mil," concludindo q*ue* ho Mexia auia de vir acabados cinquo mil anos depois da criação do mu*n*do, começandose ho sexto mil. Este doutor falou pola boca do S*piritu* Santo porq*ue* ho Mexia naquele tempo veo, começandose hos seis mil anos depois do mundo criado e feito. E aguora ia estamos no seitimo mil, por onde bem pare-ce que ia ho Mexia veo e vos, ᶠsen*h*ores, no*m* sei comoᶠ ainda esperaes por elle.

Helia Rabi, leendo ho capitolo acima aleguado, estando presente Rabi Iu*d*a, dixe: "No*m* minguoara ho mu*n*do ne*m* se perdera ates que outocentos e cinquoenta iubileus no*m* seiam acabados; mas, pore*m*, no pustumeiro e derradeiro, vira ho Mexia, filho de Dauid." Ex aqui hu*m* testimunho bem euidente pera vos demostrar ho Mexia ser ia vindo. Rabi Iosua confirma*n*do isto diz que ainda que hos iudeus no*m* fação penitentia dos seus pecados, ne*m* por isso no*m* leixara ho Mexia de vir na fim dos iubileus, que sera ho seu tempo dete*r*minado e ordenado polos p*r*ofetas, porque d'outra maneira a sua palaura seria mintirossa, ho que não pode ser.

No*m* tenhaes, senhores, ia debate ne*m* duuida da vinda do Mexia, porque ia todas as profitias dele escritas e polos profetas pronu*n*ciadas, ia são acabadas e consumidas. Escrito estaua por Zacharias, capitolo ix, que ho Mexia auia d'entrar na cidade de Ierusalem caualeiro feito, sobre a asna e ho asno. E assi ho confirma Rabi Salamão, dizendo sobre este passo que ho Mexia auia de vir pobre caualeiro sobre a asna.

---

f-f int. + *misquinhos* exp.

[49] Chapters of a talmudic tractate are named by *incipit*. The first chapter of 'Avodah Zarah begins "*sheloshah yamim li-fene 'edehen shella-goyim*" ("three days before the festivals of the gentiles"). In this context, the word *'ed* is etymologically related to the Syriac *'id* (festival). Machado, or his source, mistakenly takes this word as the biblical word *'ed* (calamity, misfortune), orthographically identical but etymologically different. This same mistranslation is found in the *Ajuda da Fé* of Mestre António written in 1486, B.N.L. MS Fundo Geral 6967, fols. 22ra, 27ra. In his *'Ezer ha-'Emunah,* Moses ha-Kohen of Tordesillas (late 14th c.) cites the complaint of his Christian adversary that Jews call Christian holidays by the name of *'ed*. R. Moses, unaware of the etymology of the word, gives an apologetic answer. See Y. Shamir, *Rabbi Moses Ha-Kohen of Tordesillas and his Book 'Ezer Ha-Emunah* (Leiden, 1975), p. 67, and for the Hebrew text, Y. Shamir, ed., *Rabbi Moses Ha-Kohen of Tor-desillas and His Book 'Ezer Ha-'Emunah — A Chapter in the History of the Judeo-Christian Controversy* (Coconut Grove, Fla., 1972), pp. 135f.

[50] B. T. Sanhedrin 97a, A.Z. 9a cited in *ACPJ*, 1, 2, p. 31. The Sonc. (Sanhedrin, p. 657; cf. A.Z., p. 43) translation reads: "The Tanna debe Eliyyahu teaches: The world is to exist six thousand years. In the first two thousand there was desolation; two thousand years the Torah

"Before their downfall"[49] in which it says the following: "We read that Elijah said that the world was to last for six thousand years and in the seventh it would be destroyed. The division is thus: Two thousand years of vanity, two thousand years of the Law, and two thousand years of misery."[50] [*fol. 13r*] Referring to these years, Rabbi Cateua[51] says: "The Lord will be strengthened on that thousandth day, which was the year six thousand,"[52] concluding that the Messiah would come five thousand years after the creation of the world at the beginning of the sixth millennium. This doctor spoke through the mouth of the Holy Spirit because the Messiah came at that time, the beginning of the year six thousand from the time of creation. Now we are in the seventh millennium and it well appears that the Messiah has come to you. I do not know, gentlemen,[53] how you still wait for Him.

When Rabbi Elijah read the above passage, he said to Rabbi Judah who was present: "The world will not decline or cease to exist until eight hundred and fifty jubilees have passed. In the last jubilee, the Messiah, the son of David, will come."[54] Here is clear evidence to prove to you that the Messiah has already come. Rabbi Joshua who confirms this says that even though the Jews do not repent their sins, the Messiah would still not fail to come at the end of the jubilees which would be the time ordained and determined by the prophets.[55] If this were the case, His word would be false and this could not be.

Therefore, gentlemen, have no qualms or doubts about the advent of the Messiah because all the prophecies that have been uttered and written by the prophets have already been fulfilled. Zechariah wrote in chapter 9 that the Messiah would ride mounted into the city of Jerusalem on a mare and an ass.[56] Rabbi Solomon[57] confirms this in his commentary by saying that the Messiah would come humbly mounted

---

flourished; and the next two thousand years is the Messianic era." Machado has apparently corrupted "Messia" (Messiah) to "miseria" (misery).

[51] Rabbi Kattina, a third century rabbinic teacher.

[52] B.T. Sanhedrin 97a and B.T. 'Avodah Zarah 9a cited in *PF*, p. 395 and in part in *FF*, fols. 36*vb*-37*ra*: "R. Qattina said: 'Six thousand shall the world exist, and one [thousand, the seventh], it shall be desolate, as it is written, *And the Lord alone shall be exalted in that day*" (Sonc., Sanhedrin, p. 657).

[53] "I do not know, gentlemen" interlinear addition replacing "wretches." See note *e*.

[54] B.T. Sanhedrin 97b. The correct reading is "eighty-five jubilees": "Elijah said to Rab Judah, the brother of R. Salla the Pious: 'The world shall exist not less than eighty-five jubilees, and in the last jubilee the son of David will come.'" (Sonc., p. 658). The passage is cited at *ACPJ*, 1, 2, p. 31; *FF*, fol. 37*ra* (quinqaginta quinque iubilei). Machado's "Rabbi Elijah" may have resulted from a misreading of such a passage as "Item dicit Helias Rabbi Iudae" (*ACPJ*, 1, 2, p. 31).

[55] The discussion is found in B.T. Sanhedrin 97b (Sonc., pp. 66of.), *PF*, p. 401.

[56] Cf. Zech. 9:9.

[57] R. Solomon ben Isaac (Rashi), 1040-1105. See Introduction.

Diguouos que este foi Christo, nosso Rredentor e Saluador, que assi entrou na cidade de Ierusalem. Este foi ho profeta do qual falou Moises no Deuteronomio, capitolo xviij, que auia de ser aleuantado dentre vossos predecessores, como foi Christo, filho de Dauid do tribu rreal de Iuda.

Esto teende por firmeza, que ho Mexia ia veo, e assi ho afirmão hos vossos doutores antepassados, posto que hos modernos rrabinos vos trazem enganados, nom vos querendo descubrir a verdade nem hos segredos do Talmud e talmudistas. Portanto, credenos e buscai medicos prudentes que vos demostrem a verdade, a qual he que ia são passados 1541 anos que ho Mexia Christo, nosso Deos, veo a este mundo.

Esta he a nossa fee e crença, p[e]çouos que esta seia a uossa. Amen.

[*fol. 13v*] Capitolo Quinto. De como ho Mexia veo antes da segunda destruição feita por Tito, e de muitos sinaes que cessarão no Templo.

A terceira propriedade que estaua escrita do Mexia era que elle auia de vir antes da destruição segunda do Templo, a qual foi communicada a Christo que veo antes da dita destruição per espaço de setenta e cinquo anos e meo. Vos outros, senhores,[a] grauemente erraes acerqua desta vinda do Mexia, nom crendo que veo, e andaes enguanados porquanto hos vossos rrabinos nom vos querem discubrir hos segredos do Talmud e dos talmudistas, onde se faz clara menção da vinda do Mexia, se vos quiserdes bem tudo especular e olhar. E eu tenho pera mym que estes vossos rrabinos estão iuramentados e esconiurados de nom vos declararem a verdade pera que vos outros nom vos conuertaes, e por isso nom fazem senão corromper ho Talmud e ho Testamento Velho, puntuandoo d'outra maneira que elle esteue no começo.

E se quiserdes saber que isto que dizemos que he verdade, tomai ho texto antiguo hebraico, coteia[i]o com ho moderno, e verees quanta diuersidade e diferença ha antre elles. E isto causa ho apontuar que vossos doutores fazem, tirando pontos e pondo pontos e mudando letras, por onde dão outro sentido e outro falso intendimento. E pera proua disto, veiãose hos setenta enterpretadores que tresladarão ho Testamento Velho de hebraico en greguo por mandado de Tholomeu,

---

a int. +*iudeus* exp.

[58] *Comm., ad. loc.; PF*, p. 848 *et passim; ACPJ*, 1, 11, pp. 104f.
[59] Cf. Deut. 18:15.

[1] See above, chap. 3, n. 29.
[2] Interlinear addition. MS reads "Jews" expunged. See note *a*.

upon an ass.[58] This, I tell you, was Christ, our Redeemer and Savior, who entered the city of Jerusalem. This was the prophet of whom Moses spoke in Deuteronomy, chapter 18, who would be raised up from among your ancestors,[59] as was Christ, the son of David of the royal tribe of Judah.

Hold it to be true then, that the Messiah has already come, as your ancient doctors affirmed, for the present-day rabbis are leading you astray. They do not want you to discover the truth or the secrets of the Talmud and the talmudists. Therefore, believe us and seek prudent physicians who will show you the truth: 1541 years have already passed since Christ, our God, came to this world.

This is our faith and belief; I ask that it also be yours. Amen.

[fol. 13v] Chapter Five. How the Messiah came before the second destruction by Titus, and of the many signs that ceased in the Temple.

The third characteristic written of the Messiah was that He would come before the second destruction of the Temple. This was fulfilled in Christ who come to this world seventy-five and a half years before this destruction.[1] But you, gentlemen,[2] are in grave error concerning this advent of the Messiah for you do not believe that He came. You go astray since your rabbis do not wish to reveal to you the secrets of the Talmud and the talmudists. There clear mention is made of His coming if you wish to examine the entire matter thoroughly. I firmly believe that your rabbis have sworn not to show you the truth so that you will not convert. For this reason, they corrupt the Talmud and the Old Testament by altering the original pointing of the letters.

If you wish to verify that what I say is true, pick up the old Hebrew text and compare it with the modern and you will see how much diversity and difference exist between the two. This is caused by your doctors pointing the individual letters differently. They take out points that were there, add points that were not, and even change letters. All of this alters the meaning and results in a false reading.[3] To prove this, look at the version of the Old Testament translated into Greek from the Hebrew by the seventy translators by order of Ptolemy, king of Egypt.[4]

---

[3] See above, chap. 4, n. 32.

[4] The tradition that the Septuagint was translated under the patronage of Ptolemy II Philadelphus (d. 246 b.c.) goes back to the *Letter of Aristeas* (*To Philocrates*), written in the second century b.c. It is adumbrated in Josephus and in such early Christian writers as Sts. Jerome and Augustine. See Moses Hadas, ed., *Aristeas to Philocrates* (New York, 1951), pp. 66ff.; Josephus, *Ant.* 17:2; Jerome, *Prefatio in Pentateuchem, PL,* 28:150; Augustine, *Civitas Dei,* 18.42. Cf. *DJC,* pp. 55f.; *Post.,* 2, CCiiir.

rrei de Egito, e veiase ho vosso hebraico e veres muito descrime e deferença.

Assi que todo ho vosso dizer nom he senão enguanos e falsidades manifestas, polo qual folguariamos que tomasseis vos a uossa briuia em hebraico e nos a nossa em latim, e que disputassemos e confirisemos, e a verdade se conheciria. Mas vos, enguanados, nom queres praticar nem communicar vossas cousas comnosco, e segundo me dixe hum iudeu, pareceme que uos he defesso no Talmud que nom disputeis comnosco pera que nom venhaes em conhicimento da verdade, ᵇassi como he defeso aos mouros que nom disputem a sua Lei.ᵇ E portanto, andaes por cantos fazendo falsos aiuntamentos e conuenticolos e sinaguoguas, enguanando ho pouo simples, sacrificando a Moises e iudaizando, afirmando que ainda ho Mexia nom veo. ᶜ(Perdoaime se diguo isto com colera.)ᶜ Hora venhão qua todos hos rrabinos e doutores e mestres das sinaguoguas de Purtugual, e respondãome a esta pergunta: Dizei de 1541 anos pera qua vos ouuistes dizer que algum milagre ou marauilha se [fol. 14r] fezesse antre vos outros, ou que algum anio falasse com Iuda, como se acontecco quando a vossa Lei teue viguor, e antes que viesse ho Mexia, ou que antes vos ouuesse profeta que pronunciasse a uinda deste Senhor?

Vos peruentura fazees tão grandes pecados e cometes tão grandes crimes e excessos ou sondes tão grandes idolatras, que Deos nom vos quer discubrir esta vinda do Mexia que esperaes. Diguouos que isto procede da vossa grande ciguidade e obstinação e incredulidade na qual andaes assi enguanados e enbibidos em muita ignorantia e em muitos errores, e por isto nom vindes em perfeito conhicimento.

Por certo, muito nos espantamos serdes vos hum pouo tão obstinado e encredolo, que tomada ha agua do baptismo e conuersando e viuendo comnosco, recalcitraes, corraes pera traz, como faz ho crangueio. Nam sabeemos se são isto fauores, mimos, e afaguos dos principes e daqueles aos quaes pertence meter a mão nesta massa, a qual tirão e não metem, pera que ho nome de Ihesus nom seia blasfemado neste Purtugual como foi, e prazera a Deos que mais nom sera.

Diguouos, senhores, que andaes muito enguanados, porque ho Mexia

---

b-b int.   c-c int.

⁵ *Brivia*, a corruption of *biblia*, was used in Spanish and Portuguese to refer to the Scriptures. See Judah ibn Verga, *Sheveṭ Yehudah*, ed. Shohat (Jerusalem, 1946), p. 26 *et passim*.

⁶ The Talmud as such does not prohibit disputation with a non-Jew although statements against teaching him the Torah may be found (B.T. Sanhedrin 59a, B.T. Ḥagigah 13; cf. *ACPJ*, 2, 6, pp.

Look at your Hebrew here and you will see considerable discrepancy and diversity.

Thus, all that you say is no more than deceit and manifest falsehood. It would please us very much if you would take your Hebrew Bible,[5] while we take our Latin, and if you would dispute and consult with us. In this way will the truth be known. Yet you, deceived as you are, do not care to discuss your writings with us. According to what a Jew told me, it appears that the Talmud prohibits you from debating with us[6] in order to prevent you from coming to know the truth just as the Moors have been prohibited from debating their law.[7] You therefore go about organizing perfidious assemblies, conventicles, and synagogues in order to deceive the simple people, sacrifice to Moses, judaize, and affirm that the Messiah has not yet come. (Pardon me if I say this with some anger).[8] Let all the doctors and rabbis and teachers of the synagogues of Portugal come and answer this question: Tell me if in the last 1541 years you have heard of some miracle or marvel [*fol. 14r*] that has happened among you; if you know of some angel who has spoken with Judah, as happened when your Law was in force before the Messiah came or before any prophet declared to you the coming of this Lord?

Perhaps God does not want to reveal to you this coming of the Messiah for whom you wait because you commit such sins, perpetrate such crimes, and are so steeped in idolatry. I say to you that this is due to your blindness, obstinacy, and incredulity which cause you to go about steeped in error and ignorance and prevented from recognizing the truth.

We are indeed astonished that you are such an obstinate and incredulous people. Even though you have been baptized and live and converse with us, you are recalcitrant and walk backwards like the crab. We do not know why such a situation is permitted to prevail. Perhaps it is due to the favors, connivings, and courting of the princes and others who fail to exercise their responsibilities that Jesus' name has been blasphemed in Portugal. May it be God's will that this no longer be so.

I say to you, gentlemen, that you are very much in error, because the

---

192f.). Occasional statements discouraging religious disputation may be found, however, elsewhere in Jewish literature. See Judah ben Samuel, *Sefer Ḥasidim*, ed. J. Wistinetzki (Frankfurt, 1924), p. 204 (sec. 811).

[7] "Just ... law." Interlinear addition. See note *b*.

[8] "(Pardon ... anger.)" Interlinear addition. See note *c*.

no*m* ouuera de difirir e prolonguar sua vinda por tanto tempo e leixar-
vos assi sem pastor e guoue*r*nador, ne*m* ho Templo ouuera de estar assi
caido como esta e a cidade destruida sem vossa habitação e morada,
ne*m* ouueres assi de andar derramados como andaes por Europa, Asia,
Africa, catiuos e suiuguados, porq*ue* hos vossos pecados no*m* são tão
enormes e feos como forão hos dos vossos antepassados. E, pore*m*, no*m*
esteuerão em catiueiro em Babilonia senão setenta anos e tornarão pera
Ierusale*m* com muita prosperidade.

E aguora ia faz 1541 anos q*ue* Iuda no*m* adorou ne*m* sacrificou em
Ierusalem. Q*u*e causou isto? A vinda do Mexia o causou, na qual no*m*
queres creer, e a sua morte. Assi, senhores, que deuees de creer q*ue* ia
ho Mexia veo. Esto saberees por c*er*teza se uos bem quiserdes especular
hos vossos doutores, hos quaes afirmão que ho Mexia auia de vir na fim
da segunda destruição do Templo, feita po*r* Tito.

*d*Como ya veo isto, irmãos muito amados, auies de crer e fundarvos
na nossa fee, como eu espero q*ue* fares. Leixai, pois, Moises. Leixai,
polo que deues a D*e*os e à v*ir*tude, porq*ue* no*m* deseio bispados ne*m* ab-
badias (posto q*ue* ya p*er*to estiue disto, mas no*m* foi D*e*os si*r*uido porq*ue*
não quiserão hos humanos), mas vossa saluação e co*nue*rtimento.*d*

[*fol. 14v*] Ho profeta Daniel asaz claramente declara no capitolo nono
esta vinda do Mexia, ho qual auia de vir antes que ho Templo fosse a
segunda vez destruido por Tito, ho que podees ver bem claro leendo
aquele capitolo nono de Daniel, porq*ue* elle pr*i*meiro fala da vinda de
Chr*i*sto e depois da destruição do Templo, onde asaz se conclude que ho
anio Guabriel demostrou ho tempo c*er*to a Daniel do Mexia. E pera
melhor proua, veiamos ho que sentirão hos vossos doutores ac*er*qua
desta vinda antes da destruição segunda da Santa Casa.

Antes que ho Mexia viesse muitos do vosso sangue, home*n*s santos e
v*ir*tuosos, vendo hos grandes pecados que se fazião antre elles, che-
guandose ia ho tempo do Mexia, começarão a dizer que ho Mexia no*m*
auia de vir no tempo det*er*minado, mas que auia de prolonguar e difirir
sua vinda porqua*n*to hos pecados que se comitião antre elles erão feos,
torpes, grandes, e enormes. Veo loguo Rabi Iosua acorrendo a este
error, dizendo: "No*m* vos enguanees, filhos de Isrrael, posto q*ue* polo
profeta seia escrito (Ezechiel, capitolo xviij°): 'Co*nue*rteiuos a my*m* e

d-d *marg.*

⁹ The doctors referred to are Saadia ben Joseph Gaon (d. 942) and Abraham ibn Ezra (d. 1167)
who both interpreted the seventy weeks of Dan. 9:24f. as referring to the period from the beginning of the first exile until the destruction of the second Temple. (*Beliefs and Opinions*, 8. 9; Ibn Ezra,

Messiah could not have postponed or delayed His coming for so long, leaving you without a shepherd or governor. Nor could the Temple have remained fallen as it is now and the city destroyed, bereft of your presence. Nor could you remain dispersed throughout the world, as you are, in Europe, Asia, and Africa, enslaved and subjugated, because your sins, after all, are not so great or ugly as those of your forefathers. They, however, were in captivity in Babylonia for only seventy years after which they returned to Jerusalem in great prosperity.

For 1541 years now Judah has neither worshiped nor sacrificed in Jerusalem. What caused this? The advent of the Messiah, in Whom you refuse to believe, and His death caused it. Thus, gentlemen, you must believe that the Messiah came. You can come to know this for a certainty if you care to consider your doctors, who affirm that the Messiah would come at the end of the second destruction of the Temple which was brought about by Titus.[9]

Since this did happen, dearly beloved brothers, you must believe and root yourselves in our faith, as I hope you will. Leave Moses. Abandon him because of what you owe God and virtue. I do not seek dioceses or abbeys (for I came close to this, but God was not served because men were not disposed to it) but only your salvation and conversion.[10]

[fol. 14v] The prophet Daniel clearly demonstrates in chapter nine the advent of the Messiah, Who was to come before the Temple was destroyed a second time by Titus. You can see this very clearly if you read chapter nine of Daniel. In this chapter he first speaks of the coming of Christ and then of the destruction of the Temple and clearly proves that the angel Gabriel showed him the exact time the Messiah was to come.[11] For even further proof, let us see what your doctors thought about this coming before the second destruction of the Holy City.

Before the arrival of the Messiah, many of your blood, saintly and virtuous men, saw the great sins that were being committed among their people at a time when the Messiah's coming was fast approaching and began to say that the Messiah would not come at the appointed time. Rather, He would delay and postpone His coming since the sins that were being committed among them were ugly, shameful, and great in number. Rabbi Joshua quickly replied to this, saying: "Do not be deceived, children of Israel, since by the prophet it is written (Ezekiel,

---

Comm. on Dan. 9:24). *ACPJ* (1, 2, pp. 43f.) and *FF* (fol. 39rb) cite these opinions along with the misconception that these scholars predicted the coming of the Messiah within this period.

[10] "Since ... conversion" marginal addition. See note *d*.

[11] Cf. Dan. 9:25ff.

fazei penitentia,' porque Deos nom ha de mudar a sua sentença de mandar ho Mexia antes da destruição segunda da Casa Santa, posto que pequees."

Duas cousas verdadeiras diz este vosso doutor. A primeira he que ho Mexia auia de vir antes que ho Templo fosse destruido a segunda vez por Tito, e assi veo Christo. A segunda cousa que diz he que hos pecados nom auião de difirir nem prolonguar a vinda de Mexia, pois que elle vinha pera rredimir ho pecado, vosso e nosso. Esto se confirma com aquilo que esta escrito numa grosa do liuro Grão Grande sobre hum texto que esta escrito no Genesis, no capitolo xxvijº, onde se diz que Iacob fugia de seu irmão Esau por amor da benção que lhe tomou, pera Labaam, seu tio, por mandado de Rrebeca, sua mãi. Fazse ali huma pergunta a Iacob, dizendo: "'Quem es tu, O monte grande diante de Zorobabel, pera fazer direito e iustiça?' E saira a pedra da cabeceira." "Soom de graça e graça auia," diz a grosa, rrespondendo à pergunta feita a Iacob. Este he ho Mexia que veem depois de Zorobabel, ho qual iulguara direitamente e fara iustiça, e tirara a pedra da cabeceira. Esta he a pedra [fol. 15r] da qual falou Dauid no psalmo cvijº. "A pedra que lançarão fora hos edificantes, foi posta nom angolo ou canto da casa." Esta pedra he ho Mexia, ho qual sera por cabeceira no canto da casa e dara graça à casa de Dauid vindo diante de Zorobabel.

Todos estes dizeres dos vossos doutores e das grosas concludem que ho Mexia auia de vir depois de Zorobabel, seendo por elle e por Neemias e Esdras a cidade edificada com ho Templo, por mandado de Ciro hum pouco antes que a segunda destruição viesse ao Templo e cidade. Este Zorobabel foi aquele grande duque que leuou ho pouo a Ierusalem, guiandoo por mandado delrrei Ciro quando saio do catiueiro e rreedificou a cidade com ho Templo, segundo se contem no Primeiro Liuro de Esdras, no primeiro capitolo, e Ieremias assi ho tinha profitizado no xxvº capitolo. Polo qual nom teendes debate sobre esta vinda do Mexia senão porque queres, pois que estes vossos doutores tão

---

[12] Ezek. 18:30. Vulg.: "Convertimini et agite poenitentiam."

[13] This passage is based upon a text in B.T. Sanhedrin 97b (cited in *PF*, p. 401) which discusses whether the coming of the Messiah is contingent upon the repentance of Israel, a view which R. Joshua opposed. A number of verses are cited in the passage but Ezek. 18:30 is not among them.

[14] Cf. Gen. 27:41ff.

[15] Zech. 4:7.

[16] Cf. Gen. 28:18.

chapter 18): *Turn to me and repent.*[12] God will not change His intention of sending the Messiah before the second destruction of the Holy Temple even though you sin."[13]

There are two truths contained in what your doctor says. The first is that the Messiah would come before the Temple was destroyed a second time by Titus, as Christ did. The second is that the sins committed neither delayed nor postponed His coming since He came to redeem sin, yours and ours. This is confirmed by that which is written in a gloss of the *Grão Grande* which treats of a passage that is contained in Genesis, chapter 27. It says there that Jacob, was ordered by his mother Rebekah, to flee from Esau because of the blessing which he stole and to go to his uncle Laban.[14] Here Jacob is asked: "*Who are you, oh great mountain before Zerubbabel, to bring right and justice?*[15] *And the headstone had gone forth.*"[16] The gloss responded to the question put to Jacob by saying: "I am and have received grace." This is the Messiah who comes after Zerubbabel and who will judge promptly and justly, and will take forth the headstone. This is the stone [*fol. 15r*] of which David spoke in Psalm 107. *The stone that the builders cast forth was placed at an angle or corner of the house.*[17] The stone is the Messiah who shall serve as the headstone in the corner of the house and will bestow grace on the house of David standing before Zerubbabel.[18]

All these sayings and glosses of your doctors conclude that the Messiah would come after Zerubbabel. The city and the Temple were to be rebuilt by him, Nehemiah, and Ezra by an order of Cyrus given shortly before the Temple and the city were to be destroyed for a second time. It was the great leader Zerubbabel who led the people to Jerusalem as was ordered by Cyrus when they went forth from their captivity and rebuilt the city and the Temple. This is in accord with what is contained in the First Book of Ezra, first chapter,[19] and in Jeremiah, as he prophesied in chapter 25.[20] For this reason, you have no real argument against the coming of the Messiah since these doctors of

[17] Ps. 118 (117):22.

[18] Based on a passage cited in *PF* (pp. 341, 389, 413f., 428, 637, 769), attributed to Genesis Rabbah but no longer extant in the Hebrew texts: "*Jacob left Beer-sheba* (Gen. 28:10). ... Scripture ... says, *Who are you, O great mountain* (Zech. 4:7). This is the Messiah. [This is said] since he goes forth in equity [play on Hebrew *mishor* (plain)] for he shall judge equitably, as it is said, *With righteousness he shall judge the poor and decide with equity for the meek of the earth* (Isa. 11:4); *And he shall bring forward the top stone* (Zech. 4:7). This is the stone of Jacob, as it is said, *He took the stone which he had put under his head*" (Gen. 28:18).

[19] Ezra 1:8.

[20] Jer. 25:12.

manifestamente afirmão a vinda dele naquele tempo determinado no qual, sen duuida, veo Christo tomar carne humana.

Assi, senhores, que depois que ho Templo foi edificada por mandado de Ciro, ates a vinda do Mexia que foi[e] antes da destruição da casa per espaço de setenta e tres anos e meo, se passarão quatrocentos e trinta e quatro anos. Beem podees, pois, creer, e beem veedes, que andaes errados, vendo que estes vossos doutores tão claramente vos denunciarão a vinda do Senhor Mexia en certo tempo. Mas vos outros, nom sei com que colores ou, diremos, enguanos, nom somentes corrompees vossos corações, mas ho que pior parece, nom daes azo aos simpli[z]es que se conuertão, mas trazes tanta astutia e prudentia que nom querees casar vossas filhas com christãos velhos mas sempre com nouos. Por onde daes a entender que queres ainda iudaizar. Este iulguar e iuizo nom he meu somentes, mas de muitos christãos velhos que ho vem polo olho. Por onde sabee que se eu teuesse mando nos reinos de Purtugual, eu nam volo consintiria. Mas christão velho se casasse com christaam noua, a fee de Christo estaria integra, porquanto a christaam noua nom ousaria de iudaizar, como proua ho nosso São Paulo escreuendo aos Chorinthios (Prime[ira], capitolo 7º), dizendo que homem infiel he santificado pola molher fiel.

Tornando, pois, ao nosso primeiro instituto, prouemos esta vinda do Mexia ia ser comprida. Ioel profeta falando da vinda do Mexia, diz no capitolo segundo: "Ho Senhor de Sion bradara e Ierusalem dara sua voz com brados, e hos ceos se mouerão com ha terra e ho Senhor [fol. 15v] he esperança do seu pouo e forteleza dos filhos de Isrrael. E sabee que eu, vosso Senhor, ei de morar no monte de Sion." Rabi Aquila, vosso doutor, grosando este passo diz que isto se entende do Mexia, ho qual vira antes da destruição do Templo. Olhai, pois, olhai, como [f]andaes, senhores, ceguos,[f] enguanados, cuidando que ainda nom veo vosso Senhor ho Mexia, ho qual demostra bem claramente este doutor ia ser vindo. Vergonha, auies d'aver vergonha, [g]irmãos muito amados,[g] de andar assi incredolos e obstinados acerqua desta vinda. Tirai por vossa

---

e MS que a foi   f-f int. + ho demo vos traz exp.   g-g int.

[21] See Chap. 3, n. 29.

[22] 1 Cor. 7:14. In contrast, Jewish writers in this period maintained that it was the women who kept their husbands faithful to Judaism. See Joseph Jabez, 'Or Ha-Ḥayyim (Lublin, 1861-2), p. 8a, and above, Introduction, p. 25.

[23] Correctly: third.

[24] Joel 3:16f. (In Hebrew Bible 4:16f.).

yours quite pointedly affirmed His coming at that appointed time in which Christ, without a doubt, came in human form.

Thus, gentlemen, from the time that the Temple was erected by order of Cyrus until the advent of the Messiah, which took place seventy-three and a half years before the destruction of the Temple, four hundred and thirty-four years passed.[21] So you can well believe and see that you are wrong, for your own doctors clearly reveal to you the coming of the Lord Messiah at the appointed time, I know not with what ruses or, shall I say, deceits, you not only corrupt your hearts but, even worse, prevent the simple from converting. You are so clever and wily that you do not want to marry your daughters to Old Christians, but always to New Christians. You thus show that you still wish to judaize. This judgment is not mine alone but is shared by many Old Christians who see it for themselves. Consequently, let it be known that were I at the head of the Kingdom of Portugal, I would not permit this situation to continue. Rather, if Old Christians married New Christians, the integrity of Christ's faith would be preserved: The New Christians would not dare to judaize. This is proven by Saint Paul writing to the Corinthians (First Epistle to the Corinthians, chapter 7) where he says that an unfaithful man is sanctified by the faithful woman.[22]

Turning now to our first intent, let us prove that the advent of Christ has already been fulfilled. The prophet Joel speaks of this coming in the second[23] chapter: *The Lord shall cry out from Zion and from Jerusalem He will utter His voice and the heavens will move with the earth, and the Lord* [fol. 15v] *is the hope of His people and the strength of the children of Israel. And know that I, your Lord, shall dwell on the mount of Zion.*[24] Your doctor, Rabbi Aquila,[25] glossed this passage and said that this is taken to refer to the Messiah who will come before the destruction of the Temple.[26] Look then! See how you go about, gentlemen — blind,[27] deceived, believing that your Lord, the Messiah, has still not come even though this doctor has clearly shown that He has. Shame! That is what you should feel, my beloved brothers:[28] shame; for you go about obstinately denying this

---

[25] Correctly: Akiba, second century rabbinic teacher.

[26] This is based on a passage from B.T. Sanhedrin 97b cited in *PF* (pp. 380f.). Martini correctly cites Hag. 2:6 (7) instead of the verse from Joel: "*R. Akiba erat exponens*, Adhuc unum modicum & ego commovens caelum, & terram, & adducam desiderium omnium gentium in Jerusalem. Glossa *R. Akiba exponebat hoc de diebus Messiae, & de Rege Messia, & de tempore quod fuit post destructionem primae domus.*"

[27] "How ... blind" interlinear addition which replaces "the devil leads you" which is expunged. See note *e*.

[28] "My ... brothers." Interlinear addition. See note *f*.

vida este dizer vosso comum "não veo ho Mexia" e fiquaruosha "veo Christo," que he a uerdade.

Rabi Salamão, escreuendo sobre ha autoridade acima aleguada, confirmando ho que ia teemos dito, diz: "E daqui a hum pouco vinra ho Rreino a Isrrael e nom tardara ho Mexia."

Vos outros, senhores,[h] teendes dous errores por amor dos quaes nom queres creer nem entender que ho Mexia he vindo. Ho primeiro erro he que teendes por fee que na vinda do Mexia hão de aparecer sinaes no sol e na lua, de maneira que a claridade da lua auia de ser nesse tempo tão grande como a do sol, e porquanto hos vossos antepassados isto ainda não virão, portanto no[m] quiserão que viera ho Mexia, a opinião e error dos quaes vos siguis. Verdade he que isto esta escrito no capitolo xxx de Isaias, no qual se diz: "A luz da lua sera como ha do sol." Porem, esta profitia nom se entende da vinda do Mexia, como vos falsamente entendes e cuidaes, que antão seria isto comprido. E que assi seia, Ionathas Rrabi, homem doutissimo assi no hebraico como no caldeu, ho qual tresladou todo ho Testamento Velho em caldeu, a qual tresladação hos vossos doutores daam tanta autoridade como ao hebraico, e ainda quando duuidão no hebraico socorremsse ao caldeu, este doutor tira este vosso falso error sobre a profitia aleguada, dizendo: "Nom creaes que a lua chegue iamais à claridade do sol, porque ho sol he aquele que daa a claridade e lume," como affirma ho nosso Aristoteles. Mas entendesse das virtudes dos iustos, hos quaes serão mais lumiosos sete vezes que ho sol, sendo elles lua antes da vinda do Mexia, e elle vindo, serão sol. Esto sera por amor dos iniustos idolatras que serão neste tempo enuerguonhados por amor da confusão que rreceberão. Mas loguo serão alumeados polo Mexia, como a lux do sol. Nom creaes, pois, que isto que dixe Isaias se deua fazer rrealmente na lua nem no sol quando viesse Christo [*fol. 16r*] mas entendesse dos iustos, hos quaes serão mais resplandecentes que não ho sol nem a lua.

Ho segundo erro que teendes he que cuidaes e pensaes que ho mundo nouamente se ha de renouar e que ho Mexia ha de catiuar

h int.

[29] This is based on the comment of Rashi on the passage from Sanhedrin cited above. In *PF* (p. 380f.): "*Alia expositio.* Adhuc unum modicum est: modicum scilicet regni venturi Israeli post destructionem domus prioris ..."

[30] Interlinear addition. See note *g*.

[31] Isa. 30:26.

[32] See above, Chap. 4, n. 17.

coming. For your sakes, cast aside your common saying: "The Messiah has not come," and replace it with "Christ has come." This is the truth.

Rabbi Solomon wrote about the above passage and confirmed what we have said: "Shortly the Kingdom shall come to Israel and the Messiah shall not delay."[29]

You, gentlemen,[30] make two errors which prevent you from believing or understanding that the Messiah has come. The first error is that you firmly believe that when the Messiah comes signs shall appear in the sun and moon, so that the brightness of the moon, at that time, would be as great as that of the sun. Since your forefathers did not see this happen, they did not deem that the Messiah had come. It is their opinion and error which you follow. This actually is written in chapter 30 of Isaiah, where we find: *The light of the moon will be as that of the sun.*[31] However, this prophecy does not refer to the coming of the Messiah as you falsely believe and maintain for then this too would have been fulfilled. That what I say is true may be seen in the writings of Rabbi Jonathan, a man as learned in Hebrew as in Chaldean,[32] who translated the entire Old Testament into Chaldean. This Chaldean translation is as highly esteemed by your doctors as is the Hebrew, so that when there is a question concerning the Hebrew, the Chaldean translation is consulted. This doctor rejects this false error concerning the above prophecy and says, "Do not believe that the moon will ever reach the brightness of the sun, because it is the sun that gives brightness and light," as our Aristotle affirms.[33] This, however, is to be understood to refer to the virtues of the just who will be seven times brighter than the sun. For they are the moon before the advent of the Messiah and the sun when He comes. This is in relation to the iniquitous idolators who will be disgraced at that time by the humiliation they will undergo. But then, they will be illuminated by the Messiah, as the light of the sun. Thus, do not believe that what Isaiah said is to be taken literally with respect to the moon and the sun when Christ comes [*fol. 16r*] for it actually refers to the just who will be more resplendent than either the sun or the moon.[34]

Your second error is that you think that the world will not only be altered but that the Messiah is to capture all the Gentiles and Christians

[33] This is not found in any version of the Targum. Machado's statement may be based on a confusion of such a passage as that in *PF*, p. 444: "*Porro erubescet luna*, etc. completum est in diebus Domini nostri Jesu Christi non solum quando in morte ipsius sol obscuratus est, et per consequens luna quae lumen habet a sole ..." The reference to Aristotle is apparently *Metaphysics* 8.4.

[34] Cf. B.T. Sanhedrin 91b; Kimhi, *ad. loc.* For a somewhat different approach to the problem, see *PF*, pp. 443f.

todos hos gentios e christãos e que vos hão de seruir como catiuos, ho
que ho vosso olho nunqua vera, nem hos vindoiros (esto diguo porque
nom pode ser nem sera yamais); e que ho Mexia ha de ser monarcha e
emperador de todo vniuerso mundo (ya ho foi, he, e sera), e porquanto
hos vossos antepassados isto nom virão (nom sol nem na lua), portanto
nom quiserão creer que veo ho Mexia.

Estes são hos vossos erros e ciguidades que trazees e andaes semeando
nos corações dos simplizes. Leede,[i] leede hos vossos doutores e entende[i]os, que não são de tal opinião nem sentença como esta. E que
assi seia, olhai aquilo que dizem. Rabi Samuel, vosso doutor, diz que
nom auera diferença no mundo alguma como muitos cuidarão, quando
vier ho Mexia; mas todo sera hum e ho mundo siguira seu estilo como
d'antes siguio. Veedes aqui ha verdade que sinte este doutor dizendo
que na do Mexia nom se faria mudança alguma neste mundo, como
nom se fez quando Christo veo, senão nas almas, as quaes elle, pola sua
morte, veo redimir e saluar.

Deixai, pois, per vossa vida, estes errores e crede que ho Mexia ia
veo, ho que podemos prouar por huma grosa dos vossos doutores sobre
aquele passo dos Cantares: "Alegrarnosemos e aueremos prazer en Ti."
Este he ho exemplo que ali se põe pera prouar a vinda do Mexia:
"Huma rrainha foi, a qual estaua muito beem casada con seu marido,
estando com seus filhos e filhas muito a sua vontade. Mas quis sua ven-
tura que ho marido se passou alem do mar com seus geenrros e filhos e
filhas, ficando ella soo. Mas, porem, depois de muito tempo passado,
vierãolhe nouas que hos seus genrros erão vindos, e rrespondeo ella,
dizendo: 'Prazer de minhas filhas.' E dali a pouco tempo, dixerãolhe:
'Senhora, vossos filhos são vindos.' Dixe ella: 'Pois que vierão, prazer de
minhas noras.' Finalmente lhe dixerão: 'Senhora, sabee que vosso
marido he vindo.' Dixe ella, alegrandosse: 'Este he ho prazer comprido.'"

Assi, antes da vinda do Mexia, vierão santos [*fol. 16v*] padres e
mesaieiros, como foi Habraam, Isaac, e Iacob, e foi prazer pequeno, e
depois veo Dauid profeta. Vierão hos quatro e doze profetas, e nom foi
grande prazer. Mas quando Zacharias profeta dixe, capitolo nono:
"Eulo teu Rrei; veem a ti iusto e saluador, homem e caualeiro, sobre a

---

i -*de* int.

[35] On this notion, see B.T. Berakhot 34b; *PF*, pp. 425f.
[36] "Samuel said: 'There is no difference between this world and the days of the Messiah, except
[that in the latter there will be no] bondage to foreign peoples,'" B.T. Shabbat 63a; *PF*, p. 434.
[37] Song of Songs 1:4 (1:3).

who in turn are to serve you. This neither you nor those coming after you will ever see (I say this because this cannot be — now or ever). You also believe that the Messiah will be monarch and emperor of the whole world (which He was and will be). But since your ancestors never saw this either in the sun or moon, they did not want to believe that the Messiah came.[35]

Such is the nature of the error and ignorance which you sow in the hearts of the simple ones. Read! Read your doctors and grasp their meaning, which is other than you believe it to be. To prove this, see what they say. Rabbi Samuel says that, contrary to what many believed, there will be no change in the world when the Messiah comes. Rather everything will be the same and the world will continue as it was.[36] Here is the truth as told by this doctor who said that no change would take place in the world. Thus, when Christ came, change took place only in souls which He came to redeem and save through His death.

By your life! Lay aside these errors and believe that the Messiah came. We can prove this by a gloss of one of your doctors which is based on that passage in the Song of Songs which says: *We shall rejoice and have pleasure in you.*[37] This is the parable used to prove the coming of the Messiah: "There once was a queen who was very happy with her husband, sons, and daughters. But such was her lot, that her husband went beyond the sea with his sons-in-law, sons, and daughters, leaving her alone. After some time had passed, she had news that her sons-in-law had returned. She replied: 'A joy for my daughters.' A short time later she was told: 'Madam, your sons have arrived.' And she answered: 'Since thay have come, my daughters-in-law are happy.' At last she was told: 'Madam, your husband has returned.' Full of happiness, she said: 'This is a joy fulfilled.'"[38]

And so was it before the coming of the Messiah that the holy [*fol. 16v*] patriarchs and messengers such as Abraham, Isaac, Jacob, and David the prophet came. This was a small pleasure. Then there were the four and the twelve prophets, and the pleasure was still small. But when Zechariah the prophet said, in chapter nine: *Here is your king; He comes to you as the Just one and the Savior, a man riding an ass,*[39] this is the perfect

[38] Song of Songs Rabbah to 1:4 (Sonc. pp. 49f.) cited in *PF*, p. 646: "WE WILL BE GLAD AND REJOICE IN THEE. They are like a queen whose husband the king, whose sons and sons-in-law went abroad. When they come and tell her, 'Your sons have returned,' she replies, 'What is that to me: Let my daughters-in-law rejoice.' When her sons-in-law return and they tell her, 'Your sons-in-law are here,' she replies, 'What is that to me? Let my daughters rejoice!' But when they say to her, 'The King your husband has returned,' she says, 'This is a real pleasure, joy on joy.'"
[39] Zech. 9:9.

asna," este he ho prazer comprido e perfeito, ho qual siguira Zorobabel, vindo antes da destruiçam segunda da Casa Santa. Assi ho dixe Deos. Diz mais a grosa: "Alegrate, filha de Sion, que eu virei," e rrespondeo ho profeta, dizendo: "Alegrarmeey em Deos; alegrarsea a minha alma em meu Deos que me visitara, e a sua vinda pouco tardara."

Destas grosas dos vossos doutores bem se demostra que ho Mexia loguo auia de vir depois de Zorobabel, antes que segundariamente ho Templo fosse destruido por Tito e polo pouo rromano. Esto confirma ainda huma grosa dos vossos doutores sobre hum passo dos Prouerbios, onde se diz: "Muitos pensamentos ha no coração do homem." Diz a grosa: "Assi como quando se põe algum sinal loguo se conhece aquel luguar, assi sera conhecida a vinda do Mexia quando a uara ou cetro for tirado do tribu de Iuda, que sera antes da destruição do Templo." Certamente esto fói comprido quando Christo naceo, porque antão estaua todo ho mundo no poder delrrei Herodes, estranieiro, e ho regimento fora do mando do tribu de Iuda, ho qual nunqua mais enfloreceo nem iamais enflorecera, ho qual tribu anda tão confuso e hos outros tambem, que com dificuldade sabees hos de qual tribo sondes, ho que Deos nom permitira se ainda este tribu ouuera de teer mando algum. Mas afirmouos que iamais sera florido como foi antes da vinda do Mexia.

Assi que posso concludir que ia vos nom esperaes polo vosso Mexia que foi Christo, mas esperaes polo antichristo, ho qual sera vosso Mexia, e Rrei, e Principe, e Monarcha, enguanandovos.

No liuro chamado Grão Grande se conta que Rrabi Samuel perguntou aos doutores do Talmud que lhe dixessem por onde afirmarão elles que ho Mexia auia de vir antes da segunda destruição da Casa Santa. Elles lhe dixerão que se prouaua polo texto do profeta Isaias, [fol. 17r] onde diz, no capitolo lxviº: "Antes que gemesse pario, e antes que lhe viessem as dores, pario macho." Dixerão hos talmudistas que na hora que a Casa Santa foy destruida por Nabuchodo[no]sor, loguo nessa hora, Isrrael bradou, como aquela que pare, e dixe: "O minha door e

---

[40] Continuation of passage from Song of Songs Rabbah cited above, n. 38: "*Rejoice greatly, O daughter of Zion* (Zech. 9:9) and it is also written, *Sing and rejoice, O daughter of Zion* (ibid. 2:14). At that moment she will say, *I will greatly rejoice in the Lord, my soul shall be joyful in my God*" (Isa. 61:10). The first sentence of the paragraph appears to be Machado's own interpretive addition. The sixteen prophets are Isaiah, Jeremiah, Ezekiel, Daniel and the twelve minor prophets.

[41] Prov. 19:21.

[42] Cf. Midrash Mishle (Midrash on Proverbs), *ad loc.* (ed. Buber, pp. 86f.): "Whence [do we know] that Israel is called a vineyard. It is written: *For the vineyard of the Lord of hosts is the house of*

and fulfilled pleasure which followed Zerubbabel before the second destruction of the Holy Temple. So said God. In addition the gloss says: *Rejoice, daughter of Zion, for I will come.* And the prophet said: *I will rejoice in the Lord; my soul shall rejoice in my God who will visit me and Whose coming shall not be delayed.*[40]

As you can see from these glosses of your doctors, the Messiah was to come after Zerubbabel and before the Temple was to be destroyed a second time by Titus and the Roman people. This is confirmed moreover in a gloss of your doctors on a passage from Proverbs which reads: *There are many thoughts in the heart of man.*[41] The gloss says: "As when a sign is placed for one to recognize a place, so will the coming of the Messiah be known when the staff or scepter is taken from the tribe of Judah, as will occur before the destruction of the Temple."[42] Certainly this occurred when Christ was born because at that time the whole world was under the rule of King Herod, a foreigner, and the dominion passed from the tribe of Judah which never flourished nor ever will flourish again. This tribe is so intermingled with the others that it is difficult for you to know to which tribe you belong.[43] God would not have allowed this to happen if this tribe was still to have any dominion. I can assure you, however, that it will never flourish as it did before the coming of the Messiah.

I can thus conclude that you are no longer waiting for your Messiah who was Christ but rather for the Antichrist who will be your Messiah, king, prince, and monarch, and who will deceive you.

In the book called the *Grão Grande,* it is told that Rabbi Samuel asked the doctors of the Talmud to tell him how they prove that the Messiah was to come before the second destruction of the Holy Temple. They told him that it can be proved by the text of the prophet Isaiah [*fol. 17r*] in chapter 66, where he says: *Before she groaned she gave birth, and before the pains came she gave birth to a son.*[44] The talmudists say that at that very moment when the Holy Temple was destroyed by Nebuchadnezzar, Israel cried out as she who gives birth and said, "Oh what pain!" as a

---

Israel (Isa. 5:7). Just as the location of a planting is evident as soon you plant it, so did the Holy One blessed be He plant the Kingdom in the tribe of Judah until [the King Messiah] appear as it is said, *The scepter shall not depart from Judah* (Gen. 49:10)." Neither this nor a similar passage has been located in Christian anti-Jewish literature.

[43] This is a frequent theme in polemical literature. See *PF*, pp. 26off. and the sixteenth-century *Faith Strengthened* (*Ḥizzuq 'Emunah*) of the Lithuanian Karaite Isaac of Troki, 1,8, ed. D. Deutsch (Breslau, 1873), pp. 75ff.; English: M. Mocatta, trans., (New York, 1970), pp. 43ff.

[44] Isa. 66:7.

coyta," como mulher que esta com doores e antes que gemesse pario. Esto afirma a grosa sobre ho texto de Isaias aleguado.

Ionathas caldeu, aquele que tresladou ho Testamento hebraico em caldeu, diz, confirmando isto acima dito: "Antes que gemesse pario, e antes que lhe viessem doores, foi discub[er]to ho Mexia." Assi que por estes ditos dos vossos^j doutores e grosadores, parece que ho Mexia auia de nacer antes da destruição da Casa Santa, como naceo.

Mas vos, misquinhos, nom queres ser enformados na verdade nem queres creer aos ditos dos vossos doutores antepassados, hos quaes, segundo parece em muitos luguares do Talmud, afirmão esto que teemos dito e prouamos, que ho Mexia ia veo segundo polos profetas estaua determinado. E pera confirmação desto, veiamos ho que diz Rrabi Samuel sobre ho passo de Isaias acima aleguado. Diz que Helias, andando por hum caminho, ouuia huma voz antes que a Casa Santa se destruisse, que dizia: "A Casa Santa cedo sera destruida." Ouuindo, porem, esto, fiquou muito atonito e espantado, e andando seu caminho achou certos lauradores que andauão trabalhando e semeando, e disselhes: "Deos se ensanhou sobre ho mundo e ho quer destruir, e vos outros andaes semeando e trabalhando." Helias, esta dizendo, ouuio outra voz, que dixe: "Leix[ai]os, que ia naceo ho Saluador do mundo." Perguntou loguo Helias: "E onde naceo?" Rrespondeo a voz dizendo que em Betleem. Helias loguo se foi pera Betleem e achou huma molher com seu filho enuolto e emburilhado no sangue diante dela. Helias dixelhe: "Filho pariste." Respondeo: "Filho parey, como vees." E Helias dixe: "Como esta assi envolto e mitido neste sangue." Rrespondeo ella: "Grande mal he este, Helias, que como naceo, loguo se destruio a Casa Santa e Templo de Ierusalem." Helias lhe dixe: "Filha, tomai o minino e esforçaiuos^k com elle porque sera grande saluação pera nos por sua mão." Esto dizendo, foisse Helias e acabados cinquo anos, dixe antre si: "Quero hir veer se este minino se criara como rrei ou como anio." E cheguando a Betleem, achou a molher à porta, e perguntandolhe polo [fol. 17v] minino, ela lhe respondeo, dizendo: "Ia vos dixe, Helias, que como naceo, loguo a Casa Santa foi destruida. Elle

---

j int. + *teus* exp.   k *-aiuos* int. + *-ate* exp.

[45] Based on a passage found in *PF* (p. 349) ascribed to *Bereschit Rabba priori*, *ACPJ* (1, 2, p. 35) ascribed to *Genesi magno antiquissimo*, and in Spina, *FF* (fol. 37va) ascribed to "Talmuth in Berexit Rabba." A portion of this passage is to be found in Gen. Rab. 85:1 and in the *Rabbati*, p. 131. Martini's Hebrew text is as follows: "Samuel bar Naḥman said: Whence do you say that on the very day that the Messiah was born, the Temple was destroyed, as it is said, *Before she was in labor she gave*

woman in labor who has already given birth before she can groan.[45] The gloss on the above text of Isaiah confirms this.

Jonathan the Chaldean who translated the Hebrew Testament into Chaldean confirmed the above and said: "Before she groaned, she gave birth and before the pains had started, the Messiah was revealed."[46] Thus, according to these statements of your doctors and commentators, it would seem that the Messiah was to have been born — as He was — before the destruction of the Holy Temple.

But you wretched ones do not want to know the truth nor do you want to believe the words of your learned forefathers who seem to affirm in the Talmud in many places all that we have said and are here trying to prove to you that the Messiah has already come as was determined by the prophets. To confirm this, let us look at what Rabbi Samuel had to say on this same passage of Isaiah. He wrote that while Elijah was walking along the way, he heard a voice as the Holy Temple was about to be destroyed. It said: "Soon the Holy Temple will be destroyed." On hearing this, he was stunned and amazed. He continued on his way and saw some men sowing. He said to them: "God has become angry with the world and wants to destroy it, and you go on sowing!" After he said this, he heard another voice that said: "Leave them be for the Savior of the world has already been born." Elijah then asked: "And where was he born?" The voice answered that it was in Bethlehem. Elijah then went to Bethlehem and there found a woman with her son lying covered with blood before her. He said to her: "You bore a son." She replied: "I bore a son, as you can see." And Elijah replied: "Why is he covered with blood?" She then said to him: "A great misfortune has come to pass, Elijah, for, when he was born, the Holy Temple was destroyed in Jerusalem." Elijah then said to her: "Daughter, take the child and strengthen yourselves, for a great salvation will be wrought for us through him." After he said this, Elijah left. Five years later, he said to himself: "I should like to go and see if this child was raised as a king or as an angel." When he arrived in Bethlehem, he found the woman at the door and he asked her about [fol. 17v] the child. She answered: "I already told you, Elijah, that when

---

birth; before her pain came upon her she was delivered of a son, who has heard such a thing? Who has seen such things? (Isa. 66:7f). When the Temple was destroyed, [Israel] cried like a woman in labor, as it is said, For I had a cry as a woman in travail" (Jer. 4:31). Machado's addition of "O minha door e coyta, etc." may be connected with the MS variant given in the margin of PF "[in omni] fervore coitus" which translates Gen. 30:41, the catch verse of the above passage.

[46] See TJ, ad loc., cited in ACPJ, 1, 2, p. 35; FF, fol. 37va.

tee*m* pees e no*m* anda, e olhos e no*m* vee, e orelhas e no*m* ouue. Esta como pedra." Estando assi Helias praticando co*m* a molher, aleuantarãose loguo grandes ventos e trouões e leuarão ho minino e lançarãono no maar. Helias, vendo estas cousas tão marauilhosas loguo rompeo ho seu vestido e depenou as barbas, e levou grande maguoa e tristeza, dizendo: "Perdida he a saluação de Isrrael." E loguo Helias ouuio hu*m*a voz que dizia: "No*m* he assi como tu cuidas, Helias. Mas ce*r*to tempo morara no maar grande, e depois no inf*er*no, e finalme*n*te na porta de Rroma andara."

   Diguouos, senhores, que esta visão de vosso Helias foi marauilhosa, e no*m* sinifiq*u*a outra cousa senão que ho Mexia auia de vir no fim da destruição segunda do Templo, como veo. E nisto no*m* deuies de teer debate, pois que hos vossos doutores antepassados assi tão manifestamente falarão desta vinda no tempo dete*r*minado. Esta visão, segundo parece, foi feita polo anio, ho qual veo descobrir este tão grande segredo ha Helias. Primeirame*n*te, lhe dixe ho anio que avia a Casa Santa s*er* destruida como ho Mexia nacesse. E assi foi, que po*r* amor da sua morte, ho Templo foi destruido por Tito em vingança dos vossos antepassados q*u*e matarão ho Mexia. Segundariamente, lhe dixe que auia de morar no maar grande. Assi foi que morou neste mundo, maar grande, trinta e tres anos e meo. Terceiramente, lhe dixe que auia de morar no inferno, no limbo, onde elle esteue por espaço de corenta horas, qua*n*do foi tirar hos padres santos do limbo. Quartame*n*te, esteue no paraiso terreal por espaço de corenta dias antes que elle subisse aos ceos, ¹indo e vindo aos discipolos, co*m*municando e falando co*m* eles.¹ Quintame*n*te, lhe dixe que auia de nacer em Betlee*m*, como naceo.

   Ce*r*tamente e sem duuida, todas estas cousas sam passadas e co*m*-

---

1-1 int. +*e vos outros desta sentença sondes, que ho paraiso esta a paar de Rroma. Assi affirmão hos talmudistas* exp.

---

⁴⁷ This passage from the *BRMD* to Gen. 30:41 is found in *PF*, p. 350; *ACPJ*, 1, 2, pp. 35ff.; añd *FF*, fols. 37*va*-38*ra* and is found in the *Rabbati* (p. 131 with references). Martini's version reads: "R. Samuel bar Naḥman said: Once Elijah of blessed memory was walking along on the day that the Temple was destroyed. He heard a heavenly voice shout: The Holy Temple is to be destroyed. When Elijah heard this, he assumed that the whole world would be destroyed. He found people plowing and planting. The Holy One, blessed be He, is wroth with the world and wishes to destroy His house and exile His sons among the nations of the world and you engage in day-to-day affairs. A heavenly voice went forth: Leave them be for a redeemer for Israel has been born. He said: Where is he? It replied: In Bethlehem of Judea. He went and found a woman sitting at the door of her house. Her son was lying before her soiled with blood. He said to her: My daughter, have you borne a son? She said to him: Yes. He said to her: Why is he soiled and lying in blood? She said to

he was born the Holy Temple was destroyed. He has feet and does not walk, eyes and does not see, ears and does not hear. He is like a stone." While Elijah was talking with the woman, loud claps of thunder were heard and strong winds picked up the child and hurled him into the sea. When Elijah saw these amazing things, he tore his clothes, plucked at his beard and said with much grief and sorrow: "The salvation of Israel is lost." Then he heard a voice saying: "It is not as you think Elijah; for he will dwell a certain time in the great sea and then in hell, and will finally appear at the gates of Rome."[47]

I tell you, gentlemen, that this vision of your Elijah was marvelous. It means nothing but that the Messiah was to come — as He did — at the second destruction of the Temple. There is no point of debate on this since your own ancient doctors spoke of His coming at the appointed time. It seems that Elijah's vision was conveyed by the angel who came to reveal this great secret to him. First, the angel told him that the Holy Temple was to be destroyed when the Messiah was born. And so it was; for on account of His death the Temple was destroyed by Titus who took vengeance upon your ancestors who killed the Messiah. Second, he said that He was to dwell in the great sea. And so it was that He lived in this world, the great sea,[48] for thirty-three and one-half years. Third, the angel said that He was to dwell in hell, in limbo, where He did remain for forty hours and from where He delivered the holy patriarchs. Fourth, He was in the terrestrial paradise for a period of forty days before He rose to heaven. During this time, He came and went and spoke with His disciples. Fifth, the angel told him that the Messiah was to be born in Bethlehem, as He was.[49]

There is certainly no doubt as to the fulfillment of these things.

---

him: The tragedy is that he was born on the day that the Temple was destroyed. He said to her: Stand and hold him for they will be well redeemed by him. She then arose and held him. [Elijah] left him and went off for five years. He said: Let me go and see whether the redeemer of Israel is growing up to look like a king or like the ministering angels. He found the woman sitting at the entrance of her house and said to her: My daughter, what is the lad like? She said to him: My master! Did I not tell you that he was doomed to begin with since the Temple was destroyed on the day he was born. For he has feet and does not walk, eyes and does not see, ears and does not hear, a mouth and does not speak and lies like a stone. While [Elijah] was speaking, a wind blew from the four corners of the earth and threw [the child] into the sea. He tore his clothes, pulled at his hair, and shouted: It is not as you think. He will live for four hundred years in the great sea, for eighty years in the smoke-chamber with the sons of Korah, and eighty years at the gate of Rome. For the rest, he shall wander throughout all lands until the appointed time."

[48] On this image, see *PF*, p. 740.

[49] This method of listing conclusions to be drawn from an 'aggadah is reminiscent of the method of Hieronymus de Sancta Fide. See *ACPJ*, *passim*.

pridas, e vos estaes obstinados e encredolos^m do que muito, senhores, me pesa.^m E pera saberdes ^nvos, senhores,^n que ho Mexia veo antes da destruição da Casa Santa, sabee por certeza, que como hos vossos antepassados matarão ho Mexia, loguo cessarão dez milagros, hos quaes erão continuos no Templo antes da sua morte.

[fol. 18r] Estes são hos sinaes que erão continuos na Casa Santa antes da paixão do Mexia, hos quaes loguo cessarão e nom parecerão mais no Templo, que he grande argumento contra vos pera se prouar que ia veo ho Mexia. Ho primeiro sinal era que nhuma molher prenhe mouia de cheiro de carne. Ho segundo era que nunqua fedeo carne (posto que fiquasse de dez dias), e per espaço de cinquo anos se guardaua no Templo Santo sem nunqua feder. Ho terceiro era que nunqua apareceo mosca nos deguoladoiros das rreses que matauão pera hos sacrifitios. Ho quarto era que nunqua sacerdote sonhou com molher, dormindo en sonhos, nem de dia nem de noite, nem caio em pulação alguma. Ho quinto era que nunqua se achou mingoa no pam que estara no Templo. Ho sexto era que nunqua cobra nem bicha mordeo a homem que fosse à Casa Santa. Ho seitimo era que nunqua chuua apagou ho foguo ordinado. Ho outauo sinal era que nunqua ho vento apagou ho foguo do sacrifitio. Ho nono era que as tripas, e moelas, e miudos das rreses tudo se consumia. Ho decimo sinal era que tantos cabião no Templo posto que fosse outocentos estando em pee como curuos en giolhos porque tanto luguar assi ocupauão dūma maneira como d'outra, ho que nom se podia fazer sem grande milagre.

Diguouos que todos estes sinaes forão grandes e marauilhosos, hos quaes sempre no Templo aparecerão ates a morte do Mexia, e loguo antão cessarão. E posto que ho Templo perseuerasse depois da morte de Christo ates que foi por Tito destruido, onde correrão quorenta e dous anos; porem, sempre ho Templo esteue sem estes dez sinaes. Hos sacerdotes vendo isto se marauilhauão e espantauão grandemente, e antre si e pubricamente diziam: "Hos nossos sinaes nam nos veemos. Profeta nom parece. Ho Mexias nam no conhecemos." Assi que andauão debachados, e atonitos, e espantados polo Templo porque elles vião tudo feito ao reues do que era.

---

m-m marg.   n-n int. + hos iudeus exp.

[50] "This … greatly" marginal addition. See note l.
[51] "You, gentlemen," interlinear addition which replaces "the Jews" expunged. See note m.
[52] B.T. Yoma 21a cited in PF, p. 371; ACPJ, 1, 2, pp. 38f.; FF, fol. 38rb. Machado interpolates and departs significantly from the original text: "Ten miracles were wrought in the Temple; no woman miscarried from the scent of the holy flesh; the holy flesh never became putrid; no fly was

Nevertheless, you are obstinate and incredulous and this, gentlemen, saddens me greatly.[50] So that you may know, gentlemen,[51] that the Messiah came before the destruction of the Holy Temple, take it as a certainty that when your ancestors killed the Messiah, the ten perpetual miracles of the Temple ceased before his death.

[fol. 18r] These are the signs that occurred continuously in the Holy Temple before the passion of the Messiah. These ceased afterwards and did not appear again in the Temple. This is important evidence to prove to you that the Messiah has already come. The first sign was that no pregnant woman aborted from the smell of meat. The second was that no meat became putrid even though it remained for [as long as] ten days. In the Holy Temple, it was kept for a period of five years without foul odor. The third was that a fly never appeared in the slaughterhouse of the cattle that were killed for sacrifices. The fourth was that a priest never dreamed of a woman either by day or by night nor became polluted. The fifth was that there was never a defect in the bread that was in the Temple. The sixth was that a man who went to the Holy Temple was never bitten by a snake or leech. The seventh was that rain never put out the flame that was ordained. The eighth sign was that the wind never put out the sacrificial fire. The ninth was that the intestines, gizzards, and viscera of the cattle were consumed. The tenth sign was that everyone fitted into the Temple inasmuch as eight hundred would take up as much space kneeling as standing. This could be nothing but a miracle.[52]

I tell you that all these great and marvelous signs appeared continuously in the Temple until the Messiah's death, after which they ceased. Although the Temple continued to exist after the death of Christ until it was destroyed by Titus — a period of forty-two years[53] — the signs never returned. The priests marveled at this and were greatly stunned, saying both among themselves and publicly: "We do not see our signs. A prophet does not appear. We do not recognize the Messiah." So they went about the Temple dumbfounded, astonished, and startled because they saw everything other than the way it had been.

---

seen in the slaughter-house; no pollution ever befell the high priest on the Day of Atonement; no rain ever quenched the fire of the wood-pile on the altar; neither did the wind overcome the column of smoke that arose therefrom; nor was there ever found any disqualifying defect in the 'Omer — or in the two loaves, or in the shew-bread; though the people stood closely pressed together, they still found wide spaces between them to prostrate themselves; never did serpent or scorpion injure anyone in Jerusalem, nor did any man ever say to his fellow: The place is too narrow for me to stay overnight in Jerusalem" (Sonc., p. 91).

[53] See above, Chap. 3, n. 29.

Estes sinaes que assi cessarão bem demostrauão ho Mexia ser vindo.
E alguns vossos doutores dizem que ho grande sacerdote sempre se
punha à parte destra no Templo. E Simeom ho iusto, como tras ho
Mexia nos braços, loguo se poos a sinistra, donde fiquou por custume.
Poromsse sempre dali por diante hos grandes sacerdotes, à parte
esquerda e nom à direita, ho que sinifiquaua a vinda do Mexia. [*fol. 18v*]
A candea que estaua da parte do oponente sempre estaua acesa, e esteue
ates a paixão do Mexia. Mas dali por diante, hora se acendia hora se
apaguaua, que era grande sinal que o Mexia era vindo. A lenha que era
ordenada pera o foguo do Templo forão dous tiçanzinhos da edificação
do Templo ates que ho iusto Simeom tomou ho Mexia nos braços, e
dali por diante, começarão hos sacerdotes de acarretarem lenha pera ho
Templo porque hos tiçanzinhos nom suprirão mais, demostrando a
vinda do Mexia.

Por vida minha que me espanto grandemente de vos outros, senhores,[o]
que sabees isto predito escrito polos vossos doutores e ainda esperaes
polo Mexia.

Hos sacerdotes, antes da morte do Mexia, fechauão as portas do
Templo, e sempre as achauão fechadas. Mas depois da morte do Mexia,
fechauamnas de noite, e pela manhaam achauamnas [abertas]. Vendo
isto tão grande milagre, Ionas Rrabi, bradando e espantandosse muito,
começou a dizer: "O santuario, O santuario, por que nos conturbas?
Bem sabemos que teu fim he cedo ser destruido," como foi por Tito.

Olhai por vossa vida, senhores,[p] e notai estes sinaes e marauilhas que
erão grandes indicios e demostrações que ho Mexia era vindo, polo
qual bem se parece polos dizeres e ditos acima postos que veo ho Mexia
no seu tempo determinado, que era antes da destruição do Templo
polos rromanos, feita como Iacob tinha predito e prenunciado quando
benzeo a Iudas (Genesis xlix), dizendo que ho guouerno nom se tiraria

---

o int.   p +*iudeus* exp.

[54] Simon the Just (early fourth century), high priest here identified with Simon of Luke 2:25.
[55] B. T. Yoma 39a cited in *PF*, pp. 369f.; *ACPJ*, 1, 2, pp. 38ff.; *FF*, fols. 38rb-39va. The original
text reads as follows: "Our Rabbis taught: Throughout the forty years that Simeon the Righteous
ministered, the lot ['For the Lord'] would always come up in the right hand; from that time on, it
would come up now in the right hand, now in the left. And [during the same time] the crimson-
coloured strap would become white. From that time on, it would at times become white, at others
not. Also: Throughout those forty years the westernmost light was shining, from that time on it was
now shining, now failing; also the fire of the pile of wood kept burning strong, so that the priests
did not have to bring to the pile any other wood besides the two logs, in order to fulfill the command about providing the wood unintermittently; from that time on it would occasionally keep

These signs which no longer appeared show that the Messiah has come. Some of your doctors say that the high priest always placed himself on the right side of the Temple. Simon the Just[54] who carried the Messiah in his arms placed himself on the left where he customarily remained. From then on, the high priests always remained on the left rather than the right side, which indicated the coming of the Messiah. [fol. 18v] The candle that was on the western side always remained lit until the passion of the Messiah. From then on, it remained now lit and now extinguished and this was a great sign that the Messiah had come. The wood that was required for the fire in the Temple had been two little firebrands, from the time that the Temple was built, up to the time that Simon the Just carried the Messiah in his arms. From then on, the priests began to cart firewood to the Temple because the little firebrands no longer sufficed.[55] This demonstrated the advent of the Messiah.

On my life, I am indeed greatly shocked, gentlemen,[56] that you should know this entire text written by your doctors and that you should still be waiting for the Messiah.

Before the death of the Messiah the priests closed the doors of the Temple and they remained closed. But after the death of the Messiah they closed them at night but found them open in the morning. On seeing this great miracle, Rabbi Jonah was astonished and shouted: "O sanctuary, sanctuary, why do you perturb us? We well know that soon you will be destroyed."[57] And so it was by Titus.

By your lives! Look, gentlemen,[58] and note these signs and wonders which were great indications and demonstrations that the Messiah had come. This is well supported by the passages cited above concerning the Messiah's coming at a determined time before the destruction of the Temple by the Romans. This is as Jacob had predicted and proclaimed when he blessed Judah (Genesis 49) and said that the scepter would

burning strongly, at other times not, so that the priests could not do without bringing throughout the day wood for the pile [on the altar]." (Soncino ed., pp. 184f.; see notes there for explanation.)

[56] Interlinear addition. See note n.

[57] B.T. Yoma 39b (Sonc., p. 186); cited in PF, p. 370; ACPJ, 1, 2, p. 40; FF, fol. 38 ra. "Ionas Rabbi" is R. Yoḥanan. Machado's version is very similar to that of ACPJ: "Et portae templi claudebantur in sero, et in mane reperiebantur apertae. Dicitque ita Rabam Ioanna filius Zachariae, templum, templum, quare terres nos, iam nouimus quod finis tuus erit in destructionem." In Sonc.: "... the doors of the Hekal [Sanctuary] would open by themselves, until R. Johanan b. Zakkai rebuked them, saying: "Hekal, Hekal, why wilt thou be the alarmer thyself? I know about thee that thou wilt be destroyed ..."

[58] Interlinear addition replacing "Jews". See note o.

da casa de Iuda ates que no*m* viesse ho Mexia. Este pod*er* foi tirado antes da destruição da Casa Santa, que he grande argume*n*to que loguo
veo ho Mexia. Esta confirmão algu*n*s vossos doutores, expondo esta
pr*o*fitia de Iacob. Diz Rrabi Samuel: "Ho cetro de Iuda fenecera," onde nos dizemos que ho cetro se tirara antes que a Casa Santa seia
destruida. Veem Rrabi Salamão grosando este passo e diz: "Cenadrim
he hu*m* luguar que esta em Ierusale*m*." Rrabi Aloim diz: "Ho qual he
onde iulguão con iuizo d'armas, ho qual se tirara antes da vinda do
Mexia que sera antes que ho Templo se destruia." Esto vos no*m* no
podees neguar se quiserdes leer hos historiadores e feitos dos emperador*e*s rroma*n*os, hos quaes tirarão todo pod*er* à cidade de Ierusalem
no*m* tempo de Tiberio, emperador de Rroma (posto que ya no tempo
de Outauiano emperador paguasse tributo), ho qual ma*n*da Pilatos por
p*r*esidente, sendo Herodes rrei, no qual tempo esta pr*o*fitia de Iacob se
compr*i*o.

[*fol. 19r*] *Rrabi Salamã*o, grosando aquilo que dixe Rrabi Aloim, que
hos iudeus no*m* auiam de iulguar iuizo d'armas qua*n*do ouuesse de vir
ho Mexia, diz: "V*e*rdade he que no*m* iulguarão en todo luguar, porque
ho poder lhes sera tirado; mas, porem, iulguarão no co*n*sistorio dos
sacerdotes." Verdade he que este consistorio sacerdotal do tr*i*bu de
Leui nom foi tirado, ho qual era sp*i*rit*u*al e no*m* temporal e pertentia
aos sac*e*rdotes por amor do pouo ser por elles enformado e ensinado,
como Moises tinha ordenado no Deut*e*ronomio, no capitolo xvi°. Assi
que ho iuizo d'armas e temporal foi tirado aos vossos antepassados
como Iacob tinha profitizado, vindo loguo ho Mexia. Esto afirma ser
v*e*rdade Rrabi Moises, ho qual dixe e ma*n*da que todo ho p*r*eguador ou
declarador e demo*n*strador da Lei deesse autoridade e fee aos doutores
do Talmud, no qual se afirma que ho Mexia auia de vir, como ho cetro
fosse tirado do tribu de Iuda.

---

[59] Gen. 49:10. On this verse in Jewish-Christian polemics, see Posnanski, *Schiloh*.

[60] The statement ascribed to Rabbi Samuel is obscure. That ascribed to R. Solomon is a corruption of a gloss of Rashi on a passage in B.T. Sanhedrin 41a cited in *PF*, p. 315; *ACPJ*, 1, 2, p. 41; *FF*,
fol. 38*vb*; and cf. Galatinus, p. 202. The talmudic passage reads: "Forty years before the destruction of the Temple, the Sanhedrin were exiled and took up residence in Hanuth. [Rashi glosses:
"There was a place so called in Jerusalem."] Whereon R. Isaac b. Abudimi said: "This is to teach
that they did not try [civil cases] ...' 'Can you really think so! Say rather, They did not try *capital*
charges'" (Sonc., p. 267).

[61] The comment of R. Solomon ben Isaac is on the above passage from B.T. Sanhedrin 41a
(Sonc., p. 267): "Capital cases (Hebrew: *dine nefashot*, lit. judgment of souls) may not be judged in
any location as long as the Sanhedrin functions in the consistory of hewn stone (*lishkat ha-gazit*) ..."

never be taken from the house of Judah until the coming of the Messiah.[59] This power was removed before the destruction of the Holy Temple which is a strong argument in favor of the Messiah's having already come. This is confirmed by some of your doctors who expound this prophecy of Jacob. Rabbi Samuel says: "The scepter of Judah will pass away," while we say that the scepter had been withdrawn before the Holy House was destroyed. In his gloss on this passage, Rabbi Solomon says: "The Sanhedrin is a place that is in Jerusalem." Rabbi Aloim says: "Which is where they judge with the judgment of souls, which will be withdrawn before the coming of the Messiah which will occur before the Temple is destroyed."[60] You cannot deny this if you read the historians and the exploits of the Roman emperors. It was they who withdrew the power from the city of Jerusalem during the time of Tiberius, emperor of Rome (for even during the time of the emperor Octavian tribute was paid), who named Pilate procurator. Herod was king at this time when this prophecy of Jacob was fulfilled.

[fol. 19r] In his gloss on what Rabbi Aloim said concerning the fact that the Jews were not to judge judgments of souls when the Messiah was to come, Rabbi Solomon says: "The truth is that they will not judge everywhere because the power has been withdrawn from them; however, they will judge in the consistory of the priests."[61] This sacerdotal consistory of the tribe of Levi — in its spiritual if not its temporal sense — was not withdrawn. It belongs to the priests because the people were instructed by them, as Moses had ordained in Deuteronomy, chapter 16.[62] Thus the judgment of souls which is temporal was withdrawn from your ancestors just as Jacob had prophesied, and when the Messiah came. Rabbi Moses confirmed this and said that every preacher, expounder, and promulgator of the Law should recognize the authority of the doctors of the Talmud in which it is affirmed that the Messiah was to come with the taking of the scepter from the tribe of Judah.[63]

In this and subsequent passages (see notes s, t, u, v, w), Machado had originally written *guazit* or *de guazit* and then changed this to "of the priests" or "of the tribe of Levi." This stems from a confusion in Machado or his source or informant between *lishkat ha-gazit*, the consistory of hewn stone, and *lishkat ha-kohanim*, the consistory of the priests. The statement of Rashi is cited in *ACPJ*, p. 40, in the name of R. Abdimi.

[62] Deut. 17:8-13.

[63] "Rrabi Moises" is R. Moses the Preacher (see Introduction), cited in this context in *PF*, p. 872; *ACPJ*, 1, 2, p. 41; *FF*, fol. 38va-b. This entire passage follows the sequence of *PF* but differs in the wording.

Mas �q vos, senhores,�q que cuidaes que este mando ainda nom he tirado, depois que tirado he, hora, dizeime, onde rreside este vosso mando? Certamente nom rreside no tribu de Iuda, porque vos nom tendes rrei nem senhor nem principe do tribu de Iuda que domine sobre vos. Assi que ʳnom ho aceitaes por falta da fee da qual careceis.ʳ

No Talmud se diz que dixe Iacob: "Nom se tirara ˢho mando spiritualˢ que esta no consistorio dos sacerdotesᵗ da parte de Iuda onde iulguauão as almas ates que nom venha ho Mexia." Este consistorio, ho qual era dos sacerdotes, cessou quando ho Templo foi por Tito destruido, nom d'antes. E assi ho afirma Rrabi Salamão, dizendo: "Quando se encubrir ᵘho mando spiritualᵘ do consistorio do ᵛtribu de Leuiᵛ e se tirar de iulguar as almas, dirão: 'Guay de nos, que se tirou ho cetro de Iuda e ho Mexia nom veo.'" Tudo isto he comprido; que todo ho poder que tinhão hos vossos antepassados, assi quanto ao temporal como ao spiritual, tudo cessou pola vinda do Mexia. Nem iamais teres poder nem mando no consistorio sacerdotalʷ nem temporal,ˣ porquanto estes mandos e poderes ia cessarão, comõ Iacob tinha dito.

E pera que saibaes por certeza que ho Mexia ia veo no tempo que lhe era determinado e ordenado, pooruosey aqui ho que se aconteceo no tempo que veo ho Mexia per[a] veerdes vossos erros, dos quaes praza ao Deos eterno que vos queira tirar, como eu deseio.

[fol. 19v] Em Cenedrim, liuro assi chamado, se conta que Bencoziba, iudeu assi chamado, rreinou trinta anos antre hos iudeus, dizendo que elle era ho Mexia promitido na Lei, e trazia consiguo hum doutor chamado Rrabi Aquiba, ho qual con suas preguações affirmaua que ho tempo era determinado e acabado pera ho Mexia vir, afirmando que Bencoziba era ho Mexia. Rrabi Moises, num liuro que fez dos iuizos nos direitos delrrei, diz que Rrabi Aquiba era dos milhores doutores que auia no Talmud, e portanto, afirmaua que elle era ho Mexia e que lhe diuião creer, pelo qual todo ho pouo cria nele e ho siguia, cuidando que era elle ho Mexia. E esto fazião porque vião ho tempo do Mexia acabado, e polos seus malos nom conhecerão a Christo, que era ho

---

q-q int. + *ho vosso enguano he grande* exp.   r-r int. + *sabees ho que dizees, nem sabes por onde andaes e haos de mil errores e de mil iudarias* exp.   s-s int. + *eeleoym* exp.   t int. + *guazit* exp.
u-u int. + *Cenedrim* exp.   v-v int. + *guazit* exp.   w int. + *de guazit* exp.   x int. + *de Cenedrim* exp.

---

[64] Interlinear addition replacing "your deception is great" expunged. See note *p*.
[65] See note *s*.
[66] "Spiritual authority" interlinear addition replacing "Sanhedrin" expunged. See note *t*.

But you, gentlemen,[64] still think that authority has not been withdrawn even though it has. Now tell me just where you think this authority of yours resides? It certainly is not in the hands of the tribe of Judah because you have no king or lord or prince in this tribe who rules over you. This you cannot accept because you lack faith.

In the Talmud it is said that Jacob said: "The spiritual authority which is in the consistory of the priests[65] of Judah where the souls were judged will not be withdrawn until the Messiah comes." This consistory, which belonged to the priests, ceased to exist when the Temple was destroyed by Titus and not before. Rabbi Solomon affirms this saying: "When the spiritual authority[66] of the consistory of the tribe of Levi[67] is withdrawn and souls will no longer be judged, they will say: 'Woe is us; for the scepter has been withdrawn from Judah and the Messiah has not come.'"[68] All this has come to pass; for all the power that your ancestors had — temporal as well as spiritual — ceased when the Messiah came. Nor will you have any power or authority — even temporal[69] — in the consistory of the priests, since these powers ceased, just as Jacob had said they would.

And so that you will know for certain that the Messiah had already come at the time prescribed and ordained for him, I will now tell you what happened when He came so that you can see your errors. May it please God eternal that these be abandoned as I seek.

[*fol. 19v*] In the book called *Sanhedrin* it is told that the Jew Ben Coziba ruled among his people for thirty years, claiming that he was the Messiah promised by the Law. The doctor Rabbi Akiba was with him and preached that the time for the coming of the Messiah had been determined; that that time had come and that Ben Coziba was he. In his book of the decisions on laws pertaining to a king, Rabbi Moses says that Rabbi Akiba was one of the best doctors in the Talmud. He therefore agreed that Ben Coziba was the Messiah and said that people should believe in him. All the people believed in him and followed him, thinking him to be the Messiah. They did this because they saw that the time for his coming has passed and because of their wickedness they failed to recognize Christ who was the true Messiah. Finally, however,

---

[67] See above, n. 61.

[68] Based on a passage ascribed not to Rashi but to R. Raḥmon in *PF*, p. 872; *ACPJ* 1, 2, pp. 41f. In *PF*: "When the Sanhedrin was banished from the chamber of hewn stone and the judging of capital cases was withdrawn from them, they put on sackcloth and shaved their heads and said: Woe to us for the scepter is departed from Judah and the son of David has not come." Machado is closer to *PF* which reads "nondum venit" than to the Zurich edition of *ACPJ* which reads "mundum venit."

[69] See above, n. 61.

Mexia. Finalmente, veo a morer maa morte Rrabi Aquiba, por onde loguo hos iudeus conhecerão ho enguano.

Trouxeuos aqui este enxemplo pera que saibaes como hos vossos doutores sabião ho tempo certo do Mexia, como sabia Rrabi Aquiba, e assi ho souberão hos talmudistas. Mas ho diabo hos enguanou, que posserão mil errores e mil enguanos no Talmud pera que vos outros nom vos conuertaes. E daes mil sintidos à Sagrada Escritura pera que nom seiaes vincidos que veo ia ho Mexia.

Estando eu isto escreuendo acertou de vir hum homem honesto e entendido, tangedor do real mosteiro d'Alcobaça, e me perguntou como se entendia huma profitia que esta em Osei, capitolo 3º (na qual vos outros vos fundaes pera nom crerdes que veo ho Mexia), onde se diz: "Per muitos dias me esperaras, e nom fornicaras nem teras varão; mas, porem, eu te esperarei. Porque por muitos dias estarão hos filhos de Isrrael sem rrei e principe e sacrifitio, e sem altar, e sem vestiduras sacerdotaes. E depois disto tornarão hos filhos de Isrrael e buscarão seu Senhor, e Dauid seu rrei."

Diguouos que este vosso fundamento he muito vão e de pouco valor, cuidando vos que ainda aues de sacrificar. Nom he esta ha entenção do profeta que vos cuidaes; mas esta he que vos careceres dos sacrifitios ates a fim do mundo, mas, porem, antão buscares ho Senhor que sera quando vier[em] Helias e Enoch pera vos converterem, porque loguo nesse tempo todos crerão no Mexia, ho qual veo antes da destruição do Templo, feita por Tito, por espaço de setenta e cinqu[o] anos e meo, onde ia se passarão 1541 anos.

Esta he a nossa fee e esta seia a vossa pera que alcanceis a gloria eterna. Amen.

[fol. 20r] Capitolo Sexto. De como ho Mexia auia de nacer dũma Virgem e na cidade de Dauid, chamada Betleem.

A quarta propriedade que estaua escrita do Mexia era que auia de nacer dũma virgem na cidade de Betleem, a qual virgem Maria foi do tribu de Iuda, desposada com Ioseph. Esta propriedade communicada foi a Christo, ho qual naceo desta virgem Maria. A profitia escrita esta

---

[70] Simon bar Kokhba or Kozba was leader of the insurrection against Rome at the time of Hadrian (132-5 A.D.) which led to the disastrous defeat at Bethar. R. Akiba (d. ca. 135), the eminent tannaitic scholar, was an enthusiastic supporter of Bar Kokhba and went as far as declaring him to be the Messiah. See Baron, *SRHJ*, 2:117 et seq. Machado's reference to a tragic death refers to his execution by the Romans for conspiracy. The passage is based on B.T. Sanhedrin 93b (Sonc., p. 627; the Talmud has him executed by the Rabbis) and Moses Maimonides, *Mishneh Torah, Hilkhot Melakhim*, 11:3 (English: *The Code of Maimonides: The Book of Judges* [New Haven, 1949], p. 239).

Rabbi Akiba suffered a tragic death after which the Jews came to recognize their mistake.[70]

I brought this example to your attention so that you could see how your doctors knew the exact time of the advent of the Messiah. Rabbi Akiba knew it and so did the talmudists. But the devil deceived them, so that they placed a thousand errors and a thousand mistakes in the Talmud just so that you would not convert. You yourselves interpret the Holy Scriptures in a thousand ways in order to keep from being convinced that the Messiah has come.

While I was writing this, an honest and perceptive man, the organist of the royal monastery of Alcobaça, came to visit me. He asked me how one interpreted the prophecy in chapter 3 of Hosea (on the basis of which you refuse to believe that the Messiah came), where it says: *You shall wait for Me for many days; and you shall not play the harlot nor know any man, for I will wait for you. Because the children of Israel will be without a king and prince for many days, and without an altar and sacerdotal vestments. Afterwards, the children of Israel will return and will seek their Lord and David their king.*[71]

I tell you that it is useless and pointless to believe that you will once again sacrifice [in the Temple]. This is not the intention of the prophet as you think it is. What is meant is that you will have no more sacrifices until the end of the world. Then you will look for the Lord when Elijah and Enoch[72] come to convert you. At that time everyone will believe in the Messiah who came seventy-five and a half years[73] before the destruction of the Temple by Titus. Since that time, 1541 years have passed.

This is our faith. May it also be yours so that you may attain eternal glory. Amen.

[*fol. 20r*] Chapter Six. How the Messiah was to be born of a virgin in the city of David, called Bethlehem.

The fourth characteristic written of the Messiah was that He was to be born of a virgin in the city of Bethlehem. This virgin, who was of the tribe of Judah, was married to Joseph and was called Mary. This characteristic was true of Christ who was born of this virgin Mary. The

These texts are cited in *PF*, pp. 872f; *ACPJ*, 1, 2, p. 43; and *FF*, fol. 39*ra*. The original passage in the Talmud gives Bar Kokhba's reign as two and a half years, *PJ* as three and a half, *FF* as thirty and a half, and *ACPJ*, like Machado, as thirty years.

[71] Hos. 3:3ff.

[72] See below, Chap. 18, n. 13.

[73] See below, Chap. 23, n. 29.

polo profeta Isaias no capitolo seitimo, onde se diz: "Ex que hu*m*a
v*i*rgem concebera e parira hum filho e ho seu nome chamarseha
Manuel." Hos nossos doutores todos expoe*m* e entendem esta profitia
do Mexia; porem, hos vossos doutores outro sentido lhe dão, muito
desconueniente do nosso, segundo aqui prouaremos.

Vos bee*m* sabees que no hebraico ha tres nomes, hos quaes quase
sinifiquão hu*m*a cousa, e sam estes: *veara, betula, alma*. Porem, deferença
ha entre estes nomes, porque *veara* dizse por molher menor de idade de
cem anos, quer tal molher desta idade seia virgem, quer seia corupta.
De maneira que Sarra se podia chamar *veara*, e se fora v*i*rgem, ho
mesmo nome lhe conuiera. *Betula* dizse por molher virge*m*, e no*m* por
corrupta. Quer seia de idade de cem anos, quer de dez, quer de vinte,
semp*r*e este nome lhe compete e co*n*uem s[cilicet] *betula*. *Alma* sinifiqua
duas cousas. A p*r*imeira que seia moça, e a segunda que seia v*i*rgem,
polo qual este nome no*m* se deue de atribuir senão à v*i*rgem, moça de
idade de quinze anos ates hos vinte, e dali passando ia no*m*
prop*r*iame*n*te este nome *alma* lhe conuira. Porem, como quer que estes
nomes no hebraico andão confusos, as vezes põese hu*m* nome polo
outro. E porque este nome *alma* he ho mais proprio de todos, e que
mais conuinha pera Nossa S*en*ho*r*a que era moça e v*i*rgem e encube*r*ta
miraculosa, po*r*tanto, tomou ella ho nome de *alma* porque *alma*
sinifiqua encube*r*ta ou çarrada, e no*m* ho nome de *veara*, ne*m* de *betula*,
hos quaes no*m* lhe co*n*uinhão tão prop*r*iame*n*te.

Quando, pois, ho profeta dixe, no capitolo vii°, "Ex hu*m*a v*i*rgem,"
no*m* poos *veara* ne*m* *betula*, que sinificão v*i*rgens e corruptas, mas poos
na profitia *alma*, que sinifica moça virgem, a qual foi Nossa S*en*ho*r*a.
Podees loguo creer que onde quer que no hebraico se põe *alma*, semp*r*e
sinifica moça v*i*rgem, que quer diz*e*r moça escondida, porq*u*e *almath* no
hebraico sinifica hu*m* escondimento donde descende *alma*, que quer
diz*e*r escondida. Esto podemosuos prouar por duas autoridades do
Testame*n*to Velho.

[*fol. 20v*] No Genesis, no capitolo xxiiij, se conta que Habraa*m* mandou Eleazer, seu p*r*ocurador, a Mesopotamia buscar molher pera Isaac.
E como chegou à cidade de Nathor onde estaua Rrebeca, começou de
dizer, chega*n*do à fonte onde as moças vinhão tirar aguoa: "S*en*hor, ia
estou a par desta fonte e as filhas desta cidade veem tirar aguoa. E, por-

---

¹ Isa. 7:14.
² *I.e.*, na'arah (young girl), *betulah* (virgin), *'almah* (young woman). The following discussion was
one of the major controversial issues since the time of the Evangelists (Matt. 1:23). Following the
Septuagint rendering of the Hebrew *'almah* as *parthenos*, Christianity viewed the verse as a testimony
of the virgin birth. It was then for the Jews to prove that *'almah* meant simply "young woman." See

prophecy referring to this was written by the prophet Isaiah in chapter seven, where it says: *Behold a virgin will conceive and bear a son and his name will be called Emmanuel.*[1] All our doctors expound and understand this prophecy to refer to the Messiah; however, your doctors give it another meaning very much opposed to ours, as we shall now show.

As you well know, in Hebrew there are three nouns which mean almost the same thing: *veara, betula, alma.*[2] There is, however, a difference between these names because *veara* refers to a woman under the age of one hundred years, whether she be a virgin or not. Sarah[3] could thus be called *veara* and if she were a virgin the name would still apply. *Betula,* on the other hand, refers only to a virgin. Whether she be ten, twenty, or a hundred years old, *betula* still applies. *Alma* signifies two things: the one that the girl is young; the other, that she is a virgin. Thus, this name can only be applied to a young virgin of from fifteen to twenty years. After twenty years of age, this name would not be appropriate. However, these nouns tend to be confused in Hebrew and at times are used interchangeably. Because the noun *alma* is the most appropriate for Our Lady who was young, a virgin, and miraculously concealed, she therefore took the name of *alma* which signifies concealed or enclosed[4] rather than *veara* or *betula* which do not apply to her.

Thus, when in chapter 7 the prophet said, *Behold a virgin,* he did not use *veara* or *betula* which mean both virgin and non-virgin, but instead used the word *alma* in his prophecy, for this signifies a young virgin girl, which Our Lady was. You can be assured that wherever *alma* is used in Hebrew, it always signifies a young virgin, which means "concealed girl," because *almath* in Hebrew signifies a concealment, from which the word *alma,* which means "concealed," is derived. We can prove this to you from two passages of the Old Testament.

[*fol. 20v*] In chapter 24 of Genesis it is told that Abraham sent Eleazar, his overseer, to Mesopotamia to look for a wife for Isaac. When he arrived at the city of Nahor where Rebekah dwelt, he went to the fountain from which the girls were drawing water and said: *Lord, I am now beside this fountain and the young girls of the city are drawing water from it.*

Covenant, pp. 54f.; B. Blumenkranz, *Juifs et Chrétiens dans le monde occidental,* p. 235. Machado's discussion follows the argumentation of *ACPJ* (1, 4, pp. 51ff.) which appears to be based largely on that of Jerome (*Comm., ad loc., CC,* 73:103f. [*PL,* 24:110f.]). Similar material is found in *PF,* pp. 739ff. and *FF,* fols. 146rb-147rb who quotes Nicholas de Lyra, *Post.* 2, BBvir. Cf. the additions of Paul of Burgos *ad loc.* Additio 5, 2, BBviivf.

³ Rebekah, not Sarah, is correct. See Gen. 24, *passim.*

⁴ Jerome (*ibid.*) derived the word 'almah from the Hebrew root 'lm in the sense of "hide" or "conceal," thereby yielding this interpretation. Cf. *FF,* fol. 147rb who cites *Post.,* 2, BBvir.

tanto, Senhor, aquela moça à qual eu dixer que dee de beber aos camelos e ella ho fezer, esta seya, Senhor, a qual aparelhastes pera meu senhor." Esto dizendo, veo Rrebeca, que era moça virgem. No hebraico sobre este passo, onde no latim esta "puella cui ego dixero" (a moça à qual eu diser), no hebraico nom se põe *veara* nem *betula*, mas põese *alma*, que sinifica moça *vir*gem.

Ha outra autoridade esta no Terceiro Liuro, capitolo *primeiro* dos Rreis, onde se diz que sendo ia Dauid muito velho, e nom se podendo aquentar, lhe buscarão huma moça Abisar Sonamitis, a qual dormia com elle, e esta moça era muito fremosa. No hebraico põese *alma* e nom *veara* nem *betula*, e isto porque era moça virgem.

Assi tambem vos diguo que na profitia de Isaias no se põe estes nomes *veara* ou *betula*, como vos cuidaes, hos quaes nomes sinificão virgem, como he *veara,* de qualquer idade que seia, e *betula* sinifica virgem e corrupta, de qualquer idade que seia. Mas ho profeta poos este nome *alma* que sinifiqua virgem moça, como Nossa Senhora foi antes do parto e depois do parto. E porquanto às vezes no Testamento Velho se põe este nome *alma* por molher manceba[a] nom[b] corrupta mas[c] virgem, por isso, nas autoridades acima aleguadas, por esta deferença se põe a *alma*, polo qual poderes sab*er* que onde no Testamento Velho se põe a *alma* como se poos na profitia de Isaias, sinifiqua moça virgem, e onde achardes *alma*, sinifiqua molher manceba, virgem e nom corrupta, como falsamente vos cuidaes, fortificandouos com a autoridade de Salamão nos Prou*er*bios, capitolo xxx, onde diz: "Tres cousas são muito dificiles e a quarta nom posso saber: ho caminho da aguia polo ceo, e ho caminho da cobra sobre a pedra, e ho caminho da nao polo maar, e ho caminho do varão pola virgem." Esta cousa quarta ignoraua Salamão. No nosso latim esta d'outra maneira que não no hebraico, porque no latim esta: "E ho caminho do varão da mocidade," e no hebraico esta: "E ho caminho do varão pola *alma*" (pola virgem).

Mas vos dizes q*ue* este [*fol. 21r*] nome *alma* neste texto esta por molher manceba corrupta, por onde afirmaes que assi esta no texto de Isaias no capitolo vij°. Certamente, muito nos espantamos dos vossos enguanos e falsidades que semeaes, dando falsos intendementos dos textos. Portanto, vos diguo que *alma* nesta autoridade nom pode estar por molher

---

a +*a qual pode ser corrupta ou* exp.   b int. +*nom* exp.   c int. +*ou* exp.

[5] Gen. 24:12ff.
[6] Jerome and *FF*, fol. 147*rb*.
[7] 1 Kings 1:1-4.

Moreover, Lord, that young woman whom I shall tell to give drink to the camels and who shall do it, she, Lord, is the one you made ready for my lord.[5] After he said this, Rebekah, who was a young virgin, arrived. This passage, in Latin, reads *puella cui ego dixero* (*the girl whom I shall tell*). In Hebrew the word used is neither *veara* nor *betula*, but *alma*, which signifies a young virgin woman.[6]

The other passage is found in Book Three, chapter 1 of Kings. There we read that because David was very old and could not warm himself, they sought him a young girl, Abishag the Shunamite, who slept with him.[7] This young girl was very beautiful. In Hebrew, she is referred to as *alma*, not *veara* or *betula*, because she was a virgin.[8]

As you can see, in the prophecy of Isaiah neither *veara* nor *betula* were used, as you think; for these signify a virgin no matter what her age. In the case of *betula* it can also refer to a non-virgin of any age. But the prophet used the noun *alma* which designates a young virgin woman, as was Our Lady before and after she gave birth. Because there are instances in the Old Testament where *alma* is used when referring to a young virgin woman, the above passages used this word. It therefore follows that when *alma* is used in the Old Testament, as in the case of the prophecy of Isaiah, it means a young virgin girl. Thus, where you find *alma* it means a young girl who is a virgin, and not otherwise, as you so falsely believe. You base your claim on Solomon's text in Proverbs, chapter 30, where he says: *Three things are very difficult for me and the fourth I do not know: the way of the eagle in the sky, the way of the serpent on the rock, the way of the ship on the sea, and the way of a man with a virgin.*[9] This fourth thing Solomon did not know. Our Latin is different from the Hebrew because in Latin we read *And the way of the man with the maiden,*[10] whereas in Hebrew it is: *And the way of the man with the* alma[11] (that is, with the virgin).

But you say that the [*fol. 21r*] word *alma* in this passage actually refers to a young woman who is not a virgin and it is in this sense that it is used in the passage from chapter 7 in Isaiah. We certainly are astonished at the deceits and falsities that you sow and at the erroneous interpretations you give to the texts. For this reason I am telling you

---

[8] Jerome, *CC*, 73:103f. (*PL*, 24:110f.).

[9] Prov. 30:18f.

[10] Vulgate: *Et viam viri in adolescentia.*

[11] See above, n. 1. Machado apparently vacillates between accepting 'almah as meaning both "virgin" and "young woman" or "virgin" alone. He does not seem to be able to reconcile the translation of 'almah as *adolescentia* and presumably assumes two different textual traditions. The question is dealt with in *Post.*, ibid.; *PF*, pp. 741f.; *FF*, fol. 117ra.

manceba corrupta, mas esta por virgem manceba, que he ho seu proprio sinificado. Porque se este texto onde se põe *alma* esteuera ou demostrara molher corrupta manceba, em balde fezera Salamão menção de molher adultera, loguo acrecentando ao texto de cima isto: "E tal he ho caminho da molher adultera." Assi que nom vos enguanes com este nome *alma*, porque nunqua se põe por molher corrupta, mas sempre por virgem. E nesta profitia de Isaias a *alma* se deue poor, que sinifica moça virgem, ho que poodemos concludir polo *m* çarrado, polo qual notai isto que se segue.

Vos no vosso hebraico tendes cinquo letras dobradas que são estas: *caph, men, nun, phe, sade,* e dũma maneira se escreuem hos principios das dições com estas cinquo letras, e d'outra maneira hos meos das dições, e d'outra sorte hos extremos e fins das dições. Antre estas letras teendes huma letra fechada que he esta *men,* e teendes outra letra *men* aberta. A letra *men* aberta sempre se põe no meo e no começo das dições mas *men* letra fechada, nunqua se põe no meo. Porem, nesta proficia de Isaias põese esta letra *men* fechada no meo da dição, ho que he contra sua natureza e contra ho modo de escreuer hebraico, ho qual nom se acha senão nesta profitia onde ho profeta peruerteo ho modo de escreuer, que sinificaua que tambem a uirgem auia de conceber contra ho modo da natureza, s[cilicet] virgem e parir virgem. Isto sinificaua ho *m* çarrado que era esta letra hebraica *men.*

Vos dizees que esta profitia nom se deue de entender do Mexia mas do filho de Achaz. Midras Telim, vosso doutor, diz concludindo como esta profitia nom se podia entender do filho de Achaz, como prouaremos. Que desdo tempo que esta proficia foi dita pola boca de Isaias, auião de correr seiscentos anos, hos quaes se prouão polo *men* çarrado, que he a quinzena letra do vosso alfabeto, a qual val corenta, e quinze vezes corenta fazem seiscentos anos. Esto se confirma no Talmud

---

¹² Prov. 30:20. Cf. *PF*, pp. 739ff.

¹³ See below.

¹⁴ The five Hebrew letters *kaf, mem, nun, pe* and *zade* take a special form in final position. In Isa. 9:6 such a final or closed *mem* appears in an apparently medial position (למרבה). Since this verse appears in the context of an allegedly messianic prophecy (see below), the "closed" *mem* was taken as an allusion to the virginity of Mary. See Jerome, *CC*, 73, 103f. (*PL*, 24:110f.); Paul of Burgos, *Add.* 5 to *Post., ibid.,* 2, BBvii*v*f.; *ACPJ*, 1, 4, p. 48; *FF*, fols. 36*rb-va,* 148*va.* Machado's reference to three forms might be due to a confusion with Arabic script.

¹⁵ See below, n. 19.

¹⁶ No such passage is found in Midrash Tehillim. There is, however, a passage in *PF* (p. 746) in which Rashi (R. Sa.) is cited as rejecting the view that Hezekiah is the one referred to in the verse, followed by a passage from Midrash Tehillim. Machado's statement may have resulted from a confusion of this material.

that *alma* here [in the passage from Proverbs] can only refer to a virgin, which was its intended meaning and not otherwise. For if in this passage *alma* meant a non-virgin, it would have been pointless for Solomon to make reference to the adulterous woman when he followed the above verse with *And so is the way of the adulterous woman.*[12] Thus, do not be deceived concerning this word *alma* because it is only used to refer to a virgin. For this reason *alma* ought to be used in this prophecy of Isaiah for it signifies a young virgin girl. We can conclude this from the closed[13] *m* as may be noted from what follows.

In Hebrew you have five letters with two different forms which are: *kaf, mem, nun, pe,* and *ẓade.* When these letters begin a word they are written in one way. When they fall in the middle of a word, they are written in another way and when they come at the end of a word, in still another.[14] Among these letters is the letter *mem* which has two forms, an open and a closed. The open form is always placed at the beginning and in the middle of a word. The closed form of the letter, however, is never placed in the middle. Nevertheless, in this prophecy of Isaiah this latter form of *mem is* placed in the middle of the word. This goes against the customary conventions of writing Hebrew. Now this happens only in this prophecy where the prophet altered the way of writing in order to signify that the virgin also was to conceive in a manner which was not natural: to remain a virgin after conception and parturition. This is borne out by the closed *m* which is the Hebrew letter *mem.*[15]

You say, however, that this prophecy refers to the son of Achaz and not to the Messiah. Your doctor, Midrash Tehillim, states that this prophecy cannot refer to the son of Achaz, as we will show.[16] For six hundred years were to have passed from the time Isaiah proclaimed his prophecy. This can be proved by the closed *mem,* which is the fifteenth letter of your alphabet and has the [numerical] value of forty, and forty times fifteen equals six hundred years.[17] This is confirmed in the

---

[17] The figure of six hundred years from Isaiah to Jesus is consistent with medieval Jewish chronologies. See Rosenthal, *Milḥamot,* p. 88. It is of note that Josephus reckoned six hundred years from Isaiah to the destruction of the Temple (*De bello judaico,* 7.10.3).

Final *mem* has the numerical value of six hundred. That final *mem* and the number six hundred are related is alluded to in *PF* (pp. 532, 536, 763) and *ACPJ* (1, 2, p. 29) but explained by neither. Martini does state, however, that initial *mem* has the numerical value of forty (p. 763). Machado, trying to derive the figure six hundred from this latter fact, posits that *mem* is the fifteenth letter of the alphabet. (In reality, it is the thirteenth.) Machado's remarks are closer to the interpretation of *PF* which takes the six hundred years to be the period from the prophecy to the nativity while *ACPJ* understands it to be from the prophecy to the crucifixion.

onde se diz e se escreue sobre huma virgem que he çarrada, que esta [fol.
21v] no meo do verbo, que nom teem outra tal en outro verbo nhũm,
que todas as letras são abertas, tirando nesta profitia de Isaias que esta a
letra çarrada.

Sobre este passo no Talmud se faz esta pergunta: "E como, Senhor, a
Ezechias, filho delrrei Achaz, queres vos fazer ho Mexia, e nom fezestes a
Dauid que vos faz tantos cantares?" E a isto no mesmo Talmud se
rresponde, onde se diz que quis ho profeta çarrar aquela letra men, nom
sem grande misterio. Pareceme a mim que hos vossos antepassados bem
entenderão estes misterios, mas, porem, nam volos quiserão declarar
nem descobrir, que foi grande mal pera vos e pera elles. E ho pior que
he que não quiserão entender este grande misterio do men çarrado, ou
se ho ente[n]derão, calarãose mui bem. Mas ainda dão hum sentido
muito falso a esta profitia dizendo que nom se entende do Mexia mas do
filho delrrei Achaz, chamado Ezechias, ho que nom traz rrezão nem
conclusão, nem sabees vos ho que⁻dizes, nem souberão hos vossos
predecessores. E assi volo prouaremos.

Rrabi Salamão sobre este passo diz que esta profitia nom se pode entender de Ezechias, filho de Achaz, dando esta rrezão, que quando Isaias
dixe a Achaz, "Huma virgem parira," ia Ezechias, seu filho, era de noue
anos, prouandoo assi. Achaz, seu pai, rreinou dezaseis anos, segundo se
contem no Quarto Liuro dos Rreis, no capitolo XVIº. E quando Achaz
começou de rreinar era ia de vinte anos, e ho filho Ezechias^d ia
cheguaua aos noue anos. E esta idade era quando Isaias falou con seu
pai que pidisse sinal, dizendo elle que não auia de pidir sinal pera que
nom tentasse ho Senhor, por onde Isaias lhe dixe: "Por amor disto Deos
vos dara hum sinal que he este: huma virgem concebera."

Por amor desta rrezão Rrabi Salamão falsamente dixe que esta
profitia se entendia do filho de Isaias. Assi que tambem este Rrabi
Salamão nom chegou ao fito nem à profundeza da profitia, e, portanto,
vos outros daes falso entendimento a esta profitia.

Sabee, pois, por certeza, que esta profitia nom se pode entender senão

---

d int. + Sedechias exp.

[18] The talmudic discussion is found in B.T. Sanhedrin 94a (PF, pp. 451, 531; FF, fol. 36rb): "Of the
increase (לםרבה) of his government and peace there shall be no end. R. Tanḥum said: Bar Kappara expounded in Sepphoris; Why is every mem in the middle of a word closed? — The Holy One, blessed
be He, wished to appoint Hezekiah as the Messiah, and Sennacherib as Gog and Magog,
whereupon the Attribute of Justice said before the Holy One, blessed be He: 'Sovereign of the
Universe: If Thou didst not make David the Messiah, who uttered so many hymns and psalms
before Thee, wilt Thou appoint Hezekiah as such, who did not hymn Thee inspite of all those
miracles which Thou wroughtest for him.' Therefore it [sc. the mem] was closed." (Sonc., p. 630,
See notes.)

Talmud where the word "virgin" is written with a closed [mem] [fol. 21v] in the middle of a word. The like is found in no other word for it is always written open except for this prophecy of Isaiah where the letter is closed.

The following question is raised concerning this passage in the Talmud: "How, Lord, can you make Hezekiah, son of King Achaz, the Messiah, rather than David who wrote so many songs for you?" In the Talmud it is said that the prophet wanted to close that letter in a most mysterious manner.[18] It seems to me that your forefathers understood these mysteries but did not want to reveal them to you — a great mistake for them and you. The worst was that they did not want to understand the great mystery of the closed mem; or, if they understood, they maintained their silence. A false meaning is still imposed on this prophecy when it is interpreted to refer to Hezekiah the son of King Achaz rather than to the Messiah. This simply does not make sense. You do not know what you are saying, nor did your forefathers know. We will now show you.

Rabbi Solomon says that this prophecy could not refer to Hezekiah the son of Achaz.[19] His reason is that when Isaiah said to Achaz, A virgin will give birth, Hezekiah was only nine years old. He proves it in this way: Achaz reigned sixteen years, according to the Fourth Book of Kings, chapter 16.[20] When he began his rule, he himself was twenty and Hezekiah was already nine.[21] It was at this time that Isaiah spoke with Achaz and told him to ask for a sign, whereupon the latter answered that he would not do so because he did not want to tempt the Lord. Isaiah then said: Because of this God will give you a sign which is this: a virgin will conceive.[22]

This is why Rabbi Solomon falsely stated that this prophecy refers to the son of Isaiah. By the same token, this same Rabbi Solomon did not fathom the true intent of this prophecy and therefore you do not interpret it correctly.[23]

This prophecy, however, can only refer to the Messiah who was

---

[19] Rashi (R. Solomon ben Isaac) cited in *Post., ad loc.,* 2, BBvir and cf. *PF,* p. 746. See below, n. 21.

[20] 2 Kings 16:2.

[21] Although some Jewish interpreters understood this passage as referring to the Messiah, many referred it to Hezekiah, the son of Achaz. See Rashi, *ad loc.;* Jacob ben Reuben, *Milḥamot,* p. 87; *Comm.* of David Kimhi, *ad loc.;* cf. Blumenkranz, *Juifs et chrétiens,* p. 238. For Christian sources, see Jerome, *Comm., ad loc., CC,* 73:104 (*PL,* 24:111f.); Justin Martyr, *Dialogue with Trypho,* 72, 81 in T.B. Falls, *Writings of St. Justin Martyr* (New York, 1948), pp. 256ff., 277ff.

[22] *Post., ibid.; FF,* fol. 147va.

[23] *Post., ibid.*

do Mexia, ho qual se chamou Emanuel que quer dizer Deos comnosco, ho qual nome nom teue Ezechias, porque nos nom achamos que elle iamais se chamasse Emanuel. Mas Christo se chamou Manuel, que he Deos comnosco, porque da parte da mãi he Deos comnosco, sem aiuntamento de varão e sem curru[p]ção de carne.

Mas, pola graça do Spiritu Santo, concebeo a Virgem o Verbo de Deos sen se fazer abertura nem corrumpimento algum na sua bendita carne. [fol. 22r] E pera poderdes cair nisto, podelo fazer mui facilmente e crer que huma virgem podia conceber sem ser corrupta, porque vos nom neguaes que Helias nom possa entrar em muitas casas, as ianelas çarradas, quando fanaes hos mininos. Pois, se Helias pode entrar polas ianelas çarradas dentro nas casas, e pode em muitos luguares estar no mesmo tempo, por que nom concederes que Deos pode fazer tambem que huma virgem conceba e paira?

Ho meu parecer he que assi como vos concedees ho primeiro, que tambem deuees de consentir no segundo, quanto mais polo profeta Isaias vos foi denunciado: "Ecce a alma concipiet." Assi que concludindo, nos teemos por fee que esta profitia de Isaias nom foi dita senão polo Mexias e por Nossa Senhora, Santa Maria Virgem. E vos assi ho deuees de crer e nom fazer iniuria a esta virgem nem ao Mexia, seu filho Christo, que ia veo.

Houtro negro error teendes acerqua desta profitia, ha qual ho nosso tresladador São Ieronimo do hebraico em latim assi tresladou: "Ecce virguo concipiet et pariet filium et vocabitur nomen eius Emanuel." Esta profitia foi dita no ano quarto do rreinado delrrei Achaz quando ia Ezechias tinha noue, ou treze anos, segundo outros. E portanto, falsamente corrompees hos vocabolos, e onde nos temos vocabitur, vos poondes vocabit, fundados nesta falsa rrezão que Achaz auia de chamar a seu filho Ezechias Emanuel, ho que nom he verdade, como ia se prouou, ou que a mãi lhe auia de poor este nome. Eu tenho pera mim que no hebraico estaua vocabitur na passiua e nom vocabit na autiua. Mas hos vossos talmudistas, pera nom confessarem ho Mexias ser vindo, poserão outros pontos e fezerão voguar as letras d'outra maneira pera nom crerdes que ho Mexia auia de ser concibido dũma virgem, sem pai. Porque se ho Mexia teuera pai, bem caira antão vocabit — ho pai chamara ao filho Emanuel (como vos outros queres contender, que deue de estar vocabit) — Achaz, pai de Ezechias, ou a mãi ao filho

---

[24] Elijah, as "angel of the covenant" (Mal. 3:1), is considered in Jewish tradition as symbolically present at every circumcision. See JE, 5:128. Machado takes this tradition quite literally in order to advance his argument. On this tradition in contemporary Castilian anti-Jewish polemics, see Yerushalmi, Court, p. 248, n. 236. See also below, Chap. 15, n. 34.

called Emmanuel, which means "God is with us." Hezekiah never had this name for there is no record of his ever having been called Emmanuel. Christ, however, was called Emmanuel, which is "God is with us" because of His mother who knew no man when she conceived Him.

Through the grace of the Holy Spirit, the Virgin conceived the Word of God without any opening or defilement of her blessed flesh. [*fol. 22r*] It should be very easy for you to believe that a virgin could conceive without knowing a man because you do not deny that Elijah can enter many houses with the windows closed when you circumcise male infants. So, if Elijah can enter houses through closed windows and be in many places at the same time, why can you not concede that God can also have a virgin conceive and bear a child?[24]

It seems to me that since you concede the first, then you also ought to admit to the second, especially since it was the prophet Isaiah who said: *Ecce a alma*[25] *concipiet*. We believe that this prophecy of Isaiah refers to the Messiah and to Our Lady the Holy Virgin Mary.[26] You ought to believe this also and not blaspheme either the Virgin or the Messiah, her son Christ, who has already come.

You make yet another egregious error. This prophecy was translated by our translator Saint Jerome from Hebrew into Latin, as follows: *Ecce virgo concipiet et pariet filium et vocabitur nomen eius Emmanuel*. It was proclaimed during the fourth year of the reign of King Achaz when Hezekiah was nine years old,[27] or thirteen, according to some.[28] Yet you falsely corrupt the words of the text so that where we have *vocabitur*, you have *vocabit*,[29] falsely assuming that Achaz was to call his son, Hezekiah, Emmanuel, or that he was to be so named by his mother. This is not true as we have already proved. I maintain that in Hebrew the passive, *vocabitur*, was written and not the active form, *vocabit*. But to avoid admitting that the Messiah has come or that the Messiah was conceived of a virgin, without a father, your talmudists vocalized the letters differently.[30] If the Messiah had had a father, *vocabit,* which you contend is the correct form, would have been appropriate; for Achaz is the father of Hezekiah, and either the father or the mother might have called him Emmanuel. But neither Mary nor Joseph gave Him His

---

[25] *I.e.,* Hebrew *ha-'almah*.
[26] *Post., ibid.*
[27] *PA*, Title 7, *PL*, 157:164.
[28] *Post., ibid.; FF*, fol. 147*vb*.
[29] Hebrew: *ve-qarat,* an active form.
[30] See above, Chap. 4, n. 31.

Emanuel. Mas nem Maria nem Ioseph nom poserão ho nome, mas foi chamado polo anio, e portanto, milhor parece *vocabitur,* e nom *vocabit.*

Estes errores prouem muitas vezes porque ha hi no hebraico dições que se escreuem com has mesmas letras no hebraico e nom sam diferentes senão polos puntinhos. Porque assi como no latim *vocabit* e[e] *vocabitur* se escreuem com as mesmas letras quasi, senão que ho verbo passiuo põe diferença no verbo autiuo, assi no vosso hebraico estas duas dições *vagitta,* que he tanto como *vocabit,* e *victare,* que he tanto como *vocabitur,* ambas se escreuem [*fol. 22v*] com as mesmas letras. Mas hos vossos puntinhos voguaes fezerão que onde nesta profitia estaua *vocabitur* ou *victare,* vossos talmudistas poserão *vocabit* ou *vagitta.* E assi como corromperão esta profitia fazendo que nom se entendesse do Mexia, assi corromperão a outra profitia do Mexia, a qual põe Isaias no capitolo nono, onde se diz: "Paruulus enim natus est nobis, et filius datus est nobis, et factus est principatus super humerum eius, et vocabitur nomen eius, Admirabilis, Consiliarius, Deus, Fortis, Pater futuri seculi, Princeps pacis." Esta profitia todos hos nossos doutores expõem do Mexia, onde concludem a sua humanidade e diuindade. Vos, porem, expõ[e]m dela falsamente de Ezechias, dizendo que tambem nesta profitia se deue de poor *vocabit:* Deos, Padre forte, Conselheiro marauilhoso, chamara a Ezechias principe da paz. E onde nos teemos *Princeps pacis,* hos vossos predecessores poserão assi, corrompendo todo ho texto: "Principem pacis vocabit Deus Pater Ezechiam." Assi que aquilo que ho profeta poos nesta profitia rreferindo ao Mexia emquanto Deos, vossos talmudistas referiramno a Deos Padre, e portanto, pera milhor quadrar sua sentença, onde no hebraico muito bem correito estaua "*vocabitur* ho Mexia, Deos forte, marauiloso Conselheiro," elles poserão *vocabit.*

Hora vede ho seu grande erro e falssidade. E de uos outros, [f]senhores, me espanto[f] que as profitias tão manifestas e tão claras que são do Mexia, as rrefires a ellrrei Ezechias, e nom olhaes que no caldeu esta ho contrairo, ho qual vos nom podes neguar, secundo ia antre vos esta concludido. No caldeu assi se põe "Deus fortis permanens in secula seculorum Messias" (Deos forte permanecera pera todo sempre Mexia). Este passo sobre ho qual assi erraes, nom leestes vos no caldeu, no qual

---

e MS *et*   f-f int.

[31] Hebrew: *va-yiqra.*
[32] Hebrew: *va-yiqqare.*
[33] Isa. 9:6.
[34] "I ... gentlemen" interlinear addition. See note *f.*

name, but He was named by the angel. For this reason *vocabitur* and not *vocabit* is more appropriate.

These errors frequently occur because there are words in Hebrew that are written with the same letters and differ only with regard to the points. In Latin, for example, the words *vocabit* and *vocabitur* are written with almost the same letters, except for the differences occurring between active and passive voice. Likewise, in your Hebrew, the two words *vagitta*[31] — the equivalent of *vocabit* — and *victare*[32] — the equivalent of *vocabitur* — are written [*fol. 22v*] with the same letters. Your vowel points, however, enabled your talmudists to read *vocabit* or *vagitta* where the prophecy has *vocabitur* or *victare*. Just as they corrupted this prophecy so that it could not be interpreted with reference to the Messiah, so did they corrupt the other prophecy of Isaiah, Chapter 9, which also refers to the Messiah: *Paruulus enim natus est nobis et filius datus est nobis, et factus est principatus super humerum eius, et vocabitur nomen eius, Admirabilis, Consiliarius, Deus, Fortis, Pater futuri seculi, Princeps pacis.*[33] All our doctors agree that this prophecy refers to the Messiah, thereby affirming His humanity and His divinity. You, however, falsely refer it to Hezekiah, and state that in this prophecy one should read *vocabit: God, mighty Father,* and *marvelous Counselor,* will call Hezekiah prince of peace. And where we have *Princeps pacis,* your ancestors corrupted the text and read: *Principem pacis vocabit Deus Pater Ezechiam.* Thus, where the prophet referred in this prophecy to the Messiah as God, your talmudists referred the expression to God the Father. Therefore, where the Hebrew *vocabit* had very correctly said "*vocabitur* the Messiah, mighty God [and] marvelous Counselor," they inserted *vocabit* in order to accomodate their views.

Now look at your great error and falsehood. I am astonished, gentlemen,[34] that you still believe that these prophecies, which so clearly and manifestly refer to the Messiah, are direct references to King Hezekiah. You fail to notice that it is just the opposite in the Chaldean, as you cannot deny, according to the following. In the Chaldean[35] we read *Deus fortis permanens in secula seculorum Messias* (God the Mighty will remain forever the Messiah). You have not read this passage (which you wrongly interpret) in the Chaldean where it is concluded that this

[35] The Targum to Isaiah. See Introduction. The full text of the Targum actually reads: "The prophet saith to the House of David, A child has been born to us, a son has been given to us; and he has taken the law upon himself to keep it and his name has been called from of old, Wonderful Counsellor, Mighty God, He who lives for ever, the Anointed one ... in whose days peace shall increase upon us." (John F. Stenning, *The Targum of Isaiah* [Oxford, 1949], p. 32).

se conclude que esta profitia do Mexia se entende, ho qual foi Principe de paz e Deos forte, e nom se pode entender de Ezechias em nhuma maneira, porque na dita profitia se diz: "In cuius diebus multiplicabitur pax" (nos dias do qual a paz sera multiplicada). Manifesto he que nos dias de Ezechias a paz nom foi multiplicada, mas antes elle teue guerra grande contra Samaria. E onde nos teemos *multiplicabitur*, vos tendes no hebraico *leuiathe,* a qual dição se escreue com [*fol. 23r*] ho *m* çarrado ou *men*, ho que he contra ho modo de escreuer no hebraico, que se nom fez senão por algum grande misterio que aqui nesta profitia se encludia, que era que ho Mexia auia de ser Deos e homem e auia de ser concibido dũma virgem, como ia teemos prouado.

Ainda ho prouaremos por outras profitias dos profetas, hos quaes tambem espirados polo Spiritu Santo, concludirão que huma virgem auia de parir ho Mexia, como pario, chamado Emanuel. Ho profeta Ieremias, no capitolo xxxi, diz: "Torna, virgem de Isrrael, tornate pera as tuas vilas. Ates quando te deleitas, companha perfiosa? Porque Deos criou cousa noua sobre a terra e a femea parira ho varão." Rrabi Iosua Naue diz sobre este passo que nom pode ser senão que grande cousa ha de vir à terra, porque molher parir varão nom he grande cousa porque cada dia se faz, mas femea virgem parir varão, cousa noua sera sobre a terra. Esta doutor quase affirmou que virgem auia de parir, e esta foi a nossa bendita Virgem Maria, que foi cousa noua porque tal nom se aconteceo iamais nem se acontecera. Assi que podemos concludir, segundo a exposição deste doutor expondo ho passo de Ieremias, que da Virgem Maria Ieremias fazia menção na profitia aleguada. Esto confirmão muitos vossos doutores talmudistas. Midras Telim sobre este passo nũma sua grosa diz que dixe Deos na hora que ho Mexia ouuer de vir: "Eu criarei criatura noua," como dixe Dauid no psalmo 2º: "Eu te gerei oie e te fiz nacer, e filho meu es tu." Assi tambem no Talmud se diz que hos filhos de Isrrael forão firidos por virgem, e serão consolados por virgem. Diguouos que esta virgem foi Maria, por amor da qual

---

[36] On the question of "corruption" of Scripture, see above, Chap. 4, n. 32. This passage was one of the classic points of contention in Jewish-Christian polemics. For a clear statement of a Jewish position, see Joseph Kimhi, *Covenant,* pp. 29f. Machado here bases himself on Lyra, *Post.,* 2, CCiiir. Note the similarity between Machado and the edition of *Post.* in the transliteration of the Hebrew *va-yiqra* and *va-yiqqare*: "Sciendum ... quod Rabbi Solomon et Iudei moderni sequentes ipsum exponunt hunc passum de Ezechia rege Iude, literam corrumpendo. Dicit enim quod haec est littera hebraica: Infans natus est nobis, filius datus est nobis, et erit principatus super humerum eius et vocabit nomen eius admirabilis consiliarius, Deus fortis, pater sempiternus, principem pacis. Et talis corruptio potest de facili fieri in hebreo quia haec dictio *victare*, quae significat: et vocabitur, et *vagitra*, quae significat: et vocabit, eisdem literis penitus scribuntur in hebreo sed varie sonant prop-

prophecy refers to the Messiah who was the Prince of Peace and God Almighty. It can in no way be taken to refer to Hezekiah because in the said prophecy we read: *In cuius diebus multiplicabitur pax (in whose days peace will be increased)*.[36] It is clear that in the days of Hezekiah peace was not increased; rather, he waged a great war against Samaria. Now where we have *multiplicabitur*, you have in Hebrew *leuiathe* which is written with [*fol. 23r*] the closed *m* or *mem*, which is not the customary way of writing Hebrew. This was done, of course, because of a great mystery which is inherent in this prophecy: that the Messiah was to be both God and man and was to be conceived of a virgin, as we have already proved.[37]

We shall prove this further through other prophecies of prophets who, inspired by the Holy Spirit as well, concluded that a virgin was to give birth to the Messiah, as did happen, and that He was to be called Emmanuel. The prophet Jeremiah says in chapter 31: *Return, virgin of Israel, return to your towns. How much longer will you seek pleasure, O faithless consort? For God created a new thing on earth, and a woman shall bring forth a male child.*[38] Rabbi Joshua Nave[39] says that this passage can only mean that a great thing will take place on earth. For a woman to give birth to a son is not a new thing — for it happens every day. Yet for a virgin to give birth to a son, would truly be a new thing on earth. This doctor almost attested that a virgin was to give birth, and this was our blessed Virgin Mary. It was a new thing because nothing like it had ever occurred before nor will it ever occur again. We can thus conclude, according to the explanation of this passage of Jeremiah given by this doctor, that the prophet was referring to the Virgin Mary. Many of your talmudists confirmed this. In his gloss on this passage, Midrash Tehillim says that God said that at the time the Messiah was to come: "I will create a new creature," as David said in Psalm 2: "*Today I created you and begot, and you are my son.*"[40] We also read in the Talmud that the children of Israel were wounded by a virgin, and will be comforted by a virgin. I

ter aliam et aliam punctuationem." The Targum is cited in *Post., ibid.* (cf. *PF*, p. 743) as is the conclusion of this section. Cf. *FF*, fol. 148*va*, who draws on Lyra as well.

[37] On the closed *mem*, see above, notes 14, 17. This passage reflects Lyra, *De probatione*, p. 182, the printed text of which has *levathe* which resembles Machado's *leuiathe*. It is interesting to note that although Machado knows that the Hebrew *le-marbeh* contains an *m*, he does not seem to notice that his *leuiathe* has none. See Introduction. Cf. also *FF*, fol. 36*rb* (*leuiarbe*).

[38] Jer. 31:21f. See Jerome, *Comm., ad loc., CC,* 74:312ff. (*PL*, 29:914). The Vulgate, in accord with the Hebrew, has "femina circumdabit virum."

[39] Joshua ben Levi, third-century rabbinic teacher, whom Machado has confused with the biblical Joshua ben Nun (Latin: Nave).

[40] Ps. 2:7.

muitos iudeus forão consolados, como forão hos apostolos de Christo, e aqueles que nele crerão.

Ezechiel tambem falou da virgindade de Maria no capitolo xliiij°, onde diz que Deos lhe dixe, estando elle en Ierusalem no tempo do catiueiro: "Esta porta sera fechada e nom se abrira, e varão nom entrara por ella porque ho Senhor Deos de Isrrael passou por ela." Certamente, se eu fora iudeu, vendo este texto tão manifesto como he da virgindade de Maria, loguo me ouuera de conuerter à fee de Christo, porque elle bem claramente demostra a virgindade de Maria. E posto que esta autoridade se entenda literalmente da porta [fol. 23v] do Templo que estaua ao oriente, porem, la teem seu sintido spiritual que esto sinificaua que a porta de Nossa Senhora auia de estar sempre fechada depois que ho filho de Deos entrou por ella, como teemos nos christãos por fee. E prouesse ao eterno Deos que foseis vos assi alomeados que ho mesmo cresseis: que Maria Virgem pario ho Mexia, sendo virgem antes do parto e depois do parto, como hos profetas dela tinhão profitizado. Esta virgem, porem, segundo teemos por fee, concebeo ho Mexia na cidade de Nazareth que estaua em Gualilea, e ho pario em Betleem no ano quadragesimo segundo do emperio do emperador Outauiano segundo, ho qual socedeo a Iulio Cesar, primeiro emperador rromano.

Esta propriedade quinta que estaua escrita do Mexia, a qual lhe auia de ser communicada, que auia de nacer em Betleem, estaua escrita no capitolo quinto do profeta Micheas, onde se diz, falando do nacimento do Mexia: "E tu, Betleem eufrata, pequeno es em hos milhares de Iuda. De ti a mim saira aquele que sera poderoso em Hisrrael, e ho saimento dele, eterno." Bem demostra esta profitia onde ho Mexia auia de nacer, em Beleem, onde naceo Christo, a qual propriedade lhe foi communicada e apropriada. E posto que alguns vossos doutores queirão atribuir esta autoridade a ellrrei Ezechias, carecem de fundamento, porque na predita profitia fazse menção da eternidade do Mexia que foi Deos e homem, ho que nom conuinha nem pertencia a Ezechias. Io-

---

[41] The statement of R. Joshua ben Levi is based on a passage attributed to the *BRMD* to Gen. 41:1 cited in *PF* (pp. 755f.) and *ACPJ*, 1, 4, pp. 46ff. In *PF*: "R. Joshua ben Levi said: Come and see how the Holy One, blessed be He, differs from men. A man strikes with a knife and heals with a bandage. This is not the art of the Holy One, blessed be He, for He heals by the same means through which He strikes. It is thus written, *For I will restore health to you and your wounds I will heal* (Jer. 30:17). You thus find that He heals Israel with the same thing with which He strikes them. They sinned through a virgin, as it is said *there their virgin breasts were handled* (Ezek. 23:3) and they were struck by a virgin, as it is said: *Women are ravished in Zion, virgins in the towns of Judah* (Lam. 5:11). They are consoled by a virgin, as it is said: *Return, O virgin Israel, return to these your cities. How long will you waver, O faithless daughter? For the Lord has created a new thing on earth; a woman protects a*

tell you that this virgin was Mary by whom many Jews, such as Christ's apostles, and those who believed in Him, were comforted.[41]

Ezekiel also spoke of the virginity of Mary in chapter 44. There he says that when he was in Jerusalem at the time of the captivity, God said to him: *This door will be closed and will not be opened, and no man will enter it because the Lord God of Israel went through it.*[42] To be sure, if I were a Jew looking at this passage, I would convert to the faith of Christ, for it clearly and manifestly shows Mary's virginity. Even though this passage is understood literally to refer to the eastern gate [*fol. 23v*] of the Temple, it has a spiritual meaning. For it signifies that the door of Our Lady was to remain forever closed after the son of God entered her, as we Christians accept on faith.[43] Would to God Eternal that you were so enlightened and believed the same: that the Virgin Mary gave birth to the Messiah remaining a virgin before and after parturition, as the prophets had foretold. This virgin, according to our faith, conceived the Messiah in the city of Nazareth in Galilee and bore him in Bethlehem in the forty-second year of the reign of the emperor Octavian the Second, who had succeeded Julius Caesar, the first Roman emperor.[44]

The fifth characteristic which was written of the Messiah and which was fulfilled in Him — that He was to be born in Bethlehem — is found in chapter five of the prophet Micah. Speaking of the birth of the Messiah, he said: *And you, Bethlehem Ephrathah, you are so small among the thousands of Judah. He who will be powerful in Israel will go forth from you to Me and his going forth shall be eternal.*[45] This prophecy shows that the Messiah was to be born in Bethlehem where Christ was born, and that this was fulfilled in Him. Even though some of your doctors wanted to attribute this text to King Hezekiah, they have no basis for it, because in the prophecy mention is made of the Messiah who was God and man. This neither applies to Hezekiah nor does it pertain to him. Jonathan, that great Chaldean who translated the entire Old Testament from

---

man (Jer. 31:21f.). R. Huna ... said: This is the Messiah, as it is said: *Today I have begotten you* (Ps. 2:7)".

The passage from Midrash Tehillim follows that from *BRMD* in *PF* (pp. 756ff.) and is found in sec. 2:9; ed. Buber, p. 28; ed. Braude, 1:41: "When the time comes, the Holy One, blessed be He, will say: 'I must create the Messiah — a new creation.' As Scripture says, *This day have I begotten thee.*"

[42] Ezek. 44:2.

[43] Jerome, *Comm., ad loc., CC,* 75:642ff. (*PL,* 25:428); *ACPJ,* 7, 4, p. 48; *FF,* fols. 148vb, 166vb.

[44] See above, Chap. 2, n. 25.

[45] Mic. 5:2.

nathas, aquele grande caldeu que tresladou todo ho Testamento Velho
em caldeu do hebraico, bem demostra que esta profitia nom se pode entender senão do Mexia. Assi, este doutor tresladou: "E tu, Beleem,
como pequeno eras, ia seras contado em hos milares de Iuda. De ti a
mim saira ho Mexia pera ser feito rrei sobre Isrrael." Bem conclude
Ionathas que esta profitia nom se pode entender senão do Mexia, como
he verdade. Nem vos nom podes neguar tal tresladação como esta
caldea, por onde me espanto muito cairem tantos errores entre vos e
passarem tantas faltas por vos, porque se hos vossos doutores leerão ho
caldeu sobre este passo, nom forão enguan[a]dos.

Creede, pois, comnosco, s[e]nhores, que Maria concebeo virgem e
pario virgem ho Mexia na cidade de Betleem, cidade de Dauid. Esta he a
nossa fee e crença, peçouos que esta seia a uossa. Amen.

[*fol. 24r*] Capitolo Seitimo. De como ho Mexia auia de ser Deos e homem
verdadeiro.

A seista propriedade que ho Mexia auia de teer era que aui[a] de ser
Deos e homem, como esta escrito polos profetas e polos vossos doutores
talmudistas, a qual propriedade a Christo, nosso Redentor, foi communicada e apropriada. Vos outros neguaes que ho Mexia deuia de ser
Deos e homem, e esto procede por nem entenderdes bem hos vossos profetas, hos quaes claramente ho demostrão. E portanto, vos
prouaremos isto ser verdade, primeiramente polos profetas, e depois
decenderemos aos vossos profetas talmudistas.

Ho profeta Micheas, no capitolo quinto, bem proua a sua diuindade
porque, como dixe que elle que auia de ser duque e principe, nom
pequeno de pouo de Isrrael, loguo aiuntou a diuindade, dizendo: "E a
sua saida eterna," por onde bem se conclude que ho Mexia, enquanto
Deos, sempre foi, e nom teem começo nem fim, senão, dizeime vos, de
que se entende isto: "Et egressus eius a diebus eternitatis"? Certamente
nom se pode entender senão do Mexia. Nem vos nom tendes outra
autoridade pera prouar que ho Mexia auia de nacer em Betleem, senão
esta. Concludindo, pois, dizemos que a entenção do profeta neste passo
he [de] demostrar que ho Messias auia de ser Deos e homem.

E venha qua Isaias, que volo proua mais euidentemente se ho vos
quiserdes bem olhar, especular, e entender, lançando de vos todo ho
falso e erroneo entendimento que lhe daes, no capitolo nono, falando
do Mexia e nom de Ezechia, como vos cuidaes, diz assi: "Ho pequeno
nos he nacido, e ho filho nos he dado, e ho dominio e principado foi

---

[46] Cited in *PF*, p. 526 *et passim*.

Hebrew into Chaldean, shows quite well that this prophecy could not refer to any other than the Messiah. In his translation we read: "And you, Bethlehem, as small as you are, will be counted among the thousands of Judah. The Messiah will go forth from Me to you to be made king over Israel."[46] Jonathan is quite correct when he concludes that this prophecy could not be interpreted to refer to one other than the Messiah. Nor can you deny such a translation as this one in Chaldean. For this reason, I am astonished that you have fallen into so much error because your doctors would not have been deceived had they read the Chaldean on this passage.

Believe along with us, gentlemen, that Mary conceived as a virgin and bore the Messiah as a virgin in Bethlehem, the city of David. This is our faith and belief: I ask that it be yours also. Amen.

[fol. 24r] Chapter Seven. How the Messiah was to be true God and man.

The sixth characteristic of the Messiah was that He was to be both God and man, as is written by the prophets and by your talmudic doctors. This property was fulfilled in Christ, our Redeemer. You, however, deny that the Messiah was to be God and man. This stems from your not understanding your prophets who show this very clearly. We will, therefore, show you that this is true, first by the prophets and then by your talmudic prophets.

The prophet Micah in chapter 5 proves Christ's divinity: When he spoke of Him Who was to be the duke and prince, not small among the people of Israel,[1] he then noted [His] divinity, saying: *And His eternal going forth.* We thus conclude that the Messiah always existed, with neither beginning nor end insofar as He is God. Now tell me, what do you make of this: *Et egressus eius a diebus eternitatis?*[2] Certainly, it can be understood as none other than the Messiah. Nor have you any text other than this to prove that the Messiah was to be born in Bethlehem. In conclusion, then, we say that the intention of the prophet in this passage is to show that the Messiah was to be both God and man.

Let Isaiah come and prove this to you even more clearly if you wish to see, perceive and understand. Let him cast off all that is false and erroneous in your understanding of Him. In chapter 9, when he speaks of the Messiah and not of Hezekiah, as you believe, he says: *The child is*

---

[1] Machado is here confusing Mic. 5:2 with Matt. 2:6. See above, Chap. 2, n. 2.

[2] See Jerome, *Comm., ad loc., CC,* 76:481ff. (*PL,* 25:1196ff.); *DPA,* title 8, *PL,* 157:621. Cf. Lyra's remarks in *De Probatione,* p. 104.

posto sobre hos seus ombros. Ho seu emperio sera multiplicado, e a
paz sua nom tera fim." Todas estas cousas demostram aquela humanidade e temporalidade do Mexia emquanto era home*m*. Porem, a sua
diuindade demostra ho profeta quando diz: "E ho nome dele chamarsea
Marauilhoso, Consilheiro, D*eo*s, Forte, Padre do mu*n*do vindoiro, Principe da paz." Todos estes seis nomes compete*m* ao Mexia emquanto
D*eo*s he e no*m* emquanto home*m*.

    Leixemos asaz prouada esta humanidade e diuindade do Mexia por
este dizer deste profeta, e veiamos ho que diz ho profeta Osee, capitolo
3°, falando como hos iudeus em algu*m* tempo buscarão ho S*en*h*o*r
Mexia, que sera antes ho dia do iuizo: "E depois disto tornarão hos
filhos de Isrrael e buscarão ho S*en*h*o*r D*eo*s e Dauid seu rei." Este he ho
[*fol. 24v*] Mexia, Filho de D*eo*s, e filho de Dauid emquanto home*m*,
porque elle auia de ser da casa e familia de Dauid, como foi. Esto se
confirma por aquilo que se diz no Leuitico, capitolo xxvi: "Andarei antre vos e serei vosso D*eo*s, e vos seres meu pouo." Esto se entende do
profeta do qual falou Moises no Deut*e*ronomio xviij que auia de ser ho
Mexia, do qual nesta autoridade se faz menção que auia de ser D*eo*s.

    E vos, Dauid, rreal profeta, que sintistes disto? Dai qua vossa proua!
Confundi estes *Senhores*[a] que ne*m* a vos querem creer ne*m* aos outros
profetas, tão obstinados são e fora de rezão e sentido humano. Vos no*m*
prouaees esta humanidade e diuindade no ps*almo* xliiij? C*er*tame*n*te,
que a vossa proua he muito patente quando vos dixestes estas palauras:
"A tua cadeira sera pera todo sempre e a uara do teu reino, vara sera
de direito. E amaste a iustiça e auorreceste a maldade, e portanto, D*eo*s
te vngio com oleo dalegria mais que todos hos outros."

    Veedes aqui como ho vosso Dauid, profeta grandissimo e maior q*ue*
todos hos outros, posto que vos lhe daes pequena autoridade, confessa e
afirma que ho Mexia auia de ser D*eo*s e home*m*. Esto confirma Dauid
no ps*almo* lxxi onde demostra a diuindade e humanidade do Mexia,
dizendo que nos seus dias auera muita paz e muita iustiça, e sera S*en*h*o*r
do maar e da terra. Concludindo no fim do ps*almo*, diz: "Bendito seia
ho S*en*h*o*r D*eo*s de Isrrael que faz gra*n*des marauilhas soo." Esto ao
Mexia pertence, do qual Dauid fala neste ps*almo*, ho qual no*m* se pode
ente*n*der de Salamão, posto que muitos vossos doutores seião desta
opinião q*ue* este ps*almo* de Salamão se deue de ente*n*der e no*m* do

    a int. +*iudeus* exp.

    [3] Isa. 9:6f. See Jerome, *Comm., ad loc., CC,* 73:125ff. (*PL,* 24:129f.); Isidore, *De Fide Catholica* 1, 5, 1,
PL, 83:460; *DPA,* Title 8, *PL,* 157:619; *DJC,* pp. 45, 58, 74.
    [4] Hos. 3:5. Cf. Jerome, *Comm., ad loc., CC,* 76:84ff. (*PL* 25:885ff.).
    [5] Lev. 26:12.

born to us, and the son is given to us, and the dominion and authority were placed on his shoulders. His rule will be increased and his peace will be eternal. All of these things show the Messiah's human and temporal nature insofar as He was man. However, the prophet demonstrates His divinity when he says: *And His name shall be called Marvelous, Counselor, God, the Mighty, everlasting Father, Prince of Peace.*[3] These six names all apply to the Messiah as God and not as man.

We have sufficiently proved the Messiah's humanity and divinity through these words of the prophet Isaiah. Let us now look at what the prophet Hosea says in chapter 3, where he speaks of how the Jews will look for their Lord the Messiah some time before the Day of Judgment: *And afterwards the children of Israel shall return and seek the Lord God and David their king.*[4] This is the [*fol. 24v*] Messiah, Son of God, and, as a man, son of David; for He was to be of the house and family of David and so He was. This is confirmed by that which is said in chapter 26 of Leviticus: *I will walk among you and will be your God and you shall be My people.*[5] This is taken to refer to the prophet, about whom Moses spoke in Deuteronomy 18, who would be the Messiah and whom Hosea states would be God.[6]

Now you, David, royal prophet, what do you think of all this? Here is your proof! Give the lie to these gentlemen who believe neither you nor the other prophets — so obstinate are they and so devoid of all reason and human feeling. Did you not prove the Messiah's humanity and divinity in Psalm 44? It is most certainly evident when you said these words: *Your throne shall be for ever and ever and the scepter of Your kingdom will be a scepter of justice. You loved justice and abhorred iniquity, and for this reason God anointed You with the oil of gladness above all the others.*[7]

You see how your very great prophet David — greater than all the others, although you fail to consider him of much authority — acknowledges and affirms that the Messiah would be both God and man. David confirms this in Psalm 71 where he demonstrates the divinity and humanity of the Messiah, saying that in His days there shall be much peace and justice, and He shall be Lord of the sea and the land.[8] At the end of the psalm, David says: *Blessed be the Lord God of Israel Who alone works great marvels.*[9] This refers to the Messiah of whom David

---

[6] Deut. 18:15, 18. Cf. *DJC*, p. 34.

[7] Ps. 45 (44): 7f. Cf. Jerome, *Comm.* on Isa. 9:6, *CC*, 73:125ff. (*PL*, 24: 129ff.); Isidore, *De Fide Catholica* 14:2, *PL*, 83:472; *DPA*, title 8, *PL*, 157:621f.; *DJC*, p. 64.

[8] Ps. 72 (71):7f.

[9] Ps. 72 (71):18.

Mexia, como se deue de entender. Porque neste psalmo fala Dauid como todos hos rreis ho auião de seruir e adorar. Claro he e manifesto que hos rreis do mundo nom adorarão a Salamão nem ho seruirão. Seguesse loguo do Mexia se entende, que foi adorado dos rreis maguos e dos rreis christãos. E se beem leerdes este psalmo e ho especulardes, achares que em nhuma maneira nom se pode entender de Salamão, senão do Mexia, onde se conclude a sua humanidade e diuindade. Ho mesmo proua Dauid no psalmo centesimo nono, quando diz: "Antes da lux te gerei." Esto pertence à diuindade porque ho Padre gera ho Filho, como mesmo Dauid proua no psalmo segundo, quando diz: "Ego hodie genui te." A humanidade demostra quando diz: "Dixe ho Senhor a meu senhor: 'Asentate a minha dextra'."

E ainda que alguns [fol. 25r] dos vossos doutores diguão que este psalmo nom foi composto por Dauid mas por Eleazer, ho procurador da casa e familia de Habraam, em louuor dele por amor do que fez quando liurou Loth das maãos dos cinquo rreis que poserão guerra a Sodoma e Guomorra, por onde assi concludem que por este psalmo nom podemos concludir que ho Mexia auia de ser Deos e homem, nos, porem, rreprobamos a vossa sentença, afirmando que Dauid fez ho predito psalmo centesimo nono com todos hos outros.

Ia algum tanto, polos ditos dos profetas, temos prouado como ho Mexia auia de ser Deos e homem. Aguora, veremos, segundo a proua dos vossos doutores, como he verdade que elles afirmarão que ho Mexia auia de ser Deos e homem.

No liuro chamado Grão Grande, no capitolo xxvi, se escreue aquilo que se contem no Genesis xxviij, onde se diz que se nom fora Rrubem, ho primogenito, que hos outros irmãos matarão a Ioseph. Mas, como Rrubem dixe que Ioseph era sua carne e seu sangue, antão desistirão e nam no matarão, mas meterãono na cisterna. Diz a grosa sobre este passo no mesmo liuro: "Isto sinifiqua ho que diz Ieremias nas suas Lamentações no capitolo 4°: 'Orfãos somos, sem padre.'" Assi ho Rredentor que Deos a de tirar d'antre vos outros não tera pai. Assi ho

[10] The Messianic interpretation of Psalm 72 was not foreign to Judaism, especially in the rabbinic period. (See the Targum on this psalm and B.T. Sanhedrin 98b.) In the Middle Ages, however, this interpretation was largely rejected in favor of the opinion that the psalm refers literally to Solomon (see Rashi, Kimhi, and cf. Ibn Ezra ad loc.), no doubt partially in reaction to the generally consistent treatment of Christian exegetes who explained it christologically. See Pseudo-Jerome, Brev., ad loc., PL, 26: 1089 ; DPA, Title 8 PL, 157:622; Post., Yviiiv; PF, p. 771.

[11] Ps. 110 (109):3. Cf. Pseudo-Jerome, PL, 26:1233f.; DJC, p. 60.

[12] Ps. 2:7.

[13] DJC, pp. 52, 60.

speaks in this psalm and not of Solomon as some of your doctors believe. In this psalm David speaks of all the kings who would serve and adore him. It is manifest and clear that the kings of the world did not adore or serve Solomon. Rather it was the Messiah Who was adored by the Magi and the Christian kings. If you read this psalm carefully and consider it, you will find that it can in no way be taken to refer to Solomon, but to the Messiah[10] and from it His humanity and divinity can be deduced. David proves precisely this in Psalm 109, when he says: *Before the light I begot You.*[11] This pertains to the divinity [of the Messiah] because the Father begets the Son, as indeed David proves in Psalm 2 when he says: *Ego hodie genui te.*[12] The Messiah's humanity is shown when David says: *The Lord said to my Lord: Sit at My right hand!*[13]

Some [*fol. 25r*] of your doctors say that this psalm[14] was not composed by David but by Eleazar, the overseer of the house and family of Abraham, in praise of that which Abraham did when he freed Lot from the hands of the five kings who waged war against Sodom and Gomorrah.[15] They therefore reason that we cannot conclude from this psalm that the Messiah would be both God and man. We, however, reject your opinion and affirm that David composed Psalm 109 along with all the others.

Through the sayings of the prophets we have already proved to some extent, how the Messiah would be God and man. Now we shall also see how true it is that your doctors also proved that the Messiah would be God and man.

In chapter 26 of the book known as the *Grão Grande* a passage in Genesis 38 is discussed: If it had not been for Reuben, the first born, the other brothers would have killed Joseph.[16] For Reuben[17] said that Joseph was of their own flesh and blood, and for this reason, they did not kill him but placed him in a well.[18] The gloss on this passage in that book states that: "This signifies that which Jeremiah says in chapter 4 of Lamentations: '*We are orphans without a father.*'"[19] So the Redeemer that God shall raise up from among you shall have no father. The prophet

---

[14] *I.e.*, Ps. 110 (109).

[15] Ps. 110 (109) was interpreted in Jewish tradition with reference to Abraham and his victory over the four kings in Genesis 14. This tradition, found in Midrash Tehillim to Ps. 110 (ed. Buber, pp. 465ff.; Braude, 2:205f.) and developed by Rashi in his commentary *ad loc.*, was cited by Lyra in *Post.*, 3, Eeviir. The latter probably served as Machado's source.

[16] Gen. 37:21.

[17] The remark of Judah, not Reuben, at Gen. 37:26f.

[18] See Gen. 37:20-22.

[19] Lam. 5:3.

confirma ho profeta Zacharias no capitolo iij°, dizendo: "Hum homem vira, e Oriente se chamara."

Tudo isto foi dito polo Mexia, que nom auia de teer pai neste mundo, pois que Deos eterno auia de ser ho pai deste Mexia emquanto Deos. Assi ho declarou Rrabi Mousem, dizendo que ho nacimento do Mexia seria antes da lux, donde parece que antes que ho mundo fosse feito, e antes que a lux fosse criada e feita, ia aquele que avia de vir por Mexias era.

Duas cousas podemos tirar destes dizeres acima postos. A primeira he, que dizendo elles que ho Mexia auia de sair d'antre vos, como Moises tinha dito, demostram que ho Mexia auia de ser homem. A segunda he, que dizendo elles que ho nacimento do Mexia era antes da lux, demostrarão a diuindade sua. Foi, loguo, ho Mexia Deos e homem.

Numidras, hum vosso doutor, expondo aquel passo dos Canticos, capitolo 4°; "Vem, amigua minha, veem, e seras coroada," diz: "Prestes estão as gentes do mundo pera trazerem doens ao Deos Mexia." Assi Isaias no capitolo lx ho confirma, que doens lhe auião de trazer e que ho auião de adorar. Donde parece que Deos e homem auia de ser ho Mexia, segundo ho dizer deste doutor.

[*fol. 25v*] Nos Canticos ou Cantares de Salamão, no capitolo 3°, se diz: "Olhai, senhoras de Sion, no rrei Salamão, e pola sua coroa com a qual sua mãi ho coroou." Sobre este passo diz hum vosso doutor, chamado Rrabi Auiana: "Busquamos toda a Lei e reuoluemos todos os liuros, e nom achamos que Bersabee, mãi de Salamão, fezese coroa alguma pera seu filho Salamão." Concludio dizendo, espantado: "Pois, que cousa he esta ou que coroa he esta?" E assi lheixou este passo e esta dificuldade sem conclusão e determinação. Porem, determinou de perguntar a Rrabi Eleazar, doutissimo na Lei, filho de Rrabi Ioseph, disertissimo e acutissimo nas dificuldades da Lei, e dixelhe: "Tu, peruentura, ouuiste de teu pai que coroa he esta, da qual fala Salamão nos Cantares? Ouuistelhe dizer se fez Bersabee alguma coroa a seu filho Salamão?" Rrespondeo Rrabi Eleazer, dizendo: "Este he Deos de Isrrael, ho Mexia promitido na Lei, chamado Salamão, por amor da paz que ha de teer

---

[20] Zech. 6:12, cf. Zech. 3:8. The Hebrew *ẓemaḥ* (shoot, branch) is translated in the Vulgate as *oriens*.

[21] The above is apparently derived from a passage ascribed to *BRMD* to Gen. 37:22 found in *PF*, p. 759 and *ACPJ*, 1, 5, p. 58. In *PF*: "Scripture says: *You would even cast lots over the fatherless and bargain over your friend* (Job 6:27). It is thus written: *We have become orphans, fatherless* (Lam. 5:33). R. Berechiah said: The Holy One, blessed be He, said to Israel: You said to Me, *We have become orphans, fatherless*. So shall the redeemer whom I shall raise up from you be fatherless, as it is said, *Behold, the man whose name is the branch; for he shall grow up in his place* ..."

Zechariah confirms this in chapter 3: *A man shall come and he shall be called Orient.* [20]

All of this was said by the Messiah who would not have a father in this world since God the Eternal would be the father of this Messiah insofar as He is God. Rabbi Moses declared that the birth of the Messiah would be before the light. [21] Thus it appears that before the world and light were created, He who would come as the Messiah already existed.

Two things are clear from the above statements. The first is that the statement that the Messiah would come from among you, as Moses had said, shows that the Messiah would be a man. The second is that the reference to the birth of the Messiah before [the creation] of light indicates His divinity. The Messiah was then God and man.

One of your doctors, Numidras, [22] explaining the passage from Song of Songs, chapter 4, which reads, *Come, my love, come, and you will be crowned,* [23] says: "The people of the world are ready to bring gifts to God the Messiah." [24] Isaiah confirms this in chapter 60 by saying that gifts would be brought to Him and that He would be adored. [25] According to the words of this doctor, then, it would appear that the Messiah would be both God and man.

[*fol. 25v*] In chapter 3 of the Canticles or Songs of Solomon, it says: *Behold, women of Zion, King Solomon and the crown with which his mother crowned him.* [26] Rabbi Aviana, another one of your doctors, commented on this passage: "We searched through the entire Law and examined all the books, and nowhere have we found that Bathsheba, the mother of Solomon, made any sort of crown for her son." He concluded in astonishment: "What is this thing; what crown is this?" He thereupon left this passage and its difficulties without making any decision or coming to any conclusion. However, he decided to consult the erudite Rabbi Eleazar, the son of Rabbi Joseph, a most learned interpreter of the Law, astute in his handling of passages of such a difficult nature. "By chance," he asked Rabbi Eleazar, "did our father ever mention just what crown it is about which Solomon speaks in the Song of Songs?" Rabbi Eleazar answered: "This is the God of Israel, the Messiah

---

The "statement" attributed to R. Moses the Preacher is actually the Vulgate rendering of Ps. 110(109):1: *ex utero ante luciferum genui te.*

[22] On the Portuguese *Numidras*, see Introduction.

[23] Song of Songs 4:8. Machado follows the Vulgate: *Veni ... sponsa mea. ... Veni ... coronaberis.*

[24] Midrash Tehillim on Ps. 87:4 (ed. Buber, p. 378; Braude, 2:77) cited in *PF*, p. 824: "And the nations will bring gifts to the King Messiah. ..."

[25] See Isa. 60:6. Cf. 72(71):10ff.; Matt. 2:11; *ACPJ*, 1,6, pp. 69ff.

[26] Song of Songs 3:11.

quando vier rredimir ho pouo de Isrrael, ho qual sera coroado da sinaguogua dos iudeus."

Tres cousas pera notardes diz este vosso doutor. A primeira, que chamou ao Mexia Deos de Isrrael, confesando a sua diuindade, a qual vos neguaes. A segunda, que ho texto aleguado nom se pode senão do Mexia contender, chamado Salamão Pacifico. A terceira, que Bersabee nom lhe fez coroa mas a sinaguogua, de espinhos com que ho coroarão. Estas cousas todas que diz este vosso doutor são verdadeiras e dinas de serem notadas, e nos vossos corações, com letras d'ouro esculpidas. Peruentura teeres duuida e algum escrupulo disto, que ho Mexia se auia de chamar Salamão?

Dimidras Rrabi, grosador do salteiro, expondo ho psalmo quinquagesimo de "miserere mei, Deus," diz que Dauid auia grande medo que ho Mexia nom descendesse dele por amor do grande pecado que cometeo adulterando com Bersabee, e matando ho primeiro marido Vrias. E ho pouo assi afirmaua, dizendo: "Quem matou ho pastor e tomou a cordeira pode teer saluação." Assi se conta no 2º Liuro dos Rreis, capitolo xiº. Nosso Senhor mandou dizer a Dauid polo profeta Natham que nom auia de morer (no 2º Liuro dos Rreis, capitolo xijº), dizendolhe: "Deos fez passar teu pecado, portanto, sabe que nom moreras. Hum filho teeras e sera homem de folguança, e darlhei sigurança de todos seus imiguos," e chamoulhe Salamão, que era ho Mexia Deos. [fol. 26r] Confessa este vosso doutor que ho Mexia era ho verdadeiro Salamão, Deos e homem.

No Talmud onde se faz menção deste pecado de Dauid, se diz sobre aquilo que ho profeta Natham dixe a Dauid por mandado de Deos (2º Regum, capitolo xijº): "Hum filho te nacera e sera homem de

---

[27] Based upon a passage from Song of Songs Rabbah to 3:11 (Sonc., p. 173) found in *PF* (pp. 698f.) and *ACPJ* (1, 5, pp. 58f.): "EVEN UPON THE CROWN WHEREWITH HIS MOTHER HATH CROWNED HIM. R. Jonathan said: R. Simeon b. Yoḥai asked R. Eleazar b. R. Jose: 'Have you perhaps heard from your father what is the meaning of THE CROWN WHEREWITH HIS MOTHER CROWNED HIM?' He replied, 'Yes.' 'How did he explain it?' he asked. He said: 'By a parable of a king who had an only daughter of whom he was exceedingly fond, so that at first he called her "daughter," till not satisfied with that he called her "sister," and still not satisfied with that he called her "mother." So the Holy One, blessed be He, loved Israel exceedingly and called them "daughter," as it says, *Hearken, O daughter, and consider* (Ps. XLV, 2); still not satisfied with that he called them "sister," as it says, *Open to me, my sister, my love* (S.S. 5:2); and still not satisfied with that He called them "mother," as it says, *Attend unto Me, O My people, and give ear unto Me, O My nation — u-le'umi* (Isa. LI, 4), where it is written *ul'immi* (and to my mother).' R. Simeon b. Yoḥai rose and kissed him on his head, saying, 'Had I come only to hear this explanation from your lips, it would have repaid me.' R. Ḥanina b. Isaac said: We have searched the whole of the Scripture, and we have not found anywhere that

promised in the Law, who will be crowned by the synagogue of the Jews. His name is Solomon because of the peace that will reign when He redeems the people of Israel."[27]

There are three things which your doctor says that you should know. The first is that he called the Messiah "God of Israel", thereby acknowledging His divinity which you deny. The second is that the text cited indisputably refers to the Messiah, called Solomon the Peaceful.[28] The third is that the Synagogue[29] and not Bathsheba made a crown of thorns for Him, with which they crowned Him. All these things that your doctor says are true and worthy of being noted, engraved in your hearts with letters of gold. Have you, by chance, any doubts or qualms about the Messiah's being called Solomon?

Expounding Psalm 50 (*miserere mei, Deus*),[30] Rabbi Dimidras,[31] commentator of the Psalter, says that David was greatly afraid that the Messiah would not be descended from him because of his sin in committing adultery with Bathsheba and killing her first husband Uriah. The people, however, said, "Whoever killed the shepherd and took the lamb can be saved." This is the way it is told in the Second Book of Kings, chapter 11.[32] Our Lord sent word to David through the prophet Nathan that he would not die (the Second Book of Kings, chapter 12), *God has let your sin pass, therefore, know that you will not die. You will have a son who will be a man of peace, and I will protect him against all his enemies.*[33] [This son] was called Solomon, who was God the Messiah. [*fol. 26r*] This doctor of yours acknowledges that the Messiah was the true Solomon, God and man.

In the Talmud, where David's sin is mentioned, that which the prophet Nathan said of him as ordained by God (Second Kings, chapter 12), is noted: "*A child will be born to you and he will be a man of peace,*" [i.e..]

Bathsheba made a crown for her son Solomon,* and yet you say, WITH THE CROWN WHEREWITH HIS MOTHER CROWNED HIM? What it means, however, is that just as a crown is set with precious stones and pearls, so the Tent of Meeting was conspicuous with blue and purple and scarlet and fine linen."

In *PF*, the passage breaks off at the asterisk. If Machado's source were based on that version, it would account for his statement that the question raised was not resolved. Note however, that Machado's "Aviana" (Hanina) is "Ahuna" in *ACPJ* but more correctly "Chanina" in *PF*.

[28] *Solomon (Shelomoh)* is related to *shalom* (peace) as expounded in the above midrashic text. Cf. 1 Chron. 22:9 in the Vulgate: "*et ob hanc causam Pacificus vocabitur.*"

[29] *I.e.,* the Jewish people.

[30] Ps. 51:1(50:3).

[31] On the Portuguese *Dimidras,* see Introduction.

[32] 2 Sam. 11 takes up the episode of David and Bathsheba and the death of her husband Uriah.

[33] 2 Sam. 12:13.

folguança": "Sera a ti nacido hum filho pera te mezinhar dos teus pecados." Bem parece que isto nom se pode entender de Salamão, ho qual nom pudia mezinhar hos pecados do pai, porque elle pecador era. Do Mexia se deue tudo isto de entender, por onde se conclude que auia de ser Deos, porque homem puro nom pudia rredimir ho pecado nem amezinhar a Dauid. Assi que isto poodes creer, que ho Mexia foi chamado Salamão que quer dizer pacifico ou quirido, e assi Natham lhe chamou *edid* que quer dizer quirido e amado, e que auia de ser Deos, pois que auia de amezinhar hos pecados.

Rrabi Midras perguntou a Rrabi Abba, estando praticando sobre a uinda do Mexia, que nome auia d'auer, ou como se auia de chamar. Rrespondeo Rrabi Abba que se auia de chamar *Adonay* porque este he ho seu nome, como Isaias dixe no capitolo xlijº: "Este nome lhe chamarão: nosso Iusto, nosso Deos." Dizei, por vossa vida, se Isaias diz que auemos de chamar nosso Deos noso Iusto. Nom vos parece que auia de ser Deos, pois que, segundo estes vossos doutores, Midras [e] Abba, ho Mexia se deue de chamar *Adonay*, que ho nome que nom conuem senão a Deos, como he tambem este nome Thetragramaton. Destes nomes todo ho Testamento Velho esta cheo onde quer que se faz menção de Deos ou do Mexia.

Estes nomes Adam, nosso primeiro parente, loguo conheceo como pecou, ou lhe forão rreuelados por Deos, ou polos anios, hos quaes elle mesmo discubrio aos seus filhos e depois, por arte caualistica, hos outros hos souberão e conhecerão porque ho pai estes nomes discubria ao filho, e ho filho a seu filho. E assi, por esta arte cabalistica, vierão em conhicimento deles. E Adam nom se pudia saluar sem estes nomes saber, que erão atribuidos ao Mexia. Deuia de crer que ho Mexia auia de vir saluar a geração humanal e redimir ho pecado, sabendo que auia

---

[34] Based on Midrash Tehillim 2:4 (ed. Buber, p. 40; Braude, 1:6of.) cited in *ACPJ*, 1, 5, pp. 6of.: "According to R. Johanan, there were three matters that David was distressed about; the site of the house of God; the taking of Bath-Sheba; and Solomon's succession to the Kingship ... And David was distressed about his taking of Bath-Sheba, for men were speaking against him in Israel and saying: 'Is it possible that he who took the ewe lamb, murdered its shepherd, and caused the people of Israel to die by the sword, can ever have help from God?' But the Holy One, blessed be He, set his mind at rest, for Nathan said to David: *The Lord also hath put away thy sin; thou shalt not die* (2 Sam. 12:13). About the third matter, Israel said: 'What does David think? That his Kingship can be continued through Bathsheba's son?' But the Holy One, blessed be He, set David's mind at rest, for the word of the Lord came to David, saying: *Behold, a son shall be born to thee, who shall be a man of rest ... his name shall be Solomon* (1 Chron. 22:9)."

[35] *I.e., yedid* (beloved). Solomon was also named Yedidyah (Jedidiah, II Sam. 12:25); in the Vulgate: *amabilis Domini*. See ACPJ, 1.5, p. 60 which does not cite the Hebrew.

[36] Based on the continuation of the midrashic passage cited in n. 34: "Concerning this verse, R.

"A child will be born to you to [cleanse] you of your sins."[34] It surely appears that this could not be taken to refer to Solomon, who could not cure the sins of his father, for he himself was a sinner. All this must refer to the Messiah. We can thereby conclude that He would be God, for a mere man could not redeem sin nor absolve David. You can believe then that the Messiah was called Solomon, which means "peaceful" or "beloved." For this reason Nathan called him *edid*,[35] which means "beloved" and "loved." You [may believe too] that the Messiah would be God because He would absolve sins.[36]

Rabbi Midrash was talking with Rabbi Abba concerning the advent of the Messiah and asked what His name would be or what He would be called. Rabbi Abba answered that He would be called *Adonay* because this was His name, as Isaiah[37] said in chapter 41: *They will call Him this name: Our Just One, Our God*.[38] Tell me, by your life, if Isaiah says that we are to call our God "Our Just One."[39] Does it not seem to you that it would be God since, according to your doctors Midrash [and] Abba, the Messiah is to be called *Adonay*, a name appropriate only to God, as is also the name tetragrammaton?[40] The Old Testament is filled with these names wherever the name of God or the Messiah is mentioned.

Our first ancestor Adam learned these names either after he sinned or they were revealed to him by God or by the angels. He in turn communicated them to his son, and others, and became well-versed in them through the kabbalistic art,[41] for these names were passed on from father to son. Thus, through this kabbalistic art, they came to know of them. Adam could not have been saved had he not known these names which were attributed to the Messiah. He must have believed that the Messiah would come to save the human race and to redeem them from

Judah the Levite said: Are not all sons born to their fathers? Why should Scripture say here *born to them*? Because *to thee* means to heal thee — that is, to heal thee of thy sin. Whence do we know this? From what Nathan the prophet said: *The Lord also hath put away thy sin; thou shalt not die* (2 Sam. 12:13), and Scripture goes on to say *Bath-Sheba ... bore a son, and called his name Solomon ... And the Lord ... sent by the hand of Nathan the prophet, and he called his name Jedidiah ..."* (2 Sam. 12:25).

[37] Correctly: Jeremiah.

[38] Jer. 23:6.

[39] Lam. Rab. to 1:16 (Sonc., pp. 135f.) cited in *PF*, p. 654: "What is the name of King Messiah? R. Abba b. Kahana said: His name is 'the Lord'; as it is stated, *And this is the name whereby he shall be called, The Lord is our righteousness* (Jer. 23:6)." See also *DE*, p. 51.

[40] The tetragrammaton is the four-letter name of God: YHVH. Since it is considered ineffable in Jewish tradition, another name, usually 'adonay, is substituted for it in reading. See *PF*, p. 654. On Machado's christological interpretation of the tetragrammaton, see below.

[41] See Introduction.

de ser Deos e homem — Deos pera saluar, e homem pera padecer. Esto souberão huns dos outros por esta cabalistica arte — huns ensinados polos outros por suas linhas como elles descendião, crendo na vinda do Mexia e tendo fe nele que elle auia de vir tomar carne humana pera nos saluar a vos.

[*fol. 26v*] Ha humanidade do Mexia proua Rrabi Midras Rrut[b] expondo aquele passo do Liuro de Ruth, onde se diz no quarto capitolo: "Estas são has geerações de Phares: Phares geerou Esrron, Esrron gerou Aram, Aram gerou Aminadab, Aminadab gerou Naason, Naason gerou Salmon, Salmon gerou Booz, Booz gerou Obed, Obed gerou Isai, Isai gerou Dauid" — "donde ho Mexia nacera," diz este doutor, concludindo a sua humanidade.

Rrabi Ona e Rrabi Iacob, confirmando ho dizer de Midras Rrut, dizem que esto he ho que se diz no Grão Grande, que Adam chamou ao filho que ouue depois de Abel, morto por Cain (Genesis, 4º capitolo), Seth, que quer dizer pastor, ou quer dizer outra semente me poos Deos em luguar de Abel. Esto he ho que se diz no liuro aleguado, sobre ho qual passo dixe estes vossos[c] doutores, que Adam dixe que Deos lhe posera outra semente, por amor do Mexia, que auia de descender de Seth e nom da geração de Cain. Vedes aqui ainda ha sua humanidade prouada por estes doutores, hos dizeres dos quaes se confirmão no Grão Grande, onde se diz que as filhas de Loth, cuidando que toda a geração humanal era perdida, dixerão: "Viuifiquemos de nosso pai semente" (Genesis, capitolo xix). Esto dixerão ellas por amor do deseio que tinhão que ho Mexia descendesse delas, ho que causaua ho conhecimento que tinhão que ho Mexia auia de vir, segundo a arte cabalistica, porque erão ia edoutas e ensinadas polo pai. E se nom fora este deseio, nunqua ellas dormirão com ho pai nem teuerão parte com elle, como teuerão, do qual ambas conceberão. Esto he ho que dizião: "Excitemos semente, viuifiquemos semente," ho Mexia, ho qual descendeo de Rruth que casou com Booz, a qual Rruth descendia dos filhos das filhas de Loth, segundo se contem no Liuro de Rruth.

b int.   c int. + *teuss* exp.

[42] Machado here personifies Midrash Ruth but the passage to which he alludes is not to be found in that work. Cf. Exod. Rab. 30:3. (Sonc., p. 349): "*Now these are the generations of Perez* (Ruth 4:18) — the word '*toledoth*' — (generations) is spelt defectively [for] ... as soon as Adam and Eve sinned, God made defective all the '*toledoth*' mentioned in the Bible [i.e. the word is spelt without the vowel letter *vav*]. But when Perez arose, his '*generations*' were spelt fully again, because from him Messiah would arise ..."

[43] Ruth 4:18ff.

[44] Machado's *pastor* may be a corruption of *positio*, the usual Latin rendering of Seth. See Jerome, *Liber Hebr. Quaest. in Genes., CC*, 72:8 (*PL*, 23:994); *Post.* 7, Dviir.

sin. He knew that He would be God and man — God in order to save, and man in order to suffer. They learned this from each other through this kabbalistic art. Each taught his direct descendants, believed in the coming of the Messiah, and had faith that he would become incarnate so that we could save you.

[*fol. 26v*] Rabbi Midrash Ruth[42] proves the humanity of the Messiah expounding that passage in the Book of Ruth, chapter four, where it says: *These are the generations of Pharez: Pharez begot Hezron, Hezron begot Ram, Ram begot Amminadab, Amminadab begot Nahshon, Nahshon begot Salmon, Salmon begot Boaz, Boaz begot Obed, Obed begot Jesse, Jesse begot David.*[43] This doctor infers His humanity by saying "the Messiah was descended from him."

Rabbi Huna and Rabbi Jacob confirm Midrash Ruth's words and say that the same is said in the *Grão Grande*: Adam called the son he had after Abel, who was killed by Cain (Genesis, chapter 4), Seth, which means "shepherd"[44] or "God has appointed for me other seed in place of Abel."[45] On this passage your doctors say in the aforementioned book that Adam said that God had given him another seed because of the Messiah who would be descended from Seth and not from the generation of Cain. Even here you see His humanity proved by these doctors. Their sayings are confirmed in the *Grão Grande,* where it says that the daughters of Lot thought that the whole human race was lost and said: *Let us give life to the seed of our father* (Genesis, chapter 19).[46] They said this because of their desire that the Messiah be descended from them.[47] This shows that they knew through the kabbalistic art that the Messiah would come, because they had been taught and instructed by their father. If it had not been for this desire, they never would have slept with their father nor had relations with him. They did this and they both conceived. This is what they said: *"Let us stimulate the seed, let us give life to the seed,"* [which was] the Messiah, Who was descended from Ruth. Ruth, who married Boaz, was descended from the children of the daughters of Lot, according to the Book of Ruth.[48]

---

[45] See Gen. 4:25.

[46] Gen. 19:32.

[47] Ruth Rabbah to 4:19 (Sonc., p. 93) cited in *PF*, p. 354; *ACPJ* 1, 5, p. 62: "R. Huna [in *PF*: R. Nehunya and R. Jacob bar Abin] said: *It is written For God hath appointed me another seed* (Gen. 4:25), that is seed from another place, referring to the Messiah."

On this passage, Machado is closer to the printed Hebrew editions than *PF* or *ACPJ*.

[48] Gen. Rab. 51:10 (ed. Albeck, p. 537; Sonc., I, 447f.) and the passage attributed to *BRMD* to Gen. 4:25 (*Rabbati*, p. 91). These two passages are cited in *PF*, p. 354, before the above passage from Ruth Rabbah (n. 47) and in *ACPJ* (I; 5, pp. 62f.) after the passage from Ruth Rabbah as in

Vedes aqui, senhores, como ho Mexia loguo no começo do mundo foi conhicido dos antiguos que auia de vir redimir ho pecado, ho que no*m* se podia fa*z*er senão sendo elle D*e*os. E hos antiguos assi ho conhi- cião que auia de ser D*e*os e home*m*, inspirados por D*e*os e ensinados pola arte cabalistica. Mas, vos outros, tão obstinados, não queres creer, ᵈ*senhores meus*,ᵈ q*u*e ho Mexia auia de ser D*e*os e homem, e tendes escritura que volos demostra. Por onde concludo que muito graueme*n*te seres punidos e afligidos no inferno, porque conheces a verdade e na*m* na queres creer ne*m* defender, mas andaes enguanados, errados, fora do caminho da verdade, porque assi ho queres. ᵉEn- formaiuos, *s*enhores irmãos, da *v*erdade, e no*m* andares duuidosos.ᵉ

[*fol. 27r*] No Grão Grande estaua escrito que hua molher auia de parir. Sabendo isto algu*n*s iudeus, e ouuindoo nas sinaguoguas, deter- minarão de p*er*guntare*m* aos sabios rrabinos que cousa era aquela, ou q*u*e sinificaua que hu*m*a molher auia de parir. Rresponderãolhes hos doutores da Lei dizendo que aquele passo dito era polo Mexia, porq*u*e assi ho tinha dito Dauid no p*salm*o lxxix, onde se diz: "Acaba, S*e*nh*o*r, aquilo que plantou a tu dextra, e sobre ho filho que esforçaste," acerqua do qual passo diz a tresladação caldaica: "E sobre ho Rrei Mexia que esforçaste." Ditas estas cousas, hos sabios concludi*n*do dixerão aos da p*er*gunta ho que se segue: "Achamos hu*m*a planta que D*e*os plantou em baixo, que foi Habraa*m*, e achamos planta debaixo, e planta de cima, que sera o Mexia." Isto, senhores, tão claro e manifesto que sinifiqua, *c*ertamente be*m* demostrão estes vossos doutores que esta planta ho Mexia auia de ser, D*e*os e home*m* — de cima D*e*os, e debaixo home*m*.

Midras Telim, nu*m* liuro que compos, faz hu*m*a p*er*gunta, à qual responde. A p*er*gunta he esta: "Q*u*e quer dizer Dauid no p*salm*o se- gundo quando diz: 'Ho S*e*nh*o*r me dixe: "Meu filho es tu, eu te gerei oie" '?" Rresponde Midras, dizendo: "Contadas são as cousas do Mexia

---

d-d int.   e-e later add.

Machado. On these passages Albeck, *Bereshit Rabbah*, p. 226, notes: The passage in Gen. Rab. reads: "*Come, Let us make our father drink wine ... that we may preserve seed of our father* [Gen. 19:32]. R. Tanhuma said in Samuel's name: It is not written, that we may preserve a child of our father, but, *that we may preserve seed of our father*: viz. the seed that comes from a different source, which is the King Messiah."

The passage in *BRMD* reads (from *PF*): "R. Tanḥuma said in the name of R. Samuel: It was that seed which came from another source which is that? The King Messiah."

⁴⁹ Interlinear addition. See note *d*.
⁵⁰ "Be ... longer." Later addition. See note *e*.

You see here, gentlemen, how the ancients recognized at the very beginning of the world that the Messiah would come to atone for our sins. This He could not have done if He were not God. So, then, the ancients knew that He would be God and man; for they were inspired by God and instructed through the art of the kabbalah. But you gentlemen,[49] who are so obstinate, do not want to believe that the Messiah would be God and man, even though you have writings that prove this. I can only conclude that you will be gravely punished and tormented in hell because you know the truth, but you neither wish to believe in it nor support it. Rather you prefer to go about in deception and error, straying from the path of truth. Be informed of the truth, brothers, and you will go about in doubt no longer.[50]

[fol. 27r] It was written in the *Grão Grande* that a woman would give birth. Some Jews, who knew this and heard about it in the synagogues, were determined to ask the wise rabbis what this meant or what the significance of a woman's giving birth was. The doctors of the Law answered them saying that that passage was said with reference to the Messiah, for David had said it in Psalm 79, where it is written: *Fulfill, Lord, that which you planted at Your right hand and the son whom You made strong.*[51] In the Chaldean translation we read: "the King Messiah whom you made strong."[52] After these things were said, the wise men concluded by saying the following to those who had asked the question: "We find a plant that God had planted below, which was Abraham, and we find a plant below and above, who will be the Messiah."[53] The significance of this, gentlemen, is clear and obvious and your doctors themselves certainly show that this plant would be the Messiah, God and man — God above, man below.

In a book composed by Midrash Tehillim, there is a question which he answers. The question is: "What does David mean in the second psalm when he says: *The Lord said to me: 'You are my son. I begot you today'?*"[54] Midrash answers by saying: "All that pertains to the Messiah is

---

[51] Ps. 80 (79):16. Machado follows the Vulgate reading: "Et perfice eam quam plantavit dextera tua et super filium hominis."

[52] Found in Targum, *ad loc.*; cited in *PF*, p. 537.

[53] Based on a passage ascribed in *BRMD* to Gen. 40:9 (see *Rabbati*, p. 185 and notes), found in *PF* (pp. 538, 880) and *ACPJ* (1, 5, pp. 62f.). The version of *PF* (p. 538) reads: "*There was a vine before me* (Gen. 40:9). This refers to Israel as it is said, *You bring a vine out of Egypt* (Ps. 80:9). Another interpretation: *There was a vine* refers to the King Messiah, as it is said, *the stock which Your right hand planted,* etc. (Ps. 80:16). There is a planting below and a planting above and below. The planting below is Abraham. The planting above and below is the King Messiah ..." In neither *PF* or *ACPJ* is there reference in this connection to a woman in labor.

[54] Ps. 2:7.

no foro da Lei do Testamento Velho, no Exodo no capitolo 4°, onde se diz: 'Ho meu filho primogenito Isrrael.' E no psalmo centisimo nono: 'Dixe ho Senhor ao meu senhor: "Ex vtero ante luciferum genui te."' E Daniel no capitolo vij° diz que en cima das nuuens do ceo vinha como filho do homem e ates ho Velho de dias cheguaua, e eralhe dado poder e honrra e rreino perpetuo, ho qual se nom tirara, mas reinara pera todo sempre." Estas são as autoridades que se aleguão pera se resoluer a pergunta acima poosta por Midras, as quaes concludem, segundo a entenção deste doutor, que ho Mexia auia de ser Deos e homem, como foi.

E rezão era que pois ho Mexia tinha pai nos ceos, que era Deos eterno; que neste mundo no teuesse senão mãi virgem, pera se concludir e conhecer milhor a sua diuindade, a qual esta bem declarada polo Testamento Velho e polos profetas, se vos hos quiserdes bem entender e especular. Ou, dizeime vos, de quem se entende aquilo de Daniel, acima posto, onde conclude que ho Mexia auia de reinar pera todo sempre, e ho seu reino nunqua auia de fenecer? Bem creo que dires que do Mexia se entende, pois assi crede que foi Deos e homem.

[*fol. 27v*] Hum iudeu num liuro chamado *Cefer Abair* diz que "Nosso Senhor teem hum iusto muito amado dele e quirido, e nelle afirmou ho mundo, ho qual este iusto guouerna e rege, cerquando e olhando muito bem. Este iusto he amado e querido en cima; amado e querido em baixo, e fremoso no alto, e fremoso no baixo. Este iusto he fundamento das almas dos iustos, neste folgou Deos, e deste iusto saem tres fontes viuas que reguão a parte destra e sinistra." Certo tenho pera mym que a entenção deste doutor foi demostrar que ho Mexia auia de ser iusto en cima nos ceos e iusto em baixo na terra, onde daa a demostrar que Deos e homem auia de ser, por onde parece que este iudeu, ou foi inspirado por Deos e conheceo isto, ou ho soube pola arte cabalistica, insinado e edouto polos seus parentes. No Talmud se confirma isto onde

---

[55] Exod. 4:22.

[56] Ps. 110 (109):1, 3.

[57] Dan. 7:13f. A corruption of a midrashic passage, the intent of which is to prove that the people of Israel are called the sons of God. Midrash Tehillim 2:9 (ed. Buber, p. 28; Braude, 1:40f.) cited in *PF*, pp. 527, 756f.; *ACPJ*, 1, 5, p. 63. The passage reads: "*I will declare of the decree of the Lord. He said unto me: 'Thou art My son'* (Ps. 2:7). The children of Israel are declared to be sons in the decree of the Law, in the decree of the Prophets, and in the decree of the Writings: In the decree of the Law it is written, *Thus saith the Lord: Israel is My son, My first-born* (Ex. 4:22) ... In the decree of the Writings it is written, *The Lord said unto my Lord: 'Sit thou at My right hand, until I make thine enemies thy footstool'* (Ps. 110:1), and it is also written, *I saw in the night visions, and behold there came with the clouds of heaven one like unto a son of man, and he came even to the Ancient of days, and he was brought near before Him. And there was given him dominion, and glory, and a kingdom that all the peoples, nations, and languages should serve him* (Dan. 7:13, 14)".

told in the law code of the Old Testament, Exodus, chapter 4, where it says: *Israel is My son, My first born.*[55] And in Psalm 109: *The Lord said to my lord: Ex utero ante luciferum genui te.*[56] And in chapter 7 Daniel says that He came on the clouds of heaven up to the Ancient of Days, and there was given to Him power and honor and perpetual reign which was never taken from Him; for He shall reign forever."[57] These are the texts that are cited to answer the question which Midrash posed. According to the opinion of this doctor, they lead to the belief that the Messiah would be God and man, as He was.

This would follow since the father of the Messiah, God Eternal, was in heaven; for in this world He had only a virgin mother, all the better to recognize His divinity which was clearly enunciated by the Old Testament and by the prophets, if you wish to understand properly and gain insight into them. If not, tell me then, to whom do you think the above passage from Daniel refers, when he concludes that the Messiah would reign forever and that His reign would never die? I am sure you will say that it refers to the Messiah: so believe that He was God and man.

[*fol. 27v*] In a book called *Cefer Abair,*[58] a Jew says, "Our Lord has a just one, loved and cherished by Him. In him He affirmed the world which this just one governs and rules, embraces and supervises very well. This just one is loved and cherished above; loved and cherished below. He is beautiful on high and beautiful below. He is the foundation of the souls of the just and in him God rejoiced. From him sprung three live fountains which water the right and the left."[59] I am sure that the intention of this doctor was to show that the Messiah would be just in the heavens above and just on earth. This serves to demonstrate that He would be God and man. It seems, therefore, that this Jew knew this either through divine inspiration or through the kabbalistic art in which he was indoctrinated by his family. This is confirmed in the Talmud where it stands written that "The son of David

---

[58] *Sefer ha-Bahir.* See Introduction.

[59] Bahir, ed. R. Margulies (Jerusalem, 1950-1), pars. 157, 159; ed. G. Scholem, *Das Buch Bahir* (Leipzig, 1923), par. 105, pp. 112f. The text as translated by Scholem reads: "Was ist der Achte? Einen 'Gerechten' hat Gott in seiner Welt und er liebt ihn, weil er die ganze Welt erhält und ihr Fundament ist. Er unterhält ihn und lässt ihn wachsen und zieht ihn auf und macht ihm Freude, beliebt und angesehen oben, beliebt und angesehen unten, gefürchtet und erhaben oben, gefürchtet und erhaben unten, schön und angenehm oben, schön und angenehm unten, und er ist das Fundament aller Seelen ... [There follows a discussion of the seven days of the week as represented by seven *sephirot*.] Das gleicht einem König der sieben Gärten hatte, und in dem mittleren Garten bewässert ein schöner, sprudelnder Quell aus einem Brunnen fliessender Wasser die drei zu seiner Rechten und die drei zu seiner Linken ..."

se diz e escreue que "Nom vira ho filho de Dauid ates que nom se acabem todas as almas que estão nos corpos." E antão merecerão as nouas de sair, e loguo ho filho de Dauid merecera de geerar. Estes dizeres concludem que ho Mexia auia de renouar as almas, tirandoas do pecado e danholhes a graça, a qual Christo mere[c]eo pola sua paixão, ho que elle nom podia fazer senão sendo Deos e homem, como foi.

Estas cousas e estes segredos vos outros nom entendes porquanto este veo de Moises nom se quer tirar d'antre vossos olhos, nem se tirara iamais senão quando a lei toda for huma e conhecerdes ho nosso pastor Christo, vosso Mexia. E pera saberdes ho que hos vossos antepassados sintirão da humanidade e diuindade do Mexia, notai isto que aqui vos traguo autorizado polos vossos talmudistas. Num liuro chamado *Desir* se escreue isto que se segue.

Huns dos cherumbins bradão e dizem diante do Principe dos principes, "Thetragramaton," outros dizem "*Adonay* dai fala a Iacob," outros dizem "Tudo aquilo que nom for selado pola mão do moço nom he nada, e a mão de Deos esta poosta sobre a cabeça do moço, e ho seu nome he Thetregramaton," e loguo dizem hos anios: "Bento, forte, e valente he ho Principe," dizendo: "Exercito, vem." Loguo vem ho moço e humildasse diante do Criador, louuando seu nome e dizendo: "Gloria e louuor a Deos," e se põe debaixo da cadeira de Deos, e da sua parte direita saem pedras de foguo e de corisco, e da esquerda saem trouões, e tempestades que todos estremecem. [*fol. 28r*] E quando ho moço entra debaixo da cadeira de Deos daa gloria, e ho Criador Deos eterno ho enfortalece com multidão de tochas que ho alomeam todo. Vem loguo todos hos outros diante do Criador, dizendo: "O Deos grande, O Deos forte, O Deos valente e temeroso"; e Deos chama loguo ho moço e dalhe poder sobre este mundo e ho faz Principe dele e senhor.

Este dizer he escuro e marauilhoso mas, porem, bem demostra que tudo acima dito se deue d'entender do Mexia. E parece que a entenção do iudeu que isto escreueu era demostrar que ho Mexia auia de ser Deos e homem, ho que este iudeu soube ou por alguma reuelação, ou foi en-

---

[60] B.T. '*Avodah Zarah* 5a: "The Son of David does not come until all the souls in *Guf* have been disposed of." The Hebrew word *guf* literally means "body" but Jewish tradition interpreted this passage with reference to *Guf* as the storehouse of all unborn souls. See the commentary of Rashi, *ad loc.* The passage is cited in *PF*, p. 441 but as an example of a Jewish "*insania*" rather than in support of a Christian doctrine.

[61] Apparently a corruption of (*sefer*) *yeẓirah*. See below, n. 64. On the *d-* prefix, cf. Dimidras, Chap. 7, n. 31 and Introduction.

will not come until all the souls that are now in bodies are exhausted."[60] At that time, the new ones will be privileged to go forth and the son of David will be privileged to bring forth. These sayings lead to the belief that the Messiah would regenerate souls, absolving them of sin and bestowing upon them the grace which Christ Himself merited through his suffering. This He could not have done unless He were God and man, as He was.

You do not understand these things and secrets inasmuch as you do not want to remove the veil of Moses from your eyes. Nor will it ever be removed except when the law will be one and you will recognize our shepherd Christ, your Messiah. So that you know what your ancestors felt about the humanity and divinity of the Messiah, note that which I bring to you here as authorized by your talmudists. The following is written in a book called *Desir*.[61]

Some of the cherubs shout before the Prince of princes and say: "Tetragrammaton." Others say: "Adonay speaks to Jacob from there." Still others say: "All that is not sealed by the hand of the lad is of naught. The hand of God is placed above the head of the lad and his name is Tetragrammaton." The angels then say: "The Prince is blessed, strong, and valiant," followed by "Come, hosts." Then the lad comes and does homage to the Creator, praising His name and saying: "Glory and praise to God," and he places himself under His chair. From the right, firestones and sparks issue forth; from the left, there break forth thunder and storms which cause everyone to tremble. [*fol. 28r*] And when the lad approaches the throne of God, he gives glory, and the Creator, God Eternal, fortifies him with a multitude of torches that completely illuminate him. Then all the others come before the Creator, saying: "O great God, O mighty God, O valiant and awesome God." Afterwards God calls the lad and gives him power over this world, making him lord and prince over it.[62]

This passage is obscure and arcane. Nevertheless, it proves that everything said above should be taken to refer to the Messiah. It seems that the intention of the Jew who wrote this was to show that the Messiah would be God and man. This Jew knew this either through revelation or through instruction in kabbalistic art, because he says that

---

[62] This passage has not been located in the Christian anti-Jewish literature nor in the Hebrew sources, although it evidently belongs to the rabbinic mystical *hekhalot* literature. (See Gershom Scholem, *Major Trends in Jewish Mysticism* [New York, 1946], pp. 40-79: idem, *Jewish Gnosticism, Merkabah Mysticism, and Talmudic Tradition* [New York, 1965]). Elements of this passage may be found throughout the literature. See especially the *Sefer ha-Hekhalot* in the translation of H. Odeberg, *3 Enoch or the Hebrew Book of Enoch* (Cambridge, U.K., 1928), pp. 39, 72ff., 140, 164ff.

sinado pola arte cabalistica, porque elle diz que Deos fez este moço Principe dos principes, ho que se nom pode entender senão do Mexia.

A este moço, do qual acima se faz menção, chamão hos cabalistas Matratom, que he principe das azes, ho qual se escreue com huma letra com, com a qual forão criados hos ceos e a terra. E he escrita com seis letras, e com vinte e dous nomes, e con sete santidades, e he dado sobre seis de seus nomes. He esculpido este nome em vinte e duas pedras, escrito com seis vozes sobre altura de seis. Esta aselado em cameras de cameras, e en segredo dos segredos, e em milagre de milagrees.

Este nome foi dado a Moises; porem, Deos nom lhe deu licença que dele se seruisse, mas deu Deos licença a Adam que dele se seruisse, ho que nom foi concidido a Seth, seu filho, nem aos outros patriarchas, saluo a Moises, dizendolhe: "Guarte que nom rreueles neste nome porque ho meu nome esta dentro dele." Este he ho nome de *Adonay*, como Deos dixe a Moises: "Ho nome meu *Adonay* nom lhes demostrei" (Exodo, vi° capitolo) porquanto este nome grande he, e enclude grandes misterios en si.

Posto que estes cabalistas falem escuramente acerqua deste[s] nome[s] Matratom, *Adonay*, Thetregramaton, hos quaes vos outros poderes milhor entender que eu; porem, esto cremos que estes nomes são grandes e fechão en si e ençarrão grandes misterios, hos quaes nom se podem atribuir nem communicar senão a Deos. E pois que estes cabalistas, vossos antepassados, affirmão que tres nomes auião de ser communicados ao Mexia, bem concludem que ho Mexia auia de ser Deos e homem pois que lhe[f] podemos chamar Matratom, *Adonay*, Tetregramaton, que são nomes de Deos. E hos vossos doutores cabalistas afirmão que com estes nomes Deos criou este mundo, que he dizer que Deos criou ho mundo com ho Filho e Spiritu Santo, aos quaes estes nomes lhes são atribuidos.

[*fol. 28v*] Em Midras Telim se põe huma pergunta sobre ho psalmo que começa no hebraico: *Eloy, Adonay* ("Deus, Deus meus"), psalmo xxi, que

f MS *lhes*

[63] The angel Metatron is the metamorphosized Enoch, (See Scholem, *Major Trends in Jewish Mysticism,* pp. 67ff.) In this literature, Metatron is termed "prince of the divine presence," "prince of the world," etc. and is referred to as "the boy" (*na'ar*) and as the "lesser Yaho" or the "lesser YHVH" (see above, n. 40); cf. B.T. Sanhedrin 38b (Sonc., p. 245): "Once a *Min* (heretic) said to R. Idith: It is written, *And unto Moses He said, Come up to the Lord* (Exod. 24:1). But surely, it should have stated *Come up unto Me*! It was Metatron [who said that], he replied, whose name is similar to that of his Master for it is written, *for My name is in him* (Exod. 23:21)." The passage which appears to come closest to that of Machado is found in the *Rabbati,* pp. 26ff. but it is by no means identical. Much

God made this youth Prince of princes, which could only mean the Messiah.

The kabbalists mentioned above call this youth Metatron,[63] prince of hosts. The name is written with the letter *com*, with which the heavens and the earth were created. It is written with six letters, twenty-two names, and seven sanctities over six of his names. This name is carved on twenty-two stones [and] is written with six words by six [words]. It is sealed in chambers within chambers, in the secret of secrets and in the miracle of miracles.[64]

This name was given to Moses. God did not give him permission to use it but He did give permission to Adam to use it. It was not known by Seth, his son, nor by the other patriarchs save Moses alone. [God] said to him: "Watch that you are not revealed in this name because My name is contained within it."[65] This name is *Adonay,* as God said to Moses: *I did not show them my name Adonay"* (Exodus, chapter 6),[66] because this name is great and contains great mysteries.

Since these kabbalists speak obscurely of these names — Metatron, *Adonay,* Tetragrammaton — which you understand better than I, we believe that these names are great and contain within them profound mysteries which can be attributed or applied to none other than God. And since these kabbalists, your forefathers, affirm that three names would be applied to the Messiah, they rightly conclude that the Messiah would be God and man — for we can call him Metatron, *Adonay,* [and] Tetragrammaton, which are names for God. Your kabbalist doctors affirm that God created this world with these names; that is, God created the world with the Son and the Holy Spirit, to Whom these names are applied.

[*fol. 28v*] There is a question in Midrash Tehillim on Psalm 21 which begins in Hebrew: *Eloy, Adonay (Deus, Deus meus).*[67] The question is:

---

material pertaining to Metatron has been collected by R. Margulies in *Malakhe 'Elyon* (Jerusalem, 1964), pp. 73-108.

[64] The only material drawn from the *Yeẓirah* in this section is that found in the passage from "that which is written" to "miracles," a mélange of scattered elements in that work, 1:13 *et passim*. The interested reader may consult the translation of Lazarus Goldschmidt, *Das Buch der Schöpfung* (Frankfurt, 1894), chs. 1 and 3, pp. 49ff. and 56. This translation must, however, be used with discretion.

Machado's reference to the "letter *com*" is probably a corruption of the three prime letters or *matres* of the *Yeẓirah, 'alef, mem* and *shin,* which would correspond to *o, m,* and *c* respectively.

[65] Cf. Exod. 23:21.

[66] Exod. 6:3.

[67] Ps. 22 (21):2. "Deus, deus meus" is not "Adonay" in Hebrew but "Eli, Eli."

diz assi: "Por que nomea Dauid tres vezes ho nome de D*eos?*" Responde
que "isto dixe Dauid pera te ensinar que com estes nomes criou D*eos* ho
ceo e a terra, criandoo ho Padre, e ho Filho, e ho S*piritu* Santo." Esto confirmarão dous teus doutores, de Rroub*em* e de Guad, assi
chamados, dizendo que tres pessoas — Padre, Filho, S*piritu* Santo —
criarão ho mu*n*do e mais, derão a Lei de Moises, hos quaes respondem
a esta p*er*gunta que lhes foi p*r*oposta: "Por que causa (dizia*m* eles) q*ue* as
tres pessoas criarão ho mu*n*do e mais, dera*m* a Lei?" Rresponde*m*
dizendo: "Porque a Lei foi trina e ho mundo trino feito e criado por
tres pessoas." Midras Telim daa autoridade a esto aleguando aquilo dos
Prou*er*bios onde se diz: "Eu escr*e*ui a ti trindades com selos pera te fa*z*er
saber a v*er*dade das verdades." Assi que estes doutores concludindo
dize*m* que tudo foi trinado, feito por tres trindades. A este fim que,
pois, este nome *Adonay* he atribuido à Trindade, e a Sagrada Escritura
ho atribui ao Mexia, que não podia ser senão sendo elle algu*m*a pessoa
desta Trindade, como foi a segunda pessoa *in diuinis.*

E se no*m* quis*er*des crer a Midras Telim, olhai ho que se diz no Grão
Grande no capitolo xxiij, aleguando aquilo do Genesis xxiij, onde se diz
que qua*n*do Habraa*m* hia pera ho mo*n*te Moria pera sacrificar Isaac,
aleua*n*tou ao t*er*ceiro dia hos olhos e dixe: "Ali, ali muitas trindades e
hahi na Lei muitas." Isto diz porq*ue* tudo he feito pola Trindade. Bem
se parece, segundo este dizer, que ho Mexia era do numero desta Trindade pois que a Lei dele faz me*n*ção em muitos passos atribuindolhe
este nome *Adonay,* ho qual he atribuido à Sacratissima Trindade. Esto
esta confirmado em *Cenadrim,* liuro assi chamado, onde se diz que Rrabi

---

[68] See below, n. 70.

[69] On "de Rroub*em*" and "de Guad," see Introduction.

[70] This passage is a rather severe corruption of Midrash Tehillim to Ps. 50 (49):1, ed. Buber, pp.
278f.; Braude, 1:468. It is cited correctly in *PF*, p. 494 and quoted in *DE*, p. 11, and by Abner of
Burgos in his *Sefer Teshuvot la-Meḥaref.* See Y. Baer, *Tarbiz,* 28 (1958), pp. 279f., n. 3. Cf. also Lyra,
De Prob., pp. 158f. The text reads: "A psalm of Asaph, God, God, the Lord, He hath spoken and he
called the earth into being (Ps. 50:1). The heretics asked R. Simlai: What is meant by the words
'God, God, the Lord, He hath spoken?' R. Simlai answered: Scripture does not say here 'They have
spoken,' or 'they called,' but 'He hath spoken,' and 'He called.' Later, his disciples said to him:
'Master, thou has put them off with a broken reed of an answer. But what answer wilt thou give
us?' He said to them: His three names are one, as a man may say: 'Artisan, builder and architect.'
And why did Scripture here mention three times the name of the Holy One, blessed be He? To
teach that the Holy One, blessed be He, created the universe by three names that stand for the
three goodly attributes of wisdom, understanding and knowledge ... So, too, the name of God is
repeated three times in the verse, For the Lord thy God is a devouring fire, a jealous God (Deut.
4:24). And again in the verse: The children of God said: God, God, the Lord, God, God, the Lord,
He knoweth (Josh. 22:22). Why does the phrase 'God, God, the Lord' occur twice here? Once to
stand for the three attributes by which the world was created; and once again to stand for the three

"Why does David state the name of God three times?"[68] The answer is that "David said this to teach you that God created the heavens and the earth, as the Father, the Son, and the Holy Spirit." Two doctors of yours, called the sons of Reuben and Gad, confirmed this and said that three persons — the Father, the Son, [and] the Holy Spirit — created the world and gave the Mosaic law.[69] They answer this question that was posed them by asking: "Why (they said) did the three Persons create the world and give the Law as well?" They then answered: "Because the Law was triune and the world triune, created by three Persons."[70] Midrash Tehillim corroborates this and cites the passage in Proverbs that says: *I wrote trinities for you with seals so that you would come to know the truth of truths*. Consequently these doctors say in conclusion that everything was in threes, formed by three trinities.[71] It is for this reason, then, that this name *Adonay* is attributed to the Trinity and the Holy Scriptures in turn apply it to the Messiah. This could not be unless He were a part of this Trinity as the second person *in divinis*.

If you are not disposed to believe Midrash Tehillim, look at what it says in the *Grão Grande*, chapter 23, which cites that part of Genesis 23 which treats of Abraham's going to Mount Moriah to sacrifice Isaac. On the third day he raised his eyes and said: "Yonder there are many trinities and in the Law there are many."[72] This he said because everything was created by the Trinity. According to this, it appears that the Messiah was a member of this Trinity since the Law mentions Him in many passages, applying to Him the name *Adonay* which refers to the Most Holy Trinity. This is confirmed in the book called *Sanhedrin* where

attributes whereby the Torah was given, as is said 'For I am the Lord, thy God, a jealous God (Deut. 5:9).'" In the version of Martini and those based upon him, the phrase "the heretics asked R. Simlai" is omitted.

[71] Prov. 22:20f. Machado's reference is not clear. This verse is treated in Midrash Mishle (ed. Buber, 1893), pp. 89f.; Tanḥuma, Yitro 10; Yalqut Shime'oni, Mishle 960, but these passages are not cited in Christian polemical literature. A verse frequently cited for proof of the existence of the Trinity is Eccl. 4:12. See *PF*, p. 495.

[72] A corruption of Genesis Rabbah 56:1 cited in *PF*, pp. 877f. (Sonc., p. 491): "On the third day, etc. [Gen. 22:4]. It is written, *After two days He will revive us, on the third day He will raise us up, that we may live in His presence* (Hos. 6:2). E.g. on the third day of the tribal ancestors: *And Joseph said unto them the third day: This do, and live* (Gen. 42:18); on the third day of Revelation: *And it came to pass on the third day when it was morning* (Ex. 19:16); on the third day of the spies: *And hide yourselves there three days* (Josh. 2:16); on the third day of Jonah: *And Jonah was in the belly of the fish three days and three nights* (Jonah 2, 5); on the third day of those returning from the Exile: *And we abode there three days* (Ezra 8:32); on the third day of resurrection: *After two days He will revive us, on the third day He will raise us up.*" Martini's text adds the words "for he is the King Messiah as it is said, *Restore us, O God of hosts; let Your face shine, that we may be saved* (Ps. 80:7)." These are generally considered to be a forgery. See Albeck, *Bereshit Rabbati*, p. 595, note.

Aya, restaurador da Lei e estandoa escreuendo, dixe a seus filhos:
"Sabee que no*m* ha de vir ho Mexia, filho de Dauid, ates que no*m* seia*m*
rendidas as duas casas de Isrrael pate*r*nas que são a cabeça do catiueiro
de Babilonia." Assi ho dixe Isaias no capitolo viij, dizendo: *"Adona[y]*
cabaot (ho D*eo*s dos ex*er*citos) santificares, e sera por santidade e por
pedra de mortidade e pena de escandalo às duas casas de Isrrael."
Rrabi Salamão sobre este passo diz: "E sera ho Mexia por santidade, ho
qual se chamara *Adonay.*" Todos estes dizeres conclude*m* q*ue* ho Mexia
se auia de chamar *Adonay* propriame*n*te, como chamamos a D*eo*s, por
onde elles conclude*m* que ho Mexia D*eo*s e home*m* auia de ser.

[*fol. 29r*] Rrabi Habraa*m* Abenazara, grosador do salteiro, expondo
aquele passo do ps*alm*o ij° onde se diz, "Serui a D*eo*s com temor e
alegraiuos com tremor, e armaiuos com limpeza," diz: "Armaiuos do
Mexia, Filho de Deos." Rrabi Midras, outro grosador, diz: "Armaiuos
do Filho," sobre este passo. Certo he que ho Mexia no*m* era Filho de
D*eo*s emquanto home*m*, mas filho da Virgem. Nomeandoo loguo aqui
ho Filho parece que entendia que ho Mexia auia de ser Filho de D*eo*s. E
que assi seia, parecesse ser v*er*dade, por amor do exemplo que elle põe,
polo qu*a*l se conclude bem clarame*n*te ser ho Mexia, Filho de D*eo*s. Este
he ho emxemplo que põe, dizendo que hu*m* rrei se ensanhou contra
hu*m*a cidade. Sabendoo hos cidadõees, tomarão ho p*r*incipe, filho do
rrei, e começarão de ho afo[l]guare*m*, dizendolhe q*ue* roguasse a seu
pai, rrei irado contra elles, por elles. Indo elles pera falare*m* a ellrrei,
disselhes que se fossem ao filho, darlhe*g* graças e aguardicim*en*tos,
"porque se elle não fora, todos foreis p*er*didos." E portanto, dixe
Dauid: "Armaiuos do Filho" — do Mexia. Diguouos q*ue* este enx*e*mplo
he muito v*er*dadeiro e que na*m* no poos este iudeu senão i[n]spirado po*r*

g MS *darlhes*

[73] R. Ḥiyya bar Abba, second century Tanna. On R. Ḥiyya as restorer of the Law, see B. T.
Sukkah 20a.

[74] B.T. Sanhedrin 38a in *PF*, pp. 343, 405; *ACPJ*, 1, 5, p. 66.

[75] Isa. 8:13f.

[76] The gloss of Rashi to this verse is cited in *PF*, p. 343 and *ACPJ*, 1, 6, p. 66.

[77] Abraham Ibn Ezra (1092-1161). See Introduction.

[78] Ps. 2:11f.

[79] Machado's "arm yourselves with purity" (*armaiuos com limpeza*) translates the Hebrew *nashequ*
bar, an obscure phrase which is variously translated by the different versions. Here the verb *nashequ*
is related to *nesheq* (arms) as found in an anonymous interpretation cited in the commentary of
Abraham Ibn Ezra. Cf. Rashi, *ad loc.* The Vulgate renders the word as *apprehendite.*
    The Hebrew *bar* may be taken as "purity" (Vulgate: *disciplinam*) or more commonly as an
Aramaism (cf. Prov. 31:2) meaning "son" (see Rashi, Ibn Ezra, Kimhi, *ad loc.*) The latter rendering
was, of course, appealing to Christian polemicists who preferred the rendering *osculamini filium* to

it is said that Rabbi Hiyya, the restorer of the Law,[73] said to his sons while writing: "Know that the Messiah, the son of David, will not come, until the paternal houses of Israel, which are the head of the Babylonian captivity, are terminated."[74] This was expressed by Isaiah, chapter 8, who said: *You shall sanctify Adonay zevaot (the Lord of hosts) and He shall be for a sanctification and for a stone of mortification and the penalty of scandal, for both houses of Israel.*[75] Rabbi Solomon says, concerning this passage: "And the Messiah shall be holy and He shall be called *Adonay*."[76] All these writings conclude that the Messiah would properly be called *Adonay,* as we call God, and that He would be both God and man.

[*fol. 29r*] Rabbi Abraham Ibn Ezra,[77] commentator on the Psalter, expounds the passage in Psalm 2 which reads: *Serve God with fear, and rejoice with trembling, and arm yourselves with purity.*[78] He says: "Arm yourselves with the Messiah, son of God." Rabbi Midrash, another commentator, says on this passage: "Arm yourselves with the Son." Of course, the Messiah, in His human aspect, was not the son of God, but rather the son of the Virgin. Calling Him "Son" here would seem to indicate that the Messiah had to be the Son of God. That it could clearly be shown as true that the Messiah would be the son of God, a parable is brought. The parable is that a king became enraged against an entire city. When the citizens found out, they took the prince, the son of the king, and began to placate him, telling him that he should plead with his irate father on their behalf. When they went to speak with the king, he told them to go to his son and express their thanks and gratitude, "for if it were not for him, you would all have been lost." Therefore David said: *Arm yourselves with the son* — that is, with the Messiah.[79] I tell you that this parable is very true and that this Jew would not have

---

the Vulgate version. Thus *PF*, pp. 887f.: "Osculamini filium: Ecce servite Domino. vers. 11. & 12. contra id quod supra dixit vers. 2. contra Dominum. & c. & osculamini Filium contra id quod dixit v. 2 & contra Messiam ejus. Expositio vero vocis בר est talis, qualis est Prov. 31. v. 2. quid ברי fili mi, & c. & sic dixit v. 7. Filius meus es tu." Cf. Pacios López, *Disputa, Actas,* p. 215.

Machado is aware of both interpretations although no Christian source known to me cites the former ("arm yourselves with purity").

The midrashic passage (Midrash Tehillim 2:17; ed. Buber, pp. 32f.; Braude, 1:47) as it appears in Machado is incomplete. It is cited in *PF*, p. 888, following Martini's citation of Ibn Ezra in *ACPJ*, 1, 5, pp. 64f.: "What parable fits here? That of a King who became angry at the inhabitants of a certain city, and the inhabitants of the city went and pleaded with the King's son to mollify the King. So he went and mollified his father. After the King was mollified by his son, the inhabitants of the city were about to sing a song of homage to the King. But the King said to them: 'Is it to me that ye would sing a song of homage? Go and sing the song of homage to my son: had it not been for him, I would long ago have destroyed the inhabitants of this city.'"

Deos, ho qual foi irado contra a geração humanal por amor do pecado de Adam. Mas, porem, polo Mexia somos reconciliados, e assi, como este vosso doutor dixe, assi se aconteceo.

Certamente eu tenho pera mym que estes segredos tão grandes e tão manifestos que demostrão que ho Mexia auia de ser Deos e homem nom forão sabidos destes doutores senão pola arte cabalistica, que era que ho pai descubria estes grandes segredos aos filhos, e elles nom hos descubrião senão muito secretamente, e com muita astutia e cautela. E que depois, vendo que hos iudeus se conuertião à fee de Christo no tempo da Igreia primitiva, fezerão algumas exconiurações onde concludirão que mais nom auião de descubrir estes segredos. Esto veo depois que ho maldito Talmud foy composto polos vossos doutores no Cairo, no qual corromperão a Sagrada Escritura, e grosando falsamente ho Testamento Velho, e ali acabarão de vos meterem no inferno.

Veede, veede estes doutores. Lede por elles, especulaesos bem, que asaz demostrão que o Mexia avia de ser Deos e homem, como se parece muito bem polo enxemplo acima posto que declara asaz que ho Mexia auia de ser Deos pois que auia de reconciliar a geração humanal com Deos Padre que foi ofendido polo pecado de Adam e polo de vos outros obstinados, encredolosos.

ʰDiguo, senhores, que fostes e ya nom soes ma[i]s muito amiguos de Deos e nossos. E [mu]yto deues primeiramente a Deos e aos senhores inquisidores doutissimos que teuerão e tem muito bom zelo e cuidado das vossas almas. Portanto, vos peço que nom vos tornes a enfrascar, mas ide de virtude en virtude pera que veiaes Deos de Seon e gostes daquela vida eterna. Amen.ʰ

[fol. 29v] No Grão Grande sobre hum texto do Genesis xli, onde se diz que elrrei Pharão fez a Ioseph preposto e rei de todo ho Egito, se diz que muitos sabios dixerão que desde começo do mundo ates ho Mexia, nom forão mais que dez rreis. Ho primeiro rrei que ouue no mundo, dizse ali que foi ho mundo, ho qual foi feito e criado, segundo diz Rrabi Eleazar, polo Verbo, como dixe ho rreal Dauid no psalmo xxxij: "Polo Verbo de Deos hos ceos forão criados." Rrabi Salamão diz que polo spiritu de Deos, por onde parece que estes doutores confessão ho Filho e ho Spiritu Santo, hos quaes vos neguaes.

Ho segundo rrei do mundo foi Menbroth tirano, do qual se faz menção no Genesis, capitolo x. Ho terceiro rrei foi Ioseph (Genesis xli), onde se conta como Pharão ho fez rrei de todo ho Egito. Ho quarto

h-h marg.

related it if he had not been inspired by God who was angered with the human race because of Adam's sin. Nevertheless, we are reconciled through the Messiah. As your doctor said, so it came to pass.

I am convinced that these very obvious allusions which clearly demonstrate that the Messiah would be God and man could not be known by these doctors except through the art of the kabbalah. Fathers would transmit them to their sons but only with the utmost caution and care. Afterwards, when they saw that the Jews were converting to the faith of Christ at the time of the early Church, they pronounced a ban against revealing these secrets. This occurred after the accursed Talmud was written by your doctors in Cairo. In it they corrupted the Holy Scriptures, falsely glossed the Old Testament, and managed to consign you to hell.

Look, look at these doctors. Read them and ponder their words for they sufficiently demonstrate that the Messiah would be God and man as is shown clearly in the aforementioned parable which declares that the Messiah would be God since He would reconcile the human race with God the Father who was offended by Adam's sin and by you who remain obstinate and disbelieving.

I tell you, gentlemen, that you were, but are no longer, our friends or God's. You owe a great deal first to God and then to the learned inquisitors who show zeal and concern for your souls. Therefore, I ask you not to give yourselves over to sin, but rather to go from virtue to virtue so that you may see the God of Zion and enjoy eternal life. Amen.

[fol. 29v] In the Grão Grande, there is reference to a passage in Genesis 41 where it says that Pharaoh made Joseph overseer and king of all Egypt.[80] It says that many wise men said that since the beginning of the world until the time of the Messiah, there had not been more than ten kings. It is said there that the first king in the world [was the Word] for the world was formed and created, according to Rabbi Eleazar, by the Word, as David said in Psalm 32: By the word of God the heavens were created.[81] Rabbi Solomon says "through the spirit of God." It seems then these doctors recognize the Son and the Holy Spirit, which you deny.

The second king of the world was the tyrant Nimrod who is mentioned in Genesis, chapter 10.[82] The third king was Joseph who, according to Genesis 41, was made king of all Egypt.[83] The fourth king

[80] Gen. 41:41.
[81] Ps. 33(32):6.
[82] Gen. 10:8f.
[83] Gen. 41:39ff.

rrei foi Salamão, do qual se faz menção no Terceiro Liuro dos Rreis no capitolo *primeiro* quando foi *primeiro* rrei coroado. Ho quinto foi Nabuchadonosor (Danielis, capitolo *primeiro*). Ho seisto rrei foi Dario (Danielis, capitolo nono). Ho seitimo foi ellrrei Ciro, ao qual Isaias (capitolo xlv) chamou Chr*isto*, vngido porquanto este auia de tirar ho pouo de Isrrael de catiueiro, segundo se contem no P*ri*meiro Liuro de Esdras, no p*ri*meiro capitolo. Ho outauo rrei foi Alexandre Macedo, do qual se faz menção no P*ri*meiro Liuro de Machabeus, capitolo *primeiro*. Este foi ho p*ri*meiro que rreinou en Grecia. Ho nono foi Outauiano Augusto Cesar no tempo do qual naceo ho Mexia, segundo contão hos historiadores. E se quiserdes creer, Sam Lucas dele faz menção no segundo capitolo do seu Eua*n*gelho. E mais. No liuro acima aleguado Grão Grande se faz deste rrei menção, ao qual vos daes mais autoridade que não aos eua*n*gelistas. Mal pecado. Ho decimo rrei foi ho Mexia, do qual fala Daniel no capitolo 2°, dizendo que nos dias destes rreis se auia de aleuantar D*eos* dos ceos, ho qual auia de rreinar e nu*n*qua ser mudado. Esto se proua pola estatua gra*n*de que ellrrei Nabucho-donosor vio en sonhos, a qual Daniel declarou que sinificaua por q*ue* esta es[ta]tua tinha a cabeça d'ouro purissimo, a qual sinificaua ho rreino dos caldeus. Tinha ho peito com hos braços de prata purissima, e sinificaua ho rreino dos P*er*sas. Tinha ho ventre, pees, e coia d'arame, sinificaua ho rreino dos Greguos antre hos quaes Alexan-dre foi ho p*ri*meiro que antre elles reinou. Tinha as pernas de ferro, sinificaua ho rreino dos rroma*n*os no tempo do qual veo ho Mexia, sendo Outauiano emperador. E estes rreinos socederão hu*n*s loguo apoos dos outros.

A pedra cortada do monte, sem mãos, firio a estatua nos pees de

---

[84] 1 Kings 1:39.
[85] Dan. 1:1ff.
[86] Dan. 9:1.
[87] Isa. 45:1ff.
[88] Ezra 1:1ff.
[89] 1 Mac. 1:1.
[90] Luke 2:1.
[91] Dan. 2:38ff.
[92] Dan. 2:44.
[93] Based on a passage attributed to *BRMD* to Gen. 42:6 cited in *PF*, pp. 397f. and in an abbreviated form in *ACPJ*, 1, 5, p. 65. It is extant in various forms in Midrash 'Aseret ha-Melakhim, Pirqe de Rabbi Eliezer and Targum Sheni to Esther. See Judah L. Eisenstein, *Oẓar ha-Midrashim* (New York, 1951), 2, 461ff. The text as translated from *PF* reads: "It is taught, Ten Kings ruled from one end of the world to the other: The first King was the Holy One, blessed be He, by Whose decree the world came into being. R. Eliezer says: The world was created only through the word of

was Solomon, mentioned in the Third Book of Kings, chapter one, when he was first crowned king.[84] The fifth king was Nebuchadnezzar (Daniel, chapter 1).[85] The sixth king was Darius (Daniel, chapter 9).[86] The seventh was King Cyrus whom Isaiah (chapter 45) called Christ.[87] He was anointed since he was to free the people of Israel from their captivity, according to the First Book of Ezra, chapter 1.[88] The eighth king was Alexander the Macedonian, who is mentioned in the First Book of Maccabees, chapter 1. He was the first to reign in Greece.[89] The ninth was Octavius Augustus Caesar during whose time the Messiah was born, according to the historians. And if you care to believe it, Saint Luke mentions him in the second chapter of his Gospel.[90] Further, in the above-mentioned *Grão Grande,* which you regard with greater authority than the Evangelists (a grave sin), this king is mentioned as well. The tenth king was the Messiah of whom Daniel speaks in chapter 2,[91] saying that in the days of these kings, the God of the heavens would be exalted and would reign, never to be changed.[92] This is proved by the large statue that King Nebuchadnezzar saw in a dream.[93] Daniel explained the dream thus: the statue had a head of purest gold which signified the reign of the Chaldeans. It had a chest with arms of purest silver which signified the reign of the Persians. It had a belly, feet, and thigh of brass, which signified the dominion of the Greeks among whom was Alexander, the first to reign among them. It had legs of iron which signified the kingdom of the Romans during whose time the Messiah came when Octavius was emperor. These kingdoms followed one after the other.[94]

The stone cut from the mountain without hands damaged the feet of

---

the Holy One, blessed be He, as it is said, *By the word of the Lord the heavens were made* (Ps. 33:6). R. Simeon says: The Lord breathed forth and the world was created as it is said, *and all their host by the breath of His mouth* (*ibid.*). The second King was the wicked Nimrod, etc. The third King was Joseph, etc. The fourth King was Solomon, etc. The fifth King was Nebuchadnezzar, King of Babylon, etc. The sixth was Darius who reigned over the kingdom of the Chaldeans. The seventh King was Cyrus who ruled from one end of the world to the other, as it is said, *Thus says Cyrus King of Persia: The Lord, the God of heaven, has given me all the Kingdoms of the earth* (Ezra 1:2) ... The eighth King was Alexander the Macedonian who ruled from one end of the world to the other ... The ninth King was Augustus Caesar King of Rome ... The tenth King is the King Messiah who will rule from one end of the world to the other ... as it is written, *But the stone that struck the image became a great mountain and filled the whole earth* (Dan. 2:35); and it says, *And in the days of those Kings the God of heaven will set up a Kingdom which shall never be destroyed* ... (Dan. 2:46). With this tenth King, the Kingdom will return to its former Master. The first King shall be the last King, as it is said, *Thus says the Lord, the King of Israel and his Redeemer, the Lord of hosts! I am the first and I am the last* (Isa. 44:6) ..."

[94] Cf. *FF,* fol. 27ra.

ferro e toda a desfez. Esta pedra cortada do monte [*fol. 30r*] sem mãos sinificaua ho Mexia ou ho seu rreino, porque elle destruio muitos rreinos quando hos rreis se conuertião a sua fee, como foi Constantino, emperador de Rroma no tempo do Papa Siluestre, ho qual se conuerteo à fee de Christo com muita sua gente. Dali por diante começou a Igreia nossa de enflorecer e a vossa Sinaguogua de se abaixar.

Assi que destes dizeres podemos concludir que este Mexia auia de ser Deos e homem, como bem proua Daniel, demostrando que elle era sinificado pola pedra cortada do monte sem mãos, afirmando que ho seu rreino era perpetuo. Rrabi Salamão esto confirma expondo este passo de Daniel, dizendo que este he ho Mexia chamado Deos e Rrei, e Saluador e Iusto, e he homem caualeiro, como afirmou ho profeta Zacharias no capitolo nono. Parece loguo, segundo ho dizer deste doutor, que se ho Mexia auia de ser Saluador, que auia de ser Deos, porque ninguem nom pode saluar do pecado, como este doutor entendia, senão sendo Deos.

Em Midras Telim se alegua hum passo do psalmista no psalmo xxxv, onde se diz: "Contiguo he a fonte da vida em cuia lux veemos a lux." Grosando isto, Rrabi Iona põe este enxemplo: "Hum homem andaua de noite com candea. Veo ho vento e apaguoulhe a candea. Tornandoa acender, apaguo[u]selhe. E como isto lhe acontecesse por muitas vezes, foi constrangido esperar a manhaam. 'Assi (diz elle), foi Deos connosco, que esteuemos em catiueiro no aliube e en outras partes catiuos, e sempre Deos nos enuiou Redentor e Saluador e nos sempre tornamos a ser catiuos.' 'Mas eu por mim mesmo (dixe Deos) vos rredimirei e nunqua iamais seres catiuos nem soieitos,' porque assi ho dixe Dauid no psalmo cento e noue: 'Deos poderoso nos alomeara.'" Sobre este passo diz Rrabi Ame que Moises se glorificaua, dizendo: "Benauenturado tu, Isrrael, pouo que seras saluo por Deos."

---

[95] This exegesis is found in Jerome, *Comm.* to Daniel, *ad loc., CC;* 75A:795 (*PL*, 25:504); cf. Isidore, *De Fide Catholica,* 70:9, *PL*, 83:470; *FF*, fol. 27ra.

[96] Zech. 9:9. The citation of Rashi is actually from his commentary to Isaiah (28:16) and is found in *PF*, p. 342.

[97] Ps. 36(35):10.

[98] Not Ps. 109 (110 *AV*), but Ps. 118(117):27. The above is based on a passage from Midrash Tehillim 36:6 (ed. Buber, pp. 250ff.; Braude, 1:417f.) cited in *PF*, pp. 641f.; *ACPJ*, 1, 5, pp. 66f.: "R. Johanan said: It happened that a man lighted a lamp which went out, and each time he lighted it, it went out, until at last the man said: 'How long shall I keep tiring myself with this lamp? I will wait for the shining of the sun and go about in its light.' Similarly, when the children of Israel were enslaved in Egypt, Moses rose up and redeemed them, but they were enslaved again in Babylon. Then Daniel, Hananiah, Mishael, and Azariah rose up and redeemed them, but they were enslaved again in Elam, in Media, and in Persia. Then Mordecai and Esther rose up and redeemed them, but

iron and broke the whole statue. This stone cut from the mountain without hands signified the Messiah or His kingdom. For He destroyed many realms when kings converted to His faith, as did Constantine, emperor of Rome, and many of his people at the time of Pope Silvester. From that time on, our Church began to prosper and your synagogue to decline.

Consequently, from these words we can conclude that this Messiah was to be God and man, as Daniel rightly proved, showing that He was represented by the stone cut from the mountain [*fol. 30r*] without hands and affirming that His kingdom was to be eternal.[95] Rabbi Solomon confirms this expounding the passage from Daniel, and says that this is the Messiah called God and King, Savior and Just One, and the one to ride on a horse as the prophet Zechariah affirmed in chapter 9.[96] It seems then, according to the words of this doctor, that if the Messiah was to be a Savior, He would be God. For no one, as this doctor understood, could redeem from sin unless He were God.

In Midrash Tehillim there is a passage cited from Psalm 35, which says: *With You is the fountain of life in Whose light we see the light.*[97] On glossing this, Rabbi Jonah relates the following parable: "A man was walking at night with a candle. A wind came along and blew it out. The man lit it again, but again it went out. Since this happened to him many times, he was compelled to wait until morning. 'In like manner (he said), God was with us for we were in captivity in prison and elsewhere God always sent us a Redeemer and Savior and we always became captives again.' 'But I myself (said God) will redeem you and nevermore will you become captives nor subjects.' For David said in Psalm 109: *God the Almighty gave us light.*"[98] Commenting on this passage, Rabbi Ammi stated that Moses gloried and said: *Blessed be you, Israel, for you will be saved by God.*[99]

---

they were enslaved again in Greece. Then the Hasmonean and his sons rose up and redeemed them, but they were enslaved again in Edom the wicked. Thereupon the children of Israel said: We have grown weary of being enslaved and redeemed, only to be enslaved once again. Now let us pray not for redemption through flesh and blood, but through our redeemer, the Lord of hosts whose name is the Holy One of Israel. Now let us pray not that flesh and blood give us light but that the Holy One, blessed be He, give us light, as is said, *For with Thee is the fountain of life; in Thy light we shall see light; and also The Lord is God and He will give us light* (Ps. 118:27)."

[99] Deut. 33:29. A fragment of a passage cited in *PF* (pp. 642f.) in the name of "Midrasch Vayiqra" to Lev. 17:3 and in *ACPJ* (1:5, p. 67) in the name of Midrash Tehillim. The passage is extant in Midrash Tanḥuma, Aḥare Mot, 12 (ed. Buber, p. 71) cited in the name of R. Meir. *PF* reads: "R. Ammi said: 'Moses praised the Congregation of Israel: *Happy are you Israel, a people delivered by the Lord.*'"

Todos estes doutores concludem que ho pouo de Isrrael auia de ser saluo do pecado por Deos, que era ho Mexia, porque elle auia de ser a saluação, como dixe Iacob (Genesis xlix), que esperaua no Mexia, que auia de ser a sua saluação. Saluou loguo ho Mexia emquanto Deos e nom enquanto homem, porque Iosue, Sansão, e outros guouernadores que hos vossos antepassados teuerão nom saluarão senão hos corpos, mas ho Mexia auia de saluar as almas, ho que não podia fazer senão emquanto Deos e nom emquanto homem. Esto eu nom volo diguo de mym, mas hos vossos doutores volo afirmão.

[*fol. 30v*] Em *Canedrim*, no capitolo viijº, se diz: "Prestes he ho Senhor pera leuar Isrrael," como diz ho profeta Osse no capitolo 3º: "Tornarão hos filhos de Isrrael, e seruirão a Deos e a Dauid rrey, e eu me aleuantarey." No caldeu esta, onde nos temos "seruirão a Deos," "seruirão ao Mexia." Seguesse loguo, bem manifestamente, que ho Mexia auia de ser Deos pois quee no caldeu se põe "ho Mexia," onde no hebraico esta "Deos," a qual tresladação vos nom podes neguar porque no capitolo ia aleguado de Osee, se proua ha humanidade do Mexia quando diz: "Buscarão hos filhos de Isrrael a Dauid rei," ao Mexia, que descen[den]do da casa de Dauid prouase a sua diuindade quando diz: "Buscarão a Deos hos filhos de Isrrael." E se nom me quiserdes crer, lede vos a profitia e achares que assi he como vos diguo.

No liuro que se chama *Lei dos Sacerdotes*, se alega aquele texto do Leuitico do capitolo xxvi, onde se diz: "Andarei antre vos e serei vosso Deos e vos seres meu pouo." Sobre isto pergunta, dizendo: "Que quer dizer isto ou que sinifiqua?" Rresponde dizendo assi, pondo este enxemplo: "Hum rrei tinha hum iardim muito fresco e indo pera entrar dentro, nom achou ho ortelão porquanto se escondera do rrey." Assi foi nosso Senhor prestes pera vir exercitarsse com hos iustos; prestes pera vir estar antre elles. Elles ouuerão temor dele, e Deos lhes dira: "Por que ouuestes medo de mym? Veedesme tal como vos outros. Nom aiaes pauor nem de mym. Sabee que eu fora vosso Deos, e vos seres meu pouo."

[100] Gen. 49:18.

[101] Machado has conflated Hos. 3:5 with Jer. 30:9. See below, notes 102, 103.

[102] The passage from B.T. Sanhedrin 98b and the Targum is cited in *PF*, p. 953: "Item ad idem in Chelek: Dixit Rab, Futurum est ut Deus statuat Israeli alium David, sicut dictum est (Jerem. 30). Et servient Domino Deo suo, & Davidi regi suo, quem statuam eis. Non dicitur statui: sed statuam. Idem in Targum: Et servient coram Domino Deo suo, & obedient vel congregabunt se ad Messiam filium David quem statuam eis." This passage is followed by a citation of Hos. 3:5.

[103] Hos. 3:5.

[104] Torat Kohanim or Sifra. See Introduction.

[105] Lev. 26:12.

All these doctors conclude that the people of Israel were to be saved from sin by God, who was the Messiah, because He would be the salvation. Thus Jacob said (Genesis 49) that he was waiting for the Messiah Who would be his salvation.[100] The Messiah did save in His divine aspect but not in His human aspect. Joshua, Samson, and other governors, which your ancestors had, only saved the body, but the Messiah was to save the soul which He could do as God but not as man. I need not tell you this for your own doctors affirm it.

[fol. 30v] In chapter 8 of Sanhedrin we read: "The Lord is ready to raise up the children of Israel," as the prophet Hosea says in chapter 3: *The children of Israel will return and will serve God and David the king, and I shall rise up.*[101] The Chaldean version has "they will serve the Messiah," where we have *they will serve God.*[102] It follows then very clearly that the Messiah would be God since in the Chaldean we read "the Messiah," where in Hebrew it is "God". You cannot deny this translation because in the above chapter from Hosea the humanity of the Messiah is proved when he says: *The children of Israel shall seek David the king,* that is, the Messiah who was descended from the house of David. His divinity is proved when he says: *The children of Israel shall seek God.*[103] Now if you do not wish to believe me, read the prophecy and you will see that it is as I tell you.

In the book entitled *Law of the Priests,*[104] a passage is cited from Leviticus, chapter 26, where it says: *I will walk among you and will be your God and you will be My people.*[105] The question is raised: "What does this mean or what does this signify?" The answer is in the form of a parable: "A king had a very cool garden. When he was about to go inside, he did not find the gardener because he had hidden himself from the king." In like manner was our Lord ready to come and take exercise with the just ones; ready to come and be among them. They were afraid of Him and God said to them: "Why were you afraid of Me? You see Me as yourselves. Do not have fear or be afraid of Me. Know that I am your God and you shall be My people."[106]

---

[106] Based on a passage from Sifra, Beḥuqqotai, 3:3, cited in *PF* (pp. 732f.) and *ACPJ* (1,5, pp. 68f.); in *PF*: "*I will walk among you, and will be Your God and you shall be My people* (Lev. 26:12). To what may this be likened? To a King who went out to stroll with his tenant in the orchard. The tenant kept hiding from him. The King said to the tenant: Why do you hide from me? I am like you. So will the Holy One, blessed be He, stroll with the righteous in the future in the Garden of Eden. The righteous will see Him and tremble before Him. He will say to them: Why do you tremble before Me. I am as one of you. Could it be that you will no longer be in awe of Me? Thus does Scripture teach, *I will be your God and you shall be My people.* If you believe Me and all these things, *I am the Lord your God Who brought you out of the Land of Egypt (ibid.,* 5:13)."

Dizei, senhores, que mais proua queres dos vossos doutores pera crerdes que ho Mexia auia de ser Deos e homem, e que auia de conuersar convosco como elle conuersou e falou com hos vossos antepassados? Olhai como no liuro acima aleguado se proua que auia de ser Deos. Crede e nom vos enguanes. Vede hos vossos doutores passados e algum bem deles alcançares.[i] Polo qual me podes crer, que se eu fora iudeu, que visto tal enxemplo e tão verdadeiro, loguo, sem mais tardança, me ouuera de tornar christão. Isto podemos confirmar com aquilo que se diz no Talmud no capitolo dos Ieiuns: "Prestes he Deos pera fazer conuite aos iustos e pera vir, e elle estara no meo, e cada hum ho demostrara com ho dedo, que sera Saluador e Redentor dos corações dos homens." Assi ho dixe Isaias no capitolo xxv, onde diz: "E dirão nesse dia: 'Vees nosso Deos, este que esperauamos, e saluarnosha. Este he ho Deos que nos [fol. 31r] esperauamos. Alegrarnosemos con sua saluação.' Pois as almas nolo amostrão com ho dedo." Diguouos que esta profitia bem demostra que ho Mexia auia de ser Deos, nossa saluação, ho qual corporalmente se auia de vir e com ho dedo ho auião [de] demostrar. E todo esto foi visto e comprido porque ho Mexia foi visto na cidade de Ierusalem. E con elle falarão e communicarão hos vossos antepassados, e São Iohão Baptista ho demostrou com ho dedo no rrio de Iurdão. Assi que bem se demostra que era Deos ho Mexia, como Isaias tinha profitizado.

Ho profeta Ieremias, no capitolo xxiij, nos demostra ha humanidade com a diuindade do Mexia quando diz: "Ex aqui hos dias veem, diz ho Senhor, e suscitarey a Dauid e reinara e sera sabedor, e fara iuizo e iustiça na terra. E nestes dias se saluara Iudas, e Isrrael morara confiadamente." Veedes aqui a humanidade do Mexia porque tudo isto lhe pertence quanto à humanidade. Diz mais ho profeta: "Este he ho nome que lhe chamarão: 'Ho Senhor, nosso Iusto.'" Aqui pinta ho profeta a sua diuindade porque onde nos temos "Dominus iustus noster," no hebraico esta "nomen domini Thetregramaton." Este nome nom conuem a pesoa humana propriamente, senão a soo Deos pois que este nome lhe auia de ser communicado. Verdade he que este nome às vezes se atribuie e se rrefere às cousas irracionaes ou rrationaes, porem, empropriamente por amor d'alguma conuenientia que teem aquelas

---

i MS *alcancancares*

[107] *Ie.*, the talmudic tractate *Ta'anit*. See Introduction.
[108] Isa. 25:9.
[109] Based on B.T. Ta'anit 31a (Sonc. pp. 164f.) cited in *PF*, p. 733, and *ACPJ*, 1,5, p. 69: 'Ulla Bira'ah said in the name of R. Eleazar: In the days to come the Holy One, blessed be He, will hold a

Tell me, gentlemen, what better witnesses do you want than your own doctors to make you believe that the Messiah would be God and man and that He would converse with you as He conversed and spoke with your forefathers? See how in the book cited above it was proved He would be God. Believe and do not deceive yourselves. Consult your doctors of yore and some good will come of it. Believe me when I say that if I had been a Jew and had seen such a parable and such a truth, I would have become a Christian without delay. This can be corroborated by what is said in the Talmud in the Chapter of Fasts:[107] "God is ready to invite the just ones and to come. He will be in the middle and each one will point at him with his finger for He will be the Savior and Redeemer of the hearts of men." Thus did Isaiah say in chapter 25: *And on that day they will say: See our God for Whom we have been waiting and Who will save us. This is the God that we [fol. 31r] have been waiting for. We will rejoice in his salvation.*[108] "Then souls will point him out to us with their finger."[109] I tell you that this prophecy clearly shows that the Messiah was to be God, our salvation, Who was to come because the Messiah was seen in the city of Jerusalem. Your ancestors spoke and conversed with Him and Saint John the Baptist pointed to Him at the river Jordan. This then does show that the Messiah was God, as Isaiah had prophesied.

In chapter 23, the prophet Jeremiah shows us the humanity and divinity of the Messiah when he says: *Behold the days come, says the Lord, and I shall raise [up] David and he shall reign and be wise, and will exercise judgment and justice in the land. And in these days shall Judah be saved and Israel will dwell without fear.*[110] You see here the humanity of the Messiah because, in this regard, all this pertains to Him. The prophet says further: *This is the name which they shall call Him: The Lord, our Just One.*[111] The prophet is here referring to His divinity because where we have *Dominus iustus noster,* the Hebrew reads *nomen domini Thetregramaton.* This name does not properly befit a human person but rather God alone since this is the name that would be applied to Him. It is true that this name at times is attributed to both rational and non-rational things. However, this imprecise usage is due to certain similarities which exist between

chorus for the righteous and He will sit in their midst in the Garden of Eden and every one of them will point with his finger toward Him, as it is said, *And it shall be said in that day: Lo, this is our God, for whom we waited, that He might save us; this is the Lord for whom we waited, we will be glad and rejoice in His salvation* [Isa. 25:9]." The phrase "then ... finger" (*pois ... dedo*) appears to be Machado's own interpolation.

[110] Jer. 23:5f.

[111] Jer. 23:6. Cf. Jerome, *Comm., ad loc., CC,* 74:215ff. (*PL,* 24:852).

cousas, as quaes conue*m* co*m* algu*m* efeito diuino. Disto temos enxe*m*-plo no Genesis, capitolo xxij°, onde se diz que Habraa*m* chamou ao luguar onde quis sacrificar Isaac "Ho S*en*hor vee" ("vocauit nome*n* loci illius 'Dominus videt'"). No hebraico esta Thetragramato*n*. E outros passos estão polo Testame*n*to Velho, onde este nome Thetregramato*n* se põe e se atribui às cr*i*aturas irracionaes. Pore*m*, isto he empropr*i*a-me*n*te. Como dizemos que este nome em plural *heloym* conue*m* aos homens, como dixe Dauid no ps*al*mo lxxxi: "Ego dixi: 'Dii estis,'" no hebraico põese *heloym*, mas isto he empropr*i*ame*n*te. Polo qual, con-cludindo diguo que este nome Thetregramatom no*m* conue*m* senão a D*e*os propriame*n*te. E porqua*n*to este nome em muitos passos da Sagrada Escritura se põe polo Mexia, podemos concluir que auia de ser D*e*os pois que tal nome no*m* conue*m* senão a Deos. Em esto no*m* tenhaes duuida algu*m*a ne*m* debate, porq*ue* esta he ha v*e*rdade, e crer ho contrario tudo he bulrra e são enguanos e falsidades. E porquanto tocamos aqui neste nome Thetregramato*n*, veiamos que sinifiqua e de que letras se compoem.

[*fol. 31v*] Este nome Thetragramato*n* se compõe de quatro letras hebraicas, que são estas: *iot, he, vau, he*. Esta letra *iot* quer diz*e*r prin-cipio, e sinifiqua ho Padre que he pr*i*ncipio e começo de todalas cousas. *He,* segunda letra, quer diz[er] śer, e sinifiqua ho V*e*rbo ete*r*no que daa ser a todalas cousas. *Vau,* terceira letra, quer dizer virtude, e sinifiqua ho Sp*irit*u Santo, ho qual inspira todas as boas v*i*rtudes. *He*, letra derradeira, sinifiqua ha humanidade do Mexia, a qual se aiuntou co*m* a diuindade. Assi que, neste nome se entende a Diuina Trindade co*m* ha humanidade do Mexia. E, portanto, esta letra *he* se põe duas vezes porque nūma sinifiqua na pr*i*meira ho Filho e sua diuindade, e na quarta letra *he* sinifiqua a sua humanidade. Onde se parece que ho Padre e ho Filho e ho Sp*irit*u Santo são *ab eterno*, sem começo e pr*i*ncipio e sem fim, e ha humanidade do Mexia feita foi em tempo e tem começo e pr*i*ncipio, e no*m* tera fim, porq*ue* ho Mexia pera todo sempre sera D*e*os e home*m* porquanto aquilo que elle tomou, q*ue* foi a carne, nu*n*qua mais aleixara.

---

[112] Gen. 22:14.

[113] Ps. 82(81):6.

[114] *I.e.,* '*elohim.*

[115] Machado follows Lyra's discussion of the divine names, '*elohim* (which is a homonym and may, according to Jewish tradition, mean "God," "gods," or "judges") and the tetragrammaton by which only God is called. Lyra, in *De Probatione,* pp. 172ff. drew from Maimonides' *Guide for the Perplexed,* 1, 61: "Item Gen. 22. c. Vocavit Abraham nomen loci illius, Dominus videt. Ubi habemus Dominus, in Hebraeo habetur, Domini tetragrammaton" (p. 172). "Hoc etiam expresse dicit Rabi Moses, in libro directionis perplexorum: dicens, quod omnia nomina divina derivata sunt ab

these things and certain aspects of the divine. We have an example of this in chapter 22 of Genesis where it says that Abraham called the place where he wanted to sacrifice Isaac "the Lord sees" (*vocauit nomen loci illius Dominus videt*).[112] In Hebrew this is the tetragrammaton. There are other passages in the Old Testament where the name "Tetragrammaton" is used and applied to non-rational creatures. However, this is not proper. The plural word *elohim* can refer to men. It is true that in Psalm 81 David said *Ego dixi: Dii estis*,[113] the Hebrew *heloym*[114] is used, but it is inappropriate. In conclusion I will say that for this reason the name "Tetragrammaton" is appropriately suited to God only. And since in many passages of the Holy Scriptures this name is used to refer to the Messiah, we can conclude that He would be God since this name is suitable only for God.[115] Do not doubt this nor debate the point for it is true. To believe the contrary is sheer deception, error, and untruth. And since we are touching on this name "Tetragrammaton," let us see what it means and of which letters it is composed.

[*fol. 31v*] The name "Tetragrammaton" is composed of four Hebrew letters, which are: *yod, he, vav,* and *he.* The letter *yod* means "beginning" and signifies the Father, Who is the origin and the beginning of all things. *He,* the second letter, means "being," and signifies the eternal Word Which gives existence to all things. *Vav,* the third letter, means "virtue" and signifies the Holy Spirit which inspired all virtues. *He,* the last letter, signifies the humanity of the Messiah which was conjoined to His divinity. Thus, it is understood that this name embraces both the divine Trinity and the humanity of the Messiah. Therefore, the letter *he* is used twice because in the first instance it signifies the Son and His divinity, and in the fourth or last it signifies His humanity. It would thus seem that the Father and the Son and the Holy Spirit are *ab eterno*, without beginning and without end. The humanity of the Messiah, on the other hand, was created in time and thus has origin and beginning, but no end, because the Messiah will forever be God and man for He will never take leave of the flesh He assumed.[116]

---

operibus divinis, preter nomen Domini tetragrammaton, quod est appropriatum altissimo Creatori ... judices & sapientes et divina sapientia praediti, aliquando nominantur Eloym, in sacra scriptura; secundum quod dicitur in Psalmo: Ego dixi dii estis. In Hebreo ponitur Eloym. Non sic autem est de nomine Domini tetragrammaton quod significat divinam essentiam, nudam et puram ... et quod sic est in Hebraeo, Ieremiae 33. [!] et hoc est, nomen ejus, quod vocabunt eum, Dominus justus noster: Ita ut nomen Domini tetragrammaton ..." (pp. 174f.). Similar material, based on rabbinic sources, is found in *PF*, pp. 655ff.

[116] The christological interpretation of the tetragrammaton has its root in such writers as Petrus Alphonsi, who divided YHVH into YH, HV, and VH so as to create a trinitarian division, although he

E se vos quiserdes saber quanta *v*irtude tee*m* este nome e como he marauilhoso, leede aquele ps*almo* de Dauid viii° e veres como se espanta de ser nome que no*m* foi feito sem grande misterio. Isaias, no capitolo xxx°, faz me*n*ção deste nome quando diz: "Ho nome do *Senh*or vee*m* de longe." No hebraico põese Thetragramato*n*, composto das quatro letras que ia dixemos, as quaes bem puntuadas e situadas soa*m* este nome *Iohesua*, ho qual se declina no greguo *Iesos*, no latim *Ihesus*, que quer diz*er* saluador. E, portanto, hos tresladores do hebraico en greguo ou em latim, onde achaua*m Iohesua* ou *Iotsua, sem*pre tresladarão *saluator* ou *saluatare* ou *Ihesus*. Estes segredos e estes misterios be*m* hos sabees vos outros e maiores ainda, mas na*m* nos queres discubrir por no*m* vos deguolardes com ho vosso mesmo cutelo. E que*m* discubrio este segredo deste nome Thetragramato*n* iudeu era. Porem, bem sei que tudo no*m* discub*r*io, mas muitas cousas pera si reseruou, no[m] querendo lançar quanto tinha fora.

Podemos ia, senhores, concludir que esta prop*r*iedade que esta escrita polos profetas e polos vossos talmudistas e polos cabalistas, que ho Mexia auia de ser D*eo*s e home*m*, foi co*m*municada e atribuida a Ch*ri*sto, noso Redentor e Saluador, e nisto no*m* tenhaes debate n*e*m duuida, por vossa vida. E pois *que* esta he a nossa fee, seia ta*m*bem a vossa. Ame*n*.

[*fol. 32r*] Capitolo Outauo. De como hos rreis auião de adorar ho Mexia e dos doo*en*s que lhe auião de apresentar.

A seitima propriedade que estaua escrita polos profetas que auia de

ascribes no particular interpretation to these three biliterals. See *PA*, Title 2, *PL*, 157:611; cf. Peter of Blois, *Contra perfidiam Judaeorum, PL*, 207:832ff. Machado's own interpretation bears a close relationship to that of *FF*, fol. 59*v*: "Scribitur enim quattuor litteris scilicet ioth, he, vaf, he, velut si nostris utamur litteris, i, h, v, h, unde et a Grecis thetragramaton dicitur ut dictum est quod Hebrei pronunciant Adonay, aliter scribentes et aliter proferentes quia non est eis datum ineffabilitatem huius nominis penetrare unde nec valent proferre. Secundum secretum est quod istud sanctum nomen significat mysterium Trinitatis et unitatis divine essentie. Tres namque littere sunt quibus ipsum sanctum nomen scribitur sed una earum bis ponitur, scīlicet he que innuit Spìritum Sanctum procedere tam a Filio quam a Patre. Ioth idem est quod principium et convenit Patri qui est principium sine principio, quia Pater a nullo sed alie persone ab eo procedunt. He interpretatur vita et convenit Spiritui Sancto qui est omnium vivificator et inspirator, sicut ipse Dominus ait (Ioann. 6): Spiritus est qui vivificat. Vaf idem sonat quod ipse quod est pronomen demonstrativum et significat Filium qui visibilis et demonstrabilis factus est in assumpta humanitate, quia in terris visus est et cum hominibus conversatus est (Baruch 3). Tertium secretum est quod istud sanctum nomen ut tradunt peritissimi Hebreorum tante virtutis est ut si distinguatur in tres dictiones quelibet significet nomen Dei per se idipsum significans quod et integrum quod ex quattuor litteris constat."
[117] Ps. 9(8):2.

And if you want to know how much virtue is contained in this name and how full of wonder it is, read Psalm 8 and you will see how amazed David is at this name that was not created without some great mystery.[117] In chapter 30, Isaiah mentions this name when he says: *The name of the Lord comes from afar.*[118] In Hebrew the word Tetragrammaton is used, composed of the four letters which we have already mentioned. These, when written in the proper order and with the correct pointing, yield the name *Iohesua*, which in Greek is declined *Iesos,* and in Latin *Ihesus*, which means "savior". Consequently, those who translated from Hebrew into Greek or Latin always rendered *Iohesua* or *Iotsua* as either *saluator, saluatare* or *Ihesus*. You know these secrets and even greater mysteries than these very well, but you refuse to disclose them for fear of cutting your throats with your own knife. Yet he who disclosed the secret of the name Tetragrammaton was a Jew. However, I know he did not disclose everything, for he kept many things to himself and did not wish to bring them forth.[119]

We can now conclude, gentlemen, that the Messiah's characteristic of being God and man, as written by the prophets and your talmudists and kabbalists, was fulfilled in Christ, our Redeemer and Savior. By your lives, neither doubt nor argue. And because this is our faith, may it also be yours. Amen.

[*fol. 32r*] Chapter Eight. How the kings would adore the Messiah and of the gifts they would offer Him.

The seventh characteristic of the Messiah which was described by the

---

[118] Isa. 30:27.

[119] *FF*: "Quintum secretum est quod in hoc Dei nomine video [*sic*] ineffabili nomen Iesu est insertum. Immo non est aliud nomen quam istud. Patet. Tres enim littere eius principales sunt ioth, he, vaf, que secundum litteras nostras idem sunt i, h, v, et patet quod iste tres littere coniuncte faciunt istud nomen Iesu. Titellus supraponitur propter titulum crucis. He vero vel h duplicatur. Significat non solum Spiritum Sanctum procedere a Patre et Filio sed etiam mysterium incarnationis designat, quia Spiritu Sancto cooperante et non ex virili semine conceptus est Messias Iesus Christus Dominus noster ut primum he referatur ad productionem Spiritus Sancti secundum vero ad conceptionem sive incarnationem verbi divini ... Quare ergo non illis [*i.e.,* the names in Isa. 9:5] sed vocari voluit Iesus? Respondetur quod secundum philosophum a fine denominatur res. (1 De anima). Christus igitur debuit denominari a fine intento qui finis fuit salvatio humani generis. Et ideo debuit nominari Iesus quod interpretatur salus vel salvatio" (fol. 60r).

"Noster benedictus salvavit in tempore sed eius salvatio durat sine tempore in eternum ... sed in Christo Iesu vero Messia fuit et est vox significativa sine tempore cum sua salvatio sine tempore; hoc est in eternum fit ..." (fol. 60v). For an additional Iberian treatment of this topic, see J. Carreras Artau, "La 'Allocutio super Tetragrammaton' de Arnaldo de Vilanova," *Sefarad*, 9 (1949), 75-105.

ser communicada ao Mexia era que hos rreis ho auião de adorar, a qual
foi communicada a Christo, segundo prouaremos polos profetas e polos
vossos doutores.

No Grão Grande esta hum texto que diz: "E sera adorado dos rreis."
Rrabi Cabet sobre este passo diz: "Eu te direi huma cousa boa dos antiguos, a qual he que todolos presentes que Iacob ofereceo a Esau,
tornando de Mesopotamia pera terra de Chanaam (segundo se contem
no Genesis, capitolo xxxvi), as gentes do mundo hos tornarão a dar ao
Mexia, como dixe Dauid no psalmo lxxi: 'Hos rreis de Tarsia e das in-
suas presentes ofrecerão, e hos reis de Arabia e de Saba ofrecerão
dooens e ofericimentos trazerão.'"

Sobre este passo ho doutor acima aleguado diz que quer dizer
trazerão. Responde que todos, assi passados como vindoiros, todos
presentarão doens ao Mexia e ho conhecerão por Rrei e Saluador. Deste
doutor podemos tirar este documento, que ho Mexia de todos auia de
ser adorado e honrrado com doens e presentes e de todos auia de ser
conhicido, sem conhicimento do qual ninguem nom se podia saluar.

Adam, nosso primeiro padre, bem conheceo ho Mexia na semente que
dele saio, que foi Seth, seu filho. Conhecerãono as filhas de Loth, que
com ho proprio pai dormirão senão pera viuificarem aquela semente
donde ho Mexia auia se sair, e conhecendoo, adoraramno. Habraam ho
adorou e conheceo quando Deos lhe deu a benção da Terra da
Promissão, que era ho paraiso, porque elle bem sabia que nhũm padre
santo hia ao paraiso, mas ao limbo descendião todos. E, portanto,
loguo Habraam perguntou a Deos como auia de herdar aquela Terra da
Promissão, segundo se contem no Genesis, capitolo xv. E Deos lhe dixe
que tomasse huma vaca de tres anos e hum carneiro do mesmo tempo,
huma rrola e huma pomba, e que tudo fezesse e diuidisse em partes, e
assi ho fez. Todas estas cousas rrepresentauão a vinda do Mexia, crendo
Habraam nele a adorandoo, como Deos lhe dixe: "Na tua semente todas
as gentes serão benditas," que forão aqueles que crerão no Mexia e ho
adorarão, como Dauid dixe que hos rreis de Arabia e Persia ho auia de
adorar, como se comprio, porque tudo foi acabado no Mexia.

Hos antiguos, por Deos inspirados, e outros ensinados pola arte
cabalistica, bem sabião que creatura pura, como foi Adam e forão hos

---

¹ Gen. 32:13ff., 33:8ff. (xxxvi is an error).
² Based on Genesis Rabbah 78:12 (Sonc., p. 724) cited in *PF*, p. 771; *ACPJ*, 1, 6, p. 70; *FF*, fol.
61*ra*. Machado's *Rabbi Cabet* is not clear. The passage reads: "One of the common people (*PF*: our
master) said to R. Hoshaya: 'If I tell you a good thing, will you repeat it in public in my name?'
'What is it?' asked he. 'All the gifts which the Patriarch Jacob made to Esau,' replied he, 'the

prophets was that the kings would adore him. This characteristic was fulfilled in Christ, as we shall prove through the prophets and through your doctors.

In the *Grão Grande,* there is a passage which says: "And he will be adored by the kings." Rabbi Cabet comments on this passage saying: "I will tell you something good [told by] the ancients: All the presents that Jacob offered Esau on his return from Mesopotamia to the land of Canaan (according to Genesis, chapter 36)[1] the peoples of the world will again give to the Messiah, as David said in Psalm 71: *The kings of Tarshish and the isles shall offer presents, and the kings of Arabia and of Sheba shall bring gifts and offerings.*"[2]

The doctor cited above interprets what "shall bring" means in this passage. It means, he says, that all who have lived or will live will bring gifts to the Messiah Whom they will recognize as their king and Savior. From this doctor we can draw this fundamental truth: that the Messiah would be adored and honored with gifts. He would be known by all and without such knowledge none could be saved.

Adam, our first ancestor, knew the Messiah well through his son Seth, the seed that came from him. The daughters of Lot knew him for they slept with their own father to bring life to the seed from which the Messiah was to spring — and knowing Him, they adored Him. Abraham adored Him and knew Him when God gave him the blessing of the Promised Land, which was Paradise. For he knew that none of the holy Patriarchs went to Paradise, but rather all descended to Limbo. Therefore Abraham asked God how he was to inherit that Promised Land, according to Genesis, chapter 15.[3] God told him to take a three-year old cow, a ram of the same age, a dove and a pigeon, and divide them all into pieces and he did so.[4] All of these things represented the advent of the Messiah in whom Abraham believed and whom he adored. Thus God said to him: *In your seed all peoples will be blessed.*[5] These were those who believed in the Messiah and adored Him; for David said that the kings of Arabia and Persia would adore Him, as they did, because everything was fulfilled in the Messiah.

The ancients, inspired by God, and others instructed in the art of the kabbalah, knew and recognized that no mere creature, such as Adam

heathens will return them to the Messiah in the Messianic era.' 'What is the proof?' *'The Kings of Tarshish and of the isles shall return tribute* (Ps. 12:10): It does not say, "shall bring," but *"shall return."* 'By thy life!' he exclaimed, 'thou hast said a good thing, and I will teach it in thy name.'

[3] Gen. 15:7.

[4] Gen. 15:8ff.

[5] Gen. 22:18.

outros, nom podião satisfaz*er* polo pecado de Ada*m*, que era quase infinito, comitido contra pessoa infinita, e portanto, foy [*fol. 32v*] necessario que viesse D*eos* e home*m* pera redimir ho pecado. Este foi ho Mexia, no qual hos passados crerão que auia de vir tomar carne humana pera redimir ho pecado, adorandoo e conhece*n*doo, como estaua dele escrito, que auia de ser adorado. Iob ta*m*bem conheceo esta vinda do Mexia, e ho adorou, como elle dixe q*ue* da sua carne viria ho seu saluador. Iacob este Mexia conheceo quando elle dixe (Genesis xlix): "A tua saluação espero, D*eos*," adorandoo e c*re*ndo nele. Assi que bem vedes como ho Mexia foi adorado, e acatado, e honrrado dos antepassados na fee e na esperança que tinhão dele, c*re*ndo que elle hos auia de saluar e redimir.

Esta mesma enca*r*nação foi discube*r*ta aos rreis maguos, hos quaes com hos seus proprios olhos virão ho Mexia e ho adorarão, como ia Dauid deles tinha profitizado no ps*almo* acima aleguado, onde se conclude que hos rreis auião de adorar ho Mexia, como temos por fee que ho adorarão. E se vos quiserdes diz*er* que este ps*almo* no*m* fala no Mexia sena*m* de Salamão, e portanto, que não podemos contra vos concludir que hos rreis auião de adorar ho Mexia, diguouos que se sondes desta opinião — que este ps*almo* no*m* se entende senão de Salamão e no*m* do Mexia — que erraes, porquanto nele se diz que todos hos rreis ho auião de adorar. Hora, prouaime vos como todos hos rreis adorarão a Salamão e como foi rrei de todo ho mundo, segu*n*do se nele conclude. Portanto, no*m* tenhaes debate ne*m* duuida, mas sabee por c*er*teza que ho dito ps*almo* foi feito por Dauid em louuor do Mexia.

Midras, vosso doutor, grosador do psalteiro, expõe todo este ps*almo* do Mexia, porque qua*n*do nos dizemos: "Senh*o*r, daa ho teu iuizo ao rrei," diz este doutor "ao teu Mexia," ho qual foi Rrei dos rreis. E temos loguo que hos rreis auião de adorar ho Mexia, como adorarão. E pera proua disto, teemos aquilo q*ue* se alegua no Grão Grande que se conte*m* no Genesis, capitolo xxv, onde se diz que Habraa*m* deu tudo quanto pusuia a Isaac, seu filho, e aos filhos das concubinas deu dooe*n*s, e hos apartou de Isaac. Esto aleguado, dizse aly no liuro aleguado que isto fez Habraa*m* por despeiar Isaac, hos quaes tomarão hos caminhos de Sabaa, que erão filhos de Hebraa*m*, que gerou Iecsam, do qual descendeo Saba (Genesis, xxv).

[6] Job 19:26. Cf. Jerome, *PL*, 26:706.
[7] Gen. 49:18.
[8] See above, chap. 7, n. 10.
[9] Ps. 72(71):2.

and others, could redeem Adam's almost infinite sin, committed against an infinite Being. [*fol. 32v*] It was therefore necessary that [One Who was] God and man come to atone for the sin. This was the Messiah Whom our forefathers believed would come in human form to expiate sin. He was adored and was known, as it was written that He would be. Job also knew of this coming of the Messiah and adored Him, for he said that from his flesh his Savior would come.[6] Jacob knew this Messiah when he said (Genesis 49): *I wait for Your salvation, God,*[7] and he adored Him and had faith in Him. So you see quite well how the Messiah was adored, respected, and honored by the ancients through the faith and hope they had in Him and that they believed that He would save and redeem them.

This very incarnation was revealed to the Magi who saw the Messiah with their own eyes and adored Him, as David has prophesied in the psalm cited above. It thus follows that the Magi would adore the Messiah as our faith maintains. But if you wish to say that this psalm speaks not of the Messiah but rather of Solomon and we are consequently unable to conclude that the Magi would adore the Messiah, then I say to you that you are in error if you believe this. For in this psalm it says that all the kings would venerate Him. Now, prove to me how all the kings adored Solomon and how he was king of the entire world, according to what was written. Therefore, neither debate nor be doubtful, but rather know as a certainty that this psalm was written by David in praise of the Messiah.[8]

Your doctor Midrash, the commentator on the Psalter, explains this psalm as referring to the Messiah. When we say: *Lord, give your judgment to the king,*[9] this doctor says "to your Messiah," who was the King of kings.[10] We hold therefore that the kings would adore the Messiah, as they did. To prove this we bring that which is cited in the *Grão Grande* concerning that found in Genesis, chapter 25, where it says that Abraham gave all that he possessed to his son Isaac, and to the sons of the concubines he gave gifts and sent them away from Isaac.[11] After this is cited in that book, we read that Abraham did this to free Isaac from [the envy of] those who took to the road of Sheba, who was descended from Abraham through Jokshan (Genesis 25).[12]

---

[10] Based on a passage from Midrash Tehillim 72:2 (ed. Buber, p. 378; Braude, 1:560) which follows the short passage from Genesis Rabbah in *PF*, pp. 771f. (cited also on pp. 420, 837): "*Give the King Thy judgments O God ...*" Here *King* means King Messiah, of whom it is said *And there shall come forth a shoot of the stock of Jesse ...* (Isa. 11:1)."

[11] Gen. 25:5f.

[12] Jokshan. Gen. 25:2.

E Habraa*m* ensinou Saba como ho Mexia auia de vir e auia de ser adorado dos rreis. E pola arte cabalistica correo esta fama ates ho tempo de Balaa*m*, ho qual profitizou do Mexia que auia de nacer hu*m*a estrela de Iacob (Numeros, capitolo xxiiii), a qual estrela pareceo qua*n*do naceo ho Mexia. [*fol. 33r*] Este Balaam ensinou hos outros, por onde assi andauão ia ensinados pola arte cabalistica, que como virão a estrela nacida, loguo conhecerão que nacido era ho Mexia, por onde determinarão de ire*m* adorar ho Mexia e de lhe leuarem presentes, como Isaias tinha profitizado no capitolo lx: "Virão todos de Saba e de Arabia e trazerão dooe*n*s, e virão co*m* camelos." Rrabi Moises do Egito, sobre este passo, diz: "Este he ho Mexia ao qual virão, e este he ho seu nome: 'D*eos*, nosa Iustiça,' ao qual hos rreis trazerão dooe*n*s e ho adorarão."

Este doutor duas cousas diz que vos neguaes. A pr*i*meira he que ho passo de Isaias se entende do Mexia e não d'outra pesoa. A segu*n*da, que hos rreis auião de adorar ho Mexia e lhe auião de trazer dooe*n*s. Tudo isto foi comprido no tempo do Mexia assi propr*i*amente como estaua profitizado por Isaias no capitolo ix° e por Dauid no ps*almo* acima aleguado. Esto confirma Rrabi Midras, que diz: "Aparelhadas são as gentes pera trazerem dooe*n*s ao Mexia." Estas gentes forão hos reis maguos que erão gentios da geração de Balaa*m*, hos quaes, como virão aquela estrela, segundo Balaa*m* hos tinha ensinados, se forão pera Betleem pera ho adorarem e pera lhe oferecere*m* doens. E lhe oferecerão doe*n*s: ouro, onde conhecerão que era rrei; mirra, onde conhecerão que era home*m*; encenso, onde conhecerão que era D*eos*. Todas estas tres cousas teue ho Mexia, que foi rrei, D*eos* e home*m*, e elles por tal ho conhecerão. Loguo ho adorarão como a D*eos*, conhecendoo por tal, segundo ia estauão enformados polos seus antepassados.

[13] Num. 24:17.

[14] Isa. 60:6.

[15] Jer. 23:6.

[16] The above material is based on a text attributed to *BRMD*, preserved in the *Rabbati*, pp. 102f., and is found in *PF*, pp. 771f. (following Genesis Rabbah 78:12 and Midrash Tehillim, 72:2 as in Machado), *ACPJ*, 1, 6, pp. 70f. and *FF*, fol. 61*r*a. The version of *PF* reads: "It is so written: *The caravans of Tema look, the travelers of Sheba hope* (Job 6:19). Sheba refers to none other than the sons of Abraham, as it is said *Jokshan was the father of Sheba and Dedan* (Gen. 25:3). When Solomon's reign became great, they said: Perhaps this is the Messiah. They came to him as it is said, *Now when the queen of Sheba heard of the fame of Solomon concerning the name of the Lord, she came to test him with questions* (1 Kings 10:1). Do not read the *queen of Sheba* (*malkat Sheva*) but the *Kingdom of Sheba* (*malkhuta di-Sheva*). *Concerning the name of the Lord* means that they had a prophet, who prophesied in the name of the Lord, his God. Their words were handed down from Abraham. How do we know that they will last until the days of the Messiah and be of use to him? It is written: *A multitude of camels shall cover you, the young of Midian and Ephah: all those from Sheba shall come. They shall bring gold and frankin-*

Abraham taught Sheba how the Messiah would come and be adored by the kings. This report continued to circulate through the kabbalistic art until the time of Balaam, who prophesied about the Messiah and said that a star would be born out of Jacob (Numbers, chapter 24).[13] This star appeared when the Messiah was born. [*fol. 33r*] Balaam told the others so that they knew that the Messiah had been born when they saw the star since they were instructed in the kabbalistic art. They therefore decided to go and adore Him and to bring Him presents as Isaiah had prophesied in chapter 60: *All shall come with camels from Sheba and Arabia, and they shall bring gifts.*[14] Rabbi Moses of Egypt commented on this passage: "The one to whom they came is the Messiah and this is His name: *God, our Righteousness*[15] whom the king adored and to whom they brought gifts."[16]

This doctor says two things which you deny. The first is that the passage from Isaiah refers to the Messiah and no other. The second is that the kings would adore Him and bring Him gifts. All of this was truly fulfilled during the time of the Messiah, as was prophesied by Isaiah in chapter 9[17] and by David in the psalm cited above.[18] Rabbi Midrash confirms this by saying: "The people are prepared to bring gifts to the Messiah."[19] These people were the Magi who were Gentiles of the generation of Balaam and who went forthwith to Bethlehem to adore Him and offer Him gifts, when they saw the star as Balaam had instructed them to do.[20] They offered him gifts: gold, for they recognized that He was king; myrrh, for they recognized that He was man; frankincense, for they recognized He was God.[21] The Messiah was these three things — king, God, and man — and as such did they recognize Him. They adored Him then as God for they so knew Him in accord with the teachings of their ancestors.

cense and proclaim the praise of the Lord (Isa. 60:6). This is the King Messiah as it is said: *This is the name by which he will be called. 'The Lord is our righteousness'* (Isa. 23:6), and Isaiah says *but the Lord will arise upon you, and His glory will be seen upon you. And nations shall come to your light, and Kings to the brightness of your rising* (Isa. 60:2f.)."

[17] Isa. 9:6.

[18] Ps. 72(71).

[19] An apparent reference to the midrash cited above.

[20] The Magi were according to tradition the spiritual disciples of Balaam but of course not his contemporaries. See Jerome, *Comm. in Matt.* 2:2, CC, 77:12-13 (*PL.*, 26:26): "Ad confusionem Judaeorum, ut nativitatem Christi a gentibus discerent, oritur in oriente stella quam futuram Balaam, cujus successores erant, vaticinio noverant Lege Numerorum librum (Cap. xxiv)."

[21] Matt. 2:11. See Jerome, *Comm.in Matt.* 2:11, ibid.: "Pulcherrime munerum sacramenta Juvencus presbiter uno versiculo comprehendit:

Thus, aurum, myrram, regique, hominique, Deoque Dona ferunt."

Cf. *Post.*, 4, biiv.

Ho mesmo veemos aguora neste tempo mode*r*no comprido, porque rreis e p*r*incipes ho adorão e seruem e cree*m* nele, que são hos rreis christãos. E ia este Mexia foi adorado em Africa, em Asia, em Europa, nas quaes partes ho seu nome foi conhecido e adorado. E se aguora no*m* he en todas estas pa*r*tes adorado, ha falta he dos rreis christãos, e largua co*n*ta darão a D*eo*s porqua*n*to no*m* se aiuntão todos p*er*a desbaratare*m* aquele grande cão do tu*r*quo que tee*m* em seu pod*er* a Terra da Promissão.

Assi, *sen*hores, que deues de ter por c*er*teza que esta prop*r*iedade que estaua escrita polos profetas e polos vossos doutores do Mexia, que auia de s*er* adorado dos rreis, foi comunicada a Chr*is*to, nosso Redentor.

Esta he a nossa fee, e seia a vossa. Ame*n*.

[*fol. 33v*] Capitolo Nono. De como todos descendião hos padres santos ao limbo, hos quaes ho Mexia auia de tirar.

A outaua propriedade do Mexia era que elle auia de tirar hos padres santos que estauão no limbo, pola sua morte, e Chr*is*to assi ho fez, segundo prouaremos polos profetas e polos vossos doutores e grosadores e talmudistas.

Nos christãos cremos que ha hi quatro luguares de pena, posto que toda não seia igual. Ho primeiro luguar he ho inferno que esta no centro da terra, onde todos aqueles descendem que vão em pecado mortal, no qual luguar no*m* ha redenção, como diz Iob: "In inferno nulla est redemptio." Ho segundo luguar loguo depois do infe*r*no, subindo pera qua pera cima pera terra, he ho limbo dos mininos que vão deste mu*n*do sen sere*m* lauados do pecado original, e estes no*m* te*m* senão a pena da*m*ni, que he care*cer* da visão de D*eo*s, hos quaes nu*n*qua iamais dali sairão. Ho t*er*ceiro luguar he ho p*ur*guatorio onde descendem aqueles que vão deste mu*n*do co*m* a graça de D*eo*s, e porquanto no*m* paguão aqui toda a pena diuida, a culpa ali ha vão paguar, a qual como he pagua, sobe*m* ao paraiso as almas assi p*ur*guadas. E isto se aconteceo depois que ho paraiso se abrio, que foi pola paixão de Christo. Mas antes que Christo padecesse estaua ho quarto luguar que era ho limbo dos padres santos, onde elles entrauão depois que saia*m* p*ur*guados do p*ur*guatorio, e depois do pecado de Ada*m* ates que ho Mexia la foi, semp*re* ali esteuerão.

---

[1] Cf. Job 7:9. Part of the Office of the Dead in the Roman Breviary (first Responsory to the third Nocturn): "Peccantem me quotidie, et non me poenitentem, timor mortis conturbat me: Quia in inferno nulla est redemptio, miserere mei." This is cited with variations in Gil Vicente's *Auto da Barca*

We see the same thing fulfilled during our own time, for Christian kings and princes worship and serve Him and believe in Him. The Messiah has already been worshiped in Africa, in Asia, and in Europe, where His name was known and venerated. And if He is not now venerated everywhere, the fault lies with the Christian kings who will have some tall explaining to do to God as to why they do not all band together to crush that great dog of a Turk who has the Promised Land under his control.

And so, gentlemen, you must believe without a doubt that this characteristic that was described by the prophets and by your doctors — that the Messiah would be venerated by the kings — was fulfilled in Christ, our Redeemer.

This is our faith; may it also be yours. Amen.

[*fol. 33v*] Chapter Nine. How all the holy patriarchs descended to Limbo to be delivered by the Messiah.

The eighth characteristic of the Messiah was that through His death He would remove the holy patriarchs from Limbo, as Christ did. We shall prove this through the prophets and through your doctors, commentators and talmudists.

We Christians believe that there are four different places of punishment. The first is Hell which is in the center of the earth and where all who have committed a mortal sin go. There is no redemption here, as Job says: *In inferno nulla est redemptio.*[1] The second place after Hell, ascending toward earth, is the Limbo of the children who go from this world without having been cleansed of original sin. They will never be able to leave there but they suffer only the *pena damni*[2] which is the deprivation of the vision of God. The third place is Purgatory where those who leave this world with the grace of God go. Since they do not pay their whole debt here on earth they are held accountable for it there. When they have completely paid their debt, their souls are then purged and they rise to Paradise. This happened only after Paradise was opened through the passion of Christ. Before Christ's passion, the fourth place was the Limbo of the holy patriarchs who entered there after they were cleansed in Purgatory and remained from the time of Adam's sin until the Messiah descended to deliver them.

---

do Purgatório in *Obras completas*, ed. Braga, 2:97 and in the same author's *Auto da Barca da Glória, ibid.,* 2:160. In *Don Quixote*, 1,25, Sancho says: "*Quien ha infierno ... nula es retencio*" to which Don Quixote replies: "*No entiendo que quiere decir retencio.*" "*Retencio es,*" replies Sancho, "*que quien está en el infierno nunca sale del, ni puede.*"

[2] *I.e.,* the *pena sensus et damni,* the deprivation of eternal beatitude.

Esta he, pois, a propriedade do Mexia, que pola sua morte auia de abrir ho paraiso, ho qual se fechara polo pecado de Adam, e auia de tirar hos padres santos que estauão no limbo e leualos ao paraiso celestrial. E porquanto Christo esto fez, portanto nos confessamos que elle foi ho Mexia promitido na Lei.

Veiamos primeiramente como todos hos padres santos descendião ao limbo, depois veremos como ho Mexia hos auia de tirar dali.

Midras de Rrut, hum vosso doutor, expondo aquilo que se escreue no quarto capitolo de Rruth, onde dizse: "Estas são as gerações de Phares, que Phares gerou Esrrom, e cet," diz assi este doutor, que en todo ho luguar da Sagrada Escritura no qual se diz ou se põe nacimentos ou gerações, sam escrituras minguadas dūma letra de maneira que fiquão minguoadas e emperfeitas. E quando no Genesis no capitolo ij° se diz: "Estas são as gerações da terra e do ceo," nom minguou letra alguma, mas tudo esta perfeito e cheo. E diz este doutor que esto nom he sem causa nem sem rrezão. [fol. 34r] A rezão de Midras he que Deos criou todas as cousas perfeitas, sem falta alguma ou desfalicimento algum. Mas como Adam pecou, todas as cousas forão minguoadas e des-falicidas. Esto causou ho seu pecado, as quaes cousas nunqua iamais tornarão a sua perfeição ates que nom venha ho filho de Phares. Este Phares se põe por cabeceira no quarto capitolo de Rruth ates cheguar a Dauid, do qual ho Mexia auia de ser filho, e assi descendia de Phares. E, portanto, este filho de Phares, que era ho Mexia, auia de vir restaurar todas as cousas e polas em perfeição, como elle fez pola sua morte, porquanto tudo estaua destruido polo pecado de Adam.

No Talmud em muitos luguares se confirma isto, nos quaes se diz que as cousas que Deos criou no começo do mundo erão perfeitas, sem falta e sem minguoa alguma. Mas como Adam pecou, loguo as cousas deste mundo perderão sua perfeição e fiquarão todas minguoadas e faltadas. Disto temos emxemplo no mesmo Adam que era varão perfeitissimo mas como pecou, loguo a sua discrição e perfeição começou a minguoar. Immortal fora, mas ho pecado ho fez mortal [e] pasiuel, soieto a todas as penalidades deste mundo. Ho paraiso esteuera aberto

---

³ See Introduction.

⁴ Ruth 4:18ff.

⁵ Gen. 2:4.

⁶ Based on a conflation of texts in Genesis Rabbah 12:6 (Sonc. 1:92, 96; cf. Exodus Rabbah 30:3) cited in *PF*, p. 604; *ACPJ*, 1, 7, pp. 73f. In *ACPJ*, the source is erroneously given as "Midres Ruth," probably on the basis of the quotation from the Book of Ruth. This may ultimately be the source of Machado's error. The passage reads in *PF*: "R. Berekiah said: Even though these things were created in their fulness, when Adam sinned, they were spoiled and they will not return to their per-

This characteristic of the Messiah then is that through His death He would reopen Paradise, which had been closed because of Adam's sin, and would deliver the holy fathers who were in Limbo and take them to the celestial Paradise. Because Christ did this, we therefore acknowledge that He is the Messiah promised by the Law.

Let us first see how all the holy patriarchs descended into Limbo and then we shall see how the Messiah was to deliver them from there.

Midrash de Ruth,[3] one of your doctors, expounded that passage in the fourth chapter of Ruth where it says: *These are the generations of Pharez: Pharez begot Hezron, et cetera.*[4] He says that wherever "births" or "generations" are mentioned anywhere in the Holy Scriptures, they are lacking one letter which renders them incomplete and imperfect. But where we read in chapter 2 of Genesis, *These are the generations of the earth and of the heavens,*[5] everything is perfect since there are no letters missing. This doctor says that this is not without some cause and reason. [*fol. 34r*] Midrash's reason is that God created everything perfect, without any deficiencies or weaknesses. But from the time Adam sinned, everything became diminished and defective because of his sin and these things never returned to their state of perfection until the time of the son of Pharez. This same Pharez is placed at the top of the list in chapter 4 of Ruth which leads to David whose son the Messiah would be. In this way, He descended from Pharez. Therefore, the Messiah, Who was the son of Pharez, would come and restore all things, rendering them perfect once again. This He did through His death since everything was destroyed by Adam's sin.[6]

This is confirmed in many places in the Talmud for we read there that all things created by God at the beginning of the world were perfect, without anything lacking or deficient. But when Adam sinned, the things of this world lost their perfection and became deficient and wanting. We have an example of this in Adam himself for Adam was flawless, but when he transgressed, his discernment and perfection began to be impaired. He had been immortal but the sin he committed made him mortal and vulnerable, subject to all the dangers of this

---

fection until the son of Perez comes [i.e., the Messiah]; [for in the verse] *These are the toledot* (generations) *of Perez* (Ruth 4:18), *toledot* is spelt fully [with a *vav*]; R. Abbahu said in the name of R[av]: *Be-hibbaram* (*when they were created*; Gen. 2:4) means, with a *he* created He them. It follows that this world was created by means of a *he*. Now the *he* is closed on all sides and open underneath; that is an indication that all the dead descend into Sheol; its upper hook is an indication that they are to ascend thence; the opening at the side is a hint of penitents. The next world was created with a *yod*; as the *yod* has a bent back, so are the wicked, their erectness shall be bent and their faces blackened [with shame] in the Messianic future, as it is written: *And the loftiness of man shall be bowed down* ..." (Isa. 2:17).

e ho seu pecado loguo ho çarrou. Esteu[er]a e morara no paraiso
terreal, porem ho pecado ho lançou fora, que sinifiquaua que assi auia
de ser lançado do paraiso celestrial ates que viesse ho Mexia, que tudo
isto auia de rrestaurar e renouar.

Assi esta escrito no Talmud, la onde se moue a questão do pecado de
Adam, e ali se conclude que ho Mexia auia de vir renouar estas cousas e
tirar hos padres santos do limbo. Esto se pode ainda prouar segundo
aquilo que esta escrito no Grão Grande, onde se diz, conformemente ao
que se diz no Genesis no capitolo 3º: "Fez Deos morar diante do paraiso
ho cherubim, e chamouo, dizendo: 'Daa a espada.'" Perguntase ali que
quer dizer "diante do paraiso." Rresponde que "diante do paraiso foi
criado ho inferno," e loguo diz: "E quem escapara deste foguo?" Rrabi
Iona responde dizendo que a espada da circumcisão e da Lei hos tirara
do inferno, leuandoos ao limbo e nom ao paraiso.

Diguouos que estes dizeres concludem que aqueles que erão fanados
e circumcidados, e que guardauam a Lei de Moises, estes erão guar-
dados do foguo do inferno. Porem, nom subião aos ceos mas descendião ao limbo onde esperauão por ho Mexia que hos auia de liurar e
tirar daquele limbo onde estauão, caricidos da visão de Deos, a qual
muito deseiauão pera serem bemauenturados.

[fol. 34v] Ho pecado de Adam causaua tudo isto, que nhuma alma, por
muito iusta que fosse, nem santa, nom pudia entrar no paraiso, mas auia
de esperar polo Mexia que avia de vir tiralo daquele limbo. Rrabi Iona
diz, confirmando isto, que quando Adam soube que toda a sua geração
nom avia de ir ao paraiso, cesou de gerar, e quando soube que ho
Mexia auia de vir pera redimir esta geração de Adam, tornou a gerar.
Esto pudia Adam saber por reuelação diuina — que todas as almas san-
tas auiam [de] descender ao limbo polo seu pecado ates que viesse ho
Mexia que as auia de liurar daquele limbo onde estauão, carecendo da
visão diuina. A isto Midras daa autoridade dizendo que toda a companha de Isrrael auia de descender ao inferno. Porem, quem guardaua a
Lei, ao limbo descendia, mas acima nom subia ates que nom fosse
rridimida pelo seu redentor, que foi ho Mexia Christo, nosso Redentor
e Saluador. Isto se pode confirmar por aquilo que Deos dixe a Habraam
(Genesis, capitolo xv): "E tu iras a teus parentes em paz, e seras

---

[7] Cf. Gen. 3:24.
[8] This is based on Genesis Rabbah 21:9, not cited in *PF* or *ACPJ*. (cf., however, *PF*, p. 572). In
Sonc. (p. 178): ... *At the east of the Garden of Eden* [Gen. 3:24] ... *Another interpretation: Mi-ḳedem* [*at the
east*] before (*ḳodem*) the Garden of Eden the Gehenna was created, the Gehenna having been created
on the second day, and the Garden of Eden not till the third ... *That turns every way* (*ibid.*): because
it [Gehenna] revolves about man and burns him up from head to foot. Said Adam: 'Who will

world. Paradise had been open but his transgression closed it. He dwelled in a terrestrial Paradise but because of his sin he was cast out. This meant that he would remain cast out of the celestial Paradise until the [coming of the] Messiah Who would restore everything as it was.

It is written in the Talmud where the question of Adam's sin is raised that the Messiah would come and restore things to their previous state and would remove the holy patriarchs from Limbo. This can be proved further from a passage in the *Grão Grande* which comments on Genesis, chapter 3, where it says: "God made the cherubim remain in front of Paradise and called to him, saying: Yield your sword."[7] It is then asked what "in front of Paradise" means. The answer is that it means "Hell was created in front of Paradise." Then, it is asked, who will escape from this fire? Rabbi Jonah answered that the sword of circumcision and of the Law will take them all out of Hell, bringing them to Limbo but not to Paradise.

I tell you that these statements maintain that those who were circumcised and kept the Law of Moses were saved from the fires of Hell. However, they did not ascend to heaven but rather descended into Limbo where they waited for the Messiah who was to free them from that place where they were deprived of the vision of God. It was this which they very much desired in order to attain bliss.

[*fol. 34v*] Adam's sin was responsible for the fact that no soul, no matter how righteous or saintly it was, could enter Paradise. Rather it had to wait for the Messiah Who would come and remove it from Limbo. Rabbi Jonah, confirming this, says that when Adam learned that his entire progeny would not go to Paradise, he ceased procreating. Then when he found out that the Messiah would come to redeem the progeny of Adam, he once again begin to procreate. Adam knew through divine revelation that all the saintly souls would descend into Limbo because of his sin and would stay there until the Messiah would come and free them from the place where they remained, deprived of divine vision. Midrash corroborates this when he says that all of Israel would descend into Hell. However, he who kept the Law[8] would descend into Limbo and would not rise until his deliverance by his Redeemer, who was Christ the Messiah, our Redeemer and Savior. This may be confirmed by what God said to Abraham (Genesis, chapter 15): *And you shall go to your kinsmen in peace and be buried in a good old age*.[9] It is clear that the an-

---

deliver my children from this flaming fire?' R. Huna said in R. Abba's name: *Sword* refers to circumcision, as it is written, *Make thee knives of flint, and circumcise again*, etc. (Josh. 5:2)."

[9] Gen. 15:15.

sob[te]rrado com boa vilhici." Manifesto he que hos parentes de Habraam nom estauão no paraiso senão no limbo, por onde parece que la foi Habraam teer, onde esteue com hos outros ates a vinda do Mexia. Assi ho afirma Rrabi Amon expondo este passo que fala da morte de Abraam, onde este doutor conclude que Abraam nom subio aos ceos mas ao limbo descendeo.

Num liuro chamado *Sabat* se escreue que dizia Rrabi Eleazar: "As almas dos iustos são guardadas debaixo da cadeira de Deos; porem, as dos maos andão vaguabundas dum cabo pera ho outro, nom tendo rrequiem nem folgança alguma." Loguo no dito liuro sobre este dizer, faz huma pergunta, dizendo: "Se as almas dos iustos estão debaixo da cadeira da gloria de Deos, as dos maos nom terão algum luguar determinado?" Rresponde este doutor e diz que as almas dos iustos e dos maos estão no inferno; porem, as almas dos iustos teem fauor e as dos maos nom teem rrefrigerio. Conclude este doutor muito bem dizendo que todas as almas, assi dos boons como dos maos, descendião ao inferno; porem, as almas dos iustos tinhão refrigerio porquanto estauão no limbo esperando polo Mexia, mas as almas dos maos nom teem refrigerio porquanto estão no inferno onde nom teem redenção.

Bem veedes, senhores, como estes vossos doutores todos concludem que as almas dos padres [*fol. 35r*] santos nom subião aos ceos mas todas hião ao limbo, por muito santos que fossem, e por muito purguados que esteuessem da pena diuida ao pecado, esperando pola vinda do Senhor Mexia que as auia de tirar dali daquele carcere. Esto he ho que dixe Dauid no psalmo xxii, onde diz : "Ainda que descenda en vale de escuridades, nom auerei medo algum, porque tu es commiguo, Senhor."

Num liuro chamado *Cifre* diz Rabi Ioa Galileu: "Vem, e aprende quanto he ho mericimento do Mexia e ho preço dos iustos. Adam nom passou mais de hum mandamento emquanto comeo do pomo vedado e fruito que lhe fora defesso, estando elle no paraiso terreal, porque

---

[10] The above follows a passage in *ACPJ* (1, 7, p. 76) cited without reference to any source. Since the passage mentions "Rabbi Ramon" (Rrabi Amon), it might be thought that the ultimate source would be *BRMD*, the only text to mention an as yet unidentified Rabbi Raḥmon. However, *PF*, the first source for passages mentioning this "sage," does not contain this text. On the identity of R. Raḥmon, see S. Lieberman, *Shki'in* (Jerusalem, 1939), p. 67; Y. F. Baer, "Ha-midrashim ha-mezuyyafim shel Raymundus Martini u-meqomam be-milḥemet ha-dat shel yeme ha-beynayim," *Sefer ha-zikkaron le-Asher Gulak ve-li-Shemuel Klein* (Jerusalem, 1941-2), pp. 46f.; A. Diez Macho, "Acerca de los Midrašim Falsificados de Raimundo Martí," *Sefarad*, 9(1949), p. 149. Diez Macho attempts to refute Baer's position that these passages are forgeries. The passage in *ACPJ* reads: "... Item (Gen.) dicit dominus Abrahae. Tu autem ibis ad patres tuos in pace, sepultus in senectute bona. Dicit Rabbi Ramon, parentes Abrahae idolorum cultores erant, Thare videlicet et Nachor, quia sic habetur in libro Iosue. Ergo ad infernum descenderunt per consequens & Abraham."

cestors of Abraham were not in Paradise but rather in Limbo. It would thus seem that there is where Abraham went and where he was with the others until the advent of the Messiah. Rabbi Amon affirms this in expounding the passage which treats of the death of Abraham. This doctor concludes that Abraham did not rise to heaven but descended into Limbo.[10]

In a book entitled *Shabbat*,[11] it is written that Rabbi Eleazar said: "The souls of the righteous are kept under the throne of God. However, those of the wicked wander about from one end to the other without any rest or peace." Afterwards the question is raised: "If the souls of the righteous are under the throne of glory of God, will those of the wicked have no fixed place?" This doctor answers that the souls of the righteous and of the wicked are in Hell. However, the souls of the righteous are favored but those of the wicked never have relief. This doctor concludes very well by stating that all the souls, both of the good and of the wicked, descended into Hell. However, the souls of the righteous experienced relief in Limbo while waiting for the Messiah, but the souls of the wicked were not refreshed since they are in Hell and will never be redeemed.[12]

You can indeed see, gentlemen, how all of these doctors of yours conclude that the souls of the holy patriarchs [*fol. 35r*] did not ascend into heaven. They went rather to Limbo, no matter how saintly they were or how greatly they were purged of the penalty due to the transgression. There they waited for the Lord Messiah who would take those souls from that prison. This is what David said in Psalm 22: *Although I descend into the valley of darkness, I shall have no fear, because you, Lord, are with me.*[13]

In a book entitled *Sifre*,[14] Rabbi Ioa the Galilean says: "Come and learn how great is the worth of the Messiah and the value of the just ones. Adam transgressed only one commandment while in the earthly Paradise, when he ate the apple which was the fruit forbidden to him.

---

[11] *I.e.*, the talmudic tractate Shabbat. See Introduction.

[12] Machado's text is apparently based on B.T. Shabbat 152b, found neither in *PF* nor in *ACPJ*. The passage reads: "It was taught, R. Eliezer said: The souls of the righteous are hidden under the Throne of Glory ... But those of the wicked continue to be imprisoned, while one angel stands at one end of the world and a second stands at the other end, and they sling their souls to each other... Rabbah asked R. Nahman: What about those who are intermediate? Had I died I could not have told you this, he replied. Thus did Samuel say: Both these and those [the wicked and the intermediate] [*sic*] are delivered to Dumah; these enjoy rest, whereas the others have no rest" (*Sonc.*, p. 779).

[13] Ps. 23(22):4.

[14] Sifra, the tannaitic midrash on Leviticus, and not Sifre, that on Numbers and Deuteronomy, is meant. However, this passage is also cited in the name of "Siphre" in *PF*. See below, n. 15.

depois pode comet*er* muitos pecados. Aguora, vee quantas mortes forão ordenadas pera elle e pera geração humanal (Genesis, capitolo iijº), e pera suas gerações, e gerações de gerações. E a parte do mal de Ada*m* foi grande, mas, porem, a parte do bem, que sera a p*ar*te do Mexia, excede todo mal, porque qua*n*to Ada*m* desmereceo, muito mais ho Mexia mereceo, porque ho Mexia vira que este mal redimira, ho qual alcançarão aqueles q*ue* descendere*m* ao limbo."

Bem conclude este doutor que todo ho mal que nos mereceo Ada*m* polo seu pecado, todo foi redimido e paguo e satisfeito polo Mexia, que muito mereceo ac*er*qua de D*eos*, que reconciliou a geração humanal com D*eos* que estaua muito irado por este pecado de Ada*m,* por amor do qual nhu*m*a alma no*m* pudia subir ao paraiso, mas ao inf*er*no todas as almas descendião — as iustas pera ho limbo e as iniustas p*er*a ho inferno.

Moises, grande amiguo foi de D*eos*, dador da Lei, tirou ho pouo do catiueiro de Pharão, falou co*m* hos anios, teue coloquio e familiaridade co*m* D*eos*, mas como morreo, loguo descendeo ao limbo e no*m* subio aos ceos. Esto confirma Midras, vosso doutor, expondo aquilo de Ecclesiastico, capitolo vijº, onde se diz: "Ho iusto pereceo e a sua iustiça," dizendo que isto se diz por Moises, ho qual semelhaua a hu*m* filho dũma molher prenhe. Esta molh[e]r estaua nu*m* carcere presa, e ac*er*tou de parir no mesmo carcere onde criou ho menino. E sendo elle ia de idade, ac*er*tou de pasar ho rrei daqu*e*la terra a par do carcere. Vendoo, ho moço começou de bradar, dizendo: "S*en*hor, aqui naci e aqui me criei e no*m* pequei porque estou aqui." Rrespondeo ellrrei, dizendolhe: "Polo pecado de tua mãi estas no carcere, porque ho iusto perece e sua iustiça." Seguesse loguo[a] do diz*er* deste vosso doutor, que posto que Moises no*m* pecasse ne*m* fosse pecador, [*fol. 35v*] porem, polo pecado de Ada*m* iazio no limbo, e polo pecado original em ho qual sua mãi ho concebeo, como diz Dauid no ps*almo* cinquo*en*ta: "Com maldades soo*m* concibido, e em maldades me concebeo minha mãi." E assi, (posto que Moises fosse muito iusto e no*m* teuesse pecado *autual* mortal ne*m* venial), posto que a natureza humana no*m* se pode pasar sem este

a +*O iudeus* exp.

---

[15] Based on Sifra, Vayiqra, Ḥovah 20:10; *PF* (cited as Siphre), pp. 866ff.; *ACPJ* 1, 11, pp. 106f. (cited as *Zifrat*). From *PF*: "R. Jose the Galilean said: Go and perceive the merit of the King Messiah and the reward of the righteous from Adam. He was given only one prohibition and transgressed it. See how many deaths were decreed upon him and his generations and his generations' generations until the end of all generations. Which is greater? A good or an evil dispensation? A good dispensation is greater and an evil dispensation the lesser. And the King Messiah who afflicts and anguishes himself for the sinners (as it is said, *But he was wounded for our transgressions* [Isa. 53:5])

This led to his being able to commit many sins. Now you see how death came to him and the whole human race (Genesis, chapter 3) and to all future generations. The evil side of Adam was great, but the good side, that related to the Messiah, exceeds all evil. For although Adam's merit diminished, the Messiah's worth was greatly enhanced, for the Messiah had seen that he had redeemed this wickedness and those who had descended into Limbo."[15]

This doctor rightly concludes that all the evil that befell us through Adam's sin was redeemed, atoned, and expiated by the Messiah Whose merit was great before God; for He reconciled the human race with God who was irate over Adam's transgression which prevented any soul from ascending into Paradise. Rather, they all descended to Hell — the righteous going to Limbo and the wicked to Hell.

Moses, the law giver and greatly beloved of God, freed his people from the captivity of Pharaoh, spoke with the angels and conversed familiarly with God. Yet, when he died, he went to Limbo and not to heaven. Your doctor Midrash confirms this when he comments on the passage from Ecclesiasticus, chapter 7, which says: *The righteous and his righteousness perished.*[16] He says that this refers to Moses who is likened to the child of a pregnant woman. This woman was a prisoner in a jail and managed to give birth there where she also raised her child. When he had come of age, the king of the land happened to pass by the jail. On seeing him, the lad begain to shout: "Sir, I was born and raised here but this is due to no fault of my own." The king answered and said: "It is because of your mother's sin that you are in jail, for the just perished with his justice."[17] It follows then[18] from these words of your doctor that although Moses had not sinned nor had he been a sinner [*fol. 35v*], he nevertheless went to Limbo because of Adam's transgression and the original sin in which his mother conceived him. It is as David says in Psalm 50: *I was conceived with iniquity and in sin did my mother conceive me.*[19] Thus, even though Moses was very righteous and committed no actual mortal or venial sin (although human nature can not be free of venial

---

will certainly bring favor upon all those generations, as it is written, *the Lord has laid upon him the iniquity of us all* (Isa. 53:6)."

[16] Not Ecclus. but Eccl. 7:15.

[17] Based on Ecclesiastes Rabbah to 7:13 (Sonc., p. 196) cited in *PF*, pp. 619f.; *ACPJ* 1, 7, pp. 76f.: "To what may our teacher Moses be likened? To a pregnant woman shut up in a prison. She gave birth there to a son, reared him there and died there. After a while the King passed by the entrance of the prison, and as he passed the son began to cry, 'My Lord King, here was I born and here I grew up. For what sin I am kept here I do not know. He answered, 'For your mother's sin.'"

[18] MS has "O Jews" expunged. See note *a*.

[19] Ps. 51:5 (50:7).

venial, porem, ho pecado original fez que ao limbo fosse Moises, onde esperou polo Mexia, como fazião hos outros padres santos que la estauão.

Ia temos prouado como todos hos padres santos descendião ao limbo por muito iustos que fossem. Aguora, com poucas palauras, veiamos como forão redimidos polo Mexia e dali tirados e leuados ao paraiso.

Esta he a uerdade. Crede, se quiserdes, senhores,[b] que Christo, nosso Redentor, Missias promitido na Lei, este tirou hos padres santos que estauão no limbo, e hos leuou ao paraiso. Ou, deuees conceder que ainda estão no limbo, ho que nom pode ser. E assi deues de crer segundo a vosso opinião, pois que esperaes polo Mexia que hos a de liurar.

Em Midras Telim se escreue que toda a companha de Isrrael ante Deos he predestinada e ordenada pera ho inferno ou limbo, em ho qual iazerão ates que venha ho Mexia e hos tirara daquele carcere. Ex aqui hum testimunho bem manifesto em ho qual se conclude que a companha de Isrrael, que estaua no limbo, auia de ser liure polo Mexia, como nos temos por fee que foy, e assi ho cremos. E gustado[c] me ouuesse loguo deste mundo partir e fosseis vos desta fee comnosco.

Ho pecado de Adam foi grauissimo sobre todolos pecados, porque elle pecou por soberba, gula, cubiça, polo qual elle nom pode satisfazer. Por este pecado foi, pois, loguo necessario que outrem satisfezesse por elle. Porem, nom se pode achar outra pesoa mais conueniente para iso que foi ho Mexia, que auia de ser Deos e homem, que auia de exceder per humildad[e], temperança, e abstinentia a Adam, ho qual foi causa que todos hos da vossa Lei fossem ao limbo, do qual ho mesmo Mexia hos auia de tirar, como tirou e liurou depois que morreo no dia da sua resurreição, estando tres dias com elles no limbo, e ao terceiro dia hos tirou pera hos leuar ao paraiso. Acabados hos corenta dias depois da sua resurreição, hos leuou comsiguo a sua Gloria, onde rreinão e triu[n]fão com elle e triunfarão pera todo sempre.

Concludindo, pois, dizemos que por amor do pecado de Adam nom entrou alma alguma no paraiso, mas as iustas esteuerão no limbo ates a uinda do Mexia que as [a]via [de] tirar de catiueiro.

Esta he a nossa fee e seia a vossa. Amen.

b int.   c uncertain reading

[20] Interlinear addition. See note *b*.
[21] Reference to passage in Midrash Tehillim 49:2 (ed. Buber, p. 277; Braude, 1:465) cited in *PF*, pp. 607f.; *ACPJ*, 1, 7, p. 74. In *PF*: "Rich and poor together (Ps. 49:3) means that he who is rich in

sin), it was nevertheless original sin which sent Moses to Limbo where he waited for the Messiah as did the other holy patriarchs who were also there.

We have already proved how all the holy patriarchs descended into Limbo no matter how righteous they were. Now, in a few words, let us see how they were redeemed from there by the Messiah and then taken to Paradise.

This is the truth. Believe, if you will, gentlemen,[20] that the Christ our Redeemer, the Messiah promised in the Law, removed the holy patriarchs from Limbo and took them to Paradise. If not, you will have to concede that they are still in Limbo, which is not possible. So must you believe according to your own opinion for you are waiting for the Messiah who is to deliver them.

It is written in Midrash Tehillim that all of Israel is predestined and ordained before God to go to either Hell or Limbo,[21] where they are to remain until the Messiah comes and takes them from that prison. Now here is very clear evidence from which one may conclude that all of Israel who were in Limbo would be freed by the Messiah. We have faith that it was so and so do we believe. And if I were to leave this world soon, it would be my hope[22] that you also would be of this faith.

Adam's sin was the gravest of all sins, since he sinned through haughtiness, gluttony [and] greed which he could not expiate. Because of this sin, it was necessary for another to expiate for him. No other more suitable than the Messiah could be found for He would be God and man and would outdo Adam in humility, temperance, and abstinence. For it was the latter who caused all those who followed your Law to go to Limbo from which the Messiah would deliver them. He did so, after He died, on the day of His resurrection. He was with them in Limbo three days and on the third He freed them and carried them to Paradise. Forty days after His resurrection, He took them with Him to His glory where they reign and triumph as they shall forever.

So in conclusion, we shall say that because of Adam's sin no soul entered Paradise and that the souls of the righteous remained in Limbo until the advent of the Messiah who was to free them from their captivity.

This is our faith; may it be yours. Amen.

Torah and he who is poor in Torah all descend to Gehenna even though they were heads of the Sanhedrin ..."

[22] The Portuguese "e gustado" is unclear.

[*fol. 36r*] Capitolo Decimo. De como ho Mexia auia de ser da casa e familia de Dauid, como ho nosso Chr*isto* foi.

A nona propriedade do Mexia era que elle auia de ser da casa e familia de Dauid, segundo estaua escrito polos profetas, a qual foi communicada a Chr*isto*.

Moises v*er*dadeiro testimunho deu que ho Mexia auia de sair d'antre vos outros s*en*ho*res.[a] Assi ho afirmou elle, segundo esta escrito no Deuteronomio no capitolo xviii°, onde se diz: "Hu*m* profeta suscitara D*eos* d'antre vos, ho qual ou[u]ires como a mi*m* mesmo," posto que hos vossos antepassados na*m* no quiserão ouuir ne*m* quiserão crer que elle era ho Mexia promitido na Lei, afirma*n*dolhes Chr*isto*, por muitas vezes, q*ue* Moises dera testimunho dele, e que esculdrinhasse*m* bem as Escrituras e que acharião que era v*er*dade que elle era ho profeta do qual falou Moises no luguar ia p*r*aleguado. E posto que algu*n*s vossos doutores queirão dizer que Moises no*m* falou do Mexia no luguar ia dito mas q*ue* falara de Iosue, diguouos q*ue* no*m* sabem ho que dizem, porque Iosue no*m* foi profeta mas som*en*tes capitão deles. Portanto, no*m* tenhaes esto em debate ou duuida, mas crede, como he v*er*dade, que este profeta, do qual aqui fala Moises, era ho Mexia, ho qual auia de sair d'antre vos outros, como saio.

Este, porem, profeta, auia de ser da casa e familia de Dauid, e auiasse de chamar "filho de Dauid," como nos lhe chamamos, que disto temos muitas testemunhas. No ps*almo* cxxxi se diz que iurou ho S*en*hor en verdade a Dauid que no*m* no auia d'enguanar "porque do fruito do teu ventre porei sobre a tua cadeira." E esto p*r*imeiro lhe foi promitido polo profeta Natha*m*, segundo se conte*m* no Segundo Liuro dos Reis, no capitolo vij°, ho que p*r*imeiramente foi comp*r*ido em Salamão que foi figura do Mexia, ho qual, loguo depois da morte de Dauid, socedeo no rreino, e depois mais p*er*feitam*en*te se comprio em Chr*isto* Mexia, que foi filho de Dauid, segundo a ca*r*ne.

No P*r*imeiro Liuro de Paralipemeno*m*, no capitolo xvij, se escre*u*e que Dauid dete*r*minou de edificar hum templo em o qual D*eos* fosse se*r*uido, pera poor nele a archa do Testame*n*to. Estando elle nesta determinação, ma*n*dou D*eos* ho profeta Natha*m* a Dauid que lhe dixesse que elle no*m* lhe auia de edificar casa. Mas dixelhe ho profeta da parte de D*eos*: "Como acabares teus dias, irteas pera teus parentes, e D*eos*

a int.

---

[1] Interlinear addition. See note *a*.
[2] Deut. 18:15.

[*fol. 36r*] Chapter Ten. How the Messiah was to be descended from the house and family of David, as Christ was.

The ninth characteristic of the Messiah was that He was to be descended from the house and family of David, according to that written in the prophets, and this was fulfilled in Christ.

Moses offered valid testimony in support of the Messiah's descent from you gentlemen.[1] He affirmed this in the text written in chapter 18 of Deuteronomy, where it says: *God will bring forth a prophet from among you, to whom you shall listen as if it were Me*.[2] But your ancestors did not want to listen to Him nor did they want to believe that He was the Messiah promised in the Law. Christ affirmed that He was many times and pointed out to them that Moses had given them proof that He was the promised Messiah. He advised them to delve into the Scriptures for there they would find that it was true that He was the prophet about whom Moses spoke in the above text. Even though some of your doctors prefer to say that Moses was not speaking of the Messiah but rather of Joshua,[3] I say that they do not know what they are talking about because Joshua was not a prophet but only their chieftain. Consequently you need neither debate this point nor have any doubt concerning it. Instead, believe the truth: This prophet, of whom Moses speaks here, was the Messiah Who came from among you.

However, this prophet was to be of the house and family of David and would be called "the son of David," as we call Him. For this, we have considerable proof. In Psalm 131 it says that the Lord swore in truth to David that He would not deceive him *because I shall place upon your throne the fruit of your womb*.[4] This was first promised him by the prophet Nathan, according to the Second Book of Kings, chapter 7,[5] and was first fulfilled in Solomon who was the figure of Christ and who became king after David's death. It was later more perfectly fulfilled in Christ the Messiah who was the son of David according to the flesh.

In the First Book of Chronicles, chapter 17, it is written that David decided to erect a Temple in which God would be worshiped and in which the ark of the Testament could be placed. At this time God sent his prophet Nathan to David to tell him that he was not to erect such a house for Him.[6] Speaking in God's name, Nathan told him instead:

---

[3] See, e.g., Ibn Ezra *ad loc.;* cf. *PF*, p. 886; *FF*, fol. 134*va*.
[4] Ps. 132 (131):11. See Isidore, *De fide catholica*, 1.9, *PL*, 83:469.
[5] 2 Sam. 7:12.
[6] 1 Chron. 17:1ff.; cf. 2 Sam. 7:1ff.

suscitara huma semente depois disto, a qual sera dos teus filhos, e eu
confirmarei ho seu reino, e este me edificara a Casa e Templo, e eu en-
fortelecerei a sua cadeira pera todo sempre. E eu serei seu pai e elle
sera meu filho, e a minha misericordia nunqua ha tirarei dele, assi
como eu tirei daquele que foi antes de ti, que foi Saul. E poloei na
minha casa e no meu reino pera todo sempre [*fol. 36v*] e ho seu trono
sera firmissimo pera todo sempre."

Certamente esto que aqui se põe, que ho profeta Natham dixe a
Dauid por mandado de Deos, nom se pode entender de Salamão, porque
Salamão nom reinou pera todo sempre. Mas antes muitos doutores são
da sentença que elle que he danado porquanto adorou os idolos,
tirando São Ieronimo que diz que he saluo. E mais, quando Natham isto
dixe a Dauid ia Salamão era nado, e ho profeta dixe a Dauid que auia
Deos de suscitar semente, a qual nom podia ser senão ho Mexia, que
auia de reinar pera todo sempre.

Assi que, concludindo, afirmamos que ho Mexia auia de ser da casa e
familia de Dauid, segundo se contem no luguar aleguado, e esta foi a
entenção de Deos do profeta Natão. E, portanto, nom dees à autoridade
outro sentido nem entendimento, porque erraes, porque São Paulo,
escreuendo huma epistola aos vossos predecessores, falando do Mexia
no primeiro capitolo, pera prouar ho nacimento do Mexia, trouxe pera
proua aquilo que acima esta aleguado: "Ego ero illi in patrem, et ipse
erit michi in filium."

No Segundo Liuro dos Reis, capitolo xii, se põe ho nacimento de
Salamão, filho de Dauid, que sinificaua ho Mexia, que auia tambem de
ser filho de Dauid, segundo a carne. Isaias isto proua euidentemente no
capitolo xi, quando diz: "Saira huma vara da raiz de Iesse" (que foi
Maria do tribu de Iuda e da familia e casa de Dauid), "e huma frol desta
raiz subira." (Ho Mexia foi filho de Maria.) Como este mesmo profeta
dixe no capitolo vij: "Audite, domus Dauid" (Ouui, casa de Dauid).
Este he ho sinal que huma virgem parira.

Bem se parece deste dizer que da casa de Dauid auia de ser este
Mexia. Vos tendes por fee que ho Mexia ha de ser monarcha e rrei de
todo ho mundo vniuerso. E pois que ha de ser rrei, he necessario que
seia do tribu de Iuda, e se ha de ser do tribu de Iuda, sera da casa e
familia de Dauid, donde descenderam hos reis de Iuda. Bem creo que
nesta propriedade, nom somos muito diferentes nem vos neguaes que ho

---

⁷ 1 Chron. 17:11ff.; cf. 2 Sam. 7:12ff.
⁸ Machado's remarks appear to be based on Isidore, *De fide catholica*, 1.9, *PL*, 83:465ff. Cf. Lyra,
Post., 1, NNiiv.

When your days come to an end and you go to your fathers, God will then raise up a seed which will be of your sons and I will affirm his kingdom. It will be he who will erect a house and Temple for Me and I shall strengthen his throne forever. And I will be his father and he shall be My son, and never will I take My mercy from him as I did from Saul who came before you. And I will place him in My house and in My kingdom forever [fol. 36v] and his throne will be secure forever.[7]

What the prophet Nathan said to David in God's name can certainly not be taken to refer to Solomon because Solomon did not reign forever. Indeed, many doctors are of the opinion that he is damned since he adored idols, save Saint Jerome who believes he was saved.[8] Furthermore, when Nathan said this to David, Solomon had already been born and the prophet said that God would raise up a seed which could be none other than the Messiah, Who would reign forever.

Thus, in conclusion, we affirm that the Messiah was to be of the house and family of David, according to the above, and that this was the intention of God and of the prophet Nathan. Therefore, do not read any other meaning into this text, for if you do, you are in error; for Saint Paul, in chapter 1 of his Epistle to your ancestors brought that which was cited above as proof of the birth of the Messiah: *Ego ero illi in patrem, et ipse erit michi in filium.*[9]

In the Second Book of Kings, chapter 12, mention is made of the birth of Solomon, the son of David,[10] who foreshadowed the Messiah Who would also be the son of David according to the flesh. Isaiah clearly proves this in chapter 11, when he says: *A shoot shall come forth from the stem of Jesse* (who was Mary from the tribe of Judah and from the family and house of David), *and a blossom shall grow out of its roots*[11] (the Messiah was the son of Mary). As this same prophet said in chapter 7: *Audite, domus Dauid (Hear, O house of David).*[12] This is the sign that a virgin will give birth.

It seems evident from these words that the Messiah would be descended from the house of David. You believe that the Messiah will be monarch and king of the whole world. Yet since he is to be king, it is necessary that he be of the tribe of Judah. If then he is to be of the tribe of Judah, it follows that he will be of the house and family of David from which the kings of Judah are descended. I do not believe we

[9] Heb. 1:5.
[10] 2 Sam. 12:24.
[11] Isa. 11:1.
[12] Isa. 7:3.

Mexia no*m* seia da casa e familia de Dauid. Mas assi esperaes que ho Mexia ha de ser da casa e familia de Dauid, mas eu quisera que creses vos que ia este Mexia foi da casa e familia de Dauid e que ia veo a este mu*n*do tomar carne humana.

Olhai, senhores, olhai, que a fim do mu*n*do se chegua, e ho Mexia no*m* ouuera tanto de prolonguar sua vinda, como vos credes, ainda esperando por elle, em luguar do qual teres ho maluado antichri*sto* que vos fara crer q*ue* [h]e ho Mexia. E eu assi ho tenho p*er*a my*m* senão vos co*n*u*er*terdes.

Esta he a nossa fee e crença, peçouos que esta seia ta*m*bem a uossa. Amen.

[*fol. 37r*] Capitolo Vndecimo. De como ho Mexia auia de ser vngido por ho Sp*iritu* do S*enh*or, auia de vir proue e no*m* com pompa ne*m* triumfo ne*m* aparato, como os iudeus esperauão.

A decima propriedade que estaua escrita do Mexia era q*ue* ele auia de ser vngido polo Sp*iritu* Santo, e avia de vir muito pobre e sem pompa e aparato; muito desp*r*ezado e vil e desp*r*eziuel. Ho profeta Isaias no capitolo lxi ho proua, dizendo em pessoa do Mexia: "Ho sp*iritu* do S*enh*or sobre mi*m*, porquè me vngio e ma*n*doume que viesse eua*n*gelizar e p*r*eguar aos pobres; e p*r*eguar aos catiuos do pecado, remissão, e aos ceguos, vista."

Tudo isto foi comprido no Mexia, que foi vngido polo Sp*iritu* Santo no seu concibime*n*to, porquanto loguo foi cheo de toda graça e de toda perfeição. E loguo foi benauenturado comp*r*ehensor, vendo semp*r*e aquela esentia diuina, na qual, como em espelho, todalas cousas via. E p*r*eguou aos pobres em Ierusalem, e deu vista aos ceguos. Assi q*ue* no*m* fiquou nada desta profitia que no*m* fosse co*m*prida no nosso Mexia Chri*sto*.

Dauid, ta*m*bem, daa testimunho q*ue* ho Mexia auia de ser vngido qua*n*do diz no ps*alm*o xliiij: "Amaste a iustiça e auorreceste a maldade, e portanto, D*eos* te vngio com oleo d'alegria mais que todos hos outros." Assi foi ho Mexia ho mais amado e querido que anios, ne*m* archa*n*ios, ne*m* cherube*n*s.

Tende, pois, por c*er*teza, que ho Mexia auia de ser vngido e consagrado polo Sp*iritu* Santo, como foi Chri*sto*, ho v*er*dadeiro Mexia. Assi ho tinha profetizado Isaias no capitolo xi, onde diz: "E ho sp*iritu* do S*enh*or folguara sobre elle: sp*iritu* da sabadoria e entendimento; sp*iritu* de conselho e de forteleza; sp*iritu* de cientia e de piedade, e encheloa ho sp*iritu* do S*enh*or de temor. No*m* iulguara segundo a uista, ne*m* segundo

differ on these points nor do you deny that the Messiah is of the house and family of David. But you hope that the Messiah is yet to come forth from the house and family of David while I should like you to believe that the Messiah has already come forth from this house and family and that He has already come to this world and become incarnate.

Look, gentlemen, look; for the end of the world is approaching and the Messiah could not have prolonged His coming by as much as you believe. You still wait for Him but, in His place, you will have the wicked Antichrist who will make you believe that he is the Messiah. I suspect this will be so unless you convert.

This is our faith and belief and I ask that it be yours as well. Amen.

[*fol. 37r*] Chapter Eleven. How the Messiah would be anointed by the Spirit of the Lord and how He would come as a pauper, without pomp, triumph, or fanfare as the Jews expected.

The tenth characteristic that was written of the Messiah was that He would be anointed by the Holy Spirit and that He would come as a poor man without pomp and splendor; disdained, scorned, and rejected. In chapter 61, the prophet Isaiah proves this in speaking of the Messiah when he says: *The Spirit of the Lord is upon me because he anointed me and commanded me to evangelize and preach to the poor; to preach absolution to those enslaved by sin, and sight to the blind.*[1]

All this was fulfilled in the Messiah Who was anointed by the Holy Spirit at His conception and was then imbued with complete grace and perfection. He then attained blessed comprehension, always seeing that divine essence in which He saw all things as in a mirror. Thus did He preach to the poor in Jerusalem and give sight to the blind. There is then nothing in this prophecy which was not fulfilled in our Messiah Christ.

David also gives testimony that the Messiah would be anointed when he says in Psalm 44: *You loved justice and abhorred evil; therefore God anointed You more than any other with the oil of gladness.*[2] Thus was the Messiah more beloved and cherished than the angels, the archangels, or the cherubs.

Believe then, without a doubt, that the Messiah would be anointed and consecrated by the Holy Spirit, as was Christ, the true Messiah. So had Isaiah prophesied in chapter 11, where he says: *And the spirit of the Lord shall rest upon him: the spirit of wisdom and understanding; the spirit of counsel and of fortitude; the spirit of knowledge and of compassion; and the spirit*

[1] Isa. 61:1.
[2] Ps. 45(44):8.

ho ouuir, mas iulguara hos pobres com iustiça e arguira segundo
direito. E antão morara ho lobo com ho cordeiro, e ho pardo com ho
cabrito, e ho bezerro e ho liom e a ouelha morarão iuntamente, e hum
moço pequeno hos guiara."

Todo este capitolo fala do Mexia, concludindo a grande paz e concordia que auia d'auer no mundo quando viesse este Mexia. E assi
antão grande era a paz e concordia que ho emperador Outauiano tinha
com todo ho mundo quando veo este Mexia, ho qual foi cheo destes
sete dooens do Spiritu Santo aqui aleguados. E, portanto, nom vos
enguanes cuidando que quando vier ho Mexia que ha de comer ho lobo
com ho cordeiro. Leixai ho sentido carnal e tomay ho spiritual, porque
isto nom sinificaua senão a grande paz e concordia que na vinda do
Mexia auia d'auer en todo ho mundo, porque antão a paz e iustiça se
beixarão (psalmo lxxxiiij).

[fol. 37v] Deste Mexia estaua profitizado que auia de vir como homem
pobre e desprezado e vil. Assi veo Christo, por onde concludimos que
elle foi ho Mexia promitido na Lei pois que todalas propriedades que
estão escritas do Mexia, quanto he à primeira vinda, forão vistas e
compridas em Christo. Ho profeta Zacharias deu euidente testimunho
disto no capitolo ix, onde diz: "Dizei à filha de Sion: 'Ex ho teu rrei.
Vem muito manso, iusto, e saluador, pobre em cima da asna.'"
Diguouos que assi como aqui nesta profitia esta escrito, a qual nom se
pode entender d'outra pessoa senão do Mexia, segundo todos hos vossos
doutores, assi se comprio na cidade de Ierusalem quando Christo entrou, subido na asna. Queres mais comprimento da profitia que este?

E vos ᵃoutros, senhores,ᵃ afirmaaes que ho Mexia ha de uir com
grande aparato e exercito pera tomar ho emperio rromano. O vos
outros, ᵇsenhores irmãos,ᵇ como vos enguanaes, nom entendendo as
profitias nem autoridades do Mexia, mas tudo confundis. Diguouos que
as autoridades e profitias que falão e demostrão que ho Mexia ha de vir
muito espantoso e com grande poder, se entendem da sua vinda quando
ha de vir iulguar hos viuos e mortos, como diz Malachias no capitolo 3º:
"E quem podera pensar no dia da sua vinda, ou quem estara pera o ver?

---

a-a marg. + *cuitados e miseros e misquinhos* exp.   b-b int.

³ Isa. 11:2ff.
⁴ Ps. 85(84):11.
⁵ Zech. 9:9. Machado's version of the verse, which adds the "dicite filiae Sion" of Isa. 62:11, is
similar to that of Isidore of Seville, *De fide catholica*, 1.15.1 as printed in *PL*, 83:473: "Dicite filiae
Sion: Ecce rex tuus venit tibi iustus, et salvator, pauper, sedens super asinum indomitum." It is to
be noted, however, that the text of *De fide catholica* found in B.N.L. MS Alc. 375, fol. 144r follows
the Vulgate.

of the Lord shall fill him with fear. He shall not judge by what he sees nor by what he hears; but shall judge the poor with equity and shall contend justly. And then the wolf shall dwell with the lamb, and the leopard with the kid, and the calf and the lion and the ewe shall dwell together and a small lad shall lead them.[3]

This chapter speaks in its entirety of the Messiah and alludes to the great peace and harmony that would reign in the world when the Messiah came. Thus was there great peace and harmony between the emperor Octavian and the rest of the world when the Messiah came, endowed by the Holy Spirit with the seven gifts mentioned above. Therefore, do not deceive yourselves into thinking that when the Messiah comes, the wolf will eat with the lamb. Look upon this in the spiritual sense and not in the corporeal sense as you do. For it signified the great peace and harmony that would reign in the whole world when the Messiah came, for then peace and justice would kiss each other (Psalm 84).[4]

[*fol. 37v*] It was prophesied that this Messiah would come as a poor man, scorned and disdained. Christ came in this manner and we therefore conclude that He was the Messiah promised in the Law since all the characteristics that are written of the Messiah regarding His first coming were seen and fulfilled in Christ. The prophet Zechariah gave evident proof of this in chapter 9 where he says: *Say to the daughter of Zion: Behold your king. He comes very meek, righteous, and a savior; a poor man upon an ass.*[5] I tell you that just as what is written here in this prophecy cannot be taken to refer to any one save the Messiah according to all your doctors, so was it fulfilled in the city of Jerusalem when Christ entered, mounted on an ass. Do you want more proof of the fulfillment of the prophecy than this?

But you, gentlemen,[6] maintain that the Messiah will come with great pomp and a large army to take over the Roman empire. O esteemed brothers,[7] how you deceive yourselves by not understanding either the prophecies or the Messianic proof-texts, all of which you confuse. I tell you that these passages and prophecies which show that the Messiah will come with awesomeness and great might are understood to refer to His coming to judge the quick and the dead as Malachi says in chapter 3: *And who will be able to think of the day of His coming? And who will be present to see Him? Because He will come like a fire.*[8] You think that the

---

[6] Marginal addition replacing "poor, miserable, wretched." See note *a*.
[7] Interlinear addition. See note *b*.
[8] Mal. 3:2.

porque elle vira como hum foguo." Vos cuidaes que esta profitia, que se entende da vinda do Mexia en carne, e ho profeta fala da vinda ao iuizo. E, portanto, sobre que ho profeta Malachias fala das duas vindas do Senhor — da vinda em carne e da vinda ao iuizo — e porque vos nom sabes discirnir antre estas duas vindas, por isto tudo confundes, afirmando, com as autoridades que falão da vinda ao iuizo que ho Mexia ha de vir com grande poder e com grande exercito. E as autoridades que falão da sua vinda com humildade e pobreza, laa lhes daes outra coor falsa, enguanados vos mesmos.

Crede, crede comnosco que ho Mexia ia veo, e são passados 1541 anos veo proue, nom com rriquezas, nem com caualarias, nem com exercito pera vencer hos christãos ᶜou iudeus, mouros ou paguãos;ᶜ mas veo com muita pobreza e humildade chamarnos a uos e a nos, ensinandonos muita pobreza e muita humildade. E Isaias [e] Ieremias em muitos passos das suas profitias, bem demostrão a pobreza do Mexia de maneira que hos vossos antepassados ho auião de leixar por amor da sua pobreza, como leixarão.

Nos cremos que foi vngido e pobre ho Mexia, e nesta fee viuemos e vos deuees de viuer. Amen.

[*fol. 40v*] Capitolo Duodecimo. De como ho Mexia auia de fazer milagres, ho qual nom auia de ser conhicido dos iudeus; porem, seria visto no mundo.

A undecima propriedade que estaua polos profetas escrita do Mexia era que elle auia de fazer milagres. Hos iudeus nom no auião de conhecer; porem, auia de ser visto Deos e homem neste mundo.

Dos milagres que ho Mexia auia de fazer (como fez Christo andando neste mundo) Isaias da testimunho no capitolo xxix, onde diz: "Naquele dia ouuirão hos surdos, e hos ceguos, tirada a escuridade dos seus olhos, verão." Bem se comprio isto na cidade de Ierusalem no tempo do Mexia, porque elle sarou hos surdos e lhes deu ouuidos pera ouuirem; sarou muitos ceguos e hos fez ver. Cheos estão hos euangelistas destes milagres, se vos lhes quiserdes daar fee. Ao menos, verdade he que do Mexia estaua escrito que auia de fazer milagres, ho que foi comprido no tempo de Christo. E assi nos acertamos e vos erraes grauemente. Isaias outro testimunho daa disto no capitolo xxxv, onde diz: "Antão se abrirão hos olhos dos ceguos, e as orelhas dos surdos se manifestarão;

c-c int.

⁹ "Or ... pagans" interlinear addition. See note *c*.

prophet and this prophecy, which refer to the coming of the Messiah in the flesh, speak of the coming in judgment. Therefore, by reason of the fact that the prophet Malachi speaks of two comings of the Lord — that in the flesh and that in judgment — and because you do not know how to distinguish between these two comings, you consequently confuse everything. You affirm, on the basis of the texts that speak of the coming in judgment, that the Messiah will come with great power and a mighty army. Yet the passages that speak of His coming humble and as a pauper you color falsely, and so deceive yourselves.

Believe, believe with us that the Messiah has already come and that 1541 years have passed since He came — not with riches, but in poverty; not with horses nor with an army to conquer the Christians or Jews, Moors or pagans;[9] but in extreme poverty and with great humility to call us and to teach us these same ways. In many passages of their prophecies, Isaiah and Jeremiah clearly show the poverty of the Messiah and the way that your ancestors would turn from Him because of His poverty, as they did.

We believe that the Messiah was anointed and was poor and it is in this belief that we live, as should you. Amen.

[*fol. 40v*] Chapter Twelve. How the Messiah would appear in this world and perform miracles but would not be recognized by the Jews.[1]

The eleventh characteristic that was written of the Messiah by the prophets was that He would perform miracles. The Jews could not know Him; however, He would appear in this world as God and man.

Isaiah gives testimony of these miracles (wrought by Christ when He was on this earth) in chapter 29 when he says: *On that day the deaf shall hear; and the blind shall see with the darkness of their eyes removed.*[2] This was clearly fulfilled in the city of Jerusalem at the time of the Messiah, because He healed the deaf by giving them ears with which to hear and cured the blind by making them see. The [writings of the] evangelists are full of these miracles if you would let yourselves believe them. The truth at least is that it was written that the Messiah would work miracles, and this was fulfilled during the time of Christ. For this reason, it is we who are right and you who gravely err. Isaiah gives further proof of this in chapter 35, where he says: *Then the eyes of the blind shall be opened and the ears of the deaf shall be made to hear; the lame shall leap*

---

[1] See Introduction.
[2] Isa. 29:18.

antão saltar ho coio como o ceruo, e a linguoa dos mudos nom sera em-
pidida." Diguouos, senhores, que esta profitia foi comprida no tempo
do Mexia, porque todos estes forão curados por elle e sãos feitos. Assi
ainda ho afirma Isaias no capitolo lxi no qual diz, falando do Mexia:
"Mandoume curar hos angustiados do coração, preguar a remissão dos
pecados, e daar vista aos ceguos."

Ia nom tenhaes debate nem duuida que todas estas profetias forão
escritas do Mexia, as quaes ia passarão e forão compridas, que he hum
grande argumento e grande inditio que ho Mexia ia veo. Todas estas
cousas acima postas se acontecerão na vinda do Mexia, no tempo do
qual loguo aparecerão grandes milagres que demostrauão manifestamente a sua vinda, como foi a estrela de Iacob que loguo pareceo aos
rreis, e ho vierão adorar.

Sendo da idade de XXX anos, começou a preguar, fazer grandes e
marauilhosos milagres, hos quaes profeta que antes delle fosse nunqua
fez de modo e maneira que elle fez, curando hos ceguos, surdos, man-
cos; resuscitou a Lazaro de quatro dias morto,[a] e viueo por muito
tempo. Por onde parece que nom pudia ser aquilo feito por arte magica,
que he grande argumento que elle era ho Mexia promitido na Lei. Andou sobre as aguoas. Pola sua morte tremeo a terra. Ho sol foi feito
escuro. Rresurgio ao terceiro dia. Foi visto em Ierusalem depois da sua
morte. "Quis vnquam talia audiuit aut vidit?"

Estas cousas certamente vos auião de cautiuar [fol. 40r] e constranger
ho entendimento pera crerdes que Christo era ho Mexia promitido na
Lei, pois que nele se comprirão has profitias es[c]ritas do Mexia. Hos
profetas muitos milagres fezerão, mas nhũm deles nom morreo e
resurgio ao terceiro dia, como Christo; nem algum deles resuscitou
morto de quatro dias da sorte e maneira que Christo resuscitou. Todas
estas cousas erão soficientes argumentos pera hos vossos antepassados
que ho matarão, ho conhecerem. Porem, as profitias estauão escritas
que nom no avião de conhecer, tanta auia de ser a sua ciguidade e
misquindade.

Disto da Ieremias testimunho no capitolo ix, onde diz: "'Leixarei meu
pouo, e sairmeey deles, porque todos são adulteros, e portanto, nom me
conhecerão,' diz ho Senhor." Palauras são do Mexia que dizia pola

a MS mortos

[3] Isa. 35:5f.
[4] Isa. 61:1.
[5] See above, Chap. 9, n. 20.
[6] John 11:17, 43ff.

as the deer, and the tongue of the mute shall no longer be silent.[3] I tell you, gentlemen, that this prophecy was fulfilled during the time of Christ because the sick were cured and made whole by him. Isaiah reaffirms this in chapter 66 in speaking of the Messiah when he says: *He sent me to heal the brokenhearted, to preach the forgiveness of sin, and to give sight to the blind.*[4]

Cease to doubt or debate for all the prophecies written of the Messiah have come to pass and have now been fulfilled. This strengthens the conviction that the Messiah has already come, for all these things happened while Christ was on this earth. During this time, His advent was made known by the occurrence of great miracles, such as Jacob's star[5] which soon appeared to the kings who [then] came to adore Him.

When he was thirty years old, [the Messiah] began to preach [and] to perform great and wondrous miracles which no prophet before Him had ever done in quite the same way. For He cured the blind, deaf, and lame [and] revived Lazarus who lived for a long time after He had been dead for four days.[6] All this could not have been brought about through the art of magic[7] but rather by Him who was the Messiah promised in the Law. He walked on water. Because of His death, the earth trembled. The sun was darkened. On the third day He rose again and was seen in Jerusalem after his death. *Quis vnquam talia audiuit aut vidit?*

These things should certainly convince [*fol. 40r*] and constrain you to believe that Christ was the Messiah promised in the Law for in Him the prophecies written of the Messiah were fulfilled. The prophets worked many miracles but not one of them died and then rose again on the third day as Christ did; nor did one of them bring back to life one who had been dead four days as Christ did. All these things should have been sufficient proof for your ancestors, who killed Christ, to have known Him. However, it was written in the prophecies that they would not recognize Him — so great was their blindness and wretchedness.

Jeremiah proves this in chapter 9, where he says: *I shall leave My people and abandon them, because they are all adulterers and have not known Me, says the Lord.*[8] These are the words of the Messiah Who spoke through the

---

[7] That Jesus performed his miracles through magic was a common theme in Jewish polemical literature. See the medieval tract *Toledot Yeshu* in J. C. Wagenseil, *Tela ignea Satanae* (Altdorf, 1681), pp. 6f. (Hebrew with Latin translation); Morris Goldstein, *Jesus in the Jewish Tradition* (New York, 1950), pp. 149f. (English).

[8] Jer. 9:2f.

boca do profeta, como depois se aconteceo, que na*m* no c[on]hecerão, e portan*t*o, D*e*os vos leixou desemparados, fora da terra vossa propria de Ierusale*m*. Ho mesmo afirma Isaias no capitolo p*r*imeir*o*, onde diz: "Ouui, ceos; e tu, terra, ouue, porq*ue* ho S*e*nhor fala: 'Eu criei filhos e hos aleua*n*tei, e elles me desp*r*ezarão. E ho boi conheceo seu S*e*nh*o*r, e ho asno a ma*n*iadoira; Isrrael, porem, no*m* me conheceo, e ho meu pouo no*m* me entendeo.'"

Esta profitia bem comp*r*ida foi no tempo dos vossos p*r*edecessores que nu*n*qua conhecerão ho Mexia; e ho boi e asno ho conhecerão quando elle naceo. Esto causou aquilo que dixe ho profeta Isaias, capitolo vi°: "Ouuires e no*m* entenderes; e veres e no*m* conheceres. Cegua ho coração deste pouo, e ag*r*aualhe as orelhas, e fechalhe[b] hos olhos pera q*ue* no*m* veião." Isto fez que hos vossos p*r*edecessores no*m* conhecerão ho Mexia, como Ieremias tinha profitizado, dizendo, capito-lo quinto: "'Pecou contra my*m* a casa de Isrrael e a casa de Iuda,' diz ho S*e*nh*o*r. Neguarão ho S*e*nh*o*r, e dixerão: 'No*m* he este, ne*m* ha de vir mal sobre nos; espada e fome no*m* auemos de veer. Hos profetas falarão ao vento, e no*m* teuerão reposta alguma.'"

Tudo isto foi comp*r*ido na paixão do Mexia porq*ue* antão neguarão hos vossos antepassados a Ch*r*is*t*o Mexia, dizendo q*ue* no*m* tinhão senão a Cesar por rrei. Porem, ho Mexia foi visto e andou no mu*n*do, e con-ue*r*sou e falou. Disto Dauid da testemunho no ps*al*mo lxxxiii: "Ho da-dor da Lei dara a benção, e irão de vi*r*tude em vi*r*tude, e ho D*e*os dos deoses sera visto em Sion." Certame*n*te no mo*n*te de Sion q*ue* estaua em Ierusalem, foi elle muitas vezes visto, como Dauid diz no ps*al*mo lxvii: "O D*e*os, vijrão as vossas passadas, e as entradas do meu rei D*e*os."

Isto he ho que cremos, que Ch*r*is*t*o Mexia fez grandes milagres, como dele estaua profitizado, andando neste mu*n*do. Porem, no*m* foi conhi-cido dos vossos p*r*edecessores, posto q*ue* andou neste mu*n*do D*e*os e home*m*. Esta ta*m*bem seia a uossa fee e acertares.

[*fol. 38r*] Capitolo Terciodecimo. Como ho Mexia auia de morrer polo pecado de Adam.

A duodecima propriedade que estaua escrita do Mexia era que elle auia de morrer polo pecado de Adam, a qual foi co*m*municada a Christo, segundo prouaremos polos profetas e polos vossos doutores talmudistas.

b MS *fechalhes*

9 Isa. 1:2f.

mouth of the prophet and said that they would not know Him, as it later happened. Consequently, God left you abandoned, exiled from your own land of Jerusalem. Isaiah also affirms this in the first chapter, where he says: *Hark, O heavens and you, earth, listen, for the Lord speaks: I raised and brought up sons, and they disregarded me. The ox knew his lord, and the ass his trough; Israel however, did not know Me; My people did not consider Me.*[9]

This prophecy was indeed fulfilled during the time of your ancestors who never recognized the Messiah; but the ox and the ass knew Him when He was born. This occasioned what the prophet Isaiah said in chapter 6: *You shall hear but not understand; and you shall look but not see. Blind the heart of this people and make their ears dull, and close their eyes so they will not see.*[10] This resulted in your ancestors' not knowing the Messiah, as Jeremiah prophesied in chapter 5: *The house of Israel and the house of Judah have sinned against Me, says the Lord. They denied the Lord and said: It is not He, nor shall evil befall us, neither shall we see the sword or famine. The prophets have spoken to the wind and have received no answer.*[11]

All this was fulfilled in the passion of the Messiah because it was at that time that your forefathers rejected Christ the Messiah and said that Caesar was their only king. Nevertheless, the Messiah walked about the earth and was seen; He spoke and conversed. David gives proof of this in Psalm 83: *The lawgiver shall bestow the blessing and they shall go from virtue to virtue and the God of gods shall be seen in Zion.*[12] Certainly He was seen many times on Mount Zion which was in Jerusalem, as David says in Psalm 67: *O God, they shall see Your goings and the comings of my king God.*[13]

This is what we believe: that Christ the Messiah worked great miracles as was prophesied He would do on this earth. Nevertheless, He was not recognized by your forefathers even though He walked in this world as God and man. May this also be your faith for then you will have attained certain truth.

[*fol. 38r*] Chapter Thirteen. How the Messiah would die because of the sin of Adam.

The twelfth characteristic of the Messiah was that He would die because of Adam's sin. This was fulfilled in Christ, as we shall prove through your prophets and through your doctors of the Talmud.

---

[10] Isa. 6:9f.
[11] Jer. 5:11ff.
[12] Ps. 84(83):8.
[13] Ps. 68(67):25.

No Gram Grande esta hum texto que diz: "Fez morar diante do paraiso ho cherubim" (Genesis, 3º)[1]. Rrabi Iosua sobre este passo diz assi: "Eu fui com hum anio diante das portas do inferno polo ver todo desdo começo ates ho fim, e não achamos naquela hora tempo pera ho podermos ver porquanto neste dia morrera Rrabam Simon, filho de Guamaliel. E depois, tornando com ho anio, achamos ho Mexia, filho de Dauid. Assi que cheguamos às portas do limbo, e quando hos presos virão a lux do Mexia, alegrarãose grandemente, e loguo começarão a dizer: 'Este he aquele que nos ha de tirar destas tenebras, escuridade, e grandes treuas em has quaes estamos.'"

Este doutor, inspirado polo Spiritu Santo, via esta visão, onde claramente se demostraua que hos padres santos estauão todos no limbo, e que ho Mexia hos auia de liurar e tirar do limbo por sua morte e paixão. Assi ho afirma ho profeta Ose no capitolo xiiiº, onde diz em luguar do Mexia: "Do poder do inferno hos liurarei, e da morte hos redimirei." Dauid disto daa testimunho quando diz no psalmo xxix: "Senhor Deos Padre, tirastes do inferno a minha alma." Isto dixe ho psalmista em pessoa do Mexia porquanto auia de descender ao limbo tirar hos padres santos pola sua morte, como fez. Porque ho corpo fiquou no sepulcro com a diuindade apartado da alma, a qual esteue no limbo acompanhada da diuindade. E, portanto, naqueles tres dias, Christo nom foi homem por amor do apartamento do corpo e da alma. E porquanto a definição do homem nom lhe conuinha naqueles tres dias; por isso, nom foi homem, que he que ho homem he animal racional.

Rrabi Ionatas expondo aquele verso do psalmo xlviij, onde se diz: "Assi como as ouelhas são poostas no inferno, e a morte hos apacentara," diz assi: "E sentai e vede que todos vaam ao limbo iustos, assi hos filhos de Adam, e filhas, como de Noe, rricos e pobres, e serão ridimidos polas iniurias que farão ao Mexia."

Bem afirma este doutor que todos auião de descender ao limbo, e nhũm nom auia de escapar, nem Adam, nem Noe, nem Seth, nem Sem, e Iaphet. Porem, nom pudião de la sair senão polas iniurias que auião de

---

[1] Gen. 3:24.
[2] Honorific title.
[3] Based on a passage ascribed to *BRMD* to Gen. 24:67 cited in *PF*, pp. 605f.; *ACPJ*, 1, 7, pp. 77f. In the version of *PF*: "R. Joshua ben Levi said: I went with the angel Kippod until I came to the gates of Gehenna. I then sent the angel Kippod to measure Gehenna from front to back. But there was not ample time for him to measure for at that time they killed R. Simeon ben Gamaliel. I wanted to go but I could not. Afterwards I went with Kippod the angel and the Messiah the son of David went with me. When those imprisoned in Gehenna saw the light of the Messiah, they began

In the *Grão Grande*, there is a passage that says: *He had made the cherubs dwell before Paradise* (Genesis, chapter 3).[1] Commenting on this passage, Rabbi Joshua says: "I went with an angel before the gates of Hell to see everything from the beginning up to the end, but there was not enough time at that moment for us to do so because on that day Rabban Simeon,[2] son of Gamaliel, died. When we later returned with the angel, we found the Messiah, the son of David. When we arrived at the gates of Limbo, the prisoners saw the light of the Messiah and they greatly rejoiced. They then began to say: "This is He who freed us from the darkness in which we find ourselves.""[3]

This doctor, who was inspired by the Holy Spirit, saw this vision which clearly shows that the holy patriarchs were all in Limbo and that the Messiah would free them by redeeming them through His passion and death. The prophet Hosea affirms this in chapter 13 where he speaks for the Messiah: *I shall free them from the power of Hell and redeem them from death.*[4] David evidences this when he says in Psalm 29: *Lord God the Father, You have brought up my soul from Hell.*[5] The psalmist was speaking for the Messiah Who would descend into Limbo and redeem the holy patriarchs through His death, as He in fact did. For His body remained in the sepulcher, separated from the soul which was in Limbo with His divine aspect. Therefore, for three days Christ was not man because of the separation of His body from His soul. Since the definition of a man could not be applied to Him during those three days (for man is a rational animal) He was consequently not a man.[6]

Rabbi Jonathan, commenting on that verse in Psalm 48, which reads: *They are placed in Hell like sheep, and Death shall lead them to pasture,*[7] says: "See and believe that all go to Limbo as righteous men — the sons and daughters of Adam as well as of Noah, the rich and poor — and all shall be redeemed through that which they afflict upon the Messiah."[8]

This doctor clearly affirms that everyone would descend into Limbo and that no one, not even Adam, Noah, Seth, Shem or Japheth would escape. Their only means of leaving was through injuries inflicted upon

---

(Latin: *fuerunt laetantes*) to receive him. They said: He will take us out of this darkness ..." The name of the angel Kippod, is omitted in *ACPJ* as in Machado.

[4] Hos. 13:14. The Vulgate reading of *De manu mortis liberabo eos, de morte redimam eos* is found in the Latin version of the *Mirror*, fol. 62.

[5] Ps. 30(29):4.

[6] *Summa theologiae*, 3, 52, 3.

[7] Ps. 49(48):15.

[8] This is not a passage from the Targum of Jonathan but a reference to the citation from Midrash Tehillim cited above. See chap. 9, n. 21. Cf. *PF*, p. 608: "Simul in unum descendunt pariter in infernum etiamsi princeps studiorum existat."

fazer ao Mexias, matandoo[a] e dandolhe mil marteiros, como a elle lhe aconteceo. Por onde parece que estes doutores, ou sabião estas cousas inspirados por Deos ou pola arte cabalistica, porque elles mui claramente predixerão aquilo que auia de acontecer ao Mexia, dizendo elles que auia de morrer polo pecado de Adam, e que auia de tirar hos padres do limbo, como elle fez. [fol. 38v] De maneira que ho Mexia, pola sua morte, liurou os iustos que estauão no limbo, assi da Lei de Moises como da Lei da natureza. Hos outros iniustos iazião no inferno pera nunqua serem redimidos.

Isaias no capitolo xli, diz: "Ho meu seruo sera alto e muito exalçado." Rrabi Ionatas sobre este passo diz que ho Mexia sera mais alto exalçado que não Moises, e altiado grandemente. Hos talmudistas grosando estes ditos de Ionatas no Talmud dizem que ho Mexia auia de ser mais alto que Habraam, mais exalçado que Moises, mais altiado que hos anios polas iniurias que deue de sofrer pera tirar hos ençarredos do limbo. Estes doutores nestes dizeres nom errarão mas acertarão porque ho Mexia auia de exceder Habraam e sobrepoiar Moises e preceder hos anios na gloria, como ao presente se faz naquela gloria, da qual vos nunqua gostares senão crerdes que ho Mexia liurou hos padres santos do limbo pola sua morte e paixão, e hos leuou à gloria.

Isaias bem proua no capitolo cinquoenta que ho Mexia auia de padecer mil doestos e mil iniurias polo pecado de Adam, como ia padeceo. Diz, pois, ho profeta em luguar do Mexia: "Ho meu corpo dei àqueles que ho querião ferir; as minhas faces àqueles que me queriam daar bofetadas e esbofetar; a minha face nom tirey diante daqueles que me querião esbofetar e eniuriar." Manifesto he que isto nom aconteceo ao profeta. Isaias dizia loguo isto por outra pessoa — polo Mexia — ho qual bem foi esbofetado dos vossos predecessores, hos quaes ho açoutarão e esbofetarão asaz.[b]

E posto que elles alguma de pequena ignorantia teuerão, mas vos, senhores, nhuma tendes, porque homens doutissimos e grandes letrados, assi no Testamento Novo, como no Velho, vos bradão com suas trombetas e bozinas, que vos conuertaes. Cada dia hos tendes nessa corte. La

a MS *mantandoo*   b +*poosto que neste tempo moderno nos aiuntamentos illictos e ... tos e nas vossas sinaguogas ho açoutãa asaz e ... lendo ainda Moises, porque quantas vezes ho leedes, tantas vezes ho açoutaes e ... mais que hos vossos passados; por* exp.

[9] Correct reference is Isa. 52:13.
[10] This text, not in the Targum, is ascribed to Genesis Rabbah to 28:10 in *PF* (pp. 389, 413, 428, 637, 769) although it is lacking in our editions. See, however, Midrash Tanḥuma, Toledot, 14; *Comm.* of Joseph Kara to Isaiah *ad loc.*, Moses ben Naḥman, *Disputation* in O. S. Rankin, *Jewish*

the Messiah which would torment and kill Him, as did (indeed) happen. It may be assumed that these doctors knew of these things either through divine inspiration or through the kabbalistic art, because they very clearly predicted what would happen to the Messiah: that He would die because of Adam's transgression and that He would redeem the patriarchs from Limbo, as He did. [*fol. 38v*] So that the Messiah, through His death, redeemed the righteous — both those under the law of Moses and those under natural law — from Limbo. The others, the sinners, remained in Hell and shall never be redeemed.

In chapter 41, Isaiah says: *My servant shall be elevated and exalted.*[9] Rabbi Jonathan comments on this and says that the Messiah shall be more highly exalted than Moses and greatly elevated.[10] The talmudists who glossed these words of Jonathan in the Talmud say that the Messiah would be higher than Abraham, more exalted than Moses, and more elevated than the angels because of the afflictions He would suffer in redeeming those confined in Limbo. These doctors did not err in their thinking but were correct, for the Messiah would surpass Abraham and be greater than Moses and take precedence over the angels in glory as is the case now; a glory which you will never enjoy unless you believe that the Messiah freed the holy patriarchs from Limbo through His passion and death, and then led them to glory.

In chapter fifty, Isaiah rightly proves that the Messiah would suffer a thousand insults and a thousand injuries through Adam's sin, as He did. The prophet speaks for the Messiah and says: *I gave my body to those who would wound me; my cheeks to those who would strike me and slap me in the face for I did not turn away from those who would hit me or insult me.*[11] It is clear of course that this did not happen to the prophet. Rather, Isaiah was speaking for some one else — for the Messiah — Who was struck repeatedly by your forefathers who severely whipped Him and struck Him.[12]

These men were rather ignorant; but you, gentlemen, are not, because learned men well versed in the New as well as the Old Testament call to you with their trumpets and horns to convert. They are at your disposal at Court every day: Vila Franca, Soares, Padilha,

---

Religious Polemic (Edinburgh, 1958), p. 193. It is cited in *ACPJ*, 1, 9, p. 96 as well. From *PF*: "My servant, the Messiah, shall prosper, he shall be exalted, and be great, and grow very mighty." *ACPJ* reads: "Supra quem textum sic habetur in Talmuth, Exaltabitur plus quam Abraham, eleuabitur plusquam Moyses, & sublimis erit plusquam angeli ..."

[11] Isa. 50:6.

[12] MS reads "Since in these modern times they whip Him heavily at illegal meetings and in your synagogues ... you still read Moses, for the more you read Moses, the more you whip Him ... even more than your ancestors ..." expunged. See note *b*.

tendes Vilafranca, Soaires, Padilha, Frias, Hulmedo, Santiaguo; Aluaro Guomez, doutor de Paris, Rromeiro, doutor de Paris. Estes buscai, com estes confiri; grandes medicos são. Estes vos sangrarão e vos tirarão estes errores nos quaes andaes enuoltos. Lançai essa eruilhaca, esse ioio fora de vos; fazeis triguo limpo pera que possamos comer do vosso pão e gostar da vossa vida, da qual ya todos guostão, como tenho sabido. Praza a Deos que seya pera seruiço de Deos e pera vossa saluação e nossa edificação.

[*fol. 39r*] Isaias no capitolo liij° euidentemente, e por hum estilo mui claro, demostra alguma cousa daquilo que auia de acontecer ao Mexia por amor do pecado de Adam, ho que do profeta em nhuma maneira se pode entender, nem taes cousas iamais lhe acontecerão. Porque se assi fora, nos anaes dos vossos predecessores disso se fezera alguma menção. Polo qual, eu creo que grande he ho vosso erro e a vossa ignorantia. Mas eu tenho pera mym que he grande obstinação e incredulidade,[c] e perdoaime que falo com colera.[c]

Hora, veiamos ho que diz ho profeta do Mexia. Verdadeiramente elle comsiguo trouxe todas as nossas infirmidades, e todas as nossas doores leuou às costas. Nos cuidauamos que era hum leproso, e que era desprezado do Senhor, e leixado d'elle; mas, porem, elle foi chaguado polos nossos pecados e vicios e maldades. Nom quero aqui mais poor da profitia pera que vos mesmos ha veiaes no vosso hebraico, a qual todo he do Mexia. Onde se conclude que por amor do pecado de Adam, Christo assi morreo pera que fosse tirar aqueles padres santos que estauão no limbo por amor do pecado de Adam que fechou ho paraiso, o qual ho Mexia abrio depois da sua morte. Por onde parece que ho pecado de Adam, segundo a uontade diuina que escolheo este modo de redemir a geração humanal, nom podia ser redimido senão pola morte e paixão do Mexia.

Esta he a redenção que todos esperauam e bradauão, dizendo: "Senhor, vemnos redimir e tirar deste catiueiro."[d] Como dixe Iacob (Genesis xlix), estando ia pera morte: "A tua saluação, Senhor, espero eu." Manifesto he que Iacob nom esperaua saluação do corpo, porque elle bem sabia que auia de morer; mas esperaua a redenção da alma, a qual bem sabia que nom a pudia fazer senão pola morte do Mexia.

Nas grossas do profeta Daniel e no Gram Grande sobre este passo de

---

c-c int.   d MS *catiuerey*

[13] On these, see Introduction.
[14] Isaiah 53, one of the "suffering servant" passages, was taken in Christian tradition to refer to

Frias, Hulmedo, Santiago, and Alvaro Gomes and Romeiro, the latter two doctors of Paris.[13] Seek them out and confer with them; they are great physicians. They will bleed you and remove the errors in which you are enveloped. Cast away the vetch and weeds; produce clean wheat so that we can eat your bread and relish your life which, as I have known, all others now savor. May it please God that it be for His service, for your salvation, and for our edification.

[*fol. 39r*] In chapter 53 Isaiah demonstrates in a clear and lucid style something of what would happen to the Messiah because of Adam's sin. This cannot in any way be interpreted as referring to the prophet himself for never did such things befall him.[14] If they had, the records of your forefathers would have made some mention of them. Consequently, I believe the error and ignorance into which you have fallen are very great indeed. I see this as stubborn obstinacy, though I ask your pardon for speaking, as I do, with some anger.[15]

Now let us see what the prophet actually says about the Messiah. He truly brought with Him all our infirmities and carried on His back all our sorrows. We believe that He was a leper and that He was scorned and abandoned by the Lord; yet, He was also wounded through our sins, vices, and evils. I prefer not discussing this prophecy any further so that you yourselves can consult the rest in your Hebrew which deals in its entirety with the Messiah. It follows then that, because of Adam's sin, Christ died so that he could free the holy patriarchs who were in Limbo because of Adam's transgression, which had closed Paradise to them but which would again be open after the Messiah's death. Thus it seems that the sin of Adam, could not be expiated except through the passion and death of the Messiah, according to the divine will which chose this mode of redeeming the human race.

This is the redemption for which all were hoping and calling. "Lord," they said, "come and free us from this bondage." It is as Jacob said (Genesis, 49), as he was about to die: *I wait for Your salvation, Lord.*[16] It is obvious that Jacob was not waiting for the salvation of his body because he knew very well that he would die; but he was waiting for the redemption of his soul which he knew all too well could not be accomplished except through the death of the Messiah.

In the glosses on the prophet Daniel and in the *Grão Grande,* there are

the passion and death of Christ. On Jewish reactions to this interpretation, see Adolf Neubauer and Samuel Driver, *The Fifty-third Chapter of Isaiah According to the Jewish Interpreters,* 2 vols. (Oxford, 1877).

[15] "Though ... anger" interlinear addition. See note *c.*

[16] Gen. 49:18.

Daniel, que diz: "E a lux com elle mora" (capitolo ijº), se diz isto que se segue, que he pera notar: "Que quer dizer: 'E a luz com elle mora'?" Rrabi Salamão responde, dizendo: "Esta he a lux do Mexia." Vem a grosa e diz: "Mostrounos Deos que olhou pera ho Mexia, e pera sua geração, e pera lux que estaua debaixo da cadeira da sua gloria, e pera Satanas, ho qual determinaua de perder a geração do Mexia." Diz mais no luguar prealeguado, que perguntou ho diabo, dizendo: "Senhor do mundo, esta lux que esta escondida debaixo da cadeira da gloria, pera quem he?" Rrespondeo Deos, dizendo: "He pera ho Mexia e pera sua geração." Dixe ho diabo: "Senhor, leixame destruir este poder deste Mexia e da sua geração." [fol. 39v] Ho Mexia, ouuindo isto, dixe: "Senhor padre, leixaime, que eu vencerei e quebrantarei ho poder deste Sathanas, e ho meterei em catiueiro, e em carceres perpetuos." Deos eterno, ouuindo estas cousas e esforço do Mexia, lhe dixe: "Meu iusto es, e meu amado e quirido; e, portanto, sabe que hos pecados dos humanos e mortaes te hão de meter em muita aguonia e trabalho e paixão porque hos teus olhos nom verão a lux; as tuas orelhas ouuirão doestos e iniurias grandes; hos teus narizes cheirarão grandes fedores; tua boca se fartara d'amargura; a tua linguoa se apeguara ao paladar, que falar nom poderas; ho couro da tua carne se peguara aos hossos; ho teu corpo se quebrantara com açoutes." Isto acabado, dixe Deos Padre ao Mexia: "A tua vontade esta prestes pera sofrer estas paixões e angustias? E senão quiseres isto sofrer, sabe que ey loguo de destruir ho mundo, e ho lançarei fora de toda a prosperidade em que elle esta." Rrespondeo ho Mexia, diz ndo: "Senhor, som muito contente e ledo de sofrer todas estas paixões pola geração humanal, com condição que resusci[te]stes e viuifiques hos mortos de Adam e aqueles, hos quaes engulirão hos liões; e aqueles que se alaguarão no maar, saluares; e hos que morrerão nos ventres de suas mãaes, e hos que esteuerão no Vosso pensamento, saluares, que nacerão depois. Estas são as cousas que Vos peço, as quaes, se me quiserdes conceder, prestes estou pera sofrer todas as paixões e iniurias por amor da geração humanal." Rrespondeo Deos, dizendolhe: "Eu te outorguo tudo isto que me pidiste." Loguo naquela hora ho Mexia tomou na sua vontade de sofrer, por amor do pecado de Adam, todas [as] paixões e iniurias.

---

[17] Dan. 2:22.

[18] Based on a passage ascribed to BRMD to Gen. 1:1 cited in PF, pp. 416f. (cf. pp. 642, 852) and ACPJ, 1, 7, pp. 78ff. Cf. Pesiḳta Rabbati 36:1, trans. Braude, [New Haven, 1968], 2: 677ff. According to PF: "In the beginning God created (Gen. 1:1)… It is written, Light is sown for the righteous (Ps. 97:11). R. Abba said: Light dwells with Him (Dan. 2:22). This refers to the light of the Messiah. It is

commentaries on the verse in Daniel, chapter 2 which reads: *And the light dwells with him.*[17] The question asked — "What does *and the light dwells with him* mean?" — is worthy of note. Rabbi Solomon answers that "this is the light of the Messiah." The gloss says: "We were shown that God beheld the Messiah and his generation and the light that was under the throne of glory and Satan who was determined to destroy the whole human race." We read further in this work that the devil asked: "Lord of the world, for whom is this light that is hidden under the throne of glory?" God answered saying "It is for the Messiah and his generation." Then the devil said: "Lord, let me destroy the power of this Messiah and his generation." [*fol. 39v*] When the Messiah heard this he said: "Father, let me overcome and break the power of this Satan, for I shall seize him and imprison him forever." God the Eternal, on hearing these things and the courage of the Messiah, said to him: "You are My righteous one; My beloved and cherished one. Know, therefore, that human, mortal sins will be the cause of much pain, travail, and suffering for you, because your eyes shall not see the light; your ears shall hear harsh offenses and insults; your nostrils shall breathe strong stenches; your mouth shall be filled with bitterness; your tongue shall stick to your palate and you shall not be able to speak; your flesh shall cling to your bones; your body shall be broken with lashings." After having said that this would befall him, God the Father then asked the Messiah "Is your will ready to suffer this torture and anguish? If not, know that I shall then destroy the world, divesting it of the prosperity in which it now finds itself." The Messiah answered saying: "Lord, I am pleased and glad to undergo these sufferings for the human race, on the condition that You resurrect and revive those who died because of Adam and those devoured by lions; I ask that You save those engulfed by the sea and children who were stillborn and those who were conceived by You to be born later. If You grant these things that I ask of You, I am ready to endure all torments and abuses for the sake of mankind." God answered him saying: "I shall grant all that you asked." Immediately afterwards the Messiah took it upon himself to bear all manner of suffering and abuse.[18]

---

also said: *For with You is the fountain of life; in Your light do we see light* (Ps. 36:10). This is the light of the Messiah. This teaches that the Holy One, blessed be He, contemplated the King Messiah and put him away under His throne of glory. Satan said to the Holy One, blessed be He: Lord of the world, for whom is this light which is hidden under Your throne of glory put away? He said to him: The Messiah and his generation. He said to him: Lord of the world, give me leave and I shall bring charges against him and his generations. The Holy One, blessed be He, said to him: You will not prevail. He said to him: Lord of the world, give me leave and I shall prevail. [God] ... said to him:

Diguouos que estes dizeres e estas grossas na*m* saie*m* muito fora da rrezão. E parece que estes home*n*s souberão estas cousas por algu*m*a reuelação ou inspiração, ou forão ensinados pola arte cabalistica, porque as mais cousas que acima se dixerão, acontecerão ao Mexia. E, portanto, estas cousas no*m* são pera se desp*r*ezare*m*. Por onde me parece q*ue* vos outros tendes grandes segredos acerqua do Mexia; pore*m*, no*m* nos queres discubrir pera q*ue* por elles no*m* seiaes conuin-cidos.

Vos fares ho que milhor vos parece. Porem, esta he a nossa fee — q*ue* ho Mexia veo padecer neste mu*n*do pera tirar hos padres santos que estauão no limbo — e esta fee seya a uossa. Ame*n*.

[*fol. 41r*] Capitolo Quartodecimo. Como ho Mexia auia de resurgir, e subir aos ceos.

A duodecima propriedade que estaua escrita do Mexia era que elle auia de resurgir, e depois, subir aos ceos, a qual foi co*m*municada a Chr*i*sto, segundo prouaremos polos profetas e polos vossos doutores talmudistas.

Ho profeta Ose no te*r*ceiro capitolo daa fee desta resurreição do Mexia, quando diz: "Vinde e tornemos a D*eo*s, porque elle nos firio e sarou, e nos tomou e amezinhounos e viuificarnosha depois de dous dias, e no terceiro dia nos suscitara e viueremos diante da sua pre-sença." Ex aqui como Ose p*r*edixe esta resurreição que auia de ser ao terceiro dia, no qual ho Mexia auia de resurgir.

E assi aconteceo a Chr*i*sto, que ao te*r*ceiro dia elle resurgio contando pa*r*te do dia por todo dia, segundo a figura senedoches. E assi iouue parte da sesta feira, toma*n*doa por todo dia e todo ho sabbado inteiro e parte do domi*n*guo, contandoo po*r* todo dia. Porem, no*m* iouue no sepulcro senão por espaço de corenta horas.

Parece logu*o* que Chr*i*sto foi ho Mexia pois que aquilo que dele estaua escrito, lhe foi communicado.

Esta resurreição confirmasse no Grão Grande no capitolo xxiij sobre

If this is your intention, I would as soon cause Satan to perish from this world but I will not allow one soul from that generation to perish. [God] ... began to recount: My righteous Messiah, the sins of those that have been put away with you will put you under a heavy yoke. Your eyes will not see light; your ears will hear abuse from the nations of the world; your nose will smell stench; your mouth will taste bitterness and your tongue will cleave to your palate; your skin will hang on your bones and your breath will grow weary and heavy. If you wish these things, it is well; if not, I banish them forthwith. He said to Him: Lord of the world, I am content to accept those sufferings on the condition that You revive in my time all those that died from Adam to the present. Indeed, not only them must You save but also all those who were devoured by wolves and lions, all those

I tell you that the words of these glosses do not transcend the bounds of reason. It seems that these men knew these things through some revelation or inspiration, or were instructed in the art of the kabbalah, for most of the things happened to the Messiah and thus are not to be disregarded. It seems to me then that you possess great secrets concerning the Messiah. However, you do not wish to divulge them, lest you become convinced [of them].

You will no doubt do what seems best for you. Nevertheless, this is our faith — that the Messiah came to this world to suffer so that He could free the holy Patriarchs from Limbo. May this also be your faith. Amen.

[*fol. 41r*] Chapter Fourteen. How the Messiah would be resurrected and ascend into heaven.

The twelfth[1] characteristic written of the Messiah was that He was to be resurrected and then ascend into heaven. This was fulfilled in Christ, as we shall prove through the prophets and through your talmudists.

In the third[2] chapter of Hosea there is an affirmation of this resurrection when the prophet says: *Come, and let us return to God, because He has wounded us and healed us. He took us and treated us and after two days He shall revive us and on the third day He shall raise us up and we shall live in His presence.*[3] This is Hosea's prediction of the resurrection which would take place on the third day when the Messiah would be resurrected.

Thus did Christ return on the third day, counting part of a day as a whole day, as in the [rhetorical] figure of synecdoche.[4] Thus, He remained in the sepulcher part of Friday — counting it a whole day — all of Saturday, and part of Sunday, also taken as a whole day. However, he lay there in all no more than forty hours.

It seems, therefore, that Christ was the Messiah, for that written about the latter was fulfilled in the former.

This resurrection is confirmed in the *Grão Grande* in chapter 23, which

---

who drowned in waters and rivers, all those who were aborted and even those whom You thought would be created and who were not created ... [God] said: Yes. The Messiah immediately accepted all these sufferings out of love, as it is said, *He was oppressed and he was afflicted* (Isa. 53:7)."

[1] The thirteenth through the sixteenth characteristics are numbered as the twelfth through the fifteenth respectively. The seventeenth through the twentieth are correctly numbered.

[2] Correctly: "sixth."

[3] Hos. 6:1ff.

[4] *I.e., synecdoche,* the figure *pars pro toto.* Modern Portuguese is *sinedoque.* Cf. Augustine, *De Doctrina Christiana,* 3:35.

ho texto do Genesis no capitolo xxij, onde se diz que Habraam ao terceiro dia aleuantou hos olhos e vio ho luguar onde auia de sacrificar a Isaac no monte Moria. Vem Rrabi Moises e diz sobre este passo: "Muitas trindades hahi na Lei, e huma he a resurreição do Mexia." Isto dixe este vosso doutor porquanto sabia que ho Mexia auia de rresurgir ao terceiro dia, como Rrabi Ionatas diz sobre ho capitolo de Ose terceiro, sobre aquele passo, onde diz: "No terceiro dia nos suscitara." Este he ho Mexia, ho qual resurgindo, muitos suscitara, como suscitou. Porque todos aqueles padres santos que iazião sepultados em Ebron, como era Adam, Eua, Habraam, Isaac, Iacobo, e outros muitos, resurgirão com elle. E, portanto, aqueles padres santos se mandauão lançar na Terra da Promissão, porque inspirados por Deos, sabião que ho Mexia auia de ser sepultado naquela terra, e que auia de resurgir. Porem, Ioseph, que morreo no Egito, rrogou a seus irmãos, segundo se contem no Genesis no capitolo cinquoenta, que quando Deos hos visitasse, que leuasse ha sua ossada pera Terra da Promissão, sabendo per diuinal inspiração que ho Mexia auia de resurgir naquela terra pera que elle resurgisse.

[*fol. 41v*] No Grão Grande esta hum texto que diz que Habraam tomou Isaac e ho leuou à tenda de Sarra pera que morasse com ella. Diz Rrabi Moises sobre este passo: "Este he ho Mexia, que por amor de Adam, morara no limbo, e ao terceiro dia, viuera." Esto quer dizer que ho Mexia auia de hir ao limbo, e depois, que auia de resurgir. E assi a Christo aconteceo, que elle esteue no limbo, e ao terceiro dia resurgio, comprindo as profitias que dele estauão escritas.

Ia temos prouado como ho Mexia auia de resurgir ao terceiro dia, como resurgia Christo. Aguora veiamos como auia de subir aos ceos e auia de estar à destra de Deos Padre, como aguora este no ceo impirio.

Dauid disto daa euidente testimunho no psalmo cix, onde diz: "Dixe ho Senhor ao meu Senhor: 'Asentate à minha destra.'" Palauras são de Deos Padre, ditas ao Mexia. Assi ho confirma Rrabi Ioda expondo este passo, e dizendo: "Este he ho rei Mexia, ho qual se asentara à destra de

---

[5] See Gen. 22:4.

[6] Based on the passage from Genesis Rabbah cited in Chap. 7, n. 72. "Embellished" by Martini, it was further distorted in *ACPJ* (1, 8, p. 82) to yield the following which is close to Machado: "Et Rabbi Moyses praedicator in Genes. magno super id (Gen. 22) dicit Autem die tertio. Elevatis oculis, videbat locum procul. Dixit, Multae sunt in sacra scriptura dierum trinitates, quarum una est resurrectio Messiae." Cf. *FF*, fol. 62va (*multe trinitates Dei*); *DE*, p. 90.

[7] Source unidentified.

[8] The burial of Adam in Hebron is commonly cited in Christian tradition on the basis of Jos. 14:15. See *DTC*, 1:381; *HS*, Gen. 59, *PL*, 198:1106. For Abraham, Isaac and Jacob, see Gen. 23:9, 25:9f., 49:30.

comments on a verse in chapter 22 of Genesis. It says that on the third day Abraham raised up his eyes and saw the place where he would sacrifice Isaac on Mount Moriah.[5] The comment of Rabbi Moses on this verse is that "there are many trinities in the Law and one is the resurrection of the Messiah."[6] Your doctor said this since he knew that the Messiah would rise on the third day. Thus did Rabbi Jonathan interpret that verse in chapter three of Hosea which reads: *On the third day He shall raise us up*.[7] This is the Messiah who would raise up many others as He rose Himself. For all the holy Patriarchs who lay buried in Hebron — Adam, Eve, Abraham, Isaac, Jacob[8] — and many others rose with Him. Therefore, the holy Patriarchs were domiciled in the Promised Land because they knew through divine inspiration that the Messiah would be buried in that land and that He would be resurrected. Therefore, according to Genesis, chapter fifty, Joseph, who died in Egypt, pleaded with his brothers that at the time of God's visitation they carry his bones to the Promised Land[9] for he knew through divine inspiration that the Messiah would rise up so that he too could be resurrected.

[*fol. 41v*] In the *Grão Grande,* there is a passage that says that Abraham took Isaac to Sarah's tent so that he could live with her.[10] Rabbi Moses comments on this passage: "This is the Messiah who had dwelled in Limbo on account of Adam but had come alive on the third day."[11] This means that the Messiah would go to Limbo and would subsequently rise up. This happened to Christ Who was in Limbo and Who rose on the third day, fulfilling the prophecies that were written of Him.

Now that we have proved how the Messiah would be resurrected on the third day as Christ was, let us see how He would ascend into heaven and be at the right hand of God the Father, as He is now in the highest heavens.

David gives clear testimony of this in Psalm 109, where he says: *The Lord said to my Lord: Sit at My right hand*.[12] These are the words God the Father said to the Messiah. Rabbi Judah confirms this in his commentary on this verse: "This is the king Messiah who will sit at the right hand of God." The Chaldean version supports this: "The Lord says to

---

[9] See Gen. 50:23f.

[10] Gen. 24:67, according to which Isaac brought Rebekah to Sarah's tent.

[11] The passage ascribed to *BRMD* to Gen. 24:67 (*PF*, pp. 535f., 862) has little to do with the above. *PF* reads: "The King Messiah was with the generation of the wicked and was determined to seek mercy for Israel and to fast and afflict himself for them, as it is said, *He was wounded for our transgressions...* (Isa. 53:5)."

[12] Ps. 110(109):1.

Deos." Isto autoriza ho caldeu, que diz: "Ho Senhor diz a seu Verbo: 'Habraam estara asentado à parte esquerda, e ho Mexia, à direita.'"

Bem se demostra por estes dizeres destes doutores vossos que ho Mexia se auia de asentar à destra de Deos, como aguora esta. Esta foi a entenção de Dauid no psalmo ia acima aleguado, ho qual Dauid todo compos do Mexia, posto que alguns vossos doutores afirmem que Dauid nom fez este psalmo, mas que foi Eleazer, ho procurador da casa e familia de Habraam, em seu louuor porquanto vencera aqueles cinquo rreis, liurando a Loth, seu sobrinho, do catiueiro deles quando vierão contra Guomorra e Sodoma, segundo se contem no Genesis no capitolo xiiij°. Porem, tudo isto he falso porque Dauid, no psalmo aleguado, diz: "Tu es sacerdos." Hora, dizeime vos a mym, onde achastes vos que Habraam fosse sacerdote, segundo a ordem de Melchesedech, como foi ho Mexia? Por tal, nom tenhaes debate nem duuida, porque do Mexia se entende ho psalmo, no qual manifestamente se demostra que ho Mexia auia de estar à destra de Deos Padre, como aguora esta Christo, verdadeiro Mexia promitido na Lei. Isto se confirma no Talmud, onde se alegua aquilo de Daniel no capitolo vii°, onde se diz: "Cadeiras são postas," e depois, diz: "Cadeira he posta." Rrabi Aquiba sobre este passo diz: "Estes textos nom são contrairos posto que diguão 'cadeiras' em plural, e 'cadeira' em singular, porque huma cadeira he pera Deos, e outra pera Dauid." Diz Rrabi Salamão: "Este Dauid he ho Mexia que estara à destra de Deos." Bem prouão estes doutores que ho Mexia auia de estar à destra de Deos Padre.

Assi esta Christo Mexia, ao qual isto que estaua profitizado do Mexia — que auia de resurgir e estar à destra de Deos — foi comunicado, como nos teemos por fee e crença verdadeira, e praza a Deos que assi ho creaes vos. Amen.

[fol. 42r] Capitolo Quintodecimo. Como todos hos sacrifitios cessarão pola morte do Mexia, e socedeo ho sacramento do altar.

A terciadecima propriedade que estaua escrita do Mexia era que pela

---

13 This passage, with a reference to Midrash Tehillim 18:29 (ed. Buber, p. 157; Braude, 1:261; cited in PF, pp. 537, 882; ACPJ, 1, 8, p. 2; FF, fol. 62r) and to the Targum appears to be a confusion of a text similar to ACPJ: "Dixit Rabbi Ioda in nomine Rabbi Hannae, futurum est quod deus Messiam sedere faciat ad dexteram suam, sicut scriptum est, Dixit dominus domino meo, sede a dextris meis. Et in Caldaica translatione sic habetur. Dixit Dominus Verbo suo." The passages from Midrash Tehillim and the Targum are similarly juxtaposed in ACPJ and PF. The passage from the Targum is no longer extant in our editions.

14 See below, n. 18.

15 ACPJ, ibid. from Midrash Tehillim 110:1ff. (ed. Buber, pp. 465ff.; ed. Braude, 2:205ff.). See also Jerome, Comm. in Matt. 22:41ff., CC, 77:209ff. (PL, 26:171ff.).

His Word: Abraham will be seated on the left, and the Messiah on the right."[13]

As you can see from all this, your doctors clearly show that the Messiah would sit at the right hand of God as He now does. This was David's intention in the aforementioned psalm which he composed about the Messiah. Some of the doctors assert, however, that David was not the author of this psalm.[14] Rather, it was written by Eleazar, the steward of the house and family of Abraham, in praise of Abraham's conquering the five kings and freeing his nephew Lot whom they captured when they waged war against Sodom and Gomorrah, as stated in Genesis, chapter 14.[15] Nevertheless, this is not true because in the same psalm David says: *You are a priest*.[16] Now, tell me, where have you found that Abraham was a priest after the order of Melchizedek,[17] as was the Messiah?[18] For this reason neither debate this nor be in doubt for this psalm refers to the Messiah and distinctly shows that he would be at the right hand of God the Father as is Christ,[19] the true Messiah as promised in the Law. This is confirmed in the Talmud where the words *thrones were placed* and *throne was placed* are cited from Daniel, chapter 7.[20] Regarding this, Rabbi Akiba says: "These passages are not contradictory even though 'thrones' is in the plural and 'throne' in the singular, for one throne is for God and the other for David." Rabbi Solomon adds: "This David is the Messiah who will be at the right hand of God."[21] These doctors [also] prove that the Messiah would be at the right hand of God the Father.

This then is Christ the Messiah in Whom was fulfilled that which was prophesied: that He would arise and be at the right hand of God. This we truly believe and attest. May it please God, that you believe as well. Amen.

[*fol. 42r*] Chapter Fifteen. How after the death of the Messiah all the sacrifices came to an end to be succeeded by the sacrament of the altar.

The thirteenth characteristic written of the Messiah was that through

[16] Ps. 110(109):4.

[17] According to the continuation of the above verse "in aeternum secundum ordinem Melchisedech."

[18] See chap. 7, n. 15. Melchizedek was first mentioned as a type of Christ in Heb. 6:20. Ps. 110:9 was consequently interpreted in a similar vein, i.e., with reference to Christ. See *Post.*, 3, EEviiir.

[19] Cf. 1 Pet. 3:21f.

[20] Dan. 7:9.

[21] Based on B.T. Ḥagigah 14a (cf. B.T. Sanhedrin 38b), cited in *PF*, p. 345; *ACPJ*, 1, 8, pp. 82f.; *FF*, fol. 62vb. "One passage says: *His throne was fiery flames* [Dan. 7:9]; and another passage says: *Till thrones were placed,* and *One that was ancient of days did sit* (Dan. 7:9f.) — There is no contradiction: one [throne] for Him, and one for David: this is the view of R. Akiba" (Sonc., p. 83; cf. notes *ad loc.*).

sua vinda, todolos sacrifitios vossos auião de cessar, e auia de soceder
ho sacrifitio do altar, segundo prouaremos polos profetas e polos talmudistas.

Na vossa Lei auia tres generos de preceitos: moraes, iudiciaes,
ceremoniaes. Hos preceitos moraes erão hos dez Mandamentos da Lei
da natureza, a qual he que nom faças à outrem ho que nom querias que
te fezessem. Estes dez Mandamentos forão renouados no monte Sinay e
dados aos vossos antepassados, nam ia nouamente instituidos, mas
repitidos (Exodi xx). E porquanto estes preceitos erão da Lei da
natureza, a qual precedeo a Lei de Moises, pola vinda do Mexia nom
cessarão, nem cessarão ates o fim do mundo. E forão declarados na
nossa Lei polo Mexia porquanto hos vossos predecessores lhes dauão
algum intendimento falso, dizendo que Deos nom difindia ho coração,[a]
mas somentes a mão acerqua do preceito nono, onde se diz: "Non con-
cupi[s]ces vxorem."

Auia hi outros preceitos chamados iudiciaes, hos quaes pertencião aos
iuizes e regedores e aos autos iudiciaes, como era que quem quebraua
hum olho a seu proximo, outro lhe quebrauão; e quem furtaua huma
ouelha, paguaua duas. E destes preceitos todo ho Exodo esta cheo.
Estes cessarão pola morte do Mexia, e dali por diante, nom teuerão
mais viguor nem forças.

Auia hi outros preceitos chamados ceremoniaes que pertencião aos
sacerdotes e às cousas do Templo, como erão as benções e vestiduras
dos sacerdotes, e hos sacrifitios, e oblações que ofericião. Todo ho
Leuitico destas cirimonias esta cheo, e todas cessarão pola morte do
Mexia porquanto todas estas cirimonias nom sinificauão outra cousa
senão a vinda do Mexia. E, portanto, falsamente hos guardaes e deles
vsaes e pequaes grauemente, sinificando a uinda do Mexia vindoira,
onde elle ia veo, e falso entendimento lhe daes. Porem, cremos que ya
disto vos cauidaes.

Isaias daa testimunho euidente de como todos estes preceitos, assi
iudiciaes como cerimoniaes, auião de cessar em algum tempo pola
vinda do Mexia, onde elle diz assi no capitolo primeiro: "Nom me
ofereças mais sacrifitio em balde, porque ho vosso encenso me he
abominação. As vossas neomenias ou cantiguas, hos vossos sabbados, as

---

a MS *caração*

[1] Lev. 19:18. The negative formulation of the "golden rule" as stated by Hillel, "What is hateful
to you, do not to another," is found in B.T. Shabbat 31a.
[2] Deut. 5:21, cf. Exod. 20:17. This section appears to follow *Post.* to Exod. 20:17, 1, Nviiiv: "Et
ad hoc facit apparentia litterae quia sub eodem versu utraque concupiscentia prohibetur; non
tamen variatur sententia, ut sit unum sive duo praecepta quantum ad intellectum nostrum sed

His coming, all your sacrifices would cease, to be superseded by the sacrifice of the altar, as we shall prove through the prophets and the talmudists.

In your Law, there were three kinds of precepts: moral, judicial, ceremonial. The moral precepts were the Ten Commandments of the law of nature, which is "Do not do to others what you would not like them to do to you."[1] These Ten Commandments were given to your forefathers on Mount Sinai, not as a new promulgation but as a restatement (Exodus 20). Since these precepts came under the law of nature, which preceded the Law of Moses, they did not cease to be valid with the coming of the Messiah, but will be in force until the end of the world. They were stated by the Messiah in our Law since your predecessors interpreted them falsely: In reference to the ninth commandment, *Non concupi<s>ces vxorem,* they said that God did not prohibit [thought of] the heart but only [deeds of] the hand.[2]

The judicial precepts came under the jurisdiction of the judges and governors, and judicial processes. Such was that which states that whoever injured the eye of his neighbor shall suffer in a like manner;[3] or whoever stole a sheep should be fined two.[4] All of Exodus is filled with these precepts. After the death of the Messiah, these ceased to have any validity or force.

The ceremonial precepts pertained to the priests and matters relating to the Temple, such as the benedictions and the vestments of the priests and the sacrifices and oblations they offered. All of Leviticus is full of these ceremonies that ceased with the death of the Messiah since they merely adumbrated His coming. For this reason you are committing a grave sin by deceitfully keeping and observing them as symbolizing the future coming of the Messiah when He has already come. You misinterpret this and are most careful to do so.

Isaiah clearly attests how all these precepts — judicial as well as ceremonial — would at some time come to an end through the advent of the Messiah, for in the first chapter he says: *Offer Me no more sacrifices in vain, because your incense is an abomination to Me. Your new moons or songs, your Sabbaths, your feasts, at no time shall I endure.*[5] I tell you that this has

---

variatur multum in hoc sive sit unum sive duo praecepta intellectus hebreorum quia dicunt quod per hoc non prohibetur concupiscentia nisi aliqualiter prorumpat in actus exteriores; sicut est cum ex concupiscentia uxoris aliene aliquis movetur ad tangendum eam impudice vel sollicitandum eam verbis vel muneribus et secundum hoc dixerunt aliqui doctores nostri quod lex vetus prohibebat manum et non animum ..." Cf. *FF*, fol. 51*va.*

[3] Exod. 21:24, cf. Lev. 24:20.
[4] Exod. 22:1 where the penalty for stealing sheep is four for every one stolen.
[5] Isa 1:13. Correctly: "I could *not* sustain you."

vossas festas en algum tempo nom sofrerei." Diguouos que ia isto he comprido, porque pola morte do Mexia, loguo lhe auorrecerão.

[fol. 42v] Dizeime, pois, pera que iudaizaes? Pera que guardaes ho sabbado e as festas da Lei de Moises? Nom veedes que todas estas cousas ia auorrecem a Deos? Nom nas quer, nem lhe aprazem. E pera confirmação disto, olhai ho que diz ho profeta Isaias no capitolo i°: "As vossas companhas e hos vossos aiuntamentos são muyto maos. As vossas kallendas, as vossas festas, auorreceo a minha alma. Sãome odiosas todas estas cousas. Sostenteiuos e trabalhei comvosco, e aguora se estenderdes as mãos, tirarei hos meus olhos de vos outros; e quando multiplicardes a oração, nom vos ouuirei."

O senhores, que queres dizer a isto? Nom vedes que tudo isto he comprido? Porque se estas cousas ainda aprouessem a Deos, como aprouerão no tempo passado, Deos vos daria luguar pera lhe fazerdes oração. Mas bem vedes que nom no tendes, nem teres iamais, e isto he porque todas estas festas cessarão.

Pois, couitados de vos e misquinhos ᵇ(perdoaime porque diguo isto com colera),ᵇ porque fazes sinaguoguas, aiuntamentos falsos, enguanosos, porque Deos hos auorrece e nam nos quer. Assi ho afirma Isaias no capitolo lx°: "Aquele que me oferece boi he tanto como se matasse homem; e aquele que me oferece guado he tanto como se me oferecesse porco; e quem me oferece sacrifitio, sangue de porco me oferece." Bem vedes como estes sacrifitios lhe auião de auorrecer, e nam nos auia de aceitar. Aguora ho veedes comprido pois que nom vos he permitido sacrificar. E se quiserdes saber como todos hos vossos sacrifitios cessarão, venha ho profeta Malachias, que foi mais cheguado à vinda do Mexia que outro profeta algum, e veiamos ho que sentio da cessação destes vossos sacrificios. No capitolo primeiro, falando com hos sacerdotes, diz assi: "'Ia me nom aprazes, nem agradaes,' diz ho Senhor dos exercitos, 'e doom algum nom tomarei mais da vossa mão, porque desde oriento ates ho ocidente, grande he ho meu nome antre has gentes. E en todo luguar sacrificão e oferecem ao meu nome, hum sacrifitio muito limpo porque ho meu nome grande he antre has gentes.'"

Diguouos que isto nom era outra cousa senão que Deos determinaua de leixar hos vossos sacrifitios, como Malachias bem proua, e determinaua de daar ho sacrifitio do altar aos gentios pera lhe oferecerem sacrifitio limpo, como aguora se oferece na christindade. Rroguouos que leaes este profeta, e hos outros intrinsecamente hos especulai, inuesti-

---

b-b int.

⁶ Isa. 1:13ff.

been fulfilled because the death of the Messiah made them abhorrent to Him.

[*fol. 42v*] Tell me, then, why do you judaize? Why do you observe the Sabbath and the feasts of the Law of Moses? Do you not see that all these things are abhorrent to God? He does not care for them nor do they please Him. As a confirmation of this, see what the prophet Isaiah says in chapter 1: *Your gatherings and assemblies are most wicked. Your new moons, your feasts, are loathsome to My soul. All these things are odious to Me. I sustained you and worked with you; but now if you extend your hands, I shall take My eyes from you; and when you increase your prayers, I shall not hear you.*[6]

O gentlemen, what do you say to all this? Do you not see that all this has come to pass? For if these things were still as pleasing to God as they were in times gone by, He would give you a place where you could pray to Him. But, as you can well see, you do not have such a place, nor will you ever have it, and this is because all these feasts no longer exist.

You wretched, miserable creatures (forgive me, for I say this with some anger)[7] who form synagogues and sinister and deceitful assemblies on account of which God hates rather than loves you! Isaiah affirms this in chapter 60: *He who offers Me an ox commits the same act as if he had killed a man; and he who offers Me a sheep offers Me the likes of a swine; and he who offers Me a sacrifice, offers Me the blood of a swine.*[8] You see how God was to abhor these sacrifices and not accept them. Now you see this fulfilled since you are no longer permitted to make sacrifices. If you would like to know how all your offerings came to an end, let us look at what the prophet Malachi has to say. For he, more than any other, was the closest to the time of the Messiah's coming. In the first chapter, in speaking with the priests, he says: *You no longer please nor delight,* says the Lord of hosts, *and I shall no longer accept any gift from your hand, because from East to West, great is My name among the nations. Everywhere they sacrifice and make oblations to My name; a very pure sacrifice because My name is great among the nations.*[9]

I tell you that this is nothing more than God's decision to renounce your sacrifices, as Malachi rightly proves, and to give the sacrifice of the altar to the Gentiles so they can offer Him a pure oblation, as is now offered in Christianity. I implore you to read this prophet and to deliberate over the others. Examine them [and] hit the mark for they

[7] Interlinear addition. See footnote *b*.
[8] The correct reference is Isa. 66:3.
[9] Mal. 1:10f. Cf. *ACPJ* 1, 9, p. 88.

guai, cheguailhe o fito, que no*m* prouão outra cousa senão q*ue* estes sacrifitios auia*m* de cessar pola vi*n*da do Mexia.

[*fol. 43r*] A uossa principal festa he ho sabado que mais corre no ano, ho qual ta*m*bem cessou pola vi*n*da do Mexia quanto ao dia, e não quanto à oração, que he amar a D*eo*s hu*m*a vez na somana — no seitimo dia — q*ue* he a cousa moral que nelle se includia. Porque no sabbado duas cousas entrauão, das quaes hu*m*a era ceremonial, que era ho seitimo dia da somana, em ho qual auião de cessar do t*r*abalho manual, assi hos iudeus como as animallias,ᶜ e auião de tomar repouso corporal e folgança, segundo se conte*m* no Exodi, capitolo xxº. E quanto a isto, cessou ho sabbado pola morte do Mexia, assi como cessarão as outras cousas ceremoniaes em luguar do qual sabbado socedeo ho domi*n*guo, em o qual ho Mexia resurgio.

Mas vos outros, senhores,ᵈ andaes com ho vosso sabbado às costas, no*m* fazendo nada nele, mas chama*n*do as molheres christãas, pobres e neiciaes, que vos fação de come*r*, metendo a vos no inferno, e as mesquinhas, que no*m* vos acusão por algu*m* interesse que de vos esperão. Pore*m*, mais imputo ei e dou culpa a que*m* volo consenti e co*n*sintio, que não a vos outros que ho fazees, assi enguanados e errados.

Ha outra cousa q*ue* no*m* sabbado se enclude. He santificar a Deos: honrralo, acuatalo, e temelo. E isto he moral, da Lei da natureza, a qual dita e manda que deemos graças e D*eo*s polos benefitios e graças q*ue* dele recebemos. E quanto a isto q*ue* era moral, no*m* cessou ho sabado, assi como no*m* cessarão hos dez Ma*n*dame*n*tos; mas quanto ao dia seitimo, cessou; por iso, tomai ho domi*n*guo e acertarees, e leixai ho sabbado, e no*m* errarees, cuida*n*do que nhu*m*a obra se pode faze*r* em tal dia.

V*er*dade he que ha obra do pecado, esta he defesa, da qual vos no*m* cessaes, e na*m* ha das mãos da qual vos tendes grande cuidado que na*m* façaes no sabbado. Leede polos liuros dos Machabeus, leede Iosue e achares que hos vossos p*r*edecessores, nos dias dos sabbados, se defenderão.

A circu*m*cisão ta*m*bem cessou pola morte do Mexia, a qual tirou ho pecado original e deu a graça ates que ho bautismo foi promulguado e

---

c uncertain reading   d int. + *miseros e misquinhos* exp.

[10] Exod. 20:8ff.
[11] Interlinear addition replacing "miserable and wretched." See note *d*.
[11A] Machado refers to fighting on the Sabbath during the time of the Maccabean revolt. See 1

prove definitively that these sacrifices would cease with the coming of the Messiah.

[fol. 43r] Your most important holiday is the Sabbath, the most frequent of the year. It too ceased with the coming of the Messiah with respect to its observance on a particular day but not with respect to prayer, viz., the love of God once during the week — on the seventh day — which is the moral aspect contained within it. Two things entered into the celebration of the Sabbath, one of which was ceremonial. This meant that on the seventh day of the week manual labor for Jews and animals would cease and they would take physical rest and relaxation, as is stated in Exodus, chapter 20.[10] The celebration of the Sabbath ended as did other ceremonies with the death of the Messiah, and Sunday, the day on which the He rose, took its place.

But you, gentlemen,[11] walk about with your Sabbath on your back, doing nothing on that day. The poor ignorant Christian women are the ones you call upon to prepare your meals and this commits you to Hell. These miserable creatures do not denounce you because of the profit they expect to gain from you. However, I impute and cast blame not on you who are wrong and in error, but on those who have permitted you to continue to do this.

Something else included in the observance of the Sabbath is the sanctification of God: to honor, respect, and fear Him. This is moral, for it is the law of nature which proclaims and demands that we give thanks to God for the benefits and favors that we receive from Him. This moral aspect of the Sabbath did not cease, just as the Ten Commandments did not; but its observance on the seventh day no longer remained. Therefore renounce the Sabbath on which you believe no work may be done, and adopt Sunday. [In this way] you will not err, but will be in the right.

It is true that there is one sinful act — that of self-defense — which you continue to practice even though it is a physical act which you take great care not to do on the Sabbath. Read the books of Maccabees[11A] and Joshua[12] and you will find that your ancestors defended themselves [against their enemies] on Sabbath days.

Circumcision, which had compensated for original sin and was a means of grace, ceased with the Messiah's death when baptism was

Mac. 9:34, 43; 2 Mac. 8:26; Josephus, Ant. 12.6.2; Isidore, De fide catholica 15.3, PL, 83:522 with reference to 1 Mac. 2:41. Cf. JR, 10:591f.

[12] Machado's reference is not clear. He may be thinking of the Christian justification for the abrogation of circumcision based on Jos. 5:2-9. Cf. José-María Millás-Vallicrosa, "Un tratado anónimo de polémica contra los Judíos," Sefarad, 13 (1953), 16.

preguado, e ali cessou. Foi dada a Habrraam e a toda sua geração, segundo se contem no Genesis, capitolo xvij, antes que a Lei de Moises fosse dada per espaço de quatrocentos e trinta anos pera hos machos, hos quaes nom se podiam saluar sem ella. E as molheres se saluaão na fee de Christo com certos sacrifitios que hos parentes ofericião — protestatiuos e declaratiuos da fee.

E a esta circumcisão socedeo ho bautismo. Assi Isaias ho tinha profitizado no capitolo xliij°, onde diz: "Nom vos lembrees das cousas passadas, nem olhees polas cousas antiguas, porque todas ia passarão, e farei todas as cousas nouas, e farei que a minha gente amada beba dum rio deleitosso." Este rrio era ho bautismo.

[fol. 43v] A estes sacrifitios que assi cessarão, socedeo ho sacrifitio do sacramento da Eucharistia, como bem proua ho profeta Malachias no capitolo primeiro no qual diz pola boca de Deos: "Da vossa mão nom ei de tomar doom; mas hos gentios conuertidos à fee do Mexia me sacrificarão sacrifitio limpo, como aguora fazem." Este sacrifitio que auia de soceder foi figurado na Lei da natureza, segundo se contem no Genesis no [capitolo] xiiij°, onde se diz que tornando Habraam com vitoria que ouuera contra hos cinquo rreis que forão contra Guomorra e Sodoma, foiho rrecebir ellrrei de Sodoma; porem, Me[l]chesedec[h], rrei de Salem, ofereceo pam e vino porque era sacerdote de Deos muito alto. Este Melchesedech, segundo ho dizer de muitos, foi Sem, ho primeiro filho de Noe, e ho primeiro sacerdote de Deos, e ho primeiro que fez templos pera Deos, e foi rrei de Ierusalem, a qual antão se chamaua Salem, e depois se chamou Luza e Iebus, e finalmente, Ierusalem. Este Melchese[de]ch sinificaua ho Mexia, ho qual auia de oferecer pão e vinho a Deos — ho seu corpo e ho seu sangue — como depois ofereceo no dia da Cea, reprouando hos vossos sacrifitios e ordenando este sacramento⁽ᵉ⁾ da Eucharistia. No Grão Grande se confirma isto no capitolo xiii°, que começa, "Melchesedech," onde se diz que este Melchese[de]ch era Sem, filho de Noe, que sinificaua ho Mexia. Assi ho afirma sobre este passo Rrabi Samuel, dizendo: "Melchesede[c]h ofere-

e MS *sacramenteo*

[13] Gen. 17:10ff.
[14] Isa. 43:18ff.
[15] Mal. 1:10f.
[16] Gen. 14:7.
[17] Gen. 14:18.
[18] See Jerome, *Liber Hebr. Quaest. in Genes., CC,* 72:19 (*PL*, 23:1010); *Epist.* 73, ed. Labourt, 4:20 (*PL*, 22:677); Comestor, *HS*, Gen. 46, *PL*, 198:1094f. For Jewish traditions, see Leviticus Rabbah 25:6; B.T. Nedarim 32b; Pirqe de Rabbi Eliezer, xxiii; Targum to Gen. 14:4.

preached and promulgated. In chapter 17 of Genesis, we read that circumcision was [originally] given to Abraham and all the males of his generation[13] — for without this rite they could not be saved four hundred and thirty years before the Law of Moses was given. The women were saved in the faith of Christ by certain sacrifices offered by their kinsmen. These served as a declaration and confirmation of faith.

Circumcision was followed by baptism. This was prophesied by Isaiah in chapter 43 where he says: *Remember not the things of the past, nor look back at the old, because they have now all passed. I shall make all things anew, and cause my beloved people to drink from a delectable river.*[14] This river was baptism.

[*fol. 43v*] These sacrifices that came to an end were followed by that of the sacrament of the Eucharist. This is clearly proved by the prophet Malachi in chapter 1 when he says through the mouth of God: *I will take no gift from your hand; but the Gentiles converted to the faith of the Messiah shall offer Me a pure sacrifice, as they do now.*[15] This sacrifice that was to supersede [the old] was prefigured in the law of nature. In Genesis, chapter 14, where it states that when Abraham returned victorious over the five kings that attacked Sodom and Gomorrah, the king of Sodom went to receive him.[16] However, Melchizedek, king of Salem, offered bread and wine because he was the priest of the most high God.[17] This Melchizedek, according to many authorities, was Shem, the first son of Noah, and the first priest of God.[18] He was the first who made temples for God and was king of Jerusalem which at that time was called Salem,[19] afterwards Luz[20] and Jebus,[21] and finally Jerusalem. Melchizedek prefigured the Messiah Who would offer bread and wine to God — His body and His blood — as He afterwards did on the day of the Supper. [Thus he] rejected your sacrifices and ordered the sacrament of the Eucharist. This is confirmed in the *Grão Grande*, chapter 13, in the passage that begins: "Melchizedek." It says here that Melchizedek was Shem, the son of Noah, who prefigured the Messiah. Rabbi Samuel affirms this passage saying: "Melchizedek offered God bread and wine and the son of David in like manner shall offer Him

[19] Melchizedek's kingdom traditionally identified with Jerusalem. See Josephus, *Ant.* 1.10.2; Comestor, *HS*, Gen. 46, *PL*, 198:1094f.

[20] Luz was the former name of Bethel. Cf. Gen. 28:19. Machado's statement may be due to a confusion of the words of Jerome: "Luza in tribu Benjamin, quam postea Jacob cognominavit Bethel. Est autem usque hodie villa in sinistra parte viae de Neapoli pergentibus Aelium [Jerusalem]." *De Situ et Nomin. Loc. Hebr., PL,* 23:954.

[21] The Canaanite name for Jerusalem. See Jos. 15:8, 18:16, 28. Jerome referred to Jerusalem by this name in Epistles 127 and 129, ed. Labourt, 7:146, 163 (*PL*, 24: 1094, 1105).

ceo pam e vinho a Deos, e ho filho de Dauid assi oferecera pão e vinho a Deos." Dauid ho afirma no psalmo cento e noue quando diz, falando do Mexia: "Tu es sacerdote pera todo sempre, segundo a ordem de Melchesedech." Ho mesmo Dauid ainda confirma este sacramento no psalmo lxxi, dizendo: "Sera firmamento de pam na terra nas cabeças dos montes." Sobre este passo no caldeu, se escreue assi: "Sera ho Mexia feito sacrifitio de pão na terra nas cabeças dos sacerdotes."

Dizeime, por vossa vida, queres vos proua mais manifesta do que esta he, onde se include que hos sacerdotes auião de ter ho pão sobre as cabeças? Sabei, pois, por certeza, que estes sam hos sacerdotes christãos que cada dia teem ho pão sobre has cabeças — ho corpo de Nosso Senhor. Se quiserdes neguar que no psalmo acima aleguado, polos montes, nom se entendem hos sacerdotes, diguouos que erraes porque ho profeta Malachias chama aos sacerdotes montes no primeiro capitolo, onde polos "montes de Seir" entende ho profeta hos sacerdotes do Templo. Portanto, nom teenhaes duuida deste sacramento ser figurado na Lei de Moises.

Se quiserdes neguar que ho Mexia nom auia de ser sacerdote, diguouos que erraes, porque posto que elle fosse do tribu de Iuda, tambem foi sacerdote porquanto estes dous tribus ambos andauão misturados, e portanto, bem podia ho Mexia ser do tribu de Iuda e ser sacerdote. [fol. 44r] Isto prouasse por aquele passo de Malachias, no capitolo segundo, onde se diz que "hos beiços dos sacerdotes guardarão a sabedoria, e a Lei eu a requerirei da sua boca, porque anio do Senhor he." Dizse no Talmud que este sacerdote he ho Mexia. Deste modo de dizer bem se conclude que ho Mexia auia de ser sacerdote, e assi Aaron nom sinificaua outra cousa senão este Mexia. Salamão nos Prouerbios

---

[22] Ps. 110(109):4.

[23] Ps. 72(71):16. See below.

[24] The above passage, based on a text of *BRMD* to Gen. 14:18 (*PF*, p. 840; *ACPJ*, 1, 9, p. 91; *FF*. fols. 54rb-54va) and to the Targum to the above verse, is close to the text of *ACPJ*: "habetur in Berescit Rabba a Rabbi Moyse praedicatore, supra illud (Genes. 14). Melchisedek, rex Salem, obtulit panem et vinum, erat enim sacerdos dei summi. Dixit Rabbi filius Enachinam [i.e., Samuel bar Nahman; Rabbi Samuel, according to Machado]: Iste Melchisedek, erat Sem, filius Noe, sed quid vult dicere, proferens panem & vinum? Ostendit quod docuit eum sacerdotii actus, qui erat panis [*sic*] et vinum sacrificare ... Quis est ille? Ille est rex Messias de quo scriptum est: Ecce Rex tuus venit ... In hoc quod dicit, proferens panem & vinum, correspondet ei quod habetur in psalmo 75. Erit placentula panis in summis montium. Et in Chaldaica translatione habetur in psalmo 75 ... Erit sacrificium panis in terra in capite montium. Synagogae." The Hebrew text of *BRMD* in *PF* reads: "*Melchizedek the King of Salem* (Gen. 14:18). This is Shem the son of Noah. What is the meaning of *brought out bread and wine (ibid.)*? R. Samuel bar Nahman said: The laws of the priesthood were transmitted to him and he offered up bread and wine as it is said, *he was priest of*

bread and wine." David confirms this in psalm one hundred and nine when he says of the Messiah: *You are a priest forever after the order of Melchizedek*.[22] David again confirms this sacrament in Psalm 71: *There shall be a firmament of bread in the land upon the heads of the mountains*.[23] The Chaldean version writes the following on this same passage: "The Messiah shall become a sacrifice of bread in the land upon the heads of the priests."[24]

Tell me, by your life, do you want more evident proof than this that the priests were to hold the bread above their heads? Know, then, for a fact, that they are the Christian priests who hold bread — the body of Our Lord — above their heads every day.[25] If you prefer to deny that the above psalm of the mountains is understood to refer to priests, then I can only say to you that you err. The prophet Malachi calls priests "mountains" in the first chapter where, by *the mountains of Seir*, the prophet means the priests of the Temple.[26] Therefore, do not doubt that this sacrament is prefigured in the Law of Moses.

If you care to deny that the Messiah would be a priest, I say to you that you err for, even though He was of the tribe of Judah, He was also a priest. Since these two tribes[27] had become mingled, the Messiah could very well be of the tribe of Judah and be a priest. [*fol. 44r*] This is proved by the verse in chapter two of Malachi which says that *the lips of the priests shall keep knowledge, and I shall ask for the Law from their mouth, because I am the angel of the Lord*.[28] The Talmud says that this priest is the Messiah.[29] This manner of speaking shows conclusively that the Messiah would be a priest; thus Aaron prefigures none other than this Messiah.[30] Solomon mentions this sacrament in Proverbs, chapter 9,

God most high (ibid.) ... Another interpretation: *Melchizedek*: Scripture said: *The Lord has sworn*; etc. (Ps. 110:4). ... This is the King Messiah. ... What is the meaning of *brought out bread and wine?* It is said: *May there be an abundance of grain in the land* (Ps. 72:16), as it is written, *he was priest of the God most high.*" The version of the Targum in *PF* (p. 838) reads "Erit sacrificium annonae in terra in capite montium Ecclesiae" based on an Aramaic "yehe qorban de-vara be-'are'a be-resh turaya kenishta" not found in our editions. The latter read: "There shall be a sustenance of bread in the land" (yehe sa'id laḥma be-'are'a).

[25] Cf. *FF*, fol. 54*va*: "qui montes synagoge et ecclesie sunt sacerdotes qui quotidie de facto eleuant Messiam super capita sua."

[26] The reference to Mal. 1 is unclear. For the interpretation of "mountains" as priests of the Temple, see *PF*, p. 838.

[27] *I.e.*, the Levites and the Judaeans.

[28] Mal. 2:7.

[29] Possible reference to Lamentations Rabbah, proem (*PF*, p. 386) where the priest is referred to as prophet and sage. Cf. *FF*, fol. 54*va*.

[30] Details of the consecration of Aaron into the priesthood are given in Exodus 29.

menção fez deste sacramento no capitolo nono, onde diz: "Vinde e
comee ho meu pam, e bebee ho vinho que uos mesturei."[31]

Certamente assi se aconteceo, que Christo todos conuidou pera este
sacramento, ho qual elle ordenou e instituio no monte de Sion em
Ierusalem huma quinta feira aos vinte e quatro dias de Março, luna
quartadecima,[32] comido ho cordeiro pascoal dia da sua Postameira Cea,
na qual transustantiou ho pam asmo no seu sacratissimo corpo, e ho
vinho no seu sacratissimo sangue, miraculo somente e contra ha ordem
da natureza.

Esta he a nossa fee, crendo que debaixo daqueles acidentes sem
suieito; debaixo daquela redondeza tamanina da hostia, esta todo
Christo, como elle esteue na cruz — diffinitiue, e nom circumscritiue.
Porque, posto que ho corpo de Christo seia quanto; porem, a rezão da
quantidade nom lhe conuem. E se a hostia se diuidir en tres partes, en
todas estaa ocultamente e miraculosamente. Porem, vos escarneces de
nos, dizendo que adoramos ho pam, e que nom podia estar Christo en
tantas hostias nem en tantos luguares. Esto uos prouaremos aqui com
hos vossos dizeres e emxemplos ser possiuel ho que vos crerdes ser im-
possiuel.

Pera prouarmos isto com rezões naturaes ou demostratiuas, nom
podemos, porque este modo excede todo ho intendimento humano, e
capasidade nossa, e todo ho curso da natureza. Porem, podemos prouar
isto por alguns emxemplos. Vos teendes no Talmud que quando algum
minino se deue de fanar, que Helias[33] esta ali presente, posto nũma
cadeira muito ornada que lhe aparelhaes, e outra pera ho rrabi que ho
a de fanar, ho qual Helias nom vedes; e entra polas ianelas, ou esteiem
fechadas ou abertas. E se mil mininos se fanarem no mesmo dia e en
diuersos luguares, dizees que en todos esta sem no verem. O misquinhos
enguanados, e se vos isto concedes que acontece a Helias, por que vos
espantais dizermos no que ho corpo do Senhor pode estar em mil
luguares e antre as mãos de mil sacerdotes no mesmo tempo, em diuersos luguares? Sabee que assi como polo poder de Deos Helias esta em

---

[31] Prov. 9:5.

[32] *Luna quartadecima* refers to the fourteenth day of Nisan, the first month in the Jewish lunar
calendar. On this date, which commences at sunset and ends at the following sunset, the paschal
lamb was sacrificed and eaten in the evening at the traditional Passover supper. Concerning the
date, March 24, see chap. 2, n. 35.

[33] *Summa Theologiae* 3, 76, 5, d. 1. On Jewish criticism of the doctrine of transubstantiation, see
Profiat Duran's "Be not like unto thy fathers," in Franz Kobler, *Letters of Jews through the Ages* (London, 1953), 1: 279; Joseph Albo, *Book of Roots (Sefer ha-'Iqqarim)* (Philadelphia, 1929-30), 3:231-34.

[34] Elijah, termed "angel of the covenant" (Mal. 3:1), figures symbolically in the circumcision
ceremony, and a chair of honor is traditionally reserved for him. On this practice, see Pirqe de

when he says: *Come and eat my bread, and drink the wine which I mixed for you.*[31]

Thus assuredly did it happen that Christ invited everyone to this sacrament which He ordained and instituted on Mount Zion in Jerusalem on Thursday March 24, the fourteenth day of the lunar month.[32] The paschal lamb was eaten on the day of the Last Supper in which the unleavened bread was transubstantiated into His most sacred body and the wine into His most sacred blood. This could only be a miracle for it is contrary to the natural order of things.

This is our faith. We believe that behind accidents without a subject, behind the tiny roundness of the Host, Christ is totally present, as He was on the Cross — *diffinitive* and not *circumscritive*.[33] For even though Christ's body is measurable, the concept of quantity cannot be applied to Him. If the Host be divided into three parts, He would mysteriously and miraculously be in each of them. Yet, you scoff at us and say that we worship the bread, and that Christ could not be in so many Hosts and in so many places. We shall prove to you here, [however], through your own statements and parables, that what you believe to be impossible is possible.

We are unable to prove this through the use of natural or demonstrative arguments because it goes beyond all human understanding, our capacity to explain it, and the natural course of things. Still, we can prove this through some parables. You have it in the Talmud that when a male child is to be circumcised, Elijah is invisibly present, seated in a very ornate chair which you have made ready for him.[34] There is another [chair] for the rabbi who is to perform the circumcision. Elijah enters through the windows, whether they be closed or open. You say that even though a thousand male children are circumcised on the same day in different places, Elijah is [still] in all of them, although he remains unseen. Oh, misguided wretches, if you concede that this happens to Elijah, then why are you astonished at our saying that the body of the Lord can be in a thousand different places and in the hands of a thousand priests all at the same time? You say that through the power of God, Elijah is in many places although I do not believe this; because,

Rabbi Eliezer, xxix; trans. G. Friedlander, pp. 213f. Cf. Yom Tov Lipmann-Mülhausen, *Sefer Nizzaḥon*, ed. T. Hackspan, Altdorf, 1644, pp. 19f. Cf. the arguments of the 15th-century German Reformer, Hans Folz, cited by Haim H. Ben-Sasson, "Jewish-Christian Disputation in the Setting of Humanism and Reformation in the German Empire," *Harvard Theological Review*, 66 (1966), 375f. For a Jewish refutation of the argument found here, see Abraham Farissol's (1452-1528) *Magen 'Avraham*, 20, Jewish Theological Seminary of America MS 2433, fols. 24r-25r.

muitos luguares, ho q*ue* eu no*m* aprouo ser ve*r*dade, porque antes q*ue* Helias fosse, ia muitos forão circu*m*cidados, assi ta*m*bem ho corpo do Mexia pode estar em muitos luguares no mesmo tempo, ho q*ue* eu creo que he ve*r*dade porq*ue* esta he a nossa ve*r*dadeira fee e crença q*ue* temos.

[*fol. 44v*] Hos vossos doutores afirmão isto ser ve*r*dade, dizendo que Helias a muitos home*n*s apareceo no mesmo tempo e hora e en diuersos luguares, como foi a Rabi Simeo*m*, dizendolhe que ho Mexia estaua en Rroma co*m* hos doentes e marteres, e que hu*n*s saluaua e outros perdia. Tudo isto he ve*r*dade, que ho Mexia esteue com hos doentes neste mundo — co*m* hos pecadores — hu*n*s perdendo, condena*n*do pera ho infe*r*no que são hos maos, do numero dos quaes vos seres se no*m* quiserdes creer — outros sarando — hu*n*s boo*n*s e iustos.

Assi que, concludindo, diguo que me parece q*ue*, pois, De*o*s esto communicou a Helias, assi ho pode co*m*municar ao Mexia q*ue* foi De*o*s e home*m*.

Vos outros iudeus pe*r*guntaes aos christãos que sinal tee*m* elles pera crere*m* que ho corpo do Mexia esta neste sacramento. Diguouos q*ue* no*m* temos sinal outro senão a fee mediante a qual cremos. Q*ue* assi como ho Mexia entrou dentro no ventre da bendita gloriosa Vi*r*gem Maria se*m* faze*r* abertura e saindo, e assi como saio do sepulcro entrou co*m* hos discipolos, sendo as po*r*tas fechadas e ianelas, assi ta*m*bem ho corpo de Ch*r*isto pode estar debaixo daqueles acidentes. E loguo esta como ho sacerdote acaba de dize*r* as palauras ordenadas e instituidas polo Mexia, loguo ho adoramos, no*m* ho pão, como vos, misquinhos, cuidaes, mas a Ch*r*isto, que ali estaua, posto q*ue* na*m* no veiamos porquanto ho olho corporal no*m* no pode ve*r*, como vos adoraes a Helias posto que na*m* no veiaes. E pera proua disto, traguouos aqui aquilo que esta escrito no liuro dos Numeros no capitolo nono, onde se diz que quando a nuue*m* se apa*r*taua do tabe*r*nacolo onde estaua a arca do Testame*n*to, loguo ho pouo se pa*r*tia; e emqua*n*to a nuue*m* no*m* se mouia, estauão naquele luguar quedos; e quando a nuue*m* se aleua*n*taua, ho pouo inclinauase, fazendo rreuere*n*tia.

Hora, dizeeme vos. Este pouo adoraua a nuue*m*? Certamente no*m*, porque antão fora idolatra. Adoraua loguo a De*o*s que estaua escondido na nuue*m*. Assi vos diguo q*ue* no*m* adoramos nos ho pão, mas a Ch*r*isto, q*ue* esta incluso naq*ue*les acidentes. Q*ue*ando vos fazees vossa oração, tres vezes tornaes pera tras, humildosame*n*te. E qua*n*do entraes

---

[35] B.T. Sanhedrin 98a cited in *PF*, p. 351; *ACPJ*, 1, 11, p. 107. The text as translated from *PF* reads: "R. Joshua ben Levi found Elijah and R. Simeon bar Yohai standing at the entrance of the Garden of Eden. He said to them: Do I come into the World to Come. They said to him: If this Lord [desires]. R. Joshua ben Levi said: I have seen two and heard the voice of three. ... He said to

even before Elijah existed, many were circumcised. Let it be known that if you do believe this, then in like manner can the body of the Messiah be in many places at the same time. This I hold to be truth, because it is our true faith and belief.

[*fol. 44v*] Your doctors affirm that this is so when they say Elijah appeared to many men at the same time and hour in various places. Such a one was Rabbi Simeon who said that the Messiah was in Rome with the sick and the martyrs, some of whom he saved and some of whom he damned.[35] All of this is true: The Messiah went among the sick in this world — i.e., among the sinners, damning some, i.e., condemning the wicked to Hell (among whom you will be included unless you believe!) — or curing others, i.e., those who were good and righteous.

Thus, in conclusion, it seems to me that since God conferred this on Elijah, he could confer the same on the Messiah Who was both God and man.

You Jews ask the Christians what proof they have that the body of the Messiah is in this sacrament. I say to you that we have no proof other than our own faith through which we believe. Just as the Messiah entered and left the unopened womb of the blessed and glorious Virgin Mary, and left the sepulcher with its locked doors and windows and joined His disciples, so also can the body of Christ be behind those accidents. Thus it is that after the priest finishes reciting the words ordained and instituted by the Messiah, we worship not the bread, as you wretches think, but Christ, Who is there even though the human eye cannot see Him, just as you adore Elijah even though you cannot see him. As evidence of this I bring you here that which is written in chapter nine of the Book of Numbers: *When the cloud moved away from the tabernacle where the Ark of the Testament was, the people moved on; when the cloud did not move, they remained in their place; and when the cloud was lifted the people bowed and paid homage.*[36]

Now tell me. Did these people worship the cloud? Of course not, for that would have been idolatry. Rather, they worshiped God Who was hidden in the cloud. So I say to you that we do not worship the bread but rather Christ Who is concealed behind the accidents. When you

---

them: When is the Messiah coming? They said to him: Go ask him. He said to them: Where is he? They said to him: At the gate of Rome. And how is he to be known? He sits among those who are poor and suffering ills ... and he is afflicted ..." The printed editions of the Talmud have been altered due to censorship so that "at the gates of Rome" was changed to read "at the entrance." See R. Rabbinowitz, *Diqduqe Soferim* (Mayence, 1878), 9:292; the notes of Elijah of Vilna to the Talmud *ad loc.*; Midrash Tanḥuma, Tazri'a 8.

[36] Numbers 9. Machado presents a paraphrase of the central idea contained in verses 15-23.

nas sinaguoguas adoraes ho purguaminho? Certo he que vos no*m*
adoraes ho pu*r*guaminho senão a D*e*os, ho qual vos rep*r*esenta aquele
pu*r*guaminho, e torna*n*do pera tras qua*n*do oraes, uos no*m* fazees
reuerentia ao luguar, mas a D*e*os que cuidaes que esta ali p*r*esente. Assi
tambem nos no*m* adoramos [ho] pa*m*, mas ho corpo de Ch*ris*to que esta
ali oculto e esco*n*dido.

Concludindo, dizemos que pola vinda do Mexia cessarão todos hos
vossos sacrifitios, em luguar dos quaes socedeo ho sacrame*n*to do altar
que excede todolos vossos sacrifitios e cerimonias da vossa Lei, hos
quaes D*e*os lançou fora de si, reprouma*n*doos e auorrecendolhe[s], como
estaua profitizado polos profetas.

Esta he a nossa v*er*dadeira fee chatolica,[f] O senhores, e esta seia a
vossa. Ame*n*.

[*fol. 45r*] Capitolo Sextodecimo. Como ho Mexia auia de daar Lei noua
ao seu pouo.

A quartadecima propriedade que estaua escrita do Mexia era que
pola sua vinda auia de daar Lei noua ao seu pouo, tirada e reprouada a
Lei velha, ho que Ch*ris*to fez, segundo prouaremos polos profetas e
polos vossos doutores.

Ho profeta Isaias daa testimunho disto no segu*n*do capitolo, dizendo:
"Nos derradeiros dias sera ho monte composto da casa de D*e*os sobre
hos mo*n*tes, e todas as gentes correrão a elle, porq*ue* de Sion ha de sair
a Lei, e de Ierusalem a palaura." Isto no*m* se pode ente*n*der da Lei de
Moises, que auia tantos anos que fora dada, porq*ue* a Lei de Moises foi
dada no monte de Sinay (Exodi xx°), e ho profeta diz q*ue* do mo*n*te de
Sion auia esta Lei de sair, e de Ierusalem; que no*m* se pode ente*n*der
senão da Lei noua que ho Mexia auia de dar, como de feito deu aos
seus discipolos, hos quaes no monte de Sion, a confirmação dela
rreceberão qua*n*do ho Sp*irit*u Santo descendeo sobre elles, como Ioel
tinha profitizado no capitolo segu*n*do, dizendo: "E nos derradeiros dias
eu derramarei ho meu sp*irit*u sobre toda a carne: hos vossos filhos e
filhas profitizarão, e hos vossos velhos sonharão, e hos vossos moços
verão visões." Tudo isto foi comprido que estaua escrito do Mexia no
tempo de Ch*ris*to; portanto, no*m* tenhaes duuida ne*m* debate algu*m*
porq*ue* assi estaua profitizado, e assi ia se comprio.

---

f MS *chatolico*

[37] On the practice of advancing three steps before the prayer of the Eighteen Benedictions and of
stepping backwards three steps upon completing it, see Eleazar ben Judah, *Ha-Roqeaḥ Ha-Gadol*
(Jerusalem, 1967-8), par. 322, p. 214.

pray, you humbly take three steps backwards.[37] Now, when you enter the synagogue, do you adore the parchment?[38] It is certain you adore God instead because He is what that parchment represents to you. And when you step backwards when you pray, you do not pay respect to the place but more properly to God Whom you believe is present there. In like manner, we do not worship the bread but the body of Christ which is concealed and hidden therein.[39]

Finally, we say that with the coming of the Messiah all your sacrifices ended and in their place there followed the sacrament of the altar. This sacrament supersedes all of the sacrifices and ceremonies of your Law, which God rejected and despised as the prophets prophesied.

This is our true Catholic faith, gentlemen. May it be yours. Amen.

[fol. 45r] Chapter Sixteen. How the Messiah would give a new Law to His people.

The fourteenth characteristic written of the Messiah was that He would give a new Law to His people when He came. The old Law was to be rejected and abrogated. This is what Christ did, as we shall prove through the prophets and through your doctors.

The prophet Isaiah testifies to this in the second chapter: *In the last days the mountain of God's house shall be established above the mountains, and all the nations shall hasten to it, because the Law shall come forth from Zion, and the word from Jerusalem.*[1] This cannot be taken to mean the Law of Moses which had been given so many years before, because this Law was given on Mount Sinai (Exodus 20), and the prophet says that the other Law would come forth from Mount Zion, from Jerusalem. Thus, this Law can only refer to the new Law which the Messiah would give as He in fact gave it to His disciples on Mount Zion. They received confirmation of it when the Holy Spirit descended upon them, as Joel had prophesied in chapter 2: *And in the last days I will pour out My spirit upon all flesh; your sons and daughters shall prophesy, your old men shall dream, and your young men shall see visions.*[2] Everything here written of the Messiah was fulfilled during the time of Christ. Therefore, do not be in doubt nor debate, because this was foretold and this has been fulfilled.

---

[38] *I.e.*, the Torah Scroll.
[39] Cf. the accusation of Isaac of Troki (1533-1594) that the Christians worship "idols of bread" (*Ḥizzuq 'Emunah*, ed. D. Deutsch [Breslau, 1873], 1, p. 280).

[1] Isa. 2:2f. See especially Jerome, *Comm. ad loc.*, CC, 73:27f. (*PL*, 24:45); ACPJ, 1, 9, p. 86.
[2] Joel 2:28.

Ho profeta Ieremias tudo isto confirma no capitolo xxxi, falando da Lei noua que ho Mexia auia de daar, dizendo: "Sabee que hão de vir dias, e farei hum partido nouo e hum concerto com a casa de Iuda, nam ia da maneira que eu fiz com hos vossos predecessores naquele dia quando hos liurei do Egito, ho qual elles quebrantarão e corromperão. Este he, pois, ho concerto e pauto ou partido do que ei de fazer com a casa de Isrrael, porque depois daqueles dias, eu lhes darei huma lei dentro nas suas entradanhas, e nos seus corações a discreuerei, e eu serei seu Deos, e elles serão meu pouo." Que proua demandaes mais clara, senhores iudeus, que esta pera se demostrar que ho Mexia auia de daar lei nos corações dos homens — noua, leue, piadossa, aceita a todos; nom escrita em pedras, como foi a primeira, mas dentro nos corações dos humanos, esculpida com letras d'ouro.

Assi que a uossa Lei velha feneceo pois que fim auia de ter, e nom era perpetua. E a noua foi entromitida nos buchos dos iustos, duradoira ates a fim do mundo; mais perfeita que a uossa, porque a vosso Lei velha foi dada a Moises polo ministerio e obra dos anios (Exodi xix), mas a nossa foi predicada e promulguada pola boca do Mexia, Deos e homem, polo qual concludimos que foi muito mais perfeita que não a uossa.

[fol. 45v] No vosso Talmud se daa autoridade a isto, onde se diz que toda a lei que homem aprende neste mundo nom he nada ates que nom venha a Lei do Mexia, que sera toda perfeição. Em Isaias esta hum texto no capitolo duedecimo, no qual se diz: "Aguoas sacarees e tirarees com prazer das fontes do saluador." Sobre este passo estaa assi escrito no caldeo: "Receberes lei noua com prazer dos escolheitos dos iustos." Diz mais Isaias no capitolo xliiij: "E sairão aguoas viuas de Ierusalem." Diz Ionathas sobre este texto: "E nesse dia saira ensinamento de lei como huma fonte de aguoa." Todos estes dizeres dos vossos doutores, fundados sobre hos ditos dos profetas, concludem que ho Mexia, na sua vinda, auia de dar Lei noua ao seu pouo nouo, como elle mesmo fez no tempo do qual todas estas cousas forão compridas e acabadas.

No liuro Cifre, que acerqua de uos he muito autorizado, se diz que

---

³ Jer. 31:31ff.
⁴ Exodus 19 treats in part of the giving of the Ten Commandments to Moses. The role played by the angels in Moses' receiving of the Law is found in Gal. 3:19.
⁵ Ecclesiastes Rabbah to 11:8 (Sonc., p. 295) cited in PF, pp. 779, 885: "The Torah which a man learns in this world is vanity in comparison with the Torah [which will be learnt in the days] of the Messiah."

The prophet Jeremiah confirms all this in chapter 31 where he speaks of the new Law that the Messiah would give: *Know that days shall come, and I will make a new agreement and covenant with the house of Judah, unlike the one I made with your predecessors on that day when I delivered them from Egypt; a covenant they corrupted and broke. This, then, is the covenant and pact or agreement which I will make with the house of Israel, because after those days I will give them a Law, in their inward parts and in their hearts I will write it; and I will be their God, and they shall be My people.*[3] What clearer proof do you want than this, esteemed Jews, to show that the Messiah would place a new Law in the hearts of men; one that is new, lenient, merciful, [and] acceptable to all, not written on stones, as was the first, but engraved with gold letters in the human heart.

Your old Law thus became invalid, for it had limited duration and was not to function in perpetuity. The new one was placed in the bellies of the righteous and will endure until the end of the world. It is more perfect than yours because your old Law was given to Moses through the ministry and work of the angels (Exodus 19)[4] while our [Law] was preached and promulgated through the mouth of the Messiah — God and man. For this reason, we infer that [our Law] was much more perfect than yours.

[*fol. 45v*] Your Talmud lends authority to this for it says that all of the Law that man learns in this world is nothing compared to the Law of the Messiah which shall be total perfection.[5] There is a verse in Isaiah, chapter 12, in which it says that *you shall draw and take out water with joy from the fountains of the Savior.*[6] In the Chaldean [version] there is a version based on this which reads: "You shall receive a new law with joy from the chosen of the righteous."[7] In chapter 44 Isaiah adds: *Living waters shall go forth from Jerusalem.*[8] In reference to this verse, Jonathan says: "And on that day a teaching of the law shall go forth like a fountain of water."[9] All these words of your doctors which are based on the sayings of the prophets conclude that at the coming of the Messiah He was to give a new Law to His new people. This He did do and at that time all these things were fulfilled and accomplished.

In the book *Sifre,* which bears much authority among you, it is said

---

[6] Isa. 12:3 in agreement with the Vulgate: "de fontibus Salvatoris."

[7] The Targum is cited in *PF*, p. 889: "et suscipietis doctrinam novam cum laetitia ab electis justi."

[8] The verse is actually Zech. 14:8. This error is corrected in the Latin Version of the *Mirror,* fol. 40v.

[9] Targum to Zech. 13:1. The Targum to this verse does not appear to be cited in *PF* or *ACPJ.*

dias virão nos quaes por Ierusalem correrão aguoas viuas de vida, as
quaes apaguarão as da Lei velha no tempo que ho Mexia esteuer na
cidade de Ierusalem. Rrabi Iosua confirma isto, dizendo: "Dias hão de
vir quando hos comeres da Lei de Moises, concedidos na Lei, cessarão."
Assi ho afirma ho Talmud, onde se diz que a Lei de Moises loguo
esquece; mas naqueles dias do Mexia, nom esquecera a Lei que elle ha
de daar quando se tirarem hos comeres defesos na Lei de Moises, con-
cididos na Lei da graça.

Bem creo que vos tendes por fee que quando viesse ho Mexia que
auia de daar Lei noua pois que hos vossos autores e doutores assi ho
afirmão. Mas pesame que nom querees creer que ia isto he comprido.
Porque assi como estas cousas estauão escritas do Mexia, assi acontecerão no tempo de Christo, que he hum grande argumento a simili que
elle foi ho Mexia promitido na Lei vossa.

No Talmud se diz, conformemente àquilo que diz Dauid no psalmo
xxxiij: "Filhos, vinde, ouuime; ho temor do Senhor vos ensinarei," que
dixe Deos a Habraam: "Tu ensinaste a teus filhos lei na tua vida; mas,
porem, no tempo do Mexia eu mesmo darei a Lei e ha ensinarei." Certamente que isto assi se aconteceo, que ho mesmo Mexia, Deos e homem,
deu a Lei noua e ensinou hos discipolos seus; e elles ensinarão ho pouo
nouo do Mexia com a Lei noua dada por elle. Isto podemos ainda
prouar por Isaias, que diz no capitolo derradeiro, falando do aiuntamento dos gentios à fee do Mexia: "'E tomarei destes pera sacerdotes
e leuitas,' diz ho Senhor. 'E assi como hos ceos e a terra eu faço estar
diante de mym.'" Diguouos que estas palauras de Deos ditas polo
profeta, nom são ditas a uossos predecessores, [fol. 46r] nem forão ditas
por elles, mas somentes polos sacerdotes cristãos, hos quaes se auião de
converter do paguanismo à fee do Mexia, do numero dos quaes ele
determinaua de escolher hos seus sacerdotes, assi como ho elle fez,
tomados primeiramente hos apostolos que elle ordenou por sacerdotes
no dia da Cea, desprezados hos sacerdotes do Templo e da Lei, dos

---

[10] This may possibly be a corruption of a passage from Ecclesiastes Rabbah to 1:9 (Sonc., p. 33)
which follows a passage from Sifre in *PF*, p. 886: "As the former redeemer made a well fo rise, so
will the latter Redeemer bring up water, as it is stated, *And a fountain shall come forth of the house of the
Lord, and shall water the valley of Shittim* (Joel 4:18)."

[11] Ecclesiastes Rabbah to 2:1 (Sonc., p. 51) cited in *PF*, pp. 778f., 885: "All the Torah which you
learn in this word is 'vanity' in comparison with Torah [which will be learnt] in the World to Come;
because in this world a man learns Torah and forgets it, but with reference to the World to Come
what is written there? *I will put My Law in their inward parts* (Jer. 31:33)."

[12] Ps. 34(33):12.

[13] Apparent reference to Song of Songs Rabbah 1:2 (Sonc., pp. 25f.) cited in *PF*, pp. 885f.; *ACPJ*,
1, **9**, p. 87: "*Let him kiss me with the kisses of his mouth* ... When Israel heard the words, *I am the Lord thy*

that there shall be days in which living waters shall flow through Jerusalem, and these shall extinguish the old Law at the time the Messiah is in the city of Jerusalem.[10] Rabbi Joshua confirms this: "Days shall come when foods [prohibited] under the Law of Moses, shall be allowed under the [new] Law." The Talmud affirms this where it says that the Law of Moses shall soon be forgotten; but in the days of the Messiah the Law that He shall gives the Law of grace, shall permit [the eating of] foods prohibited in the Law of Moses."[11]

I firmly believe that you maintain that when the Messiah comes He will give a new Law, for this is what your authors and doctors assert. But it grieves me that you refuse to believe that this has already taken place. Everything written about the Messiah took place during the time of Christ. This is important evidence *a simili* that He was the Messiah promised in your Law.

In relation to what David says in Psalm 33: *Children, come, hear me; I will teach you the fear of the Lord,*[12] it says in the Talmud that God said to Abraham: "You taught your children [the] Law during your lifetime; however, during the Messiah's time I myself shall give the Law and teach it."[13] This certainly did happen, for the Messiah Himself — God and man — gave the new Law and taught it to His disciples. They [in turn] taught the new people of the Messiah the new Law which was given by Him. We can further prove this with the last chapter of Isaiah where he speaks of the Gentiles assembling together in the faith of the Messiah: *I will take priests and Levites from among these, says the Lord. And as the heavens and the earth, I shall make them stand before Me.*[14] I tell you that these words of God related by the prophet are not directed at your forefathers [*fol. 46r*] nor were they said of them. They were declared only of Christian priests who would convert from paganism to the faith of the Messiah Who determined to select His priests from among their numbers, as He did. He first chose the apostles whom He ordained as priests on the day of the Supper. The priests of the Temple and the [old] Law were rejected and He did not want to ordain any one of them on

---

God, the knowledge of the Torah was fixed in their heart and they learnt and forgot not. They came to Moses and said, 'Our master, Moses, do thou become an intermediary between us, as it says, *"Speak thou with us, and we will hear ... now therefore why should we die* (Ex. 20:16; Deut. 5:22)." What profit is there in our perishing?' They then became liable to forget what they learnt. They said: Just as Moses, being flesh and blood, is transitory, so his teaching is transitory. Forthwith they came a second time to Moses and said: 'Our master Moses, would that God might be revealed to us a second time.' ... He replied to them: 'This cannot be now, but it will be in the days to come: as it says, *I will put My law in their inward parts and in their heart will I write it* (Jer. 31:13).'"

[14] Isa. 66:21f.

quaes no*m* quis elle ordenar algu*m* por sace*r*dote da Lei noua no dia da Cea. Pore*m*, algu*n*s do *tr*ibu de Leui serião ordenados sace*r*dotes.

No liuro *Cifre*, se diz: "E te*m*po vira que a Lei se mudara com todas as cousas ordenadas nele." Assi no Talmud esta escrito expresame*n*te no capitolo onde fala da vinda do Mexia, que qua*n*do viesse ho Mexia, que auia de soltar as pascoas e sabados, e festas com a molher me*n*struosa; e fara todas as cousas nouas, desp*r*ezando as velhas. Assi como estaua escrito do Mexia, assi se fez porqua*n*to elle soltou as pascoas e festas e sole*m*nidades da Lei velha, Lei noua dando e entremetendoa nos corações dos home*n*s. Disto daa testimunho Rraba Barezid expondo aquel passo de Dauid do ps*a*l*m*o cxlvᵒ, onde diz: "*D*e*os* desatou hos atados," dizendo que todalas quatropeas que forão enuiadas a este mundo, De*o*s as dara por li*m*pas no tempo que vier ho Mexia, como as deu aos filhos de Noe, segu*n*do se mostra no Grão Grande, con-formeme*n*te ao q*u*e se diz no Genesis no capitolo nono, que D*e*os deu licença aos filhos de Noe que comesse todas as cousas, onde antes do diluuio no*m* comião carne. E assi se diz no Grão Grande: "Como a cerua do campo, vos solto tudo," e assi se soltarão as cousas de Moises quando vier ho Mexia.

Pergunta Rrabi Salamão que quer dizer isto que se diz no Grão Grande que D*e*os desatara hos atados, tirando as q*u*atropeas. Responde dizendo que aqueles que estauão atados pola Lei serião desatados polo Mexia das quatropeas, que são hos porcos, hos quaes antão se comerão con todas has outras ca*r*nes defessas. E isto he que ho porco no hebraico quer dizer tornado, porquanto no tempo do Mexia se tornara a come*r* dos iudeus, e assi comerão de herrod que he a milhor besta q*u*e ha no mu*n*do. No Talmud se diz que De*o*s hos criou macho e femea, e

[15] The reference is probably to Sifra, Beḥuqqotai, 2, end (ed. Weiss, p. 111a) cited in *PF*, pp. 782, 884: "*I will confirm My convenant with you* (Lev. 26:9) — not like the first covenant which you violat-ed ... but a new covenant which will never be abrogated ..."

[16] The reference is probably to a passage ascribed to *BRMD* to Gen. 41:1 (*PF*, pp. 802f.; *ACPJ*, 1, 9, p. 92) which is preserved in Midrash Tehillim 146:7, ed. Buber, p. 535; Braude, 2:365f. The ver-sion of *PF* reads: "It is written: *The Lord releases the bound* (Ps. 146:7). Every beast considered unclean in this world will be declared by the Holy One, blessed be He, to be pure in the future ... What is *the Lord releases the bound*? There is no greater prohibition [binding] than the menstruous woman for a woman menstruates and [God] prohibits her to her husband. But in the future, He shall permit her ..."

[17] *I.e.*, Bereshit Rabbah (Genesis Rabbah). See Introduction.

[18] Ps. 146(145):7.

[19] A rabbinic term for Gentiles.

[20] Gen. 9:1, 3f.

[21] Gen. 9:3. The Portuguese *cerva* should probably be *herva*, *i.e.*, "the grass of the field."

[22] Based on the continuation of the passage cited in n. 16.

the day of the Supper as priest of the new Law. However, some from the tribe of Levi would be so ordained.

It says in the book *Sifre* that "the time will come when the Law will be changed along with everything commanded in it."[15] It is written explicitly in the Talmud in the chapter that discusses the advent of the Messiah that when He came He was to put to an end the [celebration of] the Passover and the Sabbath and the rules concerning sexual relations with a menstruous woman, and that he would make all things anew, rejecting the old.[16] He did that which it was written that the Messiah would do; He terminated the Passover and other feasts and ceremonies of the old Law and gave a new Law which He placed in the hearts of men. Rabbi Bereshit[17] gives evidence of this in expounding David's words in Psalm 145: *God untied those who were bound.*[18] He says that all quadrupeds sent to this world will be pronounced clean by God at the time the Messiah comes as He gave them to the children of Noah.[19] This is shown in the *Grão Grande* in accord with that written in chapter 9 of Genesis: God permitted the children of Noah to eat all things whereas before the Flood they ate no meat.[20] Thus it says in the *Grão Grande*: "As the deer of the field, I permit all to you."[21] So will all things [prohibited by] Moses be permitted when the Messiah comes.[22]

Rabbi Solomon asks what it means in the *Grão Grande* when it says that God had released those who were bound, save the quadrupeds. He answers that those who were bound by the law would be released by the Messiah from [restrictions concerning] quadrupeds. These are the swine which will then be eaten with all the other meats that were forbidden. Now swine in Hebrew means "returned,"[23] since, at the time of the Messiah, the Jews shall return to eating pork. They shall eat of the *herrod*,[24] the best animal in the world. In the Talmud, it says that God

---

[23] The Hebrew for "pig" is *ḥazir* while the verb *ḥazar* means "to return" or "turn." In a play on this, a somewhat unorthodox midrashic passage, much exploited by Christian polemicists, reads: "Why was its name called *ḥazir* [pig]? For the Holy One, blessed be He, will return it [*le-haḥaziro*] to Israel." See the reference in Judah Rosenthal, "The Concept of the Abrogation of the Commandments in Jewish Eschatology" (Hebrew), *Meyer Waxman Jubilee Volume* (Jerusalem, 1960), p. 221; Glaser, "Invitation," p. 355, n. 15; Millás-Vallicrosa, "Un tratado anónimo," *Sefarad,* 13 (1953), p. 8. It is cited in *ACPJ* (1, 9, p. 94) as follows: "quare vocatum est nomen ejus Hazin, id est Sus? quia futurum est ut deus revertatur ad Israel. Hazire etenim Hebraice, reversio dicitur latine."

On *tornado* or *tornadizo* as a term for the New Christians, see Révah, "Marranes," pp. 30f. This etymology was reinforced by the term *marrano* derived by some from a word for swine. See Révah, *ibid.*; B. Netanyahu, *The Marranos of Spain* (New York, 1966), p. 59, n. 153; A. Farinelli, *Marrano: Storia di un vituperio* (Geneva, 1925).

[24] Machado's *de herrod* is a corruption of a probable original *behemod*, i.e., *Behemoth*, the mythical animal reserved for the righteous in the world to come. See Leviticus Rabbah 13:3, 22:10. *ACPJ* (1,

fez capão do macho, e matou a femea e salguoa pera daar a comer aos iustos no tempo do Mexia. E assi ho peixe leuiatam comerão, polo qual todos hos pescados se entendem.

Concludindo, dizemos que todos estes dizeres querem dizer que no tempo que viesse ho Mexia, poderião hos iudeus comer todas as carnes e pescados defesos na Lei, e que de tudo poderião vsar. E, portanto, crede que tudo vos he concidido pois que a Lei velha cessou e a noua foi dada polo Mexia.

Esta he a nossa fee e crença, e esta seia a vossa. Amen.

[*fol. 46v*] Capitolo Seitimodecimo. Como ho Mexia auia de tirar a idolatria, chamar hos gentios, dar ha aguoa do bautismo pera se hos homens saluarem.

A quintadecima propriedade do Mexia era que ella auia de tirar ha idolatria do mundo, como Christo tirou, segundo prouaremos polos profetas e polos talmudistas.

A todos he bem manifesto e conhicido que todo ho mundo estaua cheo de muita idolatria, assi Europa como Africa e Assia. E todas has suas prouincias, e reinos, e cidades, e poucos a Deos conhicião, senão hos vossos predecessores que adorauão hum Deos. Porem, depois que ho Mexia veo, ouue no mundo maior conhicimento de Deos que d'antes auia. Porque loguo antão, por mandado de Deos Mexia, forão hos apostolos preguar a Deos e dalo a conhecer às gentes, has quaes nam no conhicião como loguo conhecerão, porquanto muitos crião pola preguação dos apostolos em Deos.

E nom fiquou luguar, nem ilha, nem prouincia na qual ho nome de Deos nom fosse declarado, como Dauid tinha profitizado no psalmo xviij. Que por todo ho mundo a trombeta destes apostolos auia de soar, e dali por diante ho poder do diabo foi muito quebrantado, e nom podia prouocar hos humanos tanto à idolatria, como fazia antes que ho Mexia viesse. Disto daa testimunho Isaias no capitolo xlvi, dizendo: "Caio Bel, idolo; desfeito he Nabo; quebradas sam as sua[s] semelhanças e figuras todas." No liuro dos Numeros, no capitolo xxiij, se diz: "Idolo nom auera na casa de Iacob." E no Deuteronomio se diz: "Hos idolos quebrantai e desfazei." Sobre estes passos diz Rrabi Midras: "Adorão

---

9, p. 94) notes: "Item, sylvestrium animalium recipiunt Bechemoth. Dicitur in Talmut, quod animal illud Bechemoth est omnium animalium maius, et quod masculus et foemina fuerunt ab initio creati. Videns autem Deus quod si filios genuissent, prae illorum magnitudine et multitudine totus mundus esset destructus, castravit masculum, et refrigerauit foeminam quam custodit, ut eam daret iustis tempore Messiae ad comedendum."

[25] On the creation of Leviathan as male and female and the future banquet for the righteous, see

created them male and female. He castrated the male and killed the female to feed the righteous at the time of the Messiah. They shall also eat the fish Leviathan which represents all fish.[25]

In conclusion, we declare that all these sayings mean that when the Messiah comes, the Jews will be able to eat and use all the meats and fish prohibited in the Law. Therefore, accept the fact that this has all been granted you, since the old Law has been replaced by the new, which was given by the Messiah.

This is our faith and belief. May it be yours. Amen.

[*fol. 46v*] Chapter Seventeen. How the Messiah would abolish idolatry, call the Gentiles to Him, and baptize mankind so that they could be saved.

The fifteenth characteristic of the Messiah was that He would abolish idolatry in the world, as Christ did, as we shall prove by the prophets and talmudists.

It is common knowledge and well known to everyone that the whole world — Europe as well as Africa and Asia — was steeped in idolatry. In the [different] domains, provinces, and cities few knew God except for your forefathers who worshiped one God. However, after the Messiah came, there was greater knowledge of God in the world than heretofore. For, soon afterwards, the apostles, sent by God the Messiah, preached about God and made Him known to the people who had not known Him before. Thus, many believed in God because of the preaching of the apostles.

There was not a place, nor an isle, nor a province in which the name of God was not proclaimed, as David had prophesied in Psalm 18.[1] Through all the world the trumpet of the apostles would sound. Henceforth, the power of the devil was shattered and unable to seduce man to idolatry as it had before the Messiah had come. Isaiah gives proof of this in chapter 46: *The idol Bel fell, Nebo is undone; all their statues and idols are broken.*[2] In chapter 23 of the Book of Numbers, it says: *There will be no idol in the house of Jacob.*[3] In Deuteronomy we read: *Break and undo the idols.*[4] Rabbi Midrash comments on these verses: "The Gentiles worship

B.T. Bava Batra 74a. *ACPJ* (7, 9, p. 94) notes: "Item piscium, squamas non habentium accipiunt majorem, quem Leviathan appellant."

[1] Ps. 19(18):2ff.
[2] Isa. 46:1.
[3] Num. 23:21.
[4] Deut. 7:5.

hos gentios hos idolos e ho pouo de Isrrael hos segue, mas vira ho
Mexia que quebrantara hos seus poderes." Bem se parece polo dizer
deste doutor, que no tempo do Mexia, auião de cair hos idolos. E se
elles cairão polo poder dos apostolos de Christo, seguesse que elle tinha
este poder, ho qual elle mesmo lhes deu.

No Terceiro Liuro dos Rreis, no capitolo xv°, se conta que ellrrei Asa
alimpou toda a cidade de Ierusalem dos idolos. Diz Rrabi Samuel: "Este
he ho Mexia que ho pouo gentio alimpara da idolatria." Esto se confirma por aquilo que se escreue no Libro de Tobias no capitolo xiiij°,
onde se diz que dixe Tobias: "E as gentes leixarão hos seus idolos e ir-
seão pera Ierusalem, e morarão nela, e todos hos rreis se alegrarão
adorando ho Deos de Ierusalem." Esto foi comprido no tempo do Mexia
quando hos rreis gentios leixarão hos idolos e se conuertirão à fee de
Christo. Ho mesmo diz Isaias no capitolo segundo: "Ho Senhor soo sera
aleuantado naquele dia, e os idolos todos cairão e serão desfeitos." Este
dia foi quando ho Mexia veo a este mundo. Assi Esaias ho confirma no
capitolo xiij, que naquele dia ho homem lançara fora de si e da sua casa
hos idolos de prata. Ieremias confirma isto dizendo no capitolo
cinquoenta: "Tomada he Babilon; confuso he Bel; vincido he
Merodach; todolos seus idolos são confusos e vincidos." Ho profeta
Ezechiel daa autoridade [fol. 47r] a isto, dizendo no capitolo vi°: "Montes
de Isrrael, ouui a palaura do Senhor Deos: 'Sabee que ei de trazer espada
sobre vos, e ei de destruir todos hos vossos altares; e hos vossos idolos
serão destruidos; e hos vossos idolos cessarão.'"

Todas estas profitias estauão escritas dos idolos que auião de ser
destruidos e auião de cessar pola vinda do Mexia. Nos Canticos, no
capitolo segundo, se diz que a uox do meu amiguo diz: "Ex aqui, vem
ho meu amiguo saltando polos montes, e passando polos vales." Rrabi
Midras sobre este passo diz: "Este he ho Mexia que fara isto no seu
tempo — que destruira hos montes, que são hos idolos."

E vos outros, na oração maior, dizes que hos idolos serão talhados
pera fazer passar as çugidades da terra pera afirmar ho mundo no reino
de Deos. Todo isto afirma que no tempo do Mexia a idolatria auia de
ser tirada e pouco auia de reinar neste mundo, como aguora vemos que

---

⁵ Source not identified.
⁶ 1 Kings 15:12.
⁷ Source not identified.
⁸ Tob. 14:8f.
⁹ Isa. 2:17f.
¹⁰ The correct reference is Isa. 2:20.
¹¹ Jer. 50:2.
¹² Ezek. 6:3f.

the idols and the people of Israel follow them; but the Messiah shall come and break their power."[5] It seems clear enough by what this doctor says that the idols would fall at the time of the Messiah. And if they are to fall through the power of the apostles of Christ, then it would follow that He had this power which he conferred upon them.

In chapter 15 of the Third Book of Kings, it is related that King Asa purged the entire city of Jerusalem of its idols.[6] Rabbi Samuel states: "This is the Messiah who will cleanse the Gentiles of idolatry."[7] This is confirmed by that written in chapter 14 of the Book of Tobit, where it states that Tobit said: *And the people shall abandon their idols and go to Jerusalem where they shall live; and all the kings shall rejoice and worship the God of Jerusalem.*[8] This was fulfilled in the time of the Messiah, when the Gentile kings abandoned their idols and converted to the faith of Christ. Isaiah says the same in chapter 2: *The Lord alone shall be exalted on that day, and all the idols shall fall and be undone.*[9] This was the day on which the Messiah came to this world. Isaiah confirms this in chapter 13: *On that day man shall cast away from himself and from his house the idols of silver.*[10] Jeremiah corroborates this in chapter 50: *Babylon is taken; Bel is confounded; Merodach is vanquished; all their idols are confounded and vanquished.*[11] The prophet Ezekiel lends authority [*fol. 47r*] to this in chapter 6: *Mountains of Israel, hear the word of the Lord God: Know that I will bring a sword upon you, and I will destroy all your altars. And your idols shall be destroyed and come to an end.*[12]

All these prophecies were written about the idols that would come to an end and be destroyed with the advent of the Messiah. In the second chapter of Song of Songs, it states that the voice of my beloved says: *Behold, my beloved comes leaping upon the mountains, and passing through the valleys.*[13] On this verse, Rabbi Midrash says: "This is the Messiah who will do this in His time. He shall destroy the mountains, which are the idols."[14]

In your major prayer you say that the idols shall be cut off to cause iniquity to pass from the earth to realize the kingdom of God in the world. This means that at the time of the Messiah, idolatry would be abolished and little of it would hold sway in the world.[15] We see this

---

[13] Song of Songs 2:8.

[14] Apparent corruption of Song of Songs Rabbah, *ad loc.* (Sonc., p. 117) cited in *PF*, pp. 369, 469 (cf. 662, 827, 855) and *ACPJ*, 1, 10, p. 99. In *PF*: "*Leaps over the mountains*, etc. The Rabbis say: 'Mountains' is nothing but a name for idolatry, as it says, *They sacrifice on the tops of the mountains and make offerings upon the hills* (Hos. 4:13)."

[15] Reference is to the *'Alenu* prayer which forms part of the service for the New Year and is used as well as a conclusion for every Jewish prayer service. For Machado's reference to it as the *oração maior*, cf. *ACPJ*, 1, 10, p. 98: "Item, si Judaeus orationem quam dicit hodie in die capitis anni sui,

hos mais dos humanos creem em Deos, posto que nom cream em Ihesu Christo, ho que não era antes que ho Mexia viesse porque antão adorauão ho sol e a lua; e aguora isto nom he tão continuo nem frequentado na gentilidade ou paguanismo.

A sextadecima propriedade era que ho Mexia auia de chamar as gentes como viesse, e Christo assi ho fez, segundo prouaremos polos profetas e talmudistas.

Iacob ho patriarcha daa boom testimunho disto no Genesis no capitolo xlix, falando da vinda do Mexia e do seu tempo determinado, dizendo: "E elle sera esperança dos gentios." Zacharias, no capitolo xiij, diz, pera confirmação disto, falando do conuertimento dos gentios: "Este pouo (ho gentio) chamara polo meu nome, e eu ho ouuirei, e dirlheei: 'Tu es meu pouo,' e ho pouo dira: 'Tu es meu Deos.'" Dauid no psalmo cxvi, diz: "Louuai, gentes, ho Senhor. E vos todo pouo, louuaiho."

Estes tres testimunhos são soficientes pera prouar que as gentes se auião de conuerter naquele dia, que auia de ser quando ho Mexia viesse a este mundo. E nom vos enguanes, que assi foi feito, como estaua profitizado polos profetas. Ho profeta Ose, no capitolo ij°, diz: "E direi a aquele que nom he meu pouo, 'Tu es meu pouo,' e elle dira, 'Tu es meu Deos.'" Assi ho afirma Dauid no psalmo lxvi°, dizendo: "Alegremse as gentes, e tomem prazer, porque tu, Senhor iulguas hos pouos com direito, e as gentes enderenças na terra." E Isaias, no capitolo ij°, diz: "Elle arguira e iulguara as gentes."

Bem sei eu que vos nom neguares isto — que ho Mexia auia de chamar hos gentios, [fol. 47v] mas neguaes isto ser comprido, do que me pesa. E porquanto todo ho Testamento Velho esta cheo destas autoridades, has quaes afirmão que no tempo do Mexia has gentes se auião de conuerter; e se auia de fazer hum pouo nouo dos gentios, como se fez; portanto, nom quero trazer mais autoridades senão afirmar isto que dos gentios se fez, e se compos hum pouo nouo christão, ho vosso desprezado e reprouado de Deos. Este pouo, que assi se auia de conuerter, foi figurado por Rruth, que casou com Booz, a qual era gentia (Rruth, primeiro), e Rraab meretrix gentia era, e destas gentias descendeo Christo, dando a notar que este pouo tambem elle auia de saluar.

---

bene consideraverit, quam orationem solemniorem omnibus orationibus reputant ..." The relevant part of the prayer referred to by Machado is "the abominations shall be removed from the earth and the false gods exterminated."

now, for most of mankind believes in God — although not in Jesus Christ. This was not the case before the Messiah came, for then they worshiped the sun and moon. This is no longer very frequent or customary among the Gentiles or pagans.

The sixteenth characteristic of the Messiah was that He would call the nations to Him when He came. Christ did this as we shall prove through the prophets and talmudists.

The patriarch Jacob gives evidence of this in chapter 49 of Genesis. Speaking of the coming of the Messiah and the time determined for it, he says: *And he shall be the hope of the Gentiles*.[16] Zechariah speaks of the conversion of the Gentiles in chapter 13 and confirms this: *This people (the Gentiles) shall call on My name, and I shall hear them, and say to them, 'you are My people,' and the people shall say, 'You are my God.'*[17] In Psalm 116, David says: *Praise the Lord, all you nations; and laud Him, all you people*.[18]

These three texts are sufficient proof to show that the people would convert on the day on which the Messiah would come to this world. Do not be deceived for it happened just as it was foretold by the prophets. In chapter 2 of Hosea, the prophet says: *And I will say to them who are not My people; You are My people, and they shall answer, You are my God*.[19] David affirms it so in Psalm 66. *Let the nations be joyful and take pleasure, because You, Lord, judge the people with justice, and guide the nations on earth*.[20] And Isaiah says in chapter 2: *He shall dispute and judge the nations*.[21]

I know quite well that you will not deny that the Messiah is to call the Gentiles to Him, [*fol. 47v*] but you do deny that this has been fulfilled and this grieves me. Now the entire Old Testament is filled with texts such as these which assert that the nations would convert at the time of the Messiah and would form a new people (as did happen). Therefore, I do not wish to cite further texts, but to affirm that the Gentiles became a new Christian people while yours was despised and rejected by God. This people which would convert was prefigured by Ruth, the Gentile, who married Boaz (Ruth, first [chapter]) and by Rahab, the Gentile harlot. [Now] Christ was descended from these Gentile women[22] which indicates that these peoples would also be saved by Him.

---

[16] Gen. 49:10.
[17] Zech. 13:9.
[18] Ps. 117(116):1.
[19] Hos. 2:24.
[20] Ps. 67(66):5.
[21] Isa. 2:4.
[22] Ruth and Rahab, considered in the tradition to be the harlot Rabah in the Book of Joshua, are mentioned in the genealogy of Jesus, Matt. 1:5.

Porem, veiamos ho que sentirão hos vossos doutores acerqua deste conuertimento dos gentios. Dauid, no psalmo xx, diz: "Con a tua força se alegrara ho rrei." Midras, grosador do salteiro, sobre este passo diz que quer dizer "e con a tua força se alegrara ho rei." Diz, este rrei he ho Mexia, ho qual se alegrara com lio seu pouo nouo que elle alcançara. Porque a raiz de Isrrael, que he ha de Iesse, estaa por sinal, na qual as gentes esperão, como Iacob tinha ia profitizado (Genesis, xlix), que este Mexia auia de ser huma grande esperança dos gentios. Rrabi Anina diz: "Nom vira ho Mexia senão quando ouuer de daar nouos preceitos às gentes que pera elle se tornarão. E antão hos perigrinos que erão mal quiridos, serão do Mexia, e amados e queridos." Estes peregrinos são os gentios, imiguos que erão de Deos, hos quaes viuião sem leis e preceitos. Mas, como veo ho Mexia, chamados loguo, obedecerão sem tardança alguma. Assi ho afirma Dauid no psalmo xvij, dizendo: "Ho pouo que eu nom conhici, me seruio, e chamado loguo, me obedeceo."

Ho pouo gentio foi este que loguo siguio a fee de Christo, como foi chamado. Mas vos outros, obstinados, sempre perseuerastes na vossa sentença falsa e enguanosa. Rrabi Moises pergunta: "Que peregrinos são estes?" Diz: "São perigrinos que farão sacerdotes do pam, ho qual Iacob pidio quando hia pera Mesopotamia, fugindo de Esau" (Genesis, xxviij°). Nom sei se este doutor entendia ho que dizia; porem, elle dixe grande verdade, porque pola vinda do Mexia, hos peregrinos, que erão hos gentios, fezerãonos sacerdotes de Deos eterno, porquanto consagrão ho corpo de Nosso Senhor, como aguora vemos.

Ex aqui como se conuerterão os gentios à fee do Mexia Christo.

[*fol. 48r*] A seitimadecima propriedade do Mexia era que elle auia de daar ho bautismo pola sua vinda, como Christo fez, segundo prouaremos polos profetas e polos talmudistas.

Ho profeta Ezechiel euidentemente proua ho bautismo no capitolo xlvij, onde fala das aguoas que elle vio em visão que saião do Templo

[23] Ps. 21(20):2.
[24] Isa. 11:10.
[25] Gen. 49:10.
[26] Ps. 18(17):45.
[27] Rabbi Moses the Preacher.
[28] Gen. 28:20. This passage is a mélange of Midrash Tehillim 21:1 (Buber, p. 177; Braude, 1:293) cited in *PF*, pp. 651f. (cf. pp. 854, 889) and one from Exodus Rabbah 19 (Sonc., pp. 232f.) cited in *PF*, pp. 459f. Machado's version appears to be closer to *ACPJ*, 1, 10, pp. 101f. which brings both passages in juxtaposition. The latter, however, incorrectly ascribes the Exodus Rabbah passage to the Mekhilta, a tannaitic midrash on Exodus. The version of Midrash Tehillim in *PF*, which differs

Still, let us see what your doctors thought about this conversion of the Gentiles. In Psalm 20, David states: *The King shall rejoice in your strength.*[23] Midrash, the commentator on the Psalter, remarks on the verse: *The King shall rejoice in your strength,* "This king is the Messiah who shall rejoice with his new people to whom he shall come. For the root of Israel, which is that of Jesse, stands as a sign in which the nations hope,[24] as Jacob had already prophesied in Genesis 49 [to the effect] that this Messiah would be [a source of] great hope among the Gentiles."[25] Rabbi Hanina says: "The Messiah shall come only when he gives new precepts to the nations who turn to him. At that time, the foreigners who were scorned, shall be loved and cherished by the Messiah." These foreigners are the Gentiles who were inimical to God while living without laws and precepts. Yet, once the Messiah came and called them to Him, they obeyed Him without hesitation. David affirms this in Psalm 17, saying: *The people whom I did not know served Me, and when called, obeyed Me.*[26]

These are the Gentiles who followed the faith of Christ without hesitation when they were called. But you who are obstinate still persisted in your false and deceitful ideas. Rabbi Moses[27] asks: "Who are these foreigners?" He answers: "They are the foreigners who shall make priests of the bread for which Jacob asked on his way to Mesopotamia as he was fleeing from Esau" (Genesis, 28).[28] I do not know if this doctor understood what he was saying; nevertheless, he uttered a profound truth. Through the coming of Christ, the foreigners, who were the Gentiles, made priests of God Eternal of us, since they consecrated the body of Our Lord, as we now see.

That is how the Gentiles converted to the faith of Christ the Messiah.

[*fol. 48r*] The seventeenth[29] characteristic of the Messiah was that he would institute baptism when He came, as Christ did, as we shall prove by the prophets and the talmudists.

The prophet Ezekiel clearly gives evidence of this baptism in chapter

---

from that of the editions, reads: "Scripture says, *In that day shall the root of Jesse stand as an ensign to the peoples; him shall the nations seek, and his dwellings shall be glorious* (Isa. 11:10). R. Hanina said: The Messiah comes for no other reason than to give the nations the commandments ..." Exodus Rabbah reads: "R. Berekiah said: Why did he say: '*The stranger did not lodge in the street*' [Job 31:32]. Because strangers will one day be ministering priests in the Temple ... And so Aquilas, the proselyte, once quoted to the Sages, the verse: *And loveth the stranger, in giving him food and raiment* (Deut. 10, 18), and asked, Are then all the promises to the stranger that he would give them food and raiment? The reply was: Jacob ... asked but this of the Lord, as it says, *And will give me bread to eat, and raiment to put on* (Gen. 28:20)..."

[29] See Chap. 14, n. 1.

de Ierusalem, e concludindo no meo do capitolo, diz: "Toda a alma que foi firida e foi lauada neste rreguato d'aguoa, loguo sera sãa, e sairão muitos peixes depois que estas aguas começarem a correr." Certamente, isto que Ezechiel diz no capitolo aleguado se entende da aguoa do bautismo, sem a qual ninguem nom se pode saluar, nem ser lauado do pecado original. Este bautismo foi por Christo instituido quando elle foi bautizado por Sam Iohão no rrio de Iurdão, e pubricado quando elle dixe aos seus discipulos, depois da sua resurreição, que fossem preguar e bautizar. E como elles receberão ho Spiritu Santo, loguo pubricamente ho declarão por todo ho vniuerso mundo. E loguo ha circumcisão cessou, nom tendo mais viguor, nem forças, nem tera iamais. E posto que na Lei da natureza hos humanos se saluauão na fee do Mexia, crendo que elle auia de vir tomar carne humana pera hos saluar do pecado de Adam con certos sacrifitios protestatiuos desta fee; porem, como ho bautismo lhes foi promulguado, nom se poderão mais saluar na fee sem a aguoa do bautismo. Isto se entende depois que elle foi suficientemente pubricado aos humanos.

Assi, tambem, nem vos outros nom vos podes saluar na circumcisão, nem hos vossos predecessores, depois daquela geral promulguação e pubricação do bautismo. Por onde sabee e tende por certeza que quantos iudeus morrerão circumcidados e fanados de 1541 anos pera qua, todos forão ao inferno por falta da aguoa do bautismo, da qual carecerão, e a ignorantia nom excusou hos vossos antepassados, nem a uos porquanto asaz a Lei noua do Mexia he declarada, e nisto, senhores, nom tenhaes duuida nem debate. Assi que pola vinda do Mexia, que foi Christo, ho bautismo foi entremitido, e a circumcisão foi lançada fora da vontade de Deos.

Venha qua ho profeta Ezechiel e veiamos ho que sente disto. No capitolo xxxvi, ex aqui ho que diz, falando deste bautismo que auia de ser ordenado polo Mexia: "Derramarei sobre vos aguoa muito limpa, e seres limpos de todas as vossas maldades, e vos alimparei de todolos vossos idolos. Daruosei hum coração nouo, e hum spiritu nouo porei sobre vos, e tirarei este coração de pedra da vossa carne e daruosei hum coração de carne, e hum spiritu nouo porei no meo de vos outros."

[fol. 48v] E vos, Isaias, que sintis acerqua disto? Ex aqui ho que diz no capitolo xliiijº, falando do bautismo: "Eu derramarei e lançarei aguoas sobre hos sequiosos que tem sede, e aguoas sobre as cousas sequas. Lançarei ho meu spiritu sobre a tua geração, e a minha benção sobre a tua semente, e pulul16arão antre as heruas, como hos salgueiros antre aguoas muito correntes."

47 when he speaks of the waters that issued from the Temple in Jerusalem which he saw in a vision.[30] In the middle of the chapter, he closes by saying: *Every soul that was hurt and washed in this brook will then be healed, and a great multitude of fish shall come forth after these waters begin to flow.*[31] Ezekiel undoubtedly refers in this chapter to the waters of baptism without which no one can be saved nor cleansed of original sin. This baptism was instituted by Christ when He was baptized by Saint John in the River Jordan and promulgated after His resurrection, when He told his disciples to go preach and baptize. When they had received the Holy Spirit, they publicly proclaimed it throughout the whole world. Circumcision then came to an end never more to have any effect or force. Now men were saved under natural law by faith in the Messiah with the belief that He would come and take human form to save them from the sin of Adam along with certain sacrifices that confirmed this faith. Nevertheless, when baptism was promulgated, they could no longer be saved by faith without the water of baptism. This is evident since it was sufficiently proclaimed to mankind.

In like manner, neither you nor your ancestors could be saved through circumcision after the general promulgation and proclamation of baptism. Know then for a fact that all the Jews who died circumcised for the last 1541 years have all gone to hell because they failed to receive the waters of baptism. Ignorance did not excuse your ancestors nor does it you since the new Law of the Messiah was sufficiently well proclaimed. This, gentlemen, you can neither debate nor doubt. Consequently, through the coming of the Messiah, Christ, baptism was introduced and the [rite of] circumcision excised from the will of God.

Let the prophet Ezekiel come forth and let us see how he feels about this. Here is what he says in chapter 36 concerning this baptism which would be ordained by the Messiah: *I will sprinkle clean water on you and you shall be cleansed of all your evils; and I will purge you of all your idols, I will give you a new heart and will place a new spirit over you. I will take away this heart of stone from your flesh and will give you a heart of flesh, and a new spirit will I place among you.*[32]

[*fol. 48v*] And you, Isaiah, how do you feel about this? Here is what he has to say about baptism in chapter 44: *I will sprinkle and scatter water over the parched ones who are thirsty and over all that is dry. I will cast My spirit over your generation and my blessing over your seed, and they will spring up among the grass, as the willows among the flowing waters.*[33]

[30] Ezek. 47:1.
[31] Ezek. 47:9.
[32] Ezek. 36:25ff.
[33] Isa. 44:3f.

E vos, Zacharias, no*m* darees algu*m* testimunho disto pera con-
fundirdes estes obstinados que forão? Ex aqui ho grande testimunho
bem patente e manifesto que põe no capitolo xiij, dize*n*do: "Naquele
dia parecera hu*m*a fonte muito manifesta à casa de Dauid e aos
moradores de Ierusalem, em rremissião dos pecados. Tirarei hos nomes
dos idolos da terra, e no*m* serão mais auidos na memoria dos humanos.
Hos profetas falsos, hos s*piritus* maos, tudo tirarei."

Diguouos, senhores, que tudo isto que estaua escrito do Mexia — que
foi Chr*isto* — tudo he comp*r*ido e acabado quanto he à p*r*imeira vinda.
A Sagrada Escritura toda esta chea de autoridades polas quaes bem se
demostra que ho Mexia auia de daar bautismo. Pore*m*, leixemolas, e
veiamos que sintirão hos vossos doutores ace*r*qua disto.

No Talmud, no capitolo que fala como auião de ir gãynhar hos
perdões, sobre hos textos acima aleguados, diz Rrabi Aquiba: "Be-
*n*aue*n*turados seres, filhos de Isrrael, daqui por diante, que ia sondes
limpos, porque ho Padre celestrial vos ha de ma*n*dar alimpar com
bainho muito limpo que alimpara a vos e às molheres me*n*struosas."
Assi ho dixe Zacharias[a] no capitolo 4°: "Saira aguoa da casa de D*eo*s que
lauara todo ho pouo." Rrabi Iofet confirma tudo isto dizendo que ho
Mexia ve*r*tera aguoas sobre hos pouos limpas, e serão limpos de todos
hos pecados." Rrabi Iosua, sobre aquele passo de Ezechiel do capitolo
xxxvi onde se diz que D*eo*s auia de tirar ho coração de pedra, e daria
s*piritu* de carne, diz que no tempo do Mexia se abrira hu*m*a fonte em
Ierusalem que sarara todos aqueles que nela se quiserem lauar.

Concludindo, pois, dizemos que ho Mexia auia de tirar a idolatria
pola sua vinda. Auia de chamar hos gentios e fazer hu*m* pouo nouo.
Auia de daar ho bautismo, no qual todos se auião de lauar q*ue*
quisese*m* ser saluos porquanto, sem esta aguoa, no*m* ha hi saude ne*m*
vita eternal. Todas estas tres propriedades forão co*m*municadas a

a int. +*Joel* exp.

[34] Zech. 13:1f.
[35] Reference is to tractate Yoma concerned chiefly with the Day of Atonement.
[36] M. Yoma 8:9; B.T. Yoma 85b (Sonc., pp. 423f.) cited in *PF*, p. 821; *ACPJ*, 1:10, p. 103: "R.
Akiba said: Happy are you, Israel! Who is it before whom you become clean? And who is it that
makes you clean? Your father which is in heaven, as it is said: And I will sprinkle clean water upon
you and you shall be clean (Ezek. 36:25). And it further says: The hope [*miqveh* meaning both
"hope" and "ritual bath"] of Israel, the Lord (Jer. 17:13)! Just as the [bath] ... renders clean the
unclean so does the Holy One, blessed be He, render clean Israel." Machado's interpolation of a
reference to menstruous woman may be based on a confusion of this passage with Zech. 13:1, cited

And you, Zechariah, do you not have some testimony to confound those who are so obstinate? Important evidence that is quite obvious and clear may be found in chapter 13, where Zechariah says: *A fountain shall appear very clearly on that day to the house of David and to the inhabitants of Jerusalem for the absolution of sins. I will remove the names of the idols on earth, and they shall no longer be remembered by mankind. The false prophets, the evil spirits — I will remove all.*[34]

I tell you, gentlemen, all this that has been written about the first coming of the Messiah, Christ, has been realized and fulfilled. The Holy Scriptures are full of evidence that proves that the Messiah would institute baptism. However, let us leave this and see what your doctors feel about this.

In the chapter in the Talmud that speaks of gaining forgiveness,[35] we read what Rabbi Akiba says concerning the above verses: "Blessed shall you be henceforward, children of Israel, for now you are pure. For the heavenly Father shall have you bathe in clean water that shall cleanse you and the menstruous women."[36] In this same vain, Zechariah says in chapter 4 that *water shall come forth from the house of God and cleanse all the people.*[37] Rabbi Iofet confirms all of this in saying that the Messiah shall pour clean water over the people and they shall be cleansed of all their sins. Concerning the verse in Ezekiel, chapter 36, that says that God would take away the heart of stone and replace flesh with spirit, Rabbi Joshua states that in the time of the Messiah a fountain shall open in Jerusalem which will heal all those who wish to wash themselves in it.[38]

In conclusion, we say then that the Messiah would abolish idolatry with His coming [and] would call the Gentiles to Him to form a new people; He would institute baptism in which all who wanted to be saved would be cleansed, for, without this water, there is neither well-being nor eternal life. All three of these characteristics were realized in

---

above, which reads in the Vulgate: "erit fons patens ... in ablutionem peccatoris, et menstruatae." In Machado's paraphrase of the verse, "menstruatae" is omitted.

[37] Cf. Joel 4(3):18, Ezek. 36:25.

[38] Ezek. 36:26f. The above may ultimately go back to a passage such as the following in *PF*, p. 820: "... Praedictis adhuc ad iiciendum, quod legitur in lib. Kudduschin dist. Hesrah Jouchasin, [*Mandaverunt*] *magistri nostri: Spurii, et Nathinaei mundi erunt in futuro, verba sunt R. Jose, sicut dictum est Ezech. 36. v. 25.* Et spargam super vos aqvas mundas, et mundabimini, etc. [B.T. Kiddushin 72b]. Hucusque Talmud. Valde etiam bene aqva *Baptismi* et virtus ejus prophetata est ibi ubi per *Zachariam* taliter scriptum est cap. 13. vers. 2 etc. *In die illo erit fons patens domui David, et habitoribus Jerusalem ... ad restituendum, vel ad peccatum, vel ad peccati purificationem, et ad elongationem, vel ad immunditiam. Et erit in die illo, dicit Dominus Exercituum, abscindam nomen idolorum de terra et non memorabuntur ultra.*"

Chr*isto*, e tudo isto comp*r*io, como estaua profitizado, por o*n*de parece
s*er* elle ho Mexia.

Esta he a nossa fee e crença, e esta seia a uossa. Ame*n*.

[*fol. 49r*] Capitolo Outauodecimo. Como a uinda do Mexia auia de ser
declarada por p*r*eguoeiros, e como ho catiueiro dos iudeus foi por
amor da morte do Mexia, por o*n*de nu*n*qua mais a sua oração foi
ouuida.

A outauadecima propriedade do Mexia era que, antes que elle viesse,
a sua vinda auia de ser pubricada e declarada por p*r*egoeyros, como foi
a uinda de Chr*isto*, como prouaremos polos profetas, e por Iosepho.

Claro e manifesto he que a uinda de Chr*isto*, Mexia v*er*dadeiro, foi
declarada hum pouco antes que elle viesse polo milhor home*m* que foi
antre hos home*n*s, chamado Rrabi Iona. E assi lhe chama Iosepho, e
nos lhe chamamos Sa*m* Iohão Bautista, filho do sace*r*dote Zacharias, ho
qual matou aquela Herodiades impiissima, comp*r*azendolhe Herodes,
tendoa por sua molher, a qual era do proprio irmão Philipo. Este foi ho
p*r*ecursor do S*en*h*or* que p*r*eguaua a uinda do Mexia, bautizando hos
iudeus no rrio de Iurdão, onde bautizou a Chr*isto* e ho demostrou ae-
les mesmos, dize*n*dolhes que aquele era ho Mexia promitido na Lei,
prouocandoos a penitentia, dizendolhes que ho rreino dos ceos era
cheguado (ho Mexia), e que fezessem penitentia dos seus pecados pera
ho recebere*m*.

Todas estas cousas que antão se fazião demostrauão claram*en*te a
uinda do Mexia, do qual Iosepho deu claro testimunho, e de São Iohão,
dizendo no Liuro xviii°, no capitolo vi°, primeiram*en*te de Chr*isto*, q*ue*
foi ho Mexia: "No mesmo tempo foi Ih*esu* Chr*isto* varão muito sabedor,
se he cousa licita chamarlhe varão. Era fazedor de cousas marauilhosas
e espantosas; ensinador e doutor daqueles que de boa uontade folguão
de ouuire*m* cousas v*er*dadeiras e boas. Aiu*n*tou muitos pera si, assi
dos iudeus como dos gentios. Este chamauase Chr*isto*. E como hos
p*r*imeiros e principaes varões da nossa gente ho acusasem diante de
Pilatos, hos seus discipolos no*m* ouuerão medo ne*m* no desempararão.
E ao t*er*ceiro dia depois da sua morte lhes apareceo viuo, assi como hos
prophetas, espirados polo Sp*iritu* Santo, delle tinhão ditas estas cousas e

---

[1] The actual source of this passage is not the Greek text of Josephus but the medieval Hebrew
version of Josephus known as the *Josippon* which refers to John the Baptist as Rabbi Yohanan. See
Abraham A. Neuman, "A Note on John the Baptist and Jesus in Josippon," *HUCA*, 23 (1950-1), pt.

Christ Who fulfilled them all as was prophesied. For this reason it would seem that He is the Messiah.

This is our faith and belief. May it be yours. Amen.

[*fol. 49r*] Chapter Eighteen. How the coming of the Messiah would be publicly preached and how the captivity of the Jews was occasioned by the death of the Messiah, so that their prayers were never more heard.

The eighteenth characteristic of the Messiah was that before He appeared, His coming would be publicly preached and announced, as was Christ's coming. We will prove this by the prophets and by Josephus.

It is quite obvious that the coming of Christ, the true Messiah, was proclaimed shortly before He appeared, by the very best among men — Rabbi Jonas by name. He was so called by Josephus[1] while we call him Saint John the Baptist, son of the priest Zechariah, He is the one whom Herod had killed to please his wife, the very impious Herodias, who had been the wife of Herod's own brother Philip.[2] He was the precursor of the Lord who preached the coming of the Messiah. He baptized the Jews in the River Jordan,[3] where he baptized Christ[4] and showed Him to them. He told them that He was the Messiah promised in the Law, called them to repentance and told them that the kingdom of heaven had come (the Messiah), and that they ought to do penance for their sins so that they could receive Him.

All these things that took place unquestionably show the advent of the Messiah. Josephus clearly attested to this and to Saint John in Book 18, chapter 6 where he spoke of Christ, who was the Messiah: "At the same time, Jesus Christ was a very learned man, if it is permissible to call him a man. He performed marvelous and wondrous things and was master and teacher of those who willingly and gladly listened to true and good things. He gathered many unto himself — Jews as well as Gentiles. He was called Christ. When the first and foremost men among our people accused Him before Pilate, His disciples were not afraid nor did they forsake Him. On the third day after His death He appeared alive before them infused by the Holy Spirit as were the prophets.

2, p. 138; Solomon Zeitlin, *Josephus on Jesus* (Philadelphia, 1931), p. 51. The *Josippon* was known to such polemicists as Martini and Petrus Galatinus.

[2] Matt. 14:3ff., Mark 6:16f., Luke 3:19f. See Josephus, *Ant.* 18.5.1; *JE*, 6:360; Scobie, *John the Baptist*, p. 181.

[3] Mark 1:5.

[4] Mark 1:9.

outras muitas, por onde, ates aguora, perseuera ho nome e geração dos christãos."

Veedes aqui, senhores, ho grande testimunho do Mexia do vosso proprio doutor que vos confundi e condennara no dia do iuizo. Este mesmo daa testimunho de Rrabi Iona no mesmo liuro, no capitolo x⁰, onde aproua a grande bondade e virtude de Sam Iohão, chamandolhe Bautista porquanto ensinaua hos iudeus a se bautizarem, que era hum grande sinal do bautismo de Christo. Deste preguoeiro e precursor do Mexia profitizarão aqueles dous profetas Isaias e Zacharias, por tal veiamos ho que dixerão.

[*fol. 49v*] Isaias, no capitolo lx⁰, dando testimunho, diz: "Voz do que brada no deserto, aparelhai ho caminho do Senhor, e enderençai hos caminhos do Nosso Senhor, porque a gloria do Senhor sera discuberta, e toda a carne" (que he todo ho homem) "vera a saude de Deos" (que era ho Mexia). Ho segundo testimunho he do profeta Malachias que diz no capitolo 3⁰: "Eu enuiarei ho meu anio messageiro, e aparelhara ho caminho diante da tua face. E loguo supitamente vira ao seu Templo ho dominador e Senhor que vos buscaes, e ho anio do testamento que vos queres." Estas duas testimunhas dão euidentes testimunhos de Rrabi Iona, que auia de vir declarar a uinda do Mexia. E assi como estaua profitizado assi foi comprido, porque loguo veo ho Mexia.

Assi como a vinda do Mexia ha de ser denunciada quando vier iulguar hos viuos e mortos, assi foi tambem esta da sua carne que auia de tomar. Malachias proua que Helias vira denunciar a uinda de Christo antes do iuizo, quando diz no capitolo 4⁰: "Eu vos enuiarei Helias, ho profeta thesbites, antes que venha aquele grande dia espantoso do Senhor, e conuertera ho coração dos pais pera hos filhos, e ho coração dos filhos pera hos pais." Este se fara antes do dia do iuizo que vira este Helias com Enoch pera conuerterem aqueles que siguirem a seita do antichristo à fee de Christo, que antão sera huma soo.[a]

Vos, porem, senhores,[b] nom fazes alguma deferença antre estas vindas

---

a + *vos porem porquanto cuidaes que auees de rreinar pera todo sempre com ho vosso Mexia e praza a Deos que nom seia como ho antichristo* exp.   b int. + *portanto* exp.

[5] *Ant.* 18.3.3. On this passage, the so-called *Testimonium Flavianum,* see Feldman, *Josephus* 9, pp. 49ff., n. 15; Eisler, *The Messiah Jesus and John the Baptist* (New York, 1931), pp. 36-73. Cf. *HS*, Evan. 29, *PL*, 198:1551f. Machado's version omits the phrase *cum Pilatus in crucem agendum esse decrevisset,* which should follow *Pilatos.*

[6] *Ant.* 18.5.2.

[7] Isa. 40:3,5. Machado's inclusion of the phrase *"vera a saude de Deos"* is probably due to the influence of Luke 3:6.

These and many other things were said about Him which is why the name and race of the Christians has persisted up till now.'"[5]

You see here, gentlemen, your own doctor's important testimony concerning the Messiah which will confound you and will condemn you on the Day of Judgment. In the same book, chapter 10, Josephus gives proof of Rabbi Jonah and commends the great goodness and virtue of Saint John, calling him "Baptist," because he taught the Jews to be baptized, which was a great symbol of Christ's baptism.[6] The two prophets Isaiah and Zechariah gave prophecies of this herald and precursor of the Messiah. Let us see then what they had to say.

[*fol. 49v*] In chapter 60, Isaiah offers evidence: *The voice of that which cries out in the desert, prepare the way of the Lord, and make straight the paths of Our Lord, because the glory of the Lord shall be revealed, and all flesh* (which is all man) *shall see the salvation of God* (which was the Messiah).[7] The second testimony is that of the prophet Malachi who says in chapter 3: *I will send My herald angel and he shall prepare the way before your face. And then the ruler and Lord whom you seek shall suddenly come to His temple, and the angel of the covenant whom you desire.*[8] These two testimonies clearly attest to Rabbi Jonah and his proclaiming the coming of the Messiah.[9] Just as it was prophesied, so was it fulfilled, for the Messiah soon appeared.[10]

And just as the coming of the Messiah shall be foretold when He comes to judge the living and the dead, so was His coming in the flesh to be foretold as well. Malachi proves that Elijah will come and proclaim the advent of the Messiah before the Day of Judgment when he says in chapter 4: *I will send you the prophet Elijah the Tishbite*[11] *before the coming of that great and dreadful day of the Lord, and he shall turn the heart of the fathers to the children, and the heart of the children to the fathers.*[12] This will take place before the Day of Judgment when Elijah will come with Enoch[13] to convert to the one faith of Christ those who follow the sect of the Antichrist.[14]

You, however, gentlemen,[15] make no distinction between these

[8] Mal. 3:1. The inclusion of the phrase *"diante da tua face"* is probably due to the influence of Mark 1:2.

[9] Mark 1:2ff.

[10] Acts 10:42, 2 Tim. 4:1, 1 Peter 4:5.

[11] The phrase "Elijah the Tishbite" is found in the Septuagint and the Mozarabic Bible. It is so cited in Isidore, *De variis quaestionibus, PL,* 76, p. 217.

[12] Mal. 4:5f.

[13] See above, Chap. 3, n. 14.

[14] MS has "you, however, think that you are to reign forever with your Messiah and please God that he not be like the Antichrist" expunged. See note *a.*

[15] Interlinear addition. See note *b.*

do Mexia, das quaes fala este profeta Malachias asaz claramente porquanto no terceiro capitolo fala da vinda do Mexia em carne, e do seu mesageiro São Iohão, chamandolhe anio quanto à vida e virtudes, e nom quanto à natureza. Esta vida ia he comprida; nom vos enguanes por vossa vida.

No quarto capitolo fala Malachias da vinda segunda do Mexia quando ha de vir ao vale de Iosaphat iulguar todos — assi boons como maos (Ioelis, capitolo 3⁰). Estas cousas queria eu que vos especulaseis bem e olhasses, pera virdes en conhicimento da verdade, que he esta: que este Sam Iohão veo denunciar esta vinda do Senhor Mexia, ho qual loguo veo depoos elle. Mas vos, enguanados polos vossos talmudistas que corrompem toda a Sagrada Escritura, dizendo que ho texto de Malachias se entende de Helias, nom podees saber esta verdade, a qual creo que ya, irmãos meus muito amados, ya conhecees, graças seião dadas a Deos.

[fol. 5or] A nonadecima propriedade do Mexia era que, como elle viesse, auiees de ser desterrados e vaguabundos, lançados fora da vossa cidade e terra, por amor da morte do Mexia. E assi vos aconteceo, que depois que ho matarão, hos vossos antepassados forão lançados fora da cidade e catiuos por Tito, emperador de Rroma, segundo prouaremos polos profetas e talmudistas.

Isaias, no capitolo primeiro, da testimunho como a cidade auia de ser destruida, ho que nom podia ser senão por algum grande pecado que auia de ser por amor da morte do Mexia: "Ha vossa terra he deserta, as vossas cidades são quemadas com foguo, a vossa região e prouintia hos estrangeiros ha comem e roeem; e sera desemparada como se acontece na destruição das grandes batalhas. E a filha de Sion sera desemparada, assi como a choupana na vinha, e assi como a casa do pipinal." Bem veedes, senhores, como isto he comprido pois que a cidade de Ierusalem de estrangeiros esta ia ocupada, e de vos e dos vossos antecessores, desemparada e desolada. Vai ia em tanto tempo, que nom pode ser senão por amor d'algum grande e feo e enorme pecado, que foi a morte do Mexia. Isaias, no capitolo iii⁰, diz: "Ho Senhor dos exercitos tirara de Ierusalem e de Iuda todo ho homem forte e robusto, e toda a fortaleza do pam e da aguoa, e todo ho batalhador e queimador, caualeiro e iuiz e profeta." De maneira, vai ho profeta neste capitolo descreuendo as miserias que auião de vir à cidade e aos vossos predecessores, que nom

---

[16] Joel 3:12.
[17] Mal. 3:1 is taken to refer to Elijah in Pirqe de Rabbi Eliezer, ch. 29, ed. Friedlander, p. 214. Cf. Mark 9:11, Rashi and Kimhi on Mal. 3:1.

comings of the Messiah of which the prophet Malachi quite clearly speaks in the third chapter. Here he speaks of the coming of the Messiah in the flesh as well as of His messenger Saint John, whom he calls an angel with respect to his life and virtues, and not to his nature. This life has been fulfilled. For your own good, do not deceive yourselves.

In the fourth chapter Malachi speaks of the second coming of the Messiah — when He shall come to the valley of Jehoshaphat to judge everyone — the good as well as the bad (Joel, chapter 3).[16] I would wish you to examine these things and consider them well, so that you could come to a knowledge of the truth: Saint John came to reveal this coming of the Lord Messiah who came after him. But you, deceived by your talmudists who corrupt the entire Sacred Scripture by saying that the verse in Malachi refers to Elijah,[17] are not able to recognize this truth. Yet, dearly beloved brothers, I believe that you know this now, praise be to God.

[fol. 50r] The nineteenth characteristic of the Messiah was that when He came, you were to be exiled and forced to wander and cast out of your city and land because of the Messiah's death. This indeed is what happened. After your forefathers killed Him, they were driven out from the city and taken prisoner by Titus, emperor of Rome, as we shall show through the prophets and talmudists.

In the first chapter, Isaiah testifies that the city would be destroyed. This could not have taken place without some great sin, which was that of the Messiah's death: *Your land is desolate, your cities are burned with fire, strangers devour and gnaw at your country and province; and it shall be abandoned and destroyed as happens during great battles. And the daughter of Zion shall be foresaken as the shack in the vineyard, and the house in the cucumber garden.*[18] You can see very well, gentlemen, how this has been fulfilled, for the city of Jerusalem is occupied by strangers and is foresaken and desolate of your ancestors. It happened in such a way that it could not be for any reason other than some great, ugly, and enormous sin. This was the death of the Messiah. Isaiah says in chapter 3 that *The Lord of hosts shall remove from Jerusalem and Judah every strong and robust man, every stronghold of bread and water, every warrior and burner, horseman, judge, and prophet.*[19] The prophet thus describes in this chapter the misfortunes that would befall the city and your forefathers as they happened. It thus ap-

---

[18] Isa. 1:7f.
[19] Isa. 3:1f. The reading "burner" is unclear.

parece senão que tudo tinha ante hos olhos, assi como se aconteceo.
Isaias, ainda concludindo esta destruição de Ierusalem, falando da torre
e cidade e vinha que D*eos* edificou, e de como a guardou por espaço de
muito tempo, finalm*ent*e vee*m* e diz: "Aguora veeres ho que ei de fazer
à minha vinha: tirarlhei a sebe e fiquara destruida; tirarlhei todo ho
cerco e muro e sera calcada e desemparada; e, finalmente, esta vin[h]a
no*m* sera estercada ne*m* cauada, nem podada, ne*m* vindimada; mas hos
cardos e hos espinhos subirão por ella."

Ex aqui como Isaias concludi como a cidade de Ierusalem auia de ser
destruida e guastada polos contrairos dela. E tudo isto, senhores,
causou quererem hos vossos antepassados matar ho Mexia sem causa e
sem rezão. [*fol.* 50*v*] E pera saberdes que a morte do Mexia foi causa do
vosso desterro, olhai ho que diz ho rreal profeta Dauid no ps*almo* lxviij:
"Derãome a come*r* fel e a beber vinagre." Ex aqui hos morteiros que
lhe derão a comer fel e a beber vin[a]gre. Hora, veede ho que diz Dauid
em luguar do Mexia: "Hos seus olhos seião escuricidos pera que no*m*
veiam, e ha sua sobe*r*ba lhe abaixa, a sua morada seia deserta e dese*m*-
parada, e no*m* aia hahi que*m* more nas suas casas." Assi que Dauid, no
ps*almo* prealeguado, vai pondo as miserias e angustias que padecerão
hos vossos p*r*edecessores por amor da morte do Mexia.

Zacharias, no capitolo xi, falando como a cidade de Ierusalem auia
de ser destruida com a sua gente polos roma*n*os, onde bem conclude
sua destruição, e bem clarame*n*te diz: "No*m* vos ei de pacer; e ho q*u*e
morrer, morra, e ho que se cortar, seia cortado; e hos outros comão e
roaa*m* a ca*r*ne do seu proximo."

Tudo isto, senhores, he comp*r*ido e acabado, e foi feito polo pouo
rroma*n*o, como Daniel mais clarame*n*te tinha profitizado no capitolo
nono, onde diz, falando da vinda e da morte do Mexia, e da pena que
auião d'aue*r* hos iudeus por matare*m* a Chr*isto*, e diz assi: "E a cidade e
ho santuario destruira ho pouo co*m* ho duque que ha de vir, e a fim da
cidade pera todo semp*r*e sera desolada e desemparada." Este foi Tito,
emperador roma*n*o que destruio a cidade e Templo co*m* ho pouo
roma*n*o, por amor da morte do Mexia, do qual daa testimunho Iosepho
no Liuro Seitimo da *Batalha Iudaica*, dizendo no capitolo xvij° que en
toda a batalha iudaica, tomou Tito nouenta e sete mil home*n*s que
antão se achauão na cidade, que erão vindos à festa da pascoa. E
emqua*n*to durou ho sitio do pouo roma*n*o contra a cidade, morerão

²⁰ Isa. 5:5f.
²¹ Ps. 69(68):22.
²² Ps. 69(68):24ff.

pears that all this was quite apparent to him. Isaiah continues to discuss this destruction of Jerusalem and speaks of the tower, the city, and the vineyard that God made and of how He watched over it for a long time. He then finally says: *Now you shall see what I will do to my vineyard. I will remove the hedge and it shall be destroyed; I will take away the fence and the wall and it shall be trampled and laid waste. Finally, this vineyard shall not be fertilized nor dug, trimmed nor harvested; but thistles and thorns shall rise up in its stead.*[20]

Thus Isaiah concludes that the city of Jerusalem would be destroyed and ravaged by her adversaries. This in turn resulted in your ancestors' desire to kill the Messiah without cause or reason. [*fol. 50v*] So that you know that the death of the Messiah was responsible for your exile, see what the royal prophet David says in Psalm 68: *They gave me gall to eat, and vinegar to drink.*[21] These are the executioners that fed Him gall and gave Him vinegar to drink. However, see what David says speaking in the name of the Messiah: *Let their eyes be darkened so they shall not see and subdue their arrogance. May their dwelling place become desolate and abandoned; and may no one live in their houses.*[22] Thus, in this psalm, David attributes the misfortunes and anguish which your forefathers suffered at the death of the Messiah.

In chapter 11, Zechariah speaks of how the city of Jerusalem and its inhabitants would be destroyed by the Romans. Of the destruction to be wrought, he clearly states: *I will not feed you; that which shall die, let it die, and that which is to be cut off, let it be cut off; and let the others eat and gnaw at the flesh of his neighbor.*[23]

This has all been realized and fulfilled, gentlemen, and accomplished by the Roman people, as Daniel had prophesied most clearly in chapter 9. Here he refers to the coming of the Messiah and to His death as well as to the suffering the Jews shall experience for having killed Christ. In this regard he says: *And the people together with the leader who shall come, shall destroy the city and the sanctuary, and the city shall remain desolate and forsaken forevermore.*[24] This was brought about by the Roman emperor Titus and the Roman people who destroyed the city and the Temple because of the death of the Messiah. Josephus bears witness to this in the Seventh Book of the *Jewish Wars*. He says in chapter 17 that throughout the entire Jewish war Titus captured ninety-seven thousand men who were in the city at that time because of the feast of Passover. While the Roman people laid siege against the city, one million one

---

[23] Zech. 11:9.
[24] Dan. 9:26.

hu*m* milhão de home*n*s e cem mil, comprendendo iudeus e outros gentios que antão se acharão dentro co*m* hos iudeus na cidade.

Bem vedes como Iosepho da testimunho desta batalha e destruição da cidade e do Templo e dos iudeus que antão forão catiuos por Tito e desnãotão nu*n*qua mais hos iudeus teuerão dominio ne*m* ma*n*do em Iuda. Esto foi feito no ano quadragesimo segundo, depois da paixão e morte do Mexia Chr*isto*, Nosso Se*n*hor.

[*fol. 51r*] Ia vimos, segundo hos ditos dos profetas, como hos vossos predecessores auião de ser vaguabundos polo mu*n*do, por amor do pecado grande e enorme que cometerão, matando a Chr*isto*, por onde no*m* some*n*tes elles padecerão desterro, mas todos hos outros padece*m*, e padecerão hos vindoiros. Portanto, veiamos que sintirão hos vossos doutores acerqua deste desterro tão prolongu[a]do e prolixo, onde se passarão ia mil e quinhentos e corenta e hu*m* anos, dos quaes, tira*n*do quorenta e dous que correrão desna paixão de Chr*isto* ates que veo Tito, q*ue* hos vossos predecessores destruio, fiquão mil e quatroce*n*tos e noventa e noue anos que Ierusalem foi destruida e ho Templo e a gente catiuada e vendida, e poosta em desterro. Por onde bem podemos concludir que este desterro causou a morte do Mexia, donde parece que iamais a Terra da Promissão sera vossa pois que, por passare*m* hos vossos antepassados hos preceitos e ma*n*damentos da Lei, e por amor da idolatria que cometerão, no*m* esteuerão senão setenta ano*s* em catiueiro, no*m* lhes falta*n*do profeta. Mas aguora ne*m* tendes profeta ne*m* varão boo*m* as orações do qual seião ouuidas.

No Deuteronomio[c] esta hu*m* texto no capitolo xxviij, que diz: "Filhos, no*m* creeão em elles." Sobre este passo em hu*m* liuro chamado *Adobarim Arrabal*, sobre ho Deuteronomio, se diz assi: "D*e*os disse aos filhos de Isrrael: 'Vos, gente sem crença, dixestes ante my*m* no mo*n*te de Sinay: Tudo ho que D*e*os fezer e disser faremos e ouiremos' (segu*n*do se co*n*tem no Exodo, capitolo xix). Depois dixestes polo bezerro, 'Este he teu D*e*os' (Exodi, xxxij°). Eu dixe: 'Como home*n*s morreres.' Mitiuos na Terra da Promissão. Fezestes templo. Dixeuos que no*m* series

---

c int. +*Leuitico* exp.

[25] *De Bello Judaico*, 6.9.3. Josephus refers not to Jews and Gentiles but to Jerusalemites and non-Jerusalemites.

[26] Correctly: Deut. 32:20. The Hebrew has "faithless children."

[27] The passage is from Sifre, 320 (ed. Finkelstein, New York, 1969, pp. 366f.), but is cited in the name of Deuteronomy Rabbah (*Devarim Rabbah*) in *PF*, pp. 261f. and *ACPJ*, 1, 12, p. 111 (cited as *addhebarim Rabba*). From ed. Finkelstein[2] (New York, 1964): "*Children in whom there is no faithfulness* (Deut. 32:20). You are children who have no faith. You stood on Mt. Sinai and said: *All that the*

hundred thousand men died, including Jews as well as non-Jews who were then within the city with them.[25]

You can plainly see how Josephus reports this battle and the destruction of the city and of the Temple and of the Jews, who at that time were taken prisoner by Titus. Since then the Jews never held control or authority over Judah. This occurred in the forty-second year after the passion and death of the Messiah Christ, Our Lord.

[*fol. 51r*] We have now seen, according to the sayings of the prophets, how your ancestors would come to wander throughout the world because of the great and enormous sin which they committed by killing Christ. For this, not only shall they suffer exile but also all those who came after and all future generations shall suffer as well. Therefore, let us see what your doctors thought about this very prolonged and extended banishment that has lasted one thousand five hundred and forty-one years. From these subtract the forty-two years from the Passion of Christ until the time of Titus who destroyed your ancestors. There remain one thousand four hundred and ninety-nine years from the time Jerusalem and the Temple were destroyed, and the people taken into captivity to be sold later and sent into exile. From this we can properly conclude that the murder of the Messiah caused this exile. It seems then that the Promised Land will never be yours; your forefathers transgressed the precepts and commandments of the Law and served idolatry; yet for that they remained in captivity only seventy years. Prophets at that time were not wanting, but now you have no prophet nor righteous man whose prayers may be heard.

There is a verse in Deuteronomy, chapter 28 that says: *Children, believe not in them.*[26] There is a comment on this verse from Deuteronomy in the book called Devarim Rabbah,[27] which says: "God said to the children of Israel: 'People without faith, you said before Me on Mount Sinai: *Everything that God does and says we will do and we will hear,*' according to Exodus, chapter 19.[28] Afterwards you said of the calf: *'This is your God'* (Exodus, 32).[29] I said: *'You shall die like men.'*[30] I placed you in the Promised Land. You built a temple. I told you that you would not be

---

Lord has said we shall do and we shall hear (Exod. 24:7). I said, you are gods (Ps. 82:6). Once you said of the calf, Here are your gods, O Israel (Exod. 24:7). I said of you, Surely as a man will you die (Ps. 82:7). I brought you into the land of your fathers and you built My chosen house. I said that you would never be exiled from it. Once you said, We have no portion in David (2 Sam. 20:1), I said Israel will be exiled from their land" (Amos 7:17).

[28] Exod. 19:8.
[29] Exod. 32:4.
[30] Ps. 82:7.

catiuos. Depois, dixestes: 'Nom teemos parte con Dauid, nem crença com ho filho de Isai' (segundo se contem no Terceiro Liuro dos Rreis, no capitolo xij°). Eu disseuos: 'Isrrael cauara. Sera catiuo, desterrado da sua terra polas iniurias que fara ao Mexia.'"

Diguouos que esta grosa bem declara que Isrrael auia de ser catiuo porquanto nom quis teer parte na casa de Isai — nom quis creer no filho de Dauid. Esto confirmasse com aquilo que dixe Isaias no capitolo primeiro: "Isrrael nom me conheceo." Dizse no Grão Grande sobre este passo: "Ho pouo de Isrrael, paruo e nescio, nom conhecera ho Mexia neste mundo, por onde vira a ser desterrado."

Todos estes dizeres são conformes aos ditos dos profetas que afirmão que o desterro de Isrrael foi por amor da morte do Mexia.

[fol. 51v] Todos aqueles que escreuerão aquela grande destruição feita por Tito, dizem e afirmão que não foi senão porquanto matarão a Christo. E muitos vossos doutores[d] são desta sentença, que este desterro nom foy senão porquanto matarão àquele grande profeta, chamado Christo. E assi como a cidade e Templo se destruirão, assi polo consiguinte, cessou a uossa oração e sacrifitio e oblação, como claramente ho predixe Daniel. Isto podemos prouar polos profetas e talmudistas. Esta era a vigesima propriedade que estaua escrita do Mexia, a qual foi conprida no tempo do Mexia.

Ordenado era na vossa Lei, segundo se contem no Leuitico, no capitolo xxiij, que cinquo festas auião de guardar solenemente os iudeus: a festa da pascoa, pinticoste, das trobentas ou cornos, da expiação, e dos tabernacolos. E nestas festas sempre erão obriguados a oferecer certas cousas e certos sacrifitios, segundo se contem polo Leuitico. Porem, nom pudião oferecer sacrifitio a Deos em todalas cidades ou vilas; mas ho luguar era ordenado em Ierusalem no Templo, segundo se contem no Deuteronomio no capitolo xvi, onde se diz que mandou Deos que nom lhe auião de sacrificar en todo luguar senão onde elle escolhesse e mandasse, ho qual luguar foi Ierusalem. Por onde se conclude que hos vossos sacrifitios aguora ia nom são aceites nem agradaueis a Deos pois que en Ierusalem se auia de oferecer e nam

---

d int. + iudeus exp.

---

[31] 1 Kings 12:16. A more correct reading would be "inheritance" rather than "belief". There appears here to be a confusion between erança and crença. Cf. DE, p. 66; Ajuda da fé, fol. 66r.

[32] Isa. 1:3.

[33] This may be based on a passage from Sifre (309) cited in PF, p. 927. The following is translated from ed. Finkelstein² (New York, 1969), p. 349:"O foolish people and unwise (Deut. 32:6), Foolish

enslaved. Afterwards you said: '*We have no portion in David, nor belief in the son of Jesse*' (according to the Third Book of Kings, chapter 12). I told you: 'Israel shall be uprooted. They shall be taken captive and banished from their land because of the injuries they shall inflict upon the Messiah.'"[31]

I tell you that this gloss rightly states that Israel would be held captive for not wanting to have a share in the house of Jesse nor believe in the son of David. This is confirmed by the statement of Isaiah in the first chapter: *Israel knew Me not*.[32] There is a comment in the *Grão Grande* on this verse: "The stupid, ignorant people of Israel shall not know the Messiah in this world and for this reason they shall be exiled."[33]

All of these words are in accord with the sayings of the prophets which maintain that Israel's banishment was as a consequence of the Messiah's death.

[*fol. 51v*] All those who wrote of the great destruction wrought by Titus affirm this by saying that it happened only because they killed Christ. Many of your doctors[34] too are of the opinion that this exile was due only to the fact that they killed that great prophet called Christ. And just when the city and Temple were destroyed, your prayers, sacrifices, and offerings ceased as Daniel clearly predicted.[35] We can prove this through the prophets and talmudists. This was the twentieth characteristic that was written of the Messiah which was fulfilled during His time.

According to Leviticus, chapter 23, it was ordained in your Law that the Jews were solemnly to keep five festivals: those of the Passover, Pentecost, the trumpets or horns,[36] Atonement, and Tabernacles. During these festivals they were obliged to offer certain sacrifices which are mentioned in Leviticus. However, they were not able to offer a sacrifice to God in all the cities or towns. Thus it was ordained that this take place in the chosen place in Jerusalem in the Temple.[37] This is attested in chapter 16 of Deuteronomy where it says that God ordered that no sacrifices be offered to Him in any place save where He chose and ordered. This place was Jerusalem. Thus it may be inferred that your sacrifices are no longer accepted by God nor pleasing to Him since it was in Jerusalem and nowhere else that such offerings would be made.

in the past and *unwise* in the future. Similarly, *But Israel does not know* in the past, *My people does not consider in the future* (Isa. 1:3)."

[34] Interlinear addition replacing "Jews."

[35] Dan. 9:26f.

[36] Reference to the New Year festival. See Lev. 23:24, Num. 29:1.

[37] Deut. 16:5f.

em outra parte. Por onde se demostra que Deos nom quer ia vossos sacrifitios, que he hum argumento (posto que pequeno) e inditio que ia veo ho Mexia. Porque d'outra maneira nom consintira que tanto tempo esteuereis fora da Santa Cidade. Polo qual se conclude que vai em 1541 anos que nunqua oração de vos outros foi de Deos ouuida, porque se ella fora ouuida, a algum varão iusto e santo da vossa Lei fora reuelado e discuberto este segredo, que vos chamaes segredo. Ou he isto, que antre vos outros nunqua mais se achou homem iusto e boom quanto a Deos? Ho que he verdade — que nhûm que iudaiza he auido por boom acerqua de Deos, porquanto Deos nom aceita ia vossas orações. Porem, aceita elle as orações daqueles que se tornarão christãos, e ho são de boa vontade, como ha muitos neste reino, boons e iu[st]os.

[fol. 52r] Ho profeta Ieremias, falando da destruição do Templo e como a Deos hos sacrifitios iudaicos em algum tempo nom lhe auião de comprazer, diz no capitolo vijº aquilo que Deos lhe dixe, reprouando as vossas orações: "Tu, Ieremias, nom queiras roguar por este pouo, nem faças oração, nem derrames prezes por elle, porque te nom ei de ouuir." E, no meo do capitolo, diz: "Esta he a gente que nom ouue a voz de seu Senhor, nem quis tomar disciplina ou ensinança alguma."

Assi que Ieremias vai concludindo tudo aquilo que aguora he comprido — que ho Templo foi destruido, e ho pouo iudaico nom he ouuido porquanto nom ouuirão a uoz do Mexia que lhes dizia que elle era aquele profeta do qual Moises falara (Deuteronomio, xviijº). Vedes aqui a pena que veo aos vossos antepassados porquanto pecarão contra ho moço.[e] Ha mesma sentença torna a confirmar Ieremias no capitolo xi, dizendo: "Tu nom rogues por este pouo porque, posto que dees brados e clamores, nom no ouuirei mais."

Aguora se cumpre contra vos aquilo que dixe Dauid no psalmo centesimo outauo: "A sua oração seia feita em pecado — ou — se torne pecado." E assi he, pois, que Deos nom ouue vossa oração. Muitas cousas que ho real profeta Dauid dixe deste desterro e desta oração, todas forão compridas no tempo do Mexia. Aguora parece ser verdade aquilo que elle predixe no psalmo xvij: "Bradarão, porem, nom teuerão quem hos saluasse e aiudasse." E no psalmo xxi: "Bradarei por todo dia e nom ouuiras, Senhor."

e uncertain reading

[38] Jer. 7:16.
[39] Jer. 7:28.
[40] Deut. 18:15ff.

This shows that God no longer wants your sacrifices. This is one reason (though small) and indication that the Messiah has already come. Otherwise, He would not have allowed your exile from the Holy City [to last] so long. It is thus concluded that for 1541 years God has not heard any of your prayers. For if they had been heard, this secret, which you call a secret, would have been revealed and disclosed to some righteous and saintly man of your Law. Or is it that among you no just and righteous man was found before God? This is the truth: No one who judaizes has been deemed good before God and therefore God does not accept your prayers any longer. Yet, He does accept the prayers of those who have become genuine Christians as have many good and righteous people in this realm.

[*fol. 52r*] In chapter 7, Jeremiah speaks of the destruction of the Temple and of how the Jewish sacrifices would at some point cease to be pleasing to God. He repeats the words of God, Who rejected your prayers: *You, Jeremiah, do not pray for these people; neither make any supplications, nor enter any pleas on their behalf, because I will not hear you.*[38] Then in the middle of the chapter, He says: *These are the people who do not listen to the voice of their Lord, nor do they want to be corrected or instructed in any way.*[39]

Jeremiah thus proceeds to affirm all that has now been fulfilled: The Temple was destroyed and the Jewish people are not heard since they did not hearken to the voice of the Messiah Who told them He was the prophet about whom Moses had spoken (Deuteronomy, 18).[40] You see here the punishment that came upon your forefathers because they sinned against the youth. Jeremiah reiterates this notion in chapter 11: *You shall not pray for these people, for, even though you shall shout and cry out, I will not hear them any more.*[41]

That which David said against you in Psalm 108 is now being fulfilled : *Let his prayer be made in sin* (or, become sin).[42] So it is that God does not hear your prayers. Many of the things that the royal prophet David said about your exile and prayers were fulfilled at the time of the Messiah. That which he predicted in Psalm 17 now appears to be true: *They cried out; however, there was no one to save and help them.*[43] And in Psalm 21: *I will cry out all day long and you will not hear, Lord.*[44]

[41] Jer. 11:14.
[42] Ps. 109(108):7.
[43] Ps. 18(17):42.
[44] Ps. 22(21):3.

Assi bradaes vos cada dia a Deos que vos ouça, e que vos tire do catiueiro, e que vos mande ho Mexia; mas elle nom ouue. Teem aguora as orelhas tapadas, e portanto, perdoailhe. Ieremias confirma isto tudo no capitolo xiiij, dizendo: "Tu nom rogues por este pouo algum bem, porquanto ainda que elles ieiuem, eu nom nos ei de ouuir. E se me oferecerem vitimas e sacrifitios e holocaustomata, nom ei de receber nada das suas mãos; mas com fome e com espada hos ei de consumir e acabar."

E pera maior confirmação disto, olhai por vossa vida ho que diz ho mesmo Ieremias no capitolo xvº: "Ho Senhor me dixe: 'Ainda que Moises e Samuel esteiem diante de mym, a minha alma nom he pera este pouo. Portanto, lanç[a]os fora de mym, e nom pareção mais diante da minha face. E se elles te [fol. 52v] dixerem, 'Pera onde iremos?,' dizelhe tu que isto diz ho Senhor: 'Aquele que he dino da morte, serlhea dada a morte, e quem merecer fome, recebera fome, e quem for dino de espada, por ella passara, e quem for dino de catiueiro, catiuado sera. E assi huns morrerão por espada, outros serão despedaçados polos cães, outros comestos polas aues. E porquanto me leixaste, teu Deos, por isso estenderei a minha mão sobre ti e matartei.'"

Tudo isto veo ao vosso pouo porquanto nom conhecerão ho Mexia, nem no adorarão, mas dixerão contra elle: "Nom temos outro rrei senão a Cesar." Veiamos aguora que sintirão hos vossos doutores acerqua desta oração que se vos fechou.

Num liuro chamado *Barahot*, no capitolo que começa, "Nom estarão," se diz por Rrabi Eleazar, sobre aquele passo de Ezechiel no capitolo xliiij, onde esta escrito: "Esta porta esta fechada, e nom se abrira": "No dia que a Casa Santa foi destruida, forão çarradas as portas da oração." Vem Ionathas e diz: "E loguo foi muro de ferro posto antre hos iudeus, e mais antre Deos." Bem dizem estes vossos doutores, porque como a Casa Santa foi destruida por Tito, loguo Deos determinou de nom ouuir mais Iuda, nem de rreceber sua oração feita no iudaismo, como muitos fazem, que posto que seião christãos, porem sam no porque mais nom podem, ou porque hão medo do foguo, ou de desterro.

Sede, senhores, sede boons christãos e catolicos, e crede ho que nos cremos, que he a uerdade, e nom vos enguanees cuidando neiciamente

45 Jer. 14:11f.
46 Jer. 15:1ff.
47 Jer. 15:6.
48 John 19:15.
49 *I.e.*, the talmudic treatise Berakhot.
50 The fifth chapter of this tractate which begins *'En 'omedin* (lit. "they do not stand," *i.e.*, "one

Thus, every day you call out to God to hear you and to free you from captivity and to send you the Messiah; but He does not hear. He has now plugged His ears, so bear with Him. Jeremiah confirms all this in chapter 14: *Do not pray for any good for these people, since even though they fast, I will not hear them. And if they present Me with victims and sacrifices and burnt offerings, I will accept nothing from their hands. But with hunger and the sword will I consume and exterminate them.*[45]

For further evidence of this, see by your life what Jeremiah says in chapter 15: *The Lord said to me: Even though Moses and Samuel stand before me, My spirit is not for these people. Therefore, cast them forth so they will no longer be before My face. And if they [fol. 52v] say to you, Where will we go?, tell them that this is what the Lord says: He who is deserving of death shall be given it, and the one who merits hunger, shall receive it; and whosoever deserve the sword, so shall he be pierced by it, and whosoever deserve captivity, may be enslaved. And so some shall die by the sword; others torn apart by dogs, and others eaten by birds.*[46] *And because you turned from Me, your God, I will therefore extend my hand over you and kill you.*[47]

All this happened to your people because they neither knew nor worshiped the Messiah. They rather spoke against Him: *We have no king but Caesar.*[48] Let us see now what your doctors thought about your prayer which has now ceased to be heard.

In a book entitled *Berakhot*[49] there is a chapter that begins "They shall not stand."[50] Here Rabbi Eleazar comments on that passage in Ezekiel, chapter 44, which states: *This gate is closed and shall not be opened:*[51] "On the day the Holy Temple was destroyed, the gates of prayer were closed."[52] Jonathan then says: "A wall of iron was then placed between the Jews and God."[53] These doctors speak truly. When the Holy Temple was destroyed by Titus, God then decided not to listen to Judah any more nor to receive any prayer of the Jewish faith such as many offer. For, although they may be Christians, they are so only because they cannot endure anymore or because they are afraid of fire or exile.

Please, gentlemen, be good Christians and Catholics, and believe what we believe, which is the truth. Do not deceive yourselves, foolishly

---

does not stand"). Cf. *ACPJ*, 1, 12, p. 115: "in capit. *Hen umdim*, id est, *non stabunt*. Dixit Rabbi Eliazer: A die quo templum fuit destructum, orationis portae clausae sunt … ."

[51] Ezek. 44:2.

[52] B.T. Berakhot 32b (Sonc., pp. 199f.) cited in *PF*, p. 911; *ACPJ* 1, 12, p. 115: "R. Eleazar also said: From the day on which the Temple was destroyed the gates of prayer have been closed … R. Eleazar also said: Since the day that the Temple was destroyed, a wall of iron has intervened between Israel and their Father in Heaven …" The Talmud has no reference to Ezek. 44:2.

[53] See above note. "Ionathas" is an error for Eleazar.

q*ue* ho Mexia ainda no*m* veo tomar ca*r*ne humana. Por vossa vida, que no*m* aia mais ceguidade antre vos, mas crede em Ih*es*u Ch*r*isto, que he ho *ver*dadeiro Mexia promitido na Lei, ao qual estas vinte propriedades que temos declaradas como podemos, escritas polos profetas e polos vossos doutores, forão co*m*municadas e apro*p*riadas a Christo, nosso Redentor, e nisto no*m* tenhaes debate ne*m* duuida.

Aqueles que ates aqui andarão errados, ia no*m* ande*m* mais, mas fação penitentia e se arrependão dos errores em que andarão, porq*ue* loguo Nosso S*en*hor hos recebera co*m* hos braços abertos. E a uossa oração que ates aqui no*m* foi ouuida, loguo de D*eos* sera recibida, com muito praze*r* e alegria que auera antre hos anios da gloria.

Esta he a nossa fee e crença, seia, senhores, e a uossa. Ame*n*.

[*fol.* 5 3r] Capitolo Nonodecimo. Como ha hi Trindade: Padre, Filho, S*piritu* Santo, tres em pesoas, e hu*m* na esse*n*tia, D*eos*.

Porquanto vos, senhores iudeus, neguaes a sac*r*atissima e indiuidua Trindade onde iaz toda a nossa saude e nosso be*m*, e toda a nossa per-feição, portanto, dete*r*minei de vola declarar polas autoridades do Testame*n*to Velho p*r*imeirame*n*te, e depois polos vossos talmudistas e doutores antiguos. Por rezões naturais, no*m* podemos prouar esta sacratissima Trindade porquanto isto excede toda a humana capacidade e forças humanas. Ne*m* aquele diuino Plato*m*, ne*m* aquele grande philosopho Aristoteles,[a], ne*m* natural algu*m*, chegou la pera pode*r* alcançar algu*m* conhicimento.

He, pois, necessario que creamos na indiuidua Trindade porquanto a Sagrada Escritura a declara a uos e a nos. Pore*m*, nos temos mais ho Testame*n*to Nouo que nola declara mui bem, e a Santa Madre Igreia que nos ma*n*da q*ue* assi ho creamos. Nesta Trindade ha hi vnidade seu em essentia ta*m*bem e personalidade. Ha vnidade Moises nola declara quando diz no Deute*r*onomio, no capitolo vi, que dixe D*eos*, ou ho anio em luguar de D*eos*: "Ouue, Isrrael, ho teu S*en*hor, D*eos* hu*m* soo he." E no Exodo no capitolo xx°, se diz: "Eu soo*m* ho S*en*hor teu D*eos* que te tirei da terra do Egito. No*m* teras outros deoses senão a mym." No capitolo ij° de Exodo se esc*r*eue que, falando Moises co*m* D*eos*, lhe dixe: "Se hos filhos de Isrrael te pe*r*guntare*m* polo meu nome, dirlhe[s]as: 'Aquele que he me ma*n*dou a uos, dizendo: 'Eu soo*m* ho que soom.'" Veedes aqui como D*eos* demostrou a Moises a unidade da esse*n*tia, dizendo que he hu*m* D*eos* e não muitos, segundo declarão estas

a MS *Aristeteles*

thinking that the Messiah still has not come incarnate. By your life, let there be no more blindness among you. Rather, believe in Jesus Christ who is the true Messiah promised in the Law. The twenty characteristics, that we have set forth as well as we could which were stated by the prophets and by your doctors, were fulfilled in and realized in Christ, our Redeemer. Do not debate this or have any doubt about it.

Those who up to now had gone astray no longer err, for they are doing penance and repenting the errors which they committed. For this, Our Lord soon shall receive them with open arms. Your prayer, which was not heard until now, shall be received before long by God with great pleasure and joy among the angels of glory.

This is our faith and belief. May it be yours, gentlemen. Amen.

[*Fol.* 53r] Chapter Nineteen. On the existence of the Trinity: Father, Son, Holy Spirit — three in person, one in essence — God.

Since you Jewish gentlemen deny the most sacred and indivisible Trinity in which our entire well-being, salvation, and perfection reside, I have therefore decided to reveal this to you firstly through passages in the Old Testament and then through your talmudists and ancient doctors. Naturally, we cannot prove this most sacred Trinity since it exceeds all human capacity and power of understanding. Neither the divine Plato nor that great philosopher Aristotle, nor any mortal, has succeeded in attaining any understanding of it.

It is necessary then that we believe in the indivisible Trinity because the Holy Scriptures reveal it to you and to us. However, we also have the New Testament which declares this to us very clearly, as does the Holy Mother Church that commands us to believe in it. In this Trinity, there is unity in essence as well as personality. Moses reveals the unity to us, in chapter 6 of Deuteronomy when he states that God or His angel for Him said: *Hear, Israel, your Lord, God is one.*[1] And in chapter 20 of Exodus, we read: *I am the Lord your God Who brought you out of the land of Egypt. You shall have no other gods but Me.*[2] In chapter 2 of Exodus it is written that when God spoke with Moses, He said to him: *If the children of Israel ask you My name, tell them: "He Who is sent me to you, saying: I am Who I am."*[3] You see here how God showed Moses the unity of essence saying that He is one God and not many, as verses cited above from the

[1] Deut. 6:4.
[2] Exod. 20:2f.
[3] Exod. 3:13f.

autoridades do Testamento Velho acima aleguadas. No Genesis, no capitolo primeiro, se descreue a Trindade e vnidade, onde se escreue que dixe Deos: "Façamos ho homem a nossa semelhança e imagem." Dizendo "façamos," declarou a pluralidade das pessoas, e dizendo "a nossa imagem" ou "semelhança," concludio a vnidade que esta na diuindade de Deos. Todos hos nossos doutores que falarão da Trindade por esta autoridade prouão a Trindade, e mais a vnidade, e nos assi ho cremos e temos por fee. E pois que ho vosso Moises assi ho proua, auies vos de lhe daar autoridade e fee porquanto elle nom dixe isto de si mesmo, mas diz que Deos assi lho ensinou e elle volo quis assi declarar.

[*fol. 53v*] Aguora veiamos a Trindade ou personalidades da Trindade com a vnidade. Moises nolo proua quando diz no começo do liuro no primeiro capitolo: "Deos criou ho ceo e a terra." No nosso latim esta: "In principio creauit Deus celum et terram." E onde nos temos *Deus*, as vossas briuias teem *heloym*, que he nome plural deste singular *hel*, que quer dizer Deos, e *heloym* "idem est pro diis" ou deoses.

Assi que por este nome *Deus*, entendemos Deos Padre, e por este nome *principium* entendemos ho Filho, em ho qual Deos faz todas as cousas. Parece pois aqui a pluralidade das pesoas, porquanto Moises poos este nome *heloym*, sinificando ho Padre e ho Filho, ho que elle nom fezera se nom ouuera pessoas na Trindade. Porque, onde este nome *heloym* se põe, sinifica pessoas diuinas. E assi no Genesis, no capitolo 2º, onde nos temos "eritis sicut dij," quando a serpente falou com Eua pera enguanar, no hebraico põese em luguar de *dij*, *heloym*, por onde conclude que a entenção de Moises era descreuer as pessoas tres da Trindade, como loguo no começo deste liuro prouou, dando testimunho do Padre e do Filho e do Spiritu Santo. Pedr'Afonso no viº titolo do seu liuro, diz que *heloym* demostra pluralidade e ho singular he *eloa* ou *heloy*, porem, este nom se acha no hebraico. Assi tambem *adonay* traz pluralidade, e *adon* he ho singular, que quer dizer senhor. Estes nomes às vezes são atribuidos a outras pessoas, tirando Deos. Loth chamou hos anios *adonay* (*dei mei*), e Labam dixe a Iacob: "Cur furatus es heloy?" (*deos meos*). E no psalmo onde nos temos: "Ego dixi: 'Dij estis," diz ho

---

⁴ Gen. 1:26.

⁵ Cf. *DE*, pp. 9ff.; Y. F. Baer, "The Kabbalistic Doctrine in the Christological Teachings of Abner of Burgos (Hebrew)," *Tarbiẓ*, 27 (1957-8), 282, 285.

⁶ Gen. 1:1.

⁷ *I.e.*, '*elohim*.

⁸ *I.e.*, '*el*. The word '*elohim* is plural in form but may function grammatically as a singular or plural. In the former case it refers to God while in the latter it means "gods." See chap. 7, n. 115.

⁹ Isidore, *De fide catholica*, 1.4.4, *PL*, 83:458; *AJ*, pp. 29, 396; *Covenant*, p. 28.

Old Testament state. In the first chapter of Genesis, the Trinity and unity are described. It is written there that God said: *Let Us make man in Our likeness and image*.[4] By saying *Let Us make,* it declared the plurality of the persons; by saying *in Our image* or *likeness*, it expressed the unity that is contained in the divinity of God.[5] All our doctors who spoke of the Trinity give proof of it by means of this passage, and we likewise believe and have faith in it. Now since your own Moses proves it, you should grant him authority and credence since he did not speak for himself but states that God so instructed him. Consequently, he in turn wanted to make it known to you.

[*fol. 53v*] Now let us look at the Trinity or personalities of the Trinity together with the unity. Moses verifies this when he says at the beginning of the book, in the first chapter: *God created the heaven and the earth*. In our Latin it is: *In principio creauit Deus celum et terram*.[6] And where we have *Deus*, your Bible has *heloym*,[7] which is the plural form of the singular *hel*,[8] which means "God," and *heloym "idem est pro diis,"* or gods.

So, we understand the name *Deus* to mean God the Father, and the word *principium* to mean the Son,[9] through Whom God does all things. The plurality of the persons is seen here then, since Moses used the word *heloym* to refer to the Father and the Son. He would not have done so were there not persons in the Trinity. Indeed, when the word *heloym* is used, it signifies divine persons. Consequently, in the second chapter of Genesis, when the serpent spoke with Eve in order to deceive her,[10] the Hebrew uses *heloym* for *dij* where we have *eritis sicut dij*. It may thus be concluded that it was the intention of Moses to express the three persons of the Trinity. These he proved right at the beginning of the book [of Genesis] by giving evidence of the Father and the Son and the Holy Spirit. In Title VI of his book,[11] Petrus Alfonsi says that *heloym* demonstrates plurality, while the singular is *eloa* or *heloy*.[12] Nevertheless, this word is not found in Hebrew. *Adonay* in like manner also carries with it the notion of plurality while *adon* is the singular which means "lord." These names are attributed to beings other than God. Lot called the angels *adonay* (*dei mei*),[13] and Laban said to Jacob: *Cur furatus es*

---

[10] Gen. 3:5.

[11] *PA*, Title 6, *PL*, 157:608ff.

[12] I.e., '*eloah*, the singular form of '*elohim*. See above, n. 8.

[13] Gen. 19.2. '*Adonai* may mean "my lords" or "Lord" depending on the pointing. (See F. Talmage, "R. David Kimḥi as Polemicist," *HUCA*, 38 [1967], 216; U. Simon, "RaBaʿ ve-RaDaQ — Shte gishot li-sheʾelat mehemanut nusaḥ ha-miqra," *Shenaton Bar Ilan*, 6 [1967-8], 210f., 220f.) In this verse, it is pointed with the vowel sign *pataḥ* so that it can only mean "my lords." The Vulgate reads *Domini*.

hebraico: *heloy matem* (*Dij estis*). Assi que estes nomes em plurar sinificão as pessoas, e en singular a vnidade.

Dauid, no psalmo lxxx°, diz: "Isrrael, se me ouuires, nom auera antre ti deos recente ou fresco, nem adoraras deos alheo." Por onde parece que naquela sacratissima Trindade nom ha tres deoses, mas hum soo Deos, como temos por fee. Veiamos aguora alguns testimunhos do Spiritu Santo pois que ia hos temos do Padre e do Filho.

Moises, no primeiro capitolo do Genesis, diz: "Ho spiritu do Senhor andaua sobre as aguoas." Este spiritu do Senhor he ho Spiritu Santo, como nos cremos que he a terceira pessoa na Diuindade que procede do Padre e do Filho, espirado por elles como dum principio, e não de dous. Porque ho Padre e ho Filho ho espirão como hum principio por espiração passiua. Porem, isto leixo eu pera hos teologuos, e nom he necessario declarar aqui estas dificuldades, nem he necessario poor aqui como ho Padre e ho Filho amandosse, espirão ho Spiritu Santo, nem he necessario poor aqui como ho Filho procede do Padre *per modum intellectus,* e ho Spiritu Santo *per modum voluntatis.*

Mas isto creede: que ho Padre gera ho Filho sem [*fol. 54r*] outra pessoa concorrer a esta geração. Ho Filho nom gera, mas he gerado; e ho Spiritu Santo nom gera nem he gerado, mas somentes espirado, procedendo do Padre e do Filho, antre has quaes pessoas nom ha hi antiguidade ou prioridade pera que huma pessoa seia primeiro que a outra. São sem começo e sem fim. Assi que a Sagrada Escritura nos daa soficientes testimunhos do Padre, e do Filho, e do Spiritu Santo, do qual ainda mais testimunhos temos.

Dauid, no psalmo cxxxviij, diz: "Onde me irei do teu spiritu?" E Salamão no Liuro de Sabedoria diz, no capitolo primeiro: "Ho Spiritu Santo da disciplina fugira ho fingido, porque ho spiritu da sabedoria he benino." E Isaias no capitolo lxi, diz: "Ho spiritu do Senhor sobre mym." Todas estas autoridades prouão a pesoa do Spiritu Santo, e con estes ditos do Testamento Velho, prouão hos uossos doutores a pesoa terceira da Diuindade que he ho Spiritu Santo.

A Trindade se proua con a vnidade por aquilo que se escreue no psalmo lxvi, onde se diz: "Benzanos ho Deos, Deos nosso, e bendiguanos

---

[14] *I.e.,* *'elohai.*
[15] Gen. 31:30.
[16] Ps. 82(81):6.
[17] *I.e.,* *'elohim 'atem.*
[18] Ps. 81(80):9f.
[19] Gen. 1:2.
[20] Aquinas, *Summa Theologiae,* 1, 27, 3f.; *FF,* fol. 139*v.*
[21] Ps. 139(138):7.

heloy?[14] (*deos meos*).[15] And in the psalm where we have: *Ego dixi: Dij estis*,[16] the Hebrew is: *heloy matem* (*Dij estis*).[17] These names thereby in the plural signify the persons; and in the singular, the unity.

David says in Psalm 80: *Israel, if you hear Me, there shall be no new or novel gods among you, nor shall you worship a foreign god.*[18] It thus appears that in that sacred Trinity there are not three gods but only one God, as we believe. Let us now look at some evidence of the existence of the Holy Spirit, since we have already had affirmation of the Father and of the Son.

In the first chapter of Genesis, Moses says: *The spirit of the Lord moved over the waters.*[19] This spirit of the Lord is the Holy Spirit, which we believe is the third person in the Divinity Who proceeds from the Father and from the Son, proceeding from them as spirit as from one source, and not two, because the Holy Spirit proceeds from the Father and the Son as from a single essence through active spiration while He in turn receives life through passive procession. However, I will leave this for the theologians for it is not necessary to mention these difficulties here. Nor is it necessary to state here how the Father and the Son, loving each other, impart life to the Holy Spirit, nor to discuss here how the Son proceeds from the Father *per modum intellectus,* and the Holy Spirit *per modum voluntatis.*

But believe in this: that the Father alone generates the Son without [*fol. 54r*] another person participating in this generation. The Son does not generate, but rather is generated. The Holy Spirit neither generates nor is generated, but proceeds as spirit[20] from the Father and the Son among Whom there is neither priority nor seniority so that one might exist before the other. They are without beginning and without end. Thus the Holy Scriptures offer us ample testimony of the Father and the Son and of the Holy Spirit and of this we have even more proof.

David says in Psalm 138: *Where shall I go from Your spirit?*[21] In the first chapter of the Book of Wisdom, Solomon says: *The Holy Spirit of instruction shall flee from deceit, because the spirit of wisdom is benevolent.*[22] Isaiah says in chapter 61: *The spirit of the Lord is upon me.*[23] All of these verses prove [the existence of] the person of the Holy Spirit, and with these statements of the Old Testament our doctors prove [the existence of] the third person of the Divinity, which is the Holy Spirit.

The Trinity together with the Unity is proved by that which is written in Psalm 66, where it says: *May God, our God, bless us. May God bless us and*

[22] Wisd. of Sol. 1:5f.
[23] Isa. 61:1.

Deos e temamno todos hos fins da terra." Enquanto Dauid nomeou tres vezes Deos prouou ho Padre, e ho Filho, e ho Spiritu Santo. E emquanto dixe que ho temessemos, declarou a vnidade.

Estas autoridades abastem pera crerdes na sacratissima Trindade, onde ha tres pessoas — Padre, Filho, e Spiritu Santo — rrealmente distintas, de maneira que ho Padre nom he ho Filho, nem ho Filho ho Spiritu Santo. Porem, ho que faz ho Padre faz ho Filho, e faz ho Spiritu Santo quanto he às obras de fora, como criar e guouernar ho mundo, e portanto, tão poderoso he ho Padre como he ho Filho e ho Spiritu Santo, e assi são iguaes. Mas quanto às obras, intramanentes são diferentes, porque ho Padre gera, e não ho Filho, e portanto, dizem hos theologuos que hos nomes notionaes, como são estes nomes "genito," "ingenito," "espirado," nom conuem a todas as pesoas igualmente. Portanto, quanto a isto, são diferentes. Porem, quanto he às operações essentiaes, a todas as tres pessoas conuem, como he crear, guouernar, reger este mundo, e por isso, dizem hos teologuos que hos nomes essentia[e]s, como são estes, *gubernatio, creatio*, a todas as pessoas tres conuem.

[*fol. 54v*] Aguora, veiamos que sintirão hos vossos doutores acerqua desta Trindade. No Grão Grande, no capitolo xxxviijº, diz Midras, grosador do salteiro, conformemente àquilo que se escreue no Genesis no capitolo xxviijº, que ho patriarcha Iacob, fugindo pera Mesopotamia com ho medo que tinha de seu irmão Esau porquanto lhe furtara a benção por mandado da mãi, e portanto lhe tomara ha herdença primogenital ou morguado, tomou tres pedras e as poos à cabeceira, dizendo: "Se nosso Senhor poser hum dos seus nomes sobre mym como poos sobre meus parentes, sempre ho seruirei; e dizymos de todas as cousas que eu posuir lhe darei e oferecerei." Sobre isto diz ho doutor: "E as tres pedras que Iacob pos à cabeceira tornarãose em huma." E assi ho afirma ho texto do Genesis no capitolo prealeguado.

Diguouos que estas tres pedras sinificauão a Trindade: Padre, Filho, e Spiritu Santo; e ha huma pedra que achou sinificaua que estas tres pessoas nom erão tres deoses mas hum soo Deos, como nos cremos com ha Santa Madre Igreia. Isto se confirma com aquilo que Moises dixe no começo do liuro, no capitolo primeiro, pondo *heloym*, onde nos temos *Deus*. Porque no Talmud sobre este passo se diz que Moises pos *heloym* e

---

[24] Ps. 67(66):7f.

[25] Aquinas, *Summa Theologiae*, 1, 45, 6.

[26] Gen. 28:11.

[27] Based on Genesis Rabbah 68:11 (Sonc., p. 623). The passage is interpreted similarly in *PF*, p. 637: "R. Nehemiah said: He took three stones, saying: 'The Holy One, blessed be He, united His

all the ends of the earth fear Him.[24] In naming God three times, David demonstrated [the existence of] the Father, the Son, and the Holy Spirit. When he said that we should fear Him, he declared the Unity.

These authorities should suffice for you to believe in the most sacred Trinity, which contains three persons — Father, Son, and Holy Spirit — truly distinct, so that the Father is not the Son, nor the Son the Holy Spirit. However, that which the Father does the Son does — as well as the Holy Spirit regarding external works — such as the creation and government of the world. Therefore, the Son and the Holy Spirit are as powerful as the Father and, consequently, are equal. As for their works, they are different, because the Father and not the Son creates and, therefore, the theologians say that the conceptual terms such as "generated," "filiated," "spirated," do not apply equally to all the persons. Therefore, in this respect, they are different. However, as for the essential works, such as creating, governing, and ruling this world, these apply to all three persons. For this reason the theologians say that the essential nouns *gubernatio* [and] *creatio* apply to all three persons.[25]

[*fol. 54v*] Let us now see what your doctors thought about this Trinity. In chapter 38 of the *Grão Grande,* Midrash, the commentator of the Psalter, refers to that written in Genesis, chapter 28. It is there related that the patriarch Jacob fled to Mesopotamia because of the fear he had of his brother Esau from whom he had stolen the blessing as his mother directed, thereby taking away from him the estate or inheritance of the first-born. He took three stones and put them at his head,[26] saying: "If our Lord were to place upon me one of His names as He did upon my forefathers, I will serve Him forever, and I will offer and give Him a tenth part of whatever I possess." [Midrash] comments on this: "And the three stones which Jacob placed at his head, became one."[27] The passage in the aforementioned chapter of Genesis so affirms it.

I tell you that these three stones signified the Trinity: Father, Son, and Holy Spirit; and the one stone he found signified that these three persons were not three gods but only one God, as we believe with Holy Mother Church. This is confirmed by Moses' use of *heloym* at the beginning of the book, chapter one, where we have *Deus.* For the Talmud refers to this passage, and says that Moses used *heloym* and not *hel,* because it is the judgment of three.[28] The expression "judgment of

name with Abraham; with Isaac too He united His name. If these three stones become joined, then I am assured that God's name will be united with me too." And when they did thus join, he knew that God would unite His name with him."

no*m hel*, que he iuizo de tres. Dizendo "iuizo de tres" asaz demostra que
tres pesoas ha hi na Trindade.

A isto se daa autoridade por amor daquilo que se esc*r*eue no Grão
Grande, onde se alegua aquilo que se diz no Genesis, no *p*rimeiro capitolo: "Façamos ho homem à nossa semelhança ou figura seu
imagem." Ali se pergunta sobre este passo: "Com que*m* falaua D*e*os
qua*n*do isto dixe? Na*m* ia co*m* hos anios porque elles no*m* forão
c*r*iadores, ne*m* ha obra da criação lhes foi co*m*municada, porque a soo
D*e*os pertence de nada fazer algu*m*a cousa. Ne*m* falaua co*m* Moises, que
ainda no*m* era criado. Falaua loguo co*m* ho Filho e co*m* ho Sp*irit*u
Santo (*suo modo*)." Por o*n*de bem parece que este doutor confessaua a
Trindade, a qual pode muito bem entende*r* deste passo aleguado. E
mais porquanto Moises asaz clarame*n*te falou desta Trindade no
começo do seu liuro, onde prouou por este nome *heloym*, ho Padre,
Filho, Sp*irit*u Sa*n*to.

[*fol. 55r*] No Grão Grande se alegua aquele passo do Genesis do
capitolo *p*rimeiro onde se diz que "ho sp*irit*u do S*e*nh*o*r andaua sobre as
aguoas." E diz que elle he ho sp*irit*u do Mexia do qual falou Isaias no
capitolo lxi, dizendo: "Ho sp*irit*u do S*e*nh*o*r sobre my*m* porqua*n*to ho
S*e*nh*o*r me vngio e me ma*n*dou *p*reguar aos humildosos." Isto se confirma no liuro chamado *Serafim*, onde se diz sobre ho passo aleguado:
"Aqui falou ho S*e*nh*o*r pola boca de Isaias, porque ho sp*irit*u do S*e*nh*o*r
e D*e*os e ho Mexia, tirado he hu*m*a cousa, hu*m*a essentia, ainda que entre si pessoalme*n*te seia*m* distintas.

Esto, senhores, auie*e*s de crer, e eu assi ho creo. Que a sacratissima
Trindade semp*r*e foi e sera e nu*n*qua começou de ser, porqua*n*to semp*r*e
foi sem começo e p*r*incipio, e fim e termi*n*o, e sera sempre co*m* D*e*os e en
D*e*os. E nu*n*qua ha vnidade esteue sem a Trindade, ne*m* a Trindade sem
a vnidade, ne*m* ho Padre sem ho Filho, ne*m* ho Filho sem ho Sp*irit*u
Santo. Assi que estes vossos doutores confessão que ho sp*irit*u do Mexia
era D*e*os, como ho Mexia era D*e*os, e polo V*e*rbo do S*e*nh*o*r entende ho
Filho, e polo sp*irit*u do S*e*nh*o*r, ho Sp*irit*u Santo.

Por este V*e*rbo todos esperauão, que era ho Mexia que avia de vir

[28] Cf. Abner of Burgos, *Sefer Teshuvot la-Meḥaref* in Baer, *Tarbiẓ*, 21 (1957-8), 282: "... the name
'*elohim* alone indicates the three attributes together, for it represents a tribunal (*bet din*) of three, as
mentioned in Sanhedrin ... Avot ..., and Berakhot." The passages referred to are B.T. Berakhot
6a, B.T. Sanhedrin 6b, M. Avot 3:6. The latter reads: "When three sit together occupying themselves with Torah, the Shekhinah [Divine Presence] abides among them, as it is said *In the midst of the
judges, He judges* (Ps. 82:1)." See Baer's comments, *ibid*.
[29] Gen. 1:26.
[30] Gen. 1:2.

three" sufficiently demonstrates that there are three persons in the Trinity.

This is verified by that written in the *Grão Grande* in reference to the verse in Genesis, chapter one, which reads: *Let Us make man in Our likeness, form, or image*.[29] The question is there raised concerning this verse: "With whom was God speaking when He said this? Not with the angels, to be sure, because they were not creators, nor was the work of creation imparted to them, because only God can fashion something from nothingness. Neither did he speak with Moses who was not as yet created. He spoke then with the Son and with the Holy Spirit *suo modo*." It seems then that this doctor confessed the Trinity which he could easily comprehend from this passage and from the fact that Moses spoke of the Trinity at the beginning of his book. This is proved by the name *heloym*, Father, Son, and Holy Spirit.

[*fol. 55r*] The *Grão Grande* affirms the passage in Genesis, chapter 1 which says: *The spirit of the Lord moved over the waters*.[30] "Spirit" is taken to mean that of the Messiah of whom Isaiah spoke in chapter 61: *The spirit of the Lord is upon me, because the Lord anointed me to preach unto the meek*.[31] This is confirmed in the book called *Seraphim*[32] which comments on the above passage: "The Lord spoke here through the mouth of Isaiah, because the spirit of the Lord and God and the Messiah are taken as one thing, one essence, even though among themselves they may be individually distinct."

Gentlemen, you must believe this as I do: That the most sacred Trinity always was and will be and never came into being, since it always existed without start or beginning, end or termination, and will always be with God and in God. The Unity never existed without the Trinity, nor the Trinity without the Unity; the Father [did not exist] without the Son, nor the Son without the Holy Spirit. Thus these doctors of yours confess that the spirit of the Messiah was God, as the Messiah was God, and the Word of the Lord is taken to mean the Son, and the Spirit of the Lord the Holy Spirit.

Everyone hoped for this Word, Who was the Messiah, that would

[31] Isa. 61:1. Based on Genesis Rabbah 8:1 (Sonc., p. 55) cited in *PF*, pp. 545, 822; cf. pp. 503f. In the original and in *PF*, Isa. 11:2 is cited instead of Isa. 61:1: "R. Simeon b. Laḳish maintained: He [Adam] was the latest in the work of the last day and the earliest in the work of the first day. That is consistent with the view of R. Simeon b. Laḳish, for he said: *And the spirit of God hovered* (*ib.* 1:2) refers to the soul of Adam, as you read, *And the spirit of the Lord shall rest upon him* (Isa. 11:2)."

[32] Machado is probably referring to chapter 6 of Isaiah in which the seraphim recite the trisagion of verse 3, considered in Christian tradition to refer to the three Persons of the Trinity. See *PA*, Title 6, *PL*, 157: 612; cf. *PF*, p. 548.

sarar todos, sem ho qual ninguem nom se podia saluar. Assi ho afirma Iacob (Genesis xlix) quando dixe: "Salutare tuum expectabo, Domine" (Senhor, a uossa saude esperarei), que era este Verbo, este Mexia Christo, nosso Redentor. No caldeu se diz: "Nom dixe isto Iacob pola saluação que elle esperasse de Gedeon, que nom durou senão huma hora; nem no dixe por Iosue que meteo ho pouo de Isrrael na Terra da Promisão; dixeo loguo polo Mexia, que era e segunda pesoa na Diuindade, que veo tomar carne humana a este mundo pola operação deste Spiritu Santo."

Dizeime, por vossa vida, porque neguaes esta Trindade pois que tendes ho Testamento cheo de autoridades que vola prouão? Tendes hos vossos doutores que vola afirmão. Pareceme que queres punar e batalhar contra a verdade tão manifesta e patente. Rroguouos que nom vos enguanees, mas isto crede — que tres cousas estão en Deos: substantia, sapientia, voluntas, e estas tres cousas nos representão ho Padre, Filho, e Spiritu Santo. Veiamos, pois, como estas tres cousas sinifiquão a sacratissima Trindade [fol. 55v] que auia de descubrir ho segredo deste nome Adonay que demostra a Trindade. Como elle mesmo dixe aos seus discipolos: "Hide e pregai ho que vos eu dixe em nome do Padre e do Filho, e do Spiritu Santo, bautizandoos." Assi ho nosso São Iohão Euangelista, que comunicou com Christo e falou e conuersou ensinado por elle, dixe que tres estauão nos ceos: ho Padre, e ho Filho, e ho Spiritu Santo, e estes tres que erão hum soo Deos.

E porquanto ho Mexia auia de vir a este mundo tomar carne humana e declara[r] esta Trindade; portanto, nom quis Deos que se fizesse expresa menção da Trindade no Testamento Velho. Mas todos, assi Moises como hos profetas, escuramente falarão da Trindade, posto que algum tanto Habraam a pode entender quando vio aqueles tres anios (Genesis xviij°), e depois adorou hum, hos quaes, ainda que obscuramente, sinifiquauão ha Trindade com a vnidade. Ho nosso Santo Augustinho, por esta autoridade contra vos outros, proua a sacratissima e indiuidua Trindade com a sua vnidade, e nos assi ho cremos e temos por fee. Eu tenho pera mym que Moises entendeo claramente a Trindade, mas porquanto sabia que vos outros ereis muito dados a idolatria e auião de ser, falou escuramente da Trindade pera que vos outros nom creseis que auia hahi tres deosses.

E por esta rezão dizem alguns que hos setenta enterpretadores do

---

[33] Gen. 49:18.
[34] Found in Targum Yerushalmi 1 and 2 with Samson mentioned instead of Joshua. I have not located this in a Christian source.

come to heal everyone and without Whom no one could be saved. Jacob affirms this in Genesis, 49 when he said: *Salutare tuum expectabo, Domine*[33] (Lord, I will wait for your salvation), which was this Word, this Messiah Christ, our Redeemer. In the Chaldean it says: "Jacob did not say this of the salvation for which he hoped from Gideon, which lasted only one hour. Nor did he say it of Joshua who brought the people of Israel into the Promised Land. He said it then of the Messiah Who was the Second Person in the Divinity Who came into this world, clothed in human flesh, by means of the Holy Spirit."[34]

Tell me, by your life, why do you deny this Trinity since you have the [Old] Testament full of passages that prove it to you? You have your doctors that verify it for you. It seems to me that you want to fight and struggle against the truth [which is] so obvious and clear. I beseech you not to deceive yourselves, but to believe this: that there are three things contained in God: *substantia, sapientia, voluntas,* and these three things represent for us the Father, the Son, and the Holy Spirit. So let us see how these three things denote the most sacred Trinity [*fol. 55v*] in order to reveal the secret of this name *Adonay,* which demonstrates the Trinity. He himself said to His disciples: *Go and preach what I told you in the name of the Father and the Son and the Holy Spirit, baptizing them.*[35] Our St. John the Evangelist who spoke and conversed with Christ and was taught by Him, said that there were three in the heavens: the Father, the Son, and the Holy Spirit, and these three were but one God.[36]

Because the Messiah would come to this world incarnate and make declaration of this Trinity, God therefore did not want the Trinity mentioned expressly in the Old Testament. Everyone, however, Moses as well as the prophets, spoke allusively of the Trinity, while Abraham could [even] understand it somewhat when he saw those three angels (Genesis 18).[37] Yet he worshiped one, even though they allusively denote the Trinity along with the Unity. Our Saint Augustine, opposing your interpretation, cites this text and proves the most sacred and indivisible Trinity with its Unity.[38] We also believe and have faith in this. I am of the opinion that Moses clearly understood the Trinity. He knew, however, that you were very much given over to idolatry and would continue to be so. Thus he spoke obscurely of the Trinity lest you think that there were three gods there.

For this reason, some say that the seventy men who translated the

---

[35] Mark 16:15f.
[36] 1 John 5:7.
[37] Gen. 18:2.
[38] *Civ. Dei,* 11.10; *De unitate sanctae trinitatis, PL,* 2:1208-1212.

Testamento Velho em hebraico, por mandado de Tolomeu, rei do
Egito, que mandou que lhe tresladassem todo ho Testamento Velho em
greguo, auendo medo que nam no fezessem idolatra, tinhão isto por
manha, que onde achauão autoridade que falaua da Trindade, escuramente falauão pera que nom cuidasse Tolomeu que auia hahi tres
deoses e idolatrasse.

Concludindo, pois, dizemos que esta Trindade indiuidua claramente
nom foi discuberta senão polo Mexia, posto que dela se fezesse menção
escura. Porem, polo Testamento Velho e polos vossos doutores se
declarou auer hi Trindade com vnidade.

Esta he a nossa fee catolica; esta seia e a uossa. Amen.

[fol. 56r] Capitolo Vigesimo. Como ho Filho de Deos tomou carne humana sem auer alguma rrepunantia.

No Liuro de Ruth, no capitolo quarto, se escreue esto que segue:
"Estas são as gerações de Phares: Phares gerou Esrrom, Esrrom gerou
Aram, Aram gerou Aminadab, Aminadab gerou Naason, Naason gerou
Salmon, Salmon gerou Booz, Booz gerou Obed, Obed gerou Isai, Isai
gerou Dauid." Todos hos vossos doutores dizem sobre este passo que
ho Mexia auia de ser filho de Dauid e da sua casa e familia, e do tribu
de Iuda, como Iacob predixe (Genesis xlix), falando de Iuda, ho quarto
seu filho, donde auia de sair aquele duque que auia de reger todo
Isrrael.

Assi que este Mexia auia de ser homem verdadeiro, pois que auia de
nacer dũma virgem (Isaie vijº). E como quer que ia soficientemente vos
temos prouado que elle auia de ser Deos, seguesse que nom auia hi
repunantia nem contradição antre a carne humana e a Diuindade, ho
que cuidaes e pensaes auer hi grande repunantia antre a Diuindade e ha
humanidade, e por isto, nom queres crer que tal vnião hipostatica se
fezesse, dizendo que repuna que a Diuindade, que he cousa sim-
plicissima e limpissima, se possa aiuntar com a carne humana, que [he]
infima e baixa.

A este vossa obieição loguo responderemos, trazendo algumas rezões
persuasiuas, porquanto demostratiuas ou euidentes nom se podem
trazer porquanto esta vnião e aiuntamento hipostatico excede e
sobrepoia todo ho intendimento e humana capacidade, e portanto, a fee
supre tudo neste neguotio. Porem, veiamos como a carne humana se

---

[39] See chap. 5, n. 4.

[40] On the "emendations" of the translators, see B. T. Megillah 9a, P. T. Megillah 71d.

Hebrew Old Testament into Greek by order of Ptolemy, king of Egypt,[39] feared that [the Greeks] might practice idolatry. They therefore cleverly translated those passages which spoke of the Trinity in a veiled manner so that Ptolemy would not think that there were three gods there and thus practice idolatry.[40]

In conclusion, then, we say that this indivisible Trinity was clearly revealed by none other than the Messiah for it had [previously] been mentioned only in a veiled manner. However, [the existence of] the one Trinity and Unity was affirmed by the Old Testament and by your doctors.

This is our Catholic faith; May it be yours. Amen.

[fol. 56r] Chapter Twenty. How the Son of God assumed human flesh without there being any incompatibility.

In the fourth chapter of the Book of Ruth, the following is written: *These are the generations of Pharez: Pharez begot Hezron, Hezron begot Ram, Ram begot Amminadab, Amminadab begot Nahshon, Nahshon begot Salmon, Salmon begot Boaz, Boaz begot Obed, Obed begot Jesse, Jesse begot David.*[1] In referring to the above passage, all your doctors say that the Messiah would be the son of David, of his house and family, and of the tribe of Judah. Jacob predicted (Genesis 49) this when speaking of Judah, his fourth son, from whom that leader who would govern all of Israel would be descended.[2]

Consequently, this Messiah would be a true man, for He would be born of a virgin (Isaiah 7).[3] And since we have sufficiently proved already that He would be God, it follows that there would be no contradiction or incompatibility between human flesh and the Divinity. You think and believe that there is great incompatibility between Divinity and humanity and thus do not want to believe that such a hypostatic union could take place, since the idea that the Divinity, which is most simple and pure, could unite with human flesh, which is mean and low, is repugnant.

We shall reply to your objection shortly and present some persuasive arguments. Since demonstrative evidence cannot be cited because this hypostatic union transcends all human capacity and understanding, faith compensates for everything in this matter. However, let us see

[1] Ruth 4:18ff.
[2] Gen. 49:10.
[3] Isa. 7:14.

pode aiuntar com a Diuindade, nom obstante que a natureza he muito baixa.

A nossa alma he hum spiritu simplissimo e limpo, nom composto de forma e materia; porem, aiuntasse com a carne composta e baixa, e muito infima. Porque a alma he criada por Deos, e feita por Elle de nada. He hum espiramento de vida que Deos da aos homens (Genesis primeiro); mas ha carne criasse do sangue humano, çuio e podre por pecado. Assi, tambem, posto que a carne humana seia baixa e infima e soieita a toda malitia, nom simplex mas composta, nem por isso nom leixo[u] Deos de a tomar e de a aiuntar assi. Porque a carne que Deos tomou foi do sacratissimo sangue da gloriosa Virgem Maria e da sua bendita carne, a qual nom era soieita a pecado nem vitio, porquanto, ella nom foi concibida em pecado original. [fol. 56v] Mas antes que ho Filho de Deos viesse ao ventre de Maria, Virgem bendita, veo aquele grande obreiro ho Spiritu Santo e com sua marauillosa operação, obrou este grande misterio, dando virtude de gerar a esta virgem que concebeo sem semente de varão, senão pola graça do Spiritu Santo. E posto que a carne de Nossa Senhora, madre de Deos, fora çuia e soieita ao pecado como a carne dos outros humanos, ho que nom foi porquanto disto foi reseruada por Deos, ainda nom ouuera hi repunantia por onde Deos nom podera tomar carne humana. Porque primeiramente ho Spiritu Santo ha alimpara, e posto que nam na alimpara, ainda Deos tomara esta carne huma[na] sen se çuiar. Porque, assi como ho sol com seus rraios passa polos luguares çuios e torpes sem se çuiar nem sentir em si alguma cousa, assi tambem Deos podera tomar carne humana sen se çuiar. Polo qual concludo que a uossa rezão nom he muito eficaz nem forte, em a qual dizes, que porquanto Deos he simplex e a carne humana çuia e torpe, que por isso Deos nom avia de tomar esta carne.

Portanto crede que este aiuntamento se pode fazer, como de feito se fez; que ho Filho proprio de Deos eterno, a segunda pessoa na Diuindade, veo tomar esta nossa carne humana pera nella nos redimir e saluar, pois que nela pecara Adam, nom auendo repunantia alguma, por onde nom se podesse fazer nem contradição.

Mas parece isto ser verdade — que todas aquelas cousas são possiues a Deos; que nom trazem consiguo alguma repunantia ou implicação de contradição. E Deos tomar carne humana nom traz consiguo contradição, segundo ia vos prouei acima. Seguesse loguo que ho pode fazer. E assi ho fez, que [não] se vestio desta nossa pele humana senão

---

⁴ Gen. 2:7.

how human flesh can be united with the Divinity, notwithstanding its base nature.

Our soul is a most simple and pure spirit, not composed of either form or matter. Yet it is conjoined with base, low, and mean flesh. The soul is created by God, fashioned by Him out of nothing; it is a breath of life that God gives to men (Genesis 1).[4] But the flesh, foul and corrupt through sin, is created from human blood. Thus, although human flesh is base, mean, subject to all manner of evil, compound and not simple, God nevertheless took it and conjoined it as He did. For the flesh that God took was from the most sacred blood and blessed flesh of the glorious Virgin Mary, who was not subject to sin or vice since she was not conceived in original sin. [*fol. 56v*] Yet before the Son of God would come to the womb of Mary, the blessed Virgin, that great operator, the Holy Spirit, brought about this remarkable mystery, with His miraculous act, making it possible for this virgin to give birth; for she conceived not with a man's seed, but through the grace of the Holy Spirit. And even if the flesh of Our Lady, mother of God, had been foul and subject to sin as is the flesh of other human beings (which was not the case since it was protected from this by God), there still would not have been any incompatibility which would have prevented God from assuming human flesh. Firstly, the Holy Spirit had cleansed it; and even if He had not cleansed it, God would still have assumed human flesh without becoming defiled. For, just as the sun with its rays passes through dirty and vile places without soiling itself or becoming affected, God too could assume human flesh without becoming soiled.[5] I therefore conclude that your notion that God would not assume human flesh because He is simple, while human flesh is impure and base, is neither effective nor forceful.

Believe then that this union can take place, as it in fact did; that God the Eternal's own Son — the Second Person in the Divinity — came and assumed our own human flesh to redeem and save us (since Adam had sinned through it). There was no sort of incompatibility and, consequently, there could exist no contradiction.

It appears that it is true that all those things are possible for God and that they bear no incompatibility or implication of contradiction. That God should take on human flesh is not intrinsically contradictory, as we already proved to you above. It follows then that He can do it, and so He did. He clothed Himself in our human skin only to show us the

---

[5] On this argument, see Athanasius, *De incarnatione verbi*, 17, ed. R. W. Thomson, pp. 176ff. (*PG*, 25:125); Maximinus, *Contra Judaeos*, *PL*, 57:747; *AJ*, p. 165.

pera nos demostrar ho grande amor e afeição que nos tinha, e pera nos reconciliar com Deos Padre, porquanto como Adam pecou, grandes imizades antre Deos e ha humana carne se siguirão. Isto he ho que diz ho real profeta Dauid no psalmo lxxxiiij°: "A misericordia e a uerdade se encontrarão, e a iustiça e a paz se beixarão. A uerdade naceo da terra" (que foi a humanidade do Mexia) "e a iustiça olhou do ceo" (que foi a diuindade do Mexia, que foi Deos e homem). [fol. 57r] No mesmo psalmo diz Dauid, falando do Mexia: "Porem, acerqua daqueles que temem a Deos esta ho Saluador delle pera que a gloria more na nossa terra."

Diguouos que isto demostra que ho Saluador auia de morar en Iuda; que auia de ser gloria pera todos. Este Saluador era Deos e homem; por ende, parece que, pois, auia de tomar carne humana que nom auia alguma repunantia pera que esta vnião e aiuntamento nom se fezesse.

Assi que da parte de Deos nom auia alguma contradição pois que todas as cousas lhe são possiuees, nem tão pouco da parte da natureza humana nom auia repunantia alguma. Porque assi como todas as cousas estão debaixo da obedientia de Deos e todas as cousas lhe seruem à vontade, assi a natureza humana auia de obedecer a Deos, polo qual ha pode assi aiuntar como aiuntou, sem auer hi repunantia nem contradição. E posto que estas rezomzinhas catiuem algum tanto ho nosso intindimento; porem, isto nom he nada, mas a fee deue aqui de suprir onde falta a rezão natural.

Aiuntouse, pois, a natureza humana com a diuina, não como materia e forma que fazem hum composto, nem como substantia e acidente, porque a natureza humana neste aiuntamento hipostatico, perdeo ho supposito proprio, e se suppositou no alheo — no Diuino — Deos determinando aquela dependentia; mas aiuntarãose estas duas naturezas — s[cilicet] a Diuina e humana — per modo e maneira de emxertar. Porque assi como ho ramo emxertado e ensirido nom perde sua natureza posto que esteie mitido no tronco d'outra aruore, nom tendo dous suppositos mas hum soo que he ho do tronco onde ho ramo esta suppositado, assi a natureza humana fiquou com seu modo e ser, tirando ho seu proprio supposito, e fiquou ho Diuino com a natureza Diuina. Por onde temde por fee e certeza que ho Mexia teue duas naturezas — s[cilicet] ha humana e diuina — e hum soo supposto diuino, porquanto ho humano nom fiquou.

Todas estas cousas são verdadeiras; porem, nom nas podemos prouar

---

[6] See above, chap. 1, n. 35.

[7] Ps. 85(84):11f.; 85(84):10.

great love and affection He had for us and to reconcile us with God the Father. For, when Adam sinned, there followed considerable enmity between God and man. In this regard, the royal prophet David says in Psalm 84: *Mercy and truth come together, and justice and peace kiss each other. Truth came forth from the earth* (which was the humanity of the Messiah), *and justice looked down from heaven*[6] (which was the Divinity of the Messiah, who was God and man). [*fol. 57r*] In the same psalm, David speaks of the Messiah: *Still, His Savior is nigh those who fear God that glory may dwell in our land.*[7]

I tell you that this shows that the Savior would dwell in Judah and that He would be a glory for all. This Savior was God and man. Consequently, it seems that He would assume human flesh without any incompatibility which would prevent this union from taking place.

Thus, there was no contradiction on the part of God since everything is possible for Him. Nor was there any incompatibility with regard to His human nature. For, since everything is subject to obedience to God and all things serve Him at will, it follows that [His] human nature would obey God. He would thus form the union, as He did, without there being either incompatibility or contradiction. While this intellectualizing may appeal to our understanding to some extent, it means nothing; for faith must compensate here where natural reason fails.

So, then, both the divine and human natures were continued but not as matter and form that make up a compound, nor as substance and accident. For in this hypostatic union the human nature lost its own individuality and united with that of another, the divine, with God himself determining that dependence. The two natures, the divine and the human, are united by the method and means of grafting.[8] For, just as the grafted and inserted branch does not lose its character even though it be placed in the trunk of another tree, there results not two distinct qualities but only one, that of the trunk where the branch is attached. So, the human nature, while relinquishing its own individuality, maintains its manner and being, as does the divine His divine nature. Believe and accept as true then that the Messiah had two natures — the human and the divine — and was only one divine person, because the human element did not remain.

All these things are true; however, we cannot prove them through natural or demonstrative reasoning. But we believe this through the

---

[8] Durand de Saint-Pourçain, *In sententias theologicas Petri Lombardi* (Venice, 1621; photoreprint, Ridgewood, NJ, 1964), 3, 6, 4; 2, 225*v*-226*r*. Machado here mentions Durand in a marginal note.

por rezões naturaes ou demonstratiuas. Mas cremos isto por fee que teemos e polos nossos doutores que assi nolo declarão, e polos euangelistas que falão deste Verbo encarnado na natureza humana.

[*fol. 57v*] Vos outros, senhores, dizees que se he verdade que ho Filho tomou carne humana, loguo quereis infirir que assi tambem ho Padre e ho Spiritu Santo tomarão carne humana. A consequentia nom val muito dinheiro, porque ia atras vos declarei como ho Padre, Filho, Spiritu Santo são tres pessoas realmente distinctas. De modo e maneira que ho Padre nom he Filho, nem ho Spiritu Santo, mas são pesoas distintas como he So[c]r[a]tes, Plato e filho e pai. E, portanto, huma pesoa pode tomar esta carne humana, nam na tomando as outras, e pera isto, tomay este emxemplo. Se tres homens tomarem huma loba e aconcertarem todos tres pera hum deles a vestir, e todos tres aiudarem a metela pola cabeça a hum deles, ho qual tambem se aiuda a vestir, nom direis vos, se sondes sabedores, que todos tres uistirão a loba, mas que hum soo a uestio. Porem, todos tres aiudarão e obrarão no vestir. Assi tambem dizemos que todas tres pessoas obrarão nesta encarnação; porem, huma soo pessoa, que foi a do Filho, vestio esta nossa camisa humana, posto que todos tres poderão iuntamente tomar esta carne humana, ou cada hum per si. Porem, nom sem misterio tomou ho Filho, segunda pesoa na Diuindade, carne humana, e não has outras duas pesoas. Isto se fez porque aquele que era Filho na Diuindade, ho fosse na humanidade. Porque, se viera ho Spiritu Santo, ouuera de ser filho, segundo a natureza humana, e assi ouuera hi dous filhos, e portanto, isto se fez.

Porem, a principal causa foi a vontade diuina que quis que assi fosse que ho Filho de Deos eterno viesse tomar carne humana per a natureza humana padecer e satisfazer por aquele grande pecado de Adam, polo qual nhuma pura creatura pode satisfazer. E posto que Deos teuesse outros muitos modos com hos quaes podera perdoar este pecado; porem, nom sem grande misterio diuino foi assi ordenado no consistorio diuino que ho Mexia morresse e padecesse. E por isto veo elle qua pera que com a sua grande humildade vencesse aquela grande soberba do nosso primeiro parente.

Esta he a nossa fee que temos: que ho Filho de Deos eterno veo a este mundo tomar carne humana, feito homem e Deos, como polos profetas estaua profitizado e milhor declarado por São Iohão Euangelista, se autoridade lhe quiserdes daar. Peçouos que esta seia tambem a vossa fee. Amen.

---

[9] Cf. Joseph Kimhi, *Book of the Covenant* (Toronto, 1972), p. 63; Profiat Duran, *Kelimat ha-Goyim*, 2,

faith we have and through our doctors who declare it to us and through the evangelists who speak of the Word incarnate, in human form.

[*fol. 57v*] You say, gentlemen, that if it is true that the Son assumed human flesh, then the Father and the Holy Spirit also did so.[9] This is what you want to infer. But your conclusion is worthless because I already explained to you above how the Father, Son, and Holy Spirit are really three distinct persons. Consequently, the Father is neither the Son nor the Holy Spirit. They are distinct persons as are Socrates or Plato or a father and a son. Therefore, one person can assume this human flesh, while the others do not. To illustrate this, take the following example: If three men take a cloak and agree that one of them shall wear it while the other two help the third to put it over his head, then you, if you are wise men, cannot say that all three put on the cloak, since only one did. However, all three helped and participated in putting it on. In like manner we also say that all three persons participated in the incarnation. However, only one person, the Son, put on this our human garment even though all three together or each one alone could have assumed our human flesh. Nevertheless, it is not without mystery that the Son, the second person in the Divinity, took on human flesh and not the other two persons. This was so because He Who was Son in Divinity was so in humanity. For if the Holy Spirit had come, He would have had to be a son in accord with human character, and in this case there would have been two sons. For this reason, all transpired as it did.

Still, the principal cause was the divine will which wanted the Son of the Eternal God to come and assume human flesh in order to suffer for mankind and atone for that great sin of Adam which no mere creature could expiate. And even though God might have had many other ways by which He would have pardoned this sin, it was nonetheless ordained in the divine consistory — not without great divine mystery — that the Messiah suffer and die. So it was that He came here, with His great humility, in order to overcome the great pride of our first ancestor.

This is our faith: that the Son of God Eternal came to this world to assume human flesh, as man and God, as was foretold by the prophets and explicitly stated by Saint John the Evangelist,[10] if you wish to grant him authority. I beg you to accept this as your faith also. Amen.

Ha-Ẓofeh le-Hokhmat Yisra'el, 3 (1919), 147; *Summa Theologiae,* 3, 3, 5; R. Lull, *Opera omnia* (Mainz, 1729; photoreprint, Frankfurt, 1965), 4:514.

[10] John 1:1,14.

[*fol. 58r*] Capitolo Vigesimo primeiro. Como hos iudeus no*m* entende*m* a Sagrada Escritura sp*irit*ualmente, mas carnalme*n*te. Ho que procede, no*m* quere*m* elles crer em Ih*esu* Chr*isto*.

Vos outros, senhores iudeus, no*m* entendes hos passos do Testame*n*to Velho ne*m* autoridades que falão do Mexia, porq*ue* na*m* queres crer en Ih*esu* Chr*isto*, e, portanto, lhes daes mil sintidos falsos e erroneos. Ho profeta Isaias da bom testimunho disto, dizendo no capitolo vij°: "No*m* auees de entende*r* senão crerdes." Polo qual, se vos quiserdes crer em Ih*esu* Chr*isto*, loguo auees de ser alomeados de modo e maneira q*ue* loguo perfeitame*n*te entenderes as cousas que são saudaue*e*s pera a uossa alma. E porque estas cousas que nos cremos são gra*n*des e dificiles pera se crere*m*; portanto, a fee q*ue* nos temos nos da grande aiuda. Esta, pois, tomay vos, e loguo entenderes.

Se Habraa*m* no*m* crera a D*eo*s, que era ia nonagenario, q*ue* auia de teer hu*m* filho, nu*n*qua elle fora amiguo de D*eo*s como foi, porquanto aquela fee e crença q*ue* elle teue lhe foi reputada pera sua iustificação (Genesis, xv), e foi dino que na sua semente todas as gentes forão benditas.

Assi vos, ta*m*bem, se quiserdes crer que ho Mexia veo loguo, seres alomeados pera entende*r*des as cousas que pertence*m* a vossa alma. D'outra maneira, teree*s* sempr*e* peneiras diante dos olhos co*m* ho veeo de Moises cube*r*tos, que nu*n*qua saberes a v*er*dade, a qual iazia escondida na uossa Lei, que no*m* era senão sombra.

Maes esta nossa he ho sol, dada em Ierusalem polo sol da iustiça, que foi ho Mexia. E porque vos no*m* queres creer comnosco; portanto, caies em mil falsos errores, no*m* entendendo a Sagrada Escritura senão carnalme*n*te, e no*m* sp*irit*ualmente, dizendo q*ue* D*eo*s que tee*m* pees, que tee*m* mãos e cabeça e corpo composto, e que se ira como hos humanos, e que no*m* esta senão no ocidente[a] e nu*n*qua no oriente,[b] e, portanto, sempr*e* fazeis vossas orações pera ho ocidente, segundo se contem no vosso liuro das doutrinas. Estes errores todos procedem por no*m* quererdes crer que Ih*esu* Chr*isto* he Filho de D*eo*s v*er*dadeiro. Assi ho confirma Isaias no capitolo vi°, dizendo q*ue* D*eo*s lhe dixe: "Dize a este pouo: 'Ou[u]ires e no*m* entenderes, e olhando veres, e no*m* saberes.' Boto esta ho coração deste pouo. Cegualhe hos olhos e agraualhos pera

---

a originally *oriente* with -*c*- written above -*r*- and -*d*- added int.   b int. + *ocidente* exp.

[1] Isa. 7:9. Machado's version is closer to the Septuagint text cited by Jerome, *CC*, 73:99 (*PL*, 24:107).

[2] Gen. 15:4.

[*fol. 58r*] Chapter twenty-one. How the Jews do not understand the Holy Scripture according to the spirit but according to the flesh. This leads to their not wanting to believe in Jesus Christ.

You Jewish gentlemen do not understand those passages or texts of the Old Testament that speak of the Messiah because you do not want to believe in Jesus Christ. You rather give them a thousand false or error-ridden interpretations. The prophet Isaiah, gives proof of this in chapter 7 when he says: *You do not have to understand; just believe.*[1] In this way, if you want to believe in Jesus Christ you will be enlightened at once in such a way that you will immediately understand perfectly the things that are salutary for your soul. Because these things in which we believe are extraordinary and difficult to believe, the faith that we have aids us greatly. So accept this and you will then understand.

If Abraham had not believed God that he would have a son at the age of ninety, he would never have been the beloved of God that he was. For the faith and belief that he had was considered for him as righteousness (Genesis 15),[2] and he was worthy of having all his posterity blessed.

Thus, if you to wish to believe that the Messiah came, you will be sufficiently enlightened to understand the things that pertain to your soul. Otherwise, you will always have a screen before your eyes and they will be covered with the veil of Moses. You will never know the truth, which lies hidden within your Law which is only a shadow.

But our [law] is the sun, given in Jerusalem by the sun of justice Who was the Messiah. Since you do not wish to believe as we, you therefore fall into a thousand false errors and understand the Holy Scriptures according to the flesh and not according to the spirit. For you say that God has feet, hands, a head, and a composite body; that He becomes angry with man;[3] that He is in only the west and never in the east[4] and for this reason, you say your prayers facing west,[5] in accordance with your book of doctrines.[6] All these errors stem from your failure to believe that Jesus Christ is the Son of the true God. Isaiah confirms this in chapter 6, when he says that God told him: *Tell this people: You shall hear, but not understand; looking, you shall see, but shall not perceive. Cast forth*

---

[3] Machado bases himself on the list of talmudic "absurdities" cited in *DPA*. See Merchavia, pp. 99ff.

[4] Cf. B.T. Bava Batra 25. The reference is to the Land of Israel which is west of Babylonia.

[5] It is the Jewish practice to face Jerusalem in prayer. See B. T. Berakhot 30a.

[6] Cf. *DPA*, Title 1, col. 543: "Iterum vestri in doctrinarum libro asserunt quod Deus in occidente est tantum" (cited in *FF*, fol. 198va). See B. T. Bava Batra 25.

que nom veia com hos seus olhos e ouça com has suas orelhas, e se conuerta." Tudo isto se cumpre em vos outros porque não queres crer em Ihesu Christo.

[fol. 58v] Ho profeta Abuch, no 2º capitolo, diz que ho iusto viue com a fee e obras. Diguouos que esta he a fee do nosso Christo que daa entendimento e vida spiritual, a qual vos nom tendes porque careceis desta nossa fee, a qual, se vos teueseis perfeitamente, guostaries spiritualmente deste maniar da Sagrada Escritura que he tão doce como mel pera'queles que crem.

Mas porque vos nom queres crer, por isso Deos vos fechou hos segredos e misterios grandes que se encludem no liuro da vida, fechado pera vos, e aberto pera nos, porquanto cremos en Ihesu. Isaias daa disto testimunho no capitolo xxix, onde diz: "Veres como em liuro que vos sera fechado, ho qual como se deer àquele que sabe letras e lhe dixerem que lea, rrespondera que nom pode porquanto ho liuro esta fechado. Porem, naqueles dias hos surdos ouuirão as palauras daquele liuro."

Esto he que hos segredos da Sagrada Escritura são fechados a uos outros iudeus, e portanto, nam nos entendes senão carnalmente. Mas aos gentios christãos tudo he discuberto, tudo he reuelado; nada nom esta fechado. Esta nossa fee tudo nos abre e descobre. Isto confirma Daniel no capitolo xijº, onde diz: "Hos sermoons e palauras estão fechados ates ho tempo da consumação; ates que muitos aprendão e auisão seia comprida pera que conheção todas as cousas." Tudo isto aguora he comprido, que a vos hos segredos estão fechados e a nos, por amor da fee, são discubertos. Diguouos, senhores, que emquanto leerdes Moises, que sempre ho seu veeo ha de estar no vosso coração.

Tomai, senhores, este nosso escudo da fee. Leixai Moises que ia cessou, ia feneceo. Leixai as sinaguoguas, vossos aiuntamentos. Gua[r]dai a aguoa do bautismo que tomastes. Armaiuos com ella, porque a circumcisão ia pereceo, ia feneceo, ia morreo na cruz com Christo. A uossa Lei, sepultada foi no sepulcro com Christo. Leixai hos sabados, nom sabbatizes, mas tomai ho dominguo. Ide às nossas igreias. Ouui as nossas preguações, e acertares. Esto, senhores, que vos diguo, tomayho bem de mym, que nom deseio senão vossa saude, vossa saluação. Folguaria de vos ver benauenturados e boons christãos, amiguos de Christo e nom de Moises, que ia nom vos traz saude mas morte, condenação, e peste pera hos corpos e almas.

[7] Isa 6:9f.
[8] Hab. 2:4.
[9] Isa. 29:11f.

the heart of this people. Make their [ears] heavy and blind them lest they see with their eyes and hear with their ears and convert.[7] All this is fulfilled in you because you do not want to believe in Jesus Christ.

[*fol. 58v*] The prophet Habakkuk says in chapter 2 that the righteous live by faith and works.[8] I tell you that this is the faith of our Christ which gives understanding and spiritual life which you do not have because you lack our faith. For if you had it perfectly, you would spiritually enjoy the food of the Holy Scriptures that is as sweet as honey for those who believe.

Yet because you do not want to believe, God did not reveal to you the great mysteries and secrets that are found in the book of life and which have been disclosed to us because we believe in Jesus. Isaiah affirms this in chapter 29, where he says: *You shall see as in a book that is closed to you which, when given to him who is learned and is asked to read, answers that he cannot since the book is closed.*[9] *However, in those days, the deaf shall hear the words of that book.*[10]

This means that the secrets of the Holy Scriptures are closed to you Jews and, therefore, you only understand them according to the flesh. But everything is disclosed and revealed to the Christian nations; nothing is closed to them. Our faith opens up and discloses everything to us. Daniel confirms this in chapter 12, where he says: *The sermons and words are closed until the end; until many learn and advise that this must be fulfilled so that they know all things.*[11] All this is now fulfilled: the secrets are not revealed to you but are disclosed to us by virtue of our faith. I tell you, gentlemen, that as long as you continue to read Moses, his veil will always be on your heart.[12]

Gentlemen, accept our shield of faith. Leave Moses who is no longer but has passed on. Leave the synagogues, your assemblies. Honor the baptismal water of which you partook. Fortify yourselves with it, because the rite of circumcision no longer exists; it expired and came to an end on the cross with Christ. Your law was buried in the sepulcher with Christ. Renounce the Sabbath, do not keep it. Take Sunday instead. Go to our churches. Listen to our sermons and be on the true path. Do not think ill of me, gentlemen, for telling you this, for I only desire your well-being and salvation. I would be happy to see you blessed and good Christians; friends of Christ and not of Moses who brings you not salvation but death — ruin and pestilence for your bodies and souls.

[10] Isa. 29:18.
[11] Dan. 12:4.
[12] See 2 Cor. 3:15.

[*fol. 59r*] Daniel daa huma muito boa rezão asinando a causa porque nom entendes, dizendo no capitolo xij°: "Hos impiadosos viuirão sem piedade e todos nom emtenderão; mas, porem, hos doutos entenderão." Diguouos que estes impiadosos, e que viuem sem piedade, sondes vos que nom tendes piedade pera vos mesmos, nom querendo vos fir-mimente crer em Christo senão fingidamente, e por isso, nom entendes ho liuro dos segredos que vos esta fechado, ho qual abrio ho Mexia e nolo deu que ho leessemos. E nos somos hos doutos, como diz Daniel, que entendemos estes segredos, polo qual a Sagrada Escritura spiritualmente e segundo ho sintido verdadeiro entendemos, e nom car-nalmente, como vos. Nos temos aquele grande fundamento e alicece, e este o forte e firme, ho qual iamais caira, que he a fee da qual vos careces, e portanto, nom entendes.

Isto, pois, crede e tende por fee, que iamais entenderes se nom crer-des, porque se vos esteueseis armados deste arnes da fee, vos entendiries aquele passo de Isaias,[c] que diz no capitolo 2°: "Do monte de Sion saira a Lei e a palaura do Senhor de Ierusalem, e iulguara as gentes e arguira muitos pouos." Certamente, isto nom entendes vos, que tendes hos sin-tidos obtusos e errados, que he que no monte de Sion a Lei noua auia de ser dada, como foi polo Mexia que a deu aos seus discipolos, dia de Pinticoste, mandandolhes que a fossem pobricar por todo ho vniuerso mundo, como elles loguo fezerão, declarando esta Lei noua em Ierusalem aos vossos antepassados. E nom querendo elles ouuila; mas persiguindo hos discipolos de Christo, tornarãose aos gentios, hos quaes a rreceberão e entenderão. Porquanto vos, senhores, careceis desta fee nossa, que he fundamento de toda bem; portanto, hos vossos doutores nom alomeados polo Spiritu Santo, dizem que muitas cousas conuem a Deos, que são falsas e erroneas, e carecem de toda rezão.

Dizem hos vossos doutores, no liuro terceiro da doutrina, que Deos teem luguar e que ocupa luguar; e que cada dia huma vez se ira contra ho mundo, e isto na primeira hora do dia, afirmando que hos reis da maldade lhe põe na cabeça naquela hora a sua diadena, e que antão Deos se ira, e ha merencoria. A isto nom sei que digua senão que aqueles vossos doutores que composerão hos liuros da doutrina (e eu chamolhes liuro[s] de falsidade) ouuerão mester, loguo castiguados, pois

c MS Israias

[13] Dan. 12:10.
[14] Isa. 2:3f.
[15] Matt. 28:16ff.

[*fol. 59r*] Daniel gives a very good reason why you do not understand in chapter 12: *The merciless ones shall live without compassion, and none shall understand; but the learned shall understand.*[13] I tell you that these impious ones that live without mercy are you who do not even have compassion for yourselves; for you do not want to believe truly in Christ but only to feign belief. It is for this reason that you do not understand the book of secrets that is closed to you and which the Messiah opened and gave to us to read. We are the learned, as Daniel says, who understand these mysteries; who understand the Holy Scriptures in its true sense, according to the spirit and not according to the flesh as you do. Our faith, which you lack and fail to understand, is that great foundation and support — strong and firm — which shall never topple.

Believe and have faith in this: You will never understand if you do not believe. If you were fitted with this armor of faith, you would understand that passage in chapter 2 of Isaiah that says: *From the Mount of Zion shall go forth the law and the word of the Lord from Jerusalem. And He shall judge the nations and rebuke many peoples.*[14] You certainly do not understand this — you whose senses have been dulled and deceived! The new Law would be given on Mount Zion, as the Messiah gave it to His disciples at Pentecost, ordering them to go and promulgate it throughout the whole world.[15] This they did afterwards, proclaiming the new Law to your ancestors in Jerusalem. Yet they did not want to hear it and instead persecuted Christ's disciples who then turned to the Gentiles who received and understood it. You, gentlemen, lack our faith which is the basis of all good. Your doctors, therefore, who were not illuminated by the Holy Spirit, say that there are many things which are true of God which are false and erroneous and devoid of all reason.

In the third book of the doctrine your doctors say that God has a place and occupies a place,[16] and that once each day, at the first hour of the day, He becomes angry at the world. They maintain that at that hour the kings of evil place God's crown on His head and it is then that He becomes angry and melancholy. I do not know what to answer to this except that those doctors of yours who composed the books of doctrine (which I call books of deception) were forthwith to be punished

[16] Cf. *DPA*, Title 1, col. 549: "Vestri doctores in doctrinae libro tertio, Deum in loco esse asserunt sex partibus terminato, affirmantes testimonio hoc Danielis qui ait [Dan. 10:20] ... On this passage, not extant in the editions of the Talmud, see Merchavia, p. 101, n. 21a. The "liber tertius" apparently refers to the talmudic order of *Neziqin* (Torts). See Merchavia, pp. 90ff., p. 93, n. 1. On God as "place," see Genesis Rabbah 68:9 and Solomon Schechter, *Aspects of Rabbinic Theology* (New York, 1909), pp. 26-28.

que em Deos poserão ira, e per consiguinte, paixão e tristeza. "Malitia eorum obsecauit eos belluas!" [*fol. 59v*] E dizem que ninguem nom sabe nem conhece ho ponto daquela primeira hora no qual Deos se ira senam Balaam, filho de Beor, do qual se faz menção no Liuro dos Numeros, no capitolo xxiiij. Nem Moises nom no soube.

O quanta paruoice e tolice iaz nesses liuros da doutrina, e pera vosso mal forão elles compostos. Hora, vede que paruoisse e falsidade he esta tão grande que Balaam magico e diabolico, tendo pauto com ho diabo, soube este ponto desta hora, na qual Deos se ira, e Moises, que foi tão santo e iusto e tão amiguo de Deos e seu familiar, nam no soube. Certamente, bem honrrarão estes doutores ho vosso Moises. Assi que estes dizeres dos vossos doutores parecem mininices e enguanos pera emlaçarem hos simplizes. Fundamsse nas autoridades, as quaes nom entendem, e portanto, lhes daam falso intendimento, porque elles mais eram carnaes que espirituaes.

Traguouos aqui estes errores pera que saibaes que andaes errados e que hos liuros que vos chamais da doutrina podees lhes chamar liuros de errores e falsidades. E mais uos diguo que nhuma verdade se contem neles. Assi ho afirma Pedr'Afonso, vosso doutor tornado christão, no seu liuro no primeiro titolo, onde traz mil errores e mil paruoices dos antepassados, as quaes elle conheceo mui bem, como elle foi lauado pola aguoa do bautismo, e como vestio a nossa fee.

Assi vos, senhores, se quiserdes vestir a nossa pelle, a nossa fee, loguo conheceres a verdade, leixando as vossas falsidades. E pera verdes as ᵈfalsidades deles,ᵈ olhai ho que afirmão. Mais estes doutores do valle tenebroso dizem blasfemias contra Deos, dizendo que Deos chora cada dia huma vez, e que dos seus olhos saiem duas lagrimas, as quaes caem no grande maar. E dizem que estas lagrimas são aquele grande resplendor que cae das estrelas. Esto he huma grande blasfemia contra Deos por onde deuem de conceder que Deos he composto de quatro ellementos, e que hos elementos são materia de Deos, porque as lagrimas nom procedem senão da superfluidade da humidade.

---

d-d int. + *vossos paruoices* exp.

[17] Based on B.T. Berakhot 7a, cf. B.T. Sanhedrin 105b. Machado's source is *DPA*, cols. 549f.: "Dicitis siquidem eum singulis diebus semel in die irasci ... Prima etiam hora diei eum irasci asseritis, causam hujus irae esse dicentes, quod in illa hora reges iniquitatis exsurgentes, diademata sibi imponunt, et solem adorant... Aiunt praeterea quod ipsius horae qua irascitur punctum nemo noverit unquam, nisi Balaam filius Beor. In hoc autem verbo vobis ipsis contrarii estis, cum ex una parte Moyses eum vocet ariolum (*Num.* xxii), vos etiam vocetis iniquum, ex altera vero parte eum prudentiorem Moyse esse significetis." Cf. *FF*, fol. 200ra.

since they ascribed ire, passion, and sadness to God. *Malitia eorum obsecauit eos belluas.* [*fol. 59v*] They say too that no one knows or is acquainted with the exact moment of that first hour in which God becomes angry except Balaam, the son of Beor, who is mentioned in the Book of Numbers, chapter 24. Not even Moses knew![17]

Oh, how much imbecility and stupidity there is in those books of doctrine which were composed for your undoing. Come now, see what great nonsense and falsity it is to say that the diabolical sorcerer Balaam, who had a pact with the devil, knew the very moment in that hour in which God became angry, and that Moses, who was so saintly, righteous, beloved of and intimate with God, did not know. Your doctors certainly honored Moses well. In short, these sayings of your doctors appear to be childish and mere deceits to trap the simple. They are founded on texts which they do not understand and which they interpret erroneously according to the flesh rather than the spirit.

I bring these errors to your attention here so that you know that you are in the wrong and that the books that you call doctrine can well be called books of error and falsity. Moreover, I will tell you that there is not one truth to be found in them. Petrus Alfonsi, a doctor of yours turned Christian, affirms this in the first title of his book. Here he brings forth a thousand errors and a thousand stupidities of your forefathers.[18] He recognized them very well when he was washed with the baptismal water and clothed himself in our faith.[19]

Therefore, gentlemen, if you wish to wear our garb and our faith, you will quickly come to know the truth and abandon your errors. In order to see their deceit,[20] just look at what they assert. These doctors from the dark valley hurl blasphemies at God and say that He cries once each day and that from His eyes two tears fall which drop into the great sea. They further say that these tears are the great splendor that falls from the stars. This is indeed blasphemy toward God of considerable magnitude, for they must then concede that God is composed of four elements and that these elements are His substance, in that the tears derive from superfluity of humidity.[21]

---

[18] Reference to "Titulus Primus" of *DPA* which "ostendit quod Judaei verba prophetarum carnaliter intelligunt et ea falso exponunt."

[19] See Introduction.

[20] MS replaces "your foolishness" with "their deceit." See note *d*.

[21] B.T. Berakhot 59a. Machado's source is *DPA*, col. 550: "Nec hoc sufficit eis de Deo dicere, sed eum etiam quotidie semel in die plorare, et ab ejus oculis duas prodeuntes lacrymas in magnum mare dicunt concidere, et has fulgorem esse affirmant illum qui tempore nocturno de stellis videtur cadere. Haec autem ratio Deum ex quatuor elementis ostendit compositum esse. Neque enim fiunt

No*m* quero mais insistir nestas pa*r*uoices *que* no*m* procede*m* senão
por falta da fee, a qual se vos teue*r*des, conheceres a ue*r*dade e loguo ho
liuro vos sera abe*r*to e discube*r*to, ho qual, sem fee, nu*n*qua conheceres
e sempre andareis boçaes e idiotas.

Esta he a nossa fee, e peçouos *que* esta seya a vossa. Ame*n*.

[*fol. 60r*] Capitolo Vigesimo segundo. Como hos iudeus falsame*n*te
esperão que hão de resurgir todos qua*n*do vier ho Mexia, e que hão de
morar outra vez em Ierusalem.

Como Ada*m* pecou e foi a D*e*os desobediente, loguo lhe foi necessario
algu*m* remedio pera se saluar. Por*que* ho doente tee*m* necessidade de
medico e mezinha, e d'outra maneira, mal iria ao doente se soubesse
que a sua chagua no*m* tinha remedio ne*m* medela ou defensiuo algu*m*.
Ada*m*, pois, como pecou, loguo adoeceo, loguo foi chaguado e vulnera-
do grauame*n*te no corpo e na alma; portanto, teue necessidade de
medico e de mezinha. Ho medico *que* foi ordenado pera mezinhar esta
chagua foi Ch*ri*sto, Mexia promitido na vossa Lei, e a mezinha ou
enxarope foi a sua fee de Ch*ri*sto, sem a qual ningue*m* no*m* pode ser
dino da benauenturança.

Esta mezinha correo desde começo do mu*n*do ates que ho Mexia
padeceo quanto foi àqueles que erão da Lei da natureza. Porem, depois
de Habraa*m*, correo, alem desta fee do Mexia, a circu*m*cisão quanto
àqueles *que* erão da sua casa e familia, e cessou pola morte do Mexia,
no*m* tendo mais viguor ne*m* virtude nem força algu*m*a porquanto D*e*os
assi tinha ordenado que ates ali auia de durar. E dali por diante veo ho
bautismo, mais perfeito *que* não a circu*m*cisão, porqua*n*to no*m* abria a
porta do paraiso, mas ho bautismo loguo abrio, por amor da paixão do
Mexia, ho qual, como resurgio loguo, hos padres santos que elle tirou
do limbo ta*m*be*m*, com elle, resurgirão. E segundo algu*n*s afirmão, com
seus proprios corpos resurgirão, subindo aos ceos onde estarão pera
todo sempe*r*.

Mas, porem, vos outros, s*e*n*h*ores,[a] ceguos, e obstinados, e incredolos
[b](e tenho porem pera mym que ia sondes muito boons christãos e
milhores que hos velhos)[b] contra rezão, no*m* entendendo as autoridades
da Sagrada Escritura, afirmais dizendo, que quando vier ho Mexia, *que*

a int.   b-b int.

lacrymae nisi ex humiditatis abundantia descendunt de capite. Si vero ita est, ergo elementa sunt
Dei materia. Omnis autem materia prior est et simplicior forma. Ergo et haec priora et simpliciora
Deo sunt, quod nefas est credere." Cf. *FF*, fol. 200r.

I do not wish to insist anymore on these absurdities which arise from a lack of faith which, if possessed, would permit you to recognize the truth. The book would then be opened to you and revealed without delay. Yet, without faith, you will never recognize it, and will always be louts and idiots.

This is our faith and I beg that it be yours. Amen.

[*fol. 60r*] Chapter twenty-two. How the Jews wrongly wait for all to be resurrected and to return again to Jerusalem when the Messiah comes.

When Adam disobeyed God and sinned, he was in need of some cure to save him, for one who is ill requires a doctor and medication. If these were not available, the patient would suffer, knowing that there was no remedy, cure, or any preventive for his affliction. Thus, when Adam transgressed he immediately fell ill, and was at once hurt and gravely wounded in his body and soul. He, therefore, was in need of a doctor and medication. The doctor who was ordained to cure this wound was Christ, the Messiah promised in your law; and the medicine or elixir was Adam's faith in Christ, without which no one is worthy of beatitude.

This medicine was used from the beginning of the world until the Messiah suffered all that He did for those who were under the Law of Nature. Then, after Abraham, there existed along with the faith of the Messiah the rite of circumcision for all those who were of [Abraham's] house and family. This came to an end with the Messiah's death, after which it was no longer in force, having no power or merit whatsoever for God had so ordered that it was not to be practiced after that time. After that, baptism was introduced. This was more perfect than circumcision, for the latter never opened the door of Paradise. [Yet baptism did so] through the passion of the Messiah Who came to life and delivered the holy Patriarchs, who also rose with Him out of Limbo. According to the assertions of some, they rose bodily and ascended the heavens, where they shall be forevermore.

Yet you, gentlemen,[1] blind, obstinate, and incredulous, (I am of the opinion, however, that you are very good Christians and better than the old),[2] opposed to reason without understanding the authoritative passages of the Holy Scriptures, state that, when the Messiah comes, all

---

[1] Interlinear addition. See note *a*.
[2] (I ... old). Interlinear addition. See note *b*.

todos aqueles que são mortos, que resurgirão e virão morar na Terra
da Promissão, e que no Templo adorarão e sacrificarão a Deos como
sacrificauão a Deos antes que ho Mexia viesse. E assi viuires pera todo
sempre com ho vosso Mexia, polo qual esperais, que ha de reinar temporalmente pera todo sempre, subiuguando hos gentios. Pera confirmação disto, trazeis ho que diz Ezechi[e]l no capitolo xxxvij, onde diz
que dixe Nosso Senhor: "Eu abrirey hos vossos moimentos, e vos tirarei
dos vossos sepulcros, e vos meterei na vossa terra, e vos farei folguar na
vossa terra de Isrrael." Hos vossos paruos e simplizes doutores, fundados nesta autoridade, afirmão que isto se ha de comprir quando vier
ho vosso Mexia, e que antão aues de resurgir e morar na terra vossa
que foi da Promissão. Por vossa vida, senhores, que nom me tenhaes a
mal se as vezes falo mais do que ei de falar, porque nom posso teer
pacientia lendo estes dizeres e enguanos dos vossos doutores que são
causa de muito mal.

[fol. 6ov] Sabees donde veem esta vossa simplicidade ᶜ(chamolhe simplicidade, e perdoaime)?ᶜ Prouem que nom sabees que ho Mexia teem
duas vindas: huma en carne com humildade, a qual que ia passou; a
outra ha de ser ao iuizo, a qual ainda nom he comprida. Mas comprirsea
por vosso mal (e nosso tambem), quando Deos quiser e for seruido. Desta
vinda no iuizo fala ho profeta Ezechiel no capitolo acima aleguado,
onde fala do dia do iuizo e como hos corpos hão de resurgir e sair dos
seus moimentos. Por onde eu concludo que grandes são hos vossos
errores, polo qual vindes a cair naquele grande error de Mafamede que
no seu Alchorão leixou que hos mouros tambem auião de resurgir pera
casarem com moças virgens e se fartarão de leite e manteiga, e morarão
nuns campos muito deliciosos. Isto procede por vos outros mal enten-
didos às autoridades da Sagrada Escritura, e porquanto este liuro vos
esta escondido e nom vos he discuberto por falta da fee que nom tendes.

Nos, em verdade, tal sentença como a vossa nom aprouamos nem
louuamos mas condenamos, crendo que ho Mexia ia veo, e porem,
ainda vira ao dia de iuizo iulguar hos viuos e hos mortos, e daar a cada
hum, segundo seus mericimentos ou desmericimentos. Polo qual falso
he ho que credes, que auees de resurgir quando vier ho Mexia. Verdade
he que vos resurgireis no dia do iuizo e tomares vossos corpos e saires
dos vossos moimentos, e ireis ao vale de Iosaphat (Ioelis 3º) onde seres

c-c int.

³ Ezek. 37:12.
⁴ Cf. Genesis Rabbah 96:5.

those who are dead shall come to life and shall dwell in the Promised Land, and that they shall worship God in the Temple and sacrifice to Him as they did before the Messiah came. So shall you live forevermore with your messiah for whom you are waiting and who shall reign temporally for all time, subjugating the Gentiles. As a confirmation of this, you refer to chapter 37 of Ezekiel, where it says that our Lord said: *I will open your graves and place you in your land, and I will make you rejoice in your Land of Israel.*[3] Your stupid and simple doctors, basing themselves on this text, state that this will come to pass when your Messiah comes. At that time, you will rise and dwell in your Promised Land.[4] By your life, gentlemen, do not think ill of me if at times I speak more than I ought; but I have no patience when I read these sayings and deceits of your doctors which are the cause of much evil.

[*fol. 60v*] Do you know the source of your simple-mindedness? (Pardon me if I call it simple-mindedness.)[5] It stems from your not knowing that the Messiah has two advents: one in the flesh with humility, which has already come to pass; the other of judgment, which is yet to be fulfilled. But fulfilled it will be — because of your evil (and ours as well) — whenever God wills it and is so pleased. The prophet Ezekiel speaks of this judgment in the above chapter when speaking of the Day of Judgment and of how bodies will rise and leave their graves. I thereby conclude that your many errors have caused you to fall into that great error of Mohammed who allowed in his Koran that the Moors would also come to life again in order to marry young virgins. They would satiate themselves with milk and butter and dwell in fields of superb delight.[6] This stems from your misinterpretation of the passages from the Holy Scriptures which are due to the fact that this book is concealed from you and not revealed because of your lack of faith.

We truly neither approve of nor praise your convictions. Rather, we condemn them and believe that the Messiah has already come and that He shall return on the Day of Judgment to judge the quick and the dead[7] and to grant each his just reward. Your belief that you shall rise again when the Messiah comes is false. It is true that you shall come to life on the Day of Judgment and shall leave your tombs bodily and go to the Valley of Jehoshaphat (Joel, 3)[8] where you shall be eternally con-

---

[5] (Pardon ... simple-mindedness). Interlinear addition. See note *c*.
[6] Koran, 56:1-38; *DPA,* col. 599.
[7] Acts 10:42, 2 Tim. 4:1, 1 Peter 4:5.
[8] Joel 3:12.

condenados eternalmente pera as penas do inferno, se nom quiserdes crer em Christo Ihesu, nosso Redentor e nosso Saluador.

Nom cuidees, pois, que aues de reinar com ho Mexia em Ierusalem, porque Ierusalem terreal foi destruida por Tito pera nela nunqua mais ent[r]ardes (Danielis ix). E ho direito que tinhees na Terra da Promissão, todo ho perdestes porque fostes tredores a Deos e matastes ho seu Filho.

Vos bem sabees que aqueles que são tredores à coroa rreal nom somentes perdem hos seus beens proprios, e honrras, e dinidades que teem, mas assi tambem hos filhos que auião de soceder nestas honrras temporaes, assi as perdem.

Ho mesmo aconteceo que hos vossos antepassados forão tredores à coroa e rreinado do Mexia, e portanto, perderão pera sy e pera vos todas has honrras e dinidades, e terras e cidades da Terra da Promissão.

[*fol. 61r*] Assi, senhores, que todo ho vosso direito foi perdido e ho Templo destruido com a cidade, pera nunqua mais se edificar. E por isso, lançai tal error de vos como este, que he feo, e torpe, e enorme; mas crede no dia do iuizo, no qual seres iulguados por boons ou por maos, assi como vos fezerdes. Portanto, nom esperees nem cuidees que auees de triunfar em Ierusalem terreal; mas esperai e tende confiança na cidade de Ierusalem celestrial, se fordes boons, e fies e leaes christãos, e amiguos de Christo, porque ali reinares com ho Mexia, pera todo sempre. E se nom quiserdes sentir comnosco e ser desta nossa sentença catolica e fiel, he necessario que caeres em muitos errores e paruoices. Como diz Aristoteles: "Vno absurdo dato, multa conti[n]gunt" (Primo *Phisicorum*).

Assi que do vosso error estes se seguem. Primeiramente, que aqueles que estão no inferno nom serão punidos eternalmente e pera todo sempre, ho que he contra Iob quen diz: "Inferno nulla est redemptio." E assi Dathan e Abiron, que viuos descenderão ao inferno (Numeros xvi°), quando vier ho Mexia virão reinar com elle, e todos aqueles iudeus que la iazem, todos sairão pera reinarem com ho Mexia. A se algum iudeu morrer em pecado mortal naquele dia que ho Mexia ouuer de vir, nom sera punido, porquanto loguo ha de resurgir. E aqueles que antão forom viuos, nom morrerão iamais, que he contra ho rreal profeta Dauid, que diz no psalmo lxxxviij°: "Quis est homo qui viuet, et non videbit mortem?"

Segundariamente, se segue do vosso dito falso que ao pecado mortal

---

⁹ Dan. 9:26f.
¹⁰ *Phys.* 1.2.

demned to the punishments of hell unless you believe in Christ Jesus, our Redeemer and our Savior.

Do not believe then that you shall reign with the Messiah in Jerusalem; because the Jerusalem of this world was destroyed by Titus so that you shall never again enter there (Daniel, 9).[9] You further lose the right you had to the Promised Land because you betrayed God and killed His Son.

You know very well that not only those who are traitors to the royal crown lose their personal goods, honors, and titles, but their children, who would normally inherit these temporal honors, also lose them.

The same happened to your forefathers who were traitors to the crown and kingdom of the Messiah. They, therefore, lost, for themselves and for you all their honors and titles as well as the lands and cities of the Promised Land.

[*fol. 61r*] Thus, gentlemen, all your rights were lost and the Temple and the city were destroyed never again to be rebuilt. For this reason, repudiate these ugly, shameful, and enormous errors and believe in the Day of Judgment on which you shall be judged as good or evil in accord with your actions. Neither expect nor believe that you shall triumph in the terrestrial Jerusalem. Rather, if you are good, faithful, and loyal Christians and beloved of Christ, have hope and confidence in the heavenly city of Jerusalem, because there you shall reign with the Messiah forevermore. However, if you do not wish to believe as we, and join our true Catholic faith, you must inevitably fall into many errors and follies. As Aristotle says: *Vno absurdo dato, multa con-ti<n>gunt* (1 *Phys.*).[10]

From your error, these others follow: Firstly, those who are in Hell shall not be eternally punished. This is contrary to what Job says: *Inferno nulla est redemptio.*[11] Thus Dathan and Abiram who descended into Hell alive (Numbers 16) shall reign with the Messiah when He comes,[12] and every single Jew that is there shall go forth to reign with the Messiah. If some Jew dies in mortal sin on the day the Messiah is to come, he shall not be punished since he is about to be resurrected. And those who were alive at that time shall never die, for if it were otherwise, it would not be in accord with what the royal prophet David says in Psalm 88: *Quis est homo qui viuet, et non videbit mortem?*[13]

Secondly, it follows from your erroneous statement that mortal sin

[11] See above, chap. 9, n. 1.
[12] Num. 16:33.
[13] Ps. 89(88):49.

no*m* he diuida pena ete*r*na, mas soo temporal pois que tal pena se deue de acabar pera depois hos vossos iudeus triu*n*fare*m* a vida.

Te*r*ceirame*n*te, se segue que confundis ho paraiso porquanto pondes hum pera vos, que sera na Terra da Promissão, e he necessario que aia hi outro pera hos home*n*s iustos e vi*r*tuosos das outras nações; ou aues de confessar que todos hos outros vão ao inferno e que nos somos hos p*r*imeiros. Mas, pore*m*, se no*m* credes em Ih*e*su, e se no*m* lançardes tal error como este fora de uos, seres hos condenados, e nos hos saluos.

Quartame*n*te, se segue que no*m* pondes dia do iuizo onde todos serão iulguados. E, porem, hos profetas estão cheos de autoridades, has quaes euidenteme*n*te prouão ho dia do iuizo quando ho Mexia ha de vir muito espa*n*toso e terriuel, com grandes poderes naquele grande dia.

[*fol. 61v*] Vos dizees que quando hos mortos iudeus resurgire*m* na vinda do Mexia, que todos hão de resurgir pera exercitare*m* hos seus ofitios como exercitauão quando erão viuos; e cada hu*m* tera sua dinidade e seu ofitio. Ce*r*tame*n*te que tal opinião me parece bestial e não racional, ha qual carece de todo fundame*n*to e de toda rezão. Hora, dizeime, se todos hos pontifices e grandes sace*r*dotes hão de resurgir pera exercitare*m* seus ofitios, dizeime, que*m* sera antão ho grande sace*r*dote? Aaro*m* ou Eleazar, seu filho, ou Phinees, ou qual destes? Manifesto he que todos iuntame*n*te na*m* no ha de ser, porq*ue* a Lei no*m* põe senão hu*m* soo sace*r*dote. E se hu*m* deue de ser sace*r*dote apos ho outro, e cada hu*m* se*r*uira ta*n*to como d'antes se*r*uio q*ue* morresse, e acabada a roda, tornarão a começar, e assi nu*n*qua acaba-rão.

E assi como dizemos do sace*r*dotio, ho mesmo se segue no rreinado e no guouerno do reino ("et sic erit processus in infinitu*m*"), por onde nu*n*qua seres bem rregidos ne*m* guoue*r*nados, porquanto aquele que for honrrado emquanto rreger, loguo acabado, ho guoue*r*no fiquara desonrrado e abatido pois que outro siguinte deue de socede*r* no reino. Pois muitos rreis no*m* pode*m* se*r* iuntame*n*te porq*ue* ho reino hu*m* soo deue de ser. E assi Ezechiel ho diz: "Vnu*m* pastore*m* omnes habebu*n*t" (capitolo xxxvij).

Ta*m*be*m* no*m* podem ser muitos grandes sace*r*dotes se ho Templo deue de ser hu*m* soo, porq*ue* se forem muitos, "confusão loguo na mão." Como diz Aristoteles no outauo da *Philosophia*: "Expedit vnum *e*sse p*r*incipem." E se forem muitos bispos, seguesse q*ue* a lei se deue

14 Joel 2:11, 31; Mal. 4:5; Romans 2:16.
15 Cf. *Summa Theologiae,* 1, 2.
16 Cf. Aquinas, *De regno,* 1, 2. (See below, chap. 23, n. 1.)

does not incur eternal but only temporal punishment since such a penalty must be paid in full for your Jews to win life.

Thirdly, it follows that you are confused about Paradise. You posit one for yourselves which is to be the Promised Land, and, by necessity, another for the just and virtuous men of other nations. Otherwise, you would have to confess that all the others go to Hell and that we are the first among them. Nevertheless, if you do not believe in Jesus and do not abandon such an error, you shall be condemned, and we saved.

Fourthly, it follows that you do not posit a day for judgment in which everyone shall be judged. Yet, the prophets are full of texts which plainly attest to the day of judgment when the Messiah shall come, most marvelously and wondrously, with great power on that day.[14]

[fol. 61v] You say that all Jews that have died shall be resurrected when the Messiah comes and that they shall come back to life so that they may exercise the same offices they did when they were alive. Each one shall have his own benefice and office. Such an opinion certainly seems imbecilic and irrational to me, based neither on fact nor reason. Tell me now, if all the priests and high priests are to rise again to exercise their offices, which one, tell me, shall be the high priest? Aaron, Eleazar his son, Phineas — which one of these? It is clear that all of them will not serve together because the Law provides for only one priest. For if one priest is to follow another, and each shall serve as he did before he died, it will continue to go around like this in a never-ending cycle.

What we say about the priesthood is also true of the rulership and government of the kingdom (et sic erit processus in infinitum).[15] Therefore, you shall never be properly ruled or governed. For he who shall be honored while he rules shall leave his government in dishonor and weakness when his rule ends, since another shall follow to take his place in the realm. For many kings cannot rule together at the same time because there can be only one rulership.[16] So do we find in Ezekiel: Vnum pastorem omnes habebunt (chapter 37).[17]

In like manner, there cannot be many high priests if there is to be one Temple. If there were many, one would have confusion on one's hands. As Aristotle says in the eighth book of the Philosophy:[18] Expedit vnum esse principem.[19] If there were many bishops, it follows that the law would

---

[17] Ezek. 37:24.

[18] Metaphys. 13.9. The "eighth book" might be a confusion with the eight books of the Physics.

[19] The quotation found in Aristotle: "The rule of many is not good; let one be the ruler," is from Homer's Iliad, Book 2, line 204.

loguo de destruir, porque todos no*m* hão de ma*n*dar ho mesmo, mas serão antre si diferentes.

Assi que me parece que mil enco*n*uenientes se segue*m* deste p*r*imeiro vosso error, que todos hos iudeus deuem de rresurgir pera exe*r*citare*m* hos mesmos offitios que se*r*uirão antes que morressem.

Na*m* vos quero, senhores, traze*r* mais enco*n*uenientes que estes. E se mais quiserdes veer, no titolo te*r*ceiro de Pedr'Afonso, vosso doutor, hos achares. Ledeos se quiserdes conhecer a ue*r*dade, que he esta. Vos no*m* auees de resurgir, como cuidaes e esperaes falsame*n*te, quando vier ho Mexia tomar ca*r*ne humana, porq*ue* ia ha tomou. Mas vira no dia do iuizo qua*n*do todos estaremos diante da Sua Magestade no vale de Iosaphat, e darnosha, segu*n*do merecidos.

Esta he a nossa fee e crença; peçouos que esta seia a vossa. Ame*n*.

[*fol. 62r*] Capitolo Vigesimo te*r*cio. Como aos pastores e inquisidores conue*m* de olhare*m* polas ouelhas a elles comitidas, das quaes darão largua co*n*ta.

Ho pastor do guado a elle comitido he obriguado a dar conta e rezão de toda perda e da*m*no que sobrevier sobre seu guado por sua falta ou nigligentia; ou por no*m* poor aquela indust*r*ia ou diligentia que se rrequere*m*, por onde he obriguado a dar rrezão de todo mao rrecado que sobrevier e acontecer. Esto procede porquanto a isso se obriguou, toma*n*do carreguo disso polo q*u*al fiqua obriguado e obnoxio a satis-faze*r* a seu se*n*hor do guado, se algu*m* mao rrecado se seguir. A proua da rrezão natural pera isto abasta que cada hu*m* he obriguado de dar rrezão das cousas q*ue* lhe são emcomendadas, e se se siguir algu*m*a falta, ia fiqua obriguad[o] a restituir ho dano.

Assi ta*m*bem dizemos que hos p*r*incipes e reis e hos p*r*elados, como bispos ou outros quaesquer que tee*m* regimento, são pastores mais altos e mais p*r*ezados que não hos do guado; e hos suditos destes são as ouelhas. E como quer que estas ouelhas são p*r*ezadas e de alto estado; portanto, hos pastores são mais obriguados de porem maior diligentia e custodia ace*r*qua do seu guado.

D*e*os ete*r*no he ho grande pastor e regedor e guoue*r*nador de todo ho mu*n*do. E porquanto no*m* conue*m* que fale comnosco, porque D*e*os ni*n*gue*m* vee ne*m* pode veer co[m] ho olho corporal, instituio D*e*os outros pastores que falasse*m* e co*m*municasse*m* comnosco — hu*n*s pera ho temporal, como são hos rreis, outros pera ho sp*irit*ual, como são hos p*r*elados. Pore*m*, todos sam ordenados por D*e*os. Assi ho afirma São Thomas no vigesimo opusculo, no capitolo xv do *Rregimento dos Principes,*

then be destroyed, because not all would rule alike but would differ one from the other.

For this reason it seems to me that there are a thousand incongruities that stem from this first error of yours that all the Jews must arise to exercise the same offices they filled before they died.

It is not necessary, gentlemen, to bring to your attention any more incongruities than these. If you do wish to see more, look at the third title of Petrus Alfonsi,[20] your own doctor, and there you will find them. Read them if you want to know this truth. You shall not rise again, as you vainly think and hope, when the Messiah comes clothed in human flesh, because he has already so appeared. But He shall come on Judgment Day when we shall all stand before His Majesty in the Valley of Jehoshaphat to be judged according to our merits.

This is our faith and belief. I ask that it be yours [also]. Amen.

[fol. 62r] Chapter Twenty-three. How it behooves the shepherds and Inquisitors to look after the sheep who have been entrusted to them, and for whom they shall render a long account.

The shepherd entrusted with a flock is obliged to explain and account for any loss or injury that befalls his flock through his own fault or negligence or failure to apply the necessary industry and diligence. In such a case every loss that is incurred must be accounted for. This arises from the responsibilities in this regard that one has taken upon himself in that he is obliged and bound to satisfy the master of his flock should some loss be incurred. An innate sense of reason is sufficient to prove that each one is obliged to give an account of the things entrusted to him and, in the case of loss, is obliged to make amends for the damage.

We say too that princes, kings, and prelates, as well as bishops or others who rule, are pastors more highly to be esteemed than shepherds of a flock. Their subjects are the sheep, and, since these sheep are esteemed and of high position, the shepherds are even more obliged to exercise greater diligence and caution in the care of their flock.

God the Eternal is the great shepherd, ruler, and governor of the whole world. Since it is not suitable that He speak with us — because no one sees God nor can He be seen with the human eye — He appointed other shepherds to speak and communicate with us. Some, the

---

[20] *DPA*, cols. 581-594, entitled "Titulus 3: De stulta Judaeorum confutanda credulitate super mortuorum resurrectione quos credunt et resurrecturos esse et iterum terram incolere."

onde conclude que hos principes e hos prelados são ordenados e por Deos instituidos, hos quaes teem as suas vezes. Esto podemos prouar polo Primeiro Liuro dos Rreis, no capitolo viij°, onde se diz que ho pouo, desprezando a Samuel que hos rregia, pidirão rrei a Deos, e como Samuel dixe ao Senhor que pidião rrei, Deos lhe dixe: "Nom desprezão a ti, mas a mym que te eligi e te pus nas minhas vezes." Disto daa testimunho Salamão nos Prouerbios, no capitolo viij, dizendo em luguar de Deos: "Por mym rreinão hos rreis." Assi leemos no Primeiro Liuro dos Rreis, no capitolo ix, que Deos ellegeo Saul, e depois a Dauid (capitolo xvi°), por onde bem parece que hos rreis nom somentes teem as vezes de Deos, mas ainda são elligidos e escolhidos por Deos pera regerem seu pouo. [fol. 62v] São Paulo, escreuendo aos rromanos, no capitolo xiiij, bem proua que ho poder dos rreis e ho dos prelados de Deos procede, dizendo: "Ho poder nom he senão de Deos, e quem rresisti a este poder, a Deos resisti."

Assi que nom temos debate nem duuida acerqua disto. Porem, assi ho principe como ho prelado são obriguados a olharem como pace seu guado, e por que campos andão suas ouelhas — se no alheo, que has tirem, e se no seu campo, que has guiem bem e enderencem — e se alguma esteuer enferma ou doente ou eibada, que ha curem e lhe deem hos enpastos e defenssiuos necessarios pera ho corpo e pera alma. Ho bom pastor, se peruentura vee que a sua ouelha se saie do seu proprio paciguo e anda pollo alheo, carea, traela pera manada; nom na leixa andar vaguabunda. Assi ho principe e prelado deue de olhar se ho cristão leixa ho seu paciguo, a fee de Christo, e trazelo pera manada per boas amoestações, enxemplos, conselhos e se não quiser siguir a manada, que lhe deem aguilhoadas que ho amearem, e quando morrer quiser, "per ignem et aquam erit refrigerium eius."

Manifesto he e claro a todos como ho nome de Ihesus nestes rreinos

---

[1] Machado may be referring to the following by St. Thomas Aquinas: "Therefore let the king recognize that such is the office which he undertakes, namely, that he is to be in the kingdom what the soul is in the body, and what God is in the world. If he reflects seriously upon this, a zeal for justice will be enkindled in him when he contemplates that he has been appointed to this position in place of God, to exercise judgment in his kingdom..." (*On Kingship to the King of Cyprus*, trans. Gerald B. Phelan, [Toronto, 1949], Book 2, chapter 1, p. 54; Latin: *De regimine principum ad regem Cypri* [Rome, 1940], pp. 11f.) It has not been possible at this point to verify our author's designation of twentieth opuscule, chapter 15. The title which he gives and which in Latin is *De regimine principum* is that given to St. Thomas' *De regno, ad regem Cypri* which is interpolated into another work, not of Aquinas' authorship, *De regimine principum*. This title was commonly applied to the two works together. The *De regno* originally contained twenty chapters, generally divided into two books (*ibid.*, p. xiv).

[2] 1 Sam. 8:5f.

kings, are in charge of temporal affairs; those who are in charge of the spiritual are the prelates. However, all are ordained by God. St. Thomas affirms this in chapter 15 of *On The Rule of Princes,* twentieth opuscule. Here he concludes that princes and prelates are appointed and ordained by God and are invested with His authority.[1] We can prove this through the First Book of Kings, chapter 8, where it says that the people rejected Samuel who was their ruler and asked God for another king.[2] When Samuel told the Lord that they wanted another king, God said to him: *They do not despise you, but rather Me Who chose you to govern in My place.*[3] Solomon testifies to this in Proverbs, chapter 8, where he speaks for God: *By Me kings reign.*[4] We read in the First Book of Kings, chapter 9, that God first chose Saul[5] and then David (chapter 16)[6] and it seems then quite obvious that kings not only have God's authority but moreover are elected and chosen by Him to govern His people. [*fol. 62v*] In writing to the Romans, St. Paul truly proves in chapter 14 that the power of kings and prelates proceeds from God[7] by stating that *there is no power but of God, and whosoever resists this power resists God.*[8]

We, therefore, have no cause for debate or doubt on this matter. However, the prince and the prelate are obliged to watch their flock while they graze and to know in which fields their sheep wander. If their flock happen to wander into strange country, they must retrieve them; if they are within their own field, they are to lead them and guide the sheep well. If one should become incapacitated, ill, or injured, they must cure it by giving it nourishment and such antidotes necessary for the body and soul. If by chance the good shepherd sees that a sheep of his is straying from its own pasture and going into that of another, he takes it and brings it back to the flock; he does not let it wander astray. In like manner, the prince and the prelate must see if the Christian is leaving his pasture, the faith of Christ, and bring him back to the flock for proper admonishing, teaching, [and] counsel. If he does not wish to follow the flock, let them goad and break him and, when he wants to die, *per ignem et aquam erit refrigerium eius.*

It is clear and manifest to everyone how the name of Jesus is shamed

[3] 1 Sam. 8:7.
[4] Prov. 8:15.
[5] 1 Sam 9:17.
[6] 1 Sam. 16:11ff.
[7] Romans 13:1.
[8] Romans 13:2.

andou baixo e abatido por todos no*m* tirare*m* por hu*m*a corda; por todos nom sere*m* dũma fee e dũma crença. E disto eu no*m* me espantaua muito, porquanto onde[a] ha mouros, negros, indios, iudeus, necessario he que cada hu*m* sigua seu caminho e sua seita. Mas, espantaua me porquanto ni*n*gue*m* no*m* hia à mão a isto; ni*n*gue*m* no*m* corrigia isto. Aguora, pore*m*, segundo ouço dize*r* e segundo fama correr, ho nome de Ih*e*s*u*s anda algu*m* tanto mais exalçado e aleuantado pois que ordenados são inquisidores disertissimos, catolicos, christianissimos, doutissimos.

A vos, pois, senhores, pertence esta uista e batalha campal. A uos conue*m* olhar por vosso exe*r*cito e por vossos caualeiros. Olhai, senhores, que esta caualaria de Christo no*m* se desfaça. Estes caualeiros de Christo que forão pola aguoa do bautismo e tornarão pera traz como coua*r*des, aguilhoaios; tornaios à militia e caualaria de Ch*r*i*s*to; no*m* nos leixeis andar vaguabu*n*dos fora da fe. Ho serenissimo e inuitissimo rrei Dom Iohão te*r*ceiro deste nome a uos este [*fol. 6 3r*] careguo encome*n*dou. A sua co*n*cientia purissima desencarreguou, e a vossa carreguo, polo qual vos dareis largua conta das ouelhas que por vossa falta se perdere*m*, ou por pouca diligentia ou i*n*dustria que poserdes.

Senhores, no*m* aia hahi fauor, ne*m* amizade, ne*m* familiaridade. Tudo isto se lance detras as costas, e vai ho dulcissimo nome de Ih*e*s*u*s diante, e co*m* elle venceres. E as ouelhas que fora do curral andão, à manada trazeres. Neste libelozinho algu*n*s defensiuos e subsidios achares pera amezinhar estas ouelhas perdidas. Fazendo vos, senhores, isto con diligentia e por amor de Ih*e*s*u*s, muitas almas sarares, e ho rreino de Pu*r*tugual da eruilhaca e ioyo alimpares [b](como cremos que ya por vossa industria esta limpo e puro)[b] e de Nosso S*e*nh*o*r ho gualardão, e p*r*emio, e me*r*ce receberes. E se ho contrairo se fe*z*er, ho que no*m* cremos, olhai ho que diz Nosso S*e*nh*o*r contra hos negligentes pastores.

Ho profeta Ezechiel, no capitolo xxxiiij, diz que Nosso S*e*nh*o*r lhe dixe: "Filho do home*m*, profeta dos pastores de Isrrael, e diras aos pastores estas cousas: 'Diz ho S*e*nh*o*r D*e*os: Couitados dos pastores de Isrrael que pacião a si mesmos. Has manadas dos guados nom pace*m* hos pastores? Vos comies ho leite, e vestieies vos de panos p*r*ezados, e tomies ho milhor bocado, mata*n*do e roendo ho milhor guado; pore*m*, no*m* pacies as minhas ouelhas, porquanto as enfermas e debeles ouelhas vos no*m* esforçaueis ne*m* sarastes, e as quebradas no*m* co*n*solidastes ne*m* aiuntastes, e has derramadas no*m* trouxestes pera manadas, as perdidas

a MS *onda*   b-b int.

and humiliated in this kingdom because everyone is at loggerheads; all are not of the same faith or belief. Yet this does not surprise me very much since where there are Moors, Negroes, Indians, [and] Jews, it is inevitable that each go his own way and follow his own sect. What I do find astonishing is that no one has put a stop to this; no one has changed this. Now, however, according to current report and what I have heard said, the name of Jesus has been exalted and dignified somewhat because very Christian, Catholic inquisitors, who are most learned and eloquent, have been appointed.

So to you, gentlemen, belongs this sight and pitched battle. It behooves you to look after your army and your cavalrymen. See to it, gentlemen, that this cavalry of Christ is not destroyed. Goad these horsemen of Christ who were baptized and then recoiled like cowards. Return them to His militia and cavalry; do not let them wander outside the faith. His most serene and invincible Highness, John the Third by name [*fol. 63r*] has entrusted this responsibility to you. His most pure conscience has been satisfied by charging you with these moral duties. You shall therefore have to give a detailed account of any sheep which go astray through your own fault, or through your lack of diligence and industry.

Do not grant any favors, gentlemen, nor be friendly or familiar. Let all be cast behind with only the most sweet name of Jesus ahead and with it you will triumph. The sheep who stray from the barnyard shall you bring back to the fold. In this manual, you will find some antidotes and remedies for treating these lost sheep. By doing this, gentlemen, with diligence and for the love of Jesus, you will heal many souls and the kingdom of Portugal shall be cleansed of vetch and darnel (as we do believe it to be clean and pure through your industry)[9] and you will receive from Our Lord grace, mercy, and recompense. Yet, if the contrary should be the case — which we do not believe — take note of what Our Lord says against negligent shepherds.

The prophet Ezekiel says in chapter 34 that Our Lord told him: *Son of man, prophet of the shepherds of Israel, tell these things to the shepherds: The Lord God says: Woe be to the shepherds of Israel who feed themselves. Do not the shepherds feed the flocks? You consume the milk, and dress yourselves in fine cloth, and take the best morsels, killing and eating away at the best flock. However, do not feed My sheep for you did not strengthen or heal the ones that were sick and the weak; neither did you mend nor blind those that were broken. The ones that were scattered you did not bring back to the fold; those that were lost you failed to*

---

[9] (As ... industry). Interlinear addition. See note *b*.

no*m* guainhastes ne*m* nas buscastes; mas afligieylas e atrome*n*taueilas
co*m* vosso pode*r* forte e austero, suiuguandoas. Portanto, as minhas
ouelhas são derramadas; no*m* ha hi pastor que has guarde; são roidas e
comidas das bestas feras dos campos. Assi que as minhas manadas
andão erradas e vaguabu*n*das polos montes e vales. No*m* ha hi que*m*
hos caree, e rega, e guoue*m*e.'"

Certame*n*te bem podemos dizer que neste tempo mode*r*no isto se
cu*m*pre porquanto no*m* ha hi pastor que se doia da perda e da*m*no das
ouelhas que andão vaguabundas e perdidas por este reino de Purtugual. Mas cada hu*m* segue a seita que quer e ho modo de viuer que
lhe vem a uontade, por onde ho nome de Ih*e*sus he desp*r*ezado e
espedaçado, e cada dia crucificado.

A vos, senhores pastores, pertence po*r* isto olhar, e vede ho q*u*e diz
Ezechiel no luguar aleguado: [*fol. 6 3v*] "Portanto, pastores, ouui a
palaura do S*en*ho*r*: 'Viuo eu,' diz ho S*en*ho*r* Deo*s*, 'pois que as minhas
ouelhas são comidas e roidas das bestas feras e no*m* ha hi pastor que
has guarde e tire da boca do lobo; mas hos pastores pace*m* a si mesmos
e no*m* curão da minha manada.' Porta*n*to ouui, pastores, a palaura do
S*en*ho*r* que diz estas palauras: 'Eu pidirei conta e rezão da minha
manada e das minhas ouelhas aos pastores, e tirarlhe[s]ei ho pode*r* que
tee*m* de pacer, e liurarei as minhas ouelhas do pode*r* deles.'" Bem
parece, s*e*nhores, que estreita conta ḍarão hos p*r*elados das suas ouelhas
se na*m* nas quisere*m* pacer e carear pera fee de Christo. E pois que vos
sondes pastores destas ouelhas vaguabu*n*das da fee de Ch*r*isto, trazeas
ao curral da Igreia, "videte ne sit populus D*o*mi*n*i absq*ue* pastore"
(Numeror*um* xxvij°). "Bonus pastor anima*m* sua*m* ponit pro ouibus
suis" (Iohannis, decimos).

Senhores, aquilo olhai, que dixe São Paulo (Actuu*s* xx°): "Olhai por
vos e polas ouelhas que vos são comitidas, pois que ho Sp*irit*u Santo vos
fez aguora[c] p*r*elados e rreitores das almas destes que andão fora da
Igreia militante e triu*n*fante." Trazeios ao caminho da v*er*dade por
vossos santissimos enxe*m*plos, p*r*eguações, e amoestações.

E vos, senhores iudeus, olhai que "erreis ouelhas erradas e vaguabu*n*-
das, e se ho fostes ates aguora, ia vos conue*r*tei pera ho vosso bispo e
pastor das vossas almas que he Ch*r*isto Ih*e*su" (E*p*istola P*r*imeira Petri ij°),
ho Mexia promitido na vossa Lei que foi, e ia no*m* he mas; a nossa Lei
seia a vossa dada pola boca de Ch*r*isto Ih*e*su na cidade de Ierusale*m*.

c +*bispos* exp.

[10] Ezek. 34:2ff.
[11] Ezek. 34:7ff.

recover or seek. Rather, you ruled over them by afflicting and tormenting them with your force and vigor. Therefore, My sheep are scattered about, there is no shepherd to watch over them; they are gnawed at and eaten by the wild beasts of the field. Thus My stray flock is wandering about through the mountains and valleys; there is no one there to lead, rule, and govern them.[10]

We can justly say that in these modern times this is being fulfilled since there is no shepherd who grieves over the loss or injury of the sheep who are wandering about lost throughout the Kingdom of Portugal. For each one follows the sect of his choice and the type of life he so desires, so that the name of Jesus is spurned, shattered and crucified every day.

It is for you shepherds, gentlemen, to examine and see what Ezekiel says at that place: [*fol. 63v*] *Therefore, shepherds, hear the word of the Lord: As I live, says the Lord God, because My sheep are eaten and gnawed at by the wild beasts and there is no shepherd there to protect them and pull them out of the wolf's mouth; but the shepherds tend themselves and do not heal My flock. Therefore, shepherds, hear the word of the Lord who says these words: I will ask the shepherds for an account and record of My flock and of My sheep, and I will take away from their authority to tend, and will deliver My sheep from their power.*[11] It seems clear, gentlemen, that the prelates will be giving an exact account of their sheep if they do not wish to tend them and lead them to Christ's faith. And since you are the shepherds of these sheep who have wandered from the faith of Christ, bring them to the corral of the Church, *videte ne sit populus Domini absque pastore* (**Numbers, 27**).[12] *Bonus pastor animam suam ponit pro ouibus suis* (**John, 10**).[13]

Gentlemen, remark what St. Paul said (Acts, 20): *Take heed of yourselves and of the sheep entrusted to you; for the Holy Spirit now makes you*[14] *prelates and rectors of the souls of those who are outside of the militant and triumphant Church.*[15] Bring them to the road of truth by your most holy examples, sermons, and counsel.

And you, Jewish gentlemen, consider that *you were errant and wandering sheep; but if you were so until now, I have already converted you for the Bishop and Shepherd of your souls who is Christ Jesus* (Peter 2),[16] the Messiah promised in your law which once was but now is no more. Let our Law, which was given through the mouth of Christ Jesus in the city of Jerusalem, be yours. I beseech you to care for your souls and con-

---

[12] Num. 27:17.
[13] John 10:11.
[14] MS has "bishops" expunged. See note *c*.
[15] Acts 20:28.
[16] I Pet. 2:25.

Peçouos que olhes por vossas almas e conscientias. Purificaiuos e alim-
paiuos das cirimonias da Lei velha. Vestiuos destas nossas armas que
são a fee de Ihesu Christo, vosso e nosso Redentor.

Rroguouos, por amor de Nosso Senhor, que nom me tenhaes a mal se
este libelozinho compos, que he em vosso fauor, e nom desonrra.
Porque lendo vos por elle, se errados andaes ou andastes, aqui achares
algumas mezinhas com que poderes curar algum tanto vossas chaguas.
Se nom for tão ornado e pulido e limado na linguoa purtugues, perdoay
a simplicidade da linguoa, porque ho meu entento he mais olhar polas
sentenças que não pola linguoa.

Começouse no começo d'Agosto da era de 1541, e acabouse nos XX
dias de Setembro nos estudos do rreal mosteiro d'Alcobaça, a louuor e
gloria de Deos e de São Bernardo, nosso padre.

---

[17] On the concern for linguistic style in inquisitorial sermons, see Edward Glaser, "Portuguese
Sermons at Autos-da-Fé: Introduction and Bibliography," *SBB*, 2(1955), 56; *DE*, pp. lxxviii, 6ff.

sciences. Purify and cleanse yourselves of the ceremonies of the old Law. Arm yourselves in our faith in Jesus Christ, your and our Redeemer.

I beg you, for the love of Our Lord, not to think ill of me because of this manual that I composed. [It was written] in order to benefit you and not to discredit you. For if you are in error, you will find in reading it some remedy with which to cure your wounds. If the Portuguese has not been so ornate, polished, or finished, forgive its plainness, because it was my intention to focus on the ideas and not on how they were expressed.[17]

Begun at the beginning of August in the year 1541, and completed on the twentieth day of September in the study of the royal Monastery of Alcobaça, for the praise and glory of God and of St. Bernard, our father.[18]

---

[18] St. Bernard, the eleventh-century reformer of the Cistercian order, was alleged to have indirectly founded the monastery of Alcobaça on the basis of Bernard's reference to "my brethren who are in your Kingdom" in his correspondence with Afonso Henriquez, Epist. 308, *PL,* 172:512; P. Jaffe-S. Loewenfeld, *Regesta pontificum romanorum* (Leipzig, 1888), 2: 561, n. 9255.

BIBLIOGRAPHY

Albo, Joseph. *Book of Roots (Sefer ha-'Iqqarim)*. Philadelphia, 1929-1930.

Alfonso X, el Sabio. *General estoria,* ed. A. Solalinde. Madrid, 1930.

Almeida, Fortunato de. *História da igreja em Portugal.* New ed. Damião Peres. 4 vols. Oporto, 1967.

Almosnino, Moses. *Regimiento de la vida.* Salonica, 1564.

Alphonsus de Spina. *Fortalitium Fidei.* Lyons, 1511.

Altmann, A. *Biblical and Other Studies.* Cambridge, Mass., 1963.

Amador de los Ríos, José. *Historia social, política, y religiosa de los Judíos de España y Portugal.* 3 vols. Madrid, 1875-1876; latest edition, 3 vols. in l, Madrid, 1973.

Anselmo, A. J. *Bibliografia das obras impressas em Portugal no século XVI.* Lisbon, 1926.

António (Mestre). Ajuda da fé [1486 A. D.] MS B.N.L., Fundo Geral 6967.

Antonio, Nicolás. *Biblioteca hispana nova.* 2 vols. Madrid, 1783. New ed. Mario Ruffini. Turin, 1963.

Aristeas to Philocrates, ed. Moses Hadas. New York, 1951.

Artau, J. Carreras. "La 'Allocutio super Tetragrammaton' de Arnaldo de Vilanova," *Sefarad,* 9 (1949), 75-105.

Athanasius. *De incarnatione,* ed. Robt. W. Thomson. Oxford, 1971. (*PG,* 25:95-198.)

Augustinus. *De doctrina christiana*, ed. Joseph Martin, *CC,* 32 (1962). (*PL,* 34:15-122).

⸺. *Quaestiones in heptateuchum*, ed. I. Fraipont, *CC,* 33 (1958). (*PL,* 34:547-824).

Pseudo-Augustine. *De unitate sanctae trinitatis, PL,* 42:1208-1212.

Azevedo, J. Lúcio de. *História dos Cristãos novos portugueses.* Lisbon, 1921.

Baer, Yitzhak F. *History of the Jews in Christian Spain.* 2 vols. Philadelphia, 1966.

⸺. "The Kabbalistic Doctrine in the Christological Teachings of Abner of Burgos" (Hebrew), *Tarbiz,* 27 (1957-1958), 278-289.

⸺. *Sefer ha-zikkaron le-Asher Gulak ve-li-Shemuel Klein.* Jerusalem, 1941-1942.

Bahir. *Das Buch Bahir,* ed. Gershom Scholem. Leipzig, 1923; photoreprint Darmstadt, 1970.

Bahir. *Sefer Ha-Bahir,* ed. R. Margulies. Jerusalem, 1950-1951.

Barbosa Machado, Diogo. *Bibliotheca lusitana.* Lisbon, 1747; photoreprint Coimbra, 1966.

Barnett, Richard D. *The Sephardi Heritage.* New York, 1971.

Baron, Salo W. *A Social and Religious History of the Jews.* 15 vols. to date. Philadelphia, 1952-.

Barreto, João Franco. Bibliotheca lusitana, MS 803 da Casa Cadaval.

Barros, João de. *Diálogo em louvor de nossa linguagem.* Coimbra, 1947.

⸺. *Diálogo evangélico sobre os artigos da fé contra o Talmud dos Judeus (Evangelical Dialogue Concerning the Articles of the Faith against the Talmud of the Jews),* written 1541. Ed. I. S. Révah. Lisbon, 1950.

⸺. *Ropica Pnefma.* Lisbon, 1952.

Ben-Sasson, Haim H. "Jewish-Christian Disputation in the Setting of Humanism and Reformation in the German Empire," *Harvard Thological Review,* 66 (1966), 369-390.

Bernard of Clairvaux. *Epistola* 308. *PL,* 182:512-513.

Besso, Henry V. "Judaeo-Spanish — Its Growth and Decline," in Rich. D. Barnett, *The Sephardi Heritage.* London, 1971, pp. 604-635.

Bieler, Ludwig. "The Grammarian's Craft: A Professional Talk," *Folia: Studies in the Christian Perpetuation of the Classics,* 10 (1958), 3-42.

Blau, Joseph L. *The Christian Interpretation of the Cabala in the Renaissance.* New York, 1944.

Blumenkranz, Bernhard. *Die Judenpredigt Augustins.* Basel, 1946.

——. *Juifs et chrétiens dans le monde occidentale.* Paris, 1960.

Borst, Arno. *Der Turmbau von Babel.* Stuttgart, 1957-1963.

Brito, Bernardo. *Chrónica de Cister.* Lisbon, 1602.

Buescu, Maria L. Carvalhão, ed. *Gramática de lingua portuguesa.* Lisbon, 1971.

Cartagena, Alonso de. *Defensorium unitatis christianae,* ed. M. Alonso. Madrid, 1943.

Castro, Américo. *The Structure of Spanish History.* Princeton, 1954.

Cassuto, Umberto. *Gli Ebrei a Firenze nell'età del Rinascimento.* Florence, 1918; photo-reprint Florence, 1965. (*Ha-Yehudim be-Firenze bi-Tequfat ha-Renesans.* Jerusalem, 1967).

Chaytor, H. J. "The Medieval Reader and Textual Criticism," *Bulletin of the John Rylands Library,* 26 (1941-1942), 49-56.

Crispin, Gilbert. *Disputatio Judei et Christiani et anonymi auctoris,* ed. Bernhard Blumenkranz. Utrecht, 1956.

Danielou, Jean. "La typologie de la semaine au IVe siècle," *Recherches des Sciences Religieuses,* 35 (1948), 382-441.

Duchesne, Louis Marie. *Christian Worship: Its Origin and Development.* London, 1927.

Duran, Profiat. *Kelimat ha-Goyim, Ha-Zofeh le-Hokhmat Yisra'el,* 3(1913-1914) 99-113, 143-180; 4(1914-1915) 37-48, 81-96, 115-132.

Durand de Saint-Pourçain. *In sententias theologicas Petri Lombardi.* Venice, 1621; photoreprint Ridgewood, N.J., 1964.

Eisenstein, Judah David. *Ozar ha-Midrashim.* New York, 1951.

Eisler, Robert. *The Messiah Jesus and John the Baptist.* New York, 1931.

Eleazar ben Judah. *Ha-Roqeah Ha-Gadol.* Jerusalem, 1967-1968.

Eusebius. *Chronica, PG,* 19:99-598.

Excerptos de um cancioneiro quinhentista: Trovas quese fizeram nas terças em tempo de Elrei D. Manoel. Evora, 1883.

Farinelli, Arturo. *Marrano: Storia di un vituperio.* Geneva, 1925.

Farissol, Abraham. Magen 'Avraham, XX, MS Jewish Theological Seminary of America 2433.

Feldman, L. H., *Josephus.* Cambridge, 1965.

Ferro, M. J. Pimenta. *Os Judeus em Portugal no século XIV.* Lisbon, 1970.

Ficino, Marsilio. *De religione christiana et fidei pietate opusculum.* Strassburg, 1507.

Ginzberg. L. *Legends of the Jews.* 7 vols. Philadelphia, 1947.

Glaser, Edward. "Portuguese Sermons at Autos-da-Fé: Introduction and Bibliography," *SBB,* 2 (1955), 53-78.

Glossa ordinaria, PL, vols. 63-64.

Goldschmidt, Lazarus. *Sepher Jesirah: Das Buch der Schöpfung.* Frankfurt, 1894.

Goldstein, Morris. *Jesus in the Jewish Tradition.* New York, 1950.

Gonçalves, Manuel Cerejeira. *Clenardo e a sociedade portuguesa do seu tempo.* Coimbra, 1949.

Gregorius. *Homiliae in Ezechielem*, *PL*, 76:785-1072.

——. *Moralia sive Expositio in Job*, *PL*, 75:515-76:782.

Halkin, A. S. "The Medieval Attitude Towards Hebrew," in Alexander Altmann, *Biblical and Other Studies*. Cambridge, Mass., 1963, pp. 233-250.

Herculano, Alexandre. *History of the Origin and Establishment of the Inquisition in Portugal*. Stanford, 1926; photoreprint New York, 1972 (Trans. of *História da origem e estabelecimento da inquisição em Portugal*. 3 vols. Lisbon, n.d.).

Hieronymus. *Commentariorum in Esaiam Libri 1-11*, ed. Marc Adriaen, *CC*, 73 (1963). (*PL*, 24:17-424).

——. *Commentariorum in Esaiam Libri 12-18*, ed. Marc Adriaen, *CC*, 73A (1963). (*PL*, 24:425-704).

——. *Commentariorum in Hieremiam Libri 6*, ed. Sigofredus Reiter, *CC*, 74 (1960). (*PL*, 24:705-934).

——. *Commentariorum in Hiezechielem Libri 14*, ed. François Glorie, *CC*, 75 (1964). (*PL*, 24:15-490).

——. *Commentariorum in Danielem Libri 3 (4)*, ed. François Glorie, *CC*, 75A (1964) (*PL*, 25:491-583).

——. *Commentariorum in Oseam*, etc. ed. Marc Adriaen, *CC*, 76 (1969). (*PL*, 25:815-1578).

——. *Commentariorum in Matheum Libri 4*, ed. D. Hurst & M. Adriaen, *CC*, 77 (1969). (*PL*, 26:15-228).

——. *Divinae Bibliothecae*, *PL*, 28:177-1520.

——. Epistulae. *Lettres*, ed. Jerome Labourt. 7 vols. Paris (Budé), 1949-.

——. *Eusebii Caesariensis De situ et nominibus locorum hebraeorum liber*, *PL*, 23:903-976.

——. *Eusebii Pamphili chronici canones*, ed. F. K. Fotheringham. London 1923.

——. *Hebreae quaestiones in libro Geneseos*, ed. Paul de Lagarde, *CC*, 72 (1959). (*PL*, 23:983-1062).

Pseudo-Hieronymus. *Breviarium in Psalmos*, *PL*, 26:863-1378.

Hieronymus de Sancta Fide (Joshua Lorki). *Contra Iudaeos* (also entitled *Ad convincendum perfidiam Judaeorum* and *Hebraeomastix*). Zurich, 1552.

Hirsch, Elizabeth F. *Damião de Gois; The Life and Thought of a Portuguese Humanist*. The Hague, 1967.

Ḥizzuq 'Emunah, ed. D. Deutsch. Breslau, 1873.

Ibn Verga, Judah. *Sheveṭ Yehuda*, ed. Y. F. Baer and A. Shohat. Jerusalem, 1946.

Imbonati, C. J. *Bibliotheca latina hebraica*. Rome, 1694.

Inventário dos códices alcobacenses, ed. A. F. de Ataíde e Melo. Lisbon, 1930-1932.

Isidore. *Chronica, PL*, 83:1017-1058.

——. *De fide catholica contra Judaeos*, *PL*, 83:449-538.

——. *Etymologiarum sive originum libri 20*, W. M. Lindsay. Oxford, 1911. (*PL*, 82:737-773).

——. *Liber de variis quaestionibus*, ed. Angel C. Vega and A. E. Anspach. Escorial, 1940.

Jabez, Joseph. *'Or Ha-Ḥayyim*. Lublin, 1861-1862.

Jacobus de Voragine. *Legenda aurea sanctorum*, ed. Johann Siber. Lyons, 1493.

Jaffe, Philipp and S. Loewenfeld. *Regesta pontificum romanorum*. Leipzig, 1888.

Jayne, Kingsley G. *Vasco da Gama and His Successors, 1460-1580*. London, 1910.

Josephus. *The Jewish Antiquities*, ed. H. St. J. Thackeray. 5 vols. in *Josephus*. London: Loeb Class. Library, 1930-1963.

Josephus, trans. Louis H. Feldman. Cambridge, U. K., 1965.

Judah ben Samuel. *Sefer Ḥasidim*, ed. Jehuda Wistinetzki. Frankfurt, 1924.

Justin Martyr. *Dialogue with Trypho*, in *Writings of St. Justin Martyr*, trans. T. B. Falls. New York, 1948.

Kayserling, Meyer. *Biblioteca española-portugueza-judaica.* Strassburg, 1890; photoreprint New York, 1971.

——. *Geschichte der Juden in Portugal.* Leipzig, 1867. (*História dos Judeus em Portugal.* São Paulo, 1971.)

Kimhi, David. *Perush.* Standard editions of Rabbinic Bible.

——. *Sefer ha-Shorashim,* ed. J. Biesenthal and F. Lebrecht. Berlin, 1847.

Kimhi, Joseph. *Book of the Covenant,* trans. Frank Talmage. Toronto, 1972.

Kobler, Franz. *Letters of Jews Through the Ages.* London, 1953.

Láfer, Celso. *O Judeu em Gil Vicente.* São Paulo, 1963.

Lieberman, Saul. *Shki'in.* Jerusalem, 1939.

Lipmann-Mülhausen, Yom Tov. *Sefer Nizzahon,* ed. T. Hackspan. Altdorf, 1644.

Lull, Ramon. *Opera Omnia.* Mainz, 1721-1742; photoreprint, Frankfurt, 1965.

Mariz, Pedro de. *Diálogos de vária história.* Lisbon, 1647.

Marmorstein, A. "David Kimhi, Apologiste," *REJ,* 66 (1913), 246-251.

Marques, Antonio H. de Oliveira. *Guia do estudante de história medieval portuguesa.* Lisbon, 1964.

Martini, Raymundus. *Pugio fidei,* ed. Carpzov. Leipzig, 1687.

Martins, Mário. "A polémica religiosa nalguns codices de Alcobaça," *Brotéria,* 42 (1946), 241-250. (*Estudos de literatura medieval.* [Braga, 1956.], pp. 307-316.)

——. "Filosofia esotérica no 'Speculum Hebreorum,'" *Estudos,* pp. 349-358.

——. "Fr. João, monge de Alcobaça e controversista," *Brotéria,* 42 (1946), 412-421. (*Estudos,* pp. 317-326.)

Maximus episcopus Gothorum. *Contra Judaeos,* PL, 57:795-806 (author given as Maximus Taurinensis).

Merchavia, Ch. *The Church Versus Talmudic and Midrashic Literature, 500-1248* (Hebrew). Jerusalem, 1970.

Midrash Tehillim. Warsaw, 1875.

Millás-Vallicrosa, José-María. "Un tratado anónimo de polémica contra los Judíos," *Sefarad,* 13 (1953), 3-34.

Monteiro, Pedro. *Claustro Dominicano.* 3 vols. Lisbon, 1729.

Nahon, Gerard. "Les Sephardim, les Marranes, les Inquisitions Peninsulaires et leurs archives dans les travaux récents de I.-S. Révah," *REJ,* 132 (1973), 38-44.

Netanyahu, Benzion. "Alonso de Espina: was he a New Christian?" *Proceedings of the American Academy for Jewish Research,* 43 (1976), 144-46.

——. *The Marranos of Spain from the Late XIVth to the Early XVIth Century according to the Hebrew Sources.* New York, 1966.

Neubauer, Adolf and Samuel R. Driver, ed. and transl. *The "Suffering Servant" of Isaiah according to the Jewish Interpreters.* 2 vols. Oxford, 1877: photoreprint New York, 1969.

Neumann, Abraham A. "A Note on John the Baptist and Jesus in Josippon," *HUCA,* 23 (1950-1951), pt. 2, pp. 137-149.

Nicolas de Lyra. *Postilla super totam Bibliam.* 4 vols. Strassburg, 1492; photoreprint Frankfurt, 1971.

——. *Quaestio de probatione adventus Christi per scripturas a Judaeis receptas.* [n.p. 1475?]

Novinsky, Anita. *Cristãos novos na Bahia.* São Paulo, 1972.

Pacios López, Antonio. *La disputa de Tortosa.* 2 vols. Madrid, 1957 (Text of the protocols in Latin).

Pereira, Gaspar de Leão, trans. *Tratado que fez mestre Hieronimo ... contra os Judeus ...* Goa, 1564.

Petrus Alfonsi, *Dialogus, PL*, 157:525-672.

Peter of Blois. *Contra perfidiam Judaeorum, PL*, 207:825-870.

Petrus Comestor. *Historia scholastica, PL*, 198:1050-1721.

Pico della Mirandola, Giovanni. *Opera Omnia*. Basel, 1572.

Pimenta, Alfredo. *D. João III*. Oporto, 1936.

Pirke de-Rabbi Eliezer, trans. Gerald Friedlander. London, 1916.

Pontes, José Maria da Cruz. *Estudo para uma edição crítica do livro da corte enperial*. Coimbra, 1957.

Posnanski, Adolf. *Schiloh; ein Beitrag zur Geschichte der Messiaslehre*. 2 vols. Leipzig, 1904.

Rabbinowitz, S. Z. *Diqduqe Soferim*. Mayence 1878.

Rankin, Oliver S. *Jewish Religious Polemic*. Edinburgh, 1958.

Remedios, Joaquim Mendes dos. *Os Judeus em Portugal*. 2 vols. Coimbra, 1895-1928.

Resende, Garcia de. *Miscellanea*, ed. J. Mendes dos Remedios. Coimbra, 1917.

Reuchlin, Johann. *De verbo mirifico*. Lyon, 1556.

Révah, I. S. *La censure inquisitoriale portugaise au XVIe siècle*. Lisbon, 1960.

——. "Les Marranes," *REJ*, 118 (1959) 27-77.

——. "Les Marranes portugais et l'inquisition au xvie siècle," in Rich. D. Barnett, *The Sephardi Heritage*. New York, 1971, pp. 479-526.

Rosenthal, Judah. "The Concept of the Abrogation of the Commandments in Jewish Eschatology" (Hebrew), *Meyer Waxman Jubilee Volume*. Jerusalem, 1960.

Rouët de Journel, Marie-Joseph. *Enchiridion patristicum*. Brescia, 1922.

Sá, Diogo de. Inquisiçam e segredos de fee contra a obstinada perfidia dos Iudeus (Inquisition and Mysteries of the Faith against the Obstinate Jewish Perfidy). A.N.T.T. MS da livraria 360 [written in the 1550s].

Sanches, A. N. Ribeiro. *Christãos novos e Christãos velhos em Portugal*, ed. R. Rego. Oporto, 1973.

Santos, António Ribeiro dos. "Ensayo de huma Biblioteca anti-rabbinica, ou Memorial dos escritores portuguesses que escreverão de controversia anti-judaica," *Memórias de litteratura portugueza publicadas pela Academia Real das Sciencias de Lisboa*, 8 (1806), 308-372.

——. "Memória sobre as origens da tipographia em Portugal no século XV," *Memórias*,[2] 8 (1856), 1-76.

Saraiva, António José. *A cultura em Portugal*. Lisbon, 1950.

——. *A inquisição portuguesa*. Lisbon, 1956.

——. *História da cultura em Portugal*. Lisbon, 1962.

——. *Inquisição e Cristãos novos*. Oporto, 1969.

Schechter, Solomon. *Aspects of Rabbinic Theology*. New York, 1909.

Schneider, Réné. *Rome: Complexité et harmonie*. 10 ed. Rome, 1908.

Scholem, Gershom. *Jewish Gnosticism, Merkabah Mysticism, and Talmudic Tradition*. New York, 1965.

——. *Major Trends in Jewish Mysticism*. New York, 1941.

Scobie, Charles H. H. *John the Baptist*. Philadelphia, 1964.

Scotus, Duns. *Reportata parisiensa* in *Opera Omnia*, vols. 22-24. Paris, 1891-1895.

Secret, François. *Le Zòhar chez les Kabbalistes chrétiens de la Renaissance*. Paris, 1958.

Sefer ha-Hekhalot, trans. Hugo Odeberg, in *3 Enoch or the Hebrew Book of Enoch*. Cambridge, U.K., 1928.

Serrão, Joel. *A emigração portuguesa; sondagem histórica*. Lisbon, 1972.

Shamir, Y. *Rabbi Moses Ha-Kohen of Tordesillas and his Book 'Ezer Ha-Emunah*. Leiden, 1975. (Hebrew text under same title adding *A Chapter in the History of the Judaeo-Christian Controversy*. Cocunut Grove, Florida, 1972).

Simon, Marcel. *Verus Israel: étude sur les relations entre chrétiens et juifs dans l'Empire romain, 135-425*. Paris, 1948.

Simon, U. "Raba' ve-RaDaQ — Shte gishot li-she'elat mehemanut nusaḥ ha-miqra," *Shenaton Bar Ilan*, 6 (1967-1968), 191-236.

Slouschz, Nahum. *Ha-'Anusim be-Porṭugal*. Tel Aviv, 1932.

Smalley, Beryl. *The Study of the Bible in the Middle Ages*. London, 1958.

Steinschneider, Moritz. "Die Kanonische Zahl der Muhammedanischen Secten und die Symbolik der Zahl 70-73," *ZDMG*, 4 (1850), 150ff.

Stenning, John F. *The Targum of Isaiah*. Oxford, 1949.

Talmage, Frank. "The New Portugal and the New Christians," *Association for Jewish Studies Newsletter*. February, 1975.

——. "R. David Kimhi as Polemicist," *Hebrew Union College Annual*, 38 (1967), 213-235.

——. "To Sabbatize in Peace: Jews and New Christians in Sixteenth-Century Portuguese Polemics," to appear in the jubilee volume honoring Professor Alexander Altmann, Duke University Press.

——. "The *Mirror of the New Christians* and Its Sources" (Hebrew), *Proceedings of the Sixth World Congress of Jewish Studies*, 2 (1976), 87-94.

Tertullian. *Adversus Judaeos*, ed. A. Gerlo, *CC*, 2 (1964), 633-682.

Thomas Aquinas. *On Kingship to the King of Cyprus*, trans. G. B. Phelan. Toronto, 1949 (Latin: *De regimine principum ad regem Cypri*).

——. *Summa theologiae*. 4 vols. Taurini: Marietti, 1948.

Vicente, Gil. *Obras completas*, ed. Marques Braga. Lisbon, 1963-1968.

Visch, Karl de. *Biblioteca scriptorum sacri ordinis cisterciensis*.[2] Cologne, 1656.

Wagenseil, Johann C. *Tela ignea Satanae*. Altdorf, 1681.

Williams, Arthur Lukyn. *Talmudic Judaism and Christianity*. London, 1933.

Wolf, Johann Christoph. *Biblioteca hebraea*. Hamburg, 1715-1733.

Yerushalmi, Yosef Hayim. *From Spanish Court to Italian Ghetto*. New York and London, 1971.

——. "Professing Jews in Post-Expulsion Spain and Portugal," *Salo Wittmayer Baron Jubilee Volume*. New York and London, 1975, pp. 1023-1058.

——. "Prolegomenon" to Herculano, *Origin*, pp. 34ff.

Zeitlin, Solomon. *Josephus on Jesus*. Philadelphia, 1931.

INDEX

INDEX OF SCRIPTURAL CITATIONS

(Hebrew Scriptures according to Masoretic Text)

INDEX OF RABBINIC SOURCES

DATE DUE

Finite
Mathematics
& Its
Applications

SEVENTH EDITION

Finite Mathematics & Its Applications

Larry J. Goldstein
Goldstein Educational Technologies

David I. Schneider
University of Maryland

Martha J. Siegel
Towson University

PRENTICE HALL
Upper Saddle River, New Jersey 07458

Library of Congress Cataloging-in-Publication Data

Goldstein, Larry Joel.
    Finite mathematics & its applications/Larry J. Goldstein,
    David I. Schneider, Martha J. Siegel—7th ed.
            p.   cm.
    Rev. ed. of: Finite mathematics and its applications. 6th ed. c1998.
    Includes index.
    ISBN 0-13-018678-3
    1. Mathematics. I. Title: Finite mathematics and its applications. II. Schnieder, David I.
    III. Siegel, Martha J. IV. Goldstein, Larry Joel. Finite mathematics and its applications.
    V. Title

QA39.2.G643 2001   CIP
510--dc21   00-036762

Acquisitions Editor: *Kathleen Boothby Sestak*
Production Editor: *Lynn Savino Wendel*
Assistant Vice President of Production and Manufacturing: *David W. Riccardi*
Editor in Chief: *Sally Yagan*
Executive Managing Editor: *Kathleen Schiaparelli*
Senior Managing Editor: *Linda Mihatov Behrens*
Manufacturing Buyer: *Alan Fischer*
Manufacturing Manager: *Trudy Pisciotti*
Marketing Manager: *Patrice Lumumba Jones*
Marketing Assistant: *Vince Jansen*
Director of Marketing: *John Tweeddale*
Associate Editor, Mathematics/Statistics Media: *Audra J. Walsh*
Editorial Assistant/Supplements Editor: *Joanne Wendelken*
Art Director: *Maureen Eide*
Assistant to Art Director: *John Christiana*
Interior Designer: *Jill Little*
Cover Designer: *Daniel Conte*
Art Editor: *Grace Hazeldine*
Art Manager: *Gus Vibal*
Director of Creative Services: *Paul Belfanti*
Cover Photo: *Timothy Hursley/Superstock, Inc.*
Art Studio: *Academy Artworks*

Printed in the United States of America
10 9 8 7 6 5 4 3 2 1

ISBN 0-13-018678-3

Material from the Uniform CPA Examination Questions and Unofficial Answers,
copyright © 1994, 1995 by American Institute of Certified Public Accountants, Inc.
is reprinted (or adapted) with permission.

Prentice-Hall International (UK) Limited, *London*
Prentice-Hall of Australia Pty. Limited, *Sydney*
Prentice-Hall Canada, Inc., *Toronto*
Prentice-Hall Hispanoamericana, S.A., *Mexico*
Prentice-Hall of India Private Limited, *New Delhi*
Prentice-Hall of Japan, Inc. *Tokyo*
Pearson Education Asia Pte. Ltd.
Editora Prentice-Hall do Brasil, Ltda., *Rio de Janeiro*

Mathematics and Its Applications

This volume is one of a collection of texts for freshman and sophomore college mathematics courses. Included in this collection are the following.

Calculus and Its Applications, ninth edition, by L. Goldstein, D. Lay, and D. Schneider. A text designed for a two-semester course in calculus for students of business and the social and life sciences. Emphasizes an intuitive approach and integrates applications into the development.

Brief Calculus and Its Applications, ninth edition, by L. Goldstein, D. Lay, and D. Schneider. Consists of the first eight chapters of the above book with some material from later chapters.

Finite Mathematics & Its Applications, seventh edition, by L. Goldstein, D. Schneider, and M. Siegel. A traditional finite mathematics text for students of business and the social and life sciences. Allows courses to begin with either linear mathematics (linear programming, matrices) or probability and statistics. Includes topics in discrete mathematics.

Applied Calculus: A Graphing Approach by D. Schneider and D. Lay. A one-semester or two-quarter technology-required reform calculus text for students majoring in business, economics, life sciences, and social sciences.

Contents

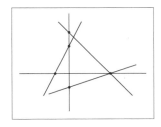

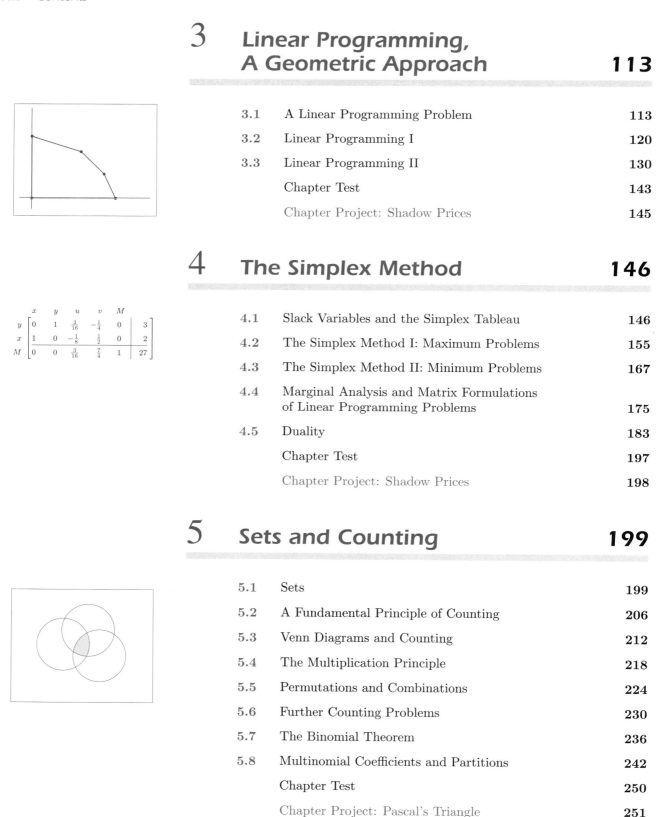

9 The Theory of Games — 427

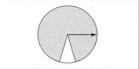
10 The Mathematics of Finance — 455

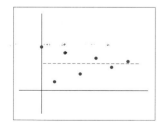
11 Difference Equations and Mathematical Models — 489

12 Logic **528**

13 Graphs **579**

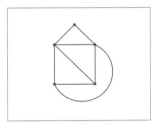

Preface

This work is the seventh edition of our text for the traditional finite mathematics course taught to first- and second-year college students, especially those majoring in business and the social and biological sciences. Finite mathematics courses exhibit tremendous diversity with respect to both content and approach. Therefore, in revising this book, we incorporated a wide range of topics from which an instructor may design a curriculum, as well as a high degree of flexibility in the order in which the topics may be presented. For the mathematics of finance, we even allow for flexibility in the approach of the presentation.

In this edition we attempt to maintain our popular student-oriented approach throughout and, in particular, through the use of the following features:

Applications

We provide realistic applications that illustrate the uses of finite mathematics in other disciplines. The reader may survey the variety of applications by referring to the Index of Applications located on the front endpapers. Wherever possible, we attempt to use applications to motivate the mathematics. For example, the concept of linear programming is introduced in Chapter 3 via a discussion of production options for a factory with a labor limitation.

Examples

We include many more worked examples than is customary in textbooks. Furthermore, we include computational details to enhance comprehension by students whose basic skills are weak.

Exercises

More than 2200 exercises comprise about one-quarter of the book, the most important part of the text in our opinion. The exercises at the ends of the sections are usually arranged in the order in which the text proceeds, so that homework assignments may be easily made after only part of a section is discussed. Interesting applications and more challenging problems tend to be located near the ends of the exercise sets. Supplementary exercises at the end of each chapter amplify the other exercise sets and provide cumulative exercises that require skills acquired from earlier chapters. Answers to the odd-numbered exercises are included at the back of the book.

Practice Problems

The practice problems are a popular and useful feature of the book. They are carefully selected exercises located at the end of each section, just before the exercise set. Complete solutions follow the exercise set. The practice problems often focus on points that are potentially confusing or are likely to be overlooked. We recommend that the reader seriously attempt to do the practice problems and study their solutions before moving on to the exercises.

Use of Technology

Although the use of technology is optional for this text, many of the topics can be enhanced with graphing calculators and computers. Also, each year more students own graphing calculators that they have used in their high school mathematics courses. Therefore, whenever relevant, we explicitly show the student how to use graphing calculators effectively to assist in understanding the fundamental concepts of the course. In addition, the text contains an appendix on the use of graphing calculators and about 200 specially designated "calculator and computer" exercises. Such exercises are denoted by GC.

In our discussions of graphing calculators, we specifically refer to the TI-82 and TI-83 since these are the two most popular graphing calculators. Therefore, *most* students will have a book customized to their calculator. Students with other graphing calculators can consult their guidebooks to learn how to make adjustments. Had the calculator material been written generically, *every student* would have to make adjustments.

Examples from Professional Exams

We have included questions similar to those found on CPA and GMAT exams to further illustrate the relevance of the material in the course. These multiple-choice questions are identified with the notation PE.

Review of Fundamental Concepts

Near the end of each chapter is a set of questions that help the student recall the key ideas of the chapter and focus on the relevance of these concepts.

New in This Edition

Among the changes in this edition, the following are the most significant.

1. *Visual Representations of Data.* A new optional section has been added to the beginning of Chapter 7 that shows several ways data are represented graphically.

2. *Chapter Summaries.* Each chapter contains a detailed summary of the important definitions and results from the chapter, serving as a handy study tool for the student.

3. *Chapter Tests.* Each chapter has a sample test that can be used by the student to help determine if he or she has mastered the important concepts of the chapter. The answers to the chapter tests are given at the back of the book.

4. *Chapter Projects.* These extended projects can be used as in-class or out-of-class group projects, or special assignments. The projects develop interesting applications or enhance key concepts of the chapters.

Minimal Prerequisites

Because of the great variation in student preparation, we keep formal prerequisites to a minimum. We assume only a first year of high school algebra. Furthermore, we review, as needed, those topics that are typically weak spots for students.

Topics Included

This edition has more material than can be covered in most one-semester courses. Therefore, the instructor can structure the course to the students' needs and interests. The book divides naturally into four parts. The first part consists of linear mathematics: linear equations, matrices, and linear programming (Chapters 1–4); the second part is devoted to probability and statistics (Chapters 5–7); the third part covers topics utilizing the ideas of the other parts (Chapters 8–10); and the fourth part explores key topics from discrete mathematics that are sometimes included in the modern finite mathematics curriculum (Chapters 11–13). We prefer to begin with linear mathematics since it makes for a smooth transition from high school mathematics and leads quickly to interesting applications, especially linear programming. Our preference notwithstanding, the instructor may begin this book with Chapter 5 (Sets and Counting) and then do either the linear mathematics or the probability and statistics.

Supplements

1. *Instructor's Solutions Manual*: Contains the solutions to every exercise in the text.

2. *Students' Solutions Manual and Explorations in Finite Mathematics Software*: Includes the solution to every odd problem in the text as well as a copy of the premier software package for finite mathematics, developed by David Schneider. "Explorations in Finite Mathematics" includes 28 routines which include an animated solution of geometric linear programming problems, student-directed solutions to Gaussian elimination and simplex method problems, interactive shading of Venn diagrams, and detailed analyses of loans and annuities. Matrix operations use rational arithmetic, and matrices are displayed on-screen with typeset quality. An animated Galton board routine shows in a dynamic fashion how the binomial distribution eventually approaches the normal distribution as n increases.

3. *Test Item File*: Contains sample test questions, both multiple-choice and standard, for each chapter of the text.

4. *TestGen-EQ* provides nearly 1000 suggested test questions, keyed to chapter and section. *TestGen-Eq* is a test-specific testing program networkable for administering tests and capturing grades online. Edit and add your own questions, or use the new "Function Plotter" to create a nearly unlimited number of tests and drill worksheets.

5. *Prentice Hall Companion Website*: (http://www.prenhall.com/goldstein) Created as an extra resource for both students and professors, the site includes the following features:

   (a) *Excel Tutorials and Projects written by Revathi Narasimhan at St. Peter's College.* Uses Excel to enhance the understanding of many of the topics in the course. Using a combination of specially designed projects and tutorials, students are able to analyze data, draw conclusions, and present their analysis in a professional format.

(b) *Net Tutor* Real time, on-line tutoring allows students to ask questions and get help on the text material from mathematics instructors.

(c) *Online Calculator Manuals* for the TI-82, TI-83, TI-85, TI-86, TI-89, TI-92, HP, Sharp and Casio graphing calculators.

Acknowledgments

While writing this book, we have received assistance from many persons—our heartfelt thanks goes out to them all. Especially, we would like to thank the following reviewers, who took the time and energy to share their ideas, preferences, and often their enthusiasm, with us.

Reviewers

Gary W. Frick, Charles County Community College; Henry J. Ricardo, Medgar Evers College of the City University of New York; Mary Pearce, Austin Community College; Elisabeth Schuster, DeVry Institute of Technology; Manoug Manougian, University of South Florida.

James F. Hurley, University of Connecticut; Sam Councilman, California State University, Long Beach; Carl D. Meyer, Jr., North Carolina State University; Stephen H. Brown, Auburn University; Bart Braden, Northern Kentucky University; James C. Thorpe, University of Missouri, St. Louis; Joseph Stampfli, Indiana University; Martin C. Tangora, University of Illinois, Chicago Circle; William D. Blair, Northern Illinois University; Richard Pellerin, Northern Virginia Community College; Roger Osborn, University of Texas, Austin; Thomas J. Hill, University of Oklahoma, Norman; Donald E. Myers, University of Arizona, Tempe.

D. R. Dunninger, Michigan State University; Hiram Paley, University of Illinois, Urbana-Champaign; Joan McCarter, Arizona State University; Robert Carmignani, University of Missouri; Philip Kutzko, University of Iowa; Juan Gatica, University of Iowa; Frank Warner, University of Pennsylvania; Richard Porter, Northeastern University; William Ramaley, Fort Lewis College; Robin G. Symonds, Indiana University at Kokomo; Elizabeth Teles, Montgomery College; Charles J. Miller, Foothill Community College; Phil Steitz, Beloit College; Barry Cipra.

Karl A. Beres, Ripon College; Larry G. Blaine, Plymouth State College; Brenda J. Bloomgarden, Chesapeake College; Paul Boisvert, Robert Morris College; Eric Chandler, Randolph-Macon Women's College; James P. Coughlin, Towson University; Karen J. Edwards, Paul Smith's College; Theodore Faticoni, Fordham College; Robert Gusalnick, University of Southern California; Ruthanne Harre, Missouri Valley College; Eric Heinz, Catonsville Community College; Ralph James, California State University at Stanislaus; Donald A. Jones, Oregon State University; Karla Karstens, University of Vermont; Juan Migliore, University of Notre Dame; Peter Majumdar, Indiana-Purdue University at Fort Wayne; Jeanette L. McGillicuddy, River College; Michael McLane, Purdue University; Richard J. O'Malley, University of Wisconsin at Milwaukee; Arthur Rosenthal, Salem State College; Linda Schultz, McHenry County College; Randy Schwartz, Schoolcraft College; Peter Williams, California State University at San Bernardino; David C. Vella, Skidmore College; Tan Vovan, Suffolk University; Hugh Walters, Contra Costa College; Chungkuang Wang, Fashion Institute of Technology; Rebecca Wells, Henderson Community College; Cynthia Wilson, Life College.

We also thank the many people at Prentice Hall who have contributed to the success of our books. We appreciate the efforts of the production, art, manufacturing, marketing, and sales departments. Our sincere thanks to production editor Lynn Savino Wendel and to copyeditor Patricia M. Daly for their most able work. We would also like to thank Amanda Lubell for her contribution of many exercises and ideas throughout the preparation of the book, Erica O'Leary for her expert proofreading, and Laurel Technical Services for their diligent accuracy checking and assistance with the supplements package.

The authors wish to extend special thanks to our editor Kathy Boothby Sestak and Senior Project Manager Gina Huck. Kathy's help in planning and Gina's execution of this new edition was greatly appreciated. We also thank our typesetter Dennis Kletzing. Dennis's considerable skills and congenial manner made for an uncomplicated and pleasant production process.

If you have comments or suggestions, we would like to hear from you. We hope that you enjoy using this book as much as we have enjoyed writing it.

Larry J. Goldstein
larry.goldstein@iln.net

David I. Schneider
dis@math.umd.edu

Martha J. Siegel
siegel@towson.edu

Finite
Mathematics
& Its
Applications

C H A P T E R

1

Linear Equations and Straight Lines

Many applications considered later in this text involve linear equations and their geometric counterparts—straight lines. So let us begin by studying the basic facts about these two important notions.

1.1 Coordinate Systems and Graphs

Often we can display numerical data by using a *Cartesian coordinate system* on either a line or a plane. We construct a Cartesian coordinate system on a line by choosing an arbitrary point O (the *origin*) on the line and a unit of distance along the line. We then assign to each point on the line a number that reflects its directed distance from the origin. Positive numbers refer to points on the right of the origin, negative numbers to points on the left. In Fig. 1 we have drawn a Cartesian coordinate system on the line and have labeled a number of points with their corresponding numbers. Each point on the line corresponds to a number (positive, negative, or zero). Conversely, every number corresponds to a point on the line.

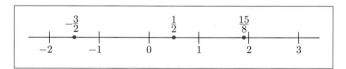

Figure 1.

A Cartesian coordinate system may be used to numerically describe points on a line. In a similar fashion, we can construct a Cartesian coordinate system to numerically locate points on a plane. Such a system consists of two perpendicular lines called the *coordinate axes*. These lines are usually drawn so that one is horizontal and one is vertical. The horizontal line is called the *x-axis*, the vertical line the *y-axis*. Their point of intersection is called the *origin* (Fig. 2). Each point of the plane is identified by a pair of numbers (a, b). The first number, a, tells the number of units from the point to the *y*-axis (Fig. 3). When a is positive,

1

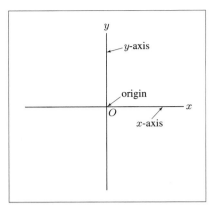

Figure 2.

the point is to the right of the y-axis; when a is negative, the point is to the left of the y-axis. The second number, b, gives the number of units from the point to the x-axis (Fig. 4). When b is positive, the point is above the x-axis; when b is negative, the point is below. The numbers a and b are called, respectively, the x- and y-*coordinates of the point.* In order to plot the point (a, b), begin at the origin and move a units in the x-direction and then b units in the y-direction.

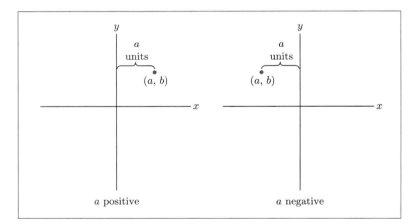

Figure 3.

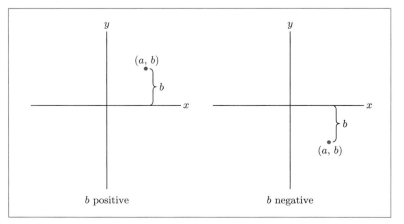

Figure 4.

▸ Example 1   Plot the following points.

(a) $(2, 1)$ (b) $(-1, 3)$ (c) $(-2, -1)$ (d) $(0, -3)$

Solution   (a)

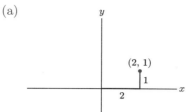

(b)

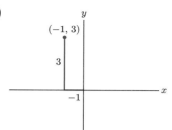

(b)

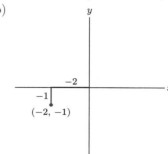

(d)

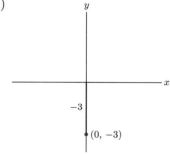

◆

In many applications one encounters equations expressing relationships between variables x and y. Some typical equations are

$$y = 2x - 1$$
$$5x^2 + 3y^3 = 7$$
$$y = 2x^2 - 5x + 8.$$

To any equation in x and y one can associate a certain collection of points in the plane. Namely, the point (a, b) belongs to the collection provided that the equation is satisfied when we substitute a for each occurrence of x and substitute b for each occurrence of y. This collection of points is usually a curve of some sort and is called the *graph of the equation*.

▸ Example 2   Are the following points on the graph of the equation $8x - 4y = 4$?

(a) $(3, 5)$ (b) $(5, 17)$

Solution   (a) Substitute 3 for each occurrence of x and 5 for each occurrence of y in the equation.

$$8x - 4y = 4$$
$$8 \cdot 3 - 4 \cdot 5 = 4$$
$$24 - 20 = 4$$
$$4 = 4$$

Since the equation is satisfied, the point $(3, 5)$ is on the graph of the equation.

(b) Replace x by 5 and y by 17 in the equation.

$$8x - 4y = 4$$
$$8 \cdot 5 - 4 \cdot 17 = 4$$
$$40 - 68 = 4$$
$$-28 = 4$$

The equation is clearly not satisfied, so the point $(5, 17)$ is *not* on the graph of the equation.   ◆

◗ **Example 3**   Sketch the graph of the equation $y = 2x - 1$.

Solution   First find some points on the graph by choosing various values for x and determining the corresponding values for y:

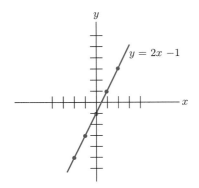

Figure 5.

x	y
-2	$2 \cdot (-2) - 1 = -5$
-1	$2 \cdot (-1) - 1 = -3$
0	$2 \cdot 0 - 1 = -1$
1	$2 \cdot 1 - 1 = 1$
2	$2 \cdot 2 - 1 = 3$

Thus the points $(-2, -5)$, $(-1, -3)$, $(0, -1)$, $(1, 1)$, and $(2, 3)$ are all on the graph. Plot these points (Fig. 5). It appears that the points lie on a straight line. By taking more values for x and plotting the corresponding points, it is easy to become convinced that the graph of $y = 2x - 1$ is indeed a straight line.   ◆

◗ **Example 4**   Sketch the graph of the equation $x = 3$.

Solution   It is clear that the x-coordinate of any point on the graph must be 3. The y-coordinate can be anything. So some points on the graph are $(3, 0)$, $(3, 5)$, $(3, -4)$, $(3, -2)$. Again the graph is a straight line (Fig. 6).   ◆

◗ **Example 5**   Sketch the graph of the equation $x = a$, where a is any given number.

Solution   The x-coordinate of any point on the graph must be a. Reasoning as in Example 4, the graph is a vertical line a units away from the y-axis (Fig. 7). (Of course, if a is negative, then the line lies to the left of the y-axis.)   ◆

The equations in Examples 3 to 5 are all special cases of the general equation

$$cx + dy = e,$$

corresponding to particular choices of the constants c, d, and e. Any such equation is called a *linear equation* (in the two variables x and y).

The *standard form* of a linear equation is obtained by solving for y if y appears and for x if y does not appear. In the former case the standard form looks like

$$y = mx + b \qquad (m, b \text{ constants}),$$

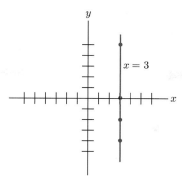

Figure 6.   **Figure 7.**

whereas in the latter it looks like

$$x = a \qquad (a \text{ constant}).$$

▶ **Example 6**   Find the standard form of the following equations.

(a) $8x - 4y = 4$ (b) $2x + 3y = 3$ (c) $2x = 6$

Solution   (a) Since y appears, we obtain the standard form by solving for y in terms of x:

$$8x - 4y = 4$$
$$-4y = -8x + 4$$
$$y = 2x - 1.$$

Thus the standard form of $8x - 4y = 4$ is $y = 2x - 1$—that is, $y = mx + b$ with $m = 2$, $b = -1$.

(b) Again y occurs, so we solve for y:

$$2x + 3y = 3$$
$$3y = -2x + 3$$
$$y = -\tfrac{2}{3}x + 1.$$

So the standard form is $y = -(2/3)x + 1$. Here $m = -2/3$ and $b = 1$.

(c) Here y does not occur, so we solve for x:

$$2x = 6$$
$$x = 3.$$

Thus the standard form of $2x = 6$ is $x = 3$—that is, $x = a$, where a is 3. ◆

We have seen that any linear equation has one of the two standard forms $y = mx + b$ and $x = a$. From Example 5, the graph of $x = a$ is a vertical line, a units from the y-axis. What can be said about the graph of $y = mx + b$? In Example 3, we saw that the graph is a straight line in the special case $y = 2x - 1$. Actually, the graph of $y = mx + b$ is always a straight line. To sketch the graph, we need only locate two points. Two convenient points to locate are the *intercepts*, the points where the line crosses the x- and y-axes. When x is 0, $y = m \cdot 0 + b = b$. Thus $(0, b)$ is on the graph of $y = mx + b$ and is the y-intercept of the line. The x-intercept is found as follows: A point on the x-axis has y-coordinate 0. So the x-coordinate of the x-intercept can be found by setting $y = 0$—that is, $mx + b = 0$—and solving this equation for x.

▶ Example 7   Sketch the graph of the equation $y = 2x - 1$.

Solution   Here $m = 2$, $b = -1$. The y-intercept is $(0, b) = (0, -1)$. To find the x-intercept, we must solve $2x - 1 = 0$. But then $2x = 1$ and $x = 1/2$. So the x-intercept is $(1/2, 0)$. Plot the two points $(0, -1)$ and $(1/2, 0)$, and draw the straight line through them (Fig. 8).   ◆

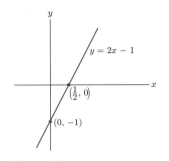

Figure 8.

Note   The line in Example 7 had different x- and y-intercepts. Two other circumstances can occur, however. First, the two intercepts may be the same, as in $y = 3x$. Second, there may be no x-intercept, as in $y = 1$. In both of these circumstances, we must plot some point other than an intercept in order to graph the line.

To summarize,

To graph the equation $y = mx + b$,

1. Plot the y-intercept $(0, b)$.

2. Plot some other point. [The most convenient choice is often the x-intercept $(x, 0)$, where x is determined by solving $mx + b = 0$.]

3. Draw a line through the two points.

The next example gives an application of linear equations.

▶ Example 8   (*Linear Depreciation*)   For tax purposes, businesses must keep track of the current values of each of their assets. A common mathematical model is to assume that the current value y is related to the age x of the asset by a linear equation. A moving company buys a 40-foot van with a useful lifetime of 5 years. After x months of use, the value y of the van is estimated by the linear equation

$$y = 25,000 - 400x.$$

(a)   Sketch the graph of this linear equation.

(b)   What is the value of the van after 5 years?

(c)   What economic interpretation can be given to the y-intercept of the graph?

Solution   (a)   The y-intercept is $(0, 25,000)$. The x-intercept is found from the equation

$$25,000 - 400x = 0$$

$$x = \frac{125}{2},$$

so the x-intercept is $(125/2, 0)$. The graph of the linear equation is sketched in Fig. 9. Note how the value decreases as the age of the truck increases. The value of the truck reaches 0 after $125/2$ months. Note also that we have sketched only the portion of the graph that has physical meaning, namely the portion for x between 0 and $125/2$.

(b)   After 5 years (or 60 months), the value of the van is

$$y = 25,000 - 400(60) = 25,000 - 24,000 = 1000.$$

Since the useful life of the van is 5 years, this value represents the *salvage value* of the van.

(c)   The y-intercept corresponds to the value of the truck at $x = 0$ months, that is, the initial value of the truck, \$25,000.   ◆

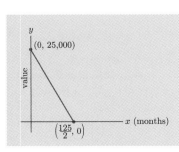

Figure 9.

GC[1] Accurate graphs of straight lines can be obtained with a *graphing utility*; that is, a graphing calculator or a computer with graphing software. The equation is usually entered in standard form. Figures 10, 11, and 12 show how the equation from Example 7 is entered and graphed on a TI-83 graphing calculator. The window setting in Fig. 11 is sometimes referred to as $[-2, 4]$ *by* $[-2, 2]$. The graphing utility also can be used to find the coordinates of points on the line (see Fig. 13) and to determine the intercepts (see Figs. 14 and 15). Vertical lines can be drawn with the VERTICAL command from the DRAW menu. For instance, to draw the vertical line through the cursor, go to the home screen and press 2nd [DRAW] **4**.

Figure 10.

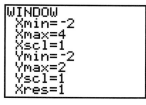

Figure 11.

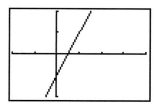

Figure 12.

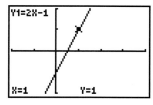

Figure 13.

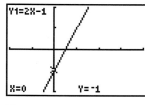

Figure 14.

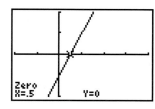

Figure 15.

Throughout this text we discuss specifics of using the TI-82 and TI-83 graphing calculators. Additional details are provided in Appendix B. For the specific details of using other calculators, consult the guidebook that comes with the calculator.

Practice Problems 1.1

1. Plot the point $(500, 200)$.

2. Is the point $(4, -7)$ on the graph of the linear equation $2x - 3y = 1$? Is the point $(5, 3)$?

3. Graph the linear equation $5x + y = 10$.

4. Graph the straight line $y = 3x$.

▶ Exercises 1.1

In Exercises 1–8, plot the given point.

1. $(2, 3)$

2. $(-1, 4)$

3. $(0, -2)$

4. $(2, 0)$

5. $(-2, 1)$

6. $\left(-1, -\frac{5}{2}\right)$

7. $(-20, 40)$

8. $(25, 30)$

9. (PE[2]) In Fig. 16, the point P has coordinates
   - (a) $(5, 3)$
   - (b) $(-3, 5)$
   - (c) $(-5, 3)$
   - (d) $(3, -5)$
   - (e) $(5, -3)$

---

[1]GC is an abbreviation for "Graphing Calculator."

[2]Exercises denoted PE are similar to questions appearing in professional exams such as GMAT and CPA exams.

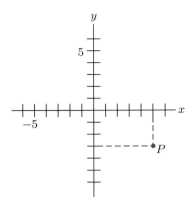

Figure 16.

10. (PE) In Fig. 17, the point P has coordinates
   (a) $(-4, 5)$ (b) $(5, -4)$ (c) $(10, -8)$
   (d) $(-8, 10)$ (e) $(4, 5)$

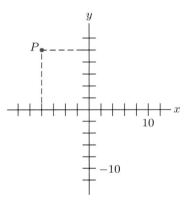

Figure 17.

In Exercises 11–14, each linear equation is in the standard form $y = mx + b$. Identify m and b.

11. $y = 5x + 8$ 12. $y = -2x - 6$

13. $y = 3$ 14. $y = \frac{2}{3}x$

In Exercises 15–18, put the linear equations into standard form.

15. $14x + 7y = 21$ 16. $x - y = 3$

17. $3x = 5$ 18. $-\frac{1}{2}x + \frac{2}{3}y = 10$

In Exercises 19–22, find the x-intercept and the y-intercept of each line.

19. $y = -4x + 8$ 20. $y = 5$

21. $x = 7$ 22. $y = -8x$

In Exercises 23–28, graph the given linear equation.

23. $y = \frac{1}{3}x - 1$ 24. $y = 2x$

25. $y = \frac{5}{2}$ 26. $x = 0$

27. $3x + 4y = 24$ 28. $x + y = 3$

29. Which of the following equations describe the same line as the equation $2x + 3y = 6$?
   (a) $4x + 6y = 12$ (b) $y = -\frac{2}{3}x + 2$
   (c) $x = 3 - \frac{3}{2}y$ (d) $6 - 2x - y = 0$
   (e) $y = 2 - \frac{2}{3}x$ (f) $x + y = 1$

30. Which of the following equations describe the same line as the equation $\frac{1}{2}x - 5y = 1$?
   (a) $2x - \frac{1}{5}y = 1$ (b) $x = 5y + 2$
   (c) $2 - 5x + 10y = 0$ (d) $y = .1(x - 2)$
   (e) $10y - x = -2$ (f) $1 + .5x = 2 + 5y$

31. Each of the lines L_1, L_2, and L_3 in Fig. 18 is the graph of one of the equations (a), (b), and (c). Match each of the equations with its corresponding line.
   (a) $x + y = 3$ (b) $2x - y = -2$ (c) $x = 3y + 3$

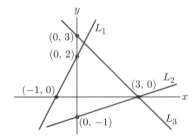

Figure 18.

32. Which of the following equations is graphed in Fig. 19?
   (a) $x + y = 3$ (b) $y = x - 1$ (c) $2y = x + 3$

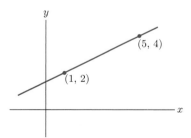

Figure 19.

33. The temperature of water in a heating tea kettle rises according to the equation $y = 30x + 72$, where y is the temperature (in degrees Fahrenheit) x minutes after the kettle was put on the burner.
   (a) After how many minutes will the water boil?
   (b) What physical interpretation can be given to the y-intercept of the graph?
   (c) Does the x-intercept have a meaningful physical interpretation?

34. The amount of tropical rainforest area in Central America has been decreasing steadily in recent years. The amount y (in thousands of square miles) x years after 1969 is estimated by the linear equation

$$y = \left(-\frac{25}{8}\right)x + 130.$$

(a) Sketch the graph of this linear equation.

(b) What interpretation can be given to the y-intercept of the graph?

(c) When were there 80,000 square miles of tropical rain forests?

(d) If this trend continues, how large will the rain forest be in the year 2004?

35. The worldwide consumption of cigarettes has been increasing steadily in recent years. The number of trillions of cigarettes, y, purchased x years after 1960, is estimated by the linear equation

$$y = .075x + 2.5.$$

(a) Sketch the graph of this linear equation.

(b) What interpretation can be given to the y-intercept of the graph?

(c) When were there 4 trillion cigarettes sold?

(d) If this trend continues, how many cigarettes will be sold in the year 2020?

36. Find an equation of the line having y-intercept $(0,5)$ and x-intercept $(4,0)$.

37. Consider an equation of the form $y = mx + b$. When the value of m remains fixed and the value of b changes, the graph is translated vertically. As the value of b increases, does the graph move up or down?

38. Can a line have more than one x-intercept?

39. What is the equation of the x-axis?

40. What is the general form of the equation of a line that is parallel to the x-axis?

41. Does every line have a y-intercept?

42. Does every line have an x-intercept?

Solutions to Practice Problems 1.1

1. Since the numbers are large, make each hatchmark correspond to 100. Then the point $(500, 200)$ is found by starting at the origin, moving 500 units to the right and then 200 units up (Fig. 20).

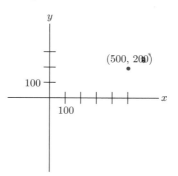

Figure 20.

2. Substitute the point $(4, -7)$ into the equation $2x - 3y = 1$.

$$2(4) - 3(-7) = 1$$
$$8 + 21 = 1$$
$$29 = 1$$

The equation does not hold, so $(4, -7)$ is not on the graph. Similarly, if we substitute $(5, 3)$ into the equation, we find that

$$2 \cdot 5 - 3 \cdot 3 = 1$$
$$10 - 9 = 1$$
$$1 = 1.$$

So the equation holds and $(5, 3)$ is on the graph.

3. The standard form is obtained by solving for y:

$$y = -5x + 10.$$

Thus $m = -5$ and $b = 10$. The y-intercept is $(0, 10)$. To get the x-intercept, set $y = 0$:

$$0 = -5x + 10$$
$$5x = 10$$
$$x = 2.$$

So the x-intercept is $(2, 0)$ (Fig. 21).

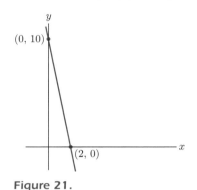

Figure 21.

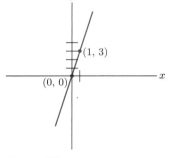

Figure 22.

4. To find the y-intercept, set $x = 0$; then $y = 3 \cdot 0 = 0$. To find the x-intercept, set $y = 0$; then $3x = 0$ or $x = 0$. The two intercepts are the same point $(0, 0)$. We must therefore plot some other point. Setting $x = 1$, we obtain $y = 3 \cdot 1 = 3$, so another point on the line is $(1, 3)$ (Fig. 22).

1.2 Linear Inequalities

In this section we study the properties of inequalities. Start with a Cartesian coordinate system on the line (Fig. 1). Recall that it is possible to associate with each point of the line a number; and conversely, with each number (positive, negative, or zero) it is possible to associate a point on the line.

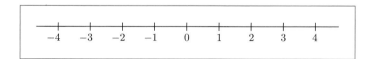

Figure 1.

Let a and b be any numbers. We say that *a is less than b* if a lies to the left of b on the line. When a is less than b, we write $a < b$ (read: a is less than b). Thus, for example, $2 < 3$, $-1 < 2$, $-3 < -1$, and $0 < 4$. When a is less than b, we also say that *b is greater than a* ($b > a$). Thus, for example, $3 > 2$, $2 > -1$, $-1 > -3$, and $4 > 0$. Sometimes it is convenient to have a notation that means that a is no larger than b. The notation used for this is $a \leq b$ (read: a is less than or equal to b). Similarly, the notation $a \geq b$ (read: a is greater than or equal to b) means that a is no smaller than b. The symbols $>$, $<$, $\geq$, and $\leq$ are called *inequality signs*. It is easiest to remember the meaning of these various symbols by noting that the symbols $>$ and $<$ always *point toward the smaller* of a and b.

An inequality expresses a relationship between the quantities on both of its sides. This relationship is very similar to the relationship expressed by an equation. And just as some problems require solving equations, others require solving inequalities. Our next task will be to state and illustrate the arithmetic operations permissible in dealing with inequalities. These permissible operations form the basis of a technique for solving the inequalities occurring in applications.

Inequality Property 1   Suppose that $a < b$ and that c is any number. Then $a + c < b + c$ and $a - c < b - c$. In other words, the same number can be added or subtracted from both sides of the inequality.

For example, start with the inequality $2 < 3$ and add 4 to both sides to get

$$2 + 4 < 3 + 4.$$

That is,

$$6 < 7,$$

a correct inequality.

▶ **Example 1**   Solve the inequality $x + 4 > 3$. That is, determine all values of x for which the inequality holds.

Solution   We proceed as we would in dealing with an equation. Isolate x on the left by subtracting 4 from both sides, which is permissible by Inequality Property 1:

$$x + 4 > 3$$
$$(x + 4) - 4 > 3 - 4$$
$$x > -1.$$

That is, the values of x for which the inequality holds are exactly those x greater than -1.   ◆

In dealing with an equation, both sides may be multiplied or divided by a number. However, multiplying or dividing an inequality by a number requires some care. The result depends on whether the number is positive or negative. More precisely,

---

Inequality Property 2

2A. If $a < b$ and c is positive, then $ac < bc$.

2B. If $a < b$ and c is negative, then $ac > bc$.

In other words, an inequality may be multiplied by a positive number, just as in the case of equations. But to multiply an inequality by a negative number, it is necessary to reverse the inequality sign. For example, the inequality $-1 < 2$ can be multiplied by 4 to get $-4 < 8$, a correct statement. But if we were to multiply by -4, it would be necessary to reverse the inequality sign, since -4 is negative. In this latter case we would get $4 > -8$, a correct statement.

Note   Inequality Properties 1 and 2 are stated using only $<$. However, exactly the same properties hold if $<$ is replaced by $>$, $\le$, or $\ge$.

▶ **Example 2**   Solve the inequality $-3x + 2 \geq -1$.

Solution   Treat the inequality as if it were an equation. The goal is to isolate x on one side. To this end, first subtract 2 from both sides (Property 1). This gives

$$(-3x + 2) - 2 \geq -1 - 2$$
$$-3x \geq -3.$$

Next, we multiply by $-\frac{1}{3}$. (This gives x on the left.) But $-\frac{1}{3}$ is negative, so by Property 2B we must reverse the inequality sign. Thus,

$$-\tfrac{1}{3}(-3x) \leq -\tfrac{1}{3}(-3)$$
$$x \leq 1.$$

Therefore, the values of x satisfying the inequality are precisely those values that are ≤ 1.   ◆

The inequalities of greatest interest to us[1] are those in two variables, x and y, and having the form $cx + dy \leq e$ or $cx + dy \geq e$, where c, d, and e are given numbers, with c and d not both 0. We will call such inequalities *linear inequalities*. When $d \neq 0$ (that is, when y actually appears), the inequality can be put into one of the *standard forms* $y \leq mx + b$ or $y \geq mx + b$. When $d = 0$, the inequality can be put into one of the *standard forms* $x \leq a$ or $x \geq a$. The procedure for putting a linear inequality into standard form is analogous to that for putting a linear equation into standard form.

▶ **Example 3**   Put the linear inequality $2x - 3y \geq -9$ into standard form.

Solution   Since we want the y-term on the left and all other terms on the right, begin by subtracting $2x$ from both sides:

$$-3y \geq -2x - 9.$$

Next, multiply by $-\frac{1}{3}$, remembering to change the inequality sign, since $-\frac{1}{3}$ is negative:

$$y \leq -\tfrac{1}{3}(-2x - 9)$$
$$y \leq \tfrac{2}{3}x + 3.$$

The last inequality is in standard form.   ◆

▶ **Example 4**   Find the standard form of the inequality $\frac{1}{2}x \geq 4$.

Solution   Note that y does not appear in the inequality. Just as was the case in finding the standard form of a linear equation when y does not appear, solve for x. To do this, multiply by 2 to get

$$x \geq 8,$$

the standard form.   ◆

---

[1] Such inequalities arise in our discussion of linear programming in Chapter 3.

Graphing Linear Inequalities   Associated with every linear inequality is a set of points of the plane, the set of all those points that satisfy the inequality. This set of points is called the *graph* of the inequality.

▶ **Example 5**   Determine whether or not the given point satisfies the inequality $y \geq -\frac{2}{3}x + 4$.

(a) $(3, 4)$ (b) $(0, 0)$

Solution   Substitute the x-coordinate of the point for x and the y-coordinate for y, and determine if the resulting inequality is correct or not.

(a) $4 \geq -\frac{2}{3}(3) + 4$ (b) $0 \geq -\frac{2}{3}(0) + 4$

$\quad\;\; 4 \geq -2 + 4$ $\quad\;\; 0 \geq 0 + 4$

$\quad\;\; 4 \geq 2$ (correct) $\quad\;\; 0 \geq 4$ (not correct)

Therefore, the point $(3, 4)$ satisfies the inequality and the point $(0, 0)$ does not.

◆

It is easiest to determine the graph of a given inequality after it has been written in standard form. Therefore, let us describe the graphs of each of the standard forms. The easiest to handle are the forms $x \geq a$ and $x \leq a$.

A point satisfies the inequality $x \geq a$ if and only if its x-coordinate is greater than or equal to a. The y-coordinate can be anything. Therefore, the graph of $x \geq a$ consists of all points to the right of and on the vertical line $x = a$. We will display the graph by crossing out the portion of the plane to the left of the line (see Fig. 2). Similarly, the graph of $x \leq a$ consists of the points to the left of and on the line $x = a$. This graph is shown in Fig. 3.

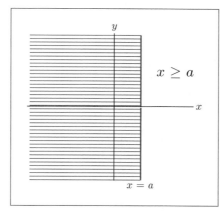

Figure 2.

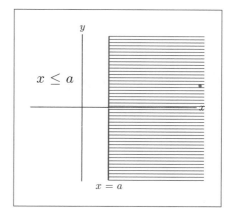

Figure 3.

Here is a simple procedure for graphing the other two standard forms.

To graph $y \geq mx + b$ or $y \leq mx + b$,

1. Draw the graph of $y = mx + b$.

2. Throw away, that is, "cross out," the portion of the plane not satisfying the inequality. The graph of $y \geq mx + b$ consists of all points above or on the line. The graph of $y \leq mx + b$ consists of all points below or on the line.

The graphs of the inequalities $y \geq mx + b$ and $y \leq mx + b$ are shown in Fig. 4. Some simple reasoning suffices to show why these graphs are correct. Draw the line $y = mx + b$, as in Fig. 5, and pick any point P above the line. Suppose that P has coordinates (x, y). Let Q be the point on the line that lies directly below P. Then Q has the same first coordinate as P, that is, x. Since Q lies on the line, the second coordinate of Q is $mx + b$. Since the second coordinate of P is clearly larger than the second coordinate of Q, we must have $y \geq mx + b$. Similarly, any point below the line satisfies $y \leq mx + b$. Thus the two graphs are as given in Fig. 4.

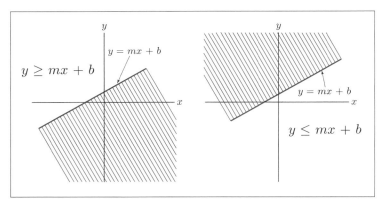

Figure 4.

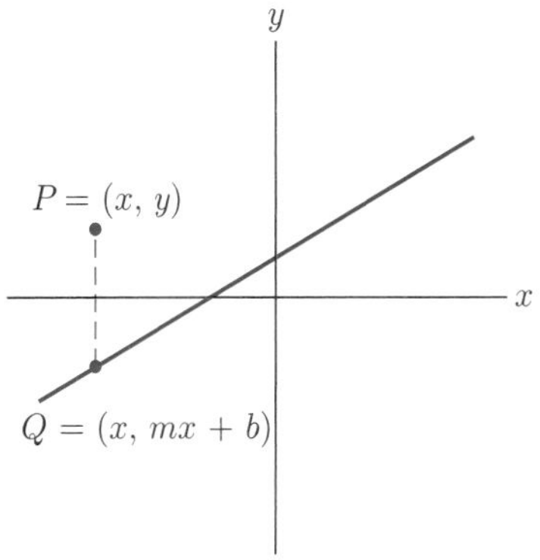

Figure 5.

▶ Example 6   Graph the inequality $2x + 3y \geq 15$.

Solution   In order to apply the aforementioned procedure, the inequality must first be put into standard form:

$$2x + 3y \geq 15$$
$$3y \geq -2x + 15$$
$$y \geq -\tfrac{2}{3}x + 5.$$

The last inequality is in standard form. Next, we graph the line $y = -\frac{2}{3}x + 5$. Its intercepts are $(0, 5)$ and $\left(\frac{15}{2}, 0\right)$. Since the inequality is "$y \geq$" we cross out the region below the line and label the region above with the inequality. The graph consists of all points above or on the line (Fig. 6).   ◆

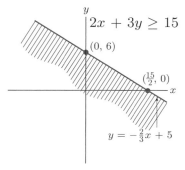

Figure 6.

▶ Example 7   Graph the inequality $4x - 2y \geq 12$.

Solution   First, put the inequality in standard form:

$$4x - 2y \geq 12$$
$$-2y \geq -4x + 12$$
$$y \leq 2x - 6$$

(note the change in the inequality sign!). Next, graph $y = 2x - 6$. The intercepts are $(0, -6)$ and $(3, 0)$. Since the inequality is "$y \leq$" the graph consists of all points below or on the line (Fig. 7).

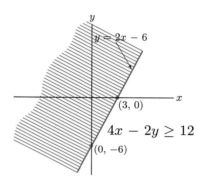

Figure 7.   ◆

So far, we have been concerned only with graphing single inequalities. The next example concerns graphing a system of inequalities. That is, it asks us to determine all points of the plane that *simultaneously* satisfy all inequalities of a system.

▶ Example 8   Graph the system of inequalities

$$\begin{cases} 2x + 3y \geq 15 \\ 4x - 2y \geq 12 \\ \qquad y \geq 0. \end{cases}$$

Solution   The first two inequalities have already been graphed in Examples 6 and 7. The graph of $y \geq 0$ consists of all points above or on the x-axis. In Fig. 8, any point that is crossed out is *not* on the graph of at least one inequality. So the points

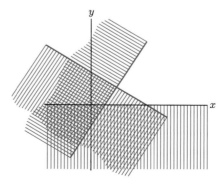

Figure 8.

that simultaneously satisfy all three inequalities are those in the remaining clear region and its border.   ◆

Remark   At first, our convention of crossing out those points *not* on the graph of an inequality (instead of shading the points *on* the graph) may have seemed odd. However, the real advantage of this convention becomes apparent when graphing a system of inequalities. Imagine trying to find the graph of the system of Example 8 if the points *on* the graph of each inequality had been shaded. It would have been necessary to locate the points that had been shaded three times. This is hard to do.

The graph of a system of inequalities is called a *feasible set*. The feasible set associated to the system of Example 8 is a three-sided, unbounded region.

Given a specific point, we should be able to decide whether or not the point lies in the feasible set. The next example shows how this is done.

◗ **Example 9**   Determine whether the points $(5, 3)$ and $(4, 2)$ are in the feasible set of the system of inequalities of Example 8.

Solution   If we had very accurate measuring devices, we could plot the points in the graph of Fig. 8 and determine whether or not they lie in the feasible set. However, there is a simpler and more reliable algebraic method. Just substitute the coordinates of the points into each of the inequalities of the system and see whether or not *all* of the inequalities are satisfied. So doing, we find that $(5, 3)$ is in the feasible set and $(4, 2)$ is not.

$$(5, 3) \qquad \begin{cases} 2(5) + 3(3) \geq 15 \\ 4(5) - 2(3) \geq 12 \\ \qquad\quad (3) \geq 0 \end{cases} \qquad \begin{cases} 19 \geq 15 \\ 14 \geq 12 \\ 3 \geq 0 \end{cases}$$

$$(4, 2) \qquad \begin{cases} 2(4) + 3(2) \geq 15 \\ 4(4) - 2(2) \geq 12 \\ \qquad\quad (2) \geq 0 \end{cases} \qquad \begin{cases} 14 \geq 15 \\ 12 \geq 12 \\ 2 \geq 0 \end{cases} \qquad\quad ◆$$

GC   Some graphing calculators will display feasible sets of inequalities. With the TI-82 and TI-83, the **Shade** command (invoked with [2nd] [DRAW] **7** from the home screen) can be used to shade one side of the straight line $\mathbf{Y}_1$. Suppose the window is $[a, b]$ *by* $[c, d]$. The region above the line can be thought of as lying between the lower function $\mathbf{Y}_1$ and the upper function $y = d + 1$. The region below the line can be thought of as lying between the lower function $y = c - 1$ and the upper function $\mathbf{Y}_1$. These regions can be shaded with the commands

$$\mathbf{Shade}(lowerfunction, upperfunction, 3) \quad \text{[TI-82]}$$
$$\mathbf{Shade}(lowerfunction, upperfunction, a, b, 2, 3) \quad \text{[TI-83]}$$

See Figs. 9 and 10, which were drawn with the window $[-5, 13]$ *by* $[-6, 6]$.

The regions to the left and right, respectively, of the vertical line $x = k$ can be shaded with the commands

$$\mathbf{Shade(c-1,d+1,3,a,k)} \quad \text{and} \quad \mathbf{Shade(c-1,d+1,3,k,b)} \quad \text{[TI-82]}$$
$$\mathbf{Shade(c-1,d+1,a,k,2,3)} \quad \text{and} \quad \mathbf{Shade(c-1,d+1,k,b,2,3)} \quad \text{[TI-83]}$$

See Figs. 11 and 12, which were drawn with the window $[-5, 13]$ *by* $[-6, 6]$.

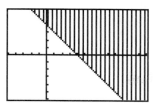

Figure 9. TI-82
`Shade(-X + 4, 7, 3)`

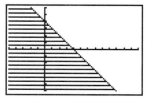

Figure 10. TI-83
`Shade(-7, -X + 4, -5, 13, 2, 3)`

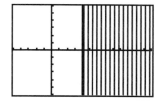

Figure 11. TI-82
`Shade(-7, 7, 3, 4, 13)`

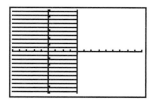

Figure 12. TI-83
`Shade(-7, 7, -5, 4, 2, 3)`

With the TI-83, there is a style icon (initially a line of four dots) to the left of each function in the **Y=** editor. To change the style icon of a function, move the cursor to the icon and press the ENTER key. Of the seven different icons, the icons ◣ and ◤ specify that the line be graphed and the points above and below the line, respectively, be crossed out. Figure 13 shows the **Y=** editor and the feasible set for Example 8.

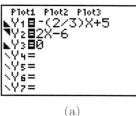

(a)

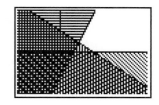

(b) $[-10, 20]$ by $[-10, 10]$

Figure 13.

Practice Problems 1.2	1. Graph the inequality $3x - y \geq 3$.

2. Graph the feasible set for the system of inequalities

$$\begin{cases} x \geq 0, \ y \geq 0 \\ x + 2y \leq \ \ 4 \\ 4x - 4y \geq -4. \end{cases}$$

▶ Exercises 1.2

In Exercises 1–4, state whether the inequality is true or false.

1. $2 \leq -3$ **2.** $-2 \leq 0$ **3.** $7 \leq 7$ **4.** $0 \geq \frac{1}{2}$

In Exercises 5–7, solve for x.

5. $2x - 5 \geq 3$ **6.** $3x - 7 \leq 2$

7. $-5x + 13 \leq -2$

8. Which of the following results from solving $-x + 1 \leq 3$ for x?

(a) $x \leq 4$ (b) $x \leq 2$

(c) $x \geq -4$ (d) $x \geq -2$

In Exercises 9–14, put the linear inequality into standard form.

9. $2x + y \leq 5$ 10. $-3x + y \geq 1$

11. $5x - \frac{1}{3}y \leq 6$ 12. $\frac{1}{2}x - y \leq -1$

13. $4x \geq -3$ 14. $-2x \leq 4$

In Exercises 15–22, determine whether or not the given point satisfies the given inequality.

15. $3x + 5y \leq 12$, $(2, 1)$ 16. $-2x + y \geq 9$, $(3, 15)$

17. $y \geq -2x + 7$, $(3, 0)$ 18. $y \leq \frac{1}{2}x + 3$, $(4, 6)$

19. $y \leq 3x - 4$, $(3, 5)$ 20. $y \geq x$, $(-3, -2)$

21. $x \geq 5$, $(7, -2)$ 22. $x \leq 7$, $(0, 0)$

In Exercises 23–26, graph the given inequality by crossing out (i.e., discarding) the points not satisfying the inequality.

23. $y \leq \frac{1}{3}x + 1$

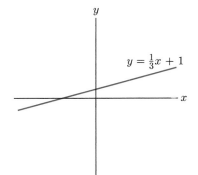

24. $y \geq -x + 1$

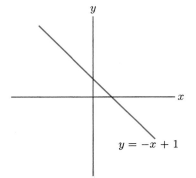

25. $x \geq 4$

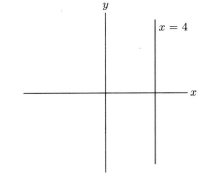

26. $y \leq 2$

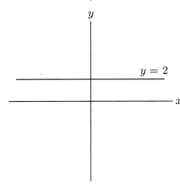

In Exercises 27–36, graph the given inequality.

27. $y \leq 2x + 1$ 28. $y \geq -3x + 6$

29. $x \geq 2$ 30. $x \geq 0$

31. $x + 4y \geq 12$ 32. $4x - 4y \geq 8$

33. $4x - 5y + 25 \geq 0$ 34. $.2y - x \geq .4$

35. $\frac{1}{2}x - \frac{1}{3}y \leq 1$ 36. $3y - 3x \leq 2y + x + 1$

In Exercises 37–42, graph the feasible set for the system of inequalities.

37. $\begin{cases} y \leq 2x - 4 \\ y \geq 0 \end{cases}$ 38. $\begin{cases} y \geq -\frac{1}{3}x + 1 \\ x \geq 0 \end{cases}$

39. $\begin{cases} x + 2y \geq 2 \\ 3x - y \geq 3 \end{cases}$ 40. $\begin{cases} 3x + 6y \geq 24 \\ 3x + y \geq 6 \end{cases}$

41. $\begin{cases} x + 5y \leq 10 \\ x + y \leq 3 \\ x \geq 0, \ y \geq 0 \end{cases}$ 42. $\begin{cases} x + 2y \geq 6 \\ x + y \geq 5 \\ x \geq 1 \end{cases}$

In Exercises 43–46, determine whether the given point is in the feasible set of this system of inequalities:

$$\begin{cases} 6x + 3y \leq 96 \\ x + y \leq 18 \\ 2x + 6y \leq 72 \\ x \geq 0, \ y \geq 0. \end{cases}$$

43. $(8, 7)$ 44. $(14, 3)$

45. $(9, 10)$ 46. $(16, 0)$

In Exercises 47–50, determine whether the given point is above or below the given line.

47. $y = 2x + 5$, $(3, 9)$ **48.** $3x - y = 4$, $(2, 3)$

49. $7 - 4x + 5y = 0$, $(0, 0)$ **50.** $x = 2y + 5$, $(6, 1)$

51. Give a system of inequalities for which the graph is the region between the pair of lines $8x - 4y - 4 = 0$ and $8x - 4y = 0$.

52. (PE) The shaded region in Fig. 14 is bounded by four straight lines. Which of the following is NOT an equation of one of the boundary lines?

   (a) $y = 0$ (b) $y = 2$ (c) $x = 0$

   (d) $2x + 3y = 12$ (e) $3x + 2y = 12$

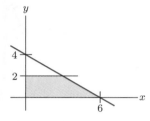

Figure 14.

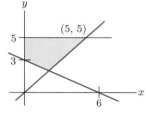

Figure 15.

53. (PE) The shaded region in Fig. 15 is bounded by four straight lines. Which of the following is NOT an equation of one of the boundary lines?

   (a) $x = 0$ (b) $y = x$ (c) $y = 5$

   (d) $y = 0$ (e) $x + 2y = 6$

54. (PE) Which quadrant in Fig. 16 contains no points that satisfy the inequality $x + 2y \ge 6$?

   (a) none   (b) I   (c) II   (d) III   (e) IV

Figure 16.

55. (PE) Which quadrant in Fig. 16 contains no points that satisfy the inequality $3y - 2x \ge 6$?

   (a) none   (b) I   (c) II   (d) III   (e) IV

Use a graphing calculator or a computer to solve Exercises 56–59.

56. Graph the line $4x - 2y = 7$.

   (a) Locate the point on the line with x-coordinate 3.6.

   (b) Does the point $(3.6, 3.5)$ lie above or below the line? Explain.

57. Graph the line $x + 2y = 11$.

   (a) Locate the point on the line with x-coordinate 6.

   (b) Does the point $(6, 2.6)$ lie above or below the line? Explain.

58. If your graphing calculator can shade feasible sets of inequalities, display the feasible set in Exercise 37.

59. If your graphing calculator can shade feasible sets of inequalities, display the feasible set in Exercise 40.

Solutions to Practice Problems 1.2

1. Linear inequalities are easiest to graph if they are first put into standard form. Subtract $3x$ from both sides and multiply by -1:

$$3x - y \ge 3$$
$$-y \ge -3x + 3$$
$$y \le 3x - 3.$$

Now graph the line $y = 3x - 3$ (Fig. 17). The graph of the inequality is the portion of the plane below and on the line ("$\le$" corresponds to below), so throw away (that is, cross out) the portion above the line.

2. Begin by putting the linear inequalities into standard form and then graphing them all on the same coordinate system.

$$\begin{cases} x \ge 0, \ y \ge 0 \\ x + 2y \le \ \ 4 \\ 4x - 4y \ge -4 \end{cases} \quad \text{has standard form} \quad \begin{cases} x \ge 0, \ y \ge 0 \\ y \le -\frac{1}{2}x + 2 \\ y \le \ \ \ \ x + 1 \end{cases}$$

A good procedure to follow is to graph all of the linear equations and then cross out the regions to be thrown away one at a time (Fig. 18). The inequalities $x \ge 0$ and $y \ge 0$ arise frequently in applications. The first has the form $x \ge a$, where $a = 0$, and the second has the form $y \ge mx + b$, where $m = 0$ and $b = 0$. To graph them, just cross out all points to the left of the y-axis and all points below the x-axis, respectively.

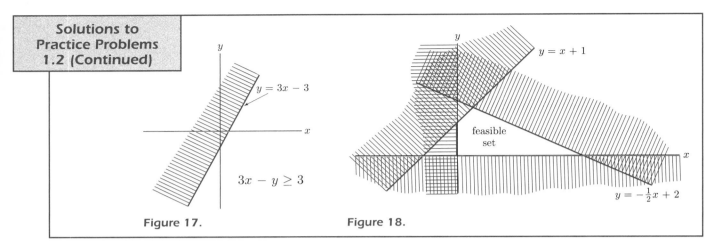

Solutions to Practice Problems 1.2 (Continued)

Figure 17.

Figure 18.

1.3 The Intersection Point of a Pair of Lines

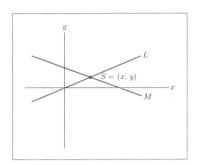

Figure 1.

Suppose that we are given a pair of intersecting straight lines L and M. Let us consider the problem of determining the coordinates of the point of intersection $S = (x, y)$ (see Fig. 1). We may as well assume that the equations of L and M are given in standard form. First, let us assume that both lines are in the first standard form — that is, that the equations are

$$L: \quad y = mx + b, \qquad M: \quad y = nx + c.$$

Since the point S is on both lines, its coordinates satisfy both equations. In particular, we have two expressions for its y-coordinate:

$$y = mx + b = nx + c.$$

The last equality gives an equation from which x can easily be determined. Then the value of y can be determined as $mx + b$ (or $nx + c$). Let us see how this works in a particular example.

▶ **Example 1** Find the point of intersection of the two lines $y = 2x - 3$ and $y = x + 1$.

Solution To find the x-coordinate of the point of intersection, equate the two expressions for y and solve for x:

$$2x - 3 = x + 1$$
$$2x - x = 1 + 3$$
$$x = 4.$$

To find the value of y, set $x = 4$ in either equation, say the first. Then

$$y = 2 \cdot 4 - 3 = 5.$$

So the point of intersection is $(4, 5)$.   ◆

▶ **Example 2** Find the point of intersection of the two lines $x + 2y = 6$ and $5x + 2y = 18$.

Solution To use the method described, the equations must be in standard form. Solving both equations for y, we get the standard forms

$$y = -\tfrac{1}{2}x + 3$$
$$y = -\tfrac{5}{2}x + 9.$$

Equating the expressions for y gives

$$-\tfrac{1}{2}x + 3 = -\tfrac{5}{2}x + 9$$
$$\tfrac{5}{2}x - \tfrac{1}{2}x = 9 - 3$$
$$2x = 6$$
$$x = 3.$$

Setting $x = 3$ in the first equation gives

$$y = -\tfrac{1}{2}(3) + 3 = \tfrac{3}{2}.$$

So the intersection point is $\left(3, \tfrac{3}{2}\right)$. ◆

The preceding method works when both equations have the first standard form. In case one equation has the standard form $x = a$, things are much simpler. The value of x is then given directly without any work, namely $x = a$. The value of y can be found by substituting a for x in the other equation.

▶ **Example 3**   Find the point of intersection of the lines $y = 2x - 1$ and $x = 2$.

Solution   The x-coordinate of the intersection point is 2, and the y-coordinate is $y = 2 \cdot 2 - 1 = 3$. Therefore, the intersection point is $(2, 3)$. ◆

The method just introduced may be used to solve systems of two equations in two variables.

▶ **Example 4**   Solve the following system of linear equations:

$$\begin{cases} 2x + 3y = 7 \\ 4x - 2y = 9. \end{cases}$$

Solution   First convert the equations to standard form:

$$2x + 3y = 7 \qquad\qquad 4x - 2y = 9$$
$$3y = -2x + 7 \qquad\qquad -2y = -4x + 9$$
$$y = -\tfrac{2}{3}x + \tfrac{7}{3}; \qquad\qquad y = 2x - \tfrac{9}{2}.$$

Now equate the two expressions for y:

$$2x - \tfrac{9}{2} = -\tfrac{2}{3}x + \tfrac{7}{3}$$
$$\tfrac{8}{3}x = \tfrac{7}{3} + \tfrac{9}{2} = \tfrac{14}{6} + \tfrac{27}{6} = \tfrac{41}{6}$$
$$x = \tfrac{3}{8} \cdot \tfrac{41}{6} = \tfrac{41}{16}$$
$$y = 2x - \tfrac{9}{2} = 2\left(\tfrac{41}{16}\right) - \tfrac{9}{2} = \tfrac{5}{8}.$$

So the solution of the given system is $x = \tfrac{41}{16}$, $y = \tfrac{5}{8}$. ◆

Supply and Demand Curves   The price p that a commodity sells for is related to the quantity q available. Economists study two sorts of graphs that express relationships between q and p. To describe these graphs, let us plot *quantity* along the horizontal axis and *price* along the vertical axis. The first graph relating q and p is called a *supply curve* (Fig. 2) and expresses the relationship between q and p from a manufacturer's point of view. For every quantity q, the supply curve specifies the price p for which the manufacturer is willing to produce the quantity q. The greater the quantity to be supplied, the higher the price must be. So supply curves rise when viewed from left to right.

Figure 2.

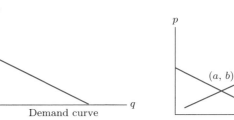

Figure 3.   **Figure 4.**

The second curve relating q and p is called a *demand curve* (Fig. 3) and expresses the relationship between q and p from the consumer's viewpoint. For each quantity q, the demand curve gives the price p that must be charged in order for q units of the commodity to be sold. The greater the quantity that must be sold, the lower the price that consumers must be asked to pay. So demand curves fall when viewed from left to right.

Suppose the supply and demand curves for a commodity are drawn on a single coordinate system (Fig. 4). The intersection point (a, b) of the two curves has an economic significance: The quantity produced will stabilize at a units and the price will be b dollars per unit.

▶ **Example 5**   Suppose the supply curve for a certain commodity is the straight line whose equation is $p = .0002q + 2$ (p in dollars). Suppose the demand curve for the same commodity is the straight line whose equation is $p = -.0005q + 5.5$. Determine both the quantity of the commodity that will be produced and the price at which it will sell.

Solution   We must solve the system of linear equations

$$\begin{cases} p = & .0002q + & 2 \\ p = & -.0005q + & 5.5 \end{cases}$$

$$.0002q + 2 = -.0005q + 5.5$$
$$.0007q = 3.5$$
$$q = \frac{3.5}{.0007} = 5000$$
$$p = .0002(5000) + 2 = 1 + 2 = 3$$

Thus 5000 units of the commodity will be produced and it will sell for $3 per unit.   ◆

GC   Graphing utilities have commands that find the intersection point of a pair of lines. Figure 5 shows the result of solving Example 4 on the TI-83 with the intersect command of the CALC menu. Since the x-coordinate of the intersection point is assigned to ANS, the x-intercept can be converted to a fraction by pressing MATH **1** ENTER from the home screen.

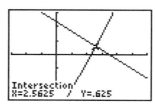

Figure 5. $[-3, 6]$ *by* $[-3, 3]$

<table>
<tr><td>

**Practice Problems
1.3**

</td><td>

Figure 6 shows the feasible set of a system of linear inequalities; its four vertices are labeled A, B, C, and D.

</td></tr>
</table>

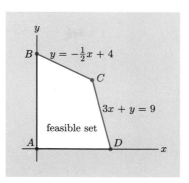

Figure 6.

1. Use the method of this section to find the coordinates of the point C.

2. Determine the coordinates of the points A and B by inspection.

3. Find the coordinates of the point D.

▶ Exercises 1.3

In Exercises 1–6, find the point of intersection of the given pair of straight lines.

1. $\begin{cases} y = 4x - 5 \\ y = -2x + 7 \end{cases}$

2. $\begin{cases} y = 3x - 15 \\ y = -2x + 10 \end{cases}$

3. $\begin{cases} x - 4y = -2 \\ x + 2y = 4 \end{cases}$

4. $\begin{cases} 2x - 3y = 3 \\ y = 3 \end{cases}$

5. $\begin{cases} y = \frac{1}{3}x - 1 \\ x = 12 \end{cases}$

6. $\begin{cases} 2x - 3y = 3 \\ x = 6 \end{cases}$

7. Does $(6, 4)$ satisfy the following system of linear equations?

$$\begin{cases} x - 3y = -6 \\ 3x - 2y = 10 \end{cases}$$

8. Does $(12, 4)$ satisfy the following system of linear equations?

$$\begin{cases} y = \frac{1}{3}x - 1 \\ x = 12 \end{cases}$$

In Exercises 9–12, solve the systems of linear equations.

9. $\begin{cases} 2x + y = 7 \\ x - y = 3 \end{cases}$

10. $\begin{cases} x + 2y = 4 \\ \frac{1}{2}x + \frac{1}{2}y = 3 \end{cases}$

11. $\begin{cases} 5x - 2y = 1 \\ 2x + y = -4 \end{cases}$

12. $\begin{cases} x + 2y = 6 \\ x - \frac{1}{3}y = 4 \end{cases}$

In Exercises 13–16, find the coordinates of the vertices of the feasible sets.

13.

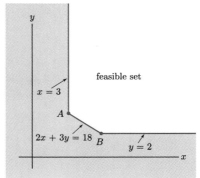

14.

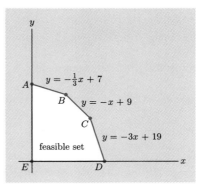

15.

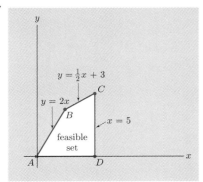

16.

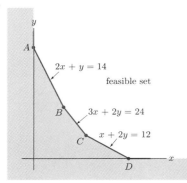

In Exercises 17–22, graph the feasible set for the system of inequalities and find the coordinates of the vertices.

17.
$$\begin{cases} 2y - x \leq 6 \\ x + 2y \geq 10 \\ x \leq 6 \end{cases}$$

18.
$$\begin{cases} 2x + y \geq 10 \\ x \geq 2 \\ y \geq 2 \end{cases}$$

19.
$$\begin{cases} x + 3y \leq 18 \\ 2x + y \leq 16 \\ x \geq 0,\ y \geq 0 \end{cases}$$

20.
$$\begin{cases} 5x + 2y \geq 14 \\ x + 3y \geq 8 \\ x \geq 0,\ y \geq 0 \end{cases}$$

21.
$$\begin{cases} 4x + y \geq 8 \\ x + y \geq 5 \\ x + 3y \geq 9 \\ x \geq 0,\ y \geq 0 \end{cases}$$

22.
$$\begin{cases} x + 4y \leq 28 \\ x + y \leq 10 \\ 3x + y \leq 24 \\ x \geq 0,\ y \geq 0 \end{cases}$$

23. The supply curve for a certain commodity is $p = .0001q + .05$.

(a) What price must be offered in order for 19,500 units of the commodity to be supplied?

(b) What prices result in no units of the commodity being supplied?

24. The demand curve for a certain commodity is $p = -.001q + 32.5$.

(a) At what price can 31,500 units of the commodity be sold?

(b) What quantities are so large that that many units of the commodity cannot possibly all be sold no matter how low the price?

25. Suppose that supply and demand for a certain commodity are described by the supply and demand curves of Exercises 23 and 24. Determine the quantity of the commodity that will be produced and the selling price.

26. The x- and y-intercepts of line L_1 are 1 unit to the left and 2 units below the x- and y-intercepts of line L_2, respectively. The equation for L_1 is $y = 3x + 6$. Find the point of intersection of L_1 and L_2.

27. A plant supervisor must apportion her 40-hour workweek between hours working on the assembly line and hours supervising the work of others. She is paid $12 per hour for working and $15 per hour for supervising. If her earnings for a certain week are $504, how much time does she spend on each task?

28. (PE) An appliance store sells a 13″ TV for $90 and a 19″ TV of the same brand for $120. During a one-week period the store sold 5 more 19″ TVs than 13″ TVs and collected $4800. What was the total number of TV sets sold?
(a) 42 (b) 43 (c) 44 (d) 45 (e) 46

29. (PE) In a wrestling competition, the total weight of the two contestants is 700 pounds. If twice the weight of the first contestant is 275 pounds more than the weight of the second contestant, what is the weight (in pounds) of the first contestant?
(a) 275 (b) 300 (c) 325 (d) 350 (e) 375

Exercises 30–35 require the use of a graphing calculator or a computer.

In Exercises 30–33, graph the lines and use the INTERSECT command to estimate the point of intersection to two decimal places.

30.
$$\begin{cases} y = -\frac{2}{3}x + 4.5 \\ y = 2x \end{cases}$$

31.
$$\begin{cases} y = .25x + 1.3 \\ y = -.5x + 4.1 \end{cases}$$

32.
$$\begin{cases} 2x + 3y = 5 \\ -4x + 5y = 1 \end{cases}$$

33.
$$\begin{cases} x - 4y = -5 \\ 3x - 2y = 4.2 \end{cases}$$

In Exercises 34 and 35, (a) draw the straight lines corresponding to the inequalities (use a window such as **ZDecimal** that gives nice values of the coordinates of points); (b) find the coordinates of the vertices of the feasible set; (c) locate the given point with the cursor; (d) determine whether or not the given point lies in the feasible set.

34.
$$\begin{cases} 2x + y \geq 5 \\ x - 2y \leq 0 \end{cases} \quad (2.2, 1.4)$$

35.
$$\begin{cases} -x + 3y \geq 3 \\ .4x + y \geq 3.2 \end{cases} \quad (3.2, 2)$$

1. Point C is the point of intersection of the lines with equations $y = -\frac{1}{2}x + 4$ and $3x + y = 9$. To use the method of this section, the second equation must be put into its standard form $y = -3x + 9$. Now equate the two expressions for y and solve.

$$-\tfrac{1}{2}x + 4 = -3x + 9$$
$$\tfrac{5}{2}x = 5$$
$$x = \tfrac{2}{5} \cdot 5 = 2$$
$$y = -\tfrac{1}{2}(2) + 4 = 3$$

Therefore, $C = (2, 3)$.

2. $A = (0, 0)$, since the point A is the origin. $B = (0, 4)$, since it is the y-intercept of the line with equation $y = -\frac{1}{2}x + 4$.

3. D is the x-intercept of the line $3x + y = 9$. Its first coordinate is found by setting $y = 0$ and solving for x.

$$3x + (0) = 9$$
$$x = 3$$

Therefore, $D = (3, 0)$.

1.4 The Slope of a Straight Line

As we have seen, any linear equation can be put into one of the two standard forms, $y = mx + b$ or $x = a$. In this section, let us exclude linear equations whose standard form is of the latter type. *Geometrically, this means that we will consider only nonvertical lines.*

Suppose that we are given a nonvertical line L whose equation is $y = mx + b$. The number m is called the *slope of L*. That is, the slope is the coefficient of x in the standard form of the equation of the line.

▶ **Example 1** Find the slopes of the lines having the following equations.

(a) $y = 2x + 1$ (b) $y = -\frac{3}{4}x + 2$ (c) $y = 3$ (d) $-8x + 2y = 4$

Solution (a) $m = 2$.
(b) $m = -\frac{3}{4}$.
(c) When we write the equation in the form $y = 0 \cdot x + 3$, we see that $m = 0$.
(d) First, we put the equation in standard form:

$$-8x + 2y = 4$$
$$2y = 8x + 4$$
$$y = 4x + 2.$$

Thus $m = 4$. ◆

The definition of the slope is given in terms of the standard form of the equation of the line. Let us give an alternative definition.

Geometric Definition of Slope Let L be a line passing through the points (x_1, y_1) and (x_2, y_2), where $x_1 \neq x_2$. Then the slope of L is given by the formula

$$m = \frac{y_2 - y_1}{x_2 - x_1}. \tag{1}$$

That is, the slope is the difference in the y-coordinates divided by the difference in the x-coordinates, with both differences formed in the same order.

Before proving this definition equivalent to the first one given, let us show how it can be used.

▶ **Example 2**   Find the slope of the line passing through the points $(1, 3)$ and $(4, 6)$.

Solution   We have

$$m = \frac{[\text{difference in } y\text{-coordinates}]}{[\text{difference in } x\text{-coordinates}]} = \frac{6 - 3}{4 - 1} = \frac{3}{3} = 1.$$

Thus $m = 1$. [Note that if we reverse the order of the points and use formula (1) to compute the slope, then we get

$$m = \frac{3 - 6}{1 - 4} = \frac{-3}{-3} = 1,$$

which is the same answer. The order of the points is immaterial. The important concern is to make sure that the differences in the x- and y-coordinates are formed in the same order.]   ◆

The slope of a line does not depend on which pair of points is chosen as (x_1, y_1) and (x_2, y_2). Consider the line $y = 4x - 3$ and two points $(1, 1)$ and $(3, 9)$, which are on the line. Using these two points, we calculate the slope to be

$$m = \frac{9 - 1}{3 - 1} = \frac{8}{2} = 4.$$

Now let's choose two other points on the line, say $(2, 5)$ and $(-1, -7)$, and use these points to determine m. We obtain

$$m = \frac{-7 - 5}{-1 - 2} = \frac{-12}{-3} = 4.$$

The two pairs of points give the same slope.

Justification of Formula (1)   Since (x_1, y_1) and (x_2, y_2) are both on the line, both points satisfy the equation of the line, which has the form $y = mx + b$. Thus

$$y_2 = mx_2 + b$$
$$y_1 = mx_1 + b.$$

Subtracting these two equations gives

$$y_2 - y_1 = mx_2 - mx_1 = m(x_2 - x_1).$$

Dividing by $x_2 - x_1$, we have

$$m = \frac{y_2 - y_1}{x_2 - x_1},$$

which is formula (1). So the two definitions of slope lead to the same number.◆

Let us now study four of the most important properties of the slope of a straight line. We begin with the *steepness property*, since it provides us with a geometric interpretation for the number m.

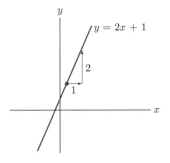

Figure 1.

> **Steepness Property** Let the line L have slope m. If we start at any point on the line and move 1 unit to the right, then we must move m units vertically in order to return to the line (Fig. 1). (Of course, if m is positive, then we move up; and if m is negative, we move down.)

▶ **Example 3** Illustrate the steepness property for each of the lines.

(a) $y = 2x + 1$ (b) $y = -\frac{3}{4}x + 2$ (c) $y = 3$

Solution (a) Here $m = 2$. So starting from any point on the line, proceeding 1 unit to the right, we must go 2 units up to return to the line (Fig. 2).

(b) Here $m = -\frac{3}{4}$. So starting from any point on the line, proceeding 1 unit to the right, we must go $\frac{3}{4}$ unit down to return to the line (Fig. 3).

(c) Here $m = 0$. So going 1 unit to the right requires going 0 units vertically to return to the line (Fig. 4).   ◆

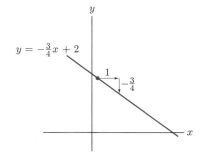

Figure 2.   **Figure 3.**   **Figure 4.**

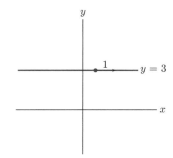

In the next example we introduce a new method for graphing a linear equation. This method relies on the steepness property and is much more efficient than finding two points on the line (e.g., the two intercepts).

▶ **Example 4** Use the steepness property to draw the graph of $y = \frac{1}{2}x + \frac{3}{2}$.

Solution   The y-intercept is $\left(0, \frac{3}{2}\right)$, as we read from the equation. We can find another point on the line using the steepness property. Start at $\left(0, \frac{3}{2}\right)$. Go 1 unit to the right. Since the slope is $\frac{1}{2}$, we must move vertically $\frac{1}{2}$ unit to return to the line. But this locates a second point on the line. So we draw the line through the two points. The entire procedure is illustrated in Fig. 5.   ◆

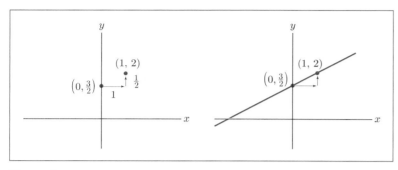   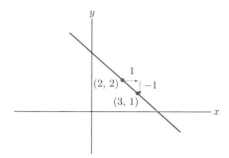

Figure 5.   **Figure 6.**

Actually, to use the steepness property to graph an equation, all that is needed is the slope plus *any* point (not necessarily the y-intercept).

▶ **Example 5**   Graph the line of slope -1 which passes through the point $(2, 2)$.

Solution   Start at $(2, 2)$, move 1 unit to the right and then -1 unit vertically, that is, 1 unit down. The line through $(2, 2)$ and the resulting point is the desired line (see Fig. 6).   ◆

Slope measures the *steepness* of a line. Namely, the slope of a line tells whether it is rising or falling, and how fast. Specifically, lines of positive slope rise as we move from left to right. Lines of negative slope fall, and lines of zero slope stay level. The larger the magnitude of the slope, the steeper the ascent or descent. These facts are directly implied by the steepness property (see Fig. 7).

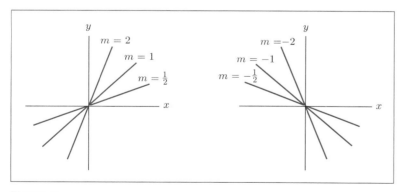   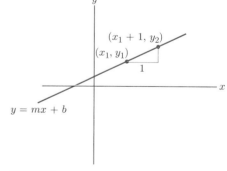

Figure 7.   **Figure 8.**

Justification of the Steepness Property   Consider a line with equation $y = mx + b$, and let (x_1, y_1) be any point on the line. If we start from this point and move 1 unit to the right, the first coordinate of the new point is $x_1 + 1$ since the x-coordinate is increased by 1. Now go far enough vertically to return to the line. Denote the y-coordinate of this new point by y_2 (see Fig. 8). We must show that to get y_2, we add m to y_1. That is, $y_2 = y_1 + m$. By equation (1), we can compute m as

$$m = \frac{[\text{difference in } y\text{-coordinates}]}{[\text{difference in } x\text{-coordinates}]} = \frac{y_2 - y_1}{1} = y_2 - y_1.$$

In other words, $y_2 = y_1 + m$, which is what we desired to show. ◆

Often the slopes of the straight lines that occur in applications have interesting and significant interpretations. An application in the field of economics is illustrated in the next example.

▶ **Example 6** (*Economics*) Suppose a manufacturer finds that the cost y of producing x units of a certain commodity is given by the formula $y = 2x + 5000$. What interpretation can be given to the slope of the graph of this equation?

Solution Suppose that the firm is producing at a certain level and increases production by 1 unit. That is, x is increased by 1 unit. By the steepness property, the value of y then increases by 2, which is the slope of the line whose equation is $y = 2x + 5000$. Thus *each additional unit of production costs $2*. (The graph of $y = 2x + 5000$ is called a *cost curve*. It relates the size of production to total cost. The graph is a straight line, and economists call its slope the *marginal cost of production*. The y-coordinate of the y-intercept is called the *fixed cost*. In this case the fixed cost is $5000, and it includes costs such as rent and insurance which are incurred even if no units are produced.) ◆

In applied problems having time as a variable, the letter t is often used in place of the letter x. If so, straight lines have equations of the form $y = mt + b$ and are graphed on a ty-coordinate system.

▶ **Example 7** (*Depreciation*) The federal government allows an income tax deduction for the decrease in value (or *depreciation*) of capital assets (such as buildings and equipment). One method of calculating the depreciation is to take equal amounts over the expected lifetime of the asset. This method is called *straight-line depreciation*. For tax purposes the value V of an asset t years after purchase is figured according to the equation $V = -100{,}000t + 700{,}000$. The expected life of the asset is 5 years.

(a) How much did the asset originally cost?

(b) What is the annual deduction for depreciation?

(c) What is the salvage value of the asset? (That is, what is the value of the asset after 5 years?)

Solution (a) The original cost is the value of V at $t = 0$, namely

$$V = -100{,}000(0) + 700{,}000 = 700{,}000.$$

That is, the asset originally cost $700,000.

(b) By the steepness property, each increase of 1 in t causes a decrease in V of 100,000. That is, the value is decreasing by $100,000 per year. So the depreciation deduction is $100,000 each year.

(c) After 5 years, the value of V is given by

$$V = -100{,}000(5) + 700{,}000 = 200{,}000.$$

The salvage value is $200,000. ◆

We have seen in Example 5 how to sketch a straight line when given its slope and one point on it. Let us now see how to find the equation of the line from this data.

> **Point-Slope Formula**   The equation of the straight line passing through (x_1, y_1) and having slope m is given by $y - y_1 = m(x - x_1)$.

▶ **Example 8**   Find the equation of the line that passes through $(2, 3)$ and has slope $\frac{1}{2}$.

Solution   Here $x_1 = 2$, $y_1 = 3$, and $m = \frac{1}{2}$. So the equation is

$$y - 3 = \tfrac{1}{2}(x - 2)$$
$$y - 3 = \tfrac{1}{2}x - 1$$
$$y = \tfrac{1}{2}x + 2.$$ ◆

▶ **Example 9**   Find the equation of the line through the points $(3, 1)$ and $(6, 0)$.

Solution   We can compute the slope from equation (1):

$$[\text{slope}] = \frac{[\text{difference in } y\text{-coordinates}]}{[\text{difference in } x\text{-coordinates}]} = \frac{1 - 0}{3 - 6} = -\frac{1}{3}.$$

Now we can determine the equation from the point-slope formula with $(x_1, y_1) = (3, 1)$ and $m = -\frac{1}{3}$:

$$y - 1 = -\tfrac{1}{3}(x - 3)$$
$$y = -\tfrac{1}{3}x + 2.$$

[*Question:* What would the equation be if we had chosen $(x_1, y_1) = (6, 0)$?]   ◆

▶ **Example 10**   For each dollar in monthly advertising expenditure, a store experiences a 6-dollar increase in sales revenue. Even without advertising, the store has $30,000 in sales revenue per month. Let x be the number of dollars of advertising expenditures per month and let y be the number of dollars in sales revenue per month.

(a) Find the equation of the line that expresses the relationship between x and y.

(b) If the store spends $10,000 in advertising, what will be the sales revenue for the month?

(c) How much would the store have to spend on advertising to attain $150,000 in sales revenue for the month?

Solution   (a) The steepness property tells us that the line has slope $m = 6$. Since $x = 0$ (no advertising expenditures) yields $y = \$30,000$, the y-intercept of the line is $(0, 30,000)$. Therefore, the standard form of the equation of the line is

$$y = 6x + 30,000.$$

(b) If $x = 10,000$, then $y = 6(10,000) + 30,000$. Therefore, the sales revenue for the month will be $90,000.

(c) We are given that $y = 150,000$, and we must find the value of x for which

$$150,000 = 6x + 30,000.$$

Solving for x, we obtain $6x = 120,000$, and hence $x = \$20,000$. To attain $150,000 in sales revenue, the store should invest $20,000 in advertising. ◆

Verification of the Point-Slope Formula   Let (x, y) be any point on the line passing through the point (x_1, y_1) and having slope m. Then, by equation (1), we have

$$m = \frac{y - y_1}{x - x_1}.$$

Multiplying through by $x - x_1$ gives

$$y - y_1 = m(x - x_1). \qquad (2)$$

Thus every point (x, y) on the line satisfies equation (2). So (2) gives the equation of the line through (x_1, y_1) and having slope m.   ◆

The next property of slope relates the slopes of two perpendicular lines.

Perpendicular Property   When two lines are perpendicular, their slopes are negative reciprocals of one another. That is, if two lines with slopes m and n are perpendicular to one another, then[1]

$$m = -\frac{1}{n}.$$

Conversely, if two lines have slopes that are negative reciprocals of one another, they are perpendicular.

A proof of the perpendicular property is outlined in Exercise 85. Let us show how it can be used to help find equations of lines.

▶ **Example 11**   Find the equation of the line perpendicular to the graph of $y = 2x - 5$ and passing through $(1, 2)$.

Solution   The slope of the graph of $y = 2x - 5$ is 2. By the perpendicular property, the slope of a line perpendicular to it is $-\frac{1}{2}$. If a line has slope $-\frac{1}{2}$ and passes through $(1, 2)$, it has the equation

$$y - 2 = -\tfrac{1}{2}(x - 1) \quad \text{or} \quad y = -\tfrac{1}{2}x + \tfrac{5}{2}$$

(by the point-slope formula).   ◆

The final property of slopes gives the relationship between slopes of parallel lines. A proof is outlined in Exercise 84.

Parallel Property   Parallel lines have the same slope. Conversely, if two lines have the same slope, they are parallel.

▶ **Example 12**   Find the equation of the line through $(2, 0)$ and parallel to the line whose equation is $y = \frac{1}{3}x - 11$.

Solution   The slope of the line having equation $y = \frac{1}{3}x - 11$ is $\frac{1}{3}$. Therefore, any line parallel to it also has slope $\frac{1}{3}$. Thus the desired line passes through $(2, 0)$ and has slope $\frac{1}{3}$, so its equation is

$$y - 0 = \tfrac{1}{3}(x - 2) \quad \text{or} \quad y = \tfrac{1}{3}x - \tfrac{2}{3}.$$ ◆

---

[1]If $n = 0$, this formula does not say anything, since $1/0$ is undefined. However, in this case, one line is horizontal and one is vertical, the vertical one having an undefined slope.

GC Figure 9 shows the perpendicular lines $y = x$ and $y = -x$ drawn on a TI calculator with the windows **ZStandard** and **ZSquare**. With the **ZSquare** window, the lines visually bisect the quadrants and appear perpendicular. Also, with the **ZSquare** window, one unit on the x-axis has the same length as one unit on the y-axis. We say that the **ZSquare** window has "true aspect." In general, a window will approximately exhibit true aspect when $(\textbf{Ymax} - \textbf{Ymin}) \approx \frac{2}{3}(\textbf{Xmax} - \textbf{Xmin})$. Only with true aspect do two lines whose slopes are negative reciprocals of each other actually look perpendicular.

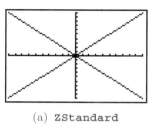

(a) **ZStandard**   (b) **ZSquare**

Figure 9.

Practice Problems 1.4	Suppose that the revenue y from selling x units of a certain commodity is given by the formula $y = 4x$. (Revenue is the amount of money received from the sale of the commodity.)

1. What interpretation can be given to the slope of the graph of this equation?

2. (See Example 6.) Find the coordinates of the point of intersection of $y = 4x$ and $y = 2x + 5000$.

3. What interpretation can be given to the value of the x-coordinate of the point found in Problem 2?

▶ Exercises 1.4

In Exercises 1–4, find the slope of the line having the given equation.

1. $y = \frac{2}{3}x + 7$ 2. $y = -4$

3. $y - 3 = 5(x + 4)$ 4. $7x + 5y = 10$

In Exercises 5–8, plot each pair of points, draw the straight line between them, and find the slope.

5. $(3, 4), (7, 9)$ 6. $(-2, 1), (3, -3)$

7. $(0, 0), (5, 4)$ 8. $(4, 17), (-2, 17)$

9. What is the slope of any line parallel to the y-axis?

10. Why doesn't it make sense to talk about the slope of the line between the two points $(2, 3)$ and $(2, -1)$?

In Exercises 11–14, graph the given linear equation by beginning at the y-intercept, moving 1 unit to the right and m units in the y-direction.

11. $y = -2x + 1$ 12. $y = 4x - 2$

13. $y = 3x$ 14. $y = -2$

In Exercises 15–22, find the equation of line L.

15.
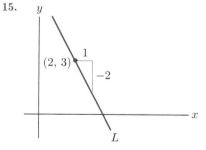

16.
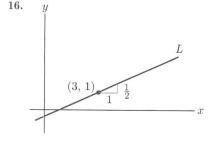

17.

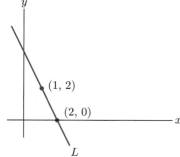

18.

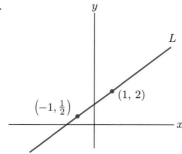

19.

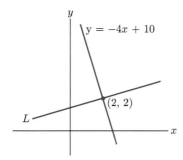

L perpendicular to $y = -4x + 10$

20.

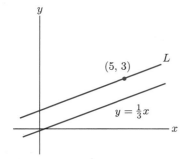

L parallel to $y = \frac{1}{3}x$

21.

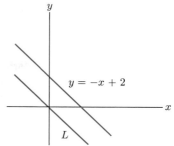

L parallel to $y = -x + 2$

22.

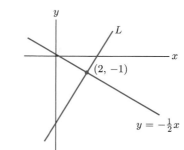

L perpendicular to $y = -\frac{1}{2}x$

23. Find the equation of the line passing through the point $(2, 3)$ and parallel to the x-axis.

24. Find the equation of the line passing through $(0, 0)$ and having slope 1.5.

25. Find the y-intercept of the line passing through the point $(5, 6)$ and having slope $\frac{3}{5}$.

26. Find the slope of the line passing through the point $(1, 4)$ and having y-intercept $(0, 4)$.

27. A salesperson's weekly pay depends on the volume of sales. If she sells x units of goods, then her pay is $y = 5x + 60$ dollars. Give an interpretation to the slope and the y-intercept of this straight line.

28. A manufacturer has fixed costs (such as rent and insurance) of \$2000 per month. The cost of producing each unit of goods is \$4. Give the linear equation for the cost of producing x units per month.

29. Suppose the price that must be set in order to sell q items is given by the equation $p = -3q + 1200$.

   (a) Find and interpret the p-intercept of the graph of the equation.

   (b) Find and interpret the q-intercept of the graph of the equation.

   (c) Find and interpret the slope of the graph of the equation.

   (d) What price must be set in order to sell 350 items?

   (e) What quantity will be sold if the price is \$300?

   (f) Sketch the graph of the equation.

30. Biologists have found that the number of chirps that crickets of a certain species make per minute is related to the temperature. The relationship is very close to linear. At $68°$F those crickets chirp about 124 times a minute. At $80°$F they chirp about 172 times a minute.

    (a) Find the linear equation relating Fahrenheit temperature F and the number of chirps c.

    (b) If you only count chirps for 15 seconds, how can you quickly estimate the temperature?

31. Suppose that the cost of making 20 radios is $6800 and the cost of making 50 radios is $9500.

    (a) Find the cost equation.

    (b) What is the fixed cost?

    (c) What is the marginal cost of production?

    (d) Sketch the graph of the equation.

Exercises 32–34 are related.

32. Suppose that the total cost y of making x coats is given by the formula $y = 40x + 2400$.

    (a) What is the cost of making 100 coats?

    (b) How many coats can be made for $3600?

    (c) Find and interpret the y-intercept of the graph of the equation.

    (d) Find and interpret the slope of the graph of the equation.

33. Suppose that the total revenue y from the sale of x coats is given by the formula $y = 100x$.

    (a) What is the revenue if 300 coats are sold?

    (b) How many coats must be sold to have a revenue of $6000?

    (c) Find and interpret the y-intercept of the graph of the equation.

    (d) Find and interpret the slope of the graph of the equation.

34. Consider a coat factory with the cost and revenue equations given in Exercises 32 and 33.

    (a) Find the equation giving the profit y resulting from making and selling x coats.

    (b) Find and interpret the y-intercept of the graph of the equation.

    (c) Find and interpret the x-intercept of the graph of the equation.

    (d) Find and interpret the slope of the graph of the equation.

    (e) How much profit will be made if 80 coats are sold?

    (f) How many coats must be sold to have a profit of $6000?

    (g) Sketch the graph of the equation found in part (a).

An apartment complex has a storage tank to hold its heating oil. The tank was filled on January 1, but no more deliveries of oil will be made until sometime in March. Let t denote the number of days after January 1 and let y denote the number of gallons of fuel oil in the tank. Current records show that y and t will be related by the equation $y = 30{,}000 - 400t$.

35. Graph the equation $y = 30{,}000 - 400t$.

36. How much oil will be in the tank on February 1?

37. How much oil will be in the tank on February 15?

38. Determine the y-intercept of the graph. Explain its significance.

39. Determine the t-intercept of the graph. Explain its significance.

A corporation receives payment for a large contract on July 1, bringing its cash reserves to $2.3 million. Let y denote its cash reserves (in millions) t days after July 1. The corporation's accountants estimate that y and t will be related by the equation $y = 2.3 - .15t$.

40. Graph the equation $y = 2.3 - .15t$.

41. How much cash does the corporation have on the morning of July 16?

42. Determine the y-intercept of the graph. Explain its significance.

43. Determine the t-intercept of the graph. Explain its significance.

44. Determine the cash reserves on July 4.

45. When will the cash reserves be $.8 million?

In a certain factory, each day the expected number of accidents is related to the number of overtime hours by a linear equation. Suppose that on one day there were 1000 overtime hours logged and 8 accidents reported, and on another day there were 400 overtime hours logged and 5 accidents.

46. Find the equation relating the number of accidents, y, to the number of overtime hours, x.

47. What are the expected number of accidents when no overtime hours are logged?

48. What are the expected number of accidents when 2000 hours of overtime are logged?

49. To what level should the number of overtime hours be restricted if the company feels it cannot tolerate more than 10 accidents a day?

A furniture salesperson earns $160 a week plus 10% commission on her sales. Let x denote her sales and y her income for a week.

50. Express y in terms of x.

51. Determine her week's income if she sells $1000 in merchandise that week.

52. How much must she sell in a week in order to earn $500?

Find the equations of the following lines.

53. Slope is 3; y-intercept is $(0, -1)$

54. Slope is $-\frac{1}{2}$; y-intercept is $(0, 0)$

55. Slope is 1; $(1, 2)$ on line

56. Slope is $-\frac{1}{3}$; $(6, -2)$ on line

57. Slope is -7; $(5, 0)$ on line

58. Slope is $\frac{1}{2}$; $(2, -3)$ on line

59. Slope is 0; $(7, 4)$ on line

60. Slope is $-\frac{2}{5}$; $(0, 5)$ on line

61. $(2, 1)$ and $(4, 2)$ on line

62. $(5, -3)$ and $(-1, 3)$ on line

63. $(0, 0)$ and $(1, -2)$ on line

64. $(2, -1)$ and $(3, -1)$ on line

In each of Exercises 65–68 we specify a line by giving the slope and one point on the line. We give the first coordinate of some points on the line. Without deriving the equation of the line, find the second coordinate of each of the points.

65. Slope is 2, $(1, 3)$ on line; $(2,\ )$; $(0,\ )$; $(-1,\ )$

66. Slope is -3, $(2, 2)$ on line; $(3,\ )$; $(4,\ )$; $(1,\ )$

67. Slope is $-\frac{1}{4}$, $(-1, -1)$ on line; $(0,\ )$; $(1,\ )$; $(-2,\ )$

68. Slope is $\frac{1}{3}$, $(-5, 2)$ on line; $(-4,\ )$; $(-3,\ )$; $(-2,\ )$

69. Each of the lines (A), (B), (C), and (D) in Fig. 10 is the graph of one of the linear equations (a), (b), (c), and (d). Match each line with its equation.

(A)

(B)
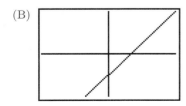

(C)
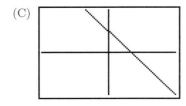

(D)
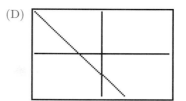

Figure 10.

(a) $x + y = 1$ (b) $x - y = 1$

(c) $x + y = -1$ (d) $x - y = -1$

70. The following table gives several points on the line $\mathbf{Y}_1 = mx + b$. Find m and b.

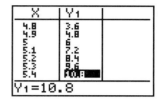

71. Celsius and Fahrenheit temperatures are related by a linear equation. Use the fact that $0°\text{C} = 32°\text{F}$ and $100°\text{C} = 212°\text{F}$ to find an equation.

72. An archaeologist dates a bone fragment discovered at a depth of 4 feet as approximately 1500 B.C. and dates a pottery shard at a depth of 8 feet as approximately 2100 B.C. Assuming there is a linear relationship between depths and dates at this archeological site, find the equation that relates depth to date. How deep should the archaeologist dig to look for relics from 3000 B.C.?

73. The average college tuition and fees at four-year public colleges increased from $2035 in 1990 to $3491 in 1998. Assuming that average tuition and fees increased linearly with respect to time, find the equation that relates the average tuition and fees, y, to the number of years after 1990, x. What were the average tuition and fees in 1994?

74. Two-year college enrollments increased from 4.5 million in 1980 to 5.8 million in 2000. Assuming that enrollments increased linearly with respect to time, find the equation that relates the enrollment, y, to the number of years after 1980, x. When was the enrollment 6 million?

75. Consider a linear equation of the form $y = mx + b$. When the value of b remains fixed and the value of m changes, the graph rotates about the point $(0, b)$. As the value of m increases, will the graph rotate in a clockwise or counterclockwise direction?

76. Write an inequality whose graph consists of the points on or below the straight line passing through the two points $(2, 5)$ and $(4, 9)$.

77. Write an inequality whose graph consists of the points on or above the line with slope 4 and y-intercept $(0, 3)$.

78. Find a system of inequalities having the feasible set in Fig. 11.

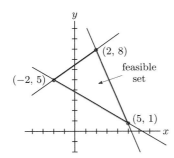

Figure 11.

79. Find a system of inequalities having the feasible set in Fig. 12.

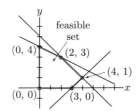

Figure 12.

80. Show that the points $(1, 3)$, $(2, 4)$, and $(3, -1)$ are *not* on the same line.

81. For what value of k will the three points $(1, 5)$, $(2, 7)$, and $(3, k)$ be on the same line?

82. Find the value of a for which the line through the points $(a, 1)$ and $(2, -3.1)$ is parallel to the line through the points $(-1, 0)$ and $(3.8, 2.4)$.

83. Rework Exercise 82, where the word "parallel" is replaced by the word "perpendicular."

84. Prove the parallel property. [*Hint*: If $y = mx + b$ and $y = m'x + b'$ are the equations of two lines, then the two lines have a point in common if and only if the equation $mx + b = m'x + b'$ has a solution x.]

85. Prove the perpendicular property. [*Hint*: Without loss of generality, assume that both lines pass through the origin. Use the point-slope formula, the Pythagorean theorem, and Fig. 13.]

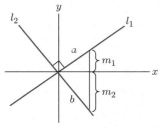

Figure 13.

86. What is the difference between having no slope and zero slope?

87. (PE) Figure 14 gives the cost of shipping a package from coast to coast. What is the cost of shipping a 20-pound package?
(a) $15.00   (b) $15.50   (c) $16.00
(d) $16.50   (e) $17.00

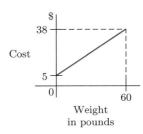

Figure 14.

88. (PE) Figure 15 gives the conversion of temperatures from Centigrade to Fahrenheit. What is the Fahrenheit equivalent of $30°\,$C?
(a) $85°\,$F   (b) $86°\,$F   (c) $87°\,$F
(d) $88°\,$F   (e) $89°\,$F

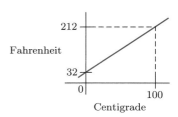

Figure 15.

89. (PE) A company produces a single product for which variable costs are $100 per unit and annual fixed costs are $1,000,000. If the product sells for $130 per unit, how many units must the company produce and sell in order to attain an annual profit of $2,000,000?
(a) 10,000   (b) 15,385   (c) 20,000
(d) 66,667   (e) 100,000

90. (PE) A T-shirt company has fixed costs of $25,000 per year. Each T-shirt costs $8.00 to produce and sells for $12.50. How many T-shirts must the company produce and sell each year in order to make a profit of $65,000?
(a) 9200   (b) 11,250   (c) 14,375
(d) 20,000   (e) 25,556

91. (PE) Suppose the number n of single-use cameras sold each month varies with the price according to the equation $n = 2200 - 25p$. What is the monthly revenue if the price of each camera is $8?

    (a) $200   (b) $2,000   (c) $16,000

    (d) $17,600   (e) $18,000

92. (PE) Suppose the quantity q of a certain brand of mountain bike sold each week depends on price according to the equation $q = 800 - 4p$. What is the total weekly revenue if a bike sells for $150?

    (a) $200   (b) $600   (c) $2000

    (d) $30,000   (e) $80,000

93. (PE) During 1999 a manufacturer produced 50,000 items that sold for $100 each. The manufacturer had fixed costs of $600,000 and made a profit before income taxes of $400,000. In 2000, rent and insurance combined increased by $200,000. Assuming that the quantity produced and all other costs were unchanged, what should the 2000 price be if the manufacturer is to make the same $400,000 profit before income taxes?

    (a) $96   (b) $100   (c) $102   (d) $104   (e) $106

94. (PE) Rework Exercise 93 with a 1999 fixed cost of $800,000 and a profit before income taxes of $300,000.

    (a) $96   (b) $100   (c) $102   (d) $104   (e) $106

Exercises 95–99 require the use of a graphing calculator or a computer.

95. Graph the two lines $y = .5x + 1$ and $y = -2x + 9$ in the standard window $[-10, 10]$ by $[-10, 10]$. Do they appear perpendicular? If not, change the window to one having true aspect, such as $[-15, 15]$ by $[-10, 10]$, and look at the graphs.

96. Graph the three lines $y = 2x - 3$, $y = 2x$, and $y = 2x + 3$ together and then identify each line without using TRACE.

97. Graph the three lines $y = 2x + 1$, $y = x + 1$, and $y = .5x + 1$ together and then identify each line without using TRACE.

98. Graph the line $y = -.5x + 2$ with the window ZDecimal. Without pressing ⎡TRACE⎤, move the cursor to a point on the line. Then move the cursor one unit to the right and down $\frac{1}{2}$ unit to return to the line. If you start at a point on the line and move 2 units to the right, how many units down will you have to move the cursor to return to the line? Test your answer.

99. Repeat Exercise 98 for the line $y = .75x - 2$, using "up" instead of "down" and $\frac{3}{4}$ instead of $\frac{1}{2}$.

Solutions to Practice Problems 1.4

1. By the steepness property, whenever x is increased by 1 unit, the value of y is increased by 4 units. Therefore, *each additional unit of production brings in $4 of revenue.* (The graph of $y = 4x$ is called a *revenue curve* and its slope is called the *marginal revenue of production.*)

2. $\begin{cases} y = 4x \\ y = 2x + 5000 \end{cases}$

    Equate expressions for y:

    $$4x = 2x + 5000$$
    $$2x = 5000$$
    $$x = 2500$$
    $$y = 4(2500) = 10,000.$$

3. When producing 2500 units, the revenue equals the cost. This value of x is called the *break-even point.* Since profit = (revenue) − (cost), the company will make a profit only if its level of production is greater than the break-even point (Fig. 16).

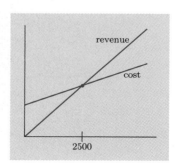

Figure 16.

1.5 The Method of Least Squares

Modern people compile graphs of literally thousands of different quantities: the purchasing value of the dollar as a function of time; the pressure of a fixed volume of air as a function of temperature; the average income of people as a function of their years of formal education; or the incidence of strokes as a function of blood pressure. The observed points on such graphs tend to be irregularly distributed due to the complicated nature of the phenomena underlying them as well as to errors made in observation (for example, a given procedure for measuring average income may not count certain groups). In spite of the imperfect nature of the data, we are often faced with the problem of making assessments and predictions based on them. Roughly speaking, this problem amounts to filtering the sources of errors in the data and isolating the basic underlying trend. Frequently, on the basis of a suspicion or a working hypothesis, we may suspect that the underlying trend is linear—that is, the data should lie on a straight line. But which straight line? This is the problem that the *method of least squares* attempts to answer. To be more specific, let us consider the following problem:

> **Problem** Given observed data points $(x_1, y_1), (x_2, y_2), \ldots, (x_N, y_N)$ in the plane, find the straight line that "best" fits these points.

In order to completely understand the statement of the problem being considered, we must define what it means for a line to "best" fit a set of points. If (x_i, y_i) is one of our observed points, then we will measure how far it is from a given line $y = ax + b$ by the vertical distance, E_i, from the point to the line. (See Fig. 1.)

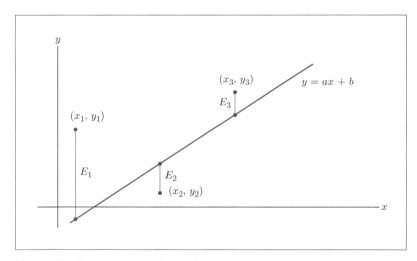

Figure 1. Fitting a line to data points

Statisticians prefer to work with the square of the vertical distance E_i. The total error in approximating the data points $(x_1, y_1), \ldots, (x_N, y_N)$ by the line $y = ax + b$ is usually measured by the sum E of the squares of the vertical distances from the points to the line,

$$E = E_1^2 + E_2^2 + \cdots + E_N^2.$$

E is called the *least-squares error* of the observed points with respect to the line. If all the observed points lie on the line $y = ax + b$, then all the E_i are zero and the error E is zero. If a given observed point is far away from the line, the corresponding E_i^2 is large and hence makes a large contribution to the error E.

▶ Example 1   Determine the least-squares error when the line $y = 1.5x + 3$ is used to approximate the data points $(1, 6)$, $(4, 5)$, and $(6, 14)$.

Solution   Figure 2 shows the line, the points, and the vertical distances. The vertical distance of a point from the line is determined by finding the second coordinate of the point on the line having the same x-coordinate as the point. For instance, for the data point $(1, 6)$, the point on the line with x-coordinate 1 has y-coordinate $y = 1.5(1) + 3 = 4.5$ and therefore vertical distance $6 - 4.5 = 1.5$. Table 1 summarizes the vertical distances. The table shows that the least-squares error is $1.5^2 + 4^2 + 2^2 = 2.25 + 16 + 4 = 22.25$. ◆

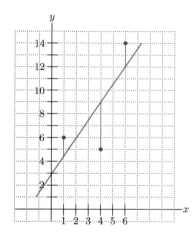

Figure 2.

Table 1	Vertical distances from the line y =1.5x + 3	
Data Point	**Point on Line**	**Vertical Distance**
$(1, 6)$	$(1, 4.5)$	1.5
$(4, 5)$	$(4, 9)$	4
$(6, 14)$	$(6, 12)$	2

In general, we cannot expect to find a line $y = mx + b$ that fits the observed points so well that the error E is zero. Actually, this situation will occur only if the observed points lie on a straight line. However, we can rephrase our original problem as follows:

Problem   Given observed data points $(x_1, y_1), (x_2, y_2), \ldots, (x_N, y_N)$ in the plane, find the straight line $y = mx + b$ for which the error E is as small as possible.

This line, called the *least-squares line* or the *regression line*, can be found from the data points with the formulas

$$m = \frac{N \cdot \sum xy - \sum x \cdot \sum y}{N \cdot \sum x^2 - \left(\sum x\right)^2}$$

$$b = \frac{\sum y - m \cdot \sum x}{N},$$

where

$$\sum x = \text{sum of the } x\text{-coordinates of the data points}$$
$$\sum y = \text{sum of the } y\text{-coordinates of the data points}$$
$$\sum xy = \text{sum of the products of the coordinates of the data points}$$
$$\sum x^2 = \text{sum of the squares of the } x\text{-coordinates of the data points}$$
$$N = \text{number of data points.}$$

That is,

$$\sum x = x_1 + x_2 + \cdots + x_N$$
$$\sum y = y_1 + y_2 + \cdots + y_N$$
$$\sum xy = x_1 \cdot y_1 + x_2 \cdot y_2 + \cdots + x_N \cdot y_N$$
$$\sum x^2 = x_1^2 + x_2^2 + \cdots + x_N^2.$$

▶ **Example 2** Find the least-squares line for the data points of Example 1.

Solution The sums are calculated in Table 2 and then used to determine the values of m and b.

Table 2			
x	y	xy	x^2
1	6	6	1
4	5	20	16
6	14	84	36
$\sum x = 11$	$\sum y = 25$	$\sum xy = 110$	$\sum x^2 = 53$

$$m = \frac{3 \cdot 110 - 11 \cdot 25}{3 \cdot 53 - 11^2} = \frac{55}{38} \approx 1.45$$

$$b = \frac{25 - \frac{55}{38} \cdot 11}{3} = \frac{38 \cdot 25 - 55 \cdot 11}{38 \cdot 3} = \frac{345}{114} = \frac{115}{38} \approx 3.03$$

Therefore, the equation of the least-squares line is $y = \frac{55}{38}x + \frac{115}{38}$. With this line, the least-squares error can be shown to be about 22.13. ◆

Obtaining the Least-Squares Line with Technology Least-squares lines can be obtained with graphing calculators, spreadsheets, or mathematics software. For instance, on the TI-83 graphing calculator screens in Fig. 3, the data points are entered into lists, the least-squares line is calculated with the item **LinReg(ax + b)** of the STAT/CALC menu, and the data points and line are plotted with [STAT PLOT] and GRAPH. The last part of this section contains the details for obtaining least-squares lines with TI-82 and TI-83 graphing calculators. For other graphing calculators, see the guidebook for that particular calculator.

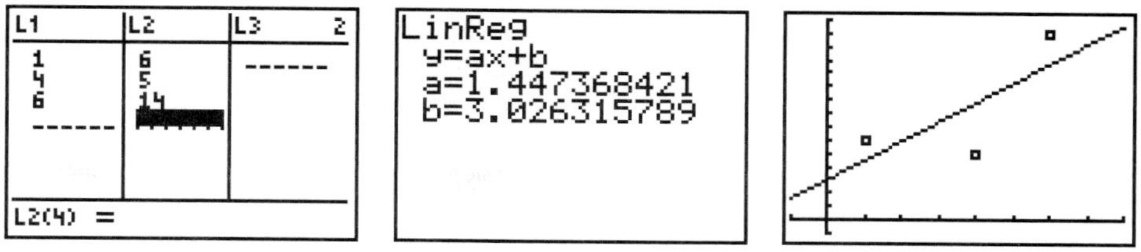

Figure 3. Obtaining a least-squares line with a TI-83.

Spreadsheet programs, such as Excel and Lotus 1-2-3, have special functions that calculate the slope and y-intercept of the least-squares line for a collection of data points. Figure 4 shows how the least-squares line of Example 2 is calculated in Excel. For those familiar with Excel, cell B4 contains the formula **"=SLOPE(B1:B3,A1:A3)"** and cell B5 contains the formula **"=INTERCEPT(B1:B3,A1:A3)"**.

	A	B
1	1	6
2	4	5
3	6	14
4	Slope	1.447368
5	Intercept	3.026316

Figure 4. Using Excel to calculate a least-squares line.

The next example obtains a least-squares line and uses the line to make projections.

▶ **Example 3** Table 3 gives the U.S. per capita health care expenditures[1] for several years.

Table 3	U.S. per Capita Health Care Expenditures				
Year	1993	1994	1995	1996	1997
Dollars	3242	3387	3525	3665	3800

(a) Find the least-squares line for this data.

(b) Use the least-squares line to predict the per capita health care expenditures for the year 2000.

(c) Use the least-squares line to predict when per capita health care expenditures will reach $5000.

Solution (a) The numbers can be made more manageable by counting years beginning with 1993 and measuring dollars in thousands. See Table 4.

Table 4	U.S. per Capita Health Care Expenditures				
Years (after 1993)	0	1	2	3	4
Dollars (in thousands)	3.242	3.387	3.525	3.665	3.800

---

[1] U.S. Health Care Financing Administration, *Health Care Financing Review*, Fall 1998.

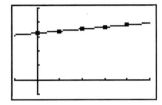

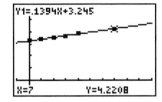

The slope and y-intercept of the least-squares line can be found with the formulas involving sums or with technology. The sums are calculated in Table 5 and then used to determine the values of m and b. The screens in the margin show the results of calculating m and b with a graphing calculator.

Table 5

x	y	xy	x^2
0	3.242	0	0
1	3.387	3.387	1
2	3.525	7.050	4
3	3.665	10.995	9
4	3.800	15.200	16
$\sum x = 10$	$\sum y = 17.619$	$\sum xy = 36.632$	$\sum x^2 = 30$

$$m = \frac{5 \cdot 36.632 - 10 \cdot 17.619}{5 \cdot 30 - 10^2} = \frac{6.97}{50} = .1394$$

$$b = \frac{17.619 - .1394 \cdot 10}{5} = \frac{16.225}{5} = 3.245$$

Therefore, the least-squares line is $y = .1394x + 3.245$.

(b) The year 2000 corresponds to $x = 7$. The value of y is

$$y = .1394(7) + 3.245 = 4.2208.$$

Therefore, an estimate of per capita health care expenditures in the year 2000 is $4220.80.

(c) Set the value of y equal to 5 and solve for x.

$$5 = .1394x + 3.245$$

$$x = \frac{5 - 3.245}{.1394} \approx 12.6$$

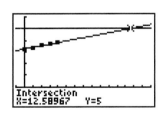

Therefore, expenditures are projected to reach $5000 in 12.6 years after 1993; that is, near the middle of the year 2005. ◆

Obtaining the Least-Squares Line with a TI-82 or TI-83   The following steps find the straight line that minimizes the least-squares error for the points $(1, 4)$, $(2, 5)$, and $(3, 8)$.

1. Press [STAT] **1** to obtain a table used for entering the data.

2. If there are no data in columns labeled $\mathbf{L}_1$ and $\mathbf{L}_2$, proceed to step 4.

3. Move the cursor up to $\mathbf{L}_1$ and press [CLEAR] [ENTER] to delete all data in $\mathbf{L}_1$'s column. Move the cursor right and up to $\mathbf{L}_2$ and press [CLEAR] [ENTER] to delete all data in $\mathbf{L}_2$'s column.

4. If necessary, move the cursor left to the first blank row of the $\mathbf{L}_1$ column. Press **1** [ENTER] **2** [ENTER] **3** [ENTER] to place the x-coordinates of the three points into the $\mathbf{L}_1$ column.

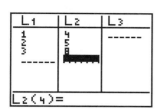

Figure 5.

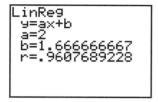

Figure 6.

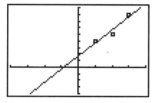

Figure 7.

5. Move the cursor right to the **L₂** column and press **4** [ENTER] **5** [ENTER] **8** [ENTER] to place the y-coordinates of the three points into the **L₂** column. The screen should now appear as in Fig. 5.

6. Press [STAT] [▶] and press the number for **LinReg(ax + b)**.

7. Press [ENTER]. The TI-82 screen should now appear as in Fig. 6. The TI-83 screen normally is missing the last line. (*Note*: The number r is called the *correlation coefficient* and is a measure of the degree of linear association between the two variables. If the absolute value of r is close to 1, then there is a high degree of linear association. To have the value of r appear with a TI-83, create a blank line on the home screen, press [2nd] [CATALOG], select DiagnosticOn, and press [ENTER] twice.) The least-squares line is $y = 2x + \frac{5}{3}$. (*Note*: $\frac{5}{3} \approx 1.666666667$.)

8. If desired, the linear function can be assigned to **Y₁** with the following steps:
   (a) Press [Y=] [CLEAR] to erase the current expression in **Y₁**.
   (b) Press [VARS] **5** [▶] [▶] and the number for **RegEQ** to assign the linear function to **Y₁**.

9. The original points can be easily plotted along with the least-squares line. Assume that the linear function has been assigned to **Y₁**, that all other functions have been cleared or deselected, and that the window has been set to $[-4, 4]$ *by* $[-4, 9]$. Press [2nd] [STAT PLOT] [ENTER] [ENTER] [GRAPH] to see the display in Fig. 7. (*Note 1*: To turn off the point-plotting feature, press [2nd] [STAT PLOT] [ENTER] [▶] [ENTER]. *Note 2*: With the TI-83, the point-plotting feature can be toggled from the function-declaration screen by moving the cursor to the word **"Plot1"** on the top line and pressing [ENTER].)

Practice Problems **1.5**	**1.** Can a vertical distance be negative?
	2. Under what condition will a vertical distance be zero?

▶ Exercises 1.5

1. Suppose the line $y = 3x + 1$ is used to fit the four data points in Table 6. Complete the table and determine the least-squares error E.

2. Suppose the line $y = -2x + 12$ is used to fit the four data points in Table 7. Complete the table and determine the least-squares error E.

Table 6

Data Point	Point on Line	Vertical Distance
$(1, 3)$		
$(2, 6)$		
$(3, 11)$		
$(4, 12)$		

Table 7

Data Point	Point on Line	Vertical Distance
$(1, 11)$		
$(2, 7)$		
$(3, 5)$		
$(4, 5)$		

3. Find the least-squares error E for the least-squares line fit to the four points in Fig. 8.

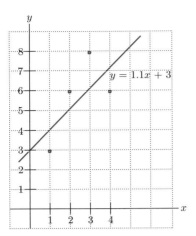

Figure 8.

4. Find the least-squares error E for the least-squares line fit to the five points in Fig. 9.

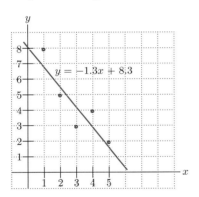

Figure 9.

5. Complete Table 8 and find the values of m and b for the straight line that provides the best least-squares fit to the data.

Table 8			
x	y	xy	x^2
1	7		
2	6		
3	4		
4	3		
$\sum x =$	$\sum y =$	$\sum xy =$	$\sum x^2 =$

6. Complete Table 9 and find the values of m and b for the straight line that provides the best least-squares fit to the data.

Table 9			
x	y	xy	x^2
1	2		
2	4		
3	7		
4	9		
5	12		
$\sum x =$	$\sum y =$	$\sum xy =$	$\sum x^2 =$

7. Consider the data points $(1, 2)$, $(2, 5)$, and $(3, 11)$. Find the straight line that provides the best least-squares fit to these data.

8. Consider the data points $(1, 8)$, $(2, 4)$, and $(4, 3)$. Find the straight line that provides the best least-squares fit to these data.

9. Consider the data points $(1, 9)$, $(2, 8)$, $(3, 6)$, and $(4, 3)$. Find the straight line that provides the best least-squares fit to these data.

10. Consider the data points $(1, 5)$, $(2, 7)$, $(3, 6)$, and $(4, 10)$. Find the straight line that provides the best least-squares fit to these data.

Since Exercises 11–16 use real data, they are best answered with a graphing calculator or spreadsheet.

11. The following table[2] gives the crude male death rate for lung cancer in 1950 and the per capita consumption of cigarettes in 1930 in various countries.
    (a) Use the method of least-squares to obtain the straight line that best fits these data.
    (b) In 1930 the per capita cigarette consumption in Finland was 1100. Use the straight line found in part (a) to estimate the male lung cancer death rate in Finland in 1950.

[2]These data were obtained from *Smoking and Health*, Report of the Advisory Committee to the Surgeon General of the Public Health Service, U.S. Department of Health, Education, and Welfare, Washington, D.C., Public Health Service Publication No. 1103, p. 176.

Country	Cigarette Consumption (per Capita)	Lung Cancer Deaths (per Million Males)
Norway	250	95
Sweden	300	120
Denmark	350	165
Australia	470	170

Year	Percent
1975	13.9
1980	16.2
1985	19.4
1990	21.3
1995	20.0
1998	24.4

12. The accompanying table shows the 1994 price of a gallon (in U.S. dollars) of fuel and the average miles driven per automobile for several countries.[3]

   (a) Find the straight line that provides the best least-squares fit to these data.

   (b) In 1994, the price of gas in Japan was $4.14 per gallon. Use the straight line of part (a) to estimate the average number of miles automobiles were driven in Japan.

Country	Price per Gallon	Average Miles per Auto
Canada	$1.57	10,371
England	$2.86	10,186
France	$3.31	8740
Germany	$3.34	7674
Sweden	$3.44	7456
United States	$1.24	11,099

13. The following table gives the percent of persons 25 years and over who have completed four or more years of college.[4]

   (a) Use the method of least squares to obtain the straight line that best fits these data.

   (b) Estimate the percent for the year 1993.

   (c) If the trend determined by the straight line in part (a) continues, when will the percent reach 27?

14. The following table gives the number (in millions) of cars in use in the United States[5] for certain years.

Year	Cars
1980	104.6
1985	114.7
1990	123.3
1991	123.3
1992	120.3
1993	121.1
1994	122.0
1995	123.2

   (a) Use the method of least squares to obtain the straight line that best fits these data.

   (b) Estimate the number of cars in use in 1983.

   (c) If the trend determined by the straight line in part (a) continues, when will the number of cars in use reach 130 million?

15. The following table gives the 2000 life expectancy at birth for several countries.[6]

Country	Men	Women
Finland	74.0	81.13
United States	73.0	79.8
Australia	77.5	83.5
Japan	77.13	83.45

---

[3]Source: Energy Information Administration, *International Energy Annual*. U.S. Highway Administration, *Highway Statistics*, 1994.
[4]U.S. Bureau of the Census.
[5]American Automobile Manufacturers Association, Inc., Detroit, MI. *Motor Vehicle Facts and Figures*.
[6]U.S. Bureau of the Census, International Database.

(a) Use the method of least squares to obtain the straight line that best fits these data.

(b) In Switzerland the life expectancy for men is 76 years. Use the least-squares line to estimate the life expectancy for women.

(c) In Denmark the life expectancy for women is 79.5 years. Use the least-squares line to estimate the life expectancy for men.

16. Two Harvard economists studied countries' relationships between the independence of banks and inflation rates from 1955 to 1990.[7] The independence of banks was rated on a scale of -1.5 to 2.5, with -1.5, 0, and 2.5 corresponding to least, average, and most independence, respectively. The following table gives the values for various countries.

Country	Independence Rating	Inflation Rate (%)
New Zealand	-1.4	7.6
Italy	$-.75$	7.2
Belgium	.3	4.0
France	.4	6.0
Canada	.9	4.5
United States	1.6	4.0
Switzerland	2.2	3.1

(a) Use the method of least squares to obtain the straight line that best fits these data.

(b) What relationship between independence of banks and inflation is indicated by the least-squares line?

(c) Japan has a .6 independence rating. Use the least-squares line to estimate Japan's inflation rate.

(d) The inflation rate for Britain is 6.8. Use the least-squares line to estimate Britain's independence rating.

17. Suppose you have found the line of best least-squares fit to a collection of points and that you edit the data by adding a point on the line to the data. Will the expanded data have the same least-squares line? Explain the rationale for your conclusion, and then experiment to test whether your conclusion is correct.

18. Find the best least-squares fit to the points $(5, 4)$ and $(7, 3)$. Show that it is the straight line through the two points.

Solutions to Practice Problems 1.5

1. No. The word "distance" implies a nonnegative number. It is the absolute value of the difference between the y-coordinate of the data point and the y-coordinate of the point on the line.

2. The vertical distance will be zero when the point actually lies on the least-squares line.

▶ Chapter 1 Summary

1. Cartesian coordinate systems associate a number with each point of a line and associate a pair of numbers with each point of a plane.

2. The collection of points in the plane that satisfy the linear equation $ax + by = c$ (where a and b are not both zero) lies on a straight line. After this equation is put into one of the standard forms $y = mx + b$ or $x = a$, the graph can be easily drawn.

3. The direction of the inequality sign in an inequality is unchanged when a number is added to or subtracted

from both sides of the inequality, or when both sides of the inequality are multiplied by the same positive number. The direction of the inequality sign is reversed when both sides of the inequality are multiplied by the same negative number.

4. The collection of points in the plane that satisfy the linear inequality $ax + by \leq c$ or $ax + by \geq c$ consists of all points on and to one side of the graph of the corresponding linear equation. After this inequality is put

---

[7] J. Bradford DeLong (Harvard) and L. H. Summers (World Bank).

into standard form, the graph can be easily pictured by crossing out the half-plane consisting of the points that do not satisfy the inequality.

5. The feasible set of a system of linear inequalities (that is, the collection of points that satisfy all the inequalities) is best obtained by crossing out the points not satisfied by each inequality.

6. The point of intersection of a pair of lines can be obtained by first converting the equations to standard form and then either equating the two expressions for y or substituting the value of x from the form $x = a$ into the other equation.

7. The slope of the line $y = mx + b$ is the number m. It is also the ratio of the difference between the y-coordinates and the difference between the x-coordinates of any pair of points on the line.

8. The steepness property states that if we start at any point on a line of slope m and move 1 unit to the right, then we must move m units vertically to return to the line.

9. The point-slope formula states that the line of slope m passing through the point (x_1, y_1) has the equation $y - y_1 = m(x - x_1)$.

10. Two lines are parallel if and only if they have the same slope. Two lines are perpendicular if and only if the product of their slopes is -1.

11. The method of least squares finds the straight line that gives the best fit to a collection of points in the sense that the sum of the squares of the vertical distances from the points to the line is as small as possible. The slope and y-intercept of the least-squares line are usually found with formulas involving sums of coordinates or by using a graphing calculator.

Review of Fundamental Concepts of Chapter 1

1. How do you determine the coordinates of a point in the plane?
2. What is meant by the graph of an equation in x and y?
3. What is the general form of a linear equation in x and y?
4. What is the standard form of a linear equation in x and y?
5. What is the y-intercept of a line? How do you find the y-intercept from an equation of a line?
6. What is the x-intercept of a line? How do you find the x-intercept from an equation of a line?
7. Give a method for graphing the equation $y = mx + b$.
8. State the inequality properties for addition, subtraction, and multiplication.
9. What are the general and standard forms of a linear inequality in x and y?
10. Explain how to obtain the graph of a linear inequality.
11. What is meant by the *feasible set* of a system of linear inequalities?
12. Describe how to obtain the point of intersection of two lines.
13. Define the slope of a line, and give a physical description.
14. Suppose you know the slope and the coordinates of a point on a line. How could you draw the line without first finding its equation?
15. What is the point-slope form of the equation of a line?
16. Describe how to find the equation for a line when you know the coordinates of two points on the line.
17. What can you say about the slopes of perpendicular lines?
18. What can you say about the slopes of parallel lines?
19. What is the least-squares line approximation to a set of data points?

▶ Chapter 1 Supplementary Exercises

1. What is the equation of the y-axis?
2. Graph the linear equation $y = -\frac{1}{2}x$.
3. Find the point of intersection of the pair of straight lines $x - 5y = 6$ and $3x = 6$.
4. Find the slope of the line having the equation $3x - 4y = 8$.
5. Find the equation of the line having y-intercept $(0, 5)$ and x-intercept $(10, 0)$.
6. Graph the linear inequality $x - 3y \geq 12$.
7. Does the point $(1, 2)$ satisfy the linear inequality $3x + 4y \geq 11$?
8. Find the point of intersection of the pair of straight lines $2x - y = 1$ and $x + 2y = 13$.
9. Find the equation of the straight line passing through the point $(15, 16)$ and parallel to the line $2x - 10y = 7$.

10. Find the y-coordinate of the point having x-coordinate 1 and lying on the line $y = 3x + 7$.

11. Find the x-intercept of the straight line with equation $x = 5$.

12. Graph the linear inequality $y \le 6$.

13. Solve the following system of linear equations:

$$\begin{cases} 3x - 2y = 1 \\ 2x + y = 24. \end{cases}$$

14. Graph the feasible set for the following system of inequalities:

$$\begin{cases} 2y + 7x \ge 30 \\ 4y - x \ge 0 \\ y \le 8. \end{cases}$$

15. Find the y-intercept of the line passing through the point $(4, 9)$ and having slope $\frac{1}{2}$.

16. The fee charged by a local moving company depends on the amount of time required for the move. If t hours are required, then the fee is $y = 35t + 20$ dollars. Give an interpretation of the slope and y-intercept of this line.

17. Are the points $(1, 2)$, $(2, 0)$, and $(3, 1)$ on the same line?

18. Write an equation of the line with x-intercept $(3, 0)$ and y-intercept $(0, -2)$.

19. (PE) If $x + 7y = 30$ and $x = -2y$, then y equals
    (a) -12 (b) 12 (c) 30/9 (d) 6 (e) -6

20. Write the inequality whose graph is the half-plane below the line with slope $\frac{2}{3}$ and y-intercept $\left(0, \frac{3}{2}\right)$.

21. Write the inequality whose graph is the half-plane above the line through $(2, -1)$ and $(6, 8.6)$.

22. Solve the system of linear equations

$$\begin{cases} 1.2x + 2.4y = .6 \\ 4.8y - 1.6x = 2.4. \end{cases}$$

23. Find the equation of the line through $(1, 1)$ and the intersection point of the lines $y = -x + 1$ and $y = 2x + 3$.

24. Find all numbers x such that $2x + 3(x - 2) \ge 0$.

25. Graph the equation $x + \frac{1}{2}y = 4$, and give the slope and both intercepts.

26. Do the three graphs of the linear equations $2x - 3y = 1$, $5x + 2y = 0$, and $x + y = 1$ contain a common point?

27. Show that the lines with equations $2x - 3y = 1$ and $3x + 2y = 4$ are perpendicular.

28. Each of the half-planes (A), (B), (C), and (D) is the graph of one of the linear inequalities (a), (b), (c) and (d). Match each half-plane with its inequality.

(A)

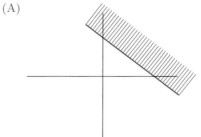

(B)

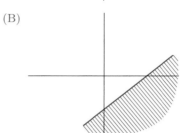

(C)

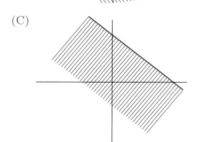

(D)

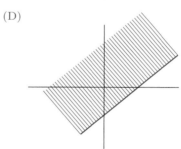

(a) $x + y \ge 1$ (b) $x + y \le 1$

(c) $x - y \le 1$ (d) $y - x \le -1$

29. Each of the lines L_1, L_2, and L_3 in Fig. 1 is the graph of one of the equations (a), (b), and (c). Match each of the following equations with its corresponding line.

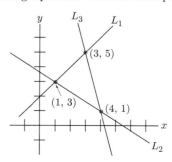

Figure 1.

(a) $4x + y = 17$

(b) $y = x + 2$

(c) $2x + 3y = 11$

30. Find a system of inequalities having the feasible set in Fig. 2 and find the coordinates of the unspecified vertex. [*Note:* There is a right angle at the vertex $\left(4, \frac{3}{2}\right)$.]

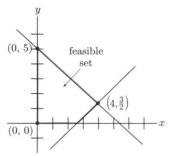

Figure 2.

31. Consider the following four equations

$$p = .01q - 5$$
$$p = .005q + .5$$
$$p = -.01q - 10$$
$$p = -.01q + 5.$$

One is the equation of a supply curve and another is the equation of a demand curve. Identify the two equations and then find the intersection point of those two curves.

32. Find the vertices of the following feasible set.

$$\begin{cases} x \geq 0 \\ y \geq 0 \\ 5x + y \leq 50 \\ 2x + 3y \leq 33 \\ x - 2y \geq -8 \end{cases}$$

33. It is not possible to draw a straight line through all three of the points $(2, 4)$, $(5, 8)$, and $(7, 9)$. However, it *is* possible for a straight line to *miss* all three points by the same amount; that is, there is a line that makes the vertical distances d_1, d_2, and d_3 in Fig. 3 equal. Find the equation of this line. [*Hint:* Let the equation of the line be $y = mx + b$. Then the point P has coordinates $(2, 2m + b)$.]

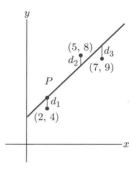

Figure 3.

34. For a certain manufacturer, the production and sale of each additional unit yields an additional profit of $10. The sale of 1000 units yields a profit of $4000.

(a) Find the profit equation.

(b) Find the y- and x-intercepts of the graph of the profit equation.

(c) Sketch the graph of the profit equation.

35. One-day car rentals cost $50 plus 10 cents per mile from company A and $40 plus 20 cents per mile from company B.

(a) For each company, give the linear equations for the cost, y, when x miles are driven.

(b) Which company offers the best value when the car is driven for 80 miles?

(c) Which company offers the best value when the car is driven for 160 miles?

(d) For what mileage do the two companies offer the same value?

36. (*Linear Depreciation*) For accounting purposes, the value of certain items is depreciated linearly over time from the purchase price to the salvage value. Suppose that a computer was purchased in 1986 for $5000 and sold in 1994 for $1000.

(a) Find the linear equation giving its value, y, after x years.

(b) How much was the computer worth in 1990?

(c) When was the computer valued at $2000?

37. Graph the linear inequality $x \leq 3y + 2$.

38. A furniture store offers its new employees a weekly salary of $200 plus a 3% commission on sales. After one year, employees receive $100 per week plus a 5% sales commission. For what weekly sales level will the two scales produce the same salary?

39. Find a system of linear inequalities having the feasible set of Fig. 4.

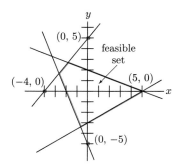

Figure 4.

40. Find a system of linear inequalities having the feasible set of Fig. 5.

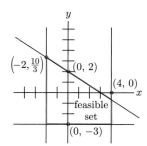

Figure 5.

41. Students entering college in 1999 expressed the greatest interest in elementary and secondary teaching careers in 30 years. The following table gives the percent of college freshmen in 1995 through 1999 who said that their probable career choice would be in elementary or secondary education.[8]

(a) Use the method of least squares to obtain the straight line that best fits these data.

(b) Estimate the percentage of students who entered college in 2000 whose probable career was in elementary or secondary education.

(c) If the trend continues, when will 12% of freshmen have elementary or secondary education as their probable career choice?

Year	Percent
1995	9.7
1996	10.2
1997	9.7
1998	10.6
1999	11.2

42. The following table[9] gives the (age-adjusted) death rate per 100,000 women from breast cancer and the daily dietary fat intake (in grams per day) for various countries.

Country	Fat Intake	Death Rate
Japan	41	4
Poland	90	10
Finland	118	13
United States	148	21

(a) Use the method of least squares to obtain the straight line that best fits these data.

(b) In Denmark women consume an average of 160 grams of fat per day. Use the least-squares line to estimate the breast cancer death rate.

(c) In New Zealand the breast cancer death rate is 22 women per 100,000. Use the least-squares line to estimate the daily fat intake in New Zealand.

▶ Chapter 1 Chapter Test

1. Graph the linear equation $y = 3x$.

2. Find the y-coordinate of the point having x-coordinate $\frac{1}{2}$ and lying on the line $y = -2x + 6$.

3. Find the equation of the line through the point $(-1, 3)$ and parallel to the line $y = -2x + 6$.

4. Solve the system of linear equations

$$\begin{cases} 2x - 3y = 9 \\ -3x + 7y = -11. \end{cases}$$

5. Show that the lines $3x - y = 1$ and $-\frac{1}{3}x - 4 = y$ are perpendicular.

6. Graph the inequality $x + y \geq 8$ in the plane.

[8] *The American Freshman: National Norms*; American Council on Education, University of California–Los Angeles.
[9] B. S. Reddy et al., "Nutrition and Its Relationship to Cancer," *Advances in Cancer Research* 32:237, 1980.

7. Find the equation of the line of slope 2 that passes through the intersection point of the lines $4x + 5y = 11$ and $2x - 3y = 7$.

8. Find the coordinates of the vertices of the feasible set for the following system of inequalities.

$$\begin{cases} x + y \geq 16 \\ -2x + y \leq 10 \\ 3x + y \leq 75 \\ x \geq 0, \ y \geq 0 \end{cases}$$

9. Fred sells carpeting. He earns $200 each week plus 5% commission on sales. His sister thinks she has a better job selling carpet because she earns $250 a week plus 3% commission on her sales. For what volume of sales is Fred's sister correct? When is she incorrect?

Chapter Project

Break-Even Analysis

We discussed linear demand curves in Section 1.3. Demand curves normally apply to an entire industry or to a monopolist; that is, a manufacturer that is so large that the quantity it supplies affects the market price of the commodity. We discussed linear cost curves and break-even analysis in Section 1.4. In this chapter project we combine demand curves and cost curves with least-squares lines to extend break-even analysis to a monopolist.

1. Table 1 can be used to obtain the demand curve for a monopolist who manufactures and sells a unique type of camera. The first column gives several production quantities in thousands of cameras and the second column gives the corresponding prices per camera. For instance, in order to sell 200 thousand cameras, the manufacturer must set the price at $79 per camera. Find the least-squares line that best fits these data; that is, find a demand curve for the camera.

Table 1	
q (thousands)	p (dollars)
100	90
200	79
300	72
400	59
500	50

2. Use the demand curve from part 1 to estimate the price that must be charged in order to sell 350 thousand cameras. Calculate the revenue for this price and quantity. (*Note:* The revenue is the amount of money received from the sale of the cameras.)

3. Use the demand curve to estimate the quantity that can be sold if the price is $75 per camera. Calculate the revenue for this price and quantity.

4. Determine the expression that gives the revenue from producing and selling q thousand cameras. (*Note:* The number of cameras sold will be $1000q$.)

5. Assuming that the manufacturer has fixed costs of $8,000,000 and that the variable cost of producing each thousand cameras is $25,000, find the equation of the cost curve.

6. Graph the revenue curve from part 4 and the cost curve from part 5 on a graphing calculator and determine the two points of intersection.

7. What is the break-even point; that is, the lowest value of q for which cost equals revenue?

8. For what values of q will the company make a profit?

C H A P T E R

Matrices

2

We begin this chapter by developing a method for solving systems of linear equations in any number of variables. Our discussion of this method will lead naturally into the study of mathematical objects called *matrices*. The arithmetic and applications of matrices are the main topics of the chapter. We discuss in detail the application of matrix arithmetic to input–output analysis, which can be (and is) used to make production decisions for large businesses and entire economies.

2.1 Solving Systems of Linear Equations, I

In Chapter 1 we presented a method for solving systems of linear equations in two variables. The method of Chapter 1 is very efficient for determining the solutions. Unfortunately, it works only for systems of linear equations having *two* variables. In many applications we meet systems having more than two variables, as the following example illustrates.

▶ Example 1   The Upside Down company specializes in making down jackets, ski vests, and comforters. The requirements for down and labor and the profits earned are given in the following chart.

	Down (pounds)	Time (labor-hours)	Profit ($)
Jacket	3	2	6
Vest	2	1	6
Comforter	4	1	2

Each week the company has available 600 pounds of down and 275 labor-hours. It wants to earn a weekly profit of $1150. How many of each item should the company make each week?

Solution   The requirements and earnings can be expressed by a system of equations. Let x be the number of jackets, y the number of vests, and z the number of comforters. If 600 pounds of down are used, then

$$[\text{down in jackets}] + [\text{down in vests}] + [\text{down in comforters}] = 600$$
$$3\,[\text{no. jackets}] \ + \ 2\,[\text{no. vests}] \ + \ 4\,[\text{no. comforters}] \ = 600.$$

That is,

$$3x + 2y + 4z = 600.$$

Similarly, the equation for labor is

$$2x + y + z = 275,$$

and the equation for the profit is

$$6x + 6y + 2z = 1150.$$

The numbers x, y, and z must simultaneously satisfy a system of three linear equations in three variables.

$$\begin{cases} 3x + 2y + 4z = \ \ 600 \\ 2x + \ y + \ z = \ \ 275 \\ 6x + 6y + 2z = 1150 \end{cases} \tag{1}$$

Later we present a method for determining the solution to this system. This method yields the solution $x = 50$, $y = 125$, and $z = 50$. It is easy to confirm that these values of x, y, and z satisfy all three equations:

$$3(50) + 2(125) + 4(50) = \ \ 600$$
$$2(50) + \ (125) + \ (50) = \ \ 275$$
$$6(50) + 6(125) + 2(50) = 1150.$$

Thus, the Upside Down company can make a profit of \$1150 by producing 50 jackets, 125 vests, and 50 comforters.   ◆

In this section we develop a step-by-step procedure for solving systems of linear equations such as (1). The procedure, called the *Gaussian elimination method*, consists of repeatedly simplifying the system, using so-called elementary row operations, until the solution stares us in the face!

In the system of linear equations (1) the equations have been written in such a way that the x-terms, the y-terms, and the z-terms lie in different columns. We shall always be careful to display systems of equations with separate columns for each variable. One of the key ideas of the Gaussian elimination method is to think of the solution as a system of linear equations in its own right. For example, we can write the solution of system (1) as

$$\begin{cases} x \qquad\quad = \ 50 \\ \quad\ y \quad\ = 125 \\ \qquad\ z = \ \ 50. \end{cases} \tag{2}$$

This is just a system of linear equations in which the coefficients of most terms are zero! Since the only terms with nonzero coefficients are arranged on a diagonal, such a system is said to be in *diagonal form*.

Our method for solving a system of linear equations consists of repeatedly using three operations that alter the system but do not change the solutions. The operations are used to transform the system into a system in diagonal form. Since the operations involve only elementary arithmetic and are applied to entire equations (i.e., rows of the system), they are called *elementary row operations.* Let us begin our study of the Gaussian elimination method by introducing these operations.

> **Elementary Row Operation 1**   Rearrange the equations in any order.

This operation is harmless enough. It certainly does not change the solutions of the system.

> **Elementary Row Operation 2**   Multiply an equation by a nonzero number.

For example, if we are given the system of linear equations

$$\begin{cases} 2x - 3y + 4z = 11 \\ 4x - 19y + z = 31 \\ 5x + 7y - z = 12, \end{cases}$$

then we may replace it by a new system obtained by leaving the last two equations unchanged and multiplying the first equation by 3. To accomplish this, multiply each term of the first equation by 3. The transformed system is

$$\begin{cases} 6x - 9y + 12z = 33 \\ 4x - 19y + z = 31 \\ 5x + 7y - z = 12. \end{cases}$$

The operation of multiplying an equation by a nonzero number does not change the solutions of the system. For if a particular set of values of the variables satisfies the original equation, it satisfies the resulting equation, and vice versa.

Elementary row operation 2 may be used to make the coefficient of a particular variable 1.

▶ **Example 2**   Replace the system

$$\begin{cases} -5x + 10y + 20z = 4 \\ x \qquad\quad - 12z = 1 \\ x + y + z = 0 \end{cases}$$

by an equivalent system in which the coefficient of x in the first equation is 1.

Solution   The coefficient of x in the first equation is -5, so we use elementary row operation 2 to multiply the first equation by $-\frac{1}{5}$. Multiplying each term of the first equation by $-\frac{1}{5}$ gives

$$\begin{cases} x - 2y - 4z = -\frac{4}{5} \\ x \qquad\quad - 12z = 1 \\ x + y + z = 0. \end{cases}$$

◆

Another operation that can be performed on a system without changing its solutions is to replace one equation by its sum with some other equation. For example, consider this system of equations:

$$A: \begin{cases} x + y - 2z = 3 \\ x + 2y - 5z = 4 \\ 5x + 8y - 18z = 14. \end{cases}$$

We can replace the second equation by the sum of the first and the second. Since

$$\begin{array}{r} x + y - 2z = 3 \\ + \quad x + 2y - 5z = 4 \\ \hline 2x + 3y - 7z = 7, \end{array}$$

the resulting system is

$$B: \begin{cases} x + y - 2z = 3 \\ 2x + 3y - 7z = 7 \\ 5x + 8y - 18z = 14. \end{cases}$$

If a particular choice of x, y, and z satisfies system A, it also satisfies system B. This is because system B results from adding equations. Similarly, system A can be derived from system B by subtracting equations. So any particular solution of system A is a solution of system B, and vice versa.

The operation of adding equations is usually used in conjunction with elementary row operation 2. That is, an equation is changed by adding to it a nonzero multiple of another equation. For example, consider the system

$$\begin{cases} x + y - 2z = 3 \\ x + 2y - 5z = 4 \\ 5x + 8y - 18z = 14. \end{cases}$$

Let us change the second equation by adding to it twice the first. Since

$$\begin{array}{ll} 2(\text{first}) & 2x + 2y - 4z = 6 \\ + \ (\text{second}) & \underline{x + 2y - 5z = 4} \\ & 3x + 4y - 9z = 10, \end{array}$$

the new second equation is

$$3x + 4y - 9z = 10$$

and the transformed system is

$$\begin{cases} x + y - 2z = 3 \\ 3x + 4y - 9z = 10 \\ 5x + 8y - 18z = 14. \end{cases}$$

Since addition of equations and elementary row operation 2 are often used together, let us define a third elementary row operation.

Elementary Row Operation 3   Change an equation by adding to it a multiple of another equation.

For reference, let us summarize the elementary row operations we have just defined.

Elementary Row Operations

1. Rearrange the equations in any order.

2. Multiply an equation by a nonzero number.

3. Change an equation by adding to it a multiple of another equation.

The idea of the Gaussian elimination method is to transform an arbitrary system of linear equations into diagonal form by repeated applications of the three elementary row operations. To see how the method works, consider the following example.

▶ **Example 3** Solve the following system by the Gaussian elimination method:

$$\begin{cases} x - 3y = 7 \\ -3x + 4y = -1. \end{cases}$$

Solution Let us transform this system into diagonal form by examining one column at a time, starting from the left. Examine the first column:

$$x$$
$$-3x$$

The coefficient of the top x is 1, which is exactly what it should be for the system to be in diagonal form. So we do nothing to this term. Now examine the next term in the column, $-3x$. In diagonal form this term must be absent. In order to accomplish this, we add a multiple of the first equation to the second. Since the coefficient of x in the second is -3, we add three times the first equation to the second equation in order to cancel the x-term. (Abbreviation: $[2] + 3[1]$. The $[2]$ means that we are changing equation 2. The expression $[2] + 3[1]$ means that we are replacing equation 2 by the original equation plus three times equation 1.)

$$\begin{cases} x - 3y = 7 \\ -3x + 4y = -1 \end{cases} \xrightarrow{\;[2]+3[1]\;} \begin{cases} x - 3y = 7 \\ -5y = 20 \end{cases}$$

The first column now has the proper form, so we proceed to the second column. In diagonal form that column will have one nonzero term, namely the second, and the coefficient of y in that term must be 1. To bring this about, multiply the second equation by $-\frac{1}{5}$ (abbreviation: $-\frac{1}{5}[2]$):

$$\begin{cases} x - 3y = 7 \\ -5y = 20 \end{cases} \xrightarrow{\;-\frac{1}{5}[2]\;} \begin{cases} x - 3y = 7 \\ y = -4. \end{cases}$$

The second column still does not have the correct form. We must get rid of the $-3y$-term in the first equation. We do this by adding a multiple of the second equation to the first. Since the coefficient of the term to be canceled is -3, we add three times the second equation to the first:

$$\begin{cases} x - 3y = 7 \\ y = -4 \end{cases} \xrightarrow{\;[1]+3[2]\;} \begin{cases} x = -5 \\ y = -4. \end{cases}$$

The system is now in diagonal form and the solution can be read off: $x = -5$, $y = -4$. ◆

▶ Example 4　Use the Gaussian elimination method to solve the system

$$\begin{cases} 2x - 6y = -8 \\ -5x + 13y = 1. \end{cases}$$

Solution　We can perform the calculations in a mechanical way, proceeding column by column from the left:

$$\begin{cases} 2x - 6y = -8 \\ -5x + 13y = 1 \end{cases} \xrightarrow{\frac{1}{2}[1]} \begin{cases} x - 3y = -4 \\ -5x + 13y = 1 \end{cases}$$

$$\xrightarrow{[2] + 5[1]} \begin{cases} x - 3y = -4 \\ -2y = -19 \end{cases}$$

$$\xrightarrow{-\frac{1}{2}[2]} \begin{cases} x - 3y = -4 \\ y = \frac{19}{2} \end{cases}$$

$$\xrightarrow{[1] + 3[2]} \begin{cases} x = \frac{49}{2} \\ y = \frac{19}{2}. \end{cases}$$

So the solution of the system is $x = \frac{49}{2}$, $y = \frac{19}{2}$.　◆

The calculation becomes easier to follow if we omit writing down the variables at each stage and work only with the coefficients. At each stage of the computation, the system is represented by a rectangular array of numbers. For instance, the original system is written[1]

$$\left[\begin{array}{cc|c} 2 & -6 & -8 \\ -5 & 13 & 1 \end{array}\right].$$

The elementary row operations are performed on the rows of this rectangular array just as if the variables were there. So, for example, the first step in the above is to multiply the first equation by $\frac{1}{2}$. This corresponds to multiplying the first row of the array by $\frac{1}{2}$ to get

$$\left[\begin{array}{cc|c} 1 & -3 & -4 \\ -5 & 13 & 1 \end{array}\right].$$

The diagonal form just corresponds to the array

$$\left[\begin{array}{cc|c} 1 & 0 & \frac{49}{2} \\ 0 & 1 & \frac{19}{2} \end{array}\right].$$

Note that this array has ones down the diagonal and zeros everywhere else on the left. The solution of the system appears on the right.

A rectangular array of numbers is called a *matrix* (plural: *matrices*). In the next example, we use matrices to carry out the Gaussian elimination method.

▶ Example 5　Use the Gaussian elimination method to solve the system

$$\begin{cases} 3x - 6y + 9z = 0 \\ 4x - 6y + 8z = -4 \\ -2x - y + z = 7. \end{cases}$$

---

[1]The vertical line between the second and third columns is a placemarker that separates the data obtained from the right- and left-hand sides of the equations. It is inserted for visual convenience.

Solution The initial array corresponding to the system is

$$\begin{bmatrix} 3 & -6 & 9 & | & 0 \\ 4 & -6 & 8 & | & -4 \\ -2 & -1 & 1 & | & 7 \end{bmatrix}.$$

We must use elementary row operations to transform this array into diagonal form—that is, with ones down the diagonal and zeros everywhere else on the left:

$$\begin{bmatrix} 1 & 0 & 0 & | & * \\ 0 & 1 & 0 & | & * \\ 0 & 0 & 1 & | & * \end{bmatrix}.$$

We proceed one column at a time.

$$\begin{bmatrix} 3 & -6 & 9 & | & 0 \\ 4 & -6 & 8 & | & -4 \\ -2 & -1 & 1 & | & 7 \end{bmatrix} \xrightarrow{\frac{1}{3}[1]} \begin{bmatrix} 1 & -2 & 3 & | & 0 \\ 4 & -6 & 8 & | & -4 \\ -2 & -1 & 1 & | & 7 \end{bmatrix} \xrightarrow{[2]+(-4)[1]}$$

$$\begin{bmatrix} 1 & -2 & 3 & | & 0 \\ 0 & 2 & -4 & | & -4 \\ -2 & -1 & 1 & | & 7 \end{bmatrix} \xrightarrow{[3]+2[1]} \begin{bmatrix} 1 & -2 & 3 & | & 0 \\ 0 & 2 & -4 & | & -4 \\ 0 & -5 & 7 & | & 7 \end{bmatrix} \xrightarrow{\frac{1}{2}[2]}$$

$$\begin{bmatrix} 1 & -2 & 3 & | & 0 \\ 0 & 1 & -2 & | & -2 \\ 0 & -5 & 7 & | & 7 \end{bmatrix} \xrightarrow{[1]+2[2]} \begin{bmatrix} 1 & 0 & -1 & | & -4 \\ 0 & 1 & -2 & | & -2 \\ 0 & -5 & 7 & | & 7 \end{bmatrix} \xrightarrow{[3]+5[2]}$$

$$\begin{bmatrix} 1 & 0 & -1 & | & -4 \\ 0 & 1 & -2 & | & -2 \\ 0 & 0 & -3 & | & -3 \end{bmatrix} \xrightarrow{(-\frac{1}{3})[3]} \begin{bmatrix} 1 & 0 & -1 & | & -4 \\ 0 & 1 & -2 & | & -2 \\ 0 & 0 & 1 & | & 1 \end{bmatrix} \xrightarrow{[1]+1[3]}$$

$$\begin{bmatrix} 1 & 0 & 0 & | & -3 \\ 0 & 1 & -2 & | & -2 \\ 0 & 0 & 1 & | & 1 \end{bmatrix} \xrightarrow{[2]+2[3]} \begin{bmatrix} 1 & 0 & 0 & | & -3 \\ 0 & 1 & 0 & | & 0 \\ 0 & 0 & 1 & | & 1 \end{bmatrix}.$$

The last array is in diagonal form, so we just put back the variables and read off the solution:

$$x = -3, \qquad y = 0, \qquad z = 1.$$

Because so much arithmetic has been performed, it is a good idea to check the solution by substituting the values for x, y, and z into each of the equations of the original system. This will uncover any arithmetic errors that may have occurred.

$$\begin{cases} 3x - 6y + 9z = 0 \\ 4x - 6y + 8z = -4 \\ -2x - y + z = 7 \end{cases} \qquad \begin{cases} 3(-3) - 6(0) + 9(1) = 0 \\ 4(-3) - 6(0) + 8(1) = -4 \\ -2(-3) - (0) + (1) = 7 \end{cases}$$

$$\begin{cases} -9 - 0 + 9 = 0 \\ -12 - 0 + 8 = -4 \\ 6 - 0 + 1 = 7 \end{cases}$$

$$\begin{cases} 0 = 0 \\ -4 = -4 \\ 7 = 7. \end{cases}$$

So we have indeed found a solution of the system. ◆

Remark Note that so far we have not had to use elementary row operation 1, which allows interchange of equations. But in some examples it is definitely needed.

Consider this system:

$$\begin{cases} y + z = 0 \\ 3x - y + z = 6 \\ 6x \quad\;\; - z = 3. \end{cases}$$

The first step of the Gaussian elimination method consists of making the x-coefficient 1 in the first equation. But we cannot do this, since the first equation does not involve x. To remedy this difficulty, just interchange the first two equations to guarantee that the first equation involves x. Now proceed as before. Of course, in terms of the matrix of coefficients, interchanging equations corresponds to interchanging rows of the matrix.

GC Graphing utilities can perform many operations with matrices, including elementary row operations. With a TI-82 or TI-83, pressing MATRX presents three menus. See Fig. 1. You define a new matrix or alter an existing matrix with the EDIT menu. You place the name of an existing matrix on the home screen with the NAMES menu. You perform operations on existing matrices with the MATH menu.

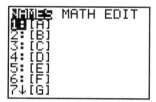
Figure 1.

Figure 2.

With the EDIT menu, you first select one of the names [A], [B], [C], ... for the matrix and then specify the size and fill in the entries as shown in Fig. 2. The three elementary row operations are carried out with commands of the following forms from the MATRX/MATH menu.

rowSwap(*matrix, rowA, rowB*)	Interchange *rowA* and *rowB* of *matrix*
*row(*value, matrix, row*)	Multiply *row* of *matrix* by *value*
*row+(*value, matrix, rowA, rowB*)	Add *value*rowA* to *rowB* of *matrix*

When one of these commands is carried out, the resulting matrix is displayed but the stored matrix is not changed. Therefore, when a sequence of commands is executed to carry out the Gaussian elimination method, each command should be followed with $\rightarrow$ *matrix* to change the stored matrix. (*Note*: To display the name of a matrix, press MATRX, cursor down to the matrix, and press ENTER. To display an arrow, press STO ▶.) For instance, if in Example 5 the original matrix is named [A], then the first three row operations are carried out with

*row(1/3,[A],1) STO ▶ **[A]**
*row+(-4,[A],1,2) STO ▶ **[A]**
*row+(2,[A],1,3) STO ▶ **[A]**.

Matrix entries are normally displayed on the calculator as decimals. From the home screen you can display the entries as fractions with a command such as **[A]** ▶ **Frac** or **Ans** ▶ **Frac**. (▶ **Frac** is displayed by pressing MATH **1**.) See Fig. 3.

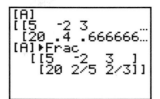

Figure 3.

**Practice Problems
2.1**

1. Determine whether the following systems of linear equations are in diagonal form.

(a) $\begin{cases} x & + z = 3 \\ & y & = 2 \\ & & z = 7 \end{cases}$ (b) $\begin{cases} x & = 3 \\ & y = 5 \\ & z = 7 \end{cases}$ (c) $\begin{cases} x & = -1 \\ & y & = 0 \\ & 3z = 4 \end{cases}$

2. Perform the indicated elementary row operation.

(a) $\begin{cases} x - 3y = 2 \\ 2x + 3y = 5 \end{cases} \xrightarrow{\;[2] + (-2)[1]\;}$ (b) $\begin{cases} x + y = 3 \\ -x + 2y = 5 \end{cases} \xrightarrow{\;[2] + (1)[1]\;}$

3. State the next elementary row operation that should be performed when applying the Gaussian elimination method.

(a) $\begin{bmatrix} 0 & 2 & 4 & | & 1 \\ 0 & 3 & -7 & | & 0 \\ 3 & 6 & -3 & | & 3 \end{bmatrix}$ (b) $\begin{bmatrix} 1 & -3 & 4 & | & 5 \\ 0 & 2 & 3 & | & 4 \\ -6 & 5 & -7 & | & 0 \end{bmatrix}$

▶ Exercises 2.1

In Exercises 1–8, perform the indicated elementary row operations and give their abbreviations.

1. Operation 2: Multiply the first equation by 2.

$$\begin{cases} \frac{1}{2}x - 3y = 2 \\ 5x + 4y = 1 \end{cases}$$

2. Operation 2: Multiply the second equation by -1.

$$\begin{cases} x + 4y = 6 \\ -y = 2 \end{cases}$$

3. Operation 3: Change the second equation by adding to it 5 times the first equation.

$$\begin{cases} x + 2y = 3 \\ -5x + 4y = 1 \end{cases}$$

4. Operation 3: Change the second equation by adding

to it $\left(-\frac{1}{2}\right)$ times the first equation.

$$\begin{cases} x - 6y = 4 \\ \frac{1}{2}x + 2y = 1 \end{cases}$$

5. Operation 3: Change the third equation by adding to it (-4) times the first equation.

$$\begin{cases} x - 2y + z = 0 \\ y - 2z = 4 \\ 4x + y + 3z = 5 \end{cases}$$

6. Operation 3: Change the third equation by adding to it 3 times the second equation.

$$\begin{cases} x + 6y - 4z = 1 \\ y + 3z = 1 \\ -3y + 7z = 2 \end{cases}$$

7. Operation 3: Change the first row by adding to it $\frac{1}{2}$ times the second row.

$$\begin{bmatrix} 1 & -\frac{1}{2} & \bigm| & 3 \\ 0 & 1 & \bigm| & 4 \end{bmatrix}$$

8. Operation 3: Change the third row by adding to it (-4) times the second row.

$$\begin{bmatrix} 1 & 0 & 7 & \bigm| & 9 \\ 0 & 1 & -2 & \bigm| & 3 \\ 0 & 4 & 8 & \bigm| & 5 \end{bmatrix}$$

In Exercises 9–16, state the next elementary row operation that should be performed in order to put the matrix into diagonal form. Do not perform the operation.

9. $\begin{bmatrix} 1 & -5 & \bigm| & 1 \\ -2 & 4 & \bigm| & 6 \end{bmatrix}$ 10. $\begin{bmatrix} 1 & 3 & \bigm| & 4 \\ 0 & 2 & \bigm| & 6 \end{bmatrix}$

11. $\begin{bmatrix} 1 & 2 & \bigm| & 3 \\ 0 & 1 & \bigm| & 4 \end{bmatrix}$ 12. $\begin{bmatrix} 1 & -2 & 5 & \bigm| & 7 \\ 0 & -3 & 6 & \bigm| & 9 \\ 4 & 5 & -6 & \bigm| & 7 \end{bmatrix}$

13. $\begin{bmatrix} 0 & 5 & -3 & \bigm| & 6 \\ 2 & -3 & 4 & \bigm| & 5 \\ 4 & 1 & -7 & \bigm| & 8 \end{bmatrix}$ 14. $\begin{bmatrix} 1 & 4 & -2 & \bigm| & 5 \\ 0 & -3 & 6 & \bigm| & 9 \\ 0 & 4 & 3 & \bigm| & 1 \end{bmatrix}$

15. $\begin{bmatrix} 1 & 0 & 3 & \bigm| & 4 \\ 0 & 1 & 2 & \bigm| & 5 \\ 0 & 0 & 1 & \bigm| & 6 \end{bmatrix}$ 16. $\begin{bmatrix} 1 & 2 & 4 & \bigm| & 5 \\ 0 & 0 & 3 & \bigm| & 6 \\ 0 & 1 & 1 & \bigm| & 7 \end{bmatrix}$

In Exercises 17–30, solve the linear system by using the Gaussian elimination method.

17. $\begin{cases} 3x + 9y = 6 \\ 2x + 8y = 6 \end{cases}$ 18. $\begin{cases} \frac{1}{3}x + 2y = 1 \\ -2x - 4y = 6 \end{cases}$

19. $\begin{cases} x - 3y + 4z = 1 \\ 4x - 10y + 10z = 4 \\ -3x + 9y - 5z = -6 \end{cases}$

20. $\begin{cases} \frac{1}{2}x + y = 4 \\ -4x - 7y + 3z = -31 \\ 6x + 14y + 7z = 50 \end{cases}$

21. $\begin{cases} 2x - 2y + 4 = 0 \\ 3x + 4y - 1 = 0 \end{cases}$ 22. $\begin{cases} 2x + 3y = 4 \\ -x + 2y = -2 \end{cases}$

23. $\begin{cases} 4x - 4y + 4z = -8 \\ x - 2y - 2z = -1 \\ 2x + y + 3z = 1 \end{cases}$

24. $\begin{cases} x + 2y + 2z - 11 = 0 \\ x - y - z + 4 = 0 \\ 2x + 5y + 9z - 39 = 0 \end{cases}$

25. $\begin{cases} .2x + .3y = 4 \\ .6x + 1.1y = 15 \end{cases}$ 26. $\begin{cases} \frac{3}{2}x + 6y = 9 \\ \frac{1}{2}x - \frac{2}{3}y = 11 \end{cases}$

27. $\begin{cases} x + y + 4z = 3 \\ 4x + y - 2z = -6 \\ -3x + 2z = 1 \end{cases}$

28. $\begin{cases} -2x - 3y + 2z = -2 \\ x + y = 3 \\ -x - 3y + 5z = 8 \end{cases}$

29. $\begin{cases} -x + y = -1 \\ x + z = 4 \\ 6x - 3y + 2z = 10 \end{cases}$

30. $\begin{cases} x + 2z = 9 \\ y + z = 1 \\ 3x - 2y = 9 \end{cases}$

31. (PE) A baked potato smothered with cheddar cheese weighs 180 grams and contains 10.5 grams of protein. If cheddar cheese contains 25% protein and a baked potato contains 2% protein, how many grams of cheddar cheese are there?

(a) 25   (b) 30   (c) 35   (d) 40   (e) 45

32. (PE) A high school math department purchased brand A calculators for $80 each and brand B calculators for $95 each. It purchased a total of 20 calculators at a total cost of $1780. How many brand A calculators did the department purchase?

(a) 7   (b) 8   (c) 9   (d) 10   (e) 11

33. A 600-seat movie theater charges $5.50 admission for adults and $2.50 for children. If the theater is full and $1911 is collected, how many adults and how many children are in the audience?

34. A baseball player's batting average is determined by dividing the number of hits by the number of times at bat and multiplying by 1000. (Batting averages are usually, but not necessarily, rounded to the nearest whole number.) For instance, if a player gets 2 hits in 5 times at bat, his batting average is 400: $\left(\frac{2}{5} \times 1000 = 400\right)$. Partway through the season, a player thinks to himself, "If I get a hit in my next time at bat, my average will go up to 250; if I don't get a hit, it will drop to 187.5." How many times has this player batted, how many hits has he had, and what is his current batting average?

35. A bank wishes to invest a $100,000 trust fund in three sources: bonds paying 8%; certificates of deposit paying 7%; and first mortgages paying 10%. The bank wishes to realize an $8000 annual income from the investment. A condition of the trust is that the total amount invested in bonds and certificates of deposit must be triple the amount invested in mortgages. How much should the bank invest in each possible category? Let x, y, and z, respectively, be the amounts invested in bonds, certificates of deposit, and first mortgages. Solve the system of equations by the Gaussian elimination method.

36. A dietitian wishes to plan a meal around three foods. Each ounce of food I contains 10% of the daily requirements for carbohydrates, 10% for protein, and 15% for vitamin C. Each ounce of food II contains 10% of the daily requirements for carbohydrates, 5% for protein, and 0% for vitamin C. Each ounce of food III contains 10% of the daily requirements for carbohydrates, 25% for protein, and 10% for vitamin C. How many ounces of each food should be served in order to supply exactly the daily requirements for each nutrient? Let x, y, and z, respectively, be the number of ounces of foods I, II, and III.

Exercises 37–40 require the use of a graphing calculator or a computer. Most graphing calculators are able to perform an elementary row operation with a single instruction.

37. Enter the matrix corresponding to the equations in Exercise 3, and change the second row by adding to it 5 times the first row.

38. Enter the matrix from Exercise 5, and change the third row by adding to it (-4) times the first row.

39. Enter the matrix in Exercise 7, and interchange the rows.

40. Enter the matrix corresponding to the linear system in Exercise 25, and multiply the first row by 5.

In Exercises 41 and 42, solve the system of linear equations by the Gaussian elimination method.

41. $\begin{cases} 2x + 2y + 2z + 4w = -12 \\ \quad\quad y + z + w = -5 \\ \quad\quad\quad z + 2w = -6 \\ x + y + z + 4w = -14 \end{cases}$

42. $\begin{cases} 2x \quad\quad - z + 5w = 19 \\ 2x + 3y - z + 5w = 28 \\ \quad\quad - z + 5w = 21 \\ 6x \quad\quad - 3z \quad\quad = -3 \end{cases}$

Solutions to Practice Problems 2.1

1. **(a)** Not in diagonal form, since the first equation contains both x and z.

(b) Not in diagonal form, since the variables are not arranged in diagonal fashion.

(c) Not in diagonal form, since the coefficient of z is not 1.

2. **(a)** Change the system into another system in which the second equation is altered by having (-2)(first equation) added to it. The new system is

$$\begin{cases} x - 3y = 2 \\ \quad\quad 9y = 1. \end{cases}$$

The equation $9y = 1$ was obtained as follows:

$$\begin{array}{ll} (-2)(\text{first equation}) & -2x + 6y = -4 \\ + \ (\text{second equation}) & \underline{2x + 3y = \ \ 5} \\ & \quad\quad 9y = \ \ 1. \end{array}$$

(b) Change the second equation by adding to it 1 times the first equation. The result is

$$\begin{cases} x + y = 3 \\ \quad\quad 3y = 8. \end{cases}$$

3. **(a)** The first row should contain a nonzero number as its first entry. This can be accomplished by interchanging the first and third rows.

(b) The first column can be put into proper form by eliminating the -6. To accomplish this, multiply the first row by 6 and add this product to the third row. The notation for this operation is

$$\underrightarrow{[3] + 6[1]}$$

2.2 Solving Systems of Linear Equations, II

In this section we introduce the operation of pivoting and consider systems of linear equations that do not have unique solutions.

Roughly speaking, the Gaussian elimination method applied to a matrix proceeds as follows: Consider the columns one at a time, from left to right. For each column use the elementary row operations to transform the appropriate entry to a one and the remaining entries in the column to zeros. (The "appropriate" entry is the first entry in the first column, the second entry in the second column, and so forth.) This sequence of elementary row operations performed for each column is called *pivoting*. More precisely,

---

Method   To pivot a matrix about a given nonzero entry,

1. Transform the given entry into a one.

2. Transform all other entries in the same column into zeros.

Pivoting is used in solving problems other than systems of linear equations. As we shall see in Chapter 4, it is the basis for the simplex method of solving linear programming problems.

▸ **Example 1**   Pivot the matrix about the circled element.

$$\left[\begin{array}{cc|c} 18 & \boxed{-6} & 15 \\ 5 & -2 & 4 \end{array}\right]$$

Solution   The first step is to transform the -6 to a 1. We do this by multiplying the first row by $-\frac{1}{6}$:

$$\left[\begin{array}{cc|c} 18 & -6 & 15 \\ 5 & -2 & 4 \end{array}\right] \quad \xrightarrow{-\frac{1}{6}[1]} \quad \left[\begin{array}{cc|c} -3 & 1 & -\frac{5}{2} \\ 5 & -2 & 4 \end{array}\right].$$

Next, we transform the -2 (the only remaining entry in column 2) into a 0:

$$\left[\begin{array}{cc|c} -3 & 1 & -\frac{5}{2} \\ 5 & -2 & 4 \end{array}\right] \quad \xrightarrow{[2]+2[1]} \quad \left[\begin{array}{cc|c} -3 & 1 & -\frac{5}{2} \\ -1 & 0 & -1 \end{array}\right].$$

The last matrix is the result of pivoting the original matrix about the circled entry.   ◆

In terms of pivoting, we can give the following summary of the Gaussian elimination method.

> **Gaussian Elimination Method to Transform a System of Linear Equations into Diagonal Form**
>
> 1. Write down the matrix corresponding to the linear system.
> 2. Make sure that the first entry in the first column is nonzero. Do this by interchanging the first row with one of the rows below it, if necessary.
> 3. Pivot the matrix about the first entry in the first column.
> 4. Make sure that the second entry in the second column is nonzero. Do this by interchanging the second row with one of the rows below it, if necessary.
> 5. Pivot the matrix about the second entry in the second column.
> 6. Continue in this manner.

All the systems considered in the preceding section had only a single solution. In this case we say that the solution is *unique*. Let us now use the Gaussian elimination method to study the various possibilities other than a unique solution. We first experiment with an example.

▶ **Example 2** Determine all solutions of the system

$$\begin{cases} 2x + 2y + 4z = 8 \\ x - y + 2z = 2 \\ -x + 5y - 2z = 2. \end{cases}$$

Solution We set up the matrix corresponding to the system and perform the appropriate pivoting operations. (The elements pivoted about are circled.)

$$\begin{bmatrix} \textcircled{2} & 2 & 4 & | & 8 \\ 1 & -1 & 2 & | & 2 \\ -1 & 5 & -2 & | & 2 \end{bmatrix} \quad \xrightarrow[\substack{\frac{1}{2}[1] \\ [2]+(-1)[1] \\ [3]+(1)[1]}]{} \quad \begin{bmatrix} 1 & 1 & 2 & | & 4 \\ 0 & \textcircled{-2} & 0 & | & -2 \\ 0 & 6 & 0 & | & 6 \end{bmatrix}$$

$$\xrightarrow[\substack{\left(-\frac{1}{2}\right)[2] \\ [1]+(-1)[2] \\ [3]+(-6)[2]}]{} \quad \begin{bmatrix} 1 & 0 & 2 & | & 3 \\ 0 & 1 & 0 & | & 1 \\ 0 & 0 & 0 & | & 0 \end{bmatrix}$$

Note that our method must terminate here, since there is no way to transform the third entry in the third column into a 1 without disturbing the columns already in appropriate form. The equations corresponding to the last matrix read

$$\begin{cases} x & + 2z = 3 \\ y & = 1 \\ 0 & = 0. \end{cases}$$

The last equation does not involve any of the variables and so may be omitted. This leaves the two equations

$$\begin{cases} x & + 2z = 3 \\ y & = 1. \end{cases}$$

Now, taking the $2z$-term in the first equation to the right side, we can write the equations

$$\begin{cases} x = 3 - 2z \\ y = 1. \end{cases}$$

The value of y is given: $y = 1$. The value of x is given in terms of z. To find a solution to this system, assign any value to z. Then the first equation gives a value for x and thereby a specific solution to the system. For example, if we take $z = 1$, then the corresponding specific solution is

$$z = 1$$
$$x = 3 - 2(1) = 1$$
$$y = 1.$$

If we take $z = -3$, the corresponding specific solution is

$$z = -3$$
$$x = 3 - 2(-3) = 9$$
$$y = 1.$$

Thus, we see that the original system has infinitely many specific solutions, corresponding to the infinitely many possible different choices for z.

We say that the *general solution* of the system is

$$z = \text{any value}$$
$$x = 3 - 2z$$
$$y = 1. \qquad \blacklozenge$$

When a linear system cannot be *completely* diagonalized,

1. Apply the Gaussian elimination method to as many columns as possible. Proceed from left to right, but do not disturb columns that have already been put into proper form.

2. Variables corresponding to columns not in proper form can assume any value.

3. The other variables can be expressed in terms of the variables of step 2.

▶ **Example 3** Find all solutions of the linear system

$$\begin{cases} x + 2y - z + 3w = 5 \\ y + 2z + w = 7. \end{cases}$$

Solution   The Gaussian elimination method proceeds as follows:

$$\begin{bmatrix} 1 & 2 & -1 & 3 & \bigm| & 5 \\ 0 & \textcircled{1} & 2 & 1 & \bigm| & 7 \end{bmatrix}$$ (The first column is already in proper form.)

$$\xrightarrow{[1] + (-2)[2]} \begin{bmatrix} 1 & 0 & -5 & 1 & \bigm| & -9 \\ 0 & 1 & 2 & 1 & \bigm| & 7 \end{bmatrix}.$$

We cannot do anything further with the last two columns (without disturbing the first two columns), so the corresponding variables, z and w, can assume any values. Writing down the equations corresponding to the last matrix yields

$$\begin{cases} x \quad - 5z + w = -9 \\ \quad y + 2z + w = \quad 7, \end{cases}$$

or

$$z = \text{any value}$$
$$w = \text{any value}$$
$$x = -9 + 5z - w$$
$$y = \quad 7 - 2z - w.$$

To determine a specific solution, let $z = 1$, $w = 2$. Then a specific solution of the original system is

$$z = 1$$
$$w = 2$$
$$x = -9 + 5(1) - (2) = -6$$
$$y = \quad 7 - 2(1) - (2) = \quad 3.$$ ◆

▶ **Example 4** Find all solutions of the system of equations

$$\begin{cases} x - \quad 7y + \quad z = 3 \\ 2x - 14y + 3z = 4. \end{cases}$$

Solution The first pivot operation is routine:

$$\begin{bmatrix} ① & -7 & 1 & | & 3 \\ 2 & -14 & 3 & | & 4 \end{bmatrix} \xrightarrow{[2] + (-2)[1]} \begin{bmatrix} 1 & -7 & 1 & | & 3 \\ 0 & 0 & 1 & | & -2 \end{bmatrix}.$$

However, it is impossible to pivot about the zero in the second column. So skip the second column and pivot about the second entry in the third column to get

$$\begin{bmatrix} 1 & -7 & 0 & | & 5 \\ 0 & 0 & 1 & | & -2 \end{bmatrix}.$$

This is as far as we can go. The variable corresponding to the second column, namely y, can assume any value, and the general solution of the system is obtained from the equations

$$\begin{cases} x - 7y \quad = \quad 5 \\ \quad\quad\quad z = -2. \end{cases}$$

Therefore, the general solution of the system is

$$y = \text{any value}$$
$$x = 5 + 7y$$
$$z = -2.$$ ◆

We have seen that a linear system may have a unique solution or it may have infinitely many solutions. But another phenomenon can occur: A system may have no solutions at all, as the next example shows.

▶ **Example 5**   Find all solutions of the system

$$\begin{cases} x - y + z = 3 \\ x + y - z = 5 \\ -2x + 4y - 4z = 1. \end{cases}$$

Solution   We apply the Gaussian elimination method to the matrix of the system.

$$\begin{bmatrix} \textcircled{1} & -1 & 1 & | & 3 \\ 1 & 1 & -1 & | & 5 \\ -2 & 4 & -4 & | & 1 \end{bmatrix} \xrightarrow[\text{[3]} + 2[1]]{[2] + (-1)[1]} \begin{bmatrix} 1 & -1 & 1 & | & 3 \\ 0 & \textcircled{2} & -2 & | & 2 \\ 0 & 2 & -2 & | & 7 \end{bmatrix}$$

$$\xrightarrow[\text{[3]} + (-2)[2]]{\begin{array}{c} \frac{1}{2}[2] \\ [1] + (1)[2] \end{array}} \begin{bmatrix} 1 & 0 & 0 & | & 4 \\ 0 & 1 & -1 & | & 1 \\ 0 & 0 & 0 & | & 5 \end{bmatrix}$$

We cannot pivot about the last zero in the third column, so we have carried the method as far as we can. Let us write out the equations corresponding to the last matrix:

$$\begin{cases} x \qquad\quad = 4 \\ \quad y - z = 1 \\ \quad 0 \qquad = 5. \end{cases}$$

Note that the last equation is a built-in contradiction. In mathematical terms, the last equation is *inconsistent*. So the last equation can never be satisfied, no matter what the values of x, y, and z. Thus, the original system has no solutions. Systems with no solutions can always be detected by the presence of inconsistent equations in the last matrix resulting from the Gaussian elimination method. ◆

At first it might seem strange that some systems have no solutions, some have one, and yet others have infinitely many. The reason for the difference can be explained geometrically. For simplicity, consider the case of systems of two equations in two variables. Each equation in this case has a graph in the xy-plane, and the graph is a straight line. As we have seen, solving the system corresponds to finding the points lying on both lines. There are three possibilities. First, the two lines may intersect. In this case the solution is unique. Second, the two lines may be parallel. Then the two lines do not intersect, and the system has no solutions. Finally, the two equations may represent the same line, as, for example, the equations $2x + 3y = 1$ and $4x + 6y = 2$ do. In this case every point on the line is a solution of the system; that is, there are infinitely many solutions (Fig. 1).

GC   With the TI-83, the complete Gaussian elimination method can be carried out in one step as shown in Fig. 2 for the matrix of Example 4. To enter the symbol **rref(**, press [MATRX] [▶] to obtain the MATRX/MATH menu, cursor down to **B:rref(** and press [ENTER]. (*Note:* **rref** stands for "row-reduced echelon

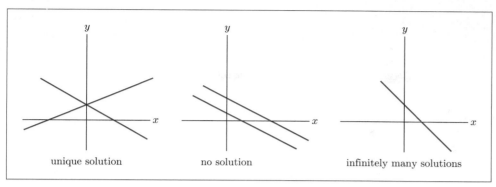

Figure 1.

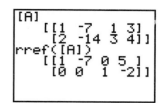

Figure 2.

form," the name given to the final form of a matrix that has been completely row reduced.)

| **Practice Problems 2.2** | **1.** Find a specific solution to a system of linear equations whose general solution is |

$$w = \text{any value}$$
$$y = \text{any value}$$
$$z = 7 + 6w$$
$$x = 26 - 2y + 14w.$$

2. Find all solutions of this system of linear equations.

$$\begin{cases} 2x + 4y - 4z - 4w = 24 \\ -3x - 6y + 10z - 18w = -8 \\ -x - 2y + 4z - 10w = 2 \end{cases}$$

▶ Exercises 2.2

In Exercises 1–8, pivot each matrix about the circled element.

1. $\begin{bmatrix} ② & -4 & 6 \\ 3 & 7 & 1 \end{bmatrix}$

2. $\begin{bmatrix} 1 & 2 & 3 \\ 4 & ⑧ & -12 \end{bmatrix}$

3. $\begin{bmatrix} 7 & 1 & 4 & 5 \\ -1 & 1 & ② & 6 \\ 4 & 0 & 2 & 3 \end{bmatrix}$

4. $\begin{bmatrix} 5 & 10 & -10 & 12 \\ 4 & 3 & 6 & 12 \\ 4 & ④ & 4 & -16 \end{bmatrix}$

5. $\begin{bmatrix} ② & 3 \\ 6 & 0 \\ 1 & 5 \end{bmatrix}$

6. $\begin{bmatrix} 2 & 1 \\ ① & 0 \end{bmatrix}$

7. $\begin{bmatrix} 4 & 3 & 0 \\ \frac{2}{3} & 0 & -2 \\ 1 & 3 & ⑥ \end{bmatrix}$

8. $\begin{bmatrix} 1 & 0 & 2 \\ -1 & 1 & ② \\ 1 & 2 & 6 \end{bmatrix}$

In Exercises 9–22, use the Gaussian elimination method to find all solutions of the systems of linear equations.

9. $\begin{cases} 2x - 4y = 6 \\ -x + 2y = -3 \end{cases}$

10. $\begin{cases} -\frac{1}{2}x + y = \frac{3}{2} \\ -3x + 6y = 10 \end{cases}$

11. $\begin{cases} x + 2y = 5 \\ 3x - y = 1 \\ -x + 3y = 5 \end{cases}$

12. $\begin{cases} x - 6y = 12 \\ -\frac{1}{2}x + 3y = -6 \\ \frac{1}{3}x - 2y = 4 \end{cases}$

13. $\begin{cases} x - y + 3z = 3 \\ -2x + 3y - 11z = -4 \\ x - 2y + 8z = 6 \end{cases}$

14. $\begin{cases} x - 3y + z = 5 \\ -2x + 7y - 6z = -9 \\ x - 2y - 3z = 6 \end{cases}$

15. $\begin{cases} x + y + z = -1 \\ 2x + 3y + 2z = 3 \\ 2x + y + 2z = -7 \end{cases}$ 16. $\begin{cases} x - 3y + 2z = 10 \\ -x + 3y - z = -6 \\ -x + 3y + 2z = 6 \end{cases}$

17. $\begin{cases} x + 2y + 3z = 4 \\ 5x + 6y + 7z = 8 \\ x + 2y + 3z = 5 \end{cases}$ 18. $\begin{cases} x + 3y = 7 \\ x + 2y = 5 \\ -x + y = 2 \end{cases}$

19. $\begin{cases} x + y - 2z + 2w = 5 \\ 2x + y - 4z + w = 5 \\ 3x + 4y - 6z + 9w = 20 \\ 4x + 4y - 8z + 8w = 20 \end{cases}$

20. $\begin{cases} 2y + z - w = 1 \\ x - y + z + w = 14 \\ -x - 9y - z + 4w = 11 \\ x + y + z = 9 \end{cases}$

21. $\begin{cases} 6x - 4y = 2 \\ -3x + 3y = 6 \\ 5x + 2y = 39 \end{cases}$ 22. $\begin{cases} 3x + 2y = 5 \\ -x + 3y = 2 \\ 5x + 2y = 6 \\ 6x + y = 39 \end{cases}$

In Exercises 23–25, find three solutions to the systems of equations.

23. $\begin{cases} x + 2y + z = 5 \\ y + 3z = 9 \end{cases}$ 24. $\begin{cases} x + 5y + 3z = 9 \\ 2x + 9y + 7z = 5 \end{cases}$

25. $\begin{cases} x + 7y - 3z = 8 \\ z = 5 \end{cases}$

26. An out-of-shape athlete runs 6 miles per hour, swims 1 mile per hour, and bikes 10 miles per hour. He entered a triathlon, which requires all three events, and finished 5 hours and 40 minutes later. A friend who runs 8 miles per hour, swims 2 miles per hour, and bikes 15 miles per hour finished the same course in 3 hours and 35 minutes. The total course was 32 miles long. How many miles was each segment (running, swimming, and biking)?

27. In a laboratory experiment, a researcher wants to provide a rabbit with exactly 1000 units of vitamin A, exactly 1600 units of vitamin C, and exactly 2400 units of vitamin E. The rabbit is fed a mixture of three foods. Each gram of food 1 contains 2 units of vitamin A, 3 units of vitamin C, and 5 units of vitamin E. Each gram of food 2 contains 4 units of vitamin A, 7 units of vitamin C, and 9 units of vitamin E. Each gram of food 3 contains 6 units of vitamin A, 10 units of vitamin C, and 14 units of vitamin E. How many grams of each food should the rabbit be fed?

28. Rework Exercise 27 with the requirement for vitamin E changed to 2000 units.

29. Granny's Custom Quilts receives an order for a patchwork quilt made from square patches of three types: solid green, solid blue, and floral. The quilt is to be 8 squares by 12 squares, and there must be 15 times as many solid squares as floral squares. If Granny's charges $3 per solid square and $5 per floral square, and if the customer wishes to spend exactly $300, how many of each type of square may be used in the quilt?

30. Amanda is decorating her new home and wants to buy some house plants. She is interested in three types of plants costing $7, $10, and $13. If she has budgeted exactly $150 for the plants and wants to buy exactly 15 of them, what are her options?

31. Find all solutions to the following system of equations.

$$\begin{cases} x^2 + y^2 + z^2 = 14 \\ x^2 - y^2 + 2z^2 = 15 \\ x^2 + 2y^2 + 3z^2 = 36 \end{cases}$$

32. For what value of k will the following system of linear equations have a solution?

$$\begin{cases} 2x + 6y = 4 \\ x + 7y = 10 \\ kx + 8y = 4 \end{cases}$$

33. For what values(s) of k will the following system of linear equations have no solution? Infinitely many solutions?

$$\begin{cases} 2x - 3y = 4 \\ -6x + 9y = k \end{cases}$$

Exercises 34–42 require the use of a graphing calculator or a computer.

In Exercises 34–37, graph the three equations together, and determine the number of solutions (exactly one, none, or infinitely many). If there is exactly one solution, estimate the solution.

34. $\begin{cases} x + y = 10 \\ 2x - 3y = 5 \\ -x + 3y = 2 \end{cases}$ 35. $\begin{cases} 2x + 3y = 5 \\ -3x + 5y = 22 \\ 2x + y = -1 \end{cases}$

36. $\begin{cases} 2x + y = 12 \\ 3x - y = 2 \\ x + 2y = 16 \end{cases}$ 37. $\begin{cases} 3x - 2y = 3 \\ -2x + 4y = 14 \\ x + y = 11 \end{cases}$

In Exercises 38–41, solve the system of linear equations by the Gaussian elimination method.

38. $\begin{cases} 4x - 3y + 2z = 3 \\ -7x + 5y = 2 \\ -10x + 7y + 2z = 4 \end{cases}$

39. $\begin{cases} 2x + 3y + 6z = 4 \\ 4x + 7y = 2 \\ 3x + 5y + 3z = 3 \end{cases}$

40. $\begin{cases} 2x - 5y - 3z = -3 \\ -5x + 12y + 3z = 11 \\ -3x + 7y \quad = 8 \end{cases}$

41. $\begin{cases} 8x + 3y - 2z = 5 \\ 12x + 5y + 2z = 3 \\ 5x + 2y \quad = 7 \end{cases}$

42. If your calculator or computer has **rref** or an analogous command, apply the command to the matrix in Example 5. How does the final matrix differ from the one appearing in the text?

Solutions to Practice Problems 2.2

1. Since w and y can each assume any value, select any numbers, say $w = 1$ and $y = 2$. Then $z = 7 + 6(1) = 13$ and $x = 26 - 2(2) + 14(1) = 36$. So $x = 36$, $y = 2$, $z = 13$, $w = 1$ is a specific solution. There are infinitely many different specific solutions since there are infinitely many different choices for w and y.

2. We apply the Gaussian elimination method to the matrix of the system.

$$\begin{bmatrix} ② & 4 & -4 & -4 & 24 \\ -3 & -6 & 10 & -18 & -8 \\ -1 & -2 & 4 & -10 & 2 \end{bmatrix} \xrightarrow[\substack{\frac{1}{2}[1] \\ [2]+3[1] \\ [3]+1[1]}]{} \begin{bmatrix} 1 & 2 & -2 & -2 & 12 \\ 0 & 0 & ④ & -24 & 28 \\ 0 & 0 & 2 & -12 & 14 \end{bmatrix}$$

$$\xrightarrow[\substack{\frac{1}{4}[2] \\ [1]+2[2] \\ [3]+(-2)[2]}]{} \begin{bmatrix} 1 & 2 & 0 & -14 & 26 \\ 0 & 0 & 1 & -6 & 7 \\ 0 & 0 & 0 & 0 & 0 \end{bmatrix}$$

The corresponding system of equations is

$$\begin{cases} x + 2y \quad - 14w = 26 \\ \quad z - 6w = 7. \end{cases}$$

The general solution is

$$w = \text{any value}$$
$$y = \text{any value}$$
$$z = 7 + 6w$$
$$x = 26 - 2y + 14w.$$

2.3 Arithmetic Operations on Matrices

We introduced matrices in Sections 2.1 and 2.2 to display the coefficients of a system of linear equations. For example, the linear system

$$\begin{cases} 5x - 3y = \frac{1}{2} \\ 4x + 2y = -1 \end{cases}$$

is represented by the matrix

$$\begin{bmatrix} 5 & -3 & \Big| & \frac{1}{2} \\ 4 & 2 & \Big| & -1 \end{bmatrix}.$$

After we have become accustomed to using such matrices in solving linear systems, we may omit the vertical line that separates the left and right sides of the equations. We need only remember that the right side of the equations is recorded in the right column. So, for example, we would write the preceding matrix in the form

$$\begin{bmatrix} 5 & -3 & \frac{1}{2} \\ 4 & 2 & -1 \end{bmatrix}.$$

A matrix is *any* rectangular array of numbers and may be of any size. Here are some examples of matrices of various sizes:

$$\begin{bmatrix} 3 & 7 \\ 0 & -1 \end{bmatrix}, \qquad \begin{bmatrix} 1 \\ 2 \end{bmatrix}, \qquad \begin{bmatrix} 2 & 1 \end{bmatrix}, \qquad \begin{bmatrix} 6 \end{bmatrix}, \qquad \begin{bmatrix} 5 & 7 & -1 \\ 0 & 3 & 5 \\ 6 & 0 & 5 \end{bmatrix}.$$

Examples of matrices abound in everyday life. For example, the newspaper stock market report is a large matrix with several thousand rows, one for each listed stock. The columns of the matrix give the various data about each stock, such as opening and closing price, number of shares traded, and so on. Another example of a matrix is a mileage chart on a road map. The rows and columns are labeled with the names of cities. The number at a given row and column gives the distance between the corresponding cities.

In these everyday examples, matrices are used only to display data. However, the most important applications involve arithmetic operations on matrices—namely, addition, subtraction, and multiplication of matrices. The major goal of this section is to discuss these operations. Before we can do so, however, we need some vocabulary with which to describe matrices.

A matrix is described by the number of rows and columns it contains. For example, the matrix

$$\begin{bmatrix} 7 & 5 \\ \frac{1}{2} & -2 \\ 2 & -11 \end{bmatrix}$$

has three rows and two columns and is referred to as a 3×2 (read: "three-by-two") *matrix*. The matrix $\begin{bmatrix} 4 & 5 & 0 \end{bmatrix}$ has one row and three columns and is a 1×3 *matrix*. A matrix with only one row is often called a *row matrix* (sometimes also called a *row vector*). A matrix, such as

$$\begin{bmatrix} 2 \\ 7 \end{bmatrix},$$

that has only one column is called a *column matrix* or *column vector*. If a matrix has the same number of rows and columns, it is called a *square matrix*. Here are some square matrices of various sizes:

$$\begin{bmatrix} 5 \end{bmatrix}, \qquad \begin{bmatrix} 1 & 2 \\ 3 & 4 \end{bmatrix}, \qquad \begin{bmatrix} 2 & -1 & 0 \\ 3 & 5 & 4 \\ 0 & 3 & -7 \end{bmatrix}.$$

The rows of a matrix are numbered from the top down, and the columns are numbered from left to right. For example, the first row of the matrix

$$\begin{bmatrix} 1 & -1 & 0 \\ 2 & 1 & 7 \\ -3 & 2 & 4 \end{bmatrix}$$

is $\begin{bmatrix} 1 & -1 & 0 \end{bmatrix}$, and its third column is

$$\begin{bmatrix} 0 \\ 7 \\ 4 \end{bmatrix}.$$

The numbers in a matrix, called *entries*, may be identified in terms of the row and column containing the entry in question. For example, the entry in the first row, third column of the following matrix is 0:

$$\begin{bmatrix} 1 & -1 & \boxed{0} \\ 2 & 1 & 7 \\ -3 & 2 & 4 \end{bmatrix};$$

the entry in the second row, first column is 2:

$$\begin{bmatrix} 1 & -1 & 0 \\ \boxed{2} & 1 & 7 \\ -3 & 2 & 4 \end{bmatrix};$$

and the entry in the third row, third column is 4:

$$\begin{bmatrix} 1 & -1 & 0 \\ 2 & 1 & 7 \\ -3 & 2 & \boxed{4} \end{bmatrix}.$$

We use double-subscripted letters to indicate the locations of the entries of a matrix. We denote the entry in the ith row, jth column by a_{ij}. For instance, in the preceding matrix we have $a_{13} = 0$, $a_{21} = 2$, and $a_{33} = 4$.

We say that two matrices A and B are *equal*, denoted $A = B$, provided that they have the same size and that all their corresponding entries are equal.

Addition and Subtraction of Matrices   We define the sum $A + B$ of two matrices A and B only if A and B are two matrices of the same size—that is, if A and B have the same number of rows and the same number of columns. In this case $A + B$ is the matrix formed by adding the corresponding entries of A and B. For example,

$$\begin{bmatrix} 2 & 0 \\ 1 & 1 \\ 5 & 3 \end{bmatrix} + \begin{bmatrix} 5 & 4 \\ 0 & 2 \\ 2 & 6 \end{bmatrix} = \begin{bmatrix} 2+5 & 0+4 \\ 1+0 & 1+2 \\ 5+2 & 3+6 \end{bmatrix} = \begin{bmatrix} 7 & 4 \\ 1 & 3 \\ 7 & 9 \end{bmatrix}.$$

We subtract matrices of the same size by subtracting corresponding entries. Thus, we have

$$\begin{bmatrix} 7 \\ 1 \end{bmatrix} - \begin{bmatrix} 3 \\ 2 \end{bmatrix} = \begin{bmatrix} 7-3 \\ 1-2 \end{bmatrix} = \begin{bmatrix} 4 \\ -1 \end{bmatrix}.$$

Multiplication of Matrices   It might seem that to define the product of two matrices, one would start with two matrices of like size and multiply the corresponding entries. But this definition is not useful, since the calculations that arise in applications require a somewhat more complex multiplication. In the interests of simplicity, we start by defining the product of a row matrix times a column matrix.

If A is a row matrix and B is a column matrix, then we can form the product $A \cdot B$ provided that the two matrices have the same length. The product $A \cdot B$ is the 1×1 matrix obtained by multiplying corresponding entries of A and B and then forming the sum.

We may put this definition into algebraic terms as follows. Suppose that A is the row matrix

$$A = \begin{bmatrix} a_1 & a_2 & \cdots & a_n \end{bmatrix},$$

and B is the column matrix

$$B = \begin{bmatrix} b_1 \\ b_2 \\ \vdots \\ b_n \end{bmatrix}.$$

Note that A and B are both of the same length, namely n. Then

$$A \cdot B = \begin{bmatrix} a_1 & a_2 & \cdots & a_n \end{bmatrix} \cdot \begin{bmatrix} b_1 \\ b_2 \\ \vdots \\ b_n \end{bmatrix}$$

is calculated by multiplying corresponding entries of A and B and forming the sum; that is,

$$A \cdot B = \begin{bmatrix} a_1 b_1 + a_2 b_2 + \cdots + a_n b_n \end{bmatrix}.$$

Notice that the product is a 1×1 matrix, namely a single number in brackets.

Here are some examples of the product of a row matrix times a column matrix:

$$\begin{bmatrix} 3 & \frac{1}{2} \end{bmatrix} \cdot \begin{bmatrix} 1 \\ 4 \end{bmatrix} = \begin{bmatrix} 3 \cdot 1 + \frac{1}{2} \cdot 4 \end{bmatrix} = \begin{bmatrix} 5 \end{bmatrix};$$

$$\begin{bmatrix} 2 & 0 & -1 \end{bmatrix} \cdot \begin{bmatrix} 6 \\ 5 \\ 3 \end{bmatrix} = \begin{bmatrix} 2 \cdot 6 + 0 \cdot 5 + (-1) \cdot 3 \end{bmatrix} = \begin{bmatrix} 9 \end{bmatrix}.$$

In multiplying a row matrix times a column matrix, it helps to use both of your hands. Use your left index finger to point to an element of the row matrix and your right to point to the corresponding element of the column. Multiply the elements you are pointing to and keep a running total of the products in your head. After each multiplication move your fingers to the next elements of each matrix. With a little practice you should be able to multiply a row times a column quickly and accurately.

The preceding definition of multiplication may seem strange. But products of this sort occur in many down-to-earth problems. Consider, for instance, the next example.

▶ Example 1 A dairy farm produces three items—milk, eggs, and cheese. The prices of the three items are $1.50 per gallon, $0.80 per dozen, and $2.00 per pound, respectively. In a certain week the dairy farm sells 30,000 gallons of milk, 2000 dozen eggs, and 5000 pounds of cheese. Represent its total revenue as a matrix product.

Solution   The total revenue equals

$$(1.50)(30{,}000) + (.80)(2000) + (2)(5000).$$

This suggests that we define two matrices: The first displays the prices of the various produce:

$$\begin{bmatrix} 1.50 & .80 & 2 \end{bmatrix}.$$

The second represents the production:

$$\begin{bmatrix} 30{,}000 \\ 2{,}000 \\ 5{,}000 \end{bmatrix}.$$

Then the revenue for the week, when placed in a 1×1 matrix, equals

$$\begin{bmatrix} 1.50 & .80 & 2 \end{bmatrix} \begin{bmatrix} 30{,}000 \\ 2{,}000 \\ 5{,}000 \end{bmatrix} = \begin{bmatrix} 56{,}600 \end{bmatrix}. \qquad \blacklozenge$$

The principle behind Example 1 is this: Any sum of products of the form $a_1 b_1 + a_2 b_2 + \cdots + a_n b_n$, when placed in a 1×1 matrix, can be written as the matrix product

$$\begin{bmatrix} a_1 b_1 + a_2 b_2 + \cdots + a_n b_n \end{bmatrix} = \begin{bmatrix} a_1 & a_2 & \cdots & a_n \end{bmatrix} \cdot \begin{bmatrix} b_1 \\ b_2 \\ \vdots \\ b_n \end{bmatrix}.$$

Let us illustrate the procedure for multiplying more general matrices by working out a typical product:

$$\begin{bmatrix} 2 & 1 \\ 0 & 1 \\ 1 & 0 \end{bmatrix} \cdot \begin{bmatrix} 1 & 1 \\ 4 & 2 \end{bmatrix}.$$

To obtain the entries of the product, we multiply the rows of the left matrix by the columns of the right matrix, taking care to arrange the products in a specific way to yield a matrix, as follows. Start with the first row on the left, $\begin{bmatrix} 2 & 1 \end{bmatrix}$, and the first column on the right, $\begin{bmatrix} 1 \\ 4 \end{bmatrix}$. Their product is $\begin{bmatrix} 6 \end{bmatrix}$, so we enter 6 as the element in the first row, first column of the product:

$$\begin{bmatrix} 2 & 1 \\ 0 & 1 \\ 1 & 0 \end{bmatrix} \cdot \begin{bmatrix} 1 & 1 \\ 4 & 2 \end{bmatrix} = \begin{bmatrix} 6 & \\ & \\ & \end{bmatrix}.$$

The product of the first row of the left matrix and the second column of the right matrix is $\begin{bmatrix} 4 \end{bmatrix}$, so we put a 4 in the first row, second column of the product:

$$\begin{bmatrix} 2 & 1 \\ 0 & 1 \\ 1 & 0 \end{bmatrix} \cdot \begin{bmatrix} 1 & 1 \\ 4 & 2 \end{bmatrix} = \begin{bmatrix} 6 & 4 \\ & \\ & \end{bmatrix}.$$

There are no more columns that can be multiplied by the first row, so let us move to the second row and shift back to the first column. Correspondingly, we move down one row in the product:

$$\begin{bmatrix} 2 & 1 \\ 0 & 1 \\ 1 & 0 \end{bmatrix} \cdot \begin{bmatrix} 1 & 1 \\ 4 & 2 \end{bmatrix} = \begin{bmatrix} 6 & 4 \\ 4 & \\ & \end{bmatrix};$$

$$\begin{bmatrix} 2 & 1 \\ 0 & 1 \\ 1 & 0 \end{bmatrix} \cdot \begin{bmatrix} 1 & 1 \\ 4 & 2 \end{bmatrix} = \begin{bmatrix} 6 & 4 \\ 4 & 2 \\ & \end{bmatrix}.$$

We have now exhausted the second row of the left matrix, so we shift to the third row and correspondingly move down one row in the product:

$$\begin{bmatrix} 2 & 1 \\ 0 & 1 \\ 1 & 0 \end{bmatrix} \cdot \begin{bmatrix} 1 & 1 \\ 4 & 2 \end{bmatrix} = \begin{bmatrix} 6 & 4 \\ 4 & 2 \\ 1 & \end{bmatrix};$$

$$\begin{bmatrix} 2 & 1 \\ 0 & 1 \\ 1 & 0 \end{bmatrix} \cdot \begin{bmatrix} 1 & 1 \\ 4 & 2 \end{bmatrix} = \begin{bmatrix} 6 & 4 \\ 4 & 2 \\ 1 & 1 \end{bmatrix}.$$

Note that we have now multiplied every row of the left matrix by every column of the right matrix. This completes the computation of the product:

$$\begin{bmatrix} 2 & 1 \\ 0 & 1 \\ 1 & 0 \end{bmatrix} \cdot \begin{bmatrix} 1 & 1 \\ 4 & 2 \end{bmatrix} = \begin{bmatrix} 6 & 4 \\ 4 & 2 \\ 1 & 1 \end{bmatrix}.$$

▶ **Example 2** Calculate the following product:

$$\begin{bmatrix} 1 & 5 \\ 3 & 2 \end{bmatrix} \cdot \begin{bmatrix} 1 & 2 \\ 1 & 0 \end{bmatrix}.$$

Solution

$$\begin{bmatrix} 1 & 5 \\ 3 & 2 \end{bmatrix} \cdot \begin{bmatrix} 1 & 2 \\ 1 & 0 \end{bmatrix} = \begin{bmatrix} 6 & \\ & \end{bmatrix}$$

$$\begin{bmatrix} 1 & 5 \\ 3 & 2 \end{bmatrix} \cdot \begin{bmatrix} 1 & 2 \\ 1 & 0 \end{bmatrix} = \begin{bmatrix} 6 & 2 \\ & \end{bmatrix}$$

$$\begin{bmatrix} 1 & 5 \\ 3 & 2 \end{bmatrix} \cdot \begin{bmatrix} 1 & 2 \\ 1 & 0 \end{bmatrix} = \begin{bmatrix} 6 & 2 \\ 5 & \end{bmatrix}$$

$$\begin{bmatrix} 1 & 5 \\ 3 & 2 \end{bmatrix} \cdot \begin{bmatrix} 1 & 2 \\ 1 & 0 \end{bmatrix} = \begin{bmatrix} 6 & 2 \\ 5 & 6 \end{bmatrix}$$

Thus,

$$\begin{bmatrix} 1 & 5 \\ 3 & 2 \end{bmatrix} \cdot \begin{bmatrix} 1 & 2 \\ 1 & 0 \end{bmatrix} = \begin{bmatrix} 6 & 2 \\ 5 & 6 \end{bmatrix}.$$

◆

Notice that we cannot use the preceding method to compute the product $A \cdot B$ of *any* matrices A and B. For the procedure to work, it is crucial that the number of entries of each row of A be the same as the number of entries of each column of B. (Or, to put it another way, the number of columns of the left matrix must equal the number of rows of the right matrix.) Therefore, in order for us to form the product $A \cdot B$, the sizes of A and B must match up in a special way. If A is $m \times n$ and B is $p \times q$, then the product $A \cdot B$ is defined only in case the "inner" dimensions n and p are equal. In that case, the size of the product is determined by the "outer" dimensions m and q. It is an $m \times q$ matrix:

$$\begin{matrix} A & \cdot & B & = & C. \\ m \times n & & p \times q & & m \times q \end{matrix}$$

equal

So, for example,

$$3 \times 4 \qquad 4 \times 2 \qquad 3 \times 2$$

$$2 \times 2 \qquad 2 \times 1 \qquad 2 \times 1$$

If the sizes of A and B do not match up in the way just described, the product $A \cdot B$ is not defined.

▶ **Example 3**   Calculate the following products, if defined.

(a) $\begin{bmatrix} 3 & -1 \\ 2 & 0 \\ 1 & 5 \end{bmatrix} \begin{bmatrix} 1 & 0 \\ 5 & -4 \\ 2 & -1 \end{bmatrix}$ (b) $\begin{bmatrix} 3 & -1 \\ 2 & 0 \\ 1 & 5 \end{bmatrix} \begin{bmatrix} 5 & 4 \\ -2 & 3 \end{bmatrix}$

Solution   (a) The matrices to be multiplied are 3×2 and 3×2. The inner dimensions do not match, so the product is undefined.

(b) We are asked to multiply a 3×2 matrix times a 2×2 matrix. The inner dimensions match, so the product is defined and has size determined by the outer dimensions, that is, 3×2.

$$\begin{bmatrix} 3 & -1 \\ 2 & 0 \\ 1 & 5 \end{bmatrix} \cdot \begin{bmatrix} 5 & 4 \\ -2 & 3 \end{bmatrix} = \begin{bmatrix} 3 \cdot 5 + (-1) \cdot (-2) & 3 \cdot 4 + (-1) \cdot 3 \\ 2 \cdot 5 + 0 \cdot (-2) & 2 \cdot 4 + 0 \cdot 3 \\ 1 \cdot 5 + 5 \cdot (-2) & 1 \cdot 4 + 5 \cdot 3 \end{bmatrix}$$

$$= \begin{bmatrix} 17 & 9 \\ 10 & 8 \\ -5 & 19 \end{bmatrix}$$

◆

Multiplication of matrices has many properties in common with multiplication of ordinary numbers. However, there is at least one important difference. With matrix multiplication, the order of the factors is usually important. For example, the product of a 2×3 matrix times a 3×2 matrix is defined: The product is a 2×2 matrix. If the order is reversed to a 3×2 matrix times a 2×3 matrix, the product is a 3×3 matrix. So reversing the order may change the size of the product. Even when it does not, reversing the order may still change the entries in the product, as the following two products demonstrate:

$$\begin{bmatrix} 1 & 5 \\ 3 & 2 \end{bmatrix} \begin{bmatrix} 1 & 2 \\ 1 & 0 \end{bmatrix} = \begin{bmatrix} 6 & 2 \\ 5 & 6 \end{bmatrix}; \quad \begin{bmatrix} 1 & 2 \\ 1 & 0 \end{bmatrix} \begin{bmatrix} 1 & 5 \\ 3 & 2 \end{bmatrix} = \begin{bmatrix} 7 & 9 \\ 1 & 5 \end{bmatrix}.$$

▶ Example 4   An investment trust has investments in three states. Its deposits in each state are divided among bonds, mortgages, and consumer loans. On January 1 the amount (in millions of dollars) of money invested in each category by state is given by the matrix

	Bonds	Mortgages	Consumer loans
State A	10	5	20
State B	30	12	10
State C	15	6	25

The current average yields are 7% for bonds, 9% for mortgages, and 15% for consumer loans. Determine the earnings of the trust from its investments in each state.

Solution   Define the matrix of investment yields by

$$\begin{bmatrix} .07 \\ .09 \\ .15 \end{bmatrix} \begin{matrix} \text{Bonds} \\ \text{Mortgages} \\ \text{Consumer loans.} \end{matrix}$$

The amount earned in state A, for instance, is

[amount of bonds][yield of bonds]

+ [amount of mortgages][yield of mortgages]

+ [amount of consumer loans][yield of consumer loans]

$$= (10)(.07) + (5)(.09) + (20)(.15).$$

And this is just the first entry of the product:

$$\begin{bmatrix} 10 & 5 & 20 \\ 30 & 12 & 10 \\ 15 & 6 & 25 \end{bmatrix} \begin{bmatrix} .07 \\ .09 \\ .15 \end{bmatrix}.$$

Similarly, the earnings for the other states are the second and third entries of the product. Carrying out the arithmetic, we find that

$$\begin{bmatrix} 10 & 5 & 20 \\ 30 & 12 & 10 \\ 15 & 6 & 25 \end{bmatrix} \begin{bmatrix} .07 \\ .09 \\ .15 \end{bmatrix} = \begin{bmatrix} 4.15 \\ 4.68 \\ 5.34 \end{bmatrix}.$$

Therefore, the trust earns $4.15 million in state A, $4.68 million in state B, and $5.34 million in state C. ◆

▶ Example 5 A clothing manufacturer has factories in Los Angeles, San Antonio, and Newark. Sales (in thousands) during the first quarter of last year are summarized in the production matrix

	Los Angeles	San Antonio	Newark
Coats	12	13	38
Shirts	25	5	26
Sweaters	11	8	8
Ties	5	0	12

During this period the selling price of a coat was $100, of a shirt $10, of a sweater $25, and of a tie $5.

(a) Use a matrix calculation to determine the total revenue produced by each of the factories.

(b) Suppose that the prices had been $110, $8, $20, and $10, respectively. How would this have affected the revenue of each factory?

Solution (a) For each factory, we wish to multiply the price of each item by the number produced to arrive at revenue. Since the production figures for the various items of clothing are arranged down the columns, we arrange the prices in a row matrix, ready for multiplication. The price matrix is

$$\begin{bmatrix} 100 & 10 & 25 & 5 \end{bmatrix}.$$

The revenues of the various factories are then the entries of the product

$$\begin{bmatrix} 100 & 10 & 25 & 5 \end{bmatrix} \begin{bmatrix} 12 & 13 & 38 \\ 25 & 5 & 26 \\ 11 & 8 & 8 \\ 5 & 0 & 12 \end{bmatrix} = \begin{array}{ccc} \text{Los Angeles} & \text{San Antonio} & \text{Newark} \\ \begin{bmatrix} 1750 & 1550 & 4320 \end{bmatrix}. \end{array}$$

Since the production figures are in thousands, the revenue figures are in thousands of dollars. That is, the Los Angeles factory has revenues of $1,750,000, the San Antonio factory $1,550,000, and the Newark factory $4,320,000.

(b) In a similar way, we determine the revenue of each factory if the price matrix had been $\begin{bmatrix} 110 & 8 & 20 & 10 \end{bmatrix}$.

$$\begin{bmatrix} 110 & 8 & 20 & 10 \end{bmatrix} \begin{bmatrix} 12 & 13 & 38 \\ 25 & 5 & 26 \\ 11 & 8 & 8 \\ 5 & 0 & 12 \end{bmatrix} = \begin{array}{ccc} \text{Los Angeles} & \text{San Antonio} & \text{Newark} \\ \begin{bmatrix} 1790 & 1630 & 4668 \end{bmatrix}. \end{array}$$

The change in revenue at each factory can be read from the difference of the revenue matrices:

$$\begin{bmatrix} 1790 & 1630 & 4668 \end{bmatrix} - \begin{bmatrix} 1750 & 1550 & 4320 \end{bmatrix} = \begin{bmatrix} 40 & 80 & 348 \end{bmatrix}.$$

If prices had been as given in (b), revenues of the Los Angeles factory would have increased by $40,000, revenues at San Antonio would have increased by $80,000, and revenues at Newark would have increased by $348,000. ◆

There are special matrices analogous to the number 1. Such matrices are called *identity matrices*. The identity matrix I_n of size n is the $n \times n$ square matrix with all zeros except for ones down the upper-left-to-lower-right diagonal. Here are the identity matrices of sizes 2, 3, and 4:

$$I_2 = \begin{bmatrix} 1 & 0 \\ 0 & 1 \end{bmatrix}; \qquad I_3 = \begin{bmatrix} 1 & 0 & 0 \\ 0 & 1 & 0 \\ 0 & 0 & 1 \end{bmatrix}; \qquad I_4 = \begin{bmatrix} 1 & 0 & 0 & 0 \\ 0 & 1 & 0 & 0 \\ 0 & 0 & 1 & 0 \\ 0 & 0 & 0 & 1 \end{bmatrix}.$$

The characteristic property of an identity matrix is that it plays the role of the number 1; that is,

$$I_n \cdot A = A \cdot I_n = A$$

for all $n \times n$ matrices A.

One of the principal uses of matrices is in dealing with systems of linear equations. Matrices provide a compact way of writing systems, as the next example shows.

▶ Example 6   Write the system of linear equations

$$\begin{cases} -2x + 4y = 2 \\ -3x + 7y = 7 \end{cases}$$

as a matrix equation.

Solution   The system of equations can be written in the form

$$\begin{bmatrix} -2x + 4y \\ -3x + 7y \end{bmatrix} = \begin{bmatrix} 2 \\ 7 \end{bmatrix}.$$

So consider the matrices

$$A = \begin{bmatrix} -2 & 4 \\ -3 & 7 \end{bmatrix}, \qquad X = \begin{bmatrix} x \\ y \end{bmatrix}, \qquad B = \begin{bmatrix} 2 \\ 7 \end{bmatrix}.$$

Notice that

$$AX = \begin{bmatrix} -2 & 4 \\ -3 & 7 \end{bmatrix} \begin{bmatrix} x \\ y \end{bmatrix} = \begin{bmatrix} -2x + 4y \\ -3x + 7y \end{bmatrix}.$$

Thus, AX is a 2×1 column matrix whose entries correspond to the left side of the given system of linear equations. Since the entries of B correspond to the right side of the system of equations, we can rewrite the given system in the form

$$AX = B$$

—that is,

$$\begin{bmatrix} -2 & 4 \\ -3 & 7 \end{bmatrix} \begin{bmatrix} x \\ y \end{bmatrix} = \begin{bmatrix} 2 \\ 7 \end{bmatrix}. \qquad \blacklozenge$$

The matrix A of the preceding example displays the coefficients of the variables x and y, and so it is called the *coefficient matrix* of the system.

GC   The arithmetic operations $+$, $-$, and $*$ can be applied to matrices in much the same way as to numbers, as Figs. 1 and 2 show. (*Note:* **[A]*[B]** also can be written as **[A][B]**.) Identity matrices are placed on the home screen with the command **identity(** from the MATRX/MATH menu, as shown in Fig. 3. The value in the ith row, jth column of the matrix **[A]** can be displayed with **[A](i,j)**. See Fig. 4.

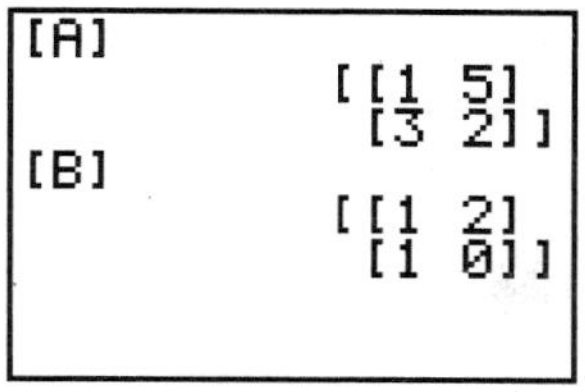

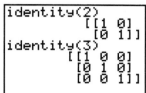

[A]
$$\begin{bmatrix} 1 & 5 \\ 3 & 2 \end{bmatrix}$$

[B]
$$\begin{bmatrix} 1 & 2 \\ 1 & 0 \end{bmatrix}$$

Figure 1.

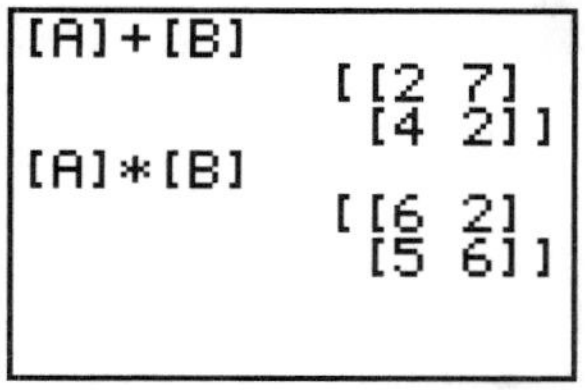

[A]+[B]
$$\begin{bmatrix} 2 & 7 \\ 4 & 2 \end{bmatrix}$$

[A]*[B]
$$\begin{bmatrix} 6 & 2 \\ 5 & 6 \end{bmatrix}$$

Figure 2.

identity(2)
$$\begin{bmatrix} 1 & 0 \\ 0 & 1 \end{bmatrix}$$

identity(3)
$$\begin{bmatrix} 1 & 0 & 0 \\ 0 & 1 & 0 \\ 0 & 0 & 1 \end{bmatrix}$$

Figure 3.

[A]
$$\begin{bmatrix} 1 & 5 & -4 \\ 3 & 2 & 25 \end{bmatrix}$$

[A](2,3)
$$25$$

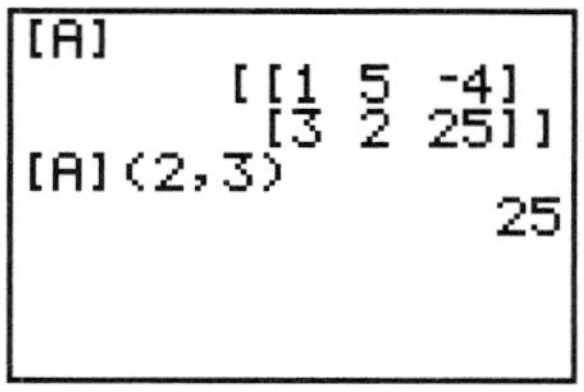

Figure 4.

**Practice Problems
2.3**

1. Compute

$$\begin{bmatrix} 3 & 1 & 2 \\ -1 & 0 & \frac{1}{2} \\ 0 & 4 & 1 \end{bmatrix} \begin{bmatrix} 7 & -1 & 0 \\ 5 & 4 & 2 \\ -6 & 0 & 4 \end{bmatrix}.$$

2. Give the system of linear equations that is equivalent to the matrix equation

$$\begin{bmatrix} 3 & -6 \\ 2 & 1 \end{bmatrix} \begin{bmatrix} x \\ y \end{bmatrix} = \begin{bmatrix} 5 \\ 0 \end{bmatrix}.$$

3. Give a matrix equation equivalent to this system of equations:

$$\begin{cases} 8x + 3y = 7 \\ 9x - 2y = -5. \end{cases}$$

▶ Exercises 2.3

In Exercises 1–6, give the size and special characteristics of the given matrix (such as square, column, row, identity).

1. $\begin{bmatrix} 3 & 2 & 4 \\ \frac{1}{2} & 0 & 6 \end{bmatrix}$

2. $\begin{bmatrix} 3 \\ -1 \end{bmatrix}$

3. $\begin{bmatrix} 2 & \frac{1}{3} & 0 \end{bmatrix}$

4. $\begin{bmatrix} 1 & 0 \\ 0 & 1 \end{bmatrix}$

5. $\begin{bmatrix} -2 \end{bmatrix}$

6. $\begin{bmatrix} 0 & 0 & 0 & 0 \\ 0 & 0 & 0 & 0 \end{bmatrix}$

In Exercises 7–14, perform the indicated matrix calculations.

7. $\begin{bmatrix} 4 & -2 \\ 3 & 0 \end{bmatrix} + \begin{bmatrix} 5 & 5 \\ 4 & -1 \end{bmatrix}$

8. $\begin{bmatrix} 8 \\ -3 \end{bmatrix} + \begin{bmatrix} 5 \\ 6 \end{bmatrix}$

9. $\begin{bmatrix} 2 & 8 \\ \frac{4}{3} & 4 \\ 1 & -2 \end{bmatrix} - \begin{bmatrix} 1 & 5 \\ \frac{1}{3} & 2 \\ -3 & 0 \end{bmatrix}$

10. $\begin{bmatrix} 1 & 0 \\ 0 & 1 \end{bmatrix} - \begin{bmatrix} .8 & .5 \\ .2 & .5 \end{bmatrix}$

11. $\begin{bmatrix} 5 & 3 \end{bmatrix} \begin{bmatrix} 1 \\ 2 \end{bmatrix}$

12. $\begin{bmatrix} 1 & 0 & 0 \end{bmatrix} \begin{bmatrix} \frac{1}{2} \\ 6 \\ 2 \end{bmatrix}$

13. $\begin{bmatrix} 6 & 1 & 5 \end{bmatrix} \begin{bmatrix} \frac{1}{2} \\ -3 \\ 2 \end{bmatrix}$

14. $\begin{bmatrix} 0 & 0 \end{bmatrix} \begin{bmatrix} 5 \\ -3 \end{bmatrix}$

In Exercises 15–20, the sizes of two matrices are given. Tell whether or not the product AB is defined. If so, give its size.

15. A, 3×4; B, 4×5
16. A, 3×3; B, 3×4
17. A, 3×2; B, 3×2
18. A, 1×1; B, 1×1
19. A, 3×3; B, 3×1
20. A, 4×2; B, 3×4

In Exercises 21–30, perform the multiplication.

21. $\begin{bmatrix} 3 & 1 \\ 0 & 2 \end{bmatrix} \begin{bmatrix} 1 & 4 \\ 3 & 5 \end{bmatrix}$

22. $\begin{bmatrix} 4 & -1 \\ 2 & \frac{1}{2} \end{bmatrix} \begin{bmatrix} 3 \\ 2 \end{bmatrix}$

23. $\begin{bmatrix} 4 & 1 & 0 \\ -2 & 0 & 3 \\ 1 & 5 & -1 \end{bmatrix} \begin{bmatrix} 5 \\ 1 \\ 2 \end{bmatrix}$

24. $\begin{bmatrix} 0 & 0 \\ 0 & 0 \\ 0 & 0 \end{bmatrix} \begin{bmatrix} 1 & 2 \\ 3 & 4 \end{bmatrix}$

25. $\begin{bmatrix} 1 & 0 \\ 0 & 1 \end{bmatrix} \begin{bmatrix} 5 & 6 \\ 7 & 8 \end{bmatrix}$

26. $\begin{bmatrix} 1 & 2 \\ 1 & 3 \end{bmatrix} \begin{bmatrix} 3 & -2 \\ -1 & 1 \end{bmatrix}$

27. $\begin{bmatrix} .6 & .3 \\ .4 & .7 \end{bmatrix} \begin{bmatrix} .6 & .3 \\ .4 & .7 \end{bmatrix}$

28. $\begin{bmatrix} 0 & 1 & 2 \\ -1 & 4 & \frac{1}{2} \\ 1 & 3 & 0 \end{bmatrix} \begin{bmatrix} 3 & -1 & 5 \\ 0 & 2 & 2 \\ 4 & -6 & 0 \end{bmatrix}$

29. $\begin{bmatrix} 2 & -1 & 4 \\ 0 & 1 & 0 \\ \frac{1}{2} & 3 & -2 \end{bmatrix} \begin{bmatrix} 4 & 8 & 0 \\ 3 & -1 & 2 \\ 5 & 0 & 1 \end{bmatrix}$

30. $\begin{bmatrix} 1 & 0 & 0 \\ 0 & 1 & 0 \\ 0 & 0 & 1 \end{bmatrix} \begin{bmatrix} 1 \\ 2 \\ 3 \end{bmatrix}$

In Exercises 31–34, give the system of linear equations that is equivalent to the matrix equation. Do not solve.

31. $\begin{bmatrix} 2 & 3 \\ 4 & 5 \end{bmatrix} \begin{bmatrix} x \\ y \end{bmatrix} = \begin{bmatrix} 6 \\ 7 \end{bmatrix}$

32. $\begin{bmatrix} -3 & 4 \\ 0 & 1 \end{bmatrix} \begin{bmatrix} x \\ y \end{bmatrix} = \begin{bmatrix} 1 \\ 1 \end{bmatrix}$

33. $\begin{bmatrix} 1 & 2 & 3 \\ 4 & 5 & 6 \\ 7 & 8 & 9 \end{bmatrix} \begin{bmatrix} x \\ y \\ z \end{bmatrix} = \begin{bmatrix} 10 \\ 11 \\ 12 \end{bmatrix}$

34. $\begin{bmatrix} 1 & 0 & 0 \\ 0 & 1 & 0 \\ 0 & 0 & 1 \end{bmatrix} \begin{bmatrix} x \\ y \\ z \end{bmatrix} = \begin{bmatrix} 1 \\ 2 \\ 3 \end{bmatrix}$

In Exercises 35–38, write the given system of linear equations in matrix form.

35. $\begin{cases} 3x + 2y = -1 \\ 7x - y = 2 \end{cases}$

36. $\begin{cases} 5x - 2y = 6 \\ -2x + 4y = 0 \end{cases}$

37. $\begin{cases} x - 2y + 3z = 5 \\ y + z = 6 \\ z = 2 \end{cases}$

38. $\begin{cases} -2x + 4y - z = 5 \\ x + 6y + 3z = -1 \\ 7x + 4z = 8 \end{cases}$

The distributive law says that $(A+B)C = AC+BC$. That is, adding A and B and then multiplying on the right by C gives the same result as first multiplying each of A and B on the right by C and then adding. In Exercises 39 and 40, verify the distributive law for the given matrices.

39. $A = \begin{bmatrix} 1 & 2 \\ 0 & 3 \end{bmatrix}$, $B = \begin{bmatrix} 3 & -2 \\ 4 & 5 \end{bmatrix}$, $C = \begin{bmatrix} 1 & 6 \\ 2 & 0 \end{bmatrix}$

40. $A = \begin{bmatrix} 1 & 0 & 0 \\ 0 & 1 & 0 \\ 0 & 0 & 1 \end{bmatrix}$, $B = \begin{bmatrix} 2 & 1 & 3 \\ 0 & 5 & -1 \\ 3 & 6 & 0 \end{bmatrix}$, $C = \begin{bmatrix} 0 \\ 3 \\ -4 \end{bmatrix}$

Two $n \times n$ matrices A and B are called *inverses* (of one another) if both products AB and BA equal I_n. Check that the pairs of matrices in Exercises 41 and 42 are inverses.

41. $\begin{bmatrix} 3 & -1 \\ -1 & \frac{1}{2} \end{bmatrix}$, $\begin{bmatrix} 1 & 2 \\ 2 & 6 \end{bmatrix}$

42. $\begin{bmatrix} 2 & 8 & -11 \\ -1 & -5 & 7 \\ 1 & 2 & -3 \end{bmatrix}$, $\begin{bmatrix} 1 & 2 & 1 \\ 4 & 5 & -3 \\ 3 & 4 & -2 \end{bmatrix}$

43. The quantities of pants, shirts, and jackets owned by Mike and Don are given by the matrix A, and the costs of these items are given by matrix B.

$$\begin{array}{c} \\ \text{Mike} \\ \text{Don} \end{array} \begin{array}{ccc} \text{Pants} & \text{Shirts} & \text{Jackets} \\ \begin{bmatrix} 6 & 8 & 2 \\ 2 & 5 & 3 \end{bmatrix} \end{array} = A$$

$$\begin{array}{c} \text{Pants} \\ \text{Shirts} \\ \text{Jackets} \end{array} \begin{bmatrix} 20 \\ 15 \\ 50 \end{bmatrix} = B$$

(a) Calculate the matrix AB.

(b) Interpret the entries of the matrix AB.

44. A company has three appliance stores that sell washers, dryers, and stoves. Matrices A and B give the wholesale and retail prices of these items, respectively. Matrices C and D give the quantities of these items sold by the three stores in September and October, respectively.

$$A = \begin{array}{ccc} \text{Washers} & \text{Dryers} & \text{Stoves} \\ [\ 300 & 250 & 450\ ] \end{array}$$

$$B = \begin{array}{ccc} \text{Washers} & \text{Dryers} & \text{Stoves} \\ [\ 500 & 450 & 750\ ] \end{array}$$

$$C = \begin{array}{c} \\ \\ \\ \\ \end{array} \begin{array}{ccc} \text{Store 1} & \text{Store 2} & \text{Store 3} \\ \begin{bmatrix} 30 & 40 & 20 \\ 20 & 30 & 10 \\ 10 & 5 & 35 \end{bmatrix} \end{array} \begin{array}{c} \text{Washers} \\ \text{Dryers} \\ \text{Stoves} \end{array}$$

$$D = \begin{bmatrix} 20 & 50 & 30 \\ 30 & 10 & 20 \\ 10 & 20 & 30 \end{bmatrix} \begin{matrix} \text{Washers} \\ \text{Dryers} \\ \text{Stoves} \end{matrix}$$

Store 1   Store 2   Store 3

Determine and interpret the following matrices.

(a) AC (b) AD

(c) BC (d) BD

(e) $B - A$ (f) $(B - A)C$

(g) $(B - A)D$ (h) $C + D$

(i) $(B - A)(C + D)$

45. Three professors teaching the same course have entirely different grading policies. The percentage of students given each grade by the professors is summarized in the matrix

Grade

	A	B	C	D	F
Prof. I	25	35	30	10	0
Prof. II	10	20	40	20	10
Prof. III	5	10	20	40	25

(a) The point values of the grades are A = 4, B = 3, C = 2, D = 1, and F = 0. Use matrix multiplication to determine the average grade given by each professor.

(b) Professor I has 240 students, professor II has 120 students, and professor III has 40 students. Use matrix multiplication to determine the numbers of A's, B's, C's, D's, and F's given.

46. A professor bases semester grades on four 100-point items: homework, quizzes, a midterm exam, and a final exam. Students may choose one of three schemes summarized in the following matrix for weighting the points from the four items. Use matrix multiplication to determine the most advantageous weighting scheme for a student who earned 97 points on homework, 72 points on the quizzes, 83 points on the midterm exam, and 75 points on the final exam.

Items

	Hw	Qu	ME	FE
Scheme I	.10	.10	.30	.50
Scheme II	.10	.20	.30	.40
Scheme III	.15	.15	.35	.35

47. In a certain town the proportions of voters voting Democratic and Republican by various age groups is summarized by this matrix:

	Dem.	Rep.
Under 30	.65	.35
30–50	.55	.45
Over 50	.45	.55

$= A.$

The population of voters in the town by age group is given by the matrix

$$B = \begin{bmatrix} \underbrace{6000}_{\substack{\text{Under} \\ 30}} & \underbrace{8000}_{\substack{\text{30–50}}} & \underbrace{4000}_{\substack{\text{Over} \\ 50}} \end{bmatrix}.$$

Interpret the entries of the matrix product BA.

48. Refer to Exercise 47.

(a) Using the given data, which party would win and what would be the percentage of the winning vote?

(b) Suppose that the population of the town shifted toward older residents as reflected in the population matrix $B = \begin{bmatrix} 2000 & 4000 & 12{,}000 \end{bmatrix}$. What would be the result of the election now?

49. Suppose that a contractor employs carpenters, bricklayers, and plumbers, working three shifts per day. The number of labor-hours employed in each of the shifts is summarized in the matrix

Shift

	1	2	3
Carpenters	50	20	10
Bricklayers	30	30	15
Plumbers	20	20	5

Labor in shift 1 costs $10 per hour, in shift 2 $15 per hour, and in shift 3 $20 per hour. Use matrix multiplication to compute the amount spent on each type of labor.

50. A flu epidemic hits a large city. Each resident of the city is either sick, well, or a carrier. The proportion of people in each of the categories is expressed by the matrix

Age

	0–10	10–30	Over 30
Well	.70	.70	.60
Sick	.10	.20	.30
Carrier	.20	.10	.10

$= A.$

The population of the city is distributed by age and sex as follows:

		Male	Female
	0–10	60,000	65,000
Age	10–30	100,000	110,000
	Over 30	200,000	230,000

$= B.$

(a) Compute AB.

(b) How many sick males are there?

(c) How many female carriers are there?

51. Mikey's diet consists of food X and food Y. The matrix N represents the number of units of nutrients 1, 2, and 3 per ounce for each of the foods.

$$N = \begin{array}{c} \\ \begin{array}{ccc} 1 & 2 & 3 \end{array} \\ \begin{bmatrix} 60 & 50 & 38 \\ 42 & 50 & 67 \end{bmatrix} \begin{array}{c} X \\ Y \end{array} \end{array}$$

The matrices B, L, and D represent the number of ounces of each food that Mikey eats each day for breakfast, lunch, and dinner, respectively.

$$B = \begin{array}{c} \begin{array}{cc} X & Y \end{array} \\ \begin{bmatrix} 2 & 1 \end{bmatrix} \end{array} \quad L = \begin{array}{c} \begin{array}{cc} X & Y \end{array} \\ \begin{bmatrix} 1 & 3 \end{bmatrix} \end{array} \quad D = \begin{array}{c} \begin{array}{cc} X & Y \end{array} \\ \begin{bmatrix} 2 & 4 \end{bmatrix} \end{array}$$

Calculate and interpret the following.

(a) BN　　　(b) LN　　　(c) DN

(d) $B + L + D$　　(e) $(B + L + D)N$

52. A bakery makes three types of cookies, I, II, and III. Each type of cookie is made from the four ingredients A, B, C, and D. The number of units of each ingredient used in each type of cookie is given by the matrix M. The cost per unit of each of the four ingredients (in cents) is given by the matrix N. The selling price for each of the cookies (in cents) is given by the matrix S. The baker receives an order for 10 type I cookies, 20 type II cookies, and 15 type III cookies, as represented by the matrix R.

$$M = \begin{array}{c} \begin{array}{cccc} A & B & C & D \end{array} \\ \begin{bmatrix} 1 & 0 & 2 & 4 \\ 3 & 2 & 1 & 1 \\ 2 & 5 & 3 & 1 \end{bmatrix} \begin{array}{c} I \\ II \\ III \end{array} \end{array} \quad N = \begin{bmatrix} 10 \\ 20 \\ 15 \\ 17 \end{bmatrix} \begin{array}{c} A \\ B \\ C \\ D \end{array}$$

$$S = \begin{bmatrix} 175 \\ 150 \\ 225 \end{bmatrix} \begin{array}{c} I \\ II \\ III \end{array} \quad R = \begin{array}{c} \begin{array}{ccc} I & II & III \end{array} \\ \begin{bmatrix} 10 & 20 & 15 \end{bmatrix} \end{array}$$

Calculate and interpret the following.

(a) RM　　　(b) MN　　　(c) RMN

(d) $S - MN$　　(e) $R(S - MN)$　　(f) RS

53. A community fitness center has a pool and a weight room. The admission prices (in dollars) for residents and nonresidents are given by the matrix

$$P = \begin{bmatrix} 4.50 \\ 5.00 \end{bmatrix} \begin{array}{c} \text{Residents} \\ \text{Nonresidents.} \end{array}$$

The average daily numbers of customers for the fitness center are given by the matrix

$$A = \begin{array}{c} \begin{array}{cc} \text{Residents} & \text{Nonresidents} \end{array} \\ \begin{bmatrix} 90 & 63 \\ 78 & 59 \end{bmatrix} \begin{array}{c} \text{Pool} \\ \text{Weight room.} \end{array} \end{array}$$

(a) Compute AP.

(b) What is the average amount of money taken in by the pool each day?

54. A company makes radios and TV sets. Each radio requires 3 hours of assembly and $\frac{1}{2}$ hour of packaging, while each TV set requires 5 hours of assembly and 1 hour of packaging.

(a) Write a matrix T representing the required time for assembly and packaging of radios and TV sets.

(b) The company receives an order from a retail outlet for 30 radios and 20 TV sets. Find a matrix S so that either ST or TS gives the total assembly time and the total packaging time required to fill the order. What is the total assembly time? What is the total packaging time?

55. The matrix equation $AX = B$, where A is a 3×3 matrix, has the solution $x = 5$, $y = 4$, $z = 3$. What will be the new solution to this equation if the first and third columns of A are interchanged?

56. Find the values of a and b for which $A \cdot B = I_3$, where

$$A = \begin{bmatrix} 3 & 2 & 0 \\ 1 & 1 & 0 \\ 0 & 0 & 1 \end{bmatrix} \quad \text{and} \quad B = \begin{bmatrix} a & b & 0 \\ -1 & 3 & 0 \\ 0 & 0 & 1 \end{bmatrix}.$$

In Exercises 57 and 58, determine the matrix B based on the screen shown.

57.
```
[A]
      [[1  5  -4]
       [3  2  25]]
[A]+[B]
      [[4   3  -3]
       [-2  8  32]]
```

58.
```
[A]
      [[1  5  -4]
       [3  2  25]]
[A]-[B]
      [[-4  1  -1]
       [3   3  23]]
```

59. If A is a 3×4 matrix and $A(BB)$ is defined, what is the size of matrix B?

60. If B is a 3×5 matrix and $(AA)B$ is defined, what is the size of matrix A?

Exercises 61–70 require the use of a graphing calculator or a computer.

In Exercises 61–69, calculate the given expression, where

$$A = \begin{bmatrix} .4 & 7 & -3 \\ 19 & .5 & 1.6 \\ -9 & 11 & 2 \end{bmatrix}, \quad B = \begin{bmatrix} 6 & -9 & .3 \\ 1.5 & 22 & -4 \\ -5 & 6.6 & 14 \end{bmatrix},$$

and

$$C = \begin{bmatrix} 2.4 & 8 & -.2 \\ -11 & .3 & 6 \\ 7 & -4 & 5.1 \end{bmatrix}.$$

61. AB **62.** BA

63. $A(B+C)$ **64.** $AB + AC$

65. Display a_{23} on the home screen.

66. Display a_{31} on the home screen.

67. A^2 (that is, AA)   **68.** A^3 (that is, AAA)

69. Calculate `[A]^2` and `[A]^3`. Compare your results with your answers in Exercises 67 and 68.

70. Try multiplying matrices A and B, where the number of columns of A differs from the number of rows of B. How does your calculator or computer respond?

Solutions to Practice Problems 2.3

1. Answer:

$$\begin{bmatrix} 3 & 1 & 2 \\ -1 & 0 & \frac{1}{2} \\ 0 & 4 & 1 \end{bmatrix} \begin{bmatrix} 7 & -1 & 0 \\ 5 & 4 & 2 \\ -6 & 0 & 4 \end{bmatrix} = \begin{bmatrix} 14 & 1 & 10 \\ -10 & 1 & 2 \\ 14 & 16 & 12 \end{bmatrix}.$$

The systematic steps to be taken are as follows:

(a) Determine the size of the product matrix. Since we have a

$$\text{(3)}\times 3 \quad \text{times a} \quad 3 \times \text{(3)},$$
$$\text{└── outer dimensions ──┘}$$

the size of the product is given by the outer dimensions or 3×3. Begin by drawing a 3×3 rectangular array.

(b) Find the entries one at a time. To find the entry in the first row, first column of the product, look at the first row of the left given matrix and the first column of the right given matrix and form their product.

$$\begin{bmatrix} 3 & 1 & 2 \\ -1 & 0 & \frac{1}{2} \\ 0 & 4 & 1 \end{bmatrix} \begin{bmatrix} 7 & -1 & 0 \\ 5 & 4 & 2 \\ -6 & 0 & 4 \end{bmatrix} = \begin{bmatrix} 14 & & \\ & & \\ & & \end{bmatrix}$$

since $3 \cdot 7 + 1 \cdot 5 + 2(-6) = 14$. In general, to find the entry in the ith row, jth column of the product, put one finger on the ith row of the left given matrix and another finger on the jth column of the right given matrix. Then multiply the row matrix times the column matrix to get the desired entry.

2. Denote the three matrices by A, X, and B, respectively. Since b_{11} (the entry of the first row, first column of B) is 5, this means that

$$\begin{bmatrix} \text{first row of } A \end{bmatrix} \begin{bmatrix} \text{first} \\ \text{column} \\ \text{of } X \end{bmatrix} = \begin{bmatrix} b_{11} \end{bmatrix}.$$

That is,

$$\begin{bmatrix} 3 & -6 \end{bmatrix} \begin{bmatrix} x \\ y \end{bmatrix} = \begin{bmatrix} 5 \end{bmatrix} \quad \text{or} \quad 3x - 6y = 5.$$

Similarly, $b_{21} = 0$ says that $2x + y = 0$. Therefore, the corresponding system of linear equations is

$$\begin{cases} 3x - 6y = 5 \\ 2x + y = 0. \end{cases}$$

Solutions to Practice Problems 2.3 (Continued)

3. The coefficient matrix is

$$\begin{bmatrix} 8 & 3 \\ 9 & -2 \end{bmatrix}.$$

So the system is equivalent to the matrix equation

$$\begin{bmatrix} 8 & 3 \\ 9 & -2 \end{bmatrix} \begin{bmatrix} x \\ y \end{bmatrix} = \begin{bmatrix} 7 \\ -5 \end{bmatrix}.$$

2.4 The Inverse of a Matrix

In Section 2.3 we introduced the operations of addition, subtraction, and multiplication of matrices. In this section let us pursue the algebra of matrices a bit further and consider equations involving matrices. Specifically, we consider equations of the form

$$AX = B, \tag{1}$$

where A and B are given matrices and X is an unknown matrix whose entries are to be determined. Such equations among matrices are intimately bound up with the theory of systems of linear equations. Indeed, we described the connection in a special case in Example 6 of Section 2.3. In that example we wrote the system of linear equations

$$\begin{cases} -2x + 4y = 2 \\ -3x + 7y = 7 \end{cases}$$

as a matrix equation of the form (1), where

$$A = \begin{bmatrix} -2 & 4 \\ -3 & 7 \end{bmatrix}, \qquad B = \begin{bmatrix} 2 \\ 7 \end{bmatrix}, \qquad X = \begin{bmatrix} x \\ y \end{bmatrix}.$$

Note that by determining the entries (x and y) of the unknown matrix X, we solve the system of linear equations. We will return to this example after we have made a complete study of the matrix equation (1).

As motivation for our solution of equation (1), let us consider the analogous equation among numbers:

$$ax = b,$$

where a and b are given numbers[1] and x is to be determined. Let us examine its solution in great detail. Multiply both sides by $1/a$. (Note that $1/a$ makes sense, since $a \neq 0$.)

$$\left(\frac{1}{a}\right) \cdot (ax) = \frac{1}{a} \cdot b$$

$$\left(\frac{1}{a} \cdot a\right) \cdot x = \frac{1}{a} \cdot b$$

$$1 \cdot x = \frac{1}{a} \cdot b$$

$$x = \frac{1}{a} \cdot b$$

---

[1] We may as well assume that $a \neq 0$. Otherwise, x does not occur.

Let us model our solution of equation (1) on the preceding calculation. To do so, we need to multiply both sides of the equation by a matrix that plays the same role in matrix arithmetic as $1/a$ plays in ordinary arithmetic. Our first task then will be to introduce this matrix and study its properties.

The number $1/a$ has the following relationship to the number a:

$$\frac{1}{a} \cdot a = a \cdot \frac{1}{a} = 1. \tag{2}$$

The matrix analog of the number 1 is an identity matrix I. This prompts us to generalize equation (2) to matrices as follows. Suppose that we are given a square matrix A. Then the *inverse* of A, denoted A^{-1}, is a square matrix with the property

$$A^{-1}A = I \quad \text{and} \quad AA^{-1} = I, \tag{3}$$

where I is an identity matrix of the same size as A. The matrix A^{-1} is the matrix analog of the number $1/a$. It can be shown that a matrix A has at most one inverse. (However, A may not have an inverse at all; see Example 3.)

If we are given a matrix A, then it is easy to determine whether or not a given matrix is its inverse. Merely check equation (3) with the given matrix substituted for A^{-1}. For example, if

$$A = \begin{bmatrix} -2 & 4 \\ -3 & 7 \end{bmatrix}, \quad \text{then} \quad A^{-1} = \begin{bmatrix} -\frac{7}{2} & 2 \\ -\frac{3}{2} & 1 \end{bmatrix}.$$

Indeed, we have

$$\underset{A^{-1}}{\begin{bmatrix} -\frac{7}{2} & 2 \\ -\frac{3}{2} & 1 \end{bmatrix}} \underset{A}{\begin{bmatrix} -2 & 4 \\ -3 & 7 \end{bmatrix}} = \begin{bmatrix} 7-6 & -14+14 \\ 3-3 & -6+7 \end{bmatrix} = \underset{I_2}{\begin{bmatrix} 1 & 0 \\ 0 & 1 \end{bmatrix}}$$

and

$$\underset{A}{\begin{bmatrix} -2 & 4 \\ -3 & 7 \end{bmatrix}} \underset{A^{-1}}{\begin{bmatrix} -\frac{7}{2} & 2 \\ -\frac{3}{2} & 1 \end{bmatrix}} = \begin{bmatrix} 7-6 & -4+4 \\ \frac{21}{2}-\frac{21}{2} & -6+7 \end{bmatrix} = \underset{I_2}{\begin{bmatrix} 1 & 0 \\ 0 & 1 \end{bmatrix}}.$$

The inverse of a matrix can be calculated using Gaussian elimination, as the next example illustrates.

▶ Example 1   Let $A = \begin{bmatrix} 3 & 1 \\ 5 & 2 \end{bmatrix}$. Determine A^{-1}.

Solution   Since A is a 2×2 matrix, A^{-1} is also a 2×2 matrix and satisfies

$$AA^{-1} = I_2 \quad \text{and} \quad A^{-1}A = I_2, \tag{4}$$

where $I_2 = \begin{bmatrix} 1 & 0 \\ 0 & 1 \end{bmatrix}$ is the 2×2 identity matrix. Suppose that

$$A^{-1} = \begin{bmatrix} x & y \\ z & w \end{bmatrix}.$$

Then the first equation of (4) reads

$$\begin{bmatrix} 3 & 1 \\ 5 & 2 \end{bmatrix} \begin{bmatrix} x & y \\ z & w \end{bmatrix} = \begin{bmatrix} 1 & 0 \\ 0 & 1 \end{bmatrix}.$$

Multiplying out the matrices on the left gives

$$\begin{bmatrix} 3x + z & 3y + w \\ 5x + 2z & 5y + 2w \end{bmatrix} = \begin{bmatrix} 1 & 0 \\ 0 & 1 \end{bmatrix}.$$

Now equate corresponding elements in the two matrices to obtain the equations

$$\begin{cases} 3x + z = 1 \\ 5x + 2z = 0, \end{cases} \qquad \begin{cases} 3y + w = 0 \\ 5y + 2w = 1. \end{cases}$$

Notice that the equations break up into two pairs of linear equations, each pair involving only two variables. Solving these two systems of linear equations yields $x = 2$, $z = -5$, $y = -1$, and $w = 3$. Therefore,

$$A^{-1} = \begin{bmatrix} 2 & -1 \\ -5 & 3 \end{bmatrix}.$$

Indeed, we may readily verify that

$$\begin{bmatrix} 3 & 1 \\ 5 & 2 \end{bmatrix} \begin{bmatrix} 2 & -1 \\ -5 & 3 \end{bmatrix} = \begin{bmatrix} 1 & 0 \\ 0 & 1 \end{bmatrix}$$

$$\begin{bmatrix} 2 & -1 \\ -5 & 3 \end{bmatrix} \begin{bmatrix} 3 & 1 \\ 5 & 2 \end{bmatrix} = \begin{bmatrix} 1 & 0 \\ 0 & 1 \end{bmatrix}. \qquad \blacklozenge$$

The preceding method can be used to calculate the inverse of matrices of any size, although it involves considerable calculation. We provide a rather efficient computational method for calculating A^{-1} in the next section. For now, however, let us be content with the above method. Using it, we can derive a general formula for A^{-1} in the case where A is a 2×2 matrix.

To determine the inverse of a 2×2 matrix, let

$$A = \begin{bmatrix} a & b \\ c & d \end{bmatrix}.$$

Let $\Delta = ad - bc$, and assume that $\Delta \neq 0$. Then A^{-1} is given by the formula

$$A^{-1} = \begin{bmatrix} \dfrac{d}{\Delta} & -\dfrac{b}{\Delta} \\[2ex] -\dfrac{c}{\Delta} & \dfrac{a}{\Delta} \end{bmatrix}. \tag{5}$$

We will omit the derivation of this formula. It proceeds along lines similar to those of Example 1. Notice that formula (5) involves division by Δ. Since division by 0 is not permissible, it is necessary that $\Delta \neq 0$ for formula (5) to be applied. We discuss the case $\Delta = 0$ in Example 3.

Obtaining equation (5) can be reduced to a simple step-by-step procedure.

To determine the inverse of $\begin{bmatrix} a & b \\ c & d \end{bmatrix}$ if $\Delta = ad - bc \neq 0$:

1. Interchange a and d to get $\begin{bmatrix} d & b \\ c & a \end{bmatrix}$.

2. Change the signs of b and c to get $\begin{bmatrix} d & -b \\ -c & a \end{bmatrix}$.

3. Divide all entries by Δ to get $\begin{bmatrix} \dfrac{d}{\Delta} & -\dfrac{b}{\Delta} \\ -\dfrac{c}{\Delta} & \dfrac{a}{\Delta} \end{bmatrix}$.

▶ **Example 2** Calculate the inverse of $\begin{bmatrix} -2 & 4 \\ -3 & 7 \end{bmatrix}$.

Solution $\Delta = (-2)\cdot 7 - 4\cdot(-3) = -2$, so $\Delta \neq 0$, and we may use the preceding computation.

1. Interchange a and d:

$$\begin{bmatrix} 7 & 4 \\ -3 & -2 \end{bmatrix}.$$

2. Change the signs of b and c:

$$\begin{bmatrix} 7 & -4 \\ 3 & -2 \end{bmatrix}.$$

3. Divide all entries by $\Delta = -2$:

$$\begin{bmatrix} -\frac{7}{2} & 2 \\ -\frac{3}{2} & 1 \end{bmatrix}.$$

Thus

$$\begin{bmatrix} -2 & 4 \\ -3 & 7 \end{bmatrix}^{-1} = \begin{bmatrix} -\frac{7}{2} & 2 \\ -\frac{3}{2} & 1 \end{bmatrix}.$$ ◆

Not every square matrix has an inverse. Indeed, it may be impossible to satisfy equation (3) for any choice of A^{-1}. This phenomenon can even occur in the case of 2×2 matrices. Here one can show that *if $\Delta = 0$, then the matrix does not have an inverse.* The next example illustrates this phenomenon in a special case.

▶ **Example 3** Show that $\begin{bmatrix} 1 & 1 \\ 1 & 1 \end{bmatrix}$ does not have an inverse.

Solution Note first that $\Delta = 1 \cdot 1 - 1 \cdot 1 = 0$, so the inverse cannot be computed via equation (5). Suppose that the given matrix did have an inverse, say

$$\begin{bmatrix} s & t \\ u & v \end{bmatrix}.$$

Then the following equation would hold:

$$\begin{bmatrix} s & t \\ u & v \end{bmatrix} \begin{bmatrix} 1 & 1 \\ 1 & 1 \end{bmatrix} = \begin{bmatrix} 1 & 0 \\ 0 & 1 \end{bmatrix}.$$

On multiplying out the two matrices on the left, we get the equation

$$\begin{bmatrix} s+t & s+t \\ u+v & u+v \end{bmatrix} = \begin{bmatrix} 1 & 0 \\ 0 & 1 \end{bmatrix},$$

so that, on equating entries in the first row:

$$s+t = 1, \qquad s+t = 0.$$

But $s+t$ cannot equal both 1 and 0. So we reach a contradiction, and therefore the original matrix cannot have an inverse. ◆

We were led to introduce the inverse of a matrix from a discussion of the matrix equation $AX = B$. Let us now return to that discussion. Suppose that A and B are given matrices and that we wish to solve the matrix equation

$$AX = B$$

for the unknown matrix X. Suppose further that A has an inverse A^{-1}. Multiply both sides of the equation on the left by A^{-1} to obtain

$$A^{-1} \cdot AX = A^{-1}B.$$

Because $A^{-1} \cdot A = I$, we have

$$IX = A^{-1}B$$
$$X = A^{-1}B.$$

Thus the matrix X is found by simply multiplying B on the left by A^{-1}, and we can summarize our findings as follows:

Solving a Matrix Equation   If the matrix A has an inverse, then the solution of the matrix equation

$$AX = B \quad \text{is given by} \quad X = A^{-1}B.$$

Matrix equations can be used to solve systems of linear equations, as illustrated in the next example.

▶ **Example 4**   Use a matrix equation to solve the system of linear equations

$$\begin{cases} -2x + 4y = 2 \\ -3x + 7y = 7. \end{cases}$$

Solution   In Example 6 of Section 2.3 we saw that the system could be written as a matrix equation:

$$\underset{A}{\begin{bmatrix} -2 & 4 \\ -3 & 7 \end{bmatrix}} \underset{X}{\begin{bmatrix} x \\ y \end{bmatrix}} = \underset{B}{\begin{bmatrix} 2 \\ 7 \end{bmatrix}}.$$

We happen to know A^{-1} from Example 2, namely

$$A^{-1} = \begin{bmatrix} -\frac{7}{2} & 2 \\ -\frac{3}{2} & 1 \end{bmatrix}.$$

So we may compute the matrix $X = A^{-1}B$:

$$X = \begin{bmatrix} x \\ y \end{bmatrix} = \begin{bmatrix} -\frac{7}{2} & 2 \\ -\frac{3}{2} & 1 \end{bmatrix} \begin{bmatrix} 2 \\ 7 \end{bmatrix} = \begin{bmatrix} 7 \\ 4 \end{bmatrix}.$$

Thus, the solution of the system is $x = 7$, $y = 4$. ◆

▶ Example 5   Let x and y denote the number of married and single adults in a certain town as of January 1. Let m and s denote the corresponding numbers for the following year. A statistical survey shows that x, y, m, and s are related by the equations

$$.9x + .2y = m$$
$$.1x + .8y = s.$$

In a given year there were found to be 490,000 married adults and 147,000 single adults.

(a) How many married adults were there in the preceding year?

(b) How many married adults were there two years ago?

Solution   (a) The given equations can be written in the matrix form

$$AX = B,$$

where

$$A = \begin{bmatrix} .9 & .2 \\ .1 & .8 \end{bmatrix}, \qquad X = \begin{bmatrix} x \\ y \end{bmatrix}, \qquad B = \begin{bmatrix} m \\ s \end{bmatrix}.$$

We are given that $B = \begin{bmatrix} 490{,}000 \\ 147{,}000 \end{bmatrix}$. So, since

$$X = A^{-1}B \quad \text{and} \quad A^{-1} = \begin{bmatrix} \frac{8}{7} & -\frac{2}{7} \\ -\frac{1}{7} & \frac{9}{7} \end{bmatrix},$$

we have

$$X = \begin{bmatrix} \frac{8}{7} & -\frac{2}{7} \\ -\frac{1}{7} & \frac{9}{7} \end{bmatrix} \begin{bmatrix} 490{,}000 \\ 147{,}000 \end{bmatrix} = \begin{bmatrix} 518{,}000 \\ 119{,}000 \end{bmatrix}.$$

Thus last year there were 518,000 married adults and 119,000 single adults.

(b) We deduce x and y for two years ago from the values of m and s for last year, namely $m = 518{,}000$, $s = 119{,}000$.

$$X = A^{-1}B = \begin{bmatrix} \frac{8}{7} & -\frac{2}{7} \\ -\frac{1}{7} & \frac{9}{7} \end{bmatrix} \begin{bmatrix} 518{,}000 \\ 119{,}000 \end{bmatrix} = \begin{bmatrix} 558{,}000 \\ 79{,}000 \end{bmatrix}.$$

That is, two years ago there were 558,000 married adults and 79,000 single adults. ◆

▶ **Example 6**   In Section 2.5 we will show that if

$$A = \begin{bmatrix} 4 & -2 & 3 \\ 8 & -3 & 5 \\ 7 & -2 & 4 \end{bmatrix}, \quad \text{then} \quad A^{-1} = \begin{bmatrix} -2 & 2 & -1 \\ 3 & -5 & 4 \\ 5 & -6 & 4 \end{bmatrix}.$$

(a) Use this fact to solve the system of linear equations

$$\begin{cases} 4x - 2y + 3z = 1 \\ 8x - 3y + 5z = 4 \\ 7x - 2y + 4z = 5. \end{cases}$$

(b) Solve the system of equations

$$\begin{cases} 4x - 2y + 3z = 4 \\ 8x - 3y + 5z = 7 \\ 7x - 2y + 4z = 6. \end{cases}$$

Solution   (a) The system can be written in the matrix form

$$\underset{A}{\begin{bmatrix} 4 & -2 & 3 \\ 8 & -3 & 5 \\ 7 & -2 & 4 \end{bmatrix}} \underset{X}{\begin{bmatrix} x \\ y \\ z \end{bmatrix}} = \underset{B}{\begin{bmatrix} 1 \\ 4 \\ 5 \end{bmatrix}}.$$

The solution of this matrix equation is $X = A^{-1}B$, or

$$\begin{bmatrix} x \\ y \\ z \end{bmatrix} = \begin{bmatrix} -2 & 2 & -1 \\ 3 & -5 & 4 \\ 5 & -6 & 4 \end{bmatrix} \begin{bmatrix} 1 \\ 4 \\ 5 \end{bmatrix} = \begin{bmatrix} 1 \\ 3 \\ 1 \end{bmatrix}.$$

Thus the solution of the system is $x = 1$, $y = 3$, $z = 1$.

(b) This system has the same left-hand side as the preceding system, so its solution is

$$\begin{bmatrix} x \\ y \\ z \end{bmatrix} = \begin{bmatrix} -2 & 2 & -1 \\ 3 & -5 & 4 \\ 5 & -6 & 4 \end{bmatrix} \begin{bmatrix} 4 \\ 7 \\ 6 \end{bmatrix} = \begin{bmatrix} 0 \\ 1 \\ 2 \end{bmatrix}.$$

That is, the solution of the system is $x = 0$, $y = 1$, $z = 2$.   ◆

Using the method of matrix equations to solve a system of linear equations is especially efficient if one wishes to solve a number of systems all having the same left-hand sides but different right-hand sides. For then A^{-1} must be computed only once for all the systems under consideration. (This point is useful in Exercises 19–22.)

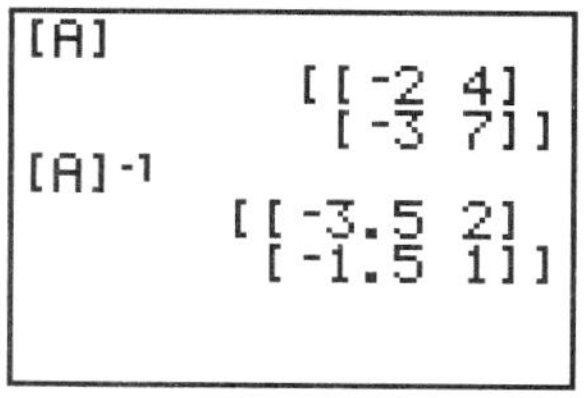

```
[A]
        [[-2  4]
         [-3  7]]
[A]-1
        [[-3.5  2]
         [-1.5  1]]
```

Figure 1.

GC   The inverse of a square matrix can be obtained directly with the inverse key [x^{-1}]. See Fig. 1. (*Note*: Do not use **[A]**^**-1**.)

1. Show that the inverse of

$$\begin{bmatrix} -4 & 1 & 2 \\ 7 & -1 & -4 \\ -\frac{1}{2} & 0 & \frac{1}{2} \end{bmatrix} \quad \text{is} \quad \begin{bmatrix} 1 & 1 & 4 \\ 3 & 2 & 4 \\ 1 & 1 & 6 \end{bmatrix}.$$

2. Use the method of this section to solve the system of linear equations

$$\begin{cases} .8x + .6y = 5 \\ .2x + .4y = 2. \end{cases}$$

▶ Exercises 2.4

In Exercises 1 and 2, use the fact that

$$\begin{bmatrix} 2 & 2 \\ \frac{1}{2} & 1 \end{bmatrix}^{-1} = \begin{bmatrix} 1 & -2 \\ -\frac{1}{2} & 2 \end{bmatrix}.$$

1. Solve $\begin{cases} 2x + 2y = 4 \\ \frac{1}{2}x + y = 1. \end{cases}$

2. Solve $\begin{cases} 2x + 2y = 14 \\ \frac{1}{2}x + y = 4. \end{cases}$

In Exercises 3–10, find the inverse of the given matrix.

3. $\begin{bmatrix} 7 & 2 \\ 3 & 1 \end{bmatrix}$ 4. $\begin{bmatrix} 2 & 3 \\ 5 & 7 \end{bmatrix}$

5. $\begin{bmatrix} 6 & 2 \\ 5 & 2 \end{bmatrix}$ 6. $\begin{bmatrix} 1 & .5 \\ 0 & .5 \end{bmatrix}$

7. $\begin{bmatrix} .7 & .2 \\ .3 & .8 \end{bmatrix}$ 8. $\begin{bmatrix} 0 & 1 \\ 1 & 0 \end{bmatrix}$

9. $\begin{bmatrix} 3 \end{bmatrix}$ 10. $\begin{bmatrix} .2 \end{bmatrix}$

In Exercises 11–14, use the method of this section to solve the system of linear equations.

11. $\begin{cases} x + 2y = 3 \\ 2x + 6y = 5 \end{cases}$ 12. $\begin{cases} 5x + 3y = 1 \\ 7x + 4y = 2 \end{cases}$

13. $\begin{cases} \frac{1}{2}x + 2y = 4 \\ 3x + 16y = 0 \end{cases}$ 14. $\begin{cases} .8x + .6y = 2 \\ .2x + .4y = 1 \end{cases}$

15. It is found that the number of married and single adults in a certain town are subject to the following statistics. Suppose that x and y denote the number of married and single adults, respectively, in a given year (say as of January 1) and let m, s denote the corresponding numbers for the following year. Then

$$.8x + .3y = m$$
$$.2x + .7y = s.$$

(a) Write this system of equations in matrix form.

(b) Solve the resulting matrix equation for $X = \begin{bmatrix} x \\ y \end{bmatrix}$.

(c) Suppose that in a given year there were found to be 100,000 married adults and 50,000 single adults. How many married (respectively, single) adults were there the preceding year?

(d) How many married (respectively, single) adults were there two years ago?

16. A flu epidemic is spreading through a town of 48,000 people. It is found that if x and y denote the numbers of people sick and well in a given week, respectively, and if s and w denote the corresponding numbers for the following week, then

$$\tfrac{1}{3}x + \tfrac{1}{4}y = s$$
$$\tfrac{2}{3}x + \tfrac{3}{4}y = w.$$

(a) Write this system of equations in matrix form.

(b) Solve the resulting matrix equation for $X = \begin{bmatrix} x \\ y \end{bmatrix}$.

(c) Suppose that 13,000 people are sick in a given week. How many were sick the preceding week?

(d) Same question as part (c), except assume that 14,000 are sick.

17. Statistics show that at a certain university, 70% of the students who live on campus during a given semester will remain on campus the following semester, and 90% of students living off campus during a given semester will remain off campus the following semester. Let x and y denote the number of students who live on and off campus this semester, and let u and v be the corresponding numbers for the next semester. Then

$$.7x + .1y = u$$
$$.3x + .9y = v.$$

(a) Write this system of equations in matrix form.

(b) Solve the resulting matrix equation for $\begin{bmatrix} x \\ y \end{bmatrix}$.

(c) Suppose that out of a group of 9000 students, 6000 currently live on campus and 3000 live off campus. How many lived on campus last semester? How many will live off campus next semester?

18. A teacher estimates that of the students who pass a test, 80% will pass the next test, while of the students who fail a test, 50% will pass the next test. Let x and y denote the number of students who pass and fail a given test, and let u and v be the corresponding numbers for the following test.

(a) Write a matrix equation relating $\begin{bmatrix} x \\ y \end{bmatrix}$ to $\begin{bmatrix} u \\ v \end{bmatrix}$.

(b) Suppose that 25 of the teacher's students pass the third test and 8 fail the third test. How many students will pass the fourth test? Approximately how many passed the second test?

In Exercises 19 and 20, use the fact that

$$\begin{bmatrix} 1 & 2 & 2 \\ 1 & 3 & 2 \\ 1 & 2 & 3 \end{bmatrix}^{-1} = \begin{bmatrix} 5 & -2 & -2 \\ -1 & 1 & 0 \\ -1 & 0 & 1 \end{bmatrix}.$$

19. Solve $\begin{cases} x + 2y + 2z = 1 \\ x + 3y + 2z = -1 \\ x + 2y + 3z = -1. \end{cases}$

20. Solve $\begin{cases} x + 2y + 2z = 1 \\ x + 3y + 2z = 0 \\ x + 2y + 3z = 0. \end{cases}$

In Exercises 21 and 22, use the fact that

$$\begin{bmatrix} 9 & 0 & 2 & 0 \\ -20 & -9 & -5 & 5 \\ 4 & 0 & 1 & 0 \\ -4 & -2 & -1 & 1 \end{bmatrix}^{-1} = \begin{bmatrix} 1 & 0 & -2 & 0 \\ 0 & 1 & 0 & -5 \\ -4 & 0 & 9 & 0 \\ 0 & 2 & 1 & -9 \end{bmatrix}.$$

21. Solve $\begin{cases} 9x \quad\;\; + 2z \quad\quad = 1 \\ -20x - 9y - 5z + 5w = 0 \\ 4x \quad\quad + z \quad\quad = 0 \\ -4x - 2y - z + w = -1. \end{cases}$

22. Solve $\begin{cases} 9x \quad\;\; + 2z \quad\quad = 2 \\ -20x - 9y - 5z + 5w = 1 \\ 4x \quad\quad + z \quad\quad = 3 \\ -4x - 2y - z + w = 0. \end{cases}$

23. Without computing Δ, show that the matrix $\begin{bmatrix} 6 & 3 \\ 2 & 1 \end{bmatrix}$ does not have an inverse.

24. If $A^{-1} = \begin{bmatrix} 2 & 7 \\ 1 & -3 \end{bmatrix}$, what is the matrix A?

25. There are two age groups for a particular species of organism. Group I consists of all organisms aged under 1 year, while group II consists of all organisms aged from 1 to 2 years. No organism survives more than 2 years. The average number of offspring per year born to each member of group I is 1, while the average number of organisms per year born to each member of group II is 2. Nine-tenths of group I survive to enter group II each year.

(a) Let x and y represent the initial number of organisms in groups I and II, respectively. Let a and b represent the number of organisms in groups I and II, respectively, after one year. Write a matrix equation relating $\begin{bmatrix} x \\ y \end{bmatrix}$ to $\begin{bmatrix} a \\ b \end{bmatrix}$.

(b) If there are initially 450,000 organisms in group I and 360,000 organisms in group II, calculate the number of organisms in each of the groups after 1 year and after 2 years.

(c) Suppose that at a certain time there were 810,000 organisms in group I and 630,000 organisms in group II. Determine the population of each group 1 year earlier.

26. If $A^2 = \begin{bmatrix} -2 & -1 \\ 2 & -1 \end{bmatrix}$ and $A^3 = \begin{bmatrix} -2 & 1 \\ -2 & -3 \end{bmatrix}$, what is A?

Exercises 27–35 require the use of a graphing calculator or a computer.

In Exercises 27–30, use the inverse key to find the inverse of the given matrix. Display the entries as fractions.

27. $\begin{bmatrix} .2 & 3 \\ 4 & 1.6 \end{bmatrix}$

28. $\begin{bmatrix} -12 & 3.3 \\ 6 & .4 \end{bmatrix}$

29. $\begin{bmatrix} .6 & 3 & -7 \\ 2.5 & -1 & 4 \\ -2 & .3 & 9 \end{bmatrix}$

30. $\begin{bmatrix} 5 & 2.3 & 6 \\ 1.2 & 5 & -7 \\ -3 & -4 & 6.5 \end{bmatrix}$

In Exercises 31–34, calculate the answer using $[\mathbf{A}]^{-1} * [\mathbf{B}]$ and give the answer using fractions.

31. $\begin{cases} 2x - 4y + 7z = 11 \\ x + 3y - 5z = -9 \\ 3x - y + 3z = 7 \end{cases}$

32. $\begin{cases} 5x + 2y - 3z = 1 \\ 4x - y + z = 22 \\ -x + 5y - 6z = 4 \end{cases}$

33. $\begin{cases} 2x \quad\quad + 7z + 5w = 10 \\ 5x - y + 3z \quad\quad = -2 \\ x + 2y \quad\quad - 2w = 0 \\ 3x - 4y + 2z - 5w = -18 \end{cases}$

$$34. \quad \begin{cases} x + 4y - z + 2w = 9 \\ 3x - 8y + 2z + 4w = -2 \\ -x - 3y + 7z - 6w = 10 \\ 4x + 2y - 3z + w = -6 \end{cases}$$

35. Try finding the inverse of a matrix that does not have an inverse. How does your calculator or computer respond?

Solutions to Practice Problems 2.4

1. To see if this matrix is indeed the inverse, multiply it by the original matrix and find out if the products are identity matrices.

$$\begin{bmatrix} 1 & 1 & 4 \\ 3 & 2 & 4 \\ 1 & 1 & 6 \end{bmatrix} \begin{bmatrix} -4 & 1 & 2 \\ 7 & -1 & -4 \\ -\frac{1}{2} & 0 & \frac{1}{2} \end{bmatrix} = \begin{bmatrix} 1 & 0 & 0 \\ 0 & 1 & 0 \\ 0 & 0 & 1 \end{bmatrix}, \quad \text{(an identity matrix)}$$

$$\begin{bmatrix} -4 & 1 & 2 \\ 7 & -1 & -4 \\ -\frac{1}{2} & 0 & \frac{1}{2} \end{bmatrix} \begin{bmatrix} 1 & 1 & 4 \\ 3 & 2 & 4 \\ 1 & 1 & 6 \end{bmatrix} = \begin{bmatrix} 1 & 0 & 0 \\ 0 & 1 & 0 \\ 0 & 0 & 1 \end{bmatrix}.$$

2. The matrix form of this system is

$$\begin{bmatrix} .8 & .6 \\ .2 & .4 \end{bmatrix} \begin{bmatrix} x \\ y \end{bmatrix} = \begin{bmatrix} 5 \\ 2 \end{bmatrix}.$$

Therefore, the solution is

$$\begin{bmatrix} x \\ y \end{bmatrix} = \begin{bmatrix} .8 & .6 \\ .2 & .4 \end{bmatrix}^{-1} \begin{bmatrix} 5 \\ 2 \end{bmatrix}.$$

To compute the inverse of the 2×2 matrix, first compute Δ.

$$\Delta = ad - bc = (.8)(.4) - (.6)(.2) = .32 - .12 = .2$$

Thus,

$$\begin{bmatrix} .8 & .6 \\ .2 & .4 \end{bmatrix}^{-1} = \begin{bmatrix} .4/.2 & -.6/.2 \\ -.2/.2 & .8/.2 \end{bmatrix} = \begin{bmatrix} 2 & -3 \\ -1 & 4 \end{bmatrix}.$$

Therefore,

$$\begin{bmatrix} x \\ y \end{bmatrix} = \begin{bmatrix} 2 & -3 \\ -1 & 4 \end{bmatrix} \begin{bmatrix} 5 \\ 2 \end{bmatrix} = \begin{bmatrix} 4 \\ 3 \end{bmatrix},$$

so the solution is $x = 4$, $y = 3$.

2.5 The Gauss–Jordan Method for Calculating Inverses

Of the several popular methods for finding the inverse of a matrix, the Gauss–Jordan method is probably the easiest to describe. It can be used on square matrices of any size. Also, the mechanical nature of the computations allows this method to be programmed for a computer with relative ease. We shall illustrate the procedure with a 2×2 matrix, whose inverse can also be calculated using the method of the previous section. Let

$$A = \begin{bmatrix} \frac{1}{2} & 1 \\ 1 & 3 \end{bmatrix}.$$

It is simple to check that

$$A^{-1} = \begin{bmatrix} 6 & -2 \\ -2 & 1 \end{bmatrix}.$$

Let us now derive this result using the Gauss–Jordan method.

Step 1   Write down the matrix A, and on its right write an identity matrix of the same size.

This is most conveniently done by placing I_2 beside A in a single matrix.

$$\begin{bmatrix} \frac{1}{2} & 1 & 1 & 0 \\ 1 & 3 & 0 & 1 \end{bmatrix}$$
$$\underbrace{\qquad}_{A} \quad \underbrace{\qquad}_{I_2}$$

Step 2   Perform elementary row operations on the left-hand matrix so as to transform it into an identity matrix. Each operation performed on the left-hand matrix is also performed on the right-hand matrix.

This step proceeds exactly like the Gaussian elimination method and may be most conveniently expressed in terms of pivoting.

$$\begin{bmatrix} \boxed{\frac{1}{2}} & 1 & 1 & 0 \\ 1 & 3 & 0 & 1 \end{bmatrix}, \quad \begin{bmatrix} 1 & 2 & 2 & 0 \\ 0 & \boxed{1} & -2 & 1 \end{bmatrix}, \quad \begin{bmatrix} 1 & 0 & 6 & -2 \\ 0 & 1 & -2 & 1 \end{bmatrix}$$

Step 3   When the matrix on the left becomes an identity matrix, the matrix on the right is the desired inverse.

So, from the last matrix of our calculation above, we have

$$A^{-1} = \begin{bmatrix} 6 & -2 \\ -2 & 1 \end{bmatrix}.$$

This is the same result obtained earlier.

   We will demonstrate why the preceding method works after some further examples.

▶ **Example 1**   Find the inverse of the matrix

$$A = \begin{bmatrix} 4 & -2 & 3 \\ 8 & -3 & 5 \\ 7 & -2 & 4 \end{bmatrix}.$$

Solution

$$\begin{bmatrix} \boxed{4} & -2 & 3 & 1 & 0 & 0 \\ 8 & -3 & 5 & 0 & 1 & 0 \\ 7 & -2 & 4 & 0 & 0 & 1 \end{bmatrix}$$

$$\left[\begin{array}{ccc|ccc} 1 & -\frac{1}{2} & \frac{3}{4} & \frac{1}{4} & 0 & 0 \\ 0 & \boxed{1} & -1 & -2 & 1 & 0 \\ 0 & \frac{3}{2} & -\frac{5}{4} & -\frac{7}{4} & 0 & 1 \end{array}\right]$$

$$\left[\begin{array}{ccc|ccc} 1 & 0 & \frac{1}{4} & -\frac{3}{4} & \frac{1}{2} & 0 \\ 0 & 1 & -1 & -2 & 1 & 0 \\ 0 & 0 & \boxed{\frac{1}{4}} & \frac{5}{4} & -\frac{3}{2} & 1 \end{array}\right]$$

$$\left[\begin{array}{ccc|ccc} 1 & 0 & 0 & -2 & 2 & -1 \\ 0 & 1 & 0 & 3 & -5 & 4 \\ 0 & 0 & 1 & 5 & -6 & 4 \end{array}\right]$$

Therefore,

$$A^{-1} = \left[\begin{array}{ccc} -2 & 2 & -1 \\ 3 & -5 & 4 \\ 5 & -6 & 4 \end{array}\right].$$

◆

Not all square matrices have inverses. If a matrix does not have an inverse, this will become apparent when applying the Gauss–Jordan method. At some point there will be no way to continue transforming the left-hand matrix into an identity matrix. This is illustrated in the next example.

▶ **Example 2** Find the inverse of the matrix

$$A = \left[\begin{array}{ccc} 1 & 3 & 2 \\ 0 & 1 & 4 \\ 1 & 5 & 10 \end{array}\right].$$

Solution

$$\left[\begin{array}{ccc|ccc} \boxed{1} & 3 & 2 & 1 & 0 & 0 \\ 0 & 1 & 4 & 0 & 1 & 0 \\ 1 & 5 & 10 & 0 & 0 & 1 \end{array}\right]$$

$$\left[\begin{array}{ccc|ccc} 1 & 3 & 2 & 1 & 0 & 0 \\ 0 & \boxed{1} & 4 & 0 & 1 & 0 \\ 0 & 2 & 8 & -1 & 0 & 1 \end{array}\right]$$

$$\left[\begin{array}{ccc|ccc} 1 & 0 & -10 & 1 & -3 & 0 \\ 0 & 1 & 4 & 0 & 1 & 0 \\ 0 & 0 & 0 & -1 & -2 & 1 \end{array}\right]$$

Since the third row of the left-hand matrix has only zero entries, it is impossible to complete the Gauss–Jordan method. Therefore, the matrix A has no inverse matrix.

◆

Verification of the Gauss–Jordan Method for Calculating Inverses   In Section 2.4 we showed how to calculate the inverse by solving several systems of linear equations. Actually, the Gauss–Jordan method is just an organized way of going about the calculation. To see why, let us consider a concrete example:

$$A = \begin{bmatrix} 4 & -2 & 3 \\ 8 & -3 & 5 \\ 7 & -2 & 4 \end{bmatrix}.$$

We wish to determine A^{-1}, so regard it as a matrix of unknowns:

$$A^{-1} = \begin{bmatrix} x_1 & x_2 & x_3 \\ y_1 & y_2 & y_3 \\ z_1 & z_2 & z_3 \end{bmatrix}.$$

The statement $AA^{-1} = I_3$ is

$$\begin{bmatrix} 4 & -2 & 3 \\ 8 & -3 & 5 \\ 7 & -2 & 4 \end{bmatrix} \begin{bmatrix} x_1 & x_2 & x_3 \\ y_1 & y_2 & y_3 \\ z_1 & z_2 & z_3 \end{bmatrix} = \begin{bmatrix} 1 & 0 & 0 \\ 0 & 1 & 0 \\ 0 & 0 & 1 \end{bmatrix}.$$

Multiplying out the matrices on the left and comparing the result with the matrix on the right give us nine equations, namely

$$\begin{cases} 4x_1 - 2y_1 + 3z_1 = 1 \\ 8x_1 - 3y_1 + 5z_1 = 0 \\ 7x_1 - 2y_1 + 4z_1 = 0 \end{cases}$$

$$\begin{cases} 4x_2 - 2y_2 + 3z_2 = 0 \\ 8x_2 - 3y_2 + 5z_2 = 1 \\ 7x_2 - 2y_2 + 4z_2 = 0 \end{cases}$$

$$\begin{cases} 4x_3 - 2y_3 + 3z_3 = 0 \\ 8x_3 - 3y_3 + 5z_3 = 0 \\ 7x_3 - 2y_3 + 4z_3 = 1. \end{cases}$$

Notice that each system of equations corresponds to one column of unknowns in A^{-1}. More precisely, if we set

$$X_1 = \begin{bmatrix} x_1 \\ y_1 \\ z_1 \end{bmatrix}, \qquad X_2 = \begin{bmatrix} x_2 \\ y_2 \\ z_2 \end{bmatrix}, \qquad X_3 = \begin{bmatrix} x_3 \\ y_3 \\ z_3 \end{bmatrix},$$

then the preceding three systems have the respective matrix forms

$$AX_1 = \begin{bmatrix} 1 \\ 0 \\ 0 \end{bmatrix}, \qquad AX_2 = \begin{bmatrix} 0 \\ 1 \\ 0 \end{bmatrix}, \qquad AX_3 = \begin{bmatrix} 0 \\ 0 \\ 1 \end{bmatrix}.$$

Now imagine the process of applying Gaussian elimination to solve these three systems. We apply elementary row operations to the matrices

$$\left[A \;\middle|\; \begin{matrix} 1 \\ 0 \\ 0 \end{matrix} \right], \qquad \left[A \;\middle|\; \begin{matrix} 0 \\ 1 \\ 0 \end{matrix} \right], \qquad \left[A \;\middle|\; \begin{matrix} 0 \\ 0 \\ 1 \end{matrix} \right].$$

The process ends when we convert A into the identity matrix, at which point the solutions may be read off the right column. So the procedure ends with the matrices

$$\begin{bmatrix} I_3 & | & X_1 \end{bmatrix}, \qquad \begin{bmatrix} I_3 & | & X_2 \end{bmatrix}, \qquad \begin{bmatrix} I_3 & | & X_3 \end{bmatrix}.$$

Realize, however, that at each step of the three Gaussian eliminations we are performing the same operations, since all three start with the matrix A on the left. So, in order to save calculations, perform the three Gaussian eliminations simultaneously by performing the row operations on the composite matrix

$$\left[\begin{array}{c|ccc} A & 1 & 0 & 0 \\ & 0 & 1 & 0 \\ & 0 & 0 & 1 \end{array}\right] = \begin{bmatrix} A & | & I_3 \end{bmatrix}.$$

The procedure ends when this matrix is converted into

$$\begin{bmatrix} I_3 & | & X_1 & X_2 & X_3 \end{bmatrix}.$$

That is, since $A^{-1} = \begin{bmatrix} X_1 & X_2 & X_3 \end{bmatrix}$, the procedure ends with A^{-1} on the right. This is the reasoning behind the Gauss–Jordan method of calculating inverses.

◆

Practice Problems 2.5

1. Use the Gauss–Jordan method to calculate the inverse of the matrix

$$\begin{bmatrix} 1 & 0 & 2 \\ 0 & 1 & -4 \\ 0 & 0 & 2 \end{bmatrix}.$$

2. Solve the system of linear equations

$$\begin{cases} x & + 2z = 4 \\ y - 4z = 6 \\ 2z = 9. \end{cases}$$

▶ Exercises 2.5

In Exercises 1–12, use the Gauss–Jordan method to compute the inverse of the matrix.

1. $\begin{bmatrix} 7 & 3 \\ 5 & 2 \end{bmatrix}$

2. $\begin{bmatrix} 5 & -2 \\ 6 & 2 \end{bmatrix}$

3. $\begin{bmatrix} 10 & 12 \\ 3 & -4 \end{bmatrix}$

4. $\begin{bmatrix} 1 & -3 \\ 0 & 1 \end{bmatrix}$

5. $\begin{bmatrix} 2 & -4 \\ -1 & 2 \end{bmatrix}$

6. $\begin{bmatrix} 1 & 3 & 1 \\ -1 & 2 & 0 \\ 2 & 11 & 3 \end{bmatrix}$

7. $\begin{bmatrix} 1 & 2 & -2 \\ 1 & 1 & 1 \\ 0 & 0 & 1 \end{bmatrix}$

8. $\begin{bmatrix} 2 & 2 & 0 \\ 0 & -2 & 0 \\ 3 & 0 & 1 \end{bmatrix}$

9. $\begin{bmatrix} -2 & 5 & 2 \\ 1 & -3 & -1 \\ -1 & 2 & 1 \end{bmatrix}$

10. $\begin{bmatrix} 1 & 0 & 0 \\ 2 & 1 & -2 \\ -1 & 2 & 1 \end{bmatrix}$

11. $\begin{bmatrix} 1 & 6 & 0 & 0 \\ 1 & 5 & 0 & 0 \\ 0 & 0 & 4 & 2 \\ 0 & 0 & 50 & 2 \end{bmatrix}$

12. $\begin{bmatrix} 6 & 0 & 2 & 0 \\ -6 & 1 & 0 & 1 \\ 1 & 0 & 1 & 0 \\ -9 & 0 & -1 & 1 \end{bmatrix}$

In Exercises 13–16, use matrix inversion to solve the system of linear equations.

13. $\begin{cases} x + y + 2z = 3 \\ 3x + 2y + 2z = 4 \\ x + y + 3z = 5 \end{cases}$

14. $\begin{cases} x + 2y + 3z = 4 \\ 3x + 5y + 5z = 3 \\ 2x + 4y + 2z = 4 \end{cases}$

15. $\begin{cases} x \quad\quad - 2z - 2w = 0 \\ \quad y \quad\quad - 5w = 1 \\ -4x \quad\quad + 9z + 9w = 2 \\ \quad 2y + \; z - 8w = 3 \end{cases}$

16. $\begin{cases} \quad\quad y + 2z = 1 \\ 2x + y + 3z = 2 \\ x + y + 2z = 3 \end{cases}$

17. Suppose that we try to solve the matrix equation $AX = B$ by using matrix inversion but find that even though the matrix A is a square matrix, it has no inverse. What can be said about the outcome from solving the associated system of linear equations by the Gaussian elimination method?

18. Find the 2×2 matrix C for which $A \cdot C = B$, where

$$A = \begin{bmatrix} 3 & 2 \\ 4 & 3 \end{bmatrix} \quad \text{and} \quad B = \begin{bmatrix} 5 & 6 \\ 1 & 7 \end{bmatrix}.$$

19. Find a 2×2 matrix A for which

$$A \cdot \begin{bmatrix} 2 \\ 1 \end{bmatrix} = \begin{bmatrix} -1 \\ 4 \end{bmatrix} \quad \text{and} \quad A \cdot \begin{bmatrix} 5 \\ 3 \end{bmatrix} = \begin{bmatrix} 0 \\ 2 \end{bmatrix}.$$

20. Let

$$A = \begin{bmatrix} 7 & 4 \\ 3 & 2 \end{bmatrix} \quad \text{and} \quad B = \begin{bmatrix} 1 & 5 \\ -3 & 4 \end{bmatrix}.$$

Each of the equations $AX = B$ and $XA = B$ has a 2×2 matrix X as a solution. Find X in each case and explain why the two answers are different.

Exercises 21–24 require the use of a graphing calculator or a computer.

In Exercises 21–24, use the Gauss–Jordan method to compute the inverse of the matrix.

21. $\begin{bmatrix} 4 & 1 \\ 7 & 2 \end{bmatrix}$ 22. $\begin{bmatrix} 8 & 3 \\ 13 & 5 \end{bmatrix}$

23. $\begin{bmatrix} 2 & 5 & 3 \\ 1 & 3 & 0 \\ 2 & 3 & 4 \end{bmatrix}$ 24. $\begin{bmatrix} 4 & -2 & -8 \\ -3 & 1 & 3 \\ 5 & 0 & 6 \end{bmatrix}$

Solutions to Practice Problems 2.5

1. First write the given matrix beside an identity matrix of the same size

$$\begin{bmatrix} 1 & 0 & 2 & | & 1 & 0 & 0 \\ 0 & 1 & -4 & | & 0 & 1 & 0 \\ 0 & 0 & 2 & | & 0 & 0 & 1 \end{bmatrix}.$$

The object is to use elementary row operations to transform the 3×3 matrix on the left into the identity matrix. The first two columns are already in the correct form.

$$\begin{bmatrix} 1 & 0 & 2 & | & 1 & 0 & 0 \\ 0 & 1 & -4 & | & 0 & 1 & 0 \\ 0 & 0 & 2 & | & 0 & 0 & 1 \end{bmatrix} \xrightarrow{\frac{1}{2}[3]} \begin{bmatrix} 1 & 0 & 2 & | & 1 & 0 & 0 \\ 0 & 1 & -4 & | & 0 & 1 & 0 \\ 0 & 0 & 1 & | & 0 & 0 & \frac{1}{2} \end{bmatrix}$$

$$\xrightarrow{[1] + (-2)[3]} \begin{bmatrix} 1 & 0 & 0 & | & 1 & 0 & -1 \\ 0 & 1 & -4 & | & 0 & 1 & 0 \\ 0 & 0 & 1 & | & 0 & 0 & \frac{1}{2} \end{bmatrix}$$

$$\xrightarrow{[2] + (4)[3]} \begin{bmatrix} 1 & 0 & 0 & | & 1 & 0 & -1 \\ 0 & 1 & 0 & | & 0 & 1 & 2 \\ 0 & 0 & 1 & | & 0 & 0 & \frac{1}{2} \end{bmatrix}$$

Thus the inverse of the given matrix is

$$\begin{bmatrix} 1 & 0 & -1 \\ 0 & 1 & 2 \\ 0 & 0 & \frac{1}{2} \end{bmatrix}.$$

Solutions to Practice Problems 2.5 (Continued)

2. The matrix form of this system of equations is $AX = B$, where A is the matrix whose inverse was found in Problem 1, and

$$B = \begin{bmatrix} 4 \\ 6 \\ 9 \end{bmatrix}.$$

Therefore, $X = A^{-1}B$, so that

$$\begin{bmatrix} x \\ y \\ z \end{bmatrix} = \begin{bmatrix} 1 & 0 & -1 \\ 0 & 1 & 2 \\ 0 & 0 & \frac{1}{2} \end{bmatrix} \begin{bmatrix} 4 \\ 6 \\ 9 \end{bmatrix} = \begin{bmatrix} -5 \\ 24 \\ \frac{9}{2} \end{bmatrix}.$$

So the solution of the system is $x = -5$, $y = 24$, $z = \frac{9}{2}$.

2.6 Input–Output Analysis

In recent years matrix arithmetic has played an ever-increasing role in economics, especially in that branch of economics called *input–output analysis*. Pioneered by the Harvard economist Vassily Leontieff, input–output analysis is used to analyze an economy in order to meet given consumption and export demands. As we shall see, such analysis leads to matrix calculations and in particular to inverses. Input–output analysis has been of such great significance that Leontieff was awarded the 1973 Nobel Prize in economics for his fundamental work in the subject.

Suppose that we divide an economy into a number of industries—transportation, agriculture, steel, and so on. Each industry produces a certain output using certain raw materials (or input). The input of each industry is made up in part by the outputs of other industries. For example, in order to produce food, agriculture uses as input the output of many industries, such as transportation (tractors and trucks) and oil (gasoline and fertilizers). This interdependence among the industries of the economy is summarized in a matrix—an *input–output matrix*. There is one column for each industry's input requirements. The entries in the column reflect the amount of input required from each of the industries. A typical input–output matrix looks like this:

Input requirments of:

		Industry 1	Industry 2	Industry 3 ...
From	Industry 1			
	Industry 2			
	Industry 3			
	⋮			

It is most convenient to express the entries of this matrix in monetary terms. That is, each column gives the dollar values of the various inputs needed by an industry in order to produce $1 worth of output.

There are consumers (other than the industries themselves) who want to purchase some of the output of these industries. The quantity of goods that these consumers want (or demand) is called the *final demand* on the economy. The final demand can be represented by a column matrix, with one entry for each industry, indicating the amount of consumable output demanded from the industry:

$$[\text{final demand}] = \begin{bmatrix} \text{amount from industry 1} \\ \text{amount from industry 2} \\ \vdots \end{bmatrix}.$$

We shall consider the situation in which the final-demand matrix is given and it is necessary to determine how much output should be produced by each industry in order to provide the needed inputs of the various industries and also to satisfy the final demand. The proper level of output can be computed using matrix calculations, as illustrated in the next example.

▶ Example 1   Suppose that an economy is composed of only three industries—coal, steel, and electricity. Each of these industries depends on the others for some of its raw materials. Suppose that to make $1 of coal, it takes no coal, but $.02 of steel and $.01 of electricity; to make $1 of steel, it takes $.15 of coal, $.03 of steel, and $.08 of electricity; and to make $1 of electricity, it takes $.43 of coal, $.20 of steel, and $.05 of electricity. How much should each industry produce to allow for consumption (not used for production) at these levels: $2 billion coal, $1 billion steel, $3 billion electricity?

Solution   Put all the data indicating the interdependence of the industries in a matrix. In each industry's column, put the amount of input from each of the industries needed to produce $1 of output in that particular industry:

$$\begin{array}{c} \\ \text{Coal} \\ \text{Steel} \\ \text{Electricity} \end{array} \begin{array}{ccc} \text{Coal} & \text{Steel} & \text{Electricity} \end{array} \\ \begin{bmatrix} 0 & .15 & .43 \\ .02 & .03 & .20 \\ .01 & .08 & .05 \end{bmatrix} = A.$$

This matrix is the *input–output matrix* corresponding to the economy. Let D denote the final-demand matrix. Then, letting the numbers in D stand for billions of dollars, we have

$$D = \begin{bmatrix} 2 \\ 1 \\ 3 \end{bmatrix}.$$

Suppose that the coal industry produces x billion dollars of output, the steel industry y billion dollars, and the electrical industry z billion dollars. Our problem is to determine the x, y, and z that yield the desired amounts left over from the production process. As an example, consider coal. The amount of coal that can be consumed or exported is just

$$x - [\text{amount of coal used in production}].$$

To determine the amount of coal used in production, refer to the input–output matrix. Production of x billion dollars of coal takes $0 \cdot x$ billion dollars of coal; production of y billion dollars of steel takes $.15y$ billion dollars of coal; and production of z billion dollars of electricity takes $.43z$ billion dollars of coal. Thus,

$$[\text{amount of coal used in production}] = 0 \cdot x + .15y + .43z.$$

This quantity should be recognized as the first entry of a matrix product. Namely, if we let

$$X = \begin{bmatrix} x \\ y \\ z \end{bmatrix},$$

then

$$\begin{bmatrix} \boxed{\text{coal}} \\ \text{steel} \\ \text{electricity} \end{bmatrix}_{\text{used in production}} = \begin{bmatrix} 0 & .15 & .43 \\ .02 & .03 & .20 \\ .01 & .08 & .05 \end{bmatrix} \begin{bmatrix} x \\ y \\ z \end{bmatrix} = AX.$$

But then the amount of each output available for purposes other than production is $X - AX$. That is, we have the matrix equation

$$X - AX = D.$$

To solve this equation for X, proceed as follows. Since $IX = X$, write the equation in the form

$$IX - AX = D$$

$$(I - A)X = D$$

$$X = (I - A)^{-1}D. \tag{1}$$

So, in other words, X may be found by multiplying D on the left by $(I - A)^{-1}$. Let us now do the arithmetic.

$$I - A = \begin{bmatrix} 1 & 0 & 0 \\ 0 & 1 & 0 \\ 0 & 0 & 1 \end{bmatrix} - \begin{bmatrix} 0 & .15 & .43 \\ .02 & .03 & .20 \\ .01 & .08 & .05 \end{bmatrix} = \begin{bmatrix} 1 & -.15 & -.43 \\ -.02 & .97 & -.20 \\ -.01 & -.08 & .95 \end{bmatrix}$$

Applying the Gauss–Jordan method, we find that

$$(I - A)^{-1} = \begin{bmatrix} 1.01 & .20 & .50 \\ .02 & 1.05 & .23 \\ .01 & .09 & 1.08 \end{bmatrix},$$

where all figures are carried to two decimal places (Exercise 5). Therefore,

$$X = (I - A)^{-1}D = \begin{bmatrix} 1.01 & .20 & .50 \\ .02 & 1.05 & .23 \\ .01 & .09 & 1.08 \end{bmatrix} \begin{bmatrix} 2 \\ 1 \\ 3 \end{bmatrix} = \begin{bmatrix} 3.72 \\ 1.78 \\ 3.35 \end{bmatrix}.$$

In other words, coal should produce \$3.72 billion worth of output, steel \$1.78 billion, and electricity \$3.35 billion. This output will meet the required final demands from each industry. ◆

The preceding analysis is useful in studying not only entire economies but also segments of economies and even individual companies.

▶ Example 2   A conglomerate has three divisions, which produce computers, semiconductors, and business forms. For each \$1 of output, the computer division needs \$.02 worth of computers, \$.20 worth of semiconductors, and \$.10 worth of business forms. For each \$1 of output, the semiconductor division needs \$.02 worth of computers, \$.01 worth of semiconductors, and \$.02 worth of business forms. For each \$1 of output, the business forms division requires \$.10 worth of computers and \$.01 worth of business forms. The conglomerate estimates the sales demand to be \$300,000,000 for the computer division, \$100,000,000 for the semiconductor division, and \$200,000,000 for the business forms division. At what level should each division produce in order to satisfy this demand?

Solution The conglomerate can be viewed as a miniature economy and its sales as the final demand. The input–output matrix for this "economy" is

$$
\begin{array}{c}
\\
\\
\begin{array}{c}
\text{Computers} \\
\text{Semiconductors} \\
\text{Business forms}
\end{array}
\end{array}
\begin{array}{ccc}
\text{Computers} & \text{Semiconductors} & \begin{array}{c}\text{Business}\\\text{forms}\end{array} \\
\left[\begin{array}{ccc}
.02 & .02 & .10 \\
.20 & .01 & 0 \\
.10 & .02 & .01
\end{array}\right] & & = A.
\end{array}
$$

The final-demand matrix is

$$
D = \begin{bmatrix} 3 \\ 1 \\ 2 \end{bmatrix},
$$

where the demand is expressed in hundreds of millions of dollars. By equation (1) the matrix X, giving the desired levels of production for the various divisions, is given by

$$
X = (I - A)^{-1} D.
$$

But

$$
I - A = \begin{bmatrix} .98 & -.02 & -.10 \\ -.20 & .99 & 0 \\ -.10 & -.02 & .99 \end{bmatrix},
$$

so that (Exercise 6)

$$
(I - A)^{-1} = \begin{bmatrix} 1.04 & .02 & .10 \\ .21 & 1.01 & .02 \\ .11 & .02 & 1.02 \end{bmatrix} \quad \text{and} \quad (I - A)^{-1}D = \begin{bmatrix} 3.34 \\ 1.68 \\ 2.39 \end{bmatrix}.
$$

Therefore,

$$
X = \begin{bmatrix} 3.34 \\ 1.68 \\ 2.39 \end{bmatrix}.
$$

That is, the computer division should produce $334,000,000, the semiconductor division $168,000,000, and the business forms division $239,000,000. ◆

Input–output analysis is usually applied to the entire economy of a country having hundreds of industries. The resulting matrix equation $(I-A)X = D$ could be solved by the Gaussian elimination method. However, it is best to find the inverse of $I - A$ and solve for X as we have done in the examples of this section. Over a short period, D might change but A is unlikely to change. Therefore, the proper outputs to satisfy the new demand can easily be determined by using the already computed inverse of $I - A$.

The Closed Leontieff Model The foregoing description of an economy is usually called the *Leontieff open model* since it views exports as an activity that takes place external to the economy. However, it is possible to consider exports as yet another industry in the economy. Instead of describing exports by a demand column D, we describe it by a column in the input–output matrix. That is, the export column describes how each dollar of exports is divided among the various industries. Since exports are now regarded as another industry, each of the original columns has an additional entry, namely the amount of output from the export industry (that is, imports) used to produce $1 of goods (of the industry corresponding to the column). If A denotes the expanded input–output matrix and X the production matrix (as before), then AX is the matrix describing the total demand experienced by each of the industries. In order for the economy to function efficiently, the total amount demanded by the various industries should equal the amount produced. That is, the production matrix must satisfy the equation

$$AX = X.$$

By studying the solutions to this equation, it is possible to determine the equilibrium states of the economy—that is, the production matrices X for which the amounts produced exactly equal the amounts needed by the various industries. The model just described is called *Leontieff's closed model.*

   We may expand the Leontieff closed model to include the effects of labor and monetary phenomena by considering labor and banking as yet further industries to be incorporated in the input–output matrix.

GC   With a graphing calculator, the matrix $(I - A)^{-1}D$ can be calculated with a single press of the ENTER key. Figure 1 shows the calculation for the matrices of Example 2.

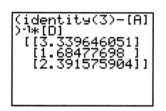

```
(identity(3)-[A]
)-1*[D]
  [[3.339646051]
   [1.68477698 ]
   [2.391575904]]
```

Figure 1.

---

1. Let

$$I = \begin{bmatrix} 1 & 0 & 0 \\ 0 & 1 & 0 \\ 0 & 0 & 1 \end{bmatrix}, \quad A = \begin{bmatrix} .1 & 0 & .1 \\ .2 & .1 & .1 \\ .1 & .2 & 0 \end{bmatrix}, \quad X = \begin{bmatrix} x \\ y \\ z \end{bmatrix}, \quad D = \begin{bmatrix} 100 \\ 200 \\ 50 \end{bmatrix}.$$

   Solve the matrix equation

$$(I - A)X = D$$

2. Let I, A, and X be as in Problem 1, but let

$$D = \begin{bmatrix} 300 \\ 100 \\ 100 \end{bmatrix}.$$

   Solve the matrix equation $(I - A)X = D$.

▶ Exercises 2.6

1. Suppose that in the economy of Example 1 the demand for electricity triples and the demand for coal doubles, whereas the demand for steel increases only by 50%. At what levels should the various industries produce in order to satisfy the new demand?

2. Suppose that the conglomerate of Example 2 is faced with an increase of 50% in demand for computers, a doubling in demand for semiconductors, and a decrease of 50% in demand for business forms. At what levels should the various divisions produce in order to satisfy the new demand?

3. Suppose that the conglomerate of Example 2 experiences a doubling in the demand for business forms. At what levels should the computer and semiconductor divisions produce?

4. A multinational corporation does business in the United States, Canada, and England. Its branches in one country purchase goods from the branches in other countries according to the matrix

Branch in:

		United States	Canada	England
Purchase from:	United States	.02	0	.02
	Canada	.01	.03	.01
	England	.03	0	.01

where the entries in the matrix represent proportions of total sales by the respective branch. The external sales by each of the offices are $800,000,000 for the U.S. branch, $300,000,000 for the Canadian branch, and $1,400,000,000 for the English branch. At what level should each of the branches produce in order to satisfy the total demand?

5. Show that to two decimal places

$$\begin{bmatrix} 1 & -.15 & -.43 \\ -.02 & .97 & -.20 \\ -.01 & -.08 & .95 \end{bmatrix}^{-1} = \begin{bmatrix} 1.01 & .20 & .50 \\ .02 & 1.05 & .23 \\ .01 & .09 & 1.08 \end{bmatrix}.$$

6. Show that to two decimal places

$$\begin{bmatrix} .98 & -.02 & -.10 \\ -.2 & .99 & 0 \\ -.10 & -.02 & .99 \end{bmatrix}^{-1} = \begin{bmatrix} 1.04 & .02 & .10 \\ .21 & 1.01 & .02 \\ .11 & .02 & 1.02 \end{bmatrix}.$$

7. A corporation has a plastics division and an industrial equipment division. For each $1 worth of output, the plastics division needs $.02 worth of plastics and $.10 worth of equipment. For each $1 worth of output, the industrial equipment division needs $.01 worth of plastics and $.05 worth of equipment. At what level should the divisions produce to meet a demand for $930,000 worth of plastics and $465,000 worth of industrial equipment?

8. Rework Exercise 7 under the condition that the demand for plastics is $1,860,000 and the demand for industrial equipment is $2,790,000.

9. An industrial system involves manufacturing, transportation, and agriculture. The interdependence of the three industries is given by the input–output matrix

$$\begin{array}{ccc} M & T & A \end{array}$$
$$\begin{bmatrix} .4 & .3 & .1 \\ .2 & .2 & .2 \\ .1 & .1 & .4 \end{bmatrix} \begin{array}{c} M \\ T \\ A \end{array}$$

At what levels must the industries produce to satisfy a demand for $100 million worth of manufactured goods, $80 million of transportation, and $200 million worth of agricultural products?

10. A town has a merchant, a baker, and a farmer. To produce $1 worth of output, the merchant requires $.30 worth of baked goods and $.40 worth of the farmer's products. To produce $1 worth of output, the baker requires $.50 worth of the merchant's goods, $.10 worth of his own goods, and $.30 worth of the farmer's goods. To produce $1 worth of output, the farmer requires $.30 worth of the merchant's goods, $.20 worth of baked goods, and $.30 worth of his own products. How much should the merchant, baker, and farmer produce to meet a demand for $20,000 worth of output from the merchant, $15,000 worth of output from the baker, and $18,000 worth of output from the farmer?

Exercises 11 and 12 require the use of a graphing calculator or a computer.

In Exercises 11 and 12, use the input–output matrix A and the final-demand matrix D to find the production matrix X for the Leontieff open model. Round your answers to two decimal places.

11. $A = \begin{bmatrix} .1 & .2 & .4 \\ .05 & .3 & .25 \\ .15 & .1 & .2 \end{bmatrix}$, $D = \begin{bmatrix} 3 \\ 7 \\ 4 \end{bmatrix}$.

12. $A = \begin{bmatrix} .2 & .35 & .15 & .05 \\ .1 & .1 & .3 & .2 \\ .075 & .2 & .05 & .1 \\ .3 & .04 & .1 & .15 \end{bmatrix}$, $D = \begin{bmatrix} 5 \\ 2 \\ 1 \\ 7 \end{bmatrix}$.

Solutions to Practice Problems 2.6

1. The equation $(I - A)X = D$ has the form $CX = D$, where C is the matrix $I - A$. From Section 2.4 we know that $X = C^{-1}D$. That is, $X = (I - A)^{-1}D$. Now

$$I - A = \begin{bmatrix} 1 & 0 & 0 \\ 0 & 1 & 0 \\ 0 & 0 & 1 \end{bmatrix} - \begin{bmatrix} .1 & 0 & .1 \\ .2 & .1 & .1 \\ .1 & .2 & 0 \end{bmatrix} = \begin{bmatrix} .9 & 0 & -.1 \\ -.2 & .9 & -.1 \\ -.1 & -.2 & 1 \end{bmatrix}.$$

Using the Gauss–Jordan method to find the inverse of this matrix, we have (to two decimal places)

$$(I - A)^{-1} = \begin{bmatrix} 1.13 & .03 & .12 \\ .27 & 1.14 & .14 \\ .17 & .23 & 1.04 \end{bmatrix}.$$

<table>
<tr><td>

**Solutions to
Practice Problems
2.6 (Continued)**

</td><td>

Therefore, rounding to the nearest integer, we have

$$X = (I - A)^{-1}D = \begin{bmatrix} 1.13 & .03 & .12 \\ .27 & 1.14 & .14 \\ .17 & .23 & 1.04 \end{bmatrix} \begin{bmatrix} 100 \\ 200 \\ 50 \end{bmatrix} = \begin{bmatrix} 125 \\ 262 \\ 115 \end{bmatrix}.$$

2. We have $X = (I - A)^{-1}D$, where $(I - A)^{-1}$ is as computed in Problem 1. So

$$X = (I - A)^{-1}D = \begin{bmatrix} 1.13 & .03 & .12 \\ .27 & 1.14 & .14 \\ .17 & .23 & 1.04 \end{bmatrix} \begin{bmatrix} 300 \\ 100 \\ 100 \end{bmatrix} = \begin{bmatrix} 354 \\ 209 \\ 178 \end{bmatrix}.$$

</td></tr>
</table>

▶ Chapter 2 Summary

1. The three elementary row operations for a system of linear equations (or a matrix) are as follows:

   (a) Rearrange the equations (rows) in any order.

   (b) Multiply an equation (row) by a nonzero number.

   (c) Change an equation (row) by adding to it a multiple of another equation (row).

2. When an elementary row operation is applied to a system of linear equations (or an augmented matrix) the solutions remain the same. The Gaussian elimination method is a systematic process that applies a sequence of elementary row operations until the solutions can be easily obtained.

3. The process of pivoting on a specific element of a matrix is to apply a sequence of elementary row operations so that the specific element becomes 1 and the other elements in its column become 0. To apply the Gaussian elimination method, proceed from left to right and perform pivots on as many columns to the left of the vertical line as possible, with the specific elements for the pivots coming from different rows.

4. After an augmented matrix has been completely reduced with the Gaussian elimination method, all the solutions to the corresponding system of linear equations can be obtained. If the matrix on the left of the vertical line is an identity matrix, then there is a unique solution. If one row of the augmented matrix is of the form $0 \quad 0 \quad 0 \cdots 0 \mid a$, where a is a nonzero number, then there are no solutions. Otherwise, there are infinitely many solutions. In this case, variables corresponding to columns that have not been pivoted can assume any values, and the values of the other variables can be expressed in terms of those variables.

5. A matrix of size $m \times n$ has m rows and n columns.

6. Matrices of the same size can be added (or subtracted) by adding (or subtracting) corresponding elements.

7. The product of an $m \times n$ matrix and an $n \times r$ matrix is the $m \times r$ matrix whose ijth element is obtained by

multiplying the ith row of the first matrix by the jth column of the second matrix. (The product of each row and column is calculated as the sum of the products of successive entries.)

8. The inverse of a square matrix A is a square matrix A^{-1} with the property that $A^{-1}A = I$ and $AA^{-1} = I$, where I is an identity matrix.

9. A 2×2 matrix $\begin{bmatrix} a & b \\ c & d \end{bmatrix}$ has an inverse if $\Delta = ad - bc \neq 0$. If so, the inverse matrix is

$$\begin{bmatrix} \dfrac{d}{\Delta} & -\dfrac{b}{\Delta} \\ -\dfrac{c}{\Delta} & \dfrac{a}{\Delta} \end{bmatrix}.$$

10. A system of linear equations can be written in the form $AX = B$, where A is a rectangular matrix of coefficients of the variables, X is a column of variables, and B is a column matrix of the constants from the right side of the system. If the matrix A has an inverse, then the solution of the equation is given by $X = A^{-1}B$.

11. To calculate the inverse of a matrix by the Gauss–Jordan method, append an identity matrix to the right of the original matrix and perform pivots to reduce the original matrix to an identity matrix. The matrix on the right will then be the inverse of the original matrix.

12. An input–output matrix has rows and columns labeled with the different industries in an economy. The ijth entry of the matrix gives the cost of the input from the industry in row i used in the production of \$1 worth of the output of industry in column j.

13. If A is an input–output matrix and D is a demand matrix giving the dollar values of the outputs from the various industries to be supplied to outside customers, then the matrix $X = (I - A)^{-1}D$ gives the amounts that must be produced by the various industries in order to meet the demand.

Review of Fundamental Concepts of Chapter 2

1. What is meant by a solution to a system of linear equations?

2. What is a matrix?

3. State three elementary row operations on equations or matrices.

4. What does it mean for a system of equations or a matrix to be in diagonal form?

5. What is meant by pivoting a matrix about a nonzero entry?

6. State the Gaussian elimination method for transforming a system of linear equations into diagonal form.

7. What is a row matrix? Column matrix? Square matrix? Identity matrix, I_n?

8. What is meant by a_{ij}, the ijth entry of a matrix?

9. Define the sum and difference of two matrices.

10. Define the product of two matrices.

11. Define the inverse of a matrix, A^{-1}.

12. Give the formula for the inverse of a 2×2 matrix.

13. Explain how to use the inverse of a matrix to solve a system of linear equations.

14. Describe the steps of the Gauss–Jordan method for calculating the inverse of a matrix.

15. What is an input–output matrix and a final-demand matrix?

16. Explain how to solve an input–output analysis problem.

▶ Chapter 2 Supplementary Exercises

In Exercises 1 and 2, pivot each matrix around the circled element.

1. $\begin{bmatrix} ③ & -6 & 1 \\ 2 & 4 & 6 \end{bmatrix}$

2. $\begin{bmatrix} -5 & -3 & 1 \\ 4 & ② & 0 \\ 0 & 6 & 7 \end{bmatrix}$

In Exercises 3–8, use the Gaussian elimination method to find all solutions of the system of linear equations.

3. $\begin{cases} \frac{1}{2}x - y = -3 \\ 4x - 5y = -9 \end{cases}$

4. $\begin{cases} 3x + 9z = 42 \\ 2x + y + 6z = 30 \\ -x + 3y - 2z = -20 \end{cases}$

5. $\begin{cases} 3x - 6y + 6z = -5 \\ -2x + 3y - 5z = \frac{7}{3} \\ x + y + 10z = 3 \end{cases}$

6. $\begin{cases} 3x + 6y - 9z = 1 \\ 2x + 4y - 6z = 1 \\ 3x + 4y + 5z = 0 \end{cases}$

7. $\begin{cases} x + 2y - 5z + 3w = 16 \\ -5x - 7y + 13z - 9w = -50 \\ -x + y - 7z + 2w = 9 \\ 3x + 4y - 7z + 6w = 33 \end{cases}$

8. $\begin{cases} 5x - 10y = 5 \\ 3x - 8y = -3 \\ -3x + 7y = 0 \end{cases}$

In Exercises 9 and 10, perform the indicated matrix operations.

9. $\begin{bmatrix} 2 \\ -1 \\ 0 \end{bmatrix} + \begin{bmatrix} 3 \\ 4 \\ 7 \end{bmatrix}$

10. $\begin{bmatrix} 1 & 3 & -2 \\ 4 & 0 & -1 \end{bmatrix} \begin{bmatrix} 3 & 5 \\ 1 & 0 \\ 0 & -6 \end{bmatrix}$

11. Find the inverse of the appropriate matrix, and use it to solve the system of equations

$$\begin{cases} 3x + 2y = 0 \\ 5x + 4y = 2. \end{cases}$$

12. The matrices

$$\begin{bmatrix} 4 & -2 & 3 \\ 8 & -3 & 5 \\ 7 & -2 & 4 \end{bmatrix} \text{ and } \begin{bmatrix} -2 & 2 & -1 \\ 3 & -5 & 4 \\ 5 & -6 & 4 \end{bmatrix}$$

are inverses of each other. Use these matrices to solve the following systems of linear equations.

(a) $\begin{cases} -2x + 2y - z = 1 \\ 3x - 5y + 4z = 0 \\ 5x - 6y + 4z = 3 \end{cases}$

(b) $\begin{cases} 4x - 2y + 3z = 0 \\ 8x - 3y + 5z = -1 \\ 7x - 2y + 4z = 2 \end{cases}$

In Exercises 13 and 14, use the Gauss–Jordan method to calculate the inverses of the following matrices.

13. $\begin{bmatrix} 2 & 6 \\ 1 & 2 \end{bmatrix}$

14. $\begin{bmatrix} 1 & 1 & 1 \\ 3 & 4 & 3 \\ 1 & 1 & 2 \end{bmatrix}$

15. Farmer Brown has 1000 acres of land on which he plans to grow corn, wheat, and soybeans. The cost of cultivating these crops is $28 per acre for corn, $40 per acre for wheat, and $32 per acre for soybeans. If Farmer

Brown wishes to use all his available land and his entire budget of $30,000, and if he wishes to plant the same number of acres of corn as wheat and soybeans combined, how many acres of each crop can he grow?

16. In an arms race between two superpowers, each nation takes stock of its own and its enemy's nuclear arsenal each year. Each nation has the policy of dismantling a certain percentage of its stockpile each year and adding that same percentage of its competitor's stockpile. Nation A uses 20% and nation B uses 10%. Suppose that the current stockpiles of nations A and B are 10,000 and 7000 weapons, respectively.

(a) What will the stockpiles be in each of the next two years?

(b) What were the stockpiles in each of the preceding two years?

(c) Show that the "missile gap" between the superpowers decreases by 30% each year under these policies. Show that the total number of weapons decreases each year if nation A begins with the most weapons, and the total number of weapons increases if nation B begins with the most weapons.

17. (PE) John pays $13 per month plus 20¢ per minute for his cell phone calls. Mary pays $19 per month plus 15¢ per minute for her calls. If during a certain month they each spoke for m minutes and paid the same amount of charges, what was the value of m?
(a) 90   (b) 100   (c) 110   (d) 120   (e) 130

18. (PE) Joe has $3.30 in his pocket made up of nickels, dimes, and quarters. There are 30 coins and there are five times as many dimes as quarters. How many quarters does Joe have?
(a) 4   (b) 5   (c) 6   (d) 7   (e) 8

19. The economy of a small country can be regarded as consisting of two industries, I and II, whose input–output matrix is

$$A = \begin{bmatrix} .4 & .2 \\ .1 & .3 \end{bmatrix}.$$

How many units should be produced by each industry in order to meet a demand for 8 units from industry I and 12 units from industry II?

▶ Chapter 2 Chapter Test

1. Solve the following system of linear equations by using the Gaussian elimination method.

$$\begin{cases} x + 2y + z = 5 \\ 2x - y + z = -5 \\ -3x + y - 2z = 8 \end{cases}$$

2. Each of the following is the final matrix of a Gaussian elimination process. Give the solutions to the corresponding systems of linear equations.

(a) $\begin{bmatrix} 1 & 0 & 0 & | & 4 \\ 0 & 1 & 0 & | & -3 \\ 0 & 0 & 1 & | & 6 \end{bmatrix}$

(b) $\begin{bmatrix} 1 & 0 & 0 & | & 2 \\ 0 & 1 & 0 & | & 3 \\ 0 & 0 & 1 & | & 5 \end{bmatrix}$

(c) $\begin{bmatrix} 1 & 0 & 0 & | & 1 \\ 0 & 1 & 0 & | & -3 \\ 0 & 0 & 1 & | & 4 \\ 0 & 0 & 0 & | & 2 \end{bmatrix}$

(d) $\begin{bmatrix} 1 & 0 & -1 & | & 2 \\ 0 & 1 & 2 & | & 2 \end{bmatrix}$

(e) $\begin{bmatrix} 1 & 2 & 0 & | & 0 \\ 0 & 0 & 1 & | & 0 \\ 0 & 0 & 0 & | & 0 \end{bmatrix}$

3. The following is the general solution to a system of linear equations. Find a *specific* solution.

$$\begin{cases} w = \text{any value} \\ z = \text{any value} \\ y = 2x + w - z \\ x = w + z \end{cases}$$

4. Find three solutions to the system

$$\begin{cases} x + y - 2z = 15 \\ y + 4z = 6. \end{cases}$$

5. Let matrices A, B, and C be defined as shown. Calculate the following matrices whenever they are defined: $A + B$, $A + C$, AB, AC, BC.

$$A = \begin{bmatrix} 2 & 1 & 0 \\ 3 & 2 & 1 \end{bmatrix} \quad B = \begin{bmatrix} -1 & 1 \\ 0 & 1 \\ 1 & -1 \end{bmatrix} \quad C = \begin{bmatrix} 0 & 1 & 2 \\ -1 & 1 & 1 \end{bmatrix}$$

6. Making a large decorative plate for retail sale takes $\frac{1}{2}$ hour molding time, 3 hours oven time, and 4 hours painting time. Vases require 1 hour molding time, 2.5 hours oven time, and 3 hours painting time. Bowls require 1 hour molding time, 2 hours oven time, and 2 hours painting time. We intend to produce x plates, y vases, and z bowls.

(a) Write three equations expressing molding time (m), oven time (v), and painting time (p) needed in terms of x, y, and z.

(b) Write the system as a matrix equation.

(c) Determine the number of hours each of molding time, oven time, and painting time to produce 100 plates, 300 vases, and 200 bowls.

7. Find A^{-1} if it exists, where

$$A = \begin{bmatrix} 1 & 2 & 1 \\ 0 & 1 & 1 \\ 1 & -1 & 0 \end{bmatrix}.$$

8. The freshman class at State University has 1500 students. Out-of-state students pay $10,000 tuition, while in-state students are charged $4500 for tuition. The school collected $12,800,000 in tuition. How many students are in-state?

9. In an economic system, each of three industries depends on the others for raw materials. To make $1 of processed wood requires 30¢ wood, 20¢ steel, and 10¢ coal. To make $1 of steel requires no wood, 30¢ steel, and 20¢ coal. To make $1 of coal requires 10¢ wood, 20¢ steel, and 5¢ coal. To allow for $1 consumption in wood, $4 consumption in steel, and $2 consumption in coal, what levels of production for wood, steel, and coal are required?

Chapter Project

Population Dynamics

In 1991 the U.S. Fish and Wildlife Service proposed logging restrictions on nearly 12 million acres of Pacific Northwest forest to help save the endangered northern spotted owl. This decision caused considerable controversy between the logging industry and environmentalists.

Mathematical ecologists created a mathematical model to analyze the population dynamics of the spotted owl.[1] They divided the female owl population into three categories—juvenile (up to one year old), subadult (1 to 2 years old), and adult (over 2 years old). Suppose that in a certain region there are currently 2950 female spotted owls made up of 650 juveniles, 200 subadults, and 2100 adults. The ecologists used matrices to project the changes in the population from year to year. The original numbers can be displayed in the column matrix

$$X_0 = \begin{bmatrix} 650 \\ 200 \\ 2100 \end{bmatrix}_0.$$

The populations after one year are given by the column matrix

$$X_1 = \begin{bmatrix} 693 \\ 117 \\ 2116 \end{bmatrix}_1.$$

The subscript 1 tells us that the matrix gives the population after one year. The column matrices for subsequent years will have subscripts 2, 3, 4, etc.

1. How many subadult females are there after one year?

2. Did the total population of females increase or decrease during the year?

Let A denote the matrix

$$\begin{bmatrix} 0 & 0 & .33 \\ .18 & 0 & 0 \\ 0 & .71 & .94 \end{bmatrix}.$$

According to the mathematical model, subsequent population distributions are generated by multiplication on the left by A. That is,

$$A \cdot X_0 = X_1, \quad A \cdot X_1 = X_2, \quad A \cdot X_2 = X_3, \dots .$$

If the population distribution at any time is given by $\begin{bmatrix} j \\ s \\ a \end{bmatrix}$, then the distribution one year later is $A \cdot \begin{bmatrix} j \\ s \\ a \end{bmatrix}$.

3. Fill in the blanks in the following statements.
   (a) Each year _____ juvenile females are born for each 100 adult females.
   (b) Each year _____% of the juvenile females survive to become subadults.
   (c) Each year _____% of the subadults survive to become adults and _____% of the adults survive.

---

[1]Lamberson, R. H., R. McKelvey, B. R. Noon, and C. Voss, "A Dynamic Analysis of Northern Spotted Owl Viability in a Fragmented Forest Landscape," *Conservation Biology*, Vol. 6, No. 4, December 1992; 505–512.

Chapter Project (Continued)

4. Calculate the column matrices X_2, X_3, X_4, and X_5. (*Note*: With a graphing calculator you can specify matrix **[A]** to be the 3×3 matrix A and specify **[B]** to be the initial 3×1 population matrix X_0. Display **[B]** in the home screen and then enter the command **[A]*Ans**. Each press of the ENTER key will generate the next population distribution matrix. *Tip*: Prior to generating the matrices invoke the MODE list and set Float to 0 so that all numbers in the population matrices will be rounded to whole numbers.)

5. Refer to item 4. Is the total female population increasing, decreasing, or neither during the first five years?

6. Explain why calculating **[A]**$^\wedge$**50*[B]** gives the column matrix for the population distribution after 50 years.

7. Find the projected population matrix after 50 years; after 100 years; after 150 years. Based on this mathematical model, what do you conclude about the prospects for the northern spotted owl?

In this model, the main impediment to the survival of the owl is the number .18 in the second row of matrix A. This number is low for two reasons. The first year of life is precarious for most animals living in the wild. In addition, juvenile owls must eventually leave the nest and establish their own territory. If much of the forest near their original home has been cleared, then they are vulnerable to predators while searching for a new home.

8. Suppose that due to better forest management, the number .18 can be increased to .26. Find the total female population for the first five years under this new assumption. Repeat item 7 and determine if extinction will be avoided under the new assumption.

C H A P T E R

Linear Programming, A Geometric Approach

3

Linear programming is a method for solving problems in which a linear function (representing cost, profit, distance, weight, or the like) is to be maximized or minimized. Such problems are called *optimization problems*. As we shall see, these problems, when translated into mathematical language, involve systems of linear inequalities, systems of linear equations, and eventually (in Chapter 4) matrices.

3.1 A Linear Programming Problem

Let us begin with a detailed discussion of a typical problem that can be solved by linear programming.

Furniture Manufacturing Problem A furniture manufacturer makes two types of furniture—chairs and sofas. For simplicity, divide the production process into three distinct operations—carpentry, finishing, and upholstery. The amount of labor required for each operation varies. Manufacture of a chair requires 6 hours of carpentry, 1 hour of finishing, and 2 hours of upholstery. Manufacture of a sofa requires 3 hours of carpentry, 1 hour of finishing, and 6 hours of upholstery. Due to limited availability of skilled labor as well as of tools and equipment, the factory has available each day 96 labor-hours for carpentry, 18 labor-hours for finishing, and 72 labor-hours for upholstery. The profit per chair is $80 and the profit per sofa $70. How many chairs and how many sofas should be produced each day to maximize the profit?

It is often helpful to tabulate data given in verbal problems. Our first step, then, is to construct a chart.

	Chair	Sofa	Available time
Carpentry	6 hours	3 hours	96 labor-hours
Finishing	1 hour	1 hour	18 labor-hours
Upholstery	2 hours	6 hours	72 labor-hours
Profit	$80	$70	

The next step is to translate the problem into mathematical language. As you know, this is done by identifying what is unknown and denoting the unknown quantities by letters. Since the problem asks for the optimal number of chairs and sofas to be produced each day, there are two unknowns—the number of chairs produced each day and the number of sofas produced each day. Let x denote the number of chairs and y the number of sofas.

To achieve a large profit, one need only manufacture a large number of chairs and sofas. But due to restricted availability of tools and labor, the factory cannot manufacture an unlimited quantity of furniture. Let us translate the restrictions into mathematical language. Each row of the chart gives one restriction. The first row says that the amount of carpentry required is 6 hours for each chair and 3 hours for each sofa. Also, there are available only 96 labor-hours of carpentry per day. We can compute the total number of labor-hours of carpentry required per day to produce x chairs and y sofas as follows:

$$\left[\text{number of labor-hours per day of carpentry}\right]$$

$$= (\text{number of hours carpentry per chair}) \cdot (\text{number of chairs per day})$$
$$+ (\text{number of hours carpentry per sofa}) \cdot (\text{number of sofas per day})$$
$$= 6 \cdot x + 3 \cdot y.$$

The requirement that at most 96 labor-hours of carpentry be used per day means that x and y must satisfy the inequality

$$6x + 3y \leq 96. \tag{1}$$

The second row of the chart gives a restriction imposed by finishing. Since 1 hour of finishing is required for each chair and sofa, and since at most 18 labor-hours of finishing are available per day, the same reasoning as used to derive inequality (1) yields

$$x + y \leq 18. \tag{2}$$

Similarly, the third row of the chart gives the restriction due to upholstery:

$$2x + 6y \leq 72. \tag{3}$$

Further restrictions are given by the fact that the numbers of chairs and sofas must be nonnegative:

$$x \geq 0, \qquad y \geq 0. \tag{4}$$

Now that we have written down the restrictions constraining x and y, let us express the profit (which is to be maximized) in terms of x and y. The profit comes from two sources—chairs and sofas. Therefore,

$$\left[\text{profit}\right] = \left[\text{profit from chairs}\right] + \left[\text{profit from sofas}\right]$$
$$= \left[\text{profit per chair}\right] \cdot \left[\text{number of chairs}\right]$$
$$+ \left[\text{profit per sofa}\right] \cdot \left[\text{number of sofas}\right] \tag{5}$$
$$= 80x + 70y.$$

Since the objective of the problem is to optimize profit, the expression $80x + 70y$ is called the *objective function*. Combining (1) to (5), we arrive at the following:

Furniture Manufacturing Problem—Mathematical Formulation   Find numbers x and y for which the objective function $80x + 70y$ is as large as possible, and for which all the following inequalities hold simultaneously:

$$\begin{cases} 6x + 3y \leq 96 \\ x + y \leq 18 \\ 2x + 6y \leq 72 \\ x \geq 0, \quad y \geq 0. \end{cases} \tag{6}$$

We may describe this mathematical problem in the following general way. We are required to maximize an expression in a certain number of variables, where the variables are subject to restrictions in the form of one or more inequalities. Problems of this sort are called *mathematical programming problems*. Actually, general mathematical programming problems can be quite involved, and their solutions may require very sophisticated mathematical ideas. However, this is not the case with the furniture manufacturing problem. What makes it a rather simple mathematical programming problem is that both the expression to be maximized and the inequalities are linear. For this reason the furniture manufacturing problem is called a *linear programming problem*. The theory of linear programming is a fairly recent advance in mathematics. It was developed over the last 50 years to deal with the increasingly more complicated problems of our technological society. The 1975 Nobel Prize in economics was awarded to Kantorovich and Koopmans for their pioneering work in the field of linear programming.

We will solve the furniture manufacturing problem in Section 3.2, where we develop a general technique for handling similar linear programming problems. At this point it is worthwhile to attempt to gain some insights into the problem and possible methods for attacking it.

It seems clear that a factory will operate most efficiently when its labor is fully utilized. Let us therefore take the operations one at a time and determine the conditions on x and y that fully utilize the three kinds of labor. The restriction on carpentry asserts that

$$6x + 3y \leq 96.$$

If x and y were chosen so that $6x + 3y$ is actually *less* than 96, we would leave the carpenters idle some of the time, a waste of labor. Thus it would seem reasonable to choose x and y to satisfy

$$6x + 3y = 96.$$

Similarly, to utilize all the finishers' time, x and y must satisfy

$$x + y = 18,$$

and to utilize all the upholsterers' time, we must have

$$2x + 6y = 72.$$

Thus, if no labor is to be wasted, then x and y must satisfy the system of equations

$$\begin{cases} 6x + 3y = 96 \\ x + y = 18 \\ 2x + 6y = 72. \end{cases} \tag{7}$$

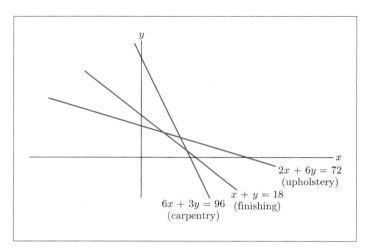

Figure 1.

Let us now graph the three equations of (7), which represent the conditions for full utilization of all forms of labor. (See the following chart and Fig. 1.)

Equation	Standard form	x-Intercept	y-Intercept
$6x + 3y = 96$	$y = -2x + 32$	$(16, 0)$	$(0, 32)$
$x + y = 18$	$y = -x + 18$	$(18, 0)$	$(0, 18)$
$2x + 6y = 72$	$y = -\frac{1}{3}x + 12$	$(36, 0)$	$(0, 12)$

What does Fig. 1 say about the furniture manufacturing problem? Each particular pair of numbers (x, y) is called a *production schedule*. Each of the lines in Fig. 1 gives the production schedules that fully utilize one of the types of labor. Notice that the three lines do not have a common intersection point. This means that there is *no* production schedule that *simultaneously* makes full use of all three types of labor. In any production schedule at least some of the labor-hours must be wasted. This is not a solution to the furniture manufacturing problem, but it is a valuable insight. It says that in the inequalities of (6) not all of the corresponding equations can hold. This suggests that we take a closer look at the system of inequalities.

The standard forms of the inequalities (6) are

$$\begin{cases} y \le -2x + 32 \\ y \le -x + 18 \\ y \le -\frac{1}{3}x + 12 \\ x \ge 0, \quad y \ge 0. \end{cases}$$

By using the techniques of Section 1.2, we arrive at a feasible set for the preceding system of inequalities, as shown in Fig. 2.

The feasible set for the furniture manufacturing problem is a bounded, five-sided region. The points on and inside the boundary of this feasible set give the production schedules that satisfy all the restrictions. In Section 3.2 we show how to pick out the particular point of the feasible set that corresponds to a maximum profit.

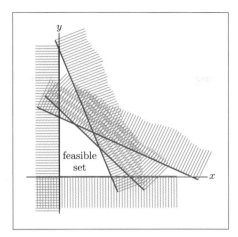

Figure 2.

**Practice Problems
3.1**

1. Determine whether the following points are in the feasible set of the furniture manufacturing problem: (a) $(10, 9)$; (b) $(14, 4)$.

2. A physical fitness enthusiast decides to devote her exercise time to a combination of jogging and cycling. She wants to earn aerobic points (a measure of the benefit of the exercise to strengthening the heart and lungs) and also to achieve relaxation and enjoyment. She jogs at 6 miles per hour and cycles at 18 miles per hour. An hour of jogging earns 12 aerobic points and an hour of cycling earns 9 aerobic points. Each week she would like to earn at least 36 aerobic points, cover at least 54 miles, and cycle at least as much as she jogs.

   (a) Fill in the chart below.

	One hour of jogging	One hour of cycling	Requirement
Miles covered			
Aerobic points			
Time required			

   (b) Let x be the number of hours of jogging and y the number of hours of cycling each week. Referring to the chart, give the inequalities that x and y must satisfy due to miles covered and aerobic points.

   (c) Give the inequalities that x and y must satisfy due to her preference for cycling and also due to the fact that x and y cannot be negative.

   (d) Express the time required as a linear function of x and y.

   (e) Graph the feasible set for the system of linear inequalities.

▶ Exercises 3.1

In Exercises 1–4, determine whether the given point is in the feasible set of the furniture manufacturing problem. (The inequalities are as follows.)

$$\begin{cases} 6x + 3y \le 96 \\ x + y \le 18 \\ 2x + 6y \le 72 \\ x \ge 0, \quad y \ge 0 \end{cases}$$

1. $(8, 7)$

2. $(14, 3)$

3. $(9, 10)$

4. $(16, 0)$

5. (*Shipping*) A truck traveling from New York to Baltimore is to be loaded with two types of cargo. Each crate of cargo A is 4 cubic feet in volume, weighs 100 pounds, and earns $13 for the driver. Each crate of

cargo B is 3 cubic feet in volume, weighs 200 pounds, and earns $9 for the driver. The truck can carry no more than 300 cubic feet of crates and no more than 10,000 pounds. Also, the number of crates of cargo B must be less than or equal to twice the number of crates of cargo A.

(a) Fill in the following chart.

	A	B	Truck capacity
Volume			
Weight			
Earnings			

(b) Let x be the number of crates of cargo A and y the number of crates of cargo B. Referring to the chart, give the two inequalities that x and y must satisfy because of the truck's capacity for volume and weight.

(c) Give the inequalities that x and y must satisfy because of the last sentence of the problem and also because x and y cannot be negative.

(d) Express the earnings from carrying x crates of cargo A and y crates of cargo B.

(e) Graph the feasible set for the shipping problem.

6. (*Mining*) A coal company owns mines in two different locations. Each day mine 1 produces 4 tons of anthracite (hard coal), 4 tons of ordinary coal, and 7 tons of bituminous (soft) coal. Each day mine 2 produces 10 tons of anthracite, 5 tons of ordinary coal, and 5 tons of bituminous coal. It costs the company $150 per day to operate mine 1 and $200 per day to operate mine 2. An order is received for 80 tons of anthracite, 60 tons of ordinary coal, and 75 tons of bituminous coal.

(a) Fill in the following chart.

	Mine 1	Mine 2	Ordered
Anthracite			
Ordinary			
Bituminous			
Daily cost			

(b) Let x be the number of days mine 1 should be operated and y the number of days mine 2 should be operated. Refer to the chart and give three inequalities that x and y must satisfy to fill the order.

(c) Give other requirements that x and y must satisfy.

(d) Find the cost of operating mine 1 for x days and mine 2 for y days.

(e) Graph the feasible set for the mining problem.

7. (*Exam Strategy*) A student is taking an exam consisting of 10 essay questions and 50 short-answer questions. He has 90 minutes to take the exam and knows he cannot possibly answer every question. The essay questions are worth 20 points each and the short-answer questions are worth 5 points each. An essay question takes 10 minutes to answer and a short-answer question takes 2 minutes. The student must do at least 3 essay questions and at least 10 short-answer questions.

(a) Fill in the following chart.

	Essay questions	Short-answer questions	Available
Time to answer			
Quantity			
Required			
Worth			

(b) Let x be the number of essay questions to be answered and y the number of short-answer questions to be answered. Refer to the chart and give the inequality that x and y must satisfy due to the amount of time available.

(c) Give the inequalities that x and y must satisfy because of the numbers of each type of question and also because of the minimum number of each type of question that must be answered.

(d) Give an expression for the score obtained from answering x essay questions and y short-answer questions.

(e) Graph the feasible set for the exam strategy problem.

8. (*Political Campaign—Resource Allocation*) A local politician has budgeted at most $80,000 for her media campaign. She plans to distribute these funds between TV ads and radio ads. Each 1-minute TV ad is expected to be seen by 20,000 viewers, and each 1-minute radio ad is expected to be heard by 4000 listeners. Each minute of TV time costs $8000 and each minute of radio time costs $2000. She has been advised to use at most 90% of her media campaign budget on television ads.

(a) Fill in the following chart. (*Note:* Fill in only the first entry of the last column.)

	One-minute TV ads	One-minute radio ads	Money available
Cost			
Audience reached			

(b) Let x be the number of minutes of TV ads and let y be the number of minutes of radio ads. Refer to the chart and give an inequality that x and y must satisfy due to the amount of money available.

(c) Give the inequality that x must satisfy due to the limitation on the amount of money to be spent on TV ads. Also, give the inequalities that x and y must satisfy because x and y cannot be negative.

(d) Give an expression for the audience reached by x minutes of TV ads and y minutes of radio ads.

(e) Graph the feasible set for the political campaign problem.

9. (*Nutrition—Dairy Cows*) A dairy farmer concludes that his small herd of cows will need at least 4550 pounds of protein in their winter feed, at least 26,880 pounds of total digestible nutrients (TDN), and at least 43,200 international units (IUs) of vitamin A. Each pound of alfalfa hay provides .13 pound of protein, .48 pound of TDN, and 2.16 IUs of vitamin A. Each pound of ground ears of corn supplies .065 pound of protein, .96 pound of TDN, and no vitamin A. Alfalfa hay costs $1 per 100-pound sack. Ground ear corn costs $1.60 per 100-pound sack.

(a) Fill in the following chart.

	Alfalfa	Corn	Requirements
Protein			
TDN			
Vitamin A			
Cost/lb			

(b) Let x be the number of pounds of alfalfa hay and y be the number of pounds of ground ears of corn to be bought. Give the inequalities that x and y must satisfy.

(c) Graph the feasible set for the system of linear inequalities.

(d) Express the cost of buying x pounds of alfalfa hay and y pounds of ground ears of corn.

Solutions to Practice Problems 3.1

1. A point is in the feasible set of a system of inequalities if it satisfies every inequality. Either the original form or the standard form of the inequalities may be used. The original form of the inequalities of the furniture manufacturing problem is

$$\begin{cases} 6x + 3y \leq 96 \\ x + y \leq 18 \\ 2x + 6y \leq 72 \\ x \geq 0, \quad y \geq 0. \end{cases}$$

(a) $(10, 9)$

$$\begin{cases} 6(10) + 3(9) \leq 96 \\ 10 + 9 \leq 18 \\ 2(10) + 6(9) \leq 72 \\ 10 \geq 0, \quad 9 \geq 0; \end{cases} \quad \begin{cases} 87 \leq 96 \\ 19 \leq 18 \\ 74 \leq 72 \\ 10 \geq 0, \quad 9 \geq 0 \end{cases} \quad \begin{matrix} \text{true} \\ \text{false} \\ \text{false} \\ \text{true} \end{matrix}$$

(b) $(14, 4)$

$$\begin{cases} 6(14) + 3(4) \leq 96 \\ 14 + 4 \leq 18 \\ 2(14) + 6(4) \leq 72 \\ 14 \geq 0, \quad 4 \geq 0; \end{cases} \quad \begin{cases} 96 \leq 96 \\ 18 \leq 18 \\ 52 \leq 72 \\ 14 \geq 0, \quad 4 \geq 0 \end{cases} \quad \begin{matrix} \text{true} \\ \text{true} \\ \text{true} \\ \text{true} \end{matrix}$$

Therefore, $(14, 4)$ is in the feasible set and $(10, 9)$ is not.

2. (a)

	One hour of jogging	One hour of cycling	Requirement
Miles covered	6	18	54
Aerobic points	12	9	36
Time required	1	1	

(b) Miles covered: $6x + 18y \geq 54$.
Aerobic points: $12x + 9y \geq 36$.

(c) $y \geq x$, $x \geq 0$. It is not necessary to list $y \geq 0$ since this is automatically assured if the other two inequalities hold.

(d) $x + y$. (An objective of the exercise program might be to minimize $x + y$.)

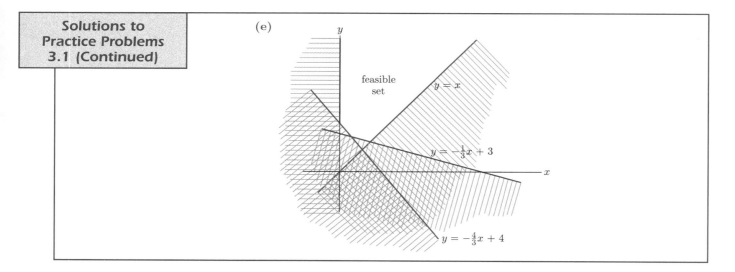

(e)

3.2 Linear Programming I

We have shown that the feasible set for the furniture manufacturing problem—that is, the set of points corresponding to production schedules satisfying all five restriction inequalities—consists of the points in the interior and on the boundary of the five-sided region drawn in Fig. 1. For reference, we have labeled

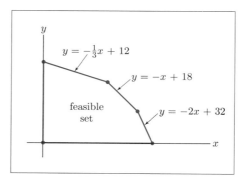

Figure 1.

each line segment with the equation of the line to which it belongs. The line segments intersect in five points, each of which is a corner of the feasible set. Such a corner is called a *vertex*. Somehow, we must pick out of the feasible set an *optimal point*—that is, a point corresponding to a production schedule that yields a maximum profit. To assist us in this task, we have the following result[1]:

Fundamental Theorem of Linear Programming The maximum (or minimum) value of the objective function is achieved at one of the vertices of the feasible set.

---

[1]For a verification, see Section 3.3.

This result does not completely solve the furniture manufacturing problem for us, but it comes close. It tells us that an optimal production schedule (a, b) corresponds to one of the five points labeled A–E in Fig. 2. So to complete the solution of the furniture manufacturing problem, it suffices to find the coordinates of the five points, evaluate the profit at each, and then choose the point corresponding to the maximum profit.

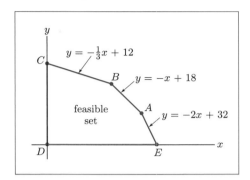

Figure 2.

Solution of the Furniture Manufacturing Problem

Let us begin by determining the coordinates of the points A–E in Fig. 2. Remembering that the x-axis has the equation $y = 0$ and the y-axis the equation $x = 0$, we see from Fig. 2 that the coordinates of A–E can be found as intersections of the following lines:

$$A : \begin{cases} y = -x + 18 \\ y = -2x + 32 \end{cases}$$

$$B : \begin{cases} y = -x + 18 \\ y = -\tfrac{1}{3}x + 12 \end{cases}$$

$$C : \begin{cases} y = -\tfrac{1}{3}x + 12 \\ x = 0 \end{cases}$$

$$D : \begin{cases} y = 0 \\ x = 0 \end{cases}$$

$$E : \begin{cases} y = 0 \\ y = -2x + 32. \end{cases}$$

The point D is clearly $(0, 0)$, and C is clearly the point $(0, 12)$. We obtain A from

$$-x + 18 = -2x + 32$$
$$x = 14$$
$$y = -14 + 18 = 4.$$

Hence $A = (14, 4)$. Similarly, we obtain B from

$$-x + 18 = -\tfrac{1}{3}x + 12$$
$$-\tfrac{2}{3}x = -6$$
$$x = 9$$
$$y = -9 + 18 = 9,$$

so $B = (9, 9)$. Finally, E is obtained from

$$0 = -2x + 32$$
$$x = 16$$
$$y = 0,$$

and thus $E = (16, 0)$. We have displayed the vertices in Fig. 3 and listed them in Table 1. In the second column we have evaluated the profit, which is given by $80x + 70y$, at each of the vertices. Note that the largest profit occurs at the vertex $(14, 4)$, so the solution of the linear programming problem is $x = 14$, $y = 4$. In other words, the factory should produce 14 chairs and 4 sofas each day in order to achieve maximum profit, and the maximum profit is $1400 per day.

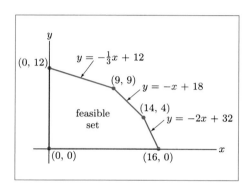

Table 1	
Vertex	Profit $= 80x + 70y$
$(14, 4)$	$80(14) + 70(4) = 1400$
$(9, 9)$	$80(9) + 70(9) = 1350$
$(0, 12)$	$80(0) + 70(12) = 840$
$(0, 0)$	$80(0) + 70(0) = 0$
$(16, 0)$	$80(16) + 70(0) = 1280$

Figure 3.

The furniture manufacturing problem is one particular example of a linear programming problem. Generally, such problems involve finding the values of x and y that maximize (or minimize) a particular linear expression in x and y and where x and y are chosen so as to satisfy one or more restrictions in the form of linear inequalities. The expression that is to be maximized (or minimized) is called the *objective function*. On the basis of our experience with the furniture manufacturing problem, we can summarize the steps to be followed in approaching *any* linear programming problem.

Step 1 Translate the problem into mathematical language.

    A. Organize the data.

    B. Identify the unknown quantities and define corresponding variables.

    C. Translate the restrictions into linear inequalities.

    D. Form the objective function.

Step 2 Graph the feasible set.

    A. Put the inequalities in standard form.

    B. Graph the straight line corresponding to each inequality.

    C. Determine the side of the line belonging to the graph of each inequality. Cross out the other side. The remaining region is the feasible set.

Step 3 Determine the vertices of the feasible set.

Step 4 Evaluate the objective function at each vertex. Determine the optimal point.

Linear programming can be applied to many problems. The Army Corps of Engineers has used linear programming to plan the location of a series of dams so as to maximize the resulting hydroelectric power production. The restrictions were to provide adequate flood control and irrigation. Public transit companies have used linear programming to plan routes and schedule buses in order to maximize services. The restrictions in this case arose from the limitations on labor, equipment, and funding. The petroleum industry uses linear programming in the refining and blending of gasoline. Profit is maximized subject to restrictions on availability of raw materials, refining capacity, and product specifications. Some large advertising firms have used linear programming in media selection. The problem consists of determining how much to spend in each medium in order to maximize the number of consumers reached. The restrictions come from limitations on the budget and the relative costs of different media. Linear programming has been also used by psychologists to design an optimal battery of tests. The problem is to maximize the correlation between test scores and the characteristic that is to be predicted. The restrictions are imposed by the length and cost of the testing.

Linear programming is also used by dietitians in planning meals for large numbers of people. The object is to minimize the cost of the diet, and the restrictions reflect the minimum daily requirements of the various nutrients considered in the diet. The next example is representative of this type of problem. Whereas in actual practice many nutritional factors are considered, we shall simplify the problem by considering only three: protein, calories, and riboflavin.

▶ Example 1   (*Nutrition—People*) Suppose a person decides to make rice and soybeans part of his staple diet. The object is to design a lowest-cost diet that provides certain minimum levels of protein, calories, and vitamin B_2 (riboflavin). Suppose that one cup of uncooked rice costs 21 cents and contains 15 grams of protein, 810 calories, and $\frac{1}{9}$ milligram of riboflavin. On the other hand, one cup of uncooked soybeans costs 14 cents and contains 22.5 grams of protein, 270 calories, and $\frac{1}{3}$ milligram of riboflavin. Suppose that the minimum daily requirements are 90 grams of protein, 1620 calories, and 1 milligram of riboflavin. Design the lowest-cost diet meeting these specifications.

Solution   We solve the problem by following steps 1–4. The first step is to translate the problem into mathematical language, and the first part of this step is to organize the data, preferably into a chart (Table 2).

Table 2

	Rice	Soybeans	Required level per day
Protein (grams/cup)	15	22.5	90
Calories (per cup)	810	270	1620
Riboflavin (milligrams/cup)	$\frac{1}{9}$	$\frac{1}{3}$	1
Cost (cents/cup)	21	14	

Now that we have organized the data, we ask for the unknowns. We wish to know how many cups each of rice and soybeans should comprise the diet, so we identify appropriate variables:

$$x = \text{number of cups of rice per day}$$
$$y = \text{number of cups of soybeans per day.}$$

Next, we obtain the restrictions on the variables. There is one restriction corresponding to each nutrient. That is, there is one restriction for each row of the chart. If x cups of rice and y cups of soybeans are consumed, the amount of protein is $15x + 22.5y$ grams. Thus, from the first row of the chart, $15x + 22.5y \geq 90$, a restriction expressing the fact that there must be at least 90 grams of protein per day. Similarly, the restrictions for calories and riboflavin lead to the inequalities $810x + 270y \geq 1620$ and $\frac{1}{9}x + \frac{1}{3}y \geq 1$, respectively. As in the furniture manufacturing problem, x and y cannot be negative, so there are two further restrictions: $x \geq 0$, $y \geq 0$. In all, there are five restrictions:

$$\begin{cases} 15x + 22.5y \geq 90 \\ 810x + 270y \geq 1620 \\ \frac{1}{9}x + \frac{1}{3}y \geq 1 \\ x \geq 0, \quad y \geq 0. \end{cases} \tag{1}$$

Now that we have the restrictions, we form the objective function, which tells us what we want to maximize or minimize. Since we wish to minimize cost, we express cost in terms of x and y. Now x cups of rice cost $21x$ cents and y cups of soybeans cost $14y$ cents, so the objective function is given by

$$[\text{cost}] = 21x + 14y. \tag{2}$$

The problem can finally be stated in mathematical form: Minimize the objective function (2) subject to the restrictions (1). This completes the first step of the solution process.

The second step requires that we graph each of the inequalities (1). In Table 3 we have summarized all the steps necessary to obtain the information from which to draw the graphs.

Table 3

Inequality	Standard form	Line	Intercepts x	y	Graph
$15x + 22.5y \geq 90$	$y \geq -\frac{2}{3}x + 4$	$y = -\frac{2}{3}x + 4$	$(6,0)$	$(0,4)$	above
$810x + 270y \geq 1620$	$y \geq -3x + 6$	$y = -3x + 6$	$(2,0)$	$(0,6)$	above
$\frac{1}{9}x + \frac{1}{3}y \geq 1$	$y \geq -\frac{1}{3}x + 3$	$y = -\frac{1}{3}x + 3$	$(9,0)$	$(0,3)$	above
$x \geq 0$	$x \geq 0$	$x = 0$	$(0,0)$	—	right
$y \geq 0$	$y \geq 0$	$y = 0$	—	$(0,0)$	above

We have sketched the graphs in Fig. 4. From Fig. 4(b) we see that the feasible set is an unbounded, five-sided region. There are four vertices, two of which are known from Table 3, since they are intercepts of boundary lines. Label the remaining two vertices A and B (Fig. 5).

The third step of the solution process consists of determining the coordinates of A and B. From Fig. 5 these coordinates can be found by solving the following

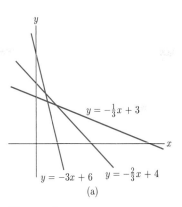

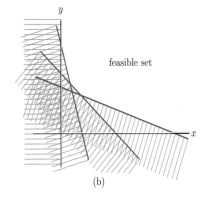

(a)   (b)

Figure 4.

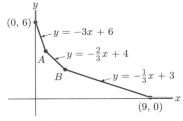

Figure 5.

systems of equations:

$$A: \begin{cases} y = -3x + 6 \\ y = -\frac{2}{3}x + 4 \end{cases} \qquad B: \begin{cases} y = -\frac{2}{3}x + 4 \\ y = -\frac{1}{3}x + 3. \end{cases}$$

To solve the first system, equate the two expressions for y:

$$-\tfrac{2}{3}x + 4 = -3x + 6$$
$$3x - \tfrac{2}{3}x = 6 - 4$$
$$\tfrac{7}{3}x = 2$$
$$x = \tfrac{6}{7}$$
$$y = -3x + 6 = -3\left(\tfrac{6}{7}\right) + 6 = \tfrac{24}{7}$$
$$A = \left(\tfrac{6}{7}, \tfrac{24}{7}\right).$$

Similarly, we find B:

$$-\tfrac{2}{3}x + 4 = -\tfrac{1}{3}x + 3$$
$$-\tfrac{1}{3}x = -1$$
$$x = 3$$
$$y = -\tfrac{2}{3}(3) + 4 = 2$$
$$B = (3, 2).$$

The fourth step consists of evaluating the objective function, in this case $21x + 14y$, at each vertex. From Table 4 we see that the minimum cost is

Table 4	
Vertex	$\boldsymbol{Cost = 21x + 14y}$
$(0, 6)$	$21 \cdot 0 + 14 \cdot 6 = \ \ 84$
$\left(\tfrac{6}{7}, \tfrac{24}{7}\right)$	$21 \cdot \tfrac{6}{7} + 14 \cdot \tfrac{24}{7} = \ \ 66$
$(3, 2)$	$21 \cdot 3 + 14 \cdot 2 = \ \ 91$
$(9, 0)$	$21 \cdot 9 + 14 \cdot 0 = 189$

achieved at the vertex $\left(\frac{6}{7}, \frac{24}{7}\right)$. So the optimal diet—that is, the one that gives nutrients at the desired levels but at minimum cost—is the one that has $\frac{6}{7}$ cup of rice per day and $\frac{24}{7}$ cups of soybeans per day.   ◆

Note   We have assumed that all linear programming problems have solutions. Although every linear programming problem presented in this text has a solution, there are problems that have no optimal feasible solution. This can happen in two ways. First, there might be no points in the feasible set. Second, feasible solutions to the system of inequalities might exist, but the objective function might not have a maximum (or minimum) value within the feasible set. See Exercises 36 and 37.

GC   Graphing calculators can draw (and often shade) a feasible set, determine the vertices of the feasible set, and evaluate the objective function at the vertices. Figures 6 to 8 show how some of these tasks can be carried out on a TI-83 for the furniture manufacturing problem. In Fig. 6, the shading was produced with the three commands **Shade(0, Y₁, 0, 9)**, **Shade(0, Y₂, 9, 14)**, and **Shade(0, Y₃, 14, 16)**, where **Y₁**, **Y₂**, and **Y₃** are the three lines in Fig. 3. In Fig. 8, the table was created by pressing ⌊STAT⌋ **1** and then entering the data for **L1** and **L2**.

Figure 6. $[0, 18]$ by $[0, 14]$

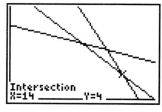

Figure 7.

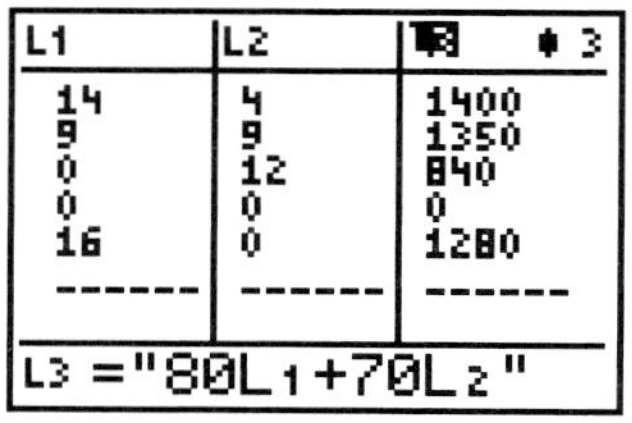

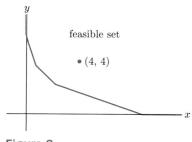

Figure 8.

**Practice Problems
3.2**

1. The feasible set for the nutrition problem is shown in Fig. 9. The cost is $21x + 14y$. *Without* using the fundamental theorem of linear programming, explain why the cost could not possibly be minimized at the point $(4, 4)$.

y

feasible set

• $(4, 4)$

x

Figure 9.

2. Rework the nutrition problem assuming that the cost of rice is changed to 7 cents per cup.

▶ Exercises 3.2

For each of the feasible sets in Exercises 1–4, determine x and y so that the objective function $4x + 3y$ is maximized.

1.

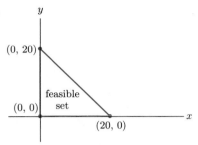

2.

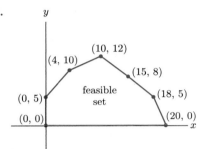

3.

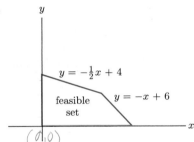

4.

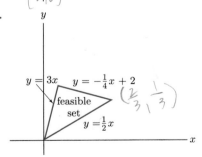

In Exercises 5–8, find the values of x and y that maximize the given objective function for the feasible set in Fig. 10.

5. $x + 2y$

6. $x + y$

7. $2x + y$

8. $3 - x - y$

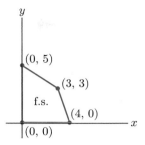

Figure 10.

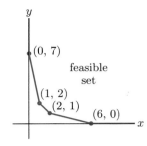

Figure 11.

In Exercises 9–12, find the values of x and y that minimize the given objective function for the feasible set in Fig. 11.

9. $8x + y$

10. $3x + 2y$

11. $2x + 3y$

12. $x + 8y$

13. (*Shipping*) Refer to Exercises 3.1, Problem 5. How many crates of each cargo should be shipped in order to satisfy the shipping requirements and yield the greatest earnings? (See the graph of the feasible set in Fig. 12.)

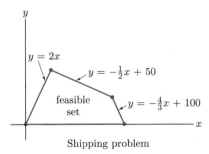

Shipping problem

Figure 12.

14. (*Mining*) Refer to Exercises 3.1, Problem 6. Find the number of days that each mine should be operated in order to fill the order at the least cost. (See the graph of the feasible set in Fig. 13.)

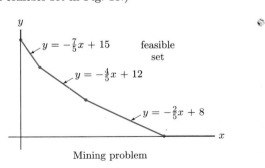

Mining problem

Figure 13.

15. (*Exam Strategy*) Refer to Exercises 3.1, Problem 7. How many of each type of question should the student do to maximize the total score? (See the graph of the feasible set in Fig. 14.)

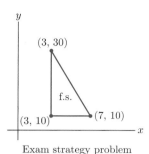

Exam strategy problem

Figure 14.

16. (*Political Campaign—Resource Allocation*) Refer to Exercises 3.1, Problem 8. How should the media funds be allocated so as to maximize the total audience? (See the graph of the feasible set in Fig. 15.)

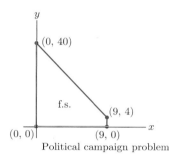

Political campaign problem

Figure 15.

In Exercises 17 and 18, rework the furniture manufacturing problem, where everything is the same except that the profit per chair is changed to the given value. (See Table 1 for vertices.)

17. $150   **18.** $60

19. Minimize the objective function $3x + 4y$ subject to the constraints

$$\begin{cases} 2x + y \ge 10 \\ x + 2y \ge 14 \\ x \ge 0, \quad y \ge 0. \end{cases}$$

20. Maximize the objective function $7x + 4y$ subject to the constraints

$$\begin{cases} 3x + 2y \le 36 \\ x + 4y \le 32 \\ x \ge 0, \quad y \ge 0. \end{cases}$$

21. Maximize the objective function $2x + 5y$ subject to the constraints

$$\begin{cases} x + 2y \le 20 \\ 3x + 2y \ge 24 \\ x \le 6 \\ x \ge 0, \quad y \ge 0. \end{cases}$$

22. Minimize the objective function $2x + 3y$ subject to the constraints

$$\begin{cases} x + y \ge 10 \\ y \le x \\ x \le 8. \end{cases}$$

23. Maximize the objective function $100x + 150y$ subject to the constraints

$$\begin{cases} x + 3y \le 120 \\ 35x + 10y \le 780 \\ x \le 20 \\ x \ge 0, \quad y \ge 0. \end{cases}$$

24. Minimize the objective function $\frac{1}{2}x + \frac{3}{4}y$ subject to the constraints

$$\begin{cases} 2x + 2y \ge 8 \\ 3x + 5y \ge 16 \\ x \ge 0, \quad y \ge 0. \end{cases}$$

25. Minimize the objective function $7x + 4y$ subject to the constraints

$$\begin{cases} y \ge -2x + 11 \\ y \le -x + 10 \\ y \le -\frac{1}{3}x + 6 \\ y \ge -\frac{1}{4}x + 4. \end{cases}$$

26. Maximize the objective function $x + 2y$ subject to the constraints

$$\begin{cases} y \le -x + 100 \\ y \ge \frac{1}{3}x + 20 \\ y \le x. \end{cases}$$

27. (*Manufacturing—Resource Allocation*) Infotron Inc. makes electronic hockey and soccer games. Each hockey game requires 2 labor-hours of assembly and 2 labor-hours of testing. Each soccer game requires 3 labor-hours of assembly and 1 labor-hour of testing. Each day there are 42 labor-hours available for assembly and 26 labor-hours available for testing. How many of each game should Infotron produce each day to maximize its total daily output?

28. (*Manufacturing—Production Planning*) An electronics company has factories in Cleveland and Toledo that manufacture three-head and four-head VCRs. Each day the Cleveland factory produces 500 three-head VCRs and 300 four-head VCRs at a cost of $18,000. Each day the Toledo factory produces 300 of each type of VCR at a cost of $15,000. An order is received for 25,000 three-head VCRs and 21,000 four-head VCRs. For how many days should each factory operate to fill the order at the least cost?

29. (*Construction—Resource Allocation*)   A contractor builds two types of homes. The first type requires one lot, $12,000 capital, and 150 labor-days to build and is sold for a profit of $2400. The second type of home requires one lot, $32,000 capital, and 200 labor-days to build and is sold for a profit of $3400. The contractor owns 150 lots and has available for the job $2,880,000 capital and 24,000 labor-days. How many homes of each type should she build to realize the greatest profit?

30. (*Nutrition—People*)   A nutritionist, working for NASA, must meet certain nutritional requirements and yet keep the weight of the food at a minimum. He is considering a combination of two foods, which are packaged in tubes. Each tube of food A contains 4 units of protein, 2 units of carbohydrates, and 2 units of fat and weighs 3 pounds. Each tube of food B contains 3 units of protein, 6 units of carbohydrates, and 1 unit of fat and weighs 2 pounds. The requirement calls for 42 units of protein, 30 units of carbohydrates, and 18 units of fat. How many tubes of each food should be supplied to the astronauts?

31. (*Packaging—Product Mix*)   The Beautiful Day Fruit Juice Company makes two varieties of fruit drink. Each can of Fruit Delight contains 10 ounces of pineapple juice, 3 ounces of orange juice, and 1 ounce of apricot juice and makes a profit of 20 cents. Each can of Heavenly Punch contains 10 ounces of pineapple juice, 2 ounces of orange juice, and 2 ounces of apricot juice and makes a profit of 30 cents. Each week the company has available 9000 ounces of pineapple juice, 2400 ounces of orange juice, and 1400 ounces of apricot juice. How many cans of Fruit Delight and of Heavenly Punch should be produced each week to maximize profits?

32. (*Manufacturing—Resource Allocation*)   The Bluejay Lacrosse Stick Company makes two kinds of lacrosse sticks. Type A sticks require 2 labor-hours for cutting, 1 labor-hour for stringing, and 2 labor-hours for finishing and are sold for a profit of $8. Type B sticks require 1 labor-hour for cutting, 3 labor-hours for stringing, and 2 labor-hours for finishing and are sold for a profit of $10. Each day the company has available 120 labor-hours for cutting, 150 labor-hours for stringing, and 140 labor-hours for finishing. How many lacrosse sticks of each kind should be manufactured each day to maximize profits?

33. (*Agriculture—Crop Planning*)   A farmer has 100 acres on which to plant oats or corn. Each acre of oats requires $18 capital and 2 hours of labor. Each acre of corn requires $36 capital and 6 hours of labor. Labor costs are $8 per hour. The farmer has $2100 available for capital and $2400 available for labor. If the revenue is $55 from each acre of oats and $125 from each

acre of corn, what planting combination will produce the greatest total profit? (Profit here is revenue plus leftover capital and labor cash reserve.) What is the maximum profit?

34. (*Agriculture—Crop Planning*)   Suppose that the farmer of Exercise 33 can allocate the $4500 available for capital and labor however he or she wants.

   (a) Without solving the linear programming problem, explain why the optimal profit cannot be less than what was found in Exercise 33.

   (b) Find the optimal solution in the new situation. Does it provide more profit than in Exercise 33?

35. (*Manufacturing—Resource Allocation*)   A company makes two items, I_1 and I_2, from three raw materials, M_1, M_2, and M_3. Item I_1 uses 3 ounces of M_1, 2 ounces of M_2, and 2 ounces of M_3. Item I_2 uses 4 ounces of M_1, 1 ounce of M_2, and 3 ounces of M_3. The profit on item I_1 is $8 and on item I_2 is $6. The company has a daily supply of 40 ounces of M_1, 20 ounces of M_2, and 60 ounces of M_3.

   (a) How many of items I_1 and I_2 should be made each day to maximize profit?

   (b) What is the maximum profit?

   (c) How many ounces of each raw material are used?

   (d) If the profit on item I_1 increases to $13, how many of items I_1 and I_2 should be made each day to maximize profit?

36. Consider the following linear programming problem: Maximize $M = 10x + 6y$ subject to the constraints

$$\begin{cases} x + y \geq 6 \\ x \geq 0, \quad y \geq 0. \end{cases}$$

   (a) Sketch the feasible set.

   (b) Determine three points in the feasible set and calculate M at each of them.

   (c) Show that the objective function attains no maximum value for points in the feasible set.

37. Consider the following linear programming problem: Minimize $M = 10x + 6y$ subject to the constraints

$$\begin{cases} x + y \geq 6 \\ 4x + 3y \leq 4 \\ x \geq 0, \quad y \geq 0. \end{cases}$$

   (a) Sketch the feasible set for the linear programming problem.

   (b) Determine a point of the feasible set.

1. The point P has a smaller value of x and a smaller value of y than $(4, 4)$ and is still in the feasible set. It therefore corresponds to a lower cost than $(4, 4)$ and still meets the requirements. We conclude that no interior point of the feasible set could possibly be an optimal point. This geometric argument indicates that an optimal point might be one that juts out far—that is, a vertex (Fig. 16).

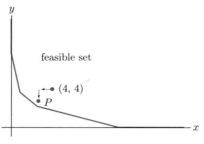

Figure 16.

2. The system of linear inequalities, feasible set, and vertices will all be the same as before. Only the objective function changes. The new objective function is $7x + 14y$. The minimum cost occurs when using 3 cups of rice and 2 cups of soybeans.

Vertex	$Cost = 7x + 14y$
$(0, 6)$	84
$\left(\frac{6}{7}, \frac{24}{7}\right)$	54
$(3, 2)$	49
$(9, 0)$	63

3.3 Linear Programming II

In this section we apply the technique of linear programming to the design of a portfolio for a retirement fund and to the transportation of goods from warehouses to retail outlets. The significant new feature of each of these problems is that, on the surface, they appear to involve more than two variables. However, they can be translated into mathematical language so that only two variables are required.

▶ Example 1 (*Investment Planning*) A pension fund has $30 million to invest. The money is to be divided among Treasury notes, bonds, and stocks. The rules for administration of the fund require that at least $3 million be invested in each type of investment, that at least half the money be invested in Treasury notes and bonds, and that the amount invested in bonds not exceed twice the amount invested in Treasury notes. The annual yields for the various investments are 7% for Treasury notes, 8% for bonds, and 9% for stocks. How should the money be allocated among the various investments to produce the largest return?

Solution First, let us agree that all numbers stand for millions. That is, we write 30 to stand for 30 million dollars. This will save us from writing many zeros. In examining the problem, we find that very little organization needs to be done. The rules for administration of the fund are written in a form from which inequalities can be read right off. Let us just summarize the remaining data in the first row of a chart (Table 1).

Table 1			
	Treasury notes	**Bonds**	**Stocks**
Yield	.07	.08	.09
Variables	x	y	$30 - (x + y)$

There appear to be three variables—the amounts to be invested in each of the three categories. However, since the three investments must total 30, we need only two variables. Let $x =$ the amount to be invested in Treasury notes and $y =$ the amount to be invested in bonds. Then the amount to be invested in stocks is $30 - (x + y)$. We have displayed the variables in Table 1.

Now for the restrictions. Since at least 3 (million dollars) must be invested in each category, we have the three inequalities

$$x \geq 3$$
$$y \geq 3$$
$$30 - (x + y) \geq 3.$$

Moreover, since at least half the money, or 15, must be invested in Treasury notes and bonds, we must have

$$x + y \geq 15.$$

Finally, since the amount invested in bonds must not exceed twice the amount invested in Treasury notes, we must have

$$y \leq 2x.$$

(In this example we do not need to state that $x \geq 0$, $y \geq 0$, since we have already required that they be greater than or equal to 3.) Thus there are five restriction inequalities:

$$\begin{cases} x \geq 3, \quad y \geq 3 \\ 30 - (x + y) \geq \ \ 3 \\ \qquad \quad x + y \geq 15 \\ \qquad \qquad y \leq 2x. \end{cases} \tag{1}$$

Next, we form the objective function, which in this case equals the total return on the investment. Since x dollars is invested at 7%, y dollars at 8%, and $30 - (x + y)$ dollars at 9%, the total return is

$$\begin{aligned} [\text{return}] &= .07x + .08y + .09[30 - (x + y)] \\ &= .07x + .08y + 2.7 - .09x - .09y \\ &= 2.7 - .02x - .01y. \end{aligned} \tag{2}$$

So the mathematical statement of the problem is: Maximize the objective function (2) subject to the restrictions (1).

The next step of the solution is to graph the inequalities (1). The necessary information is tabulated in Table 2.

Table 2

Inequality	Standard form	Line	Intercepts x	Intercepts y	Graph
$x \geq 3$	$x \geq 3$	$x = 3$	$(3, 0)$	—	Right of line
$y \geq 3$	$y \geq 3$	$y = 3$	—	$(0, 3)$	Above line
$30 - (x + y) \geq 3$	$y \leq -x + 27$	$y = -x + 27$	$(27, 0)$	$(0, 27)$	Below line
$x + y \geq 15$	$y \geq -x + 15$	$y = -x + 15$	$(15, 0)$	$(0, 15)$	Above line
$y \leq 2x$	$y \leq 2x$	$y = 2x$	$(0, 0)$	$(0, 0)$	Below line

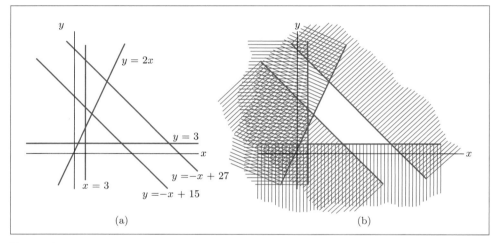

Figure 1.

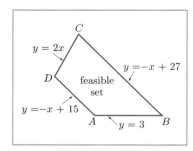

Figure 2.

One point about the chart is worth noting: It contains enough data to graph each of the lines, with the exception of $y = 2x$. The reason is that the x- and y-intercepts of this line are the same, $(0, 0)$. So to graph $y = 2x$, we must find an additional point on the line. For example, if we set $x = 2$, then $y = 4$, so $(2, 4)$ is on the line. In Fig. 1(a) we have drawn the various lines, and in Fig. 1(b) we have crossed out the appropriate regions to produce the graph of the system. The feasible set, as well as the equations of the various lines that make up its boundary, are shown in Fig. 2. From Fig. 2 we find the pairs of equations that determine each of the vertices A–D. This is the third step of the solution procedure.

$$A: \begin{cases} y = 3 \\ y = -x + 15 \end{cases} \qquad B: \begin{cases} y = 3 \\ y = -x + 27 \end{cases}$$

$$C: \begin{cases} y = -x + 27 \\ y = 2x \end{cases} \qquad D: \begin{cases} y = 2x \\ y = -x + 15 \end{cases}$$

A and B are the easiest to determine. To find A, we must solve

$$3 = -x + 15$$
$$x = 12$$
$$y = 3$$
$$A = (12, 3).$$

Similarly, $B = (24, 3)$. To find C, we must solve

$$2x = -x + 27$$
$$3x = 27$$
$$x = 9$$
$$y = 2(9) = 18$$
$$C = (9, 18).$$

Similarly, $D = (5, 10)$.

Finally, we list the four vertices and evaluate the objective function (2) at each one. The results are summarized in Table 3.

Table 3

Vertex	Return $= 2.7 - .02x - .01y$
$(5, 10)$	$2.7 - .02(5) - .01(10) = \$2.5$ million
$(9, 18)$	$2.7 - .02(9) - .01(18) = \$2.34$ million
$(24, 3)$	$2.7 - .02(24) - .01(3) = \$2.19$ million
$(12, 3)$	$2.7 - .02(12) - .01(3) = \$2.43$ million

It is clear that the largest return occurs when $x = 5$, $y = 10$. In other words, \$5 million should be invested in Treasury notes, \$10 million in bonds, and $30 - (x + y) = 30 - (5 + 10) = \$15$ million in stocks. ◆

Linear programming is of use not only in analyzing investments but in the fields of transportation and shipping. It is often used to plan routes, determine locations of warehouses, and develop efficient procedures for getting goods to people. Many linear programming problems of this variety can be formulated as *transportation problems*. A typical transportation problem involves determining the least-cost scheme for delivering a commodity stocked in a number of different warehouses to a number of different locations, say retail stores. Of course, in practical applications, it is necessary to consider problems involving perhaps dozens or even hundreds of warehouses, and possibly just as many delivery locations. For problems on such a grand scale, the methods developed so far are inadequate. For one thing, the number of variables required is usually more than two. We must wait until Chapter 4 for methods that apply to such problems. However, the next example gives an instance of a transportation problem that does not involve too many warehouses or too many delivery points. It gives the flavor of general transportation problems.

▶ Example 2   (*Transportation—Shipping*) Suppose that a Maryland TV dealer has stores in Annapolis and Rockville and warehouses in College Park and Baltimore. The cost of shipping a TV set from College Park to Annapolis is $6; from College Park to Rockville, $3; from Baltimore to Annapolis, $9; and from Baltimore to Rockville, $5. Suppose that the Annapolis store orders 25 TV sets and the Rockville store 30. Suppose further that the College Park warehouse has a stock of 45 sets and the Baltimore warehouse 40. What is the most economical way to supply the requested TV sets to the two stores?

Solution   The first step in solving a linear programming problem is to translate it into mathematical language. And the first part of this step is to organize the information given, preferably in the form of the chart. In this case, since the problem is geographic, we draw a schematic diagram, as in Fig. 3, which shows the flow of goods between warehouses and retail stores. By each route, we have written the cost. Below each warehouse we have written down its stock and below each retail store the number of TV sets it ordered.

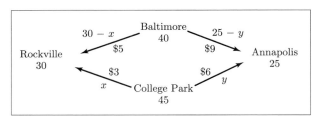

Figure 3.

Next, let us determine the variables. It appears initially that four variables are required, namely the number of TV sets to be shipped over each route. However, a closer look shows that only two variables are required. For if x denotes the number of TV sets to be shipped from College Park to Rockville, then since Rockville ordered 30 sets, the number shipped from Baltimore to Rockville is $30 - x$. Similarly, if y denotes the number of sets shipped from College Park to Annapolis, then the number shipped from Baltimore to Annapolis is $25 - y$. We have written the appropriate shipment sizes beside the various routes in Fig. 3.

As the third part of the translation process, let us write down the restrictions on the variables. Basically, there are two kinds of restrictions: None of x, y, $30 - x$, $25 - y$ can be negative, and a warehouse cannot ship more TV sets than it has in stock. Referring to Fig. 3, we see that College Park ships $x + y$ sets, so that $x + y \leq 45$. Similarly, Baltimore ships $(30 - x) + (25 - y)$ sets, so that $(30 - x) + (25 - y) \leq 40$. Simplifying this inequality, we get

$$55 - x - y \leq 40$$
$$-x - y \leq -15$$
$$x + y \geq 15.$$

The inequality $30 - x \geq 0$ can be simplified to $x \leq 30$, and the inequality $25 - y \geq 0$ can be written $y \leq 25$. So our restriction inequalities are these:

$$\begin{cases} x \geq 0, \quad y \geq 0 \\ x \leq 30, \quad y \leq 25 \\ x + y \geq 15 \\ x + y \leq 45. \end{cases} \tag{3}$$

The final step in the translation process is to form the objective function. In this problem we are attempting to minimize cost, so the objective function must express the cost in terms of x and y. Refer again to Fig. 3. There are x sets going from College Park to Rockville, and each costs \$3 to transport, so the cost of delivering these x sets is $3x$. Similarly, the costs of making the other deliveries are $6y$, $5(30 - x)$, and $9(25 - y)$, respectively. Thus the objective function is

$$\begin{aligned}[\text{cost}] &= 3x + 6y + 5(30 - x) + 9(25 - y) \\ &= 3x + 6y + 150 - 5x + 225 - 9y \\ &= 375 - 2x - 3y. \end{aligned} \tag{4}$$

So the mathematical problem we must solve is as follows: Find x and y that minimize the objective function (4) and satisfy the restrictions (3).

To solve the mathematical problem, we must graph the system of inequalities in (3). Four of the inequalities have graphs determined by horizontal and vertical lines. The only inequalities involving any work are $x + y \geq 15$ and $x + y \leq 45$. And even these are very easy to graph. The result is the graph in Fig. 4.

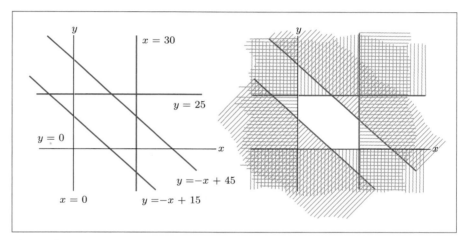

Figure 4.

In Fig. 5 we have drawn the feasible set and have labeled each boundary line with its equation. The vertices A–F are now simple to determine. First, A and F are the intercepts of the line $y = -x + 15$. Therefore, $A = (15, 0)$ and $F = (0, 15)$. Since B is the x-intercept of the line $x = 30$, we have $B = (30, 0)$. Similarly, $E = (0, 25)$. Since C is on the line $x = 30$, its x-coordinate is 30. Its y-coordinate is $y = -30 + 45 = 15$, so $C = (30, 15)$. Similarly, since D has y-coordinate 25, its x-coordinate is given by $25 = -x + 45$ or $x = 20$. Thus $D = (20, 25)$.

We have listed in Table 4 the vertices A–F as well as the cost corresponding to each one. The minimum cost of \$260 occurs at the vertex $(20, 25)$. So $x = 20$, $y = 25$ yields the minimum of the objective function. In other words, 20 TV sets should be shipped from College Park to Rockville and 25 from College Park to Annapolis, $30 - x = 10$ from Baltimore to Rockville, and $25 - y = 0$ from Baltimore to Annapolis. This solves our problem. ◆

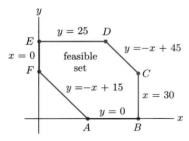

Figure 5.

Remarks Concerning the Transportation Problem   Note that the highest-cost route is the one from Baltimore to Annapolis. The solution we have obtained eliminates any shipments over this route. One might infer from this that one

Table 4

Vertex	Cost $= 375 - 2x - 3y$
$(0, 25)$	300
$(0, 15)$	330
$(15, 0)$	345
$(30, 0)$	315
$(30, 15)$	270
$(20, 25)$	260

should always avoid the most expensive route. But this is not correct reasoning. To see why, reconsider Example 2, except change the cost of transporting a TV set from Baltimore to Annapolis from \$9 to \$7. The Baltimore–Annapolis route is still the most expensive. However, in this case the minimum cost is not obtained by eliminating the Baltimore–Annapolis route. For the revised problem, the linear inequalities stay the same. So the feasible set and the vertices remain the same. The only change is in the objective function, which now is given by

$$[\text{cost}] = 3x + 6y + 5(30 - x) + 7(25 - y) = 325 - 2x - y.$$

Therefore, the costs at the various vertices are given in Table 5. So the minimum cost of \$250 is achieved when $x = 30$, $y = 15$, $30 - x = 0$, and $25 - y = 10$. Note that 10 sets are being shipped from Baltimore to Annapolis, even though this is the most expensive route.

Table 5

Vertex	Cost $= 325 - 2x - y$
$(0, 25)$	300
$(0, 15)$	310
$(15, 0)$	295
$(30, 0)$	265
$(30, 15)$	250
$(20, 25)$	260

It is even possible for the cost function to be optimized simultaneously at two different vertices. For example, if the cost from Baltimore to Annapolis is \$8 and all other data are the same as in Example 2, then the optimal cost is \$260 and is achieved at both vertices $(30, 15)$ and $(20, 25)$.

Verification of the Fundamental Theorem   The fundamental theorem of linear programming asserts that the objective function assumes its optimal value at a vertex of the feasible set. Let us verify this fact. For simplicity, we give the argument only in a special case, namely for the furniture manufacturing problem. However, this is for convenience of exposition only. The same argument as given in the following example may be used to prove the fundamental theorem in general. Our argument relies on the parallel property for straight lines, which asserts that parallel lines have the same slope.

▶ Example 3   Prove the fundamental theorem of linear programming in the special case of the furniture manufacturing problem.

Solution   The profit derived from producing x chairs and y sofas is $80x + 70y$ dollars. Let us examine all those production schedules having a given profit. As an example, consider a profit of \$2800. Then x and y must satisfy $80x + 70y = 2800$. That is, (x, y) must lie on the line whose equation is $80x + 70y = 2800$, or in standard form, $y = -\frac{8}{7}x + 40$. The slope of this line is $-\frac{8}{7}$ and its y-intercept is $(0, 40)$. We have drawn this line in Fig. 6(a), in which we have also drawn the feasible set for the furniture manufacturing problem. Note two fundamental facts: (1) Every production schedule on the line corresponds to a profit of \$2800. (2) The line lies above the feasible set. In particular, no production schedule on the line satisfies all the restrictions of the problem. The difficulty is that \$2800 is too high a profit for which to ask.

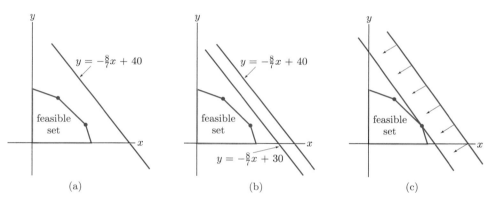

(a)   (b)   (c)

Figure 6.

So now lower the profit, say, to \$2100. In this case the production schedule (x, y) lies on the line $80x + 70y = 2100$, or in standard form, $y = -\frac{8}{7}x + 30$. This line is drawn in Fig. 6(b). Note that since both lines have slope $-\frac{8}{7}$, they are parallel by the parallel property. Actually, if we look at the production schedules yielding any fixed profit p, then they will lie along a line of slope $-\frac{8}{7}$, which is parallel to the two lines already drawn. For if the production schedule (x, y) yields a profit p, then

$$80x + 70y = p \quad \text{or} \quad y = -\frac{8}{7}x + \frac{p}{70}.$$

In other words, (x, y) lies on a line of slope $-\frac{8}{7}$ and y-intercept $(0, p/70)$. In particular, all the "lines of constant profit" are parallel to one another. So let us go back to the line of \$2800 profit. It does not touch the feasible set. So now lower the profit and therefore translate the line downward parallel to itself. Next lower the profit until we first touch the feasible set. This line now touches the feasible set at a vertex [Fig. 6(c)]. And this vertex corresponds to the optimal production schedule, since any other point of the feasible set lies on a "line of constant profit" corresponding to an even-lower profit. This shows why the fundamental theorem of linear programming is true. ◆

If the objective function is parallel to one of the boundary lines of the feasible set, there might be infinitely many solutions—all points on that boundary line provide optimal values for the objective function. Two such points are vertices of the feasible set.

▶ **Example 4**　Reconsider the TV shipping problem discussed in Example 2 with the cost of shipping from Baltimore to Annapolis now $8 and all other data the same as in Example 2. Minimize the shipping costs.

Solution　The cost function to be minimized is now

$$[\text{cost}] = 350 - 2x - 2y.$$

Note that for any fixed value of the cost, the slope of the objective function is -1. The feasible set is identical to that of Example 2 (Fig. 5). The slope of the boundary line $y = -x + 45$ is also -1. A check of the vertices of the feasible set (Table 6) shows that the minimal cost of $260 is achieved at the two vertices $C = (30, 15)$ and $D = (20, 25)$. In fact, the cost of $260 is achieved at every point on the boundary line joining these two vertices. Let's verify this in two cases. The points $(25, 20)$ and $(28, 17)$ both lie on the line $y = -x + 45$ and produce a cost of $260. Figure 7 illustrates the result.　　　◆

Table 6	
Vertex	**Cost $= 350 - 2x - 2y$**
$(0, 25)$	300
$(0, 15)$	320
$(15, 0)$	320
$(30, 0)$	290
$(30, 15)$	260
$(20, 25)$	260

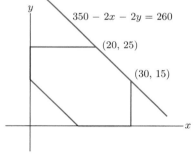

Figure 7.

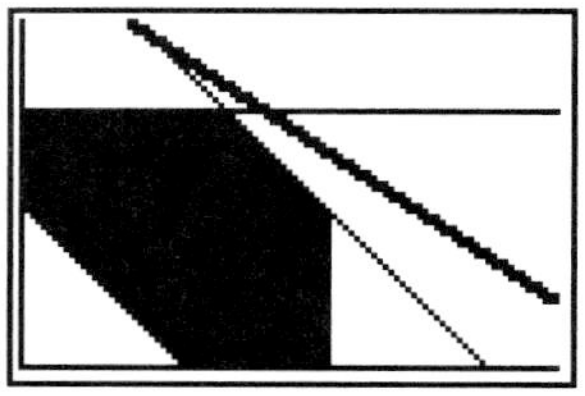

Figure 8.

GC　Graphing calculators can draw accurate feasible sets and accurate lines of constant profit (or cost). These precise drawings often permit us to select the optimal vertex by inspection. Figure 8 shows the screen for the shipping problem of Example 2. The thick line is the line of constant cost, $253. The shaded region was produced with the commands **Shade(15 − X, 25, 0, 15)**, **Shade(0, 25, 15, 20)**, and **Shade(0, 45 − X, 20, 30)**. As the thick line is lowered, the point $(20, 25)$ is selected.

Practice Problems 3.3

Problems 1–3 refer to Example 1. Translate the statement into an inequality.

1. The amount to be invested in bonds is at most $5 million more than the amount to be invested in Treasury notes.

2. No more than $25 million should be invested in stocks and bonds.

3. Rework Example 1, assuming that the yield for Treasury notes goes up to 8%.

<table>
<tr><td>

**Practice Problems
3.3 (Continued)**

</td><td>

4. A linear programming problem has objective function $[\text{cost}] = 5x + 10y$, which is to be minimized. Figure 9 shows the feasible set and the straight line of all combinations of x and y for which $[\text{cost}] = \$20$.

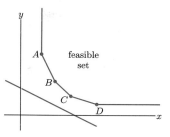

Figure 9.

(a) Give the linear equation (in standard form) of the line of constant cost c.

(b) As c increases, does the line of constant cost c move up or down?

(c) By inspection, find the vertex of the feasible set that gives the optimal solution.

</td></tr>
</table>

▶ Exercises 3.3

1. Figure 10(a) shows the feasible set of the nutrition problem of Section 3.2 and the straight line of all combinations of rice and soybeans for which the cost is 42 cents.

   (a) The objective function is $21x + 14y$. Give the linear equation (in standard form) of the line of constant cost c.

   (b) As c increases, does the line of constant cost move up or down?

   (c) By inspection, find the vertex of the feasible set that gives the optimal solution.

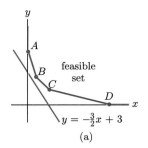

(a)

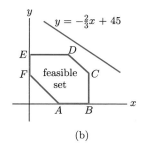

(b)

Figure 10.

2. Figure 10(b) shows the feasible set of the transportation problem of Example 2 and the straight line of all combinations of shipments for which the transportation cost is $240.

   (a) The objective function is $[\text{cost}] = 375 - 2x - 3y$. Give the linear equation (in standard form) of the line of constant cost c.

   (b) As c increases, does the line of constant cost move up or down?

   (c) By inspection, find the vertex of the feasible set that gives the optimal solution.

Consider the feasible set in Fig. 11(a). In Exercises 3–6, find an objective function of the form $ax + by$ that has its greatest value at the given point.

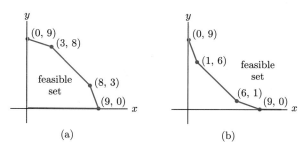

Figure 11.

3. $(9, 0)$ **4.** $(3, 8)$ **5.** $(8, 3)$ **6.** $(0, 9)$

Consider the feasible set in Fig. 11(b). In Exercises 7–10, find an objective function of the form $ax + by$ that has its least value at the given point.

7. $(9, 0)$ **8.** $(1, 6)$ **9.** $(6, 1)$ **10.** $(0, 9)$

Consider the feasible set in Fig. 12(a) on the next page, where three of the boundary lines are labeled with their slopes. In Exercises 11–14, find the point at which the given objective function has its greatest value.

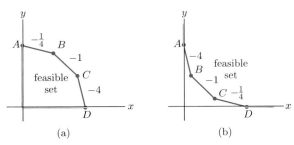

Figure 12.

11. $3x + 2y$ 12. $2x + 10y$

13. $10x + 2y$ 14. $2x + 3y$

Consider the feasible set in Fig. 12(b), where three of the boundary lines are labeled with their slopes. In Exercises 15–18, find the point at which the given objective function has its least value.

15. $2x + 10y$ **16.** $10x + 2y$

17. $2x + 3y$ **18.** $3x + 2y$

19. Consider the feasible set in Fig. 13. For what values of k will the objective function $x + ky$ be maximized at the vertex $(3, 4)$?

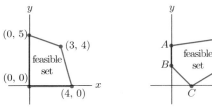

Figure 13.   **Figure 14.**

20. Consider the feasible set in Fig. 14. Explain why the objective function $ax + by$, with a and b positive, must have its maximum value at point E.

21. (*Nutrition—Animal*) Mr. Smith decides to feed his pet Doberman pinscher a combination of two dog foods. Each can of brand A contains 3 units of protein, 1 unit of carbohydrates, and 2 units of fat and costs 80 cents. Each can of brand B contains 1 unit of protein, 1 unit of carbohydrates, and 6 units of fat and costs 50 cents. Mr. Smith feels that each day his dog should have at least 6 units of protein, 4 units of carbohydrates, and 12 units of fat. How many cans of each dog food should he give to his dog each day to provide the minimum requirements at the least cost?

22. (*Oil Production*) An oil company owns two refineries. Refinery I produces each day 100 barrels of high-grade oil, 200 barrels of medium-grade oil, and 300 barrels of low-grade oil and costs $10,000 to operate. Refinery II produces each day 200 barrels of high-grade, 100 barrels of medium-grade, and 200 barrels of low-grade oil and costs $9000 to operate. An order is received for 1000 barrels of high-grade oil, 1000 barrels of medium-grade oil, and 1800 barrels of low-grade oil. How many

days should each refinery be operated to fill the order at the least cost?

23. (*Shipping—Product Mix*) A produce dealer in Florida ships oranges, grapefruits, and avocados to New York by truck. Each truckload consists of 100 crates, of which at least 20 crates must be oranges, at least 10 crates must be grapefruits, at least 30 crates must be avocados, and there must be at least as many crates of oranges as grapefruits. The profit per crate is $5 for oranges, $6 for grapefruits, and $4 for avocados. How many crates of each type should be shipped to maximize the profit? [*Hint*: Let $x =$ number of crates of oranges, $y =$ number of crates of grapefruit. Then $100 - x - y =$ number of crates of avocados.]

24. (*Investment Planning*) Mr. Jones has $9000 to invest in three types of stocks: low-risk, medium-risk, and high-risk. He invests according to three principles. The amount invested in low-risk stocks will be at most $1000 more than the amount invested in medium-risk stocks. At least $5000 will be invested in low- and medium-risk stocks. No more than $7000 will be invested in medium- and high-risk stocks. The expected yields are 6% for low-risk stocks, 7% for medium-risk stocks, and 8% for high-risk stocks. How much money should Mr. Jones invest in each type of stock to maximize his total expected yield?

25. (*Manufacturing—Production Planning*) An automobile manufacturer has assembly plants in Detroit and Cleveland, each of which can assemble cars and trucks. The Detroit plant can assemble at most 800 vehicles in one day at a cost of $1200 per car and $2100 per truck. The Cleveland plant can assemble at most 500 vehicles in one day at a cost of $1000 per car and $2000 per truck. A rush order is received for 600 cars and 300 trucks. How many vehicles of each type should each plant produce to fill the order at the least cost? (*Hint*: Let $x =$ number of cars to be produced in Detroit, $y =$ number of trucks to be produced in Detroit, $600 - x =$ number of cars to be produced in Cleveland, and $300 - y =$ number of trucks to be produced in Cleveland.)

26. (*Transportation—Shipping*) A foreign-car dealer with warehouses in New York and Baltimore receives orders from dealers in Philadelphia and Trenton. The dealer in Philadelphia needs 4 cars and the dealer in Trenton needs 7. The New York warehouse has 6 cars and the Baltimore warehouse has 8. The cost of shipping cars from Baltimore to Philadelphia is $120 per car, from Baltimore to Trenton $90 per car, from New York to Philadelphia $100 per car, and from New York to Trenton $70 per car. Find the number of cars to be shipped from each warehouse to each dealer to minimize the shipping cost.

27. (*Manufacturing—Production Planning*) An oil refinery produces gasoline, jet fuel, and diesel fuel. The profits per gallon from the sale of these fuels are $.15, $.12, and $.10, respectively. The refinery has a contract with an airline to deliver a minimum of 20,000 gallons per day of jet fuel and/or gasoline (or some of each). It has a contract with a trucking firm to deliver a minimum of 50,000 gallons per day of diesel fuel and/or gasoline (or some of each). The refinery can produce 100,000 gallons of fuel per day, distributed among the fuels in any fashion. It wishes to produce at least 5000 gallons per day of each fuel. How many gallons of each should be produced to maximize the profit?

28. (*Manufacturing—Production Planning*) Suppose that a price war reduces the profits of gasoline in Exercise 27 to $.05 per gallon and that the profits on jet fuel and diesel fuel are unchanged. How many gallons of each fuel should now be produced to maximize the profit?

29. (*Shipping—Resource Allocation*) A shipping company is buying new trucks. The high-capacity trucks cost $50,000 and hold 320 cases of merchandise. The low-capacity trucks cost $30,000 and hold 200 cases of merchandise. The company has budgeted $1,080,000 for the new trucks and has a maximum of 30 people qualified to drive the trucks. Due to availability limitations, the company can purchase at most 15 high-capacity trucks. How many of each type of truck should the company purchase to maximize the number of cases of merchandise that can be shipped simultaneously?

30. (*Shipping—Resource Allocation*) Suppose that the shipping company of Exercise 29 needs to buy enough new trucks to be able to ship 11,200 cases of merchandise. Of course, the company is willing to increase its budget.

(a) How many of each type of truck should the company purchase to minimize cost?

(b) What if the company hires 23 additional qualified drivers?

Solutions to Practice Problems 3.3

1. Amount invested in bonds $= y$. Five million dollars more than the amount invested in Treasury notes is $x + 5$. Therefore, $y \leq x + 5$.

2. Amount invested in stocks $= 30 - (x + y)$. Amount invested in bonds $= y$. Therefore,

$$30 - (x + y) + y \leq 25$$
$$30 - x \leq 25$$
$$x \geq 5.$$

3. The feasible set stays the same but the return becomes

$$\big[\text{return}\big] = .08x + .08y + .09[30 - (x + y)]$$
$$= .08x + .08y + 2.7 - .09x - .09y$$
$$= 2.7 - .01x - .01y.$$

When the return is evaluated at each of the vertices of the feasible set, the greatest return is achieved at two vertices. Either of these vertices yields an optimal solution.

(x, y)	$2.7 - .01x - .01y$
$(5, 10)$	2.55
$(12, 3)$	2.55
$(24, 3)$	2.43
$(9, 18)$	2.43

4. (a) The values of x and y for which the cost is c dollars satisfy $5x + 10y = c$. The standard form of this linear equation is $y = -\frac{1}{2}x + c/10$.

(b) The line $y = -\frac{1}{2}x + c/10$ has slope $-\frac{1}{2}$ and y-intercept $(0, c/10)$. As c increases, the slope stays the same, but the y-intercept moves up. Therefore, the line moves up.

(c) The line of constant cost \$20 does not contain any points of the feasible set, so such a low cost cannot be achieved. Increase the cost until the line of constant cost just touches the feasible set. As c increases, the line moves up (keeping the same slope) and first touches the feasible set at vertex C. Therefore, taking x and y to be the coordinates of C yields the minimum cost.

▶ Chapter 3 Summary

1. A linear programming problem asks us to find the point (or points) in the feasible set of a system of linear inequalities at which the value of a linear expression involving the variables, called the objective function, is either maximized or minimized.

2. The fundamental theorem of linear programming states that the optimal value of the objective function for a linear programming problem occurs at a vertex of the feasible set.

3. To solve a linear programming word problem, assign variables to the unknown quantities, translate the restrictions into a system of linear inequalities involving no more than two variables, form a function for the quantity to be optimized, graph the feasible set, determine the vertices of the feasible set, evaluate the objective function at each vertex, and identify the vertex that gives the optimal value.

Review of Fundamental Concepts of Chapter 3

1. What is the nature of a linear programming problem?
2. What is the role of the objective function in a linear programming problem?
3. State the fundamental theorem of linear programming.
4. Give the four-step procedure for solving a linear programming problem.

▶ Chapter 3 Supplementary Exercises

1. (*Travel—Resource Allocation*) Terrapin Airlines wants to fly 1400 members of a ski club to Colorado. The airline owns two types of planes. Type A can carry 50 passengers, requires 3 flight attendants, and costs \$14,000 for the trip. Type B can carry 300 passengers, requires 4 flight attendants, and costs \$90,000 for the trip. If the airline must use at least as many type A planes as type B and has available only 42 flight attendants, how many planes of each type should be used to minimize the cost for the trip?

2. (*Nutrition—People*) A nutritionist is designing a new breakfast cereal using wheat germ and enriched oat flour as the basic ingredients. Each ounce of wheat germ contains 2 milligrams of niacin, 3 milligrams of iron, and .5 milligram of thiamin and costs 3 cents. Each ounce of enriched oat flour contains 3 milligrams of niacin, 3 milligrams of iron, and .25 milligram of thiamin and costs 4 cents. The nutritionist wants the cereal to have at least 7 milligrams of niacin, 9 milligrams of iron, and 1 milligram of thiamin. How many ounces of wheat germ and how many ounces of enriched oat flour should be used in each serving to meet the nutritional requirements at the least cost?

3. (*Manufacturing—Resource Allocation*) An automobile manufacturer makes hardtops and sports cars. Each hardtop requires 8 labor-hours to assemble, 2 labor-hours to paint, and 2 labor-hours to upholster and is sold for a profit of \$90. Each sports car requires 18 labor-hours to assemble, 2 labor-hours to paint, and 1 labor-hour to upholster and is sold for a profit of \$100. During each day 360 labor-hours are available to assemble, 50 labor-hours to paint, and 40 labor-hours to upholster automobiles. How many hardtops and sports cars should be produced each day to maximize the profit?

4. (*Packaging—Product Mix*) A confectioner makes two raisin–nut mixtures. A box of mixture A contains 6 ounces of peanuts, 1 ounce of raisins, and 4 ounces of cashews and sells for 50 cents. A box of mixture B contains 12 ounces of peanuts, 3 ounces of raisins, and 2 ounces of cashews and sells for 90 cents. He has available 5400 ounces of peanuts, 1200 ounces of raisins, and 2400 ounces of cashews. How many boxes of each mixture should he make to maximize revenue?

5. (*Publishing—Product Mix*) A textbook publisher puts out 72 new books each year, which are classified as elementary, intermediate, and advanced. The company's policy for new books is to publish at least four advanced books, at least three times as many elementary books as intermediate books, and at least twice as many intermediate books as advanced books. On the average, the annual profits are $8000 for each elementary book, $7000 for each intermediate book, and $1000 for each advanced book. How many new books of each type should be published to maximize the annual profit while conforming to company policy?

6. (*Shipping—Resource Allocation*) A computer company has two manufacturing plants, one in Rochester and one in Queens. Transporting a computer from Rochester to the retail outlet takes 15 hours and costs $15, while transporting a computer from Queens to the retail outlet takes 20 hours and costs $30. The profit on each computer manufactured in Rochester is $40 and the profit on each computer manufactured in Queens is $30. The Rochester plant has 80 computers available and the Queens plant has 120 computers available. If there are 2100 hours and $3000 allotted for transporting the computers, how many computers should be sent to the retail outlet from each of the two plants to maximize the company's profits?

7. (*Transportation—Shipping*) An appliance company has two warehouses and two retail outlets. Warehouse A has 400 refrigerators and warehouse B has 300 refrigerators. Outlet I needs 200 refrigerators and outlet II needs 300 refrigerators. It costs $36 to ship a refrigerator from warehouse A to outlet I and $30 to ship a refrigerator from warehouse A to outlet II. It costs $30 to ship a refrigerator from warehouse B to outlet I and $25 to ship a refrigerator from warehouse B to outlet II. How should the company ship the refrigerators to minimize the cost?

▶ Chapter 3 Chapter Test

1. Describe the four main steps for solving a linear programming problem graphically.

2. Determine the objective function and the constraints for the following linear programming problems. *Do not solve the problems.*

   (a) A video game company makes two types of hockey games at two different manufacturing plants. Plant A can produce 20 type I games and 10 type II games per hour. Plant B can produce 30 type I games and 20 type II games per hour. It costs $70 per hour to operate plant A and $90 per hour to operate Plant B. The company needs 300 type I hockey games and 200 type II hockey games per day. How many hours per day should each plant spend on producing these games in order to meet the company's need and minimize production costs?

   (b) Mabel plans to invest a total of $500,000 in mutual funds, bonds, and certificates of deposit (CDs). The annual yields for mutual funds, bonds, and CDs are 7%, 6%, and 4.5%, respectively. She wishes to invest at least $150,000 in bonds and no more than $200,000 in CDs. She will invest at least half as much money in mutual funds as she does in bonds. How should she allocate the $500,000 so as to maximize her total annual yield?

3. (a) Graph the feasible set for the following linear programming problem. Maximize $3x + 2y$ subject to the constraints

$$\begin{cases} x + 2y \geq 10 \\ 2x + y \geq 8 \\ x \geq 0, \quad y \geq 0. \end{cases}$$

   (b) Does the linear programming problem in part (a) have a solution? Explain.

4. Find the coordinates of the vertices of the following feasible set.

$$\begin{cases} x + y \leq 12 \\ 5x + 7y \leq 70 \\ x \leq 9 \\ x \geq 0, \quad y \geq 0 \end{cases}$$

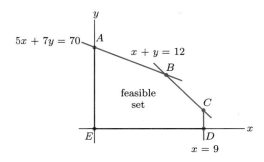

5. For the following feasible set, determine x and y so that the objective function $20x - 10y$ is

  (a) maximized

  (b) minimized

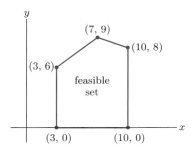

6. Suppose the objective function for a linear programming problem is $[\text{cost}] = 8x + 5y$. The feasible set for the linear programming problem is shown, along with the straight line of all combinations of x and y for which the cost is \$3200.

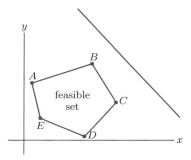

  (a) Give the linear equation (in standard form) of the line of constant cost shown in the figure.

  (b) Give the linear equation (in standard form) of the line of constant cost c.

  (c) As c decreases, does the line of constant cost move up or down?

  (d) By inspection, determine the vertex of the feasible set that results in the minimum cost.

7. Consider the feasible set shown, where three of the boundary lines are labeled with their slopes. Find the point at which the objective function $5x + 8y$ has its least value.

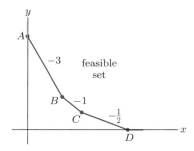

Chapter Project

Shadow Prices

When a mathematician is presented with a linear programming problem, he or she will not only determine the optimal solution but will also supply what are called *shadow prices* for each constraint. This chapter project develops the concept of a shadow price.

Consider the furniture manufacturing problem. The constraint for finishing is $x + y \leq 18$. The number 18 came from the fact that 18 hours are available for finishing each day. Suppose you could increase the number of hours available for finishing by one hour. The shadow price for the finishing constraint is the maximum price you would be willing to pay for that additional hour.

1. What is the new inequality for the finishing constraint? What is its corresponding linear equation?

2. The figure shows the graph of the original feasible set for the furniture manufacturing problem drawn with a black boundary. The blue line segments show the change in the feasible set when the new finishing constraint is used. Find the coordinates of the points A and B.

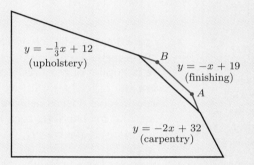

3. Determine the optimal solution for the revised linear programming problem. What is the new maximum profit? By how much was the profit increased due to the additional hour for finishing?

4. What is the shadow price for the finishing constraint?

5. Return to the original furniture manufacturing problem and assume that one additional hour is available for carpentry. Solve the altered problem and determine the shadow price for the carpentry constraint.

6. Use your knowledge of the solution of the original furniture manufacturing problem to explain why the shadow price for the upholstery constraint is 0. (*Hint*: No computation is necessary.)

7. Fill in the blanks in the following sentence. The shadow price associated with a constraint can be interpreted as the change in value of the _____ _____ per unit change of the constraint's right-hand-side resource.

The Simplex Method 4

In Chapter 3 we introduced a graphical method for solving linear programming problems. This method, although very simple, is of limited usefulness since it applies only to problems that involve (or can be reduced to) two variables. On the other hand, linear programming applications in business and economics can involve dozens or even hundreds of variables. In this chapter we describe a method for handling such applications. This method, called the *simplex method* (or *simplex algorithm*), was developed by the mathematician George B. Dantzig in the late 1940s and today is the principal method used in solving complex linear programming problems. The simplex method can be used for problems in any number of variables and is easily adapted to computer calculations.

4.1 Slack Variables and the Simplex Tableau

In this section and the next we explain how the simplex method can be used to solve linear programming problems. Let us reconsider the furniture manufacturing problem of Chapter 3. You may recall that the problem is to determine the number of chairs and the number of sofas that should be produced each day in order to maximize the profit. The requirements and availability of resources for carpentry, finishing, and upholstery determine the constraints on the production schedule. Thus, we try to find numbers x and y for which

$$80x + 70y$$

is as large as possible subject to the constraints

$$\begin{cases} 6x + 3y \leq 96 \\ x + y \leq 18 \\ 2x + 6y \leq 72 \\ x \geq 0, \quad y \geq 0. \end{cases}$$

Here x is the number of chairs to be produced each day and y is the number of sofas to be produced each day.

This problem exhibits certain features that make it particularly convenient to work with.

1. The objective function is to be maximized.
2. Each variable is constrained to be greater than or equal to 0.
3. All other constraints are of the form

$$[\text{linear polynomial}]^{*} \leq [\text{nonnegative constant}].$$

A linear programming problem satisfying these conditions is said to be in *standard form*. Our initial discussion of the simplex method will involve only such problems. Then, in Section 4.3, we consider problems in nonstandard form.

The essential feature of the simplex method is that it provides a systematic method of testing selected vertices of the feasible set until an optimal vertex is reached. The method usually begins at the origin, if it is in the feasible set, and then considers the adjacent vertex that most improves the value of the objective function. This process continues until the optimal vertex is found.

The first step of the simplex method is to convert the given linear programming problem into a system of linear *equations*. To see how this is done, consider the furniture manufacturing problem. It specifies that the variables x and y are subject to the constraint

$$6x + 3y \leq 96.$$

Let us introduce another variable, u, which turns the inequality into an equation:

$$6x + 3y + u = 96.$$

The variable u "takes up the slack" between $6x + 3y$ and 96 and is therefore called a *slack variable*. Moreover, since $6x + 3y$ is at most 96, the variable u must be greater than or equal to 0. In a similar way, the constraint

$$x + y \leq 18$$

can be turned into the equation

$$x + y + v = 18,$$

where v is a slack variable and $v \geq 0$. The third constraint,

$$2x + 6y \leq 72,$$

becomes the equation

$$2x + 6y + w = 72,$$

where w is also a slack variable and $w \geq 0$. Let us even turn our objective function $80x + 70y$ into an equation by introducing the new variable M defined by $M = 80x + 70y$. Then M is the variable we want to maximize. Moreover, it satisfies the equation

$$-80x - 70y + M = 0.$$

Thus, the furniture manufacturing problem can be restated in terms of a system of linear equations.

---

*A linear polynomial is an expression of the form $ax + by + cz + \cdots + dw$, where $a, b, c, \ldots, d$ are specific numbers and $x, y, z, \ldots, w$ are variables. Some examples are $2x - 3y + z$, $x + 2y + 3z - 4w$, and $-x + 3z - 2w$.

Furniture Manufacturing Problem   Among all the solutions of the system of linear equations

$$\begin{cases} 6x + 3y + u & = 96 \\ x + y + v & = 18 \\ 2x + 6y + w & = 72 \\ -80x - 70y + M = 0, \end{cases}$$

find one for which $x \geq 0$, $y \geq 0$, $u \geq 0$, $v \geq 0$, $w \geq 0$, and for which M is as large as possible.

In a similar way, any linear programming problem in standard form can be reduced to that of determining a certain type of solution of a system of linear equations.

◗ **Example 1**   Formulate the following linear programming problem in terms of a system of linear equations.

Maximize the objective function $3x + 4y$ subject to the constraints

$$\begin{cases} x + y \leq 20 \\ x + 2y \leq 25 \\ x \geq 0 \\ y \geq 0. \end{cases}$$

Solution   The two constraints $x + y \leq 20$ and $x + 2y \leq 25$ yield the equations

$$\begin{aligned} x + y + u & = 20 \\ x + 2y + v & = 25, \end{aligned}$$

where u and v are slack variables and $u \geq 0$ and $v \geq 0$. The objective function gives the equation $M = 3x + 4y$, or

$$-3x - 4y + M = 0.$$

So the problem can be reformulated: Among all the solutions of the system of linear equations

$$\begin{cases} x + y + u & = 20 \\ x + 2y + v & = 25 \\ -3x - 4y + M = 0, \end{cases}$$

find one for which $x \geq 0$, $y \geq 0$, $u \geq 0$, $v \geq 0$, and M is as large as possible.   ◆

◗ **Example 2**   Formulate the following linear programming problem in terms of a system of linear equations.

Maximize the objective function $x + 2y + z$ subject to the constraints

$$\begin{cases} x - y + 2z \leq 10 \\ 2x + y + 3z \leq 12 \\ x \geq 0, \quad y \geq 0, \quad z \geq 0. \end{cases}$$

Solution   The two constraints $x - y + 2z \leq 10$ and $2x + y + 3z \leq 12$ yield the equations

$$
\begin{aligned}
x - y + 2z + u \quad\quad &= 10 \\
2x + y + 3z \quad\quad + v &= 12.
\end{aligned}
$$

The objective function yields the equation $M = x + 2y + z$—that is,

$$-x - 2y - z + M = 0.$$

So the problem can be reformulated: Among all solutions of the system of linear equations

$$
\begin{cases}
x - y + 2z + u \quad\quad\quad\quad = 10 \\
2x + y + 3z \quad\quad + v \quad\quad = 12 \\
-x - 2y - z \quad\quad\quad\quad + M = 0,
\end{cases}
$$

find one for which $x \geq 0$, $y \geq 0$, $z \geq 0$, $u \geq 0$, $v \geq 0$, and M is as large as possible.   ◆

We shall now discuss a scheme for solving systems of equations like those just encountered. For the moment, we will not worry about maximizing M or keeping the variables ≥ 0. Rather, let us concentrate on a particular method for determining solutions. In order to be concrete, consider the system of linear equations from the furniture manufacturing problem:

$$
\begin{cases}
6x + 3y + u \quad\quad\quad\quad = 96 \\
x + y \quad + v \quad\quad\quad = 18 \\
2x + 6y \quad\quad + w \quad = 72 \\
-80x - 70y \quad\quad\quad + M = 0.
\end{cases}
\tag{1}
$$

This system of equations has an infinite number of solutions. We can rewrite the equations as

$$
\begin{aligned}
u &= 96 - 6x - 3y \\
v &= 18 - x - y \\
w &= 72 - 2x - 6y \\
M &= \quad\quad 80x + 70y.
\end{aligned}
$$

Given any values of x and y, we can determine corresponding values for u, v, w, and M. For example, if $x = 0$ and $y = 0$, then $u = 96$, $v = 18$, $w = 72$, and $M = 0$. These values for u, v, w, and M are precisely the numbers that appear to the right of the equality signs in our original system of linear equations. Therefore, this particular solution could have been read directly from system (1) without any computation. This method of generating solutions is used in the simplex method, so let us further explore the special properties of the system that allowed us to read off a specific solution so easily.

Note that the system of linear equations has six variables: x, y, u, v, w, and M. These variables can be divided into two groups. Group I consists of those that were set equal to 0, namely, x and y. Group II consists of those whose particular values were read from the right-hand sides of the equations, namely, u, v, w, and M. Note also that the system has a special form that allows the particular values of the group II variables to be read off: Each of the equations involves exactly one of the group II variables, and these variables always appear with coefficient 1. Thus, for example, the first equation involves the group II variable u:

$$6x + 3y + u = 96.$$

Therefore, when all group I variables (x and y) are set equal to 0, only the u-term remains on the left, and the particular value of u can be read off the right-hand side.

The special form of the system can best be described in matrix form. Write the system in the usual way as a matrix, but add column headings corresponding to the variables:

$$\begin{array}{cccccc} x & y & u & v & w & M \end{array}$$
$$\left[\begin{array}{cccccc|c} 6 & 3 & 1 & 0 & 0 & 0 & 96 \\ 1 & 1 & 0 & 1 & 0 & 0 & 18 \\ 2 & 6 & 0 & 0 & 1 & 0 & 72 \\ -80 & -70 & 0 & 0 & 0 & 1 & 0 \end{array}\right].$$

Note closely the columns corresponding to the group II variables u, v, w, and M:

$$\begin{array}{cccccc} x & y & u & v & w & M \end{array}$$
$$\left[\begin{array}{cccccc|c} 6 & 3 & 1 & 0 & 0 & 0 & 96 \\ 1 & 1 & 0 & 1 & 0 & 0 & 18 \\ 2 & 6 & 0 & 0 & 1 & 0 & 72 \\ -80 & -70 & 0 & 0 & 0 & 1 & 0 \end{array}\right].$$

The presence of these columns gives the system the special form discussed previously. Indeed, the u column asserts that u appears only in the first equation and its coefficient there is 1, and similarly for the v, w, and M columns.

The property of allowing us to read off a particular solution from the right-hand column is shared by all linear systems whose matrices contain the columns

$$\begin{array}{ccccc} 1 & 0 & 0 & \cdots & 0 \\ 0 & 1 & 0 & \cdots & 0 \\ 0 & 0 & 1 & \cdots & 0 \\ \vdots & \vdots & \vdots & & \vdots \\ 0 & 0 & 0 & \cdots & 1. \end{array}$$

(These columns need not appear in exactly the order shown.) The variables corresponding to these columns are called the group II variables. The group I variables consist of all the others. To get one particular solution to the system, set all the group I variables equal to zero and read off the values of the group II variables from the right-hand side of the system. This procedure is illustrated in the following example.

▶ Example 3   Determine by inspection one set of solutions to each of these systems of linear equations:

(a) $\begin{cases} x - 5y + u & = 3 \\ -2x + 8y \quad + v & = 11 \\ -\frac{1}{2}x \qquad\qquad + M = 0 \end{cases}$ (b) $\begin{cases} -y + 2u + v & = 12 \\ x + \frac{1}{2}y - 6u & = -1 \\ 3y + 8u \qquad + M = 4. \end{cases}$

Solution (a) The matrix of the system is

$$
\begin{array}{ccccc}
x & y & u & v & M
\end{array}
$$
$$
\left[\begin{array}{ccccc|c}
1 & -5 & 1 & 0 & 0 & 3 \\
-2 & 8 & 0 & 1 & 0 & 11 \\
-\frac{1}{2} & 0 & 0 & 0 & 1 & 0
\end{array}\right].
$$

We look for each variable whose column contains one entry of 1 and all the other entries 0.

$$
\begin{array}{ccccc}
x & y & u & v & M
\end{array}
$$
$$
\left[\begin{array}{ccccc|c}
1 & -5 & 1 & 0 & 0 & 3 \\
-2 & 8 & 0 & 1 & 0 & 11 \\
-\frac{1}{2} & 0 & 0 & 0 & 1 & 0
\end{array}\right].
$$

The group II variables should be u, v, and M, with x, y as the group I variables. Set all group I variables equal to 0. The corresponding values of the group II variables may then be read off the last column: $u = 3$, $v = 11$, $M = 0$. So one solution of the system is

$$x = 0, \qquad y = 0, \qquad u = 3, \qquad v = 11, \qquad M = 0.$$

(b) The matrix of the system is

$$
\begin{array}{ccccc}
x & y & u & v & M
\end{array}
$$
$$
\left[\begin{array}{ccccc|c}
0 & -1 & 2 & 1 & 0 & 12 \\
1 & \frac{1}{2} & -6 & 0 & 0 & -1 \\
0 & 3 & 8 & 0 & 1 & 4
\end{array}\right].
$$

The shaded columns show that the group II variables should be v, x, and M, with y, u as the group I variables. So the corresponding solution is

$$x = -1, \qquad y = 0, \qquad u = 0, \qquad v = 12, \qquad M = 4. \qquad \blacklozenge$$

A *simplex tableau* is a matrix (corresponding to a linear system) in which each of the columns

$$
\begin{array}{cccc}
1 & 0 & \cdots & 0 \\
0 & 1 & \cdots & 0 \\
\vdots & \vdots & & \vdots \\
0 & 0 & \cdots & 1
\end{array}
$$

is present (in some order) to the left of the vertical line. We have seen how to construct a simplex tableau corresponding to a linear programming problem in standard form. From this initial tableau we can read off one particular solution of the linear system by using the method described previously. This particular solution may or may not correspond to the solution of the original optimization problem. If it does not, we replace the initial tableau with another one whose corresponding solution is "closer" to the optimum. How do we replace the initial simplex tableau with another? Just pivot it about a nonzero entry! Indeed, one of the key reasons the simplex method works is that pivoting transforms one simplex tableau into another. Note also that since pivoting consists of elementary row operations, a solution corresponding to a transformed tableau is a solution of the original linear system. The next example illustrates how pivoting transforms a tableau into another one.

▶ Example 4 Consider the simplex tableau obtained from the furniture manufacturing problem:

$$
\begin{array}{cccccc}
x & y & u & v & w & M \\
\end{array}
$$
$$
\left[
\begin{array}{cccccc|c}
⑥ & 3 & 1 & 0 & 0 & 0 & 96 \\
1 & 1 & 0 & 1 & 0 & 0 & 18 \\
2 & 6 & 0 & 0 & 1 & 0 & 72 \\
-80 & -70 & 0 & 0 & 0 & 1 & 0
\end{array}
\right].
$$

(a) Pivot this tableau around the circled entry, 6.

(b) Calculate the particular solution corresponding to the transformed tableau that results from setting the new group I variables equal to 0.

Solution (a) The first step in pivoting is to replace the pivot element 6 by a 1. To do this, multiply the first row of the tableau by $\frac{1}{6}$ to get

$$
\begin{array}{cccccc}
x & y & u & v & w & M \\
\end{array}
$$
$$
\left[
\begin{array}{cccccc|c}
1 & \frac{1}{2} & \frac{1}{6} & 0 & 0 & 0 & 16 \\
1 & 1 & 0 & 1 & 0 & 0 & 18 \\
2 & 6 & 0 & 0 & 1 & 0 & 72 \\
-80 & -70 & 0 & 0 & 0 & 1 & 0
\end{array}
\right].
$$

Next we must replace all nonpivot elements in the first column by zeros. Do this by adding to the second row (-1) times the first row:

$$
\begin{array}{cccccc}
x & y & u & v & w & M \\
\end{array}
$$
$$
\left[
\begin{array}{cccccc|c}
1 & \frac{1}{2} & \frac{1}{6} & 0 & 0 & 0 & 16 \\
0 & \frac{1}{2} & -\frac{1}{6} & 1 & 0 & 0 & 2 \\
2 & 6 & 0 & 0 & 1 & 0 & 72 \\
-80 & -70 & 0 & 0 & 0 & 1 & 0
\end{array}
\right],
$$

and by adding to the third row (-2) times the first row:

$$
\begin{array}{cccccc}
x & y & u & v & w & M \\
\end{array}
$$
$$
\left[
\begin{array}{cccccc|c}
1 & \frac{1}{2} & \frac{1}{6} & 0 & 0 & 0 & 16 \\
0 & \frac{1}{2} & -\frac{1}{6} & 1 & 0 & 0 & 2 \\
0 & 5 & -\frac{1}{3} & 0 & 1 & 0 & 40 \\
-80 & -70 & 0 & 0 & 0 & 1 & 0
\end{array}
\right],
$$

and, finally, by adding to the fourth row 80 times the first row:

$$
\begin{array}{cccccc}
x & y & u & v & w & M \\
\end{array}
$$

$$
\left[\begin{array}{cccccc|c}
1 & \frac{1}{2} & \frac{1}{6} & 0 & 0 & 0 & 16 \\
0 & \frac{1}{2} & -\frac{1}{6} & 1 & 0 & 0 & 2 \\
0 & 5 & -\frac{1}{3} & 0 & 1 & 0 & 40 \\
0 & -30 & \frac{40}{3} & 0 & 0 & 1 & 1280
\end{array}\right].
$$

Note that we indeed get a new simplex tableau. The new group II variables are x, v, w, and M. The group I variables are y and u.

$$
\begin{array}{cccccc}
x & y & u & v & w & M \\
\end{array}
$$

$$
\left[\begin{array}{cccccc|c}
1 & \frac{1}{2} & \frac{1}{6} & 0 & 0 & 0 & 16 \\
0 & \frac{1}{2} & -\frac{1}{6} & 1 & 0 & 0 & 2 \\
0 & 5 & -\frac{1}{3} & 0 & 1 & 0 & 40 \\
0 & -30 & \frac{40}{3} & 0 & 0 & 1 & 1280
\end{array}\right].
$$

(b) Set the group I variables equal to 0:

$$y = 0, \qquad u = 0.$$

Read off the particular values of the group II variables from the right-hand column:

$$x = 16, \qquad v = 2, \qquad w = 40, \qquad M = 1280.$$

So the particular solution corresponding to the transformed tableau is

$$x = 16, \qquad y = 0, \qquad u = 0, \qquad v = 2, \qquad w = 40, \qquad M = 1280.$$

We see that the simplex tableau leads to the vertex $(16, 0)$ that was listed and tested in the graphical solution of the problem presented in Chapter 3.

◆

Practice Problems 4.1

1. Determine by inspection a particular solution of the following system of linear equations:

$$
\begin{cases}
x + 2y + 3u & = 6 \\
\quad y \quad\quad + v & = 4 \\
\quad 5y + 2u \quad\quad + M = 0.
\end{cases}
$$

2. Pivot the simplex tableau about the circled element.

$$
\left[\begin{array}{ccccc|c}
2 & 4 & 1 & 0 & 0 & 6 \\
3 & \boxed{1} & 0 & 1 & 0 & 0 \\
1 & 1 & 0 & 0 & 1 & 1
\end{array}\right]
$$

▶ Exercises 4.1

For each of the following linear programming problems, determine the corresponding linear system and restate the linear programming problem in terms of the linear system.

1. Maximize $8x + 13y$ subject to the constraints

$$\begin{cases} 20x + 30y \le 3500 \\ 50x + 10y \le 5000 \\ x \ge 0 \\ y \ge 0. \end{cases}$$

2. Maximize $x + 15y$ subject to the constraints

$$\begin{cases} 3x + 2y \le 10 \\ x \quad\;\; \le 15 \\ \quad\;\; y \le 3 \\ x + y \le 5 \\ x \ge 0 \\ y \ge 0. \end{cases}$$

3. Maximize $x + 2y - 3z$ subject to the constraints

$$\begin{cases} x + y + z \le 100 \\ 3x \quad\;\; + z \le 200 \\ 5x + 10y \quad\;\; \le 100 \\ x \ge 0 \\ y \ge 0 \\ z \ge 0. \end{cases}$$

4. Maximize $2x + y + 50$ subject to the constraints

$$\begin{cases} x + 3y \le 24 \\ y \le 5 \\ x + 7y \le 10 \\ x \ge 0 \\ y \ge 0. \end{cases}$$

5–8. For each of the linear programming problems in Exercises 1–4,

(a) Set up the simplex tableau.

(b) Determine the particular solution corresponding to the tableau.

In Exercises 9–12, find the particular solution corresponding to the tableau.

9.
$$\begin{array}{ccccc} x & y & u & v & M \\ \end{array}$$
$$\left[\begin{array}{ccccc|c} 0 & 2 & 1 & 0 & 0 & 10 \\ 1 & 3 & 0 & 12 & 0 & 15 \\ 0 & -1 & 0 & 17 & 1 & 20 \end{array}\right]$$

10.
$$\begin{array}{ccccc} x & y & u & v & M \\ \end{array}$$
$$\left[\begin{array}{ccccc|c} 1 & 0 & 3 & 11 & 0 & 6 \\ 0 & 1 & 10 & 17 & 0 & 16 \\ 0 & 0 & 5 & -1 & 1 & 3 \end{array}\right]$$

11.
$$\begin{array}{ccccccc} x & y & z & u & v & w & M \\ \end{array}$$
$$\left[\begin{array}{ccccccc|c} 0 & 3 & 1 & 0 & 1 & 15 & 0 & 15 \\ 1 & -1 & 0 & 0 & 2 & -5 & 0 & 10 \\ 0 & 2 & 0 & 1 & -5 & 4 & 0 & 23 \\ 0 & 11 & 0 & 0 & 11 & 6 & 1 & -11 \end{array}\right]$$

12.
$$\begin{array}{ccccccc} x & y & z & u & v & w & M \\ \end{array}$$
$$\left[\begin{array}{ccccccc|c} 6 & 0 & 1 & 0 & 5 & -1 & 0 & \frac{1}{4} \\ 5 & 1 & 0 & 0 & 3 & \frac{1}{3} & 0 & 100 \\ 4 & 0 & 0 & 1 & 8 & \frac{1}{2} & 0 & 11 \\ 2 & 0 & 0 & 0 & 6 & \frac{1}{7} & 1 & -\frac{1}{2} \end{array}\right]$$

13. Pivot the simplex tableau

$$\begin{array}{ccccc} x & y & u & v & M \\ \end{array}$$
$$\left[\begin{array}{ccccc|c} 2 & 3 & 1 & 0 & 0 & 12 \\ 1 & 1 & 0 & 1 & 0 & 10 \\ -10 & -20 & 0 & 0 & 1 & 0 \end{array}\right]$$

about the indicated element and compute the particular solution corresponding to the new tableau.

(a) 2   (b) 3

(c) 1 (second row, first column)

(d) 1 (second row, second column)

14. Pivot the simplex tableau

$$\begin{array}{ccccc} x & y & u & v & M \\ \end{array}$$
$$\left[\begin{array}{ccccc|c} 5 & 4 & 1 & 0 & 0 & 100 \\ 10 & 6 & 0 & 1 & 0 & 1200 \\ -1 & 2 & 0 & 0 & 1 & 0 \end{array}\right]$$

about the indicated element and compute the solution corresponding to the new tableau.

(a) 5   (b) 4   (c) 10   (d) 6

15. Determine which of the pivot operations in Exercise 13 increases M the most.

16. Determine which of the pivot operations in Exercise 14 increases M the most.

Solutions to Practice Problems 4.1

1. The matrix of the system is

$$
\begin{array}{ccccc}
x & y & u & v & M
\end{array}
$$
$$
\left[\begin{array}{ccccc|c}
1 & 2 & 3 & 0 & 0 & 6 \\
0 & 1 & 0 & 1 & 0 & 4 \\
0 & 5 & 2 & 0 & 1 & 0
\end{array}\right],
$$

from which we see that the group II variables are x, v, and M, and the group I variables y, u. To obtain a solution, we set the group I variables equal to 0. We obtain from the first equation that $x = 6$, from the second that $v = 4$, and from the third that $M = 0$. Thus a solution of the system is $x = 6$, $y = 0$, $u = 0$, $v = 4$, $M = 0$.

2. We must use elementary row operations to transform the second column into

$$
\begin{bmatrix} 0 \\ 1 \\ 0 \end{bmatrix}.
$$

$$
\left[\begin{array}{ccccc|c}
2 & 4 & 1 & 0 & 0 & 6 \\
3 & ① & 0 & 1 & 0 & 0 \\
1 & 1 & 0 & 0 & 1 & 1
\end{array}\right]
\xrightarrow{[1]+(-4)[2]}
\left[\begin{array}{ccccc|c}
-10 & 0 & 1 & -4 & 0 & 6 \\
3 & 1 & 0 & 1 & 0 & 0 \\
1 & 1 & 0 & 0 & 1 & 1
\end{array}\right]
$$

$$
\xrightarrow{[3]+(-1)[2]}
\left[\begin{array}{ccccc|c}
-10 & 0 & 1 & -4 & 0 & 6 \\
3 & 1 & 0 & 1 & 0 & 0 \\
-2 & 0 & 0 & -1 & 1 & 1
\end{array}\right]
$$

4.2 The Simplex Method I: Maximum Problems

We can now describe the simplex method for solving linear programming problems. The procedure will be illustrated as we solve the furniture manufacturing problem of Section 4.1. Recall that we must maximize the objective function $80x + 70y$ subject to the constraints

$$
\begin{cases}
6x + 3y \leq 96 \\
x + y \leq 18 \\
2x + 6y \leq 72 \\
x \geq 0, \quad y \geq 0.
\end{cases}
$$

Step 1 Introduce slack variables and state the problem in terms of a system of linear equations.

We carried out this step in Section 4.1. The result was the following restatement of the problem.

Furniture Manufacturing Problem Among all the solutions of the system of linear equations

$$\begin{cases} 6x + 3y + u & = 96 \\ x + y & + v & = 18 \\ 2x + 6y & + w & = 72 \\ -80x - 70y & + M = 0, \end{cases}$$

find one for which $x \geq 0$, $y \geq 0$, $u \geq 0$, $v \geq 0$, $w \geq 0$, and for which M is as large as possible.

Step 2 Construct the simplex tableau corresponding to the linear system.

This step was also carried out in Section 4.1. The tableau is

	x	y	u	v	w	M	
u	6	3	1	0	0	0	96
v	1	1	0	1	0	0	18
w	2	6	0	0	1	0	72
M	-80	-70	0	0	0	1	0

Note that we have made two additions to the previously found tableau. First, we have separated the last row from the others by means of a horizontal line. This is because the last row, which corresponds to the objective function in the original problem, will play a special role in what follows. The second addition is that we have labeled each row with one of the group II variables—namely, the variable whose value is determined by the row. Thus, for example, the first row gives the particular value of u, which is 96, so the row is labeled with a u. We will find these labels convenient.

Corresponding to this tableau, there is a particular solution to the linear system, namely the one obtained by setting all group I variables equal to 0. Reading the values of the group II variables from the last column, we obtain

$$x = 0, \qquad y = 0, \qquad u = 96, \qquad v = 18, \qquad w = 72, \qquad M = 0.$$

Our objective is to make M as large as possible. How can the value of M be increased? Look at the equation corresponding to the last row of the tableau. It reads

$$-80x - 70y + M = 0.$$

Note that two of the coefficients, -80 and -70, are negative. Or, what amounts to the same thing, if we solve for M and get

$$M = 80x + 70y,$$

then the coefficients on the right-hand side are *positive*. This fact is significant. It says that M can be increased by increasing either the value of x or the value of y. A unit change in x will increase M by 80 units, whereas a unit change in y will increase M by 70 units. And since we wish to increase M by as much as possible, it is reasonable to attempt to increase the value of x. Let us indicate this by drawing an arrow pointing to the x column of the tableau:

$$
\begin{array}{c}
\begin{array}{cccccc}
\,\, x & y & u & v & w & M
\end{array} \\
\begin{array}{c} u \\ v \\ w \\ M \end{array}
\left[
\begin{array}{cccccc|c}
6 & 3 & 1 & 0 & 0 & 0 & 96 \\
1 & 1 & 0 & 1 & 0 & 0 & 18 \\
2 & 6 & 0 & 0 & 1 & 0 & 72 \\
\hline
-80 & -70 & 0 & 0 & 0 & 1 & 0
\end{array}
\right] \\
\uparrow
\end{array}
\tag{1}
$$

To increase x (from its present value, zero), we will pivot about one of the entries (above the horizontal line) in the x column. In this way, x will become a group II variable and hence will not necessarily be zero in our next particular solution. But around which entry should we pivot? To find out, let us experiment. The results from pivoting about the 6, the 1, and the 2 in the x column are, respectively,

$$
\begin{array}{c}
\begin{array}{cccccc}
\,\, x & y & u & v & w & M
\end{array} \\
\begin{array}{c} x \\ v \\ w \\ M \end{array}
\left[
\begin{array}{cccccc|c}
1 & \frac{1}{2} & \frac{1}{6} & 0 & 0 & 0 & 16 \\
0 & \frac{1}{2} & -\frac{1}{6} & 1 & 0 & 0 & 2 \\
0 & 5 & -\frac{1}{3} & 0 & 1 & 0 & 40 \\
\hline
0 & -30 & \frac{40}{3} & 0 & 0 & 1 & 1280
\end{array}
\right]
\end{array}
$$

Pivot about 6

$$
\begin{array}{c}
\begin{array}{cccccc}
\,\, x & y & u & v & w & M
\end{array} \\
\begin{array}{c} u \\ x \\ w \\ M \end{array}
\left[
\begin{array}{cccccc|c}
0 & -3 & 1 & -6 & 0 & 0 & -12 \\
1 & 1 & 0 & 1 & 0 & 0 & 18 \\
0 & 4 & 0 & -2 & 1 & 0 & 36 \\
\hline
0 & 10 & 0 & 80 & 0 & 1 & 1440
\end{array}
\right]
\end{array}
$$

Pivot about 1

$$
\begin{array}{c}
\begin{array}{cccccc}
\,\, x & y & u & v & w & M
\end{array} \\
\begin{array}{c} u \\ v \\ x \\ M \end{array}
\left[
\begin{array}{cccccc|c}
0 & -15 & 1 & 0 & -3 & 0 & -120 \\
0 & -2 & 0 & 1 & -\frac{1}{2} & 0 & -18 \\
1 & 3 & 0 & 0 & \frac{1}{2} & 0 & 36 \\
\hline
0 & 170 & 0 & 0 & 40 & 1 & 2880
\end{array}
\right]
\end{array}
$$

Pivot about 2

Note that the labels on the rows have *changed* because the group II variables are now *different*. The solutions corresponding to these tableaux are, respectively,

$$
\begin{array}{llllll}
x = 16, & y = 0, & u = 0, & v = 2, & w = 40, & M = 1280, \\
x = 18, & y = 0, & u = -12, & v = 0, & w = 36, & M = 1440, \\
x = 36, & y = 0, & u = -120, & v = -18, & w = 0, & M = 2880.
\end{array}
$$

The second and third solutions violate the requirement that all variables be ≥ 0. Thus, we use the first solution, in which we pivoted about 6. Using this solution, we have increased the value of M to 1280 and have replaced our original tableau by

$$
\begin{array}{c}
 \\
x \\
v \\
w \\
M
\end{array}
\begin{array}{cccccc}
x & y & u & v & w & M \\
\end{array}
\left[
\begin{array}{cccccc|c}
1 & \frac{1}{2} & \frac{1}{6} & 0 & 0 & 0 & 16 \\
0 & \frac{1}{2} & -\frac{1}{6} & 1 & 0 & 0 & 2 \\
0 & 5 & -\frac{1}{3} & 0 & 1 & 0 & 40 \\
\hline
0 & -30 & \frac{40}{3} & 0 & 0 & 1 & 1280
\end{array}
\right].
$$

Can M be increased further? To answer this question, look at the last row of the tableau, which corresponds to the equation

$$-30y + \tfrac{40}{3}u + M = 1280.$$

There is a negative coefficient for the variable y in this equation. Correspondingly, when the equation is solved for M, there is a positive coefficient for y:

$$M = 1280 + 30y - \tfrac{40}{3}u.$$

Now it is clear that we should try to increase y. So we pivot about one of the entries in the y column. A calculation for each of the possible pivots shows that pivoting about the first or the third entries leads to solutions having some negative values. Therefore, we pivot about the second entry in the y column. The result is

$$
\begin{array}{c}
 \\
x \\
y \\
w \\
M
\end{array}
\begin{array}{cccccc}
x & y & u & v & w & M \\
\end{array}
\left[
\begin{array}{cccccc|c}
1 & 0 & \frac{1}{3} & -1 & 0 & 0 & 14 \\
0 & 1 & -\frac{1}{3} & 2 & 0 & 0 & 4 \\
0 & 0 & \frac{4}{3} & -10 & 1 & 0 & 20 \\
\hline
0 & 0 & \frac{10}{3} & 60 & 0 & 1 & 1400
\end{array}
\right].
$$

The corresponding solution is

$$x = 14, \qquad y = 4, \qquad u = 0, \qquad v = 0, \qquad w = 20, \qquad M = 1400.$$

Note that with this pivot operation we have increased M from 1280 to 1400.

Can we increase M any further? Let us reason as before. Use the last row of the current tableau to write M in terms of the other variables:

$$\tfrac{10}{3}u + 60v + M = 1400, \qquad M = 1400 - \tfrac{10}{3}u - 60v.$$

Note, however, that in contrast to the previous expressions for M, this one has *no positive coefficients*. And since u and v are ≥ 0, this means that M can be *at most* 1400. But M is already 1400. So M cannot be increased further. Thus, we have shown that the maximum value of M is 1400, and this occurs when $x = 14$ and $y = 4$. Thus, to maximize profits, the furniture manufacturer should be making 14 chairs and 4 sofas each day. The maximum profit is $1400. From the tableau we can read off the values of the slack variables: $u = 0$, $v = 0$, and $w = 20$. This shows that we have no slack resulting from the first inequality, so we have used all the labor-hours available for carpentry. Similarly, since $v = 0$, we have used all of the labor-hours available for finishing. But since $w = 20$, we have 20 labor-hours of upholstery remaining when we manufacture the optimal number of chairs and sofas.

Let us compare the simplex method solution of the furniture manufacturing problem with the geometric solution carried out in Chapter 3. Both solutions yield the same optimal production schedule. In the geometric solution, we found *all* of the vertices of the feasible set and then evaluated the objective function at every one of these vertices. The following table was obtained:

Vertex	Profit $= 80x + 70y$
$(14, 4)$	$80(14) + 70(4) = 1400$
$(9, 9)$	$80(9) + 70(9) = 1350$
$(0, 12)$	$80(0) + 70(12) = 840$
$(0, 0)$	$80(0) + 70(0) = 0$
$(16, 0)$	$80(16) + 70(0) = 1280$

We selected the optimal solution ($x = 14$, $y = 4$) because it produced the greatest profit.

With the simplex method, we had to consider only *some* of the vertices. In the initial tableau we first considered the vertex $(0, 0)$—that is, both x and y were 0. M was also 0. In the second tableau we looked at the vertex $(16, 0)$—that is, $x = 16$ and $y = 0$, and the tableau showed that $M = 1280$. Finally, as a result of the last pivot operation, we came to the vertex $(14, 4)$. This meant that $x = 14$ and $y = 4$. The value of the objective function was read from the tableau: $M = 1400$. Since we could not increase M any more, we did not have to consider any other vertices. In larger linear programming problems, the time saved from looking at just *some* of the vertices, rather than *all* of the vertices, can be substantial.

Based on the preceding discussion, we can state several general principles. First of all, the following criterion determines when a simplex tableau yields a maximum.

Condition for a Maximum   The particular solution derived from a simplex tableau is a maximum if and only if the bottom row contains no negative entries except perhaps the entry in the last column.[1]

We saw this condition illustrated in the previous example. Each of the first two tableaux had negative entries in the last row, and as we showed, their corresponding solutions were not maxima. However, the third tableau, with no negative entries in the last row, did yield a maximum.

The crucial point of the simplex method is the correct choice of a pivot element. In the preceding example we decided to choose a pivot element from the column corresponding to the most-negative entry in the last row. It can be proved that this is the proper choice in general; that is, we have the following rule:

---

[1] In Section 4.3 we shall encounter maximum problems whose final tableaux have a negative number in the lower right-hand corner.

Choosing the Pivot Column The pivot element should be chosen from that column to the left of the vertical line that has the most-negative entry in the last row.[2]

Choosing the correct pivot element from the designated column is somewhat more complicated. Our approach before was to calculate the tableau associated with each element and observe that only one corresponded to a solution with nonnegative elements. However, there is a simpler way to make the choice. As an illustration, let us reconsider tableau (1). We have already decided to pivot around some entry in the first column. For each *positive* entry in the pivot column we compute a ratio: the corresponding entry in the right-hand column divided by the entry in the pivot column. So, for example, for the first entry the ratio is $\frac{96}{6}$; for the second entry the ratio is $\frac{18}{1}$; and for the third entry the ratio is $\frac{72}{2}$. We write these ratios to the right of the matrix as follows:

$$
\begin{array}{c}
\begin{array}{cccccc}
x & y & u & v & w & M
\end{array} \\
\begin{array}{c}
u \\
v \\
w \\
M
\end{array}
\left[
\begin{array}{cccccc|c}
6 & 3 & 1 & 0 & 0 & 0 & 96 \\
1 & 1 & 0 & 1 & 0 & 0 & 18 \\
2 & 6 & 0 & 0 & 1 & 0 & 72 \\
\hline
-80 & -70 & 0 & 0 & 0 & 1 & 0
\end{array}
\right]
\begin{array}{l}
\frac{96}{6} = 16 \\[4pt]
\frac{18}{1} = 18 \\[4pt]
\frac{72}{2} = 36 \\[4pt]
\\
\end{array}
\end{array}
$$

It is possible to prove the following rule, which allows us to determine the pivot element from the preceding display:

Choosing the Pivot Element For each positive entry of the pivot column, compute the appropriate ratio. Choose as pivot element the one corresponding to the least-nonnegative ratio.

For instance, consider the choice of pivot element in the preceding example. The least of the ratios is 16. So we choose 6 as the pivot element.

At first, this method for choosing the pivot element might seem very odd. However, it is just a way of guaranteeing that the last column of the new tableau will have entries ≥ 0. And that is just the basis on which we chose the pivot element earlier. To obtain further insight, let us analyze the preceding example yet further.

Suppose that we pivot our tableau about the 6 in column 1. The first step in pivoting is to divide the pivot row by the pivot element (in this case, 6). This gives the array

$$
\begin{array}{c}
\begin{array}{cccccc}
x & y & u & v & w & M
\end{array} \\
\left[
\begin{array}{cccccc|c}
1 & \frac{1}{2} & \frac{1}{6} & 0 & 0 & 0 & \frac{96}{6} \\
1 & 1 & 0 & 1 & 0 & 0 & 18 \\
2 & 6 & 0 & 0 & 1 & 0 & 72 \\
\hline
-80 & -70 & 0 & 0 & 0 & 1 & 0
\end{array}
\right],
\end{array}
$$

where we have written $\frac{96}{6}$ rather than 16 to emphasize that we have divided by the pivot element. The next step in the pivot procedure is to replace the second

---

[2]In case two or more columns are tied for the honor of being the pivot column, an arbitrary choice among them may be made.

row by the second row plus (-1) times the first row. The result is

$$
\begin{array}{cccccc}
x & y & u & v & w & M \\
\end{array}
$$

$$
\left[
\begin{array}{cccccc|c}
1 & \frac{1}{2} & \frac{1}{6} & 0 & 0 & 0 & \frac{96}{6} \\
0 & \frac{1}{2} & -\frac{1}{6} & 1 & 0 & 0 & 18 - \frac{96}{6} \\
2 & 6 & 0 & 0 & 1 & 0 & 72 \\
\hline
-80 & -70 & 0 & 0 & 0 & 1 & 0
\end{array}
\right].
$$

The next step in the pivot process is to replace the third row by $[3] + (-2)[1]$ to obtain

$$
\begin{array}{cccccc}
x & y & u & v & w & M \\
\end{array}
$$

$$
\left[
\begin{array}{cccccc|c}
1 & \frac{1}{2} & \frac{1}{6} & 0 & 0 & 0 & \frac{96}{6} \\
0 & \frac{1}{2} & -\frac{1}{6} & 1 & 0 & 0 & 18 - \frac{96}{6} \\
0 & 5 & -\frac{1}{3} & 0 & 1 & 0 & 72 - 2\left(\frac{96}{6}\right) \\
\hline
-80 & -70 & 0 & 0 & 0 & 1 & 0
\end{array}
\right].
$$

The final step of the pivot process is to replace the fourth row by $[4] + 80[1]$ to obtain

$$
\begin{array}{cccccc}
x & y & u & v & w & M \\
\end{array}
$$

$$
\left[
\begin{array}{cccccc|c}
1 & \frac{1}{2} & \frac{1}{6} & 0 & 0 & 0 & \frac{96}{6} \\
0 & \frac{1}{2} & -\frac{1}{6} & 1 & 0 & 0 & 18 - \frac{96}{6} \\
0 & 5 & -\frac{1}{3} & 0 & 1 & 0 & 72 - 2\left(\frac{96}{6}\right) \\
\hline
0 & -30 & \frac{40}{3} & 0 & 0 & 1 & 1280
\end{array}
\right].
$$

The entries in the upper part of the right-hand column may be written

$$
\frac{96}{6}, \qquad \frac{18}{1} - \frac{96}{6}, \qquad 2\left(\frac{72}{2} - \frac{96}{6}\right).
$$

If we had pivoted about the 1 or 2 in the first column of the original tableau, the upper entries in the last column of the tableau would have been

$$
6\left(\frac{96}{6} - \frac{18}{1}\right), \qquad \frac{18}{1}, \qquad 2\left(\frac{72}{2} - \frac{18}{1}\right)
$$

or

$$
6\left(\frac{96}{6} - \frac{72}{2}\right), \qquad \frac{18}{1} - \frac{72}{2}, \qquad \frac{72}{2},
$$

respectively. Notice that all of the combinations of the differences of the pairs of ratios appear in these triples. In the first case, the ratio $\frac{96}{6}$ is subtracted from each of the other two ratios, whereas in the next two cases, the ratios $\frac{18}{1}$ and $\frac{72}{2}$ are subtracted. In order for the upper entries in the last column to be nonnegative, we must subtract off the smallest of the ratios. That is, we should pivot about the entry corresponding to the smallest ratio. This is the rationale governing our choice of pivot element!

Now that we have assembled all the components of the simplex method, we can summarize it as follows:

The Simplex Method for Problems in Standard Form

1. Introduce slack variables and state the problem in terms of a system of linear equations.

2. Construct the simplex tableau corresponding to the system.

3. Determine if the left part of the bottom row contains negative entries. If none are present, the solution corresponding to the tableau yields a maximum and the problem is solved.

4. If the left part of the bottom row contains negative entries, construct a new simplex tableau.

   (a) Choose the pivot column by inspecting the entries of the last row of the current tableau, excluding the right-hand entry. The pivot column is the one containing the most-negative of these entries.

   (b) Choose the pivot element by computing ratios associated with the positive entries of the pivot column. The pivot element is the one corresponding to the smallest nonnegative ratio.

   (c) Construct the new simplex tableau by pivoting around the selected element.

5. Return to step 3. Steps 3 and 4 are repeated as many times as necessary to find a maximum.

Let us now work some problems to see how this method is applied.

▶ **Example 1**   Maximize the objective function $10x + y$ subject to the constraints

$$\begin{cases} x + 2y \le 10 \\ 3x + 4y \le 6 \\ x \ge 0, \quad y \ge 0. \end{cases}$$

Solution   The corresponding system of linear equations with slack variables is

$$\begin{cases} x + 2y + u & = 10 \\ 3x + 4y \phantom{{}+u} + v & = 6 \\ -10x - y \phantom{{}+u+v} + M & = 0, \end{cases}$$

and we must find that solution of the system for which $x \ge 0$, $y \ge 0$, $u \ge 0$, $v \ge 0$, and M is as large as possible. Here is the initial simplex tableau:

$$\begin{array}{c} \\ u \\ v \\ M \end{array} \begin{array}{c} \begin{array}{ccccc} x & y & u & v & M \end{array} \\ \left[\begin{array}{ccccc|c} 1 & 2 & 1 & 0 & 0 & 10 \\ 3 & 4 & 0 & 1 & 0 & 6 \\ \hline -10 & -1 & 0 & 0 & 1 & 0 \end{array} \right] \end{array}.$$

$\uparrow$

Note that this tableau does not correspond to a maximum, since the left part of the bottom row has negative entries. So we pivot to create a new tableau. Since -10 is the most-negative entry in the last row, we choose the first column as the pivot column. To determine the pivot element, we compute ratios:

$$
\begin{array}{c}
 \\
u \\
v \\
M
\end{array}
\begin{array}{c}
\begin{array}{cccccc}
x & y & u & v & M
\end{array} \\
\left[
\begin{array}{ccccc|c}
1 & 2 & 1 & 0 & 0 & 10 \\
\boxed{3} & 4 & 0 & 1 & 0 & 6 \\
\hline
-10 & -1 & 0 & 0 & 1 & 0
\end{array}
\right]
\end{array}
\begin{array}{c}
\text{Ratios} \\
10/1 = 10 \\
6/3 = 2.
\end{array}
$$

$\uparrow$

The smallest ratio is 2, so we pivot about 3, which we have circled. The new tableau is therefore

$$
\begin{array}{c}
u \\
x \\
M
\end{array}
\begin{array}{c}
\begin{array}{ccccc}
x & y & u & v & M
\end{array} \\
\left[
\begin{array}{ccccc|c}
0 & \frac{2}{3} & 1 & -\frac{1}{3} & 0 & 8 \\
1 & \frac{4}{3} & 0 & \frac{1}{3} & 0 & 2 \\
\hline
0 & \frac{37}{3} & 0 & \frac{10}{3} & 1 & 20
\end{array}
\right]
\end{array}.
$$

Note that this tableau corresponds to a maximum, since there are no negative entries in the left part of the last row. The solution corresponding to the tableau is

$$x = 2, \qquad y = 0, \qquad u = 8, \qquad v = 0, \qquad M = 20.$$

Therefore, the objective function assumes its maximum value of 20 when $x = 2$ and $y = 0$. ◆

The simplex method can be used to solve problems in any number of variables. Let us illustrate the method for three variables.

▶ **Example 2** Maximize the objective function $x + 2y + z$ subject to the constraints

$$
\begin{cases}
x - y + 2z \leq 10 \\
2x + y + 3z \leq 12 \\
x \geq 0, \quad y \geq 0, \quad z \geq 0.
\end{cases}
$$

Solution We determined the corresponding linear system in Example 2 of Section 4.1:

$$
\begin{cases}
x - y + 2z + u = 10 \\
2x + y + 3z + v = 12 \\
-x - 2y - z + M = 0.
\end{cases}
$$

So the simplex method works as follows:

$$
\begin{array}{c}
u \\
v \\
M
\end{array}
\begin{array}{c}
\begin{array}{cccccc}
x & y & z & u & v & M
\end{array} \\
\left[
\begin{array}{cccccc|c}
1 & -1 & 2 & 1 & 0 & 0 & 10 \\
2 & \boxed{1} & 3 & 0 & 1 & 0 & 12 \\
\hline
-1 & -2 & -1 & 0 & 0 & 1 & 0
\end{array}
\right]
\end{array}
\begin{array}{l}
\\
12/1 = 12 \\
\text{(smallest} \\
\text{nonnegative ratio)}
\end{array}
$$

$\uparrow$

$$
\begin{array}{c c}
 & \begin{array}{cccccc} x & y & z & u & v & M \end{array} \\
\begin{array}{c} u \\ y \\ M \end{array} &
\left[\begin{array}{cccccc|c}
3 & 0 & 5 & 1 & 1 & 0 & 22 \\
2 & 1 & 3 & 0 & 1 & 0 & 12 \\
3 & 0 & 5 & 0 & 2 & 1 & 24
\end{array} \right]
\end{array} .
$$

Thus, the solution of the original problem $(x = 0,\ y = 12,\ z = 0)$ yields the maximum value of the objective function $x + 2y + z$. The maximum value is 24.

◆

Practice Problems 4.2

1. Which of these simplex tableaux has a solution that corresponds to a maximum for the associated linear programming problem?

(a)
$$
\begin{array}{c}
\begin{array}{ccccc} x & y & u & v & M \end{array} \\
\left[\begin{array}{ccccc|c}
3 & 1 & 0 & 1 & 0 & 5 \\
2 & 0 & 0 & 0 & 1 & 0 \\
-1 & -2 & 1 & 0 & 0 & 3
\end{array} \right]
\end{array}
$$

(b)
$$
\begin{array}{c}
\begin{array}{ccccc} x & y & u & v & M \end{array} \\
\left[\begin{array}{ccccc|c}
2 & 1 & 0 & 11 & 0 & 10 \\
1 & 0 & 1 & 7 & 0 & 1 \\
1 & 0 & 0 & 4 & 1 & -2
\end{array} \right]
\end{array}
$$

2. Suppose that in the solution of a linear programming problem by the simplex method, we encounter the following simplex tableau. What is the next step in the solution?

$$
\begin{array}{c}
\begin{array}{ccccc} x & y & u & v & M \end{array} \\
\left[\begin{array}{ccccc|c}
0 & 4 & 1 & 2 & 0 & 4 \\
1 & 5 & 0 & 1 & 0 & 9 \\
0 & 2 & 0 & -3 & 1 & 6
\end{array} \right]
\end{array}
$$

▶ Exercises 4.2

For each of the simplex tableaux in Exercises 1–4,

(a) Compute the next pivot element.

(b) Determine the next tableau.

(c) Determine the particular solution corresponding to the tableau of part (b).

1.
$$
\begin{array}{c}
\begin{array}{ccccc} x & y & u & v & M \end{array} \\
\left[\begin{array}{ccccc|c}
6 & 2 & 1 & 0 & 0 & 10 \\
1 & 3 & 0 & 1 & 0 & 6 \\
-4 & -12 & 0 & 0 & 1 & 0
\end{array} \right]
\end{array}
$$

2.
$$
\begin{array}{c}
\begin{array}{ccccc} x & y & u & v & M \end{array} \\
\left[\begin{array}{ccccc|c}
1 & 0 & 3 & 1 & 0 & 5 \\
0 & 1 & 2 & 0 & 0 & 12 \\
-6 & 0 & 5 & 0 & 1 & 10
\end{array} \right]
\end{array}
$$

3.
$$
\begin{array}{c}
\begin{array}{ccccc} x & y & u & v & M \end{array} \\
\left[\begin{array}{ccccc|c}
5 & 12 & 1 & 0 & 0 & 12 \\
15 & 10 & 0 & 1 & 0 & 5 \\
4 & -2 & 0 & 0 & 1 & 0
\end{array} \right]
\end{array}
$$

4.
$$\begin{array}{c} \begin{array}{ccccc} x & y & u & v & M \end{array} \\ \left[\begin{array}{ccccc|c} 0 & 6 & 3 & 1 & 0 & 5 \\ 1 & -5 & 2 & 0 & 0 & 8 \\ \hline 0 & 20 & -10 & 0 & 1 & 22 \end{array}\right] \end{array}$$

In Exercises 5–14, solve the linear programming problems using the simplex method.

5. Maximize $x + 3y$ subject to the constraints

$$\begin{cases} x + y \le 7 \\ x + 2y \le 10 \\ x \ge 0, \quad y \ge 0. \end{cases}$$

6. Maximize $x + 2y$ subject to the constraints

$$\begin{cases} -x + y \le 100 \\ 6x + 6y \le 1200 \\ x \ge 0, \quad y \ge 0. \end{cases}$$

7. Maximize $4x + 2y$ subject to the constraints

$$\begin{cases} 5x + y \le 80 \\ 3x + 2y \le 76 \\ x \ge 0, \quad y \ge 0. \end{cases}$$

8. Maximize $2x + 6y$ subject to the constraints

$$\begin{cases} -x + 8y \le 160 \\ 3x - y \le 3 \\ x \ge 0, \quad y \ge 0. \end{cases}$$

9. Maximize $x + 3y + 5z$ subject to the constraints

$$\begin{cases} x + 2z \le 10 \\ 3y + z \le 24 \\ x \ge 0, \quad y \ge 0, \quad z \ge 0. \end{cases}$$

10. Maximize $-x + 8y + z$ subject to the constraints

$$\begin{cases} x - 2y + 9z \le 10 \\ y + 4z \le 12 \\ x \ge 0, \quad y \ge 0, \quad z \ge 0. \end{cases}$$

11. Maximize $2x + 3y$ subject to the constraints

$$\begin{cases} 5x + y \le 30 \\ 3x + 2y \le 60 \\ x + y \le 50 \\ x \ge 0, \quad y \ge 0. \end{cases}$$

12. Maximize $10x + 12y + 10z$ subject to the constraints

$$\begin{cases} x - 2y \le 6 \\ 3x + z \le 9 \\ y + 3z \le 12 \\ x \ge 0, \quad y \ge 0, \quad z \ge 0. \end{cases}$$

13. Maximize $6x + 7y + 300$ subject to the constraints

$$\begin{cases} 2x + 3y \le 400 \\ x + y \le 150 \\ x \ge 0, \quad y \ge 0. \end{cases}$$

14. Maximize $10x + 20y + 50$ subject to the constraints

$$\begin{cases} x + y \le 10 \\ 5x + 2y \le 20 \\ x \ge 0, \quad y \ge 0. \end{cases}$$

15. Suppose that a furniture manufacturer makes chairs, sofas, and tables. The amounts of labor of various types as well as the relative availability of each type are summarized by the following chart:

	Chair	Sofa	Table	Daily labor available (labor-hours)
Carpentry	6	3	8	768
Finishing	1	1	2	144
Upholstery	2	5	0	216

The profit per chair is $80, per sofa $70, and per table $120. How many pieces of each type of furniture should be manufactured each day to maximize the profit?

16. A stereo store sells three brands of stereo systems, brands A, B, and C. It can sell a total of 100 stereo systems per month. Brands A, B, and C take up, respectively, 5, 4, and 4 cubic feet of warehouse space, and a maximum of 480 cubic feet of warehouse space is available. Brands A, B, and C generate sales commissions of $40, $20, and $30, respectively, and $3200 is available to pay the sales commissions. The profit generated from the sale of each brand is $70, $210, and $140, respectively. How many of each brand of stereo system should be sold to maximize the profit?

17. As part of a weight-reduction program, a man designs a monthly exercise program consisting of bicycling, jogging, and swimming. He would like to exercise at most 30 hours, devote at most 4 hours to swimming, and jog for no more than the total number of hours bicycling and swimming. The calories burned per hour by bicycling, jogging, and swimming are 200, 475, and 275, respectively. How many hours should be allotted to each activity to maximize the number of calories burned? If he loses 1 pound of weight for each 3500 calories burned, how many pounds will he lose each month exercising?

18. A furniture manufacturer produces small sofas, large sofas, and chairs. The profits per item are, respectively, $60, $60, and $50. The pieces of furniture require the following numbers of labor-hours for their manufacture:

	Carpentry	Upholstery	Finishing
Small sofas	10	30	20
Large sofas	10	30	0
Chairs	10	10	10

The following amounts of labor are available per month: carpentry, at most 1200 hours; upholstery, at most 3000 hours; and finishing, at most 1800 hours. How many each of small sofas, large sofas, and chairs should be manufactured to maximize the profit?

19. The XYZ Corporation plans to open three different types of fast-food restaurants. Type A restaurants require an initial cash outlay of $600,000, need 15 employees, and are expected to make an annual profit of $40,000. Type B restaurants require an initial cash outlay of $400,000, need 9 employees, and are expected to make an annual profit of $30,000. Type C restaurants require an initial cash outlay of $300,000, need 5 employees, and are expected to make an annual profit of $25,000. The XYZ Corporation has $48,000,000 available for initial outlays, does not want to hire more than 1000 new employees, and would like to open at most 70 restaurants. How many restaurants of each type should be opened to maximize the expected annual profit?

20. Maximize $60x + 90y + 300z$ subject to the constraints

$$\begin{cases} x + y + z \le 600 \\ x + 3y \le 600 \\ 2x + z \le 900 \\ x \ge 0, \quad y \ge 0, \quad z \ge 0. \end{cases}$$

21. Maximize $200x + 500y$ subject to the constraints

$$\begin{cases} x + 4y \le 300 \\ x + 2y \le 200 \\ x \ge 0, \quad y \ge 0. \end{cases}$$

In Exercises 22–25 use a graphing calculator or a computer to solve the linear programming problems by the simplex method.

22. Maximize $2x + 4y$ subject to the constraints

$$\begin{cases} 5x + y \le 8 \\ x + 2y \le 10 \\ x \ge 0, \quad y \ge 0. \end{cases}$$

23. Maximize $4x + 6y$ subject to the constraints

$$\begin{cases} x + 4y \le 4 \\ 3x + 2y \le 6 \\ x \ge 0, \quad y \ge 0. \end{cases}$$

24. Maximize $3x + 2y + 2z$ subject to the constraints

$$\begin{cases} x + y + 2z \le 6 \\ x + 5y + 2z \le 20 \\ 2x + y + z \le 4 \\ x \ge 0, \quad y \ge 0, \quad z \ge 0. \end{cases}$$

25. Maximize $16x + 4y - 20z$ subject to the constraints

$$\begin{cases} 4x + y + 5z \le 20 \\ x + 2y + 4z \le 50 \\ 4x + 10y + z \le 32 \\ x \ge 0, \quad y \ge 0, \quad z \ge 0. \end{cases}$$

Solutions to Practice Problems 4.2

1. (a) Does not correspond to a maximum, since among the entries $-1, -2, 1, 0, 0$ in the last row, at least one is negative.

(b) Corresponds to a maximum since none of the entries $1, 0, 0, 4, 1$ of the last row is negative. Note that it does not matter that the entry -2 in the right-hand corner of the matrix is negative. This number gives the value of M. In this example -2 is as large as M can become.

2. First choose the column corresponding to the most-negative entry of the final row, that is, the fourth column. For each positive entry in the fourth column that is above the horizontal line, compute the ratio with the sixth column. The smallest ratio is 2 and appears in the first row, so the next operation is to pivot around the 2 in the first row of the fourth column.

$$
\begin{bmatrix}
0 & 4 & 1 & \boxed{2} & 0 & 4 \\
1 & 5 & 0 & 1 & 0 & 9 \\
\hline
0 & 2 & 0 & -3 & 1 & 6
\end{bmatrix}
\quad
\begin{array}{l}
\frac{4}{2} = 2 \\
\frac{9}{1} = 9 \\
\\
\end{array}
$$

$$\uparrow$$

4.3 The Simplex Method II: Minimum Problems

In the preceding section we developed the simplex method and applied it to a number of problems. However, throughout we restricted ourselves to linear programming problems in standard form. Recall that such problems satisfied three properties: (1) the objective function is to be maximized; (2) each variable must be ≥ 0; and (3) all constraints other than those implied by (2) must be of the form

$$[\text{linear polynomial}] \leq [\text{nonnegative constant}].$$

In this section we do what we can to relax these restrictions.

Let us begin with restriction (3). This could be violated in two ways. First, the constant on the right-hand side of one or more constraints could be negative. Thus, for example, one constraint might be

$$x - y \leq -2.$$

A second way in which restriction (3) can be violated is for some constraints to involve $\geq$ rather than $\leq$. An example of such a constraint is

$$2x + 3y \geq 5.$$

However, we can convert such a constraint into one involving $\leq$ by multiplying both sides of the inequality by -1:

$$-2x - 3y \leq -5.$$

Of course, the right-hand constant is no longer nonnegative. Thus, if we allow negative constants on the right, we can write all constraints in the form

$$[\text{linear polynomial}] \leq [\text{constant}].$$

Henceforth, the first step in solving a linear programming problem will be to write the constraints in this form. Let us now see how to deal with the phenomenon of negative constants.

▶ Example 1   Maximize the objective function $5x + 10y$ subject to the constraints

$$
\begin{cases}
x + y \leq 20 \\
2x - y \geq 10 \\
x \geq 0, \quad y \geq 0.
\end{cases}
$$

Solution The first step is to put the second constraint into $\leq$ form. Multiply the second inequality by -1 to obtain

$$\begin{cases} x + y \leq 20 \\ -2x + y \leq -10 \\ x \geq 0, \quad y \geq 0. \end{cases}$$

Just as before, write the linear programming problem as a linear system:

$$\begin{cases} x + y + u = 20 \\ -2x + y + v = -10 \\ -5x - 10y + M = 0. \end{cases}$$

From the linear system, construct the simplex tableau:

$$\begin{array}{c} \\ u \\ v \\ M \end{array} \begin{array}{ccccc} x & y & u & v & M \\ \left[\begin{array}{ccccc|c} 1 & 1 & 1 & 0 & 0 & 20 \\ -2 & 1 & 0 & 1 & 0 & -10 \\ \hline -5 & -10 & 0 & 0 & 1 & 0 \end{array}\right]. \end{array}$$

Everything would proceed exactly as before, except that the right-hand column has a -10 in it. This means that the initial value for v is -10, which violates the condition that all variables be ≥ 0. Before we can apply the simplex method of Section 4.2, we must first put the tableau into standard form. This can be done by pivoting to remove the negative entry in the right column.

We choose the pivot element as follows. Look along the left side of the -10 row of the tableau and locate any negative entry. There is only one: -2. Use the column containing the -2 as the pivot column (that is, use column 1). Now compute ratios as before:[1]

$$\begin{array}{c} \\ u \\ v \\ M \end{array} \begin{array}{ccccc} x & y & u & v & M \\ \left[\begin{array}{ccccc|c} 1 & 1 & 1 & 0 & 0 & 20 \\ \boxed{-2} & 1 & 0 & 1 & 0 & -10 \\ \hline -5 & -10 & 0 & 0 & 1 & 0 \end{array}\right] & \begin{array}{l} \frac{20}{1} = 20 \\ \frac{-10}{-2} = 5. \end{array} \\ \uparrow \end{array}$$

The smallest positive ratio is 5, so we choose -2 as the pivot element. The new tableau is

$$\begin{array}{c} \\ u \\ x \\ M \end{array} \begin{array}{ccccc} x & y & u & v & M \\ \left[\begin{array}{ccccc|c} 0 & \frac{3}{2} & 1 & \frac{1}{2} & 0 & 15 \\ 1 & -\frac{1}{2} & 0 & -\frac{1}{2} & 0 & 5 \\ \hline 0 & -\frac{25}{2} & 0 & -\frac{5}{2} & 1 & 25 \end{array}\right]. \end{array}$$

Note that all entries in the right-hand column are now nonnegative;[2] that is, the corresponding solution has all variables ≥ 0. From here on we follow the simplex

---

[1] Note, however, that in this circumstance we compute ratios corresponding to both positive *and* negative entries (except the last) in the pivot column, considering further only positive ratios.

[2] In general, it may be necessary to pivot several times before all entries in the last column are ≥ 0.

method for tableaux in standard form:

$$
\begin{array}{c}
& \begin{array}{ccccc} x & y & u & v & M \end{array} \\
\begin{array}{c} u \\ x \\ M \end{array}
\left[
\begin{array}{ccccc|c}
0 & \boxed{\tfrac{3}{2}} & 1 & \tfrac{1}{2} & 0 & 15 \\
1 & -\tfrac{1}{2} & 0 & -\tfrac{1}{2} & 0 & 5 \\
\hline
0 & -\tfrac{25}{2} & 0 & -\tfrac{5}{2} & 1 & 25
\end{array}
\right]
\end{array}
\quad 15/\tfrac{3}{2} = 10
$$

$$\uparrow$$

$$
\begin{array}{c}
& \begin{array}{ccccc} x & y & u & v & M \end{array} \\
\begin{array}{c} y \\ x \\ M \end{array}
\left[
\begin{array}{ccccc|c}
0 & 1 & \tfrac{2}{3} & \tfrac{1}{3} & 0 & 10 \\
1 & 0 & \tfrac{1}{3} & -\tfrac{1}{3} & 0 & 10 \\
\hline
0 & 0 & \tfrac{25}{3} & \tfrac{5}{3} & 1 & 150
\end{array}
\right]
\end{array}
\; .
$$

So the maximum value of M is 150, which is attained for $x = 10$, $y = 10$. ◆

In summary,

The Simplex Method for Problems in Nonstandard Form

1. If necessary, convert all inequalities (except $x \geq 0$, $y \geq 0$) into the form

$$\big[\text{linear polynomial}\big] \leq \big[\text{constant}\big].$$

2. If a negative number appears in the upper part of the last column of the simplex tableau, remove it by pivoting.
   (a) Select one of the negative entries in its row. The column containing the entry will be the pivot column.
   (b) Select the pivot element by determining the least of the positive ratios associated with entries in the pivot column (except the bottom entry).
   (c) Pivot.

3. Repeat step 2 until there are no negative entries in the upper part of the right-hand column of the simplex tableau.

4. Proceed to apply the simplex method for tableaux in standard form.

The method we have just developed can be used to solve *minimum* problems as well as maximum problems. Minimizing the objective function f is the same as maximizing $(-1) \cdot f$. This is so since multiplying an inequality by -1 reverses the direction of the inequality sign. Thus, to apply our method to a minimum problem, we merely multiply the objective function by -1 and turn the problem into a maximum problem.

▶ **Example 2** Minimize the objective function $3x + 2y$ subject to the constraints

$$
\begin{cases}
x + y \geq 10 \\
x - y \leq 15 \\
x \geq 0, \quad y \geq 0.
\end{cases}
$$

Solution   First transform the problem so that the first two constraints are in $\leq$ form:

$$\begin{cases} -x - y \leq -10 \\ \quad x - y \leq 15 \\ \quad x \geq 0, \quad y \geq 0. \end{cases}$$

Instead of minimizing $3x + 2y$, let us maximize $-3x - 2y$. Let $M = -3x - 2y$. Then our initial simplex tableau reads

$$
\begin{array}{c c}
 & \begin{array}{c c c c c} x & y & u & v & M \end{array} \\
\begin{array}{c} u \\ v \\ M \end{array} &
\left[\begin{array}{c c c c c | c}
-1 & \boxed{-1} & 1 & 0 & 0 & -10 \\
1 & -1 & 0 & 1 & 0 & 15 \\
\hline
3 & 2 & 0 & 0 & 1 & 0
\end{array} \right]
\end{array}
\qquad \tfrac{-10}{-1} = 10.
$$

We first eliminate the -10 in the right-hand column. We have a choice of two negative entries in the -10 row. Let us choose the one in the y column. The ratios are then tabulated as before, and we pivot around the circled element. The new tableau is[3]

$$
\begin{array}{c c}
 & \begin{array}{c c c c c} x & y & u & v & M \end{array} \\
\begin{array}{c} y \\ v \\ M \end{array} &
\left[\begin{array}{c c c c c | c}
1 & 1 & -1 & 0 & 0 & 10 \\
2 & 0 & -1 & 1 & 0 & 25 \\
\hline
1 & 0 & 2 & 0 & 1 & -20
\end{array} \right]
\end{array}.
$$

Since all entries in the bottom row, except the last, are positive, this tableau corresponds to a maximum. Thus, the maximum value of $-3x - 2y$ (subject to the constraints) is -20, and this value occurs for $x = 0$, $y = 10$. Thus, the *minimum* value of $3x + 2y$ subject to the constraints is 20.   ◆

Let us now rework an applied problem previously treated (see Example 2 in Section 3.3), this time using the simplex method. For easy reference we restate the problem.

▶ Example 3   (*Transportation Problem*) Suppose that a TV dealer has stores in Annapolis and Rockville and warehouses in College Park and Baltimore. The cost of shipping sets from College Park to Annapolis is $6 per set; from College Park to Rockville, $3; from Baltimore to Annapolis, $9; and from Baltimore to Rockville, $5. Suppose that the Annapolis store orders 25 TV sets and the Rockville store 30. Further suppose that the College Park warehouse has a stock of 45 sets, and the Baltimore warehouse 40. What is the most economical way to supply the requested TV sets to the two stores?

Solution via the Simplex Method   As in the previous solution, let x be the number of sets shipped from College Park to Rockville, and y the number shipped from College Park to Annapolis. The flow of sets is depicted in Fig. 1.

---
[3]Note that we do not need the last entry in the last column to be positive. We require *only* that x, y, u, and v be ≥ 0.

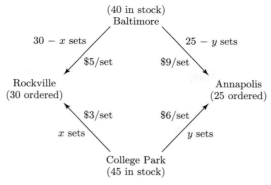

Figure 1.

Exactly as in our previous solution, we reduce the problem to the following algebraic form: Minimize $375 - 2x - 3y$ subject to the constraints

$$\begin{cases} x \le 30, \quad y \le 25 \\ x + y \ge 15 \\ x + y \le 45 \\ x \ge 0, \quad y \ge 0. \end{cases}$$

Two changes are needed. First, instead of minimizing $375 - 2x - 3y$, we maximize $-(375 - 2x - 3y) = 2x + 3y - 375$. Second, we write the constraint $x + y \ge 15$ in the form

$$-x - y \le -15.$$

With these changes made, we can write down the linear system:

$$\begin{cases} x \qquad + t \qquad\qquad\qquad\qquad = \quad 30 \\ \quad y \qquad + u \qquad\qquad\qquad = \quad 25 \\ -x - y \qquad\qquad + v \qquad\qquad = \quad -15 \\ \quad x + y \qquad\qquad\qquad + w \qquad = \quad 45 \\ -2x - 3y \qquad\qquad\qquad\qquad + M = -375. \end{cases}$$

From here on we follow our routine procedure in a mechanical way:

$$\begin{array}{c c} & \begin{array}{ccccccc} x & y & t & u & v & w & M \end{array} \\ \begin{array}{c} t \\ u \\ v \\ w \\ \\ M \end{array} & \left[\begin{array}{ccccccc|c} 1 & 0 & 1 & 0 & 0 & 0 & 0 & 30 \\ 0 & 1 & 0 & 1 & 0 & 0 & 0 & 25 \\ \boxed{-1} & -1 & 0 & 0 & 1 & 0 & 0 & -15 \\ 1 & 1 & 0 & 0 & 0 & 1 & 0 & 45 \\ \hline -2 & -3 & 0 & 0 & 0 & 0 & 1 & -375 \end{array} \right] \end{array} \quad \begin{array}{l} \frac{30}{1} = 30 \\ \\ \frac{-15}{-1} = 15 \\ \frac{45}{1} = 45 \\ \\ \end{array}$$

↑

$$
\begin{array}{c}
\begin{array}{ccccccc}
x & y & t & u & v & w & M
\end{array} \\
\begin{array}{c}
t \\ u \\ x \\ w \\ M
\end{array}
\left[
\begin{array}{ccccccc|c}
0 & -1 & 1 & 0 & ① & 0 & 0 & 15 \\
0 & 1 & 0 & 1 & 0 & 0 & 0 & 25 \\
1 & 1 & 0 & 0 & -1 & 0 & 0 & 15 \\
0 & 0 & 0 & 0 & 1 & 1 & 0 & 30 \\
\hline
0 & -1 & 0 & 0 & -2 & 0 & 1 & -345
\end{array}
\right]
\end{array}
\qquad
\begin{array}{l}
\frac{15}{1} = 15 \\[4ex] \\[2ex]
\frac{30}{1} = 30
\end{array}
$$

$\uparrow$

$$
\begin{array}{c}
\begin{array}{ccccccc}
x & y & t & u & v & w & M
\end{array} \\
\begin{array}{c}
v \\ u \\ x \\ w \\ M
\end{array}
\left[
\begin{array}{ccccccc|c}
0 & -1 & 1 & 0 & 1 & 0 & 0 & 15 \\
0 & 1 & 0 & 1 & 0 & 0 & 0 & 25 \\
1 & 0 & 1 & 0 & 0 & 0 & 0 & 30 \\
0 & ① & -1 & 0 & 0 & 1 & 0 & 15 \\
\hline
0 & -3 & 2 & 0 & 0 & 0 & 1 & -315
\end{array}
\right]
\end{array}
\qquad
\begin{array}{l}
\\[2ex]
\frac{25}{1} = 25 \\[4ex] \\
\frac{15}{1} = 15
\end{array}
$$

$\uparrow$

$$
\begin{array}{c}
\begin{array}{ccccccc}
x & y & t & u & v & w & M
\end{array} \\
\begin{array}{c}
v \\ u \\ x \\ y \\ M
\end{array}
\left[
\begin{array}{ccccccc|c}
0 & 0 & 0 & 0 & 1 & 1 & 0 & 30 \\
0 & 0 & ① & 1 & 0 & -1 & 0 & 10 \\
1 & 0 & 1 & 0 & 0 & 0 & 0 & 30 \\
0 & 1 & -1 & 0 & 0 & 1 & 0 & 15 \\
\hline
0 & 0 & -1 & 0 & 0 & 3 & 1 & -270
\end{array}
\right]
\end{array}
\qquad
\begin{array}{l}
\\[2ex]
\frac{10}{1} = 10 \\
\frac{30}{1} = 30
\end{array}
$$

$\uparrow$

$$
\begin{array}{c}
\begin{array}{ccccccc}
x & y & t & u & v & w & M
\end{array} \\
\begin{array}{c}
v \\ t \\ x \\ y \\ M
\end{array}
\left[
\begin{array}{ccccccc|c}
0 & 0 & 0 & 0 & 1 & 1 & 0 & 30 \\
0 & 0 & 1 & 1 & 0 & -1 & 0 & 10 \\
1 & 0 & 0 & -1 & 0 & 1 & 0 & 20 \\
0 & 1 & 0 & 1 & 0 & 0 & 0 & 25 \\
\hline
0 & 0 & 0 & 1 & 0 & 2 & 1 & -260
\end{array}
\right]
\end{array}
\ .
$$

The last tableau corresponds to a maximum. So $2x + 3y - 375$ has a maximum value -260, and therefore $375 - 2x - 3y$ has a minimum value 260. This value occurs when $x = 20$ and $y = 25$. This is in agreement with our previous graphical solution of the problem. ◆

The calculations used in Example 3 are not that much simpler than those in the original solution. Why, then, should we concern ourselves with the simplex method? For one thing, the simplex method is so mechanical in its execution that it is much easier to program for a computer. For another, our previous method was restricted to problems in two variables. However, suppose that the two warehouses were to deliver their TV sets to three or four or perhaps even 100 stores. Our previous method could not be applied. However, the simplex method, although yielding very large matrices and very tedious calculations, is applicable. Indeed, this is the method many industries use to optimize distribution of their products.

Some Further Comments on the Simplex Method   Our discussion has omitted some of the technical complications arising in the simplex method. A complete discussion of these is beyond the scope of this book. However, let us mention three. First, it is possible that a given linear programming problem has more than one solution. This can occur, for example, if there are ties for the choice of pivot column. For instance, if the bottom of the simplex tableau is

$$\begin{bmatrix} -3 & -7 & 4 & -7 & 1 & 3 \end{bmatrix},$$
$$\qquad\quad\uparrow\qquad\qquad\uparrow$$

then -7 is the most-negative entry and we may choose as pivot column either the second or fourth. In such a circumstance the pivot column may be chosen arbitrarily. Different choices, however, may lead to different solutions of the problem.

A second difficulty is that a given linear programming problem may have no solution at all. In this case the method will break down at some point. For example, among the ratios at a given stage there may be no nonnegative ones to consider. Then we cannot choose a pivot element. Such a breakdown of the method indicates that the associated linear programming problem has no solution.

Finally, whenever there is a tie for the choice of a pivot element, we choose one of the candidates arbitrarily. Occasionally, this may lead to a loop in which the simplex algorithm leads back to a previously encountered tableau. To prevent the loop from recurring, we should then make a different selection from the tied pivot possibilities.

Practice Problems 4.3

1. Convert the following minimum problem into a maximum problem in standard form: Minimize $3x + 4y$ subject to the constraints

$$\begin{cases} x - y \geq 0 \\ 3x - 4y \geq 0 \\ x \geq 0, \quad y \geq 0. \end{cases}$$

2. Suppose that the solution of a minimum problem yields the final simplex tableau

$$\begin{array}{ccccc} x & y & u & v & M \end{array}$$
$$\begin{bmatrix} 1 & 6 & -1 & 0 & 0 & | & 11 \\ 0 & 5 & 3 & 1 & 0 & | & 16 \\ 0 & 2 & 4 & 0 & 1 & | & -40 \end{bmatrix}.$$

What is the minimum value sought in the original problem?

▶ Exercises 4.3

In Exercises 1–6, solve the linear programming problems by the simplex method.

1. Maximize $40x + 30y$ subject to the constraints

$$\begin{cases} x + y \le 5 \\ -2x + 3y \ge 12 \\ x \ge 0, \quad y \ge 0. \end{cases}$$

2. Maximize $3x - y$ subject to the constraints

$$\begin{cases} 2x + 5y \le 100 \\ x \quad\quad \ge 10 \\ \quad\quad y \ge 0. \end{cases}$$

3. Minimize $3x + y$ subject to the constraints

$$\begin{cases} x + y \ge 3 \\ 2x \quad\quad \ge 5 \\ x \ge 0, \quad y \ge 0. \end{cases}$$

4. Minimize $3x + 5y + z$ subject to the constraints

$$\begin{cases} x + y + z \ge 20 \\ y + 2z \ge 10 \\ x \ge 0, \quad y \ge 0, \quad z \ge 0. \end{cases}$$

5. Minimize $13x + 4y$ subject to the constraints

$$\begin{cases} y \ge -2x + 11 \\ y \le -x + 10 \\ y \le -\frac{1}{3}x + 6 \\ y \ge -\frac{1}{4}x + 4 \\ x \ge 0, \quad y \ge 0. \end{cases}$$

6. Minimize $500 - 10x - 3y$ subject to the constraints

$$\begin{cases} x + y \le 20 \\ 3x + 2y \ge 50 \\ x \ge 0, \quad y \ge 0. \end{cases}$$

7. A dietitian is designing a daily diet that is to contain at least 60 units of protein, 40 units of carbohydrates, and 120 units of fat. The diet is to consist of two types of foods. One serving of food A contains 30 units of protein, 10 units of carbohydrates, and 20 units of fat and costs $3. One serving of food B contains 10 units of protein, 10 units of carbohydrates, and 60 units of fat and costs $1.50. Design the diet that provides the daily requirements at the least cost.

8. A manufacturing company has two plants, each capable of producing radios, TV sets, and stereo systems.

The daily production capacities of each plant are as follows:

	Plant I	Plant II
Radios	10	20
TV sets	30	20
Stereo systems	20	10

Plant I costs $1500 per day to operate, whereas plant II costs $1200. How many days should each plant be operated to fill an order for 1000 radios, 1800 TV sets, and 1000 stereo systems at the minimum cost?

9. An appliance store sells three brands of color TV sets, brands A, B, and C. The profit per set is $30 for brand A, $50 for brand B, and $60 for brand C. The total warehouse space allotted to all brands is sufficient for 600 sets, and the inventory is delivered only once per month. At least 100 customers per month will demand brand A, at least 50 will demand brand B, and at least 200 will demand either brand B or brand C. How can the appliance store satisfy all these constraints and earn maximum profit?

10. A citizen decides to campaign for the election of a candidate for city council. Her goal is to generate at least 210 votes by a combination of door-to-door canvassing, letter writing, and phone calls. She figures that each hour of door-to-door canvassing will generate four votes, each hour of letter writing will generate two votes, and each hour on the phone will generate three votes. She would like to devote at least seven hours to phone calls and spend at most half of her time at door-to-door canvassing. How much time should she allocate to each task in order to achieve her goal in the least amount of time?

In Exercises 11 and 12 use a graphing calculator or a computer to solve the linear programming problems by the simplex method.

11. Maximize $x - 2y$ subject to the constraints

$$\begin{cases} 4x + y \le 5 \\ x + 3y \ge 4 \\ x \ge 0, \quad y \ge 0. \end{cases}$$

12. Minimize $30x + 20y$ subject to the constraints

$$\begin{cases} 5x + 10y \ge 3 \\ 3x + 2y \ge 2 \\ x \ge 0, \quad y \ge 0. \end{cases}$$

1. To minimize $3x + 4y$, we maximize $-(3x + 4y) = -3x - 4y$. So the associated maximum problem is as follows: Maximize $-3x - 4y$ subject to the constraints

$$\begin{cases} -x + y \le 0 \\ -3x + 4y \le 0 \\ x \ge 0, \quad y \ge 0. \end{cases}$$

2. The value -40 in the lower right corner gives the solution of the associated *maximum* problem. The minimum value originally sought is the negative of the maximum value—that is, $-(-40) = 40$.

4.4 Marginal Analysis and Matrix Formulations of Linear Programming Problems

Marginal Analysis of Linear Programming Problems   The simplex method not only provides the optimal solutions to linear programming problems but also gives other useful information. As a matter of fact, each number appearing in the final simplex tableau has an interpretation that not only sheds light on the current situation but also can be used to analyze the benefits of small changes in the available resources.

Consider the final simplex tableau of the furniture manufacturing problem. Since the variable u was introduced to take up the slack in the carpentry inequality, the u column has been labeled *Carpentry*. Similarly, the v column and the w column have been labeled *Finishing* and *Upholstery*, respectively:

	x	y	($Carpentry$) u	($Finishing$) v	($Upholstery$) w	M	
x	1	0	$\frac{1}{3}$	-1	0	0	14
y	0	1	$-\frac{1}{3}$	2	0	0	4
w	0	0	$\frac{4}{3}$	-10	1	0	20
M	0	0	$\frac{10}{3}$	60	0	1	1400

The optimum profit is 1400, which occurs when $x = 14$ chairs and $y = 4$ sofas.

We now consider the following question. If additional labor becomes available, how will this change the production level and the profit? To be specific, suppose that we had 3 more labor-hours available for carpentry. The initial tableau of the furniture manufacturing problem would become

	x	y	($Carpentry$) u	($Finishing$) v	($Upholstery$) w	M	
u	6	3	1	0	0	0	$96 + 3$
v	1	1	0	1	0	0	$18 + 0$
w	2	6	0	0	1	0	$72 + 0$
M	-80	-70	0	0	0	1	$0 + 0$

Note that only the first entry of the right-hand column has been changed. The increment to the right-hand column can be written as the column

$$
\begin{array}{c}
3 \\
0 \\
0 \\
\hline
0,
\end{array}
$$

which is three times the u column and is referred to as the *increment column*. Now, when the simplex method is performed on the new initial tableau, all of the row operations will affect the increment column exactly as they affected the u column in the original initial tableau. Therefore, the final increment column will be three times the final u column. Hence, the new final tableau will be

			(Carpentry)	(Finishing)	(Upholstery)			
	x	y	u	v	w	M		
x	1	0	$\frac{1}{3}$	-1	0	0	$14 + 3\left(\frac{1}{3}\right)$
y	0	1	$-\frac{1}{3}$	2	0	0	$4 + 3\left(-\frac{1}{3}\right)$
w	0	0	$\frac{4}{3}$	-10	1	0	$20 + 3\left(\frac{4}{3}\right)$
M	0	0	$\frac{10}{3}$	60	0	1	$1400 + 3\left(\frac{10}{3}\right)$

Thus, when 3 additional labor-hours of carpentry are available,

$$
x = 14 + 3\left(\tfrac{1}{3}\right) = 15 \text{ chairs} \quad \text{and} \quad y = 4 + 3\left(-\tfrac{1}{3}\right) = 3 \text{ sofas}
$$

should be produced. The maximum profit will increase to the new value of

$$
M = 1400 + 3\left(\tfrac{10}{3}\right) = 1410 \text{ dollars.}
$$

The number 3 was arbitrary. If h is a suitable number, then adding h labor-hours of labor for carpentry to the original problem results in the final tableau:

			(Carpentry)	(Finishing)	(Upholstery)			
	x	y	u	v	w	M		
x	1	0	$\frac{1}{3}$	-1	0	0	$14 + h\left(\frac{1}{3}\right)$
y	0	1	$-\frac{1}{3}$	2	0	0	$4 + h\left(-\frac{1}{3}\right)$
w	0	0	$\frac{4}{3}$	-10	1	0	$20 + h\left(\frac{4}{3}\right)$
M	0	0	$\frac{10}{3}$	60	0	1	$1400 + h\left(\frac{10}{3}\right)$

The number h can be positive or negative. For instance, if three fewer labor-hours are available for carpentry, then setting $h = -3$ yields the optimal production schedule $x = 13$, $y = 5$ and a profit of \$1390. The only restriction on h is that the numbers in the upper part of the right-hand column of the final tableau must all be nonnegative.

Similarly, if in the original problem, the amount of labor available for finishing is increased by h labor-hours, the initial tableau becomes

		($Carpentry$)	($Finishing$)	($Upholstery$)			
	x	y	u	v	w	M	
u	6	3	1	0	0	0	$96 + 0$
v	1	1	0	1	0	0	$18 + h$
w	2	6	0	0	1	0	$72 + 0$
M	-80	-70	0	0	0	1	$0 + 0$

The right-hand column of the original tableau was changed by adding an increment column that is h times the v column, and therefore the right-hand column of the new final tableau will be the original final right-hand column plus h times the final v column:

		($Carpentry$)	($Finishing$)	($Upholstery$)			
	x	y	u	v	w	M	
x	1	0	$\frac{1}{3}$	-1	0	0	$14 + h(-1)$
y	0	1	$-\frac{1}{3}$	2	0	0	$4 + h(2)$
w	0	0	$\frac{4}{3}$	-10	1	0	$20 + h(-10)$
M	0	0	$\frac{10}{3}$	60	0	1	$1400 + h(60)$

Hence, if one additional labor-hour were available for finishing, the optimal production schedule would be $x = 13$ chairs, $y = 6$ sofas, and the profit would be $1460.

Finally, if in the original problem, the amount of labor available for upholstery is increased by h labor-hours, the initial and final tableaux become

		($Carpentry$)	($Finishing$)	($Upholstery$)			
	x	y	u	v	w	M	
u	6	3	1	0	0	0	$96 + 0$
v	1	1	0	1	0	0	$18 + 0$
w	2	6	0	0	1	0	$72 + h$
M	-80	-70	0	0	0	1	$0 + 0$

		($Carpentry$)	($Finishing$)	($Upholstery$)			
	x	y	u	v	w	M	
x	1	0	$\frac{1}{3}$	-1	0	0	$14 + h(0)$
y	0	1	$-\frac{1}{3}$	2	0	0	$4 + h(0)$
w	0	0	$\frac{4}{3}$	-10	1	0	$20 + h(1)$
M	0	0	$\frac{10}{3}$	60	0	1	$1400 + h(0)$

Therefore, a change in the amount of labor available for upholstery has no effect on the production schedule or the profit. This makes sense, since we had excess labor available for upholstery in the solution to the original problem. The slack in carpentry and finishing was used up (u and v were 0), but there was slack in the labor available for upholstery (w was 20).

In summary, each of the slack variable columns in the final tableau of the original furniture manufacturing problem gives the sensitivity to change in the production schedule and in the profit due to a suitable change in one of the factors of production. The final values in each of these columns ($u = \frac{10}{3}$, $v = 60$, and $w = 0$) are called the *marginal* values of the three factors of production—carpentry, finishing, and upholstery.

The following example shows a complete analysis of a new linear programming problem.

▸ Example 1   The Cutting Edge Knife Company manufactures paring knives and pocket knives. Each paring knife requires 3 labor-hours, 7 units of steel, and 4 units of wood. Each pocket knife requires 6 labor-hours, 5 units of steel, and 3 units of wood. The profit on each paring knife is $3, and the profit on each pocket knife is $5. Each day the company has available 90 labor-hours, 138 units of steel, and 120 units of wood.

(a) How many of each type of knife should the Cutting Edge Knife Company manufacture daily to maximize its profits?

(b) Suppose that an additional 18 units of steel were available each day. What effect would this have on the optimal solution?

(c) Generalize the result in part (b) to the case where the increase in the number of units of steel available each day is h. (The value of h can be positive or negative.) For what range of values will the result be valid?

Solution   We need to find the number of paring knives, x, and pocket knives, y, that will maximize the profit, $M = 3x + 5y$, subject to the constraints

$$\begin{cases} 3x + 6y \leq 90 \\ 7x + 5y \leq 138 \\ 4x + 3y \leq 120 \\ x \geq 0, \quad y \geq 0. \end{cases}$$

The initial tableau with slack variables u, v, and w added for labor, steel, and wood, respectively, is

			(*Labor*)	(*Steel*)	(*Wood*)			
	x	y	u	v	w	M		
u	3	⑥	1	0	0	0	90	$\frac{90}{6} = 15$
v	7	5	0	1	0	0	138	$\frac{138}{5} = 27.6$
w	4	3	0	0	1	0	120	$\frac{120}{3} = 40.$
M	-3	-5	0	0	0	1	0	

↑

The proper pivot element is the entry 6 in the y column. The next tableau is

		x	y	(Labor) u	(Steel) v	(Wood) w	M		
y		$\frac{1}{2}$	1	$\frac{1}{6}$	0	0	0	15	$15/\frac{1}{2} = 30$
v		$\boxed{\frac{9}{2}}$	0	$-\frac{5}{6}$	1	0	0	63	$63/\frac{9}{2} = 14$
w		$\frac{5}{2}$	0	$-\frac{1}{2}$	0	1	0	75	$75/\frac{5}{2} = 30.$
M		$-\frac{1}{2}$	0	$\frac{5}{6}$	0	0	1	75	

$\uparrow$

The proper pivot element is the entry $\frac{9}{2}$ in the x column. The next tableau is

		x	y	(Labor) u	(Steel) v	(Wood) w	M	
y		0	1	$\frac{7}{27}$	$-\frac{1}{9}$	0	0	8
x		1	0	$-\frac{5}{27}$	$\frac{2}{9}$	0	0	14
w		0	0	$-\frac{1}{27}$	$-\frac{5}{9}$	1	0	40
M		0	0	$\frac{20}{27}$	$\frac{1}{9}$	0	1	82

Since there are no negative entries in the last row of this tableau, the simplex method is complete.

(a) The Cutting Edge Knife Company should produce 14 paring knives and 8 pocket knives each day for a profit of $82. (Since the slack variable w has the value 40, there will be 40 excess units of wood each day.)

(b) Since 18 additional units of steel are available, the final tableau of the revised problem can be obtained from the final tableau of the original problem by adding 18 times the v column to the right-hand column:

		x	y	(Labor) u	(Steel) v	(Wood) w	M	
y		0	1	$\frac{7}{27}$	$-\frac{1}{9}$	0	0	$8 + 18\left(-\frac{1}{9}\right)$
x		1	0	$-\frac{5}{27}$	$\frac{2}{9}$	0	0	$14 + 18\left(\frac{2}{9}\right)$
w		0	0	$-\frac{1}{27}$	$-\frac{5}{9}$	1	0	$40 + 18\left(-\frac{5}{9}\right)$
M		0	0	$\frac{20}{27}$	$\frac{1}{9}$	0	1	$82 + 18\left(\frac{1}{9}\right)$

The company should make 4 more paring knives $[18\left(\frac{2}{9}\right) = 4]$ and 2 fewer pocket knives $[18\left(-\frac{1}{9}\right) = -2]$. Doing so will increase the profits by $2 $[18\left(\frac{1}{9}\right) = 2]$.

(c) With h additional units of steel available, the right-hand column of the final tableau will be similar to the preceding tableau but with 18 replaced by h:

$$
\begin{array}{c}
 \\
y \\
x \\
w \\
M
\end{array}
\begin{array}{c}
\begin{array}{cccccc}
x & y & \overset{(Labor)}{u} & \overset{(Steel)}{v} & \overset{(Wood)}{w} & M
\end{array} \\
\left[
\begin{array}{cccccc|c}
0 & 1 & \frac{7}{27} & -\frac{1}{9} & 0 & 0 & 8 + h\!\left(-\frac{1}{9}\right) \\
1 & 0 & -\frac{5}{27} & \frac{2}{9} & 0 & 0 & 14 + h\!\left(\frac{2}{9}\right) \\
0 & 0 & -\frac{1}{27} & -\frac{5}{9} & 1 & 0 & 40 + h\!\left(-\frac{5}{9}\right) \\
\hline
0 & 0 & \frac{20}{27} & \frac{1}{9} & 0 & 1 & 82 + h\!\left(\frac{1}{9}\right)
\end{array}
\right].
\end{array}
$$

Therefore, the number of paring knives made should be $14 + h\!\left(\frac{2}{9}\right)$, and the number of pocket knives made should be $8 + h\!\left(-\frac{1}{9}\right)$. The new profit will be $82 + h\!\left(\frac{1}{9}\right)$ dollars. This analysis is valid provided that each of the entries in the upper part of the right-hand column of the tableau is nonnegative. The restrictions on h given by each of these entries are as follows:

Entry	Restriction
$8 + h\!\left(-\frac{1}{9}\right)$	$h \le 72$
$14 + h\!\left(\frac{2}{9}\right)$	$h \ge -63$
$40 + h\!\left(-\frac{5}{9}\right)$	$h \le 72$

All of these restrictions will be satisfied if h is between -63 and 72. ◆

Matrix Formulations of Linear Programming Problems Linear programming problems can be neatly stated in terms of matrices. Such formulations provide a convenient way to define the *dual* of a linear programming problem, an important concept that is studied in Section 4.5. To introduce the matrix formulation of a linear programming problem, we first need the concept of inequality for matrices.

Let A and B be two matrices of the same size. We say that A is less than or equal to B (denoted $A \le B$) if each entry of A is less than or equal to the corresponding entry of B. For instance, we have the following matrix inequalities:

$$
\begin{bmatrix} 2 & -3 \\ \frac{1}{2} & 0 \end{bmatrix} \le \begin{bmatrix} 5 & -1 \\ 1 & 0 \end{bmatrix} \quad \text{and} \quad \begin{bmatrix} 5 \\ 6 \end{bmatrix} \le \begin{bmatrix} 8 \\ 9 \end{bmatrix}.
$$

The symbol $\ge$ has an analogous meaning for matrices.

▶ **Example 2** Let

$$
A = \begin{bmatrix} 6 & 3 \\ 1 & 1 \\ 2 & 6 \end{bmatrix}, \qquad B = \begin{bmatrix} 96 \\ 18 \\ 72 \end{bmatrix}, \qquad C = \begin{bmatrix} 80 & 70 \end{bmatrix}, \qquad X = \begin{bmatrix} x \\ y \end{bmatrix}.
$$

Carry out the indicated matrix multiplications in the following statement: Maximize CX subject to the constraints $AX \le B$, $X \ge \mathbf{0}$. (Here $\mathbf{0}$ is the zero matrix.)

Solution $CX = \begin{bmatrix} 80 & 70 \end{bmatrix} \begin{bmatrix} x \\ y \end{bmatrix} = \begin{bmatrix} 80x + 70y \end{bmatrix}$

$$
AX = \begin{bmatrix} 6 & 3 \\ 1 & 1 \\ 2 & 6 \end{bmatrix} \begin{bmatrix} x \\ y \end{bmatrix} = \begin{bmatrix} 6x + 3y \\ x + y \\ 2x + 6y \end{bmatrix}
$$

$$AX \leq B \text{ means } \begin{bmatrix} 6x + 3y \\ x + y \\ 2x + 6y \end{bmatrix} \leq \begin{bmatrix} 96 \\ 18 \\ 72 \end{bmatrix} \quad \text{or} \quad \begin{cases} 6x + 3y \leq 96 \\ x + y \leq 18 \\ 2x + 6y \leq 72. \end{cases}$$

$$X \geq \mathbf{0} \text{ means } \begin{bmatrix} x \\ y \end{bmatrix} \geq \begin{bmatrix} 0 \\ 0 \end{bmatrix} \quad \text{or} \quad \begin{cases} x \geq 0 \\ y \geq 0. \end{cases}$$

Hence, the statement "Maximize CX subject to the constraints $AX \leq B$, $X \geq \mathbf{0}$" is a matrix formulation of the furniture manufacturing problem. ◆

Another concept that is needed for the definition of the dual of a linear programming problem is the *transpose of a matrix*. If A is an $m \times n$ matrix, then the matrix A^T (read "A transpose") is the $n \times m$ matrix whose ijth entry is the jith entry of A. The rows of A^T are the columns of A, and vice versa.

▶ **Example 3**   Find the transpose of

(a) $\begin{bmatrix} 3 & -2 & 4 \\ 6 & 5 & 0 \end{bmatrix}$

(b) $\begin{bmatrix} 5 \\ 2 \\ 1 \end{bmatrix}$

Solution   (a) Since the given matrix has two rows and three columns, its transpose will have three rows and two columns. The entries of the first row of the transpose will be the entries in the first column of the original matrix:

$$\begin{bmatrix} 3 & 6 \\ & \\ & \end{bmatrix}.$$

The entries of the second and third rows are obtained in a similar manner from the second and third columns of the original matrix. Therefore,

$$\begin{bmatrix} 3 & -2 & 4 \\ 6 & 5 & 0 \end{bmatrix}^T = \begin{bmatrix} 3 & 6 \\ -2 & 5 \\ 4 & 0 \end{bmatrix}.$$

(b) Since the given matrix has three rows and one column, its transpose has one row and three columns. That row consists of the single column of the original matrix:

$$\begin{bmatrix} 5 \\ 2 \\ 1 \end{bmatrix}^T = \begin{bmatrix} 5 & 2 & 1 \end{bmatrix}.$$ ◆

Practice Problems 4.4

Consider the furniture manufacturing problem, whose final simplex tableau appears in Section 4.2.

1. Suppose that the number of labor-hours for finishing that are available each day is decreased by 2. What will be the effect on the optimal number of chairs and sofas produced and on the profit?

2. For what range of values of h will a marginal analysis on the effect of a change of h labor-hours for finishing be valid?

▶ **Exercises 4.4**

Exercises 1 and 2 refer to the Cutting Edge Knife Company problem of Example 1.

1. Suppose that the number of labor-hours that are available each day is increased by 54. What will be the effect on the optimal number of knives produced and on the profit?

2. For what range of values of h will a marginal analysis on the effect of a change of h labor-hours be valid?

Exercises 3 and 4 refer to the transportation problem of Example 3 in Section 4.3.

3. Suppose that the number of TV sets stocked in the College Park warehouse is increased to 50. What will be the effect on the optimal numbers of TV sets shipped from each warehouse to each store and what will be the change in the cost?

4. For what range of values of h will a marginal analysis on the effect of a change of h in the number of TV sets stocked in the College Park store be valid?

5. In the furniture manufacturing problem, for what range of values of h will a marginal analysis on the effect of a change of h labor-hours for carpentry be valid?

6. Consider the nutrition problem in Example 1 of Section 3.2. Solve the problem by the simplex method and then determine the optimal quantities of soybeans and rice in the diet, and the new cost, if the daily requirement for calories is increased to 1700. For what range of values of h will a marginal analysis on the effects of a change of h calories be valid?

In Exercises 7–10, find the transpose of the given matrix.

7. $\begin{bmatrix} 9 & 4 \\ 1 & 8 \\ 1 & -3 \end{bmatrix}$ 8. $\begin{bmatrix} 4 \\ 0 \\ 6 \end{bmatrix}$

9. $\begin{bmatrix} 7 & 6 & 5 & 1 \end{bmatrix}$ 10. $\begin{bmatrix} 5 & 2 \\ 3 & -1 \end{bmatrix}$

11. Is it true that the transpose of the transpose of a matrix is the original matrix?

12. Find an example of a matrix that is its own transpose.

In Exercises 13 and 14, give the matrix formulation of the linear programming problem.

13. Minimize $7x + 5y + 4z$ subject to

$$\begin{cases} 3x + 8y + 9z \geq 75 \\ x + 2y + 5z \geq 80 \\ 4x + y + 7z \geq 67 \\ x \geq 0, \quad y \geq 0, \quad z \geq 0. \end{cases}$$

14. Maximize $20x + 30y$ subject to

$$\begin{cases} 7x + 8y \leq 55 \\ x + 2y \leq 78 \\ x \quad\quad \leq 25 \\ x \geq 0, \quad y \geq 0. \end{cases}$$

15. Give a matrix formulation of the Cutting Edge Knife Company problem of Example 1.

16. Does every linear programming problem have a matrix formulation? If not, under what conditions will a linear programming problem have a matrix formulation?

In Exercises 17 and 18, let

$$C = \begin{bmatrix} 2 & 3 \end{bmatrix}, \quad X = \begin{bmatrix} x \\ y \end{bmatrix}, \quad A = \begin{bmatrix} 7 & 4 \\ 5 & 8 \\ 1 & 3 \end{bmatrix},$$

$$B = \begin{bmatrix} 33 \\ 44 \\ 55 \end{bmatrix}, \quad \text{and} \quad U = \begin{bmatrix} u \\ v \\ w \end{bmatrix}.$$

17. Give the linear programming problem whose matrix formulation is "Minimize CX subject to the constraints $AX \geq B$, $X \geq \mathbf{0}$."

18. Give the linear programming problem whose matrix formulation is "Maximize $B^T U$ subject to the constraints $A^T U \leq C^T$, $U \geq \mathbf{0}$."

Solutions to Practice Problems 4.4	

1. Since the finishing column in the original final tableau is

$$\begin{array}{c} -1 \\ 2 \\ -10 \\ \hline 60, \end{array}$$

the right-hand column in the new tableau is

$$14 + (-2)(-1)$$
$$4 + (-2)(2)$$
$$20 + (-2)(-10)$$
$$\overline{1400 + (-2)(60)}.$$

Therefore, the new values of x, y, and M are 16, 0, and 1280.

2. Using h instead of -2 in the marginal analysis, we find that the right-hand column of the new final tableau is

$$14 + h(-1)$$
$$4 + h(2)$$
$$20 + h(-10)$$
$$\overline{1400 + h(60)}.$$

Of course, this analysis is valid only if the three numbers above the line are not negative. That is, $14 + h(-1) \geq 0$, $4 + h(2) \geq 0$, and $20 + h(-10) \geq 0$. These three inequalities can be simplified to $h \leq 14$, $h \geq -2$, and $h \leq 2$. Therefore, in order to satisfy all three inequalities, h must be in the range $-2 \leq h \leq 2$.

4.5 Duality

Each linear programming problem may be converted into a related linear programming problem called its *dual*. The dual problem is sometimes easier to solve than the original problem and, moreover, it has the same optimum value. Furthermore, the solution of the dual problem often can provide valuable insights into the original problem. To understand the relationship between a linear programming problem and its dual, it is best to begin with a concrete example.

Problem A   Maximize the objective function $6x + 5y$ subject to the constraints

$$\begin{cases} 4x + 8y \leq 32 \\ 3x + 2y \leq 12 \\ x \geq 0, \quad y \geq 0. \end{cases}$$

The dual of Problem A is the following problem.

Problem B   Minimize the objective function $32u + 12v$ subject to the constraints

$$\begin{cases} 4u + 3v \geq 6 \\ 8u + 2v \geq 5 \\ u \geq 0, \quad v \geq 0. \end{cases}$$

The relationship between the two problems is easiest to see if we write them in their matrix formulations. Problem A is

$$\text{Maximize } \begin{bmatrix} 6 & 5 \end{bmatrix} \begin{bmatrix} x \\ y \end{bmatrix} \text{ subject to the constraints}$$

$$\begin{bmatrix} 4 & 8 \\ 3 & 2 \end{bmatrix} \begin{bmatrix} x \\ y \end{bmatrix} \leq \begin{bmatrix} 32 \\ 12 \end{bmatrix} \quad \text{and} \quad \begin{bmatrix} x \\ y \end{bmatrix} \geq \begin{bmatrix} 0 \\ 0 \end{bmatrix}.$$

Problem B is

$$\text{Minimize } \begin{bmatrix} 32 & 12 \end{bmatrix} \begin{bmatrix} u \\ v \end{bmatrix} \text{ subject to the constraints}$$

$$\begin{bmatrix} 4 & 3 \\ 8 & 2 \end{bmatrix} \begin{bmatrix} u \\ v \end{bmatrix} \geq \begin{bmatrix} 6 \\ 5 \end{bmatrix} \quad \text{and} \quad \begin{bmatrix} u \\ v \end{bmatrix} \geq \begin{bmatrix} 0 \\ 0 \end{bmatrix}.$$

Each of the numeric matrices in Problem B is the transpose of one of the matrices in Problem A. Let

$$C = \begin{bmatrix} 6 & 5 \end{bmatrix}, \quad X = \begin{bmatrix} x \\ y \end{bmatrix}, \quad A = \begin{bmatrix} 4 & 8 \\ 3 & 2 \end{bmatrix}, \quad B = \begin{bmatrix} 32 \\ 12 \end{bmatrix}, \quad U = \begin{bmatrix} u \\ v \end{bmatrix}, \quad \mathbf{0} = \begin{bmatrix} 0 \\ 0 \end{bmatrix}.$$

Problem A is

"Maximize CX subject to the constraints $AX \leq B$, $X \geq \mathbf{0}$."

Problem B is

"Minimize $B^T U$ subject to the constraints $A^T U \geq C^T$, $U \geq \mathbf{0}$."

Problem A is referred to as the *primal* problem and Problem B as its *dual*.

The Dual of a Linear Programming Problem

1. If the original (primal) problem has the form

Maximize CX subject to the constraints $AX \leq B$, $X \geq \mathbf{0}$,

then the dual problem is

Minimize $B^T U$ subject to the constraints $A^T U \geq C^T$, $U \geq \mathbf{0}$.

2. If the original (primal) problem has the form

Minimize CX subject to the constraints $AX \geq B$, $X \geq \mathbf{0}$,

then the dual problem is

Maximize $B^T U$ subject to the constraints $A^T U \leq C^T$, $U \geq \mathbf{0}$.

Note that Problem A is a standard maximization problem. That is, all of the inequalities involve $\leq$, except for $x \geq 0$ and $y \geq 0$. Problem B is a standard minimization problem in that all of its inequalities are $\geq$. The coefficients of the objective function for Problem A are the numbers on the right-hand side of the inequalities of Problem B, and vice versa. The coefficient matrices for the left-hand sides of the inequalities are transposes of one another. In an analogous way, we can start with a standard minimization problem and define its dual to be a standard maximization problem. Any linear programming problem can be put into one of these two standard forms. (If an inequality points in the wrong direction, we need only multiply it by -1.) Therefore, every linear programming problem has a dual.

▶ Example 1   Determine the dual of the following linear programming problem. Minimize $18x + 20y + 2z$ subject to the constraints

$$\begin{cases} 3x - 5y - 2z \leq 4 \\ 6x \quad\quad - 8z \geq 9 \\ x \geq 0, \quad y \geq 0, \quad z \geq 0. \end{cases}$$

Solution   We first put the problem into standard form. Since the primal problem is a minimization problem, we must write all constraints with the inequality sign $\geq$. To put the first inequality in this form, we multiply by -1 to obtain

$$-3x + 5y + 2z \geq -4.$$

We now write the problem in matrix form:

Minimize $\begin{bmatrix} 18 & 20 & 2 \end{bmatrix} \begin{bmatrix} x \\ y \\ z \end{bmatrix}$ subject to the constraints

$$\begin{bmatrix} -3 & 5 & 2 \\ 6 & 0 & -8 \end{bmatrix} \begin{bmatrix} x \\ y \\ z \end{bmatrix} \geq \begin{bmatrix} -4 \\ 9 \end{bmatrix} \quad \text{and} \quad \begin{bmatrix} x \\ y \\ z \end{bmatrix} \geq \begin{bmatrix} 0 \\ 0 \\ 0 \end{bmatrix}.$$

The dual is

Maximize $\begin{bmatrix} -4 & 9 \end{bmatrix} \begin{bmatrix} u \\ v \end{bmatrix}$ subject to the constraints

$$\begin{bmatrix} -3 & 6 \\ 5 & 0 \\ 2 & -8 \end{bmatrix} \begin{bmatrix} u \\ v \end{bmatrix} \leq \begin{bmatrix} 18 \\ 20 \\ 2 \end{bmatrix} \quad \text{and} \quad \begin{bmatrix} u \\ v \end{bmatrix} \geq \begin{bmatrix} 0 \\ 0 \end{bmatrix}.$$

Multiplying the matrices, we obtain the following:
Maximize $-4u + 9v$ subject to

$$\begin{cases} -3u + 6v \leq 18 \\ 5u \qquad \leq 20 \\ 2u - 8v \leq 2 \\ u \geq 0, \quad v \geq 0. \end{cases}$$
◆

Let us now return to Problems A and B to examine the connection between the solutions of a linear programming problem and its dual problem. Problems A and B both involve two variables and hence can be solved by the geometric method of Chapter 3. Figure 1 shows their respective feasible sets and the vertices that yield the optimum values of the objective functions. The feasible sets do not look alike, and the optimal vertices are different. However, both problems have the same optimum value, 27. The relationship between the two problems is

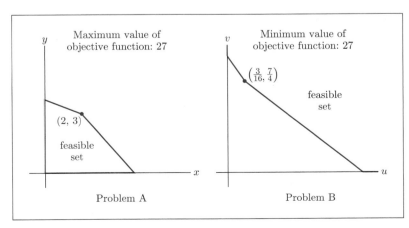

Figure 1.

brought into even sharper focus by looking at the final tableaux that arise when the two problems are solved by the simplex method. (*Note:* In Problem B, the original variables are u and v and the slack variables have been named x and y.)

FINAL TABLEAUX

Problem A

$$\begin{array}{c} \\ y \\ x \\ M \end{array} \begin{array}{c} \begin{array}{ccccc} x & y & u & v & M \end{array} \\ \left[\begin{array}{ccccc|c} 0 & 1 & \frac{3}{16} & -\frac{1}{4} & 0 & 3 \\ 1 & 0 & -\frac{1}{8} & \frac{1}{2} & 0 & 2 \\ \hline 0 & 0 & \frac{3}{16} & \frac{7}{4} & 1 & 27 \end{array} \right] \end{array}$$

Problem B

$$\begin{array}{c} \\ v \\ u \\ M \end{array} \begin{array}{c} \begin{array}{ccccc} u & v & x & y & M \end{array} \\ \left[\begin{array}{ccccc|c} 0 & 1 & -\frac{1}{2} & \frac{1}{4} & 0 & \frac{7}{4} \\ 1 & 0 & \frac{1}{8} & -\frac{3}{16} & 0 & \frac{3}{16} \\ \hline 0 & 0 & 2 & 3 & 1 & -27 \end{array} \right] \end{array}$$

The final tableau for Problem A contains the solution to Problem B ($u = \frac{3}{16}$, $v = \frac{7}{4}$) in the final entries of the u and v columns. Similarly, the final tableau for Problem B gives the solution to Problem A ($x = 2$, $y = 3$) in the final entries of its x and y columns. This situation always occurs. The solutions to a linear programming problem and its dual problem may be obtained simultaneously by solving just one of the problems using the simplex method and applying the following theorem.

Fundamental Theorem of Duality

1. If either the primal problem or the dual problem has an optimal solution, then they both have an optimal solution and their objective functions have the same values at these optimal points.

2. If both the primal and the dual problems have a feasible solution, then they both have optimal solutions and their objective functions have the same value at these optimal points.

3. The solution of one of these problems by the simplex method yields the solution of the other problem as the final entries in the columns associated with the slack variables.

▶ Example 2 Solve the linear programming problem of Example 1 by applying the simplex method to its dual problem.

Solution In the solution to Example 1, the dual problem is as follows: Maximize $-4u + 9v$ subject to the constraints

$$\begin{cases} -3u + 6v \le 18 \\ 5u \qquad\ \le 20 \\ 2u - 8v \le\ 2 \\ u \ge 0, \quad v \ge 0. \end{cases}$$

Since there are three nontrivial inequalities, the simplex method calls for three slack variables. Denote the slack variables by x, y, and z. Let $M = -4u + 9v$, and apply the simplex method.

$$
\begin{array}{c}
\begin{array}{ccccccc} & u & v & x & y & z & M \end{array} \\
\begin{array}{c} x \\ y \\ z \\ M \end{array}
\left[\begin{array}{cccccc|c}
-3 & ⑥ & 1 & 0 & 0 & 0 & 18 \\
5 & 0 & 0 & 1 & 0 & 0 & 20 \\
2 & -8 & 0 & 0 & 1 & 0 & 2 \\
\hline
4 & -9 & 0 & 0 & 0 & 1 & 0
\end{array}\right]
\end{array}
$$

$$
\begin{array}{c}
\begin{array}{ccccccc} & u & v & x & y & z & M \end{array} \\
\begin{array}{c} v \\ y \\ z \\ M \end{array}
\left[\begin{array}{cccccc|c}
-\frac{1}{2} & 1 & \frac{1}{6} & 0 & 0 & 0 & 3 \\
⑤ & 0 & 0 & 1 & 0 & 0 & 20 \\
-2 & 0 & \frac{4}{3} & 0 & 1 & 0 & 26 \\
\hline
-\frac{1}{2} & 0 & \frac{3}{2} & 0 & 0 & 1 & 27
\end{array}\right]
\end{array}
$$

$$
\begin{array}{c}
\begin{array}{ccccccc} & u & v & x & y & z & M \end{array} \\
\begin{array}{c} v \\ u \\ z \\ M \end{array}
\left[\begin{array}{cccccc|c}
0 & 1 & \frac{1}{6} & \frac{1}{10} & 0 & 0 & 5 \\
1 & 0 & 0 & \frac{1}{5} & 0 & 0 & 4 \\
0 & 0 & \frac{4}{3} & \frac{2}{5} & 1 & 0 & 34 \\
\hline
0 & 0 & \frac{3}{2} & \frac{1}{10} & 0 & 1 & 29
\end{array}\right]
\end{array}
$$

Since the maximum value of the dual problem is 29, we know that the minimum value of the original problem is also 29. Looking at the last row of the final tableau, we conclude that this minimum value is assumed when $x = \frac{3}{2}$, $y = \frac{1}{10}$, and $z = 0$. ◆

In Example 2 the dual problem was easier to solve than the original problem given in Example 1. Thus, we see how consideration of the dual problem may simplify the solution of linear programming problems in some cases.

An Economic Interpretation of the Dual Problem To illustrate the interpretation of the dual problem, let's reconsider the furniture manufacturing problem. Recall that this problem asked us to maximize the profit from the sale of x chairs and y sofas subject to limitations on the amount of labor available for carpentry, finishing, and upholstery. In mathematical terms, the problem required us to maximize $80x + 70y$ subject to the constraints

$$
\begin{cases}
6x + 3y \le 96 \\
x + y \le 18 \\
2x + 6y \le 72 \\
x \ge 0, \quad y \ge 0.
\end{cases}
$$

Its dual problem is to minimize $96u + 18v + 72w$ subject to the constraints

$$
\begin{cases}
6u + v + 2w \ge 80 \\
3u + v + 6w \ge 70 \\
u \ge 0, \quad v \ge 0, \quad w \ge 0.
\end{cases}
$$

The variables u, v, and w can be assigned a meaning so that the dual problem has a significant interpretation in terms of the original problem.

First, recall the following table of data (labor-hours except as noted):

	Chair	Sofa	Available labor-hours
Carpentry	6	3	96
Finishing	1	1	18
Upholstery	2	6	72
Profit	$80	$70	

Suppose that we have an opportunity to hire out all our workers. Suppose that hiring out carpenters will yield a profit of u dollars per hour, the finishers v dollars per hour, and the upholsterers w dollars per hour. Of course, u, v, and w all must be ≥ 0. However, there are other constraints that we should reasonably impose. Any scheme for hiring out the workers should generate at least as much profit as is currently being generated in the construction of chairs and sofas. In terms of the potential profits from hiring the workers out, the labor involved in constructing a chair will generate

$$6u + v + 2w$$

dollars of profit. And this amount should be at least equal to the $80 profit that could be earned by using the labor to construct a chair. That is, we have the constraint

$$6u + v + 2w \geq 80.$$

Similarly, considering the labor involved in building a sofa, we derive the constraint

$$3u + v + 6w \geq 70.$$

Since there are available 96 hours of carpentry, 18 hours of finishing, and 72 hours of upholstery, the total profit from hiring out the workers would be

$$96u + 18v + 72w.$$

Thus, the problem of determining the least acceptable profit from hiring out the workers is equivalent to the following: Minimize $96u + 18v + 72w$ subject to the constraints

$$\begin{cases} 6u + v + 2w \geq 80 \\ 3u + v + 6w \geq 70 \\ u \geq 0, \quad v \geq 0, \quad w \geq 0. \end{cases}$$

This is just the dual of the furniture manufacturing problem. The values u, v, and w are measures of the value of an hour's labor by each type of worker. Economists often refer to them as *shadow prices*. The fundamental theorem of duality asserts that the minimum acceptable profit that can be achieved by hiring the workers out is equal to the maximum profit that can be generated if they make furniture.

As we saw in the furniture manufacturing problem, the maximum profit, $M = 1400$, is achieved when

$$x = 14, \qquad y = 4, \qquad u = 0, \qquad v = 0, \qquad w = 20.$$

For the dual problem, we can read from the final tableau of the primal problem that the minimum acceptable profit, $M = 1400$, is achieved when

$$u = \tfrac{10}{3}, \qquad v = 60, \qquad w = 0, \qquad x = 0, \qquad y = 0.$$

The solution of the primal problem gives the activity level that meets the constraints imposed by the resources and provides the maximum profit. Such a model is called an *allocation problem*. On the other hand, the solution of the dual problem assigns values to each of the resources of production. The solution of the dual problem might be used by an insurance salesperson or by an accountant to impute a value to each resource. It is referred to as a *valuation problem*.

We summarize the situation briefly as follows:

If the original problem is a maximization problem,

$$\text{Maximize } CX \text{ subject to } AX \leq B \text{ and } X \geq \mathbf{0},$$

then we interpret the solution matrix X as the *activity matrix* in which each entry gives the optimal level of each activity. The matrix B is the *capacity* or *resources matrix*, where each entry represents the available amount of a (scarce) resource. The matrix C is the *profit matrix* whose entries are the unit profits for each activity represented in X. The dual solution matrix U is the *imputed value matrix*, which gives the imputed value of each of the resources in the production process.

If the original problem is a minimization problem,

$$\text{Minimize } CX \text{ subject to } AX \geq B \text{ and } X \geq \mathbf{0},$$

then we interpret X as the *activity matrix* in which each entry gives the optimal level of an activity. B is the *requirements matrix* in which each entry is a minimum required level of production for some commodity. C is the *cost matrix*, where each entry is the unit cost of the corresponding activity in X. The dual solution matrix U is the *imputed cost matrix* whose entries are the costs imputed to the required commodities.

We see that $x = 14 > 0$ in the solution to the primal furniture manufacturing problem, and $x = 0$ in the dual. Also, $u = \tfrac{10}{3} > 0$ in the dual and $u = 0$ in the primal problem. In general, this is the complementary nature of the solutions to the primal and dual problems. Each variable that has a positive value in the solution of the primal problem has the value 0 in the solution of the dual. Similarly, if a variable has a positive value in the solution to the dual problem, then it has the value 0 in the solution of the primal problem. This result is called the *principle of complementary slackness*.

The economic interpretation of complementary slackness is this: If a slack variable from the primal problem is positive, then having available more of the corresponding resource cannot improve the value of the objective function. For instance, since $w > 0$ in the solution of the primal problem and $2x + 6y + w = 72$, not all of the labor available for upholstery will be used in the optimal production schedule. Therefore, the marginal value of the resource is zero. As we saw in Section 4.4, the marginal value of a resource is the final value in the column of its slack variable in the primal problem. But this number is the value of the main variable in the solution of the dual problem.

When we gave an economic interpretation to the dual of the furniture manufacturing problem, we first had to assign units to each of the variables of the dual problem. For instance, u was in units of profit per labor-hour of carpentry, or

$$\frac{\text{profit}}{\text{labor-hours of carpentry}}.$$

The following systematic procedure can often be used to obtain the units for the variables of the dual problem from units appearing in the primal problem. Assume that the primal problem is stated in one of the two forms given previously.

1. Replace each entry of the matrix A by its units, written in fraction form. Label each column and row with the corresponding variable.
2. Replace each entry of the matrix C by its units, written in fraction form.
3. To find the units for a variable of the dual problem, select any entry in its row in A, divide the corresponding entry in C by the entry chosen in A, and simplify the fraction.

For the furniture manufacturing problem, the matrices are

$$
\begin{array}{c}
\quad\quad\quad\quad x \quad\quad\quad\quad\quad\quad\quad y \\[4pt]
\begin{array}{c} u \\[18pt] v \\[18pt] w \end{array}
\left[
\begin{array}{cc}
\dfrac{\text{labor-hours of carpentry}}{\text{chair}} & \dfrac{\text{labor-hours of carpentry}}{\text{sofa}} \\[12pt]
\dfrac{\text{labor-hours of finishing}}{\text{chair}} & \dfrac{\text{labor-hours of finishing}}{\text{sofa}} \\[12pt]
\dfrac{\text{labor-hours of upholstery}}{\text{chair}} & \dfrac{\text{labor-hours of upholstery}}{\text{sofa}}
\end{array}
\right] = A
\end{array}
$$

$$
\left[
\begin{array}{cc}
\dfrac{\text{profit}}{\text{chair}} & \dfrac{\text{profit}}{\text{sofa}}
\end{array}
\right] = C.
$$

Using the first entry in the row labeled u, the units for u in the dual problem are

$$\frac{\text{profit}}{\text{chair}} \div \frac{\text{labor-hours of carpentry}}{\text{chair}} = \frac{\text{profit}}{\text{chair}} \cdot \frac{\text{chair}}{\text{labor-hours of carpentry}}$$

$$= \frac{\text{profit}}{\text{labor-hours of carpentry}}.$$

Here, u is measured in dollars per labor-hour of carpentry.

▶ Example 3   A rancher needs to provide a daily dietary supplement to the minks on his ranch. He needs 6 units of protein and 5 units of carbohydrates to add to their regular feed each day. Bran X costs 32 cents per ounce and supplies 4 units of protein and 8 units of carbohydrates per ounce. Wheatchips cost 12 cents per ounce, and each ounce supplies 3 units of protein and 2 units of carbohydrates.

(a) Determine the mixture of Bran X and Wheatchips that will meet the daily requirements at minimum cost.

(b) Solve and interpret the dual problem.

Solution   (a)   Let x be the number of ounces of Bran X and y the number of ounces of Wheatchips to be added to the feed. Then we must find the values of x and y that minimize $32x + 12y$ subject to the constraints

$$\begin{cases} 4x + 3y \geq 6 \\ 8x + 2y \geq 5 \\ x \geq 0, \quad y \geq 0. \end{cases}$$

For simplicity, we solve the dual problem. Let u and v be the dual variables. We must find the values of u and v that maximize $6u + 5v$ subject to the constraints

$$\begin{cases} 4u + 8v \leq 32 \\ 3u + 2v \leq 12 \\ u \geq 0, \quad v \geq 0. \end{cases}$$

The final tableau for the dual problem (with slack variables x and y) is

	u	v	x	y	M	
v	0	1	$\frac{3}{16}$	$-\frac{1}{4}$	0	3
u	1	0	$-\frac{1}{8}$	$\frac{1}{2}$	0	2
M	0	0	$\frac{3}{16}$	$\frac{7}{4}$	1	27

The solution to the rancher's problem is to add $x = \frac{3}{16}$ ounce of Bran X and $y = \frac{7}{4} = 1\frac{3}{4}$ ounces of Wheatchips to the daily feed at a minimum cost of **27 cents per day**.

(b)   The solution of the dual problem can be read from the preceding tableau: $u = 2$ and $v = 3$. To find the units of u and v, we construct a chart from the original problem:

$$
\begin{array}{cc}
 & x & y \\
u & \dfrac{\text{units of protein}}{\text{ounce Bran } X} & \dfrac{\text{units of protein}}{\text{ounce Wheatchips}} \\
v & \dfrac{\text{units of carbohydrates}}{\text{ounce Bran } X} & \dfrac{\text{units of carbohydrates}}{\text{ounce Wheatchips}}
\end{array}
$$

$$
\begin{bmatrix} \dfrac{\text{cents}}{\text{ounce Bran } X} & \dfrac{\text{cents}}{\text{ounce Wheatchips}} \end{bmatrix}.
$$

The units for u in the dual problem are

$$\frac{\text{cents}}{\text{ounce Bran } X} \div \frac{\text{units of protein}}{\text{ounce Bran } X} = \frac{\text{cents}}{\text{ounce Bran } X} \cdot \frac{\text{ounce Bran } X}{\text{units of protein}}$$

$$= \frac{\text{cents}}{\text{units of protein}}.$$

We can interpret the dual this way: If someone were to provide the perfect daily supplement for the minks with 6 units of protein and 5 units of carbohydrates, the rancher would expect to pay 27 cents. He certainly would pay no more, since he could mix his own supplement for that price per day. The value of the protein is 2 cents per unit and the value of the carbohydrates is 3 cents per unit. ◆

A Useful Application of the Dual One type of decision that businesses must make is whether or not to introduce new products. The following example uses a linear programming problem and its dual to determine the proper course of action.

▶ Example 4   Consider the furniture manufacturing problem once again. Suppose that the manufacturer has the same resources but is considering adding a new product to his line, love seats. The manufacture of a love seat requires 3 hours of carpentry, 2 hours of finishing, and 4 hours of upholstery. What profit must he gain per love seat in order to justify adding love seats to his product line?

Solution   Let z denote the number of love seats to be produced each day, and let p be the profit per love seat. The new furniture manufacturing problem is as follows:
Maximize $80x + 70y + pz$ subject to

$$\begin{cases} 6x + 3y + 3z \leq 96 \\ x + y + 2z \leq 18 \\ 2x + 6y + 4z \leq 72 \\ x \geq 0, \quad y \geq 0, \quad z \geq 0. \end{cases}$$

What is the dual of this problem? All inequalities are $\leq$ in the original maximization problem so we may proceed directly to write the dual.
Minimize $96u + 18v + 72w$ subject to

$$\begin{cases} 6u + v + 2w \geq 80 \\ 3u + v + 6w \geq 70 \\ 3u + 2v + 4w \geq p \\ u \geq 0, \quad v \geq 0, \quad w \geq 0. \end{cases}$$

Whereas the new furniture manufacturing problem has one more variable than the original problem, its dual has one more constraint than the dual of the original problem,

$$3u + 2v + 4w \geq p.$$

If the optimal solution to the original problem (just making chairs and sofas) were to remain optimal in the new problem, the variable z would not enter the set of group II variables. If that were the case, the solution to the dual would also remain optimal. But that solution was

$$u = \tfrac{10}{3}, \qquad v = 60, \qquad w = 0.$$

And the new dual would require that $3u + 2v + 4w \geq p$. Since

$$3\left(\tfrac{10}{3}\right) + 2(60) + 4(0) = 130,$$

if the profit per love seat is at most \$130, the previous solution will remain optimal. That is, the manufacturer should make 14 chairs and 4 sofas and 0 love seats. However, if the profit per love seat exceeds \$130, the variable z will enter the set of group II variables, and we will find an optimal production schedule in which $z > 0$. ◆

A linear programming problem involving three variables and four nontrivial inequalities has the number 52 as the maximum value of its objective function.

1. How many variables and nontrivial inequalities will the dual problem have?

2. What is the optimum value for the objective function of the dual problem?

▶ Exercises 4.5

In Exercises 1–6, determine the dual problem of the given linear programming problem.

1. Maximize $4x + 2y$ subject to the constraints

$$\begin{cases} 5x + y \le 80 \\ 3x + 2y \le 76 \\ x \ge 0, \quad y \ge 0. \end{cases}$$

2. Minimize $30x + 60y + 50z$ subject to the constraints

$$\begin{cases} 5x + 3y + z \ge 2 \\ x + 2y + z \ge 3 \\ x \ge 0, \quad y \ge 0, \quad z \ge 0. \end{cases}$$

3. Minimize $10x + 12y$ subject to the constraints

$$\begin{cases} x + 2y \ge 1 \\ -x + y \ge 2 \\ 2x + 3y \ge 1 \\ x \ge 0, \quad y \ge 0. \end{cases}$$

4. Maximize $80x + 70y + 120z$ subject to the constraints

$$\begin{cases} 6x + 3y + 8z \le 768 \\ x + y + 2z \le 144 \\ 2x + 5y \le 216 \\ x \ge 0, \quad y \ge 0, \quad z \ge 0. \end{cases}$$

5. Minimize $3x + 5y + z$ subject to the constraints

$$\begin{cases} 2x - 4y - 6z \le 7 \\ y \ge 10 - 8x - 9z \\ x \ge 0, \quad y \ge 0, \quad z \ge 0. \end{cases}$$

6. Maximize $2x - 3y + 4z - 5w$ subject to the constraints

$$\begin{cases} x + y + z + w - 6 \le 10 \\ 7x + 9y - 4z - 3w \ge 5 \\ x \ge 0, \quad y \ge 0, \quad z \ge 0, \quad w \ge 0. \end{cases}$$

7. The final simplex tableau for the linear programming problem of Exercise 1 is as follows. Give the solution to the problem and to its dual.

	x	y	u	v	M	
x	1	0	$\frac{2}{7}$	$-\frac{1}{7}$	0	12
y	0	1	$-\frac{3}{7}$	$\frac{5}{7}$	0	20
M	0	0	$\frac{2}{7}$	$\frac{6}{7}$	1	88

8. The final simplex tableau for the *dual* of the linear programming problem of Exercise 2 is as follows. Give the solution to the problem and to its dual.

	u	v	x	y	z	M	
v	5	1	1	0	0	0	30
y	-7	0	-2	1	0	0	0
z	-4	0	-1	0	1	0	20
M	13	0	3	0	0	1	90

9. The final simplex tableau for the *dual* of the linear programming problem of Exercise 3 is as follows. Give the solution to the problem and to its dual.

	u	v	w	x	y	M	
x	3	0	5	1	1	0	22
v	2	1	3	0	1	0	12
M	3	0	5	0	2	1	24

10. The final simplex tableau for the linear programming problem of Exercise 4 is as follows. Give the solution to the problem and to its dual.

	x	y	z	u	v	w	M	
x	1	0	0	$\frac{5}{12}$	$-\frac{5}{3}$	$\frac{1}{12}$	0	98
z	0	0	1	$-\frac{1}{8}$	1	$-\frac{1}{8}$	0	21
y	0	1	0	$-\frac{1}{6}$	$\frac{2}{3}$	$\frac{1}{6}$	0	4
M	0	0	0	$\frac{20}{3}$	$\frac{100}{3}$	$\frac{10}{3}$	1	10,640

In Exercises 11–14, determine the dual problem. Solve either the original problem or its dual by the simplex method and then give the solutions to both.

11. Minimize $3x + y$ subject to the constraints

$$\begin{cases} x + y \ge 3 \\ 2x \ge 5 \\ x \ge 0, \quad y \ge 0. \end{cases}$$

12. Minimize $3x + 5y + z$ subject to the constraints

$$\begin{cases} x + y + \ z \geq 20 \\ \quad\ y + 2z \geq \ 0 \\ x \geq 0, \quad y \geq 0, \quad z \geq 0. \end{cases}$$

13. Maximize $10x + 12y + 10z$ subject to the constraints

$$\begin{cases} x - 2y \quad\quad \leq \ 6 \\ 3x \quad\quad + \ z \leq \ 9 \\ \quad\quad y + 3z \leq 12 \\ x \geq 0, \quad y \geq 0, \quad z \geq 0. \end{cases}$$

14. Maximize $x + 3y$ subject to the constraints

$$\begin{cases} x + \ y \leq \ 7 \\ x + 2y \leq 10 \\ x \geq 0, \quad y \geq 0. \end{cases}$$

15. Give an economic interpretation to the dual of the Cutting Edge Knife Company problem of Example 1 of Section 4.4.

16. Give an economic interpretation to the dual of Exercise 8 of Section 4.3.

17. Give an economic interpretation to the dual of the mining problem of Exercise 6 of Section 3.1 and Exercise 14 of Section 3.2.

18. Give an economic interpretation to the dual of the nutrition problem of Example 1 of Section 3.2.

19. Consider the Cutting Edge Knife Company problem of Example 1 of Section 4.4. Suppose that the company is thinking of also making table knives. If each table knife requires 4 labor-hours, 6 units of steel, and 2 units of wood, what profit must be realized per knife to justify adding this product?

In Exercises 20 and 21, use a graphing calculator or a computer to solve the linear programming problems by applying the simplex method to the dual of the problem.

20. Minimize $3x + y$ subject to the constraints

$$\begin{cases} x + y \geq 3 \\ 2x \quad\ \geq 5 \\ x \geq 0, \quad y \geq 0. \end{cases}$$

21. Minimize $16x + 42y$ subject to the constraints

$$\begin{cases} x + 3y \geq 5 \\ 2x + 4y \geq 8 \\ x \geq 0, \quad y \geq 0. \end{cases}$$

Solutions to Practice Problems 4.5

1. Four variables and three nontrivial inequalities. The number of variables in the dual problem is always the same as the number of nontrivial inequalities in the original problem. The number of nontrivial inequalities in the dual problem is the same as the number of variables in the original problem.

2. Minimum value of 52. The original problem and the dual problem always have the same optimum values. However, if this value is a maximum for one of the problems, it will be a minimum for the other.

▶ Chapter 4 Summary

1. A linear programming problem is in *standard form* if the linear objective function is to be maximized, every variable is constrained to be nonnegative, and all other constraints are of the form [linear polynomial] $\leq$ [nonnegative constant].

2. To form the *initial simplex tableau* corresponding to a linear programming problem in standard form,

   Step 1   For each constraint of the form [linear polynomial] $\leq$ [nonnegative constant], introduce a *slack variable* and write the constraint as an equation.

   Step 2   Introduce a variable M to represent the quantity to be maximized, and form the equation $-$[objective function] $+ M = 0$.

   Step 3   Form the augmented matrix corresponding to the system of linear equations from Steps 1

and 2, with the equation from Step 2 at the bottom. This matrix is the initial simplex tableau.

3. The simplex method entails pivoting around entries in the simplex tableau until the bottom row contains no negative entries except perhaps the entry in the last column. The solution can be read off the final tableau by letting the variables heading columns with 0 entries in every row but the ith row take on the value in the ith row of the right-most column, and letting the other variables equal 0.

4. The simplex method can be used to solve a linear programming problem in *nonstandard* form as follows:

   (a) If the problem is a minimization problem, convert it to a maximization problem by multiplying the objective function by -1.

(b) Form the initial tableau, and eliminate any negative entries in the upper part of the last column by pivoting.

(c) Apply the pivoting process for problems in standard form to the resulting tableau.

5. The constraints in a linear programming problem usually represent limitations in the availability of resources. *Marginal analysis* is the analysis of the effects of small changes in the constraints. The *marginal value* of a resource is the change in the optimal value of the objective function resulting from a unit increase in the availability of that resource. In the final simplex tableau, the bottom entry in each slack variable's column gives the marginal value of the resource associated with that variable.

6. A linear programming problem in standard form can be expressed in terms of matrices: Maximize CX subject to constraints $AX \leq B$ and $X \geq \mathbf{0}$, where A is the matrix of coefficients of the linear polynomials, B is the column vector of the right-hand constants, and C is a row vector of the coefficients in the objective function.

7. Given a linear programming problem in standard form, its *dual* problem is "Minimize $B^T U$ subject to $A^T U \geq C^T$, $U \geq \mathbf{0}$," where U is the column matrix consisting of the slack variables of the original problem. The original problem is called the *primal problem*. The dual of the dual is the primal problem.

8. The *fundamental theorem of duality* states that if either the primal problem or the dual problem has an optimal feasible solution, then they both have optimal feasible solutions and their objective functions have the same optimal value. Furthermore, the final simplex tableau for either of these problems yields the solution of the other as the final entries in the columns associated with the slack variables.

Review of Fundamental Concepts of Chapter 4

1. What is the standard form of a linear programming problem?

2. What is a slack variable? a group I variable? a group II variable?

3. Explain how to construct a simplex tableau corresponding to a linear programming problem in standard form.

4. Give the steps for carrying out the simplex method for linear programming problems in standard form.

5. Explain how to convert a minimization problem to a maximization problem.

6. Give the steps for carrying out the simplex method for problems in nonstandard form.

7. Describe how to obtain the dual of a linear programming problem.

8. State the fundamental theorem of duality.

9. Explain how to obtain the matrix formulation of a linear programming problem.

10. What is meant by "marginal analysis"?

11. Explain how the dual can be used to decide whether to introduce a new product.

▶ Chapter 4 Supplementary Exercises

In Exercises 1–10, use the simplex method to solve the linear programming problems.

1. Maximize $3x + 4y$ subject to the constraints

$$\begin{cases} 2x + y \leq 7 \\ -x + y \leq 1 \\ x \geq 0, \quad y \geq 0. \end{cases}$$

2. Maximize $2x + 5y$ subject to the constraints

$$\begin{cases} x + y \leq 7 \\ 4x + 3y \leq 24 \\ x \geq 0, \quad y \geq 0. \end{cases}$$

3. Maximize $2x + 3y$ subject to the constraints

$$\begin{cases} x + 2y \leq 14 \\ x + y \leq 9 \\ 3x + 2y \leq 24 \\ x \geq 0, \quad y \geq 0. \end{cases}$$

4. Maximize $3x + 7y$ subject to the constraints

$$\begin{cases} x + 2y \leq 10 \\ 4x + 3y \leq 30 \\ -2x + y \leq 0 \\ x \geq 0, \quad y \geq 0. \end{cases}$$

5. Minimize $x + y$ subject to the constraints

$$\begin{cases} 7x + 5y \geq 40 \\ x + 4y \geq 9 \\ x \geq 0, \quad y \geq 0. \end{cases}$$

6. Minimize $3x + 2y$ subject to the constraints

$$\begin{cases} x + y \geq 6 \\ x + 2y \geq 0 \\ x \geq 0, \quad y \geq 0. \end{cases}$$

7. Minimize $20x + 30y$ subject to the constraints

$$\begin{cases} x + 4y \geq 8 \\ x + y \geq 5 \\ 2x + y \geq 7 \\ x \geq 0, \quad y \geq 0. \end{cases}$$

8. Minimize $5x + 7y$ subject to the constraints

$$\begin{cases} 2x + y \geq 10 \\ 3x + 2y \geq 18 \\ x + 2y \geq 10 \\ x \geq 0, \quad y \geq 0. \end{cases}$$

9. Maximize $36x + 48y + 70z$ subject to the constraints

$$\begin{cases} x \leq 4 \\ y \leq 6 \\ z \leq 8 \\ 4x + 3y + 2z \leq 38 \\ x \geq 0, \quad y \geq 0, \quad z \geq 0. \end{cases}$$

10. Maximize $3x + 4y + 5z + 4w$ subject to the constraints

$$\begin{cases} 6x + 9y + 12z + 15w \leq 672 \\ x - y + 2z + 2w \leq 92 \\ 5x + 10y - 5z + 4w \leq 280 \\ x \geq 0, \quad y \geq 0, \quad z \geq 0, \quad w \geq 0. \end{cases}$$

11. Determine the dual problem of the linear programming problem in Exercise 3.

12. Determine the dual problem of the linear programming problem in Exercise 7.

13. The final simplex tableau for the linear programming problem of Exercise 3 is as follows. Give the solution to the problem and to its dual.

	x	y	u	v	w	M	
y	0	1	1	-1	0	0	5
x	1	0	-1	2	0	0	4
w	0	0	1	-4	1	0	2
M	0	0	1	1	0	1	23

14. The final simplex tableau for the *dual* of the linear programming problem of Exercise 7 is as follows. Give the solution to the problem and to its dual.

	u	v	w	x	y	M	
v	0	1	$\frac{7}{3}$	$\frac{4}{3}$	$-\frac{1}{3}$	0	$\frac{50}{3}$
u	1	0	$-\frac{1}{3}$	$-\frac{1}{3}$	$\frac{1}{3}$	0	$\frac{10}{3}$
M	0	0	2	4	1	1	110

15, 16. For each of the linear programming problems in Exercises 3 and 7, identify the matrices A, B, C, X, and U and state the problem and its dual in terms of matrices.

17. Consider Exercise 32 of Section 3.2.

(a) Solve the problem by the simplex method.

(b) The Bluejay Lacrosse Stick Company is considering diversifying by also making tennis rackets. A tennis racket requires 1 labor-hour for cutting, 4 labor-hours for stringing, and 2 labor-hours for finishing. How much profit must the company be able to make on each tennis racket in order to justify the diversification?

18. Consider the stereo store of Exercise 16 in Section 4.2. A fourth brand of stereo system has appeared on the market. Brand D takes up 3 cubic feet of storage space and generates a sales commission of $30. What profit would the store have to realize on the sale of each brand D stereo set in order to justify carrying it?

▶ Chapter 4 Chapter Test

1. Form the initial simplex tableau corresponding to the following linear programming problem. Maximize $2x + y - 3z$ subject to the constraints

$$\begin{cases} x + y - 2z \le 10 \\ 2x - y + 3z \le 18 \\ x + 3y + z \le 21 \\ x \ge 0, \quad y \ge 0, \quad z \ge 0. \end{cases}$$

2. Give the solution of the linear programming problem corresponding to the final tableau

$$\begin{bmatrix} x & y & z & u & v & w & M & \\ 1 & 10 & 0 & 3 & -7 & 0 & 0 & 35 \\ 0 & -7 & 0 & 8 & 14 & 1 & 0 & 42 \\ 0 & 6 & 1 & -1 & 8 & 0 & 0 & 30 \\ \hline 0 & 14 & 0 & 0 & \frac{7}{2} & 0 & 1 & 560 \end{bmatrix}.$$

Also, give the solution to the dual problem.

3. State the maximization problem corresponding to the following tableau, and solve it using the simplex method.

$$\begin{bmatrix} x & y & u & v & M & \\ 6 & 7 & 1 & 0 & 0 & 120 \\ 15 & 5 & 0 & 1 & 0 & 195 \\ \hline -3 & 4 & 0 & 0 & 1 & 0 \end{bmatrix}$$

4. Use the simplex method to solve the following linear programming problem. Minimize $12x + 5y$ subject to the constraints

$$\begin{cases} y \ge -\frac{1}{2}x + 5 \\ y \le -x + 10 \\ y \ge -3x + 10 \\ x \ge 0, \quad y \ge 0. \end{cases}$$

5. State the dual of the following linear programming problem. Minimize $3x + 2y$ subject to the constraints

$$\begin{cases} x + y \ge 6 \\ 2x - y \ge 3 \\ x \ge 0, \quad y \ge 0. \end{cases}$$

6. Consider the following linear programming problem, but do *not* solve it.

A newspaper publisher puts out a morning paper and an evening paper. He can sell all the papers he prints, but paper and labor are in short supply. Each morning paper requires 2 pounds of paper and 2 minutes of labor to print, while each evening paper requires 1 pound of paper and 3 minutes of labor to print. Each day, 6000 pounds of paper and 9600 minutes of labor are available. Morning papers sell for $.50 each, and evening papers sell for $.35 each. How many morning and evening papers should be printed in order to maximize revenue?

(a) Give the matrix formulation of the problem.

(b) Give the matrix formulation of the dual of the problem.

(c) State the dual problem without matrices. What do the variables represent?

(d) Give an economic interpretation to the dual of the problem.

Chapter Project

Shadow Prices

Jason's House of Cheese and Nuts offers two cheese assortments for holiday gift giving. In his supply refrigerator Jason has 3600 ounces of cheddar, 1498 ounces of brie, and 2396 ounces of stilton. The St. Nick assortment contains 10 ounces of cheddar, 5 ounces of brie, and 6 ounces of stilton. The Holly assortment contains 8 ounces of cheddar, 3 ounces of brie, and 8 ounces of stilton. Each St. Nick assortment sells for $4.00 and each Holly assortment sells for $3.50. How many of each assortment should be produced and sold in order to maximize Jason's revenue?

1. Solve the problem geometrically.

2. By looking at your graph from part 1, can you determine the shadow price of cheddar?

3. Solve the problem using the simplex method. The solution should be the same as in part 1. Verify your answer to part 2 by looking at your final tableau.

4. What are the shadow prices for brie and stilton?

5. What would the maximum revenue be if there were 3620 ounces of cheddar, 1500 ounces of brie, and 2400 ounces of stilton?

6. Go back to the original problem and state its dual problem. What information do the original slack variables u, v, and w give us about the dual problem? Determine the solution to the dual problem from your final tableau in part 3, and give an economic interpretation.

C H A P T E R

Sets and Counting

5

In this chapter we introduce some ideas useful in the study of probability (Chapter 6). Our first topic, the theory of sets, will provide a convenient language and notation in which to discuss probability. Using set theory, we develop a number of counting principles that can also be applied to computing probabilities.

5.1 Sets

In many applied problems one must consider collections of various sorts of objects. For example, a survey of unemployment might consider the collection of all U.S. cities with current unemployment greater than 7%. A study of birthrates might consider the collection of countries with a current birthrate less than 20 per 1000 population. Such collections are examples of sets. A *set* is any collection of objects. The objects, which may be countries, cities, years, numbers, letters, or anything else, are called the *elements* of the set. A set is often specified by a listing of its elements inside a pair of braces. For example, the set whose elements are the first six letters of the alphabet is written

$$\{a, b, c, d, e, f\}.$$

Similarly, the set whose elements are the even numbers between 1 and 11 is written

$$\{2, 4, 6, 8, 10\}.$$

We can also specify a set by giving a description of its elements (without actually listing the elements). For example, the set $\{a, b, c, d, e, f\}$ can also be written

$$\{\text{the first six letters of the alphabet}\},$$

and the set $\{2, 4, 6, 8, 10\}$ can be written

$$\{\text{all even numbers between 1 and 11}\}.$$

For convenience, we usually denote sets by capital letters, A, B, C, and so on.

The great diversity of sets is illustrated by the following examples:

1. In a linear programming problem, the feasible set is the set of all points satisfying a system of linear inequalities. The feasible set of the furniture manufacturing problem is the set of all points on or inside the five-sided region in Fig. 1.

2. Let B = {license plate numbers consisting of three letters followed by three digits}. Some typical elements of B are

SBG 602,   GXZ 179,   YHJ 006.

The number of elements in B is sufficiently large so that listing all of them is impractical. However, in this chapter we develop a technique that allows us to calculate the number of elements of B.

3. Let C = {possible sequences of outcomes of tossing a coin three times}. If we let H denote "heads" and T denote "tails," the various sequences can be easily described:

$$C = \{\text{HHH}, \text{THH}, \text{HTH}, \text{HHT}, \text{TTH}, \text{THT}, \text{HTT}, \text{TTT}\},$$

where, for instance, HTH means "first toss heads, second toss tails, third toss heads."

Sets arise in many practical contexts, as the next example shows.

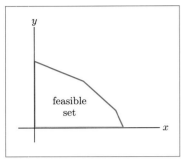

Figure 1.

▶ Example 1   Table 1 gives the rate of inflation, as measured by the percentage change in the consumer price index, for the years from 1980 to 1999. Let

$$A = \{\text{years from 1980 to 1999 in which inflation was above 6\%}\}$$
$$B = \{\text{years from 1980 to 1999 in which inflation was below 3\%}\}.$$

Determine the elements of A and B.

Solution   By reading Table 1, we see that

$$A = \{1980, 1981, 1982\}$$
$$B = \{1986, 1993, 1994, 1995, 1997, 1998, 1999\}.$$

Table 1			
Year	**Inflation (%)**	**Year**	**Inflation (%)**
1980	13.5	1990	5.4
1981	10.4	1991	4.2
1982	6.1	1992	3.0
1983	3.2	1993	2.6
1984	4.3	1994	2.6
1985	3.6	1995	2.5
1986	1.9	1996	3.4
1987	3.6	1997	1.7
1988	4.1	1998	1.6
1989	4.8	1999	2.7

◆

Suppose that we are given two sets, A and B. Then it is possible to form new sets from A and B as follows: The *union* of A and B, denoted $A \cup B$, is the set consisting of all those elements that belong to either A *or* B (or both). The *intersection* of A and B, denoted $A \cap B$, is the set consisting of those elements that belong to both A *and* B. For example, let

$$A = \{1, 2, 3, 4\} \qquad B = \{1, 3, 5, 7, 11\}.$$

Then, since $A \cup B$ consists of those elements belonging to either A or B (or both), we have

$$A \cup B = \{1, 2, 3, 4, 5, 7, 11\}.$$

Moreover, since $A \cap B$ consists of those elements that belong to both A and B, we have

$$A \cap B = \{1, 3\}.$$

▶ **Example 2**   Table 2 gives the rates of unemployment and inflation for the years from 1986 to 1999. Let

$A = \{$years from 1986 to 1999 in which unemployment is at least 6%$\}$

$B = \{$years from 1986 to 1999 in which the inflation rate is at least 4%$\}$.

(a) Describe the sets $A \cap B$ and $A \cup B$.

(b) Determine the elements of A, B, $A \cap B$, and $A \cup B$.

Solution   (a) From the descriptions of A and B, we have

$A \cap B = \{$years from 1986 to 1999 in which unemployment is
at least 6% and inflation is at least 4%$\}$

$A \cup B = \{$years from 1986 to 1999 in which either unemployment
is at least 6% or inflation is at least 4% (or both)$\}$.

Table 2

Year	Unemployment (%)	Inflation (%)
1986	6.9	1.9
1987	6.1	3.6
1988	5.4	4.1
1989	5.2	4.8
1990	5.4	5.4
1991	6.6	4.2
1992	7.4	3.0
1993	6.8	2.6
1994	6.0	2.6
1995	5.5	2.5
1996	5.4	3.4
1997	4.9	1.7
1998	4.5	1.6
1999	4.2	2.7

(b) From the table we see that

$$A = \{1986, 1987, 1991, 1992, 1993, 1994\}$$

$$B = \{1988, 1989, 1990, 1991\}$$

$$A \cap B = \{1991\}$$

$$A \cup B = \{1986, 1987, 1988, 1989, 1990, 1991, 1992, 1993, 1994\}. \qquad \blacklozenge$$

We have defined the union and the intersection of two sets. In a similar manner, we can define the union and intersection of any number of sets. For example, if A, B, and C are three sets, then their union, denoted $A \cup B \cup C$, is the set whose elements are precisely those that belong to at least one of the sets A, B, and C. Similarly, the intersection of A, B, and C, denoted $A \cap B \cap C$, is the set consisting of those elements that belong to all the sets A, B, and C. In a similar way, we may define the union and intersection of more than three sets.

Suppose that we are given a set A. We may form new sets by selecting elements from A. Sets formed in this way are called *subsets* of A. More precisely, a set B is called a *subset* of A provided that every element of B is also an element of A. For example, let $A = \{1, 2, 3\}$, $B = \{1, 3\}$. Since the elements of B (1 and 3) are also elements of A, B is a subset of A.

One set that is considered very often is the set that contains no elements at all. This set is called the *empty set* (or *null set*) and is written $\emptyset$. The empty set is a subset of every set.[1]

▶ **Example 3** Let $A = \{a, b, c\}$. Find all subsets of A.

Solution Since A contains three elements, every subset of A has at most three elements. We look for subsets according to the number of elements:

Number of elements in subset	Possible subsets
0	$\emptyset$
1	$\{a\}, \{b\}, \{c\}$
2	$\{a, b\}, \{a, c\}, \{b, c\}$
3	$\{a, b, c\}$

Thus we see that A has eight subsets, namely those listed on the right. (Note that we count A as a subset of itself.) $\blacklozenge$

It is usually convenient to regard all sets involved in a particular discussion as subsets of a single larger set. Thus, for example, if a problem involves the sets $\{a, b, c\}$, $\{e, f\}$, $\{g\}$, $\{b, x, y\}$, then we can regard all of these as subsets of the set

$$U = \{\text{all letters of the alphabet}\}.$$

Since U contains all sets being discussed, it is called a *universal set* (for the particular problem). In this book we shall always specify the particular universal set we have in mind.

Suppose that U is a universal set and A is a subset of U. The set of elements of U that are not in A is called the *complement* of A, denoted A'. For example,

---

[1] Here is why: Let A be any set. Every element of $\emptyset$ also belongs to A. If you do not agree, then you must produce an element of $\emptyset$ that does not belong to A. But you cannot, since $\emptyset$ has no elements. So $\emptyset$ is a subset of A.

if

$$U = \{1, 2, 3, 4, 5, 6, 7, 8, 9\} \quad \text{and} \quad A = \{2, 4, 6, 8\},$$

then

$$A' = \{1, 3, 5, 7, 9\}.$$

▶ **Example 4** Let $U = \{a, b, c, d, e, f, g\}$, $S = \{a, b, c\}$, and $T = \{a, c, d\}$. List the elements of the following sets.

(a) S' (b) T' (c) $(S \cap T)'$ (d) $S' \cap T'$

Solution (a) S' consists of those elements of U that are not in S, so $S' = \{d, e, f, g\}$.
(b) Similarly, $T' = \{b, e, f, g\}$.
(c) To determine $(S \cap T)'$, we must first determine $S \cap T$:

$$S \cap T = \{a, c\}.$$

Then we determine the complement of this set:

$$(S \cap T)' = \{b, d, e, f, g\}.$$

(d) We determined S' and T' in parts (a) and (b). The set $S' \cap T'$ consists of the elements that belong to both S' and T'. Therefore, referring to parts (a) and (b), we have

$$S' \cap T' = \{e, f, g\}. \qquad \blacklozenge$$

Practice Problems 5.1

1. Let $U = \{a, b, c, d, e, f, g\}$, $R = \{a, b, c, d\}$, $S = \{c, d, e\}$, and $T = \{c, e, g\}$. List the elements of the following sets.
   (a) R' (b) $R \cap S$ (c) $(R \cap S) \cap T$ (d) $R \cap (S \cap T)$

2. Let $U = \{$all Nobel Prize winners$\}$, $W = \{$women who have won Nobel Prizes$\}$, $A = \{$Americans who have won Nobel Prizes$\}$, $L = \{$winners of the Nobel Prize in literature$\}$. Describe the following sets.
   (a) W' (b) $A \cap L'$ (c) $W \cap A \cap L'$

3. Refer to Problem 2. Use set-theoretic notation to describe $\{$Nobel Prize winners who are American men or recipients of the Prize in literature$\}$.

▶ Exercises 5.1

1. Let $U = \{1, 2, 3, 4, 5, 6, 7\}$, $S = \{1, 2, 3, 4\}$, and $T = \{1, 3, 5, 7\}$. List the elements of the following sets.
   (a) S' (b) $S \cup T$ (c) $S \cap T$ (d) $S' \cap T$

2. Let $U = \{1, 2, 3, 4, 5\}$, $S = \{1, 2, 3\}$, and $T = \{5\}$. List the elements of the following sets.
   (a) S' (b) $S \cup T$ (c) $S \cap T$ (d) $S' \cap T$

3. Let $U = \{$all letters of the alphabet$\}$, $R = \{a, b, c\}$, $S = \{c, d, e, f\}$, and $T = \{x, y, z\}$. List the elements of the following sets.
   (a) $R \cup S$ (b) $R \cap S$ (c) $S \cap T$

4. Let $U = \{a, b, c, d, e, f, g\}$, $R = \{a\}$, $S = \{a, b\}$, and $T = \{b, d, e, f, g\}$. List the elements of the following sets.

   (a) $R \cup S$ (b) $R \cap S$ (c) T' (d) $T' \cup S$

5. List all subsets of the set $\{1, 2\}$.

6. List all subsets of the set $\{1\}$.

7. Let $U = \{$all college students$\}$, $M = \{$all male college students$\}$, and $F = \{$all college students who like football$\}$. Describe the elements of the following sets.
   (a) $M \cap F$ (b) M' (c) $M' \cap F'$ (d) $M \cup F$

8. Let $U = \{$all corporations$\}$, $S = \{$all corporations with headquarters in New York City$\}$, and $T = \{$all privately owned corporations$\}$. Describe the elements of the following sets.
   (a) S' (b) T' (c) $S \cap T$ (d) $S \cap T'$

9. The Standard and Poor's Index measures the price of a certain collection of 500 stocks. Table 3 compares the percentage change in the index during the first 5 days of certain years with the percentage change for the entire year. Let $U = \{$all years from 1972 to 1999$\}$, $S = \{$all years during which the index increased by 2% or more during the first 5 days$\}$, and $T = \{$all years for which the index increased by 16% or more during the entire year$\}$. List the elements of the following sets.

(a) S (b) T (c) $S \cap T$

(d) $S' \cap T$ (e) $S \cap T'$

10. Refer to Table 3. Let $U = \{$all years from 1972 to 1999$\}$, $A = \{$all years during which the index declined during the first 5 days$\}$, and $B = \{$all years during which the index declined for the entire year$\}$. List the elements of the following sets.

(a) A (b) B (c) $A \cap B$

(d) $A' \cap B$ (e) $A \cap B'$

11. Refer to Exercise 9. Describe verbally the fact that $S \cap T'$ has three elements.

12. Refer to Exercise 10. Describe verbally the fact that $A \cap B'$ has eight elements.

13. Let $U = \{a, b, c, d, e, f\}$, $R = \{a, b, c\}$, $S = \{a, c, e\}$, and $T = \{e, f\}$. List the elements of the following sets.

(a) $(R \cup S)'$ (b) $R \cup S \cup T$

(c) $R \cap S \cap T$ (d) $R \cap S \cap T'$

(e) $R' \cap S \cap T$ (f) $S \cup T$

(g) $(R \cup S) \cap (R \cup T)$

(h) $(R \cap S) \cup (R \cap T)$

(i) $R' \cap T'$

14. Let $U = \{1, 2, 3, 4, 5\}$, $R = \{1, 3, 5\}$, $S = \{3, 4, 5\}$, and $T = \{2, 4\}$. List the elements of the following sets.

(a) $R \cap S \cap T$ (b) $R \cap S \cap T'$ (c) $R \cap S' \cap T$

(d) $R' \cap T$ (e) $R \cup S$ (f) $R' \cup R$

(g) $(S \cap T)'$ (h) $S' \cup T'$

In Exercises 15–20, simplify the given expression.

15. $(S')'$ 16. $S \cap S'$ 17. $S \cup S'$

18. $S \cap \emptyset$ 19. $T \cap S \cap T'$ 20. $S \cup \emptyset$

Table 3	Percentage Change in the Standard and Poor's Index				
Year	Percent change for first 5 days	Percent change for year	Year	Percent change for first 5 days	Percent change for year
1999	3.7	19.5	1985	−1.9	26.3
1998	−1.5	26.7	1984	2.4	1.4
1997	1.0	31.0	1983	3.3	17.3
1996	0.4	20.3	1982	−2.4	14.8
1995	0.3	34.1	1981	−2.0	−9.7
1994	0.7	−1.5	1980	0.9	25.8
1993	−1.5	7.1	1979	2.8	12.3
1992	0.2	4.5	1978	−4.7	1.1
1991	−4.6	26.3	1977	−2.3	−11.5
1990	0.1	−6.6	1976	4.9	19.1
1989	1.2	27.3	1975	2.2	31.5
1988	−1.5	12.4	1974	−1.5	−29.7
1987	6.2	2.0	1973	1.5	−17.4
1986	−1.6	14.6	1972	1.4	15.6

A large corporation classifies its many divisions by their performance in the preceding year. Let P = {divisions that made a profit}, L = {divisions that had an increase in labor costs}, and T = {divisions whose total revenue increased}. Describe the sets in Exercises 21–26 using set-theoretic notation.

21. {divisions that had increases in labor costs or total revenue}

22. {divisions that did not make a profit}

23. {divisions that made a profit despite an increase in labor costs}

24. {divisions that had an increase in labor costs and either were unprofitable or did not increase their total revenue}

25. {profitable divisions with increases in labor costs and total revenue}

26. {divisions that were unprofitable or did not have increases in either labor costs or total revenue}

An automobile insurance company classifies applicants by their driving records for the previous three years. Let S = {applicants who have received speeding tickets}, A = {applicants who have caused accidents}, and D = {applicants who have been arrested for driving while intoxicated}. Describe the sets in Exercises 27–32 using set-theoretic notation.

27. {applicants who have not received speeding tickets}

28. {applicants who have caused accidents and been arrested for drunk driving}

29. {applicants who have received speeding tickets, caused accidents, or been arrested for drunk driving}

30. {applicants who have not been arrested for drunk driving but have received speeding tickets or have caused accidents}

31. {applicants who have not both caused accidents and received speeding tickets but who have been arrested for drunk driving}

32. {applicants who have not caused accidents or have not been arrested for drunk driving}

Let U = {people at Mount College}, A = {students at Mount College}, B = {teachers at Mount College}, C = {females at Mount College}, and D = {males at Mount College}. Describe verbally the sets in Exercises 33–40.

33. $A \cap D$ 34. $B \cap C$ 35. $A \cap B$ 36. $B \cup C$

37. $A \cup C'$ 38. $(A \cap D)'$ 39. D' 40. $D \cap U$

Let U = {all people}, S = {people who like strawberry ice cream}, V = {people who like vanilla ice cream}, and C = {people who like chocolate ice cream}. Describe the sets in Exercises 41–46 using set-theoretic notation.

41. {people who don't like strawberry ice cream}

42. {people who like vanilla but not chocolate ice cream}

43. {people who like vanilla or chocolate but not strawberry ice cream}

44. {people who don't like any of the three flavors of ice cream}

45. {people who like neither chocolate nor vanilla ice cream}

46. {people who like only strawberry ice cream}

47. Let U be the set of vertices in the feasible set in Fig. 2. Let R = {vertices (x, y) with $x > 0$}, S = {vertices (x, y) with $y > 0$}, and T = {vertices (x, y) with $x \le y$}. List the elements of the following sets.

   (a) R (b) S (c) T

   (d) $R' \cup S$ (e) $R' \cap T$ (f) $R \cap S \cap T$

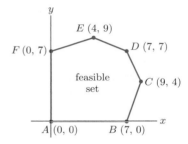

Figure 2.

48. Sam ordered a baked potato at a restaurant. The waitress offered him butter, cheese, and chives as toppings. How many different ways could he have his potato? List them.

49. Let $S = \{1, 3, 5, 7\}$ and $T = \{2, 5, 7\}$. Give an example of a subset of T that is not a subset of S.

50. Suppose that S and T are subsets of the set U. Under what circumstance will $S \cap T = T$?

51. Suppose that S and T are subsets of the set U. Under what circumstance will $S \cup T = T$?

52. Find three subsets of the set of integers from 1 through 10, R, S, and T, such that $R \cup (S \cap T)$ is different from $(R \cup S) \cap T$.

1. (a) $\{e, f, g\}$

   (b) $\{c, d\}$

   (c) $\{c\}$. This problem asks for the intersection of two sets. The first set is $R \cap S = \{c, d\}$ and the second set is $T = \{c, e, g\}$. The intersection of these sets is $\{c\}$.

   (d) $\{c\}$. Here again the problem asks for the intersection of two sets. However, now the first set is $R = \{a, b, c, d\}$ and the second set is $S \cap T = \{c, e\}$. The intersection of these sets is $\{c\}$.

   [*Note*: It should be expected that the set $(R \cap S) \cap T$ is the same as the set $R \cap (S \cap T)$, for each set consists of those elements that are in all three sets. Therefore, each of these sets equals the set $R \cap S \cap T$.]

2. (a) $W' = \{$men who have won Nobel Prizes$\}$. This is so since W' consists of those elements of U that are not in W—that is, those Nobel Prize winners who are not women.

   (b) $A \cap L' = \{$Americans who have received Nobel Prizes in fields other than literature$\}$.

   (c) $W \cap A \cap L' = \{$American women who have received Nobel Prizes in fields other than literature$\}$. This is so since to qualify for $W \cap A \cap L'$, a Nobel Prize winner must simultaneously be in W, in A, and in L'—that is, a woman, an American, and not a winner of the Nobel Prize in literature.

3. $(A \cap W') \cup L$.

5.2 A Fundamental Principle of Counting

A counting problem is one that requires us to determine the number of elements in a set S. Counting problems arise in many applications of mathematics and comprise the mathematical field of *combinatorics*. We shall study a number of different sorts of counting problems in the remainder of this chapter.

If S is any set, we will denote the number of elements in S by $n(S)$. For example, if $S = \{1, 7, 11\}$, then $n(S) = 3$, and if $S = \{a, b, c, d, e, f, g, h, i\}$, then $n(S) = 9$. Of course, if $S = \varnothing$, the empty set, then $n(S) = 0$. (The empty set contains no elements.)

Let us begin by stating one of the fundamental principles of counting, the *inclusion–exclusion principle*.

Inclusion–Exclusion Principle   Let S and T be sets. Then
$$n(S \cup T) = n(S) + n(T) - n(S \cap T). \tag{1}$$

Notice that formula (1) connects the four quantities $n(S \cup T)$, $n(S)$, $n(T)$, and $n(S \cap T)$. Given any three, the remaining quantity can be determined by using this formula.

To test the plausibility of the inclusion–exclusion principle, consider this example. Let $S = \{a, b, c, d, e\}$, $T = \{a, c, g, h\}$. Then

$$S \cup T = \{a, b, c, d, e, g, h\} \qquad n(S \cup T) = 7$$
$$S \cap T = \{a, c\} \qquad n(S \cap T) = 2.$$

In this case the inclusion–exclusion principle reads

$$n(S \cup T) = n(S) + n(T) - n(S \cap T)$$
$$7 \quad = \quad 5 \ + \ 4 \ - \quad 2,$$

which is correct.

Here is the reason for the validity of the inclusion–exclusion principle: The left side of formula (1) is $n(S \cup T)$, the number of elements in either S or T (or both). As a first approximation to this number, add the number of elements in S to the number of elements in T, obtaining $n(S) + n(T)$. However, if an element lies in both S and T, it is counted twice—once in $n(S)$ and again in $n(T)$. To make up for this double counting we must subtract the number of elements counted twice, namely $n(S \cap T)$. So doing gives us $n(S) + n(T) - n(S \cap T)$ as the number of elements in $S \cup T$.

The next example illustrates a typical use of the inclusion–exclusion principle in an applied problem.

▶ Example 1   In the year 2000, *Executive* magazine surveyed the presidents of the 500 largest corporations in the United States. Of these 500 people, 310 had degrees (of any sort) in business, 238 had undergraduate degrees in business, and 184 had graduate degrees in business. How many presidents had both undergraduate and graduate degrees in business?

Solution   Let

$$S = \{\text{presidents with an undergraduate degree in business}\}$$
$$T = \{\text{presidents with a graduate degree in business}\}.$$

Then

$S \cup T = \{\text{presidents with at least one degree in business}\}$

$S \cap T = \{\text{presidents with both undergraduate and graduate degrees in business}\}.$

From the data given we have

$$n(S) = 238 \qquad n(T) = 184 \qquad n(S \cup T) = 310.$$

The problem asks for $n(S \cap T)$. By the inclusion–exclusion principle we have

$$n(S \cup T) = n(S) + n(T) - n(S \cap T)$$
$$310 = 238 + 184 - n(S \cap T)$$
$$n(S \cap T) = 112.$$

That is, exactly 112 of the presidents had both undergraduate and graduate degrees in business.   ◆

It is possible to visualize sets geometrically by means of drawings known as *Venn diagrams*. Such graphical representations of sets are very useful tools in solving counting problems. In order to describe Venn diagrams, let us begin with a single set S contained in a universal set U. Draw a rectangle and view its points as the elements of U [Fig. 1(a)]. To show that S is a subset of U, we

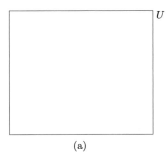
(a)

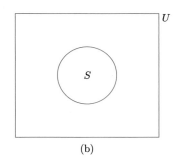
(b)

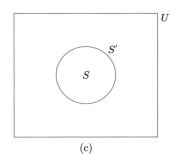
(c)

Figure 1.

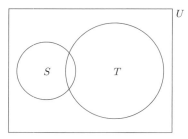

Figure 2.

draw a circle inside the rectangle and view S as the set of points in the circle [Fig. 1(b)]. The resulting diagram is called a Venn diagram of S. It illustrates the proper relationship between S and U. Since S' consists of those elements of U that are not in S, we may view the portion of the rectangle that is outside of the circle as representing S' [Fig. 1(c)].

Venn diagrams are particularly useful for visualizing the relationship between two or more sets. Suppose that we are given two sets S and T in a universal set U. As before, we represent each of the sets by means of a circle inside the rectangle (Fig. 2).

We can now illustrate a number of sets by shading in appropriate regions of the rectangle. For instance, in Fig. 3 we have shaded the regions corresponding to T, $S \cup T$, and $S \cap T$, respectively.

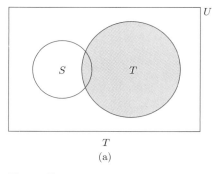

T

(a)

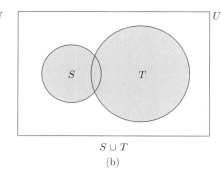

$S \cup T$

(b)

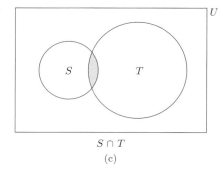

$S \cap T$

(c)

Figure 3.

▸ **Example 2** Shade the portions of the rectangle corresponding to the sets

(a) $S \cap T'$ (b) $(S \cap T')'$

Solution   (a) $S \cap T'$ consists of the points in S and in T', that is, the points in S and not in T. So we shade the points that are in the circle S but are not in the circle T [Fig. 4(a)].

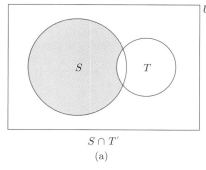

$S \cap T'$

(a)

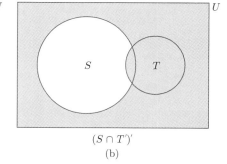

$(S \cap T')'$

(b)

Figure 4.

(b) $(S \cap T')'$ is the complement of the set $S \cap T'$. Therefore, it consists of exactly those points not shaded in Fig. 4(a). [See Fig. 4(b).]   ◆

In a similar manner, Venn diagrams can illustrate intersections and unions of three sets. Some representative regions are shaded in Fig. 5.

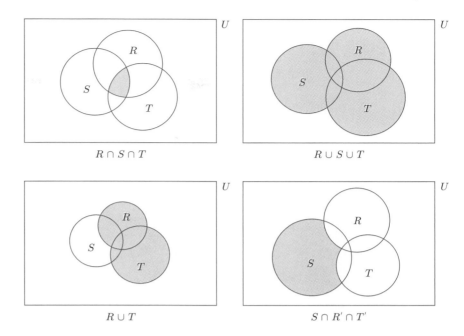

Figure 5.

There are many formulas expressing relationships between intersections and unions of sets. Possibly the most fundamental are the two formulas known as De Morgan's laws.

> **De Morgan's Laws** Let S and T be sets. Then
> $$(S \cup T)' = S' \cap T' \quad \text{and} \quad (S \cap T)' = S' \cup T'. \tag{2}$$

In other words, De Morgan's laws state that to form the complement of a union (or intersection), form the complements of the individual sets and change unions to intersections (or intersections to unions).

Verification of De Morgan's Laws Let us utilize Venn diagrams to describe $(S \cup T)'$. In Fig. 6(a) on the next page we have shaded the region corresponding to $S \cup T$. In Fig. 6(b) we have shaded the region corresponding to $(S \cup T)'$. On the other hand, in Fig. 6(c) we have shaded the region corresponding to S' and in Fig. 6(d) the region corresponding to T'. By considering the common shaded regions of Fig. 6(c) and (d), we arrive at the shaded region corresponding to $S' \cap T'$ [Fig. 6(e)]. Note that this is the same region as shaded in Fig. 6(b). Therefore,

$$(S \cup T)' = S' \cap T'.$$

This verifies the first of De Morgan's laws. The proof of the second law is similar.
◆

Practice Problems 5.2	**1.** Draw a two-circle Venn diagram and shade the portion corresponding to the set $(S \cap T') \cup (S \cap T)$.
	2. Suppose that $n(S) + n(T) = n(S \cup T)$. What can you conclude about S and T?

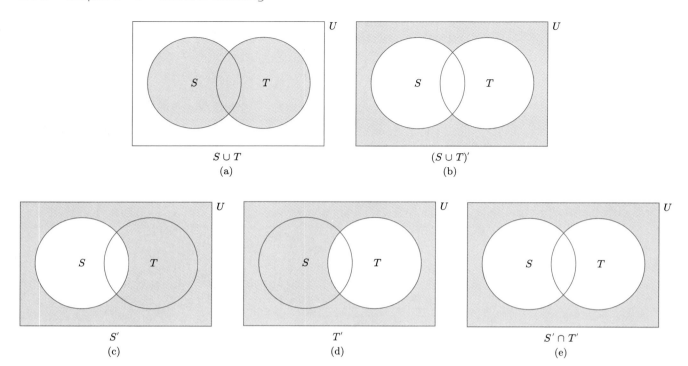

Figure 6.

▶ Exercises 5.2

1. Find $n(S \cup T)$, given that $n(S) = 5$, $n(T) = 4$, and $n(S \cap T) = 2$.

2. Find $n(S \cup T)$, given that $n(S) = 17$, $n(T) = 13$, and $n(S \cap T) = 9$.

3. Find $n(S \cap T)$, given that $n(S) = 7$, $n(T) = 8$, and $n(S \cup T) = 15$.

4. Find $n(S \cap T)$, given that $n(S) = 4$, $n(T) = 12$, and $n(S \cup T) = 15$.

5. Find $n(S)$, given that $n(T) = 7$, $n(S \cap T) = 5$, and $n(S \cup T) = 13$.

6. Find $n(T)$, given that $n(S) = 14$, $n(S \cap T) = 6$, and $n(S \cup T) = 14$.

7. If $n(S) = n(S \cap T)$, what can you conclude about S and T?

8. If $n(S) = n(S \cup T)$, what can you conclude about S and T?

9. Suppose that each of the 180 million adults in South America is fluent in Portuguese or Spanish. If 99 million are fluent in Portuguese and 95 million are fluent in Spanish, how many are fluent in both languages?

10. Suppose that all of the 1000 first-year students at a certain college are enrolled in a math or an English course. Suppose that 400 are taking both math and English and 600 are taking English. How many are taking a math course?

11. The combined membership of the MAA (Mathematical Association of America) and the AMS (American Mathematical Society) is 49,359; 28,348 people belong to the AMS and 7836 of them also belong to the MAA. How many people belong to the MAA?

12. A survey of employees in a certain company revealed that 300 people subscribe to *Newsweek*, 200 subscribe to *Time*, and 50 subscribe to both. How many people subscribe to at least one of these magazines?

13. Motors Inc. manufactured 325 cars with automatic transmissions, 216 with power steering, and 89 with both of these options. How many cars were manufactured with at least one of the two options?

14. A survey of 100 investors in stocks and bonds revealed that 80 investors owned stocks and 70 owned bonds. How many investors owned both stocks and bonds?

In Exercises 15–26, draw a two-circle Venn diagram and shade the portion corresponding to the set.

15. $S' \cap T'$

16. $S' \cap T$

17. $S \cup T'$

18. $S' \cup T'$

19. $(S \cap T)'$

20. $(S' \cap T)'$

21. $(S \cap T') \cup (S' \cap T)$

22. $(S \cap T) \cup (S' \cap T')$

23. $S \cup (S \cap T)$

24. $S \cup (T' \cup S)$

25. $S \cup S'$

26. $S \cap S'$

In Exercises 27–38, draw a three-circle Venn diagram and shade the portion corresponding to the set.

27. $R \cap S \cap T'$

28. $R' \cap S' \cap T$

29. $R \cup (S \cap T)$

30. $R \cap (S \cup T)$

31. $R \cap (S' \cup T)$

32. $R' \cup (S \cap T')$

33. $R \cap T$

34. $S \cap T'$

35. $R' \cap S' \cap T'$

36. $(R \cup S \cup T)'$

37. $(R \cap T) \cup (S \cap T')$

38. $(R \cup S') \cap (R \cup T')$

In Exercises 39–44, use De Morgan's laws to simplify the given expression.

39. $S' \cup (S \cap T)'$

40. $T \cap (S \cup T)'$

41. $(S' \cup T)'$

42. $(S' \cap T')'$

43. $T \cup (S \cap T)'$

44. $(S' \cap T)' \cup S$

In Exercises 45–50, give a set-theoretic expression that describes the shaded portion of the Venn diagram.

45.

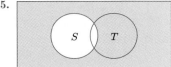

46.

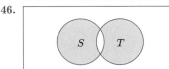

47.

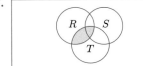

48.

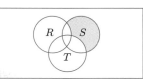

49.

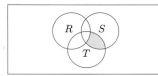

50.

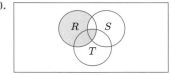

By drawing a Venn diagram, replace each of the expressions in Exercises 51–53 with one involving at most one union and the complement symbol applied only to R, S, and T.

51. $(T \cap S) \cup (T \cap R) \cup (R \cap S') \cup (T \cap R' \cap S')$

52. $(R \cap S) \cup (S \cap T) \cup (R \cap S' \cap T')$

53. $((R \cap S') \cup (S \cap T') \cup (T \cap R'))'$

Assume the universal set U is the set of all people living in the United States. Let A be the set of all citizens, B be the set of all legal aliens, and C be the set of all illegal aliens. Let D be the set of all children under 5 years of age, E be the set of children from 5 to 18 years old, and F be the set of everyone over the age of 18. Let G be the set of all people who are employed. Described in words the sets in Exercises 54–59.

54. $E \cap G \cap B$

55. $C' \cup (G \cap F)$

56. $A \cap (F \cup G)$

57. $F \cap G'$

58. $A \cap B$

59. $(A' \cup B) \cap G'$

Solutions to Practice Problems 5.2

1. $(S \cap T') \cup (S \cap T)$ is given as a union of two sets, $S \cap T'$ and $S \cap T$. The Venn diagrams for these two sets are given in Fig. 7(a) and (b). The desired set consists of the elements that are in one or the other (or both) of the two sets. Therefore, its Venn diagram is obtained by shading everything that is shaded in either Fig. 7(a) or (b) [see Fig. 7(c)]. [*Note:* Looking at Fig. 7(c) reveals that $(S \cap T') \cup (S \cap T)$ and S are the same set. Often Venn diagrams can be used to simplify complicated set-theoretic expressions.]

2. From the inclusion–exclusion principle, we obtain

$$n(S \cap T) = 0 \text{—that is, } S \cap T = \varnothing.$$

We conclude that S and T have no elements in common.

Solutions to Practice Problems 5.2 (Continued)

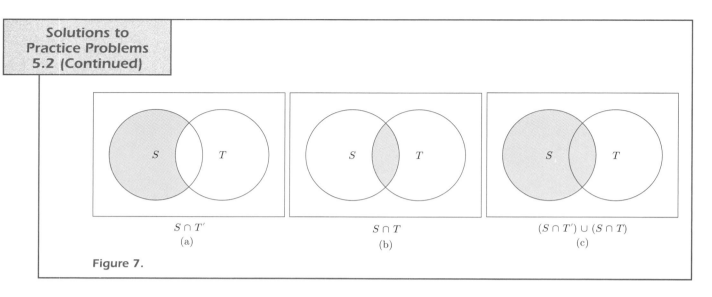

$S \cap T'$
(a)

$S \cap T$
(b)

$(S \cap T') \cup (S \cap T)$
(c)

Figure 7.

5.3 Venn Diagrams and Counting

In this section we discuss the use of Venn diagrams in solving counting problems. The techniques developed are especially useful in analyzing survey data.

Each Venn diagram divides the universal set U into a certain number of regions. For example, the Venn diagram for a single set divides U into two regions—the inside and outside of the circle [Fig. 1(a)]. The Venn diagram for two sets divides U into four regions [Fig. 1(b)]. And the Venn diagram for three sets divides U into eight regions [Fig. 1(c)]. Each of the regions is called a *basic region* for the Venn diagram. Knowing the number of elements in each basic region is of great use in many applied problems. As an illustration consider the following example.

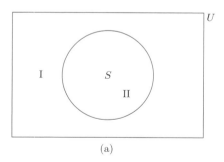

(a)

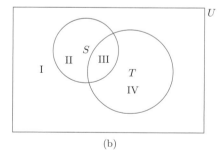

(b)

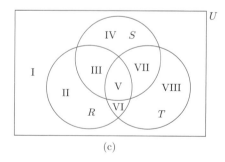

(c)

Figure 1.

▶ **Example 1**   Let

$U = \{$winners of the Nobel Prize during the period 1901–1999$\}$

$A = \{$American winners of the Nobel Prize during the period 1901–1999$\}$

$C = \{$winners of the Nobel Prize in chemistry during the period 1901–1999$\}$

$P = \{$winners of the Nobel Peace Prize during the period 1901–1999$\}$.

These sets are illustrated in the Venn diagram of Fig. 2 in which each basic region has been labeled with the number of elements in it.

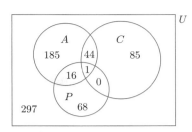

Figure 2.

(a) How many Americans received a Nobel Prize during the period 1901–1999?

(b) How many Americans received Nobel Prizes in fields other than chemistry and peace during this period?

(c) How many Americans received the Nobel Peace Prize during this period?

(d) How many people received Nobel Prizes during this period?

Solution (a) The number of Americans who received a Nobel Prize is the total contained in the circle A, which is

$$185 + 16 + 1 + 44 = 246 \quad [\text{Fig. 3(a)}].$$

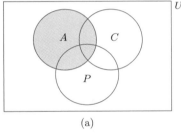 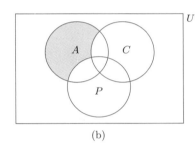 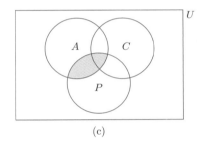

(a)   (b)   (c)

Figure 3.

(b) The question asks for the number of Nobel laureates in A but not in C and not in P. So start with the A circle and eliminate those basic regions belonging to C or P [Fig. 3(b)]. There remains a single basic region with 185 Nobel laureates. Note that this region corresponds to $A \cap C' \cap P'$.

(c) The question asks for the number of elements in both A and P—that is, $n(A \cap P)$. But $A \cap P$ comprises two basic regions [Fig. 3(c)]. Thus, to compute $n(A \cap P)$ we add the numbers in these basic regions to obtain $16 + 1 = 17$ Americans who have won the Nobel Peace Prize.

(d) The number of recipients is just $n(U)$, and we obtain it by adding together the numbers corresponding to the basic regions. We obtain

$$297 + 185 + 44 + 1 + 16 + 85 + 0 + 68 = 696. \qquad ◆$$

One need not always be given the number of elements in each of the basic regions of a Venn diagram. Very often these data can be deduced from given information.

▶ **Example 2** Consider the set of 500 corporate presidents of Example 1, Section 5.2.

(a) Draw a Venn diagram displaying the given data, and determine the number of elements in each basic region.

(b) Determine the number of presidents having exactly one degree (graduate or undergraduate) in business.

Solution   (a) Recall that we defined the following sets:

$$S = \{\text{presidents with an undergraduate degree in business}\}$$
$$T = \{\text{presidents with a graduate degree in business}\}.$$

We were given the following data:

$$n(S) = 238 \qquad n(T) = 184 \qquad n(S \cup T) = 310.$$

We draw a Venn diagram corresponding to S and T (Fig. 4). Notice that none of the given information corresponds to a basic region of the Venn diagram. So we must use our wits to determine the number of presidents in each of the regions I–IV. Region I is the complement of $S \cup T$, so it contains

$$n(U) - n(S \cup T) = 500 - 310 = 190$$

presidents. Region III is just $S \cap T$. By using the inclusion–exclusion principle, in Example 1, Section 5.2, we determined that $n(S \cap T) = 112$. Now the total number of presidents in II and III combined equals $n(S)$, or 238. Therefore, the number of presidents in II is

$$238 - 112 = 126.$$

Similarly, the number of presidents in IV is

$$184 - 112 = 72.$$

Thus we may fill in the data to obtain a completed Venn diagram (Fig. 5).

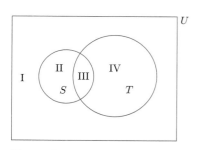

Figure 4.

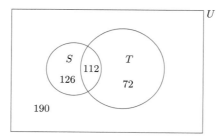

Figure 5.

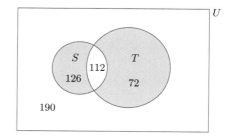

Figure 6.

(b) The number of people with exactly one business degree corresponds to the shaded region in Fig. 6. Adding together the number of presidents in each of these regions gives $126 + 72 = 198$ presidents with exactly one business degree.   ◆

Here is another example illustrating the procedure for determining the number of elements in each of the basic regions of a Venn diagram.

▶ Example 3   An advertising agency finds that of its 170 clients, 115 use television (T), 100 use radio (R), 130 use magazines (M), 75 use television and radio, 95 use radio and magazines, 85 use television and magazines, and 70 use all three. Use these data to complete a Venn diagram displaying the use of mass media (Fig. 7).

Solution   Of the various data given, only the last item corresponds to one of the eight basic regions of the Venn diagram, namely the "70" corresponding to the use of all three media. So we begin by entering this number in the diagram [Fig. 8(a)]. We can fill in the rest of the Venn diagram by working with the remaining information one piece at a time in the reverse order that it is given. Since 85 clients advertise in television and magazines, $85 - 70 = 15$ advertise in television and magazines but not on radio. The appropriate region is labeled in Fig. 8(b). In Fig. 8(c) the next

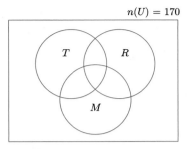

$n(U) = 170$

Figure 7.

two pieces of information have been used in the same way to fill in two more basic regions. In Fig. 8(c) we observe that three of the four basic regions comprising M have been filled in. Since $n(M) = 130$, we deduce that the number of clients advertising only in magazines is $130 - (15 + 70 + 25) = 130 - 110 = 20$ [Fig. 9(a)]. By similar reasoning the number of clients using only radio advertising and the number using only television advertising can be determined [Fig. 9(b)]. Adding together the numbers in the three circles gives the number of clients utilizing television, radio, or magazines as $25 + 5 + 0 + 15 + 70 + 25 + 20 = 160$. Since there were 170 clients in total, the remainder—or $170 - 160 = 10$ clients—use none of these media. Figure 9(c) gives a complete display of the data. ◆

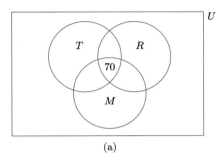

(a)

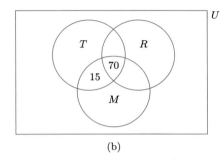

(b)

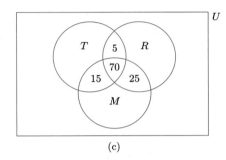

(c)

Figure 8.

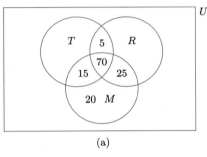

(a)

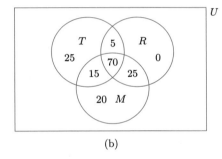

(b)

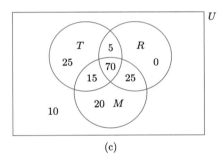

(c)

Figure 9.

Practice Problems 5.3

1. Of the 1000 first-year students at a certain college, 700 take mathematics courses, 300 take mathematics and economics courses, and 200 do not take any mathematics or economics courses. Represent these data in a Venn diagram.

2. Refer to the Venn diagram from Problem 1.

   (a) How many of the first-year students take an economics course?

   (b) How many take an economics course but not a mathematics course?

▶ Exercises 5.3

In Exercises 1–12, let R, S, and T be subsets of the universal set U. Draw an appropriate Venn diagram and use the given data to determine the number of elements in each basic region.

1. $n(U) = 14$, $n(S) = 5$, $n(T) = 6$, $n(S \cap T) = 2$.

2. $n(U) = 20$, $n(S) = 11$, $n(T) = 7$, $n(S \cap T) = 7$.

3. $n(U) = 20$, $n(S) = 12$, $n(T) = 14$, $n(S \cup T) = 18$.

4. $n(S') = 6$, $n(S \cup T) = 10$, $n(S \cap T) = 5$, $n(T) = 7$.

5. $n(U) = 75$, $n(S) = 15$, $n(T) = 25$, $n(S' \cap T') = 40$.

6. $n(S) = 9$, $n(T) = 11$, $n(S \cap T) = 5$, $n(S') = 13$.

7. $n(S) = 3$, $n(S \cup T) = 6$, $n(T) = 4$, $n(S' \cup T') = 9$.

8. $n(U) = 15$, $n(S) = 8$, $n(T) = 9$, $n(S \cup T) = 14$.

9. $n(U) = 44$, $n(R) = 17$, $n(S) = 17$, $n(T) = 17$,
   $n(R \cap S) = 7$, $n(R \cap T) = 6$, $n(S \cap T) = 5$,
   $n(R \cap S \cap T) = 2$.

10. $n(U) = 29$, $n(R) = 10$, $n(S) = 12$, $n(T) = 10$,
    $n(R \cap S) = 1$, $n(R \cap T) = 5$, $n(S \cap T) = 4$,
    $n(R \cap S \cap T) = 1$.

11. $n(R') = 22$, $n(R \cup S) = 21$, $n(S) = 14$, $n(T) = 22$,
    $n(R \cap S) = 7$, $n(S \cap T) = 9$, $n(R \cap T) = 11$,
    $n(R \cap S \cap T) = 5$.

12. $n(U) = 64$, $n(R \cup S \cup T) = 45$, $n(R) = 22$, $n(T) = 26$,
    $n(R \cap S) = 4$, $n(S \cap T) = 6$, $n(R \cap T) = 8$,
    $n(R \cap S \cap T) = 1$.

13. A survey of 70 high school students revealed that 35 like folk music, 15 like classical music, and 5 like both. How many of the students surveyed do not like either folk or classical music?

14. A total of 696 Nobel Prizes had been awarded by 1999. Fourteen of the 99 prizes in literature were awarded to Scandinavians. Scandinavians received a total of 45 awards. How many Nobel Prizes outside of literature have been awarded to non-Scandinavians?

15. Out of 35 students in a finite math class, 22 are male, 19 are business majors, 27 are first-year students, 14 are male business students, 17 are male first-year students, 15 are first-year students who are business majors, and 11 are male first-year business majors. How many upperclass female nonbusiness majors are in the class? How many female business majors are in the class?

16. A survey of 100 college faculty who exercise regularly found that 45 jog, 30 swim, 20 cycle, 6 jog and swim, 1 jogs and cycles, 5 swim and cycle, and 1 does all three. How many of the faculty members do not do any of these three activities? How many just jog?

17. One hundred college students were surveyed after voting in an election involving a Democrat and a Republican. Fifty were first-year students, 55 voted Democratic, and 25 were non–first-year students who voted Republican. How many first-year students voted Democratic?

18. A group of 100 workers were asked if they were college graduates and if they belonged to a union. Sixty were not college graduates, 20 were nonunion college graduates, and 30 were union members. How many of the workers were neither college graduates nor union members?

19. A class of 30 students was given a diagnostic test on the first day of a mathematics course. At the end of the semester, only 2 of the 21 students who had passed the diagnostic test failed the course. A total of 23 students passed the course. How many students managed to pass the course even though they had failed the diagnostic test?

20. A group of applicants for training as air-traffic controllers consisted of 35 pilots, 20 veterans, 30 pilots who were not veterans, and 50 people who were neither veterans nor pilots. How large was the group?

21. One of Shakespeare's sonnets has a verb in 11 of its 14 lines, an adjective in 9 lines, and both in 7 lines. How many lines have a verb but no adjective? An adjective and no verb? Neither an adjective nor a verb?

Of the 130 students who took a mathematics exam, 90 correctly answered the first question, 62 correctly answered the second question, and 50 correctly answered both questions. Exercises 22–26 refer to these students.

22. How many students correctly answered either the first or second question?

23. How many students did not answer either of the two questions correctly?

24. How many students answered either the first or the second question correctly, but not both?

25. How many students answered the second question correctly, but not the first?

26. How many students missed the second question?

A collector of football cards has 2200 cards. He has 1500 players from the National Football League (NFL), 900 who played defense, and 400 who played defense for the NFL. Exercises 27–32 refer to these football players.

27. How many players either were in the NFL or played defense?

28. How many players played defense but were not in the NFL?

29. How many players played offense but were not in the NFL?

30. How many players played offense in the NFL?

31. How many players either played defense or were in the NFL, but not both?

32. How many players did not play defense for the NFL?

A campus radio station surveyed 190 students to determine the types of music they liked. The survey revealed that 114 liked rock, 50 liked country, and 41 liked classical music. Moreover, 14 liked rock and country, 15 liked rock and classical, 11 liked classical and country, and 5 liked all three types of music. Exercises 33–40 refer to the students in this survey.

33. How many students like rock only?

34. How many students like country but not rock?

35. How many students like classical and country but not rock?

36. How many students like classical or country but not rock?

37. How many students like exactly one of the three types of music?

38. How many students do not like any of the three types of music?

39. How many students like at least two of the three types of music?

40. How many students do not like either rock or country?

A merchant surveyed 400 people to determine the way they learned about an upcoming sale. The survey showed that 180 learned about the sale from the radio, 190 from television, 190 from the newspaper, 80 from radio and television, 90 from radio and newspapers, 50 from television and newspapers, and 30 from all three sources. Exercises 41–46 refer to the people in this survey.

41. How many people learned of the sale from newspapers or radio, but not both?

42. How many people learned of the sale only from newspapers?

43. How many people learned of the sale from radio or television but not the newspaper?

44. How many people learned of the sale from at least two of the three media?

45. How many people learned of the sale from exactly one of the three media?

46. How many people learned of the sale from radio and television but not the newspaper?

47. One hundred and eighty business executives were surveyed to determine if they regularly read *Fortune*, *Time*, or *Money* magazines. Seventy-five read *Fortune*, 70 read *Time*, 55 read *Money*, 45 read exactly two of the three magazines, 25 read *Fortune* and *Time*, 25 read *Time* and *Money*, and 5 read all three magazines. How many read none of the three magazines?

48. A survey of the characteristics of 100 small businesses that had failed revealed that 95 of them either were undercapitalized, had inexperienced management, or had a poor location. Four of the businesses had all three of these characteristics. Forty businesses were undercapitalized but had experienced management and good location. Fifteen businesses had inexperienced management but sufficient capitalization and good location. Seven were undercapitalized and had inexperienced management. Nine were undercapitalized and had poor location. Ten had inexperienced management and poor location. How many of the businesses had poor location? Which of the three characteristics was most prevalent in the failed businesses?

Use a Venn diagram to find the number of people in the sets given in Exercises 49–53. A survey in a local high school shows that of the 4000 students in the school, 2000 take French (F), 3000 take Spanish (S), and 500 take Latin (L). The survey shows that 1500 take both French and Spanish, 300 take both French and Latin, and 200 take Spanish and Latin. Fifty students take all three languages.

49. $L \cap (F \cup S)$

50. $(L \cup F \cup S)'$

51. $L \cup S \cup F'$

52. L'

53. $F \cap S' \cap L'$

Solutions to Practice Problems 5.3	

1. Draw a Venn diagram with two circles, one for mathematics (M) and one for economics (E) [Fig. 10(a)]. This Venn diagram has four basic regions, and our goal is to label each basic region with the proper number of students. The numbers for two of the basic regions are given directly. Since "300 take mathematics and economics," $n(M \cap E) = 300$. Since "200 do not take any mathematics or economics courses," $n((M \cup E)') = 200$ [Fig. 10(b)]. Now "700 take mathematics courses." Since M is made up of two basic regions and one region has 300 elements, the other basic region of M must contain 400 elements [Fig. 10(c)]. At this point all but one of the basic regions have been labeled and $400 + 300 + 200 = 900$ students have been accounted for. Since there is a total of 1000 students, the remaining basic region has 100 students [Fig. 10(d)].

2. (a) 400. "Economics" refers to the entire circle E, which is made up of two basic regions, one having 300 elements and the other 100. (A common error is to interpret the question as asking for the number of first-year students who take economics exclusively and therefore give the answer 100. To say that a person takes an economics course does not imply anything about the person's enrollment in mathematics courses.)

   (b) 100.

**Solutions to
Practice Problems
5.3 (Continued)**

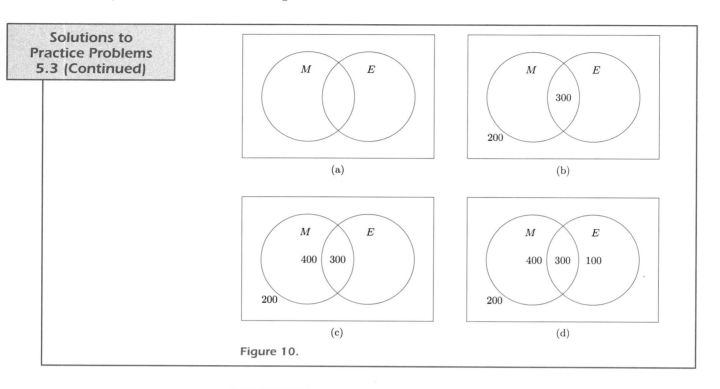

Figure 10.

5.4 The Multiplication Principle

In this section we introduce a second fundamental principle of counting, the *multiplication principle*. By way of motivation, consider the following example.

▶ Example 1

A medical researcher wishes to test the effect of a drug on a rat's perception by studying the rat's ability to run a maze while under the influence of the drug. The maze is constructed so that to arrive at the exit point C, the rat must pass through a central point B. There are five paths from the entry point A to B, and three paths from B to C. In how many different ways can the rat run the maze from A to C? (See Fig. 1.)

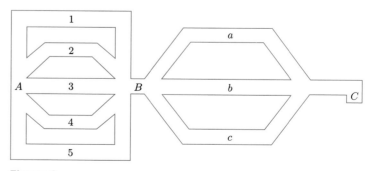

Figure 1.

Solution

The paths from A to B have been labeled 1 through 5, and the paths from B to C have been labeled a through c. The various paths through the maze can be schematically represented as in Fig. 2. The diagram shows that there are five

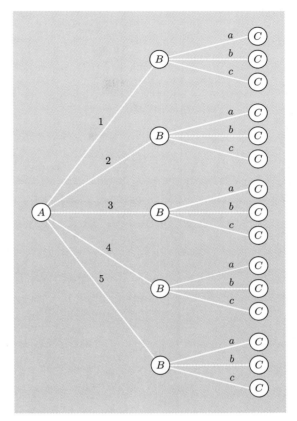

Figure 2.

ways to go from A to B. For each of these five ways, there are three ways to go from B to C. So there are five groups of three paths each, and therefore $5 \cdot 3 = 15$ possible paths from A to C. (A diagram such as Fig. 2, called a *tree diagram*, is useful in enumerating the various possibilities in counting problems.)　　◆

In the preceding problem, choosing a path is a task that can be broken up into two consecutive operations.

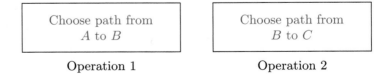

The first operation can be performed in five ways and, after the first operation has been carried out, the second can be performed in three ways. And we determined that the entire task can be performed in $5 \cdot 3 = 15$ ways. The same reasoning as just used yields the following useful counting principle:

Multiplication Principle　Suppose that a task is composed of two consecutive operations. If operation 1 can be performed in m ways and, for each of these, operation 2 can be performed in n ways, then the complete task can be performed in $m \cdot n$ ways.

▶ **Example 2**   An airline passenger must fly from New York to Frankfurt via London. There are 8 flights leaving New York for London. All of these provide connections on any one of 19 flights from London to Frankfurt. In how many different ways can the passenger book reservations?

Solution   The task "fly from New York to Frankfurt" is composed of two consecutive operations:

Fly from New York to London	Fly from London to Frankfurt
Operation 1	Operation 2

From the data given, the multiplication principle implies that the task can be accomplished in $8 \cdot 19 = 152$ ways.   ◆

It is possible to generalize the multiplication principle to tasks consisting of more than two operations.

> **Generalized Multiplication Principle**   Suppose that a task consists of t operations performed consecutively. Suppose that operation 1 can be performed in m_1 ways; for each of these, operation 2 in m_2 ways; for each of these, operation 3 in m_3 ways; and so forth. Then the task can be performed in
> $$m_1 \cdot m_2 \cdot m_3 \cdot \cdots \cdot m_t \quad \text{ways.}$$

▶ **Example 3**   A corporation has a board of directors consisting of 10 members. The board must select from among its members a chairperson, vice chairperson, and secretary. In how many ways can this be done?

Solution   The task "select the three officers" can be divided into three consecutive operations:

Select chairperson	Select vice chairperson	Select secretary

Since there are 10 directors, operation 1 can be performed in 10 ways. After the chairperson has been selected, there are 9 directors left as possible candidates for vice chairperson, so that for each way of performing operation 1, operation 2 can be performed in 9 ways. After this has been done, there are 8 directors who are possible candidates for secretary, so operation 3 can be performed in 8 ways. By the generalized multiplication principle, the number of possible ways to perform the sequence of three operations equals $10 \cdot 9 \cdot 8$, or 720. So the officers of the board can be selected in 720 ways.   ◆

In Example 3 we made important use of the phrase "for each of these" in the generalized multiplication principle. The operation "select a vice chairperson" can be performed in 10 ways, since any member of the board is eligible. However, when we view the selection process as a sequence of operations of which "select a vice chairperson" is the second operation, the situation has changed. *For each way* that the first operation is performed, one person will have been used up; hence there will be only 9 possibilities for choosing the vice chairperson.

▶ Example 4   In how many ways can a baseball team of nine members arrange themselves in a line for a group picture?

Solution   Choose the players by their place in the picture, say from left to right. The first can be chosen in nine ways; for each of these choices the second can be chosen in eight ways; for each of these choices the third can be chosen in seven ways; and so forth. So the number of possible arrangements is

$$9 \cdot 8 \cdot 7 \cdot 6 \cdot 5 \cdot 4 \cdot 3 \cdot 2 \cdot 1 = 362{,}880.$$ ◆

▶ Example 5   A certain state uses automobile license plates that consist of three letters followed by three digits. How many such license plates are there?

Solution   The task in this case, "form a license plate," consists of a sequence of six operations: three for choosing letters and three for choosing digits. Each letter can be chosen in 26 ways and each digit in 10 ways. So the number of license plates is

$$26 \cdot 26 \cdot 26 \cdot 10 \cdot 10 \cdot 10 = 17{,}576{,}000.$$ ◆

Practice Problems 5.4

1. There are six seats available in a sedan. In how many ways can six people be seated if only three can drive?

2. A multiple-choice exam contains 10 questions, each having 3 possible answers. How many different ways are there of completing the exam?

▶ Exercises 5.4

1. If there are three routes from College Park to Baltimore and five routes from Baltimore to New York, how many routes are there from College Park to New York via Baltimore?

2. How many different outfits consisting of a coat and a hat can be chosen from two coats and three hats?

3. How many different two-letter words (including nonsense words) can be formed when repetition of letters is allowed?

4. How many different two-letter words (including nonsense words) can be formed such that the two letters are distinct?

5. A railway has 20 stations. If the names of the point of departure and the destination are printed on each ticket, how many different kinds of single tickets must be printed?

6. Refer to Exercise 5. How many different kinds of tickets are needed if each ticket may be used in either direction between two stations?

7. A man has five different pairs of gloves. In how many ways can he select a right-hand glove and a left-hand glove that do not match?

8. How many license plates consisting of two letters followed by four digits are possible?

9. How many ways can five people be arranged in a line for a group picture?

10. In how many different ways can four books be arranged on a bookshelf?

11. Toss a coin six times and observe the sequence of heads or tails that results. How many different sequences are possible?

12. Refer to Exercise 11. In how many of the sequences are the first and last tosses identical?

13. Twenty athletes enter an Olympic event. How many different possibilities are there for winning the Gold Medal, Silver Medal, and Bronze Medal?

14. A sportswriter is asked to rank eight teams. How many different orderings are possible?

15. In how many different ways can a 30-member football team select a captain and an assistant captain?

16. How many different outfits can be selected from two coats, three hats, and two scarves?

17. How many different words (including nonsense words) can be formed using the four letters of the word "MATH"?

18. If you can travel from Frederick, Maryland, to Baltimore, Maryland, by car, bus, or train and from Baltimore to London by airplane or ship, how many different ways are there to go from Frederick to London?

19. An exam contains five "true or false" questions. In how many different ways can the exam be completed?

20. A company has 700 employees. Explain why there must be two people with the same pair of initials.

21. A computer manufacturer assigns serial numbers to its computers. The first symbol of a serial number is either A, B, or C, indicating the manufacturing plant. The second and third symbols taken together are one of the numbers $01, 02, \ldots, 12$, indicating the month of manufacture. The final four symbols are digits. How many possible serial numbers are there?

22. How many four-letter words (including nonsense words) can be made from the letters of "statistics," assuming that each word may not have repeated letters?

23. How many four-letter words (including nonsense words) can be made from the letters h, o, t, s, m, x, and e for each of the following conditions?

    (a) Letters can be repeated.

    (b) Letters cannot be repeated.

    (c) Words must begin with an h, and repetitions are allowed.

    (d) Words must end with a vowel, and repetitions are not allowed.

24. A group of five boys and three girls is to be photographed.

    (a) How many ways can they be arranged in one row?

    (b) How many ways can they be arranged with the girls in the front row and the boys in the back row?

25. The manager of a Little League baseball team has picked the nine starting players for a game. How many different batting orders are possible under each of the following conditions?

    (a) There are no restrictions.

    (b) The pitcher must bat last.

    (c) The pitcher must bat last, the catcher eighth, and the shortstop first.

26. How many different ways can a Venn diagram with two circles be shaded?

27. How many different ways can a Venn diagram with three circles be shaded?

28. A club can elect a member as president and a different member as treasurer in 506 different ways. How many members does the club have?

29. An exam contains six true or false statements. In how many ways can the exam be completed if leaving the answer blank is also an option?

30. A physiologist wants to test the effects of exercise and meditation on blood pressure. She devises four different exercise programs and three different meditation programs. If she wants 10 subjects for each combination of exercise and meditation program, how many volunteers must she recruit?

31. A college student eats all his meals at a restaurant offering six breakfast specials, seven lunch specials, and four dinner specials. How many days can he go without repeating an entire day's menu selection?

32. An area code is a three-digit number where the first digit cannot be 0 or 1. How many different area codes are possible?

33. A clothing store offers three styles of sweaters with each sweater available in six colors. How many different sweaters are there?

34. A furniture manufacturer makes three types of upholstered chairs and offers a choice of 20 fabrics. How many different chairs are available?

35. Six houses in a row are each to be painted with one of the colors red, blue, green, and yellow. In how many different ways can the houses be painted so that no two adjacent houses are of the same color?

36. How many three-digit odd numbers can be formed using the digits 1, 2, 3, 4, 5, 6, and 7?

37. Each of the 10 questions on a multiple-choice exam has four possible answers. How many different ways are there for a student to answer the questions? Assume that every question must be answered.

38. Fred has 10 different pairs of shoes. In how many ways can he put on a pair of shoes that do not match?

39. Suppose that Jack wants to go from Florida to Maine via New York and can travel each leg of the journey by bus, car, train, or airplane. How many different ways can Jack make the trip?

40. A restaurant menu lists 6 appetizers, 10 entrées, and 5 desserts. How many ways can a diner select a three-course meal?

41. How many ways can a milkman deliver 10 distinguishable bottles of milk on a street containing five houses?

42. A computer manufacturer offers a computer with a choice of four types of monitors, two types of keyboards, and three types of hard drives. How many different computers are offered?

43. Seven candidates for mayor, 4 candidates for city council president, and 12 propositions are being put before the electorate. How many different ballots could be cast, assuming that every voter votes on each of the items? If voters can choose to leave any item blank, how many different ballots are possible?

44. The gift-wrap desk at a large department store offers 5 box sizes, 10 wrapping papers, 7 colors of ribbon in two widths, and 9 special items to be added on the bow. How many different ways are there to gift-wrap a package assuming that the customer must choose at least a box but need not choose any of the other offerings?

45. Jose was told to get a dozen oranges, eight apples, and a half-pound of grapes. When he gets to the store he finds five varieties of oranges, five varieties of apples, and two varieties of grapes. Assuming that he buys only one variety of each type of fruit, how many different bags of fruit could he bring home?

46. Allison is preparing her applications for college. She will apply to three community colleges and has to fill out five parts to each of those applications. She will apply to three four-year schools, each of which has a six-part application. How many application segments must she complete?

47. An automobile dealer is offering five models of a particular car. On each model the customer may choose cloth or leather seats, each available in three colors, automatic or manual transmission, and a CD player or a cassette player. The car can be ordered in any one of eight exterior colors. How many different cars can be ordered?

48. In the game of *Clue*, there are six suspects in a murder that was committed in any one of nine rooms, using any one of six weapons. How many scenarios are possible?

49. James chooses a number from 1 to 100 (inclusive), Janet chooses a number between 1 and 100 that is divisible by 7, and Sandy chooses a number between 1 and 100 that is divisible by 21. How many triples of numbers are possible?

50. How many four-digit numbers can be formed using the digits $\{1, 2, 3, 4, 5, 6, 7\}$ if adjacent digits must be different?

51. A grocery store makes up fruit baskets using as many as four apples, three pears, and four oranges. A basket must contain at least one piece of fruit. How many different fruit selections are possible? (From *The Mathematics Teacher*, December 1991)

52. How many Social Security numbers are available if the only restriction is that the number 000-00-0000 cannot be assigned?

53. An art gallery has two paintings by each of four artists. In how many ways can the eight paintings be displayed in a row if paintings by the same artist must be adjacent to each other?

54. Consider the following triangular display of letters. Start with the letter T at the top and move down the triangle to a letter S at the bottom. From any given letter move only to one of the letters directly below it on the left or right. How many different paths spell *TEXAS*?

$$T$$
$$E \quad E$$
$$X \quad X \quad X$$
$$A \quad A \quad A \quad A$$
$$S \quad S \quad S \quad S \quad S$$

55. A girl dresses in the morning in a blouse, a skirt, and shoes. She always wears standard white socks. She wants to wear a different combination on every day of the year. If she has the same number of blouses, skirts, and pairs of shoes, how many of each article would she need to have a different combination every day? (From *The Mathematics Teacher*, February 1996)

56. Three couples go on a movie date. In how many ways can they be seated in a row of six seats so that each couple is seated together?

57. How many different three-letter words (including nonsense words) are there in which successive letters are different?

58. A panel of eight experts is to present opposing arguments in a discussion of legalizing marijuana for medical purposes. The four proponents arrive first and decide to sit in such a way that the panelists will alternate pro and con. In how many ways can the four proponents be seated? In how many ways can all eight panelists be seated if they adhere to the same seating rules?

Solutions to Practice Problems 5.4

1. 360. Pretend that you are given the task of seating the six people. This task consists of six operations performed consecutively, as shown in Table 1. After you have performed operation 1, five people will remain, and any one of these five can be seated in the middle front seat. After operation 2, four people remain, and so on. By the generalized multiplication principle, the task can be performed in $3 \cdot 5 \cdot 4 \cdot 3 \cdot 2 \cdot 1 = 360$ ways.

2. 3^{10}. The task of answering the questions consists of 10 consecutive operations, each of which can be performed in three ways. Therefore, by the generalized multiplication principle, the task can be performed in

$$\underbrace{3 \cdot 3 \cdot 3 \cdot \cdots \cdot 3}_{\text{10 terms}} \text{ ways.}$$

(*Note*: The answer can be left as 3^{10} or can be multiplied out to 59,049.)

Table 1	
Operation	Number of ways operation can be performed
1: Select person to drive	3
2: Select person for middle front seat	5
3: Select person for right front seat	4
4: Select person for left rear seat	3
5: Select person for middle rear seat	2
6: Select person for right rear seat	1

5.5 Permutations and Combinations

In preceding sections we have solved a variety of counting problems using Venn diagrams and the generalized multiplication principle. Let us now turn our attention to two types of counting problems that occur very frequently and that can be solved using formulas derived from the generalized multiplication principle. These problems involve what are called permutations and combinations, which are particular types of arrangements of elements of a set. The sorts of arrangements we have in mind are illustrated in two problems:

Problem A   How many words (by which we mean strings of letters) of two distinct letters can be formed from the letters $\{a, b, c\}$?

Problem B   A construction crew has three members. A team of two must be chosen for a particular job. In how many ways can the team be chosen?

Each of the two problems can be solved by enumerating all possibilities.

Solution of Problem A   There are six possible words, namely

$$ab \qquad ac \qquad ba \qquad bc \qquad ca \qquad cb.$$

Solution of Problem B   Designate the three crew members by a, b, and c. Then there are three possible two-person teams, namely

$$ab \qquad ac \qquad bc.$$

(Note that ba, the team consisting of b and a, is the same as the team ab.)

We deliberately set up both problems using the same letters in order to facilitate comparison. Both problems are concerned with counting the numbers of arrangements of the elements of the set $\{a, b, c\}$, taken two at a time, without allowing repetition (for example, aa was not allowed). However, in Problem A the order of the arrangement mattered, whereas in Problem B it did not. Arrangements of the sort considered in Problem A are called *permutations*, whereas those in Problem B are called *combinations*.

More precisely, suppose that we are given a set of n objects.[1] Then a *permutation of n objects taken r at a time* is an arrangement of r of the n objects in

---
[1] All are assumed to be different.

a specific order. So, for example, Problem A was concerned with permutations of the three objects, a, b, c ($n = 3$), taken two at a time ($r = 2$). A *combination of n objects taken r at a time* is a selection of r objects from among the n, with order disregarded. Thus, for example, in Problem B we considered combinations of the three objects a, b, c ($n = 3$), taken two at a time ($r = 2$).

It is convenient to introduce the following notation for counting permutations and combinations. Let

$$P(n, r) = \text{the number of permutations of } n \text{ objects taken } r \text{ at a time}$$

$$C(n, r) = \text{the number of combinations of } n \text{ objects taken } r \text{ at a time.}$$

Thus, for example, from our solutions to Problems A and B, we have

$$P(3, 2) = 6 \qquad C(3, 2) = 3.$$

Very simple formulas for $P(n, r)$ and $C(n, r)$ allow us to calculate these quantities for any n and r. Let us begin by stating the formula for $P(n, r)$. For $r = 1, 2, 3$ we have, respectively,

$$P(n, 1) = n$$
$$P(n, 2) = n(n - 1) \qquad \text{(two factors)}$$
$$P(n, 3) = n(n - 1)(n - 2) \qquad \text{(three factors),}$$

and, in general,

$$P(n, r) = n(n - 1)(n - 2) \cdot \cdots \cdot (n - r + 1) \qquad (r \text{ factors}). \tag{1}$$

This formula is verified at the end of this section.

▶ **Example 1** Compute the following numbers.

(a) $P(100, 2)$ (b) $P(6, 4)$ (c) $P(5, 5)$

Solution   (a) Here $n = 100$, $r = 2$. So we take the product of two factors, beginning with 100:

$$P(100, 2) = 100 \cdot 99 = 9900.$$

(b) $P(6, 4) = 6 \cdot 5 \cdot 4 \cdot 3 = 360$

(c) $P(5, 5) = 5 \cdot 4 \cdot 3 \cdot 2 \cdot 1 = 120$ ◆

In order to state the formula for $C(n, r)$, we must introduce some further notation. Suppose that r is any positive integer. We denote by $r!$ (read "r factorial") the product of all positive integers from r down to 1:

$$r! = r \cdot (r - 1) \cdot \cdots \cdot 2 \cdot 1.$$

For instance,

$$1! = 1$$
$$2! = 2 \cdot 1 = 2$$
$$3! = 3 \cdot 2 \cdot 1 = 6$$
$$4! = 4 \cdot 3 \cdot 2 \cdot 1 = 24$$
$$5! = 5 \cdot 4 \cdot 3 \cdot 2 \cdot 1 = 120.$$

In terms of this notation we can state a very simple formula for $C(n, r)$, the number of combinations of n things taken r at a time.

$$C(n,r) = \frac{P(n,r)}{r!} = \frac{n(n-1)\cdot\;\cdots\;\cdot(n-r+1)}{r(r-1)\cdot\;\cdots\;\cdot 1} \qquad (2)$$

This formula is verified at the end of this section.

▶ Example 2   Compute the following numbers.

(a) $C(100, 2)$ (b) $C(6, 4)$ (c) $C(5, 5)$

Solution   (a) $C(100, 2) = \dfrac{P(100, 2)}{2!} = \dfrac{100 \cdot 99}{2 \cdot 1} = 4950$

(b) $C(6, 4) = \dfrac{P(6, 4)}{4!} = \dfrac{6 \cdot 5 \cdot 4 \cdot 3}{4 \cdot 3 \cdot 2 \cdot 1} = 15$

(c) $C(5, 5) = \dfrac{P(5, 5)}{5!} = \dfrac{5 \cdot 4 \cdot 3 \cdot 2 \cdot 1}{5 \cdot 4 \cdot 3 \cdot 2 \cdot 1} = 1$ ◆

▶ Example 3   Solve Problems A and B using formulas (1) and (2).

Solution   The number of two-letter words that can be formed from the three letters a, b, and c is equal to $P(3, 2) = 3 \cdot 2 = 6$, in agreement with our previous solution.

The number of two-worker teams that can be formed from three individuals is equal to $C(3, 2)$, and

$$C(3, 2) = \frac{P(3, 2)}{2!} = \frac{3 \cdot 2}{2 \cdot 1} = 3,$$

in agreement with our previous result.   ◆

▶ Example 4   The board of directors of a corporation has 10 members. In how many ways can they choose a committee of 3 board members to negotiate a merger?

Solution   Since the committee of three involves no ordering of its members, we are concerned here with combinations. The number of combinations of 10 people taken 3 at a time is $C(10, 3)$, which is

$$C(10, 3) = \frac{10 \cdot 9 \cdot 8}{3 \cdot 2 \cdot 1} = 120.$$

Thus there are 120 choices for the committee.   ◆

▶ Example 5   Eight horses are entered in a race in which a first, second, and third prize will be awarded. Assuming no ties, how many different outcomes are possible?

Solution   In this example we are considering ordered arrangements of three horses, so we are dealing with permutations. The number of permutations of eight horses taken three at a time is

$$P(8, 3) = 8 \cdot 7 \cdot 6 = 336,$$

so the number of possible outcomes of the race is 336.   ◆

▶ Example 6   A political pollster wishes to survey 1500 individuals chosen from a sample of 5,000,000 adults. In how many ways can the 1500 individuals be chosen?

Solution   No ordering of the 1500 individuals is involved, so we are dealing with combinations. So the number in question is $C(5{,}000{,}000, 1500)$, a number too large to be written down in digit form. (It has several thousand digits!) But it could be calculated with the aid of a computer.   ◆

▶ **Example 7**   A club has 10 members. In how many ways can they choose a slate of four officers, consisting of a president, vice president, secretary, and treasurer?

Solution   In this problem we are dealing with an ordering of four members. (The first is the president, the second the vice president, and so on.) So we are dealing with permutations, and the number of ways of choosing the officers is

$$P(10,4) = 10 \cdot 9 \cdot 8 \cdot 7 = 5040.$$ ◆

Verification of the Formulas for P(n,r) and C(n,r)   Let us first derive the formula for $P(n,r)$, the number of permutations of n objects taken r at a time. The task of choosing r objects (in a given order) consists of r consecutive operations (Fig. 1). The first operation can be performed in n ways. For each way that the first operation is performed, one object will have been used up and so we can perform the second operation in $n - 1$ ways, and so on. For each way of performing the sequence of operations $1, 2, 3, \ldots, r - 1$, the rth operation can be performed in $n - (r - 1) = n - r + 1$ ways. By the generalized multiplication principle, the task of choosing the r objects from among the n can be performed in

$$n(n-1) \cdot \cdots \cdot (n-r+1) \quad \text{ways.}$$

That is,

$$P(n,r) = n(n-1) \cdot \cdots \cdot (n-r+1),$$

which is formula (1).

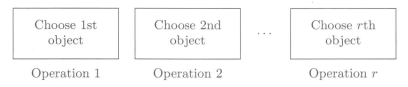

Figure 1.

Let us now verify the formula for $C(n,r)$, the number of combinations of n objects taken r at a time. Each such combination is a set of r objects and therefore can be ordered in

$$P(r,r) = r(r-1) \cdot \cdots \cdot 2 \cdot 1 = r!$$

ways by formula (1). In other words, each different combination of r objects gives rise to $r!$ permutations of the same r objects. On the other hand, each permutation of n objects taken r at a time gives rise to a combination of n objects taken r at a time, by simply ignoring the order of the permutation. Thus, if we start with the $P(n,r)$ permutations, we will have all the combinations of n objects taken r at a time, with each combination repeated $r!$ times. Thus

$$P(n,r) = r! \, C(n,r).$$

On dividing both sides of the equation by $r!$, we obtain formula (2).

GC   Most graphing calculators have commands to compute $P(n,r)$, $C(n,r)$, and $n!$. For instance, the MATH key on the TI-83 leads to the PRB menu of Fig. 2, which contains the commands **nPr**, **nCr**, and **!**. Figure 3 shows how these commands are used. *Note*: The number **8.799226775E15** represents $8.799226775 \times 10^{15}$.

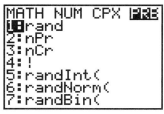

Figure 2.   Figure 3.

1. Calculate the following values.

(a) 3!   (b) 7!   (c) $P(7,3)$ (d) $C(7,3)$

2. A newborn child is to be given a first name and a middle name from a selection of 10 names. How many different possibilities are there?

▶ Exercises 5.5

For Exercises 1–20, calculate the values.

1. $P(4,2)$ 2. $P(5,1)$ 3. $P(6,3)$
4. $P(5,4)$ 5. $C(10,3)$ 6. $C(12,2)$
7. $C(5,4)$ 8. $C(6,3)$ 9. $P(5,1)$
10. $P(5,5)$ 11. $P(n,1)$ 12. $P(n,2)$
13. $C(4,4)$ 14. $C(n,2)$ 15. $C(n,n-2)$
16. $C(n,1)$ 17. $6!$ 18. $\dfrac{10!}{4!}$
19. $\dfrac{9!}{7!}$ 20. $7!$

21. In how many ways can four people line up in a row for a group picture?

22. How many different outcomes of "winner" and "runner-up" are possible if there are six contestants in a pie-eating contest?

23. How many different selections of two books can be made from a set of nine books?

24. A pizza parlor offers five toppings for the plain cheese base of the pizzas. How many different pizzas are possible that use three of the toppings?

25. How many ways are there to choose first, second, and third prizes in an art contest with 15 entrants?

26. In how many ways can six people line up at a single counter to order food at McDonald's?

27. A deluxe chocolate banana split is made with three scoops of chocolate ice cream, one banana, and a choice of 4 out of 10 possible toppings. How many different deluxe chocolate banana splits can be ordered?

28. Suppose that you own 10 sweaters. How many ways can you select four of them to take on a trip?

29. Suppose that you own 10 sweaters and are going on a trip. How many ways can you select six of them to leave at home?

30. Why do Exercises 28 and 29 have the same answer?

31. The five starting players of a basketball team are introduced one at a time. In how many different ways can they be introduced?

32. In how many different ways can the nine members of the Supreme Court reach a six-to-three decision?

33. In an eight-team football conference, each team plays every other team exactly once. How many games must be played?

34. A student is required to work exactly five problems from an eight-problem exam. In how many ways can the problems be chosen?

35. How many ways can you arrange 5 of 10 books on a shelf?

36. How many ways can you choose 5 of your 10 books to put in your backpack?

37. How many ways can you choose 5 out of 10 friends to invite to a dinner party?

38. How many ways can you distribute $1, $2, $5, $10, $20 to 5 of your 10 friends? Assume that no one gets more than one bill.

39. Suppose that you have 35 CDs and your CD player has five slots numbered 1 through 5. How many ways can you fill your CD player?

40. Of the 20 applicants for a job, 4 will be selected for intensive interviews. In how many ways can the selection be made?

41. In a batch of 100 computer diskettes, 7 are defective. A sample of three diskettes is to be selected from the batch. How many samples are possible? How many of the samples consist of all defective diskettes?

42. A student must choose five courses out of seven that he would like to take. How many possibilities are there?

43. How many different three-letter words are there having no repetition of letters?

44. A sportswriter makes a preseason guess of the top 5 football teams (in order) from among 40 major teams. How many different possibilities are there?

45. In how many different ways can a committee of 5 senators be selected from the 100 members of the U.S. Senate?

46. Theoretically, how many possibilities are there for first, second, and third places in a marathon race with 1000 entries?

Exercises 47–50 refer to poker hands. A poker hand consists of 5 cards selected from a deck of 52 cards.

47. How many different poker hands are there?

48. How many different poker hands consist entirely of aces and kings?

49. How many different poker hands consist entirely of clubs?

50. How many different poker hands consist entirely of red cards?

51. A fraternity has 20 members. In how many ways can it choose a three-person board of directors?

52. A restaurant offers an "appetizer-plate special" consisting of five selections from its list of appetizers. If there are more than 700 different possible appetizer-plate specials, what is the least possible number of appetizers?

53. Five students order different sandwiches at a campus eatery. The waiter forgets who ordered what and gives out the sandwiches at random. In how many different ways can the sandwiches be distributed?

54. A nautical signal consists of three flags arranged vertically on a flagpole. If a sailor has flags of six different colors, how many different signals are possible?

55. A high school student decides to apply to four of the eight Ivy League colleges. In how many possible ways can the four colleges be selected?

56. How many different outcomes are possible for a horse race with eight horses? Assume that there are no ties.

57. Two children, Moe and Joe, are allowed to select candy from a plate of nine pieces of candy. Moe, being younger, is allowed to choose first but can only take two candies. Joe is then allowed to take three of the remaining candies. Joe complains that he has fewer choices than Moe. Is Joe correct? How many choices will each child have?

58. In how many ways can three new basketball franchises be distributed to the five cities that have applied for them?

59. A nursery school teacher has collected a picture from each of the 12 children in the class. She wants to hang the pictures in four rows of three. How many different arrangements are possible?

60. Most racetracks have "compound" bets on two or more horses. An *exacta* is a bet in which the first and second finishers in a race are specified in order. A *quinella* is a bet on the first two finishers in a race, with order not specified. With a field of nine horses, how many different exacta bets can be placed? Quinella bets?

61. In how many ways can five mathematics books and four novels be placed on a bookshelf if the mathematics books must be together?

62. George has three books by each of his favorite four authors. In how many ways can the books be placed on a shelf if books by the same author must be together?

63. An art gallery has seven paintings by a new artist. The director wants to place four of them in a row on one wall of the gallery. How many different arrangements are possible?

64. On a children's baseball team, there are four players who can play at any of the following infield positions: catcher, first base, third base, and shortstop. There are five possible pitchers, none of whom plays any other position. And there are four players that can play any of the three outfield positions (right, left, center) or second base. In how many ways can the coach assign players to positions?

65. How many batting orders are possible for a team of nine baseball players in which the pitcher always bats last and the first baseman bats in either the third or fourth spot?

66. A cabaret show is put together by a manager who wishes to present two comedians and three singers. He can choose from 14 comedians and 20 singers. In how many ways can he select the acts for the show?

67. The cabaret show manager of Exercise 66 also controls the order of the five acts he selects. In how many ways can he organize the program once he has decided on which acts to present?

68. Seven patients are waiting to have an MRI scan, but there is time to process only three of them before the office closes for the day. In how many ways can the three patients be chosen?

69. How many five-card combinations of a standard playing-card deck have cards from exactly two suits?

70. A 10-letter word consists of 4 *A*'s and 6 *B*'s. How many different words are possible if no two *A*'s can be next to each other? *Hint*: Start with *BBBBBB* and decide where to insert the *A*'s.

71. How many five-digit ZIP codes are possible in which the product of the digits is even? (From *The Mathematics Teacher*, February 1997)

72. The streets in a town run north–south and east–west in a grid. In how many ways can Francine walk to Marion's house if Francine lives 7 blocks north and 4 blocks east of Marion's, takes the shortest route, and never cuts through a block?

Exercises 73–75 require the use of a calculator or a computer.

73. Students attending a college that operates on the semester system choose five courses each semester from a catalog containing 752 courses. The students who attend a college on the trimester system choose three courses each term from 937 courses in the catalog. Assume all courses are taught every term. In the standard four-year undergraduate program, which students have a greater number of different programs?

74. A computer manufacturer has 50 distinct microchips to place into a rectangular array that is 5 units wide by 10 units long.

(a) In how many ways can the chips be arranged?

(b) Ten of the chips control special functions. How many arrangements are possible if these must occupy the first column?

(c) Find the number of arrangements having no special-function chips in the first column.

75. (a) Calculate the number of possible lottery tickets if the player must choose five distinct numbers from 0 to 44, inclusive, where the order does not matter. The winner must match all five.

(b) Calculate the number of lottery tickets if the player must choose four distinct numbers from 0 to 99, inclusive, where the order does not matter. The winner must match all four.

(c) In which lottery does the player have a better chance of choosing the randomly selected winning numbers?

(d) Find the answer to (c) if the order in which the numbers appear on the ticket must match the order on the winning ticket.

Solutions to Practice Problems 5.5

1. (a) $3! = 3 \cdot 2 \cdot 1 = 6$

   (b) $7! = 7 \cdot 6 \cdot 5 \cdot 4 \cdot 3 \cdot 2 \cdot 1 = 5040$

   (c) $P(7,3) = \underbrace{7 \cdot 6 \cdot 5}_{3 \text{ factors}} = 210$

   [In general, $P(n,r)$ is the product of the first r factors in the descending expansion of $n!$.]

   (d) $C(7,3) = \dfrac{7 \cdot 6 \cdot 5}{3 \cdot 2 \cdot 1} = \dfrac{7 \cdot \cancel{6} \cdot 5}{\cancel{3} \cdot \cancel{2} \cdot 1} = 35$

   [A convenient procedure to follow when calculating $C(n,r)$ is first to write the product expansion of $r!$ in the denominator and then to write in the numerator an integer from the descending expansion of $n!$ above each integer in the denominator.]

2. 90. The first question to be asked here is whether permutations or combinations are involved. Two names are to be selected, and the order of the names is important. (The name Amanda Beth is different from the name Beth Amanda.) Since the problem asks for arrangements of 10 names taken 2 at a time in a *specific order*, the number of arrangements is $P(10,2) = 10 \cdot 9 = 90$. In general, order is important if a different outcome results when two items in the selection are interchanged.

5.6 Further Counting Problems

In Section 5.5 we introduced permutations and combinations and developed formulas for counting all permutations (or combinations) of a given type. Many counting problems can be formulated in terms of permutations or combinations. But to use the formulas of Section 5.5 successfully, we must be able to recognize these problems when they occur and to translate them into a form in which the formulas may be applied. In this section we practice doing that. We consider five typical applications giving rise to permutations or combinations. At first glance, the first two applications may seem to have little practical significance. However, they suggest a common way to "model" outcomes of real-life situations having two equally likely results.

As our first application, consider a coin-tossing experiment in which we toss a coin a fixed number of times. We can describe the outcome of the experiment as a sequence of "heads" and "tails." For instance, if a coin is tossed three times, then one possible outcome is "heads on the first toss, tails on the second toss, and tails on third toss." This outcome can be abbreviated as HTT. We can use the methods of the preceding section to count the number of possible outcomes having various prescribed properties.

▶ Example 1   Suppose that an experiment consists of tossing a coin 10 times and observing the sequence of heads and tails.

(a) How many different outcomes are possible?

(b) How many different outcomes have exactly four heads?

Solution   (a) Visualize each outcome of the experiment as a sequence of 10 boxes, where each box contains one letter, H or T, with the first box recording the result of the first toss, the second box recording the result of the second toss, and so forth.

$$\boxed{H}\boxed{T}\boxed{H}\boxed{T}\boxed{T}\boxed{T}\boxed{H}\boxed{T}\boxed{H}\boxed{T}$$
$$1\quad 2\quad 3\quad 4\quad 5\quad 6\quad 7\quad 8\quad 9\quad 10$$

Each box can be filled in two ways. So by the generalized multiplication principle, the sequence of 10 boxes can be filled in

$$\underbrace{2 \cdot 2 \cdot \ \cdots \ \cdot 2}_{10 \text{ factors}} = 2^{10}$$

ways. So there are $2^{10} = 1024$ different possible outcomes.

(b) An outcome with 4 heads corresponds to filling the boxes with 4 H's and 6 T's. A particular outcome is determined as soon as we decide where to place the H's. The 4 boxes to receive H's can be selected from the 10 boxes in $C(10, 4)$ ways. So the number of outcomes with 4 heads is

$$C(10, 4) = \frac{10 \cdot 9 \cdot 8 \cdot 7}{4 \cdot 3 \cdot 2 \cdot 1} = 210. \qquad \blacklozenge$$

Ideas similar to those applied in Example 1 are useful in counting even more complicated sets of outcomes of coin-tossing experiments. The second part of our next example highlights a trick that can often save time and effort.

▶ Example 2   Consider the coin-tossing experiment of Example 1.

(a) How many different outcomes have at most two heads?

(b) How many different outcomes have at least three heads?

Solution   (a) The outcomes with at most two heads are those having 0, 1, or 2 heads. Let us count the number of these outcomes separately:

0 heads: There is 1 outcome, namely T T T T T T T T T T.

1 head: To determine such an outcome, we just select the box in which to put the single H. And this can be done in $C(10, 1) = 10$ ways.

2 heads: To determine such an outcome, we just select the boxes in which to put the two H's. And this can be done in $C(10, 2) = (10 \cdot 9)/(2 \cdot 1) = 45$ ways.

Adding up all the possible outcomes, we see that the number of outcomes with at most two heads is equal to $1 + 10 + 45 = 56$.

(b) "At least three heads" refers to an outcome with either 3, 4, 5, 6, 7, 8, 9, or 10 heads. The total number of such outcomes is

$$C(10, 3) + C(10, 4) + \cdots + C(10, 10).$$

This sum can, of course, be calculated, but there is a less tedious way to solve the problem. Just start with all outcomes [1024 of them by Example 1(a)] and subtract those with at most two heads [56 of them by part (a)]. So the number of outcomes with at least three heads is $1024 - 56 = 968$. ◆

Let us now turn to a different sort of counting problem, namely one that involves counting the number of paths between two points.

▶ Example 3   In Fig. 1 we have drawn a partial map of the streets in a certain city. A tourist wishes to walk from point A to point B. We have drawn two possible routes from A to B. What is the total number of routes (with no backtracking) from A to B?

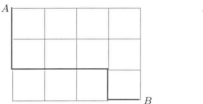   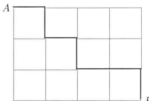

Figure 1.

Solution   Any particular route can be described by giving the directions of each block walked in the appropriate order. For instance, the route on the left of Fig. 1 is described as "a block south, a block south, a block east, a block east, a block east, a block south, a block east." Using S for south and E for east, this route can be designated by the string of letters SSEEESE. Similarly, the route on the right is ESESEES. Note that each route is then described by a string of seven letters, of which three are S's (we must go three blocks south) and four are E's (we must go four blocks east). Selecting a route is thus the same as placing three S's in a string of seven boxes:

The three boxes to receive S's can be selected in $C(7, 3) = 35$ ways. So the number of paths from A to B is 35. ◆

Let us now move on to a third type of counting problem. Suppose that we have an urn in which there are a certain number of red balls and a certain number of white balls. We perform an experiment that consists of selecting a number of balls from the urn and observing the color distribution of the sample selected. (This model may be used, for example, to describe the process of selecting people to be polled in a survey. The different colors correspond to different opinions.) By using familiar counting techniques we can calculate the number of possible samples having a given color distribution. The next example illustrates a typical computation.

▶ **Example 4** An urn contains 25 numbered balls, of which 15 are red and 10 are white. A sample of 5 balls is to be selected.

(a) How many different samples are possible?
(b) How many samples contain all red balls?
(c) How many samples contain 3 red balls and 2 white balls?
(d) How many samples contain at least 4 red balls?

Solution (a) A sample is just an unordered selection of 5 balls out of 25. There are $C(25, 5)$ such samples. Numerically, we have

$$C(25, 5) = \frac{25 \cdot 24 \cdot 23 \cdot 22 \cdot 21}{5 \cdot 4 \cdot 3 \cdot 2 \cdot 1} = 53{,}130$$

samples.

(b) To form a sample of all red balls we must select 5 balls from the 15 red ones. This can be done in $C(15, 5)$ ways—that is, in

$$C(15, 5) = \frac{15 \cdot 14 \cdot 13 \cdot 12 \cdot 11}{5 \cdot 4 \cdot 3 \cdot 2 \cdot 1} = 3003$$

ways.

(c) To answer this question we use both the multiplication principle and the formula for $C(n, r)$. We form a sample of 3 red balls and 2 white balls using a sequence of two operations:

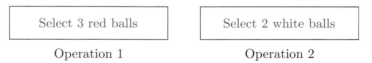

Select 3 red balls	Select 2 white balls
Operation 1	Operation 2

The first operation can be performed in $C(15, 3)$ ways and the second in $C(10, 2)$ ways. Thus the total number of samples having 3 red and 2 white balls is $C(15, 3) \cdot C(10, 2)$. That is,

$$C(15, 3) = \frac{15 \cdot 14 \cdot 13}{3 \cdot 2 \cdot 1} = 455$$

$$C(10, 2) = \frac{10 \cdot 9}{2 \cdot 1} = 45$$

$$C(15, 3) \cdot C(10, 2) = 455 \cdot 45 = 20{,}475.$$

So the number of possible samples is 20,475.

(d) A sample with at least 4 red balls has either 4 or 5 red balls. By part (b) the number of samples with 5 red balls is 3003. Using the same reasoning as in part (c), the number of samples with 4 red balls is $C(15, 4) \cdot C(10, 1) = 1365 \cdot 10 = 13{,}650$. Thus the total number of samples having at least 4 red balls is $13{,}650 + 3003 = 16{,}653$. ◆

Practice Problems 5.6	

1. A newspaper reporter wants an indication of how the 15 members of the school board feel about a certain proposal. She decides to question a sample of 6 of the board members.

   (a) How many different samples are possible?

   (b) Suppose that 10 of the board members support the proposal and 5 oppose it. How many of the samples reflect the distribution of the board? That is, in how many of the samples do 4 people support the proposal and 2 oppose it?

2. A basketball player shoots eight free throws and lists the sequence of results of each trial in order. Let S represent "success" and F represent "failure." Then, for instance, FFSSSSSS represents the outcome of missing the first two shots and hitting the rest.

   (a) How many different outcomes are possible?

   (b) How many of the outcomes have six successes?

▶ Exercises 5.6

1. An experiment consists of tossing a coin six times and observing the sequence of heads and tails.

   (a) How many different outcomes are possible?

   (b) How many different outcomes have exactly three heads?

   (c) How many different outcomes have more heads than tails?

   (d) How many different outcomes have at least two heads?

2. Refer to the map in Fig. 2. How many routes are there from A to B?

3. Refer to the map in Fig. 3. How many routes are there from A to B?

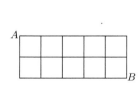

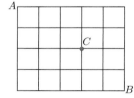

Figure 2.   **Figure 3.**

4. An urn contains 12 numbered balls, of which 8 are red and 4 are white. A sample of 4 balls is to be selected.

   (a) How many different samples are possible?

   (b) How many samples contain all red balls?

   (c) How many samples contain 2 red balls and 2 white balls?

   (d) How many samples contain at least 3 red balls?

   (e) How many samples contain a different number of red balls than white balls?

5. A bag of 10 apples contains 2 rotten apples and 8 good apples. A shopper selects a sample of 3 apples from the bag.

   (a) How many different samples are possible?

   (b) How many samples contain all good apples?

   (c) How many samples contain at least 1 rotten apple?

6. An experiment consists of tossing a coin 8 times and observing the sequence of heads and tails.

   (a) How many different outcomes are possible?

   (b) How many different outcomes have exactly 3 heads?

   (c) How many different outcomes have at least 2 heads?

   (d) How many different outcomes have 4 heads or 5 heads?

7. How many ways can a group of 100 students be assigned to dorms A, B, and C, with 25 assigned to dorm A, 40 to dorm B, and 35 to dorm C?

8. In the World Series the American League team ("A") and the National League team ("N") play until one team wins four games. If the sequence of winners is designated by letters (NAAAA means the National League won the first game and lost the next four), how many different sequences are possible?

9. Refer to the map in Fig. 3. How many of the routes from A to B pass through the point C?

10. A package contains 100 fuses, of which 10 are defective. A sample of 5 fuses is selected at random.

   (a) How many different samples are there?

   (b) How many of the samples contain 2 defective fuses?

   (c) How many of the samples contain at least 1 defective fuse?

11. In how many ways can a committee of 5 senators be selected from the 100 members of the U.S. Senate so that no two committee members are from the same state?

12. An exam contains five "true or false" questions. How many of the 32 different ways of answering these questions contain 3 or more correct answers?

13. A student is required to work exactly 6 problems from a 10-problem exam and must work exactly 3 of the first 4 problems. In how many ways can the six problems be chosen?

14. The new book shelf at a library contains two novels, six biographies, and four how-to books. In how many ways can the books be arranged on the shelf if the books for each category are placed together?

15. In how many ways can 12 jurors and 2 alternates be chosen from a group of 20 prospective jurors?

16. A committee has four male and five female members. In how many ways can a subcommittee consisting of two males and two females be selected?

17. In how many ways can an investor put together a portfolio of five stocks and six bonds selected from her favorite nine stocks and eight bonds?

18. A football team plays 10 games. In how many ways can these games result in five wins, four losses, and one tie?

19. A telemarketer makes 15 phone calls in 1 hour. In how many ways can the outcomes of the calls be three sales, eight no-sales, and four no-answers?

20. During practice, a basketball player shoots 10 free-throws. In how many ways can the outcomes result in seven hits and three misses?

21. A license plate contains six letters with no repetitions allowed. How many different license plates are possible?

22. A college mathematics department has 15 calculus classes. Five classes will use graphing calculators and four classes will use computer software. In how many different ways can the classes be selected?

23. How many different three-letter words (i.e., sequences of letters) can be formed from the letters of the word JUPITER?

24. The shortest word containing all five vowels is SEQUOIA. How many seven-letter sequences of letters, with no repeated letters, contain all five vowels?

25. Standard Maryland license plates contain three letters followed by three digits. How many different license plates are possible if no repetitions of letters or digits are allowed?

26. Out of a group of 20 senior education majors at the University of Maryland, five will be selected to student-teach in Montgomery County, four will be selected to student-teach in Prince Georges County, and three will be selected to student-teach in Howard County. In how many ways can this be done?

27. The student council at Gotham College is made up of four freshmen, five sophomores, six juniors, and seven seniors. A yearbook photographer would like to line up three council members from each class for a picture. How many different pictures are possible if each group of classmates stands together?

28. A truck driver has to deliver bread to five grocery stores. In how many different ways can he schedule the order of his stops?

29. Suppose that the stores in Exercise 28 are located in two towns far enough apart that the driver wants to make all stops in one town before going on to the next. In how many different ways can he schedule the order of his stops if the larger town has three stores?

30. Of the 14 new programmers hired by a major software company, 3 will be selected to work on programming languages, 4 will be selected to work on word processing software, and 5 will be selected to work on spreadsheet software. In how many ways can this be done?

31. How many poker hands consist of 3 aces and 2 kings?

32. How many poker hands consist of 2 aces, 2 cards of another denomination, and 1 card of a third denomination?

33. How many poker hands consist of 3 cards of one denomination and 2 cards of another denomination? (Such a poker hand is called a "full house.")

34. How many poker hands consist of 2 cards of one denomination, 2 cards of another (different) denomination, and 1 card of a third denomination? (Such a poker hand is called "two pairs.")

35. A five-digit ZIP code is said to be detour-prone if it looks like a valid and different ZIP code when read upside down (Fig. 4). For instance, 68901 and 88111 are detour-prone, whereas 32145 and 10801 are not. How many of the 10^5 possible ZIP code numbers are detour-prone?

Figure 4.

36. In how many ways can a residence director assign six students to four dormitory rooms if two rooms are doubles, two rooms are singles, and two of the students cannot be placed together?

37. A class has 12 students, of which 3 are seniors. How many committees of size 4 can be selected if at least one member of each committee must be a senior?

38. A dance team knows 15 routines of which 8 are tap, 5 are ballet, and 2 are modern. The program can consist of any five routines. In how many ways can the manager choose which routines to present if there are no restrictions?

39. Refer to Exercise 38. In how many ways can the manager choose the routines if at least one routine of each type must be included?

40. In how many ways can 6 married couples sit in a row if men and women alternate?

41. In how many ways can 6 married couples sit in a row if no 2 women sit next to each other?

42. A family has 6 members. In how many different ways can exactly three of them come to dinner? In how many different ways can no more than three of them come to dinner?

43. A family has 6 members. How many different family groups can come to dinner?

44. A family has 6 members. Each member has a place mat with his or her name on it. In how many ways can the place mats be placed around a round table?

45. There are 8 marbles in a bag, numbered 1 through 8. Three (1, 2, 3) are blue and five (4, 5, 6, 7, 8) are white. Choose three marbles from the bag. In how many samples will the number of blue marbles chosen exceed the number of white marbles chosen?

Exercises 46–49 require the use of a calculator or a computer.

46. The dean at a small college wishes to form an experimental section of General Psychology with 22 students chosen from 20 women and 18 men interested in social science.

   (a) How many different such classes are possible?

   (b) The dean decides the class should have 12 women and 10 men. Compare the number of possible classes to the solution to (a).

47. A bridge hand contains 13 cards. What percentage of bridge hands contains all four aces?

48. Which is more likely—a bridge hand with four aces or one with exactly two kings and two queens?

49. Which is more likely—a bridge hand with four aces or one with the two red kings, the two red queens, and no other kings or queens?

Solutions to Practice Problems 5.6

1. (a) $C(15, 6)$. Each sample is an unordered selection of 15 objects taken 6 at a time.

   (b) $C(10, 4) \cdot C(5, 2)$. Asking for the number of samples of a certain type is the same as asking for the number of ways that the task of forming such a sample can be performed. This task is composed of two consecutive operations. Operation 1, selecting 4 people from among the 10 that support the proposal, can be performed in $C(10, 4)$ ways. Operation 2, selecting 2 people from among the 5 people that oppose the proposal, can be performed in $C(5, 2)$ ways. Therefore, by the multiplication principle, the complete task can be performed in $C(10, 4) \cdot C(5, 2)$ ways.
   [*Note*: $C(15, 6) = 5005$ and $C(10, 4) \cdot C(5, 2) = 2100$. Therefore, less than half of the possible samples reflect the true distribution of the school board.]

2. (a) 2^8 or 256. Apply the generalized multiplication principle.

   (b) $C(8, 6)$ or 28. Each outcome having 6 successes corresponds to a sequence of 8 letters of which 6 are S's and 2 are F's. Such an outcome is specified by selecting the 6 locations for the S's from among the 8 locations, and this has $C(8, 6)$ possibilities.

5.7 The Binomial Theorem

In Sections 5.5 and 5.6 we dealt with permutations and combinations and, in particular, derived a formula for $C(n, r)$, the number of combinations of n objects taken r at a time. Namely, we have

$$C(n, r) = \frac{P(n, r)}{r!} = \frac{n(n - 1) \cdot \cdots \cdot (n - r + 1)}{r!}. \tag{1}$$

Actually, formula (1) was verified in case both n and r are positive integers. But it is useful to consider $C(n, r)$ also in case $r = 0$. In this case we are considering the number of combinations of n things taken 0 at a time. There is clearly only one such combination: the one containing no elements. Therefore,

$$C(n, 0) = 1. \tag{2}$$

Here is another convenient formula for $C(n, r)$:

$$C(n, r) = \frac{n!}{r!\,(n - r)!}. \tag{3}$$

For instance, according to formula (3),

$$C(8, 3) = \frac{8!}{3!\,(8 - 3)!} = \frac{8!}{3!\,5!} = \frac{8 \cdot 7 \cdot 6 \cdot \cancel{5} \cdot \cancel{4} \cdot \cancel{3} \cdot \cancel{2} \cdot \cancel{1}}{3 \cdot 2 \cdot 1 \cdot \cancel{5} \cdot \cancel{4} \cdot \cancel{3} \cdot \cancel{2} \cdot \cancel{1}} = \frac{8 \cdot 7 \cdot 6}{3 \cdot 2 \cdot 1},$$

which agrees with the result given by formula (1).

Verification of Formula (3)   Note that

$$n(n - 1) \cdot \,\cdots\, \cdot (n - r + 1) =$$

$$\frac{n(n - 1) \cdot \,\cdots\, \cdot (n - r + 1)\cancel{(n - r)}\cancel{(n - r - 1)} \cdot \,\cdots\, \cdot \cancel{2} \cdot \cancel{1}}{\cancel{(n - r)}\cancel{(n - r - 1)} \cdot \,\cdots\, \cdot \cancel{2} \cdot \cancel{1}} = \frac{n!}{(n - r)!}.$$

Then, by formula (1), we have

$$C(n, r) = \frac{n(n - 1) \cdot \,\cdots\, \cdot (n - r + 1)}{r!} = \frac{\dfrac{n!}{(n - r)!}}{r!} = \frac{n!}{r!\,(n - r)!},$$

which is formula (3).   ◆

Note that for $r = 0$, formula (3) reads

$$C(n, 0) = \frac{n!}{0!\,(n - 0)!} = \frac{n!}{0!\,n!} = \frac{1}{0!}.$$

Let us agree that the value of $0!$ is 1. Then the right-hand side of the equation above is 1, so that formula (3) also holds for $r = 0$.

Formula (3) can be used to prove many facts about $C(n, r)$. For example, the following formula is useful in calculating $C(n, r)$ for large values of r:

$$C(n, r) = C(n, n - r). \tag{4}$$

Suppose that we wish to calculate $C(100, 98)$. If we apply formula (4), we have

$$C(100, 98) = C(100, 100 - 98) = C(100, 2) = \frac{100 \cdot 99}{2 \cdot 1} = 4950.$$

Verification of Formula (4)   Apply formula (3) to evaluate $C(n, n - r)$:

$$C(n, n - r) = \frac{n!}{(n - r)!\,(n - (n - r))!} = \frac{n!}{(n - r)!\,r!}$$

$$= C(n, r) \quad \text{[by formula (3) again]}.$$

The formula is intuitively reasonable since each time we select a subset of r elements we are excluding a subset of $n - r$ elements. Thus there are as many subsets of $n - r$ elements as there are subsets of r elements.   ◆

An alternative notation for $C(n, r)$ is $\binom{n}{r}$. Thus, for example,

$$\binom{5}{2} = C(5, 2) = \frac{5 \cdot 4}{2 \cdot 1} = 10.$$

The symbol $\binom{n}{r}$ is called a *binomial coefficient*. To discover why, let us tabulate the values of $\binom{n}{r}$ for some small values of n and r.

$$n = 2: \quad \binom{2}{0} = 1 \quad \binom{2}{1} = 2 \quad \binom{2}{2} = 1$$

$$n = 3: \quad \binom{3}{0} = 1 \quad \binom{3}{1} = 3 \quad \binom{3}{2} = 3 \quad \binom{3}{3} = 1$$

$$n = 4: \quad \binom{4}{0} = 1 \quad \binom{4}{1} = 4 \quad \binom{4}{2} = 6 \quad \binom{4}{3} = 4 \quad \binom{4}{4} = 1$$

$$n = 5: \quad \binom{5}{0} = 1 \quad \binom{5}{1} = 5 \quad \binom{5}{2} = 10 \quad \binom{5}{3} = 10 \quad \binom{5}{4} = 5 \quad \binom{5}{5} = 1$$

Each row consists of the coefficients that arise in expanding $(x+y)^n$. To see this, inspect the results of expanding $(x + y)^n$ for $n = 2$, 3, 4, and 5:

$$(x + y)^2 = x^2 + 2xy + y^2$$
$$(x + y)^3 = x^3 + 3x^2y + 3xy^2 + y^3$$
$$(x + y)^4 = x^4 + 4x^3y + 6x^2y^2 + 4xy^3 + y^4$$
$$(x + y)^5 = x^5 + 5x^4y + 10x^3y^2 + 10x^2y^3 + 5xy^4 + y^5.$$

Compare the coefficients in any row with the values in the corresponding row of binomial coefficients. Note that they are the same. Thus we see that the binomial coefficients arise as coefficients in multiplying out powers of the binomial $x + y$; hence the name *binomial coefficient*.

What we observed for the exponents $n = 2$, 3, 4, and 5 holds true for any positive integer n. We have the following result, a proof of which is given at the end of this section.

Binomial Theorem

$$(x + y)^n = \binom{n}{0}x^n + \binom{n}{1}x^{n-1}y + \binom{n}{2}x^{n-2}y^2 + \cdots + \binom{n}{n-1}xy^{n-1} + \binom{n}{n}y^n$$

▶ Example 1   Expand $(x + y)^6$.

Solution   By the binomial theorem,

$$(x + y)^6 = \binom{6}{0}x^6 + \binom{6}{1}x^5y + \binom{6}{2}x^4y^2 + \binom{6}{3}x^3y^3$$

$$+ \binom{6}{4}x^2y^4 + \binom{6}{5}xy^5 + \binom{6}{6}y^6.$$

Furthermore,

$$\binom{6}{0} = 1 \qquad \binom{6}{1} = \frac{6}{1} = 6 \qquad \binom{6}{2} = \frac{6 \cdot 5}{2 \cdot 1} = 15$$

$$\binom{6}{3} = \frac{6 \cdot 5 \cdot 4}{3 \cdot 2 \cdot 1} = 20 \qquad \binom{6}{4} = \frac{6 \cdot 5 \cdot 4 \cdot 3}{4 \cdot 3 \cdot 2 \cdot 1} = 15$$

$$\binom{6}{5} = \frac{6 \cdot 5 \cdot 4 \cdot 3 \cdot 2}{5 \cdot 4 \cdot 3 \cdot 2 \cdot 1} = 6 \qquad \binom{6}{6} = \frac{6 \cdot 5 \cdot 4 \cdot 3 \cdot 2 \cdot 1}{6 \cdot 5 \cdot 4 \cdot 3 \cdot 2 \cdot 1} = 1.$$

Thus

$$(x + y)^6 = x^6 + 6x^5y + 15x^4y^2 + 20x^3y^3 + 15x^2y^4 + 6xy^5 + y^6. \qquad ◆$$

The binomial theorem can be used to count the number of subsets of a set, as shown in the next example.

▶ **Example 2**   Determine the number of subsets of a set with five elements.

Solution   Let us count the number of subsets of each possible size. A subset of r elements can be chosen in $\binom{5}{r}$ ways, since $C(5, r) = \binom{5}{r}$. So the set has $\binom{5}{0}$ subsets with 0 elements, $\binom{5}{1}$ subsets with 1 element, $\binom{5}{2}$ subsets with 2 elements, and so on. Therefore, the total number of subsets is

$$\binom{5}{0} + \binom{5}{1} + \binom{5}{2} + \binom{5}{3} + \binom{5}{4} + \binom{5}{5}.$$

On the other hand, the binomial theorem for $n = 5$ gives

$$(x + y)^5 = \binom{5}{0}x^5 + \binom{5}{1}x^4y + \binom{5}{2}x^3y^2 + \binom{5}{3}x^2y^3 + \binom{5}{4}xy^4 + \binom{5}{5}y^5.$$

Set $x = 1$ and $y = 1$ in this formula.

$$(1 + 1)^5 = \binom{5}{0}1^5 + \binom{5}{1}1^4 \cdot 1 + \binom{5}{2}1^3 \cdot 1^2 + \binom{5}{3}1^2 \cdot 1^3 + \binom{5}{4}1 \cdot 1^4 + \binom{5}{5}1^5$$

$$2^5 = \binom{5}{0} + \binom{5}{1} + \binom{5}{2} + \binom{5}{3} + \binom{5}{4} + \binom{5}{5}$$

Thus the total number of subsets of a set with five elements (the right side) equals $2^5 = 32$. ◆

There is nothing special about the number 5 in the preceding example. An analogous argument gives the following result:

A set of n elements has 2^n subsets.

▶ **Example 3**   A pizza parlor offers a plain cheese pizza to which any number of six possible toppings can be added. How many different pizzas can be ordered?

Solution   Ordering a pizza requires selecting a subset of the six possible toppings. Since the set of six toppings has 2^6 different subsets, there are 2^6 or 64 different pizzas. (Note that the plain cheese pizza corresponds to selecting the empty subset of toppings.) ◆

Proof of the Binomial Theorem   Note that

$$(x+y)^n = \underbrace{(x+y)(x+y) \cdot \,\cdots\, \cdot (x+y)}_{n \text{ factors}}.$$

Multiplying out these factors involves forming all products, where one term is selected from each factor, and then combining like products. For instance,

$$(x+y)(x+y)(x+y) = x \cdot x \cdot x + x \cdot x \cdot y + x \cdot y \cdot x + y \cdot x \cdot x$$
$$+ x \cdot y \cdot y + y \cdot x \cdot y + y \cdot y \cdot x + y \cdot y \cdot y.$$

The first product on the right, $x \cdot x \cdot x$, is obtained by selecting the x-term from each of the three factors. The next term, $x \cdot x \cdot y$, is obtained by selecting the x-terms from the first two factors and the y-term from the third. The next product, $x \cdot y \cdot x$, is obtained by selecting the x-terms from the first and third factors and the y-term from the second. And so on. There are as many products containing two x's and one y as there are ways of selecting the factor from which to pick the y-term—namely $\binom{3}{1}$.

In general, when multiplying the n factors $(x+y)(x+y) \cdots (x+y)$, the number of products having k y's (and therefore $(n-k)$ x's) is equal to the number of different ways of selecting the k factors from which to take the y-term—that is, $\binom{n}{k}$. Therefore, the coefficient of $x^{n-k}y^k$ is $\binom{n}{k}$. This proves the binomial theorem.   ◆

Practice Problems 5.7

1. Calculate $\binom{12}{8}$.

2. An ice cream parlor offers 10 flavors of ice cream and 5 toppings. How many different servings are possible if each choice consists of one flavor of ice cream and as many toppings as desired?

▶ Exercises 5.7

Calculate the value for each of Exercises 1–18.

1. $\binom{6}{2}$ 2. $\binom{7}{3}$ 3. $\binom{8}{1}$ 4. $\binom{9}{9}$

5. $\binom{18}{16}$ 6. $\binom{25}{24}$ 7. $\binom{7}{0}$ 8. $\binom{6}{1}$

9. $\binom{8}{8}$ 10. $\binom{9}{0}$ 11. $\binom{n}{n-1}$

12. $\binom{n}{n}$ 13. $0!$ 14. $1!$

15. $n \cdot (n-1)!$ 16. $\dfrac{n!}{n}$

17. $\binom{6}{0} + \binom{6}{1} + \binom{6}{2} + \binom{6}{3} + \binom{6}{4} + \binom{6}{5} + \binom{6}{6}$

18. $\binom{7}{0} + \binom{7}{1} + \binom{7}{2} + \binom{7}{3} + \binom{7}{4} + \binom{7}{5} + \binom{7}{6} + \binom{7}{7}$

19. Determine the first three terms in the binomial expansion of $(x+y)^{10}$.

20. Determine the first three terms in the binomial expansion of $(x+y)^{20}$.

21. Determine the last three terms in the binomial expansion of $(x+y)^{15}$.

22. Determine the last three terms in the binomial expansion of $(x+y)^{12}$.

23. Determine the middle term in the binomial expansion of $(x+y)^{20}$.

24. Determine the middle term in the binomial expansion of $(x+y)^{10}$.

25. Determine the coefficient of $x^4 y^7$ in the binomial expansion of $(x+y)^{11}$.

26. Determine the coefficient of $x^8 y^5$ in the binomial expansion of $(x+y)^{13}$.

27. How many different subsets can be chosen from a set of six elements?

28. How many different subsets can be chosen from a set of 100 elements?

29. How many different tips could you leave in a restaurant if you had a nickel, a dime, a quarter, and a half-dollar?

30. A pizza parlor offers mushrooms, green peppers, onions, and sausage as toppings for the plain cheese base. How many different types of pizzas can be made?

31. A cable TV franchise offers 20 basic channels plus a selection (at an extra cost per channel) from a collection of 6 premium channels. How many different options are available to the subscriber?

32. A salad bar offers a base of lettuce to which tomatoes, chickpeas, beets, pinto beans, olives, and green peppers can be added. Five salad dressings are available. How many different salads are possible? (Assume that each salad contains at least lettuce and at most one salad dressing.)

33. In how many ways can a selection of at least one book be made from a set of eight books?

34. In how many ways can a selection of at most five desserts be made from a dessert trolley containing six desserts?

35. Armand's Chicago Pizzeria offers thin-crust and deep-dish pizzas in 9-, 12-, and 14-inch sizes, with 15 possible toppings. How many different types of pizzas can be ordered?

36. In how many ways can a selection of at least two CDs be made from a set of seven CDs?

37. In how many ways can a selection of at most five appetizers be made from a menu containing seven appetizers?

38. An ice cream parlor offers four flavors of ice cream, three sauces, and two types of nuts. How many different sundaes consisting of a single flavor of ice cream are possible?

39. How many subsets of the set $\{a, b, c, d, e\}$ do not contain the letter c?

40. How many subsets of the set $\{1, 2, 3, 4, 5\}$ do not contain an even digit?

41. Students in a physics class are required to complete at least two out of a collection of eight lab projects. In how many ways can a student satisfy the requirement?

42. Suppose that a set has an odd number of elements. Explain why half of the subsets will have an odd number of elements.

43. How many different groups of students can show up for a seminar with an enrollment of 12?

44. In planning a menu, a dietitian must choose 2 carbohydrates from the 7 available ones, 3 vegetables from the 10 available ones, and 1 protein from the 5 available ones. How many menus are possible?

45. Show that in a Venn diagram containing three sets, there are eight possible regions. Use binomial coefficients to explain why.

46. A car dealership has 20 different models that could be placed on display in the showroom, but it has room for at most 5 of these. In how many ways can the manager choose the "show cars"?

47. A car dealership has 20 different models, of which 8 are two-door and 12 are four-door vehicles. In how many ways can the manager choose three of the two-door and two of the four-door models for a showroom display?

48. In how many ways can a car dealership with 20 cars available on a particular day make at least one sale?

49. What is the coefficient of y^4 in the expansion of $(x - 3y)^7$?

A feasible set is determined by choosing a subset from the set of five inequalities $\{x \geq 0, y \geq 0, x + y \leq 9, x + 2y \leq 12, x \geq y - 3\}$ (see Fig. 1).

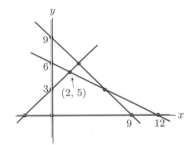

Figure 1.

50. How many feasible sets are possible?

51. How many of the possible feasible sets have $(2, 5)$ as a vertex?

Solutions to Practice Problems 5.7

1. 495. $\binom{12}{8}$ is the same as $C(12, 8)$, which equals $C(12, 12 - 8)$ or $C(12, 4)$.

$$C(12, 4) = \frac{12 \cdot 11 \cdot 10 \cdot 9}{4 \cdot 3 \cdot 2 \cdot 1} = \frac{\cancel{12} \cdot 11 \cdot \overset{5}{\cancel{10}} \cdot 9}{\cancel{4} \cdot \cancel{3} \cdot \cancel{2} \cdot 1} = 495$$

2. 320. The task of deciding what sort of serving to have consists of two operations. The first operation, selecting the flavor of ice cream, can be performed in 10 ways. The second operation, selecting the toppings, can be performed in 2^5 or 32 ways, since selecting the toppings amounts to selecting a subset from the set of 5 toppings, and a set of 5 elements has 2^5 subsets. (Notice that selecting the empty subset corresponds to ordering a plain dish of ice cream.) By the multiplication principle, the task can be performed in $10 \cdot 32 = 320$ ways.

5.8 Multinomial Coefficients and Partitions

Permutation and combination problems are only two of the many types of counting problems. By appropriately generalizing the binomial coefficients to the *multinomial coefficients*, we can consider certain generalizations of combinations, namely *partitions*. To introduce the notion of a partition, let us return to combinations and look at them from another viewpoint. Suppose that we consider combinations of n objects taken r at a time. View the n objects as the elements of a set S. Then each combination determines an ordered division of S into two subsets, S_1 and S_2, the first containing the r elements selected and the second containing the $n - r$ elements remaining (Fig. 1). We see that

$$S = S_1 \cup S_2 \quad \text{and} \quad n(S_1) + n(S_2) = n.$$

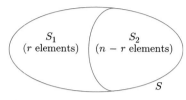

Figure 1.

This ordered division is called an *ordered partition* of type $(r, n - r)$. We know that the number of such partitions is just the number of ways of selecting the first subset, that is, $n!/[r!(n - r)!]$. If we let $n_1 = n(S_1) = r$ and $n_2 = n(S_2) = n - r$, then we find that the number of ordered partitions of type (n_1, n_2) is $n!/n_1!\,n_2!$.

We may generalize the above situation as follows: Let S be a set of n elements. An *ordered partition of S of type* $(n_1, n_2, \ldots, n_m)$ is a decomposition of S into m subsets (given in a specific order) $S_1, S_2, \ldots, S_m$, where no two of these intersect and where

$$n(S_1) = n_1, \qquad n(S_2) = n_2, \quad \ldots \quad , n(S_m) = n_m$$

(Fig. 2). Since S has n elements, we clearly must have $n = n_1 + n_2 + \cdots + n_m$.

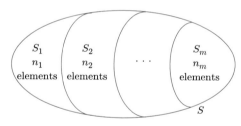

Figure 2.

▶ **Example 1** List all ordered partitions of $S = \{a, b, c, d\}$ of type $(1, 1, 2)$.

Solution

$$(\{a\}, \{b\}, \{c, d\}) \qquad (\{c\}, \{a\}, \{b, d\})$$
$$(\{a\}, \{c\}, \{b, d\}) \qquad (\{c\}, \{b\}, \{a, d\})$$
$$(\{a\}, \{d\}, \{b, c\}) \qquad (\{c\}, \{d\}, \{a, b\})$$
$$(\{b\}, \{a\}, \{c, d\}) \qquad (\{d\}, \{a\}, \{b, c\})$$
$$(\{b\}, \{c\}, \{a, d\}) \qquad (\{d\}, \{b\}, \{a, c\})$$
$$(\{b\}, \{d\}, \{a, c\}) \qquad (\{d\}, \{c\}, \{a, b\})$$

Note that the ordered partition $(\{a\}, \{b\}, \{c, d\})$ is different from the ordered partition $(\{b\}, \{a\}, \{c, d\})$, since in the first S_1 is $\{a\}$, whereas in the second S_1 is $\{b\}$. The order in which the subsets are given is significant. ◆

We saw earlier that the number of ordered partitions of type (n_1, n_2) for a set of n elements is $n!/n_1!\,n_2!$. This result generalizes.

Number of Ordered Partitions of Type (n₁, n₂, ..., nₘ) Let S be a set of n elements. Then the number of ordered partitions of S of type $(n_1, n_2, \ldots, n_m)$ is

$$\frac{n!}{n_1! \, n_2! \cdots n_m!}. \tag{1}$$

The number of ordered partitions of type $(n_1, n_2, \ldots, n_m)$ for a set of n elements is often denoted

$$\binom{n}{n_1, n_2, \ldots, n_m}.$$

Using the preceding notation, result (1) says that

$$\binom{n}{n_1, n_2, \ldots, n_m} = \frac{n!}{n_1! \, n_2! \cdots n_m!}.$$

The binomial coefficient $\binom{n}{n_1}$ can also be written $\binom{n}{n_1, n_2}$. The number

$$\binom{n}{n_1, n_2, \ldots, n_m}$$

is known as a *multinomial coefficient* since it appears as the coefficient of $x_1^{n_1} x_2^{n_2} \cdots x_m^{n_m}$ in the expansion of $(x_1 + x_2 + \cdots + x_m)^n$.

▶ **Example 2** Let S be a set of four elements. Use the formula in (1) to determine the number of ordered partitions of S of type $(1, 1, 2)$.

Solution Here $n = 4$, $n_1 = 1$, $n_2 = 1$, and $n_3 = 2$. Therefore, the number of ordered partitions of type $(1, 1, 2)$ is

$$\binom{4}{1, 1, 2} = \frac{4!}{1! \, 1! \, 2!} = \frac{4 \cdot 3 \cdot 2 \cdot 1}{1 \cdot 1 \cdot 2 \cdot 1} = 12.$$

This result is the same as obtained in Example 1 by enumeration. ◆

▶ **Example 3** A work crew consists of 12 construction workers, all having the same skills. A construction job requires four welders, three concrete workers, three heavy equipment operators, and two bricklayers. In how many ways can the 12 workers be assigned to the required tasks?

Solution Each assignment of jobs corresponds to an ordered partition of the type $(4, 3, 3, 2)$. The number of such ordered partitions is

$$\binom{12}{4, 3, 3, 2} = \frac{12!}{4! \, 3! \, 3! \, 2!} = 277{,}200. ◆$$

Sometimes all of the m subsets of an ordered partition are required to have the same number of elements. If the set has n elements and each of the m subsets has r elements, then the number of ordered partitions of type

$$(\underbrace{r, r, \ldots, r}_{m})$$

is

$$\binom{n}{r, r, \ldots, r} = \frac{n!}{r! \, r! \cdots r!} = \frac{n!}{(r!)^m}. \tag{2}$$

▶ **Example 4** In the game of bridge, four players seated in a specific order are each dealt 13 cards. How many different possibilities are there for the hands dealt to the players?

Solution   Each deal results in an ordered partition of the 52 cards of type $(13, 13, 13, 13)$. The number of such partitions is

$$\binom{52}{13, 13, 13, 13} = \frac{52!}{(13!)^4}.$$

This number is approximately 5.36×10^{28}.   ◆

Unordered Partitions   Determining the number of unordered partitions of a certain type is a complex matter. We will restrict our attention to the special case in which each subset is of the same size.

▶ **Example 5**   List all unordered partitions of $S = \{a, b, c, d\}$ of type $(2, 2)$.

Solution

$$(\{a, b\}, \{c, d\})$$
$$(\{a, c\}, \{b, d\})$$
$$(\{a, d\}, \{b, c\}) \qquad\qquad ◆$$

Note that the partition $(\{c, d\}, \{a, b\})$ is the same as the partition $(\{a, b\}, \{c, d\})$ when order is not taken into account.

Number of Unordered Partitions of Type (r, r, ..., r)   Let S be a set of n elements where $n = m \cdot r$. Then the number of unordered partitions of S of type $(r, r, \ldots, r)$ is

$$\frac{1}{m!} \cdot \frac{n!}{(r!)^m}. \qquad\qquad (3)$$

Formula (3) follows from the fact that each unordered partition of the m subsets gives rise to $m!$ ordered partitions. Therefore,

$$(m!)\,[\text{number of unordered partitions}] = [\text{number of ordered partitions}]$$

or

$$[\text{number of unordered partitions}] = \frac{1}{m!} \cdot [\text{number of ordered partitions}]$$

$$= \frac{1}{m!} \cdot \frac{n!}{(r!)^m} \quad [\text{by formula (2)}].$$

▶ **Example 6**   Let S be a set of four elements. Use formula (3) to determine the number of unordered partitions of S of type $(2, 2)$.

Solution   Here $n = 4$, $r = 2$, and $m = 2$. Therefore, the number of unordered partitions of type $(2, 2)$ is

$$\frac{1}{2!} \cdot \frac{4!}{(2!)^2} = \frac{1}{2} \cdot \frac{4 \cdot 3 \cdot 2 \cdot 1}{(2 \cdot 1)^2} = 3.$$

This result is the same as that obtained in Example 5 by enumeration.   ◆

▶ **Example 7**   A construction crew contains 12 workers, all having similar skills. In how many ways can the workers be divided into four groups of three?

Solution   The order of the four groups is not relevant. (It does not matter which is labeled S_1 and which S_2, and so on. Only the composition of the groups is important.)

Applying formula (3) with $n = 12$, $r = 3$, and $m = 4$, we see that the number of ways is

$$\frac{1}{m!} \cdot \frac{n!}{(r!)^m} = \frac{1}{4!} \cdot \frac{12!}{(3!)^4}$$

$$= \frac{1}{4 \cdot 3 \cdot 2 \cdot 1} \frac{12 \cdot 11 \cdot 10 \cdot 9 \cdot 8 \cdot 7 \cdot 6 \cdot 5 \cdot 4 \cdot 3 \cdot 2 \cdot 1}{6^4}$$

$$= \frac{2 \cdot 11 \cdot 10 \cdot 9 \cdot 8 \cdot 7 \cdot 1 \cdot 5}{6 \cdot 6} = 15,400. \qquad \blacklozenge$$

Practice Problems 5.8

1. A foundation wishes to award one grant of \$100,000, two grants of \$10,000, five grants of \$5000, and five grants of \$2000. Its list of potential grant recipients has been narrowed to 13 possibilities. In how many ways can the awards be made?

2. In how many different ways can six medical interns be put into three groups of two and assigned to
   (a) The radiology, neurology, and surgery departments?
   (b) Share living quarters?

▶ Exercises 5.8

Let S be a set of n elements. Determine the number of ordered partitions of the types in Exercises 1–10.

1. $n = 5$; $(3, 1, 1)$
2. $n = 5$; $(2, 1, 2)$
3. $n = 6$; $(2, 1, 2, 1)$
4. $n = 6$; $(3, 3)$
5. $n = 7$; $(3, 2, 2)$
6. $n = 7$; $(4, 1, 2)$
7. $n = 12$; $(4, 4, 4)$
8. $n = 8$; $(3, 3, 2)$
9. $n = 12$; $(5, 3, 2, 2)$
10. $n = 8$; $(2, 2, 2, 2)$

Let S be a set of n elements. Determine the number of unordered partitions of the types in Exercises 11–14.

11. $n = 15$; $(3, 3, 3, 3, 3)$
12. $n = 10$; $(5, 5)$
13. $n = 18$; $(6, 6, 6)$
14. $n = 12$; $(4, 4, 4)$

15. A brokerage house regularly reports the behavior of a group of 20 stocks, each stock being reported as "up," "down," or "unchanged." How many different reports can show seven stocks up, five stocks down, and eight stocks unchanged?

16. An investment advisory service rates investments as A, AA, and AAA. On a certain week, it rates 15 investments. In how many ways can it rate five investments in each of the categories?

17. In a certain month (of 30 days) it rains 10 days, snows 2 days, and is clear 18 days. In how many ways can such weather be distributed over the month?

18. A psychology experiment observes groups of four individuals. In how many ways can an experimenter choose 5 groups of 4 from among 20 subjects?

19. During orientation, new students are divided into groups of five people. In how many ways can 4 groups be chosen from among 20 people?

20. Of the nine contestants in a contest, three will receive cars, three will receive TV sets, and three will receive radios. In how many different ways can the prizes be awarded?

21. A corporation has four employees that it wants to place in high executive positions. One will become president, one will become vice president, and two will be appointed to the board of directors. In how many different ways can this be accomplished?

22. The 10 members of a city council decide to form two committees of six to study zoning ordinances and street-repair schedules, with an overlap of two committee members. In how many ways can the committees be formed? (*Hint:* Specify three groups, not two.)

23. In how many ways can the 14 children in a third-grade class be paired up for a trip to a museum?

24. A sales representative must travel to three cities twice each in the next 10 days. Her nontravel days are spent in the office. In how many different ways can she schedule her travel, assuming that she does not want to spend four consecutive days in the office?

25. Derive formula (1) using the generalized multiplication principle and the formula for $\binom{n}{r}$. (*Hint:* First select the elements of S_1, then the elements of S_2, and so on.)

Exercises 26 and 27 require the use of a calculator or a computer.

26. Calculate the number of ways that 38 students can be assigned to four seminars of size 10, 12, 10, 6, respectively.

27. Calculate the number of ways that 65 phone numbers can be distributed to 5 campaign workers if each worker gets the same number of names.

Solutions to Practice Problems 5.8

1. Each choice of recipients is an ordered partition of the 13 finalists into a first subset of one ($100,000 award), a second subset of two ($10,000 award), a third subset of five ($5000 award), and a fourth subset of five ($2000 award). The number of ways to choose the recipients is thus

$$\binom{13}{1,2,5,5} = \frac{13!}{1!\,2!\,5!\,5!}$$

$$= \frac{13 \cdot 12 \cdot 11 \cdot \overset{3}{\cancel{10}} \cdot \cancel{9} \cdot \cancel{8} \cdot 7 \cdot 6 \cdot \cancel{5} \cdot \cancel{4} \cdot \cancel{3} \cdot \cancel{2} \cdot \cancel{1}}{1 \cdot \cancel{2} \cdot 1 \cdot \cancel{5} \cdot \cancel{4} \cdot \cancel{3} \cdot \cancel{2} \cdot 1 \cdot \cancel{5} \cdot \cancel{4} \cdot \cancel{3} \cdot \cancel{2} \cdot \cancel{1}}$$

$$= 13 \cdot 12 \cdot 11 \cdot 3 \cdot 7 \cdot 6 = 216{,}216.$$

2. Each partition is of the type $(2, 2, 2)$. In part (a) the order of the subsets is important, whereas in part (b) the order is irrelevant. Consider the partitions

$$(\{\text{Dr. A, Dr. B}\}, \quad \{\text{Dr. C, Dr. D}\}, \quad \{\text{Dr. E, Dr. F}\})$$

and

$$(\{\text{Dr. C, Dr. D}\}, \quad \{\text{Dr. A, Dr. B}\}, \quad \{\text{Dr. E, Dr. F}\}).$$

With respect to part (a) these two partitions are different since in one Drs. A and B are assigned to the radiology department and in the other they are assigned to the neurology department. With respect to part (b), these two partitions are the same since, for instance, Drs. A and B are roommates in both partitions. Therefore, the answers are

(a) $\binom{6}{2,2,2} = \frac{6!}{(2!)^3} = \frac{6 \cdot 5 \cdot \cancel{4} \cdot 3 \cdot \cancel{2} \cdot 1}{\cancel{2} \cdot \cancel{2} \cdot \cancel{2}} = 90.$

(b) $\frac{1}{3!} \cdot \frac{6!}{(2!)^3} = \frac{1}{\cancel{6}} \cdot \frac{\cancel{6} \cdot 5 \cdot \cancel{4} \cdot 3 \cdot \cancel{2} \cdot 1}{\cancel{2} \cdot \cancel{2} \cdot \cancel{2}} = 15.$

▶ Chapter 5 Summary

1. A *set* is a collection of objects. Each object is called an *element* of the set. The *empty set* is the set containing no objects.

2. The *union* of two sets is the set consisting of all elements that belong to **at least one** of the sets. The *intersection* of two sets is the set consisting of all elements that belong to **both** of the sets.

3. Set A is a *subset* of set B if every element of set A is also an element of set B. In each situation or problem, all sets are considered to be subsets of a *universal set*. The set of all elements in the universal set that do not belong to the set A is called the *complement of A*, denoted A'.

4. The inclusion-exclusion principle says that the number of elements in the union of two sets is the sum of the number of elements in each set minus the number of elements in their intersection.

5. A Venn diagram consists of a rectangle containing overlapping circles and is used to depict relationships among sets. The rectangle represents the universal set and the circles represent subsets of the universal set.

6. De Morgan's laws state that the complement of the union (intersection) of two sets is the intersection (union) of their complements.

7. The multiplication principle states that the number of ways a sequence of several independent operations can be performed is the product of the number of ways each individual operation can be performed.

8. The number of ordered arrangements, each called a *permutation*, of n objects taken r at a time is $P(n, r) = n(n - 1)(n - 2) \cdots (n - r + 1)$.

9. The number of unordered arrangements, each called a *combination*, of n objects taken r at a time is

$$C(n, r) = \frac{P(n, r)}{r!} = \frac{n(n - 1)(n - 2) \cdots (n - r + 1)}{r(r - 1) \cdots 1}.$$

$C(n, r)$ is also denoted $\binom{n}{r}$.

10. The formula $C(n, r) = C(n, n - r)$ simplifies the computation of $C(n, r)$ when r is greater than $\frac{n}{2}$.

11. The binomial theorem states that

$$(x + y)^n = \binom{n}{0} x^n + \binom{n}{1} x^{n-1} y + \binom{n}{2} x^{n-2} y^2$$

$$+ \cdots + \binom{n}{n - 1} xy^{n-1} + \binom{n}{n} y^n.$$

12. A set of n elements has 2^n subsets.

13. Let S be a set of n elements, and suppose that $n = n_1 + n_2 + \cdots + n_m$ where each number in the sum is a positive integer. Then the number of ordered partitions of S into subsets of sizes $n_1, n_2, \ldots, n_m$ is

$$\frac{n!}{n_1! \, n_2! \cdots n_m!}.$$

This number is also denoted

$$\binom{n}{n_1, n_2, \ldots, n_m}.$$

14. Let S be a set of n elements, where $n = m \cdot r$. Then the number of unordered partitions of S into m subsets of size r is $\dfrac{1}{m!} \cdot \dfrac{n!}{(r!)^m}$.

Review of Fundamental Concepts of Chapter 5

1. What is a set?

2. What is a subset of a set?

3. What is an element of a set?

4. Define a universal set.

5. Define the empty set.

6. Use a Venn diagram to draw the complement of a set A.

7. Use a Venn diagram to draw the sets $A \cap B$ and $A \cup B$.

8. Use a Venn diagram to draw the sets $A \cap (B \cup C)$ and $A \cup (B \cap C)$.

9. State the generalized multiplication principle for counting.

10. What is meant by a permutation of n items taken r at a time?

11. How would you calculate the number of permutations of n items taken r at a time?

12. What is the difference between a permutation and a combination?

13. How would you calculate the number of combinations of n items taken r at a time?

14. Give a formula that can be used to calculate each of the following:

$$n! \qquad \binom{n}{r} \qquad C(n, r) \qquad P(n, r).$$

15. State the binomial theorem.

16. If a set contains n elements, how many subsets does it have?

17. Explain what is meant by an ordered partition of a set.

18. Explain how to calculate the number of ordered partitions of a set.

19. Give a formula that can be used to calculate

$$\binom{n}{n_1, n_2, \ldots, n_m}.$$

▶ Chapter 5 Supplementary Exercises

1. List all subsets of the set $\{a, b\}$.

2. Draw a two-circle Venn diagram and shade the portion corresponding to the set $(S \cup T')'$.

3. There are 16 contestants in a tennis tournament. How many different possibilities are there for the two people who will play in the final round?

4. In how many ways can a coach and five basketball players line up in a row for a picture if the coach insists on standing at one of the ends of the row?

5. Draw a three-circle Venn diagram and shade the portion corresponding to the set $R' \cap (S \cup T)$.

6. Calculate the first three terms in the binomial expansion of $(x + y)^{12}$.

7. An urn contains 14 numbered balls, of which 8 are red and 6 are green. How many different possibilities are there for selecting a sample of 5 balls in which 3 are red and 2 are green?

8. Sixty people with a certain medical condition were given pills. Fifteen of these people received placebos. Forty people showed improvement, and 30 of these people received an actual drug. How many of the people who received the drug showed no improvement?

9. An appliance store carries seven different types of washing machines and five different types of dryers. How many different combinations are possible for a customer who wants to purchase a washing machine and a dryer?

10. There are 12 contestants in a contest. Two will receive trips around the world, four will receive cars, and six will receive color TV sets. In how many different ways can the prizes be awarded?

11. Out of a group of 115 applicants for jobs at the World Bank, 70 speak French, 65 speak Spanish, 65 speak German, 45 speak French and Spanish, 35 speak Spanish and German, 40 speak French and German, and 35 speak all three languages. How many of the people speak none of the three languages?

12. Calculate $\binom{17}{15}$.

The 100 members of the Earth Club were asked what they felt the club's priorities should be in the coming year: clean water, clean air, or recycling. The responses were 45 for clean water, 30 for clean air, 42 for recycling, 13 for both clean air and clean water, 20 for clean air and recycling, 16 for clean water and recycling, and 9 for all three. Exercises 13–20 refer to this poll.

13. How many members thought the priority should be clean air only?

14. How many members thought the priority should be clean water or clean air, but not both?

15. How many members thought the priority should be clean water or recycling but not clean air?

16. How many members thought the priority should be clean air and recycling but not clean water?

17. How many members thought the priority should be exactly one of the three issues?

18. How many members thought recycling should not be a priority?

19. How many members thought the priority should be recycling but not clean air?

20. How many members thought the priority should be anything but one of these three issues?

21. How many different nine-letter words (i.e., sequences of letters) can be made using four S's and five T's?

22. Forty people take an exam. How many different possibilities are there for the set of people who pass the exam?

23. A survey at a small New England college showed that 400 students skied, 300 played ice hockey, and 150 did both. How many students participated in at least one of these sports?

24. How many different meals can be chosen if there are 6 appetizers, 10 main dishes, and 8 desserts, assuming a meal consists of one item from each category?

25. On an essay test there are 5 questions worth 20 points each. In how many ways can a student get 10 points on one question, 15 points on each of three questions, and 20 points on another question?

26. How many seven-digit numbers are even and have a 3 in the hundreds place?

27. How many telephone numbers are theoretically possible if all numbers are of the form *abc-def-ghij* and neither of the first two leading digits (*a* and *d*) is zero?

28. Calculate the number of different strings of letters of length at least 1 but less than 11.

29. How many strings of length 8 can be formed from the symbols *a*, *b*, *c*, *d*, and *e*? How many of the strings have at least one *e*?

30. How many different 5-person basketball teams can be formed from a pool of 12 players?

31. Fourteen students in the 100-student eighth grade are to be chosen to tour the United Nations. How many different groups of 14 are possible?

32. In one ZIP code, there are 40,000 households. Of them, 4000 households get *Fancy Diet Magazine*, 10,000 households get *Clean Living Journal*, and 1500 households get both publications. How many households get neither?

33. At each stage in a decision process, a computer program has three branches. There are 10 stages at which these branches appear. How many different paths could the process follow?

34. Sixty people apply for 10 job openings. In how many ways can all the jobs be filled?

35. A computerized test generator can generate any one of 5 problems for each of the 10 areas being tested. How many different tests can be generated?

36. If a string of six letters cannot contain any vowels (a, e, i, o, u), how many strings are possible?

37. How many different 4-person delegations can be chosen from 10 ambassadors?

38. In how many ways can a teacher divide a class of 21 students into groups of 7 students each?

39. In how many ways can 14 different candies be distributed to 14 scouts?

40. In how many ways can 100 senators be divided into groups of 20 each?

41. In how many ways can 100 senators be assigned to groups of 20 each if the 2 senators from the state of New York cannot be in the same group?

42. Determine the number of palindromes of length 3 that can be formed from the letters in the word PALINDROME.

43. Determine the number of palindromes of length 4 that can be formed from the letters in the word PALINDROME.

44. Determine the number of palindromes of length 5 that can be formed from the letters in the word PALINDROME.

45. A designer of a window display wants to form a pyramid with 15 hats. She wants to place the five men's hats in the bottom row, the four women's hats in the next row, next the three baseball caps, then the two berets, and a clown's hat at the top. All the hats are different. How many displays are possible?

46. In how many ways can 5 people be assigned to seats in a 12-seat room?

47. A poker hand consists of five cards. How many different poker hands contain all cards of the same suit? (Such a hand is called a "flush.")

48. How many three-digit numbers are there in which no two digits are alike?

49. How many three-digit numbers are there in which exactly two digits are alike?

50. How many hands of five cards contain exactly three aces?

51. Fraternity and sorority names consist of two or three letters from the Greek alphabet. How many different names are there in which no letter appears more than once? (The Greek alphabet contains 24 letters.)

In Exercises 52–54 suppose there are three boys and three girls at a party.

52. How many different pairings of the six into three boy-girl pairs can be formed?

53. In how many ways can they be seated in a row such that no person is seated next to someone of the same sex?

54. In how many ways can they be seated at a round table such that no person is seated next to someone of the same sex?

55. If 10 lines are drawn in the plane so that none of them are parallel and no three lines intersect at the same point, how many points of intersection are there? If each of these 10 lines forms the boundary of the bounded feasible set of a system of linear inequalities, how many of the intersections occur outside the feasible set?

56. Two elementary school teachers have 24 students each. The first teacher splits his students into four groups of six. The second teacher splits her students into six groups of four. Which teacher has more options?

57. A consulting engineer agrees to spend three days at Widgets International, four days at Gadgets Unlimited, and three days at Doodads Incorporated in the next two workweeks. In how many different ways can she schedule her consultations?

58. A set of books can be arranged on a bookshelf in 120 different ways. How many books are in the set?

59. How many batting orders are possible in a nine-member baseball team if the catcher must bat fourth and the pitcher last?

60. In how many ways can a committee of 5 people be chosen from 12 married couples if

    (a) The committee must consist of two men and three women?

    (b) A husband and wife cannot both serve on the committee?

61. Suppose that you are voting in an election for state delegate. Two state delegates are to be elected from among seven candidates. In how many different ways can you cast your ballot? (*Note:* You may vote for two candidates. However, some people "single-shoot," and others don't pull any levers.)

62. The object is to start with the letter A on top and to move down the diagram to the C at the bottom. From any given letter, move only to one of the letters directly below it on the left or right. If these rules are followed, how many different paths spell *ALGEBRAIC*?

$$A$$
$$L \quad L$$
$$G \quad G \quad G$$
$$E \quad E \quad E \quad E$$
$$B \quad B \quad B \quad B \quad B$$
$$R \quad R \quad R \quad R$$
$$A \quad A \quad A$$
$$I \quad I$$
$$C$$

63. How many four-letter call letters for a radio station can be made if the first letter must be a K or a W?

Exercises 64–66 require the use of a calculator or computer.

64. A group of students can be arranged in a row of seats in 479,001,600 ways. How many students are there?

65. There are 25 people in a department who must be deployed to work on three projects requiring 10, 9, and 6 people. All the people are eligible for all jobs. Calculate the number of ways this can be done.

66. (a) Calculate the number of license plates that can be formed using three distinct letters and three distinct numbers in any order.

    (b) Compare the solution to (a) with the number of license plates consisting of three distinct letters followed by three distinct numbers. (See Section 4, Example 5.)

▶ Chapter 5 Chapter Test

1. Calculate each of the following:
   (a) $4!$ (b) $P(7,3)$ (c) $C(18,16)$
   (d) $\begin{pmatrix} 6 \\ 0 \end{pmatrix}$ (e) $\begin{pmatrix} 5 \\ 2,1,2 \end{pmatrix}$

2. True or false?
   (a) $\{a,b\} = \{b,a,b\}$.
   (b) If $A \cup B = A$, then $A \cap B = B$.
   (c) $(A \cap B)' = A' \cap B'$.

3. Let $U = \{a,b,c,d,e\}$, $S = \{b,c,d\}$, and $T = \{a,c,e\}$. List the elements of the following sets.
   (a) $S' \cap T$ (b) $(S \cup T)'$

4. Draw a three-circle Venn diagram and shade the portion corresponding to the set $A \cap (B' \cup C)$.

5. The Choral Society and the Drama Club at State University hold a joint party. Of the 60 people attending, 40 are members of the Choral Society and 30 are members of the Drama Club. How many are members of both groups?

6. Out of a group of 100 college freshmen, 12 are education majors, 56 describe themselves as middle-of-the-road politically, and 75 did volunteer work during the past year. Of the education majors, 7 describe themselves as middle-of-the-road politically and 9 did volunteer work during the past year. Forty-two students did volunteer work during the past year and describe themselves as middle-of-the-road politically. Five freshman are education majors who describe themselves as middle-of-the-road politically and who did volunteer work during the past year. How many of the freshmen did not meet any of the three criteria? (*Note*: The data for this problem are based on a survey conducted in the fall semester of 1999 by the American Council of Education.)

7. An Internet company is considering three candidates for CEO, five candidates for CFO, and four candidates for marketing director. In how many different ways can these positions be filled?

8. (a) In choosing problems for an exam consisting of 10 true/false questions, a teacher uses a data bank of 20 easy and 30 hard questions. How many ways can he select the questions for an exam consisting of 5 questions of each type?

   (b) A student who is totally unprepared for the exam decides to answer six of the questions true and the remainder false without even reading the questions. How many different ways can he answer the questions?

9. How many three-digit numbers can be formed from the numbers $\{1,2,3,4,5,6,7\}$ if no digit is repeated?

10. A family consisting of two parents and four children is to be seated in a row for a picture. How many different arrangements are possible in which the children are seated together?

11. The 30 students in a math class consist of 10 science majors and 20 humanities majors. In how many ways can a group of 6 students be selected so that 3 students from each type of major are in the group?

12. Determine the coefficient of $x^7 y^5$ in the binomial expansion of $(x+y)^{12}$.

13. In how many ways can eight volunteers be assigned to four pairs for visiting the sick?

Chapter Project

Pascal's Triangle

In the following triangular table, known as Pascal's triangle, the entries in the nth row are the binomial coefficients $\binom{n}{0}, \binom{n}{1}, \binom{n}{2}, \ldots, \binom{n}{n}$.

$$
\begin{array}{ccccccccccccccc}
 & & & & & & & 1 & & & & & & & \text{0th row} \\
 & & & & & & 1 & & 1 & & & & & & \text{1st row} \\
 & & & & & 1 & & 2 & & 1 & & & & & \text{2nd row} \\
 & & & & 1 & & 3 & & 3 & & 1 & & & & \text{3rd row} \\
 & & & 1 & & 4 & & 6 & & 4 & & 1 & & & \text{4th row} \\
 & & 1 & & 5 & & 10 & & 10 & & 5 & & 1 & & \text{5th row} \\
 & 1 & & 6 & & 15 & & 20 & & 15 & & 6 & & 1 & \text{6th row} \\
1 & & 7 & & 21 & & 35 & & 35 & & 21 & & 7 & & 1 \quad \text{7th row}
\end{array}
$$

Observe that each number (other than the ones) is the sum of the two numbers directly above it. For example, in the 5th row the number 5 is the sum of the numbers 1 and 4 from the 4th row, and the number 10 is the sum of the numbers 4 and 6 from the 4th row. This fact is known as *Pascal's formula*. Namely, the formula says that

$$\binom{n}{r} = \binom{n-1}{r-1} + \binom{n-1}{r}.$$

1. For what values of n and r does Pascal's formula say that the number 10 in the triangle above is the sum of the numbers 4 and 6?

2. Derive Pascal's formula from the fact that $C(n,r) = \dfrac{n!}{r!\,(n-r)!}$.

3. Derive Pascal's formula from the fact that $C(n,r)$ is the number of ways of selecting r objects from a set of n objects. (*Hint*: Let x denote the nth object of the set. Count the number of ways a subset of r objects containing x can be selected and then count the number of ways a subset of r objects not containing x can be selected.)

4. Use Pascal's formula to extend Pascal's triangle to the 12th row. Determine the values of $\binom{12}{5}$ and $\binom{12}{6}$ from the extended triangle.

5. (a) Show that for any positive integer n,

$$\binom{n}{0} + \binom{n}{1} + \binom{n}{2} + \binom{n}{3} + \cdots + \binom{n}{n} = 2^n.$$

Hint: Apply the binomial theorem to $(1+1)^n$.

(b) Show that for any positive integer n,

$$\binom{n}{0} - \binom{n}{1} + \binom{n}{2} - \binom{n}{3} + \cdots \pm \binom{n}{n} = 0.$$

Hint: Apply the binomial theorem to $[1+(-1)]^n$.

(c) Show that for the 7th row of Pascal's triangle, the sum of the even-numbered elements equals the sum of the odd-numbered elements; that is,

$$\binom{7}{0} + \binom{7}{2} + \binom{7}{4} + \binom{7}{6} = \binom{7}{1} + \binom{7}{3} + \binom{7}{5} + \binom{7}{7}.$$

(d) Use the result of parts (a) and (b) to show that for any row of Pascal's triangle, the sum of the even-numbered elements equals the sum of the odd-numbered elements, and give that common sum for the nth row in terms of n. [*Hint*: Add the two equations in parts (a) and (b).]

Chapter Project   (Continued)

6. (a) Show that for any positive integer n,

$$1 + 2 + 4 + 8 + \cdots + 2^n = 2^{n+1} - 1.$$

(*Hint*: Let $S = 1 + 2 + 4 + 8 + \cdots + 2^n$, multiply both sides of the equation by 2, and subtract the first equation from the second.)

(b) Show that the sum of the elements of any row of Pascal's triangle equals one more than the sum of the elements of all previous rows.

7. (a) Consider the 7th row of Pascal's triangle. Observe that each interior number (that is, a number other than 1) is divisible by 7. For what values of n, for $1 \le n \le 12$, are the interior numbers of the nth row divisible by n?

(b) Confirm that each of the values of n from part (a) is a prime number. (*Note*: A number p is a *prime* number if the only positive integers that divide it are p and 1.) Prove that if p is a prime number, then each interior number of the pth row of Pascal's triangle is divisible by p. [*Hint*: Use the fact that $\binom{p}{r} = \frac{p(p-1)(p-2)\cdots(p-r+1)}{1 \cdot 2 \cdot 3 \cdots r}$.]

(c) Show that for any prime number p, the sum of the interior numbers of the pth row is $2^p - 2$.

(d) Calculate $2^p - 2$ for $p = 7$ and show that it is a multiple of 7.

(e) Use the results of parts (b) and (c) to show that for any prime number p, $2^p - 2$ is a multiple of p. (*Note*: This is a special case of Fermat's theorem, which states that for any prime number p and any integer a, $a^p - a$ is a multiple of p.)

8. There are 4 odd numbers in the 6th row of Pascal's triangle $(1, 15, 15, 1)$ and $4 = 2^2$ is a power of 2. For the 0th through 12th rows of Pascal's triangle, show that the number of odd numbers in each row is a power of 2.

In Fig. 1(a) each odd number in the first eight rows of Pascal's triangle has been replaced by a dot and each even number has been replaced by a space. In Fig. 1(b) the pattern for the first four rows is shown in blue. Notice that this pattern appears twice in the next four rows, with the two appearances separated by an inverted triangle. Figure 1(c) shows the locations of the odd numbers in the first 16 rows of Pascal's triangle, and Fig. 1(d) shows that the pattern for the first eight rows appears twice in the next eight rows separated by an inverted triangle. Figure 2 demonstrates that the first 32 rows of Pascal's triangle have the same property.

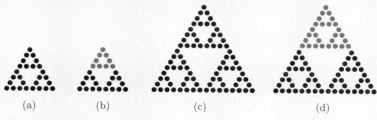

(a)   (b)   (c)   (d)

Figure 1.

9. Assume that the property shown in Figs. 1 and 2 continues to hold for subsequent rows of Pascal's triangle. Use this result to explain why the number of odd numbers in each row of Pascal's triangle is a power of 2.

Chapter Project (Continued)

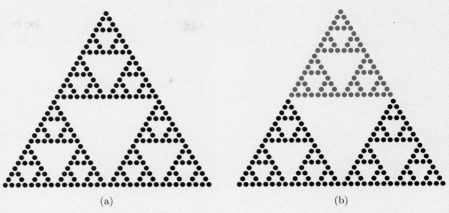

(a)　　　　　　　　　　(b)

Figure 2.

Probability 6

I n this chapter we discuss probability, the mathematics of chance. We consider the basic concepts that allow us to associate realistic probabilities to random events that we see in both our personal and professional lives.

6.1 Introduction

Uncertainty faces us every day. We wake up in the morning and check the weather report (60% chance of rain). We decide on our breakfast cereal (oatmeal might reduce cholesterol). We choose the route to school or work (average delay on Route 450 is 20 minutes, average delay on the alternate is 15 minutes). We better call our stockbroker and check the bank rates to decide how to handle our paycheck. We get a flat tire on the way to an important date (what's the chance of that?). And so on.

Many events in the world around us exhibit a random character. Yet, by repeated observations of such events we can often discern long-term patterns that persist despite random, short-term fluctuations. Probability is the branch of mathematics devoted to the study of such events.

Human beings have always been interested in games of chance and gambling. We have evidence that games such as dice have been in existence since 3000 B.C. But the mathematical treatment of such games did not begin until the fifteenth century in Italy. The French contributed to the literature in the seventeenth century in an attempt to calculate probabilities and develop the theory. The foundations of modern probability theory are generally credited to Kolomogorov, the Russian mathematician, who in 1933 proposed the axioms on which the present subject of probability rests. Even as we enter the twenty-first century, contemporary mathematicians continue to develop new ideas that are applied to such varied areas as investment and risk analysis, card shuffling, diagnostic medical procedures, cryptography, and the efficacy of treatment modalities in medical and social programs. To obtain an idea of the sorts of events that are considered, let us consider a concrete example from the field of medicine.

Suppose that we wish to analyze the reliability of a skin test for active pulmonary tuberculosis. Unfortunately, such a test is not completely reliable. On the one hand, the test may be negative even for a person with tuberculosis. On the other hand, the test may be positive for a person who does not have tuberculosis. For the moment, let us concentrate on errors of the first sort and consider only individuals actually having tuberculosis. Suppose that by observing the results of the test on increasingly large populations of tuberculosis patients we accumulate the data shown in Table 1. Note that out of each group of tuberculosis patients the test fails to identify a certain number. However, the data do exhibit a pattern. It appears that out of a very large population of tuberculosis patients the skin test will successfully identify about 98% of them. In fact, it appears that as the size of the population is increased, the relative frequency m/N more and more closely approximates the number .98. In a situation like this, we say that the skin test detects tuberculosis with a 98% likelihood or that the *probability* that the test detects tuberculosis (when present) is .98.

Table 1

Number of tuberculosis patients N	Number of positive test results m	Relative frequency of positive test results m/N
100	97	.97
500	494	.988
1000	981	.981
10,000	9806	.9806
50,000	49,008	.98016
100,000	98,005	.98005

More generally, the *probability of an event* is a number that expresses the long-run likelihood that the event will occur. Such numbers are always chosen to lie between 0 and 1. The smaller the probability, the less likely the event is to occur. So, for example, an event having probability .1 is rather unlikely to occur; an event with probability .9 is very likely to occur; and an event with probability .5 is just as likely to occur as not.

We assign probabilities to events on the following intuitive basis: The probability of an event should represent the long-run proportion of the time that the event can be expected to occur. For example, an event with probability .9 can be expected to occur 90% of the time, and an event with probability .1 can be expected to occur 10% of the time.

As we shall see, many real-life problems require us to calculate probabilities from known data. Here is one example that arises in connection with the skin test for tuberculosis.

Medical Diagnosis A clinic tests for active pulmonary tuberculosis. If a person has tuberculosis, the probability of a positive test result is .98. If a person does not have tuberculosis, the probability of a negative test result is .99. The incidence of tuberculosis in a certain city is 2 cases per 10,000 population. Suppose that an individual is tested and a positive result is noted. What is the probability that the individual actually has active pulmonary tuberculosis?

Before we can solve this problem, it will be necessary to do considerable preliminary work. We begin this work in Section 6.2, where we introduce a convenient language for discussing events and the process of observing them. In Section 6.3 we introduce probabilities of events, and in Sections 6.4, 6.5, 6.6, and 6.7 we develop methods for calculating probabilities of various sorts of events. The solution of the medical diagnosis problem is presented in Section 6.6. Section 6.8 is devoted to the simulation of simple experiments.

6.2 Experiments, Outcomes, and Events

The events whose probabilities we wish to compute all arise as outcomes of various experiments. So as our first step in developing probability theory, let us describe, in mathematical terms, the notions of experiment, outcome, and event.

For our purposes an *experiment* is an activity with an observable outcome. Here are some typical examples of experiments.

Experiment 1 Flip a coin and observe the side that faces upward.

Experiment 2 Allow a conditioned rat to run a maze, and observe which one of the three possible paths it takes.

Experiment 3 Choose a year and tabulate the amount of rainfall in New York City during that year.

We think of an experiment as being performed repeatedly. Each repetition of the experiment is called a *trial*. In each trial we observe the *outcome* of the experiment. For example, a possible outcome of Experiment 1 is "heads"; a possible outcome of Experiment 2 is "path 3"; and a possible outcome of Experiment 3 is "37.23 inches."

To describe an experiment in mathematical language, we construct a model of the experiment. It is most convenient to form the set consisting of all possible outcomes of the experiment. This set is called the *sample space* of the experiment. For example, if S_1, S_2, S_3 are the sample spaces for Experiments 1, 2, 3, respectively, then we immediately see that

$$S_1 = \{\text{heads, tails}\}$$
$$S_2 = \{\text{path 1, path 2, path 3}\}.$$

Moreover, since any nonnegative number is a candidate for the amount of rainfall, we have

$$S_3 = \{\text{all numbers} \geq 0\}.$$

We can describe an experiment in terms of the sample space as follows:

Suppose that an experiment has a sample space S. Then each trial has as its outcome one of the elements of S.

Thus, for example, each trial for Experiment 1 has as its outcome one of the elements of the set

$$S_1 = \{\text{heads, tails}\}.$$

Henceforth, we shall always describe experiments in terms of their respective sample spaces. So it is important to be able to recognize the appropriate sample space in each instance. The next few examples should help you obtain the necessary facility in doing this.

▶ **Example 1**   An experiment consists of tossing a die and observing the number on the uppermost face. Describe the sample space S for this experiment.

Solution   There are six outcomes of the experiment, corresponding to the six possible numbers on the uppermost face. Therefore,

$$S = \{1, 2, 3, 4, 5, 6\}.$$ ◆

▶ **Example 2**   Once an hour a supermarket manager observes the number of people standing in checkout lines. The store has space for at most 30 customers to wait in line. What is the sample space S for this experiment?

Solution   The outcome of the experiment is the number of people standing in checkout lines. This number may be $0, 1, 2, \ldots$, or 30. Therefore,

$$S = \{0, 1, 2, \ldots, 30\}.$$ ◆

▶ **Example 3**   An experiment consists of throwing two dice, one red and one green, and observing the uppermost face on each. What is the associated sample space S?

Solution   Each outcome of the experiment can be regarded as an ordered pair of numbers, the first representing the number on the red die and the second the number on the green die. Thus, for example, the pair of numbers $(3, 5)$ represents the outcome "3 on the red die, 5 on the green die." The sample space consists of all possible pairs of numbers (r, g), where r and g are each one of the numbers 1, 2, 3, 4, 5, 6. This sample space has 36 elements:

$$
\begin{aligned}
S = \{ &(1,1), \quad (1,2), \quad (1,3), \quad (1,4), \quad (1,5), \quad (1,6), \\
&(2,1), \quad (2,2), \quad (2,3), \quad (2,4), \quad (2,5), \quad (2,6), \\
&(3,1), \quad (3,2), \quad (3,3), \quad (3,4), \quad (3,5), \quad (3,6), \\
&(4,1), \quad (4,2), \quad (4,3), \quad (4,4), \quad (4,5), \quad (4,6), \\
&(5,1), \quad (5,2), \quad (5,3), \quad (5,4), \quad (5,5), \quad (5,6), \\
&(6,1), \quad (6,2), \quad (6,3), \quad (6,4), \quad (6,5), \quad (6,6)\}.
\end{aligned}
$$

Note that if we were interested in the *sum* of the numbers on the uppermost faces, the sample space would be quite different:

$$S = \{2, 3, 4, 5, \ldots, 12\}.$$

The preceding array helps demonstrate what the elements of this second sample space should be. Having the results of an experiment enumerated in a simple way often helps to elucidate the more complicated multistep experiment.   ◆

The sample space for an experiment should be chosen so that every outcome is included and there is no overlap. Since we will be assigning probabilities to the elements of the sample space, we choose a sample space for its utility and not for its simplicity. Personal choices might differ; there is no one right answer.

Consider the experiment of observing the number of heads on three tosses of a fair coin. One possible sample space is $\{0, 1, 2, 3\}$. But we will see later that for practical purposes we might prefer

$$S = \{\text{TTT, TTH, THT, HTT, THH, HTH, HHT, HHH}\},$$

which gives the results (heads or tails) on each of the three tosses.

▶ Example 4   The Environmental Protection Agency orders Middle States Edison Corporation to install "scrubbers" to remove the pollutants from its smokestacks. To monitor the effectiveness of the scrubbers, the corporation installs monitoring devices to record the levels of sulfur dioxide, particulate matter, and oxides of nitrogen in the smokestack emissions. Consider the monitoring operation as an experiment. Describe the associated sample space.

Solution   Each reading of the instruments consists of an ordered triple of numbers (x, y, z), where $x =$ level of sulfur dioxide, $y =$ level of particulate matter, and $z =$ level of oxides of nitrogen. The sample space thus consists of all possible triples (x, y, z), where $x \geq 0$, $y \geq 0$, and $z \geq 0$.   ◆

The sample spaces in Examples 1, 2, and 3 are *finite*. That is, the associated experiments have only a finite number of possible outcomes. However, the sample space of Example 4 is *infinite*, since there are infinitely many triples (x, y, z), where $x \geq 0$, $y \geq 0$, and $z \geq 0$.

Now that we have discussed experiments and their outcomes, let us turn our attention to the notion of "event." In connection with our preceding discussion, we can define many events whose probabilities we might wish to know. For example, in connection with Experiment 2, we can consider the event

"A conditioned rat chooses either path 2 or path 3."

Here are two events associated with Experiment 3:

"The annual rainfall in New York City exceeds 50 inches."

"The annual rainfall in New York City is less than 35 inches."

It is easy to describe events in terms of the sample space. For example, let us consider the die-tossing experiment of Example 1 and the following events.

  I. An even number occurs.
 II. A number greater than 2 occurs.

We saw previously that the sample space S for this experiment is

$$S = \{1, 2, 3, 4, 5, 6\}.$$

Assume that the experiment is performed. Then event I occurs precisely when the outcome of the experiment is 2, 4, or 6. That is, event I occurs precisely when the outcome belongs to the set

$$E_{\mathrm{I}} = \{2, 4, 6\}.$$

Note that this set is a subset of the sample space S. Similarly, we can describe event II by the set

$$E_{\mathrm{II}} = \{3, 4, 5, 6\}.$$

Event II occurs precisely when the outcome of the experiment is an element of E_{II}.

The sets E_{I} and E_{II} contain all the information we need in order to completely describe events I and II. This observation suggests the following definition of an event in terms of the sample space.

An *event* E is a subset of the sample space. We say that the event *occurs* when the outcome of the experiment is an element of E.

The next few examples provide some practice in describing events as subsets of the sample space.

▶ Example 5   Consider the supermarket of Example 2. Describe the following events as subsets of the sample space.

(a) Fewer than 5 people are waiting in line.
(b) More than 23 people are waiting in line.
(c) No people are waiting in line.

Solution   We saw that the sample space for this experiment is given by

$$S = \{0, 1, 2, \ldots, 30\}.$$

(a) If fewer than 5 people are waiting in line, then the number of people waiting is 0, 1, 2, 3, or 4. So the subset of S corresponding to event (a) is

$$\{0, 1, 2, 3, 4\}.$$

(b) In this case the number waiting must be 24, 25, 26, 27, 28, 29, or 30. So the event is just the subset

$$\{24, 25, 26, 27, 28, 29, 30\}.$$

(c) $\{0\}$.   ◆

▶ Example 6   Suppose that an experiment consists of tossing a coin three times and observing the sequence of heads and tails. (Order counts.)

(a) Determine the sample space S.
(b) Determine the event E = "exactly two heads."

Solution   (a) Denote "heads" by H and "tails" by T. Then a typical outcome of the experiment is a sequence of H's and T's. So, for instance, the sequence HTT would stand for a head followed by two tails. We exhibit all such sequences and arrive at the sample space S:

$$S = \{\text{HHH, HHT, HTH, THH, HTT, THT, TTH, TTT}\}.$$

(b) Here are the outcomes in which exactly two heads occur: HHT, HTH, THH. Therefore, event E is

$$E = \{\text{HHT, HTH, THH}\}.$$ ◆

▶ Example 7   A political poll surveys a group of people to determine their income levels and political affiliations. People are classified as either low-, middle-, or upper-level income and as either Democrat, Republican, or Independent.

(a) Find the sample space corresponding to the poll.
(b) Determine the event E_1 = "Independent."
(c) Determine the event E_2 = "low income and not Independent."
(d) Determine the event E_3 = "neither upper income nor Independent."

Solution   (a) Let us abbreviate low, middle, and upper income, respectively, by the letters L, M, and U, respectively. And let us abbreviate Democrat, Republican, and Independent by the letters D, R, and I, respectively. Then a response to the poll can be represented as a pair of letters. For example, the pair (L, D) refers to a lower-income-level Democrat. The sample space S is then given by

$$S = \{(L, D), (L, R), (L, I), (M, D), (M, R), (M, I), (U, D), (U, R), (U, I)\}.$$

(b) For event E_1 the income level may be anything, but the political affiliation is Independent. Thus

$$E_1 = \{(L, I), (M, I), (U, I)\}.$$

(c) For event E_2 the income level is low and the political affiliation may be either Democrat or Republican, so that

$$E_2 = \{(L, D), (L, R)\}.$$

(d) For event E_3 the income level may be either low or middle and the political affiliation may be Democrat or Republican. Thus

$$E_3 = \{(L, D), (M, D), (L, R), (M, R)\}. \qquad \blacklozenge$$

The *New York Times* of November 21, 1996 reported that in the New York City public schools with total enrollment of 1.06 million students, 88.1% of the students are in regular classrooms, 4.5% get part-time special education, and 7.4% get full-time special education. Students in New York City attend schools in one of the five boroughs (Manhattan, Bronx, Brooklyn, Queens, Staten Island). If we choose a student at random, we can determine if the student is in a regular classroom (C), gets part-time special education (P), or gets full-time special education (F). Likewise, for each student we can determine in what borough (M, Bx, Bk, Q, SI) the student goes to school. The sample space is

$$S = \{(C, M), (C, Bx), (C, Bk), (C, Q), (C, SI),$$
$$(P, M), (P, Bx), (P, Bk), (P, Q), (P, SI),$$
$$(F, M), (F, Bx), (F, Bk), (F, Q), (F, SI)\}.$$

A student corresponding to the sample point (F, Bk) is getting full-time special education in Brooklyn.

As we have seen, an event is a subset of the sample space. Two events are worthy of special mention. The first is the event corresponding to the empty set, $\emptyset$. This is called the *impossible event*, since it can never occur. The second special event is the set S itself. Every outcome is an element of S, so S always occurs. For this reason S is called the *certain event*.

One particular advantage of defining experiments and events in terms of sets is that it allows us to define new events from given ones by applying the operations of set theory. When so doing we always let the sample space S play the role of universal set. (All outcomes belong to the universal set.)

If E and F are events, then so are $E \cup F$, $E \cap F$, and E'. For example, consider the die-tossing experiment of Example 1. Then

$$S = \{1, 2, 3, 4, 5, 6\}.$$

Let E and F be the events given by

$$E = \{3, 4, 5, 6\} \qquad F = \{1, 4, 6\}.$$

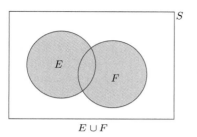

Figure 1.

Then we have

$$E \cup F = \{1, 3, 4, 5, 6\}$$
$$E \cap F = \{4, 6\}$$
$$E' = \{1, 2\}.$$

Let us interpret the events $E \cup F$, $E \cap F$, and E' using Venn diagrams. In Fig. 1 we have drawn a Venn diagram for $E \cup F$. Note that $E \cup F$ occurs precisely when the experimental outcome belongs to the shaded region—that is, to either E or F. Thus we have the following result.

The event $E \cup F$ occurs precisely when either E or F (or both) occurs.

Similarly, we can interpret the event $E \cap F$. This event occurs when the experimental outcome belongs to the shaded region of Fig. 2—that is, to both E and F. Thus we have an interpretation for $E \cap F$:

The event $E \cap F$ occurs precisely when both E and F occur.

Finally, the event E' consists of all those outcomes not in E (Fig. 3). Therefore, we have

The event E' occurs precisely when E does not occur.

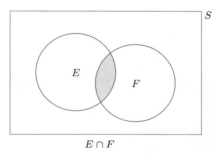

Figure 2.

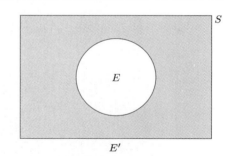

Figure 3.

▶ Example 8   Consider the pollution monitoring described in Example 4. Let E, F, and G be the events

$$E = \text{"level of sulfur dioxide} \geq 100\text{"}$$
$$F = \text{"level of particulate matter} \leq 50\text{"}$$
$$G = \text{"level of oxides of nitrogen} \leq 30\text{."}$$

Describe the following events.

(a) $E \cap F$ (b) E' (c) $E \cup G$ (d) $E' \cap F \cap G$

Solution   (a) $E \cap F$ = "level of sulfur dioxide ≥ 100 *and* level of particulate matter ≤ 50."
(b) E' = "level of sulfur dioxide < 100."
(c) $E \cup G$ = "level of sulfur dioxide ≥ 100 *or* level of oxides of nitrogen ≤ 30."

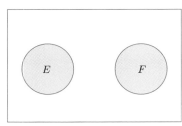

E and F are mutually exclusive

Figure 4.

(d) $E' \cap F \cap G =$ "level of sulfur dioxide < 100 *and* level of particulate matter ≤ 50 *and* level of oxides of nitrogen ≤ 30." ◆

Suppose that E and F are events in a sample space S. We say that E and F are *mutually exclusive* (or *disjoint*) provided that $E \cap F = \emptyset$. In terms of Venn diagrams, we may represent a pair of mutually exclusive events as a pair of circles with no points in common (Fig. 4). If the events E and F are mutually exclusive, then E and F cannot simultaneously occur; if E occurs, then F does not; and if F occurs, then E does not.

▶ Example 9   Let $S = \{a, b, c, d, e, f, g\}$ be a sample space, and let $E = \{a, b, c\}$, $F = \{e, f, g\}$, and $G = \{c, d, f\}$.

(a) Are E and F mutually exclusive?

(b) Are F and G mutually exclusive?

Solution   (a) $E \cap F = \emptyset$, and so E and F are mutually exclusive.

(b) $F \cap G = \{f\}$, and so F and G are *not* mutually exclusive. ◆

Practice Problems 6.2

1. A machine produces light bulbs. As part of a quality control procedure, a sample of five light bulbs is collected each hour and the number of defective light bulbs among these is observed.

   (a) What is the sample space for this experiment?

   (b) Describe the event "there are at most two defective light bulbs" as a subset of the sample space.

2. Suppose that there are two crates of citrus fruit and each crate contains oranges, grapefruit, and tangelos. An experiment consists of selecting a crate and then selecting a piece of fruit from that crate. Both the crate and the type of fruit are noted. Refer to the crates as crate I and crate II.

   (a) What is the sample space for this experiment?

   (b) Describe the event "a tangelo is selected" as a subset of the sample space.

▶ Exercises 6.2

1. A committee of two people is to be selected from five people, R, S, T, U, and V.

   (a) What is the sample space for this experiment?

   (b) Describe the event "R is on the committee" as a subset of the sample space.

   (c) Describe the event "neither R nor S is on the committee" as a subset of the sample space.

2. A letter is selected at random from the word "MISSISSIPPI."

   (a) What is the sample space for this experiment?

   (b) Describe the event "the letter chosen is a vowel" as a subset of the sample space.

3. An experiment consists of tossing a coin two times and observing the sequence of heads and tails.

   (a) What is the sample space of this experiment?

   (b) Describe the event "the first toss is a head" as a subset of the sample space.

4. A campus survey is taken to correlate the number of years that students have been on campus with their political leanings. Students are classified as first-year, sophomore, junior, or senior and as conservative or liberal.

   (a) Find the sample space corresponding to the poll.

   (b) Determine the event $E_1 =$ "conservative."

   (c) Determine the event $E_2 =$ "junior and liberal."

   (d) Determine the event $E_3 =$ "neither first-year nor conservative."

5. Suppose that we have two urns—call them urn I and urn II—each containing red balls and white balls. An experiment consists of selecting an urn and then selecting a ball from that urn and noting its color.

(a) What is a suitable sample space for this experiment?

(b) Describe the event "urn I is selected" as a subset of the sample space.

6. An experiment consists of tossing a coin four times and observing the sequence of heads and tails.

(a) What is the sample space of this experiment?

(b) Determine the event $E_1 =$ "more heads than tails occur."

(c) Determine the event $E_2 =$ "the first toss is a head."

(d) Determine the event $E_1 \cap E_2$.

7. A corporation efficiency expert records the time it takes an assembly line worker to perform a particular task. Let E be the event "more than 5 minutes," F the event "less than 8 minutes," and G the event "less than 4 minutes."

(a) Describe the sample space for this experiment.

(b) Describe the events $E \cap F$, $E \cap G$, E', F', $E' \cap F$, $E' \cap F \cap G$, and $E \cup F$.

8. A manufacturer of kitchen appliances tests the reliability of its refrigerators by recording in a laboratory test the elapsed time between consecutive failures. Let E be the event "more than nine months" and F the event "less than two years." Describe the events $E \cap F$, $E \cup F$, E', F', and $(E \cup F)'$.

9. A pair of four-sided dice, each with the numbers from 1 to 4 on their sides, are rolled and the numbers facing down are observed.

(a) List the sample space.

(b) Describe each of the following events as a subset of the sample space.

(i) Both numbers are even.
(ii) At least one number is even.
(iii) Neither number is less than or equal to 2.
(iv) The sum of the numbers is 6.
(v) The sum of the numbers is greater than or equal to 5.
(vi) The numbers are the same.
(vii) A 2 or 3 occurs, but not both 2 and 3.
(viii) No 4 appears.

10. An experiment consists of selecting a car at random from a college parking lot and observing the color and make. Let E be the event "the car is red," F be the event "the car is a Chevrolet," G be the event "the car is a green Ford," and H be the event "the car is black or a Chrysler."

(a) Which of the following pairs of events are mutually exclusive?

(i) E and F (ii) E and G
(iii) F and G (iv) E and H
(v) F and H (vi) G and H
(vii) E' and G (viii) F' and H'

(b) Describe each of the following events:

(i) $E \cap F$ (ii) $E \cup F$
(iii) E' (iv) F'
(v) G' (vi) H'
(vii) $E \cup G$ (viii) $E \cap G$
(ix) $E \cap H$ (x) $E \cup H$
(xi) $G \cap H$ (xii) $E' \cap F'$
(xiii) $E' \cup G'$

11. Let $S = \{1, 2, 3, 4, 5, 6\}$ be a sample space,

$$E = \{1, 2\} \qquad F = \{2, 3\} \qquad G = \{1, 5, 6\}.$$

(a) Are E and F mutually exclusive?

(b) Are F and G mutually exclusive?

12. Show that if E is any event, and E' its complement, then E and E' are mutually exclusive.

13. Let $S = \{a, b, c\}$ be a sample space. Determine all possible events associated with S.

14. Let S be a sample space with n outcomes. How many events are associated with S?

15. Let $S = \{1, 2, 3, 4\}$ be a sample space, $E = \{1\}$, and $F = \{2, 3\}$. Are the events $E \cup F$ and $E' \cap F'$ mutually exclusive?

16. Let S be any sample space, and E, F any events associated with S. Are the events $E \cup F$ and $E' \cap F'$ mutually exclusive? (*Hint*: Apply De Morgan's laws.)

17. Suppose that 10 coins are tossed and the number of heads observed.

(a) Describe the sample space for this experiment.

(b) Describe the event "more heads than tails" in terms of the sample space.

18. Suppose that five nickels and five dimes are tossed and the numbers of heads from each group recorded.

(a) Describe the sample space for this experiment.

(b) Describe the event "more heads on the nickels than on the dimes" in terms of the sample space.

19. An experiment consists of observing the eye color and sex of the students at a certain school. Let E be the event "blue eyes," F the event "male," and G the event "brown eyes and female."

(a) Are E and F mutually exclusive?

(b) Are E and G mutually exclusive?

(c) Are F and G mutually exclusive?

20. Consider the experiment and events of Exercise 19. Describe the following events.

(a) $E \cup F$ (b) $E \cap G$

(c) E' (d) F'

(e) $(G \cup F) \cap E$ (f) $G' \cap E$

21. Suppose that you observe the length of the line at a fast-food restaurant. Describe the sample space.

22. Suppose that you observe the time to be served at a fast-food restaurant. Describe the sample space.

23. Suppose that you observe the time between customer arrivals at a fast-food restaurant. Describe the sample space.

24. Suppose that you observe the length of the line when a customer arrives and the length of time it takes for him or her to be served in a fast-food restaurant. Describe the sample space.

25. New York, New Jersey, and Connecticut each have lotteries of various kinds; in particular, a three-digit number is chosen at random each week in each of the three states. Each week the New York papers publish all three states' winning numbers. What would the sample space look like? Let E be the event that all the numbers are even. Let F be the event that all the numbers are more than 699. Determine the events E' and $E \cap F$.

26. In the December 1, 1996 issue of *Parade* magazine, Marilyn Vos Savant discusses the following situation: "A woman and a man (who are unrelated) each has two children. At least one of the woman's children is a boy, and the man's older child is a boy."

    (a) Describe the sample space of possible families for the man and the sample space of possible families for the woman.

    (b) In the sample space describing the woman's family, let E = the event that there are two boys in the woman's family. Show the elements of E.

    (c) In the sample space describing the man's family, let F = the event that there are two boys in the man's family. Show the elements of F.

27. Anthony E. Pratt, the inventor of the game *Clue*, died in 1996. *Clue* is a board game in which players are given the opportunity to solve a murder that has six suspects, six possible weapons, and nine possible rooms where the murder may have occurred. The six suspects are Colonel Mustard, Miss Scarlet, Professor Plum, Mrs. White, Mr. Green, and Mrs. Peacock. Determine a sample space for the choice of murderer. Discuss how to form a sample space with the entire solution to the murder, giving murderer, weapon, and site.

    (a) How many points would the sample space have?

    Let E be the event that the murder occurred in the library. Let F be the event that the weapon was a gun.

    (b) Describe $E \cap F$.   (c) Describe $E \cup F$.

Solutions to Practice Problems 6.2

1. (a) $\{0, 1, 2, 3, 4, 5\}$. The sample space is the set of all outcomes of the experiment. At first glance it might seem that each outcome is a set of five light bulbs. What is observed, however, is not the specific sample but rather the number of defective bulbs in the sample. Therefore, the outcome must be a number.

   (b) $\{0, 1, 2\}$. "At most 2" means "2 or less."

2. (a) $\{(\text{crate I, orange}), (\text{crate I, grapefruit}), (\text{crate I, tangelo}), (\text{crate II, orange}), (\text{crate II, grapefruit}), (\text{crate II, tangelo})\}$. Two selections are being made and should both be recorded.

   (b) $\{(\text{crate I, tangelo}), (\text{crate II, tangelo})\}$. This set consists of those outcomes in which a tangelo is selected.

6.3 Assignment of Probabilities

In Section 6.2 we introduced the sample space of an experiment and used it to describe events. We complete our description of experiments by introducing probabilities associated to events. For the remainder of this chapter let us limit our discussion to experiments with only a finite number of outcomes.[1]

What do we mean when we say that the probability of getting a "head" on a toss of a fair coin is 50%? What is meant by the statement that the chance was 1 in 100 of choosing a particular number from the numbers $0, 1, 2, 3, \ldots, 97, 98, 99$? Similar notions are used every day. Probability occurs in the news, in strategies used in games and in war, and in decisions that involve medical treatments, insurance policies, and all kinds of risk.

---

[1] This restriction will remain in effect until our discussion of the normal distribution in Section 7.6.

Suppose that you took a coin and tossed it 152 times and kept track of the results on a chart recording the number of heads and tails as you tossed. You might try this with a real coin, or as we will see later, with a simulation device of some kind. Assume that the tally looked like this:

	Number	*Relative frequency*
Heads	67	$67/152 = 44\%$
Tails	85	$85/152 = 56\%$
Total	152	1 or 100%

How "fair" does the coin seem to be? We have computed the actual relative frequency of the two outcomes and noted that heads occurs on about 44% of the tosses, and tails on about 56% of the tosses. For this experiment, the *experimental probability*, or *relative frequency*, of heads is 44%.

This experiment is just that—an experiment—and repeating it would generally yield different tallies and different experimental probabilities. But if the coin is fair, the probability assigned to these two outcomes is the fixed theoretical value of 50% for heads and 50% for tails. What this tells us is that in theory, if a fair coin is tossed many, many times, heads will occur about 50% of the time. The experimental probability (relative frequency) of an event may be quite different from the probability.

Suppose that an experiment has a sample space S consisting of a finite number of outcomes $s_1, s_2, \ldots, s_N$. To each outcome we associate a number, called the *probability of the outcome*, which represents the relative likelihood that the outcome will occur. Suppose that to the outcome s_1 we associate the probability p_1, to the outcome s_2 the probability p_2, and so forth. We can summarize these data in a chart of the following sort:

Outcome	*Probability*
s_1	p_1
s_2	p_2
$\vdots$	$\vdots$
s_N	p_N

Such a chart is called the *probability distribution* for the experiment. The numbers $p_1, p_2, \ldots, p_N$ are chosen so that each probability represents the long-run proportion of trials in which the associated outcome can be expected to occur. Central to our assignment of probabilities is the requirement that the total probability is 1. That is,

$$p_1 + p_2 + \cdots + p_N = 1.$$

The next three examples illustrate some methods for determining probability distributions.

▶ **Example 1**   Toss an unbiased coin and observe the side that faces upward. Determine the probability distribution for this experiment.

Solution   Since the coin is unbiased, we expect each of the outcomes "heads" and "tails" to be equally likely. We assign the two outcomes equal probabilities, namely $\frac{1}{2}$.

The probability distribution is

Outcome	Probability
Heads	$\frac{1}{2}$
Tails	$\frac{1}{2}$

◆

▶ Example 2   Toss a die and observe the side that faces upward. Determine the probability distribution for this experiment.

Solution   There are six possible outcomes, namely 1, 2, 3, 4, 5, 6. Assuming that the die is unbiased, these outcomes are equally likely. So we assign to each outcome the probability $\frac{1}{6}$. Here is the probability distribution for the experiment:

Outcome	Probability	Outcome	Probability
1	$\frac{1}{6}$	4	$\frac{1}{6}$
2	$\frac{1}{6}$	5	$\frac{1}{6}$
3	$\frac{1}{6}$	6	$\frac{1}{6}$

◆

Probabilities may be assigned to the elements of a sample space using common sense about the physical nature of the experiment. The fair coin has two sides, both equally likely to be face up. The balanced die has six equally probable faces. However, it may not be possible to use intuition alone to decide on a realistic probability to assign to individual sample points. Sometimes it is necessary to conduct an experiment and use the data to shed light on the long-run relative frequency with which events occur. The following example demonstrates this technique.

▶ Example 3   Traffic engineers measure the volume of traffic on a major highway during the rush hour from 5 to 6 P.M. By observing the number of cars that pass a fixed point for 300 consecutive weekdays, they collect the following data:

Number of cars observed	Frequency observed
≤ 1000	30
1001–3000	45
3001–5000	135
5001–7000	75
> 7000	15

(a) Describe the sample space associated to this experiment.
(b) Assign a probability distribution to this experiment.

Solution   (a) The experiment consists of counting the number of cars during rush hour on 300 weekdays and assigning each day to a category depending on the number of cars observed on that day. So, for instance, if we observe 6241 cars on a particular day, we add one to the tally for the category 5001–7000. We let

$$s_1 = \text{``}\leq 1000 \text{ cars''}$$

$$s_2 = \text{``}1001\text{–}3000 \text{ cars''}$$

$$s_3 = \text{``}3001\text{–}5000 \text{ cars''}$$

$$s_4 = \text{``}5001\text{–}7000 \text{ cars''}$$

$$s_5 = \text{``}{>}7000 \text{ cars.''}$$

The sample space is

$$S = \{s_1, s_2, s_3, s_4, s_5\}.$$

(b) For each outcome we use the available data to compute its relative frequency. For example, on 30 days of the 300 observed, the number of cars passing the fixed point is ≤ 1000. So the outcome s_1 occurred in $30/300 = 10\%$ of the observations. If we assume that the 300 consecutive observations are representative of rush hours in general, it seems reasonable to assign to the outcome s_1 the probability .10. Similarly, we can assign probabilities to the other outcomes based on the percentages of observations in which they occur.

Outcome	Probability
s_1	$\frac{30}{300} = .10$
s_2	$\frac{45}{300} = .15$
s_3	$\frac{135}{300} = .45$
s_4	$\frac{75}{300} = .25$
s_5	$\frac{15}{300} = .05$

This method of assigning probabilities to outcomes is valid only insofar as the observed trials are "representative." If such probability models are to be used for planning roadways or traffic patterns, they would have to be tested extensively to be sure that the probabilities are realistic representations of the long-run frequency of events.

In fact, in many instances we cannot rely on intuition or perform such experiments to help us in assigning probabilities; instead, we must use our knowledge of sets and counting to construct a theoretical model of the experiment along with associated probabilities. We need to keep in mind that certain fundamental properties must hold when the set of outcomes (the sample space) is a finite set. These can be observed in the following probability distribution for the number of heads in four tosses of a fair coin:

Events	Probability
0 heads	$\frac{1}{16}$
1 head	$\frac{4}{16}$
2 heads	$\frac{6}{16}$
3 heads	$\frac{4}{16}$
4 heads	$\frac{1}{16}$
Total	1

Note that the column labeled "Events" contains all possible outcomes in the sample space. Also, all of the entries in the probability column are nonnegative numbers between 0 and 1. Furthermore, the sum of the probabilities is 1. These properties hold for every probability distribution.

Let an experiment have outcomes $s_1, s_2, \ldots, s_N$ with respective probabilities $p_1, p_2, p_3, \ldots, p_N$. Then the numbers $p_1, p_2, p_3, \ldots, p_N$ must satisfy two basic properties

Fundamental Property 1 Each of the numbers $p_1, p_2, \ldots, p_N$ is between 0 and 1.

Fundamental Property 2 $p_1 + p_2 + \cdots + p_N = 1$.

Roughly speaking, Fundamental Property 1 says that the likelihood of each outcome lies between 0% and 100%, whereas Fundamental Property 2 says that there is a 100% likelihood that one of the outcomes $s_1, s_2, \ldots, s_N$ will occur. The two fundamental properties may be easily verified for the probability distributions of Examples 1, 2, and 3.

▶ **Example 3**
(continued)

Verify that the probabilities assigned to the outcomes of Example 3 satisfy Fundamental Properties 1 and 2.

Solution

The probabilities are .10, .15, .45, .25, and .05. Clearly, each is between 0 and 1, so Property 1 is satisfied. Adding the probabilities shows that their sum is 1, satisfying Property 2. ◆

Suppose that we are given an experiment with a finite number of outcomes. Let us now assign to each event E a probability, which we denote by $\Pr(E)$. If E consists of a single outcome, say $E = \{s\}$, then E is called an *elementary event*. In this case we associate to E the probability of the outcome s. If E consists of more than one outcome, we may compute $\Pr(E)$ via the *addition principle*.

Addition Principle Suppose that an event E consists of the finite number of outcomes $s, t, u, \ldots, z$. That is,

$$E = \{s, t, u, \ldots, z\}.$$

Then

$$\Pr(E) = \Pr(s) + \Pr(t) + \Pr(u) + \cdots + \Pr(z).$$

We supplement the addition principle with the convention that the probability of the impossible event ∅ is 0. This is certainly reasonable, since the impossible event never occurs.

▶ **Example 4**

Observe two-child families. Describe the sample space for counting the number of boys, and assign probabilities to each outcome.

Solution

The sample space $S = \{GG, GB, BG, BB\}$ describes the sex and birth order in two-child families. If we assume that the chance of a boy (B) [or girl (G)] on any birth is $\frac{1}{2}$ and that the sex of any child does not depend on the sex of other children born to the same parents, we would conclude that each of the four outcomes in S is equally likely. Thus we would assign probability $\frac{1}{4}$ to each outcome. Then

$$\Pr(\text{no boys}) = \Pr(\text{GG}) = \tfrac{1}{4}$$
$$\Pr(\text{one boy}) = \Pr(\text{GB}) + \Pr(\text{BG}) = \tfrac{1}{4} + \tfrac{1}{4} = \tfrac{1}{2}$$
$$\Pr(\text{two boys}) = \Pr(\text{BB}) = \tfrac{1}{4}.$$

We are making a reasonable assignment of probabilities here, although U.S. statistics show that 51% of all live births are boys and 49% are girls. If we wish to take many years of census data into account for a more accurate model, we would not assign equal probabilities to each outcome in S. ◆

▶ **Example 5**   Suppose that we toss a die and observe the side that faces upward. What is the probability that an odd number will occur?

    Solution   The event "odd number occurs" corresponds to the subset of the sample space given by

$$E = \{1, 3, 5\}.$$

That is, the event occurs if a 1, 3, or 5 appears on the side that faces upward. By the addition principle,

$$\Pr(E) = \Pr(1) + \Pr(3) + \Pr(5).$$

As we observed in Example 2, each of the elementary outcomes in the die-tossing experiment has probability $\frac{1}{6}$. Therefore,

$$\Pr(E) = \tfrac{1}{6} + \tfrac{1}{6} + \tfrac{1}{6} = \tfrac{1}{2}.$$

So we expect an odd number to occur approximately half of the time. ◆

▶ **Example 6**   Consider the traffic study of Example 3. What is the probability that at most 5000 cars will use the highway during rush hour?

    Solution   The event

$$\text{"at most 5000 cars"}$$

is the same as

$$\{s_1, s_2, s_3\},$$

where we use the same notation for the outcomes as we used in Example 3. Thus the probability of the event is

$$\Pr(s_1) + \Pr(s_2) + \Pr(s_3) = .10 + .15 + .45 = .70.$$

Therefore, we expect that traffic will involve ≤ 5000 cars in approximately 70% of the rush hours. ◆

▶ **Example 7**   Suppose that we toss a red die and a green die and observe the numbers on the sides that face upward.

(a) Calculate the probabilities of the elementary events.

(b) Calculate the probability that the two dice show the same number.

Solution (a) As shown in Example 3 of Section 6.2, the sample space consists of 36 pairs of numbers:

$$S = \{(1,1), (1,2), \ldots, (6,5), (6,6)\}.$$

Each of these pairs is equally likely to occur. (How could the dice show favoritism to a particular pair?) Therefore, each outcome is expected to occur about $\frac{1}{36}$ of the time, and the probability of each elementary event is $\frac{1}{36}$.

(b) The event

$$E = \text{"both dice show the same number"}$$

consists of six outcomes:

$$E = \{(1,1), (2,2), (3,3), (4,4), (5,5), (6,6)\}.$$

Thus, by the addition principle,

$$\Pr(E) = \tfrac{1}{36} + \tfrac{1}{36} + \tfrac{1}{36} + \tfrac{1}{36} + \tfrac{1}{36} + \tfrac{1}{36} = \tfrac{6}{36} = \tfrac{1}{6}. \qquad \blacklozenge$$

▶ **Example 8** A person playing a certain lottery can win $100, $10, or $1, can break even, or can lose $10. These five outcomes with their corresponding probabilities are given by the probability distribution in Table 1.

(a) Which outcome has the greatest probability?
(b) Which outcome has the least probability?
(c) What is the probability that the person will win some money?

Solution (a) Table 1 reveals that the outcome -10 has the greatest probability, .50. (A person playing the lottery repeatedly can expect to lose $10 about 50% of the time.) This outcome is just as likely to occur as not.

(b) The outcome 100 has the least probability, .02. A person playing the lottery can expect to win $100 about 2% of the time. (This outcome is quite unlikely to occur.)

(c) We are asked to determine the probability that the event E occurs, where $E = \{100, 10, 1\}$. By the addition principle,

$$\begin{aligned} \Pr(E) &= \Pr(100) + \Pr(10) + \Pr(1) \\ &= \quad .02 \quad + \quad .05 \quad + \quad .40 \\ &= \quad .47. \end{aligned} \qquad \blacklozenge$$

Table 1

Winnings	Probability
100	.02
10	.05
1	.40
0	.03
−10	.50

Here is a useful formula that relates $\Pr(E \cup F)$ to $\Pr(E \cap F)$:

Inclusion–Exclusion Principle Let E and F be any events. Then

$$\Pr(E \cup F) = \Pr(E) + \Pr(F) - \Pr(E \cap F).$$

In particular, if E and F are mutually exclusive, then

$$\Pr(E \cup F) = \Pr(E) + \Pr(F).$$

Note the similarity of this principle to the principle of the same name that was used in Section 5.2 to count the elements in a set.

▶ Example 9   In tossing a fair die, we observe the uppermost face. What is the probability that the result is odd or greater than 4?

Solution   The event "odd number occurs" corresponds to the set

$$E = \{1, 3, 5\}.$$

The event "number greater than 4 occurs" corresponds to the set

$$F = \{5, 6\}.$$

From Example 5 we see that $\Pr(E) = \frac{1}{2}$. We use the addition principle to find $\Pr(F)$:

$$\Pr(F) = \Pr(5) + \Pr(6) = \frac{1}{6} + \frac{1}{6} = \frac{1}{3}.$$

The event "odd number or number greater than 4 occurs" is $E \cup F$. By the inclusion–exclusion principle, and the fact that $E \cap F = \{5\}$,

$$\Pr(E \cup F) = \Pr(E) + \Pr(F) - \Pr(E \cap F)$$
$$= \frac{1}{2} + \frac{1}{3} - \frac{1}{6} = \frac{4}{6} = \frac{2}{3}.$$

Of course, we could have simply found $E \cup F = \{1, 3, 5, 6\}$ and used the addition principle to get the same answer.   ◆

▶ Example 10   A factory needs two raw materials. The probability of not having an adequate supply of material A is .05, whereas the probability of not having an adequate supply of material B is .03. A study determines that the probability of a shortage of both A and B is .01. What proportion of the time can the factory operate?

Solution   Let E be the event "shortage of A" and F the event "shortage of B." We are given that

$$\Pr(E) = .05 \qquad \Pr(F) = .03 \qquad \Pr(E \cap F) = .01.$$

The factory can operate only if it has both raw materials. Therefore, we must calculate the proportion of the time in which there is no shortage of material A or material B. A shortage of A or B is the event $E \cup F$. By the inclusion–exclusion principle,

$$\Pr(E \cup F) = \Pr(E) + \Pr(F) - \Pr(E \cap F)$$
$$= \quad .05 \quad + \quad .03 \quad - \quad .01$$
$$= \quad .07.$$

Thus the factory is likely to be short of one raw material or the other 7% of the time. Therefore, the factory can expect to operate 93% of the time.   ◆

Probabilities involving unions and intersections of events are often conveniently displayed in a Venn diagram. Fig. 1 displays the probabilities from Example 10.

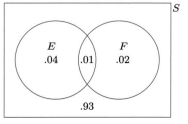

Figure 1.

Odds   Frequently in applications we meet statements like these:

The odds of a Republican victory are 3 to 2.

The odds of a recession next year are 1 to 3.

Such statements may be readily translated into the language of probability. For example, consider the first statement. It means that if the election were repeated often (a theoretical possibility), then for every two Democratic wins there would be three Republican wins. That is, the Republicans would win $\frac{3}{5}$ (or 60%) of the elections. In terms of probability, this means that the probability of a Republican win is .6. In a similar way, we can translate the second statement into probabilistic terms. The statement says that if we consider a large number of years experiencing conditions identical to this year's, then for every one that is followed by a recession, three years are not. That is, the probability of having a recession next year is $\frac{1}{4}$.

We may generalize our reasoning to obtain the following result:

If the odds in favor of an event are a to b, the probability of the event is $a/(a+b)$.

In the lottery of Example 8, the odds of winning \$100 are 1 to 49, since the probability of winning \$100 is $.02 = \frac{2}{100} = \frac{1}{50}$.

▶ **Example 11**   Suppose that the odds of rain tomorrow are 5 to 3. What is the probability that rain will occur?

Solution   The probability that rain will occur is

$$\frac{5}{5+3} = \frac{5}{8}.$$

◆

▶ **Example 12**   In the game of *Clue*, there are 6 equally likely suspects (Colonel Mustard, Miss Peacock, Professor Plum, Mr. Green, Miss Scarlet, Mrs. White), one of whom committed a murder that players are trying to solve. What are the odds that Colonel Mustard killed the victim?

Solution   The probability that Colonel Mustard committed the crime is $\frac{1}{6}$. The odds are therefore 1 to 5. We usually state odds with the larger number first, so we would more naturally claim that the odds are 5 to 1 that Colonel Mustard did *not* kill the victim.

◆

Practice Problems 6.3	

1. A mouse is put into a T-maze (a maze shaped like a "T") (Fig. 2). If he turns to the left he receives cheese, and if he turns to the right he receives a mild shock. This trial is done twice with the same mouse and the directions of the turns recorded.

   (a) What is the sample space for this experiment?

   (b) Why would it not be reasonable to assign each outcome the same probability?

2. **(a)** What are the odds in favor of an event that is just as likely to occur as not?

   (b) Is there any difference between the odds 6 to 4 and the odds 3 to 2?

3. Suppose that E and F are any events. Show that

$$\Pr(E) = \Pr(E \cap F) + \Pr(E \cap F').$$

Practice Problems 6.3 (Continued)

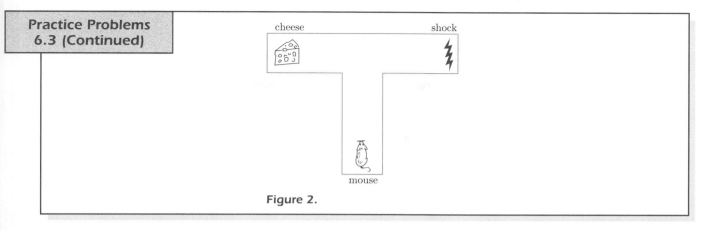

Figure 2.

▶ Exercises 6.3

1. There are 774,746 words in the Bible. The word "and" occurs 46,277 times and the word "Lord" occurs 1855 times.[2] Suppose that a word is selected at random from the Bible.

   (a) What is the probability that the word is "and"?

   (b) What is the probability that the word is "and" or "Lord"?

   (c) What is the probability that the word is neither "and" nor "Lord"?

2. An experiment consists of tossing a coin two times and observing the sequence of heads and tails. Each of the four outcomes has the same probability of occurring.

   (a) What is the probability that "HH" is the outcome?

   (b) What is the probability of the event "at least one head"?

3. Suppose that a red die and a green die are tossed and the numbers on the sides that face upward are observed. (See Example 7.)

   (a) What is the probability that the numbers add up to 8?

   (b) What is the probability that the sum of the numbers is less than 5?

4. A state is selected at random from the 50 states of the United States. What is the probability that it is one of the six New England states?

5. The modern American roulette wheel has 38 slots, which are labeled with 36 numbers evenly divided between red and black plus two green numbers 0 and 00. What is the probability that the ball lands on a green number?

6. An experiment consists of selecting a number at random from the set of numbers $\{1, 2, 3, 4, 5, 6, 7, 8, 9\}$.

   Find the probability that the number selected is
   (a) Less than 4. (b) Odd. (c) Less than 4 or odd.

7. Three horses, call them A, B, and C, are going to race against each other. The probability that A will win is $\frac{1}{3}$ and the probability that B will win is $\frac{1}{2}$.

   (a) What is the probability that C will win? (Assume that there are no ties.)

   (b) What are the odds that C will win?

8. Which of the following probabilities are feasible for an experiment having sample space $\{s_1, s_2, s_3\}$?

   (a) $\Pr(s_1) = .4$, $\Pr(s_2) = .4$, $\Pr(s_3) = .4$

   (b) $\Pr(s_1) = .5$, $\Pr(s_2) = .7$, $\Pr(s_3) = -.2$

   (c) $\Pr(s_1) = 2$, $\Pr(s_2) = 1$, $\Pr(s_3) = \frac{1}{2}$

   (d) $\Pr(s_1) = \frac{1}{4}$, $\Pr(s_2) = \frac{1}{2}$, $\Pr(s_3) = \frac{1}{4}$

9. An experiment with outcomes s_1, s_2, s_3, s_4 is described by the following probability table:

Outcome	Probability
s_1	.1
s_2	.6
s_3	.2
s_4	.1

   (a) What is $\Pr(\{s_1, s_2\})$?

   (b) What is $\Pr(\{s_2, s_4\})$?

[2] According to *The People's Almanac* by Wallechinsky and Wallace (New York: Doubleday, 1975).

10. An experiment with outcomes $s_1, s_2, s_3, s_4, s_5, s_6$ is described by the following probability table:

Outcome	Probability
s_1	.05
s_2	.25
s_3	.05
s_4	.01
s_5	.63
s_6	.01

Let $E = \{s_1, s_2\}$ and $F = \{s_3, s_5, s_6\}$.
(a) Determine $\Pr(E)$, $\Pr(F)$.
(b) Determine $\Pr(E')$.
(c) Determine $\Pr(E \cap F)$.
(d) Determine $\Pr(E \cup F)$.

11. Convert the following odds to probabilities.
(a) 10 to 1 (b) 1 to 2 (c) 4 to 5

12. In poker, the probability of being dealt a hand containing a pair of jacks or better is about $\frac{1}{6}$. What are the corresponding odds?

13. Nine percent of all candy bars sold in the United States are Snickers™ bars. What are the odds that a randomly selected candy bar purchased is a Snickers™ bar?

14. The odds of Americans living in the state where they were born is 16 to 9. What is the probability that an American selected at random lives in his or her birth state?

15. If the odds for Secretariat to win a horse race are 11:7, what is the probability that Secretariat wins? Loses?

16. Four people are running for class president, Liz, Sam, Sue, and Tom. The probabilities of Sam, Sue, and Tom winning are .18, .23, and .31, respectively.
(a) What is the probability of Liz winning?
(b) What is the probability that a boy wins?
(c) What is the probability that Tom loses?
(d) What are the odds that Sue loses?
(e) What are the odds that a girl wins?
(f) What are the odds that Sam wins?

17. Let E and F be events for which $\Pr(E) = .6$, $\Pr(F) = .5$, and $\Pr(E \cap F) = .4$. Find
(a) $\Pr(E \cup F)$
(b) $\Pr(E \cap F')$ (*Hint*: Make a Venn diagram similar to Fig. 1.)

18. Let E and F be events for which $\Pr(E) = .4$, $\Pr(F) = .5$, and $\Pr(E \cap F') = .3$. Find

(a) $\Pr(E \cap F)$ (b) $\Pr(E \cup F)$

19. A statistical analysis of the wait (in minutes) at the checkout line of a certain supermarket yields the following probability distribution:

Wait (in minutes)	Probability
At most 3	.10
More than 3 and at most 5	.20
More than 5 and at most 10	.25
More than 10 and at most 15	.25
More than 15	.20

(a) What is the probability of waiting more than 3 minutes but at most 15?
(b) If you observed the waiting times of a representative sample of 10,000 supermarket customers, approximately how many would you expect to wait for more than 3 minutes but at most 15?

20. What is the probability of the certain event?

21. The following table was derived from a survey of college freshmen.[3] Each probability is the likelihood that a randomly selected freshman applied to the specified number of colleges. For instance, 32% of the freshmen applied to just one college and therefore the probability that a student selected at random applied to just one college is .32. Convert these data into a probability distribution.

Number of Colleges Applied to	Probability
1	.32
2 or less	.46
3 or less	.61
4 or less	.72
20 or less	1

22. Refer to the data of Exercise 21. What is the probability that a student applied to three or more colleges?

23. In a study of the ages of its employees, over a period of several years a university finds the following:

Age (years)	Probability
20–34	.15
20–49	.70
20–64	.90
20–79	1.00

---

[3] *The American Freshman: National Norms for Fall 1999*, Los Angeles, Calif.: American Council on Education, 2000.

(a) Find the probability associated with each of the events: 20–34 years, 35–49 years, 50–64 years, and 65–79 years.

(b) Find the probability that an employee selected at random is at least 50 years old.

24. A realtor analyzes the office's sales over the past two years. She sorts the sales by the age of the house at the time of sale.

Age	Number of Houses Sold
1–2	1200
3–4	1570
5–6	1600
7–8	1520
9–10	1480

(a) Determine the probability that a sale chosen at random is a house between five and six years old.

(b) What are the odds that the house is less than seven years old?

25. Computer usage in a community is segmented by the kind of use:

Kind of use	Frequency
School only	20%
Work only	22%
Home computer only	20%
No computer anywhere	17%

(a) What is the probability that someone in the community uses a computer?

(b) Explain why the percentages listed above do not add up to 100%.

26. The odds in favor of event E can be calculated as

$$\frac{\Pr(E)}{1 - \Pr(E)},$$

where the odds are expressed as a ratio of whole numbers. For example, if $\Pr(E) = \frac{5}{8}$, then the odds are calculated as

$$\frac{\frac{5}{8}}{1 - \frac{5}{8}} = \frac{\frac{5}{8}}{\frac{3}{8}} = \frac{5}{3}.$$

Therefore, the odds in favor of E are 5 to 3.

(a) The probability that there will be a major earthquake in the San Francisco area during the next 30 years is .7. What are the corresponding odds?

(b) Show that if the odds in favor of event E occurring are a to b, then the odds against event E occurring are b to a.

Solutions to Practice Problems 6.3

1. (a) {LL, LR, RR, RL}. Here LL means that the mouse turned left both times, LR means that the mouse turned left the first time and right the second, and so on.

(b) The mouse will learn something from the first trial. If he turned left the first time and got rewarded, then he is more likely to turn left again on the second trial. Hence LL should have a greater probability than LR. Similarly, RL should be more likely than RR.

2. (a) 1 to 1. An event that is just as likely to occur as not has probability $\frac{1}{2}$. So if the odds are a to b, then we may set $a = 1$, $a + b = 2$. Thus $a = 1$, $b = 1$. (The odds could also be given as 2 to 2, 3 to 3, etc.)

(b) No. Odds of 6 to 4 correspond to a probability of $6/(6+4) = \frac{6}{10} = \frac{3}{5}$. Odds of 3 to 2 correspond to a probability of $3/(3 + 2) = \frac{3}{5}$. (There are always many different ways to express the same odds.)

3. The sets $(E \cap F)$ and $(E \cap F')$ have no elements in common and so are mutually exclusive. Since $E = (E \cap F) \cup (E \cap F')$, the result follows from the inclusion–exclusion principle.

6.4   Calculating Probabilities of Events

As mentioned in Section 6.3, there are several ways to assign probabilities to the events of a sample space. One way is to perform the experiment many times and assign probabilities based on empirical data. Sometimes our intuition about situations suffices, as in simple coin-tossing experiments. But we frequently are faced with forming a model of an experiment to assign probabilities consistent with Fundamental Properties 1 and 2. This section shows how the counting techniques of Chapter 5 may be used to extend these ideas to more complex situations. In addition, the exceptionally wide range of applications that make use of probability theory is illustrated.

Experiments with Equally Likely Outcomes   In the experiments associated to many common applications, all outcomes are equally likely—that is, they all have the same probability. This is the case, for example, if we toss an unbiased coin or select a person at random from a population. If a sample space has N equally likely outcomes, then the probability of each outcome is $1/N$ (since the probabilities must add up to 1). If we use this fact, the probability of any event is easy to compute. Namely, suppose that E is an event consisting of M outcomes. Then, by the addition principle,

$$\Pr(E) = \underbrace{\frac{1}{N} + \frac{1}{N} + \cdots + \frac{1}{N}}_{M \text{ times}} = \frac{M}{N}.$$

We can restate this fundamental result as follows:

Let S be a sample space consisting of N equally likely outcomes. Let E be any event. Then

$$\Pr(E) = \frac{[\text{number of outcomes in } E]}{N}. \tag{1}$$

In order to apply formula (1) in particular examples, it is necessary to compute N, the number of equally likely outcomes in the sample space, and [number of outcomes in E]. Often these quantities can be determined using the counting techniques of Chapter 5. Some illustrative computations are provided in Examples 1 through 7 here.

We should mention that, although the urn and dice problems considered in this section and the next might seem artificial and removed from applications, many applied problems can be described in mathematical terms as urn or dice-tossing experiments. We begin our discussion with two examples involving abstract urn problems. Then in two more examples we show the utility of urn models by applying them to quality control and medical screening problems (Examples 3 and 5, respectively).

▶ Example 1   An urn contains eight white balls and two green balls. A sample of three balls is selected at random. What is the probability of selecting only white balls?

Solution   The experiment consists of selecting 3 balls from the 10. Since the order in which the 3 balls are selected is immaterial, the samples are combinations of 10 balls taken three at a time. The total number of samples is therefore $\binom{10}{3}$, and this is N, the number of elements in the sample space. Since the selection of the sample is random, all samples are equally likely, and thus we can use formula (1) to compute the probability of any event. The problem asks us to compute the probability of the event $E =$ "all three balls selected are white." Since there are 8 white balls, the number of different samples in which all are white is $\binom{8}{3}$. Thus

$$\Pr(E) = \frac{[\text{number of outcomes in } E]}{N} = \frac{\binom{8}{3}}{\binom{10}{3}} = \frac{56}{120} = \frac{7}{15}.$$ ◆

▶ **Example 2**   An urn contains eight white balls and two green balls. A sample of three balls is selected at random. What is the probability that the sample contains at least one green ball?

Solution   As in Example 1, there are $N = \binom{10}{3}$ equally likely outcomes. Let F be the event "at least one green ball is selected." Let us determine the number of different outcomes in F. These outcomes contain either one or two green balls. There are $\binom{2}{1}$ ways to select one green ball from two; and for each of these, there are $\binom{8}{2}$ ways to select two white balls from eight. By the multiplication principle, the number of samples containing one green ball equals $\binom{2}{1}\binom{8}{2}$. Similarly, the number of samples containing two green balls equals $\binom{2}{2}\binom{8}{1}$. Note that although the sample size is 3, there are only two green balls in the urn. Since the sampling is done without replacement, no sample can have more than two greens. Therefore, the number of outcomes in F—namely the number of samples having at least one green ball—equals

$$\binom{2}{1}\binom{8}{2} + \binom{2}{2}\binom{8}{1} = 2 \cdot 28 + 1 \cdot 8 = 64,$$

so

$$\Pr(F) = \frac{[\text{number of outcomes in } F]}{N} = \frac{64}{\binom{10}{3}} = \frac{64}{120} = \frac{8}{15}.$$ ◆

▶ **Example 3**   (*Quality control*) A toy manufacturer inspects boxes of toys before shipment. Each box contains 10 toys. The inspection procedure consists of randomly selecting three toys from the box. If any are defective, the box is not shipped. Suppose that a given box has two defective toys. What is the probability that it will be shipped?

Solution   This problem is not really new! We solved it in disguise as Example 1. The urn can be regarded as a box of toys, and the balls as individual toys. The white balls are nondefective toys and the green balls defective toys. The random selection of three balls from the urn is just the inspection procedure. And the event "all three balls selected are white" corresponds to the box being shipped. As we calculated previously, the probability of this event is $\frac{7}{15}$. (Since $\frac{7}{15} \approx .47$, there is approximately a 47% chance of shipping a box with two defective toys. This inspection procedure is not particularly effective!) ◆

▶ **Example 4**   A professor is randomly choosing a group of three students to do an oral presentation. In her class of 10 students, 2 are on the debate team. What is the chance that the professor chooses at least one of the debaters for the group?

Solution   This is the same as Example 2. Just think of the debate team members as the green balls and the others in the class as white balls. The chance of getting at least one debate team member in the group is $\frac{8}{15} \approx .53$.   ◆

▶ Example 5   (*Medical Screening*) Suppose that a cruise ship returns to the United States from the Far East. Unknown to anyone, 4 of its 600 passengers have contracted a rare disease. Suppose that the Public Health Service screens 20 passengers, selected at random, to see whether the disease is present aboard ship. What is the probability that the presence of the disease will escape detection?

Solution   The sample space consists of samples of 20 drawn from among the 600 passengers. There are $\binom{600}{20}$ such samples. The number of samples containing none of the sick passengers is $\binom{596}{20}$. Therefore, the probability of not detecting the disease is

$$\frac{\binom{596}{20}}{\binom{600}{20}} = \frac{\dfrac{596!}{20!\,576!}}{\dfrac{600!}{20!\,580!}} = \frac{596!}{600!} \cdot \frac{580!}{576!}$$

$$= \frac{596!}{600 \cdot 599 \cdot 598 \cdot 597 \cdot 596!} \cdot \frac{580 \cdot 579 \cdot 578 \cdot 577 \cdot 576!}{576!}$$

$$= \frac{580 \cdot 579 \cdot 578 \cdot 577}{600 \cdot 599 \cdot 598 \cdot 597} \approx .87.$$

So there is approximately an 87% chance that the disease will escape detection.   ◆

The Complement Rule   The *complement rule* relates the probability of an event E to the probability of its complement E'. When applied together with counting techniques, it often simplifies computation of probabilities.

Complement Rule   Let E be any event, E' its complement. Then

$$\Pr(E) = 1 - \Pr(E').$$

For example, recall Example 1. We determined the probability of the event

$$E = \text{“all three balls selected are white”}$$

associated to the experiment of selecting three balls from an urn containing eight white balls and two green balls. We found that $\Pr(E) = \frac{7}{15}$. On the other hand, in Example 2 we determined the probability of the event

$$F = \text{“at least one green ball is selected.”}$$

The event E is the complement of F:

$$E = F'.$$

So, by the complement rule,

$$\Pr(F) = 1 - \Pr(F') = 1 - \Pr(E) = 1 - \tfrac{7}{15} = \tfrac{8}{15},$$

in agreement with the calculations of Example 2.

The complement rule is especially useful in situations where $\Pr(E')$ is easier to compute than $\Pr(E)$. One of these situations arises in the celebrated birthday problem.

▶ Example 6 — A group of five people is to be selected at random. What is the probability that two or more of them have the same birthday?

Solution — For simplicity we ignore leap years. Furthermore, we assume that each of the 365 days in a year is an equally likely birthday (not an unreasonable assumption). The experiment we have in mind is this. Pick out five people and observe their birthdays. The outcomes of this experiment are strings of five dates, corresponding to the birthdays. For example, one outcome of the experiment is

(June 2, April 6, Dec. 20, Feb. 12, Aug. 5).

Each birth date has 365 different possibilities. So, by the generalized multiplication principle, the total number N of possible outcomes of the experiment is

$$N = 365 \cdot 365 \cdot 365 \cdot 365 \cdot 365 = 365^5.$$

Let E be the event "at least two people have the same birthday." It is very difficult to calculate directly the number of outcomes in E. However, it is comparatively simple to compute the number of outcomes in E' and hence to compute $\Pr(E')$. This is because E' is the event "all five birthdays are different." An outcome in E' can be selected in a sequence of five steps:

Select a day	Select a different day	Select yet a different day	Select yet a different day	Select yet a different day

These five steps will result in a sequence of five different birthdays. The first step can be performed in 365 ways; for each of these, the next step in 364; for each of these, the next step in 363; for each of these, the next step in 362; and for each of these, the last step in 361 ways. Therefore, E' contains $365 \cdot 364 \cdot 363 \cdot 362 \cdot 361$ [or $P(365, 5)$] outcomes, and

$$\Pr(E') = \frac{365 \cdot 364 \cdot 363 \cdot 362 \cdot 361}{365^5} \approx .973.$$

By the complement rule,

$$\Pr(E) = 1 - \Pr(E') = 1 - .973 = .027.$$

So the likelihood is about 2.7% that two or more of the five people will have the same birthday. ◆

The experiment of Example 6 can be repeated using samples of 8, 10, 20, or any number of people. As before, let E be the event "at least two people have the same birthday," so that $E' =$ "all the birthdays are different." If a sample of r people is used, then the same reasoning as used previously yields

$$\Pr(E') = \frac{365 \cdot 364 \cdot \,\cdots\, \cdot (365 - r + 1)}{365^r}.$$

Table 1 gives the values of $\Pr(E) = 1 - \Pr(E')$ for various values of r. You may be surprised by the numbers in the table. Even with as few as 23 people it is more likely than not that at least two people have the same birthday. With a sample of 50 people we are almost certain to have two with the same birthday. (Try this experiment in your dormitory or class.)

Table 1	Probability that, in a randomly selected group of r people, at least two will have the same birthday								
r	5	10	15	20	22	23	25	30	40	50
$\Pr(E)$	.027	.117	.253	.411	.476	.507	.569	.706	.891	.970

▶ **Example 7**   A die is tossed five times. What is the probability of obtaining exactly three 4's?

Solution   There are $6^5 = 7776$ possible outcomes when a die is tossed five times. These are equally likely to occur. The event we seek is $E =$ "three 4's." How many outcomes are in E? There are $1 \cdot 1 \cdot 1 \cdot 5 \cdot 5 = 25$ ways to get three 4's followed by two tosses yielding anything except 4. But the three 4's need not appear in the first three tosses. What if the 4's appear as 4xx44? The number of possibilities is $1 \cdot 5 \cdot 5 \cdot 1 \cdot 1 = 25$. Thus we need to determine in how many orders these three 4's can appear in the sequence of five tosses. That is just $C(5, 3) = 10$. Therefore, E contains $(10)(25)$ elements, and

$$\Pr(\text{exactly three 4's in five tosses of a die}) = \frac{(10)(25)}{7776} \approx .03.$$

Thus there is about a 3% chance that in five tosses of a fair die we obtain three 4's.   ◆

Verification of the Complement Rule   If S is the sample space, then $\Pr(S) = 1$, $E \cup E' = S$, and $E \cap E' = \emptyset$. Therefore, by the inclusion–exclusion principle,

$$\Pr(S) = \Pr(E \cup E') = \Pr(E) + \Pr(E').$$

So we have

$$1 = \Pr(E) + \Pr(E') \quad \text{and} \quad \Pr(E') = 1 - \Pr(E).$$ ◆

Practice Problems 6.4

1. A couple decides to have four children. What is the probability that among the children there will be at least one boy and at least one girl?

2. (a) Find the probability that all the numbers are different in three spins of a roulette wheel. [*Note*: A roulette wheel has 38 numbers.]

   (b) Guess how many spins are required in order that the probability that all the numbers are different will be less than .5.

▶ **Exercises 6.4**

1. Each of three people randomly chooses one of three calculus sections to take (A, B, or C).

   (a) What is the probability that they all choose the same one?

   (b) What is the probability that they each choose a different section?

2. Michael and Christopher are among seven contestants in a race to be run on a seven-lane track. If the runners are assigned to the lanes at random, what is the probability that Michael will be assigned to the inside lane and Christopher will be assigned to the outside lane?

3. Suppose you are asked to choose a whole number between 1 and 13, inclusive.

   (a) What is the probability that it is odd?

   (b) What is the probability that it is even?

   (c) What is the probability that it is a multiple of 3?

   (d) What is the probability that it is odd or a multiple of 3?

4. Five numbers are chosen at random from the whole numbers between 1 and 13, inclusive, with replacement.

   (a) What is the probability that all the numbers are even?

   (b) What is the probability that all the numbers are odd?

   (c) What is the probability that at least one of the numbers is odd?

5. Five numbers are chosen at random from the whole numbers between 1 and 13, inclusive, without replacement.

   (a) What is the probability that all the numbers are even?

   (b) What is the probability that all the numbers are odd?

   (c) What is the probability that at least one of the numbers is odd?

6. An urn contains 40 balls, some red and some white. If the probability of selecting a red ball is .45, how many red balls are in the urn?

7. An urn contains six white balls and five red balls. A sample of four balls is selected at random from the urn. What is the probability that the sample contains two white balls and two red balls?

8. A factory produces fuses, which are packaged in boxes of 10. Three fuses are selected at random from each box for inspection. The box is rejected if at least one of these three fuses is defective. What is the probability that a box containing five defective fuses will be rejected?

9. Of the nine members of the board of trustees of a college, five agree with the president on a certain issue. The president selects three trustees at random and asks for their opinions. What is the probability that at least two of them will agree with him?

10. An urn contains five red balls and four white balls. A sample of two balls is selected at random from the urn. What is the probability that at least one of the balls is red?

Exercises 11–14 refer to a classroom of children (12 boys and 10 girls) in which seven students are chosen to go to the blackboard.

11. What is the probability that at least two girls are chosen?

12. What is the probability that no boys are chosen?

13. What is the probability that more boys than girls are chosen?

14. What is the probability that the first three children chosen are boys?

15. Without consultation, each of four organizations announces a one-day convention to be held during June. Find the probability that at least two organizations specify the same day for their convention.

16. Five letters are selected from the alphabet, one at a time with replacement, to form a five-letter "word." What is the probability that the "word" has five different letters?

17. Michael is one of seven contestants entered in two races to be run on a seven-lane track. If in each race the runners are assigned to the lanes at random, what is the probability that Michael will be assigned to the inside lane at least once?

18. An airport limousine has four passengers and stops at six different hotels. What is the probability that two or more people will be staying at the same hotel? (Assume that each person is just as likely to stay in one hotel as another.)

19. In a certain agricultural region the probability of a drought during the growing season is .2, the probability of a severe cold spell is .15, and the probability of both is .1. Find the probability of

   (a) Either a drought or a severe cold spell

   (b) Neither a drought nor a severe cold spell

   (c) Not having a drought

20. A coin is to be tossed seven times. What is the probability of obtaining four heads and three tails?

21. Let E and F be events such that

$$\Pr(E) = .3 \quad \Pr(F') = .6 \quad \text{and} \quad \Pr(E \cup F) = .7.$$

What is $\Pr(E \cap F)$?

22. In a certain manufacturing process the probability of a type I defect is .12, the probability of a type II defect is .22, and the probability of having both types of defects is .02. Find the probability of having neither type of defect.

23. A man has six different pairs of socks, from which he selects two socks at random. What is the probability that the selected socks will match?

24. Of the 15 members on a Senate committee, 10 plan to vote "yes" and 5 plan to vote "no" on an important issue. A reporter attempts to predict the outcome of the vote by questioning six of the senators. Find the probability that this sample is precisely representative of the final vote. That is, find the probability that four of the six senators questioned plan to vote "yes."

25. A man, a woman, and their three children randomly stand in a row for a family picture. What is the probability that the parents will be standing next to each other?

26. In poker the probabilities of being dealt a flush, a straight, and a straight flush are .0019654, .0039246, and .0000154, respectively. What is the probability of being dealt a straight or a flush?

27. Figure 1 shows a partial map of the streets in a certain city. A tourist starts at point A and selects at random a path to point B. (We shall assume that he walks only south and east.)

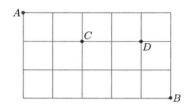

Figure 1.

Find the probability that

(a) He passes through point C.

(b) He passes through point D.

(c) He passes through point C and point D.

(d) He passes through point C or point D.

28. A couple decides to have four children. What is the probability that they will have more girls than boys?

29. A law firm has six senior and four junior partners. A committee of three partners is selected at random to represent the firm at a conference. What is the probability that at least one of the junior partners is on the committee?

30. A coin is to be tossed six times. What is the probability of obtaining exactly three heads?

31. A bag contains nine tomatoes, of which one is rotten. A sample of three tomatoes is selected at random. What is the probability that the sample contains the rotten tomato?

32. A vacationer has brought along four novels and four nonfiction books. One day the person selects two at random to take to the beach. What is the probability that both are novels?

Exercises 33 and 34[1] refer to the Illinois Lottery Lotto game. In this game, the player chooses six different integers from 1 to 40. If the six match (in any order) the six different integers drawn by the lottery, the player wins the grand prize jackpot, which starts at $1 million and grows weekly until won. Multiple winners split the pot equally. For each $1 bet, the player must pick two (presumably different) sets of six integers.

33. What is the probability of winning the Illinois Lottery Lotto with a $1 bet?

34. In the game week ending June 18, 1983, 2 million people bought $1 tickets and 78 people matched all six winning integers and split the jackpot. If all numbers were selected randomly, the likelihood of having so many joint winners would be about 10^{-115}. Can you think of any reason that such an unlikely event occurred? (*Note:* The winning numbers were 7, 13, 14, 21, 28, and 35.) What would be the best strategy in selecting the numbers to ensure that in the event you won, you would probably not have to share the jackpot with too many people?

35. The U.S. Senate consists of two senators from each of the 50 states. Five senators are to be selected at random to form a committee. What is the probability that no two members of the committee are from the same state?

36. A politician knows that a committee vote is stacked against her, 6 to 3. However, she has the option of letting a randomly selected subcommittee decide the issue. Show that the smaller the subcommittee is, the better her chances of winning the vote. (Consider only subcommittees with an odd number of members, so that tie votes are precluded.)

37. What is the probability that in a group of 25 people at least one person has a birthday on June 13? Why is your answer different from the probability displayed in Table 1 for $r = 25$?

38. What is the probability that a random arrangement of the letters in the word GEESE has all the E's adjacent to one another?

39. Fred is having a dinner party and is limited to 10 guests. He has 16 men friends and 12 women friends, including Laura and Mary.

(a) If Fred chooses his guests at random, what is the probability that Mary and Laura are invited?

(b) If Fred decides to invite 5 men and 5 women, what is the probability that Mary and Laura are invited?

40. In the American League, the East, Central, and West divisions consist of 6, 5, and 4 baseball teams, respectively. A sportswriter predicts the winner of each of the three divisions by choosing a team completely at random in each division. What is the probability that the sportswriter will predict at least one winner correctly?

41. Suppose that the sportswriter in Exercise 40 eliminates from each division one team that clearly has no chance of winning and predicts a winner at random from the remaining teams. Assuming the eliminated teams don't end up surprising anyone, what is the writer's chance of predicting at least one winner?

---

[1] The data for these exercises were taken from Allan J. Gottlieb's "Puzzle Corner" in *Technology Review*, February/March 1985.

42. Suppose that the sportswriter in Exercise 40 simply puts the 15 team names in a hat and draws 3 completely at random. Does this increase or decrease the writer's chance of picking at least one winner?

Exercises 43–47 require the use of a calculator or computer.

43. Two balls are to be selected at random without replacement from an urn that contains 40 balls, some red and some white. If the probability of selecting two red balls is .1, how many red balls are in the urn?

44. Find the probability that at least two people in a group of size $n = 5$ select the same card when drawing from a 52-card deck with replacement. Determine for what size group the probability of such a match first exceeds .5.

45. A die is tossed 24 times.
    (a) How many 3's would you expect?
    (b) Calculate the probability of getting exactly four 3's.

46. There were 16 presidents of the Continental Congresses from 1774 to 1788. Each of the five students in a seminar in American history chooses one of these on which to do a report. If all presidents are equally likely to be chosen, calculate the probability that at least two students choose the same president.

47. A political science class has 20 students, each of whom chooses a topic from a list for a term paper. How big a pool of topics is necessary for the probability of at least one duplicate to drop below 50%?

Solutions to Practice Problems 6.4

1. Each possible outcome is a string of four letters composed of B's and G's. By the generalized multiplication principle, there are 2^4 or 16 possible outcomes. Let E be the event "children of both sexes." Then $E' = \{BBBB, GGGG\}$, and

$$\Pr(E') = \frac{[\text{number of outcomes in } E']}{[\text{total number of outcomes}]} = \frac{2}{16} = \frac{1}{8}.$$

Therefore,

$$\Pr(E) = 1 - \Pr(E') = 1 - \frac{1}{8} = \frac{7}{8}.$$

So the probability is 87.5% that they will have children of both sexes.

2. (a) Each sequence of three numbers is just as likely to occur as any other. Therefore,

$$\Pr(\text{numbers different}) = \frac{[\text{number of outcomes with numbers different}]}{[\text{number of possible outcomes}]}$$
$$= \frac{38 \cdot 37 \cdot 36}{38^3} \approx .92.$$

   (b) 8

6.5 Conditional Probability and Independence

The probability of an event depends, often in a critical way, on the sample space in question. In this section we explore this dependence in some detail by introducing what are called *conditional probabilities*.

To illustrate the dependence of probabilities on the sample space, consider the following example.

▶ Example 1   Suppose that a certain mathematics class contains 26 students. Of these, 14 are economics majors, 15 are first-year students, and 7 are neither. Suppose that a person is selected at random from the class.

(a) What is the probability that the person is both an economics major and a first-year student?

(b) Suppose we are given the additional information that the person selected is a first-year student. What is the probability that he or she is also an economics major?

Solution   Let E denote the set of economics majors and F the set of first-year students. A complete Venn diagram of the class can be obtained with the techniques of Section 5.3. See Fig. 1.

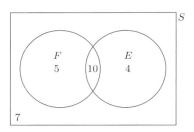

Figure 1.

(a) In selecting a student from the class, the sample space consists of all 26 students. Since the choice is random, all students are equally likely to be selected. The event "economics major and first-year student" corresponds to the set $E \cap F$ of the Venn diagram. Therefore,

$$\Pr(E \cap F) = \frac{[\text{number of outcomes in } E \cap F]}{[\text{number of possible outcomes}]} = \frac{10}{26} = \frac{5}{13}.$$

So the probability of selecting a first-year economics major is $\frac{5}{13}$.

(b) If we know that the student selected is a first-year student, then the possible outcomes of the experiment are restricted. They must belong to F. In other words, given the additional information, we must alter the sample space from "all students" to "first-year students." Since each of the 15 first-year students is equally likely to be selected, and since 10 of the 15 first-year students are economics majors, the probability of choosing an economics major under these circumstances is equal to $\frac{10}{15} = \frac{2}{3}$.   ◆

Let us consider Example 1 more carefully. In part (a) the sample space is the set of all students in the mathematics class, E is the event "student is an economics major" and F is the event "student is a first-year student." On the other hand, part (b) poses a condition, "student is a first-year student." The condition is satisfied by every element of F. We are being asked to find the conditional probability of E given F, written $\Pr(E|F)$. To do this we shall restrict our attention to the new (restricted) sample space, now just the elements of F. Thus, we consider only first-year students and ask, of these, what is the probability of choosing an economics major. We assign a value to $\Pr(E|F)$ via the following formula:

Conditional Probability

$$\Pr(E|F) = \frac{\Pr(E \cap F)}{\Pr(F)}, \qquad (1)$$

provided that $\Pr(F) \neq 0$.

We will provide an intuitive justification of this formula shortly. However, we first give two applications.

▶ Example 2   Consider all families with two children (not twins). Assume that all elements of the sample space {BB, BG, GB, GG} are equally likely. (Here, for instance, BG denotes the birth sequence "boy girl.") Let E be the event {BB} and F the event "at least one boy." Calculate $\Pr(E|F)$.

Solution   Each of the four birth sequences is equally likely and has probability $\frac{1}{4}$. In particular, since $F = \{\text{BB, BG, GB}\}$, $E \cap F = \{\text{BB}\}$, we have $\Pr(E \cap F) = \frac{1}{4}$. Also, $\Pr(F) = \frac{1}{4} + \frac{1}{4} + \frac{1}{4} = \frac{3}{4}$. The conditional probability $\Pr(E|F)$ equals the probability that a two-child family has two boys given that it has at least one. This conditional probability has the value

$$\Pr(E|F) = \frac{\Pr(E \cap F)}{\Pr(F)} = \frac{\frac{1}{4}}{\frac{3}{4}} = \frac{1}{3}.$$

[This result is contrary to many people's intuition. They reason that among families with at least one boy, the other child is just as likely to be a boy as a girl. Therefore, they conclude incorrectly that the probability $\Pr(E|F)$ is $\frac{1}{2}$.] ◆

▶ **Example 3** Twenty percent of the employees of Acme Steel Company are college graduates. Of all its employees, 25% earn more than $50,000 per year, and 15% are college graduates earning more than $50,000. What is the probability that an employee selected at random earns more than $50,000 per year, given that he or she is a college graduate?

Solution Let H and C be the events

$$H = \text{"earns more than \$50,000 per year"}$$
$$C = \text{"college graduate."}$$

We are asked to calculate $\Pr(H|C)$. The given data are

$$\Pr(H) = .25 \qquad \Pr(C) = .20 \qquad \Pr(H \cap C) = .15.$$

By formula (1), we have

$$\Pr(H|C) = \frac{\Pr(H \cap C)}{\Pr(C)} = \frac{.15}{.20} = \frac{3}{4}.$$

Thus $\frac{3}{4}$ of all college graduates at Acme Steel earn more than $50,000 per year. ◆

Suppose that an experiment has N equally likely outcomes. Then we may apply the following formula to calculate $\Pr(E|F)$.

Conditional Probability in Case of Equally Likely Outcomes

$$\Pr(E|F) = \frac{[\text{number of outcomes in } E \cap F]}{[\text{number of outcomes in } F]}, \tag{2}$$

provided that $[\text{number of outcomes in } F] \neq 0$.

For instance, in Example 2, the different birth sequences were all equally likely. Moreover, the number of outcomes in $E \cap F$ (two boys) is 1, whereas the number of outcomes in F (at least one boy) is 3. Then formula (2) gives that $\Pr(E|F) = \frac{1}{3}$, in agreement with the calculation of Example 2.

Let us now justify formulas (1) and (2).

Justification of Formula (1) Formula (1) is a definition of conditional probability and as such does not really need any justification. (We can make whatever definitions we choose!) However, let us proceed intuitively and show that the definition is reasonable, in the sense that formula (1) gives the expected long-run proportion of occurrences of E given that F occurs. Assume that our experiment is performed repeatedly, say for 10,000 trials. We would expect F to occur in approximately $10,000 \Pr(F)$ trials. Among these, the trials for which E also occurs are exactly those for which both E and F occur. In other words, the trials for which E also occurs are exactly those for which the event $E \cap F$ occurs; and this event has probability $\Pr(E \cap F)$. Therefore, out of the original 10,000 trials, there should be approximately $10,000 \Pr(E \cap F)$ in which E and F both occur.

Thus, considering only those trials in which F occurs, the proportion in which E also occurs is

$$\frac{10{,}000\,\Pr(E \cap F)}{10{,}000\,\Pr(F)} = \frac{\Pr(E \cap F)}{\Pr(F)}.$$

Thus, at least intuitively, it seems reasonable to define $\Pr(E|F)$ by formula (1).   ◆

Justification of Formula (2)   Suppose that the number of outcomes of the experiment is N. Then

$$\Pr(F) = \frac{[\text{number of outcomes in } F]}{N}$$

$$\Pr(E \cap F) = \frac{[\text{number of outcomes in } E \cap F]}{N}.$$

Therefore, using formula (1), we have

$$\Pr(E|F) = \frac{\Pr(E \cap F)}{\Pr(F)}$$

$$= \frac{\dfrac{[\text{number of outcomes in } E \cap F]}{N}}{\dfrac{[\text{number of outcomes in } F]}{N}}$$

$$= \frac{[\text{number of outcomes in } E \cap F]}{[\text{number of outcomes in } F]}.$$ ◆

From formula (1), multiplying both sides of the equation by $\Pr(F)$, we can deduce the following useful fact.

Product Rule   If $\Pr(F) \neq 0$,

$$\Pr(E \cap F) = \Pr(F) \cdot \Pr(E|F). \tag{3}$$

The next example illustrates the use of this rule.

▶ **Example 4**   Assume that a certain school contains an equal number of female and male students and that 5% of the male population is color-blind. Find the probability that a randomly selected student is a color-blind male.

Solution   Let $M =$ "male" and $B =$ "color-blind." We wish to calculate $\Pr(B \cap M)$. From the given data,

$$\Pr(M) = .5 \quad \text{and} \quad \Pr(B|M) = .05.$$

Therefore, by the product rule,

$$\Pr(B \cap M) = \Pr(M) \cdot \Pr(B|M) = (.5)(.05) = .025.$$ ◆

Often an event G can be described as a sequence of two other events E and F. That is, G occurs if F occurs and then E occurs. The product rule allows us to compute the probability of G as the probability of F times the conditional probability $\Pr(E|F)$. The next example illustrates this point.

▶ **Example 5**   A sequence of two playing cards is drawn at random (without replacement) from a standard deck of 52 cards. What is the probability that the first card is red and the second is black?

Solution   The event in question is a sequence of two events, namely,

$$F = \text{“the first card is red”}$$
$$E = \text{“the second card is black.”}$$

Since half the deck consists of red cards, $\Pr(F) = \frac{1}{2}$. If we are given that F occurs, then there are only 51 cards left in the deck, of which 26 are black, so

$$\Pr(E|F) = \tfrac{26}{51}.$$

By the product rule

$$\Pr(E \cap F) = \Pr(F) \cdot \Pr(E|F) = \tfrac{1}{2} \cdot \tfrac{26}{51} = \tfrac{13}{51}. \qquad \blacklozenge$$

The product rule may be generalized to sequences of three events E_1, E_2, and E_3:

$$\Pr(E_1 \cap E_2 \cap E_3) = \Pr(E_1) \cdot \Pr(E_2|E_1) \cdot \Pr(E_3|E_1 \cap E_2).$$

Similar formulas hold for sequences of four or more events.

One of the most important applications of conditional probability is in the discussion of independent events. Intuitively, two events are independent of each other if the occurrence of one has no effect on the likelihood that the other will occur. For example, suppose that we toss a die twice. Let the events E and F be

$$F = \text{“first throw is a 6”}$$
$$E = \text{“second throw is a 3.”}$$

Then intuitively these events are independent of one another. Throwing a 6 on the first throw has no effect whatsoever on the outcome of the second throw. On the other hand, suppose that we draw a sequence of two cards at random (without replacement) from a deck. Then the events

$$F = \text{“first card is red”}$$
$$E = \text{“second card is black”}$$

are not independent of one another, at least intuitively. Indeed, whether or not we draw a red on the first card affects the likelihood of drawing a black on the second.

The notion of independence of events is easily formulated. If E and F are events in a sample space and $\Pr(F) \neq 0$, then the product rule states that $\Pr(E \cap F) = \Pr(E|F) \cdot \Pr(F)$. However, if the occurrence of event F does not affect the likelihood of the occurrence of event E, we would expect that $\Pr(E|F) = \Pr(E)$. Substitution then shows that $\Pr(E \cap F) = \Pr(E) \cdot \Pr(F)$.

Let E and F be events. We say that E and F are *independent* provided that

$$\Pr(E \cap F) = \Pr(E) \cdot \Pr(F).$$

If $\Pr(E) \neq 0$ and $\Pr(F) \neq 0$, then our definition is equivalent to the intuitive statement of independence stated in terms of conditional probability. The two may be used interchangeably.

> Let E and F be events with nonzero probability. E and F are *independent* provided that
>
> $$\Pr(E|F) = \Pr(E) \quad \text{and} \quad \Pr(F|E) = \Pr(F).$$

▶ **Example 6**   An experiment consists of observing the outcome of two consecutive throws of a die. Let E and F be the events

$$E = \text{``the first throw is a 3''}$$
$$F = \text{``the second throw is a 6.''}$$

Show that these events are independent.

Solution   Clearly, $\Pr(E) = \Pr(F) = \frac{1}{6}$. To compute $\Pr(E|F)$, assume that F occurs. Then there are six possible outcomes:

$$F = \{(1,6),(2,6),(3,6),(4,6),(5,6),(6,6)\},$$

and all outcomes are equally likely. Moreover,

$$E \cap F = \{(3,6)\},$$

so that

$$\Pr(E|F) = \frac{[\text{number of outcomes in } E \cap F]}{[\text{number of outcomes in } F]} = \frac{1}{6} = \Pr(E).$$

similarly, $\Pr(F|E) = \Pr(F)$. So E and F are independent events, in agreement with our intuition.   ◆

▶ **Example 7**   Suppose that an experiment consists of observing the results of drawing two consecutive cards from a 52-card deck. Let E and F be the events

$$E = \text{``second card is black''}$$
$$F = \text{``first card is red.''}$$

Are these events independent?

Solution   There are the same number of outcomes with the second card red as with the second card black, so $\Pr(E) = \frac{1}{2}$. To compute $\Pr(E|F)$, note that if F occurs, then there are 51 equally likely choices for the second card, of which 26 are black, so that $\Pr(E|F) = \frac{26}{51}$. Note that $\Pr(E|F) \neq \Pr(E)$, so E and F are not independent, in agreement with our intuition.   ◆

▶ **Example 8**   Suppose that we toss a coin three times and record the sequence of heads and tails. Let E be the event "at most one head occurs" and F the event "both heads and tails occur." Are E and F independent?

Solution   Using the abbreviations H for "heads" and T for "tails," we have

$$E = \{\text{TTT, HTT, THT, TTH}\}$$
$$F = \{\text{HTT, HTH, HHT, THH, THT, TTH}\}$$
$$E \cap F = \{\text{HTT, THT, TTH}\}.$$

The sample space contains eight equally likely outcomes, so that

$$\Pr(E) = \tfrac{1}{2} \qquad \Pr(F) = \tfrac{3}{4} \qquad \Pr(E \cap F) = \tfrac{3}{8}.$$

Moreover,

$$\Pr(E) \cdot \Pr(F) = \tfrac{1}{2} \cdot \tfrac{3}{4} = \tfrac{3}{8},$$

which equals $\Pr(E \cap F)$. So E and F are independent. ◆

▶ **Example 9** Suppose that a family has four children. Let E be the event "at most one boy" and F the event "at least one child of each sex." Are E and F independent?

Solution Let B stand for "boy" and G for "girl." Then

$$E = \{\text{GGGG, GGGB, GGBG, GBGG, BGGG}\}$$
$$F = \{\text{GGGB, GGBG, GBGG, BGGG, BBBG, BBGB, BGBB,}$$
$$\text{GBBB, BBGG, BGBG, BGGB, GBBG, GBGB, GGBB}\},$$

and the sample space consists of 16 equally likely outcomes. Furthermore,

$$E \cap F = \{\text{GGGB, GGBG, GBGG, BGGG}\}.$$

Therefore,

$$\Pr(E) = \tfrac{5}{16} \qquad \Pr(F) = \tfrac{7}{8} \qquad \Pr(E \cap F) = \tfrac{1}{4}.$$

In this example

$$\Pr(E) \cdot \Pr(F) = \tfrac{5}{16} \cdot \tfrac{7}{8} \neq \Pr(E \cap F).$$

So E and F are *not* independent events. ◆

Examples 8 and 9 are similar, yet the events they describe are independent in one case and not the other. Although intuition is frequently a big help, in complex problems we shall need to use the definition of independence to verify that our intuition is correct.

▶ **Example 10** A new hand calculator is designed to be ultrareliable by having two independent calculating units. The probability that a given calculating unit fails within the first 1000 hours of operation is .001. What is the probability that at least one calculating unit will operate without failure for the first 1000 hours of operation?

Solution Let

$$E = \text{"calculating unit 1 fails in first 1000 hours"}$$
$$F = \text{"calculating unit 2 fails in first 1000 hours."}$$

Then E and F are independent events, since the calculating units are independent of one another. Therefore,

$$\Pr(E \cap F) = \Pr(E) \cdot \Pr(F) = (.001)^2 = .000001$$
$$\Pr((E \cap F)') = 1 - .000001 = .999999.$$

Since $(E \cap F)' = $ "not both calculating units fail in first 1000 hours," the desired probability is .999999. ◆

The concept of independent events can be extended to more than two events:

A set of events is said to be *independent* if, for each collection of events chosen from them, say $E_1, E_2, \ldots, E_n$, we have

$$\Pr(E_1 \cap E_2 \cap \cdots \cap E_n) = \Pr(E_1) \cdot \Pr(E_2) \cdot \cdots \cdot \Pr(E_n).$$

▶ Example 11   Three events A, B, and C are independent; $\Pr(A) = .5$, $\Pr(B) = .3$, and $\Pr(C) = .2$.

(a) Calculate $\Pr(A \cap B \cap C)$.   (b) Calculate $\Pr(A \cap C)$.

Solution   (a) $\Pr(A \cap B \cap C) = \Pr(A) \cdot \Pr(B) \cdot \Pr(C) = (.5)(.3)(.2) = .03$.

(b) $\Pr(A \cap C) = \Pr(A) \cdot \Pr(C) = (.5)(.2) = .1$.   ◆

We shall leave as an exercise the intuitively reasonable result that if E and F are independent events, so are E and F', E' and F, and E' and F'. This result also generalizes to any collection of independent events.

▶ Example 12   A company manufactures stereo components. Experience shows that defects in manufacture are independent of one another. Quality control studies reveal that

2% of CD players are defective,

3% of amplifiers are defective,

7% of speakers are defective.

A system consists of a CD player, an amplifier, and two speakers. What is the probability that the system is not defective?

Solution   Let C, A, S_1, and S_2 be events corresponding to defective CD player, amplifiers, speaker 1, and speaker 2, respectively. Then

$$\Pr(C) = .02 \qquad \Pr(A) = .03 \qquad \Pr(S_1) = \Pr(S_2) = .07.$$

We wish to calculate $\Pr(C' \cap A' \cap S_1' \cap S_2')$. By the complement rule we have

$$\Pr(C') = .98 \qquad \Pr(A') = .97 \qquad \Pr(S_1') = \Pr(S_2') = .93.$$

Since we have assumed that C, A, S_1, and S_2 are independent, so are C', A', S_1', and S_2'. Therefore,

$$\Pr(C' \cap A' \cap S_1' \cap S_2') = \Pr(C') \cdot \Pr(A') \cdot \Pr(S_1') \cdot \Pr(S_2')$$
$$= (.98)(.97)(.93)^2 \approx .822.$$

Thus there is an 82.2% chance that the system is not defective.   ◆

Practice Problems 6.5

1. Suppose there are three cards: one red on both sides; one white on both sides; and one having a side of each color. A card is selected at random and placed on a table. If the up side is red, what is the probability that the down side is red? (Try guessing at the answer before working it using the formula for conditional probability.)

2. Show that if events E and F are independent of each other, then so are E and F'. [*Hint:* Since $E \cap F$ and $E \cap F'$ are mutually exclusive, we have

$$\Pr(E) = \Pr(E \cap F) + \Pr(E \cap F').]$$

▶ Exercises 6.5

In Exercises 1–4, let S be a sample space and E and F events associated with S. Suppose that $\Pr(E) = .5$, $\Pr(F) = .3$, and $\Pr(E \cap F) = .1$.

1. Calculate $\Pr(E|F)$ and $\Pr(F|E)$.

2. Are E and F independent events? Explain.

3. Calculate $\Pr(E|F')$.

4. Calculate $\Pr(E'|F')$.

5. A doctor studies the known cancer patients in a certain town. The probability that a randomly chosen resident has cancer is found to be .001. It is found that 30% of the town works for Ajax Chemical Company. The probability that an employee of Ajax has cancer is equal to .003. Are the events "has cancer" and "works for Ajax" independent of one another?

6. The proportion of individuals in a certain city earning more than \$25,000 per year is .25. The proportion of individuals earning more than \$25,000 and having a college degree is .10. Suppose that a person is randomly chosen and he turns out to be earning more than \$25,000. What is the probability that he is a college graduate?

7. A medical screening program administers three independent fitness tests. Of the persons taking the tests, 80% pass test I, 75% pass test II, and 60% pass test III. A participant is chosen at random.
   (a) What is the probability that she will pass all three tests?
   (b) What is the probability that she will pass at least two of the three tests?

8. A stereo system contains 50 transistors. The probability that a given transistor will fail in 100,000 hours of use is .0005. Assume that the failures of the various transistors are independent of one another. What is the probability that no transistor will fail during the first 100,000 hours of use?

9. A TV set contains five circuit boards of type A, five of type B, and three of type C. The probability of failing in its first 5000 hours of use is .01 for a type A circuit board, .02 for a type B circuit board, and .025 for a type C circuit board. Assuming that the failures of the various circuit boards are independent of one another, compute the probability that no circuit board fails in the first 5000 hours of use.

10. A certain brand of a long-life bulb has probability .01 of burning out in less than 1000 hours. Suppose that we wish to light a corridor with a number of independent bulbs in such a way that at least one of the bulbs remains lit for 1000 consecutive hours. What is the minimum number of bulbs needed to ensure that the probability of success is at least .99999?

11. Let E and F be events with $\Pr(E) = \frac{1}{2}$, $\Pr(F) = \frac{1}{3}$, and $\Pr(E \cap F) = \frac{1}{4}$. Compute $\Pr(E|F)$ and $\Pr(F|E)$.

12. Let E and F be events with $\Pr(E) = .3$, $\Pr(F) = .6$, and $\Pr(E \cup F) = .7$. Find
   (a) $\Pr(E \cap F)$ (b) $\Pr(E|F)$ (c) $\Pr(F|E)$
   (d) $\Pr(E' \cap F)$ (e) $\Pr(E'|F)$

13. Of the registered voters in a certain town, 50% are Democrats, 40% favor a school loan, and 30% are Democrats who favor a school loan. Suppose that a registered voter is selected at random from the town.
   (a) What is the probability that the person is not a Democrat and opposes the school loan?
   (b) What is the conditional probability that the person favors the school loan given that he or she is a Democrat?
   (c) What is the conditional probability that the person is a Democrat given that he or she favors the school loan?

14. Of the students at a certain college, 50% regularly attend the football games, 30% are first-year students, and 40% are upper-class students who do not regularly attend football games. Suppose that a student is selected at random.
   (a) What is the probability that the person both is a first-year student and regularly attends football games?
   (b) What is the conditional probability that the person regularly attends football games given that he is a first-year student?
   (c) What is the conditional probability that the person is a first-year student given that he regularly attends football games?

15. A coin is tossed three times. What is the conditional probability that the outcome is HHH given that at least two heads occur?

16. Two balls are selected at random from an urn containing two white balls and three red balls. What is the conditional probability that both balls are white given that at least one of them is white?

17. The probabilities that a person A and a person B will live an additional 15 years are .8 and .7, respectively. Assuming that their lifespans are independent, what is the probability that A or B will live an additional 15 years?

18. A sample of two balls is drawn from an urn containing two white balls and three red balls. Are the events "the sample contains at least one white ball" and "the sample contains balls of both colors" independent?

19. Jane has two friends who do not know each other. Each of them has heard the same rumor. The probability that each will tell Jane is 60%. What is the probability that Jane does not hear the rumor from either of these friends?

20. The probability that a fisherman catches a tuna in any one excursion is .15. What is the probability that he catches a tuna on each of three excursions? on at least one of three excursions?

21. The probability that a prize appears in a box of breakfast cereal is .005. What is the probability that two boxes of cereal contain at least one prize?

22. A "true–false" exam has 10 questions. Assuming that the questions are independent and that a student is guessing, find the probability that she gets 100%.

23. Suppose that in Sleepy Valley only 30% of those over 50 years old own CD players. Find the probability that among four randomly chosen people in that age group none owns a CD player.

24. Assume that A and B are events in a sample space and that $\Pr(A) = .40$ and $\Pr(B|A) = .25$. Find $\Pr(A \cap B)$. With the further assumption that $\Pr(B) = .30$, find $\Pr(A \cup B)$, $\Pr(A' \cap B)$, and $\Pr(A|B)$.

25. Show that if events E and F are independent of each other, then so are E' and F'.

26. Show that if E and F are independent events, then

$$\Pr(E \cup F) = 1 - \Pr(E') \cdot \Pr(F').$$

27. A basketball player with a free-throw shooting average of .6 is on the line for a one-and-one free throw. (That is, a second throw is allowed only if the first is successful.) What is the probability that the player will score 0 points? 1 point? 2 points? Assume that the two throws are independent.

28. Let $\Pr(F) > 0$.
    (a) Show that $\Pr(E'|F) = 1 - \Pr(E|F)$.

    (b) Find an example for which

    $$\Pr(E|F') \neq 1 - \Pr(E|F).$$

29. Use the inclusion–exclusion principle for (nonconditional) probabilities to show that if E, F, and G are events in S, then

$$\Pr(E \cup F|G) = \Pr(E|G) + \Pr(F|G) - \Pr(E \cap F|G).$$

30. The percentage of the U.S. male population that has ever been married is given in Table 1. Explain how the table relates to the idea of conditional probability by giving a precise definition of "% ever married among 25- to 29-year-olds."

Table 1

Ages	Percent ever married
15–19	1.5
20–24	20.7
25–29	54.8
30–34	73.0
35–44	87.2
45–54	93.7

31. Two communities are being compared as to their annual death rates. Community A is in the Sunbelt and community B is in Alaska.

    Community A: Population: 120,000
    Number of deaths: 12,000
    Community B: Population: 90,000
    Number of deaths: 4500

    (a) Find the death rate in community A. Note that this is a conditional probability, namely

    $$\Pr(\text{death}|A).$$

    (b) Express the probability you found in part (a) as a death rate per 1000 in the population of community A.

    (c) Find $\Pr(\text{death}|B)$.

32. A hospital uses two tests to classify blood. Every blood sample is subjected to both tests. The first test correctly identifies blood type with probability .7, and the second test correctly identifies blood type with probability .8. The probability that at least one of the tests correctly identifies the blood type is .9.

    (a) Find the probability that both tests correctly identify the blood type.

    (b) Determine the probability that the second test is correct given that the first test is correct.

    (c) Determine the probability that the first test is correct given that the second test is correct.

    (d) Are the events "test I correctly identifies the blood type" and "test II correctly identifies the blood type" independent?

33. Sixty-five percent of the patients in the emergency room of a hospital are seen by a physician immediately. The remainder are kept waiting in the waiting room. Eighty percent of those kept waiting are seen within 2 hours. Seventy-five percent of those seen immediately are admitted to the hospital. Forty percent of those seen within 2 hours (but not immediately) are admitted to the hospital, and 10% of those who wait more than 2 hours are admitted to the hospital. Let A be the event "the patient is seen immediately." Let

B be the event "the patient is not seen immediately but is seen within 2 hours." Let C be the event "the patient waits more than 2 hours." Let H be the event "the patient is admitted to the hospital."

(a) Find $\Pr(B)$. (b) Find $\Pr(C)$. (c) Find $\Pr(H)$.

34. Out of 250 students interviewed at a community college, 90 were taking mathematics but not computer science, 160 were taking mathematics, and 50 were taking neither mathematics nor computer science. Find the probability that a student chosen at random was

   (a) Taking just computer science

   (b) Taking mathematics or computer science, but not both

   (c) Taking computer science

   (d) Not taking mathematics

   (e) Taking mathematics, given that the student was taking computer science

   (f) Taking computer science, given that the student was taking mathematics

   (g) Taking mathematics, given that the student was taking computer science or mathematics

   (h) Taking computer science, given that the student was not taking mathematics

   (i) Not taking mathematics, given that the student was not taking computer science

35. Out of 250 third-grade boys, 120 played baseball, 140 played soccer, and 50 played both. Find the probability that a boy chosen at random

   (a) Did not play either sport

   (b) Played exactly one sport

   (c) Played soccer but not baseball

   (d) Played soccer, given that he played baseball

   (e) Played baseball, given that he did not play soccer

   (f) Did not play soccer, given that he did not play baseball

36. Table 2 provides some information about students at a certain college. Find the probability that a student selected at random is

   (a) A senior

   (b) Working full time

   (c) Working part time, given that the student is a first-year student

   (d) A first-year student, given that the student does not work

   (e) A junior or senior, given that the student does not work

   (f) Working part time or full time, given that the student is a sophomore or a junior

Table 2

	Works full time	Works part time	Not working
First-year	130	460	210
Sophomore	100	500	150
Junior	80	420	100
Senior	200	300	50

37. Table 3 describes the voters in a certain district. Find the probability that a voter chosen at random is a

   (a) Democrat

   (b) Male

   (c) Independent, given that the voter is female

   (d) Male, given that the voter is a Republican

   (e) Female, given that the voter is not an Independent

   (f) Democrat, given that the voter is not a Republican

Table 3

	Democrat	Republican	Independent
Male	400	700	300
Female	600	300	200

38. Table 4 describes the incidence of a disease called the X virus.

Table 4

	White	African American	Other
Have X virus	1,000	1,200	50
Disease free	100,000	35,000	10,000

   (a) Find the probability that someone in this population is disease free.

   (b) Find the probability that a person has the X virus.

   (c) If a person is an African American, what is the probability that he or she has the X virus?

   (d) Given a person who is not African American, what is the probability that he or she has the X virus?

   (e) Would you say that race and incidence of the disease are independent? Explain.

39. Table 5 shows the numbers of officers and enlisted persons on active military duty on September 30, 1998. Let E be the event that a person selected at random from the active-duty military personnel is enlisted and

let N be the event that a person selected at random from the active-duty military personnel is in the Navy.

Table 5

	Army	Navy	Marine Corps	Air Force
Officer	78,498	54,999	17,892	71,892
Enlisted	401,188	323,120	155,250	291,590

(a) Find each of the following probabilities: $\Pr(E)$, $\Pr(N)$, $\Pr(E \cap N)$, $\Pr(E|N)$, $\Pr(N|E)$.

(b) Are the events E and N independent?

40. One interpretation of a baseball player's batting average is as the probability of getting a hit each time the player goes to bat. For instance, a player with a .300 average has probability .3 of getting a hit.

   (a) If a player with .3 probability of getting a hit bats four times in a game and each at-bat is an independent event, what is the probability of the player getting at least one hit in the game?

   (b) What is the probability of the player in part (a) starting off the season with at least one hit in each of the first 10 games?

   (c) If there are 20 players with a .300 average, what is the probability that at least one of them will start the season with a 10-game hitting streak?

41. Juan randomly chooses a positive integer that is divisible by 7 and is less than 70. Chita randomly selects a positive integer less than 70 that is divisible by 3. What is the probability that they choose the same number?

42. Juan randomly chooses a positive integer that is divisible by 7 and is less than 70. Chita randomly selects a positive integer less than 70 that is divisible by 11. What is the probability that they choose the same number?

43. A bag contains four blue marbles, three white marbles, and six red marbles. Three marbles are selected from the bag. What is the probability they are all red? What is the probability that they are all the same color?

44. A spinner on a wheel with the numbers 2, 5, 6, and 9 in segments of equal area is spun at random. Another spinner on a wheel with equal segments marked with numbers 3, 7, and 8 is also spun. What is the probability that the sum of the two numbers chosen by the spinners is odd?

45. Horatio goes to the deli for sandwiches and orders two roast beef sandwiches and two ham sandwiches. They are wrapped and put into a paper bag. What is the probability that two sandwiches chosen at random will both be roast beef? What is the probability that the two sandwiches chosen at random will be alike?

46. Ten slips of paper have numbers 1 through 10. Sue chooses two slips at random. What is the probability that the sum of the numbers chosen is even?

47. A bag contains five red marbles and eight white marbles. If a sample of four marbles contains one white marble, what is the probability that all the marbles in the sample are white?

48. Eight people each have a deck of well-shuffled cards. Each chooses a card at random from his or her own deck. What is the probability that there is at least one match?

Exercises 49–51 require the use of a calculator or computer.

49. Consider the following table, with figures in thousands, pertaining to the 1998 American civilian labor force. Determine if gender and unemployment status are independent by finding the probabilities $\Pr(W)$, $\Pr(U)$, and $\Pr(W \cap U)$.

	Employed (E)	Unemployed (U)	Totals
Men (M)	70,693	3266	73,959
Women (W)	60,771	2944	63,715
Totals	131,464	6210	137,674

Source: U.S. Bureau of Labor Statistics.

50. A diagnostic test is given to a large population to determine its efficacy. Of the 313 people for whom the test is positive, 260 are known to have the condition. The rest are free of the condition. Of the 8249 people for whom the test is negative, 14 are known to have the condition and 8235 do not.

   (a) Determine the probability of a false positive.

   (b) Determine the probability that a person with a positive test result actually has the disease.

   (c) What is the prevalence of the disease in this group?

51. (a) Find the probability of drawing four aces from a deck of 52 cards in four repeated draws without replacement.

   (b) Calculate the probability of drawing two red queens followed by two red kings in four draws from the deck without replacement.

   (c) Which of the two events in (a) or (b) is more likely?

1. $\frac{2}{3}$. Let F be the event that the up side is red and E the event that the down side is red. $\Pr(F) = \frac{1}{2}$ since half the faces are red. $F \cap E$ is the event that both sides of the card are red—that is, that the card that is red on both sides was selected, an event with probability $\frac{1}{3}$. By (2),

$$\Pr(E|F) = \frac{\Pr(E \cap F)}{\Pr(F)} = \frac{\frac{1}{3}}{\frac{1}{2}} = \frac{2}{3}.$$

(This result may seem more intuitively evident when you realize that two-thirds of the time the card will have the same color on the bottom as on the top.)

2. By the hint,

$$\begin{aligned}
\Pr(E \cap F') &= \Pr(E) - \Pr(E \cap F) \\
&= \Pr(E) - \Pr(E) \cdot \Pr(F) \qquad \text{(since E and F are independent)} \\
&= \Pr(E)[1 - \Pr(F)] \\
&= \Pr(E) \cdot \Pr(F') \qquad \text{(by the complement rule)}.
\end{aligned}$$

Therefore, E and F' are independent events.

6.6 Tree Diagrams

In solving many probability problems, it is helpful to represent the various events and their associated probabilities by a *tree diagram*. To explain this useful notion, suppose that we wish to compute the probability of an event that results from performing a sequence of experiments. The various outcomes of each experiment are represented as branches emanating from a point. For example, Fig. 1 represents an experiment with three outcomes. Notice that each branch has been labeled with the probability of the associated outcome. For example, the probability of outcome 1 is .5.

We represent experiments performed one after another by stringing together diagrams of the sort shown in Fig. 1, proceeding from left to right. For example, the diagram in Fig. 2 indicates that first we perform experiment A, having three outcomes, labeled 1–3. If the outcome is 1 or 2, we perform experiment B. If the outcome is 3, we perform experiment C. The probabilities on the right are conditional probabilities. For example, the top probability is the probability of outcome a (of B) given outcome 1 (of A). The probability of a sequence of outcomes may then be computed by multiplying the probabilities along a path. For example, to calculate the probability of outcome 2 followed by outcome b,

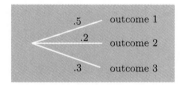

Figure 1.

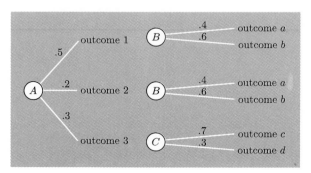

Figure 2.

we must calculate $\Pr(2 \text{ and } b) = \Pr(2) \cdot \Pr(b|2)$. To carry out this calculation, trace out the sequence of outcomes. Multiplying the probabilities along the path gives $(.2)(.6) = .12$—the probability of outcome 2 followed by outcome b.

The next example illustrates the use of tree diagrams in calculating probabilities.

▶ Example 1   (*Voting*) A pollster is hired by a presidential candidate to determine his support among the voters of Pennsylvania's two big cities: Philadelphia and Pittsburgh. The pollster designs the following sampling technique: Select one of the cities at random and then poll a voter selected at random from that city. Suppose that in Philadelphia two-fifths of the voters favor the Republican candidate and three-fifths favor the Democratic candidate. Suppose that in Pittsburgh two-thirds of the voters favor the Republican candidate and one-third favor the Democratic candidate.

(a) Draw a tree diagram describing the survey.
(b) Find the probability that the voter polled is from Philadelphia and favors the Republican candidate.
(c) Find the probability that the voter favors the Republican candidate.
(d) Find the probability that the voter is from Philadelphia, given that he or she favors the Republican candidate.

Solution   (a) The survey proceeds in two steps: First, select a city, and second, poll a voter. Figure 3(a) shows the possible outcomes of the first step and the associated probabilities. For each outcome of the first step there are two possibilities for the second step: The person selected could favor the Republican or the Democrat. In Fig. 3(b) we have represented these possibilities by drawing branches emanating from each of the outcomes of the first step. The probabilities on the new branches are actually conditional probabilities. For instance,

$$\tfrac{2}{5} = \Pr(\text{Rep}|\text{Phila}),$$

the probability that the voter favors the Republican candidate, given that the voter is from Philadelphia.

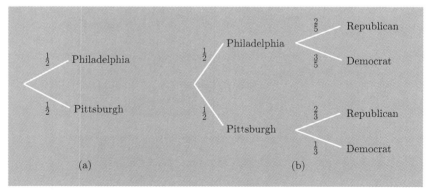

Figure 3.

(b) $\Pr(\text{Phila} \cap \text{Rep}) = \Pr(\text{Phila}) \cdot \Pr(\text{Rep}|\text{Phila}) = \tfrac{1}{2} \cdot \tfrac{2}{5} = \tfrac{1}{5}$.

That is, the probability is $\tfrac{1}{5}$ that the combined outcome corresponds to the path highlighted in Fig. 4(a). We have written the probability $\tfrac{1}{5}$ at the end of the path to which it corresponds.

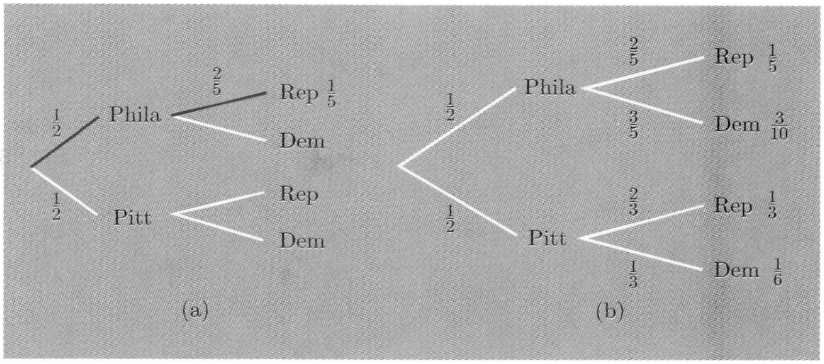

Figure 4.

(c) In Fig. 4(b) we have computed the probabilities for each path of the tree as in part (b). Namely, the probability for a given path is the product of the probabilities for each of its segments. We are asked for $\Pr(\text{Rep})$. There are two paths through the tree leading to Republican, namely

$$\text{Philadelphia} \cap \text{Republican} \quad \text{or} \quad \text{Pittsburgh} \cap \text{Republican}.$$

The probabilities of these two paths are $\frac{1}{5}$ and $\frac{1}{3}$, respectively. So the probability that the Republican is favored equals $\frac{1}{5} + \frac{1}{3} = \frac{8}{15}$.

(d) Here we are asked for $\Pr(\text{Phila}|\text{Rep})$. By the definition of conditional probability,

$$\Pr(\text{Phila}|\text{Rep}) = \frac{\Pr(\text{Phila} \cap \text{Rep})}{\Pr(\text{Rep})} = \frac{\frac{1}{5}}{\frac{8}{15}} = \frac{3}{8}. \qquad \blacklozenge$$

Note that from part (c) we might be led to conclude that the Republican candidate is leading, with $\frac{8}{15}$ of the vote. However, we must always be careful when interpreting surveys. The results depend heavily on the survey design. For example, the survey drew half of its sample from each of the cities. However, Philadelphia is a much larger city and is leaning toward the Democratic candidate—so much so, in fact, that in terms of popular vote the Democratic candidate would win, contrary to our expectations drawn from (c). A pollster must be very careful in designing the procedure for selecting people.

We now finally solve the medical diagnosis problem introduced in Section 6.1.

▶ **Example 2** (*Medical Screening*) Suppose that the reliability of a skin test for active pulmonary tuberculosis (TB) is specified as follows: Of people with TB, 98% have a positive reaction and 2% have a negative reaction; of people free of TB, 99% have a negative reaction and 1% have a positive reaction. From a large population of which 2 per 10,000 persons have TB, a person is selected at random and given a skin test, which turns out to be positive. What is the probability that the person has active pulmonary tuberculosis?

Solution The given data are organized in Fig. 5. The procedure called for is as follows: First select a person at random from the population. There are two possible outcomes: The person has TB,

$$\Pr(\text{TB}) = \frac{2}{10,000} = .0002,$$

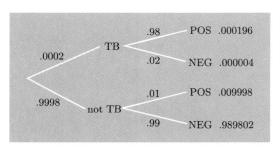

Figure 5.

or the person does not have TB,

$$\text{Pr(not TB)} = 1 - .0002 = .9998.$$

For each of these two possibilities the possible test results and conditional probabilities are given. Multiplying the probabilities along each of the paths through the tree gives the probabilities of the different outcomes. The resulting probabilities are written on the right in Fig. 5. The problem asks for the conditional probability that a person has TB, given that the test is positive. By definition,

$$\text{Pr(TB|POS)} = \frac{\text{Pr(TB} \cap \text{POS)}}{\text{Pr(POS)}} = \frac{.000196}{.000196 + .009998} = \frac{.000196}{.010194} \approx .02.$$

Therefore, the probability is .02 that a person with a positive skin test has TB. In other words, although the skin test is quite reliable, only about 2% of those with a positive test turn out to have active TB. This result must be taken into account when large-scale medical diagnostic tests are planned. Because the group of people without TB is so much larger than the group with TB, the small error in the former group is magnified to the point where it dominates the calculation.

◆

Note The numerical data presented in Example 2 are only approximate. Variations in air quality for different localities within the United States cause variations in the incidence of TB and the reliability of skin tests.

Tree diagrams come in all shapes and sizes. Three or more branches might emanate from a single point, for example, and some trees may not have the symmetry of those in Examples 1 and 2. Tree diagrams arise whenever an activity can be thought of as a sequence of simpler activities.

▶ **Example 3**   (*Quality Control*) A box contains five good light bulbs and two defective ones. Bulbs are selected one at a time (without replacement) until a good bulb is found. Find the probability that the number of bulbs selected is (i) one, (ii) two, (iii) three.

Solution   The initial situation in the box is shown in Fig. 6(a). A bulb selected at random will be good (G) with probability $\frac{5}{7}$ and defective (D) with probability $\frac{2}{7}$. If a good bulb is selected, the activity stops. Otherwise, the situation is as shown in Fig. 6(b), and a bulb selected at random has probability $\frac{5}{6}$ of being good and probability $\frac{1}{6}$ of being defective. If the second bulb is good, the activity stops. If the second bulb is defective, then the situation is as shown in Fig. 6(c). At this point a bulb has probability 1 of being good.

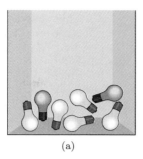 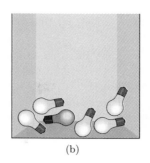 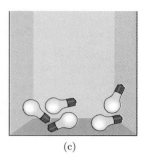

(a) (b) (c)

Figure 6.

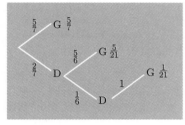

Figure 7.

The tree diagram corresponding to the sequence of activities is given in Fig. 7. Each of the three paths has a different length. The probability associated with the length of each path has been computed by multiplying the probabilities for its branches. The first path corresponds to the situation where only one bulb is selected, the second path corresponds to two bulbs, and the third path to three bulbs. Therefore,

$$\text{(i)} \ \ \Pr(1) = \tfrac{5}{7} \qquad \text{(ii)} \ \ \Pr(2) = \tfrac{5}{21} \qquad \text{(iii)} \ \ \Pr(3) = \tfrac{1}{21}. \qquad \blacklozenge$$

Practice Problems 6.6

Fifty percent of the students enrolled in a business statistics course had previously taken a finite math course. Thirty percent of these students received an A for the statistics course, whereas 20% of the other students received an A for the statistics course.

1. Draw a tree diagram and label it with the appropriate probabilities.

2. What is the probability that a student selected at random previously took a finite math course and did not receive an A in the statistics course?

3. What is the probability that a student selected at random received an A in the statistics course?

4. What is the conditional probability that a student previously took a finite math course, given that he or she received an A in the statistics course?

▶ Exercises 6.6

In Exercises 1–4, draw trees representing the sequence of experiments.

1. Experiment I is performed. Outcome a occurs with probability .3 and outcome b occurs with probability .7. Then experiment II is performed. Its outcome c occurs with probability .6 and its outcome d occurs with probability .4.

2. Experiment I is performed twice. The three outcomes of experiment I are equally likely.

3. A stereo repair shop uses a two-step diagnostic procedure to repair amplifiers. Step I locates the problem in an amplifier with probability .8. Step II (which is exe-

cuted only if step I fails to locate the problem) locates the problem with probability .6.

4. A training program is used by a corporation to direct hirees to appropriate jobs. The program consists of two steps. Step I identifies 30% as management trainees, 60% as nonmanagerial workers, and 10% as to be fired. In step II, 75% of the management trainees are assigned to managerial positions, 20% are assigned to nonmanagerial positions, and 5% are fired. In step II, 60% of the nonmanagerial workers are kept in the same category, 10% are assigned to management positions, and 30% are fired.

5. Refer to Exercise 3. What is the probability that the procedure will fail to locate the problem?

6. Refer to Exercise 4. What is the probability that a randomly chosen hiree will be assigned to a management position at the end of the training period?

7. Refer to Exercise 4. What is the probability that a randomly chosen hiree will be fired by the end of the training period?

8. Refer to Exercise 4. What is the probability that a randomly chosen hiree will be designated a management trainee but *not* be appointed to a management position?

9. Suppose that we have a white urn containing two white balls and one red ball and we have a red urn containing one white ball and three red balls. An experiment consists of selecting at random a ball from the white urn and then (without replacing the first ball) selecting at random a ball from the urn having the color of the first ball. Find the probability that the second ball is red.

10. A card is drawn from a 52-card deck. If the card is a picture card, we toss a coin. If the card is not a picture card, we toss a die. Find the probability that we end the sequence with a "6" on the die. Find the probability that we end the sequence with a "head" on the coin.

11. A card is drawn from a 52-card deck. We continue to draw until we have drawn a king or until we have drawn five cards, whichever comes first. Draw a tree diagram that illustrates the experiment. Put the appropriate probabilities on the tree. Find the probability that the drawing ends before the fourth draw.

12. Twenty percent of the library books in the fiction section are worn and need replacement. Ten percent of the nonfiction holdings are worn. The library's holdings are 40% fiction and 60% nonfiction. Draw a tree diagram to illustrate how to find the probability that a book chosen at random from this library is worn and needs replacement.

13. There are three sections of a mathematics course available at convenient times for a student. There is a 20% chance that Professor Jones gives a final exam, a 10% chance that Professor Cates gives a final exam, and a 5% chance that Professor Smithson gives a final. At other times there are two biology sections, and in those the probabilities of a final are 20% and 13%, respectively. Find the probability that a student who randomly chooses one mathematics course and one biology course has to take at least one final examination.

14. Draw a tree diagram that illustrates the following. Three-fifths of kindergarten children are bussed to school, while two-fifths of the first to fifth graders are bussed. The school has grades K through 5 and 17.5% of the students are in kindergarten. Determine the probability that a child chosen at random from the school is bussed to school.

15. Color blindness is a sex-linked, inherited condition that is much more common among men than women. Suppose that 5% of all men and .4% of all women are color-blind. A person is chosen at random and found to be color-blind. What is the probability that the person is male? (You may assume that 50% of the population are men and 50% are women.)

16. A mouse is put into a T-maze (a maze shaped like a "T"). In this maze he has the choice of turning to the left and being rewarded with cheese or going to the right and receiving a mild shock. Before any conditioning takes place (i.e., on trial 1), the mouse is equally likely to go to the left or to the right. After the first trial his decision is influenced by what happened on the previous trial. If he receives cheese on any trial, the probabilities of his going to the left or right become .9 and .1, respectively, on the following trial. If he receives the electric shock on any trial, the probabilities of his going to the left or right on the next trial become .7 and .3, respectively. What is the probability that the mouse will turn left on the second trial?

17. Refer to Exercise 16. What is the probability that the mouse will turn left on the third trial?

18. A factory has two machines that produce bolts. Machine I produces 60% of the daily output of bolts, and 3% of its bolts are defective. Machine II produces 40% of the daily output, and 2% of its bolts are defective.

    (a) What is the probability that a bolt selected at random will be defective?

    (b) If a bolt is selected at random and found to be defective, what is the probability that it was produced by machine I?

19. Three ordinary quarters and a fake quarter with two heads are placed in a hat. One quarter is selected at random and tossed twice. If the outcome is "HH," what is the probability that the fake quarter was selected?

20. Suppose that the reliability of a test for hepatitis is specified as follows: Of people with hepatitis, 95% have a positive reaction and 5% have a negative reaction; of people free of hepatitis, 90% have a negative reaction and 10% have a positive reaction. From a large population of which .05% of the people have hepatitis, a person is selected at random and given the test. If the test is positive, what is the probability that the person actually has hepatitis?

21. (*Tennis*) Kim has a strong first serve; whenever it is good (that is, in) she wins the point 75% of the time. Whenever her second serve is good, she wins the point 50% of the time. Sixty percent of her first serves and 75% of her second serves are good.

    (a) What is the probability that Kim wins the point when she serves?

    (b) If Kim wins a service point, what is the probability that her first serve was good?

22. Suppose that during any year the probability of an accidental nuclear war is .0001 (provided, of course, that there hasn't been one in a previous year). Draw a tree diagram representing the possibilities for the next three years. What is the probability that there will be an accidental nuclear war during the next three years?

23. Refer to Exercise 22. What is the probability that there will be an accidental nuclear war during the next n years?

24. A coin is to be tossed at most five times. The tosser wins as soon as the number of heads exceeds the number of tails and loses as soon as three tails have been tossed. Draw a tree diagram for this game and calculate the probability of winning.

25. Suppose that instead of tossing a coin, the player in Exercise 24 draws up to five cards from a deck consisting only of three red and three black cards. The drawer wins as soon as the number of red cards exceeds the number of black cards and loses as soon as three black cards have been drawn. Does the tree diagram for the card game have the same shape as the tree diagram for the coin game? Is there any difference in the probability of winning? If so, which game has the greater probability of winning?

26. A man has been guessing the colors of cards drawn from a standard deck. During the first 50 draws he kept track of the number of cards of each color. What is the probability of guessing the color of the fifty-first card?

27. (*Genetics*) Traits passed from generation to generation are carried by genes. For a certain type of pea plant, the color of the flower produced by the plant (either red or white) is determined by a pair of genes. Each gene is of one of the types C (dominant gene) or c (recessive gene). Plants for which both genes are of type c (said to have genotype cc) produce white flowers. All other plants—that is, plants of genotypes CC and Cc—produce red flowers. When two plants are crossed, the offspring receives one gene from each parent.

    (a) Suppose you cross two pea plants of genotype Cc. What is the probability that the offspring produces white flowers? red flowers?

    (b) Suppose you have a batch of red-flowering pea plants, of which 60% have genotype Cc and 40% have genotype CC. If you select one of these plants at random and cross it with a white-flowering pea plant, what is the probability that the offspring will produce red flowers?

28. (*Genetics*) Refer to Exercise 27. Suppose a batch of 99 pea plants contains 33 plants of each of the three genotypes.

    (a) If you select one of these plants at random and cross it with a white-flowering pea plant, what is the probability that the offspring will produce white flowers?

    (b) If you select one of the 99 pea plants at random, cross it with a white-flowering pea plant, and the offspring produces red flowers, what is the probability that the selected plant had genotype Cc?

29. At a local college, four sections of economics are taught during the day and two sections are taught at night. Seventy-five percent of the day sections are taught by full-time faculty. Forty percent of the evening sections are taught by full-time faculty. If Jane has a part-time teacher for her economics course, what is the probability that she is taking a night class?

30. Car production in the United States in 1995 was distributed among car manufacturers as follows.[1]

U.S. car production	Type		Percentage of type by brand	
71%	Domestic	Chrysler	13%
		Ford	31%
		General Motors	56%
29%	Foreign	Honda	30%
		Toyota	28%
		Other	42%

This means that 71% of the cars produced in the United States were manufactured by domestic companies; of them, 13% were Chryslers, 31% were Fords, and 56% were General Motors products.

    (a) A 1995 automobile is chosen at random. What is the probability that it is a General Motors car?

    (b) What is the probability that a randomly selected automobile is a Ford or a Toyota?

---

[1] *Information Please Almanac*, 1997, p. 79.

Solutions to Practice Problems 6.6

1.

.5 Finite math .3 A .15
.7 not A .35
.5 No finite math .2 A .10
.8 not A .40

2. The event "finite math and not A" corresponds to the second path of the tree diagram, which has probability .35.

3. This event is satisfied by the first or third paths and therefore has probability $.15 + .10 = .25$.

4. $\Pr(\text{finite math}|A) = \dfrac{\Pr(\text{finite math and A})}{\Pr(A)} = \dfrac{.15}{.25} = .6$.

6.7 Bayes' Theorem

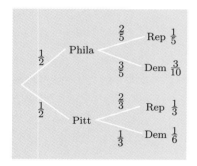

Figure 1.

Let us reconsider the polling survey in Example 1(d) of Section 6.6 (see Fig. 1). Given that the person chosen at random favors the Republican candidate, what is the probability that the respondent is from Philadelphia? We found this probability, $\Pr(\text{Phila}|\text{Rep})$, by finding

$$\frac{\Pr(\text{Phila} \cap \text{Rep})}{\Pr(\text{Rep})}.$$

Let us analyze the components of this calculation. First, recall that

$$\Pr(\text{Phila} \cap \text{Rep}) = \Pr(\text{Phila}) \cdot \Pr(\text{Rep}|\text{Phila}).$$

Second,

$$\Pr(\text{Rep}) = \Pr(\text{Phila} \cap \text{Rep}) + \Pr(\text{Pitt} \cap \text{Rep})$$

$$= \Pr(\text{Phila}) \cdot \Pr(\text{Rep}|\text{Phila}) + \Pr(\text{Pitt}) \cdot \Pr(\text{Rep}|\text{Pitt}),$$

by using the tree diagram. Denote the events "Phila," "Pitt," "Rep," and "Dem" by the letters A, B, R, and D, respectively. Then

$$\Pr(\text{Phila}|\text{Rep}) = \Pr(A|R)$$

$$= \frac{\Pr(A \cap R)}{\Pr(R)}$$

$$= \frac{\Pr(A) \cdot \Pr(R|A)}{\Pr(A) \cdot \Pr(R|A) + \Pr(B) \cdot \Pr(R|B)}.$$

This is a special case of Bayes' theorem.

We summarize a simple form of Bayes' theorem. Suppose that A is an event in S, and B_1 and B_2 are mutually exclusive events such that $B_1 \cup B_2 = S$. Then

$$\Pr(B_1|A) = \frac{\Pr(B_1) \cdot \Pr(A|B_1)}{\Pr(B_1) \cdot \Pr(A|B_1) + \Pr(B_2) \cdot \Pr(A|B_2)}.$$

We have the same type of result for the situation in which we have three mutually exclusive sets B_1, B_2, and B_3 whose union is all of S. We state Bayes' theorem for that case and leave the general case for n mutually exclusive sets for the end of the section.

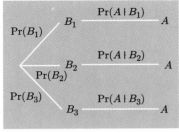

Bayes' Theorem (n = 3)   If B_1, B_2, and B_3 are mutually exclusive events, and $B_1 \cup B_2 \cup B_3 = S$, then for any event A in S,

$$\Pr(B_1|A) = \frac{\Pr(B_1) \cdot \Pr(A|B_1)}{\Pr(B_1) \cdot \Pr(A|B_1) + \Pr(B_2) \cdot \Pr(A|B_2) + \Pr(B_3) \cdot \Pr(A|B_3)}.$$

See Fig. 2.

Figure 2.

▶ Example 1   Solve the tuberculosis skin test problem of Example 2 of Section 6.6 by using Bayes' theorem.

Solution   The observed event A is "positive skin test result." There are two possible events leading to A—namely,

$$B_1 = \text{"person has tuberculosis"}$$

$$B_2 = \text{"person does not have tuberculosis."}$$

We wish to calculate $\Pr(B_1|A)$. From the data given we have

$$\Pr(B_1) = \frac{2}{10{,}000} = .0002$$

$$\Pr(B_2) = .9998$$

$$\Pr(A|B_1) = \Pr(\text{POS}|\text{TB}) = .98$$

$$\Pr(A|B_2) = \Pr(\text{POS}|\text{not TB}) = .01.$$

Therefore, by Bayes' theorem,

$$\Pr(B_1|A) = \frac{\Pr(B_1)\Pr(A|B_1)}{\Pr(B_1)\Pr(A|B_1) + \Pr(B_2)\Pr(A|B_2)}$$

$$= \frac{(.0002)(.98)}{(.0002)(.98) + (.9998)(.01)} \approx .02,$$

in agreement with our calculation of Example 2 of Section 6.6.   ◆

The advantages of Bayes' theorem over the use of tree diagrams are that (1) we do not need to draw the tree diagram to calculate the desired probability, and (2) we need not compute extraneous probabilities. These advantages become significant in dealing with experiments having many outcomes.

▶ Example 2   (*Quality Control*) A printer has seven book-binding machines. For each machine Table 1 gives the proportion of the total book production that it binds and the probability that the machine produces a defective binding. For instance, machine 1 binds 10% of the books and produces a defective binding with probability .03. Suppose that a book is selected at random and found to have a defective binding. What is the probability that it was bound by machine 1?

Solution   In this example we have seven mutually exclusive events whose union is the entire sample space (the book was bound by one, and only one, of the seven machines). Bayes' theorem can be extended to any finite number of B_i's.

	Table 1		
Machine	**Proportion of books bound**	**Probability of defective binding**
1	.10	.03
2	.05	.03
3	.20	.02
4	.15	.02
5	.25	.01
6	.15	.02
7	.10	.03

Let B_i $(i = 1, 2, \ldots, 7)$ be the event that the book was bound by machine i, and let A be the event that the book has a defective binding. Then, for example,

$$\Pr(B_1) = .10 \quad \text{and} \quad \Pr(A|B_1) = .03.$$

The problem asks for the reversed conditional probability, $\Pr(B_1|A)$. By Bayes' theorem,

$$\Pr(B_1|A) = \frac{\Pr(B_1)\Pr(A|B_1)}{\Pr(B_1)\Pr(A|B_1) + \Pr(B_2)\Pr(A|B_2) + \cdots + \Pr(B_7)\Pr(A|B_7)}$$

$$= \frac{(.10)(.03)}{(.10)(.03) + (.05)(.03) + (.20)(.02) + (.15)(.02) + (.25)(.01) + (.15)(.02) + (.10)(.03)}$$

$$= \frac{.003}{.02} = .15. \qquad \blacklozenge$$

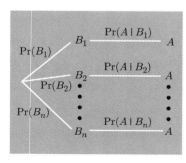

Figure 3.

Derivation of Bayes' Theorem   To derive Bayes' theorem in general, we consider a two-stage tree. Suppose that at the first stage there are the events $B_1, B_2, \ldots, B_n$, which are mutually exclusive and exhaust all possibilities. Let us examine only the paths of the tree leading to event A at the second stage of the experiment (see Fig. 3). Suppose we are given that the event A occurs. What is $\Pr(B_1|A)$? First, consider $\Pr(B_1 \cap A)$. This can be seen from Fig. 3 to be $\Pr(B_1) \cdot \Pr(A|B_1)$. Next we calculate $\Pr(A)$. Recall that A occurs at stage 2, preceded at stage 1 by either event $B_1, B_2, \ldots,$ or B_n. Since $B_1, B_2, \ldots, B_n$ are mutually exclusive,

$$\Pr(A) = \Pr(B_1 \cap A) + \Pr(B_2 \cap A) + \cdots + \Pr(B_n \cap A).$$

Each of the elements in the sum can be calculated by the product rule, or directly from Fig. 3:

$$\Pr(B_1 \cap A) = \Pr(B_1) \cdot \Pr(A|B_1)$$

$$\Pr(B_2 \cap A) = \Pr(B_2) \cdot \Pr(A|B_2)$$

$$\vdots$$

$$\Pr(B_n \cap A) = \Pr(B_n) \cdot \Pr(A|B_n).$$

The result is the following:

Bayes' Theorem If $B_1, B_2, \ldots, B_n$ are mutually exclusive events, and if $B_1 \cup B_2 \cup \cdots \cup B_n = S$, then for any event A in S,

$$\Pr(B_1|A) = \frac{\Pr(B_1) \cdot \Pr(A|B_1)}{\Pr(B_1) \cdot \Pr(A|B_1) + \Pr(B_2) \cdot \Pr(A|B_2) + \cdots + \Pr(B_n) \cdot \Pr(A|B_n)}$$

$$\Pr(B_2|A) = \frac{\Pr(B_2) \cdot \Pr(A|B_2)}{\Pr(B_1) \cdot \Pr(A|B_1) + \Pr(B_2) \cdot \Pr(A|B_2) + \cdots + \Pr(B_n) \cdot \Pr(A|B_n)},$$

and so forth.

Practice Problems 6.7

Refer to Example 2. Suppose that a book is selected at random and found to have a defective binding.

1. What is the probability that the book was bound by machine 2?

2. By what machine is the book most likely to have been bound?

▶ Exercises 6.7

1. An automobile insurance company has determined the accident rate (probability of having at least one accident during a year) for various age groups (see Table 2). Suppose that a policyholder calls in to report an accident. What is the probability that he or she is over 60?

Table 2

Age group	Proportion of total insured	Accident rate
Under 21	.05	.06
21–30	.10	.04
31–40	.25	.02
41–50	.20	.015
51–60	.30	.025
Over 60	.10	.04

2. An electronic device has six different types of transistors. For each type of transistor, Table 3 gives the proportion of the total number of transistors of that type and the failure rate (probability of failing within one year). If a transistor fails, what is the probability that it is type 1?

Table 3

Type	Proportion of total	Failure rate
1	.30	.0002
2	.25	.0004
3	.20	.0005
4	.10	.001
5	.05	.002
6	.10	.004

3. The enrollment in a certain course is 10% first-year students, 30% sophomores, 40% juniors, and 20% seniors. Past experience has shown that the likelihood of receiving an A in the course is .2 for first-year students, .4 for sophomores, .3 for juniors, and .1 for seniors. Find the probability that a student who receives an A is a sophomore.

4. A metropolitan police department maintains statistics of larcenies reported in the various precincts of the city. It records the proportion of the city population in each precinct and the precinct larceny rate (= the proportion of the precinct population reporting a larceny within the past year). These statistics are summarized in Table 4. A larceny victim is randomly chosen from

the city population. What is the probability he or she comes from Precinct 3?

Table 4

Precinct	Proportion of population	Larceny rate
1	.20	.01
2	.10	.02
3	.40	.05
4	.30	.04

5. Table 5 gives the distribution of incomes and shows the proportion of two-car families by income level for a certain suburban county. Suppose that a randomly chosen family has two or more cars. What is the probability that its income is at least $25,000 per year?

Table 5

Annual family income	Proportion of people	Proportion having two or more cars
< $10,000	.10	.2
$10,000–$14,999	.20	.5
$15,000–$19,999	.35	.6
$20,000–$24,999	.30	.75
≥ $25,000	.05	.9

6. Table 6 gives the distribution of voter registration and voter turnouts for a certain city. A randomly chosen person is questioned at the polls. What is the probability that the person is an Independent?

Table 6

	Proportion registered	Proportion turnout
Democrat	.50	.4
Republican	.20	.5
Independent	.30	.7

7. A crime investigator feels 70% certain that the suspect being held for a theft is guilty. She then discovers that the thief was left-handed. Twenty percent of the

population is left-handed, and the suspect is also left-handed. In light of this new evidence, what probability should the investigator now assign to the guilt of the suspect?

8. Table 7 shows the percentages of various portions of the U.S. population based on age and sex. Suppose that a person is chosen at random from the entire population.

Table 7

U.S. Population	Age Group	
	% of population	% male
Under 5 yrs	7	51
5–19 yrs	25	51
20–44 yrs	37	49
45–64 yrs	20	41
Over 64 yrs	11	40

(a) What is the probability that the person chosen is male?

(b) Given that the person chosen is male, find the probability that he is between 5 and 19 years old.

9. A multinational company has five divisions: A, B, C, D, and E. The percentage of employees from each division who speak at least two languages fluently is shown in Table 8.

Table 8

Division	Number of employees	Percent of employees that are bilingual
A	20,000	20
B	15,000	15
C	25,000	12
D	30,000	10
E	10,000	10
Total	100,000	

(a) Find the probability that an employee selected at random is bilingual.

(b) Find the probability that a bilingual employee selected at random works for division C.

10. A specially made pair of dice has only one- and two-spots on the faces. One of the dice has three faces with a one-spot and three faces with a two-spot. The

other die has two faces with a one-spot and four faces with a two-spot. One of the dice is selected at random and then rolled six times. If a two-spot shows up only once, what is the probability that it is the die with four two-spots?

11. The *New York Times* of January 24, 1997, discusses the recommendation of a special panel concerning mammograms for women in their 40s. About 2% of women aged 40 to 49 years old develop breast cancer in their 40s. But the mammogram used for women in that age group has a high rate of false positives and false negatives; the false positive rate is .30, and the false negative rate is .25. If a woman in her 40s has a positive mammogram, what is the probability that she actually has breast cancer?

12. A *false negative* in a diagnostic test is a test result that is negative even though the patient has the condition. A *false positive*, on the other hand, is a test result that is positive although the patient does not have the condition. A drug-testing laboratory produces false negative results 2% of the time and false positive results 5% of the time. Suppose that the laboratory has been hired by a company in which 10% of the employees use drugs.

    (a) If an employee tests positive for drug use, what is the probability that he or she actually uses drugs?

    (b) What is the probability that a non-drug user will test positive for drug use twice in a row?

    (c) What is the probability that someone who tests positive twice in a row is not a drug user?

13. Thirteen cards are dealt from a deck of 52 cards.

    (a) What is the probability that the ace of spades is one of the 13 cards?

    (b) Suppose one of the 13 cards is chosen at random and found *not* to be the ace of spades. What is the probability that *none* of the 13 cards is the ace of spades?

    (c) Suppose the experiment in part (b) is repeated a total of 10 times (replacing the card looked at each time), and the ace of spades is not seen. What is the probability that the ace of spades actually *is* one of the 13 cards?

14. There are two cookie jars on the shelf in the kitchen. The red one has 10 chocolate-chip cookies and 15 gingersnaps. The blue jar has 20 chocolate-chip cookies and 10 gingersnaps. James goes down in the middle of the night and without turning on the light chooses a jar at random and then chooses a cookie at random. If the cookie is chocolate chip, what is the probability that he got the cookie from the blue jar?

15. Twenty percent of the contestants in a scholarship competition come from Pylesville High School, 40% come from Millerville High School, and the remainder come from Lakeside High School. Two percent of the Pylesville students are among the scholarship winners; 3% of the Millerville contestants and 5% of the Lakeside contestants win.

    (a) If a winner is chosen at random, what is the probability that he or she is from Lakeside?

    (b) What percentage of the winners are from Pylesville?

16. There are three sections of English 101. In Section I there are 25 students, of whom 5 are mathematics majors. In Section II there are 20 students, of whom 6 are mathematics majors. In Section III there are 35 students, of whom 5 are mathematics majors. A student in English 101 is chosen at random. Find the probability that the student is from Section I, given that he or she is a mathematics major.

17. An over-the-counter pregnancy test claims to be 99% accurate. Actually, what the insert says is that if the test is performed properly, it is 99% sure to detect a pregnancy.

    (a) What is the probability of a false negative?

    (b) Let us assume that the probability is 98% that the test result is negative for a woman who is not pregnant. If the woman estimates that her chances of being pregnant are about 40% and the test result is positive, what is the probability that she is actually pregnant?

18. A test for a condition is very sensitive and has a high probability of false positives, say 20%. Its rate of false negatives is 10%. The condition is estimated to exist in 65% of all patients sent for screening. If the test is positive, what is the chance the patient has the condition? Suppose that the condition is much more rare in the population—say $\Pr(\text{condition}) = .30$. Given the same testing situation, what is $\Pr(\text{condition}|\text{pos})$?

19. It is estimated that 10% of Olympic athletes use steroids. The test currently being used to detect steroids is said to be 93% effective in correctly detecting steroids in users. It yields false positives in only 2% of the tests. A country's best weightlifter tests positive. What is the probability that he actually takes steroids?

20. Ten percent of the pens made by Apex are defective. Only 5% of the pens made by its competitor, B-ink, are defective. Since Apex pens are cheaper than B-ink pens, an office orders 70% of its stock from Apex and 30% from B-ink. A pen is chosen at random and found to be defective. What is the probability that it was produced by Apex?

**Solutions to
Practice Problems
6.7**

1. The problem asks for $\Pr(B_2|A)$. Bayes' theorem gives this probability as a quotient with numerator $\Pr(B_2)\Pr(A|B_2)$ and the same denominator as in the solution to Example 2. Therefore,

$$\Pr(B_2|A) = \frac{\Pr(B_2)\Pr(A|B_2)}{.02} = \frac{(.05)(.03)}{.02} = .075.$$

2. To solve this problem we must compute the seven conditional probabilities

$$\Pr(B_1|A), \quad \Pr(B_2|A), \quad \ldots, \quad \Pr(B_7|A)$$

and see which one is the largest. The first two have already been computed. Using the method of the preceding problem we find that

$$\Pr(B_3|A) = .20, \quad \Pr(B_4|A) = .15, \quad \Pr(B_5|A) = .125,$$
$$\Pr(B_6|A) = .15, \quad \text{and} \quad \Pr(B_7|A) = .15.$$

Therefore, the book was most likely bound by machine 3.

6.8 Simulation

Simulation is a method of imitating an experiment by using an artificial device to substitute for the real thing. The technique is used often in industrial and scientific applications. For example, in the 1970s Deaconess Hospital in St. Louis was planning to add an extension to the hospital with 144 medical-surgical beds. The planners knew that an increase in the number of beds would require additional operating rooms and recovery room beds. By studying the pattern of patients already being treated in the existing hospital, Homer H. Schmitz and N. K. Kwak[1] constructed a mathematical model to imitate the rate of flow of patients through the planned hospital (with the additional beds) to see what the typical operating suite schedule would look like. But they did not use patients! They used random numbers and a computer in their simulation model. They built a model in which they could vary the number of operating rooms and adjust the schedule. By repeating the experiment many times, they found the optimal number of new operating rooms and recovery room beds to complement the added beds.

Calculators have a command, usually called **rand** or **rnd**, that can be used to select a number at random from a specified set of numbers. Each number in the set is just as likely to be selected as any other. Although random number tables are generally available and many of the techniques discussed here can be used with such tables, we recommend using a graphing calculator or a computer if at all possible when doing simulations. On TI-82 and TI-83 graphing calculators, the command **rand** by itself generates a number x, where $0 \leq x < 1$, and a command of the form **seq(rand,X,1,n,1)** $\rightarrow$ **L$_1$** creates a list of n such numbers, where n can be as large as 999. The item **rand** is the first command on the MATH/PRB menu and **seq** is the fifth command on the LIST/OPS menu. Figures 1 and 2 show the menus for the TI-83 calculator. Figure 3 shows the screen of the TI-83 (set to two decimal places from the MODE menu) generating the beginning of a random sequence of 20 numbers. Move the cursor to the right to see more of the sequence. Pressing the ⌷ENTER⌷ key generates another sequence of 20 numbers.

---

[1]Homer H. Schmitz and N. K. Kwak, "Monte Carlo simulation of operating-room and recovery-room usage," *Operations Research* **20**, 1972, pp. 1171–1180.

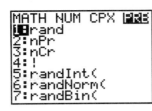

Figure 1.

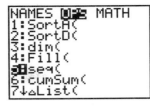

Figure 2.

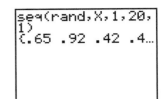

Figure 3.

▶ **Example 1**   Use a calculator to simulate 20 tosses of a fair coin. Then count the number of heads and tails.

Solution   We will generate 20 random numbers between 0 and 1. Each number less than .5 will be interpreted as a head and each number greater than or equal to .5 will be interpreted as a tail. The following steps generate and display a sorted list of 20 random numbers between 0 and 1 with a TI-82 or TI-83 calculator.

1. On the home screen, execute the command **seq(rand,X,1,20,1)→L₁** to place 20 random numbers between 0 and 1 into the list **L₁**; see Fig. 4.

2. Execute the command **SortA(L₁)** to sort the entries in the list **L₁** in ascending order. [**SortA(** is the first command in the LIST/OPS menu.] See Fig. 5.

3. Press STAT **1** to view the elements of **L₁** in a table.

4. Use the down-arrow key to scroll down the list and place the cursor on the last number less than .5. See Fig. 6. Here, the display **L1(12)** at the bottom of the screen tells us that the highlighted number is the 12th number in the list. Therefore, our simulation of 20 coin tosses yields 12 heads and 8 tails.

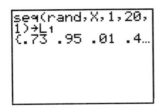

Figure 4.

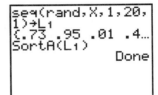

Figure 5.

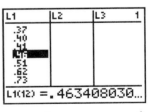

Figure 6.   ◆

Calculators can select whole numbers at random. With the TI-82 and TI-83 calculators, the command **int(n∗rand)+1** selects at random a whole number from 1 to n. (Here, **rand** produces a number from 0 to 1, $n∗$**rand** produces a number less than n, and **int**, located on the MATH/NUM screen, throws away the decimal part of the number to produce a whole number from 0 through $n-1$. Adding 1 shifts the range to 1 through n.) Therefore, the command **seq(int(n∗rand)+1,X,1,r,1)→ L₁** places a sequence of r randomly selected whole numbers from 1 to n into the list **L₁**. [*Note*: With a TI-83, this task also can be accomplished with the command **randInt(1,n,r) → L₁**, where **randInt** is the fifth item on the MATH/PRB menu.] Some examples of the use of these commands follow:

1. *Simulate the toss of a single die*: **int(6∗rand)+1** produces a random whole number from 1 to 6. Figures 7 and 8 show the results of 10 such simulated tosses.

```
seq(int(6*rand)+
1,X,1,10,1)→L₁
```

L1	L2	L3	1
3.00	------	------	
4.00			
4.00			
4.00			
4.00			
3.00			
5.00			
L1(1)=3			

Figure 7.   **Figure 8.**

2. *Simulate the toss of a pair of dice*: `int(6*rand)+1+int(6*rand)+1` produces a whole number from 2 to 12 distributed as the sum of the faces.

3. *Simulate 10 tosses of a pair of dice*: `seq(int(6*rand)+1+int(6*rand)+1,X,1,10,1)` → `L₁` produces a list of 10 random whole numbers from 2 to 12.

4. *Simulate the selection of a ball from an urn containing 7 white balls and 3 red balls*: Think of the white balls as numbered from 1 to 7, and the red balls as numbered from 8 to 10. Then `int(10*rand)+1` selects a ball at random and the number determines its color.

5. *Simulate the outcome of a free throw by Michael Jordan, who had an 83% free-throw average*: Consider each shot as a random whole number from 1 to 100, where a number from 1 to 83 represents a successful free throw and a number from 84 to 100 represents a miss. Then `int(100*rand)+1` determines whether the free throw is successful.

▶ **Example 2**   Simulate 72 tosses of a fair die, and tabulate the results by using the graphing capabilities of a graphing calculator. Compare your results with the theoretical probabilities.

Solution   Generate the 72 random whole numbers from 1 to 6 and store them in **L₁**. On the TI-82 or TI-83, you may tally the results by setting the STATPLOT as shown in Fig. 9 and adjusting the WINDOW (Fig. 10) to allow the maximum frequency to show in the bar graph. Such a result is shown in Fig. 11. The GRAPH key will sketch a special type of bar graph indicating the number of tosses resulting in each of the possible outcomes, 1, 2, 3, 4, 5, and 6. Use the TRACE command and the cursor to determine the number of items in each of the bars. In Fig. 11, for example, we can read from the graph that there are $n = 9$ tosses that are greater than or equal to 2 and less than 3 (for a die, this means exactly 2).

Figure 9.

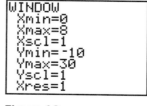

Figure 10.

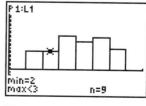

Figure 11.

Since the probability of each outcome is $\frac{1}{6}$ and the number of tosses is 72, we would expect that each of the outcomes would occur $(\frac{1}{6})(72) = 12$ times. Observations of the graph or a survey of the generated list will give us the actual number of occurrences in each simulation of 72 tosses.   ◆

▶ Example 3   Patients having surgery fall into three categories. Sixty percent of them require two hours in the recovery room, 30% require one hour in the recovery room, and the remainder require a half-hour. Simulate the number of hours of recovery room time required by 25 patients.

Solution   One technique is to generate 25 random whole numbers from 1 to 10. Numbers 1 to 6 represent a patient who requires two hours in the recovery room, numbers 7 to 9 represent a patient who requires one hour in the recovery room, and the number 10 represents a patient needing a half-hour in the recovery room. The command **seq(int(10*rand)+1,X,1,25,1)** → **L₁** followed by **SortA(L₁)** enters the random numbers in list **L₁** and sorts them in ascending order. The down-arrow key will scroll down the list so that we can count all those random entries from 1 to 6, those from 7 to 9, and the 10s. Here is one possible outcome:

$$1, 1, 2, 2, 2, 4, 4, 4, 4, 5, 5, 5, 5, 5, 6, \quad 7, 7, 8, 8, 8, 9, \quad 10, 10, 10, 10,$$

giving 15 patients who require two hours, 6 patients who require one hour, and 4 patients who require a half-hour. The total amount of time in the recovery room needed by these patients is $15(2) + 6(1) + 4(\frac{1}{2}) = 38$ hours. ◆

▶ Example 4   Customers steadily arrive at a bank during the hour from 9 A.M. to 10 A.M. so that the line of customers is never empty. There are three tellers, and each customer requires a varying amount of time with a teller. For simplicity, we assume that 40% of the customers need 3 minutes, 50% need 5 minutes, and 10% need 8 minutes. Each customer enters the queue at the end and goes to the first available teller when reaching the front of the queue. Simulate the service process.

(a) Show how many of the first 20 customers each of the tellers is able to service on a random day and in that hour.

(b) If all 20 customers were at the bank when it opened at 9 A.M., what was the average time spent at the bank once it opened?

Solution   (a) We generate 20 random whole numbers from 1 to 10. We consider numbers 1 to 4 as representing customers requiring 3 minutes, numbers 5 to 9 as customers requiring 5 minutes, and 10 as customers needing 8 minutes. We do not sort them, because we want to preserve the randomness of their arrival. Here is a typical list:

Cust. #:   1, 2, 3, 4, 5, 6, 7, 8, 9, 10, 11, 12, 13, 14, 15, 16, 17, 18, 19, 20
Random #: 10, 7, 2, 3, 1, 6, 4, 3, 1, 10, 6, 5, 2, 3, 7, 7, 10, 10, 5, 5.

To determine the schedule, let the tellers be A, B, and C. Then the first customer goes to teller A. Since her random number is 10, she requires 8 minutes, occupying teller A until 9:08. Meanwhile, the second customer, with random number 7, goes to teller B, where he needs 5 minutes. He occupies teller B until 9:05. Then customer #3, with random number 2, goes to teller C until 9:03. Since teller C finishes first, customer #4 steps up to C at 9:03. That customer (with random number 3) requires 3 minutes and leaves teller C at 9:06. In case two tellers are free at the same moment, let us use the convention that the tellers are chosen in alphabetical order, with A first. From Table 1, we see that teller A served 6 of the first 20 customers, and teller B served 6 and C served 8 customers. They completed the first 20 transactions at 9:34 A.M.

Table 1

Customer #	Random #	Time req.	Teller	Start time	End time
1	10	8	A	9:00	9:08
2	7	5	B	9:00	9:05
3	2	3	C	9:00	9:03
4	3	3	C	9:03	9:06
5	1	3	B	9:05	9:08
6	6	5	C	9:06	9:11
7	4	3	A	9:08	9:11
8	3	3	B	9:08	9:11
9	1	3	A	9:11	9:14
10	10	8	B	9:11	9:19
11	6	5	C	9:11	9:16
12	5	5	A	9:14	9:19
13	2	3	C	9:16	9:19
14	3	3	A	9:19	9:22
15	7	5	B	9:19	9:24
16	7	5	C	9:19	9:24
17	10	8	A	9:22	9:30
18	10	8	B	9:24	9:32
19	5	5	C	9:24	9:29
20	5	5	C	9:29	9:34

(b) We can find the average amount of time spent after the bank opened by totaling the time spent by all customers (use the number of minutes after 9 A.M. in the "End time" column) and dividing by 20, the number of customers. This gives $(8+5+3+6+8+11+11+11+14+19+16+19+19+22+24+24+30+32+29+34)/20 = 17.25$ minutes. Thus, on the average, a person who was at the bank at 9 A.M. required 17.25 minutes after the bank opened to be served and to complete the transaction. ◆

The simulation should be repeated many times to determine the typical outcome. So you might simulate 50 days from 9 A.M. to 10 A.M. to see how long it takes to service the first 20 customers and, on the average, how long a customer spends in the bank if he or she is one of the first 20 people there when the bank opens. It might be useful to see the effect of using four tellers or see what happens when the probabilities of the service times are defined differently.

In practice, the arrival times of the customers are also random and can be built into the simulation. A time-and-motion study would be used to determine the appropriate probabilistic model of the arrival process.

▶ Exercises 6.8

1. Simulate 72 tosses of a fair die. Give the relative frequency and the corresponding theoretical probability of each of the outcomes and compare them.

2. Simulate 96 tosses of a pair of dice where the sum is observed. Give the relative frequency and the corresponding theoretical probability of each of the outcomes. Make a table showing your results. Repeat the experiment 6 times and consider the total as if 576 tosses were simulated. [*Note*: (6)(96) = 576.]

3. Simulate 10 free throws for Michael Jordan, whose free throw average is 83%. How many of the shots were successful?

4. A baseball player has a batting average of .331. Simulate 10 at-bats for this player and tell how many hits he gets. (A batting average of .331 means that 33.1% of at-bats result in a hit.)

5. A student who has not studied for a 10-question multiple-choice test, with 4 choices among the answers (a, b, c, d) for each question, decides to simulate such a test and answer the questions according to a simulation in which each choice of answer has the same probability. Use a calculator to generate a simulated answer sheet. Assume the correct answers are a, b, b, c, d, d, a, c, b, a. What is the student's score?

6. In sampling 4 balls at random from an urn containing 30 balls, *without replacement* after each draw, we consider the balls as numbered 1 to 30. In selecting random whole numbers from 1 to 30, we ignore any number that has already been selected and continue the selection until we obtain a sample of size 4. Assume there are 20 red balls and 10 green balls in the urn. Draw 10 samples of size 4 and tabulate the number of red balls in each sample. Compare your results with the theoretical probability.

7. Students are queued up at the registrar's office when the registration windows open at 8 A.M. There are four open windows; students approach the first open window as they advance to the front of the queue. Assume that 10% of the students require 5 minutes of service time, 30% of the students require 7 minutes of service time, 40% require 10 minutes, and 20% require 15 minutes. Simulate the service of the first 20 students in a random queue. Show the schedule of service at the four windows (A, B, C, D), determine how long it takes to process these students, and give the average time from 8 A.M. to leaving the service window.

8. Simulate the bank queue of Example 4 using four tellers. Give the time needed to process the first 20 customers and the average time spent by each customer in the bank after 9 A.M.

9. A reservoir is built to hold a maximum of 6 units of water. Assume a unit is one million cubic feet. At the start of the year, the reservoir holds 1 unit of water, and at the end of every week, it disperses 2 units for drinking water. Rainfall is the only source of water for the reservoir. Records show that weekly rainfall varies with the following probabilities:

# units per week:	1	2	3	4
Probability:	.4	.3	.2	.1

Simulate 13 weeks of rainfall. Then make a chart showing the amount of water in the reservoir at the end of each week. Determine the number of weeks in which the reservoir runs dry. Determine the number of weeks in which the reservoir overflows. What is the average amount of water in the reservoir over the 13-week period?

10. Simulate 108 tosses of three dice, and show the frequency of each possible sum of the faces: $3, 4, \ldots, 18$.

▶ Chapter 6 Summary

1. The *sample space* of an experiment is the set of all possible outcomes of the experiment. Each subset of the sample space is called an *event*. We say that an event *occurs* when the outcome is an element of the event.

2. The event $E \cup F$ occurs when either E or F (or both) occurs. The event $E \cap F$ occurs when both E and F occur. The event E' occurs when E does not occur.

3. Two events are *mutually exclusive* if they cannot both occur at the same time.

4. A *probability distribution* for a finite sample space associates a probability with each outcome of the sample space. Each probability is a number between 0 and 1, and the sum of the probabilities is 1. The probability of an event is the sum of the probabilities of the outcomes in the event.

5. The inclusion-exclusion principle states that the probability of the union of two events is the sum of the probabilities of the events minus the probability of their intersection. If the two events are mutually exclusive, the probability of the union is just the sum of the probabilities of the events.

6. We say that the *odds* in favor of an event are a to b if the probability of the event is $a/(a+b)$. Intuitively, the event is expected to occur a times for every b times it does not occur.

7. For a sample space with a finite number of equally likely outcomes, the probability of an event is the number of elements in the event divided by the number of elements in the sample space.

8. The probability of the complement of an event is 1 minus the probability of the event.

9. $\Pr(E|F)$, the conditional probability that E occurs given that F occurs, is computed as $\Pr(E \cap F)/\Pr(F)$. For a sample space with a finite number of equally likely outcomes, it can be computed as $n(E \cap F)/n(F)$.

10. The product rule states that if $\Pr(F) \neq 0$, then $\Pr(E \cap F) = \Pr(F) \cdot \Pr(E|F)$.

11. E and F are *independent* events if $\Pr(E \cap F) = \Pr(E) \cdot \Pr(F)$. Equivalently, E and F [with $\Pr(F) \neq 0$] are independent events if $\Pr(E|F) = \Pr(E)$.

12. A collection of events is said to be *independent* if for each collection of events chosen from them, the probability that all the events occur equals the product of the probabilities that each occurs.

13. Tree diagrams provide a useful device for determining probabilities of combined outcomes in a sequence of experiments.

14. Bayes' theorem states that if $B_1, B_2, \ldots, B_n$ are mutually exclusive events whose union is the entire sample space and A is an event, then for each event B_i,

$$\Pr(B_i|A) = \frac{\Pr(B_i)\Pr(A|B_i)}{\Pr(B_1)\Pr(A|B_1) + \cdots + \Pr(B_n)\Pr(A|B_n)}.$$

15. The ability to generate random numbers allows us to simulate the outcomes of experiments.

Review of Fundamental Concepts of Chapter 6

1. Describe how to form a sample space for an experiment.

2. Using the language of sets and assuming that A and B are events in a sample space S, write the following events in set notation: (A or B); (A and B); not A.

3. In a sample space, what is the probability of the empty set?

4. What subset in a sample space corresponds to the certain event?

5. Draw Venn diagrams for the events A or B, A and B, not A.

6. Write a formula for the probability of the event $A \cup B$ assuming that you know $\Pr(A)$, $\Pr(B)$, and $\Pr(A \cap B)$.

7. Explain the difference between mutually exclusive events and independent events.

8. State the addition principle.

9. Suppose the probability of an event is k/n. What are the odds that the event will occur?

10. Suppose the odds that an event occurs are a to b. What is the probability that the event will occur?

11. State the inclusion–exclusion principle for two events.

12. What is the definition of $\Pr(E|F)$?

13. What is Bayes' theorem?

14. What is a tree diagram?

▶ Chapter 6 Supplementary Exercises

1. A coin is to be tossed five times. What is the probability of obtaining at least one head?

2. Suppose that we toss a coin three times and observe the sequence of heads and tails. Let E be the event that "the first toss lands heads" and F the event that "there are more heads than tails." Are E and F independent?

3. Each box of a certain brand of candy contains either a toy airplane or a toy gun. If one-third of the boxes contain an airplane and two-thirds contain a gun, what is the probability that a person who buys two boxes of candy will receive both an airplane and a gun?

4. A committee consists of five men and five women. If three people are selected at random from the committee, what is the probability that they will all be men?

5. Out of the 50 colleges in a certain state, 25 are private, 15 offer engineering majors, and 5 are private colleges offering engineering majors. If a college is selected at random, what is the conditional probability that it offers an engineering major given that it is a public college?

6. An auditing procedure for income tax returns has the following characteristics: If the return is incorrect, the probability is 90% that it will be rejected; if the return is correct, the probability is 95% that it will be accepted. Suppose that 80% of all income tax returns are correct. If a return is audited and rejected, what is the probability that the return was actually correct?

7. A number is chosen at random from the numbers 1 to 100. What is the probability that the number is divisible by 5?

8. A number is chosen at random from the numbers 1 to 10,000. What is the probability that the number is divisible by 5?

9. A number is chosen at random from the numbers 1 to 10,000. What is the probability that the number is divisible by 3 or 5?

10. A number is chosen at random from the numbers 1 to 10,000. What is the probability that the number is divisible by 3 or 12?

11. Jack and Hugo attend a party at which there are two tables of 8 for dinner. If guests are assigned to seats at random, what is the probability that Jack and Hugo will be seated at the same table?

12. Five students are to receive special honors at commencement. Of the five, two are engineering majors.

    (a) What is the probability that the two engineering majors will be called up as the first two students to receive their awards?

    (b) What is the probability that the two engineering majors will be called up consecutively to receive their awards?

13. Prior to taking an essay examination, students are given 10 questions to prepare. Six of the 10 will appear on the exam. One student decides to prepare only eight of the questions. Assume that the questions are equally likely to be chosen by the professor.

    (a) What is the probability that she has prepared every question appearing on the test?

    (b) What is the probability that both questions she did not prepare appear on the test?

14. A collection of code words consists of all strings of seven characters, where each of the first three characters can be any letter or digit and each of the last four characters must be a digit. For example, 7A32765 is allowed but 7A3B765 is not.

    (a) What is the probability that a code word chosen at random begins with ABC?

    (b) What is the probability that a code word chosen at random ends with 6578?

    (c) What is the probability that a code word chosen at random ends with a four-digit number divisible by 3?

    (d) What is the probability that a code word chosen at random consists of three letters followed by four even digits?

15. Two archers shoot at a moving target. One can hit the target with probability $\frac{1}{4}$ and the other with probability $\frac{1}{3}$. Assuming that their efforts are independent events, what is the probability that

    (a) Both will hit the target?

    (b) At least one will hit the target?

16. If the odds in favor of an event are 7 to 5, what is the probability that the event will occur?

17. In an Olympic swimming event, two of the seven contestants are American. The contestants are randomly assigned to lanes 1 through 7. What is the probability that the Americans are assigned to the first two lanes?

18. An urn contains three balls numbered 1, 2, and 3. Balls are drawn one at a time without replacement until the sum of the numbers drawn is four or more. Find the probability of stopping after exactly two balls are drawn.

19. A red die and a green die are tossed as a pair. Let E be the event that "the red die shows a 2" and let F be the event that "the sum of the numbers is 8." Are the events E and F independent?

20. Let E and F be events with $\Pr(E) = .4$, $\Pr(F) = .3$, and $\Pr(E \cup F) = .5$. Find $\Pr(E|F)$.

21. A supermarket has three employees who package and weigh produce. Employee A records the correct weight 98% of the time. Employees B and C record the correct weight 97% and 95% of the time, respectively. Employees A, B, and C handle 40%, 40%, and 20% of the packaging, respectively. A customer complains about the incorrect weight recorded on a package he has purchased. What is the probability that the package was weighed by employee C?

22. Three people are chosen at random. What is the probability that at least two of them were born on the same day of the week?

23. Let B and A be independent events for which the probability that at least one of them occurs is $\frac{1}{2}$ and the probability that B occurs but A does not occur is $\frac{1}{3}$. Find $\Pr(A)$.

24. An urn contains 10 balls numbered 1 through 10. Seven balls are drawn one at a time at random without replacement. Find the probability that exactly three odd-numbered balls are drawn and they occur on odd-numbered draws from the urn.

25. Each of three sealed opaque envelopes contains two bills. One envelope contains two $1 bills, another contains two $5 bills, and the third contains a $1 bill and a $5 bill. An envelope is selected at random and a bill is taken from the envelope at random. If it is a $5 bill, what is the probability that the other bill in the envelope is also a $5 bill?

26. A carnival huckster has placed a coin under one of three cups and asks you to guess which cup contains the coin. After you select a cup, he removes one of the unselected cups, which he guarantees does not contain the coin. You may now either stay with your original choice or switch to the other remaining cup. What decision will give you the greater probability of winning?

27. The odds of an American worker living within 20 minutes of work are 13 to 12. What is the probability that a worker selected at random lives within 20 minutes of work?

28. Twenty-six percent of all Americans are under 18 years old. What are the odds that a person selected at random is under 18?

29. If the nine letters A, C, D, E, I, N, O, T, and U are arranged to form a word, what is the probability that it will be one of the meaningful words EDUCATION, AUCTIONED, or CAUTIONED?

30. An island contains an equal number of one-headed, two-headed, and three-headed dragons. If a dragon head is picked at random, what is the likelihood of its belonging to a one-headed dragon?

31. Two players each toss a coin three times. What is the probability that they get the same number of tails?

32. Suppose that a pair of dice is tossed. Given that a double does not occur, what is the probability that one die shows a three?

33. According to *Bottom Line Personal* of March 30, 1991, the chances of having a left-handed child are 4 in 10 if both parents are left-handed, 2 in 10 if one parent is left-handed, and only 1 in 10 if neither parent is left-handed. Suppose a left-handed child is chosen at random from a population in which 25% of the adults are left-handed. What is the probability that the child's parents are both left-handed?

34. Of the 120 students in a class, 30 speak Chinese, 50 speak Spanish, 75 speak French, 12 speak Spanish and Chinese, 30 speak Spanish and French, and 15 speak Chinese and French. Seven students speak all three languages. A student is chosen at random. What is the probability that he speaks none of these languages?

35. What is the probability that a whole number between 100 and 400 contains the digit 2?

36. A committee is composed of w women and m men. If three women and two men are added to the committee, and if one person is selected at random from the enlarged committee, then the probability that a woman is selected can be represented by

    (a) $\dfrac{w}{m}$ (b) $\dfrac{w}{w+m}$ (c) $\dfrac{w+3}{m+2}$

    (d) $\dfrac{w+3}{w+m+3}$ (e) $\dfrac{w+3}{w+m+5}$

37. Of a group of people surveyed in a political poll, 60% said they would vote for candidate R. Of those who said they would vote for R, 90% actually voted for R, and of those who did not say they would vote for R, 5% actually voted for R. What percent of the group voted for R?

    (a) 56%   (b) 59%   (c) 62%

    (d) 65%   (e) 74%

Exercises 38–41 require the use of a calculator or computer.

38. How many people are needed to have the probability of at least two matching birthdays be at least 80%?

39. A drug company wants to test a drug for a chronic disease. The company wants a sample of 500 people who have the disease. It tests 12,735 people for the disease, which generally affects 5% of the population. The test is known to have a 2% false positive rate and a 4% false negative rate. Six hundred and fifty people test positive for the disease. Based on the test results, how many of the total population actually can be expected to have the disease?

40. Simulate an experiment in which either you toss a die until you get a 6 or you have tossed the die 15 times. Record the number of times you toss the die until the first 6. Find the relative frequency of each outcome in the set $\{1, 2, 3, \ldots, 15\}$. Perform the experiment at least 20 times.

41. Simulate an experiment in which you draw 3 cards from a deck of 52 cards, with replacement after each draw. Determine the number of spades in the sample and repeat the experiment 20 times. Find the relative frequency of at least 2 spades in a sample of size 3. What is the theoretical probability of at least 2 spades in a sample of size 3?

▶ Chapter 6 Chapter Test

1. A box contains a penny, a nickel, a dime, a quarter, and a half dollar. You select two coins at random from the box.

    (a) Construct a sample space for this situation.

    (b) List the elements of the event E in which the total value of the coins you have selected is an even number of cents.

2. Convert the following odds to probabilities.

    (a) 3 to 5   (b) 1,000,000 to 1

3. When Tommy plays checkers against his father, he wins 40% of the time. When he plays against his mother, he wins 30% of the time. What are the odds of him beating his father? losing to his mother?

4. Some of the candidates for president of the computer club at Riverdale High are seniors, and the rest are juniors. Let J be the event in which a junior is elected, and let F be the event in which a female is elected. Describe the following events:

    (a) $J \cap F'$ (b) $(J \cap F)'$ (c) $F' \cup J$

5. Emilio tosses a fair coin five times. What is the probability that he gets at least one head and at least one tail?

6. Fifteen percent of children attending kindergarten have not had a measles vaccine. In a class of 20 students, what is the probability that at least one has not had a measles vaccine?

7. Suppose E and F are events in a sample space, with $\Pr(E) = \frac{1}{4}$, $\Pr(F') = \frac{3}{8}$, and $\Pr(E' \cap F) = \frac{1}{2}$. Determine the following:

   (a) $\Pr(F)$ (b) $\Pr(E \cup F)$ (c) $\Pr(F|E')$

   (d) Are E and F mutually exclusive?

   (e) Are E and F independent?

8. Ten of a certain kind of gadget are tested. The probability that any given such gadget is defective is .1. What is the probability that at least one of the 10 gadgets is defective? What is the probability that exactly one of the 10 gadgets is defective?

9. Wanda has a deck of 52 cards, a box, and an urn. The box contains 5 red marbles and 10 green marbles, while the urn contains 12 red marbles and 8 green marbles. Wanda picks a card at random from the deck. If it is a face card (jack, queen, or king), she then picks a marble from the box. Otherwise, she picks a marble from the urn.

   (a) Determine the probability that she picks a red marble, given that she drew a face card from the deck.

   (b) What is the probability that she ends up with a red marble?

   (c) If E is the event in which Wanda picks a face card and F is the event in which she picks a red marble, are E and F independent? mutually exclusive?

   (d) If Wanda ends up with a green marble, what is the probability that she drew a face card?

10. The probability distribution for the result of rolling a loaded die is given in Table 1.

    (a) Determine the probability that the outcome is an odd number.

    (b) Given that the outcome is odd, what is the probability that the outcome is greater than 4?

Table 1

Outcome	1	2	3	4	5	6
Probability	.15	.20	.10	.25	.25	.05

11. A finite math class of 50 students is composed of freshmen and sophomores according to Table 2. A student from the class is selected at random.

    (a) What is the probability that the selected student is either female or a sophomore?

    (b) What is the probability that the selected student is male, given that the student is a freshman?

Table 2

	Freshmen	Sophomores
Females	12	8
Males	14	16

Chapter Project

Two Paradoxes

First Paradox: *Under certain circumstances you have your best chance of winning a tennis match if you play most of your games against the best possible opponent.*

Alice and her two sisters, Betty and Carol, are avid tennis players. Betty is the best of the three sisters and Carol plays at the same level as Alice. Alice defeats Carol 50% of the time but only defeats Betty 40% of the time.

Alice's mother offers to give her $100 if she can win two consecutive games when playing three alternating games against her two sisters. Since the games will alternate, Alice has two choices for the sequence of opponents. One possibility is to play the first game against Betty, followed by a game with Carol, and then another game with Betty. We will refer to this sequence as BCB. The other possible sequence is CBC.

1. Make a guess of the best sequence for Alice to choose; the one having the majority of the games against the weaker opponent or the one having the majority of the games against the stronger opponent.

2. Calculate the probability of Alice getting the $100 reward if she chooses the sequence CBC.

3. Calculate the probability of Alice getting the $100 reward if she chooses the sequence BCB.

4. Which sequence should Alice choose?

5. How would you explain to someone who didn't know probability why the sequence you chose is best?

Second Paradox: *The probability of a male applicant being admitted to a graduate school can be higher than the probability for a female applicant even though for each department the probability of a female being admitted is higher.* (This apparent contradiction is known as Simpson's paradox.)

To simplify matters, consider a university with two professional graduate programs, medicine and law. Suppose that last year 1000 men and 1000 women applied and the outcome was as shown in Table 1.

Table 1

	Men			Women		
	Applied	Accepted	Rejected	Applied	Accepted	Rejected
Law	700	560	140	400	340	60
Medicine	300	40	260	600	160	440

6. What is the probability that a male applicant was accepted to a professional program? female?

7. Which gender does the university appear to be favoring?

8. What is the probability that a male applicant was accepted to law school? female?

9. What is the probability that a male applicant was accepted to medical school? female?

10. Which gender do the individual professional schools appear to be favoring?

11. Without using probability, justify the apparent contradiction between the answers for part 7 and part 10.

CHAPTER

Probability and Statistics

7

S tatistics is the branch of mathematics that deals with data: their collection, description, analysis, and use in prediction. In this chapter we present some topics in statistics that can be used as a springboard to further study. Since we are presenting a series of topics rather than a comprehensive survey, we will bypass large areas of statistics without saying anything about them. However, the discussion should give you some feeling for the subject. Section 7.1 shows how bar charts, pie charts, histograms, and box plots help us turn raw data into a visual form that often allows us to see patterns in the data quickly. Section 7.2 discusses the problem of describing data by means of a distribution and a histogram. It also introduces the concept of random variables. Section 7.3 presents the binomial distribution, one of the most commonly used distributions in statistical applications. Sections 7.4 and 7.5 introduce the mean and the standard deviation, the two most frequently used descriptive statistics, and illustrate how Chebychev's inequality can be used in making estimations. Sections 7.6 and 7.7 explore the binomial distribution further and introduce the normal distribution, which has special importance in statistical analysis.

7.1 Visual Representations of Data

Data can be presented in raw form or organized and displayed in tables or charts. In this section we use various types of charts to visualize and analyze data.

In the fall of 1999, freshmen at 462 colleges in the United States answered an extensive questionnaire.[1] One question asked each student to give the highest degree they planned to pursue. Table 1 gives the tallies for the six most common responses. Such a table is often referred to as a *frequency table* since it presents the frequency with which each response occurs.

---

[1] The detailed results of the questionnaire are given in *The American Freshman: National Norms for Fall 1999* (Los Angeles: American Council on Education, 2000, UCLA).

Table 1		
Highest Degree Planned	**Number**	**Percent**
Associate	10,187	4.1
Bachelor's	69,745	27.9
Master's	104,748	41.9
Law	37,093	14.8
Medical	19,069	7.6
Doctorate	9,404	3.8
Total	250,246	

Bar Charts   The numbers from the example in Table 1 are displayed in the *bar chart* of Fig. 1. This pictorial display gives a good feel for the relative number of students planning to earn each degree.

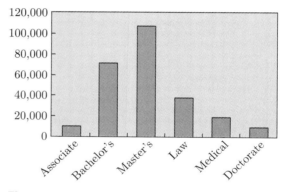

Figure 1. Bar chart for highest degree planned.

The percentages in the right column of Table 1 give the percent of the students out of this group of 250,246 students who plan to pursue each degree. The bar chart for the percentages is shown in Fig. 2. It looks exactly like the bar chart in Fig. 1. The only difference is the labeling of the tick marks along the y-axis.

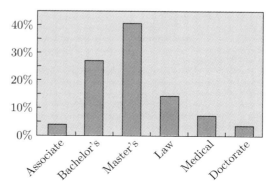

Figure 2.

Pie Charts   Another popular type of chart that can be used to display data consisting of several categories is the *pie chart*. It consists of a circle subdivided into sectors (slices of pie), where each sector corresponds to a category. The area of each sector is proportional to the percentage of items in that category. This is accomplished by making the central angle of each sector equal to 360° times the percentage associated with the segment.

▶ Example 1   Create a pie chart for the "highest degree planned" data. Label each sector with its category and percentage.

Solution   Step 1. Use the rightmost column of Table 1 to obtain the central angles for the sectors. See Table 2.

Step 2. Draw a circle, draw a horizontal radius line extending from the center of the circle, and then use a protractor to draw an angle of measure approximately 14.8° with the radius line as the initial side of the angle. See Fig. 3(a).

Step 3. Draw an angle of approximately 100.4°, using the terminal side of the angle drawn in Step 2 as the initial side. See Fig. 3(b).

Step 4. Continue as in Step 3 to draw each sector, and then label the sectors with their categories and percentages.   ◆

Table 2

Highest Degree Planned	Percent	360° × Percent
Associate	4.1	14.8°
Bachelor's	27.9	100.4°
Master's	41.9	150.8°
Law	14.8	53.3°
Medical	7.6	27.4°
Doctorate	3.8	13.7°

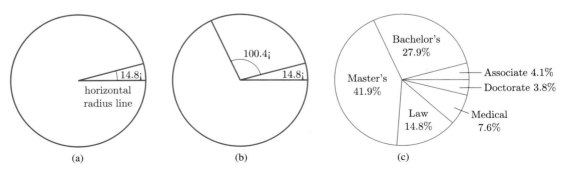

Figure 3. Pie chart for highest degree planned.

Histograms In the "highest degree planned" example, the responses to the question were words. The data to be organized consisted of six different words, where each occurred with a high frequency. In many cases to be analyzed, the data are a collection of numbers. For instance, the data could consist of ages, weights, or test scores of individuals. In such cases, the x-axis in a bar chart is labeled with numbers, as in an ordinary x-y coordinate system, and the data are referred to as *numerical data*. The bars in this type of bar chart have no space between them, and the bar chart is called a *histogram*.

▶ Example 2   Figure 4 gives the quiz scores for a class of 25 students.

$$8 \quad 7 \quad 6 \quad 10 \quad 5 \quad 10 \quad 7 \quad 1 \quad 8 \quad 0 \quad 10 \quad 5 \quad 9 \quad 3 \quad 8 \quad 6 \quad 10 \quad 4 \quad 9 \quad 10 \quad 7 \quad 0 \quad 9 \quad 5 \quad 8$$

Figure 4.

(a) Organize the data into a frequency table.

(b) Create a histogram for the data.

Solution   (a) An easy way to count the number of exams for each score is to write down the numbers from 0 through 10, and considering the quiz papers one at a time, make a slash mark alongside the score for each paper. Such a tabulation produces Table 3(a). In Table 3(b) the slash marks have been totaled.

Table 3		Tabulation of Quiz Scores		
10	⟋⟋⟋⟋		10	5
9	///		9	3
8	////		8	4
7	///		7	3
6	//		6	2
5	///		5	3
4	/		4	1
3	/		3	1
2			2	0
1	/		1	1
0	//		0	2
	(a)			(b)

(b) The histogram (see Fig. 5) is drawn on an x-y coordinate system. Note that each bar is centered over its corresponding score. This is accomplished by having the base of each bar extend one-half unit on each side of its score. For instance, the base of the bar corresponding to a score of 10 extends from 9.5 to 10.5.   ◆

The steps required to create and explore the histogram with a TI-83 graphing calculator are shown in Figures 6 through 11. (The details of carrying out the task are presented in Appendix B.) For Figs. 6 and 7, the stat list editor was invoked with $\boxed{\text{STAT}}$ **1**, the scores were placed in the L_1 column, and their frequencies

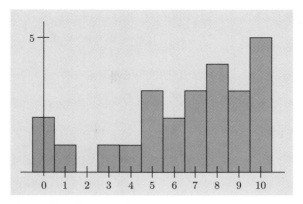

Figure 5. Histogram for quiz scores.

were placed in the L_2 column. The screen in Fig. 8 was invoked with [2nd] [STAT PLOT] **1**. "On" was selected in the On/Off row, the histogram icon was selected as the Type, Xlist was left at its default value "L_1", and Freq was set to L_2. In Fig. 9, Xmin was set to the left coordinate of the first rectangle, Xmax was set to the right coordinate of the last rectangle, Xscl was set to the length of the base of each rectangle, and Ymin and Ymax were set to be large enough to display the rectangles. Pressing [GRAPH] produced the screen in Fig. 10. In Fig. 11, [TRACE] was pressed and the cursor moved to the rectangle corresponding to a score of 8. The numbers at the bottom of the screen say that the rectangle extends from 7.5 to 8.5 on the x-axis and that $n = 4$ students had grades of 8 on the quiz.

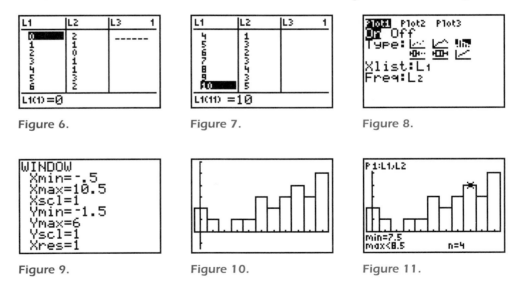

Figure 6.   Figure 7.   Figure 8.

Figure 9.   Figure 10.   Figure 11.

Median, Quartiles, and Box Plots   When an instructor returns exam papers, he or she usually gives students some indication of how they did overall. Occasionally the instructor gives the average of the grades, and perhaps the standard deviation. (These two topics are discussed extensively in the remainder of this chapter.) However, most instructors state the *median* of the grade distribution. The median grade is the grade that divides the bottom 50% of the grades from the top 50%. To find the median of a set of N numbers, first arrange the numbers in increasing or decreasing order. The median is the middle number if N is odd and the average of the two middle numbers if N is even.

▶ Example 3   Find the medians of the following two sets of data.

(a) Tiger Woods's four rounds of golf in the 1997 U.S. Masters tournament:
70   66   65   69

(b) The 25 quiz scores discussed in Example 2

Solution   (a) Here $N = 4$, an even number. Arranged in increasing order, the four scores are

$$65, \ 66, \ 69, \ 70.$$

The middle two scores are 66 and 69. The median is their average. Therefore,

$$\text{median} = \frac{66 + 69}{2} = \frac{135}{2} = 67.5.$$

(b) Here $N = 25$, an odd number. The position of the middle number is $\frac{25 + 1}{2} = 13$. The tabulation of quiz scores in Table 3 can be used instead of an ordering of the scores. The median will be the thirteenth highest score. Adding up the numbers of scores of 10's, 9's, and 8's gives 12 scores. Therefore, the thirteenth score must be a 7. That is, the median is 7.   ◆

Graphing calculators can display a picture, called a *box plot*, that analyzes a set of data and shows not only the median, but also the *quartiles*. The quartiles are the medians of the sets of data below and above the median. The median of the numbers less than the median is called the first quartile and is denoted Q_1. The median of the numbers greater than the median is called the third quartile and is denoted by Q_3. A box plot also is useful in showing pictorially the spread of the data. Figure 12 gives the box plot on a TI-83 for the set of 25 quiz scores presented in Example 1. The steps for obtaining the box plot are the same as for the histogram as shown in Figs. 6 through 10, with the exception that in Fig. 8 the fifth icon is selected.

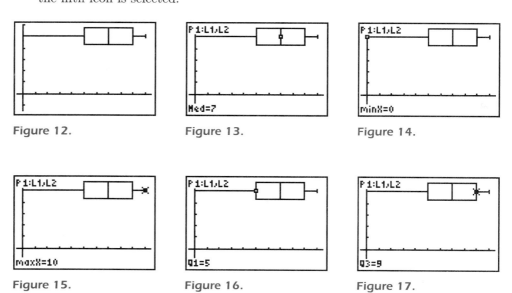

Figure 12.   Figure 13.   Figure 14.

Figure 15.   Figure 16.   Figure 17.

Figure 13, which shows the median, appears when $\boxed{\text{TRACE}}$ is pressed. Pressing the arrow keys reveals the smallest quiz score (minX), the largest quiz score (maxX), and the first and third quartiles. See Figs. 14–17.

Figure 18 shows the five pieces of information given by a box plot. This information is referred to as the *five-number summary* of the data. The median is also called the second quartile and is denoted Q_2. Essentially, the three quartiles divide the data into four approximately equal parts, each part consisting of roughly 25% of the numbers. The length of the rectangular part of the box plot, which is $Q_3 - Q_1$, is called the *interquartile range*. The quartiles provide information about the dispersion of the data. The interquartile range is the length of the interval in which approximately the middle 50% of the data lie.

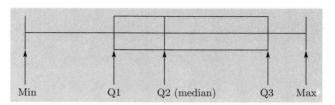

Figure 18. A general box plot.

▶ **Example 4**   Find the five-number summary and the interquartile range for the following set of numbers: 1   3   6   10   15   21   28   36   45   55.

Solution   The numbers are given in ascending order, and there are 10 numbers. Immediately we see that min = 1 and max = 55. The next number to be found is the median. Since 10 is an even number, the median is the average of the middle two numbers.

$$1 \quad 3 \quad 6 \quad 10 \quad \mathbf{15} \quad \mathbf{21} \quad 28 \quad 36 \quad 45 \quad 55$$

That is,

$$Q_2 = \text{median} = \frac{15 + 21}{2} = 18.$$

The numbers to the left of the median are 1   3   6   10   15, and the numbers to the right of the median are 21   28   36   45   55. These lists have medians 6 and 36, respectively. Therefore, $Q_1 = 6$, $Q_3 = 36$, and the interquartile range is $Q_3 - Q_1 = 30$.   ◆

| **Practice Problems 7.1** | Suppose a list consists of 17 numbers in increasing order. Clearly the first number is the min and the last number is the max. |

1. Which number in the list is the median?

2. Which numbers in the list are used to obtain the first quartile?

3. Which numbers in the list are used to obtain the third quartile?

▶ Exercises 7.1

In Exercises 1–4, display the data in a bar chart that shows frequencies on the *y*-axis.

1. 1998 School Enrollments (in millions)

Type	Enrollment
Elementary	38.1
Secondary	14.7
College	14.6

Source: U.S. Dept. of Education, National Center for Education Statistics, *Digest of Educational Statistics*, 1998.

2. 1998 U.S. Defense Employees

Branch	Officers and Enlistees
Army	483,880
Navy	382,338
Marine Corps	173,142
Air Force	367,470

Source: U.S. Dept. of Defense, *Defense '99*.

3. Areas of the Great Lakes

Lake	Area (sq mi)
Superior	31,700
Michigan	22,300
Huron	23,100
Erie	9,910
Ontario	7,550

Source: *Encyclopedia Britannica*.

4. Bachelor's Degrees Earned in 1996, by Field

Field of Study	Number of Degrees
Business	227,102
Social Sciences	126,479
Education	105,509
Health Sciences	84,036
Engineering	77,437
Psychology	73,291
Other	470,938

Source: U.S. National Center for Education Statistics, *Digest of Education Statistics*, annual.

5. Display the data from the table in Exercise 1 in a bar chart showing percentages on the *y*-axis.

6. Display the data from the table in Exercise 2 in a bar chart showing percentages on the *y*-axis.

7. Display the data from the table in Exercise 1 in a pie chart.

8. Display the data from the table in Exercise 2 in a pie chart.

9. Display the data from the table in Exercise 3 in a pie chart.

10. Display the data from the table in Exercise 4 in a pie chart.

Exercises 11 and 12 refer to the pie chart in Fig. 3(c).

11. What is the probability that a freshman selected at random in the fall of 1999 planned to obtain a Master's or Doctorate degree?

12. What is the probability that a freshman selected at random in the fall of 1999 planned to obtain a medical or law degree?

13. The ages at inauguration of the 41 presidents from George Washington to Bill Clinton are shown. Draw a histogram for the ages.

    57, 61, 57, 57, 58, 57, 61, 54, 68, 51, 49, 64, 50,
    48, 65, 52, 56, 46, 54, 49, 50, 47, 55, 54, 42, 51,
    56, 55, 51, 54, 51, 60, 62, 43, 55, 56, 61, 52, 69,
    64, 46

14. The number of tie-breaking votes cast by each of the 21 vice presidents of the United States who served during the twentieth century are shown. Draw a histogram for these data.

    0, 0, 4, 10, 0, 2, 3, 3, 4, 1, 7,
    8, 0, 4, 2, 0, 0, 1, 7, 0, 4

In Exercises 15 and 16, draw the box plot corresponding to the given five-number summary.

15. min $= 2$, $Q_1 = 5$, $Q_2 = 7$, $Q_3 = 10$, max $= 15$

16. min $= 10$, $Q_1 = 13$, $Q_2 = 17$, $Q_3 = 20$, max $= 25$

In Exercises 17–20, find the five-number summary and the interquartile range for the given set of numbers, and then draw the box plot.

17. 10, 11, 13, 14, 16, 17, 19, 20, 21, 23, 24

18. 3, 6, 8, 9, 11, 14, 18

19. 20, 25, 31, 38, 42, 47, 51, 54, 56

20. 7, 17, 26, 34, 41, 47, 52, 56, 59, 61

21. Match each of the histograms in column I with the corresponding box plot in column II.

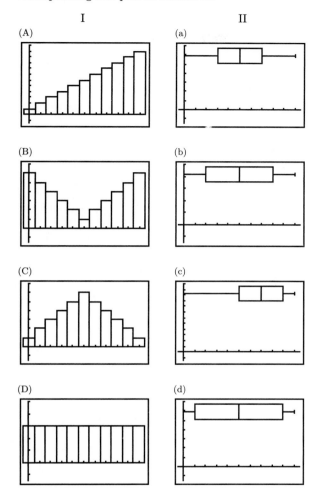

I   II

(A)   (a)

(B)   (b)

(C)   (c)

(D)   (d)

22. The box plot for the price (in cents) of a can of tomato soup is shown.

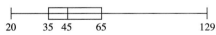

  20   35 45   65   129

(a) Approximately what percentage of the soups are priced below 35 cents?

(b) Approximately what percentage of the soups are priced above 65 cents?

(c) Approximately what percentage of the soups are priced below 45 cents?

(d) Approximately what percentage of the soups are priced between 45 and 65 cents?

(e) What is the median price of a can of soup?

23. Consider the following box plot of scores on a standardized test.

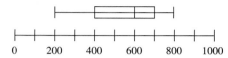

   0   200   400   600   800   1000

(a) Give the five-number summary of the data.

(b) Approximately what percentage of the scores is below 400?

(c) Approximately what percentage of the scores is between 400 and 600?

(d) Approximately what percentage of the scores is higher than 600?

(e) Approximately what percentage of the scores is between 200 and 700?

24. On April 14, 2000 the American League and National League (baseball) leaders were listed in the *New York Times* with their batting averages. Compare the data using a box plot and discuss which of the leagues seems to have the better players.

American League: .476, .457, .433, .432, .429, .414, .412, .412, .406, .400

National League: .500, .486, .433, .425, .423, .421, .389, .389, .382, .381

25. The Atlanta Braves played baseball against the Milwaukee Brewers in April 2000. The batting averages of each team's players (except for pitchers and designated hitters) on that day were as follows:

Braves: .229, .243, .317, .281, .296, .200, .345, .227, .350, .286

Brewers: .317, .150, .270, .333, .250, .200, .359, .280, .091

Draw a box plot for each team and comment on which team seems to be more likely to win. Explain your answer.

Solutions to Practice Problems 7.1

1. Since there are an odd number of numbers in the list, the middle number (that is, the ninth number) is the median. *Note:* When N, the number of numbers, is odd, the median is the $\frac{N+1}{2}$th number.

2. There are 8 numbers in the truncated list consisting of the numbers to the left of the median. Since 8 is even, the median of this truncated list is the average of the middle two numbers. That is, the first quartile is the average of the fourth and fifth numbers. *Note*: When N is even, the median of a list of N numbers is the average of the $\frac{N}{2}$th number and the number following the $\frac{N}{2}$th number.

3. There are 8 numbers in the truncated list consisting of the numbers to the right of the median. Since 8 is even, the median of this truncated list is the average of the middle two numbers of the truncated list. So the third quartile is the average of the fourth and fifth numbers of the truncated list; that is, the average of the thirteenth and fourteenth numbers of the original list.

7.2 Frequency and Probability Distributions

Our goal in this section is to describe a given set of data in terms that allow for interpretation and comparison. As we shall see, both graphical and tabular displays of data can be useful for this purpose.

Our modern technological society has a fetish about gathering statistical data. It is hardly possible to glance at a newspaper or a magazine and not be confronted with massive arrays of statistics gathered from studies of schools, churches, the economy, and so forth. One of the chief tasks confronting us is to interpret in a meaningful way the data collected and to make decisions based on our interpretations. The mathematical tools for doing this belong to that part of mathematics called statistics.

To get an idea of the problems considered in statistics, let us consider a concrete example. Mr. Jones, a businessman, is interested in purchasing a car dealership. Two dealerships are for sale, and each dealer has provided him with data describing past sales. Dealership A provided 1 year's worth of data, dealership B, 2 years' worth. The data are summarized in Table 1. The problem confronting Mr. Jones is that of analyzing the data to determine which car dealership to buy.

Table 1

Weekly sales	Number of occurrences	
	Dealership A	Dealership B
5	2	20
6	2	0
7	13	0
8	20	10
9	10	12
10	4	50
11	1	12

These data are presented in a form often used in statistical surveys. For each possible value of a statistical variable (in this case the number of cars sold weekly) we have tabulated the number of occurrences. Such a tabulation is called a *frequency distribution*. Although a frequency distribution is a very useful way of displaying and summarizing survey data, it is by no means the most efficient form in which to analyze such data. For example, it is difficult to compare dealership A with dealership B using only Table 1.

Comparisons are much more easily made if we use proportions rather than actual numbers of occurrences. For example, instead of recording that dealership A had weekly sales of 5 cars during 2 weeks of the year, let us record that the proportion of the observed weeks in which dealership A had weekly sales of 5 was $\frac{2}{52} \approx .04$. Similarly, by dividing each of the entries in the right column by 52, we obtain a new table describing the sales of dealership A (Table 2).[1] We similarly can construct a new table for dealership B (Table 3).

Table 2	
Weekly sales	**Proportion of occurrences, dealership A**
5	$\frac{2}{52} \approx .04$
6	$\frac{2}{52} \approx .04$
7	$\frac{13}{52} = .25$
8	$\frac{20}{52} \approx .38$
9	$\frac{10}{52} \approx .19$
10	$\frac{4}{52} \approx .08$
11	$\frac{1}{52} \approx .02$

Table 3	
Weekly sales	**Proportion of occurrences, dealership B**
5	$\frac{20}{104} \approx .19$
6	0
7	0
8	$\frac{10}{104} \approx .10$
9	$\frac{12}{104} \approx .12$
10	$\frac{50}{104} \approx .48$
11	$\frac{12}{104} \approx .12$

These tables are called *relative frequency distributions*. In general, consider an experiment with the numerical outcomes $x_1, x_2, \ldots, x_r$. Suppose that the number of occurrences of x_1 is f_1, the number of occurrences of x_2 is f_2, and so forth (Table 4). The frequency distribution lists all the outcomes of the experiment and the number of times each occurred. (For the sake of simplicity, we usually arrange $x_1, x_2, \ldots, x_r$ in increasing order.)

Table 4		
Outcome	**Frequency**	**Relative frequency**
x_1	f_1	f_1/n
x_2	f_2	f_2/n
$\vdots$	$\vdots$	$\vdots$
x_r	f_r	f_r/n
Total n		1

Suppose that the total number of occurrences is n. Then the relative frequency of outcome x_1 is f_1/n, the relative frequency of outcome x_2 is f_2/n, and

---

[1] For simplification we shall round off the data of this example to two decimal places.

so forth. The relative frequency distribution pairs each outcome with its relative frequency. The sum of the frequencies in a frequency distribution is n. The sum of the relative frequencies in a relative frequency distribution is 1.

The frequency or relative frequency distribution is obtained directly from the performance of an experiment and the collection of data observed at each trial of the experiment. For example, we might imagine a coin-tossing experiment in which a coin is tossed five times and the number of occurrences of heads is observed. On each performance of the experiment we might observe 0, 1, 2, 3, 4, or 5 heads. We could repeat the experiment, say 90 times, and record the outcomes. We have collected data like that in Table 5. While doing the experiment we would record the frequencies $f_0, f_1, f_2, \ldots, f_5$ of the various outcomes and then divide by 90 to obtain the relative frequencies $f_0/90, f_1/90, f_2/90, \ldots, f_5/90$. The sum of the frequency column is the number of trials of the experiment (here, 90), and the sum of the relative frequency column is 1.

Table 5

Number of heads	Frequency	Relative frequency
0	3	$\frac{3}{90} \approx .03$
1	14	$\frac{14}{90} \approx .16$
2	23	$\frac{23}{90} \approx .26$
3	27	$\frac{27}{90} = .30$
4	17	$\frac{17}{90} \approx .19$
5	6	$\frac{6}{90} \approx .07$
Total	90	$\frac{90}{90} = 1.00$

It is often possible to gain useful insight into an experiment by representing its relative frequency distribution in graphical form. For instance, let us graph the relative frequency distribution for car dealership A. Begin by drawing a number line (Fig. 1).

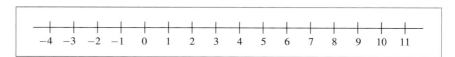

Figure 1.

The numbers that represent possible outcomes of the experiment (weekly car sales) are 5, 6, 7, 8, 9, 10, 11. Locate each of these numbers on the number line. Above each number erect a rectangle whose base is one unit wide and whose height is the relative frequency of that number. Above the number 5, for example, we draw a rectangle of height .04. The completed graph is shown in Fig. 2. For the sake of comparison we have also drawn a graph of the relative frequency distribution for dealership B.

Graphs of the type just drawn are called *histograms*. They vividly illustrate the data being considered. For example, comparison of the histograms of Fig. 2 reveals significant differences between the two dealerships. On the one hand, dealership A is very consistent. Most weeks its sales are in the middle range of 7, 8, or 9. On the other hand, dealership B can often achieve very high sales (it had

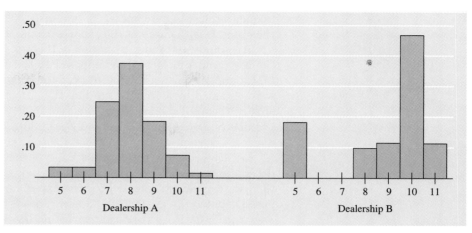

Figure 2.

sales of 10 in 48% of the weeks) at the expense of a significant number of weeks of low sales (sales of 5 in 19% of the weeks). The histogram for the coin-tossing experiment recorded previously appears in Fig. 3.

It is possible to use histograms to represent the relative frequency of events as areas. To illustrate the procedure, consider the histogram corresponding to dealership A. Each rectangle has width 1 and height equal to the relative frequency of a particular outcome of the experiment. For instance, the highest rectangle is centered over the number 8 and has height .38, the relative frequency of the outcome 8. Note that the area of the rectangle is

$$\text{area} = (\text{height})(\text{width}) = (.38)(1) = .38.$$

In other words, the area of the rectangle equals the relative frequency of the corresponding outcome. We have verified this in the case of the outcome 8, but it is true in general. In a similar fashion, we may represent the relative frequency of more complicated events as areas. Consider, for example, the event $E =$ "sales between 7 and 10, inclusive." This event consists of the set of outcomes $\{7, 8, 9, 10\}$, and so its relative frequency is the sum of the respective relative

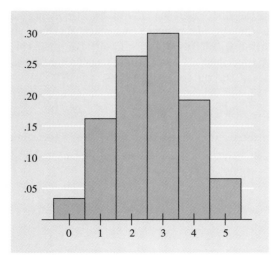

Figure 3. Relative frequency distribution for number of heads in 5 tosses—experimental results.

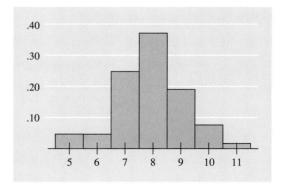

Figure 4.

frequencies of the outcomes 7, 8, 9, and 10. Therefore, the relative frequency of the event E is the area of the shaded region of the histogram in Fig. 4.

An important thing to notice is that so far we have made the tables and the histograms for actual, as opposed to theoretical, experiments. That is, the tables and the histograms were produced from collections of sample data that were obtained by actually recording the outcomes of experiments. We shall now look at theoretical experiments and continue to explore the important notion of *probability distribution*. In many cases, data of an actual experiment are best interpreted when we can construct a theoretical model for the experiment.

Let us reconsider the coin-tossing experiment in which a coin was tossed five times and the number of occurrences of heads recorded. If the coins are fair coins, then we can set up a model for the experiment by noting once again that the possible outcomes are 0, 1, 2, 3, 4, or 5 heads. We will construct the *probability distribution* for this experiment by listing the outcomes in the sample space with their probabilities. The probabilities of 0, 1, 2, 3, 4, 5 heads can be obtained with the methods of Chapter 6. The number of distinct sequences of 5 tosses is 2^5, or 32. The number of sequences having k heads (and $5 - k$ tails) is

$$C(5, k) = \binom{5}{k}.$$

Thus

$$\Pr(k \text{ heads}) = \frac{\binom{5}{k}}{2^5} \qquad (k = 0, 1, 2, 3, 4, 5).$$

The probability distribution for the experiment is shown in Table 6.

The histogram for a probability distribution is constructed in the same way as the histogram for a relative frequency distribution. Each outcome is represented on the number line, and above each outcome we erect a rectangle of width 1 and of height equal to the probability corresponding to that outcome (see Fig. 5).

We note that the histogram in Fig. 5 is based on a theoretical model of coin tossing, whereas the histogram in Fig. 3 was drawn from experimental results only available after the experiment is actually performed and observed.

Just as we used the histogram for the relative frequency distribution to picture the relative frequency of an event, we may also use the histogram of a probability distribution to picture the probability of an event. For instance, to find the probability of at least 3 heads on 5 tosses of a fair coin, we need only add the probabilities of the outcomes: 3 heads, 4 heads, 5 heads. That is,

$$\Pr(\text{at least 3 heads}) = \Pr(3 \text{ heads}) + \Pr(4 \text{ heads}) + \Pr(5 \text{ heads}).$$

Since each of these probabilities is equal to the area of a rectangle in the histogram of Fig. 5, the area of the shaded region in Fig. 6 equals the probability of the event. This result is a special case of the following fact:

In a histogram of a probability distribution, the probability of an event E is the sum of the areas of the rectangles corresponding to the outcomes in E.

Table 6

Number of heads	Probability
0	$\dfrac{\binom{5}{0}}{2^5} = \dfrac{1}{32}$
1	$\dfrac{\binom{5}{1}}{2^5} = \dfrac{5}{32}$
2	$\dfrac{\binom{5}{2}}{2^5} = \dfrac{10}{32}$
3	$\dfrac{\binom{5}{3}}{2^5} = \dfrac{10}{32}$
4	$\dfrac{\binom{5}{4}}{2^5} = \dfrac{5}{32}$
5	$\dfrac{\binom{5}{5}}{2^5} = \dfrac{1}{32}$

▶ Example 1   The histogram of a probability distribution is as given in Fig. 7. Shade in the portion of the histogram whose area is the probability of the event "more than 50."

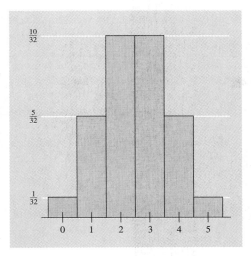

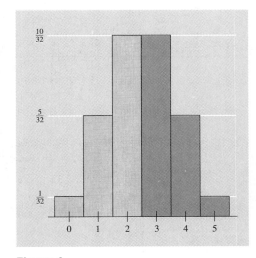

Figure 5. Probability distribution for number of heads in 5 tosses—theoretical results.

Figure 6.

Solution   The event "more than 50" is the set of outcomes $\{51, 52, 53, 54, 55, 56, 57, 58, 59\}$. So we shade in the portion of the histogram corresponding to these outcomes (Fig. 8). The area of the shaded region is the probability of the event "more than 50." ◆

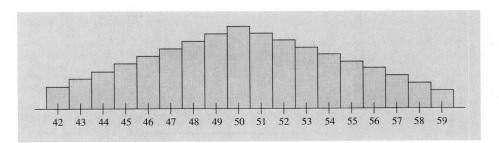

Figure 7.

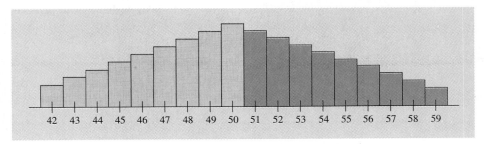

Figure 8.

Random Variables   Consider a theoretical experiment with numerical outcomes. Denote the outcome of the experiment by the letter X. For example, if the experiment consists of observing the number of heads in five tosses of a fair coin, then X assumes one of the six values 0, 1, 2, 3, 4, 5. Since the values of

X are determined by the unpredictable random outcomes of the experiment, X is called a *random variable* or, more specifically, the *random variable associated with the experiment.*

The random variable notation is often convenient and is commonly used in probability and statistics texts. In considering several different experiments, it is sometimes necessary to use letters other than X to stand for random variables. It is customary, however, to use only capital letters, such as X, Y, Z, W, U, V, for random variables.

If k is one of the possible outcomes of the experiment with associated random variable X, then we denote the probability of the outcome k by

$$\Pr(X = k).$$

For example, in the coin-tossing experiment described previously, if X is the number of heads in the five tosses, then

$$\Pr(X = 3)$$

denotes the probability of getting 3 heads. The probability distribution of the random variable X is shown in Table 7.

Rather than speak of the probability distribution associated with the model of an experiment, we can speak of the *probability distribution associated with the corresponding random variable.* Such a probability distribution is a table listing the various values of X (i.e., outcomes of the experiment) and their associated probabilities with $p_1 + p_2 + \cdots + p_r = 1$:

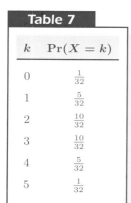

Table 7

k	$\Pr(X = k)$
0	$\frac{1}{32}$
1	$\frac{5}{32}$
2	$\frac{10}{32}$
3	$\frac{10}{32}$
4	$\frac{5}{32}$
5	$\frac{1}{32}$

k	$\Pr(X = k)$
x_1	p_1
x_2	p_2
$\vdots$	$\vdots$
x_r	p_r

▶ **Example 2**   Consider the urn of Example 2 of Section 6.4, in which there are eight white balls and two green balls. A sample of three balls is chosen at random from the urn. Let X denote the number of green balls in the sample. Find the probability distribution of X.

Solution   As in Example 2 of Section 6.4, we note that there are $N = \binom{10}{3} = 120$ equally likely outcomes. X can be 0, 1, or 2. From that example we conclude that

$$\Pr(X = 1) = \frac{56}{120} = \frac{7}{15} \quad \text{and} \quad \Pr(X = 2) = \frac{8}{120} = \frac{1}{15}.$$

$\Pr(X = 0)$ can be found by noting that there are

$$\binom{2}{0}\binom{8}{3} = (1)(56)$$

elements in the event "no greens." Hence,

$$\Pr(X = 0) = \frac{56}{120} = \frac{7}{15}.$$

The probability distribution for X is given by the following table.

k	$\Pr(X = k)$
0	$\frac{7}{15}$
1	$\frac{7}{15}$
2	$\frac{1}{15}$

◆

▶ **Example 3** Let X denote the random variable defined as the sum of the upper faces appearing when two dice are thrown. Determine the probability distribution of X and draw its histogram.

Solution The experiment of throwing two dice leads to 36 possibilities, each having probability $\frac{1}{36}$.

$$
\begin{array}{cccccc}
(1,1) & (1,2) & (1,3) & (1,4) & (1,5) & (1,6) \\
(2,1) & (2,2) & (2,3) & (2,4) & (2,5) & (2,6) \\
(3,1) & (3,2) & (3,3) & (3,4) & (3,5) & (3,6) \\
(4,1) & (4,2) & (4,3) & (4,4) & (4,5) & (4,6) \\
(5,1) & (5,2) & (5,3) & (5,4) & (5,5) & (5,6) \\
(6,1) & (6,2) & (6,3) & (6,4) & (6,5) & (6,6)
\end{array}
$$

The sum of the numbers in each pair gives the value of X. For example, the pair $(3,1)$ corresponds to $X = 4$. Note that the pairs corresponding to a given value of X lie on a diagonal, as shown in the preceding chart, where we have indicated all pairs corresponding to $X = 4$. It is now easy to calculate the number of pairs corresponding to a given value k of X and from it the probability $\Pr(X = k)$. For example, there are three pairs adding to 4, so

$$\Pr(X = 4) = \tfrac{3}{36} = \tfrac{1}{12}.$$

Performing this calculation for all k from 2 to 12 gives the following probability distribution and the histogram shown in Fig. 9.

k	$\Pr(X = k)$	k	$\Pr(X = k)$
2	$\frac{1}{36}$	8	$\frac{5}{36}$
3	$\frac{1}{18}$	9	$\frac{1}{9}$
4	$\frac{1}{12}$	10	$\frac{1}{12}$
5	$\frac{1}{9}$	11	$\frac{1}{18}$
6	$\frac{5}{36}$	12	$\frac{1}{36}$
7	$\frac{1}{6}$		

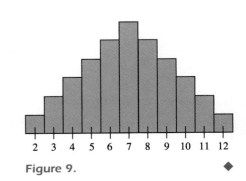

Figure 9.

◆

The advantage of the random variable notation is that the variable X can be treated algebraically and we can consider expressions such as X^2. This is just the random variable corresponding to the experiment whose outcomes are the squares of the outcomes of the original experiment. Similarly, we can consider random variables such as $X + 3$ and $(X - 2)^2$. One important example of algebraic manipulation of random variables appears in Section 7.5. There are many others.

▶ Example 4   Suppose that a random variable X has probability distribution given by the following table:

k	$\Pr(X = k)$
-1	.2
0	.3
1	.1
2	.4

Determine the probability distribution of the random variable X^2.

Solution   The outcomes of X^2 are the squares of the outcomes of X. The probabilities of the outcomes of X^2 are determined by the probabilities of the outcomes of X. The possible outcomes of X^2 are $k = 1$ (which results from the case $X = -1$ or from the case $X = 1$), $k = 0$, and $k = 4$. Since

$$\Pr(X^2 = 1) = \Pr(X = -1) + \Pr(X = 1),$$

the probability distribution of X^2 is as follows.

k	$\Pr(X^2 = k)$
0	.3
1	.3
4	.4

Practice Problems 7.2

1. In a certain carnival game a wheel is divided into five equal parts, of which two are red and three are white. The player spins the wheel until the marker lands on "red" or until three spins have occurred. The number of spins is observed. Determine the probability distribution for this experiment.

2. Refer to the carnival game of Problem 1. Suppose that the player pays $1 to play this game and receives 50 cents for each spin. Determine the probability distribution for the experiment of playing the game and observing the player's earnings.

▶ Exercises 7.2

1. Table 8 gives the frequency distribution for the final grades in a course. (Here A = 4, B = 3, C = 2, D = 1, F = 0). Determine the relative frequency distribution associated with these data and draw the associated histogram.

Table 8

Grade	Number of occurrences
0	2
1	3
2	10
3	6
4	4

2. The number of cars waiting to be served at a gas station was counted at the beginning of every minute during the morning rush hour. The frequency distribution is given in Table 9. Determine the relative frequency distribution associated with these data and draw the histogram.

Table 9

Number of cars waiting	Number of occurrences
0	0
1	9
2	21
3	15
4	12
5	3

3. The telephone company counted the number of people dialing the weather each minute on a rainy morning from 5 A.M. to 6 A.M. The frequency distribution is given in Table 10. Determine the relative frequency distribution associated with these data.

4. A production manager counted the number of items produced each hour during a 40-hour workweek. The frequency distribution is given in Table 11. Determine the relative frequency distribution associated with these data.

5. A fair coin is tossed three times and the number of heads is observed. Determine the probability distribution for this experiment and draw its histogram.

Table 10

Number of calls during minute	Number of occurrences
20	3
21	3
22	0
23	6
24	18
25	12
26	0
27	9
28	6
29	3

Table 11

Number produced during hour	Number of occurrences
50	2
51	0
52	4
53	6
54	14
55	8
56	4
57	0
58	0
59	2

6. An urn contains three red balls and four white balls. A sample of three balls is selected at random and the number of red balls observed. Determine the probability distribution for this experiment and draw its histogram.

7. An archer can hit the bull's-eye of the target with probability $\frac{1}{3}$. She shoots until she hits the bull's-eye or until four shots have been taken. The number of shots is observed. Determine the probability distribution for this experiment.

8. A die is rolled and the number on the top face is observed. Determine the probability distribution for this experiment and draw its histogram.

9. In a certain carnival game the player selects two balls at random from an urn containing two red balls and four white balls. The player receives $5 if he draws two red balls and $1 if he draws one red ball. He loses $1 if no red balls are in the sample. Determine the probability distribution for the experiment of playing the game and observing the player's earnings.

10. In a certain carnival game a player pays $1 and then tosses a fair coin until either a "head" occurs or he has tossed the coin four times. He receives 50 cents for each toss. Determine the probability distribution for the experiment of playing the game and observing the player's earnings.

11. Figure 10 is the histogram for a probability distribution. What is the probability that the outcome is between 5 and 7, inclusive?

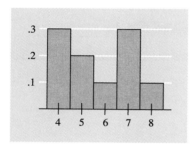

Figure 10.

12. Figure 11 is the histogram for a probability distribution. To what event do the shaded rectangles correspond?

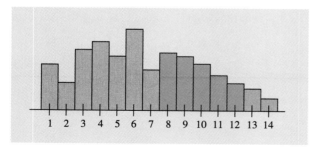

Figure 11.

Let the random variables X and Y have the probability distributions listed in Table 12. Determine the probability distributions of the random variables in Exercises 13–20.

Table 12

k	$\Pr(X = k)$	k	$\Pr(Y = k)$
0	.1	5	.3
1	.2	10	.4
2	.3	15	.1
3	.2	20	.1
4	.2	25	.1

13. X^2
14. Y^2
15. $X - 1$
16. $Y - 15$
17. $\frac{1}{5}Y$
18. $2X^2$
19. $(X + 1)^2$
20. $\left(\frac{1}{5}Y + 1\right)^2$

21. Two classes take the same examination and the grades are recorded in Table 13. We assigned the integers 0 through 4 to the grades F through A, respectively. Table 13 gives the frequency distribution of grades in each class. Find the relative frequency distribution and the histogram for each class. Describe the difference in the grade distributions for the two classes.

Table 13

		Number of students	
Grade		9 A.M. class	10 A.M. class
F	(0)	10	16
D	(1)	15	23
C	(2)	20	15
B	(3)	10	21
A	(4)	5	25

22. Using Table 13, answer the following questions.

   (a) What percentage of the students in the 9 A.M. class have grades of C or less?

   (b) What percentage of the 10 A.M. class have grades of C or less?

   (c) What percentage of the 9 A.M. class have grades of D or F?

   (d) What percentage of the students in both classes combined have grades of C or more?

Exercises 23–27 refer to the tables associated with Exercises 1–4.

23. For the data in Table 8, determine the percentage of students who get C or higher.

24. The data in Table 9 have been tabulated for every minute of the (60-minute) rush hour. What percentage of the time is the waiting line 4 or more cars?

25. Use the data in Table 10.

    (a) For what percentage of the 60 minutes from 5 A.M. to 6 A.M. are there either less than 22 or more than 27 calls to the weather number?

    (b) For what percentage of the hour are there between 23 and 25 calls (inclusive)?

    (c) Draw the histogram.

    (d) What would be your estimate of the average number of calls coming in during a minute of the hour for which the data have been tabulated? Explain.

26. Draw a histogram for the relative frequency distribution of Table 11.

27. For the data in Table 11, answer the following questions.

    (a) What is the highest number of items produced in any one hour?

    (b) What percentage of the time is that maximum number of items produced?

    (c) What number of items is produced with the highest frequency?

    (d) In what percentage of the 40 hours do production levels exceed 54 items?

    (e) Estimate the average number of items produced per hour in this week. Explain.

28. Assume that X and Y are random variables with the given probability distributions.

k	$\Pr(X = k)$	$\Pr(Y = k)$
1	.30	.20
2	.40	.20
3	.20	.20
4	.10	.40

(a) Draw the histogram for X.

(b) Draw the histogram for Y.

(c) Find $\Pr(X = 2 \text{ or } 3)$.

(d) Find $\Pr(Y = 2 \text{ or } 3)$.

(e) Find the probability that X is at least 2.

(f) Find the probability that $X + 3$ is at least 5.

(g) Find the probability that Y^2 is at most 9.

(h) Find the probability that Y is at most 10.

(i) Find the probability distribution of $2X$.

(j) Find the probability distribution of $(Y + 2)^2$.

(k) Which of X or Y has the higher average value? Why would you think so?

29. Here is the probability distribution of the random variable U.

k	$\Pr(U = k)$
0	$\frac{3}{15}$
1	$\frac{2}{15}$
2	$\frac{4}{15}$
3	$\frac{5}{15}$
4	?

(a) Determine the probability that $U = 4$.

(b) Find $\Pr(U \geq 2)$.

(c) Find the probability that U is at most 3.

(d) Find the probability that $U + 2$ is less than 4.

(e) Draw the histogram of the distribution of U.

Solutions to Practice Problems 7.2

1. Since the outcomes are the numbers of spins, there are three possible outcomes: one, two, and three spins. The probabilities for each of these outcomes can be computed from a tree diagram (Fig. 12). For instance, the outcome two (spins) occurs if the first spin lands on white and the second spin on red. The probability of this outcome is $\frac{3}{5} \cdot \frac{2}{5} = \frac{6}{25}$.

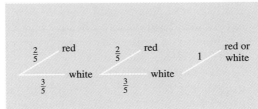

k	$\Pr(X = k)$
1	$\frac{2}{5}$
2	$\frac{6}{25}$
3	$\frac{9}{25}$

Figure 12.

Solutions to
Practice Problems
7.2 (Continued)

2. The same game is being played as in Problem 1, except that now the outcome we are concentrating on is the player's financial situation at the end of the game. The player's earnings depend on the number of spins as follows: one spin results in −$.50 earnings (i.e., a loss of 50 cents); two spins result in $0 earnings (i.e., breaking even); and three spins result in $.50 earnings (i.e., the player ends up ahead by 50 cents). The probabilities for these three situations are the same as before.

Earnings	Probability
−$.50	$\frac{2}{5}$
0	$\frac{6}{25}$
$.50	$\frac{9}{25}$

7.3 Binomial Trials

In this section we fix our attention on the simplest experiments: those with just two outcomes. These experiments, called *binomial trials* (or *Bernoulli trials*), occur in many applications. Here are some examples of binomial trials.

1. Toss a coin and observe the outcome, heads or tails.
2. Administer a drug to a sick individual and classify the reaction as "effective" or "ineffective."
3. Manufacture a light bulb and classify it as "nondefective" or "defective."

The outcomes of a binomial trial are usually called "success" and "failure." Of course, the labels "success" and "failure" need have no connection with the usual meanings of these words. For example, in experiment 2 we might label the outcome "ineffective" as "success" and "effective" as "failure." Throughout our discussion of binomial trials we will always denote the probability of "success" by p and probability of "failure" by q. Since a binomial trial has only two outcomes, we have $p + q = 1$, or

$$q = 1 - p. \tag{1}$$

Consider a particular binomial trial and the following experiment. Repeat the binomial trial n times and observe the number of successes that occur. Assume that the n successive trials are independent of one another. The fundamental problem of the theory of binomial trials is to calculate the probabilities of the outcomes of this experiment.

Let X be a random variable associated with the experiment. X is the number of "successes" in the n trials of the experiment. For example, if we toss a coin 20 times and assume that "heads" is a "success," then $X = 3$ means that the experiment resulted in 3 "heads" and 17 "tails." In an experiment of n trials, the number of "successes" can be any one of the numbers $0, 1, 2, \ldots, n$. These are the possible values of X.

We write $\Pr(X = k)$ to denote the probability that $X = k$, namely, the probability that k of the n trials result in success. As we saw in the coin-tossing experiment in Section 7.2, we can find the probability distribution of X using the methods of counting and basic probability principles developed earlier in the book.

If X is the number of "successes" in n independent trials, where in each trial the probability of a "success" is p, then

$$\Pr(X = k) = \binom{n}{k} p^k q^{n-k} \tag{2}$$

for $k = 0, 1, 2, \ldots, n$.

Note that the right side of (2) is one of the terms in the binomial expansion of $(p + q)^n$ (see Section 5.7). We say that X is a *binomial random variable* with parameters n and p. The derivation of (2) is given at the end of this section.

Let X be the number of heads in five tosses of a fair coin. Then X is a binomial random variable with parameters $p = \frac{1}{2}$ and $n = 5$. The calculation for this particular variable appears in Section 7.2. The probability distribution is

k	$\Pr(X = k)$
0	$\frac{1}{32}$
1	$\frac{5}{32}$
2	$\frac{10}{32}$
3	$\frac{10}{32}$
4	$\frac{5}{32}$
5	$\frac{1}{32}$

By (2)

$$\Pr(X = k) = \binom{5}{k} \left(\frac{1}{2}\right)^k \left(\frac{1}{2}\right)^{5-k}.$$

Substitution of the values of k (0, 1, 2, 3, 4, 5) in (2) gives the probabilities in the table.

▶ **Example 1** Each time at bat the probability that a baseball player gets a hit is .300. He comes up to bat four times in a game. Assume that his times at bat are independent trials. Find the probability that he gets (a) exactly two hits and (b) at least two hits.

Solution Each at-bat is considered an independent binomial trial. A "success" is a hit. So $p = .300$, $q = 1 - p = .700$, and $n = 4$. Therefore, X is the number of hits in four at-bats or the number of "successes" in 4 trials.

(a) We need to determine $\Pr(X = 2)$. From formula (2) with $k = 2$, we have

$$\Pr(X = 2) = \binom{4}{2}(.300)^2(.700)^{4-2} = 6(.09)(.49) = .2646.$$

(b) "At least two hits" means $X \geq 2$. Applying formula (2) with $k = 2$, 3, and 4, we have

$$\Pr(X \geq 2) = \Pr(X = 2) + \Pr(X = 3) + \Pr(X = 4)$$

$$= \binom{4}{2}(.300)^2(.700)^2 + \binom{4}{3}(.300)^3(.700)^1 + \binom{4}{4}(.300)^4(.700)^0$$

$$= 6(.09)(.49) + 4(.027)(.700) + 1(.0081)(1)$$

$$= .2646 + .0756 + .0081 = .3483.$$

So the batter can be expected to get at least two hits out of four at-bats in about 35% of the games. ◆

▶ Example 2   Statistics[1] show that 61% of all married women in the United States are in the labor force. Five married U.S. women are randomly selected. Find the probability that at least one of them is in the labor force. Assume that each selection is an independent binomial trial.

Solution   Let "success" be "in the labor force." Then

$$p = .61 \qquad q = 1 - p = .39 \quad \text{and} \quad n = 5.$$

Therefore, X is the number of women (out of the five selected) that are in the labor force. Then

$$\Pr(X \geq 1) = 1 - \Pr(X = 0) = 1 - \binom{5}{0}(.61)^0(.39)^5$$

$$\approx 1 - .009 = .991.$$

Thus, in a group of five randomly selected married U.S. women, there is about a 99.1% chance that at least one of them is in the labor force. ◆

▶ Example 3   A plumbing-supplies manufacturer produces faucet washers, which are packaged in boxes of 300. Quality control studies have shown that 2% of the washers are defective. What is the probability that a box of washers contains exactly 9 defective washers?

Solution   Deciding whether a single washer is or is not defective is a binomial trial. Since we wish to consider the number of defective washers in a box, let "success" be the outcome "defective." Then

$$p = .02 \qquad q = 1 - .02 = .98 \qquad n = 300.$$

The probability that 9 out of 300 washers are defective equals

$$\Pr(X = 9) = \binom{300}{9}(.02)^9(.98)^{291} \approx .07.$$ ◆

▶ Example 4   The recovery rate for a certain cattle disease is 25%. If 40 cattle are afflicted with the disease, what is the probability that exactly 10 will recover?

Solution   In this example the binomial trial consists of observing a single cow, with recovery as "success." Then

$$p = .25 \qquad q = 1 - .25 = .75 \qquad n = 40.$$

The probability of 10 successes is

$$\Pr(X = 10) = \binom{40}{10}(.25)^{10}(.75)^{30} \approx .14.$$ ◆

---

[1]Statistical Abstract of the United States; U.S. Census Bureau, 1999.

The numerical work in Examples 3 and 4 required a calculator [to compute, for example, $(.98)^{291}$]. In other problems the calculations can be stickier. Suppose, for example, that we return to Example 4. What is the probability that 16 or more cattle recover? Using formula (2) to compute the probabilities that $16, 17, \ldots, 40$ cattle recover, the desired probability is

$$\Pr(X = 16) + \Pr(X = 17) + \cdots + \Pr(X = 40)$$
$$= \binom{40}{16}(.25)^{16}(.75)^{24} + \binom{40}{17}(.25)^{17}(.75)^{23} + \cdots + \binom{40}{40}(.25)^{40}(.75)^{0}.$$

Each of the terms in this sum is difficult to compute. The thought of computing all of them should be sufficient motivation to seek an alternative approach. Fortunately, there is a reasonably simple method of approximating a sum of this type. We will illustrate the technique in Section 7.7.

Verification of Formula (2)   We first consider the case where $n = 3$ and then generalize. Consider a three-trial binomial experiment with two possible results (S or F) on each trial. Assume that the trials are independent and the probability of "S" on each trial is p. It follows that the probability of "F" on each trial is $1 - p$, which we denote by q. The tree in Fig. 1 represents the possible outcomes of the experiment.

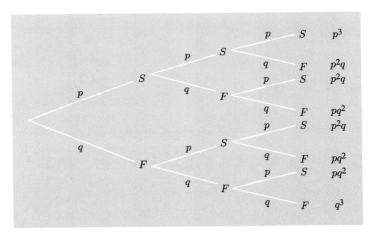

Figure 1.

The probability of each individual branch is obtained by multiplying the probabilities along the branch. Then, the probability of two successes in three trials, for example, is the sum of the probabilities of each branch representing two S's and one F. There are three such branches, each with probability p^2q. For the general case, suppose we want the probability of k successes in n trials. Each branch having k S's and $(n - k)$ F's has the associated probability $p^k q^{n-k}$. How many such branches are there in the tree? We can use the methods of Chapter 5 to count the number of branches with k S's and $(n - k)$ F's. What we want to know is the number of ways in which we can arrange k S's and $(n - k)$ F's. This is just $\binom{n}{k}$. So

$$\Pr(X = k) = \binom{n}{k} p^k q^{n-k}. \qquad \blacklozenge$$

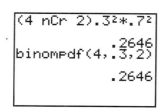

Figure 2.

GC Binomial probabilities are easily calculated on most graphing calculators. Let's solve Example 1. Figure 2 shows two ways to obtain the answer to part (a) on a TI-83. [To display **binompdf(**, press 2nd [DISTR] **0**. The general form of the command is **binompdf(n,p,x)**, where **x** is the number of successes.] With a TI-82, only the method in the first line of Fig. 2 is available.

A convenient way to work with binomial probabilities is to assign the formula for calculating probabilities to a function. In Fig. 3, the formula for **Y₁** can be used with any calculator; the formula for **Y₂** requires a TI-83. After the function has been defined, probabilities can be calculated (see Fig. 4), tables of probabilities can be displayed (see Fig. 5), and sums of consecutive probabilities can be calculated (see Fig. 6).

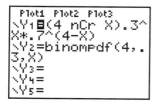

Figure 3.

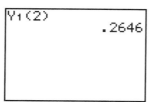

Figure 4.

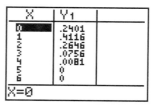

Figure 5.

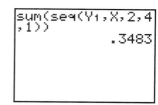

Figure 6.

To display **Y₁** on the home screen, press one of the following sequences of keys:

TI-83: VARS ▶ **1 1**

TI-82: 2nd [Y-VARS] **1 1**

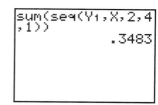

Figure 7.

To display a table, first press 2nd [TBLSET] to bring up the TABLE SETUP screen of Fig. 7. The table determined by the settings will have a column for **X** and a column for the values of each function that is selected in the **Y=** editor. The values for **X** will begin with the setting of **TblStart** (**TblMin** on the TI-82) and increase by the setting of **ΔTbl**. For our purposes, the settings for **Indpnt** and **Depend** should always be **Auto**. To see the table in Fig. 5, press 2nd [TABLE].

To add up consecutive probabilities, for instance, $\Pr(X = r)$ through $\Pr(X = s)$, use the command

$$\text{sum(seq(Y}_1\text{,X,}r\text{,}s\text{,1)).}$$

To display the word **sum**, press 2nd [LIST], move the cursor right to MATH, and press **5**. To display the word **seq**, press 2nd [LIST], if necessary move the cursor to OPS, and press **5**.

**Practice Problems
7.3**

1. A number is selected at random from the numbers 0 through 9999. What is the probability that the number is a multiple of 5?

2. If the experiment in Problem 1 is repeated 20 times, with replacement, what is the probability of getting four numbers that are multiples of 5?

▶ Exercises 7.3

1. A single die is tossed four times. Find the probability that exactly two of the tosses show a "one."

2. Find the probability of obtaining exactly three heads when tossing a fair coin six times.

3. A salesperson determines that the probability of making a sale to a customer is $\frac{1}{4}$. What is the probability of making a sale to three of the next four customers?

4. A basketball player makes free throws with probability .7. What is the probability of making exactly two out of five free throws?

5. Suppose that 60% of the voters in a state intend to vote for a certain candidate. What is the probability that a survey polling five people reveals that two or fewer intend to vote for that candidate?

6. An exam consists of six "true or false" questions. What is the probability that a person can get five or more correct by just guessing?

7. Sixty percent of all students at a university are female. A committee of five students is selected at random. Only one is a woman. Find the probability that no more than one woman is selected. What might be your conclusion about the way the committee was chosen?

8. Ten percent of all undergraduates at a university are chemistry majors. In a random sample of eight students, find the probability that exactly two are chemistry majors.

9. Thirty percent of all cars crossing a toll bridge have a commuter sticker. What is the probability that among 10 randomly selected cars waiting to cross the bridge at least 2 have commuter stickers?

10. Forty percent of a particular model of car are silver. What is the probability that in the next 10 observations of this model you observe 5 silver cars?

11. A die is tossed 12 times. What is the probability of at least two 5's?

12. Fifteen percent of the students who take a screening test are assigned to a remedial English class. In a group of eight students, what is the probability that three will be placed in the remedial class?

13. Nine customers at a supermarket are asked independently if they use brand X laundry soap. In general, 20% of the population use this brand. What is the probability that among the nine, more than two people use brand X?

14. Write the probability distribution for a binomial random variable with parameters $n = 6$, $p = \frac{1}{4}$.

15. Calculate the probability distribution for a binomial random variable with $n = 8$, $p = .40$.

16. (a) Show that
$$\binom{n}{k} = \binom{n}{n-k}$$

for $k = 0, 1, 2, \ldots, n$.

(b) Let X be the random variable associated with binomial trials with $n = 10$ and $p = \frac{1}{2}$. Show that
$$\Pr(X = k) = \Pr(X = 10 - k)$$

for $k = 0, 1, 2, \ldots, n$.

17. A jury has 12 jurors. A vote of at least 10 of 12 for "guilty" is necessary for a defendant to be convicted of a crime. Assume that each juror acts independently of the others and that the probability that any one juror makes the correct decision on a defendant is .80. If the defendant is guilty, what is the probability that the jury makes the correct decision?

18. Every offspring inherits a gene for hair color from each parent. We denote the dominant gene by A and the recessive gene by a. If a person has AA or Aa, then the person exhibits the dominant characteristic. We call a person with the genes Aa a hybrid. A person with aa exhibits the recessive characteristic. Two hybrid parents have three children. Find the probability that at least one child exhibits the recessive characteristic.

19. A single die is rolled 10 times and the number of sixes is observed. What is the probability that a six appears 9 times, given that it appears at least 9 times?

20. A coin is tossed until four heads occur. What is the probability that the fourth head occurs on the tenth toss?

Exercises 21–24 require the use of a graphing calculator or a computer.

21. Consider Example 3.
   (a) Calculate the probability that a box of washers contains exactly 12 defective washers.
   (b) What is the probability that at most 9 washers will be defective?

22. Consider Example 4.
   (a) Calculate the probability that exactly 20 cattle will recover.
   (b) Calculate the sum $\Pr(X = 16) + \Pr(X = 17) + \cdots + \Pr(X = 40)$ discussed in the paragraph following Example 4.

23. Suppose there is a .40% chance of being selected for jury duty in September. A school system has 900 teachers.
   (a) What is the probability that 8 teachers will be chosen for jury duty in September?
   (b) Create a table showing the probabilities of having 0 through 6 teachers chosen.
   (c) What is the probability that at most 9 teachers will be chosen?

24. When a pair of dice is tossed, the probability of obtaining seven is $\frac{1}{6}$. Suppose a pair of dice is tossed 25 times.

    (a) Calculate the probability that 8 sevens occur.

    (b) Create a table showing the probabilities of having 0 through 6 sevens occur.

    (c) What is the probability that 10 or more sevens will occur?

Solutions to Practice Problems 7.3

1. The number of multiples of 5 that occur in the numbers from 0 to 9999 is 2000. Since each of the 10,000 choices is as likely as any other, the probability is $2000/10,000 = .2$.

2. Let "success" be "the selected number is a multiple of 5." Then the selection of a number at random is a binomial trial. So $p = .2$ and $n = 20$.

$$\Pr(X = 4) = \binom{20}{4}(.2)^4(.8)^{16} \approx .2182.$$

7.4   The Mean

It is important at this point to recognize the difference between a *population* and a *sample*. A population is a set of all elements about which information is desired. A sample is a subset of a population that is analyzed in an attempt to estimate certain properties of the entire population. For instance, suppose that we are interested in finding out some characteristics of the automobile industry but do not have access to the entire population of dealerships in the United States. We must choose a random and representative sample of these dealerships and concentrate on gathering information from it.

A numerical descriptive measurement made on a sample is called a *statistic*. Such a measurement made on a population is called a *parameter* of the population. Usually, since we cannot have access to entire populations, we rely on our experimental results to obtain statistics, and we attempt to use the statistics to estimate the parameters of the population. One of the measurements we all have used is the arithmetic average. For instance, we could choose a representative random sample of $n = 200$ car dealerships across the country, determine the average weekly sales for these dealerships, and then use this value to estimate the average weekly sales of all car dealerships in the United States.

It is a familiar notion to find the *average* (also called the *mean*) of a set of numbers. For example, to obtain the average of 11, 17, 18, and 10, we add these numbers and divide by 4:

$$[\text{average}] = \frac{11 + 17 + 18 + 10}{4} = 14.$$

If we have gathered a sample of n numbers $x_1, x_2, \ldots, x_n$, the *sample mean* is

$$\bar{x} = \frac{x_1 + x_2 + \cdots + x_n}{n}. \tag{1}$$

▶ **Example 1**   Compute the sample mean of the weekly sales of dealership A of Section 7.2.

Solution   Recall that the weekly sales of dealership A are given in Table 1. Thus we may form the sample mean of the weekly sales figures as follows:

$$\frac{1}{52}[(5+5)+(6+6)+\underbrace{(7+\cdots+7)}_{13\text{ times}}+\underbrace{(8+\cdots+8)}_{20\text{ times}}$$

$$+\underbrace{(9+\cdots+9)}_{10\text{ times}}+\underbrace{(10+\cdots+10)}_{4\text{ times}}+11]$$

$$=\frac{5\cdot2+6\cdot2+7\cdot13+8\cdot20+9\cdot10+10\cdot4+11\cdot1}{52}\qquad(2)$$

$$=5\cdot\frac{2}{52}+6\cdot\frac{2}{52}+7\cdot\frac{13}{52}+8\cdot\frac{20}{52}+9\cdot\frac{10}{52}+10\cdot\frac{4}{52}+11\cdot\frac{1}{52}$$

$$\approx 7.96.$$

Thus the sample mean of the weekly sales is approximately 7.96 cars.   ◆

Table 1

Weekly sales	Number of occurrences
5	2
6	2
7	13
8	20
9	10
10	4
11	1

Note   We considered the data from dealership A to be a sample since it was only one year's data and we are interested in making comparisons and using them to predict the future sales of the two dealerships.

Let us reexamine the calculation above. The sample mean is given by expression (2). We did this calculation by adding together the observed sales for the 52 weeks of the year and then dividing by 52. To make the calculation more efficient, we noticed that we could group all of the weeks in which we observed five sales, all of the weeks in which there were six sales, and so on. Instead of adding 52 numbers, we simply multiplied each observed value of "sales" by its frequency of occurrence and then divided by 52. Another alternative is to multiply each observed value of "sales" by the relative frequency with which it occurred (e.g., $5\times\frac{2}{52}$), and then add. That is, to compute the mean weekly sales we need only add up the products [number of sales] · [relative frequency of occurrence] over all possible sales figures. If the data for any sample are displayed in a frequency table or a relative frequency table, the sample mean can be calculated in a similar fashion. Since the calculation of $\overline{x}$ depends on the sample values, $\overline{x}$ is a *statistic*.

Sample Mean   Suppose that an experiment has as outcomes the numbers $x_1, x_2, \ldots, x_r$. Suppose the frequency of x_1 is f_1, the frequency of x_2 is f_2, and so forth, and that

$$f_1+f_2+\cdots+f_r=n.$$

Then

$$\overline{x}=\frac{x_1f_1+x_2f_2+\cdots+x_rf_r}{n},$$

or

$$\overline{x}=x_1\left(\frac{f_1}{n}\right)+x_2\left(\frac{f_2}{n}\right)+\cdots+x_r\left(\frac{f_r}{n}\right).$$

Similar calculations are made when we work with entire populations. Assume the population size is N and that $x_1, x_2, \ldots, x_N$ are the population values. The *population mean*, denoted by the Greek letter μ (mu), is given by the formula

$$\mu = \frac{x_1 + x_2 + \cdots + x_N}{N}.$$

If the data have been grouped into a frequency or relative frequency table, a formula analogous to the one for samples is used:

$$\mu = x_1\left(\frac{f_1}{N}\right) + x_2\left(\frac{f_2}{N}\right) + \cdots + x_r\left(\frac{f_r}{N}\right).$$

To help distinguish the parameter from the statistic, all parameters are denoted by Greek letters and all statistics by English letters. We use the common convention of denoting a sample size by lowercase n and a population size by uppercase N.

▶ **Example 2**   An ecologist observes the life expectancy of a certain species of deer held in captivity. Based on a population of 1000 deer, he observes the data shown in Table 2. What is the mean life expectancy of this population of deer?

Solution   We convert the given data into a relative frequency distribution by replacing observed frequencies by relative frequencies [= (observed frequency)/1000] (Table 3). The mean of these data is

$$\mu = 1 \cdot 0 + 2 \cdot (.06) + 3 \cdot (.18) + 4 \cdot (.25) + 5 \cdot (.20) + 6 \cdot (.12)$$
$$+ 7 \cdot (.05) + 8 \cdot (.12) + 9 \cdot (.02) = 4.87.$$

So the mean life expectancy of this population of deer is 4.87 years.   ◆

▶ **Example 3**   Which car dealership should Mr. Jones buy if he wants the one that will, on the average, sell more cars?

Solution   We have seen in Example 1 that the mean of the sample data for dealership A is $\overline{x}_A \approx 7.96$. On the other hand, associated to the data for dealership B (Table 4),

Table 2	
Age at death (years)	Number observed
1	0
2	60
3	180
4	250
5	200
6	120
7	50
8	120
9	20

Table 3	
Age at death (years)	Relative frequency
1	0
2	.06
3	.18
4	.25
5	.20
6	.12
7	.05
8	.12
9	.02

Table 4	
Weekly sales	Relative frequency
5	$\frac{20}{104}$
6	0
7	0
8	$\frac{10}{104}$
9	$\frac{12}{104}$
10	$\frac{50}{104}$
11	$\frac{12}{104}$

we find the sample mean:

$$\overline{x}_{\mathrm{B}} = 5 \cdot \left(\tfrac{20}{104}\right) + 6 \cdot 0 + 7 \cdot 0 + 8 \cdot \left(\tfrac{10}{104}\right) + 9 \cdot \left(\tfrac{12}{104}\right) + 10 \cdot \left(\tfrac{50}{104}\right) + 11 \cdot \left(\tfrac{12}{104}\right)$$
$$\approx 8.85.$$

Thus the average sales of dealership A are 7.96 cars per week, whereas those of dealership B are 8.85 cars per week. If we make the assumption that past sales history predicts future sales, Mr. Jones should buy dealership B. ◆

Expected Value   The sample and population mean have analogs in the theoretical setting of random variables. Suppose that X is a random variable with the following probability distribution:

x_i	$\Pr(X = x_i)$
x_1	p_1
x_2	p_2
$\vdots$	$\vdots$
x_N	p_N

Then the values of X (namely $x_1, x_2, \ldots, x_N$) are the possible outcomes of an experiment. The expected value of X, denoted $\mathrm{E}(X)$, is defined as follows:

The expected value of the random variable X:

$$\mathrm{E}(X) = x_1 p_1 + x_2 p_2 + \cdots + x_N p_N. \tag{3}$$

Since the value of p_i represents the theoretical relative frequency of the outcome x_i, the formula for $\mathrm{E}(X)$ is similar to the formula for the mean of a relative frequency distribution. Thus the expected value of the random variable X is also called the *mean* of the probability distribution of X and may be denoted either by $\mathrm{E}(X)$ or by μ_X. Frequently, $\mathrm{E}(X)$ is used interchangeably with the Greek letter μ when the context is clear.

The expected value of a random variable is the center of the probability distribution in the sense that it is the balance point of the histogram. For example, let $X = $ the number of heads in 5 tosses of a fair coin. The probability distribution appears in Table 5 and the histogram in Fig. 1 on the next page. We can calculate the mean μ of X:

$$\mu_X = 0\left(\tfrac{1}{32}\right) + 1\left(\tfrac{5}{32}\right) + 2\left(\tfrac{10}{32}\right) + 3\left(\tfrac{10}{32}\right) + 4\left(\tfrac{5}{32}\right) + 5\left(\tfrac{1}{32}\right) = \tfrac{80}{32} = 2.5.$$

The mean is shown at the bottom of the histogram (Fig. 1). In contrast, we note that the sample mean, $\overline{x}$, for the coin-tossing experiment tabulated in Section 7.2 was 2.65 (see Table 6 on the next page). We rarely find that the sample mean x is exactly the theoretical value μ_X.

We use binomial random variables so often that it is helpful to know that we have an easy formula for $\mathrm{E}(X)$ in such cases.

If X is a binomial random variable with parameters n and p, then

$$\mathrm{E}(X) = np. \tag{4}$$

Table 5	X = Number of Heads in 5 Tosses of a Fair Coin	
k	$\Pr(X = k)$	$k \cdot \Pr(X = k)$
0	$\frac{1}{32}$	0
1	$\frac{5}{32}$	$\frac{5}{32}$
2	$\frac{10}{32}$	$\frac{20}{32}$
3	$\frac{10}{32}$	$\frac{30}{32}$
4	$\frac{5}{32}$	$\frac{20}{32}$
5	$\frac{1}{32}$	$\frac{5}{32}$
Totals 1		$\mu = \frac{80}{32} = 2.5$

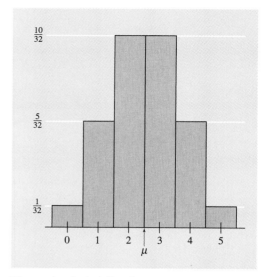

Figure 1. Probability distribution of number of heads.

If X is the number of heads in five tosses of a fair coin, then using the formula, we see that $E(X) = 5(\frac{1}{2}) = 2.5$, which is consistent with our previous calculation. Formula (4) will be verified at the end of this section.

▶ **Example 4** Consider the plumbing-supplies manufacturer of Example 3 of Section 7.3. Find the average number of defective washers per box.

Solution The number of defective washers in each box is a binomial random variable with $n = 300$ and $p = .02$. The average number of defective washers per box is the expected value of X. $E(X) = np = 300 \cdot (.02) = 6$. ◆

▶ **Example 5** Let the random variable X denote the sum of the faces appearing after tossing two dice. Determine $E(X)$.

Solution We determined the probability distribution of X in Example 3 of Section 7.2

Table 6	Observed Frequency of Heads		
Number of heads x_i	Frequency f_i	Relative frequency (f_i/n)	$x_i \cdot (f_i/n)$
0	3	.03	0
1	14	.16	.16
2	23	.26	.52
3	27	.30	.90
4	17	.18	.72
5	6	.07	.35
Totals	$n = 90$	1	$2.65 = \overline{x}$

Table 7			
k	$\Pr(X = k)$	k	$\Pr(X = k)$
2	$\frac{1}{36}$	8	$\frac{5}{36}$
3	$\frac{1}{18}$	9	$\frac{1}{9}$
4	$\frac{1}{12}$	10	$\frac{1}{12}$
5	$\frac{1}{9}$	11	$\frac{1}{18}$
6	$\frac{5}{36}$	12	$\frac{1}{36}$
7	$\frac{1}{6}$		

(Table 7). Therefore,

$$\mathrm{E}(X) = 2 \cdot \tfrac{1}{36} + 3 \cdot \tfrac{1}{18} + 4 \cdot \tfrac{1}{12} + 5 \cdot \tfrac{1}{9} + 6 \cdot \tfrac{5}{36} + 7 \cdot \tfrac{1}{6}$$

$$+ 8 \cdot \tfrac{5}{36} + 9 \cdot \tfrac{1}{9} + 10 \cdot \tfrac{1}{12} + 11 \cdot \tfrac{1}{18} + 12 \cdot \tfrac{1}{36} = 7.$$

Clearly, 7 is the balance point of the histogram shown in Section 7.2. ◆

The expected value of a random variable may be used to analyze games of chance, as the next two examples show.

▶ **Example 6**   Two people play a dice game. A single die is thrown. If the outcome is 1 or 2, then A pays B \$2. If the outcome is 3, 4, 5, or 6, then B pays A \$4. What are the long-run expected winnings for A?

Solution   Let X be the random variable representing the payoff to A. Then X assumes the possible values -2 and 4. Moreover, since the probability of 1 or 2 on the die is $\frac{1}{3}$, we have

$$\Pr(X = -2) = \tfrac{1}{3}.$$

Similarly,

$$\Pr(X = 4) = \tfrac{2}{3}.$$

Therefore,

$$\mathrm{E}(X) = (-2) \cdot \tfrac{1}{3} + 4 \cdot \tfrac{2}{3} = 2.$$

In other words, the expected payoff to A is \$2 per play. If the game is repeated a large number of times, then on the average A should profit \$2 per play. For example, in 1000 games, we expect that A will profit \$2000. ◆

In evaluating a game of chance we use the expected value of the winnings to determine how fair the game is. The expected value of a completely fair game is zero. Let us compute the expected value of the winnings for two variations of the game roulette. American and European roulette games differ in both the nature of the wheel and the rules for playing.

American roulette wheels have 38 numbers (1 through 36 plus 0 and 00), of which 18 are red, 18 are black, and 2 are green. Many different types of bets are possible. We shall consider the "red" bet. When you bet \$1 on red, you win \$1 if a red number appears and you lose \$1 otherwise.

European roulette wheels have 37 numbers (1 through 36 plus 0). The rules of European roulette differ from the American rules. One variation is as follows: When you bet \$1 on "red," you win \$1 if the ball lands on a red number and lose \$1 if the ball lands on a black number. However, if the ball lands on the green number (0), then your bet stays on the table (the bet is said to be "imprisoned") and the payoff is determined by the result of the next spin. If a red number appears, you receive your \$1 bet back, and if a black number appears, you lose your \$1 bet. However, if the green number (0) appears, you get back half of your bet, \$.50. The tree diagrams for American and European roulette are given in Fig. 2.

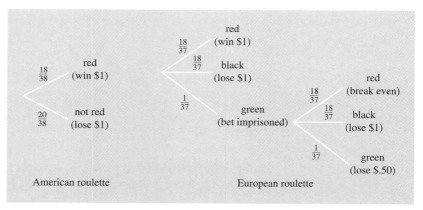

Figure 2.

▶ Example 7   (a) Set up the probability distribution tables for the earnings in American roulette and European roulette for the \$1 bet on red.

(b) Compute the expected values for the probability distributions in part (a).

Solution   (a) For American roulette there are only two possibilities: earnings of \$1 or of $-\$1$. These occur with probabilities $\frac{18}{38}$ and $\frac{20}{38}$, respectively.

For European roulette the possible earnings are \$1, \$0, $-\$.50$, or $-\$1$. There are two ways in which to lose \$1, one with probability $\frac{18}{37}$ and the other with probability $\frac{1}{37} \cdot \frac{18}{37} = \frac{18}{1369}$. Therefore,

$$\Pr(\text{lose }\$1) = \tfrac{18}{37} + \tfrac{18}{1369} = \tfrac{684}{1369}.$$

These probability distributions are tabulated in Table 8.

Table 8

American roulette	
Earnings	Probability
1	$\frac{18}{38}$
-1	$\frac{20}{38}$

European roulette	
Earnings	Probability
1	$\frac{18}{37}$
0	$\frac{18}{1369}$
$-\frac{1}{2}$	$\frac{1}{1369}$
-1	$\frac{684}{1369}$

(b) American roulette:

$$\mu = 1 \cdot \tfrac{18}{38} + (-1) \cdot \tfrac{20}{38} = -\tfrac{2}{38} \approx -.0526.$$

European roulette:

$$\mu = 1 \cdot \tfrac{18}{37} + 0 \cdot \tfrac{18}{1369} + \left(-\tfrac{1}{2}\right)\tfrac{1}{1369} + (-1)\tfrac{684}{1369}$$

$$= -\tfrac{1}{74} \approx -.0135. \qquad \blacklozenge$$

The secrets of Nicholas Dandolas, one of the famous gamblers of the twentieth century, are revealed by Ted Thackrey, Jr., in *Gambling Secrets of Nick the Greek* (Rand-McNally, 1968). The chapter entitled "Roulette" is subtitled "For Europeans Only." Looking at the probabilities of winning does not reveal any significant advantage of European roulette over American roulette: $\tfrac{18}{37}$ is not much bigger than $\tfrac{18}{38}$. Also, the chance in European roulette to break even is very small. The real difference between the two games is revealed by the expected values. Someone playing American roulette will lose, on the average, about $5\tfrac{1}{4}$ cents per \$1 bet, whereas for European roulette the average loss is about $1\tfrac{1}{3}$ cents. In both cases you expect to lose money in the long run, but in American roulette you lose nearly four times as much.

In summary, there are three things to which the mean applies: samples, populations, and probability distributions.

Verification of Formula (4)   Note that

$$\mu = 0 \cdot \Pr(X = 0) + 1 \cdot \Pr(X = 1) + \cdots + n \cdot \Pr(X = n)$$

$$= 0 \cdot \binom{n}{0} p^0 q^{n-0} + 1 \cdot \binom{n}{1} p^1 q^{n-1} + \cdots + n \cdot \binom{n}{n} p^n q^{n-n}.$$

Moreover, note that

$$k\binom{n}{k} = k \cdot \frac{n(n-1)\cdot \,\cdots\, \cdot (n-k+1)}{k(k-1)\cdot\,\cdots\,\cdot 2 \cdot 1} = \frac{n(n-1)\cdot\,\cdots\,\cdot (n-k+1)}{(k-1)\cdot\,\cdots\,\cdot 2 \cdot 1}$$

$$= n\binom{n-1}{k-1} \qquad (k = 1, 2, 3, \ldots, n).$$

Therefore,

$$\mu = 1 \cdot \binom{n}{1} p^1 q^{n-1} + 2 \cdot \binom{n}{2} p^2 q^{n-2} + \cdots + n \cdot \binom{n}{n} p^n q^0$$

$$= n\binom{n-1}{0} p^1 q^{n-1} + n\binom{n-1}{1} p^2 q^{n-2} + \cdots + n\binom{n-1}{n-1} p^n q^0$$

$$= np\left[\binom{n-1}{0} p^0 q^{n-1} + \binom{n-1}{1} pq^{n-2} + \cdots + \binom{n-1}{n-1} p^{n-1} q^0\right]$$

$$= np(p + q)^{n-1} \qquad \text{(by the binomial theorem)}$$

$$= np \qquad \text{(since } p + q = 1\text{).} \qquad \blacklozenge$$

1. A 74-year-old man pays $100 for a one-year life insurance policy, which pays $2000 in the event that he dies during the next year. According to life insurance tables, the probability of a 74-year-old man living one additional year is .95. Write down the probability distribution for the possible financial outcome and determine its expected value.

2. According to life insurance tables, the probability that a 74-year-old man will live an additional five years is .7. How much should a 74-year-old be willing to pay for a policy that pays $2000 in the event of death any time within the next 5 years?

▶ Exercises 7.4

1. Find the expected value for the probability distribution in Table 9.

Table 9

Value	Probability
0	.15
1	.2
2	.1
3	.25
4	.3

2. Find the expected value for the probability distribution in Table 10.

Table 10

Value	Probability
-1	.1
$-\frac{1}{2}$	.4
0	.25
$\frac{1}{2}$	.2
1	.05

3. A college student received the following course grades for 10 (three-credit) courses during his freshman year: 4, 4, 4, 3, 3, 3, 3, 2, 2, 1.
    (a) Find his grade point average by adding the grades and dividing by 10.
    (b) Write down the relative frequency table.
    (c) Find the mean of the relative frequency distribution in part (b).

4. An Olympic gymnast received the following scores from six judges: 9.8, 9.8, 9.4, 9.2, 9.2, 9.0.
    (a) Find the average score by adding the scores and dividing by 6.

    (b) Write down the relative frequency table.

    (c) Find the mean of the relative frequency distribution in part (b).

5. Table 11 gives the relative frequency of the number of cavities for two groups of children trying different brands of toothpaste. Calculate the sample means to determine which group had fewer cavities.

Table 11

Number of cavities	Relative frequency	
	Group A	Group B
0	.3	.2
1	.3	.3
2	.2	.3
3	.1	.1
4	0	.1
5	.1	0

6. Table 12 gives the possible returns of two different investments and their probabilities. Calculate the means of the probability distributions to determine which investment has the greater expected return.

Table 12

Investment A	
Return	Probability
$1000	.2
$2000	.5
$3000	.3

Investment B	
Return	Probability
−$3000	.1
0	.3
$4000	.6

7. In American roulette, a bettor may place a $1 bet on any one of the 38 numbers on the roulette wheel. He wins $35 (plus the return of his bet) if the ball lands on his number; otherwise, he loses his bet. Write down the probability distribution for the earnings from this type of bet and find the expected value.

8. In American roulette, a dollar may be bet on a pair of numbers. The expected earnings for this type of bet is $-\$\frac{1}{19}$. How much money does the bettor receive if the ball lands on one of the two numbers?

9. In a carnival game, the player selects balls one at a time, without replacement, from an urn containing two red and four white balls. The game proceeds until a red ball is drawn. The player pays $1 to play the game and receives $\$\frac{1}{2}$ for each ball drawn. Write down the probability distribution for the player's earnings and find its expected value.

10. In a carnival game, the player selects two coins from a bag containing two silver dollars and six slugs. Write down the probability distribution for the winnings and determine how much the player would have to pay so that he would break even, on the average, over many repetitions of the game.

11. Using life insurance tables, a retired man determines that the probability of living 5 more years is .9. He decides to take out a life insurance policy that will pay $10,000 in the event that he dies during the next 5 years. How much should he be willing to pay for this policy? (Do not take account of interest rates or inflation.)

12. Using life insurance tables, a retired couple determines that the probability of living 5 more years is .9 for the man and .95 for the woman. They decide to take out a life insurance policy that will pay $10,000 if either one dies during the next 5 years and $15,000 if both die during that time. How much should they be willing to pay for this policy? (Assume that their life spans are independent events.)

13. A pair of dice is tossed and the larger of the two numbers showing is recorded. Find the expected value of this experiment.

14. (PE) A student's exam scores are 95, 88, and 79. What score must the student earn on the fourth exam to have an average (arithmetic mean) score of 90?
    (a) 96 (b) 97 (c) 98 (d) 99 (e) 100

15. (PE) If 5, 6, and x have the same average (arithmetic mean) as 2, 7, and 9, then x equals
    (a) 4 (b) 5 (c) 6 (d) 7 (e) 8

16. (PE) A store sold an average (arithmetic mean) of x candles per day for k days, and then sold y candles on the next day. What is the average number of candles sold daily for the $(k+1)$-day period?
    (a) $x + \dfrac{y}{k}$ (b) $\dfrac{kx+y}{k+1}$ (c) $\dfrac{k(x+y)}{k+1}$
    (d) $\dfrac{x+ky}{k+1}$ (e) $x + \dfrac{y}{k+1}$

17. (PE) Last weekend a movie theater sold x adult tickets at $7 each and y children's tickets at $4 each. The average (arithmetic mean) revenue per ticket was
    (a) $\dfrac{28xy}{x+y}$ (b) $\dfrac{7x+4y}{x+y}$ (c) $\dfrac{7x+4y}{11}$
    (d) $\dfrac{28xy}{11}$ (e) $\dfrac{7x+4y}{xy}$

18. (PE) If three distinct positive integers have an average (arithmetic mean) of 70, and if the smallest of the three integers is 50, then the largest of the three integers can be at most
    (a) 70 (b) 99 (c) 100 (d) 109 (e) 159

19. (PE) If three distinct positive integers have an average (arithmetic mean) of 200, and if the smallest of the three integers is 120, then the largest of the three integers can be at most
    (a) 200 (b) 350 (c) 359 (d) 459 (e) 460

20. (PE) A small business had an average (arithmetic mean) weekly revenue of $14,000 over the past three weeks. The revenue for the first week was twice the revenue of the third week, and the revenue for the second week was half the revenue of the third week. What was the revenue for the first week?
    (a) $6000   (b) $12,000   (c) $18,000
    (d) $20,000   (e) $24,000

21. (PE) Tom, Dick, and Harry have an average (arithmetic mean) of 120 baseball cards. Tom has $1\frac{1}{2}$ times as many cards as Dick, and Harry has $\frac{1}{2}$ as many cards as Dick. How many baseball cards does Tom have?
    (a) 60 (b) 90 (c) 120 (d) 180 (e) 240

22. (PE) Three members of a study group each earned a score of 91 on an exam, and the other five members of the group each earned a score of 87. The average (arithmetic mean) score earned by the members of this study group is
    (a) 88.0 (b) 88.5 (c) 89.0 (d) 89.5 (e) 90.0

23. (PE) Five members of a baseball team have batting averages of .300, and the other four members of the team have batting averages of .350. The overall batting average among members of the team is closest to
    (a) .311 (b) .322 (c) .325 (d) .330 (e) .333

24. (PE) Half of the magazines at a newsstand sell for an average (arithmetic mean) of $2.00 and the other half sell for an average of $2.50. If the total retail value of the magazines is $135.00, how many magazines are there at the newsstand?
    (a) 56 (b) 57 (c) 58 (d) 59 (e) 60

25. (PE) A truck can carry a maximum of 75,000 pounds of cargo. How many cases of cargo can it carry if half of the cases have an average (arithmetic mean) weight of 20 pounds and the other half have an average weight of 30 pounds?
    (a) 3000 (b) 3200 (c) 3500 (d) 3750 (e) 4000

26. (PE) Bob wishes to insure a priceless family heirloom against theft. The annual premium for policy A is $150, and it will pay $75,000 if the heirloom is stolen. Policy B will pay $100,000, but the annual premium for policy B is $250. Bob estimates the probability that the heirloom will be stolen in any given year and remains undecided between the two policies. What is this estimated probability?
    (a) .001 (b) .002 (c) .003 (d) .004 (e) .005

27. (PE) The promoter of a football game is concerned that it will rain. She has the option of spending $8000 on insurance that will pay $40,000 if it rains. She estimates that the revenue from the game will be $60,000 if it does not rain and $25,000 if it does rain. What must the chance of rain be if she is ambivalent about this insurance?
    (a) 20% (b) 25% (c) 30% (d) 35% (e) 40%

Solutions to Practice Problems 7.4

1. There are two possibilities. If the man lives until the end of the year, he loses $100. If he dies during the year, his estate gains $1900 (the $2000 settlement minus the $100 premium).

Outcome	Probability
−$100	.95
$1900	.05

$$\mu = (-100)(.95) + (1900)(.05) = 0$$

(Thus, if the insurance company insures a large number of people, it should break even. Its profits will result from the interest that it earns on the money being held.)

2. Let x denote the cost of the policy. The probability distribution is as follows.

Outcome	Probability
$-x$	.7
$2000 - x$	.3

$$\mu = (-x)(.7) + (2000 - x)(.3) = -.7x + 600 - .3x = 600 - x$$

The expected value will be zero if $x = 600$. Therefore, the man should be willing to pay up to $600 for his policy.

7.5 The Variance and Standard Deviation

In Section 7.4 we introduced three analogous concepts: the mean of a sample ($\bar{x}$); the mean of a population (μ); and the mean or expected value of a random variable [$E(X)$]. The mean is probably the single most important number that can be used to describe a sample, a population, or a probability distribution of a random variable. The next most important number is the *variance*.

Roughly speaking, the variance measures the dispersal or spread of a distribution about its mean. The more closely concentrated the distribution about its mean, the smaller the variance; the more spread out, the larger the vari-

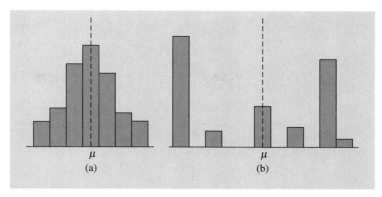

Figure 1.

ance. Thus, for example, the probability distribution whose histogram is drawn in Fig. 1(a) has a smaller variance than that in Fig. 1(b).

Let us now define the variance of a probability distribution of a random variable. Suppose X is a random variable with values $x_1, x_2, \ldots, x_N$ and respective probabilities $p_1, p_2, \ldots, p_N$. Suppose that the mean is μ. Then the deviations of the various outcomes from the mean are given by the N differences

$$x_1 - \mu, \quad x_2 - \mu, \quad \ldots, \quad x_N - \mu.$$

Since we want to give weight to the various deviations according to their likelihood of occurrence, it is tempting to multiply each deviation by its probability of occurrence. However, this will not lead to a very satisfactory measure of deviation from the mean. This is because some of the differences will be positive and others negative. In the process of addition, deviations from the mean (both positive and negative deviations) will combine to yield a zero total deviation. To correct this, we consider instead the squares of the differences:

$$(x_1 - \mu)^2, \quad (x_2 - \mu)^2, \quad \ldots, \quad (x_N - \mu)^2,$$

which are all ≥ 0. To obtain a measure of deviation from the mean, we multiply each of these expressions by the probability of the corresponding outcome. The number thus obtained is called the *variance of the probability distribution* (or of the associated random variable). That is, the variance of a probability distribution is given by the formula

$$[\text{variance}] = (x_1 - \mu)^2 p_1 + (x_2 - \mu)^2 p_2 + \cdots + (x_N - \mu)^2 p_N. \tag{1}$$

▶ **Example 1**   Compute the variance of the following probability distribution:

Outcome	Probability
0	.1
1	.3
2	.5
3	.1

Solution   The mean is given by

$$\mu = 0 \cdot (.1) + 1 \cdot (.3) + 2 \cdot (.5) + 3 \cdot (.1) = 1.6.$$

In the notation of random variables, the calculations of the variance may be summarized as follows:

k	$\Pr(X = k)$	$k - \mu$	$(k - \mu)^2$	$(k - \mu)^2 \Pr(X = k)$
0	.1	$0 - 1.6 = -1.6$	2.56	.256
1	.3	$1 - 1.6 = -.6$	.36	.108
2	.5	$2 - 1.6 = .4$	.16	.080
3	.1	$3 - 1.6 = 1.4$	1.96	.196

$$[\text{variance}] = .256 + .108 + .080 + .196 = .640. \qquad \blacklozenge$$

Actually, a much more commonly used measure of dispersal about the mean is the *standard deviation*, which is just the square root of the variance:

$$[\text{standard deviation}] = \sqrt{[\text{variance}]}.$$

The most commonly used notation for standard deviation is the Greek letter σ (sigma). Thus, for example, for the probability distribution of Example 1 we have

$$\sigma = \sqrt{[\text{variance}]} = \sqrt{.64} = .8.$$

We denote the variance by σ^2 (sigma squared). The reason for using the standard deviation as opposed to the variance is that the former is expressed in the same units of measurement as X, whereas the latter is not.

In a similar way, we can define the variance and standard deviation for a collection of data—either for an entire population or for a sample drawn from a population. If we have collected data for an entire population under study, with values $x_1, x_2, \ldots, x_N$, then the variance can be found by first finding the mean, μ, and then finding σ^2:

$$\sigma^2 = \frac{1}{N} \left[(x_1 - \mu)^2 + (x_2 - \mu)^2 + \cdots + (x_N - \mu)^2 \right].$$

If the data have been grouped into a frequency table or relative frequency table, the appropriate formulas would be

$$\sigma^2 = \frac{1}{N} \left[(x_1 - \mu)^2 (f_1) + (x_2 - \mu)^2 (f_2) + \cdots + (x_r - \mu)^2 (f_r) \right]$$

or

$$\sigma^2 = (x_1 - \mu)^2 \left(\frac{f_1}{N} \right) + (x_2 - \mu)^2 \left(\frac{f_2}{N} \right) + \cdots + (x_r - \mu)^2 \left(\frac{f_r}{N} \right),$$

where the value x_1 occurs with frequency f_1, the value x_2 occurs with frequency f_2, and so on. Recall that N denotes the population size.

▶ Example 2   Compute the variance and the standard deviation for the population of scores on a five-question quiz as tabulated in Table 1.

Solution   We first find μ.

$$\mu = \tfrac{1}{60}[0(4) + 1(9) + 2(6) + 3(14) + 4(18) + 5(9)] = \tfrac{180}{60} = 3.$$

We find σ^2 by subtracting 3 from each of the test scores, squaring the differences, weighting each with its frequency, and dividing the resulting sum by $N = 60$. The computation is shown in Table 2. Therefore, $\sigma^2 = \tfrac{132}{60} = 2.2$. The standard deviation, which is found by taking the square root of the variance, is $\sigma \approx 1.48$.

◆

Table 1

Score	Frequency
0	4
1	9
2	6
3	14
4	18
5	9
Total	60

Table 2

x_i	f_i	$(x_i - \mu)$	$(x_i - \mu)^2$	$(x_i - \mu)^2(f_i)$
0	4	-3	9	36
1	9	-2	4	36
2	6	-1	1	6
3	14	0	0	0
4	18	1	1	18
5	9	2	4	36
Totals	60			132

As we discussed in Section 7.4, we sometimes have only sample values at our disposal. If so, we must use sample statistics to estimate the population parameters. For example, we can use the sample mean $\bar{x}$ as an estimate of the population mean μ, and the sample variance as an estimate of the population variance, σ^2. In fact, if samples of size n were chosen repeatedly from a population and the sample mean were computed for each sample, then the average of these means should be close to the value of the population mean, μ. This is a desirable property for any statistic used to estimate a parameter—the averages of the statistic get arbitrarily close to the actual value of the parameter as the number of samples increases. Such an estimate is said to be *unbiased*. Thus $\bar{x}$ is an unbiased estimate of μ.

The situation with the variance is a little trickier. In order to have an unbiased estimate of the population variance σ^2, we must define the *sample variance*, s^2, in a slightly peculiar way. Suppose that $x_1, x_2, \ldots, x_n$ are the n sample values. Then the sample variance is

$$s^2 = \frac{1}{n-1}\left[(x_1 - \bar{x})^2 + (x_2 - \bar{x})^2 + \cdots + (x_n - \bar{x})^2\right],$$

and the sample standard deviation is $s = \sqrt{s^2}$. This is the usual definition and the way in which most statistical calculators do the computation of the sample variance. Note that the divisor is one less than the sample size. With this definition, s^2 is an unbiased estimate of σ^2. The formula for the sample standard deviation when the data are presented by a frequency table is analogous. For example,

$$s^2 = \frac{1}{n-1}\left[(x_1 - \bar{x})^2(f_1) + (x_2 - \bar{x})^2(f_2) + \cdots + (x_r - \bar{x})^2(f_r)\right].$$

The sample mean, $\overline{x}$, is an unbiased estimate of the population mean μ. The sample variance, s^2, is an unbiased estimate of the population variance σ^2.

▶ **Example 3**   Compute the sample standard deviations for the frequency distributions of sales in car dealerships A and B.

Solution   The frequency distribution for dealership A is given by Table 3. In Example 1 of Section 7.4, we found the sample mean of the weekly sales to be $\overline{x}_A = 7.96$. Recall that we are treating the data collected from these dealerships as samples (one year's data from dealership A and two year's data from dealership B). Therefore, the sample variance for dealership A is given by

$$s_A^2 = \tfrac{1}{51}\big[(5 - 7.96)^2 \cdot 2 + (6 - 7.96)^2 \cdot 2 + (7 - 7.96)^2 \cdot 13$$
$$+ (8 - 7.96)^2 \cdot 20 + (9 - 7.96)^2 \cdot 10 + (10 - 7.96)^2 \cdot 4$$
$$+ (11 - 7.96)^2 \cdot 1\big] \approx 1.45.$$

The sample standard deviation, s_A, for dealership A is given by

$$s_A = \sqrt{s_A^2} = \sqrt{1.45} \approx 1.20 \text{ cars.}$$

In a similar way, we find that the sample standard deviation of dealership B is $s_B \approx 2.03$ cars. Since s_A is smaller than s_B, dealership B exhibited greater variation than dealership A during the time the sales were observed. On average, dealership B had higher weekly sales, but those of dealership A showed greater consistency. The sample statistics might help Mr. Jones decide which dealership to buy. He will have to decide if consistency is more important than the size of long-term average sales per week.   ◆

There is an alternative formula for σ^2 which can simplify its calculation:

$$\sigma^2 = \mathrm{E}(X^2) - \mu^2.$$

▶ **Example 4**   Use the alternative formula for the variance to find σ^2 for X, the number of heads in five tosses of a coin.

Solution   We tabulate the essential values (Table 4). From the table we can see that

$$\mathrm{E}(X^2) = \tfrac{240}{32} = \tfrac{15}{2} \qquad \text{and} \qquad \mu = \tfrac{80}{32} = \tfrac{5}{2}.$$

Thus

$$\sigma^2 = \mathrm{E}(X^2) - \mu^2 = \tfrac{15}{2} - \left(\tfrac{5}{2}\right)^2 = \tfrac{15}{2} - \tfrac{25}{4} = \tfrac{5}{4}.$$ ◆

One of the big advantages of this alternative formula is that μ and σ^2 can be calculated at the same time; this means that we need only make one pass through the probability distribution. In addition, if the mean is an unwieldy number, we are spared the tedious task of subtracting it from the values of the variable, which sometimes produces even more unwieldy numbers that must be squared and summed.

Once again, binomial random variables are used so often that we find it convenient to have a formula for the variance that avoids messy calculations.

Table 3	
Weekly sales	**Frequency**
5	2
6	2
7	13
8	20
9	10
10	4
11	1
Total	$n = 52$

Table 4

k	$\Pr(X = k)$	k^2	$k\Pr(X = k)$	$k^2\Pr(X = k)$
0	$\frac{1}{32}$	0	0	0
1	$\frac{5}{32}$	1	$\frac{5}{32}$	$\frac{5}{32}$
2	$\frac{10}{32}$	4	$\frac{20}{32}$	$\frac{40}{32}$
3	$\frac{10}{32}$	9	$\frac{30}{32}$	$\frac{90}{32}$
4	$\frac{5}{32}$	16	$\frac{20}{32}$	$\frac{80}{32}$
5	$\frac{1}{32}$	25	$\frac{5}{32}$	$\frac{25}{32}$
			Totals $\frac{80}{32}$	$\frac{240}{32}$

If X is a binomial random variable with parameters n and p, then

$$\sigma^2 = npq.$$

For instance, the variance in Example 4 can be calculated as

$$\sigma^2 = 5 \cdot \tfrac{1}{2} \cdot \tfrac{1}{2} = \tfrac{5}{4}.$$

The variance and standard deviation are used in many sophisticated statistical analyses, which are beyond the scope of this book. For example, we can use the value of the sample mean to estimate the population mean. The sample standard deviation helps us to determine the degree of accuracy of our estimate. If the sample standard deviation is small, indicating that the population is not widely dispersed about its mean, the estimated value of μ is likely to be close to the actual value of μ.

What does the standard deviation tell us about the dispersal of the data about the mean? *Chebychev's inequality* helps us to see that the larger the standard deviation, the more likely it is that we find extreme values in the data. The probability that an outcome falls more than c units away from the mean is at most σ^2/c^2.

Chebychev's Inequality   Suppose that a probability distribution with numerical outcomes has expected value μ and standard deviation σ. Then the probability that a randomly chosen outcome lies between $\mu - c$ and $\mu + c$ is at least $1 - (\sigma^2/c^2)$.

A verification of the Chebychev inequality can be found in most elementary statistics texts.

▶ Example 5   Suppose that a probability distribution has mean 5 and standard deviation 1. Use the Chebychev inequality to estimate the probability that an outcome lies between 3 and 7.

Solution   Here $\mu = 5$, $\sigma = 1$. Since we wish to estimate the probability of an outcome lying between 3 and 7, we set $\mu - c = 3$ and $\mu + c = 7$. Thus $c = 2$. Then by the Chebychev inequality, the desired probability is at least

$$1 - \frac{\sigma^2}{c^2} = 1 - \frac{1}{4} = .75.$$

That is, if the experiment is repeated a large number of times, we expect at least 75% of the outcomes to be between 3 and 7. Also, we expect at most 25% of the outcomes to fall below 3 or above 7. ◆

The Chebychev inequality has many practical applications, one of which is illustrated in the next example.

▶ Example 6   Apex Drug Supply Company sells bottles containing 100 capsules of penicillin. Due to the bottling procedure, not every bottle contains exactly 100 capsules. Assume that the average number of capsules in a bottle is indeed 100 ($\mu = 100$) and the standard deviation is 2 ($\sigma = 2$). If the company ships 5000 bottles, estimate the number having between 95 and 105 capsules inclusive.

Solution   By Chebychev's inequality, the proportion of bottles having between $100 - 5$ and $100 + 5$ capsules should be at least

$$1 - (2^2/5^2) = \tfrac{21}{25} = .84.$$

That is, we expect at least 84% of the 5000 bottles, or 4200 bottles, to be in the desired range. ◆

Note that the estimate provided by Chebychev's inequality is crude. In more advanced statistics books, you can find sharper estimates. Also, in the case of the normal distribution, we shall provide a much more precise way of estimating the probability of falling within c units of the mean, based on using a table of areas under the normal curve (see Section 7.6).

GC   Sample means and standard deviations can be easily determined with a graphing calculator. Consider the car dealership data from Table 3. In Fig. 2 the weekly sales are entered into list **L₁** and the frequencies into **L₂**. Figure 3 was invoked by entering

$$\textbf{1–Var Stats L}_1, \textbf{L}_2$$

from the home screen. (To display **1–Var Stats**, press $\boxed{\text{STAT}}$ $\boxed{\blacktriangleright}$ **1**.) The sample mean and the standard deviation are denoted by $\overline{\textbf{x}}$ and **Sx**.

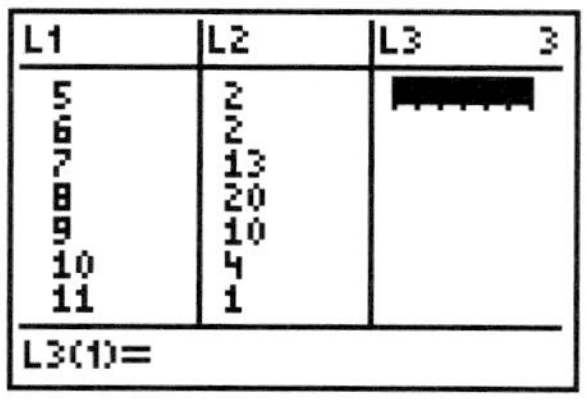

Figure 2. 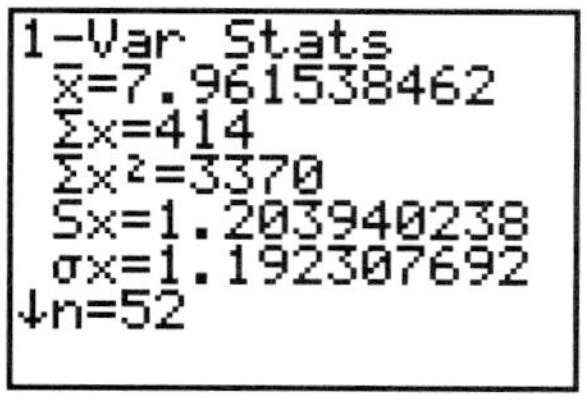   Figure 3. 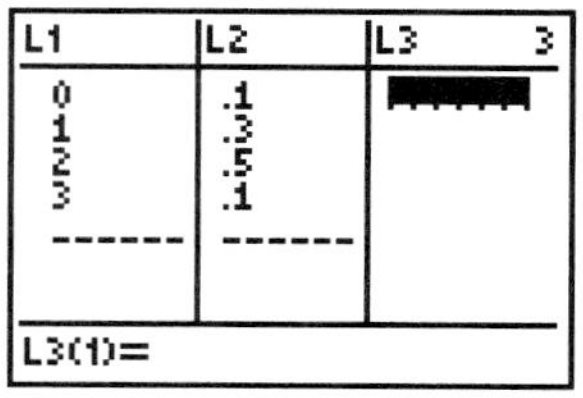   Figure 4.

With the TI-83 graphing calculator, means and standard deviations of probability distributions can be calculated in the same way by placing the probabilities in list **L₂**. See Fig. 4. Figure 5 shows the probability distribution from Example 1. The standard deviation is denoted $\sigma\textbf{x}$. Note that **n** is the sum of the entries in **L₂**.

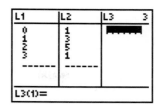

Figure 5.   **Figure 6.**   **Figure 7.**

The TI-82 will execute **1—Var Stats** L_1, L_2 only if the numbers in L_2 are integers from 0 through 99. The mean and the standard deviation for the data in Fig. 4 can be obtained by multiplying each probability in L_2 by 10 (see Fig. 6) and then executing **1—Var Stats** L_1, L_2 to obtain Fig. 7.

Practice Problems 7.5	

1. (a) Compute the variance of the probability distribution in Table 5.

   (b) Using Table 5, find the probability that the outcome is between 22 and 24, inclusive.

Table 5	
Outcome	Probability
21	$\frac{1}{16}$
22	$\frac{1}{8}$
23	$\frac{5}{8}$
24	$\frac{1}{8}$
25	$\frac{1}{16}$

2. Refer to the probability distribution of Problem 1. Use the Chebychev inequality to approximate the probability that the outcome is between 22 and 24.

▶ Exercises 7.5

1. Compute the variance of the probability distribution in Table 6.

2. Compute the variance of the probability distribution in Table 7.

Table 6	
Outcome	Probability
70	.5
71	.2
72	.1
73	.2

Table 7	
Outcome	Probability
-1	$\frac{1}{8}$
$-\frac{1}{2}$	$\frac{3}{8}$
0	$\frac{1}{8}$
$\frac{1}{2}$	$\frac{1}{8}$
1	$\frac{2}{8}$

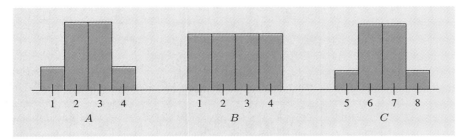

Figure 8.

3. Determine by inspection which one of the probability distributions, A or B, in Fig. 8 has the greater variance.

4. Determine by inspection which one of the probability distributions, B or C, in Fig. 8 has the greater variance.

5. Table 8 gives the probability distribution for the possible returns from two different investments.

Table 8

Investment A	
Return ($ millions)	Probability
-10	$\frac{1}{5}$
20	$\frac{3}{5}$
25	$\frac{1}{5}$

Investment B	
Return ($ millions)	Probability
0	$.3$
10	$.4$
30	$.3$

(a) Compute the mean and the variance for each investment.

(b) Which investment has the higher expected return (i.e., mean)?

(c) Which investment is less risky (i.e., has lesser variance)?

6. Two golfers recorded their scores for 20 nine-hole rounds of golf. Golfer A's scores were

$$39, 39, 40, 40, 40, 40, 40, 40,$$
$$41, 41, 41, 41, 41, 41, 41, 42, 43, 43, 43, 44.$$

Golfer B's scores were

$$40, 40, 40, 41, 41, 41, 41, 42, 42, 42, 42, 42,$$
$$43, 43, 43, 43, 43, 43, 44, 44.$$

(a) Compute the sample mean and the variance of each golfer's scores.

(b) Who is the better golfer? (*Note:* The lower the score, the better.)

(c) Who is the more consistent golfer?

7. Table 9 gives the relative frequency distribution for the weekly sales of two businesses.

(a) Compute the population mean and the variance for each business.

(b) Which business has the better sales record?

(c) Which business has the more consistent sales record?

Table 9		
	Relative frequency	
Sales	Business A	Business B
100	.1	0
101	.2	.2
102	.3	0
103	0	.2
104	0	.1
105	.2	.2
106	.2	.3

8. Student A received the following course grades during her first year of college:

$$4, 4, 4, 4, 3, 3, 2, 2, 2, 0.$$

Student B received the following course grades during her first year:

$$4, 4, 4, 4, 4, 4, 3, 1, 1, 1.$$

   (a) Write down the relative frequency distribution tables for each student, and compute the population means and variances.

   (b) Which student had the better grade point average?

   (c) Which student was more consistent?

9. Suppose that a probability distribution has mean 35 and standard deviation 5. Use the Chebychev inequality to estimate the probability that an outcome will lie between

   (a) 25 and 45.   (b) 20 and 50.   (c) 29 and 41.

10. Suppose that a probability distribution has mean 8 and standard deviation .4. Use the Chebychev inequality to estimate the probability that an outcome will lie between

    (a) 6 and 10.   (b) 7.2 and 8.8.   (c) 7.5 and 8.5.

11. For certain types of fluorescent lights the number of hours a bulb will burn before requiring replacement has a mean of 3000 hours and a standard deviation of 250 hours. Suppose that 5000 such bulbs are installed in an office building. Estimate the number that will require replacement between 2000 and 4000 hours from the time of installation.

12. An electronics firm determines that the number of defective transistors in each batch averages 15 with standard deviation 10. Suppose that 100 batches are produced. Estimate the number of batches having between 0 and 30 defective transistors.

13. Suppose that a probability distribution has mean 75 and standard deviation 6. Use the Chebychev inequality to find the value of c for which the probability that the outcome lies between $75 - c$ and $75 + c$ is at least $\frac{7}{16}$.

14. Suppose that a probability distribution has mean 17 and standard deviation .2. Use the Chebychev inequality to find the value of c for which the probability that the outcome lies between $17 - c$ and $17 + c$ is at least $\frac{15}{16}$.

15. The probability distribution for the sum of numbers obtained from tossing a pair of dice is given in Table 10.

    (a) Compute the mean and the variance of this probability distribution.

    (b) Using the table, give the probability that the number is between 4 and 10, inclusive.

   (c) Use the Chebychev inequality to estimate the probability that the number is between 4 and 10, inclusive.

Table 10

Number	Probability
2	$\frac{1}{36}$
3	$\frac{2}{36}$
4	$\frac{3}{36}$
5	$\frac{4}{36}$
6	$\frac{5}{36}$
7	$\frac{6}{36}$
8	$\frac{5}{36}$
9	$\frac{4}{36}$
10	$\frac{3}{36}$
11	$\frac{2}{36}$
12	$\frac{1}{36}$

16. The probability distribution for the number of "ones" obtained from tossing 12 dice is given in Table 11 on the next page. This probability distribution has mean 2 and standard deviation 1.291 ($\sigma^2 = \frac{5}{3}$).

    (a) Using the table, give the probability that the number of "ones" is between 0 and 4, inclusive.

    (b) Use the Chebychev inequality to estimate the probability that the number of "ones" is between 0 and 4, inclusive.

17. Redo Example 1 using the alternate formula for the variance.

18. If X is a random variable, then the variance of X equals the variance of $X - a$ for any number a. Redo Exercise 1 using this result with $a = 70$.

19. If X is a random variable, then the variance of aX equals a^2 times the variance of X. Verify this result for the random variable in Exercise 2 with $a = 2$.

20. If X is a random variable, then

$$E(X - a) = E(X) - a \quad \text{and} \quad E(aX) = aE(X)$$

for any number a. Give intuitive justifications of these results.

Table 11

Number of "ones"	Probability
0	.112
1	.269
2	.296
3	.197
4	.089
5	.028
6	.007
7	.001
8	.000
9	.000
10	.000
11	.000
12	.000

Exercises 21–24 require the use of a graphing calculator or a computer.

21. Table 12 gives the 1993–1994 enrollments of the 10 largest universities in the United States. Determine the mean and the standard deviation for these enrollments.

Table 12

University	Enrollment
University of Minnesota	51,880
Ohio State University	50,623
University of Texas	48,555
Miami Dade Community College	48,232
Texas A&M University	42,524
Arizona State	41,250
University of Wisconsin	39,999
University of Illinois	39,912
Michigan State	39,743
Houston Community College System	39,321

Source: National Center for Educational Statistics, U.S. Department of Education.

22. Table 13 gives the number of books (in millions) in the 10 largest libraries in the United States. Determine the mean and the standard deviation for the number of books.

Table 13

Library	Books
New York Public Library	10.5
Queens Borough Public Library	9.7
Chicago Public Library	6.8
Boston Public Library	6.5
Carnegie Library of Pittsburgh	6.4
Los Angeles Public Library	6.1
Free Library of Philadelphia	5.9
Brooklyn Public Library	4.7
Public Library of Cincinnati and Hamilton County	4.7
Houston Public Library	4.1

23. Table 14 summarizes the production of Ph.D. degrees in statistics at a certain university during the past 25 years. For instance, three Ph.D. degrees were awarded during 5 of the last 25 years. Determine the mean and the standard deviation for the number of degrees awarded each year.

Table 14

Number of degrees	Number of years
3	5
4	7
5	8
6	2
7	1
8	2

24. Table 15 gives the probability distribution for the possible earnings from a certain game of chance. Determine the mean and the standard deviation for the earnings.

Table 15

Earnings	Probability
−5	.23
−1	.32
1	.35
5	.07
10	.03

Solutions to Practice Problems 7.5

1. (a)

k	$\Pr(X = k)$	$k - \mu$	$(k - \mu)^2$	$(k - \mu)^2 \Pr(X = k)$
21	$\frac{1}{16}$	−2	4	$\frac{4}{16}$
22	$\frac{1}{8}$	−1	1	$\frac{1}{8}$
23	$\frac{5}{8}$	0	0	0
24	$\frac{1}{8}$	1	1	$\frac{1}{8}$
25	$\frac{1}{16}$	2	4	$\frac{4}{16}$

$$\mu = 21 \cdot \tfrac{1}{16} + 22 \cdot \tfrac{1}{8} + 23 \cdot \tfrac{5}{8} + 24 \cdot \tfrac{1}{8} + 25 \cdot \tfrac{1}{16}$$

$$= \tfrac{21}{16} + \tfrac{44}{16} + \tfrac{230}{16} + \tfrac{48}{16} + \tfrac{25}{16} = \tfrac{368}{16} = 23$$

$$[\text{variance}] = \tfrac{4}{16} + \tfrac{1}{8} + 0 + \tfrac{1}{8} + \tfrac{4}{16}$$

$$= \tfrac{2}{8} + \tfrac{1}{8} + 0 + \tfrac{1}{8} + \tfrac{2}{8} = \tfrac{6}{8} = \tfrac{3}{4}$$

(b) $\frac{7}{8}$. The probability that the outcome is between 22 and 24 is

$$\Pr(22) + \Pr(23) + \Pr(24) = \tfrac{1}{8} + \tfrac{5}{8} + \tfrac{1}{8} = \tfrac{7}{8}.$$

2. Probability $\geq \frac{1}{4}$. Here $\mu = 23$, $\sigma^2 = \frac{3}{4}$, and $c = 1$. By the Chebychev inequality, the probability that the outcome is between $23 - 1$ and $23 + 1$ is at least $1 - \left(\frac{3}{4}/1^2\right) = 1 - \frac{3}{4} = \frac{1}{4}$. [From 1(b) we obtained the actual probability of $\frac{7}{8}$, which is much greater than $\frac{1}{4}$. In the next section we will study a technique that gives better estimates. However, this technique holds only for a special type of probability distribution.]

7.6 The Normal Distribution

In this section we will see that the histogram for a binomial random variable can be approximated by a region under a smooth curve called a *normal curve*. Actually, these curves have a value in their own right in that they represent some random variables associated with experiments having infinitely many possible outcomes.

   Toss a coin 20 times and observe the number of heads. By using formula (2) of Section 7.3 with $n = 20$ and $p = .5$, we can calculate the probability of k heads. The results are displayed in Table 1 on the next page. The data of Table 1 can be displayed in histogram form, as in Fig. 1 on the next page.

   As we have seen, various probabilities may be interpreted as areas. For example, the probability that at most 9 heads occur is equal to the sum of the

Table 1	Probability of k Heads (to four places)		
k	Probability of k heads	k	Probability of k heads
0	.0000	10	.1762
1	.0000	11	.1602
2	.0002	12	.1201
3	.0011	13	.0739
4	.0046	14	.0370
5	.0148	15	.0148
6	.0370	16	.0046
7	.0739	17	.0011
8	.1201	18	.0002
9	.1602	19	.0000
		20	.0000

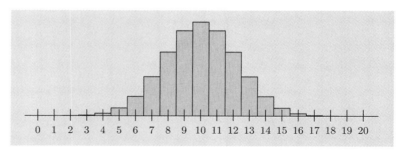

Figure 1.

areas of all the rectangles to the left of the central one (Fig. 2). The shape of the histogram in Figs. 1 and 2 suggests that we might be able to approximate such areas by using a smooth bell-shaped curve. The curve shown in Fig. 3 is a good candidate. It is called a *normal curve* and plays an important role in statistics and probability. (Tables giving the areas under normal curves have been constructed and can be used to approximate binomial probabilities.) For instance, the area of the shaded rectangles in Fig. 2 is approximately the same as the area under the normal curve to the left of 9.5 shown in Fig. 4. As another example, the probability of obtaining exactly 10 heads in 20 tosses of a coin is the area of the shaded rectangle in Fig. 5(a), which is approximated by the area under the normal curve shown in Fig. 5(b).

To be able to use normal curves in our computations, we need to study them more closely. Let us now take a glimpse into the realm of so-called continuous probability by studying appropriate experiments—namely, experiments with *normally distributed outcomes*. For such experiments, the probabilities of events are computed as areas under normal curves. It is no exaggeration to say that experiments with normally distributed outcomes are among the most significant in probability theory. Such experiments abound in the world around us. Here are a few examples:

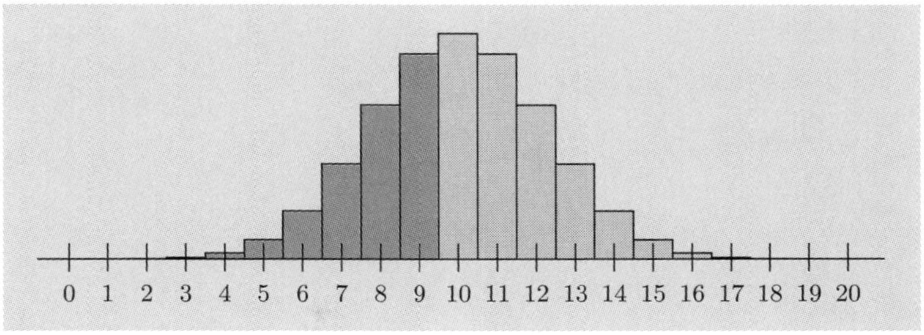

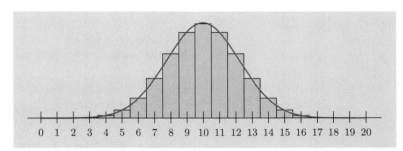

Figure 2.

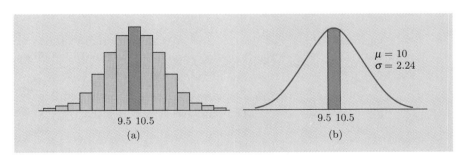

Figure 3.

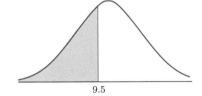

Figure 4.

1. Choose an individual at random and observe his or her IQ.

2. Choose a 1-day-old infant and observe his or her weight.

3. Choose an 8-year-old male at random and observe his height.

4. Choose a leaf at random from a particular tree and observe its length.

5. A lumber mill is cutting planks that are supposed to be 8 feet long; choose a plank at random and observe its actual length.

Figure 5.

Associated to each of the foregoing experiments is a bell-shaped curve, as shown in Fig. 6. Such a curve is called a *normal curve*. The curve is symmetric about a vertical line drawn through its highest point. This line of symmetry indicates the mean value of the corresponding experiment. The mean value is denoted as usual by the Greek letter μ. For example, if in experiment 4 above the average length of the leaves on the tree is 5 inches, then $\mu = 5$ and the corresponding bell-shaped curve is symmetric about the line $x = 5$.

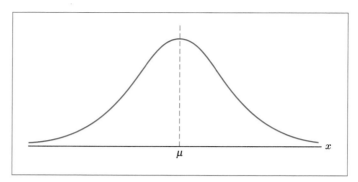

Figure 6.

The connection between an experiment with normally distributed outcomes and its associated normal curve is as follows:

> The probability that the experimental outcome is between a and b equals the area under the associated normal curve from $x = a$ to $x = b$. (This is the shaded region in Fig. 7.)

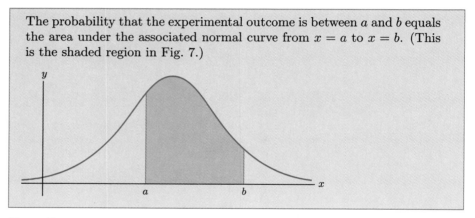

Figure 7.

The total area under a normal curve is always 1. This is due to the fact that the probability that the variable X corresponding to the distribution takes on some numerical value on the x-axis is 1.

▶ **Example 1** A certain experiment has normally distributed outcomes with mean $\mu = 1$. Shade the region corresponding to the probabilities of the following outcomes.

(a) The outcome lies between 1 and 3.
(b) The outcome lies between 0 and 2.
(c) The outcome is less than .5.
(d) The outcome is greater than 2.

Solution The outcomes are plotted along the x-axis. We then shade the appropriate area under the curve. ◆

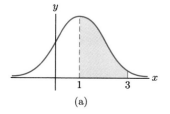
(a)

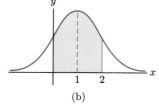
(b)

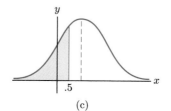
(c)

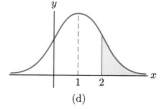
(d)

There are many different normal curves with the same mean. For instance, in Fig. 8 we have drawn three normal curves, all with $\mu = 0$. Roughly speaking, the difference between these normal curves is in the width of the center "hump."

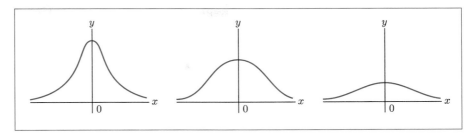

Figure 8.

A sharper hump indicates that the outcomes are more likely to be close to the mean. A flatter hump indicates a greater likelihood for the outcomes to be spread out. As we have seen, the spread of the outcomes about the mean is described by the standard deviation, denoted by the Greek letter σ. In the case of a normal curve, the standard deviation has a simple geometric meaning: The normal curve "twists" (or, in calculus terminology, "inflects") at a distance σ on either side of the mean (Fig. 9). More specifically, a normal curve may be thought of as made up of two pieces: a "cap," which looks like an upside-down bowl; and a pair of legs, which curve in the opposite direction. The places at which the cap and legs are joined are at a distance σ from the mean. Thus it is clear that the size of σ controls the sharpness of the hump.

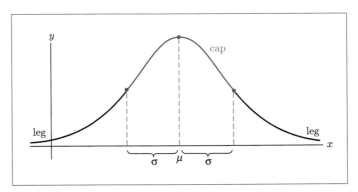

Figure 9.

A normal curve is completely described by its mean μ and standard deviation σ. In fact, given μ and σ, we may write down the equation of the associated normal curve:

$$y = \frac{1}{\sigma\sqrt{2\pi}} e^{-\left(\frac{1}{2}\right)\left(\frac{x-\mu}{\sigma}\right)^2},$$

where $\pi \approx 3.1416$ and $e \approx 2.7183$. Fortunately, we will not need this rather complicated formula in what follows. But it is only fair to say that all theoretical work on the normal curve ultimately rests on this equation.

For our purposes we will compute areas under normal curves by consulting a table. One might expect that a separate table would be needed for each normal curve, but such is not the case. Only one table is needed: the table corresponding to the *standard normal curve*, which is the one for which $\mu = 0$ and $\sigma = 1$. So let

Table 2					
z	$A(z)$	z	$A(z)$	z	$A(z)$
-4.00	.0000	-1.25	.1056	1.50	.9332
-3.75	.0001	-1.00	.1587	1.75	.9599
-3.50	.0002	$-.75$	.2266	2.00	.9772
-3.25	.0006	$-.50$	.3085	2.25	.9878
-3.00	.0013	$-.25$	.4013	2.50	.9938
-2.75	.0030	0	.5000	2.75	.9970
-2.50	.0062	.25	.5987	3.00	.9987
-2.25	.0122	.50	.6915	3.25	.9994
-2.00	.0228	.75	.7734	3.50	.9998
-1.75	.0401	1.00	.8413	3.75	.9999
-1.50	.0668	1.25	.8944	4.00	1.0000

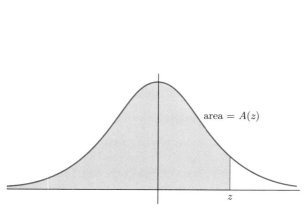

area $= A(z)$

Figure 10.

us begin our discussion of areas under normal curves by considering the standard normal curve.

We usually use the letter Z to denote a random variable having the standard normal distribution. Let z be any number and let $A(z)$ denote the area under the standard normal curve to the left of z (Fig. 10). Table 2 gives $A(z)$ for various values of z, with the values of $A(z)$ rounded to four decimal places. Thus, $A(z) = \Pr(Z \leq z)$.[1] A more extensive table can be found in Table 1 of Appendix A. The efficient use of these tables depends on the following three facts:

1. The standard normal curve is symmetric about $z = 0$.

2. The total area under the standard normal curve is 1.

3. The probability that the standard normal variable Z lies to the left of the number z is the area $A(z)$ in Fig. 10.

These facts allow us to use the tables to find the areas of various types of regions.

▶ Example 2 Use Table 2 to determine the areas of the regions under the standard normal curve pictured in Fig. 11.

Solution (a) This region is just the portion of the curve to the left of $-.5$. So its area is $A(-.5)$. Looking down the middle pair of columns of the table, we find that $A(-.5) = .3085$. This means that

$$\Pr(Z \leq -.5) = .3085.$$

---

[1]We could have said that $A(z) = \Pr(Z < z)$. However, since the region strictly to the left of z and that region with the line segment at z adjoined have the same area, $\Pr(Z < z)$ and $\Pr(Z \leq z)$ are the same. We always use the $\leq$ symbol.

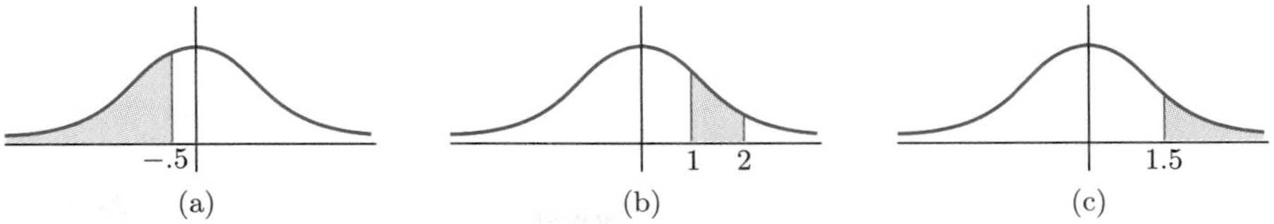

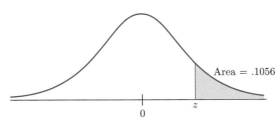

Figure 11.

(b) This region results from beginning with the region to the left of 2 and subtracting the region to the left of 1. We obtain an area of

$$A(2) - A(1) = .9772 - .8413 = .1359.$$

Thus

$$\Pr(1 \le Z \le 2) = .1359.$$

(c) This region can be thought of as the entire region under the curve, with the region to the left of 1.5 removed. Therefore, the area is

$$1 - A(1.5) = 1 - .9332 = .0668.$$

So

$$\Pr(Z \ge 1.5) = .0668. \qquad \blacklozenge$$

▶ **Example 3**   Find the value of z for which $\Pr(Z \ge z) = .1056$ (see Fig. 12).

Area = .1056

0   z

Figure 12.

Solution   Since the area under the standard normal curve is 1 and the curve is symmetric about $z = 0$, the area of the portion to the right of 0 must be .5. We draw a sketch of the standard normal curve, placing z on the axis to the right of 0. (This way, the area to the right of z will be less than .5.) Table 2 gives the values of $A(z)$, which are left tail areas. The area to the left of our z is

$$A(z) = 1 - .1056 = .8944.$$

From Table 2 we find that the value of z for which $A(z) = .8944$ is 1.25. $\qquad \blacklozenge$

Percentiles   In large-scale testing, scores are frequently reported as percentiles rather than as raw scores. What does it mean to say that a score is "the 90th percentile"? It means that, roughly speaking, the score separates the bottom 90% of the scores from the top 10%.

If a score S is the pth percentile of a normal distribution, then $p\%$ of all scores fall below S, and $(100 - p)\%$ of all scores fall above S.

▶ Example 4   What is the 50th percentile of the standard normal distribution?

Solution   The standard normal curve is symmetric about $z = 0$, and the total area under the curve is 1. Thus, 50% of the values of the standard normal variable fall below 0, and $(100 - 50)\% = 50\%$ of its values fall above 0. So 0 is the 50th percentile of the standard normal distribution.   ◆

▶ Example 5   What is the 95th percentile of the standard normal distribution?

Solution   We shall call the value that we seek z_{95} to remind us that it is a score and that the probability that an outcome is to the left of it is 95% (see Fig. 13).

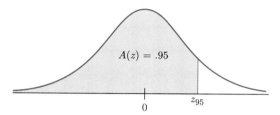

$A(z) = .95$

z_{95}

0

Figure 13.

Since Table 1 of Appendix A gives areas to the left of values of z, we should search the column marked $A(z)$ for the area we need—.95. We find that the closest value to .95 is .9505, and $A(1.65) = .9505$. Hence $z_{95} \approx 1.65$. This means that 95% of the time the standard normal variable falls below 1.65. Since $\mu = 0$ and $\sigma = 1$, another way of stating the result is that in the standard normal distribution, 95% of the values are less than 1.65 standard deviations above the mean.   ◆

The problem of finding the area of a region under any normal curve can be reduced to finding the area of a region under the standard normal curve. To illustrate the computation procedure, let us consider a numerical example.

▶ Example 6   Find the area under the normal curve with $\mu = 3$, $\sigma = 2$ from $x = 1$ to $x = 5$. This represents $\Pr(1 \leq X \leq 5)$ for a random variable X having the given normal distribution.

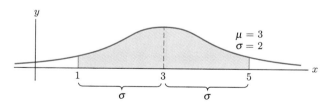

y

$\mu = 3$
$\sigma = 2$

1   3   5 x

σ σ

Figure 14.

Solution   We have sketched the described region in Fig. 14. It extends from one standard deviation below the mean to one standard deviation above. Draw the corresponding region under the standard normal curve. That is, draw the region from one standard deviation below to one standard deviation above the mean (Fig. 15). It is a theorem that this new region has the same area as the original one. But the area in Fig. 15 may be computed from Table 2 as $A(1) - A(-1)$. So our desired area is

$$A(1) - A(-1) = .8413 - .1587 = .6826.$$ ◆

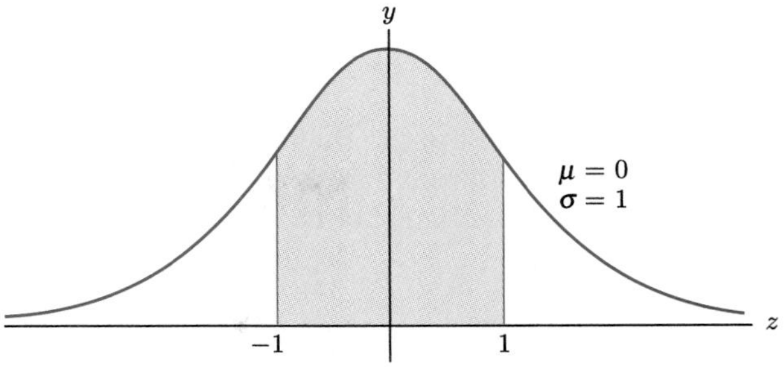

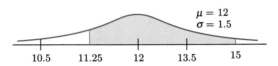

y

$\mu = 0$
$\sigma = 1$

−1   1   z

Figure 15.

▶ Example 7   Consider the normal curve with $\mu = 12$, $\sigma = 1.5$. Find the area of the region under the curve between $x = 11.25$ and $x = 15$. (Fig. 16).

$\mu = 12$
$\sigma = 1.5$

10.5   11.25   12   13.5   15

Figure 16.

Solution   Expressed as a probability, we want to find $\Pr(11.25 \leq X \leq 15)$ for a random variable X having a normal distribution with $\mu = 12$ and $\sigma = 1.5$. The number 11.25 is .75 below the mean 12. And .75 is $.75/1.5 = .5$ standard deviations. The number 15 is 3 above the mean. And 3 is $3/1.5 = 2$ standard deviations. Therefore, the region has the same area as the region under the standard normal curve from $-.5$ to 2, which is

$$A(2) - A(-.5) = .9772 - .3085 = .6687. \qquad \blacklozenge$$

Suppose that a normal curve has mean μ and standard deviation σ. Then the area under the curve from $x = a$ to $x = b$ is

$$A\left(\frac{b - \mu}{\sigma}\right) - A\left(\frac{a - \mu}{\sigma}\right).$$

The numbers $b - \mu$ and $a - \mu$, respectively, measure the distances of b and a from the mean. The numbers $(b - \mu)/\sigma$ and $(a - \mu)/\sigma$ express these distances as multiples of the standard deviation σ. So the area under the normal curve from $x = a$ to $x = b$ is computed by expressing x in terms of standard deviations from the mean and then treating the curve as if it were the standard normal curve. We summarize the procedure.

If X is a random variable having a normal distribution with mean μ and standard deviation σ, then

$$\Pr(a \leq X \leq b) = \Pr\left(\frac{a - \mu}{\sigma} \leq Z \leq \frac{b - \mu}{\sigma}\right) = A\left(\frac{b - \mu}{\sigma}\right) - A\left(\frac{a - \mu}{\sigma}\right)$$

and

$$\Pr(X \leq x) = \Pr\left(Z \leq \frac{x - \mu}{\sigma}\right) = A\left(\frac{x - \mu}{\sigma}\right),$$

where Z has the standard normal distribution and $A(z)$ is the area under that distribution to the left of z.

Let us now use our knowledge of areas under normal curves to calculate probabilities arising in some applied problems.

▶ Example 8   Suppose that for a certain population the birth weights of infants in pounds are normally distributed with $\mu = 7.75$ and $\sigma = 1.25$. Find the probability that an infant's birth weight is more than 9 pounds, 10 ounces. (*Note:* 9 pounds, 10 ounces $= 9\frac{5}{8}$ pounds.)

Solution   Let $X = $ infant's birth weight. Then X is a random variable having a normal distribution with $\mu = 7.75$ and $\sigma = 1.25$ pounds. $\Pr\left(X \geq 9\frac{5}{8}\right)$ is given by the area under the appropriate normal curve to the right of $9\frac{5}{8}$—that is, the area shaded in Fig. 17. Since $9\frac{5}{8} = 9.625$, the number $9\frac{5}{8}$ lies $9.625 - 7.75 = 1.875$ units above the mean. In turn, this is $1.875/1.25 = 1.5$ standard deviations. We can find the corresponding z-value in one calculation by finding

$$z = \frac{x - \mu}{\sigma} = \frac{9.625 - 7.75}{1.25} = 1.5.$$

Thus 9.625 is 1.5 standard deviations above the mean. The area we seek is sketched under the standard normal curve in Fig. 18 and is

$$1 - A(1.5) = 1 - .9332 = .0668.$$

So the probability that an infant weighs more than 9 pounds, 10 ounces is .0668. ◆

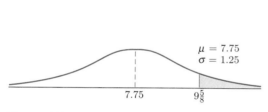

Figure 17.

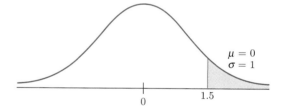

Figure 18.

▶ Example 9   A wholesale produce dealer finds that the number of boxes of bananas sold each day is normally distributed with $\mu = 1200$ and $\sigma = 100$. Find the probability that the number sold on a particular day is less than 1000.

Solution   Let $X = $ the number of boxes of bananas sold each day. Since daily sales are normally distributed, the desired probability, $\Pr(X \leq 1000)$, is the area to the left of 1000 in the normal curve drawn in Fig. 19. The number 1000 is 2 standard deviations below the mean; that is, $x = 1000$ corresponds to a z-value of

$$z = \frac{x - \mu}{\sigma} = \frac{1000 - 1200}{100} = -2.$$

Therefore, the area we seek is $A(-2) = .0228$ shown in Fig. 20. The probability that less than 1000 boxes will be sold in a day is .0228. ◆

▶ Example 10   Find the 95th percentile of infant birth weights if infant birth weights are normally distributed with $\mu = 7.75$ and $\sigma = 1.25$ pounds.

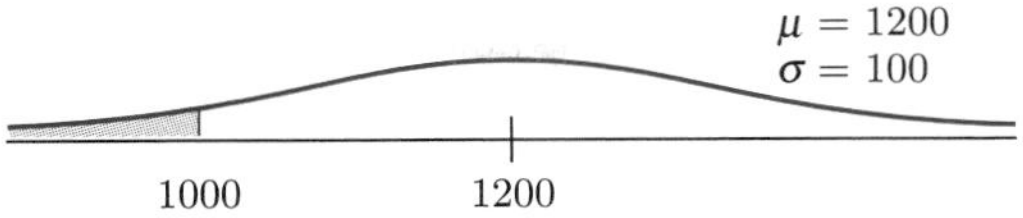

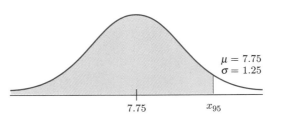

Figure 19.

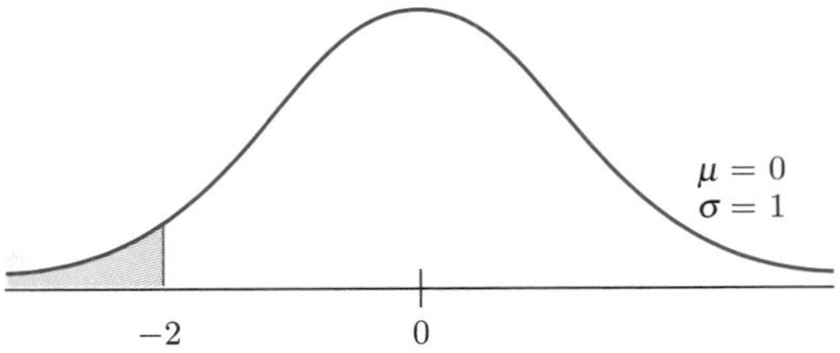

Figure 20.

Figure 21.

Solution   Let us denote the 95th percentile of the infant birth weights by x_{95}. This means that the area to the left of x_{95} under the normal curve with $\mu = 7.75$ and $\sigma = 1.25$ is 95% (Fig. 21).

The corresponding value for the standard normal random variable would be z_{95}, which we already know to be 1.65. Thus x_{95} is 1.65 standard deviations above μ. That is,

$$x_{95} = 7.75 + (1.65)(1.25) \approx 9.81 \text{ pounds.}$$

Therefore, 95% of all infants have birth weights below 9.81 pounds (9 lb, 13 oz).
◆

▶ **Example 11**   The wholesale produce dealer of Example 9 wants to be 99% sure that she has enough boxes of bananas on hand each day to meet the demand. How many should she stock each day?

Solution   Let x be the number of boxes of bananas that the produce dealer should stock. Since she wants to be 99% sure that the demand for boxes of bananas does not exceed x, we must find the 99th percentile of a normal distribution with $\mu = 1200$ and $\sigma = 100$. To help us remember what x really is, we will rename it x_{99}. The corresponding value for the standard normal random variable is z_{99}. Figures 22 and 23 on the next page show the appropriate areas—first under the given normal curve and then under the standard normal curve.

The area, $A(z)$, that we seek under the standard normal curve is .99. Referring to Table 1 of Appendix A, we get closest with $A(z) = .9906$, corresponding to $z_{99} = 2.35$. The value z_{99} is 2.35 standard deviations above the mean of its distribution. We conclude that x_{99} is also 2.35 standard deviations above its mean. Hence,

$$x_{99} = 1200 + (2.35)(100) = 1435 \text{ boxes.}$$

Therefore, we expect that on 99% of the days, 1435 boxes of bananas will meet the demand. More than 1435 boxes should be needed 1% of the time (one day out of 100).
◆

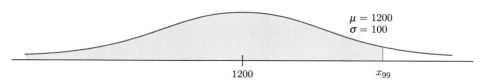

Figure 22.

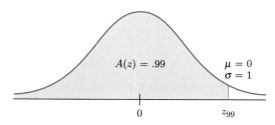

Figure 23.

We summarize the technique for finding percentiles of normal distributions.

If x_p is the pth percentile of a normal distribution with mean μ and standard deviation σ, then

$$x_p = \mu + z_p \cdot \sigma,$$

where z_p is the pth percentile of the standard normal distribution.

GC Normal curves can easily be graphed and normal probabilities calculated on most graphing calculators. Consider Example 6. Figure 24 contains the graph of the normal curve, and Fig. 25 gives the desired probability.

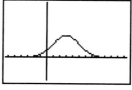

Figure 24.
$[-6.4, 12.4]$ by $[-.2, .5]$

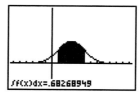

Figure 25.

Figure 26.

To graph a normal curve, you must first assign a formula to a function as in Fig. 26. (The formula for **Y₁** can be used with any calculator; the formula for **Y₂** requires a TI-83.) [To display **"normalpdf("**, press 2nd [DISTR] **1**. The general form of the command is **normalpdf(X,μ,σ).**] After the function has been defined and an appropriate window specified, the graph in Fig. 24 can be obtained by pressing GRAPH.

With a TI-82 or TI-83, an area under a normal curve can be calculated and the corresponding region of the graph shaded. Suppose **Y₁** has been set to one of the formulas in Fig. 26 and its graph appears on the screen as in Fig. 24. Suppose we want to find the area under the curve from $x = a$ to $x = b$. Press 2nd [CALC] **7** and answer the questions. Reply to **"Lower Bound?"** by moving the trace cursor to the point whose x-coordinate is a and pressing ENTER. Reply to **"Upper Bound?"** by moving the trace cursor to the point whose x-coordinate is b and pressing ENTER. [*Note:* This task is usually easiest to accomplish when the difference between **xMax** and **xMin** is a multiple of 9.4. For instance, in

Fig. 24, **xMax** − **xMin** = 12.4 − (−6.4) = 18.8 = 2(9.4).] With a TI-83, the questions can be replied to by entering numbers. For instance, after pressing 2nd [CALC] **7**, respond to **"Lower Bound?"** by typing in the number **1** and pressing ENTER, and respond to **"Upper Bound?"** by typing in the number **5** and pressing ENTER. To erase the shading under the curve, press 2nd [DRAW] **1**. To find the area of an infinite region, just select a large negative value of a or a large value of b.

The area under a normal curve also can be evaluated on the home screen with the instruction

$$\texttt{fnInt(Y}_1\texttt{,X,a,b)}$$

where **Y₁** has been set to one of the functions of the type shown in Fig. 26. For instance, the area of the shaded region in Example 6 can be evaluated by typing **fnInt(Y₁,X,1,5)** and pressing ENTER. [From the home screen, **fnInt(** is displayed with MATH **9** on a TI-82 or TI-83.]

Practice Problems 7.6

1. Refer to Fig. 27(a). Find the value of z for which the area of the shaded region is .0802.

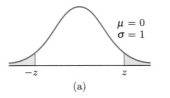
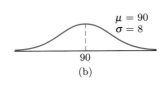

(a) (b)

Figure 27.

2. Refer to the normal curve in Fig. 27(b). Express the following numbers in terms of standard deviations from the mean.

(a) 90   (b) 82   (c) 94   (d) 104

▶ Exercises 7.6

In Exercises 1–8, use the table for $A(z)$ (Table 2) to find the areas of the shaded regions under the standard normal curve.

1.

1.25

2.

−.75   1

3.

.25

4.

−1   1

5.

.5 1.5

6.

−1

7.

−.5 .5

8.

−1.25

In Exercises 9–12, find the value of z for which the area of the shaded region under the standard normal curve is as specified.

9. Area is .0401.

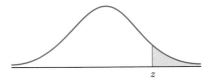
z

10. Area is .0456.

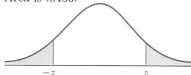

11. Area is .5468.

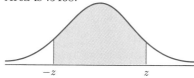

12. Area is .6915.

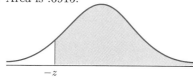

In Exercises 13–16, determine μ and σ by inspection.

13.

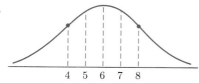

14.

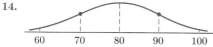

15.

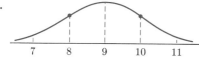

16.

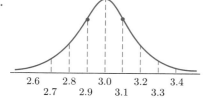

Exercises 17–20 refer to the normal curve with $\mu = 8$, $\sigma = \frac{3}{4}$.

17. Convert 6 into standard deviations from the mean.

18. Convert $9\frac{1}{4}$ into standard deviations from the mean.

19. What value of x corresponds to 10 standard deviations above the mean?

20. What value of x corresponds to 2 standard deviations below the mean?

In Exercises 21–24, find the areas of the shaded regions under the given normal curves.

21.

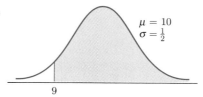

22.

23.

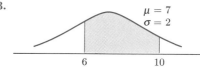

24.

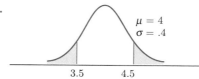

25. Suppose that the height (at the shoulder) of adult African bull bush elephants is normally distributed with $\mu = 3.3$ meters and $\sigma = .2$ meter. The elephant on display at the Smithsonian Institution has height 4 meters and is the largest elephant on record. What is the probability that an adult African bull bush elephant has height 4 meters or more?

26. At a soft-drink bottling plant, the amount of cola put into the bottles is normally distributed with $\mu = 16\frac{3}{4}$ ounces and $\sigma = \frac{1}{2}$. What is the probability that a bottle will contain less than 16 ounces?

27. Bolts produced by a machine are acceptable provided that their length is within the range from 5.95 to 6.05 centimeters. Suppose that the lengths of the bolts produced are normally distributed with $\mu = 6$ centimeters and $\sigma = .02$. What is the probability that a bolt will be of an acceptable length?

28. Suppose that IQ scores are normally distributed with $\mu = 100$ and $\sigma = 10$. What percent of the population have IQ scores of 125 or more?

29. The amount of gas sold weekly by a certain gas station is normally distributed with $\mu = 30,000$ gallons and $\sigma = 4000$. If the station has 39,000 gallons on hand at the beginning of the week, what is the probability of its running out of gas before the end of the week?

30. Suppose that the lifetimes of a certain light bulb are normally distributed with $\mu = 1200$ hours and $\sigma = 160$. Find the probability that a light bulb will burn out in less than 1000 hours.

31. Assume that SAT verbal scores for a first-year class at a university are normally distributed with mean 520 and standard deviation 75.

    (a) The top 10% of the students are placed into the honors program for English. What is the lowest score for admittance into the honors program?

    (b) What is the range of the middle 90% of the SAT verbal scores at this university?

32. A mail-order house uses an average of 300 mailing bags per day. The number of bags needed each day is approximately normally distributed with $\sigma = 50$. How many bags must the company have on hand at the beginning of a day to be 99% certain that all orders can be filled?

33. The lifetime of a certain brand of tires is normally distributed with mean $\mu = 30{,}000$ miles and standard deviation $\sigma = 5000$ miles. The company has decided to issue a warranty for the tires but does not want to replace more than 2% of the tires that it sells. At what mileage should the warranty expire?

34. Let X be a random variable with $\mu = 4$ and $\sigma = .5$.

    (a) Use the Chebyshev inequality to estimate $\Pr(3 \le X \le 5)$.

    (b) If X were normally distributed, what would be the exact probability that X is between 3 and 5 inclusive?

    (c) Reconcile the difference between the answers to (a) and (b).

35. Let X be the amount of soda released by a soft-drink dispensing machine into a 6-ounce cup. Assume that X is normally distributed with $\sigma = .25$ ounces and that the average "fill" can be set by the vendor.

    (a) At what quantity should the average "fill" be set so that no more than .5% of the releases overflow the cup?

    (b) Using the average "fill" found in part (a), determine the minimal amount that will be dispensed in 99% of the cases.

Exercises 36–39 require the use of a graphing calculator or a computer.

36. Draw the graph of the normal curve with $\mu = 10$, $\sigma = 2$ and the normal curve with $\mu = 10$, $\sigma = 3$ on the same coordinate system. Describe the effect on a normal curve of increasing σ.

37. Draw the graph of the normal curve with $\mu = 11$, $\sigma = 2$ and the normal curve with $\mu = 15$, $\sigma = 2$ on the same coordinate system. Describe the effect on a normal curve of increasing μ.

38. In a certain population, heights (in inches) are normally distributed with $\mu = 67$ and $\sigma = 3$. Find the probability that a person selected at random has a height between 63 and 71 inches.

39. In a certain manufacturing process, lengths (in cm) of widgets are normally distributed with $\mu = 5.4$ and $\sigma = .6$. Find the probability that a widget selected at random has a length greater than 5.832 cm.

Solutions to Practice Problems 7.6

1. 1.75. Due to the symmetry of normal curves, each piece of the shaded region has area $\frac{1}{2}(.0802) = .0401$. Therefore, $A(-z) = .0401$ and so by Table 2, $-z = -1.75$. Thus $z = 1.75$.

2. (a) 0. Since 90 *is* the mean, it is 0 standard deviations from the mean.

    (b) -1. Since 82 is $90 - 8$, it is 8 units or 1 standard deviation below the mean.

    (c) .5. Here $94 = 90 + 4$ is 4 units or .5 standard deviations above the mean.

    (d) 1.75. Here $104 = 90 + 14$ is 14 units or $\frac{14}{8} = 1.75$ standard deviations above the mean.

7.7 Normal Approximation to the Binomial Distribution

In Section 7.3 we saw that complicated and tedious calculations can arise from the binomial probability distribution. For instance, determining the probability of getting at least 20 threes in 100 tosses of a die requires the computation

$$\binom{100}{20}\left(\frac{1}{6}\right)^{20}\left(\frac{5}{6}\right)^{80} + \binom{100}{21}\left(\frac{1}{6}\right)^{21}\left(\frac{5}{6}\right)^{79} + \cdots + \binom{100}{100}\left(\frac{1}{6}\right)^{100}\left(\frac{5}{6}\right)^{0}.$$

Mathematicians have shown that such probabilities can be closely approximated by using normal curves.

Consider the histograms of the binomial distributions in Figures 1 and 2. The number of trials, n, increases from 5 to 40, with p fixed at .3. As n increases, the shape of the histogram more closely conforms to the shape of the region under a normal curve.

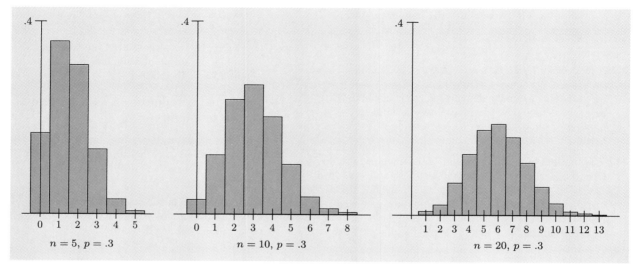

Figure 1. Binomial distribution.

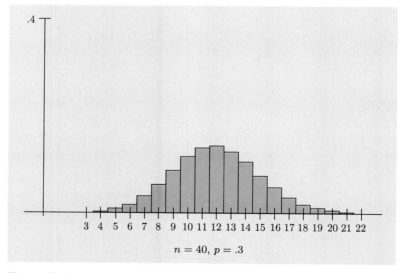

Figure 2. Binomial distribution.

We have the following result:

Suppose that we perform a sequence of n binomial trials with probability of success p and probability of failure q and observe the number of successes. Then the histogram for the resulting probability distribution may be approximated by the normal curve with $\mu = np$ and $\sigma = \sqrt{npq}$.

Note This approximation is very accurate when both $np > 5$ and $nq > 5$.

▶ Example 1 Refer to Example 3 of Section 7.3. A plumbing-supplies manufacturer produces faucet washers that are packaged in boxes of 300. Quality control studies have shown that 2% of the washers are defective. What is the probability that more than 10 of the washers in a single box are defective?

Solution Let $X =$ the number of defective washers in a box. Then X is a binomial random variable with $n = 300$ and $p = .02$. We will use the approximating normal curve with

$$\mu = np = 300(.02) = 6$$
$$\sigma = \sqrt{npq} = \sqrt{300(.02)(.98)} \approx 2.425.$$

The probability that more than 10 of the washers in a single box are defective is the sum of the areas of the rectangles centered at $11, 12, \ldots, 300$ in the histogram for the random variable X (see Fig. 3). The corresponding region under the approximating normal curve is shaded in Fig. 4. This is the area under the standard normal curve to the right of

$$z = \frac{10.5 - \mu}{\sigma} = \frac{10.5 - 6}{2.425} \approx 1.85.$$

The area of the region is $1 - A(1.85) = 1 - .9678 = .0322$. Therefore, approximately 3.22% of the boxes should contain more than 10 defective washers. ◆

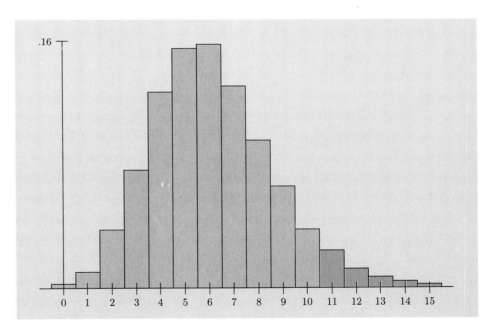

Figure 3.

Note In Fig. 4 on the next page we shaded the region to the right of 10.5 rather than to the right of 10. This gives a better approximation to the corresponding area under the histogram, since the rectangle corresponding to 11 "successes" has its left endpoint at 10.5.

Let us consider an application to medical research.

▶ Example 2 Consider the cattle disease of Example 4 of Section 7.3, from which 25% of the cattle recover. A veterinarian discovers a serum to combat the disease. In a

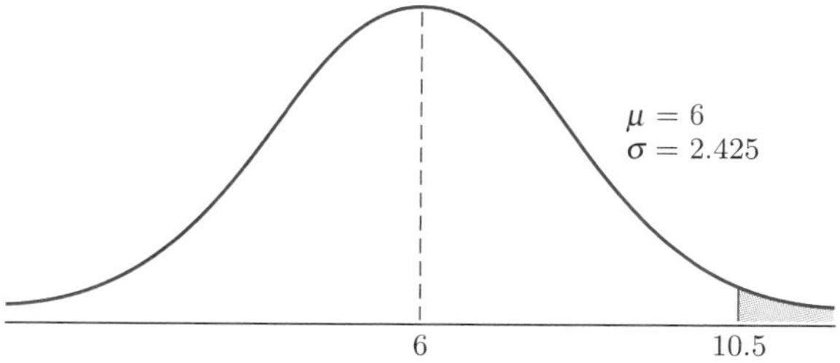

Figure 4.

test of the serum she observes that 16 of a herd of 40 recover. Suppose that the serum had not been used. What is the likelihood that at least 16 cattle would have recovered?

Solution   Let X be the number of cattle that recover. Then X is a binomial random variable with $n = 40$ independent trials. If the serum is not used, $p = .25$. The approximating normal curve has

$$\mu = np = 40(.25) = 10, \qquad \sigma = \sqrt{npq} = \sqrt{40(.25)(.75)} \approx 2.74.$$

The likelihood that at least 16 cattle would have recovered is $\Pr(X \geq 16)$. This corresponds to the area under the normal curve to the right of 15.5 (Fig. 5). The area to the right of 15.5 under a normal curve with $\mu = 10$ and $\sigma = 2.74$ is the same as the area under the standard normal curve to the right of

$$z = \frac{15.5 - \mu}{\sigma} = \frac{15.5 - 10}{2.74} \approx 2.01.$$

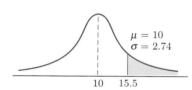

Figure 5.

We find $1 - A(2.01) \approx 1 - A(2.00) = 1 - .9772 = .0228$. Thus, if the serum were not used, the veterinarian would expect about a 2% chance that 16 or more cattle recover. Thus the 16 observed recoveries probably did not occur by chance. The veterinarian can reasonably conclude that the serum is effective against the disease.   ◆

▶ **Example 3**   Assume that a fair coin is tossed 100 times. Find the probability of observing exactly 50 heads.

Solution   Let X be the number of heads on $n = 100$ binomial trials with $p = .5$ probability of "success" on each trial. We are to find the area of the rectangle extending from 49.5 to 50.5 on the x-axis in the histogram for X. The actual probability is

$$\binom{100}{50}(.5)^{50}(.5)^{50} = \binom{100}{50}(.5)^{100}.$$

We approximate the probability with an area under the normal curve with $\mu = np = 100(.5) = 50$ and $\sigma = \sqrt{npq} = \sqrt{100(.5)(.5)} = 5$. The area we seek is sketched in Fig. 6. It is the area under the standard normal curve from

$$z = \frac{49.5 - 50}{5} = -.10 \quad \text{to} \quad z = \frac{50.5 - 50}{5} = .10.$$

Using Table 1 in Appendix A, we find that

$$A(.10) - A(-.10) = .5398 - .4602 = .0796.$$

So the likelihood of getting exactly 50 heads in 100 tosses of a fair coin is fairly small—about 8%.   ◆

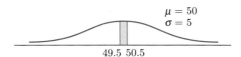

Figure 6.

▶ Example 4 Find the probability that in 100 tosses of a fair die we observe at least 20 threes.

Solution Let X be the number of threes observed in $n = 100$ trials, with $p = \frac{1}{6}$ the probability of a three on each trial. Then we need to find the area to the right of 19.5 under the normal curve with

$$\mu = np = 100\left(\tfrac{1}{6}\right) \approx 16.7 \quad \text{and} \quad \sigma = \sqrt{npq} = \sqrt{100\left(\tfrac{1}{6}\right)\left(\tfrac{5}{6}\right)} \approx 3.73.$$

This area is

$$1 - A\left(\frac{19.5 - 16.7}{3.73}\right) \approx 1 - A(.75) = 1 - .7734 = .2266.$$

Therefore, the probability of observing at least 20 threes is about .2266. ◆

Practice Problems 7.7	1. A new drug is being tested on laboratory mice. The mice have been given a disease for which the recovery rate is $\frac{1}{2}$. (a) In the first experiment the drug is given to 5 of the mice and all 5 recover. Find the probability that the success of this experiment was due to luck. That is, find the probability that 5 out of 5 mice recover in the event that the drug has no effect on the illness. (b) In a second experiment the drug is given to 25 mice and 18 recover. Find the probability that 18 or more recover in the event that the drug has no effect on the illness. 2. What conclusions can be drawn from the results in Problem 1?

▶ Exercises 7.7

In Exercises 1–14, use the normal curve to approximate the probability.

1. An experiment consists of 25 binomial trials, each having probability $\frac{1}{5}$ of success. Use an approximating normal curve to estimate the probability of

   (a) Exactly 5 successes.

   (b) Between 3 and 7 successes, inclusive.

   (c) Less than 10 successes.

2. An experiment consists of 18 binomial trials, each having probability $\frac{2}{3}$ of success. Use an approximating normal curve to estimate the probability of

   (a) Exactly 10 successes.

   (b) Between 8 and 16 successes, inclusive.

   (c) More than 12 successes.

3. Laboratory mice are given an illness for which the usual recovery rate is $\frac{1}{6}$. A new drug is tested on 20 of the mice, and 8 of them recover. What is the probability that 8 or more would have recovered if the 20 mice had not been given the drug?

4. A person claims to have ESP (extrasensory perception). A coin is tossed 16 times, and each time the person is asked to predict in advance whether the coin will land heads or tails. The person predicts correctly 75% of the time (i.e., on 12 tosses). What is the probability of being correct 12 or more times by pure guessing?

5. A wine-taster claims that she can usually distinguish between domestic and imported wines. As a test, she is given 100 wines to test and correctly identifies 63 of them. What is the probability that she accomplished that good a record by pure guessing? That is, what is the probability of being correct 63 or more times out of 100 by pure guessing?

6. In American roulette, the probability of winning when betting "red" is $\frac{9}{19}$. What is the probability of being ahead after betting the same amount 90 times?

7. A basketball player makes each free throw with probability $\frac{3}{4}$. What is the probability of making 68 or more shots out of 75 trials?

8. A bookstore determines that two-fifths of the people who come into the store make a purchase. What is the probability that of the 54 people who come into the store during a certain hour, less than 14 make a purchase?

9. A baseball player has a lifetime batting average of .310. Find the probability that he gets at least 6 hits in 20 times at bat.

10. An advertising agency, which reached 25% of its target audience with its old campaign, has devised a new advertising campaign. In a sample of 1000 people, it finds that 290 have been reached by the new advertising campaign. What is the probability that at least 290 people would have been reached by the old campaign? Does the new campaign seem to be more effective?

11. A washing machine manufacturer finds that 2% of its washing machines break down within the first year. Find the probability that less than 15 out of a lot of 1000 washers break down within 1 year.

12. The incidence of color blindness among the men in a certain country is 20%. Find the expected number of color-blind men in a random sample of 70 men. What is the probability of finding exactly that number of color-blind men in a sample of size 70?

13. In a random sample of 250 college students, 50 of them own a compact-disc player. Estimate the probability that a college student chosen at random owns a compact-disc player. If actually 25% of all college students own compact-disc players, what is the probability that in a random survey of 250 students, at most 50 of them own the devices?

14. The probabilities of failure for each of three independent components in a device are .01, .02, and .01, respectively. The device fails only if all three components fail. Out of a lot of 1 million devices, how many would be expected to fail? Find the probability that more than three devices in the lot fail.

Exercises 15–17 require the use of a graphing calculator or computer.

15. In 100 tosses of a fair coin, let X be the number of heads. Find the exact value of $\Pr(49 \le X \le 51)$, and also find the normal approximation to that probability.

16. Let X be the number of 4's in 120 tosses of a fair die. Calculate the exact probability $\Pr(17 \le X \le 21)$, and also find the normal approximation to that probability.

17. Say that there is a 20% chance that a person chosen at random from the population has never heard of John Steinbeck. Find the exact probability that in 150 people we find exactly 30 people who have not heard of Steinbeck. Compare your result with the normal approximation to that probability.

Solutions to Practice Problems 7.7

1. (a) Giving the drug to a single mouse is a binomial trial with "recovery" as "success" and "death" as "failure." If the drug has no effect, then the probability of success is $\frac{1}{2}$. The probability of five successes in five trials is given by formula (2) of Section 7.3, with $n = 5$, $p = \frac{1}{2}$, $q = \frac{1}{2}$, $k = 5$.

$$\Pr(X = 5) = \binom{5}{5}\left(\frac{1}{2}\right)^5\left(\frac{1}{2}\right)^0 = \left(\frac{1}{2}\right)^5 = \frac{1}{32} = .03125$$

(b) As in part (a), this experiment is a binomial experiment with $p = \frac{1}{2}$. However, now $n = 25$. The probability that 18 or more mice recover is

$$\Pr(X = 18) + \Pr(X = 19) + \cdots + \Pr(X = 25).$$

This probability is the area of the shaded portion of the histogram in Fig. 7(a). The histogram can be approximated by the normal curve with

$$\mu = 25 \cdot \frac{1}{2} = 12.5 \quad \text{and} \quad \sigma = \sqrt{25 \cdot \frac{1}{2} \cdot \frac{1}{2}} = \sqrt{\frac{25}{4}} = \frac{5}{2} = 2.5.$$

[Fig. 7(b)].

| Solutions to Practice Problems 7.7 (Continued) | Since the shaded portion of the histogram begins at the point 17.5, the desired probability is approximately the area of the shaded region under the normal curve. The number 17.5 is |

$$\frac{(17.5 - 12.5)}{2.5} = \frac{5}{2.5} = 2$$

standard deviations to the right of the mean. Hence, the area under the curve is $1 - A(2) = 1 - .9772 = .0228$. Therefore, the probability that 18 or more mice recover is approximately .0228.

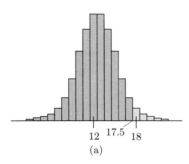 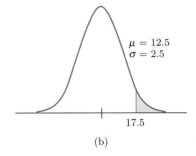

Figure 7.

2. Both experiments offer convincing evidence that the drug is helpful in treating the illness. The likelihood of obtaining the results by pure chance is slim. The second experiment might be considered more conclusive than the first, since the result, if due to chance, has a lower probability.

▶ Chapter 7 Summary

1. *Bar charts*, *pie charts*, *histograms*, and *box plots* help us turn raw data into visual forms that often allow us to see patterns in the data quickly.

2. The *median* of an ordered list of data is a number with the property that the same number of data items lie above it as below it. For an ordered list of N numbers, it is the middle number when N is odd, and the average of the two middle numbers when N is even.

3. For an ordered list of data, the *first quartile* Q_1 is the median of the list of data items below the median, and the *third quartile* Q_3 is the median of the list of data items above the median. The difference of the third and first quartiles is called the *interquartile range*. The sequence of numbers consisting of the lowest number, Q_1, the median, Q_3, and the highest number is called the *five-number summary*.

4. The probability distribution for a random variable can be displayed in a table or a histogram. With a histogram, the probability of an event is the sum of the areas of the rectangles corresponding to the outcomes in the event.

5. If the probability of success in each trial of a binomial experiment is p, then the probability of k successes in n trials is $\binom{n}{k} p^k (1-p)^{n-k}$.

6. The *sample mean* of a sample of n numbers is the sum of the numbers divided by n.

7. The *expected value* of a random variable is the sum of the products of each outcome and its probability.

8. The *variance* of a random variable is the sum of the products of the square of each outcome's distance from the expected value and the outcomes probability. The variance of the random variable X can also be computed as $E(X^2) - [E(X)]^2$.

9. A binomial random variable with parameters n and p has expected value np and variance $np(1-p)$.

10. The square root of the variance is called the *standard deviation*.

11. Chebychev's inequality states that the probability that an outcome of an experiment is within c units of the mean is at least $1 - (\sigma^2/c^2)$, where σ is the standard deviation.

12. A normal curve is identified by its mean (μ) and its standard deviation (σ). The standard normal curve has $\mu = 0$ and $\sigma = 1$. Areas of regions under the standard normal curve can be obtained with the aid of a table or graphing calculator.

13. A random variable is said to be normally distributed if the probability that an outcome lies between a and b is

the area of the region under a normal curve from $x = a$ to $x = b$. After the numbers a and b are converted to standard deviations from the mean, the sought-after probability can be obtained as an area under the standard normal curve.

14. Probabilities associated with a binomial random variable with parameters n and p can be approximated with a normal curve having $\mu = np$ and $\sigma = \sqrt{np(1-p)}$.

Review of Fundamental Concepts of Chapter 7

1. What is a bar chart? A pie chart? A histogram? A box plot?

2. What is the median of a list of numbers? The first quartile? The third quartile? The interquartile range? The five-number summary?

3. What is a frequency distribution? A relative frequency distribution? A probability distribution?

4. How is a histogram constructed from a distribution?

5. What is a random variable?

6. What is meant by the probability distribution of a discrete random variable?

7. What are the identifying features of a binomial random variable?

8. What is the formula for the probability of k successes in n independent binomial trials?

9. What is meant by the expectation (or expected value) of a random variable? Variance? Standard deviation?

10. What is the Chebychev inequality, and how is it used?

11. What is meant by a normal random variable?

12. What is meant by the pth percentile of a normal random variable?

13. How are binomial probabilities approximated with the normal distribution?

▶ Chapter 7 Supplementary Exercises

1. Display the data from the table in a bar chart that shows frequencies on the y-axis. Then display the data in a pie chart.

Table 1	U.S. Population by Region (in millions)	
Region	**Population**	
Northeast	50.8	
Midwest	59.7	
South	85.4	
West	52.8	

2. Find the five-number summary and the interquartile range for the following set of numbers, and then draw the box plot.

$$1, 2, 3, 4, 5, 9, 14, 23$$

3. An experiment consists of three binomial trials, each having probability $\frac{1}{3}$ of success.

   (a) Determine the probability distribution table for the number of successes.

   (b) Use the table to compute the mean and the variance of the probability distribution.

4. Find the area of the shaded region under the standard normal curve shown in Fig. 1(a).

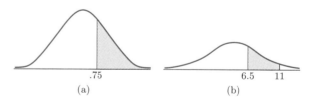

(a)   (b)

Figure 1.

5. Find the area of the shaded region under the normal curve with $\mu = 5$, $\sigma = 3$ shown in Fig. 1(b).

6. An archer has probability .3 of hitting a certain target. What is the probability of hitting the target exactly two times in four attempts?

7. Suppose that a probability distribution has mean 10 and standard deviation $\frac{1}{3}$. Use the Chebychev inequality to estimate the probability that an outcome will lie between 9 and 11.

8. Table 2 gives the probability distribution of the random variable X. Compute the mean and the variance of the random variable.

Table 2

k	$\Pr(X = k)$
0	.2
1	.3
5	.1
10	.4

9. The height of adult males in the United States is normally distributed with $\mu = 5.75$ feet and $\sigma = .2$ feet. What percent of the adult male population has height of 6 feet or greater?

10. An urn contains four red balls and four white balls. An experiment consists of selecting at random a sample of four balls and recording the number of red balls in the sample. Set up the probability distribution and compute its mean and variance.

11. In a certain city two-fifths of the registered voters are women. Out of a group of 54 voters allegedly selected at random for jury duty, 13 are women. A local civil liberties group has charged that the selection procedure discriminated against women. Use the normal curve to estimate the probability of 13 or fewer women being selected in a truly random selection process.

12. In a complicated production process, $\frac{1}{4}$ of the items produced have to be readjusted. Use the normal curve to estimate the probability that out of a batch of 75 items, between 8 and 22 (inclusive) of the items require readjustment.

13. Figure 2(a) is a normal curve with $\mu = 80$ and $\sigma = 15$. Find the value of h for which the area of the shaded region is .8664.

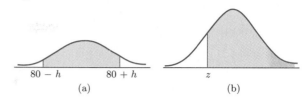

(a)   (b)

Figure 2.

14. Figure 2(b) is a standard normal curve. Find the value of z for which the area of the shaded region is .7734.

15. The World Series in baseball consists of a sequence of games that terminates when one team (the winner) wins its fourth game. If the two teams are equally likely to win any one game, what is the probability that the series will last exactly four games? Five? Six? Seven?

16. A true–false exam consists of ten 10-point questions. The instructor informs the students that six of the answers are *true* and four are *false*. An unprepared student decides to guess the answer to each question with the use of the spinner in Fig. 3, which gives *true* 60% of the time. Determine the student's expected score. Can you think of a better strategy?

Figure 3.

▶ Chapter 7 Chapter Test

1. The manager of a supermarket counts the number of customers waiting in the express checkout line at random times throughout the week. Her observations are summarized in the following frequency table.

Number Waiting in Line	Frequency
0	2
1	5
2	9
3	13
4	11
5	7
6	3

Construct the corresponding relative frequency table, and use it to estimate the probability that at most three customers are waiting in line.

2. Find the five-number summary and the interquartile range for the following set of numbers, and then draw the box plot.

20, 25, 26, 27, 29, 30, 33, 34, 37, 40, 42

3. A fair coin is tossed twice. Let X be the number of heads.
(a) Determine the probability distribution of X.
(b) Determine the probability distribution of $2X + 5$.

4. A pair of fair dice is rolled 12 times.
(a) What is $\Pr$(the result is 7 exactly twice)?
(b) What is $\Pr$(the result is 7 at least twice)?

(c) What is the expected number of times that the result is 7?

5. The probability distribution of a random variable X is given in the following table. Determine the mean, variance, and standard deviation of X.

k	$\Pr(X = k)$
-2	.3
0	.1
1	.4
3	.2

6. Lucy and Ethel play a game of chance in which a pair of fair dice is rolled once. If the result is 7 or 11, then Lucy pays Ethel $10.00. Otherwise, Ethel pays Lucy $3.00. In the long run, which player comes out ahead, and by how much?

7. Let Z be the standard normal random variable. Determine the following.

(a) $\Pr(Z \le 1)$

(b) $\Pr(Z \ge -2.25)$

(c) $\Pr(-1 \le Z \le 1.15)$

8. Assume the fasting blood glucose level among diabetics is normally distributed with mean 106 mg/100 ml and standard deviation 8 mg/100 ml.

(a) What is the probability that a randomly selected diabetic will have a fasting blood glucose level of more than 115 mg/100 ml?

(b) What is the probability that the fasting blood glucose level of a randomly selected diabetic will be between 98 and 120 mg/100 ml?

(c) For what value of c will 25% of diabetics have a fasting blood glucose level of less than c mg/100 ml? more than c mg/100 ml?

9. A new shopping mall is to be built, and 30% of the community's residents oppose the construction. A random sample of 25 residents is polled.

(a) Approximate the probability that more than 5 but at most 10 of the selected residents oppose the construction.

(b) Determine the exact probability that exactly 10 of the selected residents oppose the construction, and compare your answer with the normal approximation of that probability.

(c) Determine the exact probability that at least one of the selected residents opposes the construction, and compare your answer with the normal approximation of that probability.

Chapter Project

An Unexpected Expected Value[1]

An urn contains four red balls and six white balls. Suppose two balls are drawn at random from the urn, and let X be the number of red balls drawn. The probability of obtaining two red balls depends on whether the balls are drawn with or without replacement. The purpose of this project is to show that the expected number of red balls drawn is not affected by whether or not the first ball is replaced before the second ball is drawn.

1. Do you think the probability that both balls are red is higher if the first ball is replaced before the second ball is drawn, or if the first ball is not replaced?

2. Suppose the first ball is replaced before the second ball is drawn. Find the probability that both balls are red.

3. Suppose the first ball is not replaced before the second ball is drawn. Find the probability that both balls are red.

4. Was your intuitive guess in part 1 correct?

5. Do you think that the expected number of red balls drawn is higher if the balls are drawn with replacement or without replacement?

6. Suppose the first ball is replaced before the second ball is drawn. Find the expected number of red balls that will be drawn.

7. Suppose the first ball is not replaced before the second ball is drawn. Find the expected number of red balls that will be drawn.

8. Was your intuitive guess in part 5 correct?

9. Pretend that the balls are ping-pong balls that have been finely ground up, and that the red and white specks have been thoroughly mixed. Forty percent of the specks will be red and 60% will be white. Suppose you stir the specks and use a tablespoon to scoop out 10% of the specks. That is, suppose the tablespoon holds a quantity of specks corresponding to one ball.

    (a) What percentage of a red ball is contained in the spoon?

    (b) What percentage of the remaining specks in the urn are red?

    (c) If the spoonful of specks is replaced, does the percentage of red specks in the urn change?

    (d) Use the results from parts (b) and (c) to explain why the expected number of red balls as calculated in parts 6 and 7 is the same with and without replacement.

---

[1] The idea for this project was taken from the article "An Unexpected Expected Value," by Stephen Schwartzman, which appeared in the February 1993 issue of *The Mathematics Teacher*.

Markov Processes

8

S uppose that we perform, one after the other, a sequence of experiments that have the same set of outcomes. The probabilities of the various outcomes of a particular experiment of the sequence may depend in some way on the outcomes of preceding experiments. The nature of such a dependency may be very complicated. In the extreme, the outcome of the current experiment may depend on the entire history of the outcomes of preceding experiments. However, there is a simple type of dependency that occurs frequently in applications and that we can analyze with fair ease. Namely, we suppose that the probabilities of the various outcomes of the current experiment depend (at most) on the outcome of the preceding experiment. In this case the sequence of experiments is called a *Markov process*. In this chapter we present some of the most elementary ideas concerning Markov processes and their applications.

8.1 The Transition Matrix

Here are some Markov processes that arise in applications.

▶ Example 1   (*Investment*) A particular utility stock is very stable and, in the short run, the probability that it increases or decreases in price depends only on the result of the preceding day's trading. The price of the stock is observed at 4 P.M. each day and is recorded as "increased," "decreased," or "unchanged." The sequence of observations forms a Markov process.   ◆

▶ Example 2   (*Medicine*) A doctor tests the effect of a new drug on high blood pressure. Based on the effects of metabolism, a given dose is eliminated from the body in 24 hours. Blood pressure is measured once a day and is recorded as "high," "low," or "normal." The sequence of measurements forms a Markov process.   ◆

▶ **Example 3**   (*Sociology*) A sociologist postulates that the likelihood that, in certain countries, a woman will enter the labor force depends primarily on whether the woman's mother worked. He designs an experiment to test this hypothesis by viewing the sequence of career choices of a woman, her daughters, her granddaughters, her great-granddaughters, and so on as a Markov process.   ◆

Let us now introduce some vocabulary and mathematical machinery with which to study Markov processes. The experiments are performed at regular time intervals and have the same set of outcomes. These outcomes are called *states*, and the outcome of the current experiment is referred to as the *current state* of the process. After each time interval, the process may change its state. The transition from state to state can be described by tree diagrams, as is shown in the next example.

▶ **Example 4**   Refer to the utility stock of Example 1. Suppose that if the stock increases one day, the probability that on the next day it increases is .3, remains unchanged .2, decreases .5. On the other hand, if the stock is unchanged one day, the probability that on the next day it increases is .6, remains unchanged .1, decreases .3. If the stock decreases one day, the probability that it increases the next day is .3, is unchanged .4, decreases .3. Represent the possible transitions between states and their probabilities by tree diagrams.

Solution   The Markov process has three states: "increases," "unchanged," and "decreases." The transitions from the first state ("increases") to the other states are

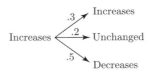

Note that each branch of the tree has been labeled with the probability of the corresponding transition. Similarly, the tree diagrams corresponding to the other two states are

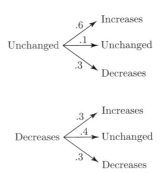

◆

The three tree diagrams of Example 4 may be summarized in a single matrix. We insert the probabilities from a given tree down a column of the matrix, so that each column of the matrix records the information about transitions from one particular state. So the first column of the matrix is

$$\begin{bmatrix} .3 \\ .2 \\ .5 \end{bmatrix},$$

corresponding to transitions from the state "increases." The complete matrix is

		Increases	Unchanged	Decreases
Next state	Increases	.3	.6	.3
	Unchanged	.2	.1	.4
	Decreases	.5	.3	.3

Current state (header spanning Increases, Unchanged, Decreases)

$$\text{Next state}\begin{array}{c}\text{Increases}\\\text{Unchanged}\\\text{Decreases}\end{array}\begin{bmatrix} .3 & .6 & .3 \\ .2 & .1 & .4 \\ .5 & .3 & .3 \end{bmatrix}.$$

This matrix, which records all data about transitions from one state to another, is called the *transition matrix of the Markov process.*

▶ Example 5 (*Women in the Labor Force*) Census studies from the 1960s reveal that in the United States 80% of the daughters of working women also work and that 30% of the daughters of nonworking women work. Assume that this trend remains unchanged from one generation to the next. Determine the corresponding transition matrix.

Solution There are two states, which we label "work" and "don't work." The first column corresponds to transitions from the first state—that is, from "work." The probability that the daughter of a working woman chooses *not* to work is $1 - .8 = .2$. Therefore, the first column is

$$\begin{bmatrix} .8 \\ .2 \end{bmatrix}.$$

In similar fashion, the second column is

$$\begin{bmatrix} .3 \\ .7 \end{bmatrix}.$$

The transition matrix is, therefore,

Current generation

$$\text{Next generation}\begin{array}{c}\text{Work}\\\text{Don't work}\end{array}\begin{bmatrix} .8 & .3 \\ .2 & .7 \end{bmatrix}.$$

with columns labeled Work, Don't work ◆

Here is the form of a general transition matrix for a Markov process:

Current state

$$\text{Next state}\begin{array}{c}\text{State 1}\\\vdots\\\text{State } i\\\vdots\\\text{State } r\end{array}\begin{bmatrix} & & & & \\ & & & & \\ & \Pr(\text{next } i\,|\,\text{current } j) & \\ & & & & \\ & & & & \end{bmatrix}.$$

with column headers State 1 ⋯ State j ⋯ State r

Note that this matrix satisfies the following two properties:

1. All entries are greater than or equal to 0.
2. The sum of the entries in each column is 1.

Any square matrix satisfying properties 1 and 2 is called a *stochastic matrix*. (The word "stochastic" derives from the Greek word "stochastices," which means a person who predicts the future.)

Let us examine further the Markov process of Example 5. In 1960 about 40% of U.S. women worked and 60% did not. This distribution is described by the column matrix

$$\begin{bmatrix} .4 \\ .6 \end{bmatrix}_0,$$

which is called a *distribution matrix*. The subscript 0 is added to denote that this matrix describes generation 0. Their daughters constitute generation 1, and their granddaughters generation 2. There is a distribution matrix for each generation: The distribution matrix for generation n is

$$\begin{bmatrix} p_W \\ p_{DW} \end{bmatrix}_n,$$

where p_W is the percentage of women in generation n who work and p_{DW} is the percentage who don't work. Of course, the numbers p_W and p_{DW} are also probabilities. The number p_W is the probability that a woman selected at random from generation n works. Similarly, p_{DW} is the probability that a woman selected at random from generation n does not work. Shortly we shall give a method for calculating the distribution matrix for generation n.

In general, whenever a Markov process applies to a group with members in r possible states, a distribution matrix of the form

$$\begin{bmatrix} p_1 \\ p_2 \\ \vdots \\ p_r \end{bmatrix}_0$$

gives the initial percentages of members in each of the r states. Similarly, a matrix of the same type (with the subscript n) gives the percentages of members in each of the r states after n time periods. Note that each of the percentages in the distribution matrix is also a probability—the probability that a randomly selected member will be in the corresponding state.

▶ Example 6   In 1960, census figures show that 40% of American women worked. Use the stochastic matrix of Example 5 to determine the percentage of working women in each of the next two generations.

Solution   Let us denote by A the stochastic matrix of Example 5:

		Current generation	
		Work	Don't work
Next generation	Work	.8	.3
	Don't work	.2	.7

The initial distribution matrix is

$$\begin{bmatrix} .4 \\ .6 \end{bmatrix}_0.$$

Our goal is to compute the distribution matrices for generations 1 and 2. With an eye toward performing similar calculations for other countries, let us use letters rather than specific numbers in these distribution matrices. Let

$$\begin{bmatrix} \quad \end{bmatrix}_0 = \begin{bmatrix} x_0 \\ y_0 \end{bmatrix}, \qquad \begin{bmatrix} \quad \end{bmatrix}_1 = \begin{bmatrix} x_1 \\ y_1 \end{bmatrix}, \qquad \begin{bmatrix} \quad \end{bmatrix}_2 = \begin{bmatrix} x_2 \\ y_2 \end{bmatrix}.$$

The state transitions from generation 0 to generation 1 may be displayed in a tree diagram.

Generation 0	*Generation 1*	*Probabilities*
	.8 — Work	$.8x_0$
x_0 — Work		
	.2 — Don't work	$.2x_0$
	.3 — Work	$.3y_0$
y_0 — Don't work		
	.7 — Don't work	$.7y_0$

Adding together the probabilities for the two paths leading to "work" in generation 1 gives

$$x_1 = .8x_0 + .3y_0. \tag{1}$$

Similarly, adding together the probabilities for the two paths leading to "don't work" in generation 1 gives

$$y_1 = .2x_0 + .7y_0. \tag{2}$$

Thus, (1) and (2) show that x_1 and y_1 can be computed from this pair of equations.

$$x_1 = .8x_0 + .3y_0$$
$$y_1 = .2x_0 + .7y_0$$

This system of equations is equivalent to the one matrix equation

$$\begin{bmatrix} .8 & .3 \\ .2 & .7 \end{bmatrix} \begin{bmatrix} x_0 \\ y_0 \end{bmatrix} = \begin{bmatrix} x_1 \\ y_1 \end{bmatrix}. \tag{3}$$

Or, to write equation (3) symbolically,

$$A \begin{bmatrix} \quad \end{bmatrix}_0 = \begin{bmatrix} \quad \end{bmatrix}_1. \tag{4}$$

Now it is easy to do the arithmetic to compute the distribution matrix for generation 1 of American women:

$$A \begin{bmatrix} \quad \end{bmatrix}_0 = \begin{bmatrix} .8 & .3 \\ .2 & .7 \end{bmatrix} \begin{bmatrix} .4 \\ .6 \end{bmatrix}_0 = \begin{bmatrix} .5 \\ .5 \end{bmatrix}_1.$$

That is, 50% of American women in generation 1 will work, and 50% will not.

To compute the distribution matrix for generation 2, we use the same reasoning as before, when we showed that to get

$$\begin{bmatrix} \quad \end{bmatrix}_1 \quad \text{from} \quad \begin{bmatrix} \quad \end{bmatrix}_0,$$

just multiply by A.

Similarly,

$$A \begin{bmatrix} \\ \end{bmatrix}_1 = \begin{bmatrix} \\ \end{bmatrix}_2.$$

However, by (4), we have a formula for $\begin{bmatrix} \\ \end{bmatrix}_1$, which we can insert into the last equation, getting[1]

$$\begin{bmatrix} \\ \end{bmatrix}_2 = A \begin{bmatrix} \\ \end{bmatrix}_1 = A \left(A \begin{bmatrix} \\ \end{bmatrix}_0 \right) = A^2 \begin{bmatrix} \\ \end{bmatrix}_0.$$

In other words,

$$A^2 \begin{bmatrix} \\ \end{bmatrix}_0 = \begin{bmatrix} \\ \end{bmatrix}_2. \tag{5}$$

A simple calculation gives

$$A^2 = \begin{bmatrix} .70 & .45 \\ .30 & .55 \end{bmatrix},$$

so that we can now compute the distribution for generation 2 of American women:

$$\begin{bmatrix} .70 & .45 \\ .30 & .55 \end{bmatrix} \begin{bmatrix} .4 \\ .6 \end{bmatrix}_0 = \begin{bmatrix} .55 \\ .45 \end{bmatrix}_2.$$

That is, after two generations 55% of American women work and 45% do not.

◆

An argument similar to that used to derive equation (5) can be used to show that

$$A^3 \begin{bmatrix} \\ \end{bmatrix}_0 = \begin{bmatrix} \\ \end{bmatrix}_3, \quad A^4 \begin{bmatrix} \\ \end{bmatrix}_0 = \begin{bmatrix} \\ \end{bmatrix}_4, \quad A^5 \begin{bmatrix} \\ \end{bmatrix}_0 = \begin{bmatrix} \\ \end{bmatrix}_5, \quad \ldots.$$

A condensed notation is

$$A^n \begin{bmatrix} \\ \end{bmatrix}_0 = \begin{bmatrix} \\ \end{bmatrix}_n \qquad (n = 1, 2, 3, \ldots). \tag{6}$$

That is, to compute the distribution matrix for generation n, merely compute the product of A^n times the distribution matrix for generation 0. Equation (6) can be used to predict the distribution matrix for any number of generations into the future, starting from any given distribution matrix. Let us now look at an entirely different type of situation that can be described by a Markov process.

▶ Example 7   Taxis pick up and deliver passengers in a city that is divided into three zones. Records kept by the drivers show that of the passengers picked up in zone I, 50% are taken to a destination in zone I, 40% to zone II, and 10% to zone III. Of the passengers picked up in zone II, 40% go to zone I, 30% to zone II, and 30% to zone III. Of the passengers picked up in zone III, 20% go to zone I, 60% to zone II, and 20% to zone III. Suppose that at the beginning of the day 60% of the taxis are in zone I, 10% in zone II, and 30% in zone III. What is the distribution of taxis in the various zones after all have had one rider? Two riders?

---

[1] Just as in elementary algebra, we define the powers $A^2, A^3, \ldots$ of the matrix A by $A^2 = A \cdot A$, $A^3 = A \cdot A \cdot A, \ldots$.

Solution   This situation is an example of a Markov process. The states are the zones. The initial distribution of the taxis gives the zeroth distribution matrix:

$$\begin{bmatrix} .6 \\ .1 \\ .3 \end{bmatrix}_0 .$$

The stochastic matrix associated to the process is the one giving the probabilities of taxis starting in any one zone and ending up in any other. There is one column for each zone:

		From zone:		
		I	II	III
To zone:	I	.5	.4	.2
	II	.4	.3	.6
	III	.1	.3	.2

$$= A.$$

After all taxis have had one passenger, the distribution matrix is just

$$A \begin{bmatrix} .6 \\ .1 \\ .3 \end{bmatrix}_0 = \begin{bmatrix} .5 & .4 & .2 \\ .4 & .3 & .6 \\ .1 & .3 & .2 \end{bmatrix} \begin{bmatrix} .6 \\ .1 \\ .3 \end{bmatrix}_0 = \begin{bmatrix} .40 \\ .45 \\ .15 \end{bmatrix}_1 .$$

That is, 40% of the taxis are in zone I, 45% in zone II, and 15% in zone III. After all taxis have had two passengers, the distribution matrix is

$$A^2 \begin{bmatrix} .6 \\ .1 \\ .3 \end{bmatrix}_0 ,$$

which, after some arithmetic, can be shown to be

$$\begin{bmatrix} .410 \\ .385 \\ .205 \end{bmatrix}_2 .$$

That is, after two passengers, 41% of the taxis are in zone I, 38.5% are in zone II, and 20.5% are in zone III.   ◆

The crucial formula used in both Examples 6 and 7 is

$$A \begin{bmatrix} \ \\ \ \\ \ \end{bmatrix}_0 = \begin{bmatrix} \ \\ \ \\ \ \end{bmatrix}_1 . \tag{7}$$

From this one follows the more general formula

$$A^n \begin{bmatrix} \ \\ \ \\ \ \end{bmatrix}_0 = \begin{bmatrix} \ \\ \ \\ \ \end{bmatrix}_n .$$

We carefully proved (7) in the special case of Example 6. Let us do the same for Example 7. Suppose that the initial distribution of taxis is

$$\begin{bmatrix} x_0 \\ y_0 \\ z_0 \end{bmatrix} .$$

How many taxis end up in zone I after one passenger? The taxis in zone I come from three sources—zones I, II, and III. And the first row of the stochastic matrix

A gives the percentages of taxis starting out in each of the zones and ending up in zone I:

$$[\text{percent of taxis going to zone I}] = [.5] \cdot [\text{percent of taxis in zone I}]$$
$$+ [.4] \cdot [\text{percent of taxis in zone II}]$$
$$+ [.2] \cdot [\text{percent of taxis in zone III}]$$
$$= .5x_0 + .4y_0 + .2z_0.$$

Indeed, the first entry, x_1, in the product

$$\begin{bmatrix} .5 & .4 & .2 \\ .4 & .3 & .6 \\ .1 & .3 & .2 \end{bmatrix} \begin{bmatrix} x_0 \\ y_0 \\ z_0 \end{bmatrix} = \begin{bmatrix} x_1 \\ \\ \end{bmatrix}$$

is just $.5x_0 + .4y_0 + .2z_0$. Similarly, the proportions of taxis in zones II and III coincide with the other two entries in the matrix product. So equation (7) really holds.

GC Let

$$A = \begin{bmatrix} .8 & .3 \\ .2 & .7 \end{bmatrix}$$

be the 2×2 matrix of Examples 5 and 6, and let

$$B = \begin{bmatrix} .4 \\ .6 \end{bmatrix}$$

be the initial distribution matrix. Successive distribution matrices are easy to obtain with a graphing calculator. The most recently displayed number or matrix becomes the value of the variable **Ans**. In Fig. 1, after matrix B is displayed, it becomes the value of the variable **Ans**. Therefore, the value of **[A]*Ans** is the matrix product AB. (In general, the variable **Ans** holds the most recent number or matrix displayed. To obtain **Ans** on a TI-82 or TI-83, press 2nd [ANS].)

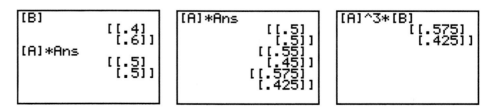

Figure 1.   Figure 2.   Figure 3.

Refer to the screen in Fig. 1. Each time the ENTER key is pressed, the instruction **[A]*Ans** is repeated. That is, the preceding matrix is multiplied on the left by the matrix A. Figure 2, which results after the ENTER key is pressed two more times, shows the additional matrices A^2B and A^3B. As a check, the matrix A^3B is computed directly in Fig. 3.

1. Is $\begin{bmatrix} \frac{2}{5} & 1 \\ \frac{3}{5} & .2 \\ \frac{2}{5} & -.3 \end{bmatrix}$ a stochastic matrix?

2. An elementary learning process consists of subjects participating in a sequence of events. Experiment shows that of the subjects not conditioned to make the correct response at the beginning of any event, 40% will be conditioned to make the correct response at the end of the event. Once a subject is conditioned to make the correct response, he stays conditioned.

   (a) Set up the 2×2 stochastic matrix with columns and rows labeled N (not conditioned) and C (conditioned) that describes this situation.

   (b) Compute A^3.

   (c) If initially all the subjects are not conditioned, what percent of them will be conditioned after three events?

▶ Exercises 8.1

In Exercises 1–6, determine whether or not the matrix is stochastic.

1. $\begin{bmatrix} 1 & .8 \\ 0 & .2 \end{bmatrix}$

2. $\begin{bmatrix} \frac{1}{3} & \frac{1}{3} \\ \frac{2}{3} & \frac{2}{3} \end{bmatrix}$

3. $\begin{bmatrix} .4 & .3 & .2 \\ .6 & .7 & .8 \end{bmatrix}$

4. $\begin{bmatrix} .4 & .5 & .1 \\ .3 & .4 & 0 \\ .3 & .2 & .9 \end{bmatrix}$

5. $\begin{bmatrix} \frac{1}{6} & \frac{5}{12} & 0 \\ \frac{1}{2} & \frac{1}{4} & .5 \\ \frac{1}{3} & \frac{1}{3} & .5 \end{bmatrix}$

6. $\begin{bmatrix} 1 & 0 & 0 \\ 0 & 1 & 0 \\ 0 & 0 & 1 \end{bmatrix}$

7. Referring to Example 5 (women in the labor force), consider a typical group of French women, of whom 45% currently work. Assume that the same percentage of daughters follow in their mothers' footsteps as with the American women—that is, those given by the matrix

$$A = \begin{bmatrix} .8 & .3 \\ .2 & .7 \end{bmatrix}.$$

Use A and A^2 to determine the proportion of working women in the next two generations. (Round off to the nearest whole percent.)

8. Repeat Exercise 7 for the women of Belgium, of whom 33% currently work. (Round off the percentage of women to the nearest whole percent.)

9. Refer to Example 7 (taxi zones). If originally 40% of the taxis start in zone I, 40% in zone II, and 20% in zone III, how will the taxis be distributed after each has taken one passenger?

10. (*T-Maze*) Each day mice are put into a T-maze (a maze shaped like a "T"; Fig. 4). In this maze they have the choice of turning to the left (rewarded with cheese) or to the right (receive cheese along with mild shock). After the first day their decision whether to turn left or right is influenced by what happened on the previous day. Of those that go to the left on a certain day, 90% go to the left on the next day and 10% go to the right. Of those that go to the right on a certain day, 70% go to the left on the next day and 30% go to the right.

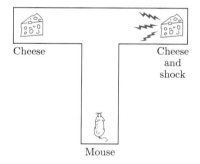

Cheese   Cheese and shock

Mouse

Figure 4.

(a) Set up the 2×2 stochastic matrix with columns and rows labeled L, R that describes this situation.

(b) Compute the second power of the matrix in part (a).

(c) Suppose that on the first day (day 0) 50% go to the left and 50% go to the right. So, the initial distribution is given by the column matrix $\begin{bmatrix} .5 \\ .5 \end{bmatrix}_0$. Using the matrices in parts (a) and (b), find the distribution matrices for the next two days, days 1 and 2.

(d) Make a guess as to the percentage of mice that will go to the left after 50 days. (Do not compute.)

11. (*Gym*) A group of physical fitness devotees works out in the gym every day. The workouts vary from strenuous to moderate to light. When their exercise routine was recorded, the following observation was made: Of the people who work out strenuously on a particular day, 40% will work out strenuously on the next day and 60% will work out moderately. Of the people who work out moderately on a particular day, 50% will work out strenuously and 50% will work out lightly on the next day. Of the people working out lightly on a particular day, 30% will work out strenuously on the next day, 20% moderately, and 50% lightly.

(a) Set up the 3×3 stochastic matrix with columns and rows labeled S, M, and L that describes these transitions.

(b) Suppose that on a particular Monday 80% have a strenuous, 10% a moderate, and 10% a light workout. What percent will have a strenuous workout on Wednesday?

12. (*Bird Migrations*) The following matrix describes the migration patterns of a species of bird from year to year among three habitats, I, II, and III.

		From habitat:		
		I	II	III
To habitat:	I	.78	.07	.15
	II	.12	.85	.05
	III	.10	.08	.80

(a) What percentage of the birds that begin the year in habitat III migrate to habitat I during the year?

(b) Explain the meaning of the percentage .85 appearing in the center of the matrix.

(c) If there are 1000 birds in each habitat at the beginning of a year, how many will be in each habitat at the end of the year? At the end of two years?

13. (*Voter Patterns*) For a certain group of states, it was observed that 70% of the Democratic governors were succeeded by Democrats and 30% by Republicans. Also, 40% of the Republican governors were succeeded by Democrats and 60% by Republicans.

(a) Set up the 2×2 stochastic matrix with columns and rows labeled D and R that displays these transitions.

(b) Compute A^2 and A^3.

(c) Suppose that all the current governors are Democrats. Assuming that the current trend holds for three elections, what percent of the governors will then be Democrats?

14. (*Market Share*) A retailer stocks three brands of breakfast cereal. A survey is taken of 5000 people who purchase cereal weekly from this retailer. Each week Crispy Flakes loses 12% of its customers to Crunchy Nuggets and 19% to Toasty Cinnamon

Twists. Crunchy Nuggets loses 16% of its customers to Crispy Flakes and 10% of its customers to Toasty Cinnamon Twists, and Toasty Cinnamon Twists loses 20% of its customers to Crispy Flakes and 14% to Crunchy Nuggets.

(a) Set up a stochastic matrix displaying these transitions.

(b) Suppose that this week 1500 people buy Crispy Flakes, 1500 buy Crunchy Nuggets, and 2000 people buy Toasty Cinnamon Twists. How many people will buy Crispy Flakes next week? How many will buy Toasty Cinnamon Twists in two weeks?

15. (*Population Movement*) A sociologist studying living patterns in a certain region determines that each year the population shifts between urban, suburban, and rural areas as shown in Fig. 5.

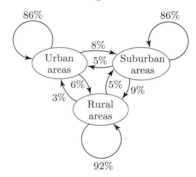

Figure 5.

(a) Set up a stochastic matrix A that displays these transitions.

(b) What percentage of people who live in urban areas in 2000 will live in rural areas in 2002?

16. Suppose that the matrices $\begin{bmatrix} .5 & .4 \\ .5 & .6 \end{bmatrix}$ and $\begin{bmatrix} .3 \\ .7 \end{bmatrix}_0$ are the stochastic and initial distribution matrices of a Markov process. Find the third and fourth distribution matrices. (Round entries to two decimal places.)

In Exercises 17–21, compute the first five powers of each matrix (round off to two decimal places).

17. $\begin{bmatrix} \frac{1}{3} & \frac{1}{3} \\ \frac{2}{3} & \frac{2}{3} \end{bmatrix}$ 18. $\begin{bmatrix} 1 & \frac{1}{2} \\ 0 & \frac{1}{2} \end{bmatrix}$

19. $\begin{bmatrix} .1 & .3 \\ .9 & .7 \end{bmatrix}$ 20. $\begin{bmatrix} 0 & 1 \\ 1 & 0 \end{bmatrix}$

21. $\begin{bmatrix} .2 & .2 & .2 \\ .3 & .3 & .3 \\ .5 & .5 & .5 \end{bmatrix}$

Stochastic matrices for which some power contains no zero entries are called *regular* matrices. In Exercises 22–24, conjecture whether or not the given matrix is regular by looking at the first few powers of the matrix.

22. $\begin{bmatrix} 0 & .4 \\ 1 & .6 \end{bmatrix}$ **23.** $\begin{bmatrix} .5 & 0 \\ .5 & 1 \end{bmatrix}$ **24.** $\begin{bmatrix} .7 & 1 \\ .3 & 0 \end{bmatrix}$

Exercises 25–30 require the use of a graphing calculator or computer.

25. Let A be the stochastic matrix $\begin{bmatrix} .1 & .6 \\ .9 & .4 \end{bmatrix}$, and let the initial distribution be $B = \begin{bmatrix} .5 \\ .5 \end{bmatrix}_0$.

(a) Generate the next four distribution matrices.

(b) Calculate $A^4 B$ and confirm that it is the same as the fourth distribution matrix.

26. Repeat Exercise 25 for the matrices $\begin{bmatrix} .4 & .2 \\ .6 & .8 \end{bmatrix}$ and $\begin{bmatrix} .7 \\ .3 \end{bmatrix}_0$.

27. Consider the matrices of Exercise 25. Beginning with the initial distribution matrix, generate 10 more distributions. Continue to generate 10 more. The matrices will get closer and closer to a certain 2×1 matrix. What is that matrix?

28. Repeat Exercise 27 for the matrices of Exercise 26.

29. Generate 35 successive powers of the matrix A from Exercise 25. (With a graphing calculator, the instruction **[A]*Ans** also can be used to compute successive powers of a square matrix.) The matrices will get closer and closer to a certain 2×2 matrix. What is that matrix? How is that matrix related to the 2×1 matrix found in Exercise 27?

30. Repeat Exercise 29 for the square matrix of Exercise 26.

Solutions to Practice Problems 8.1	

1. No. It fails on all three conditions. The matrix is not square, the entry $-.3$ is not ≥ 0, and the sum of the entries in the first (and second) column is not equal to 1.

2. (a) $\begin{array}{cc} & N \quad C \\ \begin{array}{c} N \\ C \end{array} & \begin{bmatrix} .6 & 0 \\ .4 & 1 \end{bmatrix} \end{array}$. Since there are only two possibilities and 40% of those not conditioned become conditioned, the remaining or 60% stay not conditioned. After each event 100% of the conditioned stay conditioned, and therefore 0% become not conditioned.

(b) $A^2 = \begin{bmatrix} .6 & 0 \\ .4 & 1 \end{bmatrix} \begin{bmatrix} .6 & 0 \\ .4 & 1 \end{bmatrix} = \begin{bmatrix} .36 & 0 \\ .64 & 1 \end{bmatrix}$,

$A^3 = A^2 \cdot A = \begin{bmatrix} .36 & 0 \\ .64 & 1 \end{bmatrix} \begin{bmatrix} .6 & 0 \\ .4 & 1 \end{bmatrix} = \begin{bmatrix} .216 & 0 \\ .784 & 1 \end{bmatrix}$.

(c) Here $\begin{bmatrix} \ \\ \ \end{bmatrix}_0 = \begin{bmatrix} 1 \\ 0 \end{bmatrix}$. Therefore,

$$\begin{bmatrix} \ \\ \ \end{bmatrix}_3 = A^3 \begin{bmatrix} 1 \\ 0 \end{bmatrix} = \begin{bmatrix} .216 & 0 \\ .784 & 1 \end{bmatrix} \begin{bmatrix} 1 \\ 0 \end{bmatrix} = \begin{bmatrix} .216 \\ .784 \end{bmatrix}.$$

So 78.4% will be conditioned after three events.

8.2 Regular Stochastic Matrices

In the preceding section we studied the percentages of working women in various generations in America. We showed that if $\begin{bmatrix} \ \\ \ \end{bmatrix}_0$ is the initial distribution matrix, then the distribution matrix $\begin{bmatrix} \ \\ \ \end{bmatrix}_n$ for the nth generation is given by

$$\begin{bmatrix} \ \\ \ \end{bmatrix}_n = A^n \begin{bmatrix} \ \\ \ \end{bmatrix}_0, \tag{1}$$

where A is the stochastic matrix

$$A = \begin{bmatrix} .8 & .3 \\ .2 & .7 \end{bmatrix}.$$

In this section we are interested in determining long-term trends in Markov processes. To get an idea of what is meant, consider the example of Dutch women in the labor force.

▶ Example 1   In Holland 25% of the women currently work. The effect of maternal influence of mothers on their daughters is given by the matrix

$$\begin{bmatrix} .6 & .2 \\ .4 & .8 \end{bmatrix}.$$

(a) How many women will work after $1, 2, 3, \ldots, 11$ generations?

(b) Estimate the long-term trend.

(c) Answer the same questions (a) and (b) for Denmark, assuming that 40% of all Danish women currently work and that the effect of maternal influence is the same as for Holland.

Solution   (a) The percentages of women working in generation n (for $n = 1, 2, 3, \ldots$) can be determined from equation (1):

$$\begin{bmatrix} \ \\ \ \end{bmatrix}_n = \begin{bmatrix} .6 & .2 \\ .4 & .8 \end{bmatrix}^n \begin{bmatrix} .25 \\ .75 \end{bmatrix}_0.$$

After the mildly tedious job of raising the stochastic matrix to various powers, we obtain the following results:

Generation	Percent of women working	Generation	Percent of women working
0	25	6	33.30
1	30	7	33.32
2	32	8	33.33
3	32.8	9	33.33
4	33.12	10	33.33
5	33.25	11	33.33

(b) It appears from the accompanying table that the long-term trend is for one-third or $33\frac{1}{3}\%$ of all Dutch women to work.

(c) The corresponding results for Denmark can be computed by replacing the initial distribution matrix $\begin{bmatrix} .25 \\ .75 \end{bmatrix}_0$ by $\begin{bmatrix} .40 \\ .60 \end{bmatrix}_0$, reflecting that initially 40% of all Danish women work. The results of the calculations are shown in Table 1. Again, the long-term trend is for one-third of the women to work.   ◆

From Example 1 one might begin to suspect the following: The long-term trend is always for one-third of the women to work, independent of the initial distribution.

Table 1

Generation	Percent of women working	Generation	Percent of women working
0	40	6	33.36
1	36	7	33.34
2	34.4	8	33.34
3	33.76	9	33.34
4	33.50	10	33.33
5	33.40	11	33.33

Verification   To see why this rather surprising fact should hold, it is useful to examine the powers of A:

$$A^2 = \begin{bmatrix} .44 & .28 \\ .56 & .72 \end{bmatrix} \qquad A^3 = \begin{bmatrix} .376 & .312 \\ .624 & .688 \end{bmatrix} \qquad A^4 = \begin{bmatrix} .3504 & .3248 \\ .6496 & .6752 \end{bmatrix}$$

$$A^5 = \begin{bmatrix} .3402 & .3299 \\ .6598 & .6701 \end{bmatrix} \qquad A^6 = \begin{bmatrix} .3361 & .3320 \\ .6639 & .6680 \end{bmatrix} \qquad A^7 = \begin{bmatrix} .3344 & .3328 \\ .6656 & .6672 \end{bmatrix}$$

$$A^8 = \begin{bmatrix} .3338 & .3331 \\ .6662 & .6669 \end{bmatrix} \qquad A^9 = \begin{bmatrix} .3335 & .3332 \\ .6665 & .6668 \end{bmatrix} \qquad A^{10} = \begin{bmatrix} .3334 & .3333 \\ .6666 & .6667 \end{bmatrix}.$$

As A is raised to further powers, the matrices approach

$$\begin{bmatrix} \frac{1}{3} & \frac{1}{3} \\ \frac{2}{3} & \frac{2}{3} \end{bmatrix}. \tag{2}$$

Now suppose that initially the proportion of women working is x_0. That is, the initial distribution matrix is

$$\begin{bmatrix} x_0 \\ 1 - x_0 \end{bmatrix}.$$

Then, after n generations, the distribution matrix is

$$\begin{bmatrix} \quad \\ \quad \end{bmatrix}_n = A^n \begin{bmatrix} \quad \\ \quad \end{bmatrix}_0 = A^n \begin{bmatrix} x_0 \\ 1 - x_0 \end{bmatrix}.$$

But after many generations n is large, so that A^n is approximately the matrix (2). Thus,

$$\begin{bmatrix} \quad \\ \quad \end{bmatrix}_n \approx \begin{bmatrix} \frac{1}{3} & \frac{1}{3} \\ \frac{2}{3} & \frac{2}{3} \end{bmatrix} \begin{bmatrix} x_0 \\ 1 - x_0 \end{bmatrix} = \begin{bmatrix} \frac{1}{3}x_0 + \frac{1}{3}(1 - x_0) \\ \frac{2}{3}x_0 + \frac{2}{3}(1 - x_0) \end{bmatrix} = \begin{bmatrix} \frac{1}{3} \\ \frac{2}{3} \end{bmatrix}.$$

In other words, after n generations approximately one-third of the women work and two-thirds do not.   ◆

From the preceding calculations we see that the stochastic matrix A possesses a number of very special properties. First, as n gets large, A^n approaches the matrix

$$\begin{bmatrix} \frac{1}{3} & \frac{1}{3} \\ \frac{2}{3} & \frac{2}{3} \end{bmatrix}.$$

Second, any initial distribution approaches the distribution $\begin{bmatrix} \frac{1}{3} \\ \frac{2}{3} \end{bmatrix}$ after many generations. The limiting matrix

$$\begin{bmatrix} \frac{1}{3} & \frac{1}{3} \\ \frac{2}{3} & \frac{2}{3} \end{bmatrix}$$

is called the *stable matrix* of A, and the limiting distribution

$$\begin{bmatrix} \frac{1}{3} \\ \frac{2}{3} \end{bmatrix}$$

is called the *stable distribution* of A. Finally, note that all the columns of the stable matrix are the same and are equal to the stable distribution.

The matrices that share the aforementioned properties with A are very important. For these matrices one can predict a long-term trend, and this trend is independent of the initial distribution. An important class of matrices with these properties is the class of *regular stochastic matrices*.

A stochastic matrix is said to be *regular* if some power has all positive entries.

▶ Example 2   Which of the following stochastic matrices are regular?

(a) $\begin{bmatrix} .6 & .2 \\ .4 & .8 \end{bmatrix}$ (b) $\begin{bmatrix} 0 & .5 \\ 1 & .5 \end{bmatrix}$ (c) $\begin{bmatrix} 0 & 1 \\ 1 & 0 \end{bmatrix}$

Solution   (a) All entries are positive, so the matrix is regular.

(b) Here a zero occurs in the first power. However,

$$\begin{bmatrix} 0 & .5 \\ 1 & .5 \end{bmatrix}^2 = \begin{bmatrix} .5 & .25 \\ .5 & .75 \end{bmatrix},$$

which has all positive entries. So the original matrix is regular.

(c) Note that

$$\begin{bmatrix} 0 & 1 \\ 1 & 0 \end{bmatrix}^2 = \begin{bmatrix} 1 & 0 \\ 0 & 1 \end{bmatrix} \qquad \begin{bmatrix} 0 & 1 \\ 1 & 0 \end{bmatrix}^3 = \begin{bmatrix} 0 & 1 \\ 1 & 0 \end{bmatrix}$$

$$\begin{bmatrix} 0 & 1 \\ 1 & 0 \end{bmatrix}^4 = \begin{bmatrix} 1 & 0 \\ 0 & 1 \end{bmatrix} \qquad \begin{bmatrix} 0 & 1 \\ 1 & 0 \end{bmatrix}^5 = \begin{bmatrix} 0 & 1 \\ 1 & 0 \end{bmatrix}.$$

The even powers of the matrix are the 2×2 identity matrix, and the odd powers are the original matrix. Every power has a zero in it, so the matrix is not regular.   ◆

Regular matrices share all the properties observed in the special case. Moreover, there is a simple technique for computing the stable distribution (see property 4 in the following box) that spares us from having to multiply matrices.

Let A be a regular stochastic matrix.

1. The powers A^n approach a certain matrix as n gets large. This limiting matrix is called the *stable matrix* of A.

2. For any initial distribution $\begin{bmatrix} \\ \end{bmatrix}_0$, $A^n \begin{bmatrix} \\ \end{bmatrix}_0$ approaches a certain distribution $\begin{bmatrix} \\ \end{bmatrix}$. This limiting distribution is called the *stable distribution* of A.

3. All columns of the stable matrix are the same; they equal the stable distribution.

4. The stable distribution $X = [\ ]$ can be determined by solving the system of linear equations

$$\begin{cases} \text{sum of the entries of } X = 1 \\ AX = X. \end{cases}$$

▶ Example 3   Use property 4 to determine the stable distribution of the regular stochastic matrix

$$A = \begin{bmatrix} .6 & .2 \\ .4 & .8 \end{bmatrix}.$$

Solution   Let $X = \begin{bmatrix} x \\ y \end{bmatrix}$ be the stable distribution. The condition "sum of the entries of $X = 1$" yields the equation

$$x + y = 1.$$

The condition $AX = X$ gives the equations

$$\begin{bmatrix} .6 & .2 \\ .4 & .8 \end{bmatrix} \begin{bmatrix} x \\ y \end{bmatrix} = \begin{bmatrix} x \\ y \end{bmatrix} \quad \text{or} \quad \begin{cases} .6x + .2y = x \\ .4x + .8y = y. \end{cases}$$

So we have the system

$$\begin{cases} x + \ y = 1 \\ .6x + .2y = x \\ .4x + .8y = y. \end{cases}$$

Combining terms in the second and third equations and eliminating the decimals by multiplying by 10, we have

$$\begin{cases} x + \ y = 1 \\ -4x + 2y = 0 \\ 4x - 2y = 0. \end{cases}$$

Note that the second and third equations are the same, except for a factor -1, so the last equation may be omitted. Now the system reads

$$\begin{cases} x + \ y = 1 \\ -4x + 2y = 0. \end{cases}$$

The diagonal form is obtained by the Gaussian elimination method:

$$\begin{bmatrix} 1 & 1 & | & 1 \\ -4 & 2 & | & 0 \end{bmatrix} \xrightarrow{\;[2]+4[1]\;} \begin{bmatrix} 1 & 1 & | & 1 \\ 0 & 6 & | & 4 \end{bmatrix}$$

$$\xrightarrow{\;\frac{1}{6}[2]\;} \begin{bmatrix} 1 & 1 & | & 1 \\ 0 & 1 & | & \frac{2}{3} \end{bmatrix}$$

$$\xrightarrow{\;[1]+(-1)[2]\;} \begin{bmatrix} 1 & 0 & | & \frac{1}{3} \\ 0 & 1 & | & \frac{2}{3} \end{bmatrix}$$

Thus

$$x = \tfrac{1}{3}, \qquad y = \tfrac{2}{3}.$$

So the stable distribution is

$$\begin{bmatrix} x \\ y \end{bmatrix} = \begin{bmatrix} \frac{1}{3} \\ \frac{2}{3} \end{bmatrix},$$

as we observed before. Note that once the stable distribution is determined, the stable matrix is easy to find. Just place the stable distribution in every column:

$$\begin{bmatrix} \frac{1}{3} & \frac{1}{3} \\ \frac{2}{3} & \frac{2}{3} \end{bmatrix}.$$

◆

▶ Example 4   In Section 1 we studied the distribution of taxis in three zones of a city. The movement of taxis from zone to zone was described by the regular stochastic matrix

$$A = \begin{bmatrix} .5 & .4 & .2 \\ .4 & .3 & .6 \\ .1 & .3 & .2 \end{bmatrix}.$$

In the long run, what percentage of taxis will be in each of the zones?

Solution   Let $X = \begin{bmatrix} x \\ y \\ z \end{bmatrix}$ be the stable distribution of A. Then x is the long-term percentage of taxis in zone I, y the percentage in zone II, and z the percentage in zone III. X is determined by the equations

$$\begin{cases} x + y + z = 1 \\ \qquad AX = X, \end{cases}$$

or, equivalently,

$$\begin{cases} x + \ y + \ \ z = 1 \\ .5x + .4y + .2z = x \\ .4x + .3y + .6z = y \\ .1x + .3y + .2z = z. \end{cases}$$

Rewriting the equations with all the terms involving the variables on the left, we get

$$\begin{cases} x + y + z = 1 \\ -.5x + .4y + .2z = 0 \\ .4x - .7y + .6z = 0 \\ .1x + .3y - .8z = 0. \end{cases}$$

Applying the Gaussian elimination method to this system, we get the solution $x = .4$, $y = .4$, $z = .2$. Thus, after many trips, approximately 40% of the taxis are in zone I, 40% in zone II, and 20% in zone III. ◆

We have come full circle. We began Chapter 2 by solving systems of linear equations. Matrices were developed as a tool for solving such systems. Then we found matrices to be interesting in their own right. Finally, in the current chapter, we have used systems of linear equations to answer questions about matrices.

GC If A is a square matrix, then many graphing calculators, such as the TI-82 and TI-83, can compute A^n directly for n as high as 255. (Even higher powers can then be obtained with instructions such as **Ans^255**.) For a regular stochastic matrix A, A^{255} should be an excellent approximation to the stable matrix of A. In Fig. 1, A is the matrix of Example 3 and C is the matrix of Example 4. (*Note:* ▶**Frac**, which stands for "display as a fraction," is obtained on the TI-82 and TI-83 by pressing MATH **1**.)

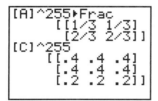

Figure 1.

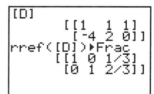

Figure 2.

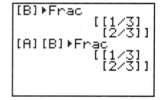

Figure 3.

Calculators or computers can be used to obtain a stable distribution by solving the system of linear equations or can be used to confirm a stable distribution by carrying out a matrix multiplication. The system of linear equations from Example 3 is solved in Fig. 2 and checked in Fig. 3.

APPENDIX Verification of Method for Obtaining the Stable Distribution

In this appendix we verify that the stable distribution X can be obtained by solving the system of equations

$$\begin{cases} \text{sum of the entries of } X = 1 \\ AX = X. \end{cases}$$

Let A be a regular stochastic matrix. Suppose that we take as the initial distribution its stable distribution X. Then the nth distribution matrix, or $A^n X$, approaches the stable distribution (by property 2), so that

$$X \approx A^n X \quad \text{for large } n.$$

Therefore,

$$AX \approx A \cdot A^n X = A^{n+1} X.$$

But $A^{n+1}X$ is the $(n+1)$st distribution matrix, which is also approximately X. Thus AX is approximately X. But the approximation can be made closer and closer by taking n large. Therefore, AX is arbitrarily close to X, or

$$AX = X. \tag{3}$$

This is a matrix equation in X. There is one other condition on X: X is a distribution matrix. Therefore,

$$\text{sum of the entries of } X = 1. \tag{4}$$

So, by (3) and (4), we find this system of linear equations for the entries of X:

$$\begin{cases} \text{sum of the entries of } X = 1 \\ AX = X. \end{cases}$$

Practice Problems 8.2

1. Is $\begin{bmatrix} 0 & .2 & .5 \\ .5 & 0 & .5 \\ .5 & .8 & 0 \end{bmatrix}$ a regular stochastic matrix? Explain your answer.

2. Find the stable matrix for the regular stochastic matrix in Problem 1.

3. In a study of cigarette smokers it was determined that of the people who smoked menthol cigarettes on a particular day, 10% smoked menthol the next day and 90% smoked nonmenthol. Of the people who smoked nonmenthol cigarettes on a particular day, the next day 30% smoked menthol and 70% smoked nonmenthol. In the long run, what percent of the people will be smoking nonmenthol cigarettes on a particular day?

▶ Exercises 8.2

In Exercises 1–6, determine whether or not the matrix is a regular stochastic matrix.

1. $\begin{bmatrix} \frac{1}{4} & \frac{2}{7} \\ \frac{3}{4} & \frac{5}{7} \end{bmatrix}$

2. $\begin{bmatrix} .6 & 0 \\ .4 & 1 \end{bmatrix}$

3. $\begin{bmatrix} .3 & 1 \\ .7 & 0 \end{bmatrix}$

4. $\begin{bmatrix} 1 & 0 & .7 \\ 0 & 1 & .2 \\ 0 & 0 & .1 \end{bmatrix}$

5. $\begin{bmatrix} 0 & .8 & 0 \\ 1 & .1 & .5 \\ 0 & .1 & .5 \end{bmatrix}$

6. $\begin{bmatrix} .6 & .6 & .6 \\ .3 & .3 & .3 \\ .1 & .1 & .1 \end{bmatrix}$

In Exercises 7–11, find the stable distribution for the given regular stochastic matrix.

7. $\begin{bmatrix} .5 & .1 \\ .5 & .9 \end{bmatrix}$

8. $\begin{bmatrix} .4 & 1 \\ .6 & 0 \end{bmatrix}$

9. $\begin{bmatrix} .8 & .3 \\ .2 & .7 \end{bmatrix}$

10. $\begin{bmatrix} .3 & .1 & .2 \\ .4 & .8 & .6 \\ .3 & .1 & .2 \end{bmatrix}$

11. $\begin{bmatrix} .1 & .4 & .7 \\ .6 & .4 & .2 \\ .3 & .2 & .1 \end{bmatrix}$

12. Refer to Exercise 10 of Section 8.1 (T-Maze). What percentage of the mice will be going to the left after many days?

13. Refer to Exercise 11 of Section 8.1 (Gym). In the long run what percentage of the people will have a strenuous workout on a particular day?

14. Refer to Exercise 13 of Section 8.1 (Voter Patterns). In the long run what proportion of the governors will be Democrats?

15. (*Genetics*) With respect to a certain gene, geneticists classify individuals as dominant, recessive, or hybrid. In an experiment, individuals are crossed with hybrids,

then their offspring are crossed with hybrids, and so on. For dominant individuals, 50% of their offspring will be dominant and 50% will be a hybrid. For the recessive individuals 50% of their offspring will be recessive and 50% hybrid. For hybrid individuals (to be crossed with hybrids) their offspring will be 25% dominant, 25% recessive, and 50% hybrid. In the long run what percent of the individuals in a generation will be dominant?

16. Commuters can get into town by car or bus. Surveys have shown that for those taking their car on a particular day, 20% take their car the next day and 80% take a bus. Also, for those taking a bus on a particular day, 50% take their car the next day and 50% take a bus. In the long run what percentage of the people take a bus on a particular day?

17. The changes in weather from day to day on the planet Xantar form a regular Markov process. Each day is either rainy or sunny. If it rains one day, there is a 90% chance that it will be sunny the following day. If it is sunny one day, there is a 60% chance of rain the next day. In the long run, what is the daily likelihood of rain?

18. A certain university has a computer room with 219 terminals. Each day there is a 3% chance that a given terminal will break and a 70% chance that a given broken terminal will be repaired. In the long run, about how many terminals in the room will be working?

19. As shown in Example 2, $\begin{bmatrix} 0 & 1 \\ 1 & 0 \end{bmatrix}$ is not a regular stochastic matrix. Show that the matrix has $\begin{bmatrix} .5 \\ .5 \end{bmatrix}$ as a

stable distribution and explain why this fact does not contradict the main premise of this section.

20. Refer to the stochastic matrix in Example 6 of Section 8.1. In the long run, what percentage of American women will work?

Exercises 21–24 require the use of a graphing calculator or a computer.

21. Consider the stochastic matrix A, where

$$A = \begin{bmatrix} .85 & .35 \\ .15 & .65 \end{bmatrix}.$$

Approximate the stable matrix of A by raising A to a high power. Then find the exact stable distribution by solving an appropriate system of linear equations. Check your answer by forming the product of A and the stable distribution.

Repeat Exercise 21 for each of the matrices in Exercises 22–24.

22. $\begin{bmatrix} .3 & .1 \\ .7 & .9 \end{bmatrix}$

23. $\begin{bmatrix} .1 & .4 & .1 \\ .3 & .2 & .8 \\ .6 & .4 & .1 \end{bmatrix}$

24. $\begin{bmatrix} .4 & .2 & .4 \\ .1 & .3 & .1 \\ .5 & .5 & .5 \end{bmatrix}$

Solutions to Practice Problems 8.2

1. Yes. It is easily seen to be stochastic. Although it has some zero entries, there are no zero entries in

$$A^2 = \begin{bmatrix} .35 & .40 & .10 \\ .25 & .50 & .25 \\ .40 & .10 & .65 \end{bmatrix}.$$

2. $\begin{cases} x + y + z = 1 \\ \begin{bmatrix} 0 & .2 & .5 \\ .5 & 0 & .5 \\ .5 & .8 & 0 \end{bmatrix} \begin{bmatrix} x \\ y \\ z \end{bmatrix} = \begin{bmatrix} x \\ y \\ z \end{bmatrix} \end{cases}$ or $\begin{cases} x + y + z = 1 \\ .2y + .5z = x \\ .5x + .5z = y \\ .5x + .8y = z \end{cases}$

or $\begin{cases} x + y + z = 1 \\ -x + .2y + .5z = 0 \\ .5x - y + .5z = 0 \\ .5x + .8y - z = 0 \end{cases}$

To simplify the arithmetic, multiply each of the last three equations of the system by 10 to eliminate the decimals. Then apply the Gaussian elimination method.

$$\begin{cases} x + y + z = 1 \\ -10x + 2y + 5z = 0 \\ 5x - 10y + 5z = 0 \\ 5x + 8y - 10z = 0 \end{cases} \qquad \begin{cases} x + y + z = 1 \\ 12y + 15z = 10 \\ -15y = -5 \\ 3y - 15z = -5 \end{cases}$$

Next interchange the second and third equations and pivot about $-15y$.

$$\begin{cases} x + y + z = 1 \\ -15y = -5 \\ 12y + 15z = 10 \\ 3y - 15z = -5 \end{cases} \qquad \begin{cases} x + z = \frac{2}{3} \\ y = \frac{1}{3} \\ 15z = 6 \\ -15z = -6 \end{cases}$$

Pivoting about $15z$ yields $x = \frac{4}{15}$, $y = \frac{5}{15}$, $z = \frac{6}{15}$, so the stable matrix is

$$\begin{bmatrix} \frac{4}{15} & \frac{4}{15} & \frac{4}{15} \\ \frac{5}{15} & \frac{5}{15} & \frac{5}{15} \\ \frac{6}{15} & \frac{6}{15} & \frac{6}{15} \end{bmatrix}.$$

3. The regular stochastic matrix describing this daily transition is

$$\begin{array}{c} \\ M \\ N \end{array} \begin{array}{cc} M & N \\ \begin{bmatrix} .1 & .3 \\ .9 & .7 \end{bmatrix} \end{array}.$$

The stable distribution is found by solving

$$\begin{cases} x + y = 1 \\ \begin{bmatrix} .1 & .3 \\ .9 & .7 \end{bmatrix} \begin{bmatrix} x \\ y \end{bmatrix} = \begin{bmatrix} x \\ y \end{bmatrix} \end{cases} \quad \text{or} \quad \begin{cases} x + y = 1 \\ .1x + .3y = x \\ .9x + .7y = y \end{cases} \quad \text{or} \quad \begin{cases} x + y = 1 \\ -.9x + .3y = 0 \\ .9x - .3y = 0. \end{cases}$$

Since the last two equations are essentially the same, we need only solve the system consisting of the first two equations. Multiply the second equation by 10:

$$\begin{cases} x + y = 1 \\ -9x + 3y = 0 \end{cases} \rightarrow \begin{cases} x + y = 1 \\ 12y = 9 \end{cases} \rightarrow \begin{cases} x = \frac{1}{4} \\ y = \frac{3}{4}. \end{cases}$$

So the stable distribution is $\begin{bmatrix} \frac{1}{4} \\ \frac{3}{4} \end{bmatrix}$. The stable distribution tells us that in the long run, 25% smoke menthol and 75% smoke nonmenthol cigarettes on any particular day.

8.3 Absorbing Stochastic Matrices

In this section we study long-term trends for a certain class of matrices which are not regular—the absorbing stochastic matrices. By way of introduction, recall some general facts about stochastic matrices.

Stochastic matrices, such as

$$\begin{bmatrix} .3 & .5 & .1 & 0 \\ .2 & .2 & .8 & 0 \\ .1 & .3 & 0 & 0 \\ .4 & 0 & .1 & 1 \end{bmatrix},$$

describe state-to-state changes in certain processes. Each column of a stochastic matrix describes the transitions (or movements) from one specific state. For example, the first column of the preceding stochastic matrix indicates that at the end of one time period the probability is .3 that an object in state 1 stays in state 1, .2 that it goes to state 2, .1 that it goes to state 3, and .4 that it goes to state 4. Similarly, the second column indicates the probabilities for transitions from state 2, the third column from state 3, and the fourth from state 4.

If A is a stochastic matrix, then the columns of A^2 describe the transitions from the various states *after two time periods*. For instance, the third column of A^2 indicates the probabilities of an object starting out in state 3 and ending up in each of the states after two time periods. Similarly, the columns of A^n indicate the transitions from the various states after n periods.

Consider the stochastic matrix just described. Its fourth column illustrates a curious phenomenon. It indicates that if an object starts out in state 4, after one time period the probabilities of going to states 1, 2, or 3 are 0 and the probability of going to state 4 is 1. In other words, all of the objects in state 4 stay in state 4. A state with this property is called an *absorbing state*. More precisely, an absorbing state is a state that always leads back to itself.

▶ Example 1   Find all absorbing states of the stochastic matrix

$$\begin{bmatrix} 1 & 0 & .3 & 0 \\ 0 & 1 & .1 & 1 \\ 0 & 0 & .5 & 0 \\ 0 & 0 & .1 & 0 \end{bmatrix}.$$

Solution   To determine which states are absorbing, one must look at the columns. The first column describes the transitions from state 1. It says that state 1 leads to state 1 100% of the time and to the other states 0% of the time. So state 1 is absorbing. Column 2 describes transitions from state 2. It says that state 2 leads to state 2 100% of the time. So state 2 is absorbing. Clearly, the third column says that state 3 is not absorbing. For example, state 3 leads to state 1 with probability .3. At first glance, column 4 seems to say that state 4 is absorbing. But it is not, because column 4 says that state 4 leads to state 2 100% of the time. ◆

Based on Example 1, we can easily determine the absorbing states of any stochastic matrix: First, the corresponding column has a single 1 and the remaining entries 0. Second, the lone 1 must be located on the main diagonal of the matrix. That is, its row and column number must be the same. So, for example, state i is an absorbing state if and only if the ith entry in the ith column is 1 and all the remaining entries in that column are 0.

An *absorbing stochastic matrix* is a stochastic matrix in which (1) there is at least one absorbing state and (2) from any state it is possible to get to at least one absorbing state, either directly or through one or more intermediate states.

▶ Example 2   Is the matrix

$$\begin{bmatrix} 1 & 0 & .3 & 0 \\ 0 & 1 & .1 & 1 \\ 0 & 0 & .5 & 0 \\ 0 & 0 & .1 & 0 \end{bmatrix}$$

an absorbing stochastic matrix?

Solution   In Example 1 we showed that states 1 and 2 were absorbing. From column 3 we see that state 3 can lead to both state 1 and state 2: state 1 with probability .3 and state 2 with probability .1. From column 4 we see that state 4 does not lead to state 1, but it does lead to state 2. Thus states 3 and 4 both lead to absorbing states, and so the matrix is an absorbing stochastic matrix.   ◆

In general, processes described by stochastic matrices can oscillate indefinitely from state to state in such a way that they exhibit no long-term trend. An example was given in Section 2 using the matrix

$$\begin{bmatrix} 0 & 1 \\ 1 & 0 \end{bmatrix}.$$

The idea of introducing absorbing states is to reduce the degree of oscillation. For when an absorbing state is reached, the process no longer changes. The main result of this section is that absorbing stochastic matrices exhibit a long-term trend. Further, we can determine this trend using a simple computational procedure.

When considering an absorbing stochastic matrix, we will always arrange the states so that the absorbing states come first, then the nonabsorbing states.

Absorbing   Nonabsorbing

$$\left[\begin{array}{c|c} & \\ & \end{array}\right]$$

When the states are ordered in this manner, an absorbing stochastic matrix can be partitioned, or subdivided, into four submatrices.

Absorbing   Nonabsorbing

$$\left[\begin{array}{c|c} I & S \\ \hline 0 & R \end{array}\right]$$

The matrix I is an identity matrix, and 0 denotes a matrix having all entries 0. The matrices S and R are the two pieces corresponding to the nonabsorbing states. For example, in the case of the absorbing stochastic matrix of Example 2, this partition is given by

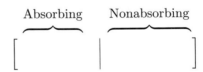

$$\left[\begin{array}{cc|cc} 1 & 0 & .3 & 0 \\ 0 & 1 & .1 & 1 \\ \hline 0 & 0 & .5 & 0 \\ 0 & 0 & .1 & 0 \end{array}\right].$$

▸ Example 3 The victims of a certain disease are classified into three states: cured, dead from the disease, or sick. Once a person is cured, he is permanently immune. Each year 70% of those sick are cured, 10% die from the disease, and 20% remain ill.

(a) Determine a stochastic matrix describing the progression of the disease.

(b) Determine the absorbing states.

Solution (a) There is one column for each state. Transferring the given data to the matrix gives the result:

$$\begin{array}{c} \\ \text{Cured} \\ \text{Dead} \\ \text{Sick} \end{array} \begin{array}{ccc} \text{Cured} & \text{Dead} & \text{Sick} \\ \begin{bmatrix} 1 & 0 & .7 \\ 0 & 1 & .1 \\ 0 & 0 & .2 \end{bmatrix} \end{array}.$$

(b) The absorbing states are "cured" and "dead," since these are the states that always lead back to themselves. The matrix is an absorbing stochastic matrix, since there is at least one absorbing state and the other state, "sick," can lead to an absorbing state. (In fact, in this case it leads to either of the absorbing states.) ◆

▸ Example 4 Find the long-term trend of the absorbing stochastic matrix

$$A = \left[\begin{array}{cc|c} 1 & 0 & .2 \\ 0 & 1 & .4 \\ 0 & 0 & .4 \end{array}\right].$$

Solution The long-term trend is found by raising A to various powers. Here are the results, accurate to three decimal places:

$$A^2 = \left[\begin{array}{cc|c} 1 & 0 & .28 \\ 0 & 1 & .56 \\ 0 & 0 & .16 \end{array}\right] \qquad A^3 = \left[\begin{array}{cc|c} 1 & 0 & .312 \\ 0 & 1 & .624 \\ 0 & 0 & .064 \end{array}\right]$$

$$A^4 = \left[\begin{array}{cc|c} 1 & 0 & .325 \\ 0 & 1 & .650 \\ 0 & 0 & .025 \end{array}\right] \qquad A^5 = \left[\begin{array}{cc|c} 1 & 0 & .330 \\ 0 & 1 & .660 \\ 0 & 0 & .010 \end{array}\right]$$

$$A^6 = \left[\begin{array}{cc|c} 1 & 0 & .332 \\ 0 & 1 & .664 \\ 0 & 0 & .004 \end{array}\right] \qquad A^7 = \left[\begin{array}{cc|c} 1 & 0 & .333 \\ 0 & 1 & .666 \\ 0 & 0 & .001 \end{array}\right].$$

Based on this numerical evidence, it appears as if the powers of A approach the matrix

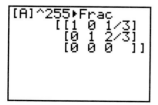

$$A = \left[\begin{array}{cc|c} 1 & 0 & \frac{1}{3} \\ 0 & 1 & \frac{2}{3} \\ 0 & 0 & 0 \end{array}\right].$$

In other words, after a large number of time intervals, 100% of those originally in state 1 remain in state 1 (column 1), 100% of those originally in state 2 remain in state 2 (column 2), and those originally in state 3 end up in state 1 with probability one-third and in state 2 with probability two-thirds. ◆

Example 4 exhibits three important features of the long-term behavior exhibited by all absorbing stochastic matrices. First, as in the case of regular stochastic matrices, the powers approach a particular matrix. This limiting matrix is called a *stable matrix*. Second, for absorbing stochastic matrices the long-term trend depends on the initial state. For example, the stable matrix just computed gives different results depending on the state in which you start. This is reflected by the fact that the three columns are different. (In the case of regular stochastic matrices, the long-term trend does not depend on the initial distribution. All columns of the stable matrix are the same. They all equal the stable distribution.) The third important point to notice is that, no matter what the initial state, all objects eventually go to absorbing states. The absorbing states act like magnets and attract all objects to themselves in the long run.

▶ **Example 5**   Find the long-term trend of the disease described in Example 3.

Solution   The stochastic matrix here is

$$\left[\begin{array}{cc|c} 1 & 0 & .7 \\ 0 & 1 & .1 \\ \hline 0 & 0 & .2 \end{array}\right].$$

Its first few powers are given by

$$A^2 = \left[\begin{array}{cc|c} 1 & 0 & .84 \\ 0 & 1 & .12 \\ \hline 0 & 0 & .04 \end{array}\right] \qquad A^3 = \left[\begin{array}{cc|c} 1 & 0 & .868 \\ 0 & 1 & .124 \\ \hline 0 & 0 & .008 \end{array}\right]$$

$$A^4 \approx \left[\begin{array}{cc|c} 1 & 0 & .874 \\ 0 & 1 & .125 \\ \hline 0 & 0 & .002 \end{array}\right] \qquad A^5 \approx \left[\begin{array}{cc|c} 1 & 0 & .875 \\ 0 & 1 & .125 \\ \hline 0 & 0 & .000 \end{array}\right].$$

It appears that the powers approach the matrix

$$A = \left[\begin{array}{cc|c} 1 & 0 & \frac{7}{8} \\ 0 & 1 & \frac{1}{8} \\ \hline 0 & 0 & 0 \end{array}\right].$$

```
[A]^255▶Frac
   [[1 0 7/8]
    [0 1 1/8]
    [0 0 0  ]]
```

This is the stable matrix. In other words, reading from column 3, of those initially in state 3, "sick," the probability is seven-eighths of eventually being cured, and one-eighth of eventually dying of the disease.   ◆

In Examples 4 and 5 we have computed the stable matrix by raising the given stochastic matrix to various powers. Actually, there is a formal computational procedure for determining the stable matrix. Suppose that we partition an absorbing stochastic matrix into submatrices

$$A = \left[\begin{array}{c|c} I & S \\ \hline 0 & R \end{array}\right].$$

The stable matrix of A is

$$\left[\begin{array}{c|c} I & S(I-R)^{-1} \\ \hline 0 & 0 \end{array}\right].$$

[*Note*: The identity matrix I in $(I-R)^{-1}$ is chosen to be the same size as R in order to make the matrix subtraction permissible.]

▶ **Example 6**   Use the preceding formula to determine the stable matrices of

(a) $\left[\begin{array}{cc|c} 1 & 0 & .2 \\ 0 & 1 & .4 \\ \hline 0 & 0 & .4 \end{array}\right]$ (b) $\left[\begin{array}{cc|c} 1 & 0 & .7 \\ 0 & 1 & .1 \\ \hline 0 & 0 & .2 \end{array}\right].$

Solution   (a)   In this case $S = \begin{bmatrix} .2 \\ .4 \end{bmatrix}$, $R = [.4]$. The stable matrix is

$$\left[\begin{array}{c|c} I & S(I-R)^{-1} \\ \hline 0 & 0 \end{array}\right] = \left[\begin{array}{cc|c} 1 & 0 & S(I-R)^{-1} \\ 0 & 1 & \\ \hline 0 & 0 & 0 \end{array}\right].$$

Since R is 1×1, to compute $I - R$ we let I be the 1×1 identity matrix $[1]$. Then

$$I - R = [1] - [.4] = [1 - .4] = [.6].$$

Now $(I-R)^{-1}$ is a matrix that when multiplied by $I - R$ or $[.6]$, gives the 1×1 identity matrix $[1]$. Thus

$$(I-R)^{-1} = [.6]^{-1} = [1/.6]$$

and

$$S(I-R)^{-1} = \begin{bmatrix} .2 \\ .4 \end{bmatrix} [1/.6] = \begin{bmatrix} .2/.6 \\ .4/.6 \end{bmatrix} = \begin{bmatrix} \frac{1}{3} \\ \frac{2}{3} \end{bmatrix}.$$

Therefore, the stable matrix is given by

$$\left[\begin{array}{cc|c} 1 & 0 & \frac{1}{3} \\ 0 & 1 & \frac{2}{3} \\ \hline 0 & 0 & 0 \end{array}\right].$$

(b)   In this case

$$S = \begin{bmatrix} .7 \\ .1 \end{bmatrix}, \quad R = [.2], \quad I - R = [1] - [.2] = [.8], \quad (I-R)^{-1} = [1/.8].$$

Therefore,

$$S(I-R)^{-1} = \begin{bmatrix} .7 \\ .1 \end{bmatrix} [1/.8] = \begin{bmatrix} .7/.8 \\ .1/.8 \end{bmatrix} = \begin{bmatrix} \frac{7}{8} \\ \frac{1}{8} \end{bmatrix}.$$

So the stable matrix is

$$\left[\begin{array}{c|c} I & S(I-R)^{-1} \\ \hline 0 & 0 \end{array}\right] = \left[\begin{array}{cc|c} 1 & 0 & \frac{7}{8} \\ 0 & 1 & \frac{1}{8} \\ \hline 0 & 0 & 0 \end{array}\right]. \qquad \blacklozenge$$

▶ Example 7   (*Gambler's Ruin*) Consider a game of chance with the following characteristics: A person repeatedly bets \$1 each play. If he wins, he receives \$1.[1] If he goes broke, he stops playing. Also, if he accumulates \$3, he stops playing. On each play the probability of winning is .4 and of losing .6. What is the probability of eventually accumulating \$3 if he starts with \$1? \$2?

Solution   There are four states, corresponding to having \$0, \$3, \$1, or \$2. The first two are absorbing states. The stochastic matrix is

$$\begin{array}{cccc} & \$0 & \$3 & \$1 & \$2 \end{array}$$
$$\begin{array}{c} \$0 \\ \$3 \\ \$1 \\ \$2 \end{array} \left[\begin{array}{cc|cc} 1 & 0 & .6 & 0 \\ 0 & 1 & 0 & .4 \\ \hline 0 & 0 & 0 & .6 \\ 0 & 0 & .4 & 0 \end{array}\right].$$

The third column is derived in this way: If he has \$1, there is a .6 probability of losing \$1, which would mean going to state \$0. Thus the first entry in the third column is .6. There is no way to get from \$1 to \$3 or from \$1 to \$1 after one play. So the second and third entries are 0. There is a .4 probability of winning \$1—that is, of going from \$1 to \$2. So the last entry is .4. The fourth column is derived similarly.

In this example

$$S = \begin{bmatrix} .6 & 0 \\ 0 & .4 \end{bmatrix} \qquad R = \begin{bmatrix} 0 & .6 \\ .4 & 0 \end{bmatrix}.$$

To compute $S(I-R)^{-1}$, observe that

$$I - R = \begin{bmatrix} 1 & 0 \\ 0 & 1 \end{bmatrix} - \begin{bmatrix} 0 & .6 \\ .4 & 0 \end{bmatrix} = \begin{bmatrix} 1 & -.6 \\ -.4 & 1 \end{bmatrix}.$$

To compute $(I-R)^{-1}$, recall that

$$\begin{bmatrix} a & b \\ c & d \end{bmatrix}^{-1} = \begin{bmatrix} d/\Delta & -b/\Delta \\ -c/\Delta & a/\Delta \end{bmatrix}, \qquad \Delta = ad - bc \neq 0.$$

So, in this example, $\Delta = 1 \cdot 1 - (-.6)(-.4) = 1 - .24 = .76$ and

$$(I - R)^{-1} = \begin{bmatrix} 1 & -.6 \\ -.4 & 1 \end{bmatrix}^{-1} \approx \begin{bmatrix} 1.32 & .79 \\ .53 & 1.32 \end{bmatrix}$$

$$S(I - R)^{-1} \approx \begin{bmatrix} .6 & 0 \\ 0 & .4 \end{bmatrix} \begin{bmatrix} 1.32 & .79 \\ .53 & 1.32 \end{bmatrix} \approx \begin{bmatrix} .79 & .47 \\ .21 & .53 \end{bmatrix}.$$

---

[1] That is, he receives his bet of \$1 plus winnings of \$1.

Thus the stable matrix is

$$\left[\begin{array}{c|c} I & S(I-R)^{-1} \\ \hline 0 & 0 \end{array}\right] = \left[\begin{array}{cc|cc} 1 & 0 & .79 & .47 \\ 0 & 1 & .21 & .53 \\ 0 & 0 & 0 & 0 \\ 0 & 0 & 0 & 0 \end{array}\right].$$

We are interested in the probability that he ends up with $3. The percentage is different for each of the two starting amounts $1 and $2. Recall the meaning of the rows and columns:

	$0	$3	$1	$2
$0	1	0	.79	.47
$3	0	1	.21	.53
$1	0	0	0	0
$2	0	0	0	0

Looking at the $1 column, we see that if he starts with $1, the probability is .21 that he ends up with $3. Looking at the $2 column, the probability is .53 that he ends up with $3. ◆

The Fundamental Matrix The matrix $(I - R)^{-1}$ used to compute the stable matrix is called the *fundamental matrix* and is denoted by the letter F. Its columns and rows should be labeled with the nonabsorbing states. The fundamental matrix directly provides certain useful probabilities for the process. Specifically, the ijth entry of F is the expected number of times the process will be in nonabsorbing state i if it starts in nonabsorbing state j. The sum of the entries of the jth column of F is the expected number of steps before absorption when the process begins in nonabsorbing state j.

The fundamental matrix for the gambler's ruin example is

$$F = \begin{array}{c} \\ \$1 \\ \$2 \end{array} \begin{array}{c} \$1 \quad \$2 \\ \left[\begin{array}{cc} 1.32 & .79 \\ .53 & 1.32 \end{array}\right]. \end{array}$$

The first column of F indicates that when the gambler begins with $1, he can expect to play $1.32 + .53 = 1.85$ times before quitting. He should have $1 for an expected number of 1.32 plays and have $2 for an expected number of .53 plays. The second column gives similar information when the gambler begins with $2.

GC A graphing utility can be used to obtain the stable matrix by raising the original stochastic matrix to a high power or by calculating $S(I-R)^{-1}$. In Figs. 1 and 2, **[A]**, **[B]**, and **[C]** are the matrices A, S, and R of Example 7. In Fig. 2, the **MODE Decimal** option was set to 2.

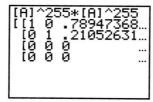

Figure 1.

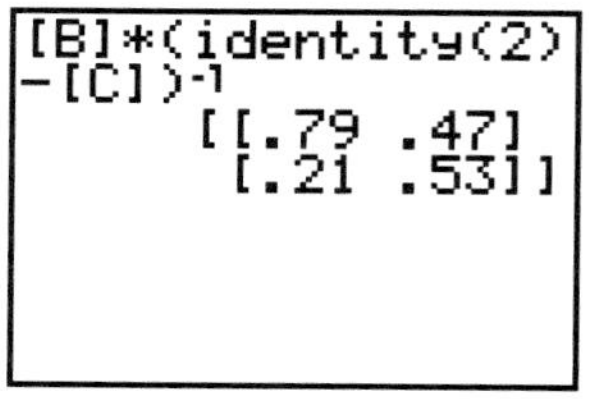

Figure 2.

<table>
<tr><td>**Practice Problems
8.3**</td><td>

1. When an absorbing stochastic matrix is partitioned, the submatrix in the upper left is an identity matrix, denoted by I. Also, when finding the stable matrix, we subtract the submatrix R from an identity matrix, also denoted by I. Are these two identity matrices the same?

2. Let A be an absorbing stochastic matrix. Interpret the entries of A^2.

3. Is $\begin{bmatrix} 1 & .4 & 0 \\ 0 & .2 & .1 \\ 0 & .4 & .9 \end{bmatrix}$ an absorbing stochastic matrix?

</td></tr>
</table>

▶ Exercises 8.3

In Exercises 1–4, determine whether the given matrix is an absorbing stochastic matrix.

1. $\begin{bmatrix} 1 & 0 & 0 & 0 \\ 0 & 1 & 0 & 0 \\ 0 & 0 & .8 & .1 \\ 0 & 0 & .2 & .9 \end{bmatrix}$

2. $\begin{bmatrix} 1 & 0 & 0 & .3 \\ 0 & 1 & 0 & .2 \\ 0 & 0 & 1 & .2 \\ 0 & 0 & 0 & .3 \end{bmatrix}$

3. $\begin{bmatrix} 1 & 0 & .4 \\ 0 & .5 & .3 \\ 0 & .5 & .3 \end{bmatrix}$

4. $\begin{bmatrix} 1 & 0 & 0 & 0 \\ 0 & 1 & 0 & 0 \\ 0 & 0 & 0 & 1 \\ 0 & 0 & 1 & 0 \end{bmatrix}$

The matrices in Exercises 5–10 are absorbing stochastic matrices. In each, identify R and S and compute the fundamental matrix and the stable matrix.

5. $\begin{bmatrix} 1 & 0 & .3 \\ 0 & 1 & .2 \\ 0 & 0 & .5 \end{bmatrix}$

6. $\begin{bmatrix} 1 & 0 & \frac{1}{2} \\ 0 & 1 & \frac{1}{6} \\ 0 & 0 & \frac{1}{3} \end{bmatrix}$

7. $\begin{bmatrix} 1 & 0 & .1 & 0 \\ 0 & 1 & .5 & .2 \\ 0 & 0 & .3 & .6 \\ 0 & 0 & .1 & .2 \end{bmatrix}$

8. $\begin{bmatrix} 1 & 0 & \frac{1}{4} & \frac{1}{6} \\ 0 & 1 & \frac{1}{6} & 0 \\ 0 & 0 & \frac{1}{4} & \frac{1}{2} \\ 0 & 0 & \frac{1}{3} & \frac{1}{3} \end{bmatrix}$

9. $\begin{bmatrix} 1 & 0 & 0 & .1 & .2 \\ 0 & 1 & 0 & .3 & 0 \\ 0 & 0 & 1 & 0 & .2 \\ 0 & 0 & 0 & .5 & 0 \\ 0 & 0 & 0 & .1 & .6 \end{bmatrix}$

10. $\begin{bmatrix} 1 & 0 & \frac{1}{4} & 0 & \frac{1}{3} \\ 0 & 1 & \frac{1}{4} & 0 & 0 \\ 0 & 0 & 0 & \frac{1}{3} & \frac{1}{6} \\ 0 & 0 & \frac{1}{2} & \frac{1}{3} & 0 \\ 0 & 0 & 0 & \frac{1}{3} & \frac{1}{2} \end{bmatrix}$

Note: $\begin{bmatrix} 1 & -\frac{1}{3} & -\frac{1}{6} \\ -\frac{1}{2} & \frac{2}{3} & 0 \\ 0 & -\frac{1}{3} & \frac{1}{2} \end{bmatrix}^{-1} = \begin{bmatrix} \frac{3}{2} & 1 & \frac{1}{2} \\ \frac{9}{8} & \frac{9}{4} & \frac{3}{8} \\ \frac{3}{4} & \frac{3}{2} & \frac{9}{4} \end{bmatrix}$.

Exercises 11 and 12 refer to Example 7, the gambler's ruin.

11. Interpret the entry .79 in the fundamental matrix.

12. If the gambler begins with \$2, what is the expected number of times that he will play before quitting?

13. Suppose that the following data were obtained from the records of a certain two-year college. Of those who were freshmen (F) during a particular year, 80% became sophomores (S) the next year and 20% dropped out (D). Of those who were sophomores during a particular year, 90% graduated (G) by the next year and 10% dropped out.

  (a) Set up the absorbing stochastic matrix with states D, G, F, S that describes this transition.

  (b) Find the stable matrix.

  (c) Determine the probability that an entering freshman will eventually graduate.

  (d) Determine the expected number of years a student entering as a freshman will attend the college before either dropping out or graduating.

14. A research article[2] on the application of stochastic matrices to mental illness considers a person to be in one of four states: state I—chronically insane and hospitalized; state II—dead, with death occurring while unhospitalized; state III—sane; state IV—mildly insane and unhospitalized. States I and II are absorbing states. Suppose that of the people in state III, after one year 1.994% will be in state II, 98% in state III, and .006% in state IV. Also, suppose that of the people in state IV, after one year 2% will be in state I, 3% in state II, and 95% in state IV.

  (a) Set up the absorbing stochastic matrix that describes this transition.

[2] A.W. Marshall and H. Goldhamer, "An Application of Markov Processes to the Study of the Epidemiology of Mental Diseases," *American Statistical Association Journal*, March 1955, pp. 99–129.

(b) Find the stable matrix.

(c) Determine the probability that a person who is currently well will eventually be chronically insane.

(d) For a person in state III, determine the expected number of years for which the person will be in state III.

15. A retailer classifies accounts as having one of four possible states: "paid up," "overdue at most 30 days," "overdue less than 60 days but more than 30 days," and "bad." If no payment is made on an overdue account by the end of the month, the status moves to the next state. When a partial payment is made on an overdue account, its improved status depends on the size of the payment. Experience shows that the following matrix describes the changes in status of accounts.

$$
\begin{array}{c}
\\
\text{Paid} \\
\leq 30 \\
< 60 \\
\text{Bad}
\end{array}
\begin{array}{cccc}
\text{Paid} & \leq 30 & < 60 & \text{Bad} \\
\left[\begin{array}{cccc}
1 & .4 & .1 & 0 \\
0 & .4 & .4 & 0 \\
0 & .2 & .4 & 0 \\
0 & 0 & .1 & 1
\end{array}\right]
\end{array}
$$

(a) What is the probability of an account eventually being paid off if it is currently overdue at most 30 days? Less than 60 days?

(b) If an account is currently overdue at most 30 days, what is the expected number of months until it is either paid or bad?

(c) If the company has $2000 in bills in the "≤ 30 day" category and $5000 in bills in the "< 60 day" category, how much can the retailer expect will eventually be paid up and how much will eventually be irretrievable bad debt?

16. The managers in a company are classified as top managers, middle managers, and first-line managers. Each year, 10% of top managers retire, 10% leave the company, 60% remain top managers, and 20% are demoted to middle managers. Each year, 5% of middle managers retire, 15% leave the company, 10% are promoted to top managers, 60% remain middle managers, and 10% are demoted to first-line managers. Each year, 5% of first-line managers retire, 25% leave the company, 10% are promoted to middle managers, and 60% remain first-line managers.

(a) What is the probability of a top manager eventually retiring? A middle manager? A first-line manager?

(b) If a person is currently a middle manager, what is the expected number of years that he or she will be with the company before either leaving or retiring?

Note:

$$
\begin{bmatrix}
.4 & -.1 & 0 \\
-.2 & .4 & -.1 \\
0 & -.1 & .4
\end{bmatrix}^{-1}
=
\begin{bmatrix}
\frac{75}{26} & \frac{10}{13} & \frac{5}{26} \\
\frac{20}{13} & \frac{40}{13} & \frac{10}{13} \\
\frac{5}{13} & \frac{10}{13} & \frac{35}{13}
\end{bmatrix}.
$$

17. As a variation of the gambler's ruin problem, suppose that on each play the probability of winning is $\frac{1}{2}$ and the gambler stops playing if he accumulates $4.

(a) What is the probability of eventually going broke if he starts with $1? $2? $3?

(b) If the gambler begins with $2, what is the expected number of times that he will play before quitting?

Note:

$$
\begin{bmatrix}
1 & -\frac{1}{2} & 0 \\
-\frac{1}{2} & 1 & -\frac{1}{2} \\
0 & -\frac{1}{2} & 1
\end{bmatrix}^{-1}
=
\begin{bmatrix}
\frac{3}{2} & 1 & \frac{1}{2} \\
1 & 2 & 1 \\
\frac{1}{2} & 1 & \frac{3}{2}
\end{bmatrix}.
$$

Exercises 18 and 19 require the use of a graphing calculator or a computer.

18. Consider the absorbing stochastic matrix A, where

$$
A = \begin{bmatrix}
1 & 0 & 0 & 0 & .6 \\
0 & 1 & 0 & .5 & .1 \\
0 & 0 & 1 & 0 & .1 \\
0 & 0 & 0 & .2 & .2 \\
0 & 0 & 0 & .3 & 0
\end{bmatrix}.
$$

Approximate the stable matrix of A by raising A to a high power. Then find the exact stable distribution by calculating $S(I - R)^{-1}$.

19. Repeat Exercise 18 for the matrix

$$
\begin{bmatrix}
1 & 0 & .5 & .4 & .2 \\
0 & 1 & 0 & .3 & .7 \\
0 & 0 & 0 & .2 & .1 \\
0 & 0 & .3 & 0 & 0 \\
0 & 0 & .2 & .1 & 0
\end{bmatrix}.
$$

Solutions to Practice Problems 8.3

1. Sometimes they are, but in general they are not. The size of the first identity matrix equals the number of absorbing states, whereas the size of the second identity matrix is the same as that of the matrix R, which equals the number of nonabsorbing states.

2. Consider the entry in the ith row, jth column of A^2. Suppose that an object begins in state j. Then the entry gives the probability that it ends up in state i after two time periods.

<table>
<tr><td>

Solutions to Practice Problems 8.3 (Continued)

</td><td>

3. Yes. (i) Its first state is absorbing. (ii) From each state it is possible to get to the first state. Note that it is possible to go directly from state 2 to state 1, since $a_{12} = .4 \neq 0$. Since $a_{13} = 0$, it is not possible to go directly from state 3 to state 1. However, this can be accomplished indirectly by going from state 3 to state 2 (possible since $a_{23} = .1 \neq 0$) and then from state 2 to state 1.

</td></tr>
</table>

▶ Chapter 8 Summary

1. A Markov process is a sequence of experiments performed at regular time intervals involving *states*. As a result of each experiment, transitions between states occur with probabilities given by a matrix called the *transition matrix*. The ijth entry in the transition matrix is the conditional probability Pr(moving to state i|in state j).

2. A *stochastic matrix* is a square matrix for which every entry is greater than or equal to 0 and the sum of the entries in each column is 1. Every transition matrix is a stochastic matrix.

3. The nth distribution matrix gives the percentage of members in each state after n time periods.

4. A^n is obtained by multiplying together n copies of A. Its ijth entry is the conditional probability Pr(moving to state i after n time periods | in state j). Also, A^n times the initial distribution matrix gives the nth distribution matrix.

5. A stochastic matrix is called *regular* if some power of the matrix has only positive entries.

6. If A is a regular stochastic matrix, as n gets large the powers of the matrix, A^n, approach a certain matrix called the *stable matrix* of A and the distribution matrices approach a certain column matrix called the *stable distribution*. Each column of the stable matrix holds the stable distribution. The stable distribution can be found by solving $AX = X$, where the sum of the entries in X is equal to 1.

7. If the probability of moving from a state to itself is 1, we call that state an *absorbing state*. An *absorbing stochastic matrix* is a stochastic matrix with at least one absorbing state and in which from any state it is possible to eventually get to an absorbing state.

8. In an absorbing process, the transition matrix should be arranged so that absorbing states are listed before nonabsorbing states. The transition matrix will have the form

$$\left[\begin{array}{c|c} I & S \\ \hline 0 & R \end{array}\right],$$

where I is an identity matrix, 0 denotes a matrix of zeros, and S and R represent the transitions from nonabsorbing to absorbing states and from nonabsorbing to nonabsorbing states, respectively.

9. The *stable matrix* of the absorbing matrix in number 8 is

$$\left[\begin{array}{c|c} I & S(I-R)^{-1} \\ \hline 0 & 0 \end{array}\right].$$

10. The *fundamental matrix* of the absorbing matrix in number 8 is the matrix $(I-R)^{-1}$. When its columns and rows are labeled with the nonabsorbing states, its ijth entry is the expected number of times the process will be in nonabsorbing state i given that it started in nonabsorbing state j. The sum of the entries in the jth column is the expected number of steps before absorption when the process begins in state j.

Review of Fundamental Concepts of Chapter 8

1. What is a Markov process?
2. What is a transition matrix? A stochastic matrix? A distribution matrix?
3. What is A^n? Give an interpretation of the entries of A^n.
4. How is the nth distribution matrix calculated from the initial distribution matrix?
5. Define *regular* stochastic matrix.
6. Define the stable matrix and stable distribution of a regular stochastic matrix.

7. Explain how to find the stable distribution of a regular stochastic matrix.
8. What is meant by an absorbing state of a stochastic matrix?
9. What is an absorbing stochastic matrix?
10. Explain how to find the stable matrix of an absorbing stochastic matrix.
11. What is the fundamental matrix of an absorbing stochastic matrix and how is it used?

▶ Chapter 8 Supplementary Exercises

In Exercises 1–6, determine whether or not the given matrix is stochastic. If so, determine if it is regular, absorbing, or neither.

1. $\begin{bmatrix} 1 & .3 & 0 & 0 \\ 0 & .1 & 0 & 0 \\ 0 & .4 & .7 & .4 \\ 0 & .2 & .3 & .6 \end{bmatrix}$
2. $\begin{bmatrix} .1 & .1 & .1 & .1 \\ .2 & .2 & .2 & .2 \\ .3 & .3 & .3 & .3 \\ .4 & .4 & .4 & .4 \end{bmatrix}$

3. $\begin{bmatrix} 0 & .3 \\ 1 & .7 \end{bmatrix}$
4. $\begin{bmatrix} 1 & 0 & 0 \\ 0 & 1 & \frac{1}{3} \\ 0 & 0 & \frac{2}{3} \end{bmatrix}$

5. $\begin{bmatrix} 1 & \frac{1}{2} & 0 \\ 0 & \frac{1}{2} & 0 \\ 0 & \frac{1}{2} & 1 \end{bmatrix}$
6. $\begin{bmatrix} 1 & 0 & 0 & .3 \\ 0 & 1 & 0 & .3 \\ 0 & 0 & .5 & .3 \\ 0 & 0 & .5 & .1 \end{bmatrix}$

7. Find the stable distribution for the regular stochastic matrix $\begin{bmatrix} .6 & .5 \\ .4 & .5 \end{bmatrix}$.

8. Find the stable matrix for the absorbing stochastic matrix

$$\begin{bmatrix} 1 & 0 & 0 & \frac{1}{8} & \frac{1}{4} \\ 0 & 1 & 0 & \frac{1}{8} & 0 \\ 0 & 0 & 1 & 0 & \frac{1}{4} \\ 0 & 0 & 0 & \frac{1}{4} & \frac{1}{2} \\ 0 & 0 & 0 & \frac{1}{2} & 0 \end{bmatrix}.$$

9. In a certain community currently 10% of the people are H (high income), 60% are M (medium income), and 30% are L (low income). Studies show that for the children of H parents, 50% also become H, 40% become M, and 10% become L. Of the children of M parents, 40% become H, 30% become M, and 30% become L. Of the children of L parents, 30% become H, 50% become M, and 20% become L.

   (a) Set up the 3×3 stochastic matrix that describes this situation.

   (b) What percent of the children of the current generation will have high incomes?

   (c) In the long run, what proportion of the population will have low incomes?

10. In a certain factory some machines are properly adjusted and some need adjusting. Technicians randomly inspect machines and make adjustments. Suppose that of the machines that are properly adjusted on a particular day, 80% will also be properly adjusted the following day and 20% will need adjusting. Also, of the machines that need adjusting on a particular day, 30% will be properly adjusted the next day and 70% will still need adjusting.

   (a) Set up the 2×2 stochastic matrix with columns labeled P (properly adjusted) and N (need adjusting) that describes this situation.

   (b) If initially all the machines are properly adjusted, what percent will need adjusting after 2 days?

   (c) In the long run, what percent will be properly adjusted each day?

11. Find the stable matrix for the absorbing stochastic matrix

$$\begin{bmatrix} 1 & 0 & \frac{1}{6} & \frac{1}{2} & \frac{2}{5} \\ 0 & 1 & 0 & 0 & \frac{2}{5} \\ 0 & 0 & 0 & 0 & 0 \\ 0 & 0 & \frac{2}{3} & \frac{1}{2} & 0 \\ 0 & 0 & \frac{1}{6} & 0 & \frac{1}{5} \end{bmatrix}.$$

12. Figure 1 gives the layout of a house with four rooms connected by doors. Room I contains a mousetrap and room II contains cheese. A mouse, after being placed in one of the rooms, will search for cheese; if unsuccessful after one minute, it will exit to another room by selecting one of the doors at random. (For instance, if the mouse is in room III, after one minute he will go to room II with probability $\frac{1}{3}$ and to room IV with probability $\frac{2}{3}$.) A mouse entering room I will be trapped and therefore no longer move. Also, a mouse entering room II will remain in that room.

II (cheese)		I (trap)
III		IV

Figure 1.

   (a) Set up the 4×4 absorbing stochastic matrix that describes this situation.

   (b) If a mouse begins in room IV, what is the probability that he will find the cheese after 2 minutes?

   (c) If a mouse begins in room IV, what is the probability that he will find the cheese in the long run?

   (d) For a mouse beginning in room III, determine the expected number of minutes that will elapse before the mouse either finds the cheese or is trapped.

13. Which of the following is the stable distribution for the regular stochastic matrix $\begin{bmatrix} .4 & .4 & .2 \\ .1 & .1 & .3 \\ .5 & .5 & .5 \end{bmatrix}$?

   (a) $\begin{bmatrix} .6 \\ .4 \\ 1 \end{bmatrix}$
   (b) $\begin{bmatrix} .2 \\ .3 \\ .5 \end{bmatrix}$
   (c) $\begin{bmatrix} .3 \\ .2 \\ .5 \end{bmatrix}$

14. A city has two competing news stations. From a survey of regular listeners it was determined that of those who listen to station A on a particular day, 90% listen to station A the next day and 10% listen to station B. Of those who listen to station B on a particular day, 20% listen to station A the next day and 80% listen to station B. If today 50% of the regular listeners listen to each station, what percentage of them would you expect to listen to station A 2 days from now?

15. Workday traffic conditions from 9 A.M. to 10 A.M. on the Baltimore Beltway can be characterized as Light, Moderate, and Heavy. The following stochastic matrix describes the day-to-day transitions.

$$\begin{array}{c@{\quad}ccc} & L & M & H \\ L & \begin{bmatrix} .70 \\ .20 \\ .10 \end{bmatrix} & \begin{matrix} .20 \\ .75 \\ .05 \end{matrix} & \begin{matrix} .10 \\ .30 \\ .60 \end{matrix} \end{array}$$

(a) Interpret the numbers in the second column of the matrix.

(b) In the long run, what percent of the workdays fall into each category?

(c) Of 20 workdays in a month, how many are expected to have Heavy traffic on the Baltimore Beltway from 9 A.M. to 10 A.M.?

16. A mental-health facility rates patients on their ability to live on their own. The state of a person's health is "able to work and considered cured (C)," or "long-term hospitalization or death (L)," or "group home (G)," or "short-term hospital care (S)." The following stochastic matrix describes the transitions from month to month. Use the fundamental matrix to determine

the expected number of months spent in state G or S before being absorbed into state C or L.

$$\begin{array}{c@{\quad}cccc} & C & L & G & S \\ C & \begin{bmatrix} 1 \\ 0 \\ 0 \\ 0 \end{bmatrix} & \begin{matrix} 0 \\ 1 \\ 0 \\ 0 \end{matrix} & \begin{matrix} .60 \\ .10 \\ .20 \\ .10 \end{matrix} & \begin{matrix} .05 \\ .40 \\ .50 \\ .05 \end{matrix} \end{array}$$

17. The contents of a reservoir depend on the available rainfall in the region and the demands on the water supply. Suppose a reservoir holds up to 4 units of water (a unit might be a million gallons) and policy for the use of the water for irrigation and drinking water never allows the contents of the reservoir to drop below 1 unit of water. The (rounded) amount of water in the reservoir from week to week seems to follow the transition matrix

$$\begin{array}{c@{\quad}cccc} & 1 & 2 & 3 & 4 \\ 1 & \begin{bmatrix} .20 \\ .30 \\ .40 \\ .10 \end{bmatrix} & \begin{matrix} .10 \\ .20 \\ .40 \\ .30 \end{matrix} & \begin{matrix} .05 \\ .20 \\ .50 \\ .25 \end{matrix} & \begin{matrix} .05 \\ .30 \\ .40 \\ .25 \end{matrix} \end{array} .$$

(a) Determine and interpret the stable distribution for the matrix.

(b) Suppose the weekly benefits to recreation in the area around the reservoir are estimated to be $4000 when there is 1 unit in the reservoir, $6000 when there are 2 units in the reservoir, $10,000 when there are 3 units, and $3000 when there are 4 units. Determine the average weekly benefits to be realized.

▶ Chapter 8 Chapter Test

1. Which of the following matrices are stochastic?

(a) $\begin{bmatrix} \frac{1}{2} & \frac{1}{3} \\ \frac{1}{2} & \frac{2}{3} \end{bmatrix}$ (b) $\begin{bmatrix} .1 & .9 \\ .5 & .5 \end{bmatrix}$

(c) $\begin{bmatrix} 1 & \frac{1}{3} \\ 0 & -\frac{2}{3} \end{bmatrix}$ (d) $\begin{bmatrix} \frac{1}{8} & \frac{1}{2} & 0 \\ \frac{3}{8} & 0 & 1 \\ \frac{1}{2} & \frac{1}{2} & 0 \end{bmatrix}$

2. Which of the following stochastic matrices are regular?

(a) $\begin{bmatrix} 1 & 0 \\ 0 & 1 \end{bmatrix}$ (b) $\begin{bmatrix} .1 & .5 \\ .9 & .5 \end{bmatrix}$

(c) $\begin{bmatrix} .4 & 1 \\ .6 & 0 \end{bmatrix}$

3. Which of the following matrices is the stable distribution for the regular stochastic matrix $\begin{bmatrix} .2 & .2 & .3 \\ .1 & .1 & .4 \\ .7 & .7 & .3 \end{bmatrix}$?

(a) $\begin{bmatrix} .3 \\ .2 \\ .5 \end{bmatrix}$ (b) $\begin{bmatrix} .25 \\ .25 \\ .50 \end{bmatrix}$

(c) $\begin{bmatrix} .35 \\ .35 \\ .30 \end{bmatrix}$ (d) $\begin{bmatrix} .2 \\ .1 \\ .7 \end{bmatrix}$

4. Find the stable distribution and the stable matrix for the regular stochastic matrix $\begin{bmatrix} \frac{1}{5} & \frac{3}{5} \\ \frac{4}{5} & \frac{2}{5} \end{bmatrix}$.

5. Students at Gotham College regularly use the two browsers Netscape® and Internet Explorer®. Of the students who use Netscape on a certain day, 70% use Netscape the next day and 30% use Internet Explorer. Of the students who use Internet Explorer on a certain day, 60% use Netscape the next day and 40% use Internet Explorer. Suppose that during the first day of a semester 50% of the students use each browser.

(a) Set up the stochastic matrix displaying these transitions.

(b) What is the initial distribution matrix?

(c) What percent of the students will use Netscape two days later?

(d) Show that $\begin{bmatrix} \frac{2}{3} \\ \frac{1}{3} \end{bmatrix}$ is the stable distribution for the stochastic matrix in part (a).

(e) Explain in a sentence the meaning of the number $\frac{2}{3}$ in the stable distribution from part (d).

6. Which of the following are absorbing stochastic matrices? For those that are not absorbing stochastic matrices, explain why.

(a) $\begin{bmatrix} 1 & 0 & .1 \\ 0 & 1 & .8 \\ 0 & 0 & .1 \end{bmatrix}$ (b) $\begin{bmatrix} 1 & 0 & 0 \\ 0 & .4 & .2 \\ 0 & .6 & .8 \end{bmatrix}$ ·(c) $\begin{bmatrix} 1 & .1 & 0 \\ 0 & .5 & 1 \\ 0 & .4 & 0 \end{bmatrix}$

7. College math departments have been rapidly establishing their own computer labs. Of the departments with no labs, each year 10% set up labs using Apple® computers, 30% set up labs using IBM® compatible computers, and the remainder do not set up labs that year. Once a lab has been established with a certain type of computer, the lab is never abandoned and the brand of computer is never changed.

(a) Set up the absorbing stochastic matrix that describes these transitions.

(b) Find the stable matrix.

(c) In the long run, what percent of the math departments will have Apple computer labs?

(d) What is the expected number of years required for a math department to decide to set up its own computer lab if it currently does not have a lab?

Chapter Project

Doubly Stochastic Matrices

A square matrix is said to be *doubly stochastic* if the sum of the entries in each column is 1 and the sum of the entries in each row is 1. Some examples of doubly stochastic matrices are

$$\begin{bmatrix} .4 & .6 \\ .6 & .4 \end{bmatrix}, \quad \begin{bmatrix} .1 & .3 & .6 \\ .6 & .1 & .3 \\ .3 & .6 & .1 \end{bmatrix}, \quad \text{and} \quad \begin{bmatrix} .1 & .2 & .3 & .4 \\ .3 & .4 & .1 & .2 \\ .2 & .3 & .4 & .1 \\ .4 & .1 & .2 & .3 \end{bmatrix}.$$

1. Give another example of a 2×2 doubly stochastic matrix.

   (a) Is your matrix symmetric? That is, does it equal its own transpose?

   (b) Prove that every 2×2 doubly stochastic matrix is symmetric.

   (c) Show that the product of your matrix and the matrix

   $$\begin{bmatrix} .4 & .6 \\ .6 & .4 \end{bmatrix}$$

   is doubly stochastic.

   (d) Show that $\begin{bmatrix} \frac{1}{2} \\ \frac{1}{2} \end{bmatrix}$ is a stable distribution for your matrix.

2. Give another example of a 3×3 doubly stochastic matrix.

   (a) Is your matrix symmetric? Are all 3×3 doubly stochastic matrices symmetric?

   (b) Show that the product of your matrix and the matrix

   $$\begin{bmatrix} .1 & .3 & .6 \\ .6 & .1 & .3 \\ .3 & .6 & .1 \end{bmatrix}$$

   is doubly stochastic.

   (c) Show that $\begin{bmatrix} \frac{1}{3} \\ \frac{1}{3} \\ \frac{1}{3} \end{bmatrix}$ is a stable distribution for your matrix.

3. Give another example of a 4×4 doubly stochastic matrix.

   (a) Is your matrix symmetric? Are all 4×4 doubly stochastic matrices symmetric?

   (b) Show that the product of your matrix and the matrix

   $$\begin{bmatrix} .1 & .2 & .3 & .4 \\ .3 & .4 & .1 & .2 \\ .2 & .3 & .4 & .1 \\ .4 & .1 & .2 & .3 \end{bmatrix}$$

   is doubly stochastic.

   (c) Show that $\begin{bmatrix} \frac{1}{4} \\ \frac{1}{4} \\ \frac{1}{4} \\ \frac{1}{4} \end{bmatrix}$ is a stable distribution for your matrix.

Chapter Project (Continued)

We will now show that the product of any two $n \times n$ doubly stochastic matrices is doubly stochastic, and that any doubly stochastic $n \times n$ matrix has

$$\begin{bmatrix} \frac{1}{n} \\ \frac{1}{n} \\ \vdots \\ \frac{1}{n} \end{bmatrix}$$

as a stable distribution. Let E_n be the $n \times n$ matrix for which each entry is 1.

4. Show that A is a doubly stochastic $n \times n$ matrix if and only if $AE_n = E_n$ and $E_nA = E_n$.

5. Show that if A and B are doubly stochastic $n \times n$ matrices, then so is AB. *Hint*: Show that $(AB)E_n = E_n$ and $E_n(AB) = E_n$.

6. Show that if A is a doubly stochastic $n \times n$ matrix, then

$$\begin{bmatrix} \frac{1}{n} \\ \frac{1}{n} \\ \vdots \\ \frac{1}{n} \end{bmatrix}$$

is a stable distribution for A. *Hint*: First show that $A \begin{bmatrix} 1 \\ 1 \\ \vdots \\ 1 \end{bmatrix} = \begin{bmatrix} 1 \\ 1 \\ \vdots \\ 1 \end{bmatrix}$.

7. A collection of $n \times n$ matrices is said to be a *convex set*[1] if whenever A and B are in the set and t is a number between 0 and 1, then $tA + (1 - t)B$ is also in the set. Show that the set of all $n \times n$ doubly stochastic matrices is a convex set.

---

[1] Convex sets are studied in advanced courses in applied matrix theory.

C H A P T E R

The Theory of Games

9

One of the more interesting developments of twentieth-century mathematics has been the theory of games, a branch of mathematics used to analyze competitive phenomena. This theory has been applied extensively in many fields, including business, economics, psychology, and sociology. The 1994 Nobel Prize in Economics was awarded to three economists for their groundbreaking work in integrating game theory into the study of economic behavior. Game theory has become one of the hottest areas of economics, with applications ranging from how the Federal Reserve sets interest rates, to how companies structure incentive pay for employees, to how companies bid on lucrative federal contracts. Mathematically, the theory of games blends the theory of matrices with probability theory. Although an extensive discussion is well beyond the scope of this book, we hope to give the flavor of the subject and some indication of the wide range of its applications.

9.1 Games and Strategies

Let us begin our study of game theory by analyzing a typical competitive situation. Suppose that in a certain town there are two furniture stores, Reliable Furniture Company and Cut-Rate Furniture Company, which compete for all furniture sales in the town. Each of the stores is planning a Labor Day sale and each has the option of marking its furniture down by 10% or 20%. The results of their decisions affect the total percentage of the market that each captures. On the basis of an analysis of past consumer tendencies, it is estimated that if Reliable chooses a 10% discount and so does Cut-Rate, then Reliable will capture 60% of the sales. If Reliable chooses a 10% discount but Cut-Rate chooses 20%, then Reliable will capture only 35% of the sales. On the other hand, if Reliable chooses a 20% discount but Cut-Rate chooses 10%, then Reliable will get 80% of the sales. If Reliable chooses a 20% discount and Cut-Rate also chooses 20%, then Reliable will get 50% of the sales. Each store is able to determine the other store's discount prior to the start of the sale and adjust its own discount accordingly. If you were a consultant to Reliable, what discount would you choose to obtain as large a share of the sales as possible?

To analyze the various possibilities, let us summarize the given data in a matrix. For the sake of brevity, denote Reliable by R and Cut-Rate by C. Then the data can be summarized as follows:

$$
\begin{array}{cc}
 & C \text{ discount} \\
R \text{ discount} & \begin{array}{c} \\ 10\% \\ 20\% \end{array} \begin{array}{cc} 10\% & 20\% \\ \left[\begin{array}{cc} .6 & .35 \\ .8 & .5 \end{array} \right] \end{array}
\end{array}.
$$

For example, the number in the second row, first column corresponds to an R discount of 20% and a C discount of 10%. In this case R will capture 80%, or .8, of the sales.

We may view R's choice of discount as choosing one of the rows of the matrix. Similarly, C's choice of discount amounts to choosing one of the columns of the matrix. Suppose that R and C both act rationally. What will be the result? Let us view things from R's perspective first. In scanning his options, he sees a .8 in the second row. So his first reaction might be to take a 20% discount and try for 80% of the sales. However, this route is very risky. As soon as C learns that R has chosen a 20% discount, C will set a 20% discount and lower R's share of the sales to 50%. So the result of choosing row 2 will be for R to capture only 50% of the sales. On the other hand, if R chooses row 1, then C will naturally choose a 20% discount to give R a 35% share of the sales. Of the options open to R, the 50% share is clearly the most desirable. So R will choose a 20% discount.

What about C? In setting his discount, C must choose a column of the matrix. Since the entries represent R's share of the sales, C wishes to make a choice resulting in as *small* a number as possible. If C chooses column 1, then R will immediately respond with a 20% discount in order to acquire 80% of the sales, a disaster for C. On the other hand, if C chooses column 2, then R will choose a 20% discount to obtain 50% of the sales. The best option open to C is to choose a 20% discount.

Thus we see that if both stores act rationally, they will each choose 20% discounts and each will capture 50% of the sales.

The preceding competitive situation is an example of a (mathematical) *game*. In such a game there are two or more players. In the example the players are R and C. Each player is allowed to make a move. In the example the moves are the choices of discount. As the result of a move by each player, there is a payoff to each player. The payoff to each player (store) is the percentage of total sales he captures. In our example, then, we have solved a problem that can be posed for any game:

Fundamental Problem of Game Theory   How should each player decide his move in order to maximize his gain?

Indeed, in our example, R and C chose moves such that each maximized his own share of sales.

Throughout this chapter we consider only games with two players, whom we shall denote by R and C. (R and C stand for row and column, respectively.) Suppose that R can make moves $R_1, R_2, \ldots, R_m$ and that C can make moves $C_1, C_2, \ldots, C_n$. Further suppose that a move R_i by R and C_j by C results in a payoff of a_{ij} to R. Then the game can be represented by the following *payoff matrix*:

$$
\begin{array}{c}
\\
\\
R \text{ moves}
\end{array}
\quad
\begin{array}{c}
\\
R_1 \\
R_2 \\
\vdots \\
R_m
\end{array}
\begin{array}{c}
C \text{ moves} \\
\begin{array}{cccc}
C_1 & C_2 & \cdots & C_n
\end{array} \\
\left[
\begin{array}{cccc}
a_{11} & a_{12} & \cdots & a_{1n} \\
a_{21} & a_{22} & \cdots & a_{2n} \\
\vdots & \vdots & & \vdots \\
a_{m1} & a_{m2} & \cdots & a_{mn}
\end{array}
\right].
\end{array}
$$

Note that the payoff matrix is an $m \times n$ matrix with a_{ij} as the entry of the ith row, jth column. In our furniture store example the payoff matrix was just the matrix we used in our analysis. Note that a move by R corresponds to a choice of a *row* of the payoff matrix, whereas a move by C corresponds to a choice of a *column*.

Suppose that a given game is played repeatedly. The players can adopt various strategies to attempt to maximize their respective gains (or minimize their losses). In what follows we shall discuss the problem of determining strategies. The simplest type of strategy is one in which a player, on consecutive plays, consistently chooses the same row (or column). Such strategies are called *pure strategies* and are discussed in this section. Strategies involving varied moves are called *mixed strategies* and are discussed in Section 9.2.

In most examples of games, the payoffs to C are related in a simple way to the corresponding payoffs to R. For example, for the furniture stores the payoff to C is 100% minus the payoff to R. In another common type of game a payoff to R of a given amount results in a loss to C of the same amount, and vice versa. For such games the sum of the gains on each play is zero; hence they are called *zero-sum games*. An illustration of such a game is provided in the next example.

▶ **Example 1** Suppose that R and C play a coin-matching game. Each player can show either heads or tails. If R and C both show heads, then C pays R \$5. If R shows heads and C shows tails, then R pays C \$8. If R shows tails and C shows heads, then C pays R \$3. If R shows tails and so does C, then C pays R \$1.

(a) Determine the payoff matrix of this game.

(b) Suppose that R and C play the game repeatedly. Determine optimal pure strategies for R and C.

Solution (a) The payoff matrix is given by

$$
\begin{array}{cc}
& C \\
& \begin{array}{cc} \text{Heads} & \text{Tails} \end{array} \\
R \quad \begin{array}{c} \text{Heads} \\ \text{Tails} \end{array} &
\left[
\begin{array}{cc}
5 & -8 \\
3 & 1
\end{array}
\right].
\end{array}
$$

Each entry specifies a payoff from C to R. The entry "-8" denotes a negative payoff to R, that is, a gain of \$8 to C.

(b) R would clearly like to choose heads so as to gain \$5. However, if R consistently chooses heads, C will retaliate by choosing tails, causing R to lose \$8. If R chooses tails, however, then the best C can do is choose tails to give a gain of \$1 to R. So R should clearly choose tails. Now we look at the game from C's point of view. Clearly, C's objective is to minimize the payment to R. If C consistently chooses heads, then R will notice the pattern and choose heads, at a cost to C of \$5. However, if C chooses tails, then the best that R can do is choose tails, thereby costing C \$1. So, clearly, the optimal move for C is to choose tails. ◆

The reasoning just described is rather cumbersome. There is, however, an easy way to summarize what we have done. Let us first describe R's reasoning. R seeks to choose a row of the matrix that will maximize his payoff. However, once a row is chosen consistently, R can expect C to counter by choosing the least element of that row. Thus R should choose his move as follows:

Optimal Pure Strategy for R

1. For each row of the payoff matrix, determine the least element.

2. Choose the row for which this element is as large as possible.

For example, in the game of Example 1 we have circled the least element of each row:

$$\begin{bmatrix} 5 & \boxed{-8} \\ 3 & \boxed{1} \end{bmatrix}.$$

The largest circled element is 1. So R should choose the second row—that is, tails.

In a similar way we may describe the optimal strategy for C. C wishes to choose a column of the payoff matrix so as to minimize the payoff to R. However, C can expect R to adjust his choice to the maximum element of the column. Therefore, we can summarize the optimal strategy for C as follows:

Optimal Pure Strategy for C

1. For each column of the payoff matrix, determine the largest element.

2. Choose the column for which this element is as small as possible.

For example, in the game of Example 1 we have circled the largest element in each column:

$$\begin{bmatrix} \boxed{5} & -8 \\ 3 & \boxed{1} \end{bmatrix}.$$

The smallest circled element is 1, so C should choose the second column, or tails.

▶ Example 2   Determine optimal pure strategies for R and C for the game whose payoff matrix is

$$\begin{bmatrix} -1 & 5 \\ 1 & 4 \\ 0 & -1 \end{bmatrix}.$$

Solution   To determine the strategy for R, we first circle the smallest element in each row:

$$\begin{bmatrix} \boxed{-1} & 5 \\ \boxed{1} & 4 \\ 0 & \boxed{-1} \end{bmatrix}.$$

The largest of these is 1, so R should play the second row. To determine the strategy for C, we circle the largest element in each column:

$$\begin{bmatrix} -1 & \boxed{5} \\ \boxed{1} & 4 \\ 0 & -1 \end{bmatrix}.$$

The smallest of these is 1, so C should play the first column. ◆

All the games considered so far have an important characteristic in common: There is an entry in the playoff matrix which is *simultaneously* the minimum element in its row and the maximum element in its column. Such an entry is called a *saddle point* for the game. As we have seen in the examples considered previously, if a game possesses a saddle point, then an optimal strategy is for R to choose the row containing the saddle point and for C to choose the column containing the saddle point.

A game need not have a saddle point. For example, the matrix

$$\begin{bmatrix} 2 & -2 \\ 0 & 1 \end{bmatrix}$$

is the payoff matrix of a game with no saddle point. The optimal pure strategy for R is to choose the row with the maximum of the circled elements in

$$\begin{bmatrix} 2 & \boxed{-2} \\ \boxed{0} & 1 \end{bmatrix}.$$

Thus, R chooses row 2. The optimal pure strategy for C is to choose the column with the minimum of the circled elements in

$$\begin{bmatrix} \boxed{2} & -2 \\ 0 & \boxed{1} \end{bmatrix}.$$

So C chooses column 2. No element is simultaneously the minimum element in its row and the maximum element in its column.

A game that has a saddle point is called a *strictly determined game*. If v is a saddle point for a strictly determined game, then if each player plays the optimal pure strategy, each repetition of the game will result in a payment of v to player R. The number v is called the *value* of the game.

▸ Example 3 Find the saddle point and the value of the strictly determined game given by the payoff matrix

$$\begin{bmatrix} -1 & -10 & 10 \\ 0 & 7 & 6 \\ 3 & 4 & 11 \\ 2 & 5 & 7 \end{bmatrix}.$$

Solution The least elements in the various rows are

$$\begin{bmatrix} -1 & \boxed{-10} & 10 \\ \boxed{0} & 7 & 6 \\ \boxed{3} & 4 & 11 \\ \boxed{2} & 5 & 7 \end{bmatrix}.$$

The maximum elements in the columns are

$$
\begin{bmatrix}
-1 & -10 & 10 \\
0 & ⑦ & 6 \\
③ & 4 & ⑪ \\
2 & 5 & 7
\end{bmatrix}.
$$

The element 3 in the third row, first column is a minimum in its row and a maximum in its column and so is a saddle point of the game. The value of the game is therefore 3: Each repetition of the game, assuming optimal strategies, results in a payoff of 3 to R.   ◆

▶ Example 4 R and C play a game in which they show 1 or 2 fingers simultaneously. It is agreed that C pays R an amount equal to the total number of fingers shown less 3 cents. Find the optimal strategy for each player and the value of the game.

Solution   The payoff matrix is given by

$$
\begin{array}{c} \\ 1 \\ 2 \end{array}
\begin{array}{cc} 1 & 2 \end{array}
\begin{bmatrix}
2-3 & 3-3 \\
3-3 & 4-3
\end{bmatrix}
=
\begin{array}{c} \\ 1 \\ 2 \end{array}
\begin{array}{cc} 1 & 2 \end{array}
\begin{bmatrix}
-1 & 0 \\
0 & 1
\end{bmatrix}.
$$

The saddle point is the element that is simultaneously the minimum of its row and the maximum of its column—so an optimal strategy is for R to show 2 fingers and for C to show 1 finger. The value of the game is 0.   ◆

A game may have more than one saddle point. Consider the game with payoff matrix

$$
\begin{bmatrix}
① & 2 & ① \\
① & 5 & ① \\
0 & -7 & -1
\end{bmatrix}.
$$

Each circled element is both the minimum element in its row and the maximum element in its column. There are four saddle points representing four optimal strategies. The value of the game, regardless of strategy, is 1. If a game has more than one saddle point, then the value of the game is the same at each of them.

Practice Problems 9.1

Which of the following matrices are the payoff matrices of strictly determined games? For those that are, determine the saddle point and optimal pure strategy for each of the players.

1. $\begin{bmatrix} 1 & -1 & -3 \\ 0 & -2 & 3 \end{bmatrix}$ 2. $\begin{bmatrix} 1 & -1 & 0 \\ 0 & -4 & 5 \end{bmatrix}$ 3. $\begin{bmatrix} 1 & -2 & 1 \\ -2 & 1 & 1 \\ 1 & 1 & -2 \end{bmatrix}$

▶ Exercises 9.1

Each of the following matrices is the payoff matrix for a strictly determined game. Determine optimal pure strategies for R and C.

1. $\begin{bmatrix} -1 & -2 \\ 0 & 3 \end{bmatrix}$

2. $\begin{bmatrix} -4 & 0 \\ 2 & 1 \end{bmatrix}$

3. $\begin{bmatrix} -2 & 4 & 1 \\ -1 & 3 & 5 \\ -3 & 5 & 2 \end{bmatrix}$

4. $\begin{bmatrix} 1 & -1 & 0 \\ 6 & 3 & 2 \\ 2 & -2 & 1 \end{bmatrix}$

5. $\begin{bmatrix} 0 & 3 \\ -1 & 1 \\ -2 & -4 \end{bmatrix}$

6. $\begin{bmatrix} 0 & -4 & 0 \\ -1 & -2 & 1 \end{bmatrix}$

Each of the following matrices is the payoff matrix for a strictly determined game. (a) Find a saddle point. (b) Determine the value of the game.

7. $\begin{bmatrix} 1 & 0 \\ 0 & -1 \end{bmatrix}$

8. $\begin{bmatrix} 2 & 3 \\ 4 & 5 \end{bmatrix}$

For each of the following games, give the payoff matrix and decide if the game is strictly determined. If so, determine the optimal strategies for R and C.

9. Suppose that R and C play a game by matching coins. On each play, C pays R the number of heads shown (0, 1, or 2) minus twice the number of tails shown.

10. In the child's game "scissor, paper, stone," each of two children calls out one of the three words. If they both call out the same word, then the game is a tie. Otherwise, "scissors" beats "paper" (since scissors can cut paper), "paper" beats "stone" (since paper can cover stone), and "stone" beats "scissors" (since stone can break scissors). Suppose that the loser pays a penny to the winner.

11. Two candidates for political office must decide to be for, against, or neutral on a certain referendum. Pollsters have determined that if candidate R comes out for the referendum, then he will gain 8000 votes if candidate C also comes out for the referendum, will lose 1000 votes if candidate C comes out against, and will gain 1000 votes if candidate C comes out neutral. If candidate R comes out against, then he will lose 7000 votes (respectively gain 4000 votes, lose 2000 votes) if candidate C comes out for (respectively against, neutral on) the referendum. If candidate R is neutral, then he will gain 3000 votes if C is for or against and will gain 2000 votes if C is neutral.

12. TV stations R and C each have a quiz show and a situation comedy to schedule for their 1 o'clock and 2 o'clock time slots. If they both schedule their quiz shows at 1 o'clock, then station R will take $3000 in advertising revenue away from station C. If they both schedule their quiz shows at 2 o'clock, then station C will take $2000 in advertising revenue from R. If they choose different hours for the quiz show, then R will take $5000 in advertising from C by scheduling it at 2 o'clock, and $2000 by scheduling it at 1 o'clock.

13. Player R has two cards: a red 5 and a black 10. Player C has three cards: a red 6, a black 7, and a black 8. They each place one of their cards on the table. If the cards are the same color, R receives the difference of the two numbers. If the cards are of different colors, C receives the minimum of the two numbers.

Solutions to Practice Problems 9.1

1. Not strictly determined. The minimum elements of the rows are

$$\begin{bmatrix} 1 & -1 & \boxed{-3} \\ 0 & \boxed{-2} & 3 \end{bmatrix};$$

the maximum elements of the columns are

$$\begin{bmatrix} \boxed{1} & \boxed{-1} & -3 \\ 0 & -2 & \boxed{3} \end{bmatrix}.$$

No element is simultaneously the minimum in its row and the maximum in its column.

Solutions to Practice Problems 9.1 (Continued)

2. Strictly determined. The least elements of the rows are

$$\begin{bmatrix} 1 & \boxed{-1} & 0 \\ 0 & \boxed{-4} & 5 \end{bmatrix}.$$

The largest elements of the columns are

$$\begin{bmatrix} \boxed{1} & \boxed{-1} & 0 \\ 0 & -4 & \boxed{5} \end{bmatrix}.$$

Thus -1 is a saddle point. The optimal strategy for R is to choose row 1; the optimal strategy for C is to choose column 2.

3. Not strictly determined. The minimum elements of the rows are

$$\begin{bmatrix} 1 & \boxed{-2} & 1 \\ \boxed{-2} & 1 & 1 \\ 1 & 1 & \boxed{-2} \end{bmatrix}.$$

The largest element for each column is 1. (Note that there are two choices for each largest element.) But none of the largest column elements is a least row element.

9.2 Mixed Strategies

In Section 9.1 we introduced strictly determined games and gave a method for determining optimal strategies for each player. However, not all games are strictly determined. For example, consider the game with payoff matrix

$$\begin{bmatrix} -1 & 5 \\ 2 & -3 \end{bmatrix}.$$

The minimum entries of the rows are

$$\begin{bmatrix} \boxed{-1} & 5 \\ 2 & \boxed{-3} \end{bmatrix},$$

whereas the maximum entries of the columns are

$$\begin{bmatrix} -1 & \boxed{5} \\ \boxed{2} & -3 \end{bmatrix}.$$

Note that no matrix entry is simultaneously the minimum in its row and the maximum in its column. Note also that no simple strategy of the type considered in Section 9.1 is sufficient to both maximize R's winnings and minimize C's losses. To see this, consider the game from R's point of view. Suppose that R repeatedly plays the strategy "first row," thereby attempting to win 5. After a few plays C will catch on to R's strategy and choose column 1, giving R a loss of 1. Similarly, if R consistently plays the strategy "second row," attempting to win 2, then C can thwart R by choosing the second column, to give R a loss of 3. It is clear that, in order to maximize his payoff, R should sometimes choose row 1 and sometimes row 2. One might expect that by choosing the rows on a probabilistic basis R can prevent C from anticipating his moves and amass enough positive payoffs to counteract the occasional negative ones. Thus we should investigate strategies of the type

$$A: \begin{cases} \text{Choose row 1 with probability .5} \\ \text{Choose row 2 with probability .5} \end{cases}$$

and

$$B: \begin{cases} \text{Choose row 1 with probability .9} \\ \text{Choose row 2 with probability .1.} \end{cases}$$

Such strategies are called *mixed strategies.* Either of the players can pursue such a strategy.

One way that R can carry out strategy A is to alternate between row 1 and row 2 on successive plays of the game. However, if C is at all clever, he will recognize this pattern and determine his play accordingly. What R should do is toss a coin and play row 1 whenever it lands heads and row 2 whenever it lands tails. Then there is no way that C can anticipate R's choice.

To carry out strategy B, R might use a card with a spinner attached at the center of a circle that is 90% blue and 10% white. R would then determine his play by spinning the spinner and choosing row 1 if the spinner landed on the blue part of the circle and row 2 if it landed on the white part. (See Fig. 1.)

It will be convenient to write mixed strategies in matrix form. Mixed strategies for R will be row matrices, and mixed strategies for C will be column matrices. Thus, for example, mixed strategy A above (for R) corresponds to the matrix

$$A: \begin{bmatrix} .5 & .5 \end{bmatrix},$$

whereas mixed strategy B (for R) corresponds to

$$B: \begin{bmatrix} .9 & .1 \end{bmatrix}.$$

The mixed strategy in which C chooses column 1 with probability .6 and column 2 with probability .4 corresponds to the column matrix

$$\begin{bmatrix} .6 \\ .4 \end{bmatrix}.$$

In comparing different mixed strategies, we use a number called their *expected value.* This number is just the average amount per game paid to R if the players pursue the given mixed strategies. The next example illustrates the computation of the expected value in a special case.

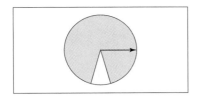

Figure 1.

▶ **Example 1** Suppose that a game has payoff matrix

$$\begin{bmatrix} -1 & 5 \\ 2 & -3 \end{bmatrix}.$$

Further suppose that R pursues the mixed strategy $\begin{bmatrix} .9 & .1 \end{bmatrix}$ and that C pursues the mixed strategy $\begin{bmatrix} .6 \\ .4 \end{bmatrix}$. Calculate the expected value of this game.

Solution   Let us view each repetition of the game as an experiment. There are four possible outcomes:

(row 1, column 1)   (row 1, column 2)

(row 2, column 1)   (row 2, column 2).

Let us compute the probability (relative frequency) with which each of the outcomes occurs. For example, consider the outcome (row 1, column 1). According to our assumptions about the strategies of R and C, R chooses row 1 with probability .9 and C chooses column 1 with probability .6. Since R and C make their respective choices independently of one another, the events "row 1" and "column 1" are independent. Therefore, we can compute the probability of the outcome (row 1, column 1) as follows:

$$\text{Pr(row 1, column 1)} = \text{Pr(row 1)} \cdot \text{Pr(column 1)} = (.9)(.6) = .54.$$

That is, the outcome "row 1, column 1" will occur with probability .54. Similarly, we compute the probabilities of the other three outcomes. Table 1 gives the probability and the amount won by R for each outcome. The average amount that R wins per play is then given by

$$(-1)(.54) + (5)(.36) + (2)(.06) + (-3)(.04) = 1.26.$$

Hence the expected value of the given strategies is 1.26.

Table 1

Outcome	R wins	Probability
Row 1, column 1	-1	$(.9)(.6) = .54$
Row 1, column 2	5	$(.9)(.4) = .36$
Row 2, column 1	2	$(.1)(.6) = .06$
Row 2, column 2	-3	$(.1)(.4) = .04$

◆

We may generalize the preceding computations. To see the pattern, let us first stick to 2×2 games. Suppose that a game has payoff matrix

$$\begin{bmatrix} a_{11} & a_{12} \\ a_{21} & a_{22} \end{bmatrix}.$$

Further suppose that R pursues a strategy $\begin{bmatrix} r_1 & r_2 \end{bmatrix}$. That is, R randomly chooses row 1 with probability r_1 and row 2 with probability r_2. Similarly, suppose that C pursues a strategy $\begin{bmatrix} c_1 \\ c_2 \end{bmatrix}$. Then the probabilities of the various outcomes can be tabulated as shown in Table 2. Thus, by following the reasoning used in the special case above, we see that the expected value of the strategies is the sum of the products of the payoffs times the corresponding probabilities:

$$a_{11}(r_1 c_1) + a_{12}(r_1 c_2) + a_{21}(r_2 c_1) + a_{22}(r_2 c_2).$$

On the average, R gains this amount for each play. A somewhat tedious (but easy) calculation shows that

$$\begin{bmatrix} r_1 & r_2 \end{bmatrix} \begin{bmatrix} a_{11} & a_{12} \\ a_{21} & a_{22} \end{bmatrix} \begin{bmatrix} c_1 \\ c_2 \end{bmatrix} = \begin{bmatrix} r_1 & r_2 \end{bmatrix} \begin{bmatrix} a_{11}c_1 + a_{12}c_2 \\ a_{21}c_1 + a_{22}c_2 \end{bmatrix}$$
$$= \begin{bmatrix} a_{11}(r_1 c_1) + a_{12}(r_1 c_2) + a_{21}(r_2 c_1) + a_{22}(r_2 c_2) \end{bmatrix}. \quad (1)$$

Table 2

Outcome	Payoff to R	Probability
Row 1, column 1	a_{11}	$r_1 c_1$
Row 1, column 2	a_{12}	$r_1 c_2$
Row 2, column 1	a_{21}	$r_2 c_1$
Row 2, column 2	a_{22}	$r_2 c_2$

Formula (1) is a special case of the following general fact:

Expected Value of a Pair of Strategies   Suppose that a game has payoff matrix

$$\begin{bmatrix} a_{11} & a_{12} & \cdots & a_{1n} \\ a_{21} & a_{22} & \cdots & a_{2n} \\ \vdots & \vdots & & \vdots \\ a_{m1} & a_{m2} & \cdots & a_{mn} \end{bmatrix}.$$

Suppose that R plays the strategy $\begin{bmatrix} r_1 & r_2 & \cdots & r_m \end{bmatrix}$ and that C plays the strategy

$$\begin{bmatrix} c_1 \\ c_2 \\ \vdots \\ c_n \end{bmatrix}.$$

Let e be the expected value of the pair of strategies. Then

$$\begin{bmatrix} r_1 & r_2 & \cdots & r_m \end{bmatrix} \begin{bmatrix} a_{11} & a_{12} & \cdots & a_{1n} \\ a_{21} & a_{22} & \cdots & a_{2n} \\ \vdots & \vdots & & \vdots \\ a_{m1} & a_{m2} & \cdots & a_{mn} \end{bmatrix} \begin{bmatrix} c_1 \\ c_2 \\ \vdots \\ c_n \end{bmatrix} = \begin{bmatrix} e \end{bmatrix}.$$

▶ **Example 2**   Suppose that a game has payoff matrix

$$\begin{bmatrix} 2 & 0 & -1 \\ -1 & 3 & 4 \end{bmatrix}$$

and that R plays the strategy $\begin{bmatrix} .5 & .5 \end{bmatrix}$. Which of the following strategies is more advantageous for C?

$$A = \begin{bmatrix} .6 \\ .3 \\ .1 \end{bmatrix} \quad \text{or} \quad B = \begin{bmatrix} .3 \\ .3 \\ .4 \end{bmatrix}$$

Solution   We compare the expected value with C using strategy A to that with C using strategy B. With strategy A we have

$$\begin{bmatrix} .5 & .5 \end{bmatrix} \begin{bmatrix} 2 & 0 & -1 \\ -1 & 3 & 4 \end{bmatrix} \begin{bmatrix} .6 \\ .3 \\ .1 \end{bmatrix} = \begin{bmatrix} .90 \end{bmatrix}.$$

Using strategy B, we have

$$\begin{bmatrix} .5 & .5 \end{bmatrix} \begin{bmatrix} 2 & 0 & -1 \\ -1 & 3 & 4 \end{bmatrix} \begin{bmatrix} .3 \\ .3 \\ .4 \end{bmatrix} = \begin{bmatrix} 1.20 \end{bmatrix}.$$

Thus strategy A will yield an average payment per play of .90 to R, whereas strategy B will yield an average payment per play of 1.20. Clearly, it is to C's advantage to choose strategy A. ◆

▶ Example 3 The Acme Chemical Corporation has two plants, each situated on the banks of the Blue River, 10 miles from one another. A single inspector is assigned to check that the plants do not dump waste into the river. If he discovers plant A dumping waste, Acme is fined \$20,000. If he discovers plant B dumping waste, Acme is fined \$50,000. Suppose that the inspector visits one of the plants each day and that he chooses, on a random basis, to visit plant B 60% of the time. Acme schedules dumping from its two plants on a random basis, one plant per day, with plant B dumping waste on 70% of the days. How much is Acme's average fine per day?

Solution The competition between Acme and the inspector can be viewed as a game, whose matrix is

$$\begin{array}{c} \\ \text{Plant } A \text{ dumps} \\ \text{Plant } B \text{ dumps} \end{array} \begin{array}{cc} \text{Inspect } A & \text{Inspect } B \\ \begin{bmatrix} -20{,}000 & 0 \\ 0 & -50{,}000 \end{bmatrix} \end{array}.$$

The strategy of Acme is given by the row matrix $\begin{bmatrix} .3 & .7 \end{bmatrix}$. The strategy of the inspector is given by the column matrix $\begin{bmatrix} .4 \\ .6 \end{bmatrix}$. The expected value of the strategies is the matrix product

$$\begin{bmatrix} .3 & .7 \end{bmatrix} \begin{bmatrix} -20{,}000 & 0 \\ 0 & -50{,}000 \end{bmatrix} \begin{bmatrix} .4 \\ .6 \end{bmatrix} = \begin{bmatrix} -6000 & -35{,}000 \end{bmatrix} \begin{bmatrix} .4 \\ .6 \end{bmatrix}$$

$$= \begin{bmatrix} -23{,}400 \end{bmatrix}.$$

In other words, Acme will be fined an average of \$23,400 per day for polluting the river. ◆

In Section 9.3 we will alter payoff matrices by adding a fixed constant to each entry so that all entries become positive numbers. This does not alter the essential character of the game, in that good strategies for the original matrix will also be good strategies for the new matrix. The only difference is that the expected value is increased by the constant added. This procedure enables us to apply the methods of linear programming to the determination of optimal mixed strategies for zero-sum games that are not strictly determined.

▶ Example 4 In Example 1 we saw that for the game with payoff matrix

$$\begin{bmatrix} -1 & 5 \\ 2 & -3 \end{bmatrix}$$

and strategies $\begin{bmatrix} .9 & .1 \end{bmatrix}$, $\begin{bmatrix} .6 \\ .4 \end{bmatrix}$, the expected value was 1.26. Compute the expected value of those strategies for the matrix obtained by adding 4 to each entry.

Solution   The new matrix is

$$\begin{bmatrix} -1+4 & 5+4 \\ 2+4 & -3+4 \end{bmatrix} \quad \text{or} \quad \begin{bmatrix} 3 & 9 \\ 6 & 1 \end{bmatrix}.$$

The expected value of the strategies for the new matrix is

$$\begin{bmatrix} .9 & .1 \end{bmatrix}\begin{bmatrix} 3 & 9 \\ 6 & 1 \end{bmatrix}\begin{bmatrix} .6 \\ .4 \end{bmatrix} = \begin{bmatrix} 3.3 & 8.2 \end{bmatrix}\begin{bmatrix} .6 \\ .4 \end{bmatrix} = 5.26.$$

As it should, the expected value has also increased by 4.   ◆

Suppose that the payoff matrix is

$$\begin{bmatrix} -\frac{1}{2} & \frac{5}{2} \\ 1 & -\frac{3}{2} \end{bmatrix}.$$

What is the expected value of the strategies $\begin{bmatrix} .9 & .1 \end{bmatrix}$ and $\begin{bmatrix} .6 \\ .4 \end{bmatrix}$? We see that

$$\begin{bmatrix} .9 & .1 \end{bmatrix}\begin{bmatrix} -\frac{1}{2} & \frac{5}{2} \\ 1 & -\frac{3}{2} \end{bmatrix}\begin{bmatrix} .6 \\ .4 \end{bmatrix} = .63.$$

We note that multiplying each element in the payoff matrix by 2 and adding 4 gives the matrix

$$\begin{bmatrix} 3 & 9 \\ 6 & 1 \end{bmatrix},$$

which with the preceding strategies gives the expected value 5.26 (see the solution to Example 4). Multiplying each element of the payoff matrix by 2 and adding 4 to each element produces the same effect on the expected value:

$$5.26 = 2(.63) + 4.$$

Practice Problems 9.2

1. Suppose that the payoff matrix of a game is

$$\begin{bmatrix} 4 & -2 \\ -3 & 1 \end{bmatrix}.$$

Suppose that R plays the strategy $\begin{bmatrix} .6 & .4 \end{bmatrix}$. Which of the two strategies $\begin{bmatrix} .5 \\ .5 \end{bmatrix}$ or $\begin{bmatrix} .7 \\ .3 \end{bmatrix}$ is better for C?

2. Answer the question in Problem 1 for the game whose payoff matrix is

$$\begin{bmatrix} 9 & 3 \\ 2 & 6 \end{bmatrix}.$$

(This matrix is obtained by adding 5 to each entry of the matrix in Problem 1.)

▶ Exercises 9.2

1. Suppose that a game has payoff matrix

$$\begin{bmatrix} 3 & -1 \\ -7 & 5 \end{bmatrix}.$$

Calculate the expected values for the following strategies and determine which of the following situations is most advantageous to R.

(a) R plays $[.5 \quad .5]$, C plays $\begin{bmatrix} .5 \\ .5 \end{bmatrix}$.

(b) R plays $[1 \quad 0]$, C plays $\begin{bmatrix} .5 \\ .5 \end{bmatrix}$.

(c) R plays $[.3 \quad .7]$, C plays $\begin{bmatrix} .6 \\ .4 \end{bmatrix}$.

(d) R plays $[.75 \quad .25]$, C plays $\begin{bmatrix} .2 \\ .8 \end{bmatrix}$.

2. Suppose that a game has payoff matrix

$$\begin{bmatrix} 1 & 0 & 2 \\ -1 & 2 & 0 \\ 0 & -1 & -1 \end{bmatrix}.$$

Calculate the expected values for the following strategies and determine which of the following situations is most advantageous to C.

(a) R plays $[1 \quad 0 \quad 0]$, C plays $\begin{bmatrix} .5 \\ .4 \\ .1 \end{bmatrix}$.

(b) R plays $[.3 \quad .3 \quad .4]$, C plays $\begin{bmatrix} .4 \\ .4 \\ .2 \end{bmatrix}$.

(c) R plays $[0 \quad .5 \quad .5]$, C plays $\begin{bmatrix} .4 \\ 0 \\ .6 \end{bmatrix}$.

(d) R plays $[.1 \quad .1 \quad .8]$, C plays $\begin{bmatrix} .2 \\ .2 \\ .6 \end{bmatrix}$.

3. Refer to Example 3. Suppose that the inspector changes his strategy and visits plant B 80% of the time. How much is Acme's average fine per day?

4. Refer to Example 3. Suppose that the inspector visits plant B 30% of the time. How much is Acme's average fine per day?

5. Suppose that two players, R and C, write down letters of the alphabet. If both write vowels or both write consonants, then there is no payment to either player. If R writes a vowel and C writes a consonant, then C pays R \$2. If R writes a consonant and C writes a vowel, then R pays C \$1. Suppose that R chooses a consonant 75% of the plays and C chooses a vowel 40% of the plays. What is the average loss (or gain) of R per play?

6. A small business owner must decide whether to carry flood insurance. She may insure her business for \$2 million for \$100,000, \$1 million for \$50,000, or \$.5 million for \$30,000. Her business is worth \$2 million. There is a flood serious enough to destroy her business an average of once every 10 years. In order to save insurance premiums, she decides each year on a probabilistic basis how much insurance to carry. She chooses \$2 million 20% of the time, \$1 million 20% of the time, \$.5 million 20% of the time, and no insurance 40% of the time. What is her average annual loss?

Solutions to Practice Problems 9.2

1. If C plays $\begin{bmatrix} .5 \\ .5 \end{bmatrix}$, the expected value (to R) is

$$[.6 \quad .4]\begin{bmatrix} 4 & -2 \\ -3 & 1 \end{bmatrix}\begin{bmatrix} .5 \\ .5 \end{bmatrix} = [1.2 \quad -.8]\begin{bmatrix} .5 \\ .5 \end{bmatrix} = [.2].$$

If C plays $\begin{bmatrix} .7 \\ .3 \end{bmatrix}$, the expected value (to R) is

$$[.6 \quad .4]\begin{bmatrix} 4 & -2 \\ -3 & 1 \end{bmatrix}\begin{bmatrix} .7 \\ .3 \end{bmatrix} = [1.2 \quad -.8]\begin{bmatrix} .7 \\ .3 \end{bmatrix} = [.6].$$

Thus in the first case R gains an average of .2 per play, whereas in the second R gains .6. Since C wishes to minimize R's winnings, C should clearly play the first strategy.

2. The answer is the same as in Problem 1, since the new expected values will be 5 more than the original expected values and the first strategy will be better for C.

9.3 Determining Optimal Mixed Strategies

As we have seen, each choice of strategies by R and C results in an expected value, representing the average payoff to R per play. In this section we shall give a method for choosing the best strategies. Let us begin by clarifying our notion of optimality.

> **Optimal Strategy for R**   To every choice of a strategy for R there is a best counterstrategy—that is, a strategy for C that results in the least expected value e. An *optimal mixed strategy for R* is one for which the expected value against C's best counterstrategy is as large as possible.

In a similar way we can define the optimal strategy for C.

> **Optimal Strategy for C**   To every choice of a strategy for C there is a best counterstrategy—that is, a strategy for R that results in the largest expected value e. An *optimal mixed strategy for C* is one for which the expected value against R's best counterstrategy is as small as possible.

It is most surprising that the optimal strategies for R and C may be determined using linear programming. To see how this is done, let us consider a particular problem.

▶ **Example 1**   Suppose that a game has payoff matrix

$$\begin{bmatrix} 5 & 3 \\ 1 & 4 \end{bmatrix}.$$

Reduce the determination of an optimal strategy for R to a linear programming problem.

Solution   Suppose that R plays the strategy $\begin{bmatrix} r_1 & r_2 \end{bmatrix}$. What is C's best counterstrategy? If C plays $\begin{bmatrix} c_1 \\ c_2 \end{bmatrix}$, then the expected value of the game is

$$\begin{bmatrix} r_1 & r_2 \end{bmatrix}\begin{bmatrix} 5 & 3 \\ 1 & 4 \end{bmatrix}\begin{bmatrix} c_1 \\ c_2 \end{bmatrix} = \begin{bmatrix} 5r_1 + r_2 & 3r_1 + 4r_2 \end{bmatrix}\begin{bmatrix} c_1 \\ c_2 \end{bmatrix}$$

$$= \begin{bmatrix} (5r_1 + r_2)c_1 + (3r_1 + 4r_2)c_2 \end{bmatrix}.$$

If C pursues his best counterstrategy, then he will try to minimize the expected value of the game. That is, C will try to minimize

$$(5r_1 + r_2)c_1 + (3r_1 + 4r_2)c_2.$$

Since $c_1 \geq 0$, $c_2 \geq 0$, $c_1 + c_2 = 1$, this expression has as its minimum value the smaller of the terms $5r_1 + r_2$ or $3r_1 + 4r_2$. That is, if $5r_1 + r_2$ is the smaller, then C should choose the strategy $c_1 = 1$, $c_2 = 0$; whereas if $3r_1 + 4r_2$ is the smaller, then C should choose the strategy $c_1 = 0$, $c_2 = 1$. In any case the expected value of the game if C adopts his best counterstrategy is the smaller of $5r_1 + r_2$ and $3r_1 + 4r_2$. The goal of R is to maximize this expected value. In other words, the mathematical problem R faces is this:

Maximize the minimum of $5r_1 + r_2$ and $3r_1 + 4r_2$,

where $r_1 \geq 0$, $r_2 \geq 0$, $r_1 + r_2 = 1$.

Let v denote the minimum of $5r_1 + r_2$ and $3r_1 + 4r_2$. Clearly, $v > 0$. Then

$$
\begin{aligned}
5r_1 + r_2 &\geq v \\
3r_1 + 4r_2 &\geq v.
\end{aligned}
\tag{1}
$$

Maximizing v is the same as minimizing $1/v$. Moreover, the inequalities (1) may be rewritten in the form

$$
\begin{aligned}
5\frac{r_1}{v} + \frac{r_2}{v} &\geq 1 \\
3\frac{r_1}{v} + 4\frac{r_2}{v} &\geq 1.
\end{aligned}
\tag{2}
$$

Moreover, since $r_1 \geq 0$, $r_2 \geq 0$, and $r_1 + r_2 = 1$, we see that

$$
\frac{r_1}{v} \geq 0 \qquad \frac{r_2}{v} \geq 0 \qquad \frac{r_1}{v} + \frac{r_2}{v} = \frac{1}{v}.
\tag{3}
$$

This suggests that we introduce new variables:

$$
y_1 = \frac{r_1}{v} \qquad y_2 = \frac{r_2}{v}.
$$

Then (3) and (2) may be rewritten as

$$
\begin{aligned}
y_1 + y_2 &= \frac{1}{v} \\
5y_1 + y_2 &\geq 1 \\
3y_1 + 4y_2 &\geq 1 \\
y_1 \geq 0, \quad y_2 &\geq 0.
\end{aligned}
$$

We wish to minimize $1/v$, so we may finally state our original question in terms of a linear programming problem: Minimize $y_1 + y_2$ subject to the constraints

$$
\begin{cases}
5y_1 + y_2 \geq 1 \\
3y_1 + 4y_2 \geq 1 \\
y_1 \geq 0, \quad y_2 \geq 0.
\end{cases}
$$
◆

In terms of the solution to this linear programming problem we may calculate R's optimal strategy as follows:

$$
r_1 = vy_1 \qquad r_2 = vy_2, \qquad \text{where} \quad v = \frac{1}{y_1 + y_2}.
$$

In the preceding derivation it was essential that the entries of the matrix were positive numbers, for this is how we derived that $v > 0$. The same reasoning used in Example 1 can be used in general to convert the determination of R's optimal strategy to a linear programming problem, *provided that the payoff matrix has positive entries*. If the payoff matrix does not have positive entries, then just add a large positive constant to each of the entries so as to give a matrix with positive entries. The new matrix will have the same optimal strategy as the original one. However, since all its entries are positive, we may use the previous reasoning to reduce determination of the optimal strategy to a linear programming problem.

Optimal Strategy for R   Let the payoff matrix of a game be

$$
\begin{bmatrix}
a_{11} & a_{12} & \cdots & a_{1n} \\
a_{21} & a_{22} & \cdots & a_{2n} \\
\vdots & \vdots & & \vdots \\
a_{m1} & a_{m2} & \cdots & a_{mn}
\end{bmatrix},
$$

where all entries of the matrix are positive numbers. Let $y_1, y_2, \ldots, y_m$ be chosen so as to minimize

$$y_1 + y_2 + \cdots + y_m$$

subject to the constraints

$$
\begin{cases}
y_1 \geq 0,\ y_2 \geq 0,\ \ldots,\ y_m \geq 0 \\
a_{11}y_1 + a_{21}y_2 + \cdots + a_{m1}y_m \geq 1 \\
a_{12}y_1 + a_{22}y_2 + \cdots + a_{m2}y_m \geq 1 \\
\qquad\qquad \vdots \\
a_{1n}y_1 + a_{2n}y_2 + \cdots + a_{mn}y_m \geq 1.
\end{cases}
$$

Let

$$
v = \frac{1}{y_1 + y_2 + \cdots + y_m}.
$$

Then an optimal strategy for R is $\begin{bmatrix} r_1 & r_2 & \cdots & r_m \end{bmatrix}$, where

$$r_1 = vy_1, \quad r_2 = vy_2, \quad \ldots, \quad r_m = vy_m.$$

Furthermore, if C adopts the best counterstrategy, then the expected value is v.

Note that the determination of $y_1, y_2, \ldots, y_m$ is a linear programming problem whose solution can be obtained using either the method of Chapter 3 (if $m = 2$) or the simplex method of Chapter 4 (any m). The next example illustrates the preceding result.

▶ **Example 2**   Suppose that a game has payoff matrix

$$
\begin{bmatrix}
5 & 3 \\
1 & 4
\end{bmatrix}.
$$

(a) Determine an optimal strategy for R.

(b) Determine the expected payoff to R if C uses the best counterstrategy.

Solution   (a) The associated linear programming problem asks us to minimize $y_1 + y_2$ subject to the constraints

$$
\begin{cases}
y_1 \geq 0, \quad y_2 \geq 0 \\
5y_1 + y_2 \geq 1 \\
3y_1 + 4y_2 \geq 1.
\end{cases}
$$

In Fig. 1 we have sketched the feasible set for this problem and evaluated the objective function at each vertex.

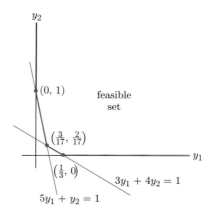

Vertex	$y_1 + y_2$
$(0, 1)$	1
$\left(\frac{3}{17}, \frac{2}{17}\right)$	$\frac{5}{17}$
$\left(\frac{1}{3}, 0\right)$	$\frac{1}{3}$

Figure 1.

The minimum value of $y_1 + y_2$ is $\frac{5}{17}$ and occurs when $y_1 = \frac{3}{17}$ and $y_2 = \frac{2}{17}$. Further,

$$v = \frac{1}{y_1 + y_2} = \frac{1}{\frac{5}{17}} = \frac{17}{5}$$

$$r_1 = vy_1 = \frac{17}{5} \cdot \frac{3}{17} = \frac{3}{5}$$

$$r_2 = vy_2 = \frac{17}{5} \cdot \frac{2}{17} = \frac{2}{5}.$$

Thus the optimal strategy for R is $\begin{bmatrix} \frac{3}{5} & \frac{2}{5} \end{bmatrix}$.

(b) The expected value against the best counterstrategy is $v = \frac{17}{5}$. ◆

There is a similar linear programming technique for determining the optimal strategy for C.

Optimal Strategy for C   Let the payoff matrix of a game be

$$\begin{bmatrix} a_{11} & a_{12} & \cdots & a_{1n} \\ a_{21} & a_{22} & \cdots & a_{2n} \\ \vdots & \vdots & & \vdots \\ a_{m1} & a_{m2} & \cdots & a_{mn} \end{bmatrix},$$

where all entries of the matrix are positive numbers. Let $z_1, z_2, \ldots, z_n$ be chosen so as to maximize

$$z_1 + z_2 + \cdots + z_n$$

subject to the constraints

$$\begin{cases} z_1 \geq 0, \quad z_2 \geq 0, \quad \ldots, \quad z_n \geq 0 \\ a_{11}z_1 + a_{12}z_2 + \cdots + a_{1n}z_n \leq 1 \\ a_{21}z_1 + a_{22}z_2 + \cdots + a_{2n}z_n \leq 1 \\ \qquad\qquad\qquad \vdots \\ a_{m1}z_1 + a_{m2}z_2 + \cdots + a_{mn}z_m \leq 1. \end{cases}$$

Let $v = 1/(z_1 + z_2 + \cdots + z_n)$. Then an optimal strategy for C is

$$\begin{bmatrix} c_1 \\ c_2 \\ \vdots \\ c_n \end{bmatrix},$$

where $c_1 = vz_1$, $c_2 = vz_2$, $\ldots$, $c_n = vz_n$.

▶ **Example 3** Determine the optimal strategy for C for the game with payoff matrix

$$\begin{bmatrix} 5 & 3 \\ 1 & 4 \end{bmatrix}.$$

Solution We must maximize $z_1 + z_2$ subject to the constraints

$$\begin{cases} z_1 \geq 0, \quad z_2 \geq 0 \\ 5z_1 + 3z_2 \leq 1 \\ z_1 + 4z_2 \leq 1. \end{cases}$$

The solution is as follows: The maximum value is $\frac{5}{17}$ and it occurs when $z_1 = \frac{1}{17}$, $z_2 = \frac{4}{17}$. Therefore, $v = \frac{17}{5}$, and the optimal strategy for C is $\begin{bmatrix} c_1 \\ c_2 \end{bmatrix}$, where

$$c_1 = vz_1 = \tfrac{17}{5} \cdot \tfrac{1}{17} = \tfrac{1}{5}$$

$$c_2 = vz_2 = \tfrac{17}{5} \cdot \tfrac{4}{17} = \tfrac{4}{5}. \qquad \blacklozenge$$

Notice that in both Examples 2 and 3 we obtained $v = \frac{17}{5}$. This was not just a coincidence. This phenomenon always occurs, and the number v is called the *value* of the game. An easy computation shows that for the matrix of Examples 2 and 3, when R and C each use their optimal strategies, the expected value is $v = \frac{17}{5}$. That is,

$$\begin{bmatrix} \tfrac{3}{5} & \tfrac{2}{5} \end{bmatrix} \begin{bmatrix} 5 & 3 \\ 1 & 4 \end{bmatrix} \begin{bmatrix} \tfrac{1}{5} \\ \tfrac{4}{5} \end{bmatrix} = \begin{bmatrix} \tfrac{17}{5} \end{bmatrix}.$$

Let us briefly reconsider the calculations of optimal strategies for R and C. We begin in every case with the matrix for the game, A. Let us assume that A is an $m \times n$ matrix and that each entry of A is a positive number. To find the optimal strategy for C, we find the matrix Z that maximizes the objective function EZ subject to the constraints $AZ \leq B$ and $Z \geq \mathbf{0}$, where

$$E = \begin{bmatrix} 1 & 1 & 1 & \cdots & 1 \end{bmatrix}$$
$$\underbrace{\hphantom{\begin{bmatrix} 1 & 1 & 1 & \cdots & 1 \end{bmatrix}}}_{n \text{ entries}}$$

$$Z = \begin{bmatrix} z_1 \\ z_2 \\ \vdots \\ z_n \end{bmatrix} \quad \text{and} \quad B = \left.\begin{bmatrix} 1 \\ 1 \\ \vdots \\ 1 \end{bmatrix}\right\} m \text{ entries.}$$

The dual of the linear programming problem associated with finding an optimal strategy for C is to find the matrix Y that minimizes the objective function $B^T Y$ subject to the constraints $A^T Y \geq E^T$ and $Y \geq \mathbf{0}$, where

$$Y = \begin{bmatrix} y_1 \\ y_2 \\ \vdots \\ y_m \end{bmatrix}.$$

But this is exactly the problem of finding an optimal strategy for R.

The problem of finding the optimal strategy for R is a linear programming problem whose dual is the problem of finding an optimal strategy for C, and vice versa.

Our previous work with duality leads us to conclude the following:

1. If there exists an optimal strategy for R, then there exists an optimal strategy for C, and vice versa.

2. The minimum of the objective function $y_1 + y_2 + \cdots + y_m$ and the maximum of the objective function $z_1 + z_2 + \cdots + z_n$ are equal—since the linear programming problems are duals of each other. Hence, the value of the optimal strategy for C is the same as the value of the optimal strategy for R, that is,

$$\frac{1}{z_1 + z_2 + \cdots + z_n} = \frac{1}{y_1 + y_2 + \cdots + y_m}.$$

▶ Example 4   Determine the optimal strategies for R and C for the game with payoff matrix

$$\begin{bmatrix} 1 & -1 \\ -3 & 0 \end{bmatrix}.$$

Solution   We cannot apply our technique directly, since only one of the entries of the given matrix is a positive number. However, if we add 4 to each entry, then the new matrix will be

$$\begin{bmatrix} 5 & 3 \\ 1 & 4 \end{bmatrix},$$

which does have all positive entries. These two payoff matrices have the same optimal strategies. The only difference is that the values in the new matrix are 4 more than that of the given matrix. Now, the optimal strategies and the value of the new matrix were found in Examples 2 and 3 to be

$$\begin{bmatrix} \frac{3}{5} & \frac{2}{5} \end{bmatrix}, \qquad \begin{bmatrix} \frac{1}{5} \\ \frac{4}{5} \end{bmatrix}, \qquad \text{and} \qquad \frac{17}{5}.$$

Therefore, the optimal strategies for the given matrix are

$$\begin{bmatrix} \frac{3}{5} & \frac{2}{5} \end{bmatrix} \qquad \text{and} \qquad \begin{bmatrix} \frac{1}{5} \\ \frac{4}{5} \end{bmatrix},$$

and the value is $\frac{17}{5} - 4 = -\frac{3}{5}$.   ◆

▶ **Example 5** Use the simplex method and the resulting tableau to determine the optimal strategies for the game of Example 4.

Solution As in Example 4, add 4 to each entry to get a matrix with positive entries, and set up the tableau for finding the optimal strategy for C. (We choose this linear programming problem because it is a maximization problem.) The transformed matrix A is

$$\begin{bmatrix} 5 & 3 \\ 1 & 4 \end{bmatrix}.$$

To find the optimal strategy for C, we need to find the values of z_1 and z_2 that maximize $z_1 + z_2$ subject to the constraints

$$\begin{cases} 5z_1 + 3z_2 \leq 1 \\ z_1 + 4z_2 \leq 1 \\ z_1 \geq 0, \quad z_2 \geq 0. \end{cases}$$

We set up the tableau using slack variables t and u and display the initial and final tableaux:

	z_1	z_2	t	u	M	
t	5	3	1	0	0	1
u	1	4	0	1	0	1
M	-1	-1	0	0	1	0

	z_1	z_2	t	u	M	
z_1	1	0	$\frac{4}{17}$	$-\frac{3}{17}$	0	$\frac{1}{17}$
z_2	0	1	$-\frac{1}{17}$	$\frac{5}{17}$	0	$\frac{4}{17}$
M	0	0	$\frac{3}{17}$	$\frac{2}{17}$	1	$\frac{5}{17}$

Thus the solution is $z_1 = \frac{1}{17}$, $z_2 = \frac{4}{17}$ with $M = z_1 + z_2 = \frac{5}{17}$. Then $v = \frac{17}{5}$, and the optimal strategy for C is

$$\begin{bmatrix} vz_1 \\ vz_2 \end{bmatrix} = \begin{bmatrix} \frac{1}{5} \\ \frac{4}{5} \end{bmatrix}.$$

This agrees with previous solutions, and the value of the matrix is $\frac{17}{5}$, which is 4 more than the original matrix. Thus the value of the game is $\frac{17}{5} - 4 = -\frac{3}{5}$.

But the optimal strategy for R can be read from the final tableau since y_1 and y_2 are the values of the variables in the dual of the problem we solved. So $y_1 = t = \frac{3}{17}$, $y_2 = u = \frac{2}{17}$, and $M = \frac{5}{17}$. Then $v = \frac{17}{5}$ and the optimal strategy for R is $\begin{bmatrix} vy_1 & vy_2 \end{bmatrix} = \begin{bmatrix} \frac{3}{5} & \frac{2}{5} \end{bmatrix}$. ◆

We actually have a very useful fact.

Fundamental Theorem of Game Theory Every two-person zero-sum game has a solution.

Verification of the Fundamental Theorem of Game Theory If the given two-person game has a saddle point, then the game is strictly determined, and optimal strategies for R and C are given by the position of the saddle point.

If the game is not strictly determined, then let us assume that the $m \times n$ payoff matrix A has only positive entries. We let B be an $m \times 1$ column matrix in which each entry is 1, and let E be a $1 \times n$ row matrix of 1's. Then

1. There is an optimal feasible solution to the problem:

$$\text{Maximize } M = EZ \text{ subject to } AZ \leq B \text{ and } Z \geq \mathbf{0}. \tag{P}$$

2. There is an optimal feasible solution to the problem:

$$\text{Minimize } M = B^T Y \text{ subject to } A^T Y \geq E^T \text{ and } Y \geq \mathbf{0}. \tag{D}$$

3. The solutions to (P) and (D) give a solution to the game.

To see that characteristics 1 and 2 hold, we note that there is a feasible solution for the inequalities of the primal problem (P). The $n \times 1$ matrix of zeros, $Z = \mathbf{0}$, satisfies $AZ \leq B$. Also, there is a feasible solution for the inequalities of the dual problem (D). This can be seen by noting that since every element of the matrix A is positive, we can find an $m \times 1$ matrix $Y \geq \mathbf{0}$ with sufficiently large entries to guarantee that $A^T Y \geq E^T$. Since the inequalities of both (P) and (D) have a feasible solution, the fundamental theorem of duality (Chapter 4) tells us that both (P) and (D) have optimal feasible solutions.

Let Z^* and Y^* be optimal feasible solutions of (P) and (D), respectively. Say that

$$Z^* = \begin{bmatrix} z_1^* \\ z_2^* \\ \vdots \\ z_n^* \end{bmatrix} \quad \text{and} \quad Y^* = \begin{bmatrix} y_1^* \\ y_2^* \\ \vdots \\ y_m^* \end{bmatrix}.$$

The maximum for (P),

$$M = z_1^* + z_2^* + \cdots + z_n^*,$$

equals the minimum for (D),

$$M = y_1^* + y_2^* + \cdots + y_m^*,$$

and

$$AZ^* \leq B \quad \text{and} \quad A^T Y^* \geq E^T.$$

Recall that B is an $m \times 1$ matrix of 1's and E^T is an $n \times 1$ matrix of 1's.

M must be strictly greater than zero since at least one of the y_i^* must be >0 in order for $A^T Y \geq E^T$ to hold. Therefore, $1/M$ is defined. We let

$$C = \begin{bmatrix} \dfrac{1}{M} z_1^* \\ \dfrac{1}{M} z_2^* \\ \vdots \\ \dfrac{1}{M} z_n^* \end{bmatrix} = \begin{bmatrix} c_1 \\ c_2 \\ \vdots \\ c_n \end{bmatrix}$$

and

$$R = \begin{bmatrix} \dfrac{1}{M} y_1^* & \dfrac{1}{M} y_2^* & \cdots & \dfrac{1}{M} y_m^* \end{bmatrix} = \begin{bmatrix} r_1 & r_2 & \cdots & r_m \end{bmatrix}.$$

Furthermore, C and R represent optimal strategies for players C and R, respectively. To verify that C and R are legitimate strategies, we note that since $M > 0$, $Z^* \geq \mathbf{0}$, and $Y^* \geq \mathbf{0}$, every entry in C and R is nonnegative. We only need to check that

$$c_1 + c_2 + \cdots + c_n = 1 \qquad r_1 + r_2 + \cdots + r_m = 1.$$

This follows directly from the definitions of M, C, and R. ◆

**Practice Problems
9.3**

1. Determine the optimal strategy for C for the game with payoff matrix
$$\begin{bmatrix} 2 & 14 \\ 6 & 12 \\ 8 & 6 \end{bmatrix}.$$

2. Determine by inspection the optimal strategies for C for the games whose payoff matrices are given.

(a) $\begin{bmatrix} 0 & 12 \\ 4 & 10 \\ 6 & 4 \end{bmatrix}$ (b) $\begin{bmatrix} 6 & 0 \\ 4 & 3 \\ 8 & -1 \end{bmatrix}$

▶ Exercises 9.3

In Exercises 1–6, determine optimal strategies for R and for C for the games whose payoff matrices are given.

1. $\begin{bmatrix} 2 & 4 \\ 5 & 3 \end{bmatrix}$

2. $\begin{bmatrix} 2 & 3 \\ 3 & 2 \end{bmatrix}$

3. $\begin{bmatrix} 3 & -6 \\ -5 & 4 \end{bmatrix}$

4. $\begin{bmatrix} 5 & 2 \\ 7 & 1 \end{bmatrix}$

5. $\begin{bmatrix} 4 & 1 \\ 2 & 4 \end{bmatrix}$

6. $\begin{bmatrix} 5 & -8 \\ 3 & 6 \end{bmatrix}$

In Exercises 7 and 8, determine optimal strategies for R for the games whose payoff matrices are given.

7. $\begin{bmatrix} 3 & 5 & -1 \\ 4 & -1 & 6 \end{bmatrix}$

8. $\begin{bmatrix} -2 & 1 & 0 \\ 2 & 0 & 1 \end{bmatrix}$

In Exercises 9 and 10, determine optimal strategies for C for the games whose payoff matrices are given.

9. $\begin{bmatrix} -3 & 1 \\ 4 & 2 \\ 1 & 0 \end{bmatrix}$

10. $\begin{bmatrix} 0 & 2 \\ 2 & -1 \\ 1 & 0 \end{bmatrix}$

11. A rumrunner attempts to smuggle rum into a country having two ports. Each day the coast guard is able to patrol only one of the ports. If the rumrunner enters via an unpatrolled port, he will be able to sell his rum for a profit of $7000. If he enters the first port and it is patrolled that day, he is certain to be caught and will have his rum (worth $1000) confiscated and be fined $1000. If he enters the second port (which is big and

crowded) and it is patrolled that day, he will have time to jettison his cargo and thereby escape a fine.

(a) What is the optimal strategy for the rumrunner?

(b) What is the optimal strategy for the coast guard?

(c) How profitable is rumrunning? That is, what is the value of the game?

12. (*Which Hand?*) Ralph puts a coin in one of his hands and Carl tries to guess which hand holds the coin. If Carl guesses incorrectly, he must pay Ralph $2. If Carl guesses correctly, then Ralph must pay him $3 if the coin was in the left hand and $1 if it was in the right.

(a) What is the optimal strategy for Ralph?

(b) What is the optimal strategy for Carl?

(c) Whom does this game favor?

13. The Carter Company can choose between two advertising strategies (I and II). Its most important competitor, Rosedale Associates, has a choice of three advertising strategies (a, b, c). The estimated payoff to Rosedale Associates away from the Carter Company is given by the payoff matrix

$$\begin{array}{c} \\ a \\ b \\ c \end{array} \begin{array}{cc} \text{I} & \text{II} \\ \begin{bmatrix} -2 & 1 \\ 2 & -3 \\ 1 & -2 \end{bmatrix}, \end{array}$$

where the entries represent thousands of dollars per week. Determine the optimal strategies for each company.

Solutions to Practice Problems 9.3

1. The associated linear programming problem is: Maximize $z_1 + z_2$ subject to the constraints

$$\begin{cases} z_1 \geq 0, \quad z_2 \geq 0. \\ 2z_1 + 14z_2 \leq 1 \\ 6z_1 + 12z_2 \leq 1 \\ 8z_1 + 6z_2 \leq 1. \end{cases}$$

In Fig. 2 we have sketched the feasible set and evaluated the objective function at each vertex. The maximum value of $z_1 + z_2$ is $\frac{4}{30}$, which is achieved at the vertex $\left(\frac{3}{30}, \frac{1}{30}\right)$. Therefore,

$$v = \frac{1}{z_1 + z_2} = \frac{1}{\frac{4}{30}} = \frac{30}{4}$$

$$c_1 = v \cdot z_1 = \frac{30}{4} \cdot \frac{3}{30} = \frac{3}{4}$$

$$c_2 = v \cdot z_2 = \frac{30}{4} \cdot \frac{1}{30} = \frac{1}{4}.$$

That is, the optimal strategy for C is $\begin{bmatrix} \frac{3}{4} \\ \frac{1}{4} \end{bmatrix}$.

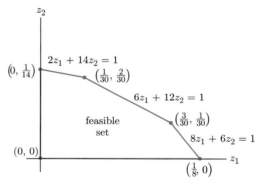

Vertex	$z_1 + z_2$
$(0,0)$	0
$\left(0, \frac{1}{14}\right)$	$\frac{1}{14}$
$\left(\frac{1}{30}, \frac{2}{30}\right)$	$\frac{3}{30}$
$\left(\frac{3}{30}, \frac{1}{30}\right)$	$\frac{4}{30}$
$\left(\frac{1}{8}, 0\right)$	$\frac{1}{8}$

Figure 2.

2. (a) $\begin{bmatrix} \frac{3}{4} \\ \frac{1}{4} \end{bmatrix}$. If we add 2 to each entry, we obtain the payoff matrix of Problem 1, so these two games have the same optimal strategies.

   (b) Always play column 2. This game is strictly determined and has the entry 3 as saddle point. It is a good idea always to check for a saddle point before looking for a mixed strategy.

▶ Chapter 9 Summary

1. A *zero-sum* game is one in which a payoff to one player results in a loss of the same amount to the other player.

2. The entry in the ith row and jth column of a payoff matrix gives the payoff to the row player (equivalently, the loss to the column player) when the row player chooses row i and the column player chooses column j.

3. A *pure strategy* is one in which the player consistently chooses the same row or column. Strategies involving varied moves are called *mixed strategies*.

4. The *optimal pure strategy* for the row player is to choose the row whose least element is maximal. The

optimal pure strategy for the column player is to choose the column whose greatest element is minimal.

5. A *saddle point* is an entry in a payoff matrix that is simultaneously the least element of its row and the greatest element of its column. A game need not have a saddle point. If a game has more than one saddle point, then the saddle points are equal.

6. A game with a saddle point is called a *strictly determined game*. In a strictly determined game, the optimal pure strategy for each player is to choose a row or column containing a saddle point.

7. In a strictly determined game, if both players use optimal pure strategies, then the saddle point gives the payoff to the row player. The value of the saddle point is called the *value of the game*.

8. If a game is not strictly determined, then the players should use mixed strategies. A *mixed strategy* for the row player is a row matrix whose ith entry is the probability that the row player will choose row i on any repetition of the game. A mixed strategy for the column player is a column matrix whose jth entry is the probability that the column player will choose column j on any repetition of the game.

9. The expected value of a pair of mixed strategies

$$R = \begin{bmatrix} r_1 & r_2 & \cdots & r_m \end{bmatrix} \quad \text{and} \quad C = \begin{bmatrix} c_1 \\ c_2 \\ \vdots \\ c_n \end{bmatrix}$$

is the average payoff per game to the row player if these mixed strategies are used. The expected value of the pair R, C of mixed strategies is found by computing the product RAC, where A is the payoff matrix for the game.

10. An *optimal mixed strategy* for the row player is one for which the column player's best counterstrategy results in the greatest possible expected value. Similarly, an optimal mixed strategy for the column player is one for which the row player's best counterstrategy results in the least possible expected value. Optimal mixed strategies for each player are found by solving a pair of dual linear programming problems, as described on pages 443–445.

Review of Fundamental Concepts of Chapter 9

1. What do the individual entries of a payoff matrix represent?

2. What is the difference between a pure strategy and a mixed strategy?

3. What is a zero-sum game?

4. Describe the optimal pure strategies for R and for C.

5. When is an entry of a payoff matrix a saddle point?

6. What is a strictly determined game and what is its value?

7. What is the expected value of a pair of mixed strategies, and how is it computed?

8. What is meant by the optimal mixed strategies of R and C, and how are they computed?

▶ Chapter 9 Supplementary Exercises

In Exercises 1–4, state whether or not the games having the given payoff matrices are strictly determined. If so, give the optimal pure strategies and the values of the strategies.

1. $\begin{bmatrix} 5 & -1 & 1 \\ -3 & 5 & 1 \\ 4 & 3 & 2 \end{bmatrix}$

2. $\begin{bmatrix} 1 & 2 & 3 \\ 3 & 2 & 1 \end{bmatrix}$

3. $\begin{bmatrix} 0 & 1 \\ 1 & 0 \\ 2 & -1 \end{bmatrix}$

4. $\begin{bmatrix} 2 & 1 & 2 \\ -1 & 0 & 3 \\ 4 & 1 & -4 \end{bmatrix}$

In Exercises 5–8, determine the expected value of each pair of mixed strategies for the given payoff matrix.

5. $\begin{bmatrix} \frac{3}{4} & \frac{1}{4} \end{bmatrix}$, $\begin{bmatrix} \frac{1}{3} \\ \frac{2}{3} \end{bmatrix}$; $\begin{bmatrix} 0 & 24 \\ 12 & -36 \end{bmatrix}$

6. $\begin{bmatrix} \frac{1}{2} & \frac{1}{2} \end{bmatrix}$, $\begin{bmatrix} \frac{1}{3} \\ \frac{1}{3} \\ \frac{1}{3} \end{bmatrix}$; $\begin{bmatrix} -6 & 6 & 0 \\ 0 & -12 & 24 \end{bmatrix}$

7. $\begin{bmatrix} .2 & .3 & .5 \end{bmatrix}$, $\begin{bmatrix} .4 \\ .6 \end{bmatrix}$; $\begin{bmatrix} 1 & 0 \\ -3 & 1 \\ 0 & 5 \end{bmatrix}$

8. $\begin{bmatrix} .1 & .1 & .8 \end{bmatrix}$, $\begin{bmatrix} .4 \\ .3 \\ .3 \end{bmatrix}$; $\begin{bmatrix} 0 & 1 & 3 \\ -1 & 0 & 2 \\ -3 & -2 & 0 \end{bmatrix}$

Determine the optimal strategies for R and for C for the games with the payoff matrices of Exercises 9 and 10.

9. $\begin{bmatrix} -3 & 4 \\ 2 & -2 \end{bmatrix}$

10. $\begin{bmatrix} 3 & -6 \\ -4 & 4 \end{bmatrix}$

11. Determine the optimal strategy for R for the game with payoff matrix
$$\begin{bmatrix} 5 & -2 & 0 \\ 1 & 4 & 1 \end{bmatrix}.$$

12. Determine the optimal strategy for C for the game with payoff matrix
$$\begin{bmatrix} 1 & 3 \\ 3 & 1 \\ 4 & 2 \end{bmatrix}.$$

13. Ruth and Carol play the following game. Both have two cards, a two and a six. Each puts one of her cards on the table. If both put down the same denomination, Ruth pays Carol $3. Otherwise, Carol pays Ruth as many dollars as the denomination of Carol's card.

    (a) Find the optimal strategies for Ruth and Carol.

    (b) Whom does this game favor?

14. An investor is considering purchasing one of three stocks. Stock A is regarded as conservative, stock B as speculative, and stock C as highly risky. If the economic growth during the coming year is strong, then stock A should increase in value by $3000, stock B by $6000, and stock C by $15,000. If the economic growth during the next year is average, then stock A should increase in value by $2000, stock B by $2000, and stock C by $1000. If the economic growth is weak, then stock A should increase in value by $1000 and stocks B and C decrease in value by $3000 and $10,000, respectively.

    (a) Set up the 3 × 3 payoff matrix showing the investing gains for the possible stock purchases and levels of economic growth.

    (b) What is the investor's optimal strategy?

▶ Chapter 9 Chapter Test

1. Consider a game with payoff matrix $\begin{bmatrix} 5 & -1 & 6 \\ -2 & 5 & -8 \\ 8 & -10 & 5 \end{bmatrix}$.

    (a) What is the meaning of the entry 6 in the upper right?

    (b) What is the meaning of the entry -10 in the bottom row?

    (c) Is this game strictly determined? Why or why not?

2. Describe the difference between a pure strategy and a mixed strategy.

3. Each of the following is a payoff matrix for a strictly determined game. Give the value of the game and the optimal pure strategies for each player.

    (a) $\begin{bmatrix} -1 & 0 \\ 2 & -2 \\ 3 & 2 \end{bmatrix}$

    (b) $\begin{bmatrix} 0 & 2 & 4 \\ -4 & 0 & 3 \\ -2 & -3 & 0 \end{bmatrix}$

4. Consider the following game. Each player chooses a number from 1 to 5. If the row player's number is higher, then he wins. If the column player's number is higher or if the two numbers match, then the column player wins. The loser must pay the winner as many dollars as the number chosen by the row player. Construct a payoff matrix for this game. Is the game strictly determined? If so, what is the value of the game? Which player would you rather be?

5. Suppose a game has payoff matrix $\begin{bmatrix} 2 & -2 & 3 \\ -1 & 1 & -3 \end{bmatrix}$.

    (a) Suppose the row player uses the mixed strategy $R = \begin{bmatrix} .4 & .6 \end{bmatrix}$ and the column player uses the mixed strategy $C = \begin{bmatrix} .3 \\ .5 \\ .2 \end{bmatrix}$. Calculate and interpret the expected value for this pair of mixed strategies.

    (b) If the row player uses the mixed strategy from part (a), then is the column player better off using the mixed strategy from part (a) or the mixed strategy $C = \begin{bmatrix} .4 \\ .1 \\ .5 \end{bmatrix}$?

6. Consider a game with payoff matrix $\begin{bmatrix} 0 & -1 \\ -4 & 5 \end{bmatrix}$.

    (a) Determine optimal mixed strategies for each player.

    (b) Whom does this game favor?

Chapter Project

Simulating the Outcomes of Mixed-Strategy Games

A mixed strategy requires the use of a device that will randomly select a row (or column) of the payoff matrix subject to a specified probability. For instance, if the strategy for R is $\begin{bmatrix} .6 & .4 \end{bmatrix}$, the device should select the first row 60% of the time and select the second row 40% of the time. A graphing calculator is well-suited to handle this task by using its *rand* function along with *relational operators*.

Each time the rand function is called, a number between 0 and 1 is generated. See Fig. 1. A relational operator, often an inequality statement, returns the value 1 when true and the value 0 when false. See Fig. 2. The instructions[1] in Fig. 3 are used to select a row from a matrix with two rows.

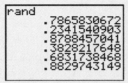

Figure 1.

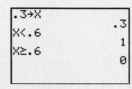

Figure 2.

Figure 3.

1. Explain why 60% of the time the instructions in Fig. 3 return a 1 and 40% of the time they return a 2. Type the instructions into your calculator, press the ENTER key twenty times, and count the number of 1's and 2's. Are there approximately twelve 1's and eight 2's?

2. Explain why the instructions in Fig. 3 should not be replaced with

$$\texttt{(rand<.6)1+(rand ≥ .6)2.}$$

Type this line into your calculator and press the ENTER key several times to convince yourself that it does not always produce 1's and 2's.

In part 1 you pressed the ENTER key repeatedly and manually kept track of the outcomes. Some graphing calculators, such as the TI-83 and TI-83 Plus can carry out the instructions many times, store the outcomes in a list, and analyze the list. The first line in Fig. 4 generates 100 random numbers between 0 and 1 and places them in the list L_1. The third and fourth lines of Fig. 4 convert each number in the list L_1 to a row number using the strategy $\begin{bmatrix} .6 & .4 \end{bmatrix}$ and place the 100 row choices into the list L_3. Fig. 6 uses the window settings shown in Fig. 5 to display the histogram for L_3. We see that the second row was selected 39 times out of 100 times. This is very close to the expected 40%.

Figure 4.

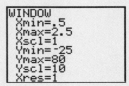

Figure 5.

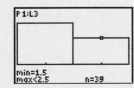

Figure 6.

---

[1]The decision of whether to use $\leq$ instead of $<$, or whether to use $>$ instead of $\geq$ is arbitrary. Theoretically, if x is a real number between 0 and 1 selected at random then $\Pr(x < .6)$ is the same as $\Pr(x \leq .6)$, and $\Pr(x > .6)$ is the same as $\Pr(x \geq .6)$. We use the inequality symbols $<$ and $\geq$ in this book.

Chapter Project   (Continued)

3. Simulate 100 column selections using the strategy $\begin{bmatrix} .2 \\ .8 \end{bmatrix}$ and create a histogram showing the number of times each column was selected. How many times was the second column selected?

   In Section 9.3, the optimal mixed strategies for the payoff matrix $\begin{bmatrix} 5 & 3 \\ 1 & 4 \end{bmatrix}$ were found to be $\begin{bmatrix} .6 & .4 \end{bmatrix}$ for R and $\begin{bmatrix} .2 \\ .8 \end{bmatrix}$ for C and the value of the game was found to be $\frac{17}{5}$. In Figs. 7 and 8, 100 games are simulated and the payoffs for the games are stored in the list L_3. Fig. 10 shows the histogram for L_3 using the window settings in Fig. 9. For instance, we see that a payoff of 3 occurred in 50 of the 100 games. Fig. 11 shows that the average of the 100 payoffs, 3.35, is very close to the value of the game, 3.4.

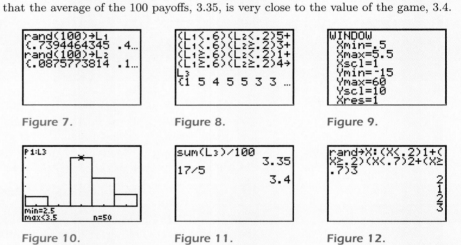

Figure 7.   Figure 8.   Figure 9.

Figure 10.   Figure 11.   Figure 12.

4. Explain in detail what is being calculated in Fig. 8.

5. Create a list of the payoffs for playing 100 games with the payoff matrix $\begin{bmatrix} 5 & 3 \\ 1 & 4 \end{bmatrix}$ using the strategies $\begin{bmatrix} .5 & .5 \end{bmatrix}$ for R and $\begin{bmatrix} .3 \\ .7 \end{bmatrix}$ for C, and compute the average of the payoffs.

6. Suppose a payoff matrix has three rows and that R's strategy is $\begin{bmatrix} .2 & .5 & .3 \end{bmatrix}$. Explain why Fig. 12 simulates the selection of a row by R. Type the instructions into your calculator, press the ENTER key forty times, and count the number of 1's, 2's, and 3's. Are there approximately eight 1's, twenty 2's, and twelve 3's?

7. Consider the 3×2 matrix in the first practice problem of Section 9.3. Suppose the strategies for R and C are $\begin{bmatrix} .2 & .5 & .3 \end{bmatrix}$ and $\begin{bmatrix} .75 \\ .25 \end{bmatrix}$ respectively. Simulate the payoffs for 100 games, display the histogram for the payoffs, and calculate the average value of the payoffs.

The Mathematics of Finance 10

This chapter presents several topics in the mathematics of finance, including compound and simple interest, annuities, and amortization. They are presented in the classical way, using methods that are centuries old but that lend themselves to modern computing techniques.

10.1 Interest

When you deposit money into a savings account, the bank pays you a fee for the use of your money. This fee is called *interest* and is determined by the amount deposited, the duration of the deposit, and the quoted interest rate. The amount deposited is called the *principal*, and the amount to which the principal grows (after the addition of interest) is called the *compound amount* or *balance*.

The entries in a hypothetical bank passbook are shown in Table 1.

Table 1

Date	Deposits	Withdrawals	Interest	Balance
1/1/00	$100.00			$100.00
4/1/00			$1.00	101.00
7/1/00			1.01	102.01
10/1/00			1.02	103.03
1/1/01			1.03	104.06

Note the following facts about this passbook:

1. The principal is $100.00. The compound amount after 1 year is $104.06.

2. Interest is being paid four times per year (or, in financial language, *quarterly*).

3. Each quarter, the interest is 1% of the previous balance. That is, $1.00 is 1% of $100.00, $1.01 is 1% of $101.00, and so on. Since $4 \times 1\%$ is 4%, we say that the money is earning 4% *annual interest compounded quarterly.*

As in the passbook shown in Table 1, interest rates are usually stated as annual percentage rates, with the interest to be *compounded* (i.e., computed) a certain number of times per year. Some common frequencies for compounding are listed in Table 2. Of special importance is the *interest rate per period*, denoted i, which is calculated by dividing the annual percentage by the number of interest periods per year.

Table 2

Number of interest periods per year	Length of each interest period	Interest compounded
1	One year	Annually
2	Six months	Semiannually
4	Three months	Quarterly
12	One month	Monthly
52	One week	Weekly
365	One day	Daily

For example, in our passbook in Table 1, the annual percentage rate was 4%, the interest was compounded quarterly, and the interest per period was $4\%/4 = 1\%$.

If interest is compounded m times per year and the annual interest rate is r, then the interest rate per period is

$$i = \frac{r}{m}.$$

▶ Example 1   Determine the interest rate per period for each of the following interest rates.

(a) 5% interest compounded semiannually

(b) 6% interest compounded monthly

Solution   (a) The annual percentage rate is 5% and the number of interest periods is 2. Therefore,

$$i = \frac{5\%}{2} = 2\tfrac{1}{2}\%.$$

Note: In decimal form, $i = .025$.

(b) The annual percentage rate is 6% and the number of interest periods is 12. Therefore,

$$i = \frac{6\%}{12} = \frac{1}{2}\%.$$

Note: In decimal form, $i = .005$.   ◆

Consider a savings account in which the interest rate per period is i. Then the interest earned during a period is i times the previous balance. That is, at the end of an interest period, the new balance, B_{new}, is computed by adding this interest to the previous balance, $B_{previous}$. Therefore,

$$B_{new} = B_{previous} + i \cdot B_{previous}. \tag{1}$$

▶ **Example 2** Compute the interest and the balance for the first two interest periods for a deposit of $1000 at 4% interest compounded semiannually.

Solution Here $i = 2\%$, or .02. The interest for the first period is 2% of $1000, or $20. Let B_1 be the balance at the end of the first interest period and B_2 the balance after two interest periods. By formula (1),

$$B_1 = 1000 + .02(1000) = 1000 + 20 = \$1020.$$

Similarly, since 2% of $1020 is $20.40, the interest for the second period is $20.40 and the balance is

$$B_2 = B_1 + .02B_1 = 1020 + .02(1020) = 1020 + 20.40 = \$1040.40.$$

Let us compute B_2 using another method:

$$\begin{aligned} B_2 &= B_1 + .02B_1 = 1 \cdot B_1 + .02B_1 = (1 + .02)B_1 \\ &= (1.02)B_1 = (1.02)1020 = \$1040.40. \end{aligned} \qquad \blacklozenge$$

The alternative method for computing B_2 just presented can be generalized. Namely, we always have

$$B_{new} = B_{previous} + i \cdot B_{previous} = 1 \cdot B_{previous} + i \cdot B_{previous}.$$

Therefore,

$$B_{new} = (1 + i)B_{previous}.$$

This last result says that balances for successive time periods are computed by multiplying by $1 + i$.

The formula for the balance after any number of interest periods is now easily derived:

Principal	P
Balance after 1 interest period	$(1 + i)P$
Balance after 2 interest periods	$(1 + i) \cdot (1 + i)P$ or $(1 + i)^2 P$
Balance after 3 interest periods	$(1 + i) \cdot (1 + i)^2 P$ or $(1 + i)^3 P$
Balance after 4 interest periods	$(1 + i)^4 P$
$\vdots$	$\vdots$
Balance after n interest periods	$(1 + i)^n P.$

Denote the compound amount by the letter F (suggestive of "future value"). Then the compound amount after n interest periods is given by the formula

$$F = (1 + i)^n P, \tag{2}$$

where i is the interest rate per period and P is the principal.

Values of $(1 + i)^n$ for specific values of i and n are easily determined using either a calculator or a table. A brief table of useful values has been included as Table 2 of Appendix A. Financial calculators have a designated key to compute $(1 + i)^n$. On an ordinary calculator, the following keystrokes will compute the value of $(1 + .005)^{24}$.

$$\boxed{1}\; \boxed{+}\; \boxed{.005}\; \boxed{=}\; \boxed{x^y}\; \boxed{24}\; \boxed{=}$$

On the home screen of a graphing calculator such as the TI-82 or TI-83, use

$$\boxed{(}\; \boxed{1}\; \boxed{+}\; \boxed{.005}\; \boxed{)}\; \boxed{\char`\^}\; \boxed{24}\; \boxed{\text{ENTER}}$$

▶ **Example 3** Apply formula (2) to the savings account passbook discussed at the beginning of this section and calculate the compound amount after 1 year and after 5 years.

Solution The principal P is \$100. Since the interest rate is 4% compounded quarterly, we have $i = 1\%$, or .01. One year consists of four interest periods, so $n = 4$. Therefore, the compound amount after 1 year is

$$F = (1 + .01)^4 \cdot 100 = (1.01)^4 \cdot 100 = (1.04060401) \cdot 100 \qquad \text{(from Appendix A)}$$

$$= 104.060401 = \$104.06 \qquad \text{(after rounding to the nearest cent)}.$$

Five years consists of $n = 5 \times 4 = 20$ interest periods. Therefore, the compound amount after 5 years is

$$F = (1.01)^{20} \cdot 100 = (1.22019004) \cdot 100 = \$122.02. \qquad \blacklozenge$$

The Excel spreadsheet in Table 3 shows the effects of interest rates (compounded quarterly) on the compound amount. [For those familiar with Excel, the entries in cells B5 and C5 are **\$B\$1*(1+A5/4)^20** and **\$B\$1*(1+A5/4)^40**, respectively. The remaining entries in the B and C columns were created with the AutoFill option from the Edit/Fill/Series dialog box. The dollar signs in **\$B\$1** prevents references to this location from being changed by AutoFill.]

The next example is a variation of the previous one and introduces a new concept, present value.

Table 3

	A	B	C
1	Principal	\$100.00	
2			
3		Compound	Amount
4	Interest Rate	5 Years	10 Years
5	3.00%	\$116.12	\$134.83
6	3.50%	\$119.03	\$141.69
7	4.00%	\$122.02	\$148.89
8	4.50%	\$125.08	\$156.44
9	5.00%	\$128.20	\$164.36
10	5.50%	\$131.41	\$172.68
11	6.00%	\$134.69	\$181.40
12	6.50%	\$138.04	\$190.56
13	7.00%	\$141.48	\$200.16
14	7.50%	\$144.99	\$210.23
15	8.00%	\$148.59	\$220.80

▶ Example 4

How much money must be deposited now in order to have $1000 after 5 years if interest is paid at a 4% annual rate compounded quarterly?

Solution

As in Example 3, we have $i = .01$ and $n = 20$. However, now we are given F and are asked to solve for P.

$$F = (1+i)^n P$$
$$1000 = (1.01)^{20} P$$
$$P = \frac{1000}{(1.01)^{20}}$$

From Table 2 of Appendix A, $(1.01)^{20} = 1.22019004$. However, the cumbersome arithmetic can be avoided by using Table 3 of Appendix A, which tabulates values of $1 \div (1+i)^n$ for various values of i and n.

$$P = \frac{1}{(1.01)^{20}} \cdot 1000 = (.81954447) \cdot 1000 = \$819.54$$

We say that $819.54 is the present value of $1000, 5 years from now, at 4% interest compounded quarterly. ◆

In general, the *present value* of F dollars at a given interest rate and given length of time is the amount of money P that must be deposited now in order for the compound amount to grow to F dollars in the given length of time. From formula (2), we see that the present value P may be computed from the following formula:

$$P = \frac{1}{(1+i)^n} \cdot F. \tag{3}$$

▶ Example 5

Determine the present value of a $10,000 payment to be received on January 1, 2004, if it is now May 1, 1995, and money can be invested at 6% interest compounded monthly.

Solution

Here $F = 10{,}000$, $n = 104$ (the number of months between the two given dates), and $i = \frac{1}{2}\% = .005$. By formula (3),

$$P = \frac{1}{(1+i)^n} \cdot F = (.59529136)10{,}000 = \$5952.91.$$

Therefore, $5952.91 invested on May 1, 1995, will grow to $10,000 by January 1, 2004. ◆

The interest that we have been discussing so far is the most prevalent type of interest and is known as *compound interest*. There is another type of interest, called *simple interest*, which is used in some financial circumstances. Let us now discuss this type of interest.

Interest rates for simple interest are given as an annual percentage rate r. Interest is earned *only* on the principal P and the interest is rP for each year. Therefore, the interest earned in n years is nrP. So the amount F after n years is the original amount plus the interest earned. That is,

$$F = P + nrP = 1 \cdot P + nrP = (1+nr)P. \tag{4}$$

▶ Example 6   Calculate the amount after 4 years if $1000 is invested at 5% simple interest.

Solution   Apply formula (4) with $P = \$1000$, $n = 4$, and $r = 5\%$ or .05.

$$F = (1 + nr)P = [1 + 4(.05)]1000 = (1.2)1000 = \$1200.$$ ◆

In Example 6, had the money been invested at 5% compound interest with annual compounding, then the compound amount would have been $1215.51. Money invested at simple interest is earning interest only on the principal amount. However, with compound interest, after the first interest period, the interest is also earning interest. Thus, if we compare two savings accounts, each earning interest at the same stated annual rate, but with one earning simple interest and the other earning compound interest, the latter will grow at a faster rate.

Effective Rate of Interest   The annual rate of interest is also known as the *nominal rate* or the *stated rate*. Its true worth depends on the number of compounding periods. The nominal rate does not help you decide, for instance, whether a savings account paying 3.65% interest compounded quarterly is better than a savings account paying 3.6% interest compounded monthly. A better measure of worth is the *effective rate of interest*. The effective rate is the simple interest rate that yields the same amount after one year as the annual rate of interest. For example, a savings account paying 3.65% interest compounded quarterly has an effective rate of 3.7%, whereas a savings account paying 3.6% compounded monthly has an effective rate of 3.66%. Therefore, the first savings account is better.

Suppose the annual rate of interest r is compounded m times per year. Then with compound interest P dollars will grow to $P(1 + i)^m$ in one year, where $i = r/m$. With simple interest r_{eff}, the balance after one year will be $P(1 + r_{\text{eff}})$. Equating the two balances,

$$P(1 + r_{\text{eff}}) = P(1 + i)^m$$
$$1 + r_{\text{eff}} = (1 + i)^m$$
$$r_{\text{eff}} = (1 + i)^m - 1. \tag{5}$$

▶ Example 7   Calculate the effective rate of interest for a savings account paying 3.65% compounded quarterly.

Solution   Apply formula (5) with $r = .0365$ and $m = 4$. Then $i = r/m = .0365/4 = .009125$ and

$$r_{\text{eff}} = (1 + .009125)^4 - 1 \approx .037.$$

Therefore, the effective rate is approximately 3.7%.   ◆

Let us summarize the key formulas developed so far.

Compound Interest

Compound amount:	$F = (1 + i)^n P$
Present value:	$P = \left[\dfrac{1}{(1 + i)^n}\right] F$
Effective rate:	$r_{\text{eff}} = (1 + i)^m - 1$

where i is the interest rate per period, n is the total number of interest periods, and m is the number of times interest is compounded per year.

Simple Interest

Amount:	$F = (1 + nr)P$

where r is the interest rate and n is the number of years.

GC Graphing calculators can easily display successive balances in a savings account. Consider the situation from Table 1, in which $100 is deposited at 4% interest compounded quarterly. In Fig. 1 successive balances are displayed in the home screen. In Fig. 2 successive balances are graphed, and in Fig. 3 they are displayed in a table.

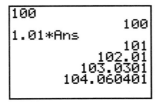
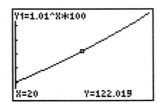
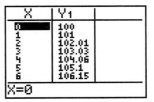

Figure 1.   Figure 2.   Figure 3.

Displaying successive balances on the home screen   Successive balances can be determined with the relation $B_{\text{new}} = (1 + i)B_{\text{previous}}$. In Fig. 1, after the principal (**100**) is entered, the last displayed value (**100**) is assigned to **Ans**. The instruction **1.01*Ans** generates the next balance (**101**) and assigns it to **Ans**. Each subsequent press of the ⎡ENTER⎤ key generates another balance.

Graphs with the TI-82 or TI-83   Figure 4 shows the **Y=** editor, where Y_1 has been set equal to **1.01^X*100**; that is, $(1 + i)^X \cdot P$. Here **X**, instead of n, is used to represent the number of interest periods. In Fig. 5, the function Y_1 is used in two ways to calculate future values (after 40 interest periods) in the home screen. (*Note*: To display the arrow, press ⎡STO ▶⎤. To display Y_1 with a TI-83, press

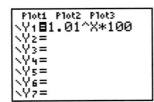
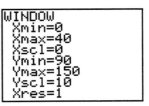

Figure 4.   Figure 5.   Figure 6.

Figure 7.

$\boxed{\text{VARS}}$ $\boxed{\blacktriangleright}$ **1 1**. With a TI-82 press $\boxed{\text{2nd}}$ [Y-VARS] **1 1**.) In Fig. 6, the $\boxed{\text{WINDOW}}$ screen is set up to display the growth of the balance for 10 years, that is, 40 interest periods. **Xscl** was set to 0 since the x-axis is not being displayed. **Ymin** was set less than 100 to allow room for coordinates of points to be displayed at the bottom of the screen. Pressing $\boxed{\text{GRAPH}}$ produces the screen of Fig. 2.

Tables with the TI-82 or TI-83   Pressing $\boxed{\text{2nd}}$ [TBLSET] brings up the TABLE SETUP screen of Fig. 7. The table determined by the settings will have a column for **X** and a column for the values of each function that is selected in the **Y=** editor. The values for **X** will begin with the setting of **TblStart** (**TblMin** on the TI-82) and increase by the setting of Δ**Tbl**. For our purposes, the settings for **Indpnt** and **Depend** should always be **Auto**. After you press $\boxed{\text{2nd}}$ [TABLE] to display the table (see Fig. 3), you can use the down-arrow key to generate further balances.

▶ **Example 8**   Consider the situation from Table 1, in which $100 is deposited at 4% interest compounded quarterly. Determine when the balance will exceed $130.

Solution   There are three ways to answer this question with a graphing calculator—with the home screen, with a graph, and with a table.

1. (Home screen)   Generate successive balances (while keeping track of the number of times the $\boxed{\text{ENTER}}$ key has been pressed) until a balance exceeding 130 is reached. See Fig. 8.

2. (Graph)   Set **Y₂ = 130** and find its intersection with the graph of **Y₁ = 1.01^X*100**. See Fig. 9.

3. (Table)   Scroll down the table for **Y₁** until the balance exceeds 130. See Fig. 10.

In each case we see that the balance will exceed $130 after 27 interest periods.◆

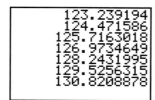

Figure 8.

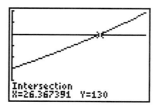

Figure 9.

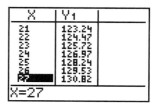

Figure 10.

Practice Problems 10.1

1. (a) In Table 3 of Appendix A, look up the value of $1/(1+i)^n$ for $i = 6\%$ and $n = 10$.

   (b) Calculate the present value of $1000 to be received 10 years in the future at 6% interest compounded annually.

2. Calculate the compound amount after 2 years of $1 at 26% interest compounded weekly.

3. Calculate the future amount of $2000 after 6 months if invested at 6% simple interest.

▶ Exercises 10.1

1. Determine i and n for the following situations.
   (a) 12% interest compounded monthly for 2 years
   (b) 8% interest compounded quarterly for 5 years
   (c) 10% interest compounded semiannually for 20 years

2. Determine i and n for the following situations.
   (a) 6% interest compounded annually for 3 years
   (b) 6% interest compounded monthly from January 1, 1998, to July 1, 2002
   (c) 9% interest compounded quarterly from January 1, 1998, to October 1, 2001

3. Determine i, n, P, and F for the following situations.
   (a) $500 invested at 6% interest compounded annually grows to $631.24 in 4 years.
   (b) $800 invested on January 1, 2001, at 6% interest compounded monthly grows to $1455.52 by January 1, 2011.
   (c) $6177.88 is deposited on January 1, 2001. The balance on July 1, 2010, is $9000 and the interest is 4% interest compounded semiannually.

4. Determine i, n, P, and F for the following situations.
   (a) The amount of money that must be deposited now at 4.5% interest compounded weekly in order to have $7500 in 1 year is $7170.12.
   (b) $3000 deposited at 6% interest compounded monthly will grow to $18,067.73 in 30 years.
   (c) In 1626, Peter Minuit, the first director-general of New Netherlands province, purchased Manhattan Island for trinkets and cloth valued at about $24. Had this money been invested at 8% interest compounded quarterly, it would have amounted to $190,751,905,000,000 by 2001.

5. Calculate the compound amount of $1000 after 2 years if deposited at 6% interest compounded monthly.

6. Calculate the present value of $10,000 payable in 5 years at 4% interest compounded semiannually.

7. Calculate the present value of $100,000 payable in 25 years at 6% interest compounded monthly.

8. Calculate the compound amount of $1000 after 1 year if deposited at 7.3% interest compounded daily.

9. Six thousand dollars is deposited in a savings account at 6% interest compounded monthly. Find the balance after 3 years and the amount of interest earned during that time.

10. Two thousand dollars is deposited in a savings account at 4% interest compounded semiannually. Find the balance after 7 years and the amount of interest earned during that time.

11. (a) How much money would have to be deposited now at 6% interest compounded monthly to accumulate to $4000 in 2 years?
    (b) How much of the $4000 would be interest?
    (c) Prepare a table showing the growth of the account for the first 3 months.

12. (a) How much money would have to be deposited now at 8% interest compounded quarterly to accumulate to $10,000 in 15 years?
    (b) How much of the $10,000 would be interest?
    (c) Prepare a table showing the growth of the account for the first 3 quarters.

13. If you had invested $10,000 on January 1, 1997, at 4% interest compounded quarterly, how much would you have on April 1, 2003?

14. In order to have $10,000 on his 25th birthday, how much would a person just turned 21 have to invest if the money will earn 6% interest compounded monthly?

15. Mr. Smith wishes to purchase a $10,000 sailboat upon his retirement in 3 years. He has just won the state lottery and would like to set aside enough cash in a savings account paying 4% interest compounded quarterly to buy the boat upon retirement. How much should he deposit?

16. Ms. Jones has just invested $100,000 at 6% interest compounded annually. How much money will she have in 20 years?

17. Consider the following savings account passbook:

	Date		
	1/1/01	2/1/01	3/1/01
Deposit	$1000.00		
Withdrawal			
Interest		$5.00	$5.03
Balance	$1000.00	$1005.00	$1010.03

(a) What annual interest rate is this bank paying?
(b) Give the interest and balance on 4/1/01.
(c) Give the interest and balance on 1/1/03.

18. Consider the following savings account passbook:

	Date		
	1/1/00	7/1/00	1/1/01
Deposit	$10,000.00		
Withdrawal			
Interest		$200.00	$204.00
Balance	$10,000.00	$10,200.00	$10,404.00

(a) Give the interest and balance on 7/1/01.

(b) Give the interest and balance on 1/1/09.

19. Is it more profitable to receive $1000 now or $1700 in 9 years? Assume that money can earn 6% interest compounded annually.

20. Is it more profitable to receive $7000 now or $10,000 in 9 years? Assume that money can earn 4% interest compounded quarterly.

21. In 1999 the Nasdaq index grew at a rate of 62.2% compounded weekly. Is this rate better or worse than 85% compounded annually?

22. Would you rather earn 8% interest compounded annually or 7.3% interest compounded daily?

23. On January 1, 1998, a deposit was made into a savings account paying interest compounded quarterly. The balance on January 1, 2001 was $10,000 and the balance on April 1, 2001, was $10,100. How large was the deposit?

24. During the 1980s a deposit was made into a savings account paying 4% interest compounded quarterly. On January 1, 2001, the balance was $2020. What was the balance on October 1, 2000?

Exercises 25–36 concern simple interest.

25. Determine r, n, P, and F for each of the following situations.
    (a) $500 invested at 4% simple interest grows to $510 in 6 months.
    (b) In order to have $550 after 2 years at 5% simple interest, $500 must be deposited.

26. Determine r, n, P, and F for each of the following situations.
    (a) At 6% simple interest, $1000 deposited on January 1, 2001, will be worth $1040 on September 1, 2001.
    (b) At 4% simple interest, in order to have $3600 in 5 years, $3000 must be deposited now.

27. Calculate the amount after 3 years if $1000 is deposited at 5% simple interest.

28. Calculate the amount after 18 months if $2000 is deposited at 6% simple interest.

29. Find the present value of $3000 in 2 years at 10% simple interest.

30. Find the present value of $2000 in 4 years at 7% simple interest.

31. Determine the (simple) interest rate at which $980 grows to $1000 in 6 months.

32. How many years are required for $1000 to grow to $1210 at 7% simple interest?

33. Determine the amount of time required for money to double at 5% simple interest.

34. Derive the formula for the (simple) interest rate at which P dollars grows to F dollars in n years. That is, express r in terms of P, F, and n.

35. Derive the formula for the present value of F dollars in n years at simple interest rate r.

36. Derive the formula for the number of years required for P dollars to grow to F dollars at simple interest rate r.

37. Suppose a principal of $100 is deposited for 5 years in a savings account at 6% interest compounded semiannually. Which of items (a)–(d) can be used to fill in the blank in the following statement? (*Note*: Before computing, use your intuition to guess the correct answer.)

    If the _____ is doubled, then the compound amount will double.
    (a) principal
    (b) interest rate
    (c) number of interest periods per year
    (d) number of years

38. Suppose a principal of $100 is deposited for 5 years in a savings account at 6% simple interest. Which of items (a)–(c) can be used to fill in the blank in the following statement? (*Note*: Before computing, use your intuition to guess the correct answer.)

    If the _____ is doubled, then the amount will double.
    (a) principal
    (b) interest rate
    (c) number of years

39. Compute the compound amount after 1 year for $100 invested at 4% interest compounded quarterly. What simple interest rate will yield the same amount in 1 year?

40. Compute the compound amount after 1 year for $100 invested at 6% interest compounded monthly. What simple interest rate will yield the same amount in 1 year?

41. Calculate the effective rate for 4% interest compounded semiannually.

42. Calculate the effective rate for 8.45% interest compounded weekly.

43. Calculate the effective rate for 4.4% interest compounded monthly.

44. Calculate the effective rate for 7.95% interest compounded quarterly.

45. Find the nominal rate corresponding to an effective rate of 4.06% if interest is compounded quarterly.

46. Find the nominal rate corresponding to an effective rate of 6.91% if interest is compounded monthly.

Exercises 47–50 require the use of a graphing calculator or a computer.

47. One thousand dollars is deposited into a savings account at 6.5% interest compounded annually. What are the balances after 1, 2, and 3 years? How many years are required for the balance to reach $1655? After how many years will the balance exceed $2000?

48. Ten thousand dollars is deposited into a savings account at 6% interest compounded monthly. What are the balances after 5, 10, and 15 months? How many months are required for the balance to reach $11,614? After how many months will the balance exceed $13,000?

49. Tom invests $100,000 at 8% interest compounded annually. When will Tom be a millionaire?

50. How many years are required for $100 to double if deposited at 6% interest compounded quarterly?

Solutions to Practice Problems 10.1

1. (a) Look up the entry in Table 3 in Appendix A in the row labeled "10" and the column labeled "6%." That entry is .55839478.

(b) Here we are given the value in the future $F = \$1000$ and are asked to find the present value P. Interest compounded annually has just one interest period per year, so $n = 10 \cdot 1 = 10$ and $i = 6\%/1 = 6\%$. By formula (3),

$$P = \frac{1}{(1+i)^n}F$$

$$= \frac{1}{(1+i)^n} \cdot 1000 \qquad \text{(with } i = 6\% \text{ and } n = 10)$$

$$= (.55839478) \cdot 1000 \qquad \text{[from part (a)]}$$

$$= 558.39478$$

$$= \$558.39 \qquad \text{(rounding to the nearest cent).}$$

2. Here we are given the present value, $P = 1$, and are asked to find the value F at a future time. Interest compounded weekly has 52 interest periods each year, so $n = 2 \times 52 = 104$ and $i = 26\%/52 = \frac{1}{2}\%$. By formula (2), we have

$$F = (1+i)^n P$$

$$= (1+i)^n \cdot 1 \qquad \text{(with } i = 1/2\% \text{ and } n = 104)$$

$$= (1.67984969) \cdot 1 \qquad \text{(using Table 2)}$$

$$= \$1.68.$$

[*Note*: In general, whenever $P = \$1$, then $F = (1+i)^n \cdot 1 = (1+i)^n$. This explains why $(1+i)^n$ is often referred to as the *compound amount* of $1.]

3. In simple interest problems, time should be expressed in terms of years. Since 6 months is $\frac{1}{2}$ of a year, formula (4) gives

$$A = (1 + nr)P = [1 + \tfrac{1}{2}(.06)]2000 = (1.03)2000 = \$2060.$$

10.2 Annuities

An annuity is a sequence of equal payments made at regular intervals of time. Here are two illustrations.

1. As the proud parent of a newborn daughter, you decide to save for her college education by depositing $100 at the end of each month into a savings account paying 6% interest compounded monthly. Eighteen years from now, after you make the last of 216 payments, the account will contain $38,735.32.

2. Having just won the state lottery, you decide not to work for the next 5 years. You want to deposit enough money into the bank so that you can withdraw $5000 at the end of each month for 60 months. If the bank pays 6% interest compounded monthly, you must deposit $258,627.80.

The payments in the foregoing financial transactions are called *rent*. The amount of a typical rent payment is denoted by the letter R. Thus, in the preceding examples, we have $R = \$100$ and $R = \$5000$, respectively.

In illustration 1, you make equal payments to a bank in order to generate a large sum of money in the future. This sum, namely $38,735.32, is called the *future value of the annuity*. Since the amount of money in the savings account is increased each time a payment is made, we refer to this type of annuity as an *increasing annuity*.

In illustration 2, the bank will make equal payments to you in order to pay back the sum of money that you currently deposit. The value of the current deposit, namely $258,627.80, is called the *present value* of the annuity. Since the amount of money in the savings account is decreased each time a payment is made, we refer to this type of annuity as a *decreasing annuity*.

We now derive formulas for future values and present values of annuities. Suppose that an increasing annuity consists of a sequence of n equal payments, each of R dollars. Suppose that the annuity payments are deposited into an account paying compound interest at the rate of i per interest period. We will further suppose that there is a single annuity payment per interest period and that the payment is made at the end of the interest period. Let us derive a formula for the future value of the annuity: that is, a formula for the balance of the account immediately after the last payment.

Each payment accumulates interest for a different number of interest periods, so let us calculate the balance in the account as the sum of n compound amounts, one corresponding to each payment (Table 1). Denote the future value of the annuity by F. Then F is the sum of the numbers in the right-hand column:

$$F = R + (1+i)R + (1+i)^2 R + (1+i)^3 R + \cdots + (1+i)^{n-1} R.$$

A compact expression for F can be obtained by multiplying both sides of this equation by $(1+i)$ and then subtracting the original equation from the new equation.

$$(1+i)F = \quad (1+i)R + (1+i)^2 R + (1+i)^3 R + \cdots + (1+i)^{n-1} R + (1+i)^n R$$
$$\underline{F = R + (1+i)R + (1+i)^2 R + (1+i)^3 R + \cdots + (1+i)^{n-1} R \qquad\qquad}$$
$$iF = (1+i)^n R - R$$

The last equation can be written $iF = [(1+i)^n - 1] \cdot R$. Dividing both sides by

Table 1

Payment	Amount	Number of interest periods on deposit	Compound amount
1	R	$n-1$	$(1+i)^{n-1}R$
2	R	$n-2$	$(1+i)^{n-2}R$
$\vdots$	$\vdots$	$\vdots$	$\vdots$
$n-2$	R	2	$(1+i)^2R$
$n-1$	R	1	$(1+i)R$
n	R	0	R

i yields

$$F = \frac{(1+i)^n - 1}{i} \cdot R.$$

The expression $[(1+i)^n - 1]/i$ occurs often in financial analysis and is denoted by the special symbol $s_{\overline{n}|\,i}$ (read "s sub n angle i"). We may summarize our calculations as follows.

Suppose that an increasing annuity consists of n payments of R dollars each, deposited at the ends of consecutive interest periods into an account with interest compounded at a rate i per period. Then the future value F of the annuity is given by the formula

$$F = s_{\overline{n}|\,i}R. \qquad (1)$$

Values of $s_{\overline{n}|\,i}$ may be computed using a calculator or looked up in an appropriate table. We have included a brief table as Table 4 of Appendix A. Financial calculators have a designated key to compute $s_{\overline{n}|\,i}$. On a typical ordinary calculator, the following keystrokes will compute the value of $s_{\overline{24}|\,.005}$.

$$\boxed{1.005} \; \boxed{x^y} \; \boxed{24} \; \boxed{=} \; \boxed{-} \; \boxed{1} \; \boxed{=} \; \boxed{\div} \; \boxed{.005} \; \boxed{=}$$

On the home screen of a graphing calculator such as the TI-82 or TI-83, use

$$\boxed{(} \; \boxed{(} \; \boxed{1.005} \; \boxed{\wedge} \; \boxed{24} \; \boxed{)} \; \boxed{-} \; \boxed{1} \; \boxed{)} \; \boxed{\div} \; \boxed{.005} \; \boxed{\text{ENTER}}$$

▶ **Example 1**   Calculate the future value of an increasing annuity of $100 per month for 5 years at 6% interest compounded monthly.

Solution   Here $R = 100$ and $i = \frac{1}{2}\%$. Since a payment is made at the end of each month for 5 years, there will be $5 \times 12 = 60$ payments. So $n = 60$. Therefore,

$$F = s_{\overline{n}|\,i}R = s_{\overline{60}|\,1/2\%} \cdot 100 = (69.77003051) \cdot 100 \qquad \text{(by Table 4)}$$
$$= \$6977.00.$$

◆

We can easily derive a formula that illustrates exactly how the future value of an increasing annuity changes from period to period. Each new balance can be computed from the previous balance with the formula

$$B_{\text{new}} = (1 + i)B_{\text{previous}} + R.$$

That is, the new balance equals the growth of the previous balance due to interest, plus the amount paid. So, for instance, if B_1 is the balance after the first payment is made, B_2 is the balance after the second payment is made, and so on, then

$$B_1 = R$$
$$B_2 = (1 + i)B_1 + R$$
$$B_3 = (1 + i)B_2 + R$$
$$\vdots$$

Successive unpaid balances are computed by multiplying by $(1 + i)$ and adding R.

If $\$R$ is deposited into an increasing annuity at the end of each interest period with interest rate i per period,

$$B_{\text{new}} = (1 + i)B_{\text{previous}} + R \tag{2}$$

can be used to calculate each new balance, B_{new}, from the previous balance, B_{previous}.

▶ **Example 2**   Consider the annuity of Example 1. Determine the future value after 61 months.

Solution   From Example 1, $i = .005$, the balance after 60 months is $\$6977.00$, and $R = 100$. Therefore, by (2)

$$[\text{balance after 61 months}] = (1 + .005)[\text{balance after 60 months}] + 100$$
$$= 1.005(6977) + 100 = 7111.89.$$

Therefore, the annuity will have accumulated to $\$7111.89$ after 61 months.   ◆

Formula (1) can also be used to determine the rent necessary to achieve a certain future value:

$$F = s_{\overline{n}|i}R$$
$$R = \frac{F}{s_{\overline{n}|i}} = \frac{1}{s_{\overline{n}|i}}F.$$

Thus we have established the following result.

Suppose that an increasing annuity of n payments has future value F and has interest compounded at the rate i per period. Then the rent R is given by

$$R = \frac{1}{s_{\overline{n}|i}} \cdot F. \tag{3}$$

Table 5 of Appendix A gives values of $1/s_{\overline{n}|i}$ for various values of n and i.

▶ Example 3   Ms. Adams would like to buy a $30,000 airplane when she retires in 8 years. How much should she deposit at the end of each half-year into an account paying 4% interest compounded semiannually so that she will have enough money to purchase the airplane?

Solution   For this increasing annuity, $n = 16$, $i = 2\%$, and $F = 30,000$. Therefore,

$$R = \frac{1}{s_{\overline{n}|i}} \cdot F = \frac{1}{s_{\overline{16}|2\%}} \cdot 30,000 = (.05365013) \cdot 30,000 \qquad \text{(by Table 5)}$$

$$= \$1609.50.$$

She should deposit $1609.50 at the end of each half-year period.   ◆

The *present value* of a decreasing annuity is the amount of money necessary to finance the sequence of annuity payments. More specifically, the present value of the annuity is the amount you would need to deposit in order to provide the desired sequence of annuity payments and leave a balance of zero at the end of the term. Let us now find a formula for the present value of the annuity. There are two ways to proceed. On the one hand, the desired present value could be computed as the sum of the present values of the various annuity payments. This computation would make use of the formula for the sum of the first n terms of a geometric progression. However, there is a much "cleaner" derivation that proceeds indirectly to obtain a formula relating the present value P and the rent R.

As before, let us assume that our annuity consists of n payments made at the ends of interest periods, with interest compounded at a rate i per interest period.

Situation 1: Suppose that the P dollars were just left in the account and that the annuity payments were not withdrawn. At the end of the n interest periods, there would be $(1 + i)^n P$ dollars in the account.

Situation 2: Suppose that the payments are withdrawn but are immediately redeposited into another account having the same rate of interest. At the end of the n interest periods, there would be $s_{\overline{n}|i}R$ dollars in the new account.

In both of these situations, P dollars is deposited and it, together with all the interest generated, is earning income at the same interest rate for the same amount of time. Therefore, the final amounts of money in the accounts should be the same. That is,

$$(1 + i)^n P = s_{\overline{n}|i}R, \qquad \text{so that} \qquad P = \frac{s_{\overline{n}|i}}{(1 + i)^n} \cdot R.$$

Let us now substitute the value of $s_{\overline{n}|i}$, namely $[(1+i)^n - 1]/i$, into the preceding formula. If we denote by $a_{\overline{n}|i}$ the expression

$$a_{\overline{n}|i} = \frac{(1 + i)^n - 1}{i(1 + i)^n},$$

then the preceding formula may be written in the simple form

$$P = a_{\overline{n}|i}R, \qquad \text{or} \qquad R = \frac{1}{a_{\overline{n}|i}}P.$$

Tables 6 and 7 of Appendix A give, respectively, the values of $a_{\overline{n}|i}$ and $1/a_{\overline{n}|i}$ for various values of n and i. Let us record the main result of our preceding discussion.

The present value P and the rent R of a decreasing annuity of n payments with interest compounded at a rate i per interest period are related by the formulas

$$P = a_{\overline{n}|i} R, \qquad R = \frac{1}{a_{\overline{n}|i}} P.$$

▶ **Example 4** How much money must you deposit now at 6% interest compounded quarterly in order to be able to withdraw $3000 at the end of each quarter year for 2 years?

Solution For this decreasing annuity, $R = 3000$, $i = 1.5\%$, and $n = 8$. We are asked to calculate the present value of the sequence of payments.

$$P = a_{\overline{n}|i} R = a_{\overline{8}|1.5\%} \cdot 3000 = (7.48592508) \cdot 3000 \qquad \text{(by Table 6)}$$
$$= \$22{,}457.78 \qquad\qquad ◆$$

The Excel spreadsheet in Table 2 shows the effect of interest rates (compounded quarterly) on the present value where the duration of the decreasing annuity is two years. [For those familiar with Excel, the entry in cell B5 was set to `=PV(A5/4,8,-$B$1)`. The form of the present value function is `PV(`*rate, nper, pmt*`)`. The payment was specified as a negative number since money is being withdrawn from the account. The remainder of the B column was created with the AutoFill option from the Edit/Fill/Series dialog box. The dollar signs in `$B$1` prevents references to this location from being changed by AutoFill.]

Table 2

	A	B
1	Rent	$3,000.00
2		
3	Interest	Present
4	rate	value
5	3.00%	$23,209.84
6	3.50%	$23,081.91
7	4.00%	$22,955.03
8	4.50%	$22,829.19
9	5.00%	$22,704.37
10	5.50%	$22,580.57
11	6.00%	$22,457.78
12	6.50%	$22,335.97
13	7.00%	$22,215.16
14	7.50%	$22,095.32
15	8.00%	$21,976.44

▶ **Example 5** If you deposit $10,000 into a fund paying 6% interest compounded monthly, how much can you withdraw at the end of each month for 1 year?

Solution For this decreasing annuity, $P = 10{,}000$, $i = \frac{1}{2}\%$, and $n = 12$. We are asked to calculate the rent for the sequence of payments.

$$R = \frac{1}{a_{\overline{n}|i}} P = \frac{1}{a_{\overline{12}|1/2\%}} \cdot 10{,}000 = (.08606643) \cdot 10{,}000 \qquad \text{(by Table 7)}$$
$$= \$860.66 \qquad\qquad ◆$$

Remark In this section we have considered only annuities with payments made at the end of each interest period. Such annuities are called *ordinary annuities*. Annuities that have payments at the beginning of the interest period are called *annuities due*. Annuities whose payment period is different from the interest period are called *general annuities*.

GC As a time-saving device, the formulas for $s_{\overline{n}|i}$, $\frac{1}{s_{\overline{n}|i}}$, $a_{\overline{n}|i}$, and $\frac{1}{a_{\overline{n}|i}}$ can be assigned to functions in the **Y=** editor. In Fig. 1, the formulas have been stored in **Y₄** through **Y₇** to correspond to the table numbers in Appendix A. Here **X**, instead of n, is used to represent the number of periods. (*Note*: To display **Y₄** with a TI-83, press [VARS] [▶] **1 4**. With a TI-82, press [2nd] [Y-VARS] **1 4**.) These functions have been deselected since we want to use them, but not graph them. Figure 2 shows two ways the value of $s_{\overline{60}|1/10\%}$ can be displayed on the home screen.

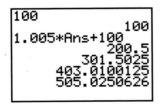

Figure 1.

Figure 2.

Graphing calculators can easily display successive balances in an annuity[1]. Consider the situation from Example 1 in which $100 is deposited at the end of each month at 6% interest compounded monthly. In Fig. 3 successive balances are displayed in the home screen. In Fig. 4 successive balances are graphed, and in Fig. 5 they are displayed in a table.

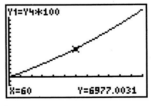
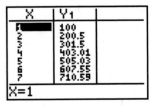

Figure 3.   **Figure 4.**   **Figure 5.**

Displaying successive balances of an increasing annuity on the home screen Successive balances can be determined with the relation $B_{\text{new}} = (1 + i)B_{\text{previous}} + R$. In Fig. 3, after the first payment (**100**) is entered, the last displayed value (**100**) is assigned to **Ans**. The instruction **1.005*Ans+100** generates the next balance (**200.5**) and assigns it to **Ans**. Each subsequent press of the [ENTER] key generates another balance.

Graphing successive balances of an increasing annuity with the TI-82 or TI-83 Figure 6 shows the **Y=** editor, where **Y₁** has been set equal to **Y₄*100**, that is, $s_{\overline{n}|i} \cdot R$. In Fig. 7 the value **.005** is assigned to **I** from the home screen.

---

[1]We limit our discussion here to increasing annuities. The corresponding analysis for decreasing annuities is similar to the analysis for the amortization of loans presented in detail in Section 10.3.

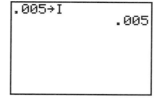

Figure 6.

Figure 7.

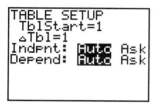

Figure 8.

(*Note*: To display the arrow, press $\boxed{\text{STO} \blacktriangleright}$.) In Fig. 8 the WINDOW screen is set up to display the growth of the balance for 10 years, that is, 120 months. **Ymin** was set to a negative value to allow room for coordinates of points to be displayed at the bottom of the screen. Pressing $\boxed{\text{GRAPH}}$ produces the screen of Fig. 4.

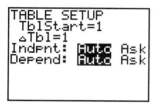

Figure 9.

Obtaining a table of successive balances of an increasing annuity with the TI-82 or TI-83   Pressing $\boxed{\text{2nd}}$ [TBLSET] brings up the TABLE SETUP screen of Fig. 9. The table determined by the settings will have a column for **X** and a column for the values of each function that is selected in the **Y=** editor. The values for **X** will begin with the setting of **TblStart** (**TblMin** on the TI-82) and increase by the setting of **ΔTbl**. For our purposes, the settings for **Indpnt** and **Depend** should always be **Auto**. After you press $\boxed{\text{2nd}}$ [TABLE] to display the table (see Fig. 5), you can use the down-arrow key to generate further balances.

▶ **Example 6**   Consider the situation from Example 1 in which $100 is deposited monthly at 6% interest compounded monthly. Determine when the balance will exceed $10,000.

Solution   There are three ways to answer this question with a graphing calculator—with the home screen, with a graph, and with a table.

1. (Home screen)   Generate successive balances (while keeping track of the number of times the $\boxed{\text{ENTER}}$ key has been pressed) until a balance exceeding 10,000 is reached. See Fig. 10.

2. (Graph)   Set $\mathbf{Y_2 = 10000}$ and find its intersection with the graph of $\mathbf{Y_1 = Y_4*100}$. See Fig. 11.

3. (Table)   Scroll down the table for $\mathbf{Y_1}$ until the balance exceeds 10,000. See Fig. 12.

In each case we see that the balance will exceed $10,000 after 82 months; that is, after 6 years and 10 months.   ◆

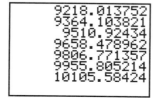

Figure 10.

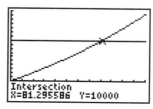

Figure 11.

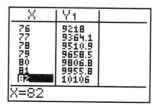

Figure 12.

| Practice Problems 10.2 | Decide whether or not each of the following annuities is an ordinary annuity, that is, the type of annuity considered in this section. If so, identify n, i, and R and calculate the present value or the future value, whichever is appropriate. |

1. You make a deposit at 9% interest compounded monthly into a fund that pays you $1 at the end of each month for 5 years.

2. At the end of each week for 2 years you deposit $10 into a savings account earning 6% interest compounded monthly.

3. At the end of each month for 2 years, you deposit $10 into a savings account earning 6% interest compounded monthly.

▶ Exercises 10.2

1. For each of the following increasing annuities, specify i, n, R, and F.

   (a) If at the end of each month, $50 is deposited into a savings account paying 6% interest compounded monthly, the balance after 10 years will be $8193.97.

   (b) Mr. Smith is saving to buy a $65,000 yacht in the year 2000. Since 1990, he has been depositing $2675.19 at the end of each half-year into a fund paying 4% interest compounded semiannually.

2. For each of the following decreasing annuities, specify i, n, R, and P.

   (a) A retiree deposits $72,582 into a bank paying 6% interest compounded monthly and withdraws $520 at the end of each month for 20 years.

   (b) In order to receive $700 at the end of each quarter-year from 1998 until 2003, Ms. Jones deposited $11,446 into a savings account paying 8% interest compounded quarterly.

3. Calculate the future value of an increasing annuity of $100 per month for 5 years at 6% interest compounded monthly.

4. Calculate the rent of an increasing annuity at 4% interest compounded semiannually if payments are made every half-year and the future value after 7 years is $10,000.

5. Calculate the rent of a decreasing annuity at 8% interest compounded quarterly with payments made every quarter-year for 7 years and present value $100,000.

6. Calculate the present value of a decreasing annuity of $1000 per year for 10 years at 6% interest compounded annually.

7. A person deposits $500 into a savings account at the end of every month for 4 years at 6% interest compounded monthly.

   (a) Find the balance at the end of 4 years.

   (b) How much interest will be earned during the 4 years?

   (c) Prepare a table showing the deposits, balance, and interest for the first three months.

8. A person deposits $800 into a savings account at the end of every quarter-year for 5 years at 6% interest compounded quarterly.

   (a) Find the balance at the end of 5 years.

   (b) How much interest will be earned during the 5 years?

   (c) Prepare a table showing the deposits, balance, and interest for the first three quarters.

9. How much must Jim save each month in order to have $12,000 to buy a new car in 3 years if the interest rate is 6% compounded monthly? How much of the $12,000 does Jim actually deposit and how much of it is interest?

10. Valerie needs $5000 3 years from now in order to pay off a loan. How much must she save each quarter for the next 3 years if interest rates are 8% compounded quarterly? How much of the $5000 will be interest?

11. When Bridget takes a new job, she is offered a $2000 bonus now or the option of an extra $200 each month for the next year. If interest rates are 6% compounded monthly, which choice is better and by how much?

12. When Michael started college, his father gave him $5000 deposited in a savings account earning 6% interest compounded monthly. Michael withdraws $500 a month starting at the beginning of the second month. Prepare a schedule showing the monthly balance in the account for the first four months.

13. A city has a debt of $1,000,000 falling due in 15 years. How much money must it deposit at the end of each half-year into a savings fund at 4% interest compounded semiannually in order to raise this amount?

14. On January 1, 2000, Tom decided to save for exactly 1 year for a 10-speed bike by depositing $10 at the end of each month into a savings account paying 6% interest compounded monthly. How much did he accumulate?

15. During Jack's first year at college, his father had been sending him $100 per month for incidental expenses. For the sophomore year, his father decided instead to make a deposit into a savings account on August 1 and have his son withdraw $100 on the first of each month from September 1 to May 1. If the bank pays 6% interest compounded monthly, how much should Jack's father deposit?

16. Suppose that a magazine subscription costs $9 per year and that you receive a magazine at the end of each month. At an interest rate of 6% compounded monthly, how much are you actually paying for each issue?

17. Is it more profitable to receive $1000 at the end of each month for 10 years or to receive a lump sum of $163,000 at the end of 10 years? Assume that money can earn 6% interest compounded monthly.

18. Is it more profitable to receive a lump sum of $10,000 at the end of 3 years or to receive $750 at the end of each quarter-year for 3 years? Assume that money can earn 8% interest compounded quarterly.

19. Suppose that you deposited $1000 into a savings account on January 1, 1993, and deposited an additional $100 into the account at the end of each quarter-year. If the bank pays 8% interest compounded quarterly, how much will be in the account on January 1, 2002?

20. Suppose that you opened a savings account on January 1, 1998, and made a deposit of $100. In 1999 you began depositing $10 into the account at the end of each month. If the bank pays 6% interest compounded monthly, how much money will be in the account on January 1, 2003?

21. Ms. Jones deposited $100 at the end of each month for 10 years into a savings account earning 6% interest compounded monthly. However, she deposited an additional $1000 at the end of the seventh year. How much money was in the account at the end of the tenth year?

22. Redo Exercise 21 for the situation where Ms. Jones withdrew $1000 at the end of the seventh year instead of depositing it.

23. Suppose you deposit $600 every six months for 5 years into an annuity at 4% interest compounded semiannually. Which of items (a)–(d) can be used to fill in the blank in the following statement? (*Note*: Before computing, use your intuition to guess the correct answer.)

If the _____ doubles, then the amount accumulated will double.

(a) rent

(b) interest rate

(c) number of interest periods per year

(d) number of years

24. Suppose you deposit $100,000 into an annuity at 4% interest compounded semiannually and withdraw an equal amount at the end of each interest period so that the account is depleted after 10 years. Which of items (a)–(d) can be used to fill in the blank in the following statement? (*Note*: Before computing, use your intuition to guess the correct answer.)

If the _____ doubles, then the total amount withdrawn each year will double.

(a) amount deposited

(b) interest rate

(c) number of interest periods per year

(d) number of years

A *perpetuity* is similar to a decreasing annuity, except that the payments continue forever. Exercises 25 and 26 concern such annuities.

25. A grateful alumnus decides to donate a permanent scholarship of $1200 per year. How much money should be deposited in the bank at 5% interest compounded annually in order to be able to supply the money for the scholarship at the end of each year?

26. Show that to establish a perpetuity paying R dollars at the end of each interest period, it requires a deposit of R/i dollars, where i is the interest rate per interest period.

A *deferred annuity* is a type of decreasing annuity whose term is to start at some future date. Exercises 27–30 concern such annuities.

27. On his tenth birthday, a boy inherits $10,000, which is to be used for his college education. The money is deposited into a trust fund that will pay him R dollars on his 18th, 19th, 20th, and 21st birthdays. Find R if the money earns 6% interest compounded annually.

28. Refer to Exercise 27. Find the size of the inheritance that would result in $10,000 per year during the college years (ages 18–21, inclusive).

29. On December 1, 1993, a philanthropist set up a permanent trust fund to buy Christmas presents for needy children. The fund will provide $6000 each year beginning on December 1, 2003. How much must have been set aside in 1993 if the money earns 6% interest compounded annually?

30. Show that the rent paid by a deferred annuity of n payments that are deferred by m interest periods is given by the formula

$$R = \frac{i(1+i)^{n+m}}{(1+i)^n - 1} \cdot P.$$

31. One dollar is deposited in a savings account with an interest rate of i per interest period. At the end of each interest period, the earned interest is withdrawn from the account and deposited into a second account earning the same rate of interest.

(a) How much money will be in the first account after n interest periods?

(b) How much money will be in the second account after n interest periods?

(c) Since both the original deposit and the interest are all on deposit and earning interest throughout the entire n interest periods, the amounts in parts (a) and (b) must add up to $(1+i)^n$. Use this fact to derive

$$s_{\overline{n}|i} = \frac{(1+i)^n - 1}{i}.$$

32. Show that $\dfrac{1}{a_{\overline{n}|i}} - \dfrac{1}{s_{\overline{n}|i}} = i.$

33. Show that $s_{\overline{n+1}|i} = (1+i)s_{\overline{n}|i} + 1.$

34. One hundred dollars is deposited in the bank at the end of each year for 20 years. During the first 5 years, the bank paid 6% interest compounded annually and after that paid 7% interest compounded annually. Show that the account balance after 20 years is

$$(1.07)^{15} \cdot 100s_{\overline{5}|6\%} + 100s_{\overline{15}|7\%}.$$

35. A municipal bond pays 8% interest compounded semi-annually on its face value of $5000. The interest is paid at the end of every half-year period. Fifteen years from now the face value of $5000 will be returned. The current market interest rate is 12% compounded semi-annually. How much should you pay for the bond?

36. A businessperson wishes to lend money for a second mortgage on some local real estate. Suppose that the mortgage pays $500 per month for a 5-year period. Suppose that you can invest your money in certificates of deposit paying 6% interest compounded monthly. How much should you offer for the mortgage?

37. Suppose that a business note for $50,000 carries an interest rate of 18% compounded monthly. Suppose that the business pays only interest for the first 5 years

and then repays the loan amount plus interest in equal monthly installments for the next 5 years.

(a) Calculate the monthly payments during the second 5-year period.

(b) Assume that the current market interest rate for such loans is 12%. How much should you be willing to pay for such a note?

38. A lottery winner is to receive $1000 a month for the next 5 years. How much is this sequence of payments worth today if interest rates are 6% compounded monthly? How is the difference between this amount and the $60,000 paid out beneficial to the agency running the lottery?

Exercises 39–42 require the use of a graphing calculator or a computer.

39. A person deposits $1000 at the end of each year into an annuity earning 5% interest compounded annually. What are the balances (that is, future values) after 1, 2, and 3 years? How many years are required for the balance to reach $30,539? After how many years will the balance exceed $50,000?

40. A person deposits $700 at the end of each quarter-year into an annuity earning 8% interest compounded quarterly. What are the balances (that is, future values) after 1, 2, and 3 quarters? How many quarters are required for the balance to reach $5204? After how many quarters will the balance exceed $10,000?

41. Jane has taken a part-time job to save for a $503 racing bike. If she puts $15 each week into a savings account paying 5.2% interest compounded weekly, when will she be able to buy the bike?

42. Bob needs $3228 to have some repairs done on his house. He decides to deposit $100 at the end of each month into an annuity earning 6% interest compounded monthly. When will he be able to do the repairs?

Solutions to Practice Problems 10.2

1. An ordinary decreasing annuity with $n = 60$, $i = \frac{3}{4}\%$, and $R = 1$. You will make a deposit now, in the present, and then withdraw money each month. The amount of this deposit is the present value of the annuity.

$$P = a_{\overline{n}|i}R = a_{\overline{60}|.75\%} \cdot 1 = (48.17337352) \cdot 1 \quad \text{(by Table 6)}$$
$$= \$48.17$$

[*Notes:* (1) When $R = 1$, we have $P = a_{\overline{n}|i}$. This explains why $a_{\overline{n}|i}$ is often called the *present value of $1*. (2) For this transaction, the future value of the annuity has no significance. At the end of 5 years, the fund will have a balance of 0.]

2. Not an ordinary annuity since the payment period (1 week) is different from the interest period (1 month).

3. An ordinary increasing annuity with $n = 24$, $i = .5\%$, and $R = \$10$. There is no money in the account now, in the present. However, in 2 years, in the future, money will have accumulated. So for this annuity, only the future value has significance.

$$F = s_{\overline{n}|i}R = s_{\overline{24}|.5\%} \cdot 10 = (25.43195524) \cdot 10 \quad \text{(by Table 4)}$$
$$= \$254.32$$

10.3 Amortization of Loans

In this section we analyze the mathematics of paying off loans. The loans we shall consider all will be repaid in a sequence of equal payments at regular time intervals, with the payment intervals coinciding with the interest periods. The process of paying off such a loan is called *amortization*. In order to obtain a feeling for the amortization process, let us consider a particular case, the amortization of a $563 loan to buy a television set. Suppose that this loan charges interest at a 12% rate with interest compounded monthly and that the monthly payments are $116 for 5 months. The repayment process is summarized in Table 1.

Table 1

Payment number	Amount	Interest	Applied to principal	Unpaid balance
1	$116	$5.63	$110.37	$452.63
2	116	4.53	111.47	341.16
3	116	3.41	112.59	228.57
4	116	2.29	113.71	114.85
5	116	1.15	114.85	0.00

Note the following facts about the financial transactions.

1. Payments are made at the end of each month. The payments have been carefully calculated to pay off the debt, with interest, in the specified time interval.

2. Since $i = 1\%$, the interest to be paid each month is 1% of the unpaid balance at the end of the previous month. That is, 5.63 is 1% of 563, 4.53 is 1% of 452.63, and so on.

3. Although we write just one check each month for $116, we regard part of the check as being applied to payment of that month's interest. The remainder, namely $116 - [\text{interest}]$, is regarded as being applied to repayment of the principal amount.

4. The unpaid balance at the end of each month is the previous unpaid balance minus the portion of the payment applied to the principal. A loan can be paid off early by paying just the current unpaid balance.

The four factors that describe the amortization process just described are as follows:

the principal	$563
the interest rate	12% compounded monthly
the term	5 months
the monthly payment	$116

The important fact to recognize is that the sequence of payments in the preceding amortization constitutes a decreasing annuity, with the person taking out the loan paying the interest. Therefore, the mathematical tools developed in Section 10.2 suffice to analyze the amortization. In particular, we could determine the monthly payment or the principal once the other three factors have been specified.

▶ Example 1   Suppose that a loan has an interest rate of 12% compounded monthly and a term of 5 months.

(a) Given that the principal is $563, calculate the monthly payment.
(b) Given that the monthly payment is $116, calculate the principal.
(c) Given that the monthly payment is $116, calculate the unpaid balance after 3 months.

Solution   The sequence of payments constitutes a decreasing annuity with the monthly payments as rent and the principal as the present value. Also, $n = 5$ and $i = 1\%$.

(a) Since $R = (1/a_{\overline{n}|\,i})P$, we see that

$$R = \frac{1}{a_{\overline{5}|\,1\%}} \cdot 563 = (.20603980) \cdot 563 \qquad \text{(by Table 7)}$$
$$= \$116.$$

(b) Since $P = a_{\overline{n}|\,i}R$, we see that

$$P = a_{\overline{5}|\,1\%} \cdot 116 = (4.85343124) \cdot 116 = \$563.00. \quad \text{(by Table 6)}$$

(c) The unpaid balance is most easily calculated by regarding it as the amount necessary to retire the debt. Therefore, it must be sufficient to generate, with interest, the sequence of two remaining payments. That is, the unpaid balance is the present value of a decreasing annuity of two payments of $116. So we see that

$$[\text{unpaid balance after 3 months}] = a_{\overline{2}|\,1\%} \cdot 116 = (1.97039506) \cdot 116$$
$$= \$228.57. \qquad \blacklozenge$$

A mortgage is a long-term loan used to purchase real estate. The real estate is used as collateral to guarantee the loan.

▶ Example 2   On December 31, 1990, a house was purchased with the buyer taking out a 30-year, $112,475 mortgage at 9% interest, compounded monthly. The mortgage payments are made at the end of each month.

(a) Calculate the amount of the monthly payment.
(b) Calculate the unpaid balance of the loan on December 31, 2016, just after the 312th payment.
(c) How much interest will be paid during the month of January 2017?
(d) How much of the principal will be paid off during the year 2016?

(e) How much interest will be paid during the year 2016?

Solution   (a) Denote the monthly payment by R. Then \$112,475 is the present value of an annuity of $n = 360$ payments, with $i = \frac{3}{4}\%$. Therefore,

$$R = \frac{1}{a\,\overline{n}|\,i} P = \frac{1}{a\,\overline{360}|\,.75\%} \cdot 112{,}475$$

$$= (.00804623) \cdot 112{,}475 \qquad \text{(by Table 7)}$$

$$= \$905.00.$$

(b) The remaining payments constitute an annuity of 48 payments. Therefore, the unpaid balance is the present value of that annuity.

$$[\text{unpaid balance}] = a\,\overline{n}|\,i\,R = a\,\overline{48}|\,.75\% \cdot 905$$

$$= (40.18478189) \cdot 905 \qquad \text{(by Table 6)}$$

$$= \$36{,}367.23$$

(c) The interest paid during 1 month is i, the interest rate per month, times the unpaid balance at the end of the preceding month. Therefore,

$$[\text{interest for January 2017}] = \tfrac{3}{4}\% \text{ of } \$36{,}367.23$$

$$= .0075 \cdot 36{,}367.23$$

$$= \$272.75.$$

(d) Since the portions of the monthly payments applied to repay the principal have the effect of reducing the unpaid balance, this question may be answered by calculating how much the unpaid balance will be reduced during 2016. Reasoning as in part (b), we determine that the unpaid balance on December 31, 2015 (just after the 300th payment), is equal to \$43,596.90. Therefore,

[amount of principal repaid in 2016]

$$= [\text{unpaid balance Dec. 31, 2015}] - [\text{unpaid balance Dec. 31, 2016}]$$

$$= \$43{,}596.90 - \$36{,}367.23 = \$7229.67.$$

(e) During the year 2016, the total amount paid is $12 \times 905 = \$10{,}860$. But by part (d), \$7229.67 is applied to repayment of principal, the remainder being applied to interest.

$$[\text{interest in 2016}] = [\text{total amount paid}] - [\text{principal repaid in 2016}]$$

$$= \$10{,}860 - \$7229.67 = \$3630.33 \qquad \blacklozenge$$

In the early years of a mortgage, most of each monthly payment is applied to interest. For the mortgage described in Example 2, the interest portion will exceed the principal portion until the twenty-third year.

Each new (unpaid) balance can be computed from the previous balance with the formula

$$B_{\text{new}} = (1 + i)B_{\text{previous}} - R.$$

That is, the new balance equals the growth of the previous balance due to interest, minus the amount paid. Successive balances are computed by multiplying by $(1 + i)$ and subtracting R.

If \$$P$ is borrowed at interest rate i per period and \$$R$ is paid back at the end of each interest period, then the formula

$$B_{\text{new}} = (1+i)B_{\text{previous}} - R \qquad (1)$$

can be used to calculate each new balance, B_{new}, from the previous balance, B_{previous}.

The Excel spreadsheet in Table 2 calculates the payment per period and shows the successive balances for the annuity of Example 2. [For those familiar with Excel, the entry in cell B4 was set to =PMT(B1,B2,-B3). The form of the payment function is PMT(*rate*,*nper*,*pv*). The present value, that is, the principal, was specified as a negative number since the money is owed to the bank. B10 was set to B3 and B11 was set to (1+\$B\$1)*B10-\$B\$4. The remainder of the B column was created with the AutoFill option from the Edit/Fill/Series dialog box. C11 was set to \$B\$1*B10 and D11 was set to \$B\$4-C11. The remainder of the C and D columns was created with the AutoFill option.]

▶ **Example 3** Refer to Example 2. Compute the unpaid balance of the loan on January 31, 2017, just after the 313th payment.

Solution By formula (1),

$$B_{\text{Jan}} = (1+i)B_{\text{Dec}} - R = (1.0075) \cdot 36{,}367.23 - 905$$
$$= \$35{,}734.98.$$

Sometimes amortized loans stipulate a *balloon payment* at the end of the term. For instance, you might pay \$200 at the end of each quarter-year for 3 years and an additional \$1000 at the end of the third year. The \$1000 is a balloon payment.

Table 2 **Amortization Table**

	A	B	C	D
1	Interest rate	0.75%		
2	Number of periods	360		
3	Principal	\$112,475.00		
4	Payment per period	\$905.00		
5				
6		Amortization Table		
7				
8		Unpaid		Applied to
9	Payment number	balance	Interest	principal
10	0	\$112,475.00		
11	1	\$112,413.56	\$843.56	\$61.44
12	2	\$112,351.66	\$843.10	\$61.90
13	3	\$112,289.30	\$842.64	\$62.36
14	4	\$112,226.47	\$842.17	\$62.83
15	5	\$112,163.17	\$841.70	\$63.30
16	6	\$112,099.39	\$841.22	\$63.78
17	7	\$112,035.14	\$840.75	\$64.25
18	8	\$111,970.40	\$840.26	\$64.74
19	9	\$111,905.18	\$839.78	\$65.22
20	10	\$111,839.47	\$839.29	\$65.71
21	11	\$111,773.27	\$838.80	\$66.20
22	12	\$111,706.57	\$838.30	\$66.70

	A	B	C	D
359	349	\$9,521.20	\$77.61	\$827.38
360	350	\$8,687.61	\$71.41	\$833.59
361	351	\$7,847.77	\$65.16	\$839.84
362	352	\$7,001.63	\$58.86	\$846.14
363	353	\$6,149.14	\$52.51	\$852.49
364	354	\$5,290.26	\$46.12	\$858.88
365	355	\$4,424.94	\$39.68	\$865.32
366	356	\$3,553.13	\$33.19	\$871.81
367	357	\$2,674.78	\$26.65	\$878.35
368	358	\$1,789.84	\$20.06	\$884.94
369	359	\$898.26	\$13.42	\$891.58
370	360	\$0.00	\$6.74	\$898.26
371		Unpaid		Applied to
372	Payment number	balance	Interest	principal

▶ **Example 4**   How much money can you borrow at 8% interest compounded quarterly if you agree to pay $200 at the end of each quarter-year for 3 years and in addition a balloon payment of $1000 at the end of the third year?

Solution   Here you are borrowing in the present and repaying in the future. The amount of the loan will be the present value of *all* the future payments. The future payments consist of an annuity and a lump-sum payment. Let us calculate the present values of each of these separately. Now, $i = 2\%$ and $n = 12$.

$$[\text{present value of annuity}] = a_{\overline{n}\rceil i} R = a_{\overline{12}\rceil 2\%} \cdot 200$$
$$= (10.57534122) \cdot 200 \quad (\text{by Table 6})$$
$$= \$2115.07$$

$$[\text{present value of balloon payment}] = \frac{1}{(1+i)^n} \cdot F$$
$$= \frac{1}{(1+i)^n} \cdot 1000 \quad (\text{for } i = 2\% \text{ and } n = 12)$$
$$= .78849318 \cdot (1000) = \$788.49$$

Therefore, the amount you can borrow is

$$\$2115.07 + \$788.49 = \$2903.56. \qquad \blacklozenge$$

GC   As in Section 10.2, we will assume that the formulas for $s_{\overline{n}\rceil i}$, $\frac{1}{s_{\overline{n}\rceil i}}$, $a_{\overline{n}\rceil i}$, and $\frac{1}{a_{\overline{n}\rceil i}}$ have been assigned to the functions $\mathbf{Y_4}$ through $\mathbf{Y_7}$.

Graphing calculators can easily display successive balances for a loan. Consider the situation from Example 2 in which $112,475 is borrowed at 9% interest compounded monthly and repaid with 360 monthly payments of $905. In Fig. 1 successive balances are displayed in the home screen. In Fig. 2 successive balances are graphed, and in Fig. 3 they are displayed as part of an amortization table. (The $\mathbf{Y_2}$ column gives the interest portion of the monthly payment.)

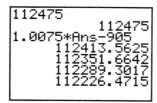   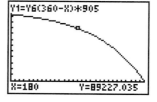

Figure 1.   Figure 2.   Figure 3.

Displaying successive balances on the home screen   Successive balances can be determined with the relation $B_{\text{new}} = (1 + i)B_{\text{previous}} - R$. In Fig. 1, after the principal (**112475**) is entered, the last displayed value (**112475**) is assigned to **Ans**. The instruction **1.0075*Ans-905** generates the next balance (**112413.5625**) and assigns it to **Ans**. Each subsequent press of the ENTER key generates another balance.

Graphing successive balances with the TI-82 or TI-83   Figure 4 shows the $\mathbf{Y=}$ editor where $\mathbf{Y_1}$ has been set equal to $\mathbf{Y_6(360-X)*905}$, that is, $a_{\overline{360-n}\rceil i} \cdot R$. In Fig. 5 the value .0075 is assigned to $\mathbf{I}$ from the home screen. In Fig. 6 the WINDOW screen is set up to display the decline of the balance for 30 years, that is, 360 months. **Ymin** was set to a negative value to allow room for coordinates of points to be displayed at the bottom of the screen. Pressing GRAPH produces the screen of Fig. 2.

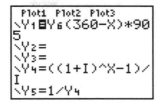

Figure 4.

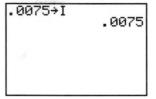

Figure 5.

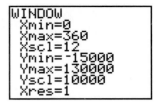

Figure 6.

Obtaining a table of successive balances with the TI-82 or TI-83   In the **Y=** editor, set $Y_2 = I*Y_1(X-1)$, that is, the interest rate times the amount of the previous balance. Also, set $Y_3 = 905 - Y_2$. Then the columns for Y_2 and Y_3 will give the interest and debt-reduction portions of the monthly payment. In Fig. 7 we have set **TblStart=354** to view the final 7 months of the mortgage. Figure 3 shows the resulting table. If you press ▶ three times, you also will see a column for Y_3. See Fig. 8. (*Note:* The values shown in Fig. 3 agree with the values in the Excel spreadsheet of Table 2. However, early values for the balance in the calculator table will differ slightly from those generated by the Excel spreadsheet and those shown in Fig. 1. This is due both to the effects of roundoff and the different methods used to generate the numbers. The values for interest and debt reduction will be the same throughout.)

Figure 7.   **Figure 8.**

▶ **Example 5**   Consider the situation from Example 2 in which $112,475 is borrowed at 9% interest compounded monthly and repaid with 360 monthly payments of $905. When will the debt-reduction portion of the payment surpass the interest portion?

Solution   The question can be answered with a table or a graph.

  1. (Table)   Consider the table of Fig. 3. Scroll up until an interest greater than half the monthly payment, that is, 452.50 is reached. Then press ▶ three times to obtain Fig. 9.

  2. (Graph)   Let Y_2 and Y_3 be the interest and debt-reduction functions as in part 1. Set the window as in Fig. 10, graph the two functions, and find their point of intersection. See Fig. 11.

In each case we see that debt reduction will exceed interest after 269 months; that is, after 22 years and 5 months.   ◆

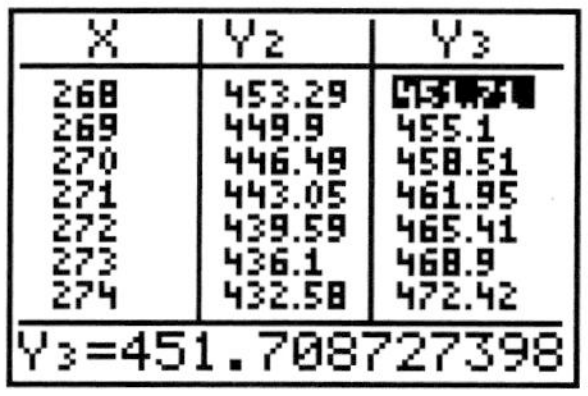

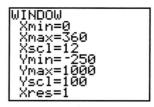

Figure 9.

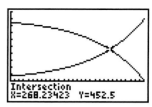

Figure 10.

Figure 11.

**Practice Problems
10.3**

1. The word "amortization" comes from the French "a mort," meaning "at the point of death." Justify the word.

2. Explain why only present values and not future values arise in amortization problems.

▶ **Exercises 10.3**

1. A loan of $10,000 is to be repaid with monthly payments for 5 years at 6% interest compounded monthly. Calculate the monthly payment.

2. Find the monthly payment on a $100,000, 25-year mortgage at 12% interest compounded monthly.

3. How much money can you borrow at 12% interest compounded semiannually if the loan is to be repaid at half-year intervals for 10 years and you can afford to pay $1000 per half-year?

4. You buy a car with a down payment of $500 and $100 per month for 3 years. If the interest rate is 9% compounded monthly, how much did the car cost?

5. Consider a $58,331, 30-year mortgage at interest rate 12% compounded monthly with a $600 monthly payment.

   (a) How much interest is paid the first month?

   (b) How much of the first month's payment is applied to paying off the principal?

   (c) What is the unpaid balance after 1 month?

   (d) What is the unpaid balance at the end of 25 years?

   (e) How much of the principal is repaid during the 26th year?

   (f) How much interest is paid during the 301st month?

6. Consider a $21,281.27 loan for 7 years at 8% interest compounded quarterly and a payment of $1000 per quarter-year.

   (a) Compute the unpaid balance after 5 years.

   (b) How much interest is paid during the fifth year?

   (c) How much principal is repaid in the first payment?

   (d) What is the total amount of interest paid on the loan?

7. Susie takes out a car loan for $8000 for a term of 3 years at 12% interest compounded monthly.

   (a) Find her monthly payments.

   (b) Find the total amount she pays for the car.

   (c) Find the total amount of interest she pays.

   (d) Find the amount she still owes after 1 year.

   (e) Find the amount she still owes after 2 years.

   (f) Find the total interest she pays in year 2.

   (g) Prepare an amortization schedule for the first 4 months.

8. James buys a house for $90,000. He puts $10,000 down and then finances the rest at 9% interest compounded monthly for 25 years.

   (a) Find his monthly payments.

   (b) Find the total amount he pays for the house.

   (c) Find the total amount of interest he pays.

   (d) Find the amount he still owes after 23 years.

   (e) Find the amount he still owes after 24 years.

   (f) Find the total amount of interest he pays in year 24.

   (g) Prepare the amortization schedule for the first 3 months.

9. A mortgage at 9% interest compounded monthly with a monthly payment of $1125 has an unpaid balance of $10,000 after 350 months. Find the unpaid balance after 351 months.

10. A loan with a quarterly payment of $1500 has an unpaid balance of $10,000 after 30 quarters and an unpaid balance of $9000 after 31 quarters. If interest is compounded quarterly, find the interest rate.

11. A loan is to be amortized over an 8-year term at 12% interest compounded semiannually, payments of $1000 every 6 months, and a balloon payment of $10,000 at the end of the term. Calculate the amount of the loan.

12. A loan of $105,504.50 is to be amortized over a 5-year term at 12% interest compounded monthly with monthly payments and a $10,000 balloon payment at the end of the term. Calculate the monthly payment.

13. Write out a complete amortization schedule (as in Table 1 at the beginning of this section) for the amortization of a $1000 loan with monthly payments at 12% interest compounded monthly for 4 months.

14. Write out a complete schedule (as in Table 1) for the amortization of a $10,000 loan with payments every 6 months at 12% interest compounded semiannually for 1 year.

15. You purchase a $120,000 house, pay $20,000 down, and take out a 30-year mortgage with monthly payments, at an interest rate of 9% compounded monthly. How much money will you be paying each month?

16. In 1990 you purchased a house and took out a 25-year, $50,000 mortgage at 6% interest compounded monthly. In 2000 you sold the house for $150,000. How much money did you have left after you paid the bank the unpaid balance on the mortgage?

17. You are considering the purchase of a condominium to use as a rental property. You estimate that you can rent the condominium for $1200 per month and that taxes, insurance, and maintenance costs will run about $200 per month. If interest rates are 9% compounded monthly, how large a 25-year mortgage can you assume and still have the rental income cover the monthly expenses?

18. Consider formula (1). Derive an analogous formula for the balance of an annuity for which regular payments are deposited into a savings account and accrue with interest.

19. A car is purchased for $6287.10 with $2000 down and a loan to be repaid at $100 a month for 3 years followed by a balloon payment. If the interest rate is 6% compounded monthly, how large will the balloon payment be?

20. A real estate speculator purchases a tract of land for $1 million and assumes a 25-year mortgage at 12% interest compounded monthly.

    (a) What is his monthly payment?

    (b) Suppose that at the end of 5 years the mortgage is changed to a 10-year term for the remaining balance. What is the new monthly payment?

    (c) Suppose that after 5 more years, the mortgage is required to be repaid in full. How much will then be due?

21. Suppose you borrow $10,000 at 4% interest compounded semiannually and pay off the loan in 7 years. Which of items (a)–(d) can be used to fill in the blank in the following statement? (*Note*: Before computing, use your intuition to guess the correct answer.)

If the _____ is doubled, then the total amount paid will double.

(a) amount of the loan

(b) interest rate

(c) number of interest periods per year

(d) duration of the loan

22. Suppose you borrow money at 4% interest compounded semiannually and pay off the loan in payments of $1000 per interest period for 5 years. Which of items (a)–(d) can be used to fill in the blank in the following statement? (*Note*: Before computing, use your intuition to guess the correct answer.)

If the _____ is doubled, then the amount that can be borrowed will double.

(a) amount paid per interest period

(b) interest rate

(c) number of interest periods per year

(d) duration of the loan

23. Suppose that you make annual payments of $5000 for 20 years into an annuity paying 6% interest compounded annually.

    (a) What is the value of the annuity at the end of the 20th year?

    (b) Suppose that you elect to have your annuity repaid to you over a 10-year period in annual installments. What is the annual payment you will receive?

    (c) Suppose that after you receive payments for 5 years you elect to have the remainder of your annuity paid to you in a lump sum. How much will you receive?

A *sinking fund* is a pool of money accumulated by a corporation or government to repay a specific debt at some future date.

24. A corporation wishes to deposit money into a sinking fund at the end of each half-year in order to repay $50 million in bonds in 10 years. It can expect to receive a 12% (compounded semiannually) return on its deposits to the sinking fund. How much should the deposits be?

25. The Federal National Mortgage Association ("Fannie Mae") puts $30 million at the end of each month into a sinking fund paying 12% interest compounded monthly. The sinking fund is to be used to repay debentures that mature 15 years from the creation of the fund. How large is the face amount of the debentures assuming the sinking fund will exactly pay them off?

26. A corporation borrows $5 million to erect a new headquarters. The financing is arranged using industrial development bonds, to be repaid in 15 years. How much should it deposit into a sinking fund at the end

of each quarter if the sinking fund earns 8% interest compounded quarterly?

27. A corporation sets up a sinking fund to replace some aging machinery. It deposits $100,000 into the fund at the end of each month for 10 years. The sinking fund earns 12% interest compounded monthly. The equipment originally cost $6 million. However, the cost of the equipment is rising 6% each year. Will the sinking fund be adequate to replace the equipment? If not, how much additional money is needed?

28. A corporation sets up a sinking fund to replace an aging warehouse. The cost of the warehouse today would be $8 million. However, the corporation plans to replace the warehouse in 5 years. It estimates that the cost of the warehouse will increase by 10% annually. The sinking fund will earn 12% interest compounded monthly. What should be the monthly payments to the sinking fund?

Exercises 29–34 require the use of a graphing calculator or a computer.

29. Bill buys a computer for $2188.91 and pays off the loan (at 9% interest compounded monthly) by paying $100 at the end of each month. Determine the balance after 1, 2, and 3 months. After how many months will the loan be paid off?

30. Alice borrows $20,000 to buy some medical equipment and pays off the loan (at 7% interest compounded annually) by paying $4195.92 at the end of each year. Determine the balance after 1, 3, and 5 years. After how many years will the loan be paid off?

31. A loan of $10,000 at 9% interest compounded monthly is repaid in 80 months with monthly payments of $166.68. How much of the loan will have been paid off after 40 months? When will more than half of the loan have been repaid?

32. A loan of $4000 at 6% interest compounded monthly is repaid in 8 years with monthly payments of $52.57. After how many months will the loan be one-quarter paid off? One-half? Three-quarters?

33. A 25-year mortgage of $124,188.57 at 8.5% interest compounded monthly has monthly payments of $1000. After how many months will at least 75% of the monthly payment go toward debt reduction?

34. A 30-year mortgage of $118,135.40 at 8.4% interest compounded monthly has monthly payments of $900. After how many months will the amount applied to debt reduction be more than twice the amount applied to interest?

Solutions to Practice Problems 10.3

1. A portion of each payment is applied to reducing the debt, and by the end of the term the debt is totally annihilated.

2. The debt is formed when the creditor gives you a lump sum of money now, in the present. The lump sum of money is gradually repaid by you, with interest, thereby generating the annuity. At the end of the term, in the future, the loan is totally paid off, so there is no more debt. That is, the future value is always zero!

   Remark You are actually functioning like a savings bank, since you are paying the interest. Think of the creditor as depositing the lump sum with you and then making regular withdrawals until the balance is 0.

▶ Chapter 10 Summary

1. Money deposited into a *savings account* earns interest at regular time periods. Interest paid on the initial deposit only is called *simple interest*. Interest paid on the current balance (that is, on the initial deposit *and* the accumulated interest) is called *compound interest*.

2. An *increasing* (*decreasing*) *annuity* is a sequence of equal deposits (withdrawals) made at the ends of regular time intervals.

3. A *mortgage* is a type of loan that is paid off in equal payments at the ends of regular time periods.

4. The following letters and symbols are used to describe savings accounts, annuities, and loans.

   P *principal*, the initial amount of money deposited

   into a savings account *or* the amount of money borrowed in a loan. P also represents the *present value* of a sum of money to be received in the future; that is, the amount of money needed to generate the future money.

   r *annual rate of interest*, interest rate stated by the bank and used to calculate the interest rate per period.

   m *number of* (*compound*) *interest periods per year*, most commonly 1, 4, or 12.

   i *compound interest rate per period*, calculated as $\frac{r}{m}$.

n *number of interest periods.*

F *future value, compound amount,* or *balance,* value in a savings account or an annuity at some point in the future. For a savings account, $F = (1 + i)^n P$ with compound interest, and $F = (1+nr)P$ with simple interest.

r_{eff} *effective rate of interest,* the simple interest rate that yields the same amount after one year as the annual rate of interest. $r_{\text{eff}} = (1 + i)^m - 1$.

R *rent,* periodic deposit into or withdrawal from an annuity *or* periodic payment on a loan.

$s_{\overline{n}|i}$ *s sub n angle i,* future value of an increasing annuity of n \$1 payments at compound interest rate i per period. For an annuity, $F = s_{\overline{n}|i}R$ and $R = \dfrac{1}{s_{\overline{n}|i}}F$.

$$s_{\overline{n}|i} = \frac{(1+i)^n - 1}{i}$$

$a_{\overline{n}|i}$ *a sub n angle i,* present value of a decreasing annuity of n \$1 payments at compound interest rate

i per period. For an annuity or loan, $P = a_{\overline{n}|i}R$ and $R = \dfrac{1}{a_{\overline{n}|i}}P$.

$$a_{\overline{n}|i} = \frac{(1+i)^n - 1}{i(1+i)^n}$$

5. At any time, the *balance* of a loan is the amount of money needed to retire (that is, pay off) the loan. It is calculated as the present value of all future payments. A payment used to retire a loan is called a *balloon payment.*

6. Successive balances can be calculated with the following formulas.

$$B_{\text{new}} = (1+i)B_{\text{previous}} \qquad \text{savings account with compound interest}$$

$$B_{\text{new}} = (1+i)B_{\text{previous}} + R \quad \text{increasing annuity}$$

$$B_{\text{new}} = (1+i)B_{\text{previous}} - R \quad \text{loan or decreasing annuity}$$

Review of Fundamental Concepts of Chapter 10

1. What is meant by *principal*?
2. What is the difference between compound interest and simple interest?
3. What is meant by the *compound amount* or *balance*?
4. How is interest per period determined from annual interest?
5. Explain how compound interest works.
6. Explain how simple interest works.
7. What is meant by the *present value* of a sum of money to be received in the future?
8. Explain the difference between the *nominal* and *effective* rates for compound interest.
9. What is an annuity?
10. What is meant by the *future value* of an annuity? *present value*? *rent*?

11. Describe the two types of annuities discussed in this chapter. In each case, identify the present and future values.
12. Give the formula for computing a new balance from a previous balance for each type of annuity.
13. Define $s_{\overline{n}|i}$ and $a_{\overline{n}|i}$.
14. State the four formulas involving $s_{\overline{n}|i}$, $a_{\overline{n}|i}$, and their reciprocals.
15. What are the components of an amortization table of a loan, and how are they calculated?
16. Give the formula for computing a new balance from a previous balance for a loan.
17. What is a balloon payment?

▶ Chapter 10 Supplementary Exercises

1. (PE) If \$100 earns 6% interest compounded annually, the compound amount after 10 years is
   (a) $(100.06)^{10}$ (b) $100 + 10(1.06)$ (c) $100(1.6)^{10}$
   (d) $100(1.06)^{10}$ (e) $100 + (0.06)^{10}$

2. Mr. West wishes to purchase a condominium for \$80,000 cash upon his retirement 10 years from now. How much should he deposit at the end of each month into an annuity paying 6% interest compounded monthly in order to accumulate the required savings?

3. The income of a typical family in a certain city is currently \$19,200 per year. Family finance experts recommend that mortgage payments not exceed 25% of a family's income. Assuming a current mortgage interest rate of 9% compounded monthly for a 30-year mortgage with monthly payments, how large a mortgage can the typical family in that city afford?

4. Calculate the compound amount of \$50 after a year if deposited at 7.3% compounded daily.

5. Which is a better investment: 10% compounded annually or 9% compounded daily?

6. Ms. Smith deposits $200 per month into a bond fund yielding 6% interest compounded monthly. How much are her holdings worth after 5 years?

7. A real estate investor takes out a $200,000 mortgage subject to the following terms: For the first 5 years, the payments will be the same as the monthly payments on a 15-year mortgage at 12% interest compounded monthly. The balance will then be payable in full.

   (a) What are the monthly payments for the first 5 years?

   (b) What balance will be owed after 5 years?

8. College expenses at a private college currently average $24,000 per year. It is estimated that these expenses are increasing at the rate of $\frac{1}{2}$% per month. What is the estimated cost of a year of college 10 years from now?

9. What is the present value of $50,000 in 10 years at 6% interest compounded monthly?

10. An investment will pay $10,000 in 2 years and then $5,000 in 3 years. If the current market interest rate is 6% compounded monthly, what should a rational person be willing to pay for the investment?

11. A woman purchases a car for $12,000. She pays $3,000 as a down payment and finances the remaining amount at 6% interest compounded monthly for 4 years. What is her monthly car payment?

12. A businessman buys a $100,000 piece of manufacturing equipment on the following terms: Interest will be charged at a rate of 4% compounded semiannually, but no payments will be made until 2 years after purchase. Starting at that time, equal semiannual payments will be made for 5 years. Determine the semiannual payment.

13. A retired person has set aside a fund of $105,003.50 for his retirement. This fund is in a bank account paying 6% interest compounded monthly. How much can he draw out of the account at the end of each month so that there is a balance of $30,000 at the end of 15 years? (*Hint*: First compute the present value of the $30,000.)

14. A business loan of $509,289.22 is to be paid off in monthly payments for 10 years with a $100,000 balloon payment at the end of the 10th year. The interest rate on the loan is 12% compounded monthly. Calculate the monthly payment.

15. Ms. Jones saves $100 per month for 30 years at 6% interest compounded monthly. How much are her accumulated savings worth?

16. An apartment building is currently generating an income of $2000 per month. Its owners are considering a 10-year second mortgage at 12% interest compounded monthly in order to pay for repairs. How large a second mortgage can the income of the apartment house support?

17. Investment A generates $1000 at the end of each year for 10 years. Investment B generates $5000 at the end of the fifth year and $5000 at the end of the tenth year. Assume a market rate of interest of 6% compounded annually. Which is the better investment?

18. A 5-year bond has a face value of $1000 and is currently selling for $800. The bond pays $5 interest at the end of each month and, in addition, will repay the $1000 face value at the end of the fifth year. The market rate of interest is currently 9% compounded monthly. Is the bond a bargain? Why or why not?

19. Calculate the effective rate for 10% interest compounded semiannually.

20. Calculate the effective rate for 18% interest compounded monthly.

21. A person makes an initial deposit of $10,000 into a savings account and then deposits $1000 at the end of each quarter-year for 15 years. If the interest rate is 8% compounded quarterly, how much money will be in the account after 15 years?

22. A $10,000 car loan at 6% interest compounded monthly is to be repaid with 36 equal monthly payments. Write out an amortization schedule for the first 6 months of the loan.

23. A person pays $200 at the end of each month for 10 years into a fund paying 1% interest per month compounded monthly. At the end of the 10th year, the payments cease, but the balance continues to earn interest. What is the value of the balance at the end of the 20th year?

24. A savings fund currently contains $300,000. It is decided to pay out this amount with 6% interest compounded monthly over a 5-year period. What are the monthly payments?

25. What is the monthly payment on a $150,000, 30-year mortgage at 9% interest?

▶ Chapter 10 Chapter Test

1. If $500 is deposited into an account earning 6.5% simple interest, what is the balance in the account after 9 months?

2. Calculate the present value of $5000 payable in 3 years at 4% simple interest.

3. A principal of $1025 is deposited into an account paying 5% interest compounded quarterly for 3 years. What is the compound amount? How much interest is earned?

4. What is the present value of $25,000 payable in 10 years at 8% interest compounded monthly?

5. Victoria is planning for her retirement by depositing $250 at the end of each month into an annuity paying 5.25% interest compounded monthly. How much money will have accumulated in 15 years?

6. Find the present value of a decreasing annuity that pays $500 per month for 4 years if the money earns 5% interest compounded monthly.

7. Calculate the rent of an increasing annuity at 5% interest compounded semiannually if payments are made every 6 months and the future value after 5 years is $12,000.

8. Calculate the rent of a decreasing annuity at 7% interest compounded monthly with payments made every month for 10 years and present value $200,000.

9. Graham opens an account with $300 and then deposits an additional $50 at the end of each month. What is the balance after 4 years if the money earns 5.5% interest compounded monthly?

10. After making the fifth semiannual payment of $350 on a loan, Wanda's unpaid balance is $2499.93. If the interest rate is 7% compounded semiannually, what will Wanda's unpaid balance be after she makes her sixth payment?

11. Nigel takes out a 5-year loan for $8000 at 8.25% interest compounded monthly.
    (a) What is his monthly payment?
    (b) How much interest is paid the first month?
    (c) What is the unpaid balance after the first month?
    (d) After 4 years, Nigel wishes to retire the loan by making a balloon payment. How much does he owe?

12. If you make a $15,000 down payment on a house and take out a 25-year mortgage with quarterly payments of $500 at 6% interest compounded quarterly, what was the price of the house?

Chapter Project

Individual Retirement Accounts

The IRA (Individual Retirement Account) is the most common tax-deferred savings plan in the United States. Earned income deposited into an IRA is not taxed in the current year and no taxes are incurred on the interest paid in subsequent years. However, when you withdraw the money from the account after age $59\frac{1}{2}$, you pay taxes on the entire amount. The first set of exercises shows that IRAs effectively earn tax-free interest. The second set of exercises shows the value of starting an IRA early.

1. Suppose you deposit $2000 of earned income into an IRA, you can earn an annual interest rate of 8% compounded annually, and you are in a 40% tax bracket. (We recognize that interest rates and tax brackets are subject to change over a long period of time, but some assumptions must be made in order to evaluate the investment.) Also, suppose you deposit the $2000 at age 25 and withdraw it at age 60.

    (a) How much money will you have remaining after you pay the taxes at age 60?

    (b) Suppose that instead of depositing the money into an IRA, you pay taxes on the money and on the yearly interest. How much money will you have at age 60? *Note*: You effectively start with $1200 (60% of $2000) and the money earns 4.8% (60% of 8%) interest after taxes.

    (c) How much additional money will you earn with the IRA?

    (d) Suppose you pay taxes on the original $2000 but are then able to earn 8% in a tax-free investment. Compare your balance at age 60 with the IRA balance.

    (e) Suppose you deposit $2000 into an IRA earning annual interest rate r, the balance is withdrawn after n years, and then the taxes are paid.

       (i) Show that if your tax bracket is k (in the discussion above $k = .40$), then the amount of money you will have is $2000(1 + r)^n(1 - k)$.

       (ii) Rewrite the expression in part (i) as $[2000(1 - k)](1 + r)^n$ and then fill in the blank in the following sentence.

    > The net earnings from $2000 deposited into an IRA account is the same amount as would result from paying taxes on the $2000 but then earning _____ tax free.

2. Earl and Larry each begin full time jobs in January 2001 and plan to retire in January 2045 after working for 44 years. For simplicity, let's assume that they are both in the 40% tax bracket throughout their lives. Also, we will assume that any money they deposit into saving accounts earns 8% interest compounded annually.

    (a) Suppose Earl opens an IRA account immediately and deposits $2000 into the account on January 1 of each year for 10 years; that is, from 2001 through 2010. After that he makes no further deposits and just lets the money earn interest. How much money will Earl have in his account when he retires in January 2045?

    (b) Suppose Larry waits ten years before opening his IRA account and then deposits $2000 into the account every January 1 during the years 2011 through 2045. How much money will Larry have in his account after his last deposit on January 1, 2045?

    (c) How much money did Earl and Larry each pay into their IRA accounts?

    (d) Who had more money in his account upon retirement?

CHAPTER 11

Difference Equations and Mathematical Models

In this chapter we discuss a number of topics from the mathematics of finance—compound interest, mortgages, and annuities. As we shall see, all such financial transactions can be described by a single type of equation, called a *difference equation*. Furthermore, the same type of difference equation can be used to model many other phenomena, such as the spread of information, radioactive decay, and population growth, to mention a few.

11.1 Introduction to Difference Equations I

To understand what difference equations are and how they arise, consider two examples concerned with financial transactions in a savings account.

Example 1 Suppose that a savings account initially contains \$40 and earns 6% interest, compounded annually. Determine a formula that describes how to compute each year's balance from the previous year's balance.

Solution The balances in the account for the first few years can be given as in the following chart, where y_0 is the initial balance (balance after zero years), y_1 is the balance after one year, and so on.

Year	*Balance*	*Interest for year*
0	$y_0 = \$40$	$(.06)40 = 2.40$
1	$y_1 = 42.40$	$(.06)42.40 = 2.54$
2	$y_2 = 44.94$	$(.06)44.94 = 2.70$
3	$y_3 = 47.64$	

Once the balance is known for a particular year, the balance at the end of the next year is computed as follows:

[balance at end of next year] = [balance at end of this year]
$$+ \text{[interest on balance at end of this year]}.$$

That is,

$$y_1 = y_0 + .06y_0$$
$$y_2 = y_1 + .06y_1$$
$$y_3 = y_2 + .06y_2.$$

(Notice that since $2 = 3 - 1$, the last equation is $y_3 = y_{3-1} + .06y_{3-1}$.) In general, if y_n is the balance after n years, then y_{n-1} is the balance at the end of the preceding year, so

$$y_n = y_{n-1} + .06y_{n-1} \qquad \text{for} \quad n = 1, 2, 3, \ldots.$$

This equation can be simplified:

$$y_n = y_{n-1} + .06y_{n-1} = 1 \cdot y_{n-1} + .06y_{n-1} = (1 + .06)y_{n-1} = 1.06y_{n-1}. \qquad (1)$$

In other words, the balance after n years is 1.06 times the balance after $n - 1$ years. This formula describes how the balance is computed in successive years. For instance, using this formula, we can compute y_4. Indeed, setting $n = 4$ and using the value of y_3 from the preceding chart,

$$y_4 = 1.06y_{4-1} = 1.06y_3 = 1.06(47.64) = \$50.50.$$

In a similar way we can compute all of the year-end balances, one after another, by using formula (1). ◆

◗ **Example 2** Suppose that a savings account contains $40 and earns 6% interest, compounded annually. At the end of each year a $3 withdrawal is made. Determine a formula that describes how to compute each year's balance from the previous year's balance.

Solution As in Example 1, we compute the first few balances in a straightforward way and organize the data in a chart.

Balance	+ *Interest for year*	− *Withdrawal*
$y_0 = \$40$	$(.06)40 = 2.40$	$3
$y_1 = 39.40$	$(.06)39.40 = 2.36$	3
$y_2 = 38.76$		

Reasoning as in Example 1, let y_n be the balance after n years. Then, by analyzing the calculations of the preceding chart, we see that

$$y_n = y_{n-1} + .06y_{n-1} - 3$$
$$\text{[new balance]} = \text{[old balance]} + \text{[interest on old balance]} - \text{[withdrawal]}$$

or

$$y_n = 1.06y_{n-1} - 3. \qquad (2)$$

This formula allows us to compute the values of y_n successively. For example, the preceding chart gives $y_2 = 38.76$. Therefore, from equation (2) with $n = 3$,

$$y_3 = (1.06)y_2 - 3 = (1.06)(38.76) - 3 = 38.09. \qquad ◆$$

Equations of the form (1) and (2) are examples of what are called difference equations. More precisely, a *difference equation* is an equation of the form

$$y_n = ay_{n-1} + b,$$

where a and b are specific numbers. For example, for the difference equation (1) we have $a = 1.06$ and $b = 0$. For the difference equation (2) we have $a = 1.06$ and $b = -3$. A difference equation gives a procedure for calculating the term y_n from the preceding term y_{n-1}, thereby allowing one to compute all the terms—provided, of course, that a place to start is given. For this purpose one is usually given a specific value for y_0. Such a value is called an *initial value*. In both of the previous examples the initial value was 40.

Whenever we are given a difference equation, our goal is to determine as much information as possible about the terms y_0, y_1, y_2, and so on. To this end there are three things we can do:

1. *Generate the first few terms.* This is useful in giving us a feeling for how successive terms are generated.

2. *Graph the terms.* The terms that have been generated can be graphed by plotting the points $(0, y_0)$, $(1, y_1)$, $(2, y_2)$, and so on. Corresponding to the term y_n, we plot the point (n, y_n). The resulting graph (Fig. 1) depicts how the terms increase or decrease as n increases. In Figs. 2 and 3 we have drawn the graphs corresponding to the difference equations of Examples 1 and 2.

3. *Solve the difference equation.* By a *solution* of a difference equation we mean a general formula from which we can directly calculate any terms without first having to calculate all of the terms preceding it. One can always write down a solution using the values of a, b, and y_0. Assume for now that $a \neq 1$. Then a solution of $y_n = ay_{n-1} + b$ is given by

$$y_n = \frac{b}{1-a} + \left(y_0 - \frac{b}{1-a}\right)a^n, \qquad a \neq 1. \tag{3}$$

(This formula will be derived in Section 11.2.)

▶ **Example 3**   Solve the difference equation $y_n = 1.06y_{n-1}$, $y_0 = 40$.

Solution   Here $a = 1.06$, $b = 0$, $y_0 = 40$. So $b/(1-a) = 0$, and from equation (3),

$$y_n = 0 + (40 - 0)(1.06)^n$$
$$y_n = 40(1.06)^n. \qquad \blacklozenge$$

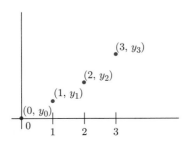

Figure 1.

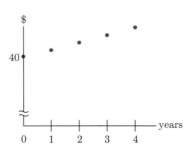

Figure 2.

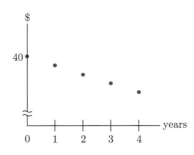

Figure 3.

▶ **Example 4**   Solve the difference equation $y_n = 1.06y_{n-1} - 3$, $y_0 = 40$. Determine y_{21}.

Solution   Here $a = 1.06$, $b = -3$, $y_0 = 40$. So $b/(1-a) = -3/(1-1.06) = -3/-.06 = 50$. Therefore,

$$y_n = 50 + (40 - 50)(1.06)^n$$
$$y_n = 50 - 10(1.06)^n.$$

In particular,

$$y_{21} = 50 - 10(1.06)^{21}.$$

Using a calculator, we find that $(1.06)^{21} \approx 3.4$, so that

$$y_{21} = 50 - 10(3.4) = 50 - 34 = 16.$$

So, after 21 years, the bank account of Example 2 will contain about \$16. [If we did not have the solution $y_n = 50 - 10(1.06)^n$, we would need to perform 21 successive calculations in order to determine y_{21}.]   ◆

In the next two examples we apply our entire three-step procedure to analyze some specific difference equations.

▶ **Example 5**   Apply the three-step procedure to study the difference equation $y_n = .2y_{n-1} + 4.8$, $y_0 = 1$.

Solution   First we compute a few terms:

$$y_0 = 1$$
$$y_1 = .2(1) + 4.8 = 5$$
$$y_2 = .2(5) + 4.8 = 5.8$$
$$y_3 = .2(5.8) + 4.8 = 5.96$$
$$y_4 = .2(5.96) + 4.8 = 5.992.$$

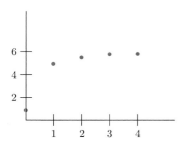

Figure 4.

Next, we graph these terms (Fig. 4). That is, we plot $(0, 1)$, $(1, 5)$, $(2, 5.8)$, $(3, 5.96)$, $(4, 5.992)$. Note that the values of y_n increase. Finally, we solve the difference equation. Here $a = .2$, $b = 4.8$, $y_0 = 1$. Thus,

$$\frac{b}{1-a} = \frac{4.8}{1-.2} = \frac{4.8}{.8} = 6$$
$$y_n = 6 + (1 - 6)(.2)^n = 6 - 5(.2)^n.$$ ◆

▶ **Example 6**   Apply the three-step procedure to study the difference equation $y_n = -.8y_{n-1} + 9$, $y_0 = 10$.

Solution   The first few terms are

$$y_0 = 10$$
$$y_1 = -.8(10) + 9 = -8 + 9 = 1$$
$$y_2 = -.8(1) + 9 = -.8 + 9 = 8.2$$
$$y_3 = -.8(8.2) + 9 = 2.44$$
$$y_4 = -.8(2.44) + 9 = 7.048.$$

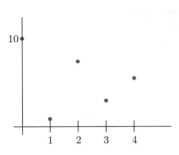

Figure 5.

The graph in Fig. 5 corresponds to these terms. Notice that in this case the points oscillate up and down. To solve the difference equation, note that

$$\frac{b}{1-a} = \frac{9}{1-(-.8)} = \frac{9}{1.8} = 5.$$

Thus

$$y_n = 5 + (10 - 5)(-.8)^n = 5 + 5(-.8)^n. \qquad \blacklozenge$$

Difference equations can be used to describe many real-life situations. The solution of a particular difference equation in such instances yields a mathematical model of the situation. For example, consider the banking problem of Example 2. We described the activity in the account by a difference equation, where y_n represents the amount of money in the account after n years. Solving the difference equation, we found that

$$y_n = 50 - 10(1.06)^n.$$

And this formula gives a mathematical model of the bank account.

Here is another example of a mathematical model derived using difference equations.

▶ **Example 7**   Suppose that the population of a certain country is currently 6 million. The growth of this population attributable to an excess of births over deaths is 2% per year. Further, the country is experiencing immigration at the rate of 40,000 people per year.

(a) Find a mathematical model for the population of the country.

(b) What will be the population of the country after 35 years?

Solution   (a) Let y_n denote the population (in millions) of the country after n years. Then $y_0 = 6$. The growth of the population in year n due to an excess of births over deaths is $.02y_{n-1}$. There are .04 (million) immigrants each year. Therefore,

$$y_n = y_{n-1} + .02y_{n-1} + .04 = 1.02y_{n-1} + .04.$$

So the terms satisfy the difference equation

$$y_n = 1.02y_{n-1} + .04 \qquad y_0 = 6.$$

Here

$$\frac{b}{1-a} = \frac{.04}{1 - 1.02} = \frac{.04}{-.02} = -2$$

$$y_n = -2 + (6 - (-2))(1.02)^n \qquad \text{or}$$

$$y_n = -2 + 8(1.02)^n.$$

This last formula is our desired mathematical model for the population.

(b) To determine the population after 35 years, merely compute y_{35}:

$$y_{35} = -2 + 8(1.02)^{35} \approx -2 + 8(2) = 14,$$

since $(1.02)^{35} \approx 2$. So the population after 35 years will be about 14 million.

◆

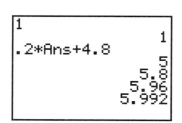

Figure 6.

GC Graphing calculators can easily display the terms and graphs of difference equations as well as tables of values. Figure 6 shows the first five terms of the difference equation $y_n = .2y_{n-1} + 4.8$, $y_0 = 1$ of Example 5. After the initial value (**1**) is entered, the last displayed value (**1**) is assigned to **Ans**. The instruction **.2*Ans+4.8** generates the next term (**5**) and assigns it to **Ans**. Each subsequent press of the ENTER key generates another term.

Graphs (see Fig. 12) and tables (see Fig. 18) for difference equations require that the calculator be set in "sequence" (as opposed to "function") mode. See the fourth lines of Figs. 7 and 8. (Also, on the TI-82, the fifth line should be set to "**Dot**.") Difference equations are defined with letters such as u and v instead of y and differ in notation from calculator to calculator. For instance, the difference equation $y_n = .2y_{n-1} + 4.8$ is written **u(n)=.2u(n-1)+4.8** on the TI-83 and is written **Uₙ=.2Uₙ₋₁+4.8** on the TI-82.

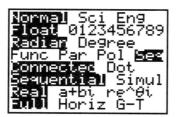

Figure 7. *TI-83*
MODE screen

Figure 8. *TI-82*
MODE screen

The minimum value of n, always 0 for our purposes, is denoted by **nMin**. The maximum value of n to appear when specifying a graph is denoted by **nMax**. The variables **Xmin**, **Xmax**, **Xscl**, **Ymin**, **Ymax**, and **Yscl** have the same meanings as with graphs of functions.

Graphs with the TI-83 When the Y= key is pressed with the calculator in Seq mode, the screen in Fig. 9 appears. In Seq mode, pressing 2nd [u] (the second function of **7**) generates u and pressing X, T, θ, n generates n. The initial value is assigned to **u(nMin)**. (*Note*: In line 5 of Fig. 9, after 1 was entered, the calculator automatically added the braces.) In Fig. 10, PlotStart is the first point to be graphed and PlotStep is the increment in the values of n. When PlotStart is set to 1, graphing begins with y_0. When PlotStep is set to 1, no points are skipped. Normally, the values of **Xmin** and **Xmax** should be set to the same values as **nMin** and **nMax**. Setting **Ymin** below the actual y-values needed creates room for coordinates of points to be displayed at the bottom of the screen. Setting **Ymax** above the actual y-values needed creates room for the display of the difference equation at the top of the screen. When you press the TRACE key, the points will be graphed and the trace cursor will be on the leftmost point. See Fig. 11. Each time the right-arrow key is pressed, the trace cursor will move to the next point and display its value. See Fig. 12. (You can also move the trace cursor to a desired point by pressing 2nd [CALC] ENTER, typing the desired value of n, and again pressing ENTER.)

Figure 9. *TI-83* Y= editor

Graphs with the TI-82 When the Y= key is pressed with the calculator in Seq mode, the screen in Fig. 13 appears. In Seq mode, pressing 2nd[Uₙ₋₁] (the second function of **7**) generates **Uₙ₋₁**. In Fig. 14, **nStart** is the initial value of n (for our purposes always 0) and **UnStart** should be set to the initial value y_0. Plotting begins at the setting for **nMin** and ends at the setting for **nMax**. We usually leave **nMin** at its default value 0. Normally, the values of **Xmin** and

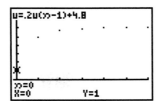

Figure 10. TI-83 WINDOW screen

Figure 11. Initial location of trace cursor

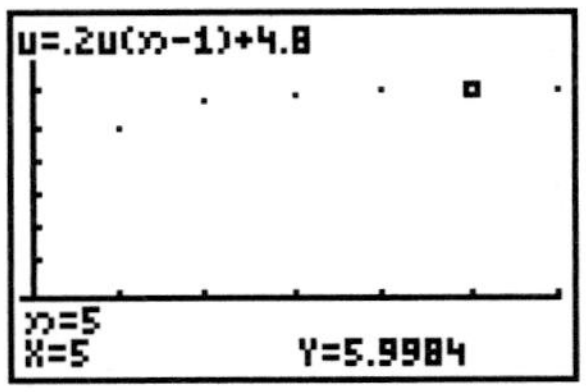

Figure 12. Trace cursor after being moved several times

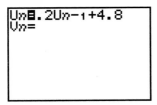

Figure 13. TI-82 **Y=** editor

Xmax should be set to the same values as **nMin** and **nMax**. Setting **Ymin** below the actual y-values needed creates room for coordinates of points to be displayed at the bottom of the screen. When you press the TRACE key, the points will be graphed and the trace cursor will be on the leftmost point. See Fig. 15. Each time the right-arrow key is pressed, the trace cursor will move to the next point and display its value. See Fig. 16. (You can also move the trace cursor to a desired point by pressing 2nd [CALC] ENTER, typing the desired value of n, and pressing ENTER.)

Figure 14. TI-82 WINDOW screen

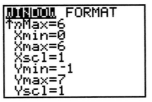

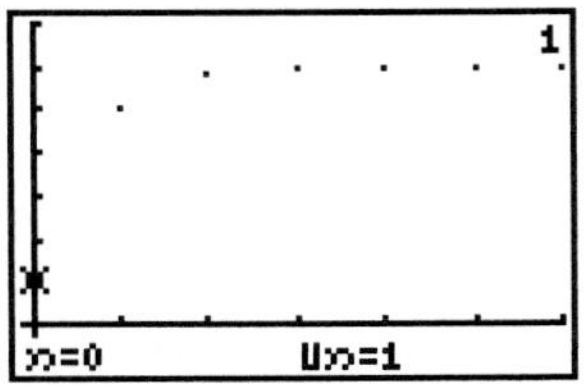

Figure 15. Initial location of trace cursor

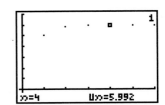

Figure 16. Trace cursor after being moved several times

Tables with the TI-82 or TI-83   Pressing 2nd [TBLSET] brings up the TABLE SETUP screen of Fig. 17. The table determined by the settings will have a column for n and a column for the values of each difference equation that is selected in the **Y=** editor. The values for n will begin with the setting of **TblStart** (**TblMin** on the TI-82) and increase by the setting of Δ**Tbl**. For our purposes, the settings for **Indpnt** and **Depend** should always be **Auto**. After you press 2nd [TABLE] to display the table (see Fig. 18), you can use the down-arrow key to generate further terms.

Figure 17.

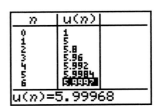

Figure 18.

Practice Problems 11.1	1. Consider the difference equation $y_n = -2y_{n-1} + 21$, $y_0 = 7.5$.

1. Consider the difference equation $y_n = -2y_{n-1} + 21$, $y_0 = 7.5$.

   (a) Generate y_0, y_1, y_2, y_3, and y_4 from the difference equation.

   (b) Graph these first few terms.

   (c) Solve the difference equation.

2. Use the solution in Problem 1(c) to obtain the terms y_0, y_1, and y_2.

▸ Exercises 11.1

For each of the difference equations in Exercises 1–6, identify a and b and compute $b/(1-a)$.

1. $y_n = 4y_{n-1} - 6$
2. $y_n = -3y_{n-1} + 16$
3. $y_n = -\frac{1}{2}y_{n-1}$
4. $y_n = \frac{1}{3}y_{n-1} + 4$
5. $y_n = -\frac{2}{3}y_{n-1} + 15$
6. $y_n = .5y_{n-1} - 4$

In Exercises 7–14, (a) Generate y_0, y_1, y_2, y_3, y_4 from the difference equation. (b) Graph these first few terms. (c) Solve the difference equation.

7. $y_n = \frac{1}{2}y_{n-1} - 1$, $y_0 = 10$
8. $y_n = .5y_{n-1} + 5$, $y_0 = 2$
9. $y_n = 2y_{n-1} - 3$, $y_0 = 3.5$
10. $y_n = 5y_{n-1} - 32$, $y_0 = 8$
11. $y_n = -.4y_{n-1} + 7$, $y_0 = 17.5$
12. $y_n = -2y_{n-1}$, $y_0 = \frac{1}{2}$
13. $y_n = 2y_{n-1} - 16$, $y_0 = 15$
14. $y_n = 2y_{n-1} + 3$, $y_0 = -2$
15. The solution to $y_n = .2y_{n-1} + 4.8$, $y_0 = 1$ is $y_n = 6 - 5(.2)^n$. Use the solution to compute y_0, y_1, y_2, y_3, y_4.
16. The solution to $y_n = -.8y_{n-1} + 9$, $y_0 = 10$ is $y_n = 5 + 5(-.8)^n$. Use the solution to compute y_0, y_1, y_2.
17. One thousand dollars is deposited into a savings account paying 5% interest compounded annually. Let y_n be the amount after n years. What is the difference equation showing how to compute y_n from y_{n-1}?
18. The population of a certain country is currently 70 million but is declining at the rate of 1% each year. Let y_n be the population after n years. Find a difference equation showing how to compute y_n from y_{n-1}.
19. One thousand dollars is deposited into an account paying 5% interest compounded annually. At the end of each year $100 is added to the account. Let y_n be the amount in the account after n years. Find a difference equation satisfied by y_n.
20. The population of a certain country is currently 70 million but is declining at the rate of 1% each year due to an excess of deaths over births. In addition, the country is losing one million people each year due to emigration. Let y_n be the population after n years. Find a difference equation satisfied by y_n.

21. Consider the difference equation $y_n = y_{n-1} + 2$, $y_0 = 1$.

    (a) Generate y_0, y_1, y_2, y_3, y_4.

    (b) Sketch the graph.

    (c) Why cannot formula (3) be used to obtain the solution?

22. Rework Exercise 21 for $y_n = y_{n-1} - 2$, $y_0 = 10$.

23. Suppose that you take a consumer loan for $55 at 20% annual interest and pay off $36 at the end of each year for two years. Compute the balance on the loan immediately after you make the first payment (i.e., the amount you would pay if you wanted to settle the account at the beginning of the second year).

24. Refer to Exercise 23. Set up the difference equation for y_n, the balance after n years.

Exercises 25–32 require the use of a graphing calculator or a computer.

In these exercises,

(a) Generate y_1 through y_7 on the home screen of a calculator.

(b) Create a table displaying y_0 through y_7.

(c) Graph the first 25 terms of the difference equation.

(d) Use the table or graph to answer the questions.

25. $y_n = .75y_{n-1} + 1.25$, $y_0 = 2$. What is y_{10}? For what value of n is y_n within .01 units of 5?

26. $y_n = 1.2y_{n-1} - 2$, $y_0 = 12.5$. What is y_{11}? For what value of n does y_n first exceed 100?

27. $y_n = 1.05y_{n-1} - 7.8$, $y_0 = 102.67$. What is y_{14} (rounded to two decimal places)? For what value of n does $y_n = 0$ (rounded to two decimal places)?

28. $y_n = .8y_{n-1} + .6$, $y_0 = 10$. What is y_{12}? For what value of n is y_n within .1 units of 3?

29. $y_n = -.85y_{n-1} + 11.1$, $y_0 = 4$. What is y_{12}? For what value of n is y_n within .1 units of 6?

30. $y_n = -1.3y_{n-1} + 1.5$, $y_0 = 1$. What is y_{14}? For what value of n is y_n approximately 39.77?

31. $y_n = y_{n-1} + .2$, $y_0 = 1$. What is y_9? For what value of n does $y_n = 4.6$?

32. $y_n = -y_{n-1} + .2$, $y_0 = 1$. What special behavior do the terms exhibit?

1. (a) $y_0 = 7.5$.

$y_1 = -2(7.5) + 21 = -15 + 21 = 6$.

$y_2 = -2(6) + 21 = -12 + 21 = 9$.

$y_3 = -2(9) + 21 = -18 + 21 = 3$.

$y_4 = -2(3) + 21 = -6 + 21 = 15$.

(b) We graph the points $(0, 7.5)$, $(1, 6)$, $(2, 9)$, $(3, 3)$, $(4, 15)$ in Fig. 19. (In order to accommodate the points, we use a different scale for each axis.)

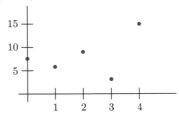

Figure 19.

(c) $y_n = \dfrac{b}{1-a} + \left(y_0 - \dfrac{b}{1-a}\right)a^n$.

Since $a = -2$ and $b = 21$, $\dfrac{b}{1-a} = \dfrac{21}{1-(-2)} = \dfrac{21}{3} = 7$.

$y_n = 7 + (7.5 - 7)(-2)^n = 7 + \frac{1}{2}(-2)^n$.

2. $y_n = 7 + \frac{1}{2}(-2)^n$.

$y_0 = 7 + \frac{1}{2}(-2)^0 = 7 + \frac{1}{2} = 7.5$. (Here we have used the fact that any number to the zeroth power is 1.)

$y_1 = 7 + \frac{1}{2}(-2)^1 = 7 + \frac{1}{2}(-2) = 7 - 1 = 6$.

$y_2 = 7 + \frac{1}{2}(-2)^2 = 7 + \frac{1}{2}(4) = 7 + 2 = 9$.

11.2 Introduction to Difference Equations II

The main result of Section 11.1 is the following:

The difference equation $y_n = ay_{n-1} + b$, with $a \neq 1$, has solution

$$y_n = \frac{b}{1-a} + \left(y_0 - \frac{b}{1-a}\right)a^n. \tag{1}$$

When $a = 1$, the difference equation $y_n = a \cdot y_{n-1} + b$ is $y_n = 1 \cdot y_{n-1} + b$ or just $y_n = y_{n-1} + b$. In this case the solution is given by a formula different from (1):

The difference equation $y_n = y_{n-1} + b$ has the solution

$$y_n = y_0 + bn. \tag{2}$$

▶ Example 1 (a) Solve the difference equation $y_n = y_{n-1} + 2$, $y_0 = 3$.

(b) Find y_{100}.

Solution (a) Since $a = 1$, the solution is given by (2). Here $b = 2$, $y_0 = 3$. Therefore,

$$y_n = 3 + 2n.$$

(b) $y_{100} = 3 + 2(100) = 203$.

Note: Without (2), determining y_{100} would require 100 computations. ◆

Both (1) and (2) are derived at the end of this section. Before deriving them, however, let us see what they tell us about simple interest, compound interest, and consumer loans.

Simple Interest Suppose that a certain amount of money is deposited in a savings account. If interest is paid only on the initial deposit (and not on accumulated interest), then the interest is called *simple*. For example, if $40 is deposited at 6% simple interest, then each year the account earns .06(40), or $2.40. So the bank balance accumulates as follows:

Year	Amount	Interest
0	$40.00	$2.40
1	42.40	2.40
2	44.80	2.40
3	47.20	

▶ Example 2 (a) Find a formula for y_n, the amount in the account above at the end of n years.

(b) Find the amount at the end of 10 years.

Solution (a) Let y_n = the amount at the end of n years. So $y_0 = 40$. Moreover,

[amount at end of n years] = [amount at end of $n - 1$ years] + [interest].
y_n = y_{n-1} + 2.40.

This difference equation has $a = 1$, $b = 2.40$, so from formula (2),

$$y_n = y_0 + bn = 40 + (2.40)n.$$

This is the desired formula.

(b) $y_{10} = 40 + (2.40)10 = 40 + 24.00 = \$64$. ◆

Compound Interest When interest is calculated on the current amount in the account (instead of on the amount initially deposited), the interest is called *compound*. The interest discussed in Section 11.1 was compound, being computed on the balance at the end of each year. Such interest is called *annual* compound interest. Often interest is compounded more than once a year. For example, interest might be stated as 6% compounded *semiannually*. This means that interest is computed every 6 months, with 3% given for each 6-month period. At the end of each such period the interest is added to the balance, which is then used to compute the interest for the next 6-month period. Similarly, 6% *interest compounded quarterly* means .06/4 or .015 interest four times a year. And 6% interest compounded six times a year means .06/6 or .01 interest each interest period of 2 months. Or, in general, if 6% interest is compounded k times a year, then .06/k interest is earned k times a year. This illustrates the following general principle:

If interest is at a yearly rate r and is compounded k times per year, then the interest rate per period (denoted i) is $i = r/k$.

▶ **Example 3**   Suppose that the interest rate is 6% compounded monthly. Find a formula for the amount after n months.

Solution   Here $r = .06$, $k = 12$, so that the monthly interest rate is $i = .005$. Let y_n denote the amount after n months. Then, reasoning as in Section 11.1,

$$y_n = y_{n-1} + .005y_{n-1} = 1.005y_{n-1}.$$

The solution of this difference equation is obtained as follows:

$$\frac{b}{1-a} = 0 \qquad y_n = 0 + (y_0 - 0)(1.005)^n = y_0(1.005)^n. \qquad ◆$$

▶ **Example 4**   Suppose that interest is computed at the rate i per interest period. Find a general formula for the balance y_n after n interest periods under (a) simple interest, (b) compound interest.

Solution   (a)   With simple interest, the interest each period is just i times the initial amount—that is, $i \cdot y_0$. Therefore,

$$y_n = y_{n-1} + iy_0.$$

Apply (2) with $b = iy_0$. Then

$$y_n = y_0 + (iy_0)n.$$

(b)   With compound interest, the interest each period is i times the current balance, or $i \cdot y_n$. Therefore,

$$y_n = y_{n-1} + iy_{n-1} = (1+i)y_{n-1}.$$

Here $b/(1-a) = 0$, so that

$$y_n = 0 + (y_0 - 0)(1+i)^n = y_0(1+i)^n. \qquad ◆$$

Summarizing,

If y_0 dollars is deposited at interest rate i per period, then the amount after n interest periods is

Simple interest:	$y_n = y_0 + (iy_0)n$	(3)
Compound interest:	$y_n = y_0(1+i)^n.$	(4)

▶ **Example 5**   How much money will you have after seven years if you deposit $40 at 8% interest compounded quarterly?

Solution   Apply formula (4). Here a period is a quarter, or 3 months. In 7 years there are $7 \cdot 4 = 28$ periods. The interest rate per period is

$$i = \frac{.08}{4} = .02.$$

The amount after 28 periods is

$$y_{28} = 40(1.02)^{28} = \$69.64.$$

[To compute $(1.02)^{28}$, we used a calculator. The answer could have been left in the form $40(1.02)^{28}$.] ◆

Consumer Loans It is common for people to buy cars or appliances "on time." Basically, they are borrowing money from the dealer and repaying it (with interest) with several equal payments until the loan is paid off. Each time period, part of the payment goes toward paying off the interest and part goes toward reducing the balance of the loan. A consumer loan used to purchase a house is called a *mortgage*.

▶ **Example 6** Suppose that a consumer loan of $2400 carries an interest rate of 12% compounded annually and a yearly payment of $1000.

(a) Write down a difference equation for y_n, the balance owed after n years.
(b) Compute the balances after 1, 2, and 3 years.

Solution (a) At the end of each year the new balance is computed as follows:

$$[\text{new balance}] = [\text{previous balance}] + [\text{interest}] - [\text{payment}].$$

Since the interest is compound, it is computed on the previous balance:

$$y_n = y_{n-1} + .12y_{n-1} - 1000.$$

Thus

$$y_n = 1.12y_{n-1} - 1000, \qquad y_0 = 2400$$

is the desired difference equation.

(b) $y_1 = 1.12y_0 - 1000 = (1.12)(2400) - 1000 = \$1688.$
$y_2 = 1.12y_1 - 1000 = (1.12)(1688) - 1000 = 891.$
$y_3 = 1.12y_2 - 1000 = (1.12)(891) - 1000 \approx 0.$ ◆

Although savings accounts using simple interest are practically unheard of, consumer loans are often computed using simple interest. Under simple interest, interest is paid on the entire amount of the initial loan, not just on the outstanding balance.

▶ **Example 7** Rework Example 6, except assume that the interest is now simple.

Solution (a) As before,

$$[\text{new balance}] = [\text{previous balance}] + [\text{interest}] - [\text{payment}].$$

Now, however, since the interest is simple, it is computed on the original loan y_0. So

$$y_n = y_{n-1} + .12y_0 - 1000, \qquad y_0 = 2400.$$

(b) $y_1 = y_0 + .12y_0 - 1000 = \$1688.$
$y_2 = y_1 + .12y_0 - 1000 = 976.$
$y_3 = y_2 + .12y_0 - 1000 = 264.$ ◆

Remark Note that after three years the loan of Example 7 is not yet paid off, whereas the loan of Example 6 is. Therefore, the loan at 12% simple interest is more expensive than the one at 12% compound interest. Actually, a 12% simple interest loan is equivalent to a 16% compound interest loan. At one time it was a common practice to advertise loans in terms of simple interest to make the interest rate seem cheaper. But the Federal Truth in Lending Law now requires that all loans be stated in terms of their equivalent compound interest rate.

Verification of Formula (1) From the difference equation $y_n = ay_{n-1} + b$ we get

$$y_1 = ay_0 + b$$
$$y_2 = ay_1 + b = a(ay_0 + b) + b$$
$$= a^2 y_0 + ab + b$$
$$y_3 = ay_2 + b = a(a^2 y_0 + ab + b) + b$$
$$= a^3 y_0 + a^2 b + ab + b$$
$$y_4 = ay_3 + b = a(a^3 y_0 + a^2 b + ab + b) + b$$
$$= a^4 y_0 + a^3 b + a^2 b + ab + b.$$

The pattern that clearly develops is

$$y_n = a^n y_0 + a^{n-1} b + a^{n-2} b + \cdots + a^2 b + ab + b. \tag{5}$$

Multiply both sides of (5) by a and then subtract the new equation from (5). Notice that many terms drop out.

$$y_n = \quad a^n y_0 + \quad\quad a^{n-1} b + a^{n-2} b + \cdots + a^2 b + ab + b$$
$$ay_n = a^{n+1} y_0 + a^n b + a^{n-1} b + a^{n-2} b + \cdots + a^2 b + ab$$
$$\overline{y_n - ay_n = a^n y_0 - a^{n+1} y_0 - a^n b + b}$$

The last equation can be written

$$(1 - a)y_n = (1 - a)a^n y_0 - ba^n + b.$$

Now, divide both sides of the equation by $(1 - a)$. [*Note:* Since $a \neq 1$, $1 - a \neq 0$.]

$$y_n = y_0 a^n - \frac{b}{1-a} \cdot a^n + \frac{b}{1-a}$$
$$= \frac{b}{1-a} + \left(y_0 - \frac{b}{1-a} \right) a^n,$$

which is formula (1). ◆

Verification of Formula (2) Formula (1) gives the solution of the difference equation $y_n = ay_{n-1} + b$ in the case $a \neq 1$. The preceding reasoning also gives the solution in case $a = 1$—namely equation (5) holds for any value of a. In particular, for $a = 1$ equation (5) reads

$$y_n = a^n y_0 + a^{n-1} b + a^{n-2} b + \cdots + a^2 b + ab + b$$
$$= 1^n y_0 + 1^{n-1} b + 1^{n-2} b + \cdots + 1^2 b + 1b + b$$
$$= y_0 + b + b + \cdots + b + b + b$$
$$= y_0 + bn.$$

Thus we have derived formula (2). ◆

Practice Problems 11.2

1. Solve the following difference equations.

   (a) $y_n = -.2y_{n-1} + 24$, $y_0 = 25$ (b) $y_n = y_{n-1} - 3$, $y_0 = 7$

2. In 1626, Peter Minuit, the first director-general of New Netherlands Province, purchased Manhattan Island for trinkets and cloth valued at about \$24. Suppose that this money had been invested at 7% interest compounded quarterly. How much would it have been worth by the U.S. bicentennial year, 1976?

▶ Exercises 11.2

1. Solve the difference equation $y_n = y_{n-1} + 5$, $y_0 = 1$.

2. Solve the difference equation $y_n = y_{n-1} - 2$, $y_0 = 50$.

In Exercises 3–8, find an expression for the amount of money in the bank after five years when the initial deposit is $80 and the annual interest rate is as given.

3. 9% compounded monthly

4. 4% simple interest

5. 100% compounded daily

6. 8% compounded quarterly

7. 7% simple interest

8. 12% compounded semiannually

9. Find the general formula for the amount of money accumulated after t years when A dollars is invested at annual interest rate r compounded k times per year.

10. Determine the amount of money accumulated after one year when $1 is deposited at 40% interest compounded:
   (a) Annually   (b) Semiannually   (c) Quarterly

11. For the difference equation $y_n = 2y_{n-1} - 10$, generate y_0, y_1, y_2, y_3 and draw the graph corresponding to the initial condition:
   (a) $y_0 = 10$ (b) $y_0 = 11$ (c) $y_0 = 9$

12. For the difference equation $y_n = \frac{1}{2}y_{n-1} + 5$, generate y_0, y_1, y_2, y_3 and draw the graph corresponding to the initial condition:
   (a) $y_0 = 10$ (b) $y_0 = 18$ (c) $y_0 = 2$

In Exercises 13–16, solve the difference equation and, by inspection, determine the long-run behavior of the terms (i.e., the behavior of the terms as n gets large).

13. $y_n = .4y_{n-1} + 3$, $y_0 = 7$

14. $y_n = 3y_{n-1} - 12$, $y_0 = 10$

15. $y_n = -5y_{n-1}$, $y_0 = 2$

16. $y_n = -.7y_{n-1} + 3.4$, $y_0 = 3$

17. A bank loan of $38,900 at 9% interest compounded monthly is made in order to buy a house and is paid off at the rate of $350 per month for 20 years. (Such a loan is called a mortgage.) The balance at any time is the amount still owed on the loan, that is, the amount that would have to be paid out to repay the loan all at once at that time. Find the difference equation for y_n, the balance after n months.

18. Refer to Exercise 17. Express in mathematical notation the fact that the loan is paid off after 20 years.

19. A house is purchased for $50,000 and depreciated over a 25-year period. Let y_n be the (undepreciated) value of the house after n years. Determine and solve the difference equation for y_n, assuming straight-line depreciation (i.e., each year the house depreciates by $\frac{1}{25}$ of its original value).

20. Refer to Exercise 19. Determine and solve the difference equation for y_n, assuming the double-declining balance method of depreciation (i.e., each year the house depreciates by $\frac{2}{25}$ of its value at the beginning of that year).

21. (PE) If a population of 500 bacteria doubles in size every 5 minutes, approximately how many minutes will it take for the population to grow to 500,000?
   (a) 45   (b) 50   (c) 55   (d) 60   (e) 65

22. (PE) The balance in a savings account doubles every 12 years. Approximately how many years will it take for the balance to grow from $100 to $25,000?
   (a) 60   (b) 72   (c) 84   (d) 96   (e) 108

23. (PE) By how much does the value of an investment increase in 2 weeks if it grows at the rate of $50 per day?
   (a) $100   (b) $640   (c) $700
   (d) $1000   (e) $1400

24. (PE) A city's population grows at the rate of one person every 20 minutes. By how many people does the population grow in 6 hours?
   (a) 18   (b) 20   (c) 60   (d) 120   (e) 180

25. (PE) A population doubles every year for 5 years. If the size of the population after the 5 years is 100,000, what was the population at the end of the second year?
   (a) 7500   (b) 10,000   (c) 12,500
   (d) 25,000   (e) 50,000

26. (PE) The value of an investment doubles every month for 8 months. After the eighth month, the investment was worth $400,000. What was the investment worth after the fourth month?
   (a) $25,000   (b) $50,000   (c) $75,000
   (d) $100,000   (e) $200,000

27. (PE) If a culture of 10^5 bacteria doubles in size every 15 minutes, how many bacteria are present after 1 hour?
   (a) $10^4(10^5)$ (b) $(10^5)^4$ (c) $2^4(10^5)$
   (d) $2(10^5)$ (e) $4(10^5)$

28. (PE) A population of 10^7 doubles in size every 6 months. How big is the population after 8 years?
   (a) $(10^7)^{16}$ (b) $10^{16}(10^7)$ (c) $16(10^7)$
   (d) $2(10^7)$ (e) $2^{16}(10^7)$

Exercises 29–34 require the use of a graphing calculator or a computer.

In these exercises, answer the questions by generating a table or graph of an appropriate difference equation.

29. One thousand dollars is deposited into a savings account at 6% interest compounded quarterly. Determine the balance after 3 years. When will the balance reach $1659? How many quarters are required for the initial deposit to double?

30. Redo Exercise 29 for simple interest of 1.5% per quarter-year.

31. Two hundred dollars is deposited into a savings account at simple interest of 4.5% annually. Determine the balance after 5 years. When will the balance reach or exceed $308? How many years are required for the initial deposit to double?

32. Redo Exercise 31 for compound interest of 4.5% compounded annually.

33. Consider the difference equation $y_n = .85y_{n-1} + 9$, $y_0 = 5$. What value do the terms approach as n gets large?

34. Consider the difference equation $y_n = -.9y_{n-1} + 19$, $y_0 = 5$. What value do the terms approach as n gets large?

Solutions to Practice Problems 11.2

1. (a) Since $a = -.2 \neq 1$, use formula (1).

$$\frac{b}{1-a} = \frac{24}{1-(-.2)} = \frac{24}{1.2} = \frac{240}{12} = 20$$

$$y_n = 20 + (25 - 20)(-.2)^n = 20 + 5(-.2)^n$$

(b) Since $a = 1$, use formula (2).

$$y_n = 7 + (-3)n = 7 - 3n$$

2. Since interest is compounded quarterly, the interest per period is $.07/4 = .0175$. Three hundred and fifty years consists of $4(350) = 1400$ interest periods. Therefore, by (4), the amount accumulated is

$$y_{1400} = 24(1.0175)^{1400}.$$

(This amount is approximately $850 billion, which is more than Manhattan Island was worth in 1976.)

11.3 Graphing Difference Equations

In this section we introduce a method for sketching the graph of the difference equation $y_n = ay_{n-1} + b$ (with initial value y_0) directly from the three numbers a, b, and y_0. As we shall see, the graphs arising from difference equations can be described completely by two characteristics—vertical direction and long-run behavior. To begin we introduce some vocabulary to describe graphs.

The *vertical direction* of a graph refers to the up-and-down motion of successive terms. A graph *increases* if it rises when read from left to right—that is, if the terms get successively larger. A graph *decreases* if it falls when read from left to right—that is, if the terms get successively smaller. Figure 1 shows the graphs of two difference equations. Both graphs increase. Figure 2 shows two examples of decreasing graphs. A graph that is either increasing or decreasing is called *monotonic*. That is, a graph is monotonic if it always heads in one direction—up or down.

The extreme opposite of a monotonic graph is one that changes its direction with every term. Such a graph is called *oscillating*. Figure 3 shows two examples of oscillating graphs. A difference equation having an oscillating graph has terms y_n that alternately increase and decrease.

In addition to the monotonic and oscillating graphs, there are the *constant* graphs, which always remain at the same height. That is, all the terms y_n are the same. A constant graph is illustrated in Fig. 4.

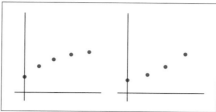

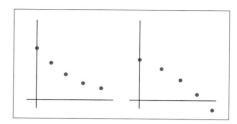

Figure 1. Increasing graphs   **Figure 2.** Decreasing graphs

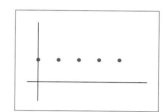

Figure 3. Oscillating graphs   **Figure 4.** Constant graph

One of the main results of this section is that the graph of a difference equation $y_n = ay_{n-1} + b$ is always either monotonic, oscillating, or constant. This threefold classification gives us all the possibilities for the vertical direction of the graph.

Long-run behavior refers to the eventual behavior of the graph. Most graphs of difference equations exhibit one of two types of long-run behavior. Some approach a horizontal line and are said to be *asymptotic* to the line. Some go indefinitely high or indefinitely low and are said to be *unbounded*. These phenomena are illustrated in Figs. 5 and 6.

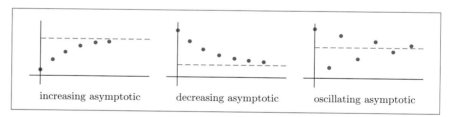

increasing asymptotic   decreasing asymptotic   oscillating asymptotic

Figure 5. Asymptotic graphs

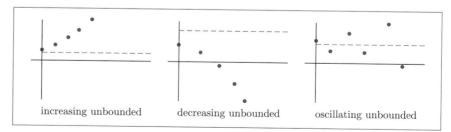

increasing unbounded   decreasing unbounded   oscillating unbounded

Figure 6. Unbounded graphs

The dashed horizontal lines in Figs. 5 and 6 each have the equation $y = b/(1-a)$. Note that in Fig. 5 the terms move steadily closer to the dashed line and in Fig. 6 they move steadily farther away from the dashed line. In the first case we say that the terms are *attracted* to the dashed line and in the second case we say that they are *repelled* by it.

Constant Graphs The general formula for the nth term of a difference equation where $a \neq 1$ is

$$y_n = \frac{b}{1-a} + \left(y_0 - \frac{b}{1-a}\right)a^n.$$

It is clear that as n varies so does a^n, and this makes y_n vary with n—unless, of course, the coefficient of a^n is 0, in which case the graph is constant. Thus we have the following result:

The graph of $y_n = ay_{n-1} + b$ $(a \neq 1)$ is constant if $y_0 - b/(1-a) = 0$; that is, if $y_0 = b/(1-a)$.

Thus, when the graph starts out on the line $y = b/(1-a)$, it stays on the line.

▶ **Example 1** Sketch the graph of the difference equation $y_n = 2y_{n-1} - 1$, $y_0 = 1$.

Solution First compute $b/(1-a)$:

$$\frac{b}{1-a} = \frac{-1}{1-2} = 1.$$

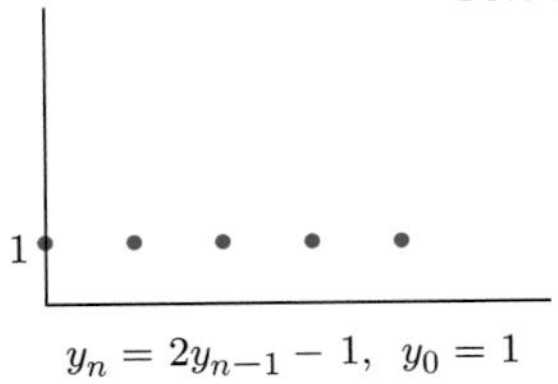

But $y_0 = 1$. So $b/(1-a)$ and y_0 are the same and the graph is constant, always equal to 1 (Fig. 7). ◆

$y_n = 2y_{n-1} - 1, \quad y_0 = 1$

Figure 7.

Throughout this section assume that $a \neq \pm 1$. Then the graph of a given difference equation either is constant or is one of the types shown in Figs. 5 and 6. We can determine the nature of the graph by looking at the coefficients a and b and the initial value y_0. We have seen how constant graphs are handled. Thus, assume that we are dealing with a nonconstant graph—that is, the graph of a difference equation for which a^n actually affects the formula for y_n. Monotonic graphs may be differentiated from oscillating graphs by the following test.

Test 1 If $a > 0$, then the graph of $y_n = ay_{n-1} + b$ is monotonic.
If $a < 0$, then the graph is oscillating.

The next two examples provide a convincing argument for Test 1.

▶ **Example 2** Discuss the vertical direction of the graph of $y_n = -.8y_{n-1} + 9$, $y_0 = 50$.

Solution The formula for y_n yields

$$y_n = 5 + 45(-.8)^n.$$

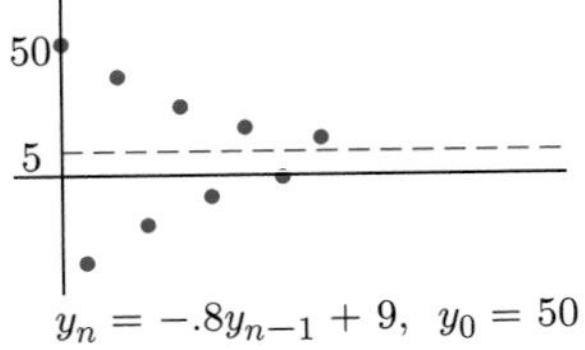

$y_n = -.8y_{n-1} + 9, \quad y_0 = 50$

Figure 8.

Note that the term $(-.8)^n$ is alternately positive and negative, since any negative number to an even power is positive and any negative number to an odd power is negative. Therefore, the expression $45(-.8)^n$ is alternately positive and negative. So $y_n = 5 + 45(-.8)^n$ is computed by alternately adding and subtracting something from 5. Thus y_n oscillates around 5. In this example $a = -.8$ (a negative number), so that the behavior just observed is consistent with that predicted by Test 1. The graph is sketched in Fig. 8. Note that in this case 5 is just $b/(1-a)$, so the graph oscillates about the line $y = b/(1-a)$. ◆

The reasoning of Example 2 works whenever $a < 0$. The oscillation of a^n from positive to negative and back forces the term

$$\left(y_0 - \frac{b}{1-a} \right) a^n$$

to swing up and back from positive to negative. So the value of

$$y_n = \frac{b}{1-a} + \left(y_0 - \frac{b}{1-a} \right) a^n$$

swings up and back, above and below $b/(1-a)$. In other words, the graph oscillates about the line $y = b/(1-a)$.

▶ **Example 3**   Discuss the vertical direction of the graph of $y_n = .8y_{n-1} + 9$, $y_0 = 50$.

Solution   In this case $b/(1-a) = 45$, and the formula for y_n gives

$$y_n = 45 + 5(.8)^n.$$

The expression $5(.8)^n$ is always positive. As n gets larger, $5(.8)^n$ gets smaller, so that y_n decreases to 45. That is, the graph is steadily decreasing to $y = 45$ (Fig. 9). Here $a = .8 > 0$, so Test 1 correctly predicts that the graph is monotonic.   ◆

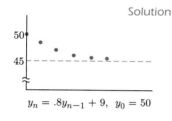

$y_n = .8y_{n-1} + 9, \ y_0 = 50$

Figure 9.

Using the following result, it is possible to determine whether a graph is asymptotic or unbounded.

Test 2   If $|a| < 1$, then the graph of $y_n = ay_{n-1} + b$ is asymptotic to the line $y = b/(1-a)$. If $|a| > 1$, then the graph is unbounded and moves away from the line $y = b/(1-a)$.

Let us examine some difference equations in light of Test 2.

▶ **Example 4**   Discuss the graphs of the difference equation $y_n = .2y_{n-1} + 4.8$, with $y_0 = 1$ and with $y_0 = 11$.

Solution   The graphs are shown in Fig. 10. Since $a = .2$, which has absolute value less than 1, Test 2 correctly predicts that each graph is asymptotic to the line $y = b/(1-a) = 4.8/(1 - .2) = 6$. When the initial value is less than 6, the graph increases and moves toward the line $y = 6$. When the initial value is greater than 6, the graph decreases toward the line $y = 6$. In each case the graph is *attracted* to the line $y = 6$.   ◆

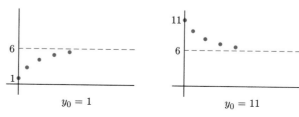

$y_0 = 1$ $y_0 = 11$

Figure 10.

▶ **Example 5**   Apply Test 2 to the difference equation $y_n = -.8y_{n-1} + 9$, $y_0 = 50$.

Solution $|a| = |-.8| = .8 < 1$. So by Test 2 the graph is asymptotic to the line $y = b/(1-a) = 5$. This agrees with the graph as drawn in Fig. 8.   ◆

▶ **Example 6**   Discuss the graphs of $y_n = 1.4y_{n-1} - 8$, with $y_0 > 20$ and with $y_0 < 20$.

Solution   The graphs are shown in Fig. 11. Since $a = 1.4 > 0$, Test 1 predicts that the graphs are monotonic. Since $|a| = |1.4| = 1.4 > 1$, Test 2 predicts that the graphs are unbounded. Here

$$\frac{b}{1-a} = \frac{-8}{1-(1.4)} = \frac{-8}{-.4} = 20.$$

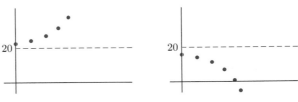

Figure 11.

Both graphs move away from the line $y = 20$ as if being *repelled* by a force.   ◆

▶ **Example 7**   Discuss the graph of the difference equation $y_n = -2y_{n-1} + 60$, where $y_0 > 20$.

Solution   A graph is drawn in Fig. 12. Since $a = -2 < 0$, Test 1 predicts that the graph is oscillating. Since $|a| = |-2| = 2 > 1$, Test 2 predicts that the graph is unbounded. Here

$$\frac{b}{1-a} = \frac{60}{1-(-2)} = \frac{60}{3} = 20.$$

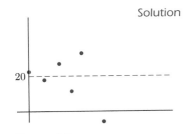

Figure 12.

Notice that successive points move farther away from $y = 20$; that is, they are repelled by the line.   ◆

Verification of Test 2   The key to verifying Test 2 is to make the following two observations:

1. If $|a| < 1$, then the powers a, a^2, a^3, a^4, ... become successively smaller and approach 0. For example, if $a = .4$, then this sequence of powers is

$$.4, .16, .064, .0256, \ldots .$$

2. If $|a| > 1$, then the powers $a, a^2, a^3, a^4, \ldots$ become unbounded; that is, they become arbitrarily large. For example, if $a = 3$, then this sequence is $3, 9, 27, 81, \ldots$.

To verify Test 2, look at the formula for y_n:

$$y_n = \frac{b}{1-a} + \boxed{\left(y_0 - \frac{b}{1-a}\right)a^n}.$$

If $|a| < 1$, then the powers of a get smaller and smaller; so the boxed term approaches 0. That is, y_n approaches $b/(1-a)$ and the graph is asymptotic to $y = b/(1-a)$. If $|a| > 1$, the powers of a are unbounded, so that the boxed term becomes arbitrarily large in magnitude. Thus y_n is unbounded, and so is the graph. ◆

In the case where $|a| < 1$, the graphs (whether oscillating or monotonic) are *attracted* steadily to the line $y = b/(1-a)$. In the case where $|a| > 1$, the graphs are *repelled* by the line $y = b/(1-a)$. Thinking of graphs as being attracted or repelled helps us in making a rough sketch.

Sign of a: $\begin{cases} \text{Positive} & \text{Monotonic} \\ \text{Negative} & \text{Oscillating} \end{cases}$

Size of a: $\begin{cases} |a| < 1 & \text{Attract} \\ |a| > 1 & \text{Repel} \end{cases}$

Figure 13 shows some of the graphs already examined with the appropriate descriptive words labeling the line $y = b/(1-a)$.

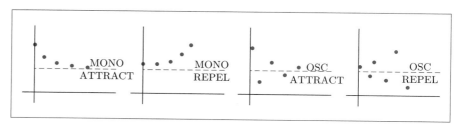

Figure 13.

Based on Tests 1 and 2 and the discussion of constant graphs, we can state a procedure for making a rough sketch of a graph without solving or generating terms.

To sketch the graph of $y_n = ay_{n-1} + b$, $a \neq 0, \pm 1$:

1. Draw the line $y = b/(1-a)$ as a dashed line.

2. Plot y_0. If y_0 is on the line $y = b/(1-a)$, the graph is constant and the procedure terminates.

3. If a is positive, write MONO, since the graph is then monotonic. If a is negative, write OSC, since the graph is then oscillating.

4. If $|a| < 1$, write ATTRACT, since the graph is attracted to the line $y = b/(1-a)$. If $|a| > 1$, write REPEL, since the graph is repelled from the line.

5. Use all the information to sketch the graph.

▶ **Example 8**   Sketch the graph of $y_n = .6y_{n-1} + 8$, $y_0 = 50$.

Solution   **1.** $\dfrac{b}{1-a} = \dfrac{8}{1-(.6)} = \dfrac{8}{.4} = 20.$ So draw the

line $y = 20$.

2. $y_0 = 50$, which is not on the line $y = 20$. So the graph is not constant.

3. $a = .6$, which is positive. Write MONO above the dashed line.

4. $|a| = |.6| = .6 < 1$. Write ATTRACT below the dashed line.

5.   The preceding information tells us to start at 50 and move monotonically toward the line $y = 20$.   ◆

▶ **Example 9**   Sketch the graph of $y_n = -1.5y_{n-1} + 5$, $y_0 = 2.6$.

Solution   **1.** $\dfrac{b}{1-a} = \dfrac{5}{1-(-1.5)} = \dfrac{5}{2.5} = 2.$ So draw the line $y = 2$.

2. $y_0 = 2.6$, which is not on the line $y = 2$. So the graph is not constant.

3. $a = -1.5$, which is negative. Write OSC above the dashed line.

4. $|a| = |-1.5| = 1.5 > 1$. Write REPEL below the dashed line.

5.   The preceding information says that the graph begins at 2.6, oscillates about, and is steadily repelled by the line $y = 2$.   ◆

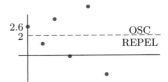

The preceding procedure does not give an exact graph, but it shows the nature of the graph. This is exactly what is needed in many applications.

▶ Example 10   Suppose that the yearly interest rate on a mortgage is 9% compounded monthly and that you can afford to make payments of $300 per month. How much can you afford to borrow?

Solution   Let i = the monthly interest rate, R = the monthly payment, and y_n = the balance after n months. Recall that y_0 = the initial amount of the loan. Then the balance after n months equals the balance after $n-1$ months plus the interest on that balance minus the monthly payment. That is,

$$y_n = y_{n-1} + iy_{n-1} - R = (1+i)y_{n-1} - R.$$

In this particular example, $i = .09/12 = .0075$ and $R = 300$, so the difference equation reads

$$y_n = 1.0075y_{n-1} - 300.$$

Apply our graph-sketching technique to this difference equation. Here

$$\frac{b}{1-a} = \frac{-300}{1-(1.0075)} = \frac{-300}{-.0075} = 40{,}000.$$

Since $a = 1.0075$ is positive and $|a| = 1.0075 > 1$, the words MONO and REPEL describe the graphs.

Let us see what happens for various initial values. If $y_0 > 40{,}000$, the balance increases indefinitely.

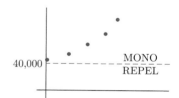

If $y_0 = 40{,}000$, the balance will always be 40,000.

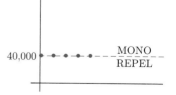

If $y_0 < 40{,}000$, the balance decreases steadily and eventually reaches 0, at which time the mortgage is paid off.

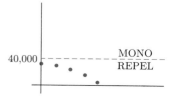

Therefore, the loan must be less than $40,000 in order for it to be paid off eventually.   ◆

<table>
<tr><td>

**Practice Problems
11.3**

</td><td>

1. A parachutist opens her parachute after reaching a speed of 100 feet per second. Suppose that y_n, the speed n seconds after opening the parachute, satisfies $y_n = .1y_{n-1} + 14.4$. Sketch the graph of y_n.

2. Rework Problem 1 if the parachute opens when the speed is 10 feet per second.

3. Upon retirement, a person deposits a certain amount of money into the bank at 6% interest compounded monthly and withdraws \$100 at the end of each month.

   (a) Set up the difference equation for y_n, the amount in the bank after n months.

   (b) How large must the initial deposit be so that the money will never run out?

</td></tr>
</table>

▶ Exercises 11.3

Each of the graphs in Fig. 14 comes from a difference equation of the form $y_n = ay_{n-1} + b$. In Exercises 1–8, list all graphs that have the stated property.

1. Monotonic   **2.** Increasing

3. Unbounded   **4.** Constant

5. Repelled from $y = b/(1-a)$

6. Decreasing   **7.** $|a| < 1$ **8.** $a < 0$

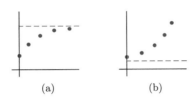

(a)   (b)

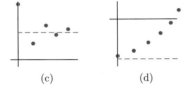

(c)   (d)

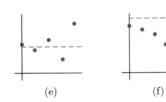

(e)   (f)

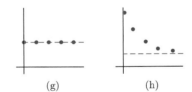

(g)   (h)

Figure 14.

In Exercises 9–14, sketch a graph having the given characteristics.

9. $y_0 = 4$, monotonic, repelled from $y = 2$

10. $y_0 = 5$, monotonic, attracted to $y = -3$

11. $y_0 = 2$, oscillating, attracted to $y = 6$

12. $y_0 = 7$, monotonic, repelled from $y = 10$

13. $y_0 = -2$, monotonic, attracted to $y = 5$

14. $y_0 = 1$, oscillating, repelled from $y = 2$

In Exercises 15–20, make a rough sketch of the graph of the difference equation without generating terms or solving the difference equation.

15. $y_n = 3y_{n-1} + 4$, $y_0 = 0$

16. $y_n = .3y_{n-1} + 3.5$, $y_0 = 2$

17. $y_n = .5y_{n-1} + 3$, $y_0 = 6$

18. $y_n = 4y_{n-1} - 18$, $y_0 = 5$

19. $y_n = -2y_{n-1} + 12$, $y_0 = 5$

20. $y_n = -.6y_{n-1} + 6.4$, $y_0 = 1$

21. A particular news item was broadcast regularly on radio and TV. Let y_n be the number of people who had heard the news within n hours after broadcasting began. Sketch the graph of y_n, assuming that it satisfies the difference equation $y_n = .7y_{n-1} + 3000$, $y_0 = 0$.

22. The radioactive element strontium 90 emits particles and slowly decays. Let y_n be the amount left after n years. Then y_n satisfies the difference equation $y_n = .98y_{n-1}$. Sketch the graph of y_n if initially there are 10 milligrams of strontium 90.

23. Laws of supply and demand cause the price of oats to fluctuate from year to year. Suppose that the current price is $1.25 per bushel and that the price n years from now, p_n, satisfies the difference equation $p_n = -.6p_{n-1} + 1.6$. (Prices are assumed to have been adjusted for inflation.) Sketch the graph of p_n.

24. Under ideal conditions a bacteria population satisfies the difference equation $y_n = 1.4y_{n-1}$, $y_0 = 1$, where y_n is the size of the population (in millions) after n hours. Sketch a graph that shows the growth of the population.

25. Suppose that the interest rate on a mortgage is 9% compounded monthly. If you can afford to pay $450 per month, how much money can you borrow?

26. A municipal government can take out a long-term construction loan at 8% interest compounded quarterly. Assuming that it can pay back $100,000 per quarter, how much money can it borrow?

27. A person makes an initial deposit into a savings account paying 6% interest compounded annually. He plans to withdraw $120 at the end of each year.

    (a) Find the difference equation for y_n, the amount after n years.

    (b) How large must y_0 be such that the money will not run out?

28. Suppose that a loan of $10,000 is to be repaid at $120 per month and that the annual interest rate is 12% compounded monthly. Then the interest for the first month is $.01 \cdot (10{,}000)$, or $100. The $120 paid at the end of the first month can be thought of as paying the $100 interest and paying $20 toward the reduction of the loan. Therefore, the balance after 1 month is $10{,}000 - $20 = $9980. How much of the $120 paid at the end of the second month goes for interest and how much is used to reduce the loan? What is the balance after 2 months?

Exercises 29–34 require the use of a graphing calculator or a computer.

In these exercises, find a difference equation with the given properties. Then confirm your answer by graphing the difference equation on a calculator or computer.

29. The terms begin at 1 and monotonically approach 8.

30. The terms begin at 9 and monotonically approach 4.

31. The terms begin at 1 and monotonically increase without bound.

32. The terms begin at 12, oscillate, and approach 6.

33. The terms begin at 5, oscillate, and are unbounded.

34. The terms begin at 50 and monotonically decrease without bound.

Solutions to Practice Problems 11.3

1. $\dfrac{b}{1-a} = \dfrac{14.4}{1-(.1)} = \dfrac{14.4}{.9} = \dfrac{144}{9} = 16.$ $y_0 = 100$, which is greater than $b/(1-a)$. Since $a = .1$ is positive, the terms y_n are monotonic. Since $|a| = .1 < 1$, the terms are attracted to the line $y = 16$. Now, plot $y_0 = 100$, draw the line $y = 16$, and write in the words MONO and ATTRACT [Fig. 15(a)]. Since the terms are attracted to the line monotonically they must move downward and asymptotically approach the line [Fig. 15(b)]. (Notice that the terminal speed, 16 feet per second, does not depend on the speed of the parachutist when the parachute is opened.)

(a)   (b)

Figure 15.

2. Everything is the same as before except that now $y_0 < 16$. The speed increases to a terminal speed of 16 feet per second.

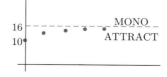

3. (a) $i = .06/12 = .005$

$$y_n = y_{n-1} + (\text{interest}) - (\text{withdrawal})$$
$$= y_{n-1} + .005y_{n-1} - 100$$
$$= (1.005)y_{n-1} - 100$$

(b) $\dfrac{b}{1-a} = \dfrac{-100}{1-(1.005)} = \dfrac{-100}{-.005} = 20,000.$ Since $a = 1.005 > 0$, the graph is monotonic. Since $|a| = 1.005 > 1$, the graph is repelled from the line $y = 20,000$.

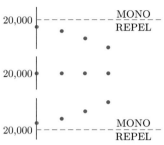

If $y_0 < 20,000$, the amount of money in the account decreases and eventually runs out.

If $y_0 = 20,000$, the amount of money in the account stays constant at 20,000.

If $y_0 > 20,000$, the amount of money in the account grows steadily and is unbounded.

Answer: $y_0 \geq 20,000$.

11.4 Mathematics of Personal Finance

In this section we apply the theory of difference equations to the study of mortgages and annuities.

Mortgages   Most families take out bank loans to pay for a new house. Such a loan, called a mortgage, is used to purchase the house and then is repaid with interest in monthly installments over a number of years, usually 25 or 30. The monthly payments are computed so that after exactly the correct length of time the unpaid balance[1] is 0 and the loan is thereby paid off.

Mortgages can be described by difference equations, as follows. Let y_n be the unpaid balance on the mortgage after n months. In particular, y_0 is the initial amount borrowed. Let i denote the monthly interest rate and R the monthly mortgage payment. Then

$$\begin{bmatrix} \text{balance after} \\ n \text{ months} \end{bmatrix} = \begin{bmatrix} \text{balance after} \\ n-1 \text{ months} \end{bmatrix} + \begin{bmatrix} \text{interest for} \\ \text{month} \end{bmatrix} - \begin{bmatrix} \text{payment} \end{bmatrix}$$

$$y_n \qquad = \qquad y_{n-1} \qquad + \qquad iy_{n-1} \qquad - \qquad R$$

$$y_n = (1+i)y_{n-1} - R. \tag{1}$$

▶ Example 1   Suppose that you can afford to pay $300 per month and the yearly interest rate is 9% compounded monthly. Exactly how much can you borrow if the mortgage is to be paid off in 30 years?

Solution   The monthly interest rate is $.09/12 = .0075$, so equation (1) becomes in this case

$$y_n = 1.0075y_{n-1} - 300.$$

[1]The balance after n months is the amount that would have to be paid at that time in order to retire the debt.

Further, we are given that the mortgage runs for 30 years, or 360 months. Thus

$$y_{360} = 0. \tag{2}$$

Our problem is to determine y_0, the amount of the loan. From our general theory we first compute $b/(1-a)$:

$$\frac{b}{1-a} = \frac{-300}{1-(1.0075)} = 40,000.$$

The formula for y_{360} is then given by

$$y_{360} = \frac{b}{1-a} + \left(y_0 - \frac{b}{1-a}\right)a^{360}$$

$$= 40,000 + (y_0 - 40,000)(1.0075)^{360}.$$

Using a calculator, we find that

$$(1.0075)^{360} = 14.73057612.$$

Therefore,

$$y_{360} = 40,000 + (y_0 - 40,000)(14.73057612).$$

However, by equation (2), $y_{360} = 0$, so that

$$0 = 40,000 + (y_0 - 40,000)(14.73057612) = 14.73057612 y_0 - 549,223.0449$$

$$y_0 = \frac{549,223.0449}{14.73057612} = 37,284.56.$$

Thus, the initial amount, that is, the amount that can be borrowed, is $37,284.56.
◆

Table 1 shows the status of the mortgage after selected payments. After the first payment of $300 is made, the balance of the loan is $y_1 = \$37,264.19$. This payment consists of $279.63 interest and $20.37 repayment of the loan. In the early months almost all of the monthly payment goes toward interest. With each passing month, however, the amount of interest declines and the amount applied to reducing the debt increases.

Table 1

Payment Number	1	2	120	240	348	360
Balance on loan	$37,264.19	$37,243.68	$33,343.49	$23,682.51	$3430.48	$0
Interest	279.63	279.48	250.45	178.53	27.77	2.23
Reduction of debt	20.37	20.52	49.55	121.47	272.23	297.77

▶ **Example 2** Suppose that we have a 30-year mortgage for $140,000 at 7.5% interest, compounded monthly. Find the monthly payment.

Solution Here the monthly interest rate i is just $.075/12 = .00625$ and $y_0 = 140,000$. Since the mortgage is for 30 years, we have

$$y_{360} = 0.$$

The difference equation for the mortgage is

$$y_n = 1.00625y_{n-1} - R \qquad y_0 = 140{,}000.$$

Now

$$\frac{b}{1-a} = -\frac{R}{1-1.00625} = \frac{R}{.00625} = 160R.$$

The formula for y_n is

$$y_n = 160R + (140{,}000 - 160R)(1.00625)^n$$

Thus

$$0 = y_{360} = 160R + (140{,}000 - 160R)(1.00625)^{360}.$$

To complete the problem, solve this equation for R. Using a calculator, $(1.00625)^{360} = 9.421533905$. Thus

$$160R + (140{,}000 - 160R)(9.421533905) = 0$$
$$1347.445425R = 1{,}319{,}014.747$$
$$R = \$978.90. \qquad \blacklozenge$$

Annuities The term *annuity* has several meanings. For our purposes an annuity is a bank account into which equal sums are deposited at regular intervals, either weekly, monthly, quarterly, or annually. The money draws interest and accumulates for a certain number of years, after which it becomes available to the investor. Annuities are often used to save for a child's college education or to generate funds for retirement.

The growth of money in an annuity can be described by a difference equation. Let $y_n = $ [the amount of money in the annuity after n time periods], $i = $ [the interest rate per time period], $D = $ [the deposit per time period]. Then $y_0 = $ [the amount after 0 time periods] $= 0$.[2] Moreover,

$$y_n = [\text{previous amount}] + [\text{interest}] + [\text{deposit}]$$
$$= \qquad y_{n-1} \qquad + \quad iy_{n-1} \quad + \quad D$$
$$= \quad (1+i)y_{n-1} + D.$$

This last equation is the difference equation of the annuity.

▶ **Example 3**   Suppose that $20 is deposited into an annuity at the end of every quarter-year and that interest is earned at the annual rate of 8%, compounded quarterly. How much money is in the annuity after 10 years?

Solution   Since 10 years = 40 quarters, the problem is to compute y_{40}. Now $D = 20$ and $i = .08/4 = .02$. So the difference equation reads

$$y_n = 1.02y_{n-1} + 20.$$

In this case

$$\frac{b}{1-a} = \frac{20}{1-1.02} = -1000.$$

---

[2]One model for the situation $y_0 = 0$ is a payroll savings plan, where a person signs up at time zero and has the first deduction made at the end of the next pay period.

Thus

$$y_n = -1000 + [0 - (-1000)](1.02)^n$$
$$= -1000 + 1000(1.02)^n.$$

In particular, setting $n = 40$,

$$y_{40} = -1000 + 1000(1.02)^{40}.$$

Using a calculator, $(1.02)^{40} = 2.208039664$. Thus

$$y_{40} = -1000 + 1000(2.208039664) = -1000 + 2208.039664 = 1208.039664.$$

Thus after 10 years the account contains $1208.04. ◆

▶ **Example 4** How much money must be deposited at the end of each quarter into an annuity at 8% interest compounded quarterly in order to have $10,000 after 15 years?

Solution Here D is unknown. But $i = .02$. Also, 15 years = 60 quarters, so that $y_{60} = 10,000$. The difference equation in this case reads

$$y_n = 1.02y_{n-1} + D \qquad y_0 = 0.$$

Then

$$\frac{b}{1-a} = \frac{D}{1-1.02} = \frac{D}{-.02} = -50D$$

and

$$y_n = -50D + (0 - (-50D))(1.02)^n$$
$$= -50D + 50D(1.02)^n.$$

Set $n = 60$. Then

$$y_{60} = -50D + 50D(1.02)^{60}.$$

However, from the statement of the problem, $y_{60} = 10,000$. Thus we have the equation

$$10,000 = -50D + 50D(1.02)^{60}$$

to be solved for D. But $(1.02)^{60} = 3.281030788$, so that

$$-50D + 50(3.281030788)D = 10,000$$
$$-50D + 164.0515394D = 10,000$$
$$114.0515394D = 10,000$$
$$D = \frac{10,000}{114.0515394} = \$87.68. \qquad ◆$$

GC A complete table similar to Table 1 is called an *amortization table* and is easily created with a graphing calculator. Consider the mortgage of Example 1 with difference equation $y_n = 1.0075y_{n-1} - 300$, $y_0 = 37284.56$. Let v_n be the interest portion of the nth payment. Then $v_n = .0075y_{n-1}$ for $n = 1, 2, 3, \ldots$. Figures 1 and 2 show these two equations defining sequences in the **Y=** editor. If both sequences are selected, then each will have a column when 2nd [TABLE] is pressed. See Fig. 3. For each value of **n**, **u(n)** is the balance after the nth payment and **v(n)** is the interest portion of the payment. For instance, the first row of the table says that after the first payment is made, the balance is $37,264.19 and $279.63 of the $300 payment consists of interest.

Figure 1. TI-83   **Figure 2.** TI-82   **Figure 3.**

Practice Problems 11.4

1. Suppose that you deposit $650,000 into a bank account paying 5% interest compounded annually and you withdraw $50,000 at the end of each year. Find a difference equation for y_n, the amount in the account after n years.

2. Refer to Problem 1. How much money will be in the account after 20 years?

3. Refer to Problem 1. Assume that the money is tax-free and that you could earn 5% interest compounded annually. Would you rather have $650,000 now or $50,000 a year for 20 years?

▶ Exercises 11.4

In Exercises 1–4, give the difference equation for y_n, the amount (or balance) after n interest periods.

1. A mortgage loan of $32,500 at 9% interest compounded monthly and having monthly payments of $261.50.

2. A bank deposit of $1000 at 6% interest compounded semiannually.

3. An annuity for which $4000 is deposited into an account at 6% interest compounded quarterly and $200 is added to the account at the end of each quarter.

4. A bank account into which $20,000 is deposited at 6% interest compounded monthly and $100 is withdrawn at the end of each month.

5. How much money can you borrow at 12% interest compounded monthly if the loan is to be paid off in monthly installments for 10 years and you can afford to pay $660 per month?

6. Find the monthly payment on a $38,000, 25-year mortgage at 12% interest compounded monthly.

7. Find the amount accumulated after 20 years if, at the end of each year, $300 is deposited into an account paying 6% interest compounded annually.

8. How much money would you have to deposit at the end of each month into an annuity paying 6% interest compounded monthly in order to have $6000 after 12 years?

9. How much money would you have to put into an account initially at 8% interest compounded quarterly in order to have $6000 after 14 years?

10. How much money would you have to put into a bank account paying 6% interest compounded monthly in order to be able to withdraw $150 each month for 30 years?

11. In order to buy a used car, a person borrows $4000 from the bank at 12% interest compounded monthly. The loan is to be paid off in 3 years with equal monthly payments. What will the monthly payments be?

12. How much money would you have to deposit at the end of each month into an annuity paying 6% interest

compounded monthly in order to have $1620 after 4 years?

Exercises 13–16 require the use of a graphing calculator or a computer.

In these exercises, use a table or graph of an appropriate difference equation to answer the questions.

13. The ABC Corporation borrows $45 million (at 8% interest compounded annually) to buy a shopping center. The loan is repaid with annual payments of $4 million per year. Determine the balance after 10 years. After how many years will the loan be paid off?

14. John buys a stereo system for $605.54 and pays for it with monthly payments of $90. The interest rate is 12% compounded monthly. Determine the amount

still owed after 4 months. After how many months will the loan be repaid?

15. A person deposits $100 at the end of each month into an annuity earning 6% interest compounded monthly. What are the balances (that is, future values) after 5, 10, and 15 months? How many months are required for the balance to reach $3228? After how many months will the balance exceed $4000?

16. Alice embarks on a savings routine. She decides to deposit $75 at the end of every three months into a savings account paying 6% interest compounded quarterly. How much money will she have accumulated after 5 years? When will she have accumulated $2474? After how many quarters will her savings exceed $4000?

Solutions to Practice Problems 11.4

1. $$\begin{bmatrix} \text{amount after} \\ n \text{ years} \end{bmatrix} = \begin{bmatrix} \text{amount after} \\ n-1 \text{ years} \end{bmatrix} + \begin{bmatrix} \text{interest for} \\ n\text{th year} \end{bmatrix} - \begin{bmatrix} \text{withdrawal at} \\ \text{end of year} \end{bmatrix}$$

$$y_n = y_{n-1} + .05y_{n-1} - 50{,}000 = (1.05)y_{n-1} - 50{,}000 \qquad y_0 = 650{,}000$$

2. Solve the difference equation and set $n = 20$.

$$\frac{b}{1-a} = \frac{-50{,}000}{1-(1.05)} = \frac{-50{,}000}{-.05} = 1{,}000{,}000$$

$$y_n = 1{,}000{,}000 + (650{,}000 - 1{,}000{,}000)(1.05)^n$$

$$= 1{,}000{,}000 - 350{,}000(1.05)^n$$

$$y_{20} = 1{,}000{,}000 - 350{,}000(2.653297705) = 71{,}345.80$$

3. $650,000. According to Problem 2, this money could be deposited into the bank. You could take out $50,000 per year and still have $71,345.80 left over after 20 years.

11.5 Modeling with Difference Equations

In this section we show how difference equations may be used to build mathematical models of a number of phenomena. Since the difference equation describing a situation contains as much data as the formula for y_n, we shall regard the difference equation itself as a mathematical model. We demonstrate in this section that the difference equation and a sketch of its graph can often be of more use than an explicit solution.

The concept of proportionality will be needed to develop some of these models.

Proportionality   To say that quantities are proportional is the same as saying that one quantity is equal to a constant times the other quantity. For instance, in a state having a 4% sales tax, the sales tax on an item is proportional to the price of the item, since

$$[\text{sales tax}] = .04[\text{price}].$$

Here, the constant of proportionality is .04. In general, for two proportional quantities we have

$$[\text{first quantity}] = k[\text{second quantity}],$$

where k is some fixed constant of proportionality. Note that if both quantities are positive and if the first quantity is known always to be smaller than the second, then k is a positive number less than 1; that is, $0 < k < 1$.

▶ Example 1   (*Radioactive Decay*) Certain forms of natural elements, such as uranium 238, strontium 90, and carbon 14, are radioactive. That is, they decay, or dissipate, over a period of time. Physicists have found that this process of decay obeys the following law: Each year the amount that decays is proportional to the amount present at the start of the year. Construct a mathematical model describing radioactive decay.

Solution   Let $y_n =$ the amount left after n years. The physical law states that

$$[\text{amount that decays in year } n] = k \cdot y_{n-1},$$

where $k \cdot y_{n-1}$ represents a constant of proportionality times the amount present at the start of that year. Therefore,

$$
y_n \quad = \quad y_{n-1} \quad - \quad k \cdot y_{n-1}
$$

$$
\begin{bmatrix} \text{amount after} \\ \text{year } n \end{bmatrix} = \begin{bmatrix} \text{amount after} \\ \text{year } n-1 \end{bmatrix} - \begin{bmatrix} \text{amount that decays} \\ \text{in year } n \end{bmatrix}
$$

or

$$y_n = (1-k)y_{n-1},$$

where k is a constant between 0 and 1. This difference equation is the mathematical model for radioactive decay. ◆

▶ Example 2   Experiment shows that for cobalt 60 (a radioactive form of cobalt used in cancer therapy) the decay constant k is given by $k = .12$.

(a) Write the difference equation for y_n in this case.
(b) Sketch the graph of the difference equation.

Solution   (a) Setting $k = .12$ in the result of Example 1, we get

$$y_n = (1 - .12)y_{n-1} \quad \text{or} \quad y_n = .88y_{n-1}.$$

(b) Since .88 is positive and less than 1, the graph is monotonic and attracted to the line $y = b/(1-a) = 0/(1-.88) = 0$. The graph is sketched in Fig. 1. ◆

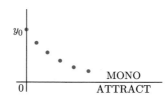

Figure 1.

▶ **Example 3** (*Growth of Bacteria*) A bacteria culture grows in such a way that each hour the increase in the number of bacteria in the culture is proportional to the total number present at the beginning of the hour. Sketch a graph depicting the growth of the culture.

Solution Let y_n = the number of bacteria present after n hours. Then the increase from the previous hour is ky_{n-1}, where k is a positive constant of proportionality. Therefore,

$$y_n = y_{n-1} + ky_{n-1}$$

$$\begin{bmatrix}\text{number after}\\ n \text{ hours}\end{bmatrix} = \begin{bmatrix}\text{number after}\\ n-1 \text{ hours}\end{bmatrix} + \begin{bmatrix}\text{increase during}\\ n\text{th hour}\end{bmatrix}$$

or

$$y_n = (1+k)y_{n-1}.$$

This last equation gives a mathematical model of the growth of the culture. Since $a = 1+k > 0$ and $|a| > 1$, the graph is monotonic and repelled from $b/(1-a) = 0$. Thus the graph is as drawn in Fig. 2. ◆

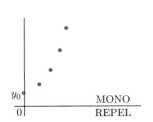

y_0 MONO
0   REPEL

Figure 2.

▶ **Example 4** (*Spread of Information*) Suppose that at 8 A.M. on a Saturday the local radio and TV stations in a town start broadcasting a certain piece of news. The number of people learning the news each hour is proportional to the number who had not yet heard it by the end of the preceding hour.

(a) Write a difference equation describing the spread of the news through the population of the town.

(b) Sketch the graph of this difference equation for the case where the constant of proportionality is .3 and the population of the town is 50,000.

Solution The example states that two quantities are proportional. The first quantity is the number of people learning the news each hour and the second is the number who have not yet heard it by the end of the preceding hour.

(a) Let y_n = the number of people who have heard the news after n hours. The terms $y_0, y_1, y_2, \ldots$ are increasing.

Let P = the total population of the town. Then the number of people who have not yet heard the news after $n - 1$ hours is $P - y_{n-1}$. Thus the assumption can be stated in the mathematical form

$$y_n = y_{n-1} + k(P - y_{n-1})$$

$$\begin{bmatrix}\text{number who know}\\ \text{after } n \text{ hours}\end{bmatrix} = \begin{bmatrix}\text{number who know}\\ \text{after } n-1 \text{ hours}\end{bmatrix} + \begin{bmatrix}\text{number who learn}\\ \text{during } n\text{th hour}\end{bmatrix},$$

where k is a constant of proportionality. The constant k tells how fast the news is traveling. It measures the percentage of the uninformed population that hears the news each hour. It is clear that $0 < k < 1$.

(b) For part (b) we assume that $k = .3$ and that the town has a population of 50,000. Further, we measure the number of people in thousands. Then $P = 50$ and the mathematical model of the spread of the news is

$$y_n = y_{n-1} + .3(50 - y_{n-1}) = y_{n-1} + 15 - .3y_{n-1} = .7y_{n-1} + 15.$$

Suppose that initially no one had heard the news, so that

$$y_0 = 0.$$

Now we may sketch the graph:

$$\frac{b}{1-a} = \frac{15}{1-.7} = \frac{15}{.3} = 50.$$

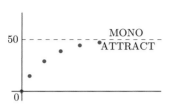

Figure 3.

Since $a = .7$, the graph is monotonic and attracted to the line $y = 50$ (Fig. 3). Note that the number of people who hear the news increases and approaches the population of the entire town. The increases between consecutive terms are large at first and then become smaller. This coincides with the intuitive impression that the news spreads rapidly at first and then progressively slower.   ◆

▶ **Example 5** (*Supply and Demand*) This year's level of production and price for most agricultural products greatly affect the level of production and price next year. Suppose that the current crop of soybeans in a certain country is 80 million bushels. Let q_n denote the quantity[3] of soybeans grown n years from now, and let p_n denote the market price in n years. Suppose experience has shown that q_n and p_n are related by the following equations:

$$p_n = 20 - .1q_n \qquad q_n = 5p_{n-1} - 10.$$

Draw a graph depicting the changes in production from year to year.

Solution   What we seek is the graph of a difference equation for q_n.

$$q_n = 5p_{n-1} - 10 = 5(20 - .1q_{n-1}) - 10 = 100 - .5q_{n-1} - 10 = -.5q_{n-1} + 90$$

This is a difference equation for q_n with

Figure 4.

$$a = -.5 \qquad b = 90 \qquad \frac{b}{1-a} = \frac{90}{1-(-.5)} = 60.$$

Since a is negative, the graph is oscillating. Since $|a| = .5 < 1$, the graph is attracted to the line $y = b/(1-a) = 60$. The initial condition is $q_0 = 80$. So the graph is as drawn in Fig. 4. Note that the graph oscillates and approaches 60. That is, the crop size fluctuates from year to year and eventually gets close to 60 million bushels.   ◆

Practice Problems 11.5

1. (*Glucose Infusion*) Glucose is being given to a patient intravenously at the rate of 100 milligrams per minute. Let y_n be the amount of glucose in the blood after n minutes, measured in milligrams. Suppose that each minute the body takes from the blood 2% of the amount of glucose present at the beginning of that minute. Find a difference equation for y_n and sketch its graph. (*Hint:* Each minute the amount of glucose in the blood is increased by the intravenous infusion and decreased by the absorption into the body.)

2. (*Light at Ocean Depths*) Sunlight is absorbed by water and so, as one descends into the ocean, the intensity of light diminishes. Suppose that at each depth, going down one more meter causes a 20% decrease in the intensity of the sunlight. Find a difference equation for y_n, the intensity of the light at a depth of n meters, and sketch its graph.

---

[3]q_n in terms of millions of bushels, p_n in terms of dollars per bushel.

▶ Exercises 11.5

1. In a certain country with current population 100 million, each year the number of births is 3% and the number of deaths 1% of the population at the beginning of the year. Find the difference equation for y_n, the population after n years. Sketch its graph.

2. A small city with current population 50,000 is experiencing an emigration of 600 people each year. Assuming that each year the increase in population due to natural causes is 1% of the population at the start of that year, find the difference equation for y_n, the population after n years. Sketch its graph.

3. After a certain drug is injected, each hour the amount removed from the bloodstream by the body is 25% of the amount in the bloodstream at the beginning of the hour. Find the difference equation for y_n, the amount in the bloodstream after n hours, and sketch the graph.

4. The atmospheric pressure at sea level is 14.7 pounds per square inch. Suppose that at any elevation an increase of 1 mile results in a decrease of 20% of the atmospheric pressure at that elevation. Find the difference equation for y_n, the atmospheric pressure at elevation n miles, and sketch its graph.

5. A sociological study[4] was made to examine the process by which doctors decide to adopt a new drug. Certain doctors who had little interaction with other physicians were called "isolated." Out of 100 isolated doctors, each month the number who adopted the new drug that month was 8% of those who had not yet adopted the drug at the beginning of the month. Find a difference equation for y_n, the number of isolated physicians using the drug after n months, and sketch its graph.

6. A cell is put into a fluid containing an 8 milligram/liter concentration of a solute. (This concentration stays constant throughout.) Initially, the concentration of the solute in the cell is 3 milligrams/liter. The solute passes through the cell membrane at such a rate that each minute the increase in concentration in the cell is 40% of the difference between the outside concentration and the inside concentration. Find the difference equation for y_n, the concentration of the solute in the cell after n minutes, and sketch its graph.

7. Psychologists have found that in certain learning situations in which there is a maximum amount that can be learned, the additional amount learned each minute is proportional to the amount yet to be learned at the beginning of that minute. Let 12 units of information be the maximum amount that can be learned and let the constant of proportionality be 30%. Find a difference equation for y_n, the amount learned after n minutes, and sketch its graph.

8. Consider two genes A and a in a population, where A is a dominant gene and a is a recessive gene controlling the same genetic trait. (That is, A and a belong to the same locus.) Suppose that initially 80% of the genes are A and 20% are a. Suppose that in each generation .003% of genes A mutate to gene a. Find a difference equation for y_n, the percentage of genes a after n generations, and sketch its graph. [*Note*: The percentage of genes $A = 1 -$ (the percentage of genes a).]

9. Thirty thousand dollars is deposited in a savings account paying 5% interest compounded annually, and $1000 is withdrawn from the account at the end of each year. Find the difference equation for y_n, the amount in the account after n years, and sketch its graph.

10. Rework Exercise 9 where $15,000 is deposited initially.

11. When a cold object is placed in a warm room, each minute its increase in temperature is proportional to the difference between the room temperature and the temperature of the object at the beginning of the minute. Suppose that the room temperature is 70°F, the initial temperature of the object is 40°F, and the constant of proportionality is 20%. Find the difference equation for y_n, the temperature of the object after n minutes, and sketch its graph.

12. Suppose that the annual amount of electricity used in the United States will increase at a rate of 7% each year and that this year 2.6 trillion kilowatt-hours are being used. Find a difference equation for y_n, the number of kilowatt-hours to be used during the year that is n years from now, and sketch its graph.

13. Suppose that in Example 5 the current price of soybeans is $10 per bushel. Find the difference equation for p_n and sketch its graph.

Exercises 14–16 require the use of a graphing calculator or a computer.

In these exercises, answer the questions by generating successive terms of the appropriate difference equation.

14. A steel rod of temperature 600° is immersed in a large vat of water at temperature 75°. Each minute its decrease in temperature is proportional to the difference between the water temperature and the temperature of the rod at the beginning of the minute, where the constant of proportionality is .3. What is the temperature after 2 seconds? When will the temperature drop below 80°?

15. The birth rate in a certain city is 3.5% per year and the death rate is 2% per year. Also, there is a net movement of population out of the city at a steady rate of 300 people per year. The population in 2000 was 5 million. Estimate the 2005 population. When will the population exceed 6 million? When will the population have doubled to 10 million?

---

[4] James S. Coleman, Elihu Katz, and Herbert Menzel, "The Diffusion of an Innovation Among Physicians," *Sociometry*, 20, 1957, pp. 253–270.

16. Consider the sociological study of Exercise 5. Out of a group of *nonisolated* doctors, let y_n be the percent who adopted the new drug after n months. Then y_n satisfies the difference equation

$$y_n = .0025y_{n-1}(500 - y_{n-1}) \qquad y_0 = 3.$$

That is, initially 3% were using the drug. What percent were using the drug after 1 year? When were over half of the doctors using the drug? When were over 99% using the drug?

Solutions to Practice Problems 11.5

1. The amount of glucose in the blood is affected by two factors. It is being increased by the steady infusion of glucose; each minute the amount is increased by 100 milligrams. On the other hand, the amount is being decreased each minute by $.02y_{n-1}$. Therefore,

$$y_n = y_{n-1} + 100 - .02y_{n-1}$$

$$\begin{bmatrix} \text{amount after} \\ n \text{ minutes} \end{bmatrix} = \begin{bmatrix} \text{amount after} \\ n-1 \text{ minutes} \end{bmatrix} + \begin{bmatrix} \text{increase due} \\ \text{to infusion} \end{bmatrix} - \begin{bmatrix} \text{amount taken} \\ \text{by the body} \end{bmatrix}$$

or

$$y_n = .98y_{n-1} + 100.$$

To sketch the graph, first compute $b/(1-a)$.

$$\frac{b}{1-a} = \frac{100}{1-.98} = \frac{100}{.02} = 5000.$$

The amount of glucose in the blood rises and approaches 5000 milligrams (Fig. 5).

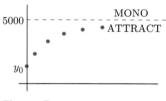

Figure 5.

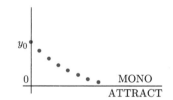

Figure 6.

2. The change in intensity in going from depth $n-1$ meters to n meters is 20% of the intensity at $n-1$ meters. Therefore,

$$y_n = y_{n-1} - .20y_{n-1}$$

$$\begin{bmatrix} \text{intensity at} \\ n \text{ meters} \end{bmatrix} = \begin{bmatrix} \text{intensity at} \\ n-1 \text{ meters} \end{bmatrix} - \begin{bmatrix} \text{change in} \\ \text{intensity} \end{bmatrix}$$

$$y_n = .8y_{n-1}.$$

Thus $b/(1-a) = 0$, and the graph is as shown in Fig. 6.

▶ Chapter 11 Summary

1. A *difference equation* of the form $y_n = ay_{n-1} + b$, where a, b, and y_0 are specified, determines a sequence of numbers in which each of the numbers (that is, $y_1, y_2, \dots$) is obtained from the preceding number by multiplying the preceding number by a and adding b.

The first number in the sequence, y_0, is called the *initial value.*

2. The graph of a difference equation is obtained by graphing the points $(0, y_0), (1, y_1), (2, y_2), \dots$.

3. The value of the nth term of a difference equation $y_n = ay_{n-1} + b$ (y_0 given) can be obtained directly (that is, without generating the preceding terms) with one of the following formulas:

$$y_n = \frac{b}{1-a} + \left(y_0 - \frac{b}{1-a}\right)a^n \quad (a \neq 1)$$

$$y_n = y_0 + bn \quad (a = 1).$$

4. Money deposited in a savings account is called the *principal*. The amount of money earned by the deposit is determined by the type of interest (*simple* or *compound*), the yearly rate of interest, and, for compound interest, the number of times interest is compounded annually. Suppose P dollars is deposited at yearly interest rate r. With simple interest, the balance after n years, y_n, satisfies the difference equation

$$y_n = y_{n-1} + rP, \quad y_0 = P.$$

With interest compounded k times per year, the *interest rate per period* is $i = k/r$ and the balance after n years, y_n, satisfies the difference equation

$$y_n = (1+i)y_{n-1}, \quad y_0 = P.$$

5. Terminology has been developed to describe the behavior of graphs of difference equations.

increasing	rises when read from left to right
decreasing	falls when read from left to right
monotonic	either increasing or decreasing
oscillating	changes its direction from rising to falling with every term
constant	always has the same value, y_0
attracted	moves closer and closer to the line $y = b/(1-a)$
repelled	moves farther and farther away from the line $y = b/(1-a)$ without bound

6. The five-step procedure for sketching the graph of a difference equation appears on page 508.

7. A *mortgage* is a loan that is paid off in equal payments. The sequence of successive balances (that is, amounts still owed) satisfies a difference equation of the form

$$y_n = (1+i)y_{n-1} - R,$$

where i is the interest rate per period and R is the payment per period.

8. An *annuity* is a sequence of equal deposits into a savings account. The sequence of successive balances satisfies a difference equation of the form

$$y_n = (1+i)y_{n-1} + D,$$

where i is the interest rate per period and D is the payment per period.

Review of Fundamental Concepts of Chapter 11

1. Explain how a sequence of numbers is generated by a difference equation of the form $y_n = ay_{n-1} + b$.

2. What is meant by an initial value for the difference equation in Question 1?

3. How do you obtain the graph of the difference equation in Question 1?

4. Give the formula that is the solution of the difference equation $y_n = ay_{n-1} + b$ with $a \neq 1$ and then with $a = 1$.

5. Explain how both simple interest and compound interest work.

6. What does it mean for a graph to be increasing? decreasing? monotonic? oscillating? constant?

7. Describe the possible long-run behaviors of the graph of the difference equation $y_n = ay_{n-1} + b$, $a \neq 1$.

8. Give the five-step procedure for sketching the graph of $y_n = ay_{n-1} + b$, $a \neq 1$.

9. What is a mortgage, and how are its successive balances calculated?

10. What is an annuity, and how are its successive balances calculated?

▶ Chapter 11 Supplementary Exercises

1. Consider the difference equation $y_n = -3y_{n-1} + 8$, $y_0 = 1$.
   (a) Generate y_1, y_2, y_3 from the difference equation.
   (b) Solve the difference equation.
   (c) Use the solution in part (b) to obtain y_4.

2. Consider the difference equation $y_n = y_{n-1} - \frac{3}{2}$, $y_0 = 10$.
   (a) Generate y_1, y_2, y_3 from the difference equation.
   (b) Solve the difference equation.
   (c) Use the solution in part (b) to obtain y_6.

3. How much money would you have to put into a savings account initially at 8% interest compounded quarterly in order to have $6600 after 10 years?

4. How much money would you have in the bank after 2 years if you deposited $1000 at 5.2% interest compounded weekly?

5. Make a rough sketch of the graph of the difference equation $y_n = -\frac{1}{3}y_{n-1} + 8$, $y_0 = 10$, without generating terms.

6. Make a rough sketch of the graph of the difference equation $y_n = 1.5y_{n-1} - 2$, $y_0 = 5$, without generating terms.

7. The population of a certain city is currently 120,000. The growth rate of the population due to more births than deaths is 3% per year. Furthermore, each year 600 people move out of the city. Let y_n be the population after n years.

   (a) Find the difference equation for the population growth.

   (b) What will be the population after 20 years?

8. The monthly payment on a $35,000, 30-year mortgage at 12% interest compounded monthly is $360. Let y_n be the unpaid balance of the mortgage after n months.

   (a) Give the difference equation expressing y_n in terms of y_{n-1}. Also, give y_0.

   (b) What is the unpaid balance after 7 years?

9. How much money must be deposited at the end of each week into an annuity at $5\frac{1}{5}\%$ (= .052) interest

compounded weekly in order to have $40,000 after 21 years?

10. Find the monthly payment on a $33,100, 20-year mortgage at 6% interest compounded monthly.

11. How much money can you borrow at 8% interest compounded annually if the loan is to be paid off in yearly installments for 18 years and you can afford to pay $2400 per year?

12. A college alumnus pledges to give his alma mater $5 at the end of each month for 4 years. If the college puts the money in a savings account earning 6% interest compounded monthly, how much money will be in the account at the end of 4 years?

13. An unknown candidate for governor in a state having 1,000,000 voters mounts an extensive media campaign. Each day, 10% of the voters who do not yet know about him become aware of his candidacy. Let y_n be the number of voters who are aware of his candidacy after n days. Find a difference equation for y_n, and sketch its graph.

14. Suppose that 100 people were just elected to a certain state legislature and that after each term 8% of those still remaining from this original group will either retire or not be reelected. Let y_n be the number of legislators from the original group of 100 who are still serving after n terms. Find a difference equation for y_n, and sketch its graph.

▶ Chapter 11 Chapter Test

1. Consider the difference equation $y_n = \frac{1}{2}y_{n-1} + 3$, $y_0 = -2$.

   (a) Determine y_1, y_2, y_3.

   (b) Solve the difference equation.

   (c) Use the solution in part (b) to determine y_4.

2. Consider the difference equation $y_n = y_{n-1} + 50$, $y_0 = 60$.

   (a) Determine y_1, y_2, y_3.

   (b) Solve the difference equation.

   (c) Use the solution in part (b) to determine y_4.

3. Make a rough sketch of the graph of each difference equation without generating terms or solving the difference equation.

   (a) $y_n = .6y_{n-1} + 20$, $y_0 = 10$

   (b) $y_n = -1.25y_{n-1} + 9$, $y_0 = 2$

4. Ideally, the concentration of chlorine in a swimming pool should be between 1 and 2 parts per million (ppm). Due to the sun and bacteria, about 20% of the chlorine dissipates each day. Suppose that initially

a swimming pool has a concentration of 1 ppm. How much chlorine, in ppm, should be added to the pool at the end of each day so that the concentration will approach 1.5 ppm as the days progress?

5. Brittany takes out a loan from a bank and repays it in quarterly payments. The balance after n quarters, y_n, satisfies the difference equation $y_n = 1.02y_{n-1} - 3000$, $y_0 = 31{,}726$.

   (a) How much money did Brittany borrow?

   (b) What was the yearly rate of interest?

   (c) How much did Brittany pay each quarter?

   (d) What will the balance of the loan be after the first quarterly payment?

6. The following table shows partial data for the initial status of a 2-year loan with monthly payments.

Payment Number	1	2	3
Balance	A	$8,888.01	B
Interest	$100	$96.31	$92.58
Reduction of debt	$354.15	$357.84	C

(a) What is the monthly payment?

(b) What is the yearly rate of interest?

(c) Find A, B, and C.

7. I plan to take out a 25-year mortgage at 9% interest compounded monthly. If I am able to pay $1000 per month, how much can I borrow?

8. Suppose that $500 is deposited into an annuity at the end of each year and that interest is 6% compounded annually. Let y_n be the balance at the end of n years.

(a) Give the difference equation for y_n. (Include the initial value.)

(b) How much money will be in the annuity after 17 years?

9. How much money would you have to deposit at the end of each month into an annuity paying 6% interest compounded monthly in order to have $20,000 after 10 years?

10. Patients with certain heart problems are often treated with digitoxin, a derivative of the digitalis plant. The rate at which a person's body eliminates digitoxin is proportional to the amount of digitoxin present. Each day about 10% of any given amount of the drug will be eliminated. Suppose that a dose of .05 milligram is given daily to a patient. Find the difference equation for y_n, the amount in the bloodstream after n doses, and sketch the graph.

Chapter Project

Connections to Markov Processes

This chapter project uses difference equations to find the stable distribution for a Markov process and gain insights into the rate with which distribution matrices approach the stable distribution.

1. Show that any 2×2 stochastic matrix can be written in the form

$$A = \begin{bmatrix} 1 - s & r \\ s & 1 - r \end{bmatrix},$$

where r and s are numbers between 0 and 1.

In this discussion, we will make the assumption that r and s are not both zero. Denote the successive distribution matrices associated with matrix A as

$$\begin{bmatrix} x_0 \\ y_0 \end{bmatrix}, \quad \begin{bmatrix} x_1 \\ y_1 \end{bmatrix}, \quad \begin{bmatrix} x_2 \\ y_2 \end{bmatrix}, \dots,$$

where

$$\begin{bmatrix} x_n \\ y_n \end{bmatrix} = A \cdot \begin{bmatrix} x_{n-1} \\ y_{n-1} \end{bmatrix} \quad \text{for } n = 1, 2, 3, \dots.$$

2. Show that $x_n = [1 - (r + s)]x_{n-1} + r$ and $y_n = [1 - (r + s)]y_{n-1} + s$. (*Hint*: Use the fact that $x_{n-1} + y_{n-1} = 1$.)

3. Show that the values of x_n approach $\dfrac{r}{r + s}$ as n gets large.

4. Show that the values of y_n approach $\dfrac{s}{r + s}$ as n gets large.

5. Express the stable distribution for A in terms of r and s.

6. Apply the result in part 5 to the 2×2 matrix in Example 1 of Section 8.2 to obtain the stable distribution for the working women Markov process.

7. Use the result in part 2 to solve for $\begin{bmatrix} x_n \\ y_n \end{bmatrix}$. That is, obtain an explicit formula for each entry that does not depend directly on A or on the preceding terms in the sequence other than the initial terms x_0 and y_0.

8. Explain why successive distribution matrices approach the stable distribution rapidly when $r + s$ is close to 1.

9. When will successive distributions oscillate about the stable distribution as they approach it?

Logic 12

In this chapter we introduce logic: the foundation for mathematics, coherent argument, and computing. The idea of logical argument was introduced in writing by Aristotle. For centuries his principles have formed the basis for systematic thought, communication, debate, law, mathematics, and science. More recently, the concept of a computing machine and the essence of programming are applications of the ancient ideas we present here. Also, new developments in mathematical logic have helped to promote significant advances in artificial intelligence.

12.1 Introduction to Logic

The building blocks of logic are statements, connectives, and the rules for calculating the truth or falsity of compound statements. We begin with statements.

A *statement* is a declarative sentence whose truth can be determined. Here are some examples of statements:

1. George Washington was the first president of the United States.
2. The New York Knicks won the NBA basketball championship in 1989.
3. The number of atoms in the universe is 10^{75}.
4. Ronald Reagan knew what Oliver North was doing.
5. If x is a positive real number and $x^2 = 9$, then $x = 3$.

We know that statement 1 is true. Statement 2 is false. Statements 3 and 4 are either true or false, but we do not know which. Neither is both true *and* false. Statement 5 is true.

To better understand what a statement is, we list below some nonstatements.

6. He is a real nice guy.
7. Do your homework!

8. If $x^2 = 9$, then $x = 3$.

9. Is this course fun?

Items 6 and 8 are not statements because the person "he" and the variable x are not specified. There are circumstances under which we would claim that item 6 is true and others under which we would claim that item 6 is false; clearly, it depends on who "he" is. Similarly, if x were a positive real number, item 8 would be true. If x were -3, item 8 would be false. Items 7 and 9 are not declarative sentences.

The *truth value* of a statement is either *true* or *false*. The problem of deciding the truth value of a declarative sentence will be dealt with in a simple manner, although it is far from simple. The assignment of a truth value to a statement may be obvious, as in the statement "George Washington was the first president of the United States." The truth value of the statement "The number of atoms in the universe is 10^{75}," on the other hand, is much more problematic. Logic cannot be used to determine the truth value of a simple statement. However, if there is agreement on the truth value of simple statements that are components of a compound statement, the rules of mathematical logic determine the truth value of the compound statement.

Logic forms the basis for analyzing legal briefs, political rhetoric, and family discussions. It allows us to understand another's point of view as well as to expose weaknesses in an argument that lead to unfounded conclusions. We combine statements naturally when we speak, using connective words like "and" and "or." We state implications with the words "if" and "then." Frequently, we negate statements with the word "not." A *compound statement* is formed by combining statements using the words "and," "or," "not," or "if, then." A *simple statement* is a statement that is not a compound statement. A compound statement is analyzed as a combination of simple statements. Its truth value is determined according to mathematical rules given in the next sections.

▶ **Example 1** Give the simple statements in each of the following compound statements.

(a) The number 6 is even and the number 5 is odd.

(b) Tom Jones does a term paper or takes the final exam.

(c) If England is in the Common Market, then the British eat Spanish oranges and Italian melons.

Solution (a) The simple statements are "The number 6 is even" and "The number 5 is odd."

(b) The simple statements are "Tom Jones does a term paper" and "Tom Jones takes the final exam."

(c) The simple statements are "England is in the Common Market," "The British eat Spanish oranges," and "The British eat Italian melons."

It is sometimes helpful to add English words to clarify the implied meaning in simple statements. ◆

To be able to develop the rules of logic and logical argument, we need to deal with any logical statement, rather than specific examples. We use the letters p, q, r, and so on to represent simple statements. They are not really the statements themselves, but variables for which a statement may be substituted. For example, we can let p represent a statement in general. Then, if we wish, we can specify that for the moment p will represent the statement "The number 5 is odd." In this particular case, p has the truth value *true*. We might decide to let p represent the statement "There are 13 states in the United States today." Then the truth value of the statement p is *false*.

The use of these logical variables is similar to the use of variables x, y, z, and so on to represent unspecified numbers in algebra. In algebra, we manipulate the symbols (such as x, y, $+$, and the implied multiplication and exponentiation) in expressions according to specified rules to establish identities such as

$$(x + y)^2 = x^2 + 2xy + y^2,$$

which are true no matter which numbers are substituted for x and y. In logic, we will manipulate the symbols in compound statements (p, q, r, "and," "or," "not," and "if, then") to look for expressions that are true no matter which statements are substituted for p, q, r, and so on.

It is useful to be able to write a compound statement in terms of its component parts and to use symbols to represent the connectives. We use $\wedge$ to represent the word "and" and $\vee$ to represent the word "or."

▶ **Example 2**   Write the compound statement "Ina likes popcorn and Fred likes peanuts" in symbolic form.

Solution   We first let p represent the statement "Ina likes popcorn" and we let q represent the statement "Fred likes peanuts." We use the symbol $\wedge$ to represent the word "and." Thus, we represent our compound statement symbolically as $p \wedge q$.   ◆

▶ **Example 3**   Write the compound statement "The United States trades with Japan or Germany trades with Japan" in symbolic form.

Solution   We use the letter p to represent the statement "The United States trades with Japan" and the letter q to represent the statement "Germany trades with Japan." We use the symbol $\vee$ to represent the word "or." Then the compound sentence is of the form $p \vee q$.   ◆

The symbol $\sim$ represents "not" so that, with p as defined in the previous example, we would use $\sim p$ to represent the statement "The United States does not trade with Japan."

▶ **Example 4**   Let p represent "Fred likes Cindy" and let q represent "Cindy likes Fred." Use the connectives $\wedge$, $\vee$, and $\sim$ to represent the following compound sentences:

(a) Fred and Cindy like each other.
(b) Fred likes Cindy but Cindy does not like Fred.
(c) Fred and Cindy dislike each other.
(d) Fred likes Cindy or Cindy likes Fred.

Solution   (a) "Fred and Cindy like each other" should be rewritten as "Fred likes Cindy and Cindy likes Fred." This is expressed symbolically as $p \wedge q$. Statement (b) can be written $p \wedge \sim q$. Note that the word "but" here means "and." Statement (c) can be rewritten as "Fred dislikes Cindy and Cindy dislikes Fred." This is written symbolically as $\sim p \wedge \sim q$. The last statement (d) is simply $p \vee q$.   ◆

▶ **Example 5**   Let p represent the statement "The interest rate is 10%" and let q be the statement "The Dow Jones average is over 10,000." Write the English statements corresponding to each of the following.

(a) $p \vee q$ (b) $p \wedge q$ (c) $p \wedge \sim q$ (d) $\sim p \vee \sim q$

Solution   (a) The statement $p \lor q$ can be written, "The interest rate is 10% or the Dow Jones average is over 10,000."

     (b) We write $p \land q$ as "The interest rate is 10% and the Dow Jones average is over 10,000."

     (c) The statement $p \land \sim q$ becomes "The interest rate is 10% and the Dow Jones average is less than or equal to 10,000."

     (d) The statement $\sim p \lor \sim q$ can be written as "The interest rate is not 10% or the Dow Jones average is less than or equal to 10,000."   ◆

     The symbol $\rightarrow$ represents an implication. The statement $p \rightarrow q$ is read "p implies q" or "if p, then q." Thus, using the representations of Example 5, the English sentence "If the interest rate is 10%, then the Dow Jones average is over 10,000" can be written as $p \rightarrow q$.

▶ Example 6   Let p denote the statement "The train stops in Washington" and let q denote the statement "The train stops in New York." Write the following statements in symbolic form.

     (a) The train stops in New York and Washington.

     (b) The train stops in Washington but not in New York.

     (c) The train does not stop in New York.

     (d) The train stops in New York or Washington.

     (e) The train stops in New York or Washington but not in both.

     (f) If the train stops in New York, it does not stop in Washington.

Solution   (a) $p \land q$. (b) $p \land \sim q$. (c) Negate q to get $\sim q$. (d) $p \lor q$. (e) $(p \lor q) \land \sim(p \land q)$. The parentheses make the statement clear. We discuss the need for them in a later section. (f) $q \rightarrow \sim p$.   ◆

     How are truth values assigned to compound statements? The assignment depends on the truth values of the simple statements and the connectives in the compound form. The rules are discussed in the next section.

Practice Problems 12.1

1. Determine which of the following sentences are statements.

     (a) The earnings of IBM went up from 1993 to 1994.

     (b) The national debt of the United States is $6 trillion.

     (c) What an exam that was!

     (d) Abraham Lincoln was the sixteenth president of the United States.

     (e) Lexington is the capital of Kentucky or Albany is the capital of the United States.

     (f) When was the Civil War?

2. Let p denote the statement "Sally is the class president" and let q denote "Sally is an accounting major." Translate the symbolic statements into proper English.

     (a) $p \land q$ **(b)** $\sim p$ **(c)** $p \lor q$

     (d) $(\sim p) \lor q$ **(e)** $p \land \sim q$ **(f)** $\sim p \lor \sim q$

▶ Exercises 12.1

In Exercises 1–15, determine which sentences are statements.

1. The number 3 is even.
2. The 1939 World's Fair was held in Miami.
3. The price of coffee depends on the rainfall in Brazil.
4. The Nile River flows through Asia.
5. What a way to go!
6. If snow falls on the Rockies, people are skiing in Aspen.
7. Why is the sky blue?
8. Moisture in the atmosphere determines the type of cloud formation.
9. No aircraft carrier is assigned to the Indian Ocean.
10. The number of stars in the universe is 10^{60}.
11. $x + 3 \geq 0$.
12. He is a brave fellow.
13. Let us pray.
14. The Louvre and the Metropolitan Museum of Art contain paintings by Leonardo da Vinci.
15. If a United States coin is fair, the chance of getting a head is $\frac{1}{3}$.
16. Let p denote the statement "Arizona has the largest U.S. Indian population" and let q denote the statement "Arizona is the site of the O.K. Corral." Write out the following statements in proper English sentences.

(a) $\sim p$ (b) $\sim p \vee q$ (c) $\sim q \wedge p$
(d) $p \vee q$ (e) $\sim p \wedge \sim q$ (f) $\sim (p \vee q)$

17. Let p denote the statement "Ozone is opaque to ultraviolet light" and let q denote the statement "Life on earth requires ozone." Write out the following statements in proper English.
(a) $p \wedge q$ (b) $\sim p \vee q$ (c) $\sim p \vee \sim q$ (d) $\sim(\sim q)$

18. Let p denote the statement "Papyrus is the earliest form of paper" and let q denote "The papyrus reed is found in Africa." Put the following statements into symbolic form.

(a) Papyrus is not the earliest form of paper.

(b) The papyrus reed is not found in Africa or papyrus is not the earliest form of paper.

(c) Papyrus is the earliest form of paper and the papyrus reed is not found in Africa.

19. Let p denote the statement "Florida borders Alabama" and let q denote the statement "Florida borders Mississippi." Put the following into symbolic form.

(a) Florida borders Alabama or Mississippi.

(b) Florida borders Alabama but not Mississippi.

(c) Florida borders Mississippi but not Alabama.

(d) Florida borders neither Alabama nor Mississippi.

Solutions to Practice Problems 12.1	

1. Statements appear in (a), (b), (d), and (e). Both (c) and (f) are not statements.
2. (a) "Sally is the class president and Sally is an accounting major."
   (b) "Sally is not the class president."
   (c) "Sally is the class president or Sally is an accounting major."
   (d) "Sally is not the class president or Sally is an accounting major."
   (e) "Sally is the class president and Sally is not an accounting major."
   (f) "Sally is not the class president or Sally is not an accounting major."

12.2 Truth Tables

In this section we discuss how the truth values of the statements $p \wedge q$, $p \vee q$, and $\sim p$ depend on the truth values of p and q.

The simple statements will be denoted p, q, r, and so on. A *statement form* is an expression formed from simple statements and connectives according to the following rules.

A simple statement is a statement form.

If p is a statement form, $\sim p$ is a statement form.

If p and q are statement forms, then so are $p \wedge q$, $p \vee q$, and $p \rightarrow q$.

▶ **Example 1** Show that each of the following is a statement form according to the definition. Assume that p, q, and r are simple statements.

(a) $(p \wedge \sim q) \to r$ (b) $\sim(p \to (q \vee \sim r))$

Solution (a) Since p, q, and r are simple statements, they are statement forms. Since q is a statement form, so is $\sim q$. Then $p \wedge \sim q$ is a statement form. Since r is a statement form, $(p \wedge \sim q) \to r$ is a statement form.

(b) Since r is a statement form, so is $\sim r$. Since both q and $\sim r$ are statement forms, $q \vee \sim r$ is a statement form. However, p is also a statement form; thus $p \to (q \vee \sim r)$ is a statement form. The negation of a statement form is a statement form, so $\sim(p \to (q \vee \sim r))$ is also. ◆

The *propositional calculus* is the manipulation, verification, and simplification of logical statement forms. It allows us to see for example whether two different statement forms are logically equivalent in the sense that they have the same truth values.

The main mechanism for determining the truth values of statement forms is known as a *truth table*. It is also possible to use tree diagrams (see Chapter 6) to determine the truth values of statement forms. We begin with truth tables.

Consider any simple statement p. Then p has one of the two truth values T (TRUE) or F (FALSE). We can list the possible values of p in a table:

p
T
F

Clearly, $\sim p$ (not p) is a form derived from p and has two possible values also. When p has the truth value T, $\sim p$ has the truth value F, and vice versa. We represent the truth value of $\sim p$ in a truth table.

p	$\sim p$
T	F
F	T

The statement form $p \wedge q$ (p and q) is made up of two statements represented by p and q and the connective $\wedge$. The statement p can have one of the truth values T or F. Similarly, q can have one of the truth values T or F. Hence, by the multiplication principle, there are four possible pairs of truth values for p and q.

Their *conjunction*, $p \wedge q$, is true if and only if both p is true *and* q is true. The truth table for conjunction is

p	q	$p \wedge q$
T	T	T
T	F	F
F	T	F
F	F	F

The *disjunction* of p and q, $p \vee q$ (p or q), is true if either p is true *or* q is true or both p and q are true. In English, the word "or" is ambiguous; we have to distinguish between the exclusive and inclusive "or." For example, in the sentence "Ira will go to either Princeton or Stanford," the word "or" is assumed to be exclusive since Ira will choose one of the schools, but not both. On the other hand, in the sentence, "Diana is smart or she is rich," the "or" probably is inclusive since either Diana is smart, Diana is rich, or Diana is both smart and rich. The mathematical statement form $p \vee q$ uses the inclusive "or" and is unambiguous, as the truth table makes clear.

p	q	$p \vee q$
T	T	T
T	F	T
F	T	T
F	F	F

Note that T stands for TRUE and F stands for FALSE. Each line of the truth table corresponds to a combination of truth values for the components p and q. There are only two lines in the table for $\sim p$, while for the others there are four.

What we have described so far is a system of calculating the truth value of a statement form based on the truth of its component statement forms. The beauty of truth tables is that they can be used to determine the truth values of more elaborate statement forms by reapplying the basic rules.

▶ Example 2   Construct a truth table for the statement form

$$\sim(p \vee q).$$

Solution   We write all the components of the statement form so that they can be evaluated for the four possible pairs of values for p and q. Note that we enter the truth values for p and q in the same order as in the previous tables. It is a good idea to use this order all the time; that is,

p	q
T	T
T	F
F	T
F	F

The truth table for the form $\sim(p \vee q)$ contains a column for each calculation.

p	q	$p \vee q$	$\sim(p \vee q)$
T	T	T	F
T	F	T	F
F	T	T	F
F	F	F	T

The third column represents the truth values of the disjunction of the first two columns, and the fourth column represents the negation of the third column. The statement form $\sim(p \vee q)$ is TRUE in one case: when both p and q are FALSE. Otherwise, $\sim(p \vee q)$ is FALSE.   ◆

▶ Example 3   Construct a truth table for the statement form

$$\sim(p \wedge \sim q) \vee p.$$

Solution

p	q	$\sim q$	$p \wedge \sim q$	$\sim(p \wedge \sim q)$	$\sim(p \wedge \sim q) \vee p$
T	T	F	F	T	T
T	F	T	T	F	T
F	T	F	F	T	T
F	F	T	F	T	T
(1)	(2)	(3)	(4)	(5)	(6)

We fill in each column by using the rules already established. Column 3 is the negation of the truth values in column 2. Column 4 represents the conjunction of columns 1 and 3. Column 5 is the negation of the statement form whose values appear in column 4. Finally, column 6 is the disjunction of columns 5 and 1. We see that this statement form has truth value TRUE no matter what the truth values of the statements p and q are. Such a statement is called a tautology. ◆

A statement form that has truth value TRUE regardless of the truth values of the individual statement variables it contains is called a *tautology*.

A statement form that has truth value FALSE regardless of the truth values of the individual statement variables it contains is called a *contradiction*.

There is a more efficient way to prepare the truth table of Example 3. Use the same order for entering possible truth values of p and q. Put the statement form at the top of the table. Fill in columns under each operation as you need them, working from the inside out. We label the columns in the order in which we fill them in.

p	q	$\sim$	$(p$	$\wedge$	$\sim q)$	$\vee$	p
T	T	T		F	F		T
T	F	F		T	T		T
F	T	T		F	F		T
F	F	T		F	T		T
(1)	(2)	(5)		(4)	(3)		(6)

We entered the values of p and q in columns 1 and 2 and then entered the values for $\sim q$ in column 3. We used the conjunction of columns 1 and 3 to fill in column 4, applied the negation to column 4 to get column 5, and the disjunction of columns 5 and 1 to get the values in column 6.

▶ Example 4   Construct the truth table for the statement form

$$(\sim p \vee \sim q) \wedge (p \wedge \sim q).$$

Solution   Again, we will use the short form of the table, putting the statement form at the top of the table, and labeling each column in the order in which it was completed.

p	q	$(\sim p$	$\vee$	$\sim q)$	$\wedge$	$(p$	$\wedge$	$\sim q)$
T	T	F	F	F	F	T	F	F
T	F	F	T	T	T	T	T	T
F	T	T	T	F	F	F	F	F
F	F	T	T	T	F	F	F	T
(1)	(2)	(3)	(5)	(4)	(7)		(6)	

There are some unlabeled columns. These were just recopied for convenience and clarity. It is not necessary to include them. Column 7, the conjunction of columns 5 and 6, tells us that the statement form is TRUE if and only if p is TRUE and q is FALSE. ◆

▶ **Example 5** Find the truth table for the statement form

$$(p \vee q) \wedge \sim(p \wedge q).$$

Solution

p	q	$(p$	$\vee$	$q)$	$\wedge$	$\sim$	$(p$	$\wedge$	$q)$
T	T		T		F	F		T	
T	F		T		T	T		F	
F	T		T		T	T		F	
F	F		F		F	T		F	
(1)	(2)		(3)		(6)	(5)		(4)	

Column 6, the conjunction of columns 3 and 5, gives the truth values of the statement form. ◆

We note that the statement form in Example 5 can be read as "p or q but not both p and q." This is the exclusive p "or" q. We will find it a useful connective and denote it by $\oplus$. The statement form $p \oplus q$ is true exactly when p is true or q is true but not both p and q are true. The truth table of $p \oplus q$ is

p	q	$p \oplus q$
T	T	F
T	F	T
F	T	T
F	F	F

If there are three simple statements in a statement form and we denote them p, q, and r, then each could take on the truth values TRUE or FALSE. Hence, by the multiplication principle, there are $2 \times 2 \times 2 = 8$ different assignments to the three variables together. There are eight lines in a truth table for such a statement form. Again, in the truth table we will list all the T's and then all the F's for the first variable. Then we alternate TT followed by FF in the second column. Finally, for the third variable we alternate T with F. This ensures that we have listed all the possibilities and facilitates comparison of the final results.

▶ **Example 6**   Construct a truth table for $(p \lor q) \land [(p \lor r) \land \sim r]$.

Solution   Note the order in which the T's and F's are listed in the first three columns. The columns are numbered in the order in which they were filled.

p	q	r			$(p \lor q) \land [(p \lor r) \land \sim r]$			
T	T	T	T	F	T		F	F
T	T	F	T	T	T		T	T
T	F	T	T	F	T		F	F
T	F	F	T	T	T		T	T
F	T	T	T	F	T		F	F
F	T	F	T	F	F		F	T
F	F	T	F	F	T		F	F
F	F	F	F	F	F		F	T
(1)	(2)	(3)	(4)	(8)	(5)		(7)	(6)

The statement form has truth value TRUE if and only if p is TRUE and r is FALSE (regardless of the truth value of q). ◆

The formal evaluation of the truth table of a statement form can help in deciding the truth value when particular sentences are substituted for the statement variables.

▶ **Example 7**   Let p denote the statement "London is the capital of England" and let q denote the statement "Venice is the capital of Italy." Determine the truth value of each of the following statements.

(a) $p \land q$ (b) $p \lor q$ (c) $\sim p \land q$
(d) $\sim p \lor \sim q$ (e) $\sim (p \land q)$ (f) $p \oplus q$

Solution   First, we note that p has truth value TRUE and q has truth value FALSE. (Rome is the capital of Italy.) Thus the conjunction in (a) is FALSE. The disjunction in (b) is TRUE because p is TRUE. In (c), both $\sim p$ and q are false, so their conjunction is FALSE. Since $\sim q$ is TRUE, statement (d) is TRUE. Since (a) is FALSE, and the statement in (e) is its negation, (e) is TRUE. Since p is TRUE and q is FALSE, $p \oplus q$ is TRUE. ◆

Logic and Computer Languages   In many computer languages, such as BASIC, the logical connectives are incorporated into programs that depend on logical decision making. The symbols are replaced by their original English words in the BASIC language; for example,

AND	$\land$
OR	$\lor$
NOT	$\sim$
XOR	$\oplus$ (XOR stands for "exclusive or").

If the statements p and q are assigned truth values T and F, then the truth tables for the connectives AND, OR, XOR, and NOT are as shown in Fig. 1.

Use of a Tree to Represent a Statement Form   Another method of describing a statement form is by using a mathematical structure called a *tree*. We have already seen tree diagrams in Chapter 6. The statement form $(p \land \sim q) \lor r$ is

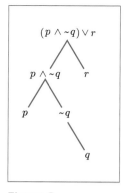

Figure 2.

p	q	p AND q	p OR q	p XOR q		p	NOT p
T	T	T	T	F		T	F
T	F	F	T	T		F	T
F	T	F	T	T			
F	F	F	F	F			

Figure 1.

diagrammed in Fig. 2. We begin by writing the statement form at the top of the tree. Two branches are then required, one for each of the operands: $(p \wedge \sim q)$ and r. We continue until we get to forms involving only a simple statement alone. From $(p \wedge \sim q)$, we require two branches, one for each of the operands p and $\sim q$. Finally, one branch is needed to perform the negation of q.

If we have specific truth values for the statement variables, the tree can be used to determine the truth value of the statement form by entering the values for all the variables and filling in truth values for the forms, working from the bottom to the top of the tree. Suppose that we are interested in the value of the statement form $(p \wedge \sim q) \vee r$ when p is TRUE, q is FALSE, and r is FALSE. Figure 3 shows how we fill in values at the nodes and proceed up the tree to its top for the truth value of the statement form.

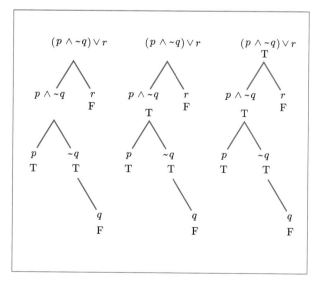

Figure 3.

GC Graphing calculators can evaluate logical expressions involving the following four logical operators: AND, OR, XOR, NOT. See Fig. 4, which was obtained by pressing [2nd] [TEST] [▶]. TRUE and FALSE are represented by the numbers 1 and 0, respectively. See Figs. 5 and 6.

With a TI-83, an entire truth table can be displayed by creating lists of zeros and ones for the variables and attaching a formula containing logical operators to a list name (see Fig. 7). (The lists **P** and **Q** can be created from the home screen as in Fig. 8. A formula is attached to **L1** by entering a logical expression surrounded by quotation marks. The list names L**P** and L**Q** are displayed from the LIST menu.)

Figure 4.

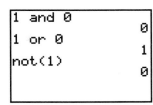

Figure 5.

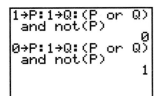

Figure 6.

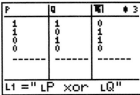

Figure 7.

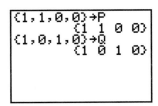

Figure 8.

**Practice Problems
12.2**

1. Construct the truth table for $(p \lor \sim r) \land q$.

2. Construct the truth table for $p \oplus \sim q$.

3. Let p denote "May follows April" and let q denote "June follows May." Determine the truth values of the following.

   (a) $p \land \sim q$ (b) $\sim(p \lor \sim q)$

   (c) $p \oplus q$ (d) $\sim[(p \land q) \oplus \sim q]$

▶ Exercises 12.2

In Exercises 1–18, construct truth tables for the given statement forms.

1. $p \land \sim q$

2. $(p \oplus q) \land r$

3. $(p \land \sim r) \lor q$

4. $\sim(p \land r) \lor q$

5. $\sim[(p \land r) \lor q]$

6. $p \land \sim p$

7. $p \lor \sim p$

8. $(p \lor q) \land \sim r$

9. $p \oplus (q \lor r)$

10. $p \lor (q \land r)$

11. $(p \lor q) \land (p \lor r)$

12. $(p \lor q) \land (p \lor \sim r)$

13. $(p \lor q) \land \sim(p \lor q)$

14. $(\sim p \lor q) \land r$

15. $\sim(p \lor q) \land r$

16. $\sim[(p \lor q) \land r]$

17. $\sim p \lor (q \land r)$

18. $(p \oplus q) \oplus \sim(p \oplus q)$

19. Compare the truth tables of $\sim p \lor \sim q$ and $\sim(p \land q)$.

20. Compare the truth tables of $p \land (q \lor r)$ and $(p \land q) \lor (p \land r)$.

21. Compare the truth tables of $p \oplus q$ and $(p \lor q) \land \sim(p \land q)$.

22. How many possible truth tables can you construct for statement forms involving two variables, p and q? (*Hint*: Consider the number of ways to complete the last column of a truth table for each of the four possible pairs of values for p and q.)

23. Compare the truth tables of $(p \land q) \lor r$ and $p \land (q \lor r)$.

24. Define the connective $\ominus$ by the truth table

p	q	$p \ominus q$
T	T	T
T	F	F
F	T	F
F	F	T

Construct the truth tables of the following.

(a) $p \ominus \sim q$ (b) $(p \ominus q) \ominus r$

(c) $p \ominus (q \ominus r)$ (d) $\sim(p \ominus q) \wedge (p \oplus q)$

25. Define $p|q$ by the truth table

p	q	$p|q$
T	T	F
T	F	T
F	T	T
F	F	T

This connective is called the *Sheffer stroke* (or NAND). Construct truth tables for the following.

(a) $p|p$ (b) $(p|p)|(q|q)$

(c) $(p|q)|(p|q)$ (d) $p|((p|q)|q)$

26. Compare the truth tables of the connectives $\sim$, $\vee$, and $\wedge$ with those constructed in Exercise 25. Do you see any similarities?

27. Let p denote "John Lennon was a member of the Beatles" and let q be the statement "The Beatles came from Spain." Determine the truth values of the following.

(a) $p \vee \sim q$ (b) $\sim p \wedge q$

(c) $p \oplus q$ (d) $\sim p \oplus q$

(e) $\sim(p \oplus q)$ (f) $(p \vee q) \oplus \sim q$

28. Let p be the statement "There were 14 original American colonies" and let q denote "Utah was one of the original colonies." Determine the truth value of each of the following.

(a) $p \vee q$ (b) $\sim p \vee q$

(c) $\sim p \wedge \sim q$ (d) $p \oplus \sim q$

29. Let p be the statement "A rectangle has three sides" and q be the statement "A right angle has 90 degrees." Determine the truth value of each of the following.

(a) $p \wedge \sim q$ (b) $\sim(p \oplus q)$

30. Draw a tree for the statement form given in Exercise 1. Assuming p has truth value T and q has value F, use the tree to find the truth value of the statement form.

31. Draw a tree for the statement form given in Exercise 2. Assuming that p has truth value T, q has truth value F, and r has truth value F, use the tree to find the truth value of the statement form.

32. Repeat Exercise 31 for the statement in Exercise 9.

33. Repeat Exercise 31 for the statement in Exercise 12.

In Exercises 34 and 35, what value will be displayed when the Enter key is pressed?

34.
```
1→P:0→Q:(P xor Q
) and not(Q)
```

35.
```
1→P:0→Q:(P and Q
) or not(P)
```

Exercises 36–41 require the use of a graphing calculator.

In Exercises 36 and 37, use a graphing calculator to determine the value of the logical expression when (a) p is TRUE, q is TRUE, and (b) p is TRUE, q is FALSE.

36. $(p \oplus q) \wedge \sim q$ **37.** $(p \vee q) \oplus \sim p$

38. $\sim p \vee (p \wedge q)$ **39.** $(p \wedge \sim q) \oplus p$

In Exercises 40 and 41, if your calculator can display a truth table, generate a truth table for the given expression.

40. $(p \vee \sim q) \oplus p$ **41.** $\sim(p \oplus q) \vee (p \wedge q)$

Solutions to Practice Problems 12.2

1.

p	q	r	$(p \vee \sim r) \wedge q$
T	T	T	T F T
T	T	F	T T T
T	F	T	T F F
T	F	F	T T F
F	T	T	F F F
F	T	F	T T T
F	F	T	F F F
F	F	F	T T F
(1)	(2)	(3)	(5) (4) (6)

2.

p	q	$p \oplus \sim q$
T	T	T F
T	F	F T
F	T	F F
F	F	T T
(1)	(2)	(4) (3)

3. Both p and q are TRUE. Thus (a) is FALSE. Item (b) is the negation of the statement $(p \vee \sim q)$, which is TRUE since p is TRUE. Hence, the statement in (b) is FALSE. Since both p and q are TRUE, $p \oplus q$ is FALSE. To analyze (d), we consider that $(p \wedge q)$ is TRUE and $\sim q$ is FALSE, so $[(p \wedge q) \oplus \sim q]$ is TRUE. Its negation is FALSE.

We are quite familiar with implications. For example, "If Jay is caught smoking in the restroom, he is suspended from school" is an implication. Note that, although Jay may avoid being caught smoking in the restroom, he still might be suspended for some other infraction. Symbolically, we can represent the statement "Jay is caught smoking in the restroom" by p, while we represent "Jay is suspended from school" by q. The implication is represented by the *conditional* connective $\rightarrow$ and we write $p \rightarrow q$. The truth table for the statement form using the conditional is as follows:

p	q	$p \rightarrow q$
T	T	T
T	F	F
F	T	T
F	F	T

The *conditional* statement form $p \rightarrow q$ has truth value FALSE only when p has truth value TRUE and q has truth value FALSE.

In the preceding case, if p is TRUE, then "Jay is caught smoking in the restroom" is TRUE, while if q were FALSE, then "Jay is not suspended" is TRUE. The implication $p \rightarrow q$ is FALSE in this case.

We call p the *hypothesis* and q the *conclusion*. Note that if the hypothesis is FALSE, then the implication $p \rightarrow q$ is TRUE. There are several ways to read $p \rightarrow q$ in English:

1. p implies q.

2. If p, then q.

3. p only if q.

4. q, if p.

5. p is sufficient for q.

6. q is a necessary condition for p.

Note that $p \rightarrow q$ means that p is sufficient for q, so if you have a true p, then you get a true q. On the other hand, $q \rightarrow p$ means that p is necessary for q, so if you want a true q, then you must have a true p.

▶ **Example 1**   In each of the following statements, determine the hypothesis and the conclusion.

(a) Bill goes to the party only if Greta goes to the party.

(b) Sue goes to the party if Craig goes to the party.

(c) For 6 to be even, it is sufficient that its square, 36, be even.

Solution   (a) The statement is in the form of p only if q. Thus the hypothesis is "Bill goes to the party" and the conclusion is "Greta goes to the party." We could rewrite the statement as "If Bill goes to the party, then Greta goes to the party." The statement "If Bill goes to the party, then Greta goes to the party" seems to mean that Greta is following Bill around, whereas the statement "Bill goes to the party only if Greta goes to the party" makes the romance seem quite the opposite. However, the second statement should be interpreted as follows: If "Bill goes to the party" is true, then that means

Greta must also have gone—for that was the ONLY reason he would go. The unemotional interpretation of the logical form shows the equivalence of the two statements.

(b) The statement is of the form q, if p. It has hypothesis "Craig goes to the party" and conclusion "Sue goes to the party."

(c) This is of the form p is sufficient for q, with the hypothesis p of the form "The square of the integer 6 is even" and the conclusion q of the form "The integer 6 is even."   ◆

▶ **Example 2**   Determine whether each of the following statements is true or false.

(a) If Paris is in France, then the Louvre is in Paris.
(b) If the Louvre is in Paris, then $2 + 3 = 7$.
(c) If $2 + 3 = 7$, then the Louvre is in Paris.
(d) If $2 + 3 = 7$, then Paris is in Spain.
(e) Paris is in Spain only if $2 + 3 = 7$.

Solution   The statement (a) is TRUE because both the hypothesis and the conclusion are TRUE. The statement (b) is FALSE because the hypothesis is TRUE but the conclusion is FALSE. The last three statements are TRUE because the hypothesis in each is FALSE. Note that the last statement has hypothesis "Paris is in Spain" and conclusion "$2 + 3 = 7$."   ◆

▶ **Example 3**   Construct the truth table of the statement "If the president dies or becomes incapacitated, then the vice president becomes president."

Solution   We let p be the statement "The president dies"; we let q be the statement "The president becomes incapacitated." We let r be the statement "The vice president becomes president." The statement form is $(p \vee q) \rightarrow r$. A truth table for the statement form is as follows:

p	q	r	$(p \vee q)$	$\rightarrow r$
T	T	T	T	T
T	T	F	T	F
T	F	T	T	T
T	F	F	T	F
F	T	T	T	T
F	T	F	T	F
F	F	T	F	T
F	F	F	F	T
(1)	(2)	(3)	(4)	(5)

The statement is FALSE only in the case where the president dies or becomes incapacitated but the vice president does not become president.   ◆

It is important to note that $p \rightarrow q$ is not the same as $q \rightarrow p$. We should not confuse the hypothesis and the conclusion in an implication. An example will demonstrate the difference between $p \rightarrow q$ and $q \rightarrow p$. Consider the implication

"If the truck carries ice cream, then it is refrigerated." If the implication is in the form $p \to q$, then $q \to p$ is the implication "If the truck is refrigerated, then it carries ice cream." These implications need not have the same truth values. The first implication is probably true; the second need not be. The truth tables of $p \to q$ and $q \to p$ show the differences.

p	q	$p \to q$	$q \to p$
T	T	T	T
T	F	F	T
F	T	T	F
F	F	T	T

The implication $q \to p$ is called the *converse* of the statement $p \to q$. Thus, given the statement "If the Los Angeles Dodgers won the pennant, some games of the World Series are in California," its converse is "If some games of the World Series are in California, then the Los Angeles Dodgers won the pennant." While the original statement is true, the converse is not. There are situations in which the hypothesis of the converse is true, but the conclusion is false. Some games of the World Series may be in California because the San Francisco Giants, the Oakland Athletics, or the Anaheim Angels, rather than the Los Angeles Dodgers, won the pennant.

▶ **Example 4**   Construct the truth table for the conjunction of $p \to q$ and its converse. That is, find the truth table of the statement form $(p \to q) \land (q \to p)$.

Solution

p	q	$(p \to q)$	$\land$	$(q \to p)$
T	T	T	T	T
T	F	F	F	T
F	T	T	F	F
F	F	T	T	T
(1)	(2)	(3)	(5)	(4)

We note that the statement form has truth value TRUE whenever p and q have the same truth value: either both TRUE or both FALSE.   ◆

The statement form $(p \to q) \land (q \to p)$ is referred to as the *biconditional*, which we write as $p \leftrightarrow q$. The statement $p \leftrightarrow q$ is read as "p, if and only if q" or "p is necessary and sufficient for q." The truth table for the biconditional is as follows:

p	q	$p \leftrightarrow q$
T	T	T
T	F	F
F	T	F
F	F	T

The biconditional is a statement form simply because it can be expressed as $(p \to q) \land (q \to p)$. In some sense, which we will discuss further in the next section, the biconditional expresses a kind of equivalence of p and q. That is, the biconditional statement form is TRUE whenever p and q are both TRUE or both FALSE. The biconditional is FALSE whenever p and q have different truth values.

Using connectives, we have seen how to string together several simple statements into compound and fairly complex statement forms. Such forms should not be confusing: What is the meaning of $\sim p \vee q$? Do we mean $\sim(p \vee q)$ or do we mean $(\sim p) \vee q$? To clarify matters and to avoid the use of too many parentheses, we define an order of *precedence* for the connectives. This dictates which of the connectives should be applied first.

The order of precedence for logical connectives is

$$\sim, \qquad \wedge, \qquad \vee, \qquad \rightarrow, \qquad \leftrightarrow.$$

One applies $\sim$ first, then $\wedge$, and so on. If there is any doubt, insert parentheses to clarify the statement form. Using the order of precedence, we see that $\sim p \vee q$ is $(\sim p) \vee q$.

▶ **Example 5**   Compare the truth tables of $(\sim p) \vee q$ and $\sim(p \vee q)$.

Solution

p	q	$(\sim p)$	$\vee$	q	$\sim$	$(p \vee q)$
T	T	F	T		F	T
T	F	F	F		F	T
F	T	T	T		F	T
F	F	T	T		T	F
(1)	(2)	(3)	(4)		(6)	(5)

Note that columns 4 and 6 are different.   ◆

▶ **Example 6**   Insert parentheses in the statement to show the proper order for the application of the connectives.

$$p \wedge q \vee r \rightarrow \sim s \wedge r$$

Solution   Reading from the left, we apply the $\sim$ first, so $\sim s \wedge r$ becomes $(\sim s) \wedge r$. We then scan for the connective $\wedge$, since that is next in the precedence list. So $p \wedge q \vee r$ becomes $(p \wedge q) \vee r$. We apply the $\rightarrow$ last, and the statement can be written

$$[(p \wedge q) \vee r] \rightarrow [(\sim s) \wedge r].$$ ◆

Parentheses have highest priority in the precedence. Clearly,

$$p \wedge (q \vee (r \rightarrow \sim s)) \wedge r$$

has the same symbols as the statement of Example 6, but the parentheses have defined a different statement form.

That the statement form $p \vee q \vee r$ may be written either as $(p \vee q) \vee r$ or as $p \vee (q \vee r)$ is shown in another section. The statement form $p \wedge q \wedge r$ can be written as $(p \wedge q) \wedge r$ or as $p \wedge (q \wedge r)$, as is shown later.

Implications and Computer Languages   The logical connective $\rightarrow$ is used in writing computer programs, although in some programming languages it is expressed with the words IF, THEN. Thus we might see an instruction of the form "IF $a = 3$ THEN LET $s = 0$." Strictly speaking, this is not a statement form, because "LET $s = 0$" is not a statement. However, that command means "the computer will set $s = 0$." Thus, if the value of a is 3, the computer sets s to 0. If $a \neq 3$, the program just continues. The instruction

$$\text{"IF } \ldots \text{ THEN } \ldots \text{ ELSE"}$$

allows for a branch in the program. For example,

$$\text{"IF } a = 3 \text{ THEN LET } s = 0 \text{ ELSE LET } s = 1\text{"}$$

assigns value 0 to s if $a = 3$ and assigns value 1 to s if $a \neq 3$.

▶ **Example 7**   For the given input values of A and B, use the program to determine the value of C. The asterisk ($*$) denotes multiplication.

$$\text{IF } (A * B) + 6 \geq 10$$
$$\text{THEN LET } C = A * B$$
$$\text{ELSE LET } C = 10$$

(a) A = −2, B = −7   (b) A = −2, B = 3   (c) A = 2, B = 2

Solution   (a) We determine that $(A * B) + 6 = 14 + 6 = 20$. Hence, we set C = 14.
(b) In this case, $(A * B) + 6 = 0$. So we set C = 10.
(c) $(A * B) + 6 = 10$. Hence, C = 4.   ◆

Implication and Common Language   The mathematical uses of the conditional and the biconditional are very precise. However, colloquial speech is rarely as precise. For example, consider the statement "Peter gets dessert only if he eats his broccoli." Technically, this means that if Peter gets dessert, he eats his broccoli. However, Peter and his parents probably interpret the statement to mean that Peter gets dessert if and only if he eats his broccoli. This imprecision in language is sometimes confusing; we make every effort to avoid confusion in mathematics by adhering to strict rules for using the conditional and biconditional.

Practice Problems 12.3

1. Using

p: "A square is a rectangle"   and q: "A rectangle has four sides,"

write out the statements in symbolic form. Name the hypothesis and the conclusion in each statement.

(a) A square is a rectangle if a rectangle has four sides.

(b) A rectangle has four sides if a square is a rectangle.

(c) A rectangle has four sides only if a square is a rectangle.

(d) A square is a rectangle is sufficient to show that a rectangle has four sides.

(e) For a rectangle to have four sides, it is necessary for a square to be a rectangle.

Practice Problems 12.3 (Continued)

2. Let p denote the statement "There are 48 states in the United States," let q denote the statement "The American flag is red, white, and blue," and let r be the statement "Maine is on the East Coast." Determine the truth value of each of the following statement forms.

   (a) $p \wedge q \to r$ **(b)** $p \vee q \to r$ **(c)** $\sim p \wedge q \leftrightarrow r$ **(d)** $p \wedge \sim q \to \sim r$

3. Use the program to assign a value to D in each of the cases listed.

   $$\text{LET } C = A + B$$
   $$\text{IF } (C > 0) \text{ OR } (A > 0)$$
   $$\text{THEN LET } \quad D = 1$$
   $$\text{ELSE LET } \quad D = -1$$

   (a) $A = 4, B = 6$ **(b)** $A = 4, B = -6$ **(c)** $A = 4, B = -4$

   (d) $A = -2, B = 4$ **(e)** $A = -6, B = 4$ **(f)** $A = -2, B = -2$

▶ Exercises 12.3

Construct a truth table for each of the statement forms in Exercises 1–15.   ●

1. $p \to \sim q$
2. $p \vee (q \to \sim r)$
3. $(p \oplus q) \to q$
4. $(p \oplus q) \to r$
5. $(\sim p \wedge q) \to r$
6. $\sim (p \to q)$
7. $(p \to q) \leftrightarrow (\sim p \vee q)$
8. $p \oplus (q \to r)$
9. $(p \to q) \to r$
10. $p \to (q \to r)$
11. $\sim (p \vee q) \to (\sim p \wedge r)$
12. $p \to (p \oplus q)$
13. $(p \vee q) \leftrightarrow (p \wedge q)$
14. $[(\sim p \wedge q) \oplus q] \to p$
15. $[p \wedge (q \vee r)] \leftrightarrow [(p \wedge q) \vee (p \wedge r)]$

Let p be the statement "Abraham Lincoln was the sixteenth president of the United States" and let q be the statement "The battle of Gettysburg took place at the O.K. Corral." Determine the truth value of each of the statement forms in Exercises 16–25.

16. $p \to q$
17. $\sim p \to q$
18. $p \to \sim q$
19. $q \to p$
20. $p \leftrightarrow q$
21. $(p \oplus q) \to p$
22. $(p \vee q) \to q$
23. $(p \wedge \sim q) \to (\sim p \oplus q)$
24. $[p \wedge (\sim q \to \sim p)] \oplus q$
25. $p \to [p \wedge (p \oplus q)]$

In Exercises 26–33, write the statement forms in symbols using the conditional ($\to$) or the biconditional ($\leftrightarrow$) connective. Name the hypothesis and the conclusion in each conditional form. Let p be the statement "Sally studied" and q be the statement "Sally passes."

26. If Sally studied, then she passes.
27. Sally studied if and only if Sally passes.
28. If Sally passes, then Sally studied.
29. Sally passes only if Sally studied.
30. That Sally studied is sufficient for Sally to pass.
31. Sally's studying is necessary for Sally to pass.
32. Sally passes implies that Sally studied.
33. If Sally did not study, then Sally does not pass.

In Exercises 34–38, let p denote the TRUE statement "The die is fair" and let q be the TRUE statement "The probability of a 2 is $\frac{1}{6}$." Write each of the statement forms in symbols, name the hypothesis and the conclusion in each, and determine whether the statement is TRUE or FALSE.

34. If the die is fair, the probability of a 2 is $\frac{1}{6}$.
35. If the die is not fair, the probability of a 2 is not $\frac{1}{6}$.
36. The probability of a 2 is $\frac{1}{6}$ only if the die is fair.
37. The die is not fair if the probability of a 2 is not $\frac{1}{6}$.
38. The die is fair implies that the probability of a 2 is $\frac{1}{6}$.
39. Give the hypothesis and the conclusion in each statement.
    (a) Healthy people live a long life.
    (b) The train stops at the station only if a passenger requests it.
    (c) For the plant to grow, it is necessary that it be exposed to sunlight.
    (d) Only if Jane goes to the store, I will go to the store.
40. State the converse of each of the following statements.
    (a) If Jane runs 20 miles, Jane is tired.
    (b) Cindy loves Fred only if Fred loves Cindy.
    (c) Jon cashes a check if the bank is open.
    (d) Errors are clear only if the documentation is complete.

(e) Sally's eating the vegetables is a necessary condition for Sally's getting dessert.

(f) Sally's eating the vegetables is sufficient for Sally's getting dessert.

41. State the converse of each of the following statements.

(a) City Sanitation collects the garbage if the mayor calls.

(b) The price of beans goes down only if there is no drought.

(c) If goldfish swim in Lake Erie, Lake Erie is fresh water.

(d) If tap water is not salted, then it boils slowly.

42. State the hypothesis and conclusion in each statement form.

(a) Copa Beach is crowded if the weather is hot and sunny.

(b) Our team wins a game only if I carry a rabbit's foot.

(c) If I carry a rabbit's foot, our team wins a game.

(d) Ivy is green is sufficient for it to be healthy.

43. Determine the output value of A in the program for the given input values of X and Y.

$$\text{LET } Z = X + Y$$
$$\text{IF } (Z \neq 0) \text{ AND } (X > 0)$$
$$\text{THEN LET } A = 6$$
$$\text{ELSE LET } A = 4$$

(a) X = 0, Y = 0   (b) X = 8, Y = −8

(c) X = −3, Y = 3   (d) X = −3, Y = 8

(e) X = 8, Y = −3   (f) X = 3, Y = −8

44. For the given input values of A and B, use the program to find the output values of X.

$$\text{LET } C = A + B$$
$$\text{IF } ((A > 0) \text{ OR } (B > 0)) \text{ AND } (C > 0)$$
$$\text{THEN LET } X = 100$$
$$\text{ELSE LET } X = -100$$

(a) A = 2, B = 2   (b) A = 2, B = −2

(c) A = 2, B = −5   (d) A = −2, B = −5

(e) A = −5, B = 3   (f) A = −5, B = 8

45. For the input values of A and B, use the program to determine the value of Y.

$$\text{LET } C = A * B$$
$$\text{IF } ((C \geq 10) \text{ AND } (A < 0)) \text{ OR } (B < 0)$$
$$\text{THEN LET } Y = 7$$
$$\text{ELSE LET } Y = 0$$

(a) A = −2, B = −6   (b) A = −1, B = −6

(c) A = −2, B = 6   (d) A = 6, B = −1

(e) A = 4, B = 3   (f) A = 3, B = 1

46. For the given input values of X and Y, use the program to determine the output value of Z.

$$\text{IF } Y \neq 0$$
$$\text{THEN LET } Z = X/Y$$
$$\text{ELSE LET } Z = -1,000,000$$

(a) X = 6, Y = 2   (b) X = 10, Y = 5

(c) X = 5, Y = 10   (d) X = 0, Y = 10

(e) X = 10, Y = 0   (f) X = −1,000,000, Y = 1

47. For the given input values of A and B, use the program to determine the value of C.

$$\text{IF } ((A < 0) \text{ AND } (B < 0)) \text{ OR } (B \geq 6)$$
$$\text{THEN LET } C = (A * B) + 4$$
$$\text{ELSE LET } C = 0$$

(a) A = −1, B = −2   (b) A = −2, B = 8

(c) A = −2, B = 3   (d) A = 3, B = −2

(e) A = 3, B = 8   (f) A = 3, B = −3

48. For the given input values for A and B, use the program to determine the output value of C.

$$\text{IF } ((A \geq 5) \text{ OR } (B \geq 5)) \text{ AND } (B \leq 10)$$
$$\text{THEN LET } C = A - B$$
$$\text{ELSE LET } C = -30$$

(a) A = 7, B = 7   (b) A = 7, B = 3

(c) A = 7, B = 12   (d) A = 4, B = 7

(e) A = 4, B = 3   (f) A = 4, B = 12

49. For the given input values of A and B, find the value of X in the program.

$$\text{LET } C = A - B$$
$$\text{IF } (C < 0) \text{ OR } (B < 0)$$
$$\text{THEN LET } D = 5 * C$$
$$\text{ELSE LET } D = 0$$
$$\text{LET } X = D + 3$$

(a) A = 0, B = 0   (b) A = 6, B = 3

(c) A = −5, B = 3   (d) A = 3, B = 5

(e) A = 5, B = −3   (f) A = −5, B = −3

50. We let S be the weekly salary for a consultant who works H hours at a rate of R dollars per hour. We take a deduction of 4% on salaries up to $1000 per week and deduct the maximum of $40 from salaries above $1000. Use the following program to find the pay P for

each of the consultants given the rate and the number of hours worked in a week.

LET $S = R * H$

IF $S < 1000$

THEN LET $D = .04 * S$

ELSE LET $D = 40$

LET $P = S - D$

(a) R = 10, H = 40   (b) R = 20, H = 40

(c) R = 25, H = 20   (d) R = 25, H = 40

(e) R = 30, H = 40   (f) R = 35, H = 40

Solutions to Practice Problems 12.3

1. (a) This is of the form $q \to p$ with hypothesis q and conclusion p. Statement (b) is of the form $p \to q$, where p is the hypothesis and q is the conclusion. Statement (c) is of the form $q \to p$, since it states that "If a rectangle has four sides, then a square is a rectangle." Note that "only if" signals the clause that is the conclusion. In (c), q is the hypothesis and p is the conclusion. Statement (d) is of the form $p \to q$ with hypothesis p and conclusion q. Statement (e) is the converse of (d) and is of the form $q \to p$ with hypothesis q and conclusion p.

2. First, we note that p, q, and r have truth values FALSE, TRUE, and TRUE, respectively. Use the order of precedence to decide which connectives are applied first.

   (a) TRUE. Since $p \wedge q$ is FALSE, the implication $(p \wedge q) \to r$ is TRUE.

   (b) TRUE. Here $p \vee q$ is TRUE and r is TRUE, so $(p \vee q) \to r$ is TRUE.

   (c) TRUE. Since p is FALSE and q is TRUE, $(\sim p) \wedge q$ is TRUE. Since r is also TRUE, $(\sim p \wedge q) \leftrightarrow r$ is TRUE.

   (d) TRUE. Since p is FALSE and $\sim q$ is also FALSE, $p \wedge (\sim q)$ is FALSE. Thus, $(p \wedge \sim q) \to r$ is TRUE.

3.

	A	B	C	D
(a)	4	6	10	1
(b)	4	−6	−2	1
(c)	4	−4	0	1
(d)	−2	4	2	1
(e)	−6	4	−2	−1
(f)	−2	−2	−4	−1

   For example, in (b) we check first to see if $(C > 0)$ is TRUE. It is not. We check to see if $(A > 0)$ is TRUE. It is. So we let $D = 1$. In (e), however, both $(C > 0)$ and $(A > 0)$ are FALSE, so we let $D = -1$.

12.4   Logical Implication and Equivalence

Different statement forms may have the same truth tables. Suppose, for example, that p and q are simple statements and we construct the truth tables of both $p \to q$ and $\sim p \vee q$.

p	q	$p \to q$	$\sim p$	$\vee$	q
T	T	T	F		T
T	F	F	F		F
F	T	T	T		T
F	F	T	T		T
(1)	(2)	(3)	(4)		(5)

We may compare columns 3 and 5 to see that, for any given pair of truth values assigned to p and q, the statement forms $p \rightarrow q$ and $\sim p \vee q$ have the same truth values.

Two statement forms that have the same truth tables are called *logically equivalent*.

Recall that we defined a *tautology* to be a statement form that has truth value TRUE regardless of the truth values of its component statements. We denote a tautology with the letter t. A statement form that always has truth value FALSE regardless of the truth values of its component statements is called a *contradiction*. We use the letter c to denote a contradiction.

▶ **Example 1**   Show that $p \vee \sim p$ is a tautology and that $p \wedge \sim p$ is a contradiction.

Solution   We construct the truth tables for the statement forms.

p	$\sim p$	$p \vee \sim p$	$p \wedge \sim p$
T	F	T	F
F	T	T	F

No matter what the value of p, $p \vee \sim p$ is TRUE and $p \wedge \sim p$ is FALSE.   ◆

▶ **Example 2**   Show that $\sim(p \wedge q)$ is logically equivalent to $\sim p \vee \sim q$.

Solution   We construct a truth table to demonstrate that $\sim(p \wedge q)$ is logically equivalent to $\sim p \vee \sim q$.

p	q	$\sim(p \wedge q)$		$\sim p \vee \sim q$		
T	T	F	T	F	F	F
T	F	T	F	F	T	T
F	T	T	F	T	T	F
F	F	T	F	T	T	T
(1)	(2)	(4)	(3)	(5)	(7)	(6)

Since columns 4 and 7 are the same, $\sim(p \wedge q)$ and $\sim p \vee \sim q$ have the same truth tables and therefore are logically equivalent.   ◆

For convenience, we denote compound statement forms by capital letters. We will use P, Q, and R, and so on, to denote statement forms such as $p \rightarrow q$, $p \wedge (q \rightarrow \sim r)$, $r \vee (p \wedge \sim(r \vee q))$, and so on. As we saw in the last section, $P \leftrightarrow Q$ is TRUE whenever P and Q have the same truth values (either both TRUE or both FALSE). And $P \leftrightarrow Q$ is FALSE if the truth values of P and Q differ. Thus P is logically equivalent to Q if and only if $P \leftrightarrow Q$ is a tautology. We write $P \Leftrightarrow Q$ when P and Q are logically equivalent. In other words,

P and Q are logically equivalent, and we write $P \Leftrightarrow Q$, whenever $P \leftrightarrow Q$ is a tautology.

We note that in comparing columns 4 and 7 in Example 2 we find that $\sim(p \wedge q)$ has the same truth table as $\sim p \vee \sim q$. This is reflected in the entries in column 8 of the following table; $\sim(p \wedge q) \leftrightarrow \sim p \vee \sim q$ is a tautology.

p	q	$\sim$	$(p \wedge q)$	$\leftrightarrow$	$\sim p$	$\vee$	$\sim q$
T	T	F	T	T	F	F	F
T	F	T	F	T	F	T	T
F	T	T	F	T	T	T	F
F	F	T	F	T	T	T	T
(1)	(2)	(4)	(3)	(8)	(5)	(7)	(6)

This particular logical equivalence is important and is one of *De Morgan's laws*. We summarize some important logical equivalences in Table 1.

The logical equivalences are important for understanding common English as well as for more formal analysis of mathematical statements and applications to computing. For example, the *contrapositive rule* is used frequently in speech. It states the equivalence of $p \rightarrow q$ with $\sim q \rightarrow \sim p$.

The *contrapositive* of the statement form $p \rightarrow q$ is the statement form $\sim q \rightarrow \sim p$.

Table 1	**Logical Equivalences**	
1.	$\sim \sim p \Leftrightarrow p$	Double negation
2a.	$(p \vee q) \Leftrightarrow (q \vee p)$	Commutative laws
b.	$(p \wedge q) \Leftrightarrow (q \wedge p)$	
c.	$(p \leftrightarrow q) \Leftrightarrow (q \leftrightarrow p)$	
3a.	$[(p \vee q) \vee r] \Leftrightarrow [p \vee (q \vee r)]$	Associative laws
b.	$[(p \wedge q) \wedge r] \Leftrightarrow [p \wedge (q \wedge r)]$	
4a.	$[p \vee (q \wedge r)] \Leftrightarrow [(p \vee q) \wedge (p \vee r)]$	Distributive laws
b.	$[p \wedge (q \vee r)] \Leftrightarrow [(p \wedge q) \vee (p \wedge r)]$	
5a.	$(p \vee p) \Leftrightarrow p$	Idempotent laws
b.	$(p \wedge p) \Leftrightarrow p$	
6a.	$(p \vee c) \Leftrightarrow p$	Identity laws
b.	$(p \vee t) \Leftrightarrow t$	
c.	$(p \wedge c) \Leftrightarrow c$	
d.	$(p \wedge t) \Leftrightarrow p$	
7a.	$(p \vee \sim p) \Leftrightarrow t$	
b.	$(p \wedge \sim p) \Leftrightarrow c$	
8a.	$\sim(p \vee q) \Leftrightarrow (\sim p \wedge \sim q)$	De Morgan's laws
b.	$\sim(p \wedge q) \Leftrightarrow (\sim p \vee \sim q)$	
9.	$(p \rightarrow q) \Leftrightarrow (\sim q \rightarrow \sim p)$	Contrapositive
10a.	$(p \rightarrow q) \Leftrightarrow (\sim p \vee q)$	Implication
b.	$(p \rightarrow q) \Leftrightarrow \sim(p \wedge \sim q)$	
11.	$(p \leftrightarrow q) \Leftrightarrow [(p \rightarrow q) \wedge (q \rightarrow p)]$	Equivalence
12.	$(p \rightarrow q) \Leftrightarrow [(p \wedge \sim q) \rightarrow c]$	Reductio ad absurdum

▶ **Example 3** State the contrapositive of "If Jay does not play Lotto, Jay will not win the Lotto jackpot."

Solution We let p be the statement "Jay does not play Lotto" and q be the statement "Jay will not win the Lotto jackpot." We use the *double negation* rule from Table 1 to see that the negation of p is the statement "Jay plays Lotto," while the negation of q is the statement "Jay will win the Lotto jackpot." The contrapositive is the statement "If Jay will win the Lotto jackpot, then Jay plays Lotto." It is logically equivalent to the original statement form (see rule 9). ◆

To prove the *contrapositive* rule, we use the truth table to show that $(p \rightarrow q) \Leftrightarrow (\sim q \rightarrow \sim p)$.

p	q	$(p \rightarrow q)$	$\leftrightarrow$	$(\sim q$	$\rightarrow$	$\sim p)$
T	T	T	T	F	T	F
T	F	F	T	T	F	F
F	T	T	T	F	T	T
F	F	T	T	T	T	T
(1)	(2)	(3)	(7)	(4)	(6)	(5)

A comparison of columns 3 and 6 shows that $p \rightarrow q$ and $\sim q \rightarrow \sim p$ have the same truth tables. Column 7 shows that the biconditional is a tautology. Hence

$$p \rightarrow q$$

is logically equivalent to its contrapositive

$$\sim q \rightarrow \sim p.$$

▶ **Example 4** A recent Associated Press article quoted a prominent official as having said, "If Mr. Jones is innocent of a crime, then he is not a suspect." State the contrapositive. Do you think the statement is TRUE or FALSE?

Solution The contrapositive of the statement is "If Mr. Jones is a suspect, then he is guilty of a crime." That seems FALSE, so the original statement is also FALSE. ◆

De Morgan's laws allow us to negate statements having the disjunctive or conjunctive connectives. It is important to recognize that when the negation is brought inside the parentheses it changes the connective from $\wedge$ to $\vee$, or vice versa.

▶ **Example 5** Negate the statement "The earth's orbit is round and a year has 365 days."

Solution We are asked to negate a statement of the form $p \wedge q$. By rule 8b, the negation can be written as "The earth's orbit is not round or a year does not have 365 days." This is TRUE whenever the original statement is FALSE. ◆

▶ **Example 6** Rewrite the statement "It is false that Jack and Jill went up the hill."

Solution We use De Morgan's laws to negate a statement of the form $(p \wedge q)$ to get "Jack did not go up the hill or Jill did not go up the hill." ◆

▶ Example 7   Use De Morgan's laws to negate the statement form $(p \wedge q) \wedge r$.

Solution $\sim((p \wedge q) \wedge r) \Leftrightarrow (\sim(p \wedge q) \vee (\sim r)) \Leftrightarrow ((\sim p \vee \sim q) \vee \sim r)$. Note that each time the negation is applied to the conjunction or the disjunction, the connective changes.   ◆

The rules in Table 1 allow us to simplify statement forms in a variety of ways. In place of any of the simple statements p, q, and r, we may substitute any compound statement. Provided we substitute consistently throughout, the equivalence holds. The rules are similar to the rules of algebra in that the need and the purpose for simplification depend on the situation. Frequently, however, we can simplify statement forms containing $\rightarrow$ by eliminating the implication. As the *implication* rule

$$(p \rightarrow q) \Leftrightarrow (\sim p \vee q)$$

shows, we can reduce a statement involving $\rightarrow$ to one involving other connectives. In fact, as the next examples demonstrate, we may express statements involving any of the connectives using only $\sim$ and $\vee$ or only $\sim$ and $\wedge$.

▶ Example 8   Eliminate the connective $\rightarrow$ in the statement form and simplify as much as possible.

$$(\sim p \wedge \sim q) \rightarrow (q \rightarrow r).$$

Solution   Eliminate both implications and simplify by first replacing p by $(\sim p \wedge \sim q)$ and q by $(q \rightarrow r)$ in rule 10a. Then reapply 10a to the implication $(q \rightarrow r)$. We have

$(\sim p \wedge \sim q) \rightarrow (q \rightarrow r)$

$\Leftrightarrow \sim(\sim p \wedge \sim q) \vee (q \rightarrow r)$ Implication

$\Leftrightarrow \sim(\sim p \wedge \sim q) \vee (\sim q \vee r)$ Implication

$\Leftrightarrow (\sim \sim p \vee \sim \sim q) \vee (\sim q \vee r)$ De Morgan's law

$\Leftrightarrow (p \vee q) \vee (\sim q \vee r)$ Double negation

$\Leftrightarrow [p \vee (q \vee \sim q) \vee r]$ Associative law

$\Leftrightarrow [(q \vee \sim q) \vee p \vee r]$ Commutative law

$\Leftrightarrow [t \vee (p \vee r)]$ Rule 7a

$\Leftrightarrow t$ Identity rule

Thus the original statement is a tautology.   ◆

We used the principle of *substitution* in the solution to the previous example. This allowed us to substitute statement forms for the simple statements in the rules of Table 1. We also substituted equivalent statement forms in interpreting the rules. The *substitution principles* are formally stated as follows:

Substitution principles:

Suppose P and R are statement forms and $P \Leftrightarrow R$. If R is substituted for P in a statement form Q, the resulting statement form Q' is logically equivalent to Q.

Suppose that P and Q are statement forms containing the simple statement p. Assume that $P \Leftrightarrow Q$. If R is any statement form and is substituted for every p in P to yield P' and for every p in Q to yield Q', then $P' \Leftrightarrow Q'$.

▶ Example 9   Rewrite the statement form

$$(p \rightarrow q) \wedge (q \vee r)$$

(a) using only the connectives $\sim$ and $\vee$.
(b) using only the connectives $\sim$ and $\wedge$.

Solution   (a) $(p \rightarrow q) \wedge (q \vee r)$

$\Leftrightarrow (\sim p \vee q) \wedge (q \vee r)$ Implication
$\Leftrightarrow (q \vee \sim p) \wedge (q \vee r)$ Commutative law
$\Leftrightarrow q \vee (\sim p \wedge r)$ Distributive law
$\Leftrightarrow q \vee (\sim p \wedge \sim \sim r)$ Double negation
$\Leftrightarrow q \vee \sim (p \vee \sim r)$ De Morgan's law

(b) $(p \rightarrow q) \wedge (q \vee r)$

$\Leftrightarrow (\sim p \vee q) \wedge (q \vee r)$ Implication
$\Leftrightarrow (\sim p \vee \sim \sim q) \wedge (q \vee r)$ Double negation
$\Leftrightarrow \sim (p \wedge \sim q) \wedge (q \vee r)$ De Morgan's law
$\Leftrightarrow \sim (p \wedge \sim q) \wedge \sim \sim (q \vee r)$ Double negation
$\Leftrightarrow \sim (p \wedge \sim q) \wedge \sim (\sim q \wedge \sim r)$ De Morgan's law ◆

▶ Example 10   Use the implication rule to show that

$$[(p \wedge \sim r) \rightarrow (q \rightarrow r)] \Leftrightarrow [\sim (p \wedge \sim r) \vee (q \rightarrow r)].$$

Solution   The implication rule states that $p \rightarrow q \Leftrightarrow \sim p \vee q$. Substitute the statement form $p \wedge \sim r$ for each p on both sides of the logical equivalence. Substitute $q \rightarrow r$ for each q in the logical equivalence. ◆

Recall that we have already seen De Morgan's laws in another form in Chapter 5. In that case, S and T were sets and

$$(S \cup T)' = S' \cap T' \qquad \text{and} \qquad (S \cap T)' = S' \cup T'.$$

De Morgan's laws for unions and intersections of sets are closely related to De Morgan's laws for the connectives $\vee$ and $\wedge$. In Section 12.6, we explore this further.

We have seen in this section how statement forms that look quite different can be logically equivalent. Statement forms sometimes can be simplified by using the logical equivalences of Table 1. Logical argument is based not only on logical equivalences, but also on those statements that logically imply others.

Given statement forms P and Q, we say that P *logically implies* Q whenever $P \rightarrow Q$ is a tautology. We write this as $P \Rightarrow Q$. $P \Rightarrow Q$ means that $P \rightarrow Q$ is a tautology.

This means that $P \Rightarrow Q$ if, whenever P is TRUE, then Q is TRUE. To determine whether a statement form P logically implies a statement form Q, we only need to consider those rows of the truth table for which P is TRUE or those for which Q is FALSE.

Table 2 summarizes some useful logical implications.

Table 2	Logical Implications	
1.	$p \Rightarrow (p \vee q)$	Addition
2.	$(p \wedge q) \Rightarrow p$	Simplification
3.	$[(p \wedge (p \rightarrow q)] \Rightarrow q$	Modus ponens
4.	$[(p \rightarrow q) \wedge \sim q] \Rightarrow \sim p$	Modus tollens
5.	$[(p \vee q) \wedge \sim q] \Rightarrow p$	Disjunctive syllogism
6.	$[(p \rightarrow q) \wedge (q \rightarrow r)] \Rightarrow (p \rightarrow r)$	Hypothetical syllogism
7a.	$[(p \rightarrow q) \vee (r \rightarrow s)] \Rightarrow [(p \vee r) \rightarrow (q \vee s)]$	Constructive dilemmas
7b.	$[(p \rightarrow q) \wedge (r \rightarrow s)] \Rightarrow [(p \wedge r) \rightarrow (q \wedge s)]$	

▶ **Example 11**   Verify $[(p \vee q) \wedge \sim q] \Rightarrow p$.

Solution   Let statement form $P = (p \vee q) \wedge \sim q$ and statement form $Q = p$. We are interested in verifying that $P \rightarrow Q$ is a tautology. In a straightforward approach, we can construct the entire truth table.

p	q	$[(p \vee q)$	$\wedge$	$\sim q]$	$\rightarrow$	p
T	T	T	F	F	T	
T	F	T	T	T	T	
F	T	T	F	F	T	
F	F	F	F	T	T	
(1)	(2)	(3)	(5)	(4)	(6)	

Column 6 shows that the implication is a tautology. We could have shortened our work. The only situation in which an implication $P \rightarrow Q$ is FALSE is when P is TRUE and Q is FALSE. We check out these possibilities by first letting P be TRUE. This requires that both $(p \vee q)$ and $\sim q$ be TRUE. This occurs when q is FALSE and p is TRUE, and this is the only possibility for P to be TRUE. The only row of the truth table we must consider is

p	q	$[(p \vee q)$	$\wedge$	$\sim q]$	$\rightarrow$	p
T	F	T	T	T	T.	

In this example it was simple to construct the entire truth table, but, in general, we can save a lot of work by considering only the relevant cases.   ◆

▶ **Example 12**   Verify modus ponens (logical implication 3).

Solution   We must show that

$$[p \wedge (p \rightarrow q)] \rightarrow q$$

is a tautology. The first row of the truth table will suffice.

p	q	$[(p \wedge (p \to q)]$	$\to$	q
T	T	T	T	T
T	F	F	F	T
F	T	F	T	T
F	F	F	T	T
(1)	(2)	(4)	(3)	(5)

Looking at the last column, we see that the implication is a tautology. ◆

Practice Problems 12.4

1. Prove $(p \to q) \Leftrightarrow (\sim p \vee q)$.

2. Rewrite the statement

$$(p \to \sim q) \to (r \wedge p)$$

eliminating the connective $\to$ and simplifying if possible.

3. Assume that the statement "Jim goes to the ballgame only if Ted gets tickets" is TRUE.

   (a) Write the contrapositive and give its truth value.

   (b) Write the converse and give its truth value.

   (c) Write the negation and give its truth value.

▶ **Exercises 12.4**

1. Show that $[(p \to q) \wedge q] \to p$ is not a tautology.

2. Show that the distributive laws hold:

   (a) $[p \vee (q \wedge r)] \Leftrightarrow [(p \vee q) \wedge (p \vee r)]$

   (b) $[p \wedge (q \vee r)] \Leftrightarrow [(p \wedge q) \vee (p \wedge r)]$.

3. Show that the second law of implication holds:

$$(p \to q) \Leftrightarrow \sim(p \wedge \sim q).$$

4. Write a statement equivalent to

$$\sim(p \wedge \sim q) \to (r \wedge p)$$

using only $\sim$ and $\wedge$.

5. The Sheffer stroke is defined by the truth table

p	q	$p\vert q$
T	T	F
T	F	T
F	T	T
F	F	T

   (a) Show that $\sim p \Leftrightarrow p\vert p$.

   (b) Show that $p \vee q \Leftrightarrow (p\vert p)\vert(q\vert q)$.

   (c) Show that $p \wedge q \Leftrightarrow (p\vert q)\vert(p\vert q)$.

   (d) Write $p \to q$ using only the Sheffer stroke.

   (e) Write $p\vert q$ using only $\sim$ and $\wedge$.

6. Without using truth tables, show that

$$[(p \vee \sim q) \wedge r] \to p \Leftrightarrow (p \vee q) \vee \sim r.$$

7. Show that

$$(p \to q) \Leftrightarrow [(p \wedge \sim q) \to c]$$

using the fact that c denotes a contradiction; that is, c is always FALSE. Read the statement aloud.

8. (a) Prove that

$$p \Rightarrow [q \to (p \wedge q)].$$

   (b) True or false?

$$p \Leftrightarrow [q \to (p \wedge q)]$$

9. True or false?

$$(p \vee q) \Rightarrow [q \to (p \wedge q)]$$

10. True or false?

$$[p \vee (p \wedge q)] \Leftrightarrow p$$

11. Write an equivalent form of $p \oplus q$ using only $\sim$ and $\vee$.

12. Write each statement using only the connectives $\sim$ and $\vee$.

    (a) $p \wedge \sim q \rightarrow p$ (b) $(p \rightarrow r) \wedge (q \vee r)$

    (c) $p \rightarrow [r \wedge (p \vee q)]$ (d) $(p \wedge q) \rightarrow (\sim q \vee r)$

13. Negate the following statements.

    (a) Arizona borders California and Arizona borders Nevada.

    (b) There are tickets available or the agency can get tickets.

    (c) The killer's hat was either white or gray.

14. Negate the following statements.

    (a) Montreal is a province in Canada and Ottawa is a province in Canada.

    (b) The salesman goes to the customer or the customer calls the salesman.

    (c) The hospital does not admit psychiatric patients or orthopedic patients.

15. Negate the following statements.

    (a) If I have a ticket to the theater, I spent a lot of money.

    (b) Basketball is played on an indoor court only if the players wear sneakers.

    (c) The stock market is going up implies that the interest rates are going down.

    (d) For humans to stay healthy, it is sufficient that humans have enough water.

16. For each statement, give the contrapositive, the converse, and the negation. Determine the truth value in each case.

    (a) If a rectangle has equal sides, it is a square.

    (b) An airplane flies faster than the speed of sound only if it is a Concorde.

    (c) If the intersection of two sets is not empty, then the union of the two sets is not empty.

    (d) If a coin is fair, the probability of a head is $\frac{1}{2}$.

17. Give the contrapositive and the converse of each statement and then give the truth value of each.

    (a) If a bird is small, it is a hummingbird.

    (b) If two nonvertical lines have the same slope, they are parallel.

    (c) If we are in Paris, we must be in France.

    (d) If a road is one-way, you cannot legally make a U-turn.

18. Bill, Sue, and Alice are lined up facing forward with Bill first, then Sue, then Alice. From a collection that they know contains three blue and two red hats, hats are placed on their heads while they are blindfolded. Blindfolds are removed, but they continue to face forward and see only those hats in front of them. Bill sees none, Sue sees Bill's, and Alice sees both Sue's and Bill's. Alice claims she does not know what color her hat is. Sue also claims that she does not know what color her hat is. Now Bill knows what color his hat is. What is it?

19. A prisoner is given one chance for freedom. He may ask one yes-or-no question of either of two guards. Each guard allows access to one of two unmarked doors. One is the door to freedom, the other the door to death. One guard always tells the truth, the other always lies. What question should the prisoner ask?

1. We show that $(p \to q) \leftrightarrow (\sim p \vee q)$ is a tautology.

p	q	$(p \to q)$	$\leftrightarrow$	$(\sim p$	$\vee$	$q)$
T	T	T	T	F	T	
T	F	F	T	F	F	
F	T	T	T	T	T	
F	F	T	T	T	T	
(1)	(2)	(3)	(6)	(4)	(5)	

2. $(p \to \sim q) \to (r \wedge p)$
   $\Leftrightarrow (\sim p \vee \sim q) \to (r \wedge p)$ Implication
   $\Leftrightarrow [\sim(\sim p \vee \sim q)] \vee (r \wedge p)$ Implication
   $\Leftrightarrow (p \wedge q) \vee (r \wedge p)$ De Morgan's law, Double negation
   $\Leftrightarrow (p \wedge q) \vee (p \wedge r)$ Commutative law
   $\Leftrightarrow p \wedge (q \vee r)$ Distributive law

3. (a) Contrapositive: "If Ted does not get tickets, Jim does not go to the ballgame." TRUE.

   (b) Converse: "If Ted gets tickets, Jim goes to the ballgame." Truth value is unknown.

   (c) We negate a statement of the form $p \to q$. We use the implication law $(p \to q) \Leftrightarrow (\sim p \vee q)$, form the negative, and apply De Morgan's law to get $[\sim(p \to q)] \Leftrightarrow (p \wedge \sim q)$. Negation: "Jim goes to the ballgame and Ted does not get tickets." FALSE.

12.5 Valid Argument

In this section we study methods of valid argument. We rely heavily on Table 2, the table of logical implications, presented in Section 12.4. Let us begin with an example.

▶ Example 1   Analyze the argument, given that the first two statements are true.

If Marvin studies mathematics, then he is smart.
Marvin is not smart.
Therefore, Marvin does not study mathematics.

Solution   Let p denote "Marvin studies mathematics" and let q denote "Marvin is smart." The argument is of the form

$$\text{If } [(p \to q) \wedge \sim q], \text{ then } \sim p.$$

Note that

$$[(p \to q) \wedge \sim q] \Rightarrow \sim p$$

is the rule of modus tollens of Table 2 of the previous section. Thus the implication

$$[(p \to q) \wedge \sim q] \to \sim p$$

is a tautology and, therefore, always TRUE. The argument presented is valid. ◆

The technique used in the example can be extended to more complex arguments.

An *argument* or a *proof* is a set of statements

$$H_1, H_2, \ldots, H_n$$

each of which is assumed to be true and a statement C that is claimed to have been deduced from them. The statements

$$H_1, H_2, \ldots, H_n$$

are called *hypotheses* and the statement C is called the *conclusion*. We say that the argument is *valid* if and only if

$$H_1 \wedge H_2 \wedge \cdots \wedge H_n \Rightarrow C.$$

The statement $H_1 \wedge H_2 \wedge \cdots \wedge H_n \rightarrow C$ is a tautology provided it is never false; if each hypothesis is true, the conclusion is also true.

In the example just given, the argument is valid because, for the hypotheses

$$H_1 = (p \rightarrow q) \quad \text{and} \quad H_2 = \sim q \quad \text{and the conclusion} \quad C = \sim p,$$

we have the logical implication $H_1 \wedge H_2 \Rightarrow C$.

There are several important points to make here. First, although the conclusion may be a true statement, the argument presented may or may not be valid. Also, if one or more of the premises is false, it is possible for a valid argument to result in a conclusion that is false. The logical implications stated earlier in this chapter can be restated in the form of *rules of inference*, as given in Table 1.

Table 1	Rules of Inference		
	From:	**Conclude:**	
1.	P	$P \vee Q$	Addition
2.	$P \wedge Q$	P	Subtraction
3.	$P \wedge (P \rightarrow Q)$	Q	Modus ponens
4.	$(P \rightarrow Q) \wedge \sim Q$	$\sim P$	Modus tollens
5.	$(P \vee Q) \wedge \sim P$	Q	Disjunctive syllogism
6.	$(P \rightarrow Q) \wedge (Q \rightarrow R)$	$P \rightarrow R$	Hypothetical syllogism
7a.	$(P \rightarrow Q) \vee (R \rightarrow S)$	$(P \vee R) \rightarrow (Q \vee S)$	Constructive dilemmas
b.	$(P \rightarrow Q) \wedge (R \rightarrow S)$	$(P \wedge R) \rightarrow (Q \wedge S)$	

▶ Example 2   Suppose that the following statements are true.

Pat is going to the office or to dinner with Jan.

If Pat is going to the office, then it is not sunny.

It is sunny.

Prove: Pat is going to dinner with Jan.

Solution   Let s, p, and d denote the statements

$$s = \text{``It is sunny.''}$$
$$p = \text{``Pat is going to the office.''}$$
$$d = \text{``Pat is going to dinner with Jan.''}$$

We write the argument step by step. Numbers in parentheses refer to the previous steps used in the argument

1.	$p \vee d$	Hypothesis
2.	$p \rightarrow \sim s$	Hypothesis
3.	s	Hypothesis
4.	$\sim p$	Modus tollens (2, 3)
5.	d	Disjunctive syllogism (1, 4)

Step 4 results from the implication $[(p \rightarrow \sim s) \wedge s] \Rightarrow \sim p$. And step 5 results from the implication $[(p \vee d) \wedge \sim p] \Rightarrow d$. We have made convenient substitutions in the rules in Table 1. ◆

▶ **Example 3**   Show that the following argument is valid.

I study either mathematics or economics.

If I have to take English, then I do not study economics.

I do not study mathematics.

Therefore, I do not have to take English.

Solution   Let p, q, and r represent the statements

$$p = \text{``I study mathematics.''}$$
$$q = \text{``I study economics.''}$$
$$r = \text{``I have to take English.''}$$

The hypotheses are

$$p \vee q, \quad r \rightarrow \sim q, \quad \text{and} \quad \sim p.$$

We write the argument step by step. Numbers in parentheses refer to the previous steps used in the argument.

1.	$p \vee q$	Hypothesis
2.	$r \rightarrow \sim q$	Hypothesis
3.	$\sim p$	Hypothesis
4.	q, since $[(p \vee q) \wedge \sim p] \Rightarrow q$	Disjunctive syllogism (1, 3)
5.	$\sim r$, since $[(r \rightarrow \sim q) \wedge q] \Rightarrow \sim r$	Modus tollens (2, 4)

Thus we have shown that r can be proven false by a valid argument from the given hypotheses. ◆

▶ Example 4 Verify that the following argument is valid.

If it is raining, then my car stalls or will not start.

If my car stalls, then I arrive late for school.

If my car does not start, I do not go to school.

Therefore, if it is raining, either I arrive late for school or I do not go to school.

Solution Let p, q, r, s and u be the following statements.

$$p = \text{``It is raining.''}$$
$$q = \text{``My car stalls.''}$$
$$r = \text{``My car starts.''}$$
$$s = \text{``I arrive late for school.''}$$
$$u = \text{``I go to school.''}$$

The argument proceeds as follows.

1. $p \to (q \vee \sim r)$		Hypothesis
2. $q \to s$		Hypothesis
3. $\sim r \to \sim u$		Hypothesis
4. $(q \vee \sim r) \to (s \vee \sim u)$		Constructive dilemma (2, 3)
5. $p \to (s \vee \sim u)$		Hypothetical syllogism (1, 4)

Therefore, a valid conclusion is "If it rains, either I arrive late for school or I do not go to school." ◆

In trying to deduce that

$$H_1 \wedge H_2 \wedge \cdots \wedge H_n \Rightarrow C,$$

we sometimes find it easier to prove that the contrapositive of

$$H_1 \wedge H_2 \wedge \cdots \wedge H_n \to C$$

is a tautology. Thus we would need to show that

$$\sim C \to \sim(H_1 \wedge H_2 \wedge \cdots \wedge H_n)$$

is a tautology. If we assume that $\sim C$ is TRUE, then, of course, the premise is that C is FALSE. The only case we need to consider to prove the tautology is the case where $\sim C$ is TRUE. In that case, we must show that $\sim(H_1 \wedge H_2 \wedge \cdots \wedge H_n)$ is TRUE also. This requires that the statement

$$(\sim H_1) \vee (\sim H_2) \vee \cdots \vee (\sim H_n)$$

be TRUE (use De Morgan's law). The disjunction is TRUE if and only if at least one of its components is TRUE. So we must show that $(\sim H_i)$ is TRUE for some subscript i. Hence, we are required to show that H_i is FALSE for at least one i. This is called an *indirect proof*.

We summarize the idea.

Indirect Proof   To prove

$$(H_1 \wedge H_2 \wedge \cdots \wedge H_n) \Rightarrow C,$$

we assume the conclusion C is FALSE and then prove that at least one of the hypotheses H_i must be FALSE.

▶ **Example 5**   Use an indirect proof to show that the following argument is valid.

If I am happy, then I do not eat too much.
I eat too much or I spend money.
I do not spend money.
Therefore, I am not happy.

Solution   We will begin symbolically. Let

$$p = \text{"I am happy."}$$
$$q = \text{"I eat too much."}$$
$$r = \text{"I spend money."}$$

We wish to show that $[(p \to {\sim}q) \wedge (q \vee r) \wedge {\sim}r] \Rightarrow {\sim}p$.   Assume, by way of indirect proof, that the conclusion is FALSE.

1. p		Negation of conclusion
2. $p \to {\sim}q$		Hypothesis
3. ${\sim}q$		Modus ponens (1, 2)
4. $q \vee r$		Hypothesis
5. r		Disjunctive syllogism (3, 4)

Therefore, the given hypothesis ${\sim}r$ is FALSE. We express the proof in words. Let us assume the negative of the conclusion; that is, we assume "I am happy." Then "I do not eat too much" (modus ponens). We were to assume "I eat too much or I spend money"; hence (disjunctive syllogism), it is true that "I spend money." This means that the hypothesis "I do not spend money" cannot be true. Assumption of the negation of the conclusion leads us to claim one of the hypotheses is false. Thus we have a valid indirect proof.   ◆

Practice Problems 12.5

1. Show that the argument is valid.

   If goldenrod is yellow, then violets are blue.
   Either pine trees are not green or goldenrod is yellow.
   Pine trees are green.
   Therefore, violets are blue.

2. Show by indirect proof that the argument is valid.

   If I go to the beach, I cannot study.
   Either I study or I work as a waiter.
   I go to the beach.
   Therefore, I work as a waiter.

▶ **Exercises 12.5**

In Exercises 1–10, show that the argument is valid.

1. Either Sue goes to the movies or she reads. Sue does not go to the movies. Therefore, Sue reads.

2. If the class votes for an oral final, the teacher is glad. If the exam is not scheduled for a Monday, the teacher is sad. The exam is scheduled for a Friday. Therefore, the class doesn't vote for an oral final.

3. If my allowance comes this week and I pay the rent, then my bank account will be in the black. If I do not pay the rent, I will be evicted. I am not evicted and my allowance comes. Therefore, my bank account is in the black.

4. Either Jane is in sixth grade implies that Jane understands fractions or Jane is in sixth grade implies that Jane is in a remedial math class. Jane is in sixth grade. Therefore, either Jane understands fractions or she is in a remedial math class.

5. If the price of oil increases, the OPEC countries are in agreement. If there is no U.N. debate, the price of oil increases. The OPEC countries are in disagreement. Therefore, there is a U.N. debate.

6. If Jill wins, then Jack loses. If Peter wins, then Paul loses. Either Jill wins or Peter wins. Therefore, either Jack loses or Paul loses.

7. If the germ is present, then the rash and the fever are present. The fever is present. The rash is not present. Therefore, the germ is not present.

8. If Hal is a politician, he is a liar or a fraud. Hal is not a liar. He is not a fraud. Therefore, Hal is not a politician.

9. If the material is cotton or rayon, it can be made into a dress. The material cannot be made into a dress. Therefore, it is not rayon.

10. If there is money in my account and I have a check, then I will pay the rent. If I do not have a check, then I am evicted. Therefore, if I am not evicted and if I do not pay the rent, then there is no money in my account.

In Exercises 11–20, test the validity of the arguments.

11. If the salaries go up, then more people apply. Either more people apply or the salaries go up. Therefore, the salaries go up.

12. If Rita studies, she gets good grades. Rita gets bad grades. Therefore, Rita does not study.

13. Either the balloon is yellow or the ribbon is pink. If the balloon is filled with helium, then the balloon is a green one. The balloon is filled with helium. Therefore, the ribbon is pink.

14. If the job offer is for at least $30,000 or has 5 weeks vacation, I will accept the position. If the offer is for less than $30,000, then I will not accept the job and I will owe rent money. I will not accept the job. Therefore, I will owe rent.

15. If the papa bear sits, the mama bear stands. If the mama bear stands, the baby bear crawls on the floor. The baby bear is standing. Therefore, the papa bear is not sitting.

16. If it is snowing, I wear my boots. It is not snowing. Therefore, I am not wearing boots.

17. If wheat prices are steady, exports will increase or the GNP will be steady. Wheat prices are steady and the GNP is steady. Therefore, exports will increase.

18. If we eat out, either Mom or Dad will treat. I pay for dinner. Therefore, we do not eat out.

19. If Tim is industrious, then Tim is in line for a promotion. Either Tim is in line for a promotion or he is thinking of leaving. Therefore, if Tim is thinking of leaving, Tim is industrious.

20. If I pass history, then I do not go to summer school. If I go to summer school, I will take a course in French. Therefore, if I go to summer school, then either I do not pass history or I take a course in French.

In Exercises 21–24, use indirect proof to show the argument is valid.

21. Sam goes to the store only if he needs milk. Sam does not need milk. Therefore, Sam does not go to the store.

22. If it rains hard, there will be no picnic. If Dave brings the Frisbee, the kids will be happy. The kids are not happy and there is a picnic. Therefore, it does not rain hard and Dave did not bring the Frisbee.

23. If the newspaper and television both report a crime, then it is a serious crime. If a person was killed, then the newspaper reports the crime. A person is killed. Television reports the crime. Therefore, the crime is serious.

24. If Linda feels ill, she takes aspirin. If she runs a fever, she does not take a bath. If Linda does not feel ill, she takes a bath. Linda runs a fever. Therefore, she takes aspirin.

<table>
<tr><td>

Solutions to Practice Problems 12.5

</td><td>

1. Let

$$g = \text{``Goldenrod is yellow.''}$$
$$v = \text{``Violets are blue.''}$$
$$p = \text{``Pine trees are green.''}$$

The following steps show the argument is valid.

1.	$g \rightarrow v$	Hypothesis
2.	$\sim p \vee g$	Hypothesis
3.	p	Hypothesis
4.	g	Disjunctive syllogism (2, 3)
5.	v	Modus ponens (1, 4)

2. Let

$$p = \text{``I go to the beach.''}$$
$$q = \text{``I study.''}$$
$$r = \text{``I work as a waiter.''}$$

Begin by assuming the negation of the conclusion.

1.	$\sim r$	Negation of conclusion
2.	$p \rightarrow \sim q$	Hypothesis
3.	$q \vee r$	Hypothesis
4.	q	Disjunctive syllogism (1, 3)
5.	$\sim p$	Modus tollens (2, 4)

Since one of the hypotheses has been shown to be false, the argument is valid.

</td></tr>
</table>

12.6   Predicate Calculus

In a previous discussion, we noted that a sentence of the form

"The number x is even"

is not a statement. Although the sentence is a declarative one, we cannot determine whether the statement is TRUE or FALSE because we do not know to what x refers. For example, if $x = 3$, then the statement is FALSE. If $x = 6$, then the statement is TRUE.

We define an *open sentence* $p(x)$ to be a declarative sentence that becomes a statement when x is given a particular value chosen from a universe of values. An open sentence is also known as a *predicate*.

Consider the open sentence $p(x) = $ "If x is even, $x - 6 > 8$." Let us consider as possible values for x all integers greater than zero, so the universe $U = \{1, 2, 3, 4, \dots\}$. Then the open sentence $p(x)$ represents many statements, one for each value of x chosen from U. Let us state $p(x)$ and record its truth value for several possible values of x. We note that the open sentence $p(x)$ becomes the statement $p(1)$ when we substitute the specific value 1 for the indeterminate letter x. Recall that an implication $p \rightarrow q$ is false if and only if p is true and q is false.

$$p(1) = \text{"If 1 is even, } -5 > 8\text{"}\ \text{is TRUE (since the hypothesis is FALSE).}$$
$$p(2) = \text{"If 2 is even, } -4 > 8\text{"}\ \text{is FALSE.}$$
$$p(3) = \text{"If 3 is even, } -3 > 8\text{"}\ \text{is TRUE.}$$
$$p(4) = \text{"If 4 is even, } -2 > 8\text{"}\ \text{is FALSE.}$$
$$p(20) = \text{"If 20 is even, } 14 > 8\text{"}\ \text{is TRUE.}$$
$$p(21) = \text{"If 21 is even, } 15 > 8\text{"}\ \text{is TRUE.}$$

In fact, $p(x)$ is TRUE for any odd integer x. And $p(x)$ is TRUE for all values of x such that x is even and $x > 14$. The only values of x for which $p(x)$ is FALSE are x even and between 2 and 14, inclusive. That is, $p(2)$, $p(4)$, $p(6)$, $p(8)$, $p(10)$, $p(12)$, and $p(14)$ are FALSE . All other values of x make $p(x)$ a TRUE statement.

▶ **Example 1**   Let
$$p(x) = \text{"If } x > 4, \text{ then } x + 10 > 14\text{"}$$
be an open sentence. Let $x \in U$ (that is, x is an element of U), where $U = \{1, 2, 3, 4, \dots\}$. Find the truth value of each statement formed when these values are substituted for x in $p(x)$.

Solution $p(1)$ is TRUE because if $x = 1$, the hypothesis is FALSE.
$p(2)$ is TRUE because if $x = 2$, the hypothesis is FALSE.
$p(3)$ is TRUE because if $x = 3$, the hypothesis is FALSE.
$p(4)$ is TRUE because if $x = 4$, the hypothesis is FALSE.
$p(5)$ is TRUE because if $x = 5$, then the hypothesis is TRUE and $x + 10 > 14$.

In fact, $p(x)$ is TRUE for all values of $x \in U$. We say that "for all $x \in U$, if $x > 4$, then $x + 10 > 14$." ◆

The statement
$$\text{For all } x \in U,\ p(x)$$
is symbolized by
$$\forall x \in U\ p(x).$$

The statement $\forall x \in U\ p(x)$ is TRUE if and only if $p(x)$ is TRUE for every $x \in U$.

We call the symbol $\forall$ the *universal quantifier* and we read it as "for all," "for every," or "for each." The universal set must be known in order to decide if $\forall x \in U\ p(x)$ is TRUE or FALSE. We emphasize that, whereas $p(x)$ is an open sentence with no assignable truth value, $\forall x \in U\ p(x)$ is a legitimate logical statement. At times, the notation will be abbreviated to $\forall x\ p(x)$ when the universe U is clear, or to $\forall x\ [p(x)]$ for further clarity.

From the example, we can see that the statement "For all $x \in U$, if $x > 4$, then $x + 10 > 14$" is a TRUE statement for $U = \{1, 2, 3, \dots\}$.

▶ **Example 2**   Let $U = \{1, 2, 3, 4, 5, 6\}$. Determine the truth value of the statement
$$\forall x\ [(x - 4)(x - 8) > 0].$$

Solution   We let $p(x)$ be the open statement "$(x-4)(x-8) > 0$." We consider the truth values of $p(1)$, $p(2)$, $p(3)$, $p(4)$, $p(5)$, and $p(6)$. We note that $p(1)$ is TRUE because $(1-4)(1-8) = (-3)(-7) = 21$ and $21 > 0$. We find that $p(2)$ and $p(3)$ are also TRUE. However, $p(4)$ is FALSE because $(4-4)(4-8) = 0$. We need not check any other values from U. Already, we know that

$$[\forall x \in U \; p(x)] \text{ is FALSE.}$$

We note that there are values of x in U for which $p(x)$ is TRUE.   ◆

The statement

$$\text{There exists an } x \text{ in } U \text{ such that } p(x)$$

is symbolized by

$$\exists x \in U \; p(x).$$

> The statement $\exists x \in U \; p(x)$ is TRUE if and only if there is at least one element $x \in U$ such that $p(x)$ is TRUE.

The symbol $\exists$ is called the *existential quantifier*. We read the existential quantifier as "there exists x such that $p(x)$," "for some x, $p(x)$," or "there is some x for which $p(x)$." We may write $\exists x \, p(x)$ when the universal set is clear. When the universal set does not appear explicitly in the statement, U must be made clear in order for $\exists x \, p(x)$ to be a statement and to have a truth value.

▶ **Example 3**   Determine the truth value of the following statements where $U = \{1, 2, 3, 4, 5, 6, 7, 8\}$.

(a) $\forall x \; (x + 3 < 15)$ (b) $\exists x \; (x > 5)$

(c) $\exists x \; (x^2 = 0)$ (d) $\forall x \; (0 < x < 10)$

(e) $\forall x \; [(x + 2 > 5) \lor (x \leq 3)]$ (f) $\exists x \; [(x - 1)(x + 2) = 0]$

Solution   (a) is TRUE because for every $x \in U$, $x + 3$ is less than 15. The statement in (b) is TRUE because, for example, $7 \in U$ and $7 > 5$. Statement (c) is FALSE because there is no $x \in U$ that satisfies the equation $x^2 = 0$. Statement (d) is TRUE. Statement (e) is TRUE because for each $x \in U$ either $x + 2 > 5$ or $x \leq 3$. Statement (f) is TRUE because $1 \in U$ and $(1-1)(1+2) = 0$.   ◆

Sometimes it is convenient to let U be a very large set—the real numbers, for example—and to restrict U within the statement itself. Consider the statement

$$\text{For every positive integer } x, \text{ either } x \text{ is even or } x + 1 \text{ is even.}$$

One way to write this is to let U be the set of positive integers and to write

$$\forall x \in U \; [(x \text{ is even}) \lor (x + 1 \text{ is even})].$$

An equivalent statement that more explicitly shows the universal set would be

$$\forall x \in U \; [(x \text{ is a positive integer}) \to ((x \text{ is even}) \lor (x + 1 \text{ is even}))].$$

The universal set can then be the set of all integers. The universe is restricted by using an implication with the hypothesis that x is a positive integer in the open sentence $p(x)$. We can allow U to be any set containing the positive integers and restrict U by using such an implication.

A statement with the existential quantifier can be rephrased to include the universe in the statement. For example, let U be the set of positive integers, and consider the statement

$$\exists x \in U \left[(x - 3)(x + 6) = 0 \right].$$

We can rewrite the statement as

$$\exists x \in U \;\; [(x \text{ is a positive integer}) \wedge ((x - 3)(x + 6) = 0)].$$

We could let U be the set of all integers or the reals, if we wish. Any set containing the positive integers would be an acceptable choice for U. The existential operator and the connective $\wedge$ can be used to restrict the universe to the positive integers.

We frequently have reason to negate a quantified statement. Of course, the negation changes the truth value from TRUE to FALSE or from FALSE to TRUE. The negations should be properly worded.

▶ **Example 4**   Negate the statement

"For every positive integer x, either x is even or $x + 1$ is even."

Solution   We could say, "It is not the case that for every positive integer x, either x is even or $x + 1$ is even." That is not entirely satisfactory, however. What we mean is that there exists a positive integer for which it is not the case that x is even or $x + 1$ is even. Assuming that U is the set of positive integers, this is written symbolically as

$$\sim[\forall x \; ((x \text{ is even}) \vee (x + 1 \text{ is even}))] \Leftrightarrow \exists x \; [\sim((x \text{ is even}) \vee (x + 1 \text{ is even}))]$$
$$\Leftrightarrow \exists x \; [(x \text{ is odd}) \wedge (x + 1 \text{ is odd})].$$

The last equivalence follows from De Morgan's laws, which allow us to rewrite a statement of the form $\sim(p \vee q)$ as $(\sim p \wedge \sim q)$. The negation of the original statement then is "There exists a positive integer x such that x is odd and $x + 1$ is odd."   ◆

▶ **Example 5**   Negate the statement "There exists a positive integer x such that $x^2 - x - 2 = 0$."

Solution   One way to negate the statement is to say, "It is not the case that there exists a positive integer x such that $x^2 - x - 2 = 0$." A better way is to say, "For all positive integers x, $x^2 - x - 2 \neq 0$." Note that

$$\sim[\exists x \; (x^2 - x - 2 = 0)] \Leftrightarrow [\forall x \; (x^2 - x - 2 \neq 0)].$$ ◆

We summarize the rules for the negation of quantified statements. The negation of a quantified statement can be rewritten by bringing the negation inside the open statement and replacing $\exists$ by $\forall$, or vice versa.

$$\sim [\exists x \; p(x)] \Leftrightarrow [\forall x \; \sim p(x)]$$
$$\sim [\forall x \; p(x)] \Leftrightarrow [\exists x \; \sim p(x)]$$

These rules are also called De Morgan's laws.

▶ **Example 6**   Write the negation of each of the following statements.

(a) All university students like football.
(b) There is a mathematics textbook that is both short and clear.
(c) For every positive integer x, if x is even, then $x + 1$ is odd.

Solution
(a) Here the universe is "university students" and $p(x)$ is the statement "Student x likes football." We negate $\forall x\, p(x)$ to get $\exists x\, [\sim p(x)]$, which in words is "There exists a university student who does not like football."

(b) The universe is the set of all mathematics textbooks. We have a statement of the form $\exists x\, [p(x) \wedge q(x)]$, where $p(x)$ denotes "The mathematics textbook is short" and $q(x)$ denotes "The mathematics textbook is clear." The negation of the statement is of the form $\sim[\exists x\, (p(x) \wedge q(x))] \Leftrightarrow [\forall x \sim(p(x) \wedge q(x))] \Leftrightarrow [\forall x\, (\sim p(x) \vee \sim q(x))]$. This translates into the English sentence "Every mathematics textbook is either not short or not clear."

(c) The universe is the set of positive integers. The statement is of the form

$$\forall x\ (p(x) \to q(x)),$$

where $p(x)$ is the statement "x is even" and $q(x)$ is "$x + 1$ is odd." We write the negation

$$\sim[\forall x\, (p(x) \to q(x))] \Leftrightarrow [\exists x \sim(p(x) \to q(x))] \Leftrightarrow [\exists x \sim(\sim p(x) \vee q(x))]$$
$$\Leftrightarrow [\exists x\, (p(x) \wedge \sim q(x))].$$

In English, this is "There exists a positive integer x such that x is even and $x + 1$ is also even." ◆

We sometimes have occasion to use sentences that have two open variables. For example, the sentence "For every child there exists an adult who cares for him or her" has two variables: the child and the adult. We can write the statement symbolically using two variables x and y. We let the universe for the x variable be the set of all children and the universe for the y variable be the set of all adults. Then we let $p(x, y) = $ "y cares for x." The statement can be written symbolically as

$$\forall x\, \exists y\, p(x, y).$$

Binding each of the variables with the universal or existential quantifier and a universal set gives a legitimate logical statement.

▶ **Example 7**   Let the universe for each of the variables be the set of all Americans. Let

$$p(x, y) = x \text{ is taller than } y$$
$$q(x, y) = x \text{ is heavier than } y.$$

Write the English sentences from the symbolic statements.

(a) $\forall x\, \forall y\, [p(x, y) \to q(x, y)]$
(b) $\forall x\, \exists y\, [p(x, y) \wedge q(x, y)]$
(c) $\forall y\, \exists x\, [p(x, y) \vee q(x, y)]$
(d) $\exists x\, \exists y\, [p(x, y) \wedge q(x, y)]$
(e) $\exists x\, \exists y\, [p(x, y) \wedge q(y, x)]$

Solution
(a) For all Americans x and y, if x is taller than y, then x is heavier than y.

(b) For every American x, there is an American y such that x is taller and heavier than y.

(c) For every American y, there is an American x such that x is taller than y or x is heavier than y.

(d) There are Americans x and y such that x is taller than y and x is heavier than y.

(e) There are Americans x and y such that x is taller than y and y is heavier than x. ◆

The rules for the negation of statements with more than one variable are just repeated applications of De Morgan's laws mentioned for single-variable statements. We have

$$\sim [\forall x\ \forall y\ p(x, y)] \Leftrightarrow \exists x\ [\sim\forall y\ p(x, y)] \Leftrightarrow \exists x\ \exists y\ [\sim p(x, y)]$$

and

$$\sim [\exists x\ \exists y\ p(x, y)] \Leftrightarrow \forall x\ [\sim\exists y\ p(x, y)] \Leftrightarrow \forall x\ \forall y\ [\sim p(x, y)].$$

We summarize these rules and several others in Table 1.

Table 1

$$1.\ \sim [\forall x\ \forall y\ p(x, y)] \Leftrightarrow \exists x\ \exists y\ [\sim p(x, y)]$$
$$2.\ \sim [\forall x\ \exists y\ p(x, y)] \Leftrightarrow \exists x\ \forall y\ [\sim p(x, y)]$$
$$3.\ \sim [\exists x\ \forall y\ p(x, y)] \Leftrightarrow \forall x\ \exists y\ [\sim p(x, y)]$$
$$4.\ \sim [\exists x\ \exists y\ p(x, y)] \Leftrightarrow \forall x\ \forall y\ [\sim p(x, y)]$$

$\Bigg\}$ De Morgan's laws

$$5.\ \forall x\ \forall y\ p(x, y) \Leftrightarrow \forall y\ \forall x\ p(x, y)$$
$$6.\ \exists x\ \exists y\ p(x, y) \Leftrightarrow \exists y\ \exists x\ p(x, y)$$
$$7.\ \exists x\ \forall y\ p(x, y) \Rightarrow \forall y\ \exists x\ p(x, y)$$

Notice that rule 7 is a logical implication and not a logical equivalence. Any other exchanges of $\exists$ and $\forall$ should be handled very carefully. They are unlikely to give equivalent statements even in specific cases.

▶ Example 8   Let the universe for both variables be the nonnegative integers $0, 1, 2, 3, 4, \ldots$. Write out the statements in words and decide on the truth value of each.

(a) $\forall x\ \forall y\ [2x = y]$ (b) $\forall x\ \exists y\ [2x = y]$

(c) $\exists x\ \forall y\ [2x = y]$ (d) $\exists x\ \forall y\ [2y = x]$

(e) $\exists y\ \forall x\ [2x = y]$ (f) $\exists x\ \exists y\ [2x = y]$

(g) $\forall y\ \exists x\ [2x = y]$

Solution   (a) For every pair of nonnegative integers x and y, $2x = y$. This is FALSE because, for example, it is FALSE in the case $x = 3$, $y = 10$.

(b) For every nonnegative integer x, there is a nonnegative integer y such that $2x = y$. This is TRUE because, once having chosen any nonnegative number x, we can let y be the double of x.

(c) There exists a nonnegative integer x such that, for every nonnegative integer y, $2x = y$. This statement is FALSE because, no matter what x we choose, $2x = y$ is TRUE only for y equal to twice x and for no other nonnegative number.

(d) There is a nonnegative number x such that, for all nonnegative numbers y, $2y = x$. This is FALSE for similar reasons as in (c).

(e) There exists a nonnegative integer y such that, for all nonnegative integers x, $2x = y$. The statement is FALSE. For it to be TRUE, we would need to find a specific value of y that can be fixed and for which, no matter what nonnegative integer x we choose, $2x = y$. This is the same as (d).

(f) There exist nonnegative integers x and y such that $2x = y$. This is TRUE. One choice that makes the statement $2x = y$ TRUE is $x = 4$ and $y = 8$.

(g) For every nonnegative integer y, there exists a nonnegative integer x such that $2x = y$. This is FALSE because if $y = 5$ there exists no nonnegative integer x such that $2x = 5$. ◆

A statement of the form $\forall x\, p(x)$ is FALSE if $\exists x\, [\sim p(x)]$ is TRUE. If we want to show that the statement $\forall x\, p(x)$ is FALSE, we need only find a value for x for which $p(x)$ is FALSE. Such an example is called a *counterexample*. We used such a counterexample in parts (a) and (g) of Example 8.

Analogy Between Sets and Statements   Actually, the symbols and the truth values in the tables are suggestive of set theory definitions introduced in Chapter 5. Recall that we use U to denote the universe and the letters S and T to denote sets in that universe. Then the union of the sets S and T is defined as

$$S \cup T = \{x \in U : x \in S \text{ or } x \in T\}.$$

If we allow $p(x)$ to represent "$x \in S$" and $q(x)$ to represent "$x \in T$," then it is TRUE that $x \in S \cup T$ if and only if the statement $p(x) \lor q(x)$ is TRUE. Thus

$$\forall x\, [x \in S \cup T \leftrightarrow p(x) \lor q(x)].$$

Similarly, we recall the definition of the intersection of two sets:

$$S \cap T = \{x \in U : x \in S \text{ and } x \in T\}.$$

It is TRUE that $x \in S \cap T$ if and only if the statement $p(x) \land q(x)$ is TRUE, where $p(x)$ and $q(x)$ are as above. Thus

$$\forall x\, [x \in S \cap T \leftrightarrow p(x) \land q(x)].$$

Using the symbol $\notin$ for "is not an element of," in addition, we have

$$S' = \{x \in U : x \notin S\}.$$

Thus $x \in S'$ if and only if $\sim p(x)$ is TRUE. Hence,

$$\forall x\, [x \in S' \leftrightarrow \sim p(x)].$$

The exclusive "or" corresponds to the *symmetric difference of S and T* defined by

$$S \oplus T = \{x \in U : x \in S \cup T \quad \text{but} \quad x \notin S \cap T\}.$$

That is, it is TRUE that $x \in S \oplus T$ if and only if the statement $p(x) \oplus q(x)$ is TRUE or

$$\forall x\, [x \in S \oplus T \leftrightarrow p(x) \oplus q(x)].$$

As with the connectives ∨ and ∧, the connectives → and ↔ have counterparts in set theory. We will assume that the universe is U and that S and T are subsets of U. We let $p(x)$ be the statement "$x \in S$" and let $q(x)$ be the statement "$x \in T$." Then we have seen that S is a subset of T if and only if every element of S is also an element of T. We say that

S is a subset of T if and only if $(x \in S) \to (x \in T)$ is TRUE for all x,

or, equivalently

S is a subset of T if and only if $\forall x \, [p(x) \to q(x)]$ is TRUE.

Two sets are equal if they have the same elements. We claim that

$S = T$ if and only if $(x \in S) \leftrightarrow (x \in T)$ is TRUE for all x,

that is,

$S = T$ if and only if $\forall x \, [p(x) \leftrightarrow q(x)]$ is TRUE.

▶ Example 9   Let $U = \{1, 2, 3, 4, 5, 6\}$, let $S = \{x \in U : x \leq 3\}$, and let $T = \{x \in U : x \text{ divides } 6\}$. Show $S \subseteq T$.

Solution   We must show that $\forall x \, [(x \in S) \to (x \in T)]$ is TRUE. An implication is FALSE only in the case where the hypothesis is TRUE and the conclusion is FALSE. Let us suppose then that the hypothesis is TRUE and show that the conclusion must also be TRUE in that case. We assume that $x \in S$. By the definition of the set S, this means that x is 1 or 2 or 3. Then $x \in T$, since in each of the cases x divides 6 and is therefore an element of T. Hence, $(x \in S) \to (x \in T)$ cannot be FALSE and must be TRUE for all $x \in U$.   ◆

Recall that we have already seen De Morgan's laws in another form in Chapter 5. In that case, we assumed that S and T were sets and showed that

$$(S \cup T)' = S' \cap T' \quad \text{and} \quad (S \cap T)' = S' \cup T'.$$

We know that $x \in S \cup T$ if and only if $(x \in S) \vee (x \in T)$ is TRUE. So $x \notin S \cup T$ if and only if the negation of the statement is TRUE. Thus

$x \in (S \cup T)'$ if and only if $\sim [(x \in S) \vee (x \in T)]$ is TRUE.

By De Morgan's law in Table 1 of Section 12.4, we know that

$x \in (S \cup T)'$ if and only if $\sim(x \in S) \wedge \sim(x \in T)$ is TRUE.

Thus

$x \in (S \cup T)'$ if and only if $(x \notin S) \wedge (x \notin T)$ is TRUE.

This means that $x \in S' \cap T'$. The De Morgan laws for unions and intersections of sets are closely related to the De Morgan laws for the connectives ∨ and ∧.

Colloquial Usage   Again, we point out that colloquial usage is frequently not precise. For example, the statement "All students in finite mathematics courses do not fail" is strictly interpreted to mean that $\forall x \in U$ [x does not fail] with U = the set of students in finite mathematics courses. This means, of course, that no one fails. On the other hand, some might loosely interpret this to mean that not every student in finite mathematics courses fails. This is the statement $\exists x \in U$ [x does not fail]. We require precision of language in mathematics and do *not* accept the second interpretation as correct.

Practice Problems 12.6	**1.** Write the following statement symbolically and write out its negation in English: "There exists a flower that can grow in sand and is not subject to mold."

1. Write the following statement symbolically and write out its negation in English: "There exists a flower that can grow in sand and is not subject to mold."

2. For the universe $U = \{0, 1, 2, 3, 4, 5, 6, 7, 8\}$, determine the truth values of the following statements.

    (a) $\forall x\,(x > 2)$ **(b)** $\exists x\,(x > 2)$

    (c) $\forall x\,(x^2 < 100)$ **(d)** $\exists x\,[(x - 1 = 4) \wedge (3x + 5 = 20)]$

3. Consider the universe for both variables x and y to be the set of nonnegative integers $\{0, 1, 2, 3, 4, \dots\}$. Write out the statements in English and determine the truth value of each.

    (a) $\forall x\,\forall y\,[x < y]$ **(b)** $\forall x\,\exists y\,[x < y]$

    (c) $\forall y\,\exists x\,[x < y]$ **(d)** $\exists x\,\forall y\,[x < y]$

    (e) $\exists x\,\exists y\,[x < y]$ **(f)** $\forall x\,\forall y\,[(x < y) \vee (y < x)]$

▶ Exercises 12.6

1. Let $U = \{1, 2, 3, 4, 5, 6\}$. Determine the truth value of

$$p(x) = [(x \text{ is even}) \text{ or } (x \text{ is divisible by } 3)]$$

for the given values of x.

    (a) $x = 1$ (b) $x = 4$

    (c) $x = 3$ (d) $x = 6$

    (e) $x = 5$

2. Determine the truth value of $p(x)$ for the values of x chosen from the universe of all letters of the alphabet where

$$p(x) = [(x \text{ is a vowel}) \text{ and } (x \text{ is in the word ABLE})].$$

    (a) $x = a$ (b) $x = d$

    (c) $x = b$ (d) $x = i$

3. Consider the universe of all college students. Let $p(x)$ denote the open statement "x takes a writing course."

    (a) Write the statement "Every college student takes a writing course" in symbols.

    (b) Write the statement "Not all college students take a writing course" symbolically.

    (c) Write the statement "Every college student does not take a writing course" symbolically.

    (d) Do any of the statements in (a), (b), or (c) imply one another? Explain.

4. Recently, as the Amtrak train pulled into the Baltimore station, the conductor announced, "All doors do not open." Since passengers were permitted to get off at the station, what do you think the conductor meant to say?

5. An alert California teacher chided "Dear Abby" (*Baltimore Sun*, March 1, 1989) for her statement "Confidential to Eunice: All men do not cheat on their wives." Let $p(x)$ be the statement "x cheats on his wife" in the universe of all men. Write out Abby's statement symbolically. Rewrite the statement using the existential quantifier. Do you think the statement is TRUE or FALSE? What do you think Abby really meant to say?

6. Consider the universe of all orange juice. Write the following symbolically, using $p(x) =$ "x comes from Florida."

    (a) All orange juice does not come from Florida.

    (b) Some orange juice comes from Florida.

    (c) Not all orange juice comes from Florida.

    (d) Some orange juice does not come from Florida.

    (e) No orange juice comes from Florida.

    (f) Are any of the statements (a) through (e) equivalent to one another? Explain.

7. Let the universe be all university professors. Let $p(x)$ be the open statement "x likes poetry." Write the following statements symbolically.

  (a) All university professors like poetry.

  (b) Some university professors do not like poetry.

  (c) Some university professors like poetry.

  (d) Not all university professors like poetry.

  (e) All university professors do not like poetry.

  (f) No university professors like poetry.

  (g) Are any of the statements in (a) through (f) equivalent? Explain.

8. Let $U = \{0, 1, 2, 3, 4\}$. Let

$$p(x) = [x^2 > 9].$$

  Find the truth value of

  (a) $\exists x \; p(x)$ (b) $\forall x \; p(x)$

9. Let $U = \{1, 2, 3, 4, 5, 6, 7, 8, 9\}$. Let

$$p(x) = \left[(x \text{ is prime}) \rightarrow (x^2 + 1 \text{ is even})\right].$$

  Find the truth value of

  (a) $\exists x \; p(x)$ (b) $\forall x \; p(x)$

10. Let $U = \{3, 4, 5, 6, \dots\}$. Let

$$p(x) = \left[(x \text{ is prime}) \rightarrow (x^2 + 1 \text{ is even})\right].$$

  Find the truth value of

  (a) $\exists x \, p(x)$ (b) $\forall x \, p(x)$

11. Let the universe consist of all nonnegative integers. Let $p(x)$ be the statement "x is even." Let $q(x)$ be the statement "x is odd." Determine the truth value of

  (a) $\forall x \; [p(x) \lor q(x)]$ (b) $[\forall x \, p(x)] \lor [\forall x \, q(x)]$

  (c) $\exists x \; [p(x) \lor q(x)]$ (d) $\exists x \; [p(x) \land q(x)]$

  (e) $\forall x \; [p(x) \land q(x)]$ (f) $[\exists x \, p(x)] \land [\exists x \, q(x)]$

  (g) $\forall x \; [p(x) \rightarrow q(x)]$ (h) $[\forall x \, p(x)] \rightarrow [\forall x \, q(x)]$

12. Let the universe consist of all real numbers. Let

$$p(x) = (x \text{ is positive})$$

  and

$$q(x) = (x \text{ is a perfect square}).$$

  Determine the truth value of

  (a) $\forall x \, p(x)$ (b) $\forall x \, q(x)$

  (c) $\exists x \, p(x)$ (d) $\exists x \, q(x)$

  (e) $\exists x \; [p(x) \rightarrow q(x)]$ (f) $\exists x \; [q(x) \rightarrow p(x)]$

  (g) $\forall x \; [p(x) \rightarrow q(x)]$ (h) $\forall x \; [q(x) \rightarrow p(x)]$

  (i) $\forall x \, p(x) \rightarrow \exists x \, q(x)$ (j) $[\forall x \, p(x)] \rightarrow [\forall x \, q(x)]$

13. Negate the following statements.

  (a) Every dog has its day.

  (b) Some men fight wars.

  (c) All mothers are married.

  (d) For every pot, there is a cover.

  (e) Not all children have pets.

  (f) Not every month has 30 days.

14. Negate each statement by changing existential quantifiers to universal quantifiers, or vice versa.

  (a) Every stitch saves time.

  (b) All books have hard covers.

  (c) Some children are afraid of snakes.

  (d) Not all computers have a hard disk.

  (e) Some chairs do not have arms.

15. Consider the universe of nonnegative integers $= \{0, 1, 2, 3, 4, \dots\}$. Write the English sentence for each symbolic statement. Determine the truth value of each statement. If the statement is FALSE, give a counterexample and write its negation out in words.

  (a) $\forall x \, \forall y \, [x + y > 12]$ (b) $\forall x \, \exists y \, [x + y > 12]$

  (c) $\exists x \, \forall y \, [x + y > 12]$ (d) $\exists x \, \exists y \, [x + y > 12]$

16. Consider the universe of all subsets of the set $A = \{a, b, c\}$. Let the variables x and y denote subsets of A. Find the truth value of each of the following statements and explain your answer. If the statement is FALSE, give a counterexample.

  (a) $\forall x \, \forall y \, [x \subseteq y]$

  (b) $\forall x \, \forall y \, [(x \subseteq y) \lor (y \subseteq x)]$

  (c) $\exists x \, \forall y \, [x \subseteq y]$

  (d) $\forall x \, \exists y \, [x \subseteq y]$

17. Let the universe for both variables x and y be the set $\{1, 2, 3, 4, 5, 6\}$. Let $p(x, y) = $ "x divides y." Give the truth values of each of the following statements; explain your answer, and give a counterexample in case the statement is FALSE.

  (a) $\forall x \, \forall y \, p(x, y)$ (b) $\forall x \, \exists y \, p(x, y)$

  (c) $\exists x \, \forall y \, p(x, y)$ (d) $\exists y \, \forall x \, p(x, y)$

  (e) $\forall y \, \exists x \, p(x, y)$ (f) $\forall x \, p(x, x)$

18. If $p(x)$ denotes "$x \in S$" and $q(x)$ denotes "$x \in T$," describe the following using logical statement forms with $p(x)$ and $q(x)$.

  (a) $x \in S' \cup T$ (b) $x \in S \oplus T'$

  (c) $x \in S' \cap T'$ (d) $x \in (S \cup T)'$

19. Let

$$U = \{0, 1, 2, 3, 4, 5, 6, 7, 8, 9, 10, 11, 12, 13\},$$

  let $S = \{x \in U : x \geq 8\}$, and let $T = \{x \in U : x \leq 10\}$.

  (a) What implication must be TRUE if and only if S is a subset of T?

  (b) Is S a subset of T? Explain.

20. Is S a subset of T? Let

$$U = \{1, 2, 3, 4, 5, 6, 7, 8, 9, 10, 11, 12\}$$
$$S = \{x \in U : x \text{ divides } 12 \text{ evenly}\}$$
$$T = \{x \in U : x \text{ is a multiple of } 2\}.$$

21. Prove that S is a subset of T, where

$$U = \{1, 2, 3, 4, 5, 6, 7, 8, 9\}$$
$$S = \{x \in U : x \text{ is a multiple of } 2\}$$
$$T = \{x \in U : x \text{ divides } 24 \text{ evenly}\}.$$

22. Prove that S is a subset of T, where

$$U = \{a, b, c, d, e, f, g, h\}$$
$$S = \{x \in U : x \text{ is a letter in } bad\}$$
$$T = \{x \in U : x \text{ is a letter in } badge\}.$$

23. Prove that $S = T$, where

$$U = \{1, 2, 3, 4, 5, 6\}$$
$$S = \{x \in U : x \text{ is a solution to } (x-8)(x-3) = 0\}$$
$$T = \{x \in U : x \text{ is a solution to } x^2 = 9\}.$$

Solutions to Practice Problems 12.6	

1. Let the universe be the collection of all flowers. Let $p(x)$ be the open sentence "x can grow in sand" and let $q(x)$ be "x is subject to mold." The statement is then

$$\exists x \, [p(x) \wedge {\sim} q(x)].$$

The negation is

$$\forall x \, [{\sim}p(x) \vee q(x)].$$

This can be stated in English as

"Every flower cannot grow in sand or is subject to mold."

2. (a) FALSE. As a counterexample, consider $x = 2$.

(b) TRUE. Consider $x = 3$.

(c) TRUE. In fact, for every $x \in U$, $x^2 \le 64$.

(d) TRUE. Consider $x = 5$.

3. (a) For all nonnegative integers x and y, $x < y$. FALSE.

(b) For every nonnegative integer x, there exists a nonnegative integer y such that $x < y$. TRUE. For any nonnegative integer x, we can let $y = x + 1$.

(c) For every nonnegative integer y, there exists a nonnegative integer x such that $x < y$. FALSE. A counterexample is found by letting $y = 0$. Then there is no nonnegative integer x such that $x < y$.

(d) There exists a nonnegative integer x such that, for all nonnegative integers y, $x < y$. FALSE. No matter what x is selected, letting $y = 0$ gives a counterexample.

(e) There exist nonnegative integers x and y such that $x < y$. TRUE. Just let $x = 3$ and $y = 79$.

(f) For every pair of nonnegative integers x and y, either $x < y$ or $y < x$. FALSE. Consider $x = y$; say, $x = 4$ and $y = 4$.

▶ Chapter 12 Summary

1. A logical statement (proposition) is a declarative sentence that is either TRUE or FALSE.

2. Logical statements frequently have connectives such as *and* $\wedge$, *or* $\vee$, *not* $\sim$, *implies* $\rightarrow$, *if and only if* $\leftrightarrow$. The order of precedence for the connectives is $\sim$, $\wedge$, $\vee$, $\rightarrow$, $\leftrightarrow$. A statement without any connectives is called a *simple statement*. The truth value of a statement depends only on the truth values of the simple statements it contains, as summarized in the following truth table.

p	q	$\sim p$	$p \vee q$	$p \wedge q$	$p \rightarrow q$	$p \leftrightarrow q$
T	T	F	T	T	T	T
T	F	F	T	F	F	F
F	T	T	T	F	T	F
F	F	T	T	F	T	T

3. A statement that is TRUE no matter what truth values are assigned to the simple statements of which it is constructed is called a *tautology*. A *contradiction* is a statement that is always FALSE.

4. The statement $p \rightarrow q$ is the implication "if p, then q (or p implies q)." It is FALSE only when p is TRUE and q is FALSE. The two-way implication $p \leftrightarrow q$ is TRUE whenever p and q have the same truth value and FALSE otherwise.

5. We say two statements p and q are *logically equivalent* and write $p \Leftrightarrow q$ if they have the same truth table, that is, if $p \leftrightarrow q$ is a tautology. We say that p *logically implies* q and write $p \Rightarrow q$ if $p \rightarrow q$ is a tautology.

6. There are several statements related to $p \rightarrow q$: The converse is $q \rightarrow p$ and the contrapositive is $\sim q \rightarrow \sim p$. If the statement is TRUE, the converse may be TRUE or FALSE. However, every statement is logically equivalent to its contrapositive. That is, $(p \rightarrow q) \leftrightarrow (\sim q \rightarrow \sim p)$ is a tautology.

7. We define the connective $\oplus$ in terms of the other connectives as follows: $p \oplus q \Leftrightarrow (p \wedge \sim q) \vee (\sim p \wedge q)$. Therefore, the statement $p \oplus q$ is TRUE if and only if p and q have opposite truth values (one is TRUE and the other is FALSE).

8. The logical connectives used in computer languages AND, OR, NOT, IF...THEN, and XOR correspond to the logical symbols $\wedge$, $\vee$, $\sim$, $\rightarrow$, $\oplus$, respectively.

9. Rules for simplifying statements containing connectives follow algebraic principles so that there is a "calculus" of propositions. To simplify statements, we usually use either the truth table or the propositional calculus. The most common laws of propositional calculus are the commutative, associative, and distributive laws:

$$p \wedge q \Leftrightarrow q \wedge p \qquad\qquad p \vee q \Leftrightarrow q \vee p$$
$$p \wedge (q \wedge r) \Leftrightarrow (p \wedge q) \wedge r \qquad p \vee (q \vee r) \Leftrightarrow (p \vee q) \vee r$$
$$p \wedge (q \vee r) \Leftrightarrow (p \wedge q) \vee (p \wedge r)$$
$$p \vee (q \wedge r) \Leftrightarrow (p \vee q) \wedge (p \vee r)$$

10. De Morgan's laws are

$$\sim(p \vee q) \Leftrightarrow \sim p \wedge \sim q$$
$$\sim(p \wedge q) \Leftrightarrow \sim p \vee \sim q.$$

11. The most common rules of inference are given in Table 1 on page 558.

12. Statements containing variables are called *predicates* and can be made into logical statements with *quantifiers*. The quantifiers are the symbols $\forall$ ("for all") and $\exists$ ("there exists"). These symbols refer to the particular universal set for the variables in the predicate.

13. Important rules of predicate calculus include the following laws:

$$\left.\begin{array}{l} \sim[\forall x\, p(x)] \Leftrightarrow [\exists x \sim p(x)] \\ \sim[\exists x\, p(x)] \Leftrightarrow [\forall x \sim p(x)] \end{array}\right\} \text{ De Morgan's laws}$$

$$\forall x \,\forall y\, p(x, y) \Leftrightarrow \forall y\, \forall x\, p(x, y)$$
$$\exists x \,\exists y\, p(x, y) \Leftrightarrow \exists y\, \exists x\, p(x, y)$$
$$\exists x \,\forall y\, p(x, y) \Rightarrow \forall y\, \exists x\, p(x, y).$$

14. To prove the statement

$$(H_1 \wedge H_2 \wedge \cdots \wedge H_n) \Rightarrow C$$

by the method of indirect proof, we assume that the conclusion C is FALSE and prove that at least one of the hypotheses H_i must be FALSE.

Review of Fundamental Concepts of Chapter 12

1. What is a logical statement? How do you decide if a collection of words is or is not a logical statement?

2. Write down the truth tables of the simple logical connectives $\wedge$, $\vee$, $\sim$, $\rightarrow$, $\leftrightarrow$.

3. When is $p \rightarrow q$ a TRUE statement?

4. What do we mean by "logical equivalence"? Explain how you might use a truth table to establish logical equivalence.

5. Explain how you might use the "algebraic" nature of the rules of Table 2, Section 12.4, to establish logical equivalence.

6. State De Morgan's laws. When should you use them?

7. Given the implication $p \rightarrow q$, what is the hypothesis? What is the conclusion?

8. Given the implication $p \rightarrow q$, write down the contrapositive and the converse. If the implication is TRUE, what can we say about the truth of the contrapositive and that of the converse?

9. Give an example (in words) of an implication that is TRUE and write its contrapositive and converse, making sure you know the difference.

10. Write the negation of $p \rightarrow q$ without using the arrow symbol.

11. Associate each of the logical connectives AND, OR, NOT, IF...THEN, and XOR with the logical symbols and an appropriate truth table.

12. Draw a logic tree for each of the symbols $\wedge$, $\vee$, $\rightarrow$, and $\leftrightarrow$ when the input has a TRUE p and a FALSE q.

13. What is a tautology? Describe how you would prove that a statement is a tautology.

14. Demonstrate each rule of inference in Table 1 of Section 12.5 with an English statement.

15. Write an English statement corresponding to $\forall x\, p(x)$. Write its negation.

16. Write an English statement corresponding to $\exists x\, [p(x) \rightarrow q(x)]$. Write its negation.

17. State De Morgan's laws for quantified statements.

18. Write an English statement of the form $\forall x\, \exists y\, p(x, y)$. Write the negation of the statement.

▶ Chapter 12 Supplementary Exercises

1. Determine which of the following are statements.
   (a) The universe is 1 billion years old.
   (b) What a beautiful morning!
   (c) Mathematics is an important part of our culture.
   (d) He is a gentleman and a scholar.
   (e) All poets are men.

2. Write each of the following statements in "if ..., then ..." format.
   (a) The lines are perpendicular implies that their slopes are negative reciprocals of each other.
   (b) Goldfish can live in a fish bowl only if the water is aerated.
   (c) Jane uses her umbrella if it rains.
   (d) Only if Morris eats all his food does Sally give him a treat.

3. Write the contrapositive and the converse of each of the statements.
   (a) The Yankees are playing in Yankee Stadium if they are in New York City.
   (b) If the Richter scale indicates the earthquake is a 7, then the quake is considered major.
   (c) If a coat is made of fur, it is warm.
   (d) If Jane is in Russia, she is in Moscow.

4. Negate the statements.
   (a) If two triangles are similar, their sides are equal.
   (b) There exists a real number x such that $x^2 = 5$.
   (c) For every positive integer n, if n is even, then n^2 is even also.
   (d) There exists a real number x such that $x^2 + 4 = 0$.

5. Determine which of the statements are tautologies.
   (a) $p \vee \sim p$
   (b) $(p \rightarrow q) \leftrightarrow (\sim p \vee q)$
   (c) $(p \wedge \sim q) \leftrightarrow \sim(\sim p \wedge q)$
   (d) $[p \rightarrow (q \rightarrow r)] \leftrightarrow [(p \rightarrow q) \rightarrow r]$

6. Construct a truth table for each of the following statements.
   (a) $p \rightarrow (\sim q \vee r)$
   (b) $p \wedge (q \leftrightarrow (r \wedge p))$

7. Which of the logical implications are true?
   (a) $[p \wedge (\sim p \vee q)] \Rightarrow q$
   (b) $[(p \rightarrow q) \wedge q] \Rightarrow p$

8. True or false?
   (a) $(\sim q \rightarrow \sim p) \Leftrightarrow (p \rightarrow q)$
   (b) $[(p \rightarrow q) \wedge (r \rightarrow p)] \Leftrightarrow q$

9. True or false?
   (a) $[(p \rightarrow q) \wedge \sim p] \Rightarrow \sim q$
   (b) $[(p \rightarrow q) \wedge \sim q] \Rightarrow \sim p$

10. For the given input for A and B, determine the output for Z.

    > LET C $= 3 * $ A $+$ B
    > IF $((\text{C} > 0)$ AND $(\text{B} > 3))$
    >   THEN LET Z $=$ C
    >   ELSE LET Z $= 100$

    (a) A $= 4$, B $= 5$
    (b) A $= 10$, B $= 2$
    (c) A $= -4$, B $= 5$
    (d) A $= -10$, B $= -2$

11. For the given inputs, determine the output for Z.

    > IF $((\text{X} > 0)$ AND $(\text{Y} > 0))$ OR $(\text{C} \geq 10)$
    >   THEN LET Z $=$ X $*$ Y
    >   ELSE LET Z $=$ X $+$ Y

    (a) X $= 5$, Y $= 10$, C $= 10$
    (b) X $= 5$, Y $= -5$, C $= 10$
    (c) X $= -10$, Y $= -5$, C $= 2$
    (d) X $= 2$, Y $= 5$, C $= 4$

12. The following statement is TRUE.

    > If the deduction is allowed,
    > then the tax law has been revised.

    Give the truth value of each of the following statements if it can be determined directly from the truth of the original.

    (a) If the tax law has been revised, the deduction is allowed.

(b) If the tax law has not been revised, the deduction is not allowed.

(c) The deduction is allowed only if the tax law has been revised.

(d) The deduction is allowed if the tax law has been revised.

(e) The deduction is allowed or the tax law has been revised.

13. Assume the following statement is TRUE.

   If the voter is over the age of 21 and has a driver's license, the voter is eligible for free driver education. Determine the truth value of each of the following directly from the original, if possible.

   (a) If the voter is eligible for free driver education, the voter is over 21 and has a driver's license.

   (b) If the voter is not eligible for free driver education, the voter is not over 21 and does not have a driver's license.

   (c) If the voter is not eligible for free driver education, the voter either is not over 21 or does not hold a driver's license.

14. Assume the statement "All mathematicians like rap music" is TRUE. Determine the truth value of the following from this assumption, if possible.

   (a) Some mathematicians like rap music.

   (b) Some mathematicians do not like rap music.

   (c) There exists no mathematician who does not like rap music.

15. Assume the statement "Some apples are not rotten" is TRUE. Determine the truth value of each of the following using only that fact, if possible.

   (a) Some apples are rotten.

   (b) All apples are not rotten.

   (c) Not all apples are rotten.

16. Show that the argument is valid: If taxes go up, I sell the house and move to India. I do not move to India. Therefore, taxes do not go up.

17. Show that the argument is valid: I study mathematics and I study business. If I study business, I cannot write poetry or I cannot study mathematics. Therefore, I cannot write poetry.

18. Show that the argument is valid: If I shop for a dress, I wear high heels. If I have a sore foot, I do not wear high heels. I shop for a dress. Therefore, I do not have a sore foot.

19. Show that the argument is valid: Asters or dahlias grow in the garden. If it is spring, asters do not grow in the garden. It is spring. Therefore, dahlias grow in the garden.

20. Use indirect proof to show the argument is valid: If the professor gives a test, Nancy studies hard. If Nancy has a date, she takes a shower. If the professor does not give a test, she does not take a shower. Nancy has a date. Therefore, Nancy studies hard.

▶ Chapter 12 Chapter Test

1. Derive the truth table for the statement

$$(p \wedge \sim q) \rightarrow q.$$

2. Which of the following expressions are statements?

   (a) Books belong in libraries.

   (b) Are mathematicians poets?

   (c) All trains from New York to Washington stop at Philadelphia.

   (d) There is a teacher at each middle school in Los Angeles who tells bad jokes.

   (e) What a terrific poem!

3. Write the contrapositive of

   If Bob hits a triple or a home run, then the coach buys him ice cream.

4. Assume the universe is the set of all integers. Write the negation of

   There exists an integer that is neither even nor greater than 8.

5. Let $U = \{1, 2, 3, 4, 5, 6, 7, 8, 9\}$. Let $p(x)$ be the open statement

$$x^2 \text{ is even} \rightarrow x^3 + 1 \text{ is prime.}$$

   Determine the truth values of the following:

$$\forall x \, [p(x)]$$
$$\exists x \, [\sim p(x)].$$

6. Classify each statement form as a tautology, a contradiction, or neither.

   (a) $(p \wedge \sim q) \vee (q \rightarrow \sim p)$

   (b) $(p \oplus \sim q) \leftrightarrow (p \leftrightarrow q)$

   (c) $\sim(p \rightarrow q) \wedge q$

7. Tell whether the following statements are TRUE or FALSE and give a reason for your answer.

   (a) If Chicago is in Illinois, then Toronto is in Canada.

   (b) If Toronto is in Canada, then Chicago is in Louisiana.

(c) If Chicago is in Louisiana, then $7 + 4 = 15$.

(d) If $7 + 4 = 15$ or Chicago is in Illinois, then Louisiana is in Canada.

8. Assume that the following statements are TRUE.

If you win the lottery or have a good job, you will have a lot of money.

If you get robbed, you will not have a lot of money.

You get robbed.

Can you conclude that you do not have a good job?

9. Write the negation of the following:

(a) There is an English dictionary that does not contain the word "Internet."

(b) Every student at the university listens to jazz.

(c) The elevator stops at all floors.

10. Let p be the statement "Spanish textbooks are expensive." Let q be the statement "Publishing costs are high." Write the following in symbolic "if, then" form:

(a) Spanish books are expensive is sufficient for publishing costs to be high.

(b) Publishing costs are high is a sufficient condition for Spanish books to be expensive.

(c) Spanish books are expensive only if publishing costs are high.

(d) Only if publishing costs are high are Spanish books expensive.

(e) Spanish books are expensive if publishing costs are high.

11. Use the following program to assign a value to the variable G for each of the inputs given.

$$\text{LET } D = A - (B * C)$$
$$\text{IF } D = 5 \text{ OR } C = 0$$
$$\text{THEN } G = 0$$
$$\text{ELSE } G = D + A$$

(a) $A = 4$, $B = 9$, $C = 3$

(b) $A = 185$, $B = 30$, $C = 6$

(c) $A = 0$, $B = 30$, $C = -6$

(d) $A = 10$, $B = 9$, $C = 0$

12. True or false:

(a) $p \wedge (q \vee r) \Leftrightarrow (p \wedge q) \vee r$

(b) $p \wedge (q \vee r) \Rightarrow (\sim q \rightarrow r)$

Chapter Project

A Logic Puzzle

Denise, Miriam, Sally, Nelson, and Bob are students at the same university. Each is in a different mathematics course and each is in a different year at the university. From the clues given, determine what mathematics course each is enrolled in and the year (freshman, sophomore, junior, senior, graduate student) each is in.

A. Sally is a sophomore.

B. Miriam (who is neither a junior nor a freshman) is taking a statistics course.

C. Neither the person who is taking calculus (who is not Bob) nor the one taking finite math is the person who is a freshman.

D. The student who is a senior is enrolled in algebra.

E. Neither Nelson (who is not a junior) nor Bob is taking precalculus.

Solve the puzzle by filling in the chart below with O to signify "yes" and X to signify "no." For example, clue A indicates that Sally is a sophomore, so put an O at the intersection of the "Sally" column and the "Sophomore" row. Notice that you can conclude that the other four students are not sophomores and that Sally is not a freshman, junior, senior, or graduate student, so that you can put eight X's in the chart to represent these conclusions. Solve the problem by working with both the clues and the chart.

	Bob	Denise	Miriam	Nelson	Sally	Freshman	Sophomore	Junior	Senior	Graduate
Algebra										
Finite Math										
Statistics										
Precalculus										
Calculus										
Freshman										
Sophomore										
Junior										
Senior										
Graduate										

C H A P T E R

Graphs 13

I n this chapter we discuss a special part of finite mathematics called graph theory. Many practical problems can be represented effectively with a mathematical structure called a graph. A detailed discussion will reveal the underlying
theory and its usefulness in arriving at solutions to these common problems in
business, sociology, geography, computer science, and management.

13.1 Graphs as Models

We begin with a few of the problems that lend themselves to solutions using the
pictorial representation that we will call a graph.

▶ Example 1 A field worker for a company that conducts polls is directed to
visit all the houses in the two neighborhoods of the city pictured
in Fig. 1. The streets are represented by line segments, the
intersection of the streets by dots. The field worker wants to
optimize her path through each neighborhood by parking her
car at A, traversing each street exactly once, and returning to
her car. What route should she choose in each case?

Solution With pencil and paper we try to solve the pollster's problem.
We try to trace a path beginning and ending at A that covers
each street exactly once. One such path is shown (Fig. 2) for
the neighborhood in Fig. 1(a). There is no route that meets the

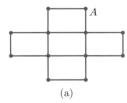

(a)

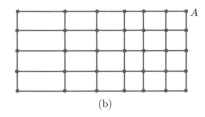

(b)

Figure 1.

579

pollster's requirements for the neighborhood of Fig. 1(b). The nonexistence of such a path will be explained later. Could we have inspected the pictures quickly and known whether such a route could be found?   ◆

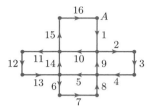

Figure 2.

▶ Example 2   A complex component is to be manufactured by a microelectronics company. The company receives raw material, makes several parts from the material, installs the parts, sometimes in sequential order, and assembles the component. Table 1 indicates each activity, its required time, and the immediate predecessors of the activity required before it can begin. What is the minimum amount of time needed for the entire job? On which days should specific jobs be done to attain this minimum?

Table 1

	Activity	Time (days)	Immediate predecessors
s.	Start	0	None
a.	Order material 1	3	None
b.	Order material 2	2	None
c.	Produce item 1	4	a
d.	Produce item 2	3	a, b
e.	Produce item 3	2	a
f.	Produce item 4	5	c, e
g.	Assemble final product	3	d, f
x.	End	0	g

Solution   We draw a diagram (Fig. 3) of the manufacturing process by representing each activity with a dot. We draw a line connecting two dots if one of the activities

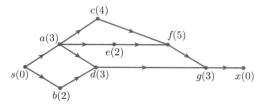

Figure 3.

represented is the immediate predecessor of the other activity, and we draw an arrow to indicate the direction of the process. Thus, since a is an immediate predecessor of d, we draw a line joining a to d with the arrow in the direction from a to d.

We can see that the minimum amount of time in which we can complete the manufacturing process of this component is the longest path (in time) through this graph from s to x. This will require 0 days for s, 3 days for a, 4 days for c, 5 days for f, and 3 days for g. We would need at least $0+3+4+5+3 = 15$ days. Note that tasks such as b may be performed while others are being completed.

Assuming that we begin the process on day 1, we should perform a on day 1 and begin b by day 2. We may begin tasks c, d, and e on day 4. Task f begins on day 8, while task g begins on day 13. That task requires 3 days, so the process arrives at x at the end of day 15. ◆

▶ **Example 3**   The police force in a large city wants to set up a communication network so that various people in the group can communicate with each other. The question is how to design the network efficiently. We might also try to satisfy other criteria while we are at it, such as making the network invulnerable to sabotage via interruption. Figure 4 is an example of such a network, in which a line joining A to B indicates that A is able to communicate with B directly. Can this network be interrupted by a cut in a line? Can it be interrupted if there is a failure in someone's telephone?

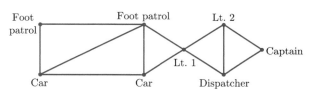

Figure 4.

Solution   Again, we can inspect the diagram and figure out what would happen if we removed any one line segment. Each person is able to communicate with everyone else no matter which line we might choose to cut. On the other hand, if we remove the telephone for Lieutenant 1, the communication network is disrupted. ◆

The essential features of the objects we have been drawing are dots and the lines that connect them. We define a *graph* to be a finite collection of *vertices* (dots) and a finite collection of *edges* (line segments) where each edge connects two vertices or connects a vertex to itself. Some of the graphs we have drawn have directions indicated on the edges. Such graphs are called *directed graphs* or *digraphs*. We first concentrate our discussion on graphs; in Section 13.4 we discuss digraphs.

A *graph* consists of two finite sets: the set V of vertices and the set E of edges such that each edge in E connects two vertices in V or connects one vertex in V to itself.

The graph in Fig. 5(a) has 5 vertices and 8 edges. Thus,

$$V = \{x, y, u, v, w\} \quad \text{and} \quad E = \{a, b, c, d, e, f, g, h\}.$$

Although the edge g joining x and v crosses the edge h joining w and y, the point of intersection of the two edges is not a vertex. In fact, we could have been a bit

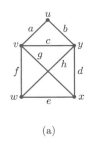

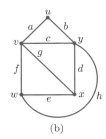

(a)   (b)

Figure 5.

more creative to avoid that problem. Figure 5(b) is an equivalent graph drawn so that the edges intersect only at vertices of the graph. Note that the edge from w to y still appears in the pictoral representation. A graph for which it is possible to draw all edges so that two edges intersect only at vertices is called a *planar graph*. We will return to a discussion of equivalence and planar graphs later.

We turn our attention to Fig. 6. Note (see vertex w) that it is possible that a vertex has no edges identified with it. Such a vertex is called an *isolated vertex*. There are two edges connecting vertices x and y. These are called *parallel edges*. The edge that connects z to itself is called a *loop*. The graph has two loops.

We are naturally interested in those properties that characterize a graph. The *degree* of a vertex v is the number of edges with vertex v. If there is a loop at vertex v, that edge is counted twice in determining the degree of v. Let us record the degrees of each of the vertices in the graph of Fig. 6.

Figure 6.

Vertex	Degree
u	4
w	0
x	4
y	4
z	4

We note that in this case the number of edges in the graph is 8 and the sum of the degrees of the vertices is $16 = 2 \times 8$. This is no accident. There is a formula that links the number of edges to the sum of the degrees of the vertices in any graph. Note that each edge has two vertices. Thus each edge contributes twice to the sum of the degrees of the vertices. Even if the edge is a loop, we agreed to count the loop twice in calculating the degree of the vertex. Thus the sum of the degrees of the vertices is twice the number of edges in the graph.

Graph Property 1   Let G be a graph. The sum of the degrees of the vertices of G is twice the number of edges of G.

We note that Graph Property 1 implies that the sum of the degrees of the vertices of a graph is an even integer. A vertex is called *even* if its degree is an even number. A vertex is called *odd* if its degree is an odd number.

▶ **Example 4**   Find the degree of each of the vertices in the graph of Fig. 7. Verify Graph Property 1. How many of the vertices are even; how many are odd?

Solution

Vertex	Degree	Odd/Even
a	5	Odd
b	5	Odd
c	2	Even
d	6	Even
e	2	Even

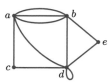

Figure 7.

The sum of the degrees is 20, which is twice 10, the number of edges. There are 2 vertices of odd degree and 3 of even degree. ◆

It is helpful to recall several simple facts about integers.

1. If we add any number of even integers, the sum is even.
2. If we add an even integer to an odd integer, the sum is odd.
3. If we add an even number of odd integers, the sum is even.
4. If we add an odd number of odd integers, the sum is odd.

▶ **Example 5** Use the graph drawn in Fig. 8 to help explain why the number of vertices of odd degree in any graph must be even.

Solution The number in parentheses at each vertex is the degree of the vertex. The sum of the degrees of the vertices is even (here $3 + 4 + 2 + 4 + 3 = 16$). Vertices have either even or odd degree. We group vertices of the same type:

$$3 + 3 \quad + \quad 2 + 4 + 4 \quad = \quad 16$$

$$\left(\begin{array}{c}\text{sum of odd}\\\text{integers}\end{array}\right) + \left(\begin{array}{c}\text{sum of even}\\\text{integers}\end{array}\right) = \left(\begin{array}{c}\text{even}\\\text{integer}\end{array}\right)$$

$$N \quad + \quad \text{even} \quad = \quad \text{even.}$$

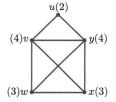

Figure 8.

Refer to the facts about integers listed previously; we know that any sum of even integers is even. The sum of all the degrees of the vertices is also even. We have denoted the even sums on the equation. The other term in the sum, labeled N, is the sum of the odd degrees. N must be even. For if N were odd, the sum on the right of the equation would also be odd. To summarize, N is even and also is the sum of odd integers. The sum of odd numbers is even only if there are an even number of terms in the sum, so N is the sum of an even number of odd numbers. (In this example, we have 2 odd vertices, giving $N = 6$.) This means the number of vertices of odd degree must be even. ◆

Graph Property 2 Let G be a graph. The number of vertices of odd degree is always even.

▶ **Example 6** Show that it is impossible to have a group of seven people such that each person has met exactly three other people in the group. Assume A has met B if and only if B has met A.

Solution If we drew a graph with seven vertices (one for each member of the group) and an edge joining two vertices if and only if the people represented by the vertices have met each other, we would have a graph with 7 vertices, each of degree 3. But the number of vertices of odd degree must be even. So no such graph can be drawn. There can be no such group of seven people.   ◆

◗ Example 7   Can we construct a graph with 6 vertices of degrees 1, 3, 5, 4, 2, and 2, respectively?

Solution   The answer is no. The sum of the degrees of the vertices is

$$1 + 3 + 5 + 4 + 2 + 2 = 17,$$

which is not even, in violation of Graph Property 1. Furthermore, three vertices would have to be odd. That violates Graph Property 2.   ◆

We note that if one has a graph G, the sum of the degrees of its vertices must be even. However, if we do not allow graphs that have more than one loop at a single vertex, it is possible to specify vertices and their degrees such that the sum of the degrees is even and yet be unable to draw the graph. Try, for example, to draw a graph (at most one loop at any vertex) with 1 vertex of degree 8 and 2 vertices of degree 2. The sum of the degrees of the vertices is 12, which is even, but no such graph exists.

◗ Example 8   How many vertices will a graph have if (a) it has 18 edges and each vertex has degree 3, (b) it has 18 edges, 4 vertices of degree 4, and the other vertices of degree 5?

Solution   (a) We know that the sum of the degrees of the vertices is twice the number of edges. A graph with 18 edges has a total degree of 36. Since each vertex has degree 3, the graph has $\frac{36}{3} = 12$ vertices.

(b) The sum of the degrees of the 4 vertices of degree 4 is 16. We let n be the number of vertices of degree 5 and note that the total of the degrees of all vertices in the graph must be

$$16 + 5n.$$

This is twice the number of edges in the graph; hence, we have

$$16 + 5n = 2(18).$$

We find that $n = 4$. Thus there are 4 vertices of degree 5 and the 4 given vertices of degree 4. The graph has a total of 8 vertices.   ◆

We have been using the term "graph" to include those with parallel edges. *We will now limit our discussion to simple graphs*—those without parallel edges.

Each branch of mathematics has a concept of equivalence, that is, being essentially the same. In geometry, two triangles are equivalent if they are congruent. In algebra, two equations are equivalent if they have the same solutions. We say that two simple graphs are *equivalent* if the vertices of the graphs can be paired so that whenever two vertices in one graph are connected by an edge, then so are the corresponding vertices of the other graph.

Consider the simple graphs in Fig. 9(a) and (b). These graphs are equivalent. It is possible to see this easily by rotating the first graph through 180° [Fig. 9(c)] and flipping the edge from c to e [Fig. 9(d)]. Of course, we also could go through systematic steps to verify that the graphs are equivalent by actually finding the pairing of the vertices in $\{a, b, c, d, e, f\}$ and $\{u, v, w, x, y, z\}$. We note that the two vertex sets have the same number of elements. This will be necessary for

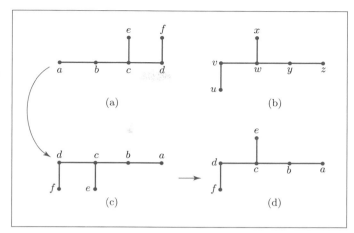

Figure 9.

finding the pairing. Second, we note that the graphs each have 5 edges. If we mark the degree of each vertex, we have 3 vertices of degree 1, 2 vertices of degree 2, and 1 vertex of degree 3 in each of the graphs.

Vertex	a	b	c	d	e	f	u	v	w	x	y	z
Degree	1	2	3	2	1	1	1	2	3	1	2	1

Thus the graphs have the same number of vertices of each degree. It is necessary to pair the vertex of degree 3 in one graph with the vertex of degree 3 in the other graph. So we pair c and w. Then we would pair e with x, since the edge from w to x can be paired to the edge from c to e. Note that x and e are each of degree 1. There are 2 vertices of degree 2 connected to each of c and w. A little experimentation reveals that d could be paired with v or y. We pair d with v. Then, clearly, we should pair f with u. The pairing of a with z and b with y follows by looking at their degrees. Here are the pairings:

$$a \to z \qquad b \to y \qquad c \to w \qquad d \to v \qquad e \to x \qquad f \to u.$$

Check that the 5 edges pair up properly:

$$\text{edge from } a \text{ to } b \to \text{edge from } z \text{ to } y$$
$$\text{edge from } b \text{ to } c \to \text{edge from } y \text{ to } w$$
$$\text{edge from } c \text{ to } d \to \text{edge from } w \text{ to } v$$
$$\text{edge from } d \text{ to } f \to \text{edge from } v \text{ to } u$$
$$\text{edge from } c \text{ to } e \to \text{edge from } w \text{ to } x.$$

Sometimes it is easy to show that two graphs are not equivalent.

▶ **Example 9**   (a) Decide if the simple graphs in Fig. 10(a) are equivalent.

(b) Do the same for the simple graphs of Fig. 10(b) and (c).

Solution   (a) We count the number of vertices in each graph. There are 6 vertices in one and 5 in the other. The graphs cannot be equivalent.

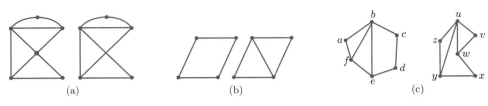

Figure 10.

(b) We count the number of edges in each graph. One has 4 edges; the other has 5 edges. The graphs cannot be equivalent.

(c) These graphs each have 6 vertices and 8 edges. We inspect the degrees of the vertices:

Vertices	a	b	c	d	e	f	u	v	w	x	y	z
Degrees	2	4	2	2	3	3	4	2	3	2	3	2

They each have 1 vertex of degree 4, 2 of degree 3, and 3 of degree 2. However, if we try to pair them up, we see that in the first graph there is an edge joining f and e (both of degree 3), but in the second graph there is no edge joining the vertices y and w (their counterparts of degree 3). The graphs are not equivalent. ◆

To check for graph equivalence in simple graphs, we can use the following checklist. If the answer to any question is "no," the graphs are not equivalent. If the answer to every question is "yes," the graphs are equivalent.

1. Do the graphs have the same number of vertices?
2. Do the graphs have the same number of edges?
3. Do the graphs have the same number of vertices of each degree?
4. Can you find a pairing of vertices of the same degree so that if there is an edge joining a pair in one graph, there is an edge in the other graph joining the corresponding pair?

For large graphs, the process of deciding whether two graphs are equivalent or not and verifying the answer may require a lot of work. For example, the graph G_1 with 15 vertices in Fig. 11 can be shown to be equivalent to G_2. You may use the following table to verify this.

v_1	v_2	v_3	v_4	v_5	v_6	v_7	v_8	v_9	v_{10}	v_{11}	v_{12}	v_{13}	v_{14}	v_{15}
u_7	u_6	u_5	u_4	u_3	u_2	u_{15}	u_{14}	u_1	u_{13}	u_{11}	u_{12}	u_{10}	u_9	u_8

However, G_1 is not equivalent to G_3. In G_3, the vertex of degree 5 (w_9) is joined by an edge to a vertex of degree 3, but v_6 in G_1 is not joined to a vertex of degree 3.

We note that in each of the graphs there are 15 vertices, of which 1 is of degree 1, 9 are of degree 2, 4 are of degree 3, and 1 is of degree 5. If we simply try to match vertices without regard to their degrees, there are 15! ways to match the 15 vertices on any two graphs. Since 15! is 1,307,674,368,000, this can be a

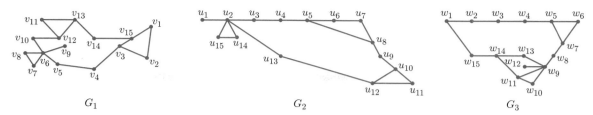

Figure 11.

daunting procedure. We should match those vertices of the same degree. In any two of the graphs of Fig. 11, we have 1 way to match the vertices of degree 1, 9! ways of matching the vertices of degree 2, 4! ways of matching vertices of degree 3, and 1 way of matching the vertices of degree 5. Thus there are

$$(1)(9!)(4!)(1) = 8{,}709{,}120$$

ways to match vertices of the same degree. Of course, the matching of vertices is not sufficient. We must also make sure that the edges match as well. Later in this chapter, we will see that representing graphs by matrices may help somewhat.

It is not always possible to avoid having the intersection of edges occur at nonvertices. To see that it may be impossible, see Fig. 12(a) and (b). In Fig. 12(c) we show a graph equivalent to the graph of Fig. 12(a) redrawn so that intersections of edges occur only at vertices. However, no graph equivalent to the graph in Fig. 12(b) can be drawn in which edges intersect only at vertices. Try it! Graphs that can be drawn so that edges intersect only at vertices are called *planar graphs*.

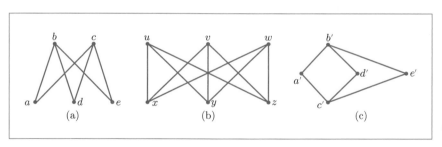

Figure 12.

▶ Example 10   Show that the graphs in Fig. 13 on the next page are equivalent.

Solution   We go through the checklist. Both graphs have 4 vertices; both have 5 edges. We tabulate the degrees of the vertices.

Vertices	u	v	w	x		a	b	c	d
Degree	2	3	2	3		2	2	3	3

Pair u with a and pair w with b. Try pairing v with c and x with d.

$$u \to a \qquad w \to b \qquad v \to c \qquad x \to d.$$

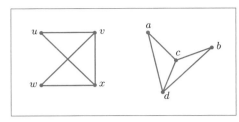

Figure 13.

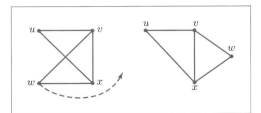

Figure 14.

Does it work? Check the edges.

$$\text{edge from } u \text{ to } v \rightarrow \text{edge from } a \text{ to } c$$
$$\text{edge from } v \text{ to } x \rightarrow \text{edge from } c \text{ to } d$$
$$\text{edge from } x \text{ to } w \rightarrow \text{edge from } d \text{ to } b$$
$$\text{edge from } w \text{ to } v \rightarrow \text{edge from } b \text{ to } c$$
$$\text{edge from } u \text{ to } x \rightarrow \text{edge from } a \text{ to } d$$

We have verified that the graphs are equivalent. We could also have used our geometric intuition to see that if we could pick up the corner at w and rotate it 180° to the right, the two graphs would look more alike (Fig. 14). ◆

The appearance of differences in the drawing of graphs that are actually equivalent can cause some difficulty. We hope that understanding the idea of equivalence will help to avoid confusion.

**Practice Problems
13.1**

1. Draw all simple graphs without loops that contain 4 vertices in which all the vertices have the same degree.

2. Determine whether the given situation contradicts Graph Property 1 or 2. If not, try to draw the graph.

   (a) Graph has 3 vertices of degree 1, 2 of degree 2, and 1 of degree 3.

   (b) Graph has 2 vertices of degree 1, 3 of degree 2, and 1 of degree 3.

   (c) Graph has 21 edges and 4 vertices of degree 4; all other vertices are of degree 5.

   (d) Determine whether the graphs in Fig. 15 are equivalent.

Figure 15.

▶ Exercises 13.1

Unless specifically stated, graphs in the following exercises may have parallel edges and loops.

1. For each of the graphs in Fig. 16:
   (a) Identify the loops and parallel edges.
   (b) Determine the degree of each of the vertices.
   (c) Determine the number of vertices of odd degree.
   (d) Verify that the sum of the degrees of the vertices is twice the number of edges in the graph.

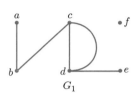

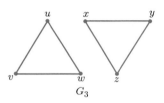

Figure 16.

2. For each of the graphs in Fig. 17, find the degree of each of the vertices. Verify that the number of vertices of odd degree is even, and show that the sum of the degrees of the vertices is twice the number of edges in the graph.

 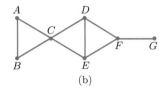

Figure 17.

3. An *acquaintance* table is shown in Fig. 18. In it we place a ▮ in the row labeled x and the column labeled y if and only if x and y are acquainted with one another. If we represent each person with a vertex and join vertices if and only if the respective people are acquainted with one another, we can represent the table with a graph. Draw the graph for the given acquaintance table.

Figure 18.

4. In the graph in Fig. 19, the vertices represent countries and an edge is drawn between two vertices if and only if a direct rail link exists between the countries they represent. Which country is connected by rail to the largest number of countries? Which country is isolated? In how many ways can we travel from A to D without returning to any country once it has been visited?

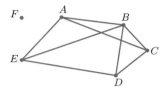

Figure 19.

5. Show that it is impossible to have a group of 13 people, each of whom is related to exactly 3 other people in the group.

6. Is it possible to draw a graph (may have parallel edges and loops) with 4 vertices where the degrees of the vertices are
   (a) 1, 1, 1, 4?
   (b) 1, 2, 3, 4?
   (c) 1, 2, 3, 3?

7. Draw graphs (they need not be simple) with 3 vertices having the given degrees if it is possible for such a graph to exist. If such a graph cannot be drawn, explain.
   (a) 1, 4, 5
   (b) 2, 4, 4
   (c) 3, 4, 4

8. Can we draw a graph having 5 vertices of degrees 1, 3, 3, 4, 4? Why?

9. If a graph has 15 edges and each vertex has degree 3, how many vertices must it have?

10. A graph has 12 edges, 2 vertices of degree 5, and all other vertices of degree 2.
    (a) How many vertices does the graph have?
    (b) Draw such a graph.

11. Each of the graphs in Fig. 20 is planar; redraw each so that edges intersect only at vertices of the graph.

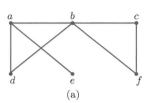

(a)

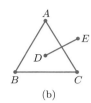

(b)

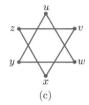

(c)

Figure 20.

12. Each of the graphs in Fig. 21 is planar. Show that each can be redrawn so that edges intersect only at vertices of the graph.

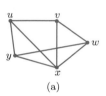

(a)

(b)

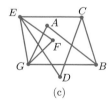

(c)

Figure 21.

13. Show that the graphs in Fig. 22 are not equivalent.

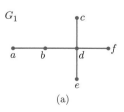

(a)

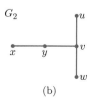

(b)

Figure 22.

14. Show that the graphs in Fig. 23 are not equivalent.

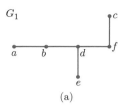

(a)

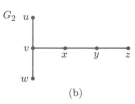

(b)

Figure 23.

15. Show that the graphs in Fig. 24 are equivalent.

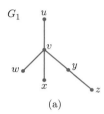

(a)

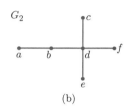

(b)

Figure 24.

16. Show that the graphs in Fig. 25 are equivalent by giving a pairing of the vertices.

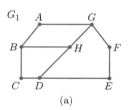

(a)

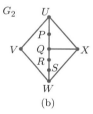

(b)

Figure 25.

In Exercises 17–21, decide if graphs G_1 and G_2 are equivalent. Explain by giving a property that holds in one and not the other or by giving a pairing of the vertices.

17.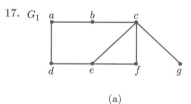

(a)

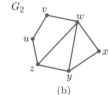

(b)

18.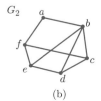

(a)

(b)

19. G_1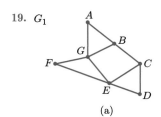

(a)

G_2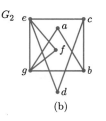

(b)

20. G_1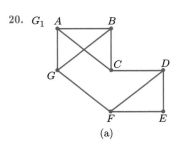

(a)

G_2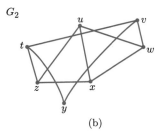

(b)

21. G_1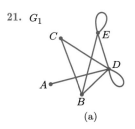

(a)

G_2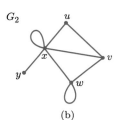

(b)

22. (a) If two graphs have the same number of vertices of the same degree, do they have the same number of edges?

(b) Do they have to be equivalent? Why?

23. A snow plow must plow all the streets represented on the grid displayed in Fig. 26. Construct a route so that the plow begins at A, exits at B, and goes down each street exactly once. If the garage is at A, can the plow begin and end at A, traversing each street exactly once?

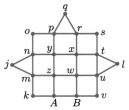

Figure 26.

24. Draw all simple graphs (no parallel edges) with 2 vertices.

25. Draw all simple graphs having 3 vertices and 5 edges.

26. Draw all simple graphs with 4 vertices and 6 edges.

Solutions to Practice Problems 13.1

1. Simple graphs have no parallel edges. We are also excluding graphs with loops. The graphs on 4 vertices where each vertex has degree 0 through 3 are given in Fig. 27.

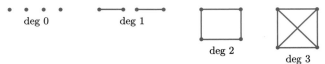

Figure 27.

2. (a) $(3)(1) + (2)(2) + (1)(3) = 10$, which is even. There are an even number of vertices of odd degree. The graph appears in Fig. 28.

(b) There are an odd number of vertices of odd degree. Also, $(2)(1) + (3)(2) + (1)(3) = 11$, which is odd. Both Graph Properties are violated. No such graph exists.

(c) We would require n vertices of degree 5, where $(4)(4) + (n)(5) = (2)(21)$. This means we must find an integer solution to the equation $5n + 16 = 42$. There is no such solution. No such graph exists.

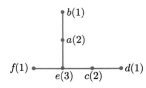

Figure 28.

(d) Yes. Use the pairings $a \to y$, $b \to u$, $c \to x$, $d \to v$, $e \to z$, $f \to w$.

13.2 Paths and Circuits

Let us consider the police communication system presented in Section 13.1. We reproduced the graph in Fig. 1, labeling the vertices with letters A through H and the edges with letters e_1 through e_{12}.

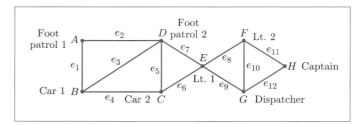

Figure 1.

We consider several paths of communication from Foot Patrol 1 at vertex A to Lieutenant 1 at E. One route through which a message could be sent is $e_2 e_7$. Some others are $e_1 e_4 e_6$ and $e_1 e_3 e_5 e_6$. Each is a sequence of edges that links together the vertices A and E.

A *path* in a graph G is a sequence of edges that links together two vertices.

Paths might repeat edges; for example, $e_1 e_3 e_2 e_1 e_4 e_6$ is a path from A to E in which edge e_1 is repeated. The *length of a path* is the number of edges in the path. The path $e_1 e_3 e_2 e_1 e_4 e_6$ has length 6.

Associated with each path is a sequence of adjacent edges. Since adjacent edges have a vertex in common, a path also defines a sequence of vertices. For the graph of Fig. 1, the vertex sequence corresponding to the path $e_1 e_2 e_5 e_6$ is $BADCE$. The number of vertices in the vertex sequence is one larger than the length of the path. In addition, if there are parallel edges, two different paths may have the same vertex sequence. Loops contribute a vertex twice to the sequence. We may always use the edge sequence to describe the path, but if there are parallel edges, the vertex sequence may not define a unique path. To simplify matters, *we limit discussion in this section to simple graphs*—those having no parallel edges. A sequence of vertices suffices to uniquely define a path in a simple graph.

Let us look at the simple graph in Fig. 2. Consider the vertex sequence $uywx$. This defines a simple path from u to x. A *simple path* is a path in which no vertex is repeated. Of course, there are other simple paths from u to x, such as uvx or $uvwx$. The path $uvuyx$ is not simple, because the vertex u is repeated.

Suppose we want to trace a path from u back to itself. That is, we are seeking a *closed path* in the graph. The vertex sequence $uyxwvu$ defines such a closed path. A *closed path* is a path in which the first and last vertices are the same. There are several closed paths starting and ending at u. Can you find some? We will have particular interest in closed paths that are *circuits* (sometimes called *cycles*)—closed paths in which no edge is repeated. The path $uyxvyu$ is a closed path, but it is not a circuit because the edge b is used twice. We point out that the vertex y is also repeated, so the path is not simple.

A *simple circuit* is a circuit with no repeated vertices except for the first and the last. A simple circuit then is a closed path with no repeated edges or vertices. Question: In simple graphs, must a circuit be a simple circuit? Any circuit necessarily uses no edge twice. Is it possible to have a circuit that repeats

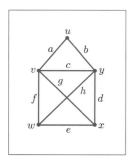

Figure 2.

a vertex? The answer is yes. Consider the circuit

$$uvwyvxyu$$

in the graph of Fig. 2. This is a circuit because no edges are repeated; however, clearly several vertices are repeated.

A graph is called *acyclic* if and only if it contains no circuits. The graphs of Figs. 1 and 2 are clearly not acyclic. We have already demonstrated several circuits. What does an acyclic graph look like?

▶ **Example 1**   Draw all acyclic graphs having 4 vertices.

Solution   See the six graphs in Fig. 3.   ◆

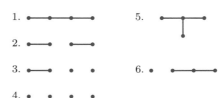

Figure 3.

▶ **Example 2**   Refer to the graph in Fig. 4 and determine whether each of the given paths is a simple path, a closed path, a circuit, or a simple circuit.

(a) *xyzuvx*   (b) *xyzuvzyx*

(c) *zwvzuyz*   (d) *uvzy*

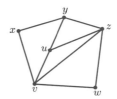

Figure 4.

Solution   (a) This is a closed path and a simple circuit. It begins and ends at x and no edges or vertices are repeated.

(b) This is a closed path because it begins and ends at x. However, it is not a circuit, because the edge joining y to z is repeated.

(c) This is a circuit that begins and ends at the vertex z. However, although no edges are repeated, the vertex z appears three times in the sequence. Thus this circuit is not a simple one.

(d) This is a simple path.   ◆

The graph given in Fig. 1 represents the communications network for a small police department. In Section 13.1 we asked whether the network is vulnerable to disruption. That is, will the removal of any person from the communication network disrupt the entire network? The removal of the vertex E corresponding to Lieutenant 1 will disrupt the entire network (Fig. 5). We say that the graph becomes *disconnected*.

A graph is *connected* if and only if given any pair of distinct vertices, there is a path between them. The graph in Fig. 1 is connected. Removal of the vertex E representing Lieutenant 1 produces a disconnected graph.

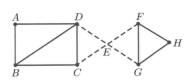

Figure 5.

▶ Example 3   Which of the graphs in Fig. 6 are connected?

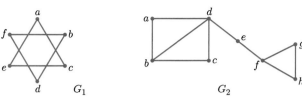

Figure 6.

Solution G_1 is not connected. There is no path from vertex a to vertex b. G_2 is connected.   ◆

▶ Example 4   Name the vertices in graph G_2 of Fig. 6 whose removal would disconnect the graph.

Solution   The removal of any one of the vertices d, e, or f would result in a disconnected graph.   ◆

Turning once again to G_2 of Fig. 6, we note that we can eliminate some edges yet retain the connectedness of the network, and we can define a path using each of the vertices of G_2. The network is connected as long as each person can communicate along some path to every other person. If we eliminate the edges from b to d, from c to d, and from f to g, we have a path through every vertex. The resulting graph has 7 edges. Is that the smallest number of edges in any path of G_2 through each vertex?

Given a connected graph G, our goal is to find a simple path using all the vertices of G and having a minimum number of edges. We call such a path a *path of minimal length* in G.

▶ Example 5   Find the path of minimal length needed to link any person in the network of Fig. 7 to any other person in the network. How many edges are in the path?

Solution   You might start anywhere on the graph and try to trace a path that hits every vertex without lifting your pen. Since we are looking for a path with a minimal number of edges, we would want to avoid any duplications, so we avoid circuits. As we will see later, a path of minimal length must contain at least 6 edges. One example is the path $yxwszuv$ (see Fig. 8). If all other edges were removed, we would still have a connected graph.   ◆

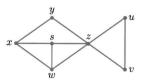

Figure 7.

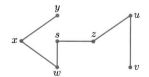

Figure 8.

The graph in Fig. 7 has 7 vertices. In order for us to have a connected graph using the 7 vertices, we must have at least 6 edges. Can you see why?

Let us try to see what is going on. Think about a connected graph with 2 vertices. Begin to trace a path from any vertex. Since the graph is connected, this vertex is not isolated, so we can follow an edge to the other vertex. Thus the connected graph with two vertices must have at least one edge. Now consider a connected graph with 3 vertices (refer to Fig. 9). Start at any vertex. It is not isolated, so there is an edge connecting it to another of the vertices. There must

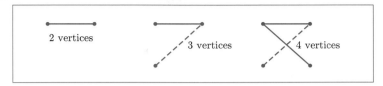

Figure 9.

be an edge joining the third vertex to one of the other two since the third vertex is not isolated either. Thus, if we have a connected graph with 3 vertices, we must have at least 2 edges. Try to draw the picture for a connected graph with 4 vertices. One is drawn in Fig. 9. The smallest number of edges possible for that graph is 3. In fact, we have a general result.

A connected graph with n vertices must have at least $n - 1$ edges.

▶ Example 6   Refer to the simple graphs in Fig. 10(a) and (b). Without lifting your pencil from the paper, try to trace a path in each graph from vertex u back to vertex u traversing each edge exactly once.

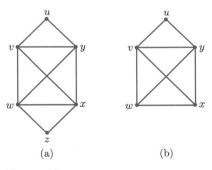

(a)   (b)

Figure 10.

Solution   There are several correct solutions for Fig. 10(a). Here is one:

$$uyxzwxvwyvu.$$

Try as you may on Fig. 10(b), there is no circuit starting at u and ending at u, using each edge exactly once. Let us analyze what goes wrong. The key is the fact that the graph has vertices of odd degree. For example, the vertex x has degree 3. Hence, if we enter on one edge at x and exit via another edge at x, we are left with still another edge with vertex x that eventually must be included in the circuit. But if we later enter toward x on that edge, there is no unused edge on which to exit. If we ever return to vertex x, we have no way out.   ◆

An *Euler path* is a path in which every edge of the graph is used exactly once. An *Euler circuit* is an Euler path that begins and ends at the same vertex.

If a graph has an Euler circuit, then all its vertices are of even degree.

The easiest way to understand this property is to imagine that we begin at a vertex on the Euler (pronounced Oiler) circuit and begin to traverse the edges. At each stage, erase the edge as we progress. What has happened? At every vertex we have erased the edge leading in and the edge leading out. This means we have erased 2 edges at each vertex. Even if we have erased a loop, we have erased 2 edges at that vertex. As we progress, we reduce the degree of each vertex by 2 and we erase all the edges, so the degree of each of the vertices is eventually 0. Thus each vertex must have had an even degree. The starting vertex must also have even degree because every time we leave the vertex (and erase an edge) we must later come back along another edge to eventually complete the circuit.

Do you think that the converse of the theorem is true? That is, if every vertex in a graph has even degree, can we find an Euler circuit? A trivial counterexample shows that this is not true (see Fig. 11). However, the Swiss mathematician Leonhard Euler (1707–1783) proved a theorem that gives conditions that are both necessary and sufficient for the existence of an Euler circuit.

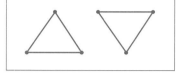

Figure 11.

> **Euler's Theorem** Let G be a graph. Then G contains an Euler circuit if and only if
>
> *1.* G is connected, and
>
> *2.* every vertex of G is of even degree.

We will not give a proof of Euler's theorem, but we will consider the practical matter of how to find an Euler circuit when we know one exists. We present a procedure (or *algorithm*) that accomplishes this.

▶ **Example 7**   (a) Explain why the graph in Fig. 12 has an Euler circuit, and (b) find an Euler circuit starting and ending at x.

Solution   (a) The graph is connected and the degree of each vertex is even, so the graph has an Euler circuit.

(b) One Euler circuit starting and ending at x is $xyvuyzx$.   ◆

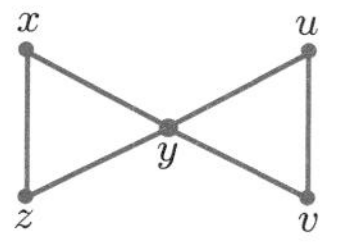

Figure 12.

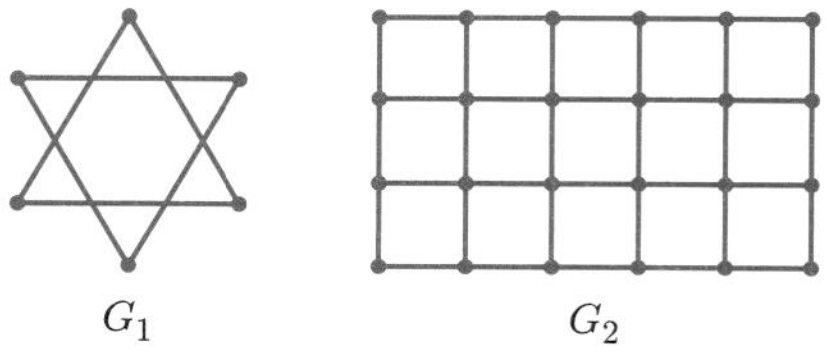

G_1

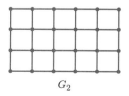

G_2

Figure 13.

▶ **Example 8**   Explain why the graphs in Fig. 13 do not have Euler circuits.

Solution   Graph G_1 is not connected, so it cannot have an Euler circuit. Graph G_2 has several vertices of odd degree and therefore has no Euler circuit. Note that G_2 is similar to the rectangular street grids in many cities. A route beginning and ending at the same point, traversing every street exactly once, is not possible for such a city.   ◆

Figure 14.

What procedure did we use to find the Euler circuit in Example 7? It seemed as if we just followed the edges around the graph. But consider what would have happened if we had begun with x, proceeded to y, and then to z (see Fig. 14). We see rather quickly that this is a bad choice, for we are forced to choose the edge from z to x and we are stranded at x; we cannot get to the other edges. An Euler circuit includes all the edges of the graph, so we want to be sure we can get to them. Notice (see Fig. 14) that, having chosen the edge from x to y and then the edge from y to z, we disconnected the graph. We want to avoid that. With this in mind, we state Fleury's algorithm for finding an Euler circuit whenever one exists.

Fleury's Algorithm for Finding an Euler Circuit   Suppose G is a graph that contains an Euler circuit.

1. Select any vertex to begin.

2. From this vertex, select an edge whose removal will not disconnect the graph. Add the edge to the Euler circuit, and erase the edge from the graph.

3. If an edge described in step 2 does not exist, there is only one choice of edge. Add the edge to the circuit, and erase it and the isolated vertex from the graph.

4. Continue from the next vertex.

▶ Example 9   Use Fleury's algorithm to find an Euler circuit for the graph of Fig. 15.

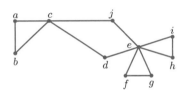

Figure 15.

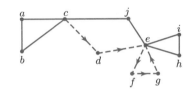

Figure 16.

Solution   Let us begin at vertex c. Proceed to vertex d. Erase the edge from the graph; include it in the circuit. Continue on to vertex e. Erase the edge; include it in the circuit. At vertex e we have several choices. We note that proceeding to j disconnects the graph. We may choose to proceed to vertex f, then g, and return to e. We include the edges in the circuit and erase the edges from the graph. Figure 16 shows our progress so far. Dashed edges are in the circuit but have been removed from the graph. As before, we cannot go from vertex e to vertex j, since the removal of the edge from e to j would disconnect the graph. Fleury's algorithm forces us to reconsider. We proceed instead to vertex i (or h) and continue. Our Euler circuit is

$$cdefgeihejcabc.$$ ◆

▶ Example 10   (a) Is it possible to trace an Euler path from x to w on the graph of Fig. 17?
(b) From u to x?

Solution   An Euler path must use every edge in the graph exactly once. In (a) we are proceeding from vertex x to vertex w. One such path is given by

$$xyuvywxvw.$$

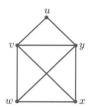

Figure 17.

In (b), after trying for a while, we wonder if it is possible to find an Euler path from u to x; we see that it is not. We analyze the situation. There is a problem at w. Vertex w has odd degree. Thus we would have to enter twice and exit once or enter once and exit twice. Since the path neither starts nor ends at w, this is impossible. If there are exactly two vertices of odd degree, there is an Euler path from one to the other. ◆

We mention an additional theorem that can be used for determining if Euler paths exist.

Euler Path Property   Let G be a graph with 3 or more vertices. Then G contains an Euler path that is not a circuit if and only if

1. G is connected,

2. two vertices are of odd degree, and

3. every other vertex is of even degree.

We note that if there are 2 vertices of odd degree, then the path proceeds from one of the vertices to the other.

◗ Example 11   Consider the problem of plowing the snow from the streets of a small subdivision. Figure 18 is a map of the region; the vertices indicate where streets intersect. An edge indicates a street that must be plowed. Can we find a route that traverses each street exactly once?

Figure 18.

Solution   To ensure that an Euler circuit exists, we have marked each vertex with its degree (Fig. 19). The graph is indeed connected and all vertices have even degree. We have marked the edges of the graph with arrows and the vertices sequentially to indicate one Euler circuit. ◆

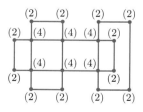   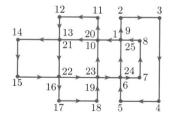

Figure 19.

One of the most famous problems in graph theory involved the famous bridges of Königsberg across the Pregel River. The town, formerly part of Prussia and later a part of the USSR, is now called Kaliningrad. Part of the town is shown in Fig. 20(a). On Sundays, it is said, the people of Königsberg would stroll from their home and try to take a walk crossing each bridge exactly once and returning home. In 1736 Euler showed that such a stroll was impossible (Euler's theorem). We will represent the land masses by points (vertices) and the bridges by edges in a graph representation of Königsberg. Although the graph is not simple (it has parallel edges), the problem is of such historical importance that we temporarily lift our restriction to consider it.

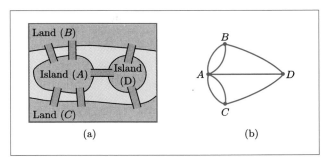

Figure 20.

We point out that the degrees of the vertices in the Königsberg bridge problem are all odd. Thus it is not possible to cross every bridge exactly once and return to the starting point!

An interesting addendum to the Königsberg bridge problem is that during World War II all seven bridges were destroyed. They were replaced by seven bridges placed roughly the way they were originally and one additional bridge. The graph representation has exactly 2 vertices of odd degree. Thus, although an Euler circuit does not exist, we could construct an Euler path that would begin at one of the vertices of odd degree and terminate at the other.

**Practice Problems
13.2**

1. Use the graph in Fig. 21 to find the length of the paths in (a) through (d). Determine if the given path is a simple path, a closed path, a circuit, or a simple circuit.

   (a) *ABHGF*   (b) *ABCHBA*

   (c) *ABCDFGCHA*   (d) *BCDFGHB*

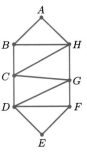

Figure 21.

Practice Problems 13.2 (Continued)

2. Determine if an Euler circuit exists in the graph in Fig. 22.

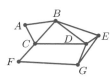

Figure 22.   **Figure 23.**

3. Show that an Euler circuit exists in the graph in Fig. 23. Find one.

▶ Exercises 13.2

Assume that all graphs are simple (no parallel edges).

1. Use the graph in Fig. 24 to find the length of the given paths.

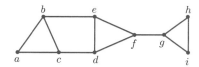

Figure 24.

 (a) *abca*   (b) *bcdefd*
 (c) *abcdfghi*   (d) *abedca*
 (e) *bcdeb*   (f) *edfghigf*

2. For each of the paths given in Exercise 1, determine if the path is

 a simple path (sp)

 a closed path (cp)

 a circuit (c)

 a simple circuit (sc).

 Justify your answers.

3. Find the lengths of each of the given paths in the graph in Fig. 25. Determine whether each is a simple path, a closed path, a circuit, or a simple circuit.

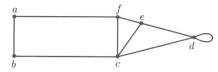

Figure 25.

 (a) *afede*   (b) *afcb*
 (c) *afcdde*   (d) *afecba*
 (e) *afcef*   (f) *abcdefa*

4. For the graph in Fig. 26, find
 (a) Four different simple paths
 (b) Five different simple circuits
 (c) Two different circuits that are not simple

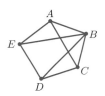   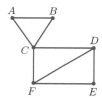

Figure 26.   **Figure 27.**

5. (a) Find four simple paths from *A* to *D* in the graph of Fig. 27.

 (b) Find three simple circuits that begin and end at *C*. Are there any more?

6. Draw all acyclic connected graphs with 5 vertices.

7. Which of the graphs in Fig. 28 is connected? Explain.

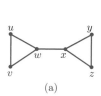   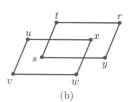

 (a)   (b)

 (c)

Figure 28.

8. Suppose that *G* is a graph with 6 vertices and 4 edges. Can *G* be connected? Why?

9. Suppose G is a graph with no loops or parallel edges. It has 5 vertices and 7 edges. Can G be disconnected? Why? What if G has 5 vertices and 5 edges?

10. Why are there no Euler circuits in the graphs in Fig. 29?

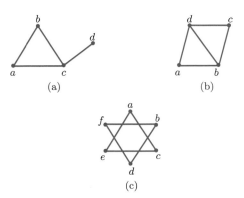

Figure 29.

11. Which of the graphs shown in Fig. 30 are acyclic? Explain.

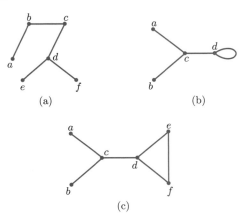

Figure 30.

12. For which of the graphs in Fig. 31 can we find an Euler circuit? Explain.

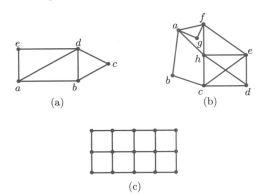

Figure 31.

13. Use Fleury's algorithm, beginning with vertex v, to find an Euler circuit in the graphs in Fig. 32.

Figure 32.

14. Use the floor plan of the house shown in Fig. 33 to draw a graph where each room and the area outside the house are represented by vertices and each door by an edge. Is it possible to begin outside the house and go through each doorway exactly once, returning to the outside? Find a route if it is possible.

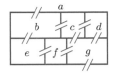

Figure 33.

15. Use the floor plan in Fig. 34 to answer the question posed in Exercise 14.

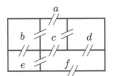

Figure 34.

16. A road inspector must investigate the roads in the area pictured in Fig. 35. Is there a route he can take that begins at city A, traverses each road exactly once, and allows him to return to A? If so, find the route. If not, why not?

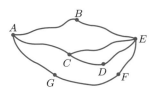

Figure 35.

17. The road inspector of Exercise 16 needs to visit the area pictured in Fig. 36. Can he find a route that begins and ends at A and traverses each road exactly

once? If so, find the route. If not, why not?

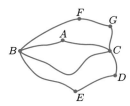

Figure 36.

18. Can an Euler path be found in the graphs in Fig. 37? Find one if you can. Otherwise, explain why one does not exist.

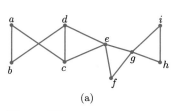

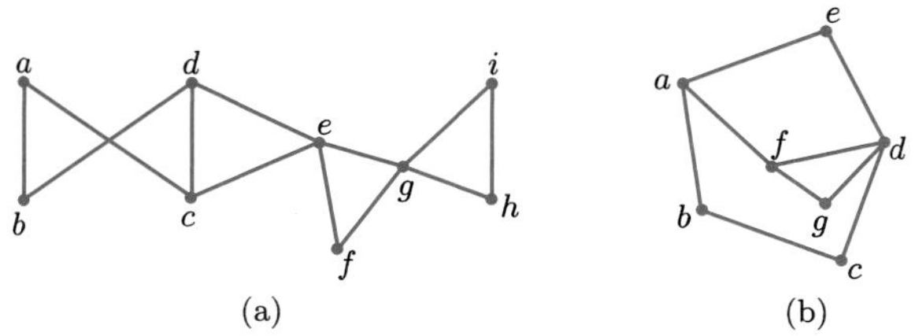

(a)　　　　　(b)

Figure 37.

19. In Fig. 38, can you construct an Euler path so as to cross over each bridge exactly once? If one exists,

where must it begin and end?

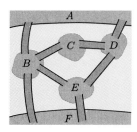

Figure 38.

20. Draw a simple graph in which every vertex has even degree but for which no Euler circuit exists.

21. For the graph in Fig. 39, find the shortest path joining the given vertices and find its length.

b to d　　d to g　　c to g

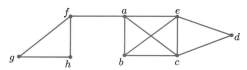

Figure 39.

Solutions to Practice Problems 13.2

1. (a) $ABHGF$ is a simple path of length 4, not closed and not a circuit.

   (b) $ABCHBA$ is a nonsimple closed path of length 5 but is not a circuit, because the edge BA is repeated.

   (c) $ABCDFGCHA$ is a closed path of length 8, not a simple circuit, but a circuit nonetheless.

   (d) $BCDFGHB$ is a simple closed path of length 6 that is also a simple circuit.

2. Since vertices E and G have odd degree, no Euler circuit exists. However, there is an Euler path beginning at E and ending at G.

3. Since the graph is connected and all vertices are of even degree, an Euler circuit exists. One example is

$$ABCDEFAGCHDGFHA.$$

13.3 Hamiltonian Circuits and Spanning Trees

▶ Example 1.　Consider a school bus company planning a route. For the graph in Fig. 1, let us indicate by a vertex each of those corners at which the bus must pick up children. There is an edge between vertices if and only if there is a path the bus can take between the two corners. Is there a route that visits each corner exactly once and for which the bus begins and ends the route at school?

Solution　One circuit is indicated on the graph in Fig. 2.　　　　◆

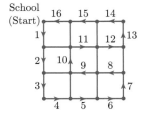

Figure 1.   Figure 2.

Example 1 shows a Hamiltonian circuit, that is, a circuit starting and ending at the same vertex that visits each other **vertex** exactly once. Sir William Rowan Hamilton (1805–1865) was born in Ireland. As a mathematician, he made significant contributions to algebra. His name is associated with circuits of this type because in 1857 he invented a game in which the player was to trace out the edges of a dodecahedron, visiting each of the 20 vertices without a repetition, and returning to the starting point. You might try Hamilton's puzzle on the dodecahedron drawn in Fig. 3. (Actually, in 1855 an English mathematician named Thomas R. Kirkman posed a similar problem to the Royal Society.) A *Hamiltonian path* is a path that is not closed and visits each vertex exactly once.

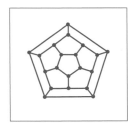

Figure 3.

Finding an Euler circuit and finding a Hamiltonian circuit is the difference in the two problems:

1. Find a route for a snow plow that traverses every street exactly once and returns to its starting point (Euler circuit).

2. Find a route for the mail truck that stops exactly once at each mail box to pick up outgoing mail and returns to the post office from which it began (Hamiltonian circuit).

In general, the problem of deciding whether a graph has a Hamiltonian circuit is more difficult than deciding on the existence of an Euler circuit. The traveling salesperson problem is a problem of this type. It is concerned with a salesperson who must visit each of several cities. The cost involved in traveling between any two cities is known, and the salesperson wishes to construct a route that minimizes cost and visits each city exactly once before returning home. No satisfactory simple procedure is known for solving the general problem.

There are a few facts that can help us decide whether a graph has a Hamiltonian circuit. We mention a few of them without proof. First, a graph G with n vertices that has a Hamiltonian circuit must have at least n edges. This allows us to say that if a graph with n vertices has fewer than n edges, it cannot have a Hamiltonian circuit. However, the fact that a graph with n vertices has at least n edges does not guarantee that the graph has a Hamiltonian circuit. We draw

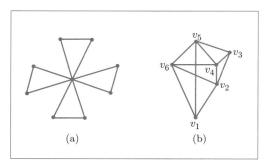

Figure 4.

one such counterexample in Fig. 4(a). The graph has 9 vertices and 12 edges, but there is no way to trace a path that begins and ends at the same vertex and includes every other vertex exactly once.

Principle 1   If

1. G is a simple graph

2. G has no loops

3. G has n vertices, where $n \geq 3$, and

4. the degree of each vertex of G is at least $n/2$,

then G has a Hamiltonian circuit.

Again, we remind the reader that if the conditions are satisfied, the graph has a Hamiltonian circuit. However, we may have graphs with Hamiltonian circuits that do not satisfy the criteria. The graph in Fig. 4(b) satisfies the criteria of Principle 1 and therefore has a Hamiltonian circuit. Can you find it?

Principle 2   If

1. G is a simple graph

2. G has no loops

3. G has n vertices, and

4. G has at least $\frac{1}{2}(n-1)(n-2)+2$ edges,

then G has a Hamiltonian circuit.

We note that the graph of Fig. 4(b) does not satisfy the criteria of Principle 2 because $n = 6$, but the number of edges is 11, while

$$\tfrac{1}{2}(n-1)(n-2)+2 = \tfrac{1}{2}(5)(4)+2 = 12.$$

However, as we have already noted, the graph does have a Hamiltonian circuit.

Principle 3   Let G be a simple graph with no loops and n vertices, where $n \geq 3$. If, for any two vertices in G not connected by an edge, the sum of their degrees is at least n, then G has a Hamiltonian circuit.

Let us analyze the graph of Fig. 4(b) in light of Principle 3. We make a chart of all those vertex pairs that are not connected and calculate the sum of the degrees of their vertices:

Vertex pairs that are not connected	Sum of degrees of vertices
$v_1 v_3$	6
$v_1 v_4$	7
$v_2 v_5$	8
$v_3 v_6$	7

There are 6 vertices in the graph, and the sums of the degrees of those pairs not connected with an edge is ≥ 6 for all such pairs. The graph is guaranteed by Principle 3 to have a Hamiltonian circuit.

Principle 3 tells us that, for example, if we have a simple graph G on 5 vertices with no loops, then in order for G to have a Hamiltonian circuit, it is sufficient that the degrees of any 2 vertices not connected with an edge sum to at least 5.

▶ **Example 2**   Which of the graphs in Fig. 5 have Hamiltonian circuits? Use the three principles if possible.

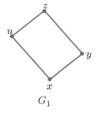 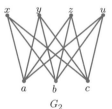 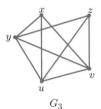

Figure 5.

Solution   We can see that the circuit $uxyzu$ is a Hamiltonian circuit in G_1. Graph G_1 has $n = 4$ vertices, each with degree $n/2 = 2$. We could have come to the same conclusion by applying Principle 1. There is no way to draw a Hamiltonian circuit in G_2. We can draw a path using every vertex, but there is no way to close the path to form a circuit. We note that this is not a violation of Principle 1, even though $n = 7$ and not every vertex has degree at least $7/2$. In particular, x, y, z, and u have degree 3. A Hamiltonian circuit exists in G_3 because it satisfies Principle 1. Note that G_3 also satisfies Principles 2 and 3. Since $n = 5$, Principle 2 requires that G_3 have at least $\frac{1}{2}(n-1)(n-2) + 2 = 8$ edges. Since the degree of each vertex is either 3 or 4, the sum of the degrees of any two vertices not connected by an edge is 6, 7, or 8. In any case, the sum is at least $n = 5$. One Hamiltonian circuit in G_3 is $xyzuvx$.   ◆

There is a whole class of problems similar to the traveling salesperson problem but much easier to solve. These involve connected graphs with weighted edges. The problem is to find a connected subgraph using all the vertices and having minimal total weight. Consider the weighted graph in Fig. 6. We could think of the graph as the representation of a pipeline through which we need to reach every customer (vertex). The weights might represent the unit cost of transmission of, say, natural gas through the pipeline. We try to find a pipeline

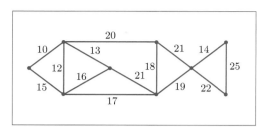

Figure 6.

system that will deliver gas to each vertex at the lowest possible unit cost. A *weighted graph* is a graph in which each edge has an associated positive number representing its weight.

A *subgraph* of a graph G is a graph whose vertex set is a subset of the vertex set of G and whose edge set is a subset of the edge set of G. There is an easy algorithm for finding a connected subgraph of a graph G with minimal total weight that includes each vertex of G. We first note that we are not looking for a path, only a subgraph of the original graph. Also, we would certainly not have any cycles (circuits) in our solution since we are trying to minimize the total weight while including every vertex of G. A graph with no cycles is called *acyclic*. Thus our goal is to find a connected acyclic subgraph of G. A connected acyclic graph is called a *tree*. Since we wish to include every vertex of G, we say we want to *span* the graph G. In graph theory parlance, we are trying to find a *minimal spanning tree* of the graph G.

A connected acyclic graph is called a *tree* because the structure can always be redrawn to look like a natural tree with its branches and limbs. We study trees in more detail in Section 13.6.

Here is the algorithm for finding the minimal spanning tree:

Minimal Spanning Tree Algorithm

1. Label the edges of the graph G: $e_1, e_2, \ldots, e_n$ in order of increasing weight. Thus,

$$\text{weight of } e_1 \leq \text{weight of } e_2 \leq \text{weight of } e_3 \leq \cdots.$$

2. Choose edge e_1 to begin the tree. Then choose the next edge in the sequence whose addition does not create a cycle.

3. Continue until no more edges must be added.

Why does the algorithm work? It operates in a greedy fashion, choosing the edges with smallest weight first. It ensures against cycles by stopping us from choosing edges that form them. It is possible that if several edges have the same weight, the algorithm could result in different minimal spanning trees. All would have the same total minimal weight, however.

▶ **Example 3**   Find the minimal spanning tree for the graph in Fig. 6.

Solution   In Fig. 7 we show the graph labeled with edges in increasing order of weight. If two edges are tied, it does not matter which comes first (although different labeling might result in a different tree). We begin with e_1, which has weight 10. We then add e_2, e_3, and e_4. However, we note that e_5 would complete a cycle

$(e_1 e_2 e_5)$, so we skip e_5 and check e_6. But we omit e_6 as well, since e_6 taken with e_2 and e_3 would form a cycle. We include e_7, e_8, and e_9 but omit e_{10}, e_{11}, and e_{12}. We conclude by including e_{13}. The algorithm gives the tree consisting of edges $e_1 e_2 e_3 e_4 e_7 e_8 e_9 e_{13}$. The total weight of this tree is

$$10 + 12 + 13 + 14 + 17 + 18 + 19 + 22 = 125.$$

Natural gas sent along this pipeline will cost the minimal amount per unit and reach each of the vertices. Note that because the graph is connected we could pump gas from any vertex to any other. In Fig. 7(c) we have drawn the resulting graph to show its treelike structure. ◆

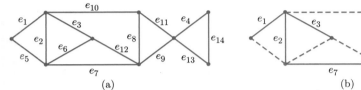
(a)

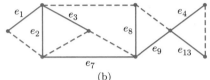
(b)

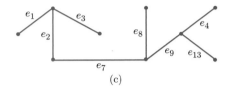
(c)

Figure 7.

▶ Example 4   A technician for a cosmetics company must plan a telephone network linking distributors in cities A, B, C, D, E, and F. Tariffs are variable, and she would like to plan a network for the lowest possible total cost. Using the map of Fig. 8(a) with the intercity tariffs (in \$1000s) shown on each edge, determine the minimal cost network.

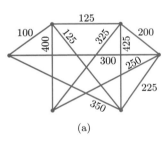
(a)

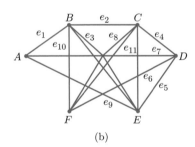
(b)

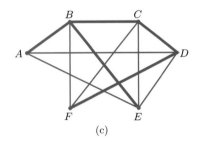
(c)

Figure 8.

Solution   We have marked the edges in order of increasing weight by assigning e_1 to the edge of lowest weight, e_2 to the next-weightier edge, and so on. Figure 8(b) is one such representation. Include e_1, e_2, e_3, and e_4, but since e_5 would complete a cycle, we omit e_5. Of the other vertices, we include only e_6. The minimal spanning tree is drawn in Fig. 8(c). Its cost is \$800,000. ◆

There is another whole class of problems called *coloring problems*; these involve applications as diverse as coloring maps, describing relationships in social groups, and planning parties. One famous problem, which was first proposed in 1852, is the *four-color problem*. To describe this problem, picture a section of an atlas map of the southeastern United States as in Fig. 9. We assign a color to each state in such a way that any two adjacent states have different colors. What is the least number of colors required to color all the states in the map?

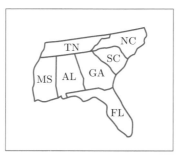

Figure 9.

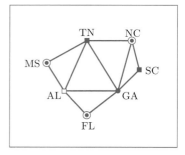

Figure 10.

For a long time mathematicians believed that any map, no matter how complex, would require no more than four colors. This was finally proved in 1976 by Kenneth Appel and Wolfgang Haken of the University of Illinois using an enormous amount of computer time for the many thousands of cases they investigated. Interest in the problem persists as mathematicians seek a more elegant proof (independent of computers). We can see that the four-color problem is a graph theory problem by representing the map with a planar graph in which each state is represented by a vertex. An edge is drawn between two vertices if and only if their corresponding states are adjacent on the map. A representation of the map in Fig. 9 with a coloring appears in Fig. 10. Different symbols represent different colors. The coloring problem is then to find the least number of colors with which we can color the vertices so that no two vertices joined by an edge are the same color.

▶ Example 5   In each of the graphs of Fig. 11, determine whether you can color the vertices using exactly two colors in such a way that no pair of vertices joined by an edge are the same color. How many colors are necessary if two do not suffice?

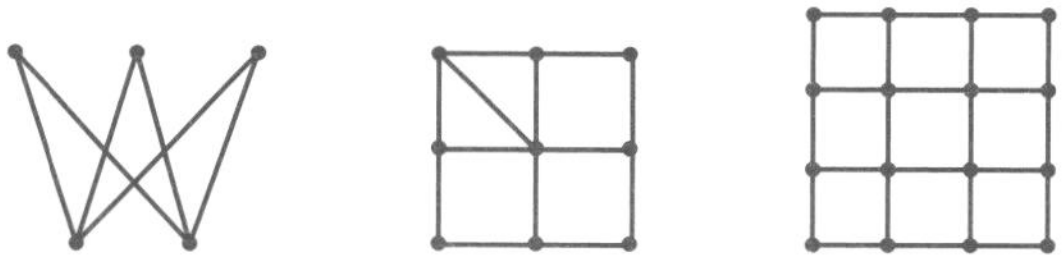

(a)   (b)   (c)

Figure 11.

Solution   Two colors are sufficient to color the graphs in (a) and in (c). The graph in (b) requires three colors.   ◆

We add that from the graph in Fig. 11(b) we might conclude (try it) that any graph with a circuit consisting of an odd number of vertices cannot be colored with only two colors. Rectangular grids, such as in Fig. 11(c), can always be colored with two colors. (To see why, think of a checkerboard.) Each vertex in the first row of the grid can be marked alternately with white and black, for example, starting with white. Then begin the next row with black, alternating white and black on the vertices of the second row. Since all the rows have the same number of vertices, adjacent vertices in the columns will have opposite colors. This can be repeated for any number of rows.

A graph G is called *bipartite* if and only if the vertices can be colored with two colors in such a way that no pair of vertices joined by an edge has the same color.

An interesting fact is the following: In a bipartite graph with a Hamiltonian circuit, the number of vertices of one color must be the same as the number of vertices of the other color. To see why, list the vertices in the Hamiltonian circuit. Except for the first and the last they must all be different. Furthermore, the color associated with any vertex differs from the color of its successor and the color of its predecessor in the circuit (since vertices connected by an edge have opposite colors). Thus vertices alternate between the two colors, with no repeated vertices except the first and the last. There must be equal numbers of each color.

▶ **Example 6**   The chairperson of a department of eight faculty members wants to invite all eight to dinner, but there are ideological rifts in the department and some people do not speak to other people in the department. In the graph in Fig. 12(a), we have represented each of the department members by a vertex and have drawn an edge between two vertices if the people they represent cannot attend together. How many parties must the department chairperson give so as to ensure that any two people who will not attend together are invited to different dinners? Who should be invited to each party?

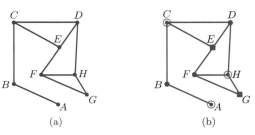

(a)   (b)

Figure 12.

Solution   We note that if two vertices represent people who cannot attend together, they are joined by an edge. Let's color those vertices different colors to indicate that they cannot attend the same party. Thus we can find out how many parties we need by finding the fewest number of colors needed to color the graph. From Fig. 12(b), we see that three colors will color the graph. Vertices of the same color represent people who can be invited together. Possible guest lists are

$$\{A, C, H\}, \quad \{E, G\}, \quad \text{and} \quad \{B, D, F\}. \qquad \blacklozenge$$

▶ **Example 7**   Suppose you are planning a meeting schedule for a day-long meeting. Several workshops are being planned for each time slot, and you want to schedule them so that you can maximize the satisfaction of the attendees. In the preregistration materials, those planning to attend indicate at most five workshops in which they would like to participate. What is the minimum number of time slots needed for the schedule if every person is to get his or her choice?

Solution   Here is a plan for the solution. Let each workshop be denoted by a vertex. Join two vertices with an edge if and only if at least one person wishes to take both workshops. The minimum number of time slots that can be used is the least number of colors needed to color the resulting graph. Since this could result in a large graph, we will leave the solution in this theoretical form.   ◆

▶ Example 8　What is the minimal number of colors needed to color the diagram in Fig. 13(a) so that adjacent regions are different colors?

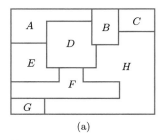
(a)

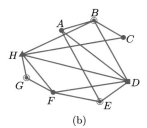
(b)

Figure 13.

Solution　Draw a graph with a vertex for each area and an edge joining the vertices of adjacent areas [Fig. 13(b)]. Color the graph so that no two vertices joined by an edge are the same color. Four colors are needed as indicated by the symbols at the vertices.　　　◆

The *chromatic number* of a graph is the minimum number of colors needed to color the graph so that no two vertices joined by an edge are the same color. Clearly, a bipartite graph has chromatic number 2. The graph in Example 8 has chromatic number 4. What is the chromatic number of a cycle? If the cycle contains no loops and no parallel edges, the chromatic number is 2 or 3. This can be seen in Fig. 14. If the cycle has an even number of vertices, two colors will suffice. Otherwise, three are required.

Figure 14.

▶ Example 9　The floor plan of the first level of a house is shown in Fig. 15.

(a) Is it possible to enter the house at the front, exit from the rear, and travel through the house going through each doorway exactly once?

(b) Can one enter the house at the front and exit from the rear, going through each room exactly once?

(c) If adjacent rooms are to be painted different colors, how many colors are necessary to paint the rooms of the house?

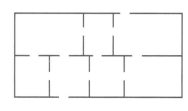

Figure 15.

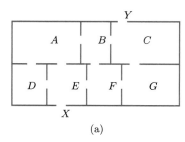
(a)

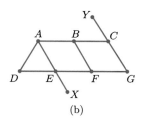
(b)

Figure 16.

Solution   Figure 16(a) and (b) show the plan and the graph representation of it. We represent the rooms with vertices and the doorways with edges.

(a) Is there an Euler path from X to Y? There are 6 vertices of odd degree, so no such path exists.

(b) Can we find a Hamiltonian path from X to Y? We construct such a path:

$$XEDABFGCY.$$

(c) How many colors do we need to color the graph? Three colors are needed to color the graph; we need three colors of paint.   ◆

Practice Problems 13.3

1. Find a Hamiltonian circuit for the graph in Fig. 17.

2. Find a minimal spanning tree for the graph in Fig. 18. The amount on each edge represents the cost of transportation of goods along the edge. What is the minimal cost?

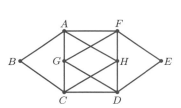

Figure 17.

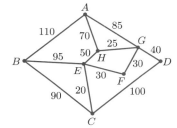

Figure 18.

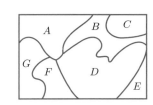

Figure 19.

3. Find the smallest number of colors needed to color the map in Fig. 19 so that no two adjacent regions are the same color.

▶ Exercises 13.3

1. Find a Hamiltonian circuit in the graphs of Fig. 20.

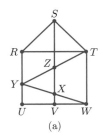

(a)

(b)

Figure 20.

2. Find a Hamiltonian circuit in the graphs of Fig. 21.

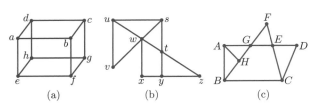

(a)   (b)   (c)

Figure 21.

3. For each graph in Fig. 22, tell whether an Euler circuit or a Hamiltonian circuit exists.

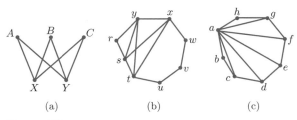

(a)   (b)   (c)

Figure 22.

4. Let G be a simple graph on 5 vertices all of degree at least 3. Must G have a Hamiltonian circuit? Explain.

5. Let G be a simple graph on 6 vertices, one of which has degree 2. Must G have a Hamiltonian circuit? Explain.

6. Let G be a simple graph with 6 vertices and 13 edges. Must G have a Hamiltonian circuit? Explain.

7. Let G be a simple graph on 8 vertices. Find the smallest number of edges that guarantee that G has a Hamiltonian circuit.

8. Draw a simple graph on 6 vertices with 10 edges in which there is a Hamiltonian circuit.

9. Find a minimal spanning tree for the graph in Fig. 23.

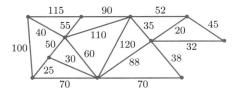

Figure 23.

10. A communication line that must reach each of the locations represented by vertices is to be laid so as to require a minimal cost. How should this be done? The cost of each connection is marked on the graph in Fig. 24.

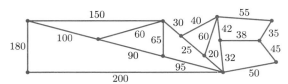

Figure 24.

11. For each graph in Fig. 25, tell if the graph is bipartite. If not, what is the minimal number of colors necessary to color the graph?

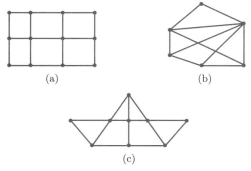

Figure 25.

12. The table in Fig. 26 uses the symbol ▮ to indicate those people who do not like each other. Draw a graph with vertices representing people and draw an edge between two vertices if and only if the people represented do not like each other.
    (a) How many colors are needed to color the graph?
    (b) All vertices colored the same color represent those people who can be invited to the same party. How many parties are needed to entertain all the people and to be assured that any two people who do not like each other will not be invited to the same party?

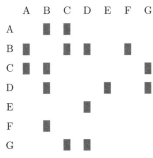

Figure 26.

13. Show that the graphs in Fig. 27 have no Hamiltonian circuits.

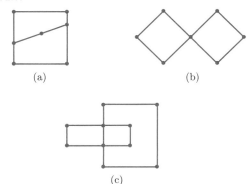

Figure 27.

14. (a) Show that each of the graphs in Fig. 28 is bipartite.
    (b) Show that each does not have a Hamiltonian circuit.

Figure 28.

15. There are 12 senior students who need to complete their major in accounting this semester. The courses, $a, b, \ldots, g$, each needs are tabulated as follows. How many time periods are needed so that they all can fulfill their requirements?

Allan:	a, c, g	Greg:	f, g
Brad:	a, b, d	Helen:	d, f
Carol:	b, e	Ira:	a, d, g
David:	a, c	Jane:	a, g
Evan:	a, b	Karen:	b, c
Ferne:	c, e	Larry:	e, f

1. A Hamiltonian circuit is $ABCHFEDGA$.
2. The minimal cost is \$305 and the minimal spanning tree appears in Fig. 29.

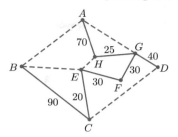

Figure 29.

3. The number of colors necessary to color the map is three.

13.4 Directed Graphs

Let us consider the problem of landing and refueling an aircraft. The aircraft lands, passengers deplane, luggage and other cargo are unloaded, the plane is replenished with food, and it is cleaned and serviced. The new cargo is loaded, passengers board, and the plane takes off again. How much time must be allocated to this process? There are several stages in the operation, some of which are dependent on others. For example, incoming cargo must be unloaded before new cargo is loaded. Some jobs can be done simultaneously: Passengers can deplane while cargo is unloaded. Table 1 shows which tasks must precede others and the time required for each task.

Table 1

Task		Immediate predecessor(s)	Time required for task (min)
S	(start)	None	0
A_1	(prepare to unload cargo and deplane passengers)	S	10
A_2	(deplane passengers)	A_1	20
A_3	(unload cargo)	A_1	30
A_4	(cleaning and food)	A_2	20
A_5	(maintenance and fuel)	A_1	30
A_6	(load cargo)	A_3	15
A_7	(board passengers)	A_4	20
E	(end)	$A_5\ A_6\ A_7$	0

This process can be represented by a graph. We indicate the required order by directing the edges to obtain a *directed graph* or *digraph*. A directed graph D is a set of vertices and a set of edges for which each edge has an initial vertex and a terminal vertex. The digraph in Fig. 1 represents the aircraft problem. There is a directed edge from vertex A_i to vertex A_j if and only if activity A_i is an immediate predecessor of activity A_j. The times required for the activities

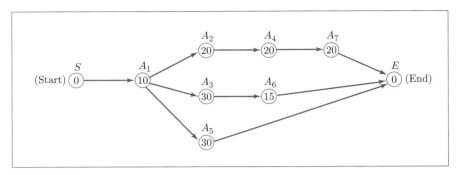

Figure 1.

appear in the large circles at the vertices. For convenience, we have a start (S) and an end (E) that require no time.

The time we need to allocate between arrival and departure is the length of the longest (time) path on Fig. 1 from start to end. There are three paths from start to end:

$$SA_1A_2A_4A_7E: \qquad \text{time} = 10 + 20 + 20 + 20 = 70 \text{ minutes}$$
$$SA_1A_3A_6E: \qquad \text{time} = 10 + 30 + 15 = 55 \text{ minutes}$$
$$SA_1A_5E: \qquad \text{time} = 10 + 30 = 40 \text{ minutes.}$$

The longest (time) path is 70 minutes, so we should allow 1 hour and 10 minutes between arrival and departure of the aircraft. The path $SA_1A_2A_4A_7E$ is called the *critical path*, and the directed graph used to represent the process is called the *activity digraph*. We should take note of the fact that, to reduce the amount of time necessary between arrival and departure of the aircraft, we first need to focus on reducing the time necessary for those activities on the critical path. For example, we can try to reduce the amount of time needed for A_4, cleaning the craft and loading the food. That would reduce the time length of the critical path. Reducing the time needed for maintenance and refueling of the aircraft (A_5) has no effect on the required time between arrival and departure, because the activity A_5 is not on the critical path. Note, however, that if we were able to reduce the time needed for A_2 to 10 minutes and the time allocated to A_7 to 12 minutes, the path $SA_1A_2A_4A_7E$ would be $10 + 10 + 20 + 12 = 52$ minutes. But that does not mean that we can turn the aircraft around in 52 minutes. We would need 55 minutes because the critical path would then become $SA_1A_3A_6E$. The digraph allows us not only to see where time savings can reduce the total time for a complicated process of interrelated activities, but also helps us to schedule those activities to minimize the necessary time.

From the activity digraph for the aircraft, we can see that the times, in minutes, to begin each task are given by

A_1	A_2	A_3	A_4	A_5	A_6	A_7	E
0	10	10	30	10	40	50	70.

▶ Example 1   Use Table 2 to draw an activity digraph. Determine the critical path and give the beginning times for each activity to ensure the minimum time from start to end.

Solution   The activity digraph appears in Fig. 2(a). From the digraph we see that activities S, A_1, A_2, A_3, and E are common to all paths from S to E. The total amount of

Table 2

Activity	Immediate predecessor(s)	Time required for task (days)
S	None	0
A_1	S	3
A_2	A_1	4
A_3	A_2	15
A_4	A_3	5
A_5	A_3	4
A_6	A_3	11
A_7	A_4, A_5	7
A_8	A_6	4
A_9	A_6, A_7	2
E	A_8, A_9	0

time for these activities is 22 days. The total times required on the paths from S to E are

$$SA_1A_2A_3A_4A_7A_9E: \qquad 22 + 5 + 7 + 2 = 36 \text{ days}$$
$$SA_1A_2A_3A_5A_7A_9E: \qquad 22 + 4 + 7 + 2 = 35 \text{ days}$$
$$SA_1A_2A_3A_6A_9E: \qquad 22 + 11 + 2 = 35 \text{ days}$$
$$SA_1A_2A_3A_6A_8E: \qquad 22 + 11 + 4 = 37 \text{ days}.$$

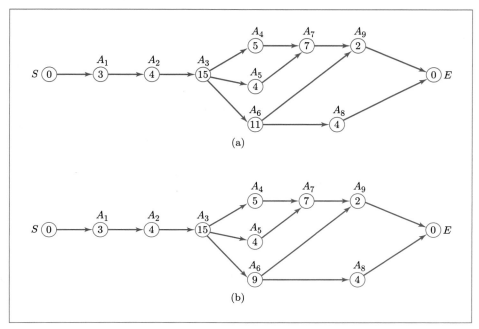

Figure 2.

The last of these paths is the critical path. The entire project will take a minimum of 37 days. We can schedule the work by following the digraph. We find the starting time of each activity by determining the length (in time) of the longest path from the start (S) to the activity in question.

Activity	A_1	A_2	A_3	A_4	A_5	A_6	A_7	A_8	A_9	E
Starting time (days)	0	3	7	22	22	22	27	33	34	37

We note that to find the time to begin A_7 we consider the two paths from start to a vertex preceding A_7. One is $SA_1A_2A_3A_4$, which requires 27 days. The other path is $SA_1A_2A_3A_5$, which requires 26 days. We use the longer of the two paths. ◆

In fact, since it is frequently difficult to count all paths from start to finish, we can use this technique to calculate both the critical path and the starting time of each activity.

▶ **Example 2**   Suppose that in the project discussed previously we are able to reduce the time required to do A_6 to 9 days. Determine the critical path then and find a schedule for the activities.

Solution   The schedule is determined from Fig. 2(b).

Activity	A_1	A_2	A_3	A_4	A_5	A_6	A_7	A_8	A_9	E
Starting time (days)	0	3	7	22	22	22	27	31	34	36

The critical path is now $SA_1A_2A_3A_4A_7A_9E$, which has length 36 days.   ◆

In actuality, the schedule of very large and complicated projects, like the building of office buildings and shopping centers, requires far more complicated activity digraphs. To find the critical path may not be as simple as in our small example. An interesting feature of critical path analysis is that it can be set up in such a way that we can use the methods of linear programming to find the longest path.

Sophisticated activity digraphs are used internally in large computer systems. For a given number of processing units in the computer, and a list of priorities for the activities we expect the computer to accomplish, digraphs help the computer plan its own processing schedule. This technique is used in what is known as the *list-processing algorithm* and is used on computers with several processors.

Another example for which a digraph is useful is given by a street pattern in which the direction of traffic is indicated. We can plan for one- and two-way streets by marking each edge (street) with appropriate arrows. We might consider the city pictured in Fig. 3(a) and ask whether a one-way street pattern exists that will allow us to get from A to B and back again. We would need to assign directions to the digraph so as to get a circuit without using any two-way streets. Can you find a solution? We have indicated one in Fig. 3(b).

A solution is not always possible. Look at the street pattern in Fig. 3(c). Try to find a one-way street pattern on which you can construct a circuit starting at A, passing through B, and returning to A.

We will use the letter D to designate a digraph. A *path* in a digraph is a sequence of edges linking two vertices. A *closed path* is a path in which the first and the last vertices are the same. A closed path in which no edge is repeated

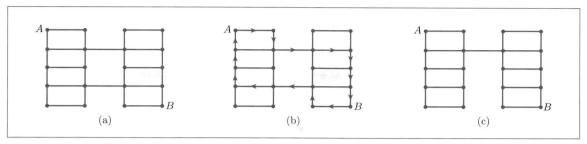

Figure 3.

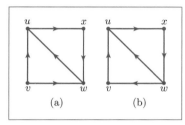

Figure 4.

is called a *circuit* (or a *cycle*). A digraph with no circuits is called *acyclic*. The digraph in Fig. 4(a) has a circuit ($wuxw$) and hence is not acyclic.

A digraph is said to be *connected* if the graph we get by omitting the directions on the edges is connected. We say that a digraph is *strongly connected* if, given any two vertices u and v, there is a path *from u to v*. We observe that the digraph in Fig. 4(a) is connected, but it is not strongly connected. There is no path from vertex u to vertex v, for example. By changing the direction on the edge joining v and w, we have the strongly connected digraph shown in Fig. 4(b).

The *outdegree* of a vertex v (od v) is the number of edges in the digraph D having v as an initial point. The *indegree* of a vertex v (id v) is the number of edges in D having v as a terminal point. Then

$$\deg(v) = \text{od } v + \text{id } v.$$

We observe in Fig. 4(a) that the indegree of vertex u is 2 and the outdegree of u is 1. Clearly, its degree is 3. The vertex v has indegree 0, which naturally means that there is no way to reach v from any other vertex in the graph.

Property 1 If D is a digraph with p vertices $v_1, v_2, \ldots, v_p$, then

$$\text{od } v_1 + \text{od } v_2 + \cdots + \text{od } v_p = \text{id } v_1 + \text{id } v_2 + \cdots + \text{id } v_p$$
$$= \text{number of edges in } D.$$

▶ **Example 3**

A small subdivision of homes is being planned with a street pattern of one-way streets represented by the digraph D in Fig. 5.

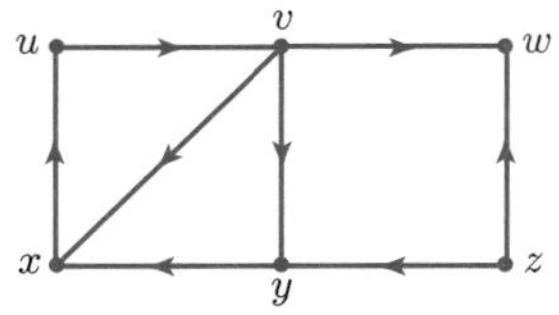

(a) Is D acyclic? If not, give at least one circuit. That is, can we drive along at least one route beginning and ending at the same vertex?

(b) Is D connected? Is D strongly connected; that is, can we begin at any vertex and drive to any other vertex?

(c) Find the id and od of each vertex of D and verify that Property 1 holds.

Solution

(a) The graph is not acyclic since $uvxu$ is a circuit.

(b) The digraph is connected, but it is not strongly connected since there is no path from vertex w to any other vertex.

(c) We note that the number of edges in the digraph is 8. The id and od of each vertex are tabulated below. In each case the sum is 8.

Vertex	u	v	w	x	y	z	*Sum*
id	1	1	2	2	2	0	8
od	1	3	0	1	1	2	8

◆

Figure 5.

We might want to determine if an Euler circuit exists in a digraph. That is, given a connected digraph D, is it possible to find a path starting at any vertex, passing along each edge exactly once, and returning to our starting point? We recall that if an undirected connected graph G has an Euler circuit, then every vertex has even degree. On the other hand, given a connected graph G, we only need to verify that each vertex has even degree to guarantee the existence of an Euler circuit in G. A similar argument can be used to prove the comparable theorem for digraphs.

Property 2   Let D be a connected digraph. Then D has an Euler circuit if and only if, for every vertex of D, od $v =$ id v.

Let us try to see why Property 2 holds. We assume that D is a digraph with an Euler circuit C. Choose an arbitrary vertex v of D. If v is not the initial or terminal vertex of the circuit C, then every time v occurs in the circuit, it is entered and exited by different edges. We can imagine that as we traverse an edge we erase it from the graph (so it cannot be used again). Each time we encounter v, we can imagine erasing the edge entering v and the edge exiting v, thus reducing both id v and od v by 1. Since all edges are eventually used, we eventually have id $v = 0$ and od $v = 0$. Thus we must have had id $v =$ od v in D. If v is the initial vertex of the circuit C, then at the start of C we reduce od v by 1 and at the end of the circuit also reduce id v by 1.

Further inspection of Fig. 5 will reveal that there is no Euler circuit in the digraph. As we scan the vertices, we see that, except at vertex u, the indegree is unequal to the outdegree.

The proof of the converse requires that we assume D is connected and, for each v, od $v =$ id v. Then we need to show that an Euler circuit exists. We do not present the proof here.

The following statement is helpful in constructing an Euler path in D, that is, finding a path from a vertex u to a vertex v that traverses every edge of the digraph exactly once.

Property 3   Let D be a connected digraph. Then D has an Euler path if and only if D contains vertices u and v such that

1. od $u =$ id $u + 1$

2. id $v =$ od $v + 1$, and

3. id $w =$ od w for every other vertex in D.

When an Euler path exists, the path begins at u and ends at v.

▶ Example 4   For the digraphs D_1 and D_2 given in Fig. 6, determine if an Euler circuit exists. Does an Euler path exist? If they do exist, find them.

Solution   We mark the id and od of each vertex. By Property 3, there are no Euler circuits and no Euler paths for the digraph for (a). There is no Euler circuit for the digraph in (b), but an Euler path indicated with numbers on the edges (in the order of traversal) can be traced from u to v because od $u =$ id $u + 1$ and id $v =$ od $v + 1$, while the outdegree and indegree of every other vertex are equal [see Fig. 7(b)].   ◆

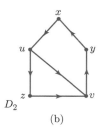

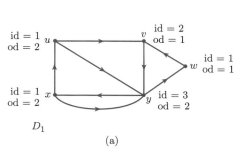

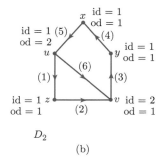

Figure 6.

Figure 7.

The theory of *Hamiltonian circuits* or *paths* for digraphs is similar to and as complex as that for graphs. The problem is to find a circuit beginning and ending at the same vertex and visiting every other vertex of the digraph exactly once. A *Hamiltonian path* is a nonclosed path that visits each vertex of the digraph exactly once. We will not mention any theorems here, but we do present an example for a trial-and-error solution. There is one application that arises naturally and for which we always have a Hamiltonian path—tournaments.

A *tournament* is a digraph in which, given any two vertices v_i and v_j, there is either a directed edge from v_i to v_j or a directed edge from v_j to v_i, but not both. If a digraph represents a tournament, then the digraph has a Hamiltonian path. This property can be used to rank teams or to rank options in a preference list. Although we shall not treat these examples here, situations in which there are a large number of choices can be effectively handled by having a computer apply the appropriate graph-theoretic procedure to obtain a ranking. The ranking is unique in the case where the digraph has no cycles.

| **Practice Problems 13.4** | **1.** Determine the id and od of each vertex in the digraph in Fig. 8. Does an Euler circuit or an Euler path exist in this digraph? Explain. |

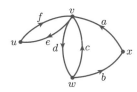

Figure 8.

**Practice Problems
13.4 (Continued)**

2. Draw the digraph and find the critical path for the writing of a grant proposal (Table 3). How much time do we need? If the time required to do A_2 can be reduced to 16 days, what other task must be accomplished faster to ensure that we can get the grant proposal ready in 30 days?

Table 3

	Task	Immediate predecessor(s)	Time for task (days)
S	start	None	0
A_1	initial meeting	S	7
A_2	write narrative	A_1	21
A_3	solicit matching funds	A_1	14
A_4	invite consultants	A_1	12
A_5	get support letters	A_3, A_4	7
A_6	proofread narrative	A_2	3
A_7	write budget	A_3	5
A_8	write time table	A_2, A_5, A_7	3
A_9	type narrative	A_6	2
A_{10}	collate and submit	A_8, A_9	1
E	end	A_{10}	0

3. **(a)** Determine whether the digraphs in Fig. 9 are (i) acyclic, (ii) connected, and/or (iii) strongly connected.

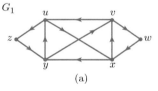
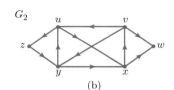
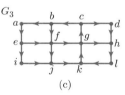

Figure 9.

(b) Determine whether the digraphs have (i) an Euler circuit, (ii) an Euler path, (iii) a Hamiltonian circuit, and/or (iv) a Hamiltonian path. Explain.

▶ Exercises 13.4

1. Determine whether each of the digraphs in Fig. 10 is connected, strongly connected, neither, or both.

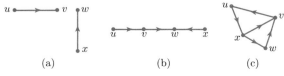

Figure 10.

2. Determine whether each of the digraphs in Fig. 11 is connected, strongly connected, neither, or both.

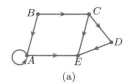
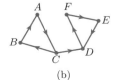

Figure 11.

3. In a computer program one procedure frequently calls another, which in turn calls other procedures. The digraph in Fig. 12 shows the relationship of six modules of a large program. An edge is directed from a procedure to one that calls it. Thus (D, E) is a directed edge because procedure D is called by E.

Figure 12.

(a) Find the indegree and the outdegree of each vertex.

(b) What do these numbers mean in terms of the computer program?

4. Which of the digraphs in Fig. 13 are acyclic? If the graph has a cycle, tell what it is.

(a)   (b)

Figure 13.

5. Which of the digraphs in Fig. 14 is acyclic? If the graph is not acyclic, demonstrate some cycle.

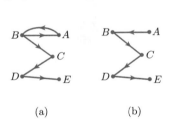
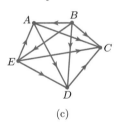

(a)   (b)   (c)

Figure 14.

6. Which of the digraphs in Fig. 15 have Euler circuits? If one exists, give it. If none exists, why not? Is there an Euler path? Explain.

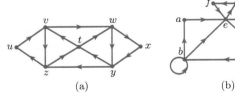

(a)   (b)

Figure 15.

7. For the graphs in Fig. 16, tell if an Euler circuit exists. If one exists, tell what it is. If none exists, explain why. Is there an Euler path? Explain.

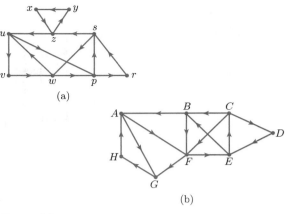

(a)

(b)

Figure 16.

8. Decide if the digraphs in Fig. 17 are connected, strongly connected, acyclic, have an Euler circuit, and/or have an Euler path. Explain your answers.

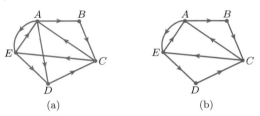

(a)   (b)

Figure 17.

9. Find an Euler circuit in the digraph of Fig. 18 if such a circuit exists.

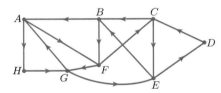

Figure 18.

10. Which of the digraphs of Fig. 19 are connected, strongly connected, acyclic, have Euler paths, and/or have Euler circuits?

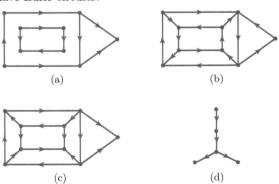

(a)   (b)

(c)   (d)

Figure 19.

11. The process of packing to go away to college is sometimes a lengthy one. From Table 4, determine the shortest possible time in which this person can be ready to leave. What is the critical path?

Table 4

	Task	Immed. predec.(s)	Time to do task (days)
S	start	None	0
A_1	talk to roommate	S	2
A_2	make list	A_1	2
A_3	shop for clothes	A_2	8
A_4	shop for toiletries	A_2	2
A_5	buy trunk	A_3	1
A_6	wash clothes	A_3	3
A_7	mend and iron	A_6	4
A_8	pack trunk	A_4, A_5, A_7	3
A_9	send trunk	A_8	1
A_{10}	pack other things	A_8	2
A_{11}	load car	A_{10}	1
E	end	A_9, A_{11}	0

12. Given the digraph in Fig. 20 representing a scheduling problem, find the critical path. Numbers in circles represent the time (in minutes) necessary for the task. If the task A_3 can be done in 5 minutes, can we reduce the total time needed? If so, what is the new time? If A_8 can be done in 10 minutes, can we reduce the total time needed? If so, what is the new total time needed?

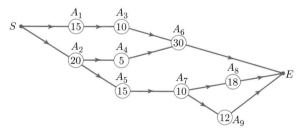

Figure 20.

13. Draw a digraph representing the precedence table (Table 5) and determine the critical path.

14. (a) Find the critical path for the digraph in Fig. 21.

    (b) How long does the entire job take?

    (c) If A_5 could be reduced to 10 minutes, is the critical path the same?

    (d) If the answer to (c) is no, give the new critical path and its time to completion.

Table 5

Job	Immediate predecessor(s)	Completion time (days)
Start		0
A	Start	15
B	Start	12
C	A	22
D	A, C	10
E	B, D	13
F	C, E	5
End	F	0

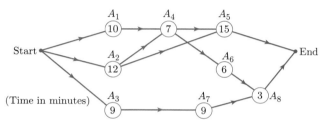

(Time in minutes)

Figure 21.

15. Draw the digraph with six vertices labeled 1, 2, 3, 4, 5, 6, where there is a directed edge from vertex u to vertex v if and only if u divides v (with remainder 0).

16. Draw the digraph with seven vertices labeled 2, 3, 4, 5, 6, 7, 8, where there is a directed edge from vertex u to vertex v if and only if u divides v but $u \neq v$.

17. Draw the digraph with nine vertices labeled 0, 1, 2, 3, 4, 5, 6, 7, 8, where there is a directed edge from vertex u to vertex v if and only if $v - u$ is a multiple of 3 and $u < v$.

18. Draw the digraph with five vertices labeled 0, 1, 2, 3, 4, where there is a directed edge from vertex u to vertex v if and only if $0 < u - v < 3$.

19. A *transition table* is a table that describes the states of a machine where certain inputs cause a change of state. Table 6 is such a table. Erroneous inputs have been left blank. Usually, when such tables control the operating system of a computer, an error message is generated when an incorrect input is used. We can draw a digraph to represent such a transition table by letting the vertices represent machine states and edges represent the inputs. An edge (labeled a) is directed from vertex A to vertex C since input of a into the machine in state A causes the transition of the machine to state C.

(a) Draw the digraph representing the transition table.

(b) If the process begins in state C and the inputs are b, b, a, what is the final state?

(c) If the process begins in state B and the inputs are b, b, a, what is the final state?

Table 6

	Inputs		
State	a	b	c
A	C		
B	A	C	
C	C	A	
D	D	E	C
E			C

Solutions to Practice Problems 13.4

1.

Vertex	u	v	w	x
id	1	3	1	1
od	1	2	2	1

The connected digraph does not satisfy the requirements of Property 2. Hence, no Euler circuit exists. Since

$$\text{od } w = \text{id } w + 1$$
$$\text{id } v = \text{od } v + 1$$
$$\text{id } u = \text{od } u$$
$$\text{id } x = \text{od } x,$$

Property 3 states that an Euler path exists. It begins at w and ends at v.

2. The digraph is given in Fig. 22. The paths from S to E and the necessary times to complete them are as follows:

$SA_1A_2A_6A_9A_{10}E$:	time $= 7 + 21 + 3 + 2 + 1 = 34$ days
$SA_1A_2A_8A_{10}E$:	time $= 7 + 21 + 3 + 1 = 32$ days
$SA_1A_3A_7A_8A_{10}E$:	time $= 7 + 14 + 5 + 3 + 1 = 30$ days
$SA_1A_3A_5A_8A_{10}E$:	time $= 7 + 14 + 7 + 3 + 1 = 32$ days
$SA_1A_4A_5A_8A_{10}E$:	time $= 7 + 12 + 7 + 3 + 1 = 30$ days.

Clearly, the critical path is the one taking 34 days. If A_2 can be reduced to 16 days' duration, then the original critical path has duration 29 days. We would need to reduce the time needed for A_1, A_3, A_5, or A_8 by 2 days to accomplish the entire process within 30 days.

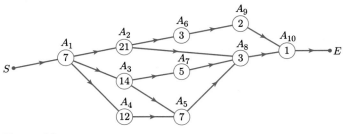

Figure 22.

3. (a) All the graphs have cycles. In both G_1 and G_2, $yuzy$ is a cycle. In G_3, $aeijkgcba$ is a cycle. All graphs are connected. But G_2 is not strongly connected. There is no path from w to y in G_2, for example.

   (b) In G_1, the indegree and the outdegree of each vertex are equal. Property 2 states there is an Euler circuit. Property 3 states there is no Euler path. There is no Hamiltonian circuit, because the cycles in G_1 force us to repeat vertices in any circuit we choose. However, $uzyvwx$ is a Hamiltonian path in G_1.

   The graph G_2 has no Euler circuit or path. Properties 2 and 3 can be used to show this, since id $v = 1$ and od $v = 3$, and id $w = 2$ and od $w = 0$. There is a Hamiltonian path in G_2: $uzyxvw$. There is no Hamiltonian circuit, because we can never leave vertex w.

   In G_3, there are neither Euler circuits nor Euler paths. A calculation of the id and od of each vertex shows that, for example, id $b \neq$ od b. Furthermore, many vertices have odd degree with b, c, e, h, j, and k having id and od differing by 1. There are no Hamiltonian paths and no Hamiltonian circuits in G_3.

13.5   Matrices and Graphs

It would be helpful to have a bookkeeping device for storing the information provided by a graph. We can use a square matrix for this purpose. We list the vertices, in the same order, along the top and side margins of the matrix. The *adjacency matrix $A(G)$ of a graph G* is the matrix obtained by letting the entry in the ith row, jth column be the number of edges joining the ith vertex with the jth vertex. A 0 denotes that the vertices are not joined by an edge. An adjacency matrix is not unique but depends on the order of the vertices in the row and column headings.

▶ Example 1   Write out the adjacency matrix $A(G)$ of the graph G in Fig. 1.

Solution   We note in the matrix below that the loop at u is recorded with a 1 in the first row, first column. No other vertex has a loop.

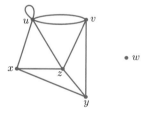

Figure 1.

$$
A(G) = \begin{array}{c} \\ u \\ v \\ w \\ x \\ y \\ z \end{array}
\begin{array}{c} \begin{array}{cccccc} u & v & w & x & y & z \end{array} \\
\left[\begin{array}{cccccc}
1 & 2 & 0 & 1 & 0 & 1 \\
2 & 0 & 0 & 0 & 1 & 1 \\
0 & 0 & 0 & 0 & 0 & 0 \\
1 & 0 & 0 & 0 & 1 & 1 \\
0 & 1 & 0 & 1 & 0 & 1 \\
1 & 1 & 0 & 1 & 1 & 0
\end{array} \right] \end{array}.
$$

We now consider only graphs with no parallel edges; that is, we restrict ourselves to simple graphs in the remainder of this section. The adjacency matrix of a simple graph has some special properties. Each entry a_{ij} must be either 0 or 1, since there is at most one edge from vertex v_i to vertex v_j. Since there is an edge from v_i to v_j if and only if there is an edge from v_j to v_i, the matrix $A(G)$ is *symmetric*; that is, $a_{ij} = a_{ji}$. If there is a loop at v_i, then $a_{ii} = 1$; otherwise, $a_{ii} = 0$.

If G is a simple graph, then $A(G)$ is a symmetric matrix of 0's and 1's.

What can we do with these matrices? First, we can store a graph in a computer in a form that can be handled mathematically. That is, instead of storing a picture of the graph, we can store all the relevant information from which the graph can be drawn.

▶ Example 2 Draw the graph whose adjacency matrix is A.

$$
A = \begin{array}{c} \\ u \\ v \\ w \\ x \\ y \end{array}
\begin{array}{c} \begin{array}{ccccc} u & v & w & x & y \end{array} \\
\left[\begin{array}{ccccc}
0 & 1 & 1 & 0 & 1 \\
1 & 0 & 1 & 1 & 1 \\
1 & 1 & 0 & 1 & 0 \\
0 & 1 & 1 & 0 & 1 \\
1 & 1 & 0 & 1 & 0
\end{array} \right] \end{array}.
$$

Solution The solution appears in Fig. 2. ◆

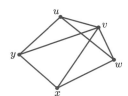

Figure 2.

We can read the degree of each vertex of a graph from an adjacency matrix. It is simply the sum of the entries in the row (or the column) corresponding to that vertex if there is no loop there. If there is a loop, we need to add 1 to the row (or column) sum, since a loop adds 2 to the degree of a vertex.

Recall that two graphs are equivalent if the vertices of the graphs can be paired in such a way that whenever two vertices of one graph are connected by an edge, then so are the corresponding vertices of the other graph. To determine if two graphs are equivalent, we can inspect the representations we have drawn and try to establish the identifications described in the definition. An alternative is to try to reorder the headings of the rows and columns in the adjacency matrices of the graphs so that the resulting matrices are identical.

▶ Example 3 Show that G_1 and G_2 (Fig. 3) are equivalent graphs by (a) establishing the identities described in the definition of equivalent graphs and (b) investigating their adjacency matrices $A(G_1)$ and $A(G_2)$.

Solution (a) There are 4 vertices in each of the vertex sets and 5 edges in each edge set. A little trial and error will show that we can identify vertices in the following way:

$$a \leftrightarrow w \qquad b \leftrightarrow u \qquad c \leftrightarrow v \qquad \text{and} \qquad d \leftrightarrow x.$$

To show that the edge identification is correct, check the 5 edges of G_1 and the 5 edges of G_2 (Table 1).

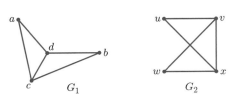

Figure 3.

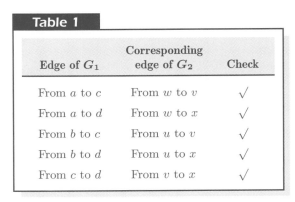

	Table 1		
		Corresponding	
	Edge of G_1	**edge of G_2**	**Check**
	From a to c	From w to v	✓
	From a to d	From w to x	✓
	From b to c	From u to v	✓
	From b to d	From u to x	✓
	From c to d	From v to x	✓

(b) The adjacency matrices of the graphs G_1 and G_2 are

$$
A(G_1) = \begin{array}{c} \\ a \\ b \\ c \\ d \end{array}
\begin{array}{c}
\begin{array}{cccc} a & b & c & d \end{array} \\
\begin{bmatrix} 0 & 0 & 1 & 1 \\ 0 & 0 & 1 & 1 \\ 1 & 1 & 0 & 1 \\ 1 & 1 & 1 & 0 \end{bmatrix}
\end{array}
\qquad
A(G_2) = \begin{array}{c} \\ u \\ v \\ w \\ x \end{array}
\begin{array}{c}
\begin{array}{cccc} u & v & w & x \end{array} \\
\begin{bmatrix} 0 & 1 & 0 & 1 \\ 1 & 0 & 1 & 1 \\ 0 & 1 & 0 & 1 \\ 1 & 1 & 1 & 0 \end{bmatrix}
\end{array}.
$$

If the rows and columns of $A(G_2)$ are ordered $u\,w\,v\,x$, the resulting matrix will be identical to $A(G_1)$. ◆

▶ Example 4 (a) Find the number of paths of length 2 from v_2 to v_4 in the graph G of Fig. 4.
(b) Write down an adjacency matrix $A(G)$ of the graph of Fig. 4.
(c) Find the square of the adjacency matrix $A(G)$.

Solution (a) We can trace the paths of length 2 from v_2 to v_4. There are two such paths: $v_2 v_1 v_4$ and $v_2 v_3 v_4$.

(b) We saw (in Example 3) that an adjacency matrix of this graph is given by

$$
A = \begin{array}{c} \\ v_1 \\ v_2 \\ v_3 \\ v_4 \end{array}
\begin{array}{c}
\begin{array}{cccc} v_1 & v_2 & v_3 & v_4 \end{array} \\
\begin{bmatrix} 0 & 1 & 0 & 1 \\ 1 & 0 & 1 & 1 \\ 0 & 1 & 0 & 1 \\ 1 & 1 & 1 & 0 \end{bmatrix}
\end{array}.
$$

Figure 4.

(c) We calculate the square of the matrix:

$$
A^2 = \begin{array}{c} \\ v_1 \\ v_2 \\ v_3 \\ v_4 \end{array}
\begin{array}{c}
\begin{array}{cccc} v_1 & v_2 & v_3 & v_4 \end{array} \\
\begin{bmatrix} 2 & 1 & 2 & 1 \\ 1 & 3 & 1 & 2 \\ 2 & 1 & 2 & 1 \\ 1 & 2 & 1 & 3 \end{bmatrix}
\end{array}.
$$

What does this matrix represent? The entry in the ith row, jth column of A^2 represents the number of paths of length 2 from v_i to v_j. Let us see why.

The entry in row 2, column 4 of A^2 is 2. Denote the entry by $a_{24}^{(2)}$. How was $a_{24}^{(2)}$ obtained? Recall from the definition of matrix multiplication that

$$a_{24}^{(2)} = a_{21}a_{14} + a_{22}a_{24} + a_{23}a_{34} + a_{24}a_{44}.$$

Thus,

$$a_{24}^{(2)} = 1 \cdot 1 + 0 \cdot 1 + 1 \cdot 1 + 1 \cdot 0 = 2.$$

Each a_{ij} in the sum represents the number of edges between the ith vertex and the jth vertex. The number a_{21} represents the number of edges from v_2 to v_1, and the number a_{14} represents the number of edges going from v_1 to v_4. The multiplication principle of Section 5.4 tells us that the product $a_{21}a_{14}$ is the number of two-edge paths from v_2 to v_4 with a stopover at v_1 (see Fig. 5).

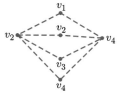

Figure 5.

Similarly, $a_{22}a_{24}$ is the number of two-edge paths from v_2 to v_4 with a stopover at v_2. Since there are no loops at v_2 in this graph ($a_{22} = 0$), there are no such paths. So $a_{22}a_{24}$ is zero. Again, $a_{23}a_{34}$ is the number of two-edge paths from v_2 to v_4 with a stopover at v_3, and $a_{24}a_{44}$ is the number of two-edge paths from v_2 to v_4 with a stopover at v_4 (why is this zero?).

The sum $a_{24}^{(2)}$ is the total number of two-edge paths from v_2 to v_4. We have found all such paths by looking at all possible stopovers. The two-edge paths from v_2 to v_4 were enumerated in (a): $v_2v_1v_4$ and $v_2v_3v_4$. ◆

Assume that a graph has n vertices $v_1, v_2, \ldots, v_n$. The typical entry in the ith row, jth column of the square of the adjacency matrix is

$$a_{ij}^{(2)} = a_{i1}a_{1j} + a_{i2}a_{2j} + \cdots + a_{in}a_{nj}.$$

The sum $a_{ij}^{(2)}$ is 0 if and only if all the terms in the sum are 0, since each a_{ij} can take on only nonnegative values. Hence, if the sum is 0, there is no two-edge path from the ith vertex to the jth vertex. On the other hand, if the sum is not 0, then some term in the sum is not 0. Hence, for at least one of the values of $k = 1, 2, \ldots, n$, both a_{ik} and a_{kj} are not 0. Thus, there is a two-edge path from v_i to v_j with a stopover at v_k, giving at least one two-edge path from v_i to v_j.

If $A = A(G)$ is the adjacency matrix of G, it represents the number of one-edge paths between vertices of G. Its square, A^2, represents the number of two-edge paths between vertices. If the i, j entry in A^2 is 0, there is no such path; otherwise, there is at least one such two-step path. In a similar way, the entries of A^3 can be interpreted as the number of three-step paths, and so on, for $A^4, A^5, \ldots, A^n$.

The i, j entry in A^m indicates the number of paths of length m between the ith vertex and the jth vertex.

Although we can tell by looking at a graph whether it is connected, if the graph information is stored in matrix form rather than as a picture, we need criteria related to the matrix representation of the graph to decide if the graph is connected. The i, j entry in A^m is 0 if and only if no path of length m exists. This leads to the following theorems.

Theorem 1 If G is a graph with adjacency matrix A, and there exists a positive integer m such that A^m has only nonzero entries, then G is connected.

The converse of Theorem 1 is false; that is, although G may be connected, it is possible that there is no positive integer m such that A^m has only nonzero entries. Exercise 6 provides such an example.

Theorem 2 Let A be the adjacency matrix of a simple graph G. Then G is connected if and only if there exists an integer m such that every entry in $A + A^2 + \cdots + A^m$ is nonzero.

▶ Example 5   Find an adjacency matrix of the graph in Fig. 6. Find the number of paths of length 4 from v_4 to v_2. Give two of them. Use the adjacency matrix to show that the graph is connected.

Solution   The matrix $A = A(G)$ is given by

$$A(G) = A = \begin{bmatrix} 0 & 0 & 0 & 1 \\ 0 & 0 & 1 & 1 \\ 0 & 1 & 0 & 1 \\ 1 & 1 & 1 & 0 \end{bmatrix}.$$

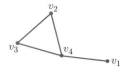

Figure 6.

We find A^2 and then $A^4 = A^2 A^2$.

$$A^4 = \begin{bmatrix} 3 & 4 & 4 & 2 \\ 4 & 7 & 6 & 6 \\ 4 & 6 & 7 & 6 \\ 2 & 6 & 6 & 11 \end{bmatrix}$$

Since all the entries are nonzero, the graph is connected. Of course, when we have the picture in front of us, the connectedness is obvious. The entry in the 4th row, 2nd column is 6. Thus there are 6 paths of length 4 from v_2 to v_4. Here are two of them:

$$v_4 v_1 v_4 v_3 v_2 \qquad \text{and} \qquad v_4 v_2 v_3 v_4 v_2.$$

Alternatively, we could have found $A + A^2$, where

$$A^2 = \begin{bmatrix} 1 & 1 & 1 & 0 \\ 1 & 2 & 1 & 1 \\ 1 & 1 & 2 & 1 \\ 0 & 1 & 1 & 3 \end{bmatrix},$$

and shown that $A + A^2$ has only nonzero entries. This is another way to verify that the graph is connected.   ◆

Although Theorems 1 and 2 seem to indicate that, theoretically, we might have to calculate A^m for large values of m to determine if a graph is connected, this is not quite so. If a graph has 4 vertices, for example, then any path of length at least 3 will either contain a cycle or contain every vertex. If we disregard the paths with cycles, then if there is a path between two distinct vertices there must be one of length less than or equal to 3. Thus we need calculate at most A, A^2, and A^3. If a graph has n vertices, then to check its connectivity using Theorem 2, we need calculate at most $A, A^2, \ldots, A^{n-1}$. It is frequently the case that fewer powers of A will be needed.

We can use another matrix to record whether there exists a path between two distinct vertices in a graph. Inspection of the graph tells us whether such a path exists. The *reachability matrix of a graph G with n vertices* is the $n \times n$ matrix whose entry in the ith row, jth column is 1 if there is a path from v_i to v_j, and 0 if no such path exists. Denote the reachability matrix of the graph G as $R(G)$. Assume v_i is reachable from itself; the entries on the diagonal of $R(G)$ are all 1.

Given a graph such as that in Fig. 6, the reachability matrix is a 4×4 matrix of 1's since every vertex can be reached from any other along some path. We say that each vertex is *clearly reachable from itself* (use a path of length 0). The reachability matrix has a zero entry whenever there is no path between two vertices. In that case, the graph is disconnected.

It is possible to find the reachability matrix of a graph from an adjacency matrix. Let I denote the $n \times n$ identity matrix [it contains 1's on the main diagonal (upper left to lower right) and 0's elsewhere]. The identity matrix represents the 0-edge paths between vertices (there is always one such path from any vertex to itself). We can obtain the reachability matrix $R(G)$ of a graph G with n vertices by first finding the matrix

$$M = I + A + A^2 + \cdots + A^{n-1}$$

and then letting $r_{ij} = 1$, the entry in the ith row, jth column of $R(G)$, if M has a nonzero entry in the ith row, jth column and letting $r_{ij} = 0$ otherwise. The reachability matrix of a graph is a symmetric matrix of 0's and 1's with 1's along the main diagonal. Clearly, in Example 5, $I + A + A^2 + A^3$ has no zero entries, so the reachability matrix is a matrix of 1's.

> **Theorem 3** A simple graph is connected if and only if its reachability matrix is a matrix consisting only of 1's.

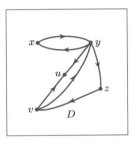

Figure 7.

As we have already discussed, a *directed graph* or a *digraph* is a graph in which every edge is given a direction. We will use the letter D to denote a digraph. If D is a digraph, it has a set of vertices and a set of directed edges, actually denoted as ordered pairs of vertices, describing the direction of the edges. Thus the edge (u, v) is the edge directed from u to v. It is possible to have edges directed between two vertices in opposite directions. For example, Fig. 7 shows a directed graph on 5 vertices. The directed edges are (x, y), (y, x), (y, z), (z, v), (v, u), (v, y), and (y, u). We assume that there is no ambiguity in giving the edge as (z, v). In our digraphs there are no parallel edges; so no other edge goes from z to v.

The *adjacency matrix of a digraph* D, $A(D)$, is formed by letting $a_{ij} = 1$ if there is a directed edge from the ith vertex to the jth vertex of D and $a_{ij} = 0$ if there is not.

▶ **Example 6** Find the adjacency matrix $A(D)$ for the digraph D in Fig. 7.

Solution The adjacency matrix for D is

$$
\begin{array}{c c}
 & \begin{array}{ccccc} u & v & x & y & z \end{array} \\
\begin{array}{c} u \\ v \\ x \\ y \\ z \end{array} &
\left[\begin{array}{ccccc}
0 & 0 & 0 & 0 & 0 \\
1 & 0 & 0 & 1 & 0 \\
0 & 0 & 0 & 1 & 0 \\
1 & 0 & 1 & 0 & 1 \\
0 & 1 & 0 & 0 & 0
\end{array} \right].
\end{array}
$$

Note that the adjacency matrix of a digraph need not be symmetric. The digraph in Fig. 7 contains an edge from v to y but does not contain an edge from y to v. Consequently, the matrix $A(D)$ contains a 1 in the 2nd row, 4th column but contains a 0 in the 4th row, 2nd column. ◆

The sum of entries in the row corresponding to any vertex v is the outdegree of v; the sum of the entries in the column corresponding to any vertex v is the indegree of v. The sum of the entries in the matrix $A(D)$ is the total number of edges in the digraph.

As in the matrix representation of graphs, the matrix representation of digraphs provides a great deal of information about the structure of the digraph. If $A = A(D)$ is the adjacency matrix of a digraph, there is a path of length m from vertex v_i to vertex v_j whenever the entry in the ith row, jth column of

A^m is nonzero. In working with digraphs, it can be extremely helpful to have a matrix representation of the graph, since it may be difficult to follow the paths to ascertain how many routes of length m lead from one vertex to another.

▶ Example 7 Find an adjacency matrix of the digraph representing the streets in one area of a city (Fig. 8). Note that some streets are one-way and others are two-way. Determine if there is a path of length 4 from the corner marked X to the corner marked Y. How many such paths are there?

Solution An adjacency matrix of the digraph is

$$
\begin{array}{c c}
 & \begin{array}{cccccc} a & b & c & d & X & Y \end{array} \\
\begin{array}{c} a \\ b \\ c \\ d \\ X \\ Y \end{array} &
\left[\begin{array}{cccccc}
0 & 1 & 0 & 0 & 1 & 0 \\
0 & 0 & 1 & 0 & 1 & 0 \\
0 & 1 & 0 & 0 & 0 & 1 \\
0 & 0 & 1 & 0 & 0 & 1 \\
1 & 0 & 0 & 0 & 0 & 0 \\
0 & 0 & 0 & 1 & 0 & 0
\end{array} \right].
\end{array}
$$

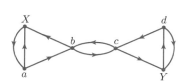

Figure 8.

To determine if there is a path of length 4 from X to Y, find the matrix A^4 and check the entry in the 5th row, last column. To calculate A^4, first find A^2 and then find $A^2 \cdot A^2$.

$$
A^2 =
\begin{array}{c c}
 & \begin{array}{cccccc} a & b & c & d & X & Y \end{array} \\
\begin{array}{c} a \\ b \\ c \\ d \\ X \\ Y \end{array} &
\left[\begin{array}{cccccc}
1 & 0 & 1 & 0 & 1 & 0 \\
1 & 1 & 0 & 0 & 0 & 1 \\
0 & 0 & 1 & 1 & 1 & 0 \\
0 & 1 & 0 & 1 & 0 & 1 \\
0 & 1 & 0 & 0 & 1 & 0 \\
0 & 0 & 1 & 0 & 0 & 1
\end{array} \right]
\end{array}
$$

$$
A^4 =
\begin{array}{c c}
 & \begin{array}{cccccc} a & b & c & d & X & Y \end{array} \\
\begin{array}{c} a \\ b \\ c \\ d \\ X \\ Y \end{array} &
\left[\begin{array}{cccccc}
1 & 1 & 2 & 1 & 3 & 0 \\
2 & 1 & 2 & 0 & 1 & 2 \\
0 & 2 & 1 & 2 & 2 & 1 \\
1 & 2 & 1 & 1 & 0 & 3 \\
1 & 2 & 0 & 0 & 1 & 1 \\
0 & 0 & 2 & 1 & 1 & 1
\end{array} \right].
\end{array}
$$

Since the entry in the 5th row, last column is 1, there is one path of length 4 from X to Y. ◆

The reachability matrix of a digraph is formed by inspecting the digraph. If there is a path from vertex v_i to v_j, a 1 appears in the ith row, jth column. If there is no such path, a 0 appears. Assume that each vertex can be reached from itself (by a path of length 0), so the diagonal entries in the reachability matrix are all 1's.

From an adjacency matrix for the digraph, we can determine if one vertex is reachable from another by calculating the *reachability matrix* $R(D)$ for the digraph D. If D has n vertices and adjacency matrix A, we first calculate the sum of the identity matrix with the first $n-1$ powers of A:

$$I + A + A^2 + \cdots + A^{n-1}.$$

We form $R(D)$ by letting $r_{ij} = 1$ whenever the sum is nonzero in the ith row, jth column. We let $r_{ij} = 0$ otherwise.

▸ Example 8   For the digraph in Fig. 9(a), find an adjacency matrix and the corresponding reachability matrix.

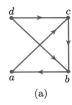

(a)   (b)

Figure 9.

Solution   An adjacency matrix A is given by

$$
\begin{array}{c@{\quad}cccc}
 & a & b & c & d \\
a & \begin{bmatrix} 0 & 0 & 1 & 0 \\ 1 & 0 & 0 & 0 \\ 0 & 1 & 0 & 0 \\ 0 & 1 & 1 & 0 \end{bmatrix}
\end{array}.
$$

The powers of A are

$$
A^2 = \begin{bmatrix} 0 & 1 & 0 & 0 \\ 0 & 0 & 1 & 0 \\ 1 & 0 & 0 & 0 \\ 1 & 1 & 0 & 0 \end{bmatrix}
\qquad
A^3 = \begin{bmatrix} 1 & 0 & 0 & 0 \\ 0 & 1 & 0 & 0 \\ 0 & 0 & 1 & 0 \\ 1 & 0 & 1 & 0 \end{bmatrix}.
$$

Finally, we add the 4×4 identity matrix to $A + A^2 + A^3$. The sum and the reachability matrix are

$$
\text{sum} = \begin{bmatrix} 2 & 1 & 1 & 0 \\ 1 & 2 & 1 & 0 \\ 1 & 1 & 2 & 0 \\ 2 & 2 & 2 & 1 \end{bmatrix}
\quad \text{and} \quad
R(D) = \begin{bmatrix} 1 & 1 & 1 & 0 \\ 1 & 1 & 1 & 0 \\ 1 & 1 & 1 & 0 \\ 1 & 1 & 1 & 1 \end{bmatrix}.
$$

In the last column of the matrix, all entries except in the last row of $R(D)$ are 0; hence the vertex d cannot be reached from any other vertex. Once we exit from d, there is no way to return, no matter how long the path.   ◆

Recall that a digraph is said to be *connected* if the graph obtained from it by ignoring the directions on the edges is a connected (undirected) graph. A digraph is *strongly connected* if, for any pair of vertices u and v, there is a path from u to v. We note that the digraph of Fig. 9(a) is connected but not strongly connected. There are no paths from vertex a to vertex d, for example.

Theorem 4   A digraph D is strongly connected if and only if its reachability matrix $R(D)$ has no zeros.

▶ **Example 9**   Determine if the digraph D given in Fig. 9(b) on the previous page is strongly connected by using the reachability matrix. Are there any four-step paths from y to w? If so, how many?

Solution   An adjacency matrix for the digraph is given by

$$
A = \begin{array}{c c}
 & \begin{array}{c c c c c c} u & v & w & x & y & z \end{array} \\
\begin{array}{c} u \\ v \\ w \\ x \\ y \\ z \end{array} & \left[\begin{array}{c c c c c c}
0 & 1 & 0 & 0 & 0 & 1 \\
0 & 0 & 1 & 0 & 0 & 1 \\
0 & 0 & 0 & 0 & 0 & 0 \\
0 & 1 & 1 & 0 & 0 & 0 \\
1 & 0 & 0 & 1 & 0 & 1 \\
0 & 0 & 0 & 1 & 0 & 0
\end{array} \right]
\end{array},
$$

and from this we can calculate the powers of A and the reachability matrix. In the matrix A we note that the row corresponding to w contains only zeros. Thus we can never leave the vertex w. Similarly, we can never enter the vertex y (the column corresponding to y contains only zeros). Thus the graph cannot be strongly connected. Calculation of A^4 reveals that there are 2 four-step paths from y to w:

$$
A^4 = \begin{array}{c c}
 & \begin{array}{c c c c c c} u & v & w & x & y & z \end{array} \\
\begin{array}{c} u \\ v \\ w \\ x \\ y \\ z \end{array} & \left[\begin{array}{c c c c c c}
0 & 1 & 2 & 0 & 0 & 1 \\
0 & 0 & 1 & 0 & 0 & 1 \\
0 & 0 & 0 & 0 & 0 & 0 \\
0 & 1 & 1 & 0 & 0 & 0 \\
0 & 1 & 2 & 2 & 0 & 1 \\
0 & 0 & 0 & 1 & 0 & 0
\end{array} \right]
\end{array}.
$$

◆

▶ **Example 10**   Show that a digraph with a directed Hamiltonian circuit must be strongly connected.

Solution   Suppose that D is a digraph with a directed Hamiltonian circuit. Then there is a cycle that passes through each vertex of the graph exactly once. Thus, if there are n vertices, there is a circuit of $n - 1$ edges containing each of the vertices. This generates a path leading from any vertex to any other. Hence, the digraph is strongly connected.   ◆

Practice Problems 13.5

1. Let A be the adjacency matrix of a simple graph.

$$
A = \begin{array}{c c}
 & \begin{array}{c c c c} a & b & c & d \end{array} \\
\begin{array}{c} a \\ b \\ c \\ d \end{array} & \left[\begin{array}{c c c c}
1 & 1 & 0 & 0 \\
1 & 0 & 1 & 0 \\
0 & 1 & 0 & 1 \\
0 & 0 & 1 & 0
\end{array} \right]
\end{array}
$$

(a) Determine the number of paths of length 3 from b to c by using the adjacency matrix.

(b) Determine from the adjacency matrix whether the graph is connected.

(c) Draw the graph for which A is the adjacency matrix.

(d) Find all the paths of length 3 from b to c.

Practice Problems 13.5 (Continued)	2. For the digraph of Fig. 10,

2. For the digraph of Fig. 10,

   (a) Find the adjacency matrix A.

   (b) Find the number of paths of length 3 from v_3 to v_4 using the matrix A.

   (c) Write out the paths of length 3 from v_3 to v_4.

   (d) Find the reachability matrix of the digraph.

   (e) Is D connected? Is D strongly connected? Explain.

Figure 10.

▶ Exercises 13.5

1. (a) Find the adjacency matrix of the graph in Fig. 11.

   (b) Find the number of paths of length 2 from v_1 to v_4 in the graph of Fig. 11.

   (c) Find the reachability matrix of the graph in Fig. 11.

Figure 11.

2. Let $A(G)$ be the adjacency matrix of a simple graph:

$$A(G) = \begin{array}{c} v_1 \\ v_2 \\ v_3 \\ v_4 \\ v_5 \end{array} \begin{array}{ccccc} v_1 & v_2 & v_3 & v_4 & v_5 \\ \left[\begin{array}{ccccc} 0 & 1 & 1 & 1 & 0 \\ 1 & 0 & 1 & 0 & 1 \\ 1 & 1 & 0 & 1 & 0 \\ 1 & 0 & 1 & 0 & 0 \\ 0 & 1 & 0 & 0 & 0 \end{array}\right] \end{array}.$$

   (a) Draw the corresponding graph.

   (b) Determine from $A(G)$ the number of paths of length 3 from v_1 to v_4.

   (c) Determine from $A(G)$ whether G is connected. Explain.

   (d) Find all the paths of length 3 from v_1 to v_4.

3. Let $A(G)$ be the adjacency matrix of a graph:

$$A(G) = \begin{array}{c} v_1 \\ v_2 \\ v_3 \\ v_4 \\ v_5 \end{array} \begin{array}{ccccc} v_1 & v_2 & v_3 & v_4 & v_5 \\ \left[\begin{array}{ccccc} 0 & 1 & 1 & 0 & 0 \\ 1 & 0 & 1 & 0 & 0 \\ 1 & 1 & 0 & 0 & 0 \\ 0 & 0 & 0 & 0 & 1 \\ 0 & 0 & 0 & 1 & 1 \end{array}\right] \end{array}.$$

   (a) Determine from the adjacency matrix whether G is a connected graph.

   (b) Draw the graph represented by $A(G)$.

4. (a) Find the adjacency matrix $A(G)$ for the graph G in Fig. 12.

   (b) What is the *smallest* power of $A(G)$ that has no zero entries?

   (c) Explain what your answer to (b) tells us about the graph.

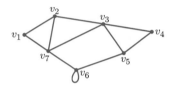

Figure 12.

5. (a) Find the adjacency matrix of the graph in Fig. 13.

   (b) Find the number of paths of length 3 from v_1 to v_4 by using the adjacency matrix.

   (c) Find the reachability matrix of the graph.

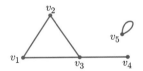

Figure 13.

6. Give an example of a graph on 3 vertices that is connected but for which A^3 contains at least one zero entry. Show A^3 for the graph you drew.

7. (a) Find the adjacency matrix A of the graph in Fig. 14.

   (b) Find the *smallest* power of A that has no zero entries.

   (c) How could you have determined the answer to part (b) directly from the graph and without reference to the adjacency matrix? Explain.

Figure 14.

8. Draw a simple graph that has reachability matrix R:

$$R = \begin{bmatrix} 1 & 1 & 1 & 0 & 1 \\ 1 & 1 & 1 & 0 & 1 \\ 1 & 1 & 1 & 0 & 1 \\ 0 & 0 & 0 & 1 & 0 \\ 1 & 1 & 1 & 0 & 1 \end{bmatrix}.$$

9. Draw a simple graph for which $A^2(G)$ is given by the matrix

$$\begin{bmatrix} 1 & 0 & 1 & 0 \\ 0 & 2 & 0 & 0 \\ 1 & 0 & 1 & 0 \\ 0 & 0 & 0 & 1 \end{bmatrix}.$$

10. (a) Find the adjacency matrix for the digraph D in Fig. 15.

(b) Find the number of paths of length 2 from a to d.

(c) Write out those paths of length 2 from a to d.

(d) Find A^4.

(e) What can you say about paths of length 4 in this digraph?

(f) Find the reachability matrix of D.

(g) Is D connected? Is D strongly connected? Explain.

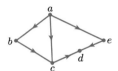

Figure 15.

11. (a) Find the adjacency matrix for the digraph in Fig. 16.

(b) Find the number of paths of length 4 from a to b.

(c) Write out those paths.

(d) Find the reachability matrix for the digraph.

(e) Is the digraph connected? Is it strongly connected? Explain.

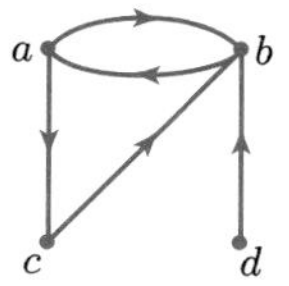

Figure 16.

12. Let $A = A(D)$ be the adjacency matrix of a digraph D.

$$A = \begin{bmatrix} 0 & 0 & 1 & 1 \\ 1 & 0 & 1 & 0 \\ 0 & 1 & 0 & 1 \\ 1 & 0 & 0 & 0 \end{bmatrix}$$

(a) From the matrix, determine the indegree and the outdegree of each vertex.

(b) Draw the digraph.

(c) Is the digraph connected? Is it strongly connected?

(d) Is there an Euler circuit in this digraph?

13. Let $A = A(D)$ be the adjacency matrix of a digraph D.

$$A = \begin{array}{c c} & \begin{array}{c c c c c} v_1 & v_2 & v_3 & v_4 & v_5 \end{array} \\ \begin{array}{c} v_1 \\ v_2 \\ v_3 \\ v_4 \\ v_5 \end{array} & \begin{bmatrix} 1 & 1 & 0 & 0 & 0 \\ 0 & 0 & 1 & 1 & 0 \\ 1 & 0 & 0 & 0 & 1 \\ 1 & 1 & 0 & 1 & 0 \\ 0 & 0 & 1 & 1 & 0 \end{bmatrix} \end{array}$$

(a) For each of the vertices, find the indegree and the outdegree directly from the matrix.

(b) Draw the digraph.

(c) Determine the number of paths of length 3 from v_1 to v_4.

(d) Write out all the paths of length 3 from v_1 to v_4.

Solutions to Practice Problems 13.5

1. (a) The matrix A^3 appears below. The entry corresponding to the number of paths of length 3 from b to c is in row 2, column 3. Thus there are three such paths.

(b) The reachability matrix can be shown to have no zeros by finding $I + A + A^2 + A^3$. Thus, the graph is connected.

(c) A graph represented by the matrix A is shown in Fig. 17.

(d) The paths of length 3 from b to c are $babc, bcdc,$ and $bcbc$.

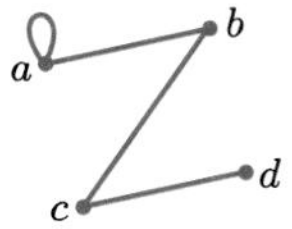

Figure 17.

$$A^2 = \begin{bmatrix} 2 & 1 & 1 & 0 \\ 1 & 2 & 0 & 1 \\ 1 & 0 & 2 & 0 \\ 0 & 1 & 0 & 1 \end{bmatrix} \qquad A^3 = \begin{bmatrix} 3 & 3 & 1 & 1 \\ 3 & 1 & 3 & 0 \\ 1 & 3 & 0 & 2 \\ 1 & 0 & 2 & 0 \end{bmatrix}$$

2. **(a)** The adjacency matrix A appears below.

(b) We show A^3. There is one path of length 3 from v_3 to v_4. This is the entry in row 3, column 4 of A^3.

(c) The only path of length 3 from v_3 to v_4 is $v_3 v_2 v_1 v_4$.

$$A = \begin{bmatrix} 0 & 0 & 0 & 1 \\ 1 & 0 & 1 & 0 \\ 0 & 1 & 0 & 0 \\ 0 & 0 & 1 & 0 \end{bmatrix} \qquad A^2 = \begin{bmatrix} 0 & 0 & 1 & 0 \\ 0 & 1 & 0 & 1 \\ 1 & 0 & 1 & 0 \\ 0 & 1 & 0 & 0 \end{bmatrix} \qquad A^3 = \begin{bmatrix} 0 & 1 & 0 & 0 \\ 1 & 0 & 2 & 0 \\ 0 & 1 & 0 & 1 \\ 1 & 0 & 1 & 0 \end{bmatrix}$$

(d) To find the reachability matrix, we add $I + A + A^2 + A^3$ to find the sum matrix has no zeros. So, the reachability matrix is a matrix containing nothing but 1's.

$$I + A + A^2 + A^3 = \begin{bmatrix} 1 & 1 & 1 & 1 \\ 2 & 2 & 3 & 1 \\ 1 & 2 & 2 & 1 \\ 1 & 1 & 2 & 1 \end{bmatrix}$$

(e) Since the reachability matrix has no zeros, the digraph is strongly connected. The digraph is connected because it is strongly connected.

13.6 Trees

In Section 13.3 we introduced the notion of a minimal spanning tree. In fact, trees have many applications.

▶ **Example 1** Suppose that your friend is thinking of an integer between 1 and 10, inclusive. Describe an efficient procedure for guessing the number if you can ask questions that can be answered only yes or no.

Solution One procedure is to ask first if the number is less than or equal to 5. If the answer is yes, we know that the number is in the set $\{1, 2, 3, 4, 5\}$. If the answer is no, we know that the number is in the set $\{6, 7, 8, 9, 10\}$. In either case, we have reduced the search to a set that is half the size of the original. We continue in that way, dividing the set in half (or as close to half as we can) as we proceed. Figure 1 contains a schematic diagram of this process. Note that at most four questions are necessary to determine the chosen number. ◆

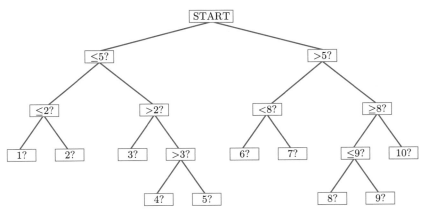

Figure 1.

The diagram representing the procedure above is an example of a tree. It is called a tree because it has several branches, some branches have branches of their own, and so on, and the picture looks something like a tree (not necessarily growing in the standard direction). In the language of graph theory, a *tree* is a connected acyclic graph. A characterization of trees follows:

Tree Property 1   Let G be a simple graph with at least two vertices. The following statements are equivalent:

1. G is a tree.

2. Each pair of distinct vertices is joined by exactly one simple path.

3. G is connected but would be disconnected if any edge were removed.

4. G is acyclic but would contain a cycle if any edge were added.

▶ Example 2   Which of the graphs in Fig. 2 are trees? If the graph is not a tree, explain how it violates the definition.

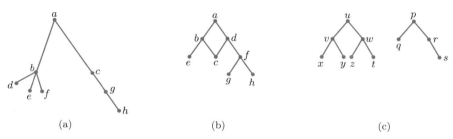

(a)   (b)   (c)

Figure 2.

Solution   The graph of Fig. 2(a) is a tree. The graph of Fig. 2(b) is not a tree because it contains a cycle. The graph of Fig. 2(c) is not connected; hence it is not a tree.

◆

▶ Example 3   Sketch all trees having 6 vertices. There are 6 of them.

Solution   Note that in each of the trees with 6 vertices (Fig. 3), there are exactly 5 edges. Also, in each tree there are some vertices of degree 1. Those vertices with degree 1 are called *leaves*. Every tree with at least one edge has at least 2 leaves. To see this, just write down the longest acyclic path in the graph. The first and last vertices in this path cannot be equal (otherwise we would have a cycle). Each of those vertices is a *leaf*.

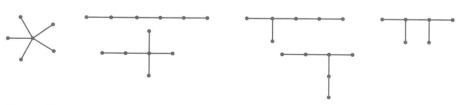

Figure 3.

◆

Tree Property 2   Let G be a simple graph with n vertices. The following statements are equivalent:

1. G is a tree.

2. G is acyclic and has $n - 1$ edges.

3. G is connected and has $n - 1$ edges.

▶ Example 4   A tree has 4 vertices of degree 3 and 3 vertices of degree 2. The remaining vertices have degree 1. Find the number of vertices in this tree.

Solution   Let n be the number of vertices of the tree.

Degree of vertex	Number of vertices	Sum of degrees
3	4	12
2	3	6
1	$n - 7$	$n - 7$
Totals n		$18 + (n - 7)$

Recall that the sum of the degrees of the vertices in any graph is equal to twice the number of edges in the graph. Since we are working with a tree with n vertices, this graph has $n - 1$ edges. Thus the sum of the degrees of the vertices is $2(n - 1) = 2n - 2$. We then get the following equation:

$$18 + (n - 7) = 2n - 2.$$

Solving this equation for n, we find that $n = 13$. Thus there are 13 vertices in the tree, and 6 of them have degree 1. Exercise 20 asks for verification that such a tree exists.   ◆

The tree introduced in the solution to the first example is called a *rooted tree*. It is a tree in which a special vertex is designated to be the *root* of the tree. The root in the tree of Fig. 1 is START; it is assumed that edges are directed down from START to other vertices. In this way, a rooted tree is actually a directed graph that is connected and acyclic and for which there is a specified, unique vertex with indegree 0. The root may appear at the top, bottom, or side of the tree. We can omit the directional arrows on the edges when the direction is clear. A familiar example of a rooted tree is an organizational chart of a company.

Suggestive terms are used to describe the parts of a tree. If there is a directed edge from u to v, we say that u is the *parent* of v and that v is the *child* of u. A leaf is a vertex that has no children. Every child in a tree has one parent, although a parent can have several children. A root has no parent and is the only vertex in the tree with this property.

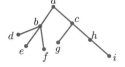

Figure 4.

▶ Example 5   In the tree of Fig. 4, identify the root and the leaves. Find all the children of c.

Solution   The root is a. The leaves are all vertices with outdegree 0: d, e, f, g, and i. The children of c are g and h.   ◆

A tree in which every parent has at most two children is called a *binary tree.* The search procedure pictured in the graph of Fig. 1 is a binary tree. A search procedure whose graph representation is a binary tree is called a *binary search.* There are many opportunities to use binary trees.

▶ Example 6   Use a binary tree to store the following words in alphabetical order:

bad   even   guppy   apple   bear   dog   fish   whale.

Solution   Here is the algorithm we will use.

  1. Start with any element in the list. (We will begin with *bad.*) That is the root. Label the root and draw two children [Fig. 5(a)].

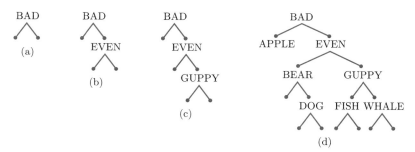

Figure 5.

  2. Choose the next element in the list. If it precedes the root in alphabetical order, label the left child with its value. If it succeeds the root in alphabetical order, label the right child with its value. Draw left and right children for the newly labeled vertex. Continue.

  Say the root is *bad.* The next word is *even.* It succeeds *bad,* so it is the label on the right child [Fig. 5(b)]. We draw two children from the vertex at *even.* The next word is *guppy.* That succeeds *even,* so *guppy* is the label on the right child of *even* [Fig. 5(c)]. We draw two children from the vertex at *guppy.* Now, the word *apple* precedes *bad,* so *apple* is the label on the left child of *bad.* Add left and right children to that vertex. Continue. The tree that results from working through the entire list appears in Fig. 5(d). ◆

  The tree we formed to store our alphabetical list can be used to search for a word in our "dictionary." If the word is not in our dictionary, we can add it to the list in the proper place.

▶ Example 7   (a) Use the tree of Fig. 5(d) to determine if the word *elk* is in the stored list. If not, add it to the tree in its proper alphabetical order. (b) Do the same for the word *asp.*

Solution   We compare *elk* with *bad.* Since *elk* succeeds *bad,* we proceed to the right child of *bad.* We compare *elk* with *even.* Since *elk* precedes *even,* we pass to the left child of *even.* The word *elk* succeeds *bear,* so we pass to the right child of *bear,* which is *dog,* and again, since *elk* succeeds *dog,* we pass the right child of *dog.* The word *elk* does not appear in the dictionary, so we add it as the right child of *dog.* Figure 6 shows the new tree. In answer to (b), the search reveals that we should add the word *asp* as the right child of *apple,* as shown in Fig. 7. ◆

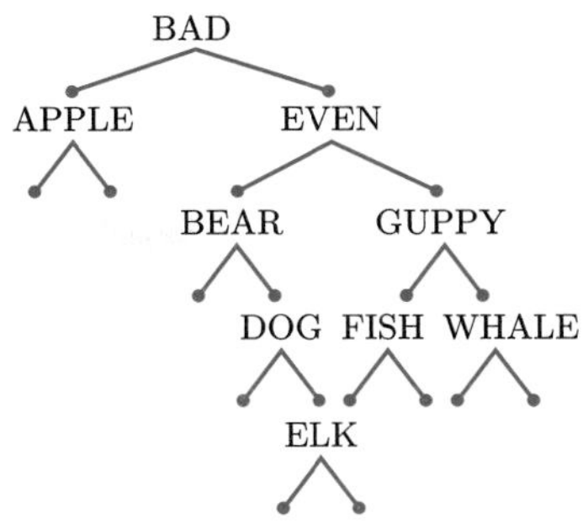

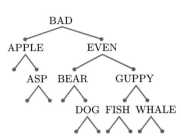

Figure 6.

Figure 7.

Another way of using trees is in showing the structure of algebraic expressions. The operators we will use here are $+$ (add), $-$ (subtract), $*$ (multiply), $\div$ (divide), and $\wedge$ (exponentiation). An algebraic expression of the form $(x+y)^\wedge 3$, commonly written as $(x+y)^3$, can be analyzed with a tree. The root of the tree representing the expression is the central operator, which indicates the last operation to be performed (in the preceding expression the root would be the exponentiation operator $\wedge$). Other vertices are labeled with operators, variables, or constants. The leaves cannot be operators. We do not put parentheses on the tree.

▶ **Example 8**   Find the algebraic expression represented by the tree in Fig. 8.

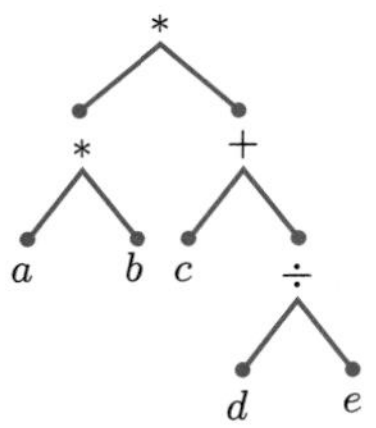

Solution   We read from the bottom up, using the parent to get the operation to be performed on the children. From the left, we have $(a*b)$, which will be multiplied by the result of the operations on the right. Again, reading from the bottom, we have c, which is added to $d \div e$. The final expression is

$$(a*b)*[c+(d \div e)].$$ ◆

Figure 8.

We assume in every algebraic expression that in order for the operations $+$, $-$, $*$, $\div$, and $\wedge$ to be performed, all of the arguments must have been evaluated. To find the value of $(a+b)$, a and b must be evaluated first. To find $(a+b) \div (b*c)$, we cannot use the operation $\div$ until both $a+b$ and $b*c$ have been evaluated. The root of the tree representing the expression is the central operation (the last operation that is to be performed). In labeling a tree to represent an algebraic expression, we work from the central operator down. The root is the central operator. We then enter the arguments of the operator (variables or constants along with operators on them). Continue the process until the symbols (except parentheses) in the expression are all on the tree.

▶ **Example 9**   Use a tree to represent the following algebraic expressions.

(a) $x+y$ (b) $(x*y)+z$ (c) $[x+(y \div z)]^\wedge (4*y)$

Solution   We use the operations $+$, $-$, $*$, $\div$, and $\wedge$ (exponentiation) to label any vertices except leaves. Leaves are labeled with variables or constants. The operation denoted on a vertex operates on the left and right subtrees emanating from that vertex, reading from left to right.

(a) Note that the central operator is $+$. The left and right branches have vertices x and y, respectively. See Fig. 9(a).

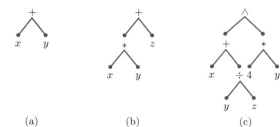

(a)   (b)   (c)

Figure 9.

(b) The central operator here is $+$, so it is the root. We must calculate both arguments in order to use the central operator. One is $x * y$; the other is z. We indicate this by having the left subtree show $x * y$, and a right branch show the variable z. See Fig. 9(b).

(c) Here the central operator is $\wedge$. To use this operation, we first must evaluate the expressions $x + (y \div z)$ and $4 * y$. The expression $x + (y \div z)$ has central operator $+$, so we have a subtree with root $+$. In turn, we must evaluate $y \div z$ before we can proceed. This requires an additional subtree. See Fig. 9(c).◆

Practice Problems 13.6

1. Draw three distinct trees with 5 vertices. How many are there?

2. Is it possible to have a tree with 2 vertices of degree 3, 1 vertex of degree 2, 6 vertices of degree 1, and 9 edges? Explain.

3. Find the tree that creates a dictionary by adding each of the words in the following list:

   daily   milk   baby   silly   bib   crib   blanket   rattle.

▶ Exercises 13.6

1. Draw all trees with 4 vertices.

2. Draw four distinct binary trees with 6 vertices.

3. Draw three distinct binary trees with 7 vertices.

4. Determine which of the graphs in Fig. 10 are trees. For those that are not trees, explain why not.

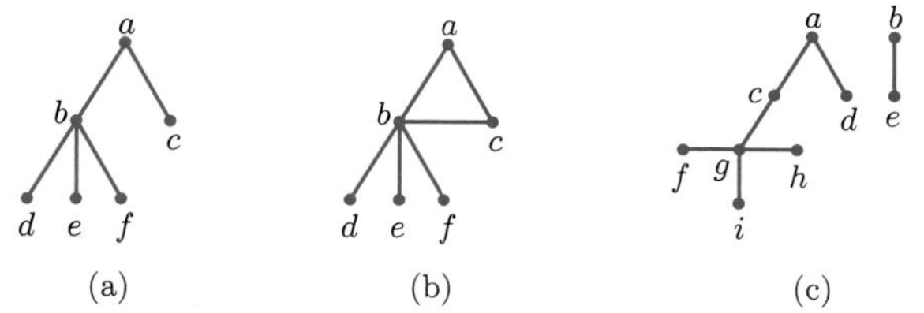

(a)   (b)   (c)

Figure 10.

5. Name the leaves in each of the trees in Fig. 11.

6. Find (a) all the children of x and (b) all the descendants of x in each of the trees of Fig. 11.

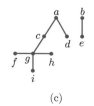

(a)   (b)   (c)

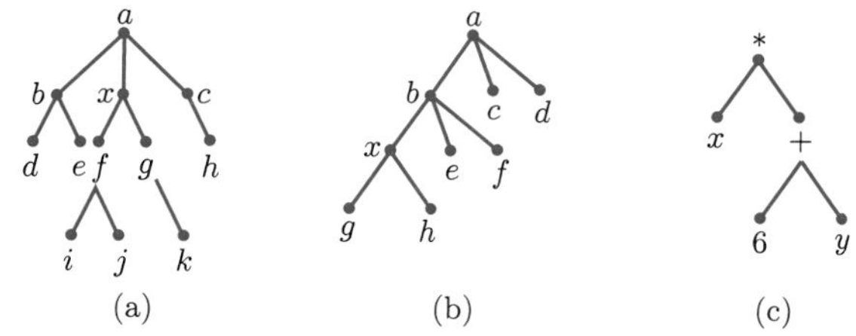

Figure 11.

7. Find the parent of x in each of the trees in Fig. 11.

8. Identify the root in each of the trees of Fig. 11.

In Exercises 9–13, draw the graph with the given properties or tell why it cannot be drawn.

9. A tree that has 7 vertices and 12 edges.

10. A tree that has vertices of degree 4, 3, 3, 3, 2, and 2.

11. A connected graph with 3 edges and 4 vertices that is not a tree.

12. A disconnected acyclic graph with 5 vertices and 4 edges.

13. A tree with 3 vertices and 1 edge.

14. Draw the binary tree that creates the dictionary from the following list: guppy, hamster, dog, cat, snake, canary, parakeet, pony.

15. Make a binary tree showing the numerical ordering of 43, 67, 58, 2, 31, 91, and 34.

16. Read the algebraic formula from the tree in Fig. 12.

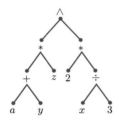

Figure 12.

17. Read the algebraic formula from the tree in Fig. 13.

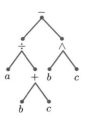

Figure 13.

18. Construct the tree that represents the algebraic expression

$$[3 \div (a * c)] + (b - d).$$

19. Construct the tree that represents the algebraic expression

$$\left[(x * y)^{\wedge}3\right] \div (a + b).$$

20. Draw the tree described by Example 4.

21. Using the scheme described in Example 1, what is the maximum number of questions needed to determine the number if your friend can choose any integer between 1 and 100, inclusive? Between 1 and 1000, inclusive?

Solutions to Practice Problems 13.6

1. There are three different trees having 5 vertices.

2. The sum of the degrees of the vertices is 14. The graph cannot have 9 edges; it must have 7 edges. A tree with 7 edges would have to have 8 vertices. There is no such tree.

3.

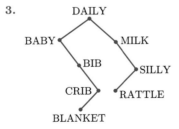

▶ Chapter 13 Summary

1. A *graph* is a finite set of vertices and a finite set of edges, where each edge connects two vertices or connects a vertex to itself. A graph is *simple* if each pair of vertices is connected by at most one edge.

2. The *degree* of a vertex is the number of edges associated with that vertex. Loops count as two edges.

3. The sum of the degrees of all vertices in a graph is even and is twice the number of edges in the graph.

4. In any graph, the number of vertices of odd degree is even.

5. A *circuit* is a closed path in which no edge is repeated. A graph is called *acyclic* if it has no circuits.

6. A graph is *connected* if and only if given any pair of vertices, there is a path between them. A directed graph, or *digraph*, is connected if the edges without direction connect the graph. It is *strongly connected* if there is a directed path from any given vertex to any other given vertex.

7. In a connected graph, a simple path using all the vertices and having a minimal number of edges is called a *path of minimal length*.

8. An *Euler path* is a path that traverses every edge in the graph exactly once. An *Euler circuit* is a closed Euler path. A graph contains an Euler circuit if and only if it is connected and every vertex of the graph has even degree.

9. Fleury's algorithm for finding an Euler circuit appears on page 597.

10. A *Hamiltonian circuit* is a circuit in which every vertex of the graph is visited exactly once (except for the endpoint, which is visited twice).

11. Suppose G is a simple graph with n vertices, no loops, and $n \geq 3$. Then G has a Hamiltonian circuit if
    (i) the degree of G is at least $\frac{n}{2}$, or
    (ii) G has at least $\frac{1}{2}(n-1)(n-2) + 2$ edges, or
    (iii) for any two vertices not connected by an edge, the sum of their degrees is at least n.

12. *Minimal Spanning Tree Algorithm*: List the edges of a weighted graph in order of increasing weight; choose the first edge in the sequence. Choose the next edge in the sequence that does not create a cycle. Continue until no more edges can be added.

13. In a digraph, the *outdegree* of a vertex is the number of edges going out from that vertex. The *indegree* of a vertex is the number of edges coming in to that vertex. The sum of the outdegrees of the vertices = the sum of the indegrees of all the vertices. A connected digraph has an Euler circuit if and only if for every one of its vertices, the indegree equals the outdegree.

14. The *adjacency matrix* of a graph with n vertices $v_1, v_2, \ldots, v_n$, is an $n \times n$ matrix in which the i, j entry is 1 if an edge joins vertex v_i with vertex v_j and is 0 otherwise.

15. The i, j entry in the kth power of the adjacency matrix A of a graph G is the number of paths in G of length k between vertex v_i and vertex v_j. If there exists a positive integer m such that A^m has only positive entries then G is connected. G is connected if and only if there exists a positive integer m such that every entry in $A + A^2 + \cdots + A^m$ is positive.

16. A *tree* is a connected acyclic graph. A simple graph with n vertices is a tree if and only if it is connected and has $n - 1$ edges, or equivalently, if and only if it is acyclic and has $n - 1$ edges.

Review of Fundamental Concepts of Chapter 13

1. Define the degree of a vertex.

2. Draw a planar graph with four vertices and draw a nonplanar graph with four vertices.

3. What is the relationship between the number of edges and the degrees of the vertices of a graph?

4. How many vertices of odd degree can a graph have?

5. Give some ways in which you can determine if two graphs are equivalent.

6. Define *simple path*, *closed path*, and *simple circuit*. Draw a graph that has each of these features and identify them.

7. What is an Euler path? Does the graph you drew in response to Question 6 have an Euler path? An Euler circuit?

8. Give a simple criterion for determining if a connected graph has an Euler circuit.

9. A connected graph with n vertices must have at least a certain number of edges. How many?

10. Explain the steps in using Fleury's algorithm to find an Euler circuit for a graph.

11. Give simple criteria for determining if a connected graph with three or more vertices has an Euler path.

12. Explain the terms *Hamiltonian path* and *Hamiltonian circuit*.

13. Write down two real-world examples in which we might want to know if there is an Euler circuit in a graph. Explain what the Euler circuit tells about each situation.

14. Write down two real-world examples in which we might want to know if there is a Hamiltonian circuit in a graph. Explain what the Hamiltonian circuit tells about each situation.

15. What is the purpose of trying to find a minimal spanning tree for a graph?

16. Explain the procedure for finding a minimal spanning tree for a graph.

17. What is a digraph? When does a connected digraph have an Euler circuit?

18. Give a real-world example of a connected digraph. Explain why you might want to know if the digraph has an Euler circuit.

19. What is a bipartite graph?

20. Explain how a matrix can be used to represent a graph. What characteristics of the graph can be determined from the matrix representation?

▶ Chapter 13 Supplementary Exercises

1. For each of the graphs in Fig. 1, give the degree of each vertex. Count the number of edges of each graph and verify the basic relationship between the sum of the degrees of the vertices and the number of edges in the graph.

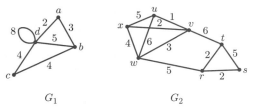

Figure 1.

2. For each of the graphs in Fig. 1, give

   (a) A simple path that is not closed

   (b) A closed path that is not a circuit

   (c) A circuit that is not a simple circuit

3. Assume that each edge of the graphs in Fig. 1 is weighted with the value given on the edge. Find a minimal spanning tree for each graph and find its weight.

4. For each graph in Fig. 1, find an Euler circuit if one exists. If none exists, explain why.

5. For each of the graphs in Fig. 2, find the degree of each vertex. Verify that the number of vertices of odd degree is even in each case.

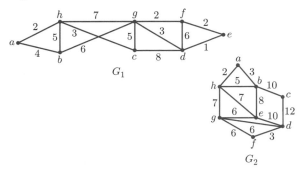

Figure 2.

6. For each of the graphs in Fig. 2, determine

   (a) A simple path that is not closed

   (b) A closed path that is not simple

   (c) A closed path that is not a circuit

   (d) A circuit that is not a simple circuit

7. Weights have been assigned to the edges of each of the graphs in Fig. 2. Use the algorithm to find a minimal spanning tree in each case and give its weight.

8. For each of the graphs in Fig. 2, determine if there is an Euler circuit. If one exists, describe it. If none exists, explain why.

9. For each of the graphs in Fig. 3, find an adjacency matrix. Find the number of paths of length 3 from v_1 to v_4 in each case.

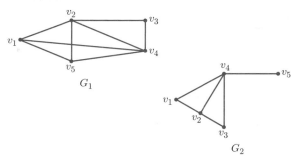

Figure 3.

10. Determine which of the three graphs G_2, G_3, G_4 in Fig. 4 are equivalent to G_1.

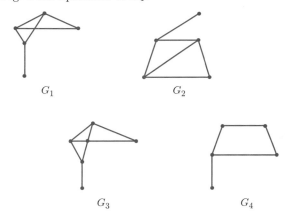

Figure 4.

11. Draw the graph G with adjacency matrix $A(G)$. Determine if the graph G' in Fig. 5 is equivalent to G. Explain.

$$A(G) = \begin{bmatrix} 0 & 1 & 1 & 1 \\ 1 & 0 & 0 & 1 \\ 1 & 0 & 0 & 0 \\ 1 & 1 & 0 & 0 \end{bmatrix}$$

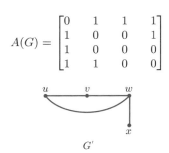

Figure 5.

12. For the floor plan of a house given in Fig. 6 on the next page, determine if there is a path starting from the outside in which you can pass through each doorway exactly once and return outside. Show the path if it exists. If it does not exist, explain why.

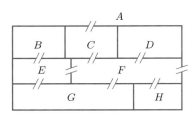

Figure 6.

13. A house painter wishes to paint the interior of the house in Fig. 6 so that no two rooms joined by a doorway are the same color. What minimal number of colors does she need?

14. Determine the critical path for the publication of a magazine given the activity digraph in Fig. 7.

15. Construct a binary tree that shows the numerical ordering of the numbers 120, 187, 230, 102, 115, 134, and 190. Show how you would search the tree for the number 127. Insert it in the proper place on the tree.

16. Construct the binary trees that represent the following algebraic expressions.
    (a) $[(4 * x) + y]^\wedge 6$ (b) $(4 * x) + y^\wedge 6$
    (c) $[4 * (x + y)]^\wedge 6$

17. Find the critical path for the activity digraph given in Fig. 8.

18. The graph in Fig. 9 represents the following: The vertices represent the people in a family; there is an edge between two members of the family if they need a car at the same time during the week. What is the minimal number of cars this family must own for everyone to have a car when it is needed?

19. What is the minimal number of colors needed to color the map in Fig. 10? No two countries with a common border can be the same color.

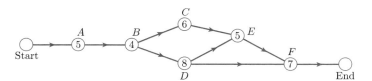

Figure 7.

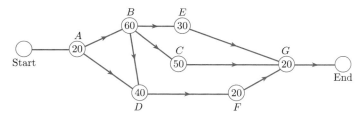

Figure 8.

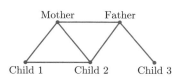

Figure 9.

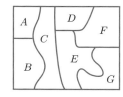

Figure 10.

▶ Chapter 13 Chapter Test

1. For the graph G in Fig. 1, give (a) a simple closed path, (b) a circuit, and (c) an acyclic, connected subgraph.

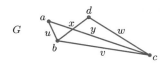

Figure 1.

2. Determine if the graph G in Fig. 1 has an Euler circuit. Explain your answer.

3. Find the minimal spanning tree for the graph in Fig. 2.

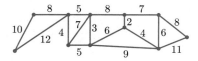

Figure 2.

4. (a) Find the adjacency matrix of the graph in Fig. 1.

   (b) Determine the number of paths of length 3 from vertex a to vertex c.

5. (a) Draw the digraph D with adjacency matrix $A(D)$.

   (b) Determine if the graph D' is equivalent to D. Explain.

   (c) Is the digraph D connected? Is it strongly connected? Explain.

$$A(D) = \begin{bmatrix} 0 & 1 & 1 & 1 \\ 1 & 0 & 1 & 1 \\ 0 & 0 & 0 & 0 \\ 0 & 1 & 1 & 0 \end{bmatrix}$$

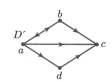

6. For the floor plan of the house in Fig. 3 determine the minimal number of colors that can be used to paint the house so that no two rooms joined by a door will be the same color.

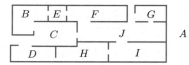

Figure 3.

7. For the floor plan of the house in Fig. 3 determine if there is a path that starts outside the house, passes through each doorway exactly once, and returns to the outside of the house. Show the path if it exists. If such a path does not exist, explain why.

8. Construct a binary tree that represents the algebraic expression

$$\sqrt{\frac{(x-3)}{(x^4+9)}}.$$

9. Find the critical path in the task starting at $\boxed{\text{Start}}$ and ending at $\boxed{\text{End}}$.

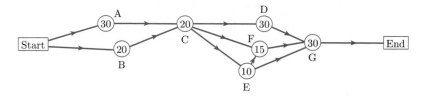

Appendix A

TABLES

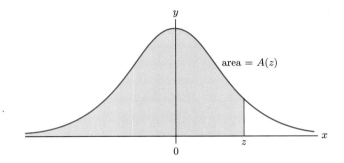

Table 1   Areas under the standard normal curve

z	$A(z)$	z	$A(z)$	z	$A(z)$	z	$A(z)$	z	$A(z)$
−3.50	.0002	−2.00	.0228	−.50	.3085	1.00	.8413	2.50	.9938
−3.45	.0003	−1.95	.0256	−.45	.3264	1.05	.8531	2.55	.9946
−3.40	.0003	−1.90	.0287	−.40	.3446	1.10	.8643	2.60	.9953
−3.35	.0004	−1.85	.0322	−.35	.3632	1.15	.8749	2.65	.9960
−3.30	.0005	−1.80	.0359	−.30	.3821	1.20	.8849	2.70	.9965
−3.25	.0006	−1.75	.0401	−.25	.4013	1.25	.8944	2.75	.9970
−3.20	.0007	−1.70	.0446	−.20	.4207	1.30	.9032	2.80	.9974
−3.15	.0008	−1.65	.0495	−.15	.4404	1.35	.9115	2.85	.9978
−3.10	.0010	−1.60	.0548	−.10	.4602	1.40	.9192	2.90	.9981
−3.05	.0011	−1.55	.0606	−.05	.4801	1.45	.9265	2.95	.9984
−3.00	.0013	−1.50	.0668	.00	.5000	1.50	.9332	3.00	.9987
−2.95	.0016	−1.45	.0735	.05	.5199	1.55	.9394	3.05	.9989
−2.90	.0019	−1.40	.0808	.10	.5398	1.60	.9452	3.10	.9990
−2.85	.0022	−1.35	.0885	.15	.5596	1.65	.9505	3.15	.9992
−2.80	.0026	−1.30	.0968	.20	.5793	1.70	.9554	3.20	.9993
−2.75	.0030	−1.25	.1056	.25	.5987	1.75	.9599	3.25	.9994
−2.70	.0035	−1.20	.1151	.30	.6179	1.80	.9641	3.30	.9995
−2.65	.0040	−1.15	.1251	.35	.6368	1.85	.9678	3.35	.9996
−2.60	.0047	−1.10	.1357	.40	.6554	1.90	.9713	3.40	.9997
−2.55	.0054	−1.05	.1469	.45	.6736	1.95	.9744	3.45	.9997
−2.50	.0062	−1.00	.1587	.50	.6915	2.00	.9772	3.50	.9998
−2.45	.0071	−.95	.1711	.55	.7088	2.05	.9798		
−2.40	.0082	−.90	.1841	.60	.7257	2.10	.9821		
−2.35	.0094	−.85	.1977	.65	.7422	2.15	.9842		
−2.30	.0107	−.80	.2119	.70	.7580	2.20	.9861		
−2.25	.0122	−.75	.2266	.75	.7734	2.25	.9878		
−2.20	.0139	−.70	.2420	.80	.7881	2.30	.9893		
−2.15	.0158	−.65	.2578	.85	.8023	2.35	.9906		
−2.10	.0179	−.60	.2743	.90	.8159	2.40	.9918		
−2.05	.0202	−.55	.2912	.95	.8289	2.45	.9929		

Table 2	$(1 + i)^n$ Compounded amount of \$1 invested for n interest periods at interest rate i per period

n	1/50 %	1/2 %	1 %	2 %	6 %
1	1.000200000	1.00500000	1.01000000	1.02000000	1.06000000
2	1.000400040	1.01002500	1.02010000	1.04040000	1.12360000
3	1.000600120	1.01507513	1.03030100	1.06120800	1.19101600
4	1.000800240	1.02015050	1.04060401	1.08243216	1.26247696
5	1.001000400	1.02525125	1.05101005	1.10408080	1.33822558
6	1.001200600	1.03037751	1.06152015	1.12616242	1.41851911
7	1.001400840	1.03552940	1.07213535	1.14868567	1.50363026
8	1.001601120	1.04070704	1.08285671	1.17165938	1.59384807
9	1.001601447	1.04591058	1.09368527	1.19509257	1.68947896
10	1.002001806	1.05114013	1.10462213	1.21899442	1.79084770
11	1.002202201	1.05639583	1.11566835	1.24337431	1.89829856
12	1.002402642	1.06167781	1.12682503	1.26824179	2.01219647
13	1.002603122	1.06698620	1.13809328	1.29360663	2.13292826
14	1.002803643	1.07232113	1.14947421	1.31947876	2.26090396
15	1.003004204	1.07768274	1.16096896	1.34586834	2.39655819
16	1.003204804	1.08307115	1.17257864	1.37278571	2.54035168
17	1.003405445	1.08848651	1.18430443	1.40024142	2.69277279
18	1.003505100	1.09392894	1.19614748	1.42824625	2.85433915
19	1.003806848	1.09939858	1.20810895	1.45681117	3.02559950
20	1.004007609	1.10489558	1.22019004	1.48594740	3.20713547
21	1.004208411	1.11042006	1.23239194	1.51566634	3.39956360
22	1.004409252	1.11597216	1.24471586	1.54597967	3.60353742
23	1.004610134	1.12155202	1.25716302	1.57689926	3.81974966
24	1.004811056	1.12715978	1.26973465	1.60843725	4.04893464
25	1.005012018	1.13279558	1.28243200	1.64060599	4.29187072
26	1.005213022	1.13845955	1.29525631	1.67341811	4.54938296
27	1.005414063	1.14415185	1.30820888	1.70688648	4.82234594
28	1.005615146	1.14987261	1.32129097	1.74102421	5.11168670
29	1.005816269	1.15562197	1.33450388	1.77584469	5.41838790
30	1.006017433	1.16140008	1.34784892	1.81136158	5.74349117
36	1.007225257	1.19668052	1.43076878	2.03988734	8.14725200
48	1.009645259	1.27048916	1.61222608	2.58707039	16.39387173
52	1.010453217	1.29609015	1.67768892	2.80032819	20.69688534
60	1.012071075	1.34885015	1.81669670	3.28103079	32.98769085
104	1.021015784	1.67984969	2.81464012	7.84183795	428.36106292
120	1.024287860	1.81939673	3.30038689	10.76516303	1,088.18774784
180	1.036652115	2.45409356	5.99580198	35.32083136	35,896.80101597
240	1.049165620	3.31020448	10.89255365	115.88873515	
300	1.061830136	4.46496981	19.78846626	380.23450806	
360	1.074647608	6.02257521	35.94964133	1,247.56112775	
365	1.075722685	6.17465278	37.78343433	1,377.40829197	

Table 3	1/(1 + i)ⁿ Present value of $1. Principal that will accumulate to $1 in n interest periods at a compound rate of i per period

			i		
n	1/50 %	1/2 %	1 %	2 %	6 %
1	.99980004	.99502488	.99009901	.98039216	.94339623
2	.99960012	.99007450	.98029605	.96116878	.88999644
3	.99940024	.98514876	.97059015	.94232233	.83961928
4	.99920040	.98024752	.96098034	.92384543	.79209366
5	.99900060	.97537067	.95146569	.90573081	.74725817
6	.99880084	.97051808	.94204524	.88797138	.70496054
7	.99860112	.96568963	.93271805	.87056018	.66505711
8	.99840144	.96088520	.92348322	.85349037	.62741237
9	.99820180	.95610468	.91433982	.83675527	.59189846
10	.99800220	.95134794	.90528695	.82034830	.55839478
11	.99780264	.94661487	.89632372	.80426304	.52678753
12	.99760312	.94190534	.88744923	.78849318	.49696936
13	.99740364	.93721924	.87866260	.77303253	.46883902
14	.99720420	.93255646	.86996297	.75787502	.44230096
15	.99700479	.92791688	.86134947	.74301473	.41726506
16	.99680543	.92330037	.85282126	.72844581	.39364628
17	.99660611	.91870684	.84437749	.71416256	.37136442
18	.99640683	.91413616	.83601731	.70015937	.35034379
19	.99620759	.90958822	.82773992	.68643076	.33051301
20	.99600839	.90506290	.81954447	.67297133	.31180473
21	.99580923	.90056010	.81143017	.65977582	.29415540
22	.99561010	.89607971	.80339621	.64683904	.27750510
23	.99541102	.89162160	.79544179	.63415592	.26179726
24	.99521198	.88718567	.78756613	.62172149	.24697855
25	.99501298	.88277181	.77976844	.60953087	.23299863
26	.99481401	.87837991	.77204796	.59757928	.21981003
27	.99461509	.87400986	.76440392	.58586204	.20736795
28	.99441621	.86966155	.75683557	.57437455	.19563014
29	.99421736	.86533488	.74934215	.56311231	.18455674
30	.99401856	.86102973	.74192292	.55207089	.17411013
36	.99282657	.83564492	.69892495	.49022315	.12274077
48	.99044688	.78709841	.62026041	.38653761	.06099840
52	.98965492	.77155127	.59605806	.35710100	.04831645
60	.98807290	.74137220	.55044962	.30478227	.03031434
104	.97941686	.59529136	.35528521	.12752113	.00233448
120	.97628805	.54963273	.30299478	.09289223	.00091896
180	.96464377	.40748243	.16678336	.02831190	.00002786
240	.95313836	.30209614	.09180584	.00862897	.00000084
300	.94177018	.22396568	.05053449	.00262996	.00000003
360	.93053759	.16604193	.02781669	.00080156	.00000000
365	.92960762	.16195243	.02646663	.00072600	.00000000

| Table 4 | $s_{\overline{n}|i}$ | Future value of an ordinary annuity of n $1 payments each, immediately after the last payment at compound interest rate of i per period |

				i		
n	1/2 %	3/4 %	1 %	1.5 %	2 %	6 %
1	1.00000000	1.00000000	1.00000000	1.00000000	1.00000000	1.00000000
2	2.00500000	2.00750000	2.01000000	2.01500000	2.02000000	2.06000000
3	3.01502500	3.02255625	3.03010000	3.04522500	3.06040000	3.18360000
4	4.03010013	4.04522542	4.06040100	4.09090337	4.12160800	4.37461600
5	5.05025063	5.07556461	5.10100501	5.15226693	5.20404016	5.63709296
6	6.07550188	6.11363135	6.15201506	6.22955093	6.30812096	6.97531854
7	7.10587939	7.15948358	7.21353521	7.32299419	7.43428338	8.39383765
8	8.14140879	8.21317971	8.28567056	8.43283911	8.58296905	9.89746791
9	9.18211583	9.27477856	9.36852727	9.55933169	9.75462843	11.49131598
10	10.22802641	10.34433940	10.46221254	10.70272167	10.94972100	13.18079494
11	11.27916654	11.42192194	11.56683467	11.86326249	12.16871542	14.97164264
12	12.33556237	12.50758636	12.68250301	13.04121143	13.41208973	16.86994120
13	13.39724018	13.60139325	13.80932804	14.23682960	14.68033152	18.88213767
14	14.46422639	14.70340370	14.94742132	15.45038205	15.97393815	21.01506593
15	15.53654752	15.81367923	16.09689554	16.68213778	17.29341692	23.27596988
16	16.61423026	16.93228183	17.25786449	17.93236984	18.63928525	25.67252808
17	17.69730141	18.05927394	18.43044314	19.20135539	20.01207096	28.21287976
18	18.78578791	19.19471849	19.61474757	20.48937572	21.41231238	30.90565255
19	19.87971685	20.33867888	20.81089504	21.79671636	22.84055863	33.75999170
20	20.97911544	21.49121897	22.01900399	23.12366710	24.29736980	36.78559120
21	22.08401101	22.65240312	23.23919403	24.47052211	25.78331719	39.99272668
22	23.19443107	23.82229614	24.47158598	25.83757994	27.29898354	43.39229028
23	24.31040322	25.00096336	25.71630183	27.22514364	28.84496321	46.99582769
24	25.43195524	26.18847059	26.97346485	28.63352080	30.42186247	50.81557735
25	26.55911502	27.38488412	28.24319950	30.06302361	32.03029972	54.86451200
26	27.69191059	28.59027075	29.52563150	31.51396896	33.67090572	59.15638272
27	28.83037015	29.80469778	30.82088781	32.98667850	35.34432383	63.70576568
28	29.97452200	31.02823301	32.12909669	34.48147867	37.05121031	68.52811162
29	31.12439461	32.26094476	33.45038766	35.99870085	38.79223451	73.63979832
30	32.28001658	33.50290184	34.78489153	37.53868137	40.56807921	79.05818622
36	39.33610496	41.15271612	43.07687836	47.27596921	51.99436719	119.12086666
48	54.09783222	57.52071111	61.22260777	69.56521929	79.35351927	256.56452882
52	59.21803075	63.31106835	67.76889215	77.92489152	90.01640927	328.28142239
60	69.77003051	75.42413693	81.66966986	96.21465171	114.05153942	533.12818089
104	135.96993732	156.68432202	181.46401172	246.93411381	342.09189731	7,122.68438195
120	163.87934681	193.51427708	230.03868946	331.28819149	488.25815171	18,119.79579725
180	290.81871245	378.40576900	499.58019754	905.62451261	1,716.04156785	
240	462.04089516	667.88686993	989.25536539	2,308.85437027	5,744.43675765	
300	692.99396243	1,121.12193732	1,878.84662619	5,737.25330834	18,961.72540308	
360	1,004.51504245	1,830.74348307	3,494.96413277	14,113.58539279	62,328.05638744	
365	1,034.93055669	1,905.50947396	3,678.34343329	15,209.49204803	68,820.41459830	

Table 5	1/s $_{\overline{n}|i}$ Rent per period for an ordinary annuity of n payments, with compound interest rate i per period, and future value $1

				i		
n	1/2 %	3/4 %	1 %	1.5 %	2 %	6 %
1	1.00000000	1.00000000	1.00000000	1.00000000	1.00000000	1.00000000
2	.49875312	.49813200	.49751244	.49627792	.49504950	.48543689
3	.33167221	.33084579	.33002211	.32838296	.32675467	.31410981
4	.24813279	.24720501	.24628109	.24444479	.24262375	.22859149
5	.19800997	.19702242	.19603980	.19408932	.19215839	.17739640
6	.16459546	.16356891	.16254837	.16052521	.15852581	.14336263
7	.14072854	.13967488	.13862828	.13655616	.13451196	.11913502
8	.12282886	.12175552	.12069029	.11858402	.11650980	.10103594
9	.10890736	.10781929	.10674036	.10460982	.10251544	.08702224
10	.09777057	.09667123	.09558208	.09343418	.09132653	.07586796
11	.08865903	.08755094	.08645408	.08429384	.08217794	.06679294
12	.08106643	.07995148	.07884879	.07667999	.07455960	.05927703
13	.07464224	.07352188	.07241482	.07024036	.06811835	.05296011
14	.06913609	.06801146	.06690117	.06472332	.06260197	.04758491
15	.06436436	.06323639	.06212378	.05994436	.05782547	.04296276
16	.06018937	.05905879	.05794460	.05576508	.05365013	.03895214
17	.05650579	.05537321	.05425806	.05207966	.04996984	.03544480
18	.05323173	.05209766	.05098205	.04880578	.04670210	.03235654
19	.05030253	.04916740	.04805175	.04587847	.04378177	.02962086
20	.04766645	.04653063	.04541531	.04324574	.04115672	.02718456
21	.04528163	.04414543	.04303075	.04086550	.03878477	.02500455
22	.04311380	.04197748	.04086372	.03870332	.03663140	.02304557
23	.04113465	.03999846	.03888584	.03673075	.03466810	.02127848
24	.03932061	.03818474	.03707347	.03492410	.03287110	.01967900
25	.03765186	.03651650	.03540675	.03326345	.03122044	.01822672
26	.03611163	.03497693	.03386888	.03173196	.02969923	.01690435
27	.03468565	.03355176	.03244553	.03031527	.02829309	.01569717
28	.03336167	.03222871	.03112444	.02900108	.02698967	.01459255
29	.03212914	.03099723	.02989502	.02777878	.02577836	.01357961
30	.03097892	.02984816	.02874811	.02663919	.02464992	.01264891
36	.02542194	.02429973	.02321431	.02115240	.01923285	.00839483
48	.01848503	.01738504	.01633384	.01437500	.01260184	.00389765
52	.01688675	.01579503	.01475603	.01283287	.01110909	.00304617
60	.01433280	.01325836	.01224445	.01039343	.00876797	.00187572
104	.00735457	.00638226	.00551073	.00404966	.00292319	.00014040
120	00610205	.00516758	.00434709	.00301852	.00204810	.00005519
180	.00343857	.00264267	.00200168	.00110421	.00058274	.00000167
240	.00216431	.00149726	.00101086	.00043312	.00017408	.00000005
300	.00144301	.00089196	.00053224	.00017430	.00005274	.00000000
360	.00099551	.00054623	.00028613	.00007085	.00001604	.00000000
365	.00096625	.00052479	.00027186	.00006575	.00001453	.00000000

Table 6	$a_{\overline{n}|i}$ Present value of an ordinary annuity of n payments of $1 one period before the first payment, with interest compounded at i per period

				i		
n	1/2%	3/4%	1%	1.5%	2%	6%
1	.99502488	.99255583	.99009901	.98522167	.98039216	.94339623
2	1.98509938	1.97772291	1.97039506	1.95588342	1.94156094	1.83339267
3	2.97024814	2.95555624	2.94098521	2.91220042	2.88388327	2.67301195
4	3.95049566	3.92611041	3.90196555	3.85438465	3.80772870	3.46510561
5	4.92586633	4.88943961	4.85343124	4.78264497	4.71345951	4.21236379
6	5.89638441	5.84559763	5.79547647	5.69718717	5.60143089	4.91732433
7	6.86207404	6.79463785	6.72819453	6.59821396	6.47199107	5.58238144
8	7.82295924	7.73661325	7.65167775	7.48592508	7.32548144	6.20979381
9	8.77906392	8.67157642	8.56601758	8.36051732	8.16223671	6.80169227
10	9.73041186	9.59957958	9.47130453	9.22218455	8.98258501	7.36008705
11	10.67702673	10.52067452	10.36762825	10.07111779	9.78684805	7.88687458
12	11.61893207	11.43491267	11.25507747	10.90750521	10.57534122	8.38384394
13	12.55615131	12.34234508	12.13374007	11.73153222	11.34837375	8.85268296
14	13.48870777	13.24302242	13.00370304	12.54338150	12.10624877	9.29498393
15	14.41662465	14.13699495	13.86505252	13.34323301	12.84926350	9.71224899
16	15.33992502	15.02431261	14.71787378	14.13126405	13.57770931	10.10589527
17	16.25863186	15.90502492	15.56225127	14.90764931	14.29187188	10.47725969
18	17.17276802	16.77918107	16.39826858	15.67256089	14.99203125	10.82760348
19	18.08235624	17.64682984	17.22600850	16.42616837	15.67846201	11.15811649
20	18.98741915	18.50801969	18.04555297	17.16863879	16.35143334	11.46992122
21	19.88797925	19.36279870	18.85698313	17.90013673	17.01120916	11.76407662
22	20.78405896	20.21121459	19.66037934	18.62082437	17.65804820	12.04158172
23	21.67568055	21.05331473	20.45582113	19.33086145	18.29220412	12.30337898
24	22.56286622	21.88914614	21.24338726	20.03040537	18.91392560	12.55035753
25	23.44563803	22.71875547	22.02315570	20.71961120	19.52345647	12.78335616
26	24.32401794	23.54218905	22.79520366	21.39863172	20.12103576	13.00316619
27	25.19802780	24.35949286	23.55960759	22.06761746	20.70689780	13.21053414
28	26.06768936	25.17071251	24.31644316	22.72671671	21.28127236	13.40616428
29	26.93302423	25.97589331	25.06578530	23.37607558	21.84438466	13.59072102
30	27.79405397	26.77508021	25.80770822	24.01583801	22.39645555	13.76483115
36	32.87101624	31.44680525	30.10750504	27.66068431	25.48884248	14.62098713
48	42.58031778	40.18478189	37.97395949	34.04255365	30.67311957	15.65002661
52	45.68974664	42.92761812	40.39419423	35.92874185	32.14494992	15.86139252
60	51.72556075	48.17337352	44.95503841	39.38026889	34.76088668	16.16142771
104	80.94172854	72.03438325	64.47147918	52.49436634	43.62394373	16.62775868
120	90.07345333	78.94169267	69.70052203	55.49845411	45.35538850	16.65135068
180	118.50351467	98.59340884	83.32166399	62.09556231	48.58440478	16.66620237
240	139.58077168	111.14495403	90.81941635	64.79573209	49.56855168	16.66665259
300	155.20686401	119.16162216	94.94655125	65.90090069	49.86850220	16.66666624
360	166.79161439	124.28186568	97.21833108	66.35324174	49.95992180	16.66666665
365	167.60951473	124.61379021	97.35333747	66.37572674	49.96369994	16.66666666

| Table 7 | 1/a$_{\overline{n}|i}$ Rent per period for an ordinary annuity of n payments whose present value is $1, with interest compounded at i per period |

			i			
n	1/2 %	3/4 %	1 %	1.5 %	2 %	6 %
1	1.00500000	1.00750000	1.01000000	1.01500000	1.02000000	1.06000000
2	.50375312	.50563200	.50751244	.51127792	.51504950	.54543689
3	.33667221	.33834579	.34002211	.34338296	.34675467	.37410981
4	.25313279	.25470501	.25628109	.25944479	.26262375	.28859149
5	.20300997	.20452242	.20603980	.20908932	.21215839	.23739640
6	.16959546	.17106891	.17254837	.17552521	.17852581	.20336263
7	.14572854	.14717488	.14862828	.15155616	.15451196	.17913502
8	.12782886	.12925552	.13069029	.13358402	.13650980	.16103594
9	.11390736	.11531929	.11674036	.11960982	.12251544	.14702224
10	.10277057	.10417123	.10558208	.10843418	.11132653	.13586796
11	.09365903	.09505094	.09645408	.09929384	.10217794	.12679294
12	.08606643	.08745148	.08884879	.09167999	.09455960	.11927703
13	.07964224	.08102188	.08241482	.08524036	.08811835	.11296011
14	.07413609	.07551146	.07690117	.07972332	.08260197	.10758491
15	.06936436	.07073639	.07212378	.07494436	.07782547	.10296276
16	.06518937	.06655879	.06794460	.07076508	.07365013	.09895214
17	.06150579	.06287321	.06425806	.06707966	.06996984	.09544480
18	.05823173	.05959766	.06098205	.06380578	.06670210	.09235654
19	.05530253	.05666740	.05805175	.06087847	.06378177	.08962086
20	.05266645	.05403063	.05541531	.05824574	.06115672	.08718456
21	.05028163	.05164543	.05303075	.05586550	.05878477	.08500455
22	.04811380	.04947748	.05086372	.05370332	.05663140	.08304557
23	.04613465	.04749846	.04888584	.05173075	.05466810	.08127848
24	.04432061	.04568474	.04707347	.04992410	.05287110	.07967900
25	.04265186	.04401650	.04540675	.04826345	.05122044	.07822672
26	.04111163	.04247693	.04386888	.04673196	.04969923	.07690435
27	.03968565	.04105176	.04244553	.04531527	.04829309	.07569717
28	.03836167	.03972871	.04112444	.04400108	.04698967	.07459255
29	.03712914	.03849723	.03989502	.04277878	.04577836	.07357961
30	.03597892	.03734816	.03874811	.04163919	.04464992	.07264891
36	.03042194	.03179973	.03321431	.03615240	.03923285	.06839483
48	.02348503	.02488504	.02633384	.02937500	.03260184	.06389765
52	.02188675	.02329503	.02475603	.02783287	.03110909	.06304617
60	.01933280	.02075836	.02224445	.02539343	.02876797	.06187572
104	.01235457	.01388226	.01551073	.01904966	.02292319	.06014040
120	.01110205	.01266758	.01434709	.01801852	.02204810	.06005519
180	.00843857	.01014267	.01200168	.01610421	.02058274	.06000167
240	.00716431	.00899726	.01101086	.01543312	.02017408	.06000005
300	.00644301	.00839196	.01053224	.01517430	.02005274	.06000000
360	.00599551	.00804623	.01028613	.01507085	.02001604	.06000000
365	.00596625	.00802479	.01027186	.01506575	.02001453	.06000000

Appendix B

USING THE TI-82 AND TI-83* GRAPHING CALCULATORS

B.1 Functions

Functions are graphed in a rectangular window like the one shown in Fig. 1. The numbers on the x-axis range from **Xmin** to **Xmax**, and the numbers on the y-axis range from **Ymin** to **Ymax**. The distances between tick marks are **Xscl** and **Yscl** on the x- and y-axes, respectively. To specify these quantities, press $\boxed{\text{WINDOW}}$ and type in the values of the six variables. Figure 2 gives the settings associated with the window in Fig. 4. The axis ranges corresponding to this setting are often denoted by $[-4, 4]$ *by* $[-5, 8]$. (*Note*: To enter a negative number, use the $\boxed{(-)}$ key on the bottom row of the calculator.)

To specify functions, press the $\boxed{\text{Y=}}$ key and type expressions next to the function names $\mathbf{Y_1}, \mathbf{Y_2}, \ldots$. (*Note*: To erase an expression, use the arrow keys to move the cursor anywhere on the expression, and press $\boxed{\text{CLEAR}}$.) In the screen of Fig. 3, called the "**Y=** editor," several functions have been specified. (The TI-82 **Y=** editor does not have the first row or the slash marks shown in Fig. 3.) The expressions were produced with the following keystrokes on the TI-83:

---

*All instructions for the TI-83 graphing calculator also apply to the TI-83 Plus.

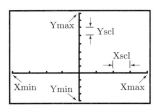

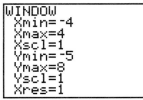

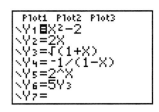

Figure 1. Typical window

Figure 2. TI-83 Settings for Fig. 4

Figure 3. TI-83 Function declarations

Y_1: $\boxed{\text{X,T,}\theta,n}$ $\boxed{x^2}$ $\boxed{-}$ **2**

Y_2: **2** $\boxed{\text{X,T,}\theta,n}$ (Notice that a multiplication sign is not needed.)

Y_3: $\boxed{\text{2nd}}$ $\boxed{\sqrt{\ }}$ **1** $\boxed{+}$ $\boxed{\text{X,T,}\theta,n}$ $\boxed{)}$

Y_4: $\boxed{(-)}$ **1** $\boxed{\div}$ $\boxed{(}$ **1** $\boxed{-}$ $\boxed{\text{X,T,}\theta,n}$ $\boxed{)}$

Y_5: **2** $\boxed{\wedge}$ $\boxed{\text{X,T,}\theta,n}$ ($\wedge$ is the symbol for exponentiation.)

Y_6: **5** $\boxed{\text{VARS}}$ $\boxed{\blacktriangleright}$ **1 3**   (The standard method for entering a function.)

The analogous keystrokes with the TI-82 are

Y_1: $\boxed{\text{X,T,}\theta}$ $\boxed{x^2}$ $\boxed{-}$ **2**

Y_2: **2** $\boxed{\text{X,T,}\theta}$ (Notice that a multiplication sign is not needed.)

Y_3: $\boxed{\text{2nd}}$ $\boxed{\sqrt{\ }}$ $\boxed{(}$ **1** $\boxed{+}$ $\boxed{\text{X,T,}\theta}$ $\boxed{)}$

Y_4: $\boxed{(-)}$ **1** $\boxed{\div}$ $\boxed{(}$ **1** $\boxed{-}$ $\boxed{\text{X,T,}\theta}$ $\boxed{)}$

Y_5: **2** $\boxed{\wedge}$ $\boxed{\text{X,T,}\theta}$ ($\wedge$ is the symbol for exponentiation.)

Y_6: **5** $\boxed{\text{2nd}}$ $\boxed{\text{Y-VARS}}$ **1 3**   (The standard method for entering a function.)

Notice that in Fig. 3 the equal sign in Y_1 is highlighted, whereas the other equal signs are not highlighted. This highlighting can be toggled by moving the cursor to an equal sign and pressing $\boxed{\text{ENTER}}$. Functions with highlighted equal signs are said to be *selected*. Pressing the $\boxed{\text{GRAPH}}$ key instructs the calculator to graph all selected functions. (*Note*: On the TI-83, the words **Plot1 Plot2 Plot3** on the first row are used for statistical plots. The backslash symbol preceding each function is used to specify one of seven possible styles for the graph of the function.)

Press $\boxed{\text{GRAPH}}$ to obtain Fig. 4. Then press $\boxed{\text{TRACE}}$ and press $\boxed{\blacktriangleright}$, the right-arrow, 29 times to obtain Fig. 5. (On the TI-82 the function definition in the upper left corner does not appear. Instead, the number 1 appears in the upper right corner.) Each time a right- or left-arrow key is pressed, the trace cursor moves along the curve and the coordinates of the trace cursor are displayed.

To approximate the function value for a specific value of x, move the trace cursor as close as possible to the value of x and read the y-coordinate of the point. For a more precise function value, press $\boxed{\text{2nd}}$ [CALC] **1**, type in a value for **X** (such as 2.5), and press $\boxed{\text{ENTER}}$. See Fig. 6. (With a TI-83, you can just enter 2.5 without first pressing $\boxed{\text{2nd}}$ [CALC] **1**.)

A point where the graph crosses the x-axis is called an *x-intercept*. The coordinates of an x-intercept can be approximated by tracing. The x-coordinate of an x-intercept is called a *zero* of the function Y_1 or a *root* of the equation $Y_1 = 0$. Figure 4 shows that Y_1 has a zero between 1 and 2 and the value of the zero is about 1.5. For a precise value of the zero, press $\boxed{\text{2nd}}$ [CALC] **2** and answer the questions. Reply to **"Left Bound?"** by moving the trace cursor to a point whose x-coordinate is less than the root and pressing $\boxed{\text{ENTER}}$. See Fig. 7. Reply

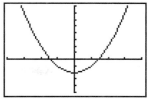
Figure 4.
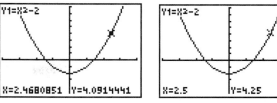
Figure 5.   Figure 6.

to **"Right Bound?"** by moving the trace cursor to a point whose x-coordinate is greater than the root and pressing ENTER. See Fig. 8. Reply to **"Guess?"** by moving the trace cursor near the x-intercept and pressing ENTER. Figure 9 shows the resulting display. (With the TI-83, an alternate way to find a zero of a function is to reply to the questions by entering appropriate numbers. For instance, after pressing 2nd [CALC] **2**, respond to **"Left Bound?"** by typing in the number 1 and pressing ENTER, respond to **"Right Bound?"** by typing in the number 2 and pressing ENTER, and respond to **"Guess?"** by typing in the number 1.5 and pressing ENTER. The final screen will be identical to Fig. 9.)

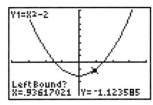
Figure 7.
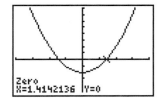
Figure 8.   Figure 9.

So far, all operations were carried out while looking at the graph of a function. These same operations also can be carried out in the home screen, which is invoked by pressing 2nd [QUIT]. For instance, the function Y_1 can be evaluated at 4 by entering $Y_1(4)$ and pressing ENTER.

Return to the **Y=** editor by pressing Y= and then select Y_2 so that now both Y_1 and Y_2 are selected. Press GRAPH to obtain the graphs of the two functions. Press TRACE and then press the right-arrow key several times. Now press the down-arrow key several times. Each time the down-arrow key is pressed, the trace cursor moves from one curve to the other. The identity of the function containing the cursor is given in the upper left or upper right part of the screen. Move the cursor as close as possible to the point of intersection of the two curves to approximate the coordinates of the intersection point. For more precise values, press 2nd [CALC] **5** and answer the questions. Reply to **"First curve?"** by moving the trace cursor to one of the curves and pressing ENTER. Reply to **"Second curve?"** by moving the trace cursor to the other curve and pressing ENTER. Reply to **"Guess?"** by either moving the trace cursor near the point of intersection or typing in a number close to the x-coordinate of the point and pressing ENTER. Figure 10 shows the resulting display.

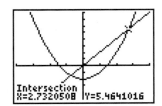
Figure 10.

B.2 Tables

When you press 2nd [TABLE], a table of function values is displayed with a column for each selected function. (If more than two functions are selected, you must press the right-arrow key to see the third and later functions.) Prior to invoking a table, you should press $\boxed{\text{2nd}}$ [TblSet] to specify certain properties of the table. See Fig. 11. The values for **X** will begin with the setting of **TblStart** (**TblMin** on the TI-82) and increase by the setting of ΔTbl. For our purposes, the settings for **Indpnt** and **Depend** should always be **Auto**. After you press $\boxed{\text{2nd}}$ [TABLE] to display the table (see Fig. 12), you can use the up- and down-arrow keys to generate further terms.

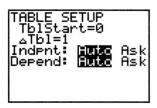

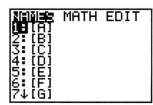

Figure 11.   Figure 12.   Figure 13.

B.3 Matrices

The TI-82 can store up to 5 matrices, and the TI-83 can store as many as 10. The matrices are referred to as $[\mathbf{A}], [\mathbf{B}], [\mathbf{C}], \ldots$. Pressing $\boxed{\text{MATRX}}$ produces the screen in Fig. 13 with the three menus **NAMES**, **MATH**, and **EDIT**. The **NAMES** menu is used to display the name of a matrix on the home screen, the **MATH** menu is used to perform certain operations on a single matrix, and the **EDIT** menu is used to define a new matrix or alter an existing matrix.

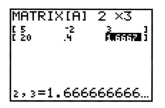

Figure 14.

To create a new matrix   Press $\boxed{\text{MATRX}}$ $\boxed{\blacktriangleleft}$ to call up the **MATRIX EDIT** menu, and then press a number corresponding to one of the unused matrix names to obtain a matrix-entry screen. Type in the number of rows, press $\boxed{\text{ENTER}}$, type in the number of columns, and press $\boxed{\text{ENTER}}$ to specify the size of the matrix. Then type in the first entry of the matrix, press $\boxed{\text{ENTER}}$, type in the next entry of the matrix, press $\boxed{\text{ENTER}}$, and so on until all entries have been entered. See Fig. 14.

To alter an existing matrix   Press $\boxed{\text{MATRX}}$ $\boxed{\blacktriangleleft}$ to call up the **MATRIX EDIT** menu, and then press a number corresponding to one of the matrix names to be altered. Move the cursor to any entry you want to change, type in the new number, and press $\boxed{\text{ENTER}}$. You can change as many entries as you like, even the number of rows and columns.

To delete a matrix   With a TI-83, press $\boxed{\text{2nd}}$ [MEM] **2 5** to obtain a list of all matrices that have been created. (On a TI-82, press $\boxed{\text{2nd}}$ [MEM] **2 4**.) Use the down-arrow key to select the desired matrix, and then press $\boxed{\text{ENTER}}$.

To display the name of a matrix on the home screen   Press $\boxed{\text{MATRX}}$ to obtain a list of all matrix names. Use the down-arrow key to select the desired matrix, and then press $\boxed{\text{ENTER}}$. Alternately, from the **MATRX NAMES** menu, type the number associated with the matrix.

B.4 Lists

A list can be thought of as a sequence or an ordered set of up to 999 numbers. Although lists can have custom names, we will use the built-in names $\mathbf{L_1}, \mathbf{L_2}, \ldots, \mathbf{L_6}$ that are found above the numeric keys. To display $\mathbf{L_1}$ on the home screen, press

2nd [L₁]. The elements of list **L₁** can be referred to as $L_1(1), L_1(2), L_1(3), \ldots$. A set of numbers can be placed into a list by enclosing them with parentheses and storing them in the list. However, often the stat list editor provides the best way to place numbers into lists and to view lists.

To invoke the stat list editor, press STAT **1**. Initially, the stat list editor has columns labeled **L₁**, **L₂**, and **L₃**. See Fig. 15. Three more columns for lists are off the screen.

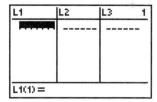

Figure 15.

Figure 16.

To place a number into a list in the stat list editor   Move the cursor to the dashed line, type in the number, and press either the down-arrow key or the ENTER key.

To remove a number from a list in the stat list editor   Move the cursor to the number and press DEL.

To delete all numbers in a list from the stat list editor   Move the cursor to the list name at the top of the screen and press CLEAR ENTER.

To create a scatterplot of a set of points whose x-coordinates are in L₁ and whose y-coordinates are in L₂   Press 2nd [STAT PLOT] **1**, create the screen in Fig. 16, and press GRAPH. (*Note*: Check that the window settings are adequate for displaying the points.)

B.5 Histograms

The following steps display a frequency histogram with rectangles centered above the integers $a, a + 1, \ldots, b$.

- Press STAT **1** to invoke the list editing screen shown in Fig. 15.
- Enter each number from a to b having nonzero frequency in the **L₁** column and its associated frequency to its right in the **L₂** column. Or, ignore the **L₂** column and place each number (repeated according to its frequency) in the **L₁** column.
- Press 2nd [STAT PLOT] **1** to invoke a screen similar to Fig. 16.
- Select "On" in the second line, the histogram icon in the Type line, and **L₁** in the Xlist line. If you ignored the **L₂** column in the second step, place 1 in the Ylist line; otherwise, place **L₂** in the Ylist line.
- Press WINDOW to invoke the window screen in Fig. 2.
- Set Xmin = $a - .5$, Xmax = $b + .5$, Xscl = 1, Ymin ≈ $-.3*$(greatest frequency), Ymax ≈ $1.2*$(greatest frequency), Yscl ≈ $.1*$(greatest frequency). *Note*: The Y settings allow ample space for the display of values while tracing.

- Press $\boxed{\text{GRAPH}}$ to view the histogram.
- To view the height of a rectangle, press $\boxed{\text{TRACE}}$ and use the arrow keys to move the cursor to the top center of the rectangle. The values of *min*, *max*, and n will be the x-coordinate of the left side of the rectangle, the x-coordinate of the right side of the rectangle, and the height of the rectangle, respectively.

With a TI-83 graphing calculator, a relative frequency histogram can be displayed by placing the relative frequencies in the $\mathbf{L}_2$ column of the list editor. If so, the *greatest relative frequency* should be used in place of the *greatest frequency* when setting the values of Ymin, Ymax, and YScl.

Answers to Exercises

CHAPTER 1

Exercises 1.1

1., 3., 5.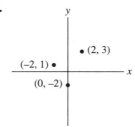

7.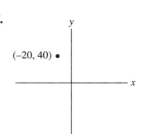

9. (e)

11. $m = 5, b = 8$ **13.** $m = 0, b = 3$ **15.** $y = -2x + 3$ **17.** $x = \dfrac{5}{3}$

19. $(2, 0), (0, 8)$ **21.** $(7, 0)$, none

23. 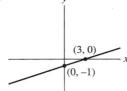   **25.**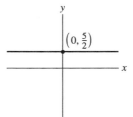

27.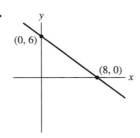

29. (a), (b), (c), (e)   **31.** (a) L_3 (b) L_1 (c) L_2

33. (a) 4 minutes, 40 seconds   (b) 72° water was placed in the kettle.   (c) No

35. (a)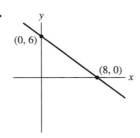

(b) In 1960, 2.5 trillion cigarettes were sold.

(c) 1980   (d) 7 trillion

37. Up   **39.** $y = 0$ **41.** No

Exercises 1.2

1. False   **3.** True   **5.** $x \geq 4$ **7.** $x \geq 3$ **9.** $y \leq -2x + 5$ **11.** $y \geq 15x - 18$ **13.** $x \geq -\dfrac{3}{4}$ **15.** Yes

17. No   **19.** Yes   **21.** Yes

23. 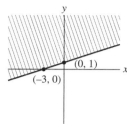   **25.** 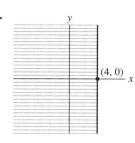   **27.** 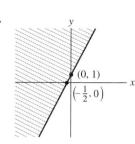   **29.**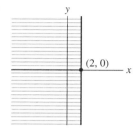

31. 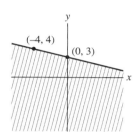   **33.** 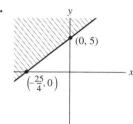   **35.** 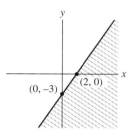   **37.**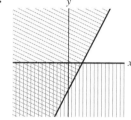

39. 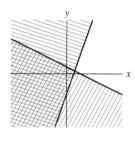   **41.**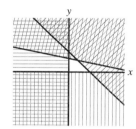

43. Yes   **45.** No   **47.** Below   **49.** Above   **51.** $\begin{cases} y \geq 2x - 1 \\ y \leq 2x \end{cases}$ **53.** (d)   **55.** (e)   **57.** (a) $(6, 2.5)$ (b) Above

59.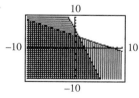

Exercises 1.3

1. $(2, 3)$ **3.** $(2, 1)$ **5.** $(12, 3)$ **7.** Yes   **9.** $x = \dfrac{10}{3}, y = \dfrac{1}{3}$ **11.** $x = -\dfrac{7}{9}, y = -\dfrac{22}{9}$ **13.** $A = (3, 4), B = (6, 2)$

15. $A = (0, 0), B = (2, 4), C = \left(5, \dfrac{11}{2}\right), D = (5, 0)$

17. 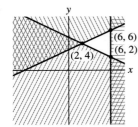   **19.** 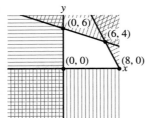   **21.**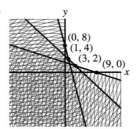

23. (a) $2.00   (b) $.05 or less   **25.** 29,500 units; $3.00   **27.** Working: 32; Supervising: 8   **29.** (c)   **31.** (3.73, 2.23)

33. (2.68, 1.92)   **35.** (a)   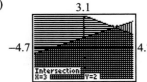   (b) (3, 2)   (c)   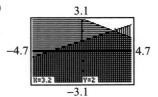   (d) No

Exercises 1.4

1. $\dfrac{2}{3}$ **3.** 5   **5.** 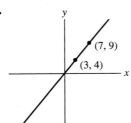 $\dfrac{5}{4}$ **7.** 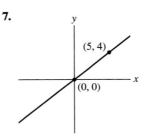 $\dfrac{4}{5}$ **9.** Undefined

11. 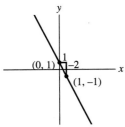   **13.** 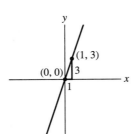   **15.** $y = -2x + 7$ **17.** $y = -2x + 4$

19. $y = \dfrac{1}{4}x + \dfrac{3}{2}$ **21.** $y = -x$ **23.** $y = 3$ **25.** (0, 3)

27. Each unit sold yields a commission of $5. In addition, she receives $60 per week base pay.

29. (a) (0, 1200); at $1200 no one will buy the item.   (b) (400, 0); even if the item is given away, only 400 will be taken.

(c) -3; to sell an additional item, the price must be reduced by $3.   (d) $150   (e) 300 items

(f)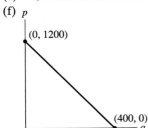

31. (a) $y = 90x + 5000$ (b) $5000   (c) $90   (d)

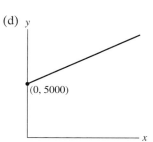
(0, 5000)

33. (a) $30,000   (b) 60 coats   (c) $(0, 0)$; if no coats are sold, there is no revenue.
(d) 100; each additional coat yields an additional $100 in revenue.   **35.**

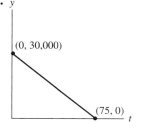
(0, 30,000)
(75, 0)

37. 12,000 gallons

39. $(75, 0)$; the tank is empty after 75 days.   **41.** $50,000   **43.** $\left(15\frac{1}{3}, 0\right)$; the cash reserves will be depleted after $15\frac{1}{3}$ days.

45. July 11   **47.** 3   **49.** 1400 hours   **51.** $260   **53.** $y = 3x - 1$ **55.** $y = x + 1$ **57.** $y = -7x + 35$ **59.** $y = 4$

61. $y = \frac{1}{2}x$ **63.** $y = -2x$ **65.** 5; 1; -1 **67.** $-\frac{5}{4}; -\frac{3}{2}; -\frac{3}{4}$ **69.** (a) (C)   (b) (B)   (c) (D)   (d) (A)

71. $F = \frac{9}{5}C + 32$ **73.** $y = 182x + 2035$; $2763   **75.** Counterclockwise   **77.** $y \geq 4x + 3$ **79.** $\begin{cases} y \leq -\frac{1}{2}x + 4 \\ y \leq -x + 5 \\ y \geq x - 3 \\ x \geq 0, y \geq 0 \end{cases}$

81. $k = 9$ **83.** $a = -.05$ **87.** (c)   **89.** (e)   **91.** (c)   **93.** (d)

95.
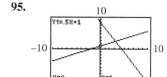
Do not appear perpendicular   **97.**
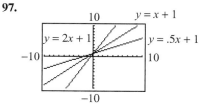
99. 1.5 units

Exercises 1.5

1. 4   **3.** 6.70   **5.** $m = -1.4; b = 8.5$ **7.** $y = 4.5x - 3$ **9.** $y = -2x + 11.5$
11. (a) $y = .338x + 21.6$ (b) About 393   **13.** (a) $y = .394x + 14.4$ (b) About 21.5%   (c) 2007
15. (a) $y = .804x + 21.3$ (b) About 82.4 years   (c) About 72.4 years   **17.** Yes

Chapter 1: Supplementary Exercises

1. $x = 0$ **2.** 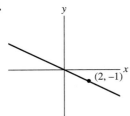   **3.** $\left(2, -\dfrac{4}{5}\right)$ **4.** $\dfrac{3}{4}$ **5.** $y = -\dfrac{1}{2}x + 5$ **6.**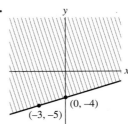

7. Yes   **8.** $(3, 5)$ **9.** $y = \dfrac{1}{5}x + 13$ **10.** 10 **11.** $(5, 0)$ **12.** 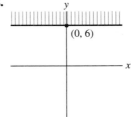   **13.** $(7, 10)$

14. 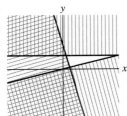   **15.** $(0, 7)$ **16.** The rate is \$35 per hour plus a flat fee of \$20.   **17.** No

18. $y = \dfrac{2}{3}x - 2$ **19.** (d)   **20.** $y \le \dfrac{2}{3}x + \dfrac{3}{2}$ **21.** $y \ge 2.4x - 5.8$ **22.** $x = -.3, y = .4$ **23.** $y = -\dfrac{2}{5}x + \dfrac{7}{5}$

24. $x \ge \dfrac{6}{5}$ **25.** $m = -2$; y-intercept: $(0, 8)$; x-intercept: $(4, 0)$;   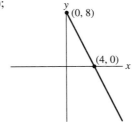   **26.** No

28. (a) (C)   (b) (A)   (c) (B)   (d) (D)   **29.** (a) L_3 (b) L_1 (c) L_2 **30.** $\begin{cases} y \le -\frac{7}{8}x + 5 \\ y \ge \frac{8}{7}x - \frac{43}{14} \\ x \ge 0, y \ge 0 \end{cases}$; $\left(\dfrac{43}{16}, 0\right)$

31. 300 units; \$2   **32.** $(0, 0), (10, 0), (9, 5), (6, 7), (0, 4)$ **33.** $y = x + \dfrac{5}{2}$

34. (a) $y = 10x - 6000$ (b) x-intercept: $(600, 0)$, y-intercept: $(0, -6000)$ (c)

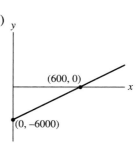

35. (a) A: $y = .1x + 50$; B: $y = .2x + 40$ (b) B   (c) A   (d) 100 miles   **36.** (a) $y = -500x + 5000$

(b) \$3000   (c) 1992   **37.**   **38.** \$5000   **39.** $\begin{cases} y \le \frac{5}{4}x + 5 \\ y \le -\frac{2}{5}x + 2 \\ y \ge \frac{3}{5}x - 3 \\ y \ge -\frac{5}{2}x - 5 \end{cases}$ **40.** $\begin{cases} y \le -\frac{2}{3}x + 2 \\ y \ge -3 \\ x \ge -2 \\ x \le 4 \end{cases}$

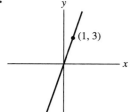

41. (a) $y = .34x + 9.6$ (b) 11.3%   (c) 2002   **42.** (a) $y = .152x - 3.063$ (b) About 21   (c) About 165 grams

Chapter 1: Chapter Test

1.

2. 5   **3.** $y = -2x + 1$ **4.** $(6, 1)$ **6.**

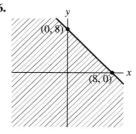

7. $y = 2x - \dfrac{71}{11}$ **8.** $(16, 0)$; $(25, 0)$; $(13, 36)$; $(2, 14)$ **9.** Less than \$2500; greater than \$2500

CHAPTER 2

Exercises 2.1

1. $\xrightarrow{\ 2[1]\ } \begin{cases} x - 6y = 4 \\ 5x + 4y = 1 \end{cases}$ **3.** $\xrightarrow{\ [2]+5[1]\ } \begin{cases} x + 2y = 3 \\ 14y = 16 \end{cases}$ **5.** $\xrightarrow{\ [3]+(-4)[1]\ } \begin{cases} x - 2y + z = 0 \\ y - 2z = 4 \\ 9y - z = 5 \end{cases}$

7. $\xrightarrow{\ [1]+\frac{1}{2}[2]\ } \begin{bmatrix} 1 & 0 & 5 \\ 0 & 1 & 4 \end{bmatrix}$ **9.** $[2] + 2[1]$ **11.** $[1] + (-2)[2]$ **13.** Interchange rows 1 and 2 or rows 1 and 3

15. $[1] + (-3)[3]$ **17.** $x = -1, y = 1$ **19.** $x = -\dfrac{8}{7}, y = -\dfrac{9}{7}, z = -\dfrac{3}{7}$ **21.** $x = -1, y = 1$ **23.** $x = 1, y = 2, z = -1$

25. $x = -2.5, y = 15$ **27.** $x = 1, y = -6, z = 2$ **29.** $x = -1, y = -2, z = 5$ **31.** (b)   **33.** 137 adults, 463 children
35. $x = \$25{,}000, y = \$50{,}000, z = \$25{,}000$ **41.** $x = 3, y = -3, z = 2, w = -4$

Exercises 2.2

1. $\begin{bmatrix} 1 & -2 & 3 \\ 0 & 13 & -8 \end{bmatrix}$ **3.** $\begin{bmatrix} 9 & -1 & 0 & -7 \\ -\frac{1}{2} & \frac{1}{2} & 1 & 3 \\ 5 & -1 & 0 & -3 \end{bmatrix}$ **5.** $\begin{bmatrix} 1 & \frac{3}{2} \\ 0 & -9 \\ 0 & \frac{7}{2} \end{bmatrix}$ **7.** $\begin{bmatrix} 4 & 3 & 0 \\ 1 & 1 & 0 \\ \frac{1}{6} & \frac{1}{2} & 1 \end{bmatrix}$ **9.** y = any value, $x = 3 + 2y$

11. $x = 1, y = 2$ **13.** No solution   **15.** z = any value, $x = -6 - z, y = 5$ **17.** No solution
19. z = any value, w = any value, $x = 2z + w, y = 5 - 3w$ **21.** $x = 5, y = 7$
23. Possible answers: $z = 0, x = -13, y = 9; z = 1, x = -8, y = 6; z = 2, x = -3, y = 3$
25. Possible answers: $y = 0, x = 23, z = 5; y = 1, x = 16, z = 5; y = 2, x = 9, z = 5$
27. x = food 1, y = food 2, z = food 3: z = any amount, $x = 300 - z, y = 100 - z$ $(0 \le z \le 100)$
29. 6 floral squares, the other 90 any mix of solid green and solid blue.   **31.** $x = \pm1, y = \pm2, z = \pm3$
33. No solution if $k \ne -12$. Infinitely many if $k = -12$.   **35.** None   **37.** $(5, 6)$
39. z = any value, $x = 11 - 21z, y = -6 + 12z$ **41.** No solution

Exercises 2.3

1. 2×3 **3.** 1×3, row matrix   **5.** 1×1, square matrix   **7.** $\begin{bmatrix} 9 & 3 \\ 7 & -1 \end{bmatrix}$ **9.** $\begin{bmatrix} 1 & 3 \\ 1 & 2 \\ 4 & -2 \end{bmatrix}$ **11.** $[11]$ **13.** $[10]$

15. Yes; 3×5 **17.** No   **19.** Yes; 3×1 **21.** $\begin{bmatrix} 6 & 17 \\ 6 & 10 \end{bmatrix}$ **23.** $\begin{bmatrix} 21 \\ -4 \\ 8 \end{bmatrix}$ **25.** $\begin{bmatrix} 5 & 6 \\ 7 & 8 \end{bmatrix}$ **27.** $\begin{bmatrix} .48 & .39 \\ .52 & .61 \end{bmatrix}$

29. $\begin{bmatrix} 25 & 17 & 2 \\ 3 & -1 & 2 \\ 1 & 1 & 4 \end{bmatrix}$ **31.** $\begin{cases} 2x + 3y = 6 \\ 4x + 5y = 7 \end{cases}$ **33.** $\begin{cases} x + 2y + 3z = 10 \\ 4x + 5y + 6z = 11 \\ 7x + 8y + 9z = 12 \end{cases}$ **35.** $\begin{bmatrix} 3 & 2 \\ 7 & -1 \end{bmatrix}\begin{bmatrix} x \\ y \end{bmatrix} = \begin{bmatrix} -1 \\ 2 \end{bmatrix}$

37. $\begin{bmatrix} 1 & -2 & 3 \\ 0 & 1 & 1 \\ 0 & 0 & 1 \end{bmatrix}\begin{bmatrix} x \\ y \\ z \end{bmatrix} = \begin{bmatrix} 5 \\ 6 \\ 2 \end{bmatrix}$ **43.** (a) $\begin{bmatrix} 340 \\ 265 \end{bmatrix}$ (b) Mike's clothes cost \$340; Don's clothes cost \$265.

45. (a) I: 2.75, II: 2, III: 1.3   (b) A: 74, B: 112, C: 128, D: 64, F: 22   **47.** 10,100 voting Democratic, 7900 voting Republican
49. Carpenters: \$1000, bricklayers: \$1050, plumbers: \$600   **51.** (a) [162 150 143], number of units of each nutrient
consumed at breakfast   (b) [186 200 239], number of units of each nutrient consumed at lunch
(c) [288 300 344], number of units of each nutrient consumed at dinner   (d) [5 8], total number of ounces of each food
that Mikey eats during a day   (e) [636 650 726], number of units of each nutrient consumed per day

53. (a) $\begin{bmatrix} 720 \\ 646 \end{bmatrix}$ (b) \$720   **55.** $x = 3, y = 4, z = 5$ **57.** $\begin{bmatrix} 3 & -2 & 1 \\ -5 & 6 & 7 \end{bmatrix}$ **59.** 4×4

61. $\begin{bmatrix} 27.9 & 130.6 & -69.88 \\ 106.75 & -149.44 & 26.1 \\ -47.5 & 336.2 & -18.7 \end{bmatrix}$ **63.** $\begin{bmatrix} -69.14 & 147.9 & -43.26 \\ 158.05 & -3.69 & 33.46 \\ -176.1 & 259.5 & 59.3 \end{bmatrix}$ **65.** $\begin{bmatrix} [A](2,3) \\ \qquad\qquad 1.6 \\ \ \end{bmatrix}$

67. $\begin{bmatrix} 160.16 & -26.7 & 4 \\ 2.7 & 150.85 & -53 \\ 187.4 & -35.5 & 48.6 \end{bmatrix}$ **69.** They match.

Exercises 2.4

1. $x = 2, y = 0$ **3.** $\begin{bmatrix} 1 & -2 \\ -3 & 7 \end{bmatrix}$ **5.** $\begin{bmatrix} 1 & -1 \\ -\frac{5}{2} & 3 \end{bmatrix}$ **7.** $\begin{bmatrix} 1.6 & -.4 \\ -.6 & 1.4 \end{bmatrix}$ **9.** $\begin{bmatrix} 1 \\ 3 \end{bmatrix}$ **11.** $x = 4, y = -\frac{1}{2}$

13. $x = 32, y = -6$ **15.** (a) $\begin{bmatrix} .8 & .3 \\ .2 & .7 \end{bmatrix}\begin{bmatrix} x \\ y \end{bmatrix} = \begin{bmatrix} m \\ s \end{bmatrix}$ (b) $\begin{bmatrix} x \\ y \end{bmatrix} = \begin{bmatrix} 1.4 & -.6 \\ -.4 & 1.6 \end{bmatrix}\begin{bmatrix} m \\ s \end{bmatrix}$ (c) 110,000 married; 40,000 single

d. 130,000 married; 20,000 single   **17.** (a) $\begin{bmatrix} .7 & .1 \\ .3 & .9 \end{bmatrix}\begin{bmatrix} x \\ y \end{bmatrix} = \begin{bmatrix} u \\ v \end{bmatrix}$ (b) $\begin{bmatrix} x \\ y \end{bmatrix} = \begin{bmatrix} \frac{3}{2} & -\frac{1}{6} \\ -\frac{1}{2} & \frac{7}{6} \end{bmatrix}\begin{bmatrix} u \\ v \end{bmatrix}$ (c) 8500; 4500

19. $x = 9, y = -2, z = -2$ **21.** $x = 1, y = 5, z = -4, w = 9$ **25.** (a) $\begin{bmatrix} 1 & 2 \\ .9 & 0 \end{bmatrix}\begin{bmatrix} x \\ y \end{bmatrix} = \begin{bmatrix} a \\ b \end{bmatrix}$

(b) After 1 year: 1,170,000 in group I and 405,000 in group II. After 2 years: 1,980,000 in group I and 1,053,000 in group II.

(c) 700,000 in group I and 55,000 in group II.   **27.** $\begin{bmatrix} -\frac{10}{73} & \frac{75}{292} \\ \frac{25}{73} & -\frac{5}{292} \end{bmatrix}$ **29.** $\begin{bmatrix} \frac{1020}{8887} & \frac{2910}{8887} & -\frac{500}{8887} \\ \frac{3050}{8887} & \frac{860}{8887} & \frac{1990}{8887} \\ \frac{125}{8887} & \frac{618}{8887} & \frac{810}{8887} \end{bmatrix}$ **31.** $x = -\frac{4}{5}, y = \frac{28}{5}, z = 5$

33. $x = 0, y = 2, z = 0, w = 2$ **35.** Displays ERR:SINGULAR MAT.

Exercises 2.5

1. $\begin{bmatrix} -2 & 3 \\ 5 & -7 \end{bmatrix}$ **3.** $\begin{bmatrix} \frac{1}{19} & \frac{3}{19} \\ \frac{3}{76} & -\frac{5}{38} \end{bmatrix}$ **5.** No inverse   **7.** $\begin{bmatrix} -1 & 2 & -4 \\ 1 & -1 & 3 \\ 0 & 0 & 1 \end{bmatrix}$ **9.** No inverse   **11.** $\begin{bmatrix} -5 & 6 & 0 & 0 \\ 1 & -1 & 0 & 0 \\ 0 & 0 & -\frac{1}{46} & \frac{1}{46} \\ 0 & 0 & \frac{25}{46} & -\frac{1}{23} \end{bmatrix}$

13. $x = 2, y = -3, z = 2$ **15.** $x = 4, y = -4, z = 3, w = -1$ **17.** Either no solutions or infinitely many solutions.

19. $\begin{bmatrix} -3 & 5 \\ 10 & -16 \end{bmatrix}$ **21.** $\begin{bmatrix} 2 & -1 \\ -7 & 4 \end{bmatrix}$ **23.** $\begin{bmatrix} -2.4 & 2.2 & 1.8 \\ .8 & -.4 & -.6 \\ .6 & -.8 & -.2 \end{bmatrix}$

Exercises 2.6

1. Coal: \$8.84 billion, steel: \$3.725 billion, electricity: \$9.895 billion
3. Computers: \$354 million, semiconductors: \$172 million   **7.** Plastics: \$955,000, industrial equipment: \$590,000

9. Manufacturing: \$398 million, transportation: \$313 million, agriculture: \$452 million   **11.** $\begin{bmatrix} 10.25 \\ 13.82 \\ 8.65 \end{bmatrix}$

Chapter 2: Supplementary Exercises

1. $\begin{bmatrix} 1 & -2 & \frac{1}{3} \\ 0 & 8 & \frac{16}{3} \end{bmatrix}$ **2.** $\begin{bmatrix} 1 & 0 & 1 \\ 2 & 1 & 0 \\ -12 & 0 & 7 \end{bmatrix}$ **3.** $x = 4, y = 5$ **4.** $x = 50, y = 2, z = -12$

5. $x = -1$, $y = \dfrac{2}{3}$, $z = \dfrac{1}{3}$ **6.** No solution   **7.** z = any value, $x = 1 - 3z$, $y = 4z$, $w = 5$ **8.** $x = 7$, $y = 3$ **9.** $\begin{bmatrix} 5 \\ 3 \\ 7 \end{bmatrix}$

10. $\begin{bmatrix} 6 & 17 \\ 12 & 26 \end{bmatrix}$ **11.** $x = -2$, $y = 3$ **12.** (a) $x = 13$, $y = 23$, $z = 19$ (b) $x = -4$, $y = 13$, $z = 14$ **13.** $\begin{bmatrix} -1 & 3 \\ \frac{1}{2} & -1 \end{bmatrix}$

14. $\begin{bmatrix} 5 & -1 & -1 \\ -3 & 1 & 0 \\ -1 & 0 & 1 \end{bmatrix}$ **15.** Corn: 500 acres; wheat: 0 acres; soybeans: 500 acres   **16.** (a) A: 9400, 8980; B:7300, 7510

(b) A: 10,857, 12,082; B: 6571, 5959   **17.** (d)   **18.** (a)   **19.** Industry I: 20; industry II: 20

Chapter 2: Chapter Test

1. $x = 2$, $y = 4$, $z = -5$ **2.** (a) $x = 4$, $y = -3$, $z = 6$ (b) $x = 2$, $y = 3$, $z = 5$ (c) No solution
(d) z = any value; $x = z + 2$, $y = -2z + 2$ (e) y = any value; $x = -2y$, $z = 0$ **3.** $w = 1$, $z = 2$, $x = 3$, $y = 5$
4. (1) $z = 0$, $y = 6$, $x = 9$; (2) $z = 1$, $y = 2$, $x = 15$; (3) $z = -1$, $y = 10$, $x = 3$

5. Not defined; $\begin{bmatrix} 2 & 2 & 2 \\ 2 & 3 & 2 \end{bmatrix}$; $\begin{bmatrix} -2 & 3 \\ -2 & 4 \end{bmatrix}$; not defined; $\begin{bmatrix} -1 & 0 & -1 \\ -1 & 1 & 1 \\ 1 & 0 & 1 \end{bmatrix}$

6. (a) $.5x + y + z = m$; $3x + 2.5y + 2z = v$; $4x + 3y + 2z = p$ (b) $\begin{bmatrix} .5 & 1 & 1 \\ 3 & 2.5 & 2 \\ 4 & 3 & 2 \end{bmatrix} \cdot \begin{bmatrix} x \\ y \\ z \end{bmatrix} = \begin{bmatrix} m \\ v \\ p \end{bmatrix}$

(c) 550 hours molding time, 1450 hours oven time, 1700 hours painting time

7. $\begin{bmatrix} \frac{1}{2} & -\frac{1}{2} & \frac{1}{2} \\ \frac{1}{2} & -\frac{1}{2} & -\frac{1}{2} \\ -\frac{1}{2} & \frac{3}{2} & \frac{1}{2} \end{bmatrix}$ **8.** 400 students   **9.** Wood: $1.98, steel: $7.39, coal: $3.87

CHAPTER 3

Exercises 3.1

1. Yes   **3.** No   **5.** (a)

	A	B	Truck capacity
Volume	4 cubic feet	3 cubic feet	300 cubic feet
Weight	100 pounds	200 pounds	10,000 pounds
Earnings	$13	$9	

(b) $4x + 3y \leq 300$; $100x + 200y \leq 10{,}000$

(c) $y \leq 2x, x \geq 0, y \geq 0$ (d) $13x + 9y$ (e)

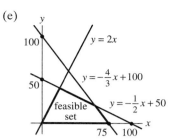

7. (a)

	Essay questions	Short-answer questions	Available
Time to answer	10 minutes	2 minutes	90 minutes
Quantity	10	50	
Required	3	10	
Worth	20 points	5 points	

(b) $10x + 2y \leq 90$
(c) $x \geq 3, x \leq 10, y \geq 10, y \leq 50$

(d) $20x + 5y$ (e)

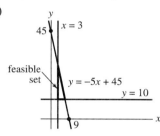

9. (a)

	Alfalfa	Corn	Requirements
Protein	.13 pound	.065 pound	4550 pounds
TDN	.48 pound	.96 pound	26,880 pounds
Vitamin A	2.16 IUs	0	43,200 IUs
Cost/lb	$0.01	$0.016	

(b) $.13x + .065y \geq 4550; .48x + .96y \geq 26,880; 2.16x \geq 43,200; y \geq 0$ (c)   (d) $.01x + .016y$

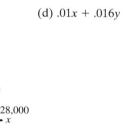

Exercises 3.2

1. $(20, 0)$ **3.** $(6, 0)$ **5.** $(0, 5)$ **7.** $(3, 3)$ **9.** $(0, 7)$ **11.** $(2, 1)$ **13.** Ship 75 crates of cargo A and no crates of cargo B.
15. Answer 3 essay questions and 30 short-answer questions.   **17.** Make 16 chairs and no sofas.
19. The minimum value is 30 and occurs at $(2, 6)$.   **21.** The maximum value is 49 and occurs at $(2, 9)$.
23. The maximum value is 6600 and occurs at $(12, 36)$.   **25.** The minimum value is 40 and occurs at $(4, 3)$.
27. Produce 9 hockey games and 8 soccer games each day.
29. Make 80 homes of the first type and 60 homes of the second type.
31. Make 400 cans of Fruit Delight and 500 cans of Heavenly Punch.

33. The farmer should plant $83\frac{1}{3}$ acres of oats and $16\frac{2}{3}$ acres of corn to make a profit of $6933.33.

35. (a) Make 8 of item I_1 and 4 of item I_2.   (b) $88   (c) 40 ounces of M_1, 20 ounces of M_2, and 28 ounces of M_3 are used.
(d) Make 10 of item I_1 and 0 of item I_2.   **37.** The feasible set contains no points.

Exercises 3.3

1. (a) $y = -\dfrac{3}{2}x + \dfrac{c}{14}$ (b) Up   (c) B **3.** Possible answer: $5x + y$ **5.** Possible answer: $2x + y$

7. Possible answer: $x + 5y$ **9.** Possible answer: $2x + 3y$ **11.** C **13.** D **15.** D **17.** C **19.** $\dfrac{1}{4} \le k \le 3$

21. Feed 1 can of brand A and 3 cans of brand B.

23. Ship 35 crates of oranges, 35 crates of grapefruits, and 30 crates of avocados.

25. In Detroit make 100 cars and 300 trucks. In Cleveland make 500 cars and 0 trucks.

27. Produce 90,000 gallons of gasoline, 5000 gallons of jet fuel, and 5000 gallons of diesel fuel.

29. Buy 9 high-capacity trucks and 21 low-capacity trucks.

FEASIBLE SETS FOR CHAPTER 3

Exercises 3.2

19.
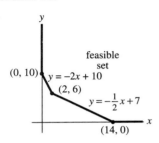

21.
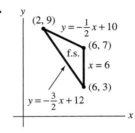

23.
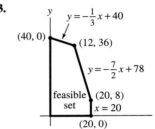

25.
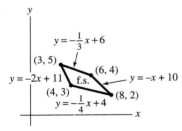

27.
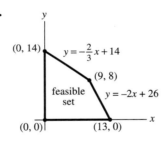

29.
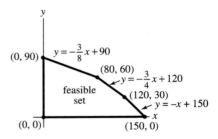

31.
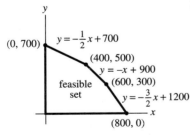

33.
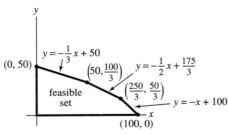

35.
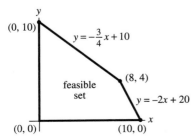

Exercises 3.3

21.

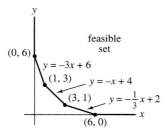

23.

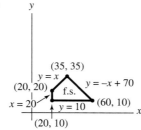

25.

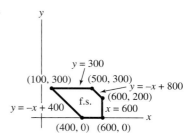

27.

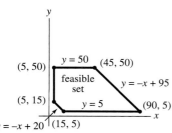

29.

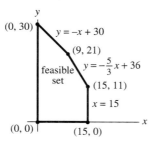

Chapter 3: Supplementary Exercises

1.

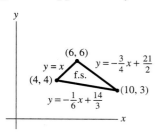

2.

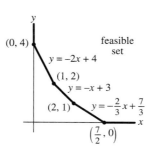

3.

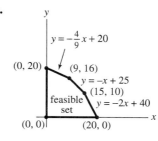

4.

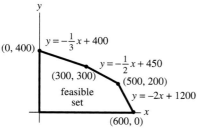

5.

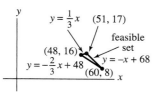

6.

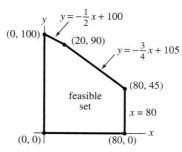

7.

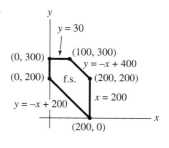

Chapter 3: Supplementary Exercises

1. Use 10 type A planes and 3 type B planes.   **2.** Use 2 ounces of wheat germ and 1 ounce of enriched oat flour.

3. Produce 9 hardtops and 16 sports cars.   **4.** Make 500 boxes of mixture A and 200 boxes of mixture B.

5. Publish 60 elementary books, 8 intermediate books, and 4 advanced books.

6. Transport 80 computers from Rochester and 45 computers from Queens.

7. Transport no computers from warehouse A to outlet I, 200 computers from warehouse A to outlet II, 200 computers from warehouse B to outlet I, and 100 computers from warehouse B to outlet II.

Chapter 3: Chapter Test

1. Step 1: Translate the problem into mathematical language. Identify variables and write the inequalities and objective function.

Step 2: Graph the feasible set.

Step 3: Determine the vertices of the feasible set.

Step 4: Evaluate the objective function at each vertex. Determine the optimal point.

2. (a) Minimize $70x + 90y$ subject to $\begin{cases} 20x + 30y \geq 300 \\ 10x + 20y \geq 200 \\ x \geq 0, y \geq 0 \end{cases}$

(b) Maximize $.07x + .06y + .045z$ subject to $\begin{cases} y \geq 150{,}000 \\ z \leq 200{,}000 \\ x + y + z \leq 500{,}000 \\ x \geq .5y \\ x \geq 0, y \geq 0, z \geq 0 \end{cases}$

3. (a)

(b) No

4. $(0, 10); (7, 5); (9, 3); (9, 0)$

5. (a) $x = 10, y = 0$ (b) $x = 3, y = 6$

6. (a) $y = -\dfrac{8}{5}x + 640$ (b) $y = -\dfrac{8}{5}x + \dfrac{c}{5}$ (c) down   (d) E

7. C

CHAPTER 4

Exercises 4.1

1. $\begin{cases} 20x + 30y + u \qquad\qquad\quad = 3500 \\ 50x + 10y \qquad + v \qquad = 5000 \\ -8x - 13y \qquad\qquad + M = 0 \end{cases}$ Maximize M given $x \geq 0, y \geq 0, u \geq 0, v \geq 0$.

3. $\begin{cases} x + y + z + u \qquad\qquad\qquad = 100 \\ 3x \qquad + z \qquad + v \qquad = 200 \\ 5x + 10y \qquad\qquad + w \qquad = 100 \\ -x - 2y + 3z \qquad\qquad + M = 0 \end{cases}$ Maximize M given $x \geq 0, y \geq 0, z \geq 0, u \geq 0, v \geq 0,$ $w \geq 0$.

5. (a)

	x	y	u	v	M	
	20	30	1	0	0	3500
	50	10	0	1	0	5000
	-8	-13	0	0	1	0

(b) $x = 0, y = 0, u = 3500, v = 5000, M = 0$

7. (a)

	x	y	z	u	v	w	M	
	1	1	1	1	0	0	0	100
	3	0	1	0	1	0	0	200
	5	10	0	0	0	1	0	100
	-1	-2	3	0	0	0	1	0

(b) $x = 0, y = 0, z = 0, u = 100, v = 200, w = 100, M = 0$

9. $x = 15, y = 0, u = 10, v = 0, M = 20$ **11.** $x = 10, y = 0, z = 15, u = 23, v = 0, w = 0, M = -11$

13. (a)

	x	y	u	v	M	
	1	$\frac{3}{2}$	$\frac{1}{2}$	0	0	6
	0	$-\frac{1}{2}$	$-\frac{1}{2}$	1	0	4
	0	-5	5	0	1	60

(b)

	x	y	u	v	M	
	$\frac{2}{3}$	1	$\frac{1}{3}$	0	0	4
	$\frac{1}{3}$	0	$-\frac{1}{3}$	1	0	6
	$\frac{10}{3}$	0	$\frac{20}{3}$	0	1	80

(c)

	x	y	u	v	M	
	0	1	1	-2	0	-8
	1	1	0	1	0	10
	0	-10	0	10	1	100

$x = 6, y = 0, u = 0, v = 4, M = 60$ $x = 0, y = 4, u = 0, v = 6, M = 80$ $x = 10, y = 0, u = -8, v = 0, M = 100$

(d)

	x	y	u	v	M	
	-1	0	1	-3	0	-18
	1	1	0	1	0	10
	10	0	0	20	1	200

15. (d)

$x = 0, y = 10, u = -18, v = 0, M = 200$

Exercises 4.2

1. (a) 3   **(b)**

	x	y	u	v	M	
u	$\frac{16}{3}$	0	1	$-\frac{2}{3}$	0	6
y	$\frac{1}{3}$	1	0	$\frac{1}{3}$	0	2
M	0	0	0	4	1	24

(c) $x = 0, y = 2, u = 6, v = 0; M = 24$

3. (a) 10   **(b)**

	x	y	u	v	M	
u	-13	0	1	$-\frac{6}{5}$	0	6
y	$\frac{3}{2}$	1	0	$\frac{1}{10}$	0	$\frac{1}{2}$
M	7	0	0	$\frac{1}{5}$	1	1

(c) $x = 0, y = \frac{1}{2}, u = 6, v = 0, M = 1.$

5. $x = 0, y = 5; M = 15$ **7.** $x = 12, y = 20; M = 88$ **9.** $x = 0, y = \frac{19}{3}, z = 5; M = 44$ **11.** $x = 0, y = 30; M = 90$

13. $x = 50, y = 100; M = 1300$ **15.** 98 chairs, 4 sofas, 21 tables

17. 11 hours bicycling, 4 hours swimming, 15 hours jogging; 3 pounds   **19.** 65 type A restaurants and 5 type C restaurants

21. $x = 100, y = 50; M = 45,000$ **23.** $x = \frac{8}{5}, y = \frac{3}{5}; M = 10$ **25.** $x = 5, y = 0, z = 0; M = 80$

Exercises 4.3

1. $x = \dfrac{3}{5}$, $y = \dfrac{22}{5}$; 156   **3.** $x = \dfrac{5}{2}$, $y = \dfrac{1}{2}$; 8   **5.** $x = 3, y = 5$; 59   **7.** 1 serving of food A, 3 servings of food B

9. Stock 100 of brand A, 50 of brand B, and 450 of brand C.   **11.** $x = 1, y = 1; M = -1$

Exercises 4.4

1. $x = 4, y = 22$; profit $= \$122$ **3.** $x = 25, y = 25$; cost $= \$250$ **5.** $-15 \le h \le 12$ **7.** $\begin{bmatrix} 9 & 1 & 1 \\ 4 & 8 & -3 \end{bmatrix}$ **9.** $\begin{bmatrix} 7 \\ 6 \\ 5 \\ 1 \end{bmatrix}$

11. Yes   **13.** Minimize $\begin{bmatrix} 7 & 5 & 4 \end{bmatrix} \begin{bmatrix} x \\ y \\ z \end{bmatrix}$ subject to the constraints $\begin{bmatrix} 3 & 8 & 9 \\ 1 & 2 & 5 \\ 4 & 1 & 7 \end{bmatrix} \begin{bmatrix} x \\ y \\ z \end{bmatrix} \ge \begin{bmatrix} 75 \\ 80 \\ 67 \end{bmatrix}$ and $\begin{bmatrix} x \\ y \\ z \end{bmatrix} \ge \begin{bmatrix} 0 \\ 0 \\ 0 \end{bmatrix}$.

15. Maximize $\begin{bmatrix} 3 & 5 \end{bmatrix} \begin{bmatrix} x \\ y \end{bmatrix}$ subject to the constraints $\begin{bmatrix} 3 & 6 \\ 7 & 5 \\ 4 & 3 \end{bmatrix} \begin{bmatrix} x \\ y \end{bmatrix} \le \begin{bmatrix} 90 \\ 138 \\ 120 \end{bmatrix}$ and $\begin{bmatrix} x \\ y \end{bmatrix} \ge \begin{bmatrix} 0 \\ 0 \end{bmatrix}$.

17. Minimize $2x + 3y$ subject to the constraints $\begin{cases} 7x + 4y \ge 33 \\ 5x + 8y \ge 44 \\ x + 3y \ge 55 \\ x \ge 0, y \ge 0 \end{cases}$

Exercises 4.5

1. Minimize $80u + 76v$ subject to the constraints   **3.** Maximize $u + 2v + w$ subject to the constraints

$\begin{cases} 5u + 3v \ge 4 \\ u + 2v \ge 2 \\ u \ge 0, v \ge 0 \end{cases}$ $\begin{cases} u - v + 2w \le 10 \\ 2u + v + 3w \le 12 \\ u \ge 0, v \ge 0, w \ge 0 \end{cases}$

5. Maximize $-7u + 10v$ subject to the constraints   **7.** $x = 12, y = 20, M = 88; u = \dfrac{2}{7}, v = \dfrac{6}{7}, M = 88$

$\begin{cases} -2u + 8v \le 3 \\ 4u + v \le 5 \\ 6u + 9v \le 1 \\ u \ge 0, v \ge 0 \end{cases}$

9. $x = 0, y = 2, M = 24; u = 0, v = 12, w = 0, M = 24$

11. Maximize $3u + 5v$ subject to the constraints $\begin{cases} u + 2v \le 3 \\ u \quad\ \le 1 \\ u \ge 0, v \ge 0 \end{cases}$ $x = \dfrac{5}{2}, y = \dfrac{1}{2}$, minimum $= 8; u = 1, v = 1$, maximum $= 8$

13. Minimize $6u + 9v + 12w$ subject to the constraints
$u = 0, v = \dfrac{10}{3}, w = 12$, minimum $= 174$ $\begin{cases} u + 3v \quad\ \ge 10 \\ -2u \quad\ + w \ge 12 \\ v + 3w \ge 10 \\ u \ge 0, v \ge 0, w \ge 0 \end{cases}$ $x = 3, y = 12, z = 0$, maximum $= 174$;

15. Suppose we can hire workers out at a profit of u dollars per hour, sell the steel at a profit of v dollars per unit, and sell the wood at a profit of w dollars per unit. To find the minimum profit at which that should be done, minimize $90u + 138v + 120w$ subject to the constraints
$$\begin{cases} 3u + 7v + 4w \geq 3 \\ 6u + 5v + 3w \geq 5 \\ u \geq 0, v \geq 0, w \geq 0 \end{cases}.$$

17. Suppose we can buy anthracite at u dollars per ton, ordinary coal at v dollars per ton, and bituminous coal at w dollars per ton. To find the maximum cost at which this should be done, maximize $80u + 60v + 75w$ subject to the constraints
$$\begin{cases} 4u + 4v + 7w \leq 150 \\ 10u + 5v + 5w \leq 200 \\ u \geq 0, v \geq 0, w \geq 0 \end{cases}.$$

19. \$3.63   **21.** $x = 2, y = 1$, maximum $= 74$

Chapter 4: Supplementary Exercises

1. $x = 2, y = 3$, max. $= 18$ **2.** $x = 0, y = 7$, max. $= 35$ **3.** $x = 4, y = 5$, max. $= 23$ **4.** $x = 2, y = 4$, max. $= 34$
5. $x = 5, y = 1$, min. $= 6$ **6.** $x = 0, y = 6$, min. $= 12$ **7.** $x = 4, y = 1$, min. $= 110$ **8.** $x = 4, y = 3$, min. $= 41$
9. $x = 1, y = 6, z = 8$, max. $= 884$ **10.** $x = 60, y = 8, z = 20, w = 0$, max. $= 312$
11. Minimize $14u + 9v + 24w$ subject to the constraints   **12.** Maximize $8u + 5v + 7w$ subject to the constraints
$$\begin{cases} u + v + 3w \geq 2 \\ 2u + v + 2w \geq 3 \\ u \geq 0, v \geq 0, w \geq 0 \end{cases}. \qquad \begin{cases} u + v + 2w \leq 20 \\ 4u + v + w \leq 30 \\ u \geq 0, v \geq 0, w \geq 0 \end{cases}.$$

13. Primal: $x = 4, y = 5$, max. $= 23$; Dual: $u = 1, v = 1, w = 0$, min. $= 23$ **14.** Primal: $x = 4, y = 1$, min. $= 110$;

Dual: $u = \dfrac{10}{3}, v = \dfrac{50}{3}, w = 0$, max. $= 110$ **15.** $A = \begin{bmatrix} 1 & 2 \\ 1 & 1 \\ 3 & 2 \end{bmatrix}, B = \begin{bmatrix} 14 \\ 9 \\ 24 \end{bmatrix}, C = [2 \ \ 3], X = \begin{bmatrix} x \\ y \end{bmatrix}$ Primal: Maximize CX subject to:

$AX \leq B, X \geq \mathbf{0}$. Dual: $U = \begin{bmatrix} u \\ v \\ w \end{bmatrix}$ Minimize $B^T U$ subject to $A^T U \geq C^T, U \geq \mathbf{0}$.   **16.** $A = \begin{bmatrix} 1 & 4 \\ 1 & 1 \\ 2 & 1 \end{bmatrix}, B = \begin{bmatrix} 8 \\ 5 \\ 7 \end{bmatrix}, C = [20 \ \ 30],$

$X = \begin{bmatrix} x \\ y \end{bmatrix}$ Primal: Minimize CX subject to $AX \geq B, X \geq \mathbf{0}$. Dual: $U = \begin{bmatrix} u \\ v \\ w \end{bmatrix}$ Maximize $B^T U$ subject to $A^T U \leq C^T, U \geq \mathbf{0}$.

17. (a) 30 type A sticks, 40 type B sticks   (b) \$11   **18.** \$210

Chapter 4: Chapter Test

1.

x	y	z	u	v	w	M	
1	1	−2	1	0	0	0	10
2	−1	3	0	1	0	0	18
1	3	1	0	0	1	0	21
−2	−1	3	0	0	0	1	0

2. $x = 35, y = 0, z = 30, u = 0, v = 0, w = 42, M = 560$

$x = 0, y = 14, z = 0, u = 0, v = \dfrac{7}{2}, w = 0, M = 560$

3. Maximize $3x - 4y$ subject to $\begin{cases} 6x + 7y \leq 120 \\ 15x + 5y \leq 195 \\ x \geq 0, y \geq 0 \end{cases}$; $x = 13, y = 0, u = 42, v = 0, M = 39$

4. $x = 2, y = 4, u = 0, v = 4, w = 0, M = 44$ **5.** Maximize $6u + 3v$ subject to $\begin{cases} u + 2v \leq 3 \\ u - v \leq 2 \\ u \geq 0, v \geq 0 \end{cases}$

6. (a) Maximize $[.50 \quad .35]\begin{bmatrix} x \\ y \end{bmatrix}$ subject to the constraints $\begin{bmatrix} 2 & 1 \\ 2 & 3 \end{bmatrix}\begin{bmatrix} x \\ y \end{bmatrix} \leq \begin{bmatrix} 6000 \\ 9600 \end{bmatrix}$ and $\begin{bmatrix} x \\ y \end{bmatrix} \geq \begin{bmatrix} 0 \\ 0 \end{bmatrix}$

(b) Minimize $[6000 \quad 9600]\begin{bmatrix} u \\ v \end{bmatrix}$ subject to the constraints $\begin{bmatrix} 2 & 2 \\ 1 & 3 \end{bmatrix}\begin{bmatrix} u \\ v \end{bmatrix} \geq \begin{bmatrix} .50 \\ .35 \end{bmatrix}$ and $\begin{bmatrix} u \\ v \end{bmatrix} \geq \begin{bmatrix} 0 \\ 0 \end{bmatrix}$

(c) Minimize $6000u + 9600v$ subject to the constraints

$\begin{cases} 2u + 2v \geq .50 \\ u + 3v \geq .35 \\ u \geq 0, v \geq 0 \end{cases}$

u is a measure of the value of a pound of paper

v is a measure of the value of a minute of labor

(d) The dual gives the minimum acceptable profit that can be achieved by selling the paper and hiring out the workers.

CHAPTER 5

Exercises 5.1

1. (a) $\{5, 6, 7\}$ (b) $\{1, 2, 3, 4, 5, 7\}$ (c) $\{1, 3\}$ (d) $\{5, 7\}$ **3.** (a) $\{a, b, c, d, e, f\}$ (b) $\{c\}$ (c) $\varnothing$ **5.** $\varnothing, \{1\}, \{2\}, \{1, 2\}$
7. {all male college students who like football}   (b) {all female college students}   (c) {all female college students who don't like football}   (d) {all male college students or all college students who like football}
9. (a) $S = \{1975, 1976, 1979, 1983, 1984, 1987, 1999\}$
(b) $T = \{1975, 1976, 1980, 1983, 1985, 1989, 1991, 1995, 1996, 1997, 1998, 1999\}$ (c) $S \cap T = \{1975, 1976, 1983, 1999\}$
(d) $S' \cap T = \{1980, 1985, 1989, 1991, 1995, 1996, 1997, 1998\}$ (e) $S \cap T' = \{1979, 1984, 1987\}$
11. From 1972 to 1999, during only three years did the Standard and Poor's Index increase by 2% or more during the first five days and also increase by 16% or more for that year.   **13.** (a) $\{d, f\}$ (b) $\{a, b, c, e, f\}$ (c) $\varnothing$ (d) $\{a, c\}$
(e) $\{e\}$ (f) $\{a, c, e, f\}$ (g) $\{a, b, c, e\}$ (h) $\{a, c\}$ (i) $\{d\}$ **15.** S **17.** U **19.** $\varnothing$ **21.** $L \cup T$ **23.** $L \cap P$
25. $P \cap L \cap T$ **27.** S' **29.** $S \cup A \cup D$ **31.** $(A \cap S)' \cap D$ **33.** {male students at Mount College}
35. {people who are both teachers and students at Mount College}   **37.** {males or students at Mount College}
39. {females at Mount College}   **41.** S' **43.** $(V \cup C) \cap S'$ **45.** $(V \cup C)'$ **47.** (a) $\{B, C, D, E\}$ (b) $\{C, D, E, F\}$
(c) $\{A, D, E, F\}$ (d) $\{A, C, D, E, F\}$ (e) $\{A, F\}$ (f) $\{D, E\}$ **49.** Possible answer: $\{2\}$ **51.** S is a subset of T.

Exercises 5.2

1. 7   **3.** 0   **5.** 11   **7.** S is a subset of T.   **9.** 14 million   **11.** 28,847   **13.** 452
15.   **17.**   **19.**   **21.**

23.   **25.**   **27.**   **29.**

31.   **33.**   **35.**   **37.**

39. $S' \cup T'$ **41.** $S \cap T'$ **43.** U **45.** S' **47.** $R \cap T$ **49.** $R' \cap S \cap T$ **51.** $T \cup (R \cap S')$
53. $(R \cap S \cap T) \cup (R' \cap S' \cap T')$ **55.** People who are not illegal aliens or everyone over the age of 18 who is employed
57. Everyone over the age of 18 who is unemployed **59.** Noncitizens who are unemployed

Exercises 5.3

1. 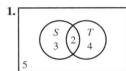 **3.** 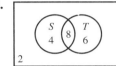 **5.** 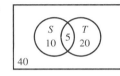 **7.**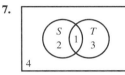

9. 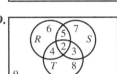 **11.**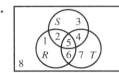

13. 25 **15.** 2, 5 **17.** 30 **19.** 4 **21.** 4, 2, 1
23. 28 **25.** 12 **27.** 2000 **29.** 200 **31.** 1600
33. 90 **35.** 6 **37.** 140 **39.** 30 **41.** 190
43. 180 **45.** 210 **47.** 35 **49.** 450 **51.** 3750
53. 250

Exercises 5.4

1. 15 **3.** 676 **5.** 380 **7.** 20 **9.** 120 **11.** 64 **13.** 6840 **15.** 870 **17.** 24 **19.** 32 **21.** 360,000
23. (a) 2401 (b) 840 (c) 343 (d) 240 **25.** (a) 362,880 (b) 40,320 (c) 720 **27.** 256 **29.** 729
31. 168 **33.** 18 **35.** 972 **37.** 1,048,576 **39.** 16 **41.** 9,765,625 **43.** 336; 520 **45.** 50 **47.** 960
49. 5600 **51.** 99 **53.** 384 **55.** 8 **57.** 16,250

Exercises 5.5

1. 12 **3.** 120 **5.** 120 **7.** 5 **9.** 5 **11.** n **13.** 1 **15.** $\dfrac{n(n-1)}{2}$ **17.** 720 **19.** 72 **21.** 24 **23.** 36
25. 2730 **27.** 210 **29.** 210 **31.** 120 **33.** 28 **35.** 30,240 **37.** 252 **39.** 38,955,840 **41.** 161,700; 35
43. 15,600 **45.** 75,287,520 **47.** 2,598,960 **49.** 1287 **51.** 1140 **53.** 120 **55.** 70 **57.** Yes; Moe: 36; Joe: 35
59. 479,001,600 **61.** 14,400 **63.** 840 **65.** 10,080 **67.** 120 **69.** 379,236 **71.** 96,875 **73.** semester system
75. (a) 1,221,759 (b) 3,921,225 (c) first lottery (d) second lottery

Exercises 5.6

1. (a) 64 (b) 20 (c) 22 (d) 57 **3.** 126 **5.** (a) 120 (b) 56 (c) 64 **7.** $C(100, 25) \cdot C(75, 40)$ **9.** 60
11. 67,800,320 **13.** 80 **15.** 3,527,160 **17.** 3528 **19.** 225,225 **21.** 165,765,600 **23.** 210 **25.** 11,232,000
27. 870,912,000 **29.** 24 **31.** 24 **33.** 3744 **35.** 3050 **37.** 369 **39.** 1500 **41.** 3,628,800 **43.** 64 **45.** 16
47. .264% **49.** four aces

Exercises 5.7

1. 15   **3.** 8   **5.** 153   **7.** 1   **9.** 1   **11.** n **13.** 1   **15.** $n!$ **17.** 64   **19.** $x^{10}, 10x^9y, 45x^8y^2$
21. $105x^2y^{13}, 15xy^{14}, y^{15}$ **23.** $184{,}756x^{10}y^{10}$ **25.** 330   **27.** 64   **29.** 16   **31.** 64   **33.** 255   **35.** 196,608
37. 120   **39.** 16   **41.** 247   **43.** 4096   **47.** 3696   **49.** $2835x^3$ **51.** 8

Exercises 5.8

1. 20   **3.** 180   **5.** 210   **7.** 34,650   **9.** 166,320   **11.** 1,401,400   **13.** 2,858,856   **15.** 99,768,240
17. 5,708,552,850   **19.** 488,864,376   **21.** 12   **23.** 135,135   **27.** 8.81×10^{41}

Chapter 5: Supplementary Exercises

1. $\varnothing, \{a\}, \{b\}, \{a, b\}$ **2.**   **3.** 120   **4.** 240   **5.**   **6.** $x^{12} + 12x^{11}y + 66x^{10}y^2$ **7.** 840

8. 15   **9.** 35   **10.** 13,860   **11.** 0   **12.** 136   **13.** 6   **14.** 49   **15.** 47   **16.** 11   **17.** 46   **18.** 58   **19.** 22
20. 23   **21.** 126   **22.** 2^{40} **23.** 550   **24.** 480   **25.** 20   **26.** 450,000   **27.** 8,100,000,000
28. 146,813,779,479,510   **29.** 390,625; 325,089   **30.** 792   **31.** C(100, 14)   **32.** 27,500   **33.** 59,049

34. C(60, 10)   **35.** 9,765,625   **36.** 85,766,121   **37.** 210   **38.** 66,512,160   **39.** 14!   **40.** $\dfrac{1}{5!} \cdot \dfrac{100!}{(20!)^5}$

41. $\dfrac{80}{99} \cdot \dfrac{1}{5!} \cdot \dfrac{100!}{(20!)^5}$ **42.** 100   **43.** 100   **44.** 1000   **45.** 34,560   **46.** 95,040   **47.** 5148   **48.** 648   **49.** 243
50. 4512   **51.** 12,696   **52.** 6   **53.** 72   **54.** 12   **55.** 45; 35   **56.** second teacher   **57.** 4200   **58.** 5   **59.** 5040
60. (a) 14,520   (b) 25,344   **61.** 29   **62.** 70   **63.** 35,152   **64.** 12   **65.** 16,360,143,800   **66.** (a) 224,640,000
(b) There are 20 times as many plates in (a).

Chapter 5: Chapter Test

1. (a) 24   (b) 210   (c) 153   (d) 1   (e) 30   **2.** (a) True   (b) True   (c) False   **3.** (a) {a, e}   (b) $\varnothing$
4.   **5.** 10   **6.** 10   **7.** 60
8. (a) 2,209,413,024   (b) 210
9. 210   **10.** 144   **11.** 136,800   **12.** 792   **13.** 2520

CHAPTER 6

Exercises 6.2

1. (a) {RS, RT, RU, RV, ST, SU, SV, TU, TV, UV}   (b) {RS, RT, RU, RV}   (c) {TU, TV, UV}
3. (a) {HH, HT, TH, TT}   (b) {HH, HT}   **5.** (a) {(I, red), (I, white), (II, red), (II, white)}   (b) {(I, red), (I, white)}
7. (a) S = {All positive numbers of minutes}   (b) "More than 5 minutes but less than 8 minutes," $\varnothing$, "5 minutes or less,"
"8 minutes or more," "5 minutes or less," "Less than 4 minutes," S
9. (a) {(1, 1), (1, 2), (1, 3), (1, 4), (2, 1), (2, 2), (2, 3), (2, 4), (3, 1), (3, 2), (3, 3), (3, 4), (4, 1), (4, 2), (4, 3), (4, 4)}
(b) (i) {(2, 2), (2, 4), (4, 2), (4, 4)}   (ii) {(1, 2), (1, 4), (2, 1), (2, 2), (2, 3), (2, 4), (3, 2), (3, 4), (4, 1), (4, 2), (4, 3), (4, 4)}
(iii) {(3, 3), (3, 4), (4, 3) (4, 4)}   (iv) {(2, 4), (3, 3), (4, 2)}   (v) {(1, 4), (2, 3), (2, 4), (3, 2), (3, 3), (3, 4), (4, 1), (4, 2), (4, 3), (4, 4)}
(vi) {(1, 1), (2, 2), (3, 3), (4, 4)}   (vii) {(1, 2), (1, 3), (2, 1), (2, 2), (2, 4), (3, 1), (3, 3), (3, 4), (4, 2), (4, 3)}
(viii) {(1, 1), (1, 2), (1, 3), (2, 1), (2, 2), (2, 3), (3, 1), (3, 2), (3, 3)}   **11.** (a). No   (b) Yes

13. $\varnothing, \{a\}, \{b\}, \{c\}, \{a, b\}, \{a, c\}, \{b, c\}, S$ **15.** Yes **17.** (a) $\{0, 1, 2, 3, 4, 5, 6, 7, 8, 9, 10\}$ (b) $\{6, 7, 8, 9, 10\}$ **19.** (a) No
(b) Yes (c) Yes **21.** The set of nonnegative integers **23.** The set of nonnegative numbers
25. $\{(000, 000, 000), (000, 000, 001), \ldots (999, 999, 999)\}$; E' = the event that at least one number is odd; $E \cap F$ = the event that all numbers are even and are more than 699 **27.** (a) 324 (b) "The murder occured in the library with a gun."
(c) "Either the murder occured in the library or it was done with a gun."

Exercises 6.3

1. (a) $\dfrac{46,277}{774,746}$ (b) $\dfrac{48,132}{774,746}$ (c) $\dfrac{726,614}{774,746}$ **3.** (a) $\dfrac{5}{36}$ (b) $\dfrac{1}{6}$ **5.** $\dfrac{1}{19}$ **7.** (a) $\dfrac{1}{6}$ (b) 1 to 5 **9.** (a) .7 (b) .7

11. (a) $\dfrac{10}{11}$ (b) $\dfrac{1}{3}$ (c) $\dfrac{4}{9}$ **13.** 9 to 91 **15.** $\dfrac{11}{18}; \dfrac{7}{18}$ **17.** (a) .7 (b) .2 **19.** (a) .7 (b) 7000

21.

Number of Colleges Applied to	Probability
1	.32
2	.14
3	.15
4	.11
5 to 20	.28

23. (a) .15, .55, .20, .10 (b) .30
25. (a) 83%
(b) Some categories are left out—people who use a computer for both school and work, for example.

Exercises 6.4

1. (a) $\dfrac{1}{9}$ (b) $\dfrac{2}{9}$ **3.** (a) $\dfrac{7}{13}$ (b) $\dfrac{6}{13}$ (c) $\dfrac{4}{13}$ (d) $\dfrac{9}{13}$ **5.** (a) $\dfrac{2}{429}$ (b) $\dfrac{7}{429}$ (c) $\dfrac{427}{429}$ **7.** $\dfrac{5}{11}$ **9.** $\dfrac{25}{42}$

11. $\dfrac{16}{17}$ **13.** $\dfrac{199}{323}$ **15.** $\dfrac{47}{250}$ **17.** $\dfrac{2}{7}$ **19.** (a) .25 (b) .75 (c) .8 **21.** 0 **23.** $\dfrac{1}{11}$ **25.** $\dfrac{2}{5}$ **27.** (a) $\dfrac{15}{28}$

(b) $\dfrac{15}{56}$ (c) $\dfrac{9}{56}$ (d) $\dfrac{9}{14}$ **29.** $\dfrac{5}{6}$ **31.** $\dfrac{1}{3}$ **33.** $\dfrac{1}{1,919,190}$ **35.** .90055 **37.** .066 **39.** (a) .119 (b) .152
41. .6 **43.** 13 **45.** (a) 4 (b) .2139 **47.** 281

Exercises 6.5

1. $\dfrac{1}{3}, \dfrac{1}{5}$ **3.** $\dfrac{4}{7}$ **5.** No **7.** (a) .36 (b) .81 **9.** .7967 **11.** $\dfrac{3}{4}, \dfrac{1}{2}$ **13.** (a) .4 (b) .6 (c) .75 **15.** $\dfrac{1}{4}$

17. .94 **19.** .16 **21.** .009975 **23.** .2401 **27.** .4, .24, .36 **31.** (a) $\dfrac{1}{10}$ (b) 100 per 1000 (c) $\dfrac{1}{20}$

33. (a) .28 (b) .07 (c) .6065 **35.** (a) .16 (b) .64 (c) .36 (d) .42 (e) .64 (f) .31
37. (a) .40 (b) .56 (c) .18 (d) .70 (e) .45 (f) .67 **39.** (a) .8399; .2712; .2317; .8545; .2759 (b) No
41. $\dfrac{1}{69}$ **43.** $\dfrac{10}{143}; \dfrac{25}{286}$ **45.** $\dfrac{1}{6}; \dfrac{1}{3}$ **47.** .0986 **49.** not independent
51. (a) 3.69×10^{-6} (b) 6.16×10^{-7} (c) (a)

Exercises 6.6

1. 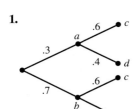   **3.** 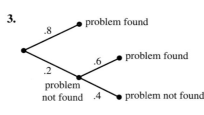   **5.** .08   **7.** .295   **9.** $\frac{7}{12}$

11. 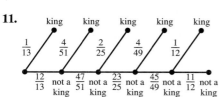 $\frac{1201}{5525} \approx .22$ **13.** .262   **15.** $\frac{25}{27}$ **17.** .86   **19.** $\frac{4}{7}$ **21.** (a) .60   (b) .75

23. $1 - (.9999)^n$

25. Same shape; probability of winning card game is greater.

27. (a) $\frac{1}{4}; \frac{3}{4}$ (b) .7   **29.** $\frac{6}{11}$

Exercises 6.7

1. $\frac{8}{53}$ **3.** $\frac{3}{7}$ **5.** .075   **7.** $\frac{35}{38} \approx 92\%$ **9.** (a) .1325   (b) $\frac{12}{53} \approx .23$ **11.** $\frac{5}{103} \approx .049$

13. (a) $\frac{1}{4}$ (b) $\frac{13}{17} \approx .765$ (c) .130   **15.** (a) $\frac{5}{9}$ (b) 11%   **17.** (a) .01   (b) $\frac{33}{34} \approx .971$ **19.** $\frac{31}{37} \approx .838$

Exercises 6.8

1. Theoretical probabilities: $\frac{1}{6}$ for each face.

Chapter 6: Supplementary Exercises

1. $\frac{31}{32}$ **2.** No   **3.** $\frac{4}{9}$ **4.** $\frac{1}{12}$ **5.** $\frac{2}{5}$ **6.** $\frac{2}{11}$ **7.** $\frac{1}{5}$ **8.** $\frac{1}{5}$ **9.** .4667   **10.** .3333   **11.** $\frac{7}{15}$ **12.** (a) $\frac{1}{10}$

(b) $\frac{2}{5}$ **13.** (a) $\frac{2}{15}$ (b) $\frac{1}{3}$ **14.** (a) $\left(\frac{1}{36}\right)^3$ (b) $\left(\frac{1}{10}\right)^4$ (c) $\frac{167}{500}$ (d) $\left(\frac{13}{18}\right)^3\left(\frac{1}{2}\right)^4$ **15.** (a) $\frac{1}{12}$ (b) $\frac{1}{2}$ **16.** $\frac{7}{12}$

17. $\frac{1}{21}$ **18.** $\frac{2}{3}$ **19.** No   **20.** $\frac{2}{3}$ **21.** $\frac{1}{3}$ **22.** $\frac{19}{49}$ **23.** $\frac{1}{6}$ **24.** $\frac{1}{21}$ **25.** $\frac{2}{3}$ **26.** Switch   **27.** $\frac{13}{25}$

28. 13 to 37   **29.** $\frac{1}{120,960}$ **30.** $\frac{1}{6}$ **31.** $\frac{5}{16}$ **32.** $\frac{1}{3}$ **33.** $\frac{4}{25}$ **34.** $\frac{1}{8}$ **35.** $\frac{138}{301}$ **36.** (e)   **37.** (a)   **38.** 35

39. 421   **41.** Theoretical probability: $\frac{5}{32}$

Chapter 6: Chapter Test

1. (a) $S = \{$PN, PD, PQ, PH, ND, NQ, NH, DQ, DH, QH$\}$ (b) $E = \{$PN, PQ, NQ, DH$\}$ **2.** (a) $\frac{3}{8}$ (b) $\frac{1,000,000}{1,000,001}$

3. (a) 2 to 3   (b) 7 to 3   **4.** (a) A male junior is elected.   (b) A female junior is not elected.

(c) A male or a junior is elected.   **5.** $\frac{15}{16}$ **6.** .9612   **7.** (a) $\frac{5}{8}$ (b) $\frac{3}{4}$ (c) $\frac{2}{3}$ (d) No   (e) No   **8.** .6513; .3874

9. (a) $\frac{1}{3}$ (b) $\frac{7}{13}$ (c) No; No   (d) $\frac{1}{3}$ **10.** (a) .50   (b) .50   **11.** (a) $\frac{18}{25}$ (b) $\frac{7}{13}$

CHAPTER 7

Exercises 7.1

1.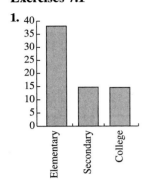

3.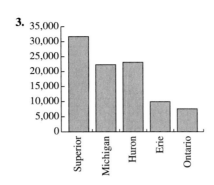

5.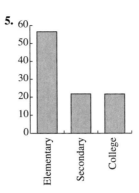

7.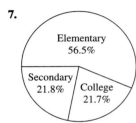

9.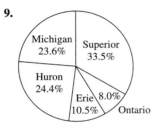

11. .457

13.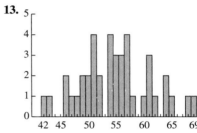

15.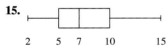

17.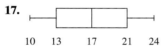

19.

21. (A)−(c), (B)−(d), (C)−(a), (D)−(b)

23. (a) min = 200, Q_1 = 400, Q_2 = 600, Q_3 = 700, max = 800   (b) 25%   (c) 25%   (d) 50%   (e) 75%

25.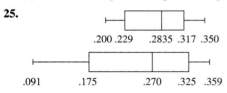

Exercises 7.2

1.

Grade	Relative frequency
0	.08
1	.12
2	.40
3	.24
4	.16

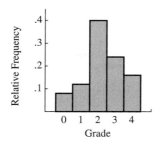

3.

Number of calls during minute	Relative frequency
20	.05
21	.05
22	0
23	.10
24	.30
25	.20
26	0
27	.15
28	.10
29	.05

5.

Number of heads	Probability
0	$\frac{1}{8}$
1	$\frac{3}{8}$
2	$\frac{3}{8}$
3	$\frac{1}{8}$

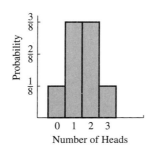

7.

Number of shots	Probability
1	$\frac{1}{3}$
2	$\frac{2}{9}$
3	$\frac{4}{27}$
4	$\frac{24}{81}$

9.

Number of red balls	Player's earnings	Probability
2	$5	$\frac{1}{15}$
1	$1	$\frac{8}{15}$
0	−$1	$\frac{6}{15}$

11. .6

13.

k	$Pr(X^2 = k)$
0	.1
1	.2
4	.3
9	.2
16	.2

15.

k	$Pr(X - 1 = k)$
−1	.1
0	.2
1	.3
2	.2
3	.2

17.

k	$Pr\left(\frac{1}{15}Y = k\right)$
1	.3
2	.4
3	.1
4	.1
5	.1

19.

k	$Pr((X + 1)^2 = k)$
1	.1
4	.2
9	.3
16	.2
25	.2

21.

Grade	Relative frequency	
	9 a.m. class	10 a.m. class
F	.17	.16
D	.25	.23
C	.33	.15
B	.17	.21
A	.08	.25

9 a.m. Class

10 a.m. Class

The 9 a.m. class has the distribution centered on the C grade with relatively few A's. The 10 a.m. class has a large percentage of A's and D's with fewer C's.   **23.** 80%

25. (a) 25%   (b) 60%   (c)   (d) ≈ 25   **27.** (a) 59   (b) 5%   (c) 54   (d) 35%   (e) ≈ 54

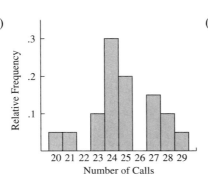

29. (a) $\Pr(U = 4) = \dfrac{1}{15}$ (b) $\dfrac{2}{3}$ (c) $\dfrac{14}{15}$ (d) $\dfrac{1}{3}$ (e)

Exercises 7.3

1. $\dfrac{25}{216}$ **3.** $\dfrac{3}{64}$ **5.** .3174   **7.** .0870; The selection may not have been random.   **9.** .8507   **11.** .6187   **13.** .2618

15.

k	Pr(X = k)
0	.0168
1	.0896
2	.2090
3	.2787
4	.2322
5	.1239
6	.0413
7	.0079
8	.0007

17. .5583   **19.** .9804   **21.** (a) .0108   (b) .9182

23. (a) 0.0190   (b)

k	Pr(X = k)
0	.0271
1	.0981
2	.1770
3	.2128
4	.1916
5	.1379
6	.0826

(c) .9961

Exercises 7.4

1. 2.35   **3.** (a) 2.9   (b)

Grade	Relative Frequency
4	.3
3	.4
2	.2
1	.1

(c) 2.9   **5.** $\bar{x}_A = 1.5, \bar{x}_B = 1.6$ **7.**

Earnings	Probability
−$1	$\frac{37}{38}$
$35	$\frac{1}{38}$

$E(X) \approx -.0526$

9.

Earnings	Probability
−50¢	$\frac{1}{3}$
0¢	$\frac{4}{15}$
50¢	$\frac{1}{5}$
$1	$\frac{2}{15}$
$1.50	$\frac{1}{15}$

$E(X) \approx .1667$ **11.** $1000   **13.** 4.47   **15.** (d)   **17.** (b)
19. (c)   **21.** (d)   **23.** (b)   **25.** (a)   **27.** (a)

Exercises 7.5

1. 1.4   **3.** B   **5.** (a) $\mu_A = 15, \mu_B = 13, \sigma_A^2 = 160, \sigma_B^2 = 141$ (b) A   (c) B
7. (a) $\mu_A = 103, \sigma_A^2 = 4.6, \mu_B = 104, \sigma_B^2 = 3.4$ (b) B   (c) B   **9.** (a) ≥ .75   (b) ≥ .89   (c) ≥ .31   **11.** ≥ 4688
13. 8   **15.** (a) $\mu = 7, \sigma^2 = \frac{35}{6}$ (b) $\frac{5}{6}$ (c) ≥ $\frac{19}{54}$ **17.** .64   **21.** $\bar{x} = 44{,}203.9, s \approx 5018.59$ **23.** $\bar{x} = 4.72, s \approx 1.43$

Exercises 7.6

1. .8944   **3.** .4013   **5.** .2417   **7.** .6170   **9.** 1.75   **11.** .75   **13.** $\mu = 6, \sigma = 2$ **15.** $\mu = 9, \sigma = 1$ **17.** $-\frac{8}{3}$

19. $15\frac{1}{2}$ **21.** .9772   **23.** .6247   **25.** .0002   **27.** .9876   **29.** .0122   **31.** (a) 618   (b) Between 396 and 644

33. 19,750 miles   **35.** (a) 5.35 ounces   (b) 4.76 ounces   **37.** The normal curve is translated to the right.   **39.** .2358

Exercises 7.7

1. (a) .1974   (b) .7888   (c) .9878   **3.** .0062   **5.** .0062   **7.** .0013   **9.** .6368   **11.** .1056   **13.** .2; .0401
15. Exact: .2356; normal approximation: .2358   **17.** Exact: .0812; normal approximation: .0813

Chapter 7: Supplementary Exercises

1.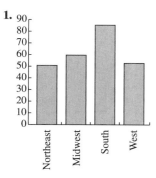

2.

3. (a)

k	$\Pr(X = k)$
0	$\frac{8}{27}$
1	$\frac{12}{27}$
2	$\frac{6}{27}$
3	$\frac{1}{27}$

(b) $\mu = 1, \sigma^2 = \frac{2}{3}$ **4.** .2266   **5.** .2857   **6.** .2646   **7.** $\geq \frac{8}{9}$ **8.** $\mu = 4.8, \sigma^2 = 19.76$

9. 10.56%   **10.**

k	$\Pr(X = k)$
0	$\frac{1}{70}$
1	$\frac{16}{70}$
2	$\frac{36}{70}$
3	$\frac{16}{70}$
4	$\frac{1}{70}$

$, \mu = 2, \sigma^2 = \frac{4}{7}$ **11.** .0122

12. .84   **13.** 22.5   **14.** −.75   **15.** $\frac{1}{8}; \frac{1}{4}; \frac{5}{16}; \frac{5}{16}$ **16.** 52; choose true for all the questions.

Chapter 7: Chapter Test

1. .58   **2.**

3. (a)

Number of Heads, k	$\Pr(X = k)$
0	.25
1	.50
2	.25

(b)

k	$\Pr(2X + 5 = k)$
5	.25
7	.50
9	.25

4. (a) 0.296   (b) 0.619   (c) 2   **5.** .4, 3.24, 1.8   **6.** Lucy; ≈11 cents per roll   **7.** (a) .8413   (b) .9878   (c) .7162
8. (a) .1587   (b) .7745   (c) 99 mg/100 ml, 113 mg/100 ml
9. (a) .3983   (b) .0118; .0092; difference is .0026   (c) .9962; .9878; difference is .0084

CHAPTER 8

Exercises 8.1

1. Yes   **3.** No   **5.** Yes   **7.** 53%; 56%   **9.** 40% will be in zone I, 40% will be in zone II, and 20% will be in zone III.

11. (a) $\begin{array}{c} \\ S \\ M \\ L \end{array}\overset{\begin{array}{ccc} S & M & L \end{array}}{\begin{bmatrix} .4 & .5 & .3 \\ .6 & 0 & .2 \\ 0 & .5 & .5 \end{bmatrix}}$ (b) 44%   **13.** (a) $\begin{array}{c} \\ D \\ R \end{array}\overset{\begin{array}{cc} D & R \end{array}}{\begin{bmatrix} .7 & .4 \\ .3 & .6 \end{bmatrix}}$ (b) $\begin{bmatrix} .61 & .52 \\ .39 & .48 \end{bmatrix}$; $\begin{bmatrix} .583 & .556 \\ .417 & .444 \end{bmatrix}$ (c) 58.3%

15. (a) $\begin{array}{c} \\ U \\ S \\ R \end{array}\overset{\begin{array}{ccc} U & S & R \end{array}}{\begin{bmatrix} .86 & .05 & .03 \\ .08 & .86 & .05 \\ .06 & .09 & .92 \end{bmatrix}}$ (b) 11.4%   **17.** All powers are $\begin{bmatrix} \frac{1}{3} & \frac{1}{3} \\ \frac{2}{3} & \frac{2}{3} \end{bmatrix}$.

19. $\begin{bmatrix} .1 & .3 \\ .9 & .7 \end{bmatrix}$; $\begin{bmatrix} .28 & .24 \\ .72 & .76 \end{bmatrix}$; $\begin{bmatrix} .24 & .25 \\ .76 & .75 \end{bmatrix}$; $\begin{bmatrix} .25 & .25 \\ .75 & .75 \end{bmatrix}$; $\begin{bmatrix} .25 & .25 \\ .75 & .75 \end{bmatrix}$ **21.** All powers are $\begin{bmatrix} .2 & .2 & .2 \\ .3 & .3 & .3 \\ .5 & .5 & .5 \end{bmatrix}$.

23. No   **25.** (a) $\begin{bmatrix} .35 \\ .65 \end{bmatrix}$; $\begin{bmatrix} .425 \\ .575 \end{bmatrix}$; $\begin{bmatrix} .3875 \\ .6125 \end{bmatrix}$; $\begin{bmatrix} .40625 \\ .59375 \end{bmatrix}$ (b) $\begin{bmatrix} .40625 \\ .59375 \end{bmatrix}$ **27.** $\begin{bmatrix} .4 \\ .6 \end{bmatrix}$ **29.** $\begin{bmatrix} .4 & .4 \\ .6 & .6 \end{bmatrix}$

Exercises 8.2

1. Yes   **3.** Yes   **5.** Yes   **7.** $\begin{bmatrix} \frac{1}{6} \\ \frac{5}{6} \end{bmatrix}$ **9.** $\begin{bmatrix} .6 \\ .4 \end{bmatrix}$ **11.** $\begin{bmatrix} \frac{5}{14} \\ \frac{3}{7} \\ \frac{3}{14} \end{bmatrix}$ **13.** 40%   **15.** 25%

17. 40%   **19.** $\begin{bmatrix} .5 \\ .5 \end{bmatrix}$ is a stable distribution for the matrix $A = \begin{bmatrix} 0 & 1 \\ 1 & 0 \end{bmatrix}$ because $.5 + .5 = 1$ and $\begin{bmatrix} 0 & 1 \\ 1 & 0 \end{bmatrix}\begin{bmatrix} .5 \\ .5 \end{bmatrix} = \begin{bmatrix} .5 \\ .5 \end{bmatrix}$.

However, given an arbitrary initial distribution $\begin{bmatrix} \\ \end{bmatrix}_0 \neq \begin{bmatrix} .5 \\ .5 \end{bmatrix}$, $A^n \begin{bmatrix} \\ \end{bmatrix}_0$ will not approach $\begin{bmatrix} .5 \\ .5 \end{bmatrix}$ as n gets large, so the

existence of a stable distribution for A does not contradict the main premise of this section.   **21.** $\begin{bmatrix} .7 & .7 \\ .3 & .3 \end{bmatrix}$; $\begin{bmatrix} .7 \\ .3 \end{bmatrix}$

23. $\begin{bmatrix} \frac{8}{35} & \frac{8}{35} & \frac{8}{35} \\ \frac{3}{7} & \frac{3}{7} & \frac{3}{7} \\ \frac{12}{35} & \frac{12}{35} & \frac{12}{35} \end{bmatrix}$; $\begin{bmatrix} \frac{8}{35} \\ \frac{3}{7} \\ \frac{12}{35} \end{bmatrix}$

Exercises 8.3

1. No   **3.** Yes   **5.** $R = [.5]; S = \begin{bmatrix} .3 \\ .2 \end{bmatrix}; F = [2];$ $\begin{bmatrix} 1 & 0 & | & .6 \\ 0 & 1 & | & .4 \\ \hline 0 & 0 & | & 0 \end{bmatrix}$

7. $R = \begin{bmatrix} .3 & .6 \\ .1 & .2 \end{bmatrix}; S = \begin{bmatrix} .1 & 0 \\ .5 & .2 \end{bmatrix}; F = \begin{bmatrix} 1.6 & 1.2 \\ .2 & 1.4 \end{bmatrix};$ $\begin{bmatrix} 1 & 0 & | & .16 & .12 \\ 0 & 1 & | & .84 & .88 \\ \hline 0 & 0 & | & 0 & 0 \\ 0 & 0 & | & 0 & 0 \end{bmatrix}$

9. $R = \begin{bmatrix} .5 & 0 \\ .1 & .6 \end{bmatrix}; S = \begin{bmatrix} .1 & .2 \\ .3 & 0 \\ 0 & .2 \end{bmatrix}; F = \begin{bmatrix} 2 & 0 \\ .5 & 2.5 \end{bmatrix};$ $\begin{bmatrix} 1 & 0 & 0 & | & .3 & .5 \\ 0 & 1 & 0 & | & .6 & 0 \\ 0 & 0 & 1 & | & .1 & .5 \\ \hline 0 & 0 & 0 & | & 0 & 0 \\ 0 & 0 & 0 & | & 0 & 0 \end{bmatrix}$

11. If the gambler begins with \$2, he should have \$1 for an expected number of .79 plays.

13. (a)
$\begin{array}{c} \\ D \\ G \\ F \\ S \end{array} \begin{array}{cccc} D & G & F & S \end{array}$
$\begin{array}{c} D \\ G \\ F \\ S \end{array} \begin{bmatrix} 1 & 0 & | & .2 & .1 \\ 0 & 1 & | & 0 & .9 \\ \hline 0 & 0 & | & 0 & 0 \\ 0 & 0 & | & .8 & 0 \end{bmatrix}$

(b)
$\begin{array}{cccc} & D & G & F & S \end{array}$
$\begin{array}{c} D \\ G \\ F \\ S \end{array} \begin{bmatrix} 1 & 0 & | & .28 & .1 \\ 0 & 1 & | & .72 & .9 \\ \hline 0 & 0 & | & 0 & 0 \\ 0 & 0 & | & 0 & 0 \end{bmatrix}$

(c) .72   (d) 1.8 years

15. (a) $\dfrac{13}{14}; \dfrac{11}{14}$ (b) $\dfrac{20}{7}$ months   (c) \$5786; \$1214

17. (a) $\dfrac{3}{4}; \dfrac{1}{2}; \dfrac{1}{4}$ (b) 4

19. $\begin{bmatrix} 1 & 0 & \frac{666}{917} & \frac{75}{131} & \frac{250}{917} \\ 0 & 1 & \frac{251}{917} & \frac{56}{131} & \frac{667}{917} \\ 0 & 0 & 0 & 0 & 0 \\ 0 & 0 & 0 & 0 & 0 \\ 0 & 0 & 0 & 0 & 0 \end{bmatrix}$

Chapter 8: Supplementary Exercises

1. Stochastic, neither   **2.** Stochastic, regular   **3.** Stochastic, regular   **4.** Stochastic, absorbing   **5.** Not stochastic

6. Stochastic, absorbing   **7.** $\begin{bmatrix} \frac{5}{9} \\ \frac{4}{9} \end{bmatrix}$ **8.** $\begin{bmatrix} 1 & 0 & 0 & | & \frac{1}{2} & \frac{1}{2} \\ 0 & 1 & 0 & | & \frac{1}{4} & \frac{1}{8} \\ 0 & 0 & 1 & | & \frac{1}{4} & \frac{3}{8} \\ \hline 0 & 0 & 0 & | & 0 & 0 \\ 0 & 0 & 0 & | & 0 & 0 \end{bmatrix}$ **9.** (a)
$\begin{array}{ccc} & H & M & L \end{array}$
$\begin{array}{c} H \\ M \\ L \end{array} \begin{bmatrix} .5 & .4 & .3 \\ .4 & .3 & .5 \\ .1 & .3 & .2 \end{bmatrix}$ (b) 38%   (c) $\dfrac{19}{97}$

10. (a)
$$\begin{array}{c} \\ P \\ N \end{array} \begin{array}{cc} P & N \\ \begin{bmatrix} .8 & .3 \\ .2 & .7 \end{bmatrix} \end{array}$$
(b) 30%   (c) 60%   **11.**
$$\left[\begin{array}{cc|ccc} 1 & 0 & \frac{11}{12} & 1 & \frac{1}{2} \\ 0 & 1 & \frac{1}{12} & 0 & \frac{1}{2} \\ \hline 0 & 0 & 0 & 0 & 0 \\ 0 & 0 & 0 & 0 & 0 \\ 0 & 0 & 0 & 0 & 0 \end{array}\right]$$
12. (a)
$$\begin{array}{c} I \;\; II \\ \begin{array}{c} I \\ II \\ III \\ IV \end{array} \left[\begin{array}{cc} 1 & 0 \\ 0 & \\ 0 & \\ 0 & \end{array}\right. \end{array}$$

(d) 3 minutes   **13.** (c)   **14.** 58.5%   **15.** (a) If the traffic is moderate on a particular day then for the probability of Light is .2, the probability of Moderate is .75, and the probability of Heavy is .05.   (b) About 37.0%, Light; 47.8%, Moderate; 15.2%, Heavy   (c) About 3 days   **16.** State G: ≈ 1.48 months; state S: ≈ 1.83 months.

17. (a)
$$\begin{bmatrix} \frac{122}{1683} \\ \frac{23}{99} \\ \frac{4}{9} \\ \frac{422}{1683} \end{bmatrix}$$
; In the long run, the probability of having 1, 2, 3, or 4 units of water in the reservoir at any given time

will be $\dfrac{122}{1683}, \dfrac{23}{99}, \dfrac{4}{9},$ or $\dfrac{122}{1683}$, respectively.   (b) About $6881

Chapter 8: Chapter Test

1. (a) stochastic   (b) not stochastic   (c) not stochastic   (d) stochastic   **2.** (a) not regular   (b) regular

(c) regular   **3.** (b)   **4.** $\begin{bmatrix} \frac{3}{7} \\ \frac{4}{7} \end{bmatrix}$; $\begin{bmatrix} \frac{3}{7} & \frac{3}{7} \\ \frac{4}{7} & \frac{4}{7} \end{bmatrix}$ **5.** (a) $\begin{bmatrix} .70 & .60 \\ .30 & .40 \end{bmatrix}$ (b) $\begin{bmatrix} .50 \\ .50 \end{bmatrix}$ (c) 66.5%   (d) $\begin{bmatrix} .70 & .60 \\ .30 & .40 \end{bmatrix}\begin{bmatrix} \frac{2}{3} \\ \frac{1}{3} \end{bmatrix} = \begin{bmatrix} \frac{2}{3} \\ \frac{1}{3} \end{bmatrix}$

6. (a) absorbing   (b) not absorbing   (c) absorbing   **7.** (a)
$$\begin{array}{c} \;\;\;\text{IBM} \;\;\; \text{App} \;\;\; \text{None} \\ \begin{bmatrix} 1 & 0 & .3 \\ 0 & 1 & .1 \\ 0 & 0 & .6 \end{bmatrix} \end{array}$$
(b) $\left[\begin{array}{cc|c} 1 & 0 & \frac{3}{4} \\ 0 & 1 & \frac{1}{4} \\ \hline 0 & 0 & 0 \end{array}\right]$ (c) 25%

(d) 2.5 years

CHAPTER 9

Exercises 9.1

1. R: row 2; C: column 1   **3.** R: row 2; C: column 1   **5.** R: row 1; C: column 1   **7.** (a) row 1, column 2   (b) 0

9.
$$\begin{array}{c} \;\;\; H \;\;\;\; T \\ \begin{array}{c} H \\ T \end{array} \begin{bmatrix} 2 & -1 \\ -1 & -4 \end{bmatrix} \end{array}$$
; strictly determined; R shows heads, C shows tails

11.
$$\begin{array}{c} \;\;\;\;\; F \;\;\;\;\;\;\; A \;\;\;\;\;\; N \\ \begin{array}{c} F \\ A \\ N \end{array} \begin{bmatrix} 8000 & -1000 & 1000 \\ -7000 & 4000 & -2000 \\ 3000 & 3000 & 2000 \end{bmatrix} \end{array}$$
; strictly determined; both should be neutral

$$\begin{bmatrix} & & 8 \\ & -5 & -5 \\ 6 & 3 & 2 \end{bmatrix} ; \text{not strictly determined}$$

Exercises 9.2

1. (a) 0   (b) 1   (c) -1.12 (d) .5 [(b) is most advantageous to R]   **3.** \$29,200   **5.** 0

Exercises 9.3

1. $\begin{bmatrix} 1 & 1 \\ 2 & 2 \end{bmatrix}$; $\begin{bmatrix} \frac{1}{4} \\ \frac{3}{4} \end{bmatrix}$ **3.** $\begin{bmatrix} 1 & 1 \\ 2 & 2 \end{bmatrix}$; $\begin{bmatrix} \frac{5}{9} \\ \frac{4}{9} \end{bmatrix}$ **5.** $\begin{bmatrix} 2 & 3 \\ 5 & 5 \end{bmatrix}$; $\begin{bmatrix} \frac{3}{5} \\ \frac{2}{5} \end{bmatrix}$ **7.** $\begin{bmatrix} 7 & 6 \\ 13 & 13 \end{bmatrix}$ **9.** $\begin{bmatrix} 0 \\ 1 \end{bmatrix}$

11. (a) $\begin{bmatrix} \frac{8}{17} & \frac{9}{17} \end{bmatrix}$ (b) $\begin{bmatrix} \frac{8}{17} \\ \frac{9}{17} \end{bmatrix}$ (c) about \$2,765   **13.** $\begin{bmatrix} \frac{5}{8} & \frac{3}{8} & 0 \end{bmatrix}$; $\begin{bmatrix} \frac{1}{2} \\ \frac{1}{2} \end{bmatrix}$

Chapter 9: Supplementary Exercises

1. Strictly determined; $R\ 3, C\ 3; 2$ **2.** Not strictly determined   **3.** Not strictly determined

4. Strictly determined; $R\ 1, C\ 2; 1$ **5.** 7   **6.** 2   **7.** 1.4   **8.** -1.3 **9.** $\begin{bmatrix} \frac{4}{11} & \frac{7}{11} \end{bmatrix}$; $\begin{bmatrix} \frac{6}{11} \\ \frac{5}{11} \end{bmatrix}$ **10.** $\begin{bmatrix} \frac{8}{17} & \frac{9}{17} \end{bmatrix}$; $\begin{bmatrix} \frac{10}{17} \\ \frac{7}{17} \end{bmatrix}$

11. $[0\ 1]$ **12.** $\begin{bmatrix} \frac{1}{4} \\ \frac{3}{4} \end{bmatrix}$ **13.** (a) Ruth should play the two $\frac{9}{14}$ of the time and the six $\frac{5}{14}$ of the time. Carol should play the

two $\frac{5}{14}$ of the time and the six $\frac{9}{14}$ of the time.   (b) Ruth   **14.** (a)

	S	A	W
A	3000	2000	1000
B	6000	2000	−3000
C	15,000	1000	−10,000

(b) Buy stock A

Chapter 9: Chapter Test

1. (a) A move R_1 by R and C_3 by C results in a payoff of 6 to R.   (b) A move R_3 by R and C_2 by C results in a payoff of 10 to C.   (c) No   **3.** (a) row 3, column 2, value = 2   (b) row 1, column 1, value = 0

4.
$$\begin{array}{c|ccccc} & 1 & 2 & 3 & 4 & 5 \\\hline 1 & -1 & -1 & -1 & -1 & -1 \\ 2 & 2 & -2 & -2 & -2 & -2 \\ 3 & 3 & 3 & -3 & -3 & -3 \\ 4 & 4 & 4 & 4 & -4 & -4 \\ 5 & 5 & 5 & 5 & 5 & -5 \end{array}$$; yes; -1; C **5.** (a) On average, C gains .16 every time the ga

6. (a) $C = \begin{bmatrix} \frac{3}{5} \\ \frac{2}{5} \end{bmatrix}$; $R = \begin{bmatrix} \frac{9}{10} & \frac{1}{10} \end{bmatrix}$ (b) C

CHAPTER 10

Exercises 10.1

1. (a) $i = .01, n = 24$ (b) $i = .02, n = 20$ (c) $i = .05, n = 40$ **3.** (a) $i = .06, n = 4, P = \$500, F = \$631.24$
(b) $i = .005, n = 120, P = \$800, F = \$1455.52$ (c) $i = .02, n = 19, P = \$6177.88, F = \$9000$ **5.** $1127.16   **7.** $22,396.57
9. $7180.08; \$1180.08   **11.** (a) $3548.74   (b) $451.26   (c)

Month	Interest	Balance
0		$3548.74
1	$17.74	$3566.48
2	$17.83	$3584.31
3	$17.92	$3602.23

13. $12,824.32   **15.** $8874.49   **17.** (a) 6%   (b) $5.05; \$1015.08   (c) $5.61; \$1127.16   **19.** $1700 in 9 years

21. better   **23.** $8874.49   **25.** (a) $r = .04, n = \frac{1}{2}, P = \$500, A = \$510$

(b) $r = .05, n = 2, P = \$500, A = \$550$ **27.** $1150   **29.** $2500   **31.** 4.08%   **33.** 20 years   **35.** $P = \dfrac{A}{1 + nr}$

37. (a)   **39.** $104.06; 4.06%   **41.** 4.04%   **43.** 4.49%   **45.** 4%   **47.** $1065; \$1134.23; \$1207.95; 8; 12

49. 30 years

Exercises 10.2

1. (a) $i = .005, n = 120, R = \$50, F = \$8193.97$ (b) $i = .02, n = 20, R = \$2675.19, F = \$65,000$
3. $6977   **5.** $4698.97   **7.** (a) $27,048.92   (b) $3048.92   (c)

Month	Interest	Balance
1		500
2	2.50	1002.50
3	5.01	1507.51

9. $305.06; \$10,982.16; \$1017.84   **11.** $200 each month; $343.75   **13.** $24,649.92   **15.** 877.91
17. $1000 at the end of each month   **19.** $7239.32   **21.** $17,584.62   **23.** (a)   **25.** $24,000   **27.** $4339.35
29. $59,189.85   **31.** (a) $1   (b) $s_{\overline{n}|i} \cdot i$ **35.** $3623.52   **37.** (a) $1269.67   (b) $65,134.88
39. $1000, \$2050, \$3152.50; 19; 26   **41.** After 33 weeks

3. $11,469.92 **5.** (a) $583.31 (b) $16.69 (c) $58,314.31 (d) $26,973.02 (e) $4188.65
7. (a) $265.71 (b) $9565.56 (c) $1565.56 (d) $5644.58 (e) $2990.59 (f) $534.53
9. $8950 **11.** $14,042.36

Payment number	Amount	Interest	Applied to principal	Unpaid balance
1	$265.71	$80.00	$185.71	$7814.29
2	265.71	78.14	187.57	7626.72
3	265.71	76.27	189.44	7437.28
4	265.71	74.37	191.34	7245.94

13.

Payment number	Amount	Interest	Applied to principal	Unpaid balance
1	$256.28	$10.00	$246.28	$753.72
2	256.28	7.54	248.74	504.98
3	256.28	5.05	251.23	253.74
4	256.28	2.54	253.74	0.00

15. $804.62 **17.** $119,161.62 **19.** $1196.68 **21.** (a)
23. (a) $183,927.96 (b) $24,989.92 (c) $105,266.63
25. $2.5 billion **27.** Yes
29. $2105.33, $2021.12, $1936.28, 24 months.
31. $4258.21; after 46 months **33.** 261

Chapter 10: Supplementary Exercises

1. (d) **2.** $488.16 **3.** $49,712.75 **4.** $53.79 **5.** 10% compounded annually **6.** $13,954.01 **7.** (a) $2400.34
(b) $167,304.68 **8.** $43,665.52 **9.** $27,481.64 **10.** $13,050.08 **11.** $211.37 **12.** $12,050.34 **13.** $782.92
14. $6872.11 **15.** $100,451.50 **16.** 139,401.04 **17.** Investment A **18.** Yes, it is a bargain since the present value is
$879.57. **19.** 10.25% **20.** 19.56% **21.** $146,861.85

22.

Payment number	Amount	Interest	Applied to principal	Unpaid balance
1	$304.22	$50.00	$254.22	$9745.78
2	304.22	48.73	255.49	9490.29
3	304.22	47.45	256.77	9233.52
4	304.22	46.17	258.05	8975.47
5	304.22	44.88	259.34	8716.13
6	304.22	43.58	260.64	8455.49

23. $151,843.34 **24.** $5799.84 **25.** $1206.93

Chapter 10: Chapter Test

1. $524.38 **2.** $4464.29 **3.** $1189.77; $164.77 **4.** $11,263.09 **5.** $68,235.59 **6.** $21,711.48 **7.** $1071.11
8. $2322.17 **9.** $3051.28 **10.** $2237.43 **11.** (a) $163.17 (b) $55 (c) $7891.83 (d) $1873.28
12. $40,812.35

CHAPTER 11

Exercises 11.1

1. $4, -6; 2$ **3.** $-\frac{1}{2}, 0; 0$ **5.** $-\frac{2}{3}, 15; 9$ **7.** (a) $10, 4, 1, -\frac{1}{2}, -\frac{5}{4}$ **9.** (a) $3.5, 4, 5, 7, 11$

(b)

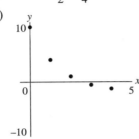

(b)

(c) $y_n = -2 + 12\left(\frac{1}{2}\right)^n$ (c) $y_n = 3 + (.5)2^n$

11. (a) $17.5, 0, 7, 4.2, 5.32$ **13.** (a) $15, 14, 12, 8, 0$ **15.** $1, 5, 5.8, 5.96, 5.992$ **17.** $y_n = 1.05y_{n-1}, y_0 = 1000$

(b)

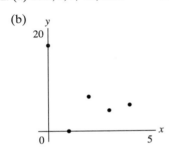

(b)

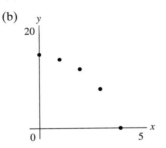

(c) $y_n = 5 + 12.5(-.4)^n$ (c) $y_n = 16 - 2^n$

19. $y_n = 1.05y_{n-1} + 100, y_0 = 1000$ **21.** (a) $1, 3, 5, 7, 9$ **23.** $\$30$ **25.** $4.8310595; 20$ **27.** $50.41; 22$

29. $5.7155165; 19$ **31.** $2.8; 18$

(b)

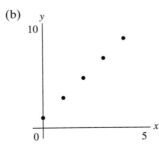

(c) $a = 1$, so the denominator of $\dfrac{b}{1 - a}$ is zero.

Exercises 11.2

1. $y_n = 1 + 5n$ **3.** $80(1.0075)^{60}$ **5.** $80\left(1 + \dfrac{1}{365}\right)^{1825}$ **7.** 108 **9.** $A\left(1 + \dfrac{r}{k}\right)^{kt}$ **11.** (a) $10; 10; 10; 10$

(b) 11; 12; 14; 18   (c) 9; 8; 6; 2

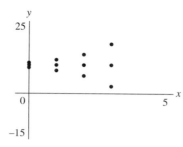

13. $y_n = 5 + 2(.4)^n$; y_n approaches 5

15. $y_n = 2(-5)^n$; y_n gets arbitrarily large, alternating between being positive and negative.   **17.** $y_n = 1.0075y_{n-1} - 350$,

$y_0 = 38,900$ **19.** $y_n = y_{n-1} - 2000$, $y_0 = 50,000$; $y_n = 50,000 - 2000n$ **21.** (b)   **23.** (c)   **25.** (c)   **27.** (c)

29. $1195.62; $8\frac{1}{2}$ years; 47   **31.** $245; 12 years; 23 years   **33.** 60

Exercises 11.3

1. (a), (b), (d), (f), (h)   **3.** (b), (d), (e), (f)   **5.** (b), (d), (e), (f)   **7.** (a), (c), (h), possibly (g)

9. Possible answer: **11.** Possible answer: **13.** Possible answer: **15.**

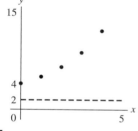
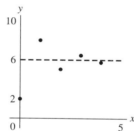
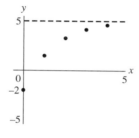
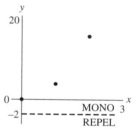

17.

19.

21.

23.

25. less than $60,000   **27.** (a) $y_n = 1.06y_{n-1} - 120$ (b) at least $2000
29. Possible answer: $y_n = .5y_{n-1} + 4$, $y_0 = 1$ **31.** Possible answer: $y_n = 2y_{n-1}$, $y_0 = 1$
33. Possible answer: $y_n = -2y_{n-1}$, $y_0 = 5$

Exercises 11.4

1. $y_n = 1.0075y_{n-1} - 261.50, y_0 = 32,500$ **3.** $y_n = 1.015y_{n-1} + 200, y_0 = 4000$ **5.** \$46,002.34   **7.** \$11,035.68
9. \$1979.44   **11.** \$132.86   **13.** \$39.205 million; 30   **15.** \$505.03; \$1022.80; \$1553.65; 30; 37

Exercises 11.5

1. $y_n = 1.02y_{n-1}, y_0 = 100$ million   **3.** $y_n = .75y_{n-1}$ **5.** $y_n = .92y_{n-1} + 8, y_0 = 0$

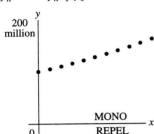   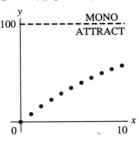

7. $y_n = .7y_{n-1} + 3.6, y_0 = 0$ **9.** $y_n = 1.05y_{n-1} - 1000, y_0 = 30,000$ **11.** $y_n = .8y_{n-1} + 14, y_0 = 40$

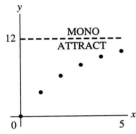   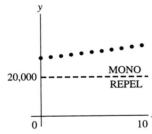   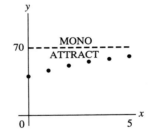

13. $p_n = -.5p_{n-1} + 21, p_0 = 10$ **15.** 5.38 million; 2013; 2047

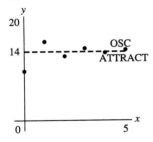

Chapter 11: Supplementary Exercises

1. (a) $5; -7; 29$ (b) $y_n = 2 - (-3)^n$ (c) -79 **2.** (a) $\dfrac{17}{2}; 7; \dfrac{11}{2}$ (b) $y_n = 10 - \dfrac{3}{2}n$ (c) 1   **3.** \$2989.08

4. \$1109.54   **5.**   **6.**   **7.** (a) $y_n = 1.03y_{n-1} - 600, y_0 = 120,000$
                                                                          (b) 200,611

8. (a) $y_n = 1.01y_{n-1} - 360$, $y_0 = 35,000$ (b) $33,693.28   **9.** $20.22   **10.** $237.14   **11.** $22,492.53
12. $270.49   **13.** $y_n = .9y_{n-1} + 100,000$, $y_0 = 0$ **14.** $y_n = .92y_{n-1}$, $y_0 = 100$

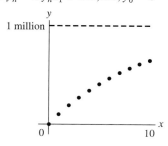
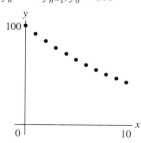

Chapter 11: Chapter Test

1. (a) $2, 4, 5$ (b) $y_n = 6 - 8\left(\dfrac{1}{2}\right)^n$ (c) 5.5 **2.** (a) $110, 160, 210$ (b) $y_n = 60 + 50n$ (c) 260

3. (a)

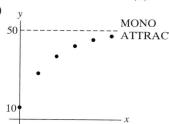

   (b)

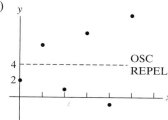

   4. .3 ppm

5. (a) $31,726   (b) 8%   (c) $3000   (d) $29,360.52   **6.** (a) $454.15   (b) 12.5%   (c) $9,245.85; $8,526.44; $361.57
7. $119,161.62   **8.** (a) $y_n = 1.06y_{n-1} + 500$; $y_0 = 0$ (b) $14,106.44   **9.** $122.04
10. $y_n = .9y_{n-1} + .05$; $y_0 = 0$

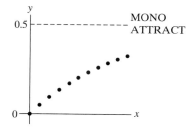

CHAPTER 12

Exercises 12.1

1. Statement   **3.** Statement   **5.** Not a statement   **7.** Not a statement   **9.** Statement   **11.** Not a statement
13. Not a statement   **15.** Statement   **17.** (a) Ozone is opaque to ultraviolet light, and life on earth requires ozone.
(b) Ozone is not opaque to ultraviolet light, or life on earth requires ozone.   (c) Ozone is not opaque to ultraviolet light,
or life on earth does not require ozone.   (d) It is not the case that life on earth does not require ozone.   **19.** (a) $p \vee q$
(b) $p \wedge \sim q$ (c) $q \wedge \sim p$ (d) $\sim p \wedge \sim q$

Exercises 12.2

1.

p	q	$p \wedge \sim q$
T	T	F
T	F	T
F	T	F
F	F	F

3.

p	q	r	$(p \wedge \sim r) \vee q$
T	T	T	T
T	T	F	T
T	F	T	F
T	F	F	T
F	T	T	T
F	T	F	T
F	F	T	F
F	F	F	F

5.

p	q	r	$\sim [(p \wedge r) \vee q]$
T	T	T	F
T	T	F	F
T	F	T	F
T	F	F	T
F	T	T	F
F	T	F	F
F	F	T	T
F	F	F	T

7.

p	$p \vee \sim p$
T	T
F	T

9.

p	q	r	$p \oplus (q \vee r)$
T	T	T	F
T	T	F	F
T	F	T	F
T	F	F	T
F	T	T	T
F	T	F	T
F	F	T	T
F	F	F	F

11.

p	q	r	$(p \vee q) \wedge (p \vee r)$
T	T	T	T
T	T	F	T
T	F	T	T
T	F	F	T
F	T	T	T
F	T	F	F
F	F	T	F
F	F	F	F

13.

p	q	$(p \vee q) \wedge \sim (p \vee q)$
T	T	F
T	F	F
F	T	F
F	F	F

15.

p	q	r	$\sim (p \vee q) \wedge r$
T	T	T	F
T	T	F	F
T	F	T	F
T	F	F	F
F	T	T	F
F	T	F	F
F	F	T	T
F	F	F	F

17.

p	q	r	$\sim p \vee (q \wedge r)$
T	T	T	T
T	T	F	F
T	F	T	F
T	F	F	F
F	T	T	T
F	T	F	T
F	F	T	T
F	F	F	T

19. They are identical.   **21.** They are identical.

23. $(p \wedge q) \vee r$ is T and $p \wedge (q \vee r)$ is F when p is F and r is T. Otherwise, the tables are identical.

25. (a)

p	$p \mid p$
T	F
F	T

(b)

p	q	$(p \mid p) \mid (q \mid q)$
T	T	T
T	F	T
F	T	T
F	F	F

(c)

p	q	$(p \mid q) \mid (p \mid q)$
T	T	T
T	F	F
F	T	F
F	F	F

(d)

p	q	$p \mid ((p \mid q) \mid q)$
T	T	F
T	F	F
F	T	T
F	F	T

27. (a) T   (b) F   (c) T   (d) F   (e) F   (f) F

29. (a) F   (b) F   (c) F   (d) F   **31.**

$$(p \oplus q) \wedge r$$
F

$p \oplus q$ r
T   **F**

p q
T   **F**

33.

$$(p \vee q) \wedge (p \vee \sim r)$$
T

$p \vee q$ $p \vee \sim r$
T   **T**

p q p $\sim r$
T   **F**   **T**   **T**

r
F

35. 0

37. (a) T   (b) T   **39.** (a) T   (b) F   **41.**

P	q		◆ 3
1	1		1
1	0		0
0	1		0
0	0		1
------	------		------
L1 ="not(LP xor L

Exercises 12.3

1.

p	q	$p \rightarrow \sim q$
T	T	F
T	F	T
F	T	T
F	F	T

3.

p	q	$(p \oplus q) \rightarrow q$
T	T	T
T	F	F
F	T	T
F	F	T

5.

p	q	r	$(\sim p \wedge q) \rightarrow r$
T	T	T	T
T	T	F	T
T	F	T	T
T	F	F	T
F	T	T	T
F	T	F	F
F	F	T	T
F	F	F	T

7.

p	q	$(p \rightarrow q) \leftrightarrow (\sim p \vee q)$
T	T	T
T	F	T
F	T	T
F	F	T

9.

p	q	r	$(p \rightarrow q) \rightarrow r$
T	T	T	T
T	T	F	F
T	F	T	T
T	F	F	T
F	T	T	T
F	T	F	F
F	F	T	T
F	F	F	F

11.

p	q	r	$\sim (p \vee q) \rightarrow (\sim p \wedge r)$
T	T	T	T
T	T	F	T
T	F	T	T
T	F	F	T
F	T	T	T
F	T	F	T
F	F	T	T
F	F	F	F

13.

p	q	$(p \vee q) \leftrightarrow (p \wedge q)$
T	T	T
T	F	F
F	T	F
F	F	T

15.

p	q	r	$[p \wedge (q \vee r)] \leftrightarrow [(p \wedge q) \vee (p \wedge r)]$
T	T	T	T
T	T	F	T
T	F	T	T
T	F	F	T
F	T	T	T
F	T	F	T
F	F	T	T
F	F	F	T

17. T   **19.** T **21.** T   **23.** F   **25.** T   **27.** $p \leftrightarrow q$ **29.** $q \rightarrow p$; hyp: q; con: p **31.** $q \rightarrow p$; hyp: q; con: p
33. $\sim p \rightarrow \sim q$; hyp: $\sim p$; con: $\sim q$ **35.** $\sim p \rightarrow \sim q$; hyp: $\sim p$; con: $\sim q$; TRUE   **37.** $\sim q \rightarrow \sim p$; hyp: $\sim q$; con: $\sim p$; TRUE

39. (a) hyp: A person is healthy; con: The person lives a long life.   (b) hyp: The train stops at the station; con: A passenger requests the stop.   (c) hyp: The plant grows; con: The plant is exposed to sunlight.   (d) hyp: I will go to the store; con: Jane goes to the store.   **41.** (a) If City Sanitation collects the garbage, then the mayor calls. (b) The price of beans goes down if there is no drought.   (c) Goldfish swim in Lake Erie if Lake Erie is fresh water. (d) Tap water is not salted if it boils slowly.   **43.** (a) 4   (b) 4   (c) 4   (d) 4   (e) 6   (f) 6   **45.** (a) 7   (b) 7 (c) 0   (d) 7   (e) 0   (f) 0   **47.** (a) 6   (b) −12   (c) 0   (d) 0   (e) 28   (f) 0   **49.** (a) 3   (b) 3 (c) −37   (d) −7   (e) 43   (f) −7

Exercises 12.4

1. When p is false and q is true, the statement is FALSE.   **5.** (d) $p \mid (q \mid q)$ (e) $\sim (p \wedge q)$

7.

p	q	c	$(p \to q) \leftrightarrow [(p \wedge \sim q) \to c]$
T	T	F	T
T	F	F	T
F	T	F	T
F	F	F	T

9. False   **11.** $\sim [\sim (p \vee q) \vee \sim (\sim p \vee \sim q)]$

13. (a) Arizona does not border California or Arizona does not border Nevada.   (b) There are no tickets available, and the agency cannot get tickets.   (c) The killer's hat was neither white nor gray.   **15.** (a) I have a ticket to the theater, and I did not spend a lot of money.   (b) Basketball is played on an indoor court, and the players do not wear sneakers. (c) The stock market is going up, and interest rates are not going down.   (d) Humans have enough water, and humans are not staying healthy.   **17.** (a) Contrapositive: If a bird is not a hummingbird, then it is not small (F)., Converse: If a bird is a hummingbird, then it is small (T).   (b) Contrapositive: If two nonvertical lines are not parallel, they do not have the same slope (T)., Converse: If two nonvertical lines are parallel, they have the same slope (T).   (c) Contrapositive: If we are not in France, then we are not in Paris (T)., Converse: If we are in France, we must be in Paris (F).   (d) Contrapositive: If you can legally make a U-turn, then the road is not one-way (T)., Converse: If you cannot legally make a U-turn, then the road is one-way (F).   **19.** Ask either guard, "If I asked you whether your door was the door to freedom, would you say yes?"

Exercises 12.5

1. m = "Sue goes to the movies."
     r = "Sue reads."

1. $m \vee r$	hyp.
2. $\sim m$	hyp.
3. r	disj. syll. (1, 2)

3. a = "My allowance comes this week."
     p = "I pay the rent."
     b = "My bank account will be in the black."
     e = "I will be evicted."

1. $(a \wedge p) \to b$	hyp.
2. $\sim p \to e$	hyp.
3. $\sim e \wedge a$	hyp.
4. $\sim e$	subtr. (3)
5. p	mod. tollens (2, 4)
6. a	subtr. (3)
7. b	mod. ponens (5, 6, 1)

5. p = "The price of oil increases."
     a = "The OPEC countries are in agreement."
     d = "There is a U.N. debate."

1. $p \to a$	hyp.
2. $\sim d \to p$	hyp.
3. $\sim a$	hyp.
4. $\sim p$	mod. tollens (1, 3)
5. d	mod. tollens (2, 4)

7. g = "The germ is present."
     r = "The rash is present."
     f = "The fever is present."

1. $g \to (r \wedge f)$	hyp.
2. f	hyp.
3. $\sim r$	hyp.
4. $\sim r \vee \sim f$	addition (3)
5. $\sim (r \wedge f)$	DeMorgan (4)
6. $\sim g$	mod. tollens (1, 5)

9. c = "The material is cotton."
r = "The material is rayon."
d = "The material can be made into a dress."

1. $(c \lor r) \to d$	hyp.
2. $\sim d$	hyp.
3. $\sim (c \lor r)$	mod. tollens $(1, 2)$
4. $\sim c \land \sim r$	DeMorgan (3)
5. $\sim r$	subtraction (4)

11. Invalid   **13.** Valid   **15.** Valid   **17.** Invalid   **19.** Invalid

21. s = "Sam goes to the store."
m = "Sam needs milk."
$H_1 = s \to m$
$H_2 = \sim m$
$C = \sim s$

1. s	$\sim C$
2. $s \to m$	H_1
3. m	$\sim H_2$; mod. ponens $(1, 2)$

23. n = "The newspaper reports the crime."
t = "Television reports the crime."
s = "The crime is serious."
k = "A person is killed."
$H_1 = (n \land t) \to s$
$H_2 = k \to n$
$H_3 = k$
$H_4 = t$
$C = s$

1. $\sim s$	$\sim C$
2. $(n \land t) \to s$	H_1
3. $\sim (n \land t)$	mod. tollens $(1, 2)$
4. $\sim n \lor \sim t$	DeMorgan (3)
5. t	H_4
6. $\sim n$	disj. syllogism $(4, 5)$
7. $k \to n$	H_2
8. $\sim k$	$\sim H_3$; mod. tollens $(6, 7)$

Exercises 12.6

1. (a) F   (b) T   (c) T   (d) T   (e) F   **3.** (a) $\forall x\, p(x)$ (b) $\sim [\forall x\, p(x)]$ (c) $\forall x \sim p(x)$
(d) (c) implies (b)   **5.** $\forall x \sim p(x)$, or $\sim [\exists x\, p(x)]$. This is FALSE. Abby meant to say, "Not all men cheat on their wives."
7. (a) $\forall x\, p(x)$ (b) $\exists x \sim p(x)$ (c) $\exists x\, p(x)$ (d) $\sim [\forall x\, p(x)]$ (e) $\forall x \sim p(x)$ (f) $\sim [\exists x\, p(x)]$
(g) (b) and (d); (e) and (f)   **9.** (a) T   (b) F   **11.** (a) T   (b) F   (c) T   (d) F   (e) F   (f) T   (g) F   (h) T
13. (a) Not every dog has his day.   (b) No men fight wars.   (c) Some mothers are unmarried.
(d) There exists a pot without a cover.   (e) All children have pets.   (f) Every month has 30 days.
15. (a) "The sum of any two nonnegative integers is greater than 12." FALSE: let $x = 1, y = 2$. "There exists two nonnegative integers whose sum is not greater than 12."   (b) "For any nonnegative integer, there is another nonnegative integer which, added to the first, makes a sum greater than 12." TRUE.   (c) "There is a nonnegative integer which, added to any other nonnegative integer, makes a sum greater than 12." TRUE.   (d) "There are two nonnegative integers the sum of which is greater than 12." TRUE.   **17.** (a) FALSE: let $x = 2, y = 3$.   (b) TRUE: for any x, let $y = x$.   (c) TRUE: let $x = 1$.
(d) FALSE: no y is divisible by every x.   (e) TRUE: for any y, let $x = y$.   (f) TRUE: any x divides itself.
19. (a) $\forall x\, [x \geq 8 \to x \leq 10]$ (b) No; consider $x = 11$.   **21.** $S = \{2, 4, 6, 8\}$, $T = \{1, 2, 3, 4, 6, 8\}$. So $\forall x [x \in S \to x \in T]$.
23. The solutions to $(x - 8)(x - 3) = 0$ are 8 and 3. The solutions to $x^2 = 9$ are -3 and 3. So, $\forall x (x \in S \leftrightarrow x \in T)$. Therefore, $S = T = \{3\}$.

Chapter 12: Supplementary Exercises

1. (a) Statement   (b) Not a statement   (c) Statement   (d) Not a statement   (e) Statement
2. (a) If two lines are perpendicular, then their slopes are negative reciprocals of each other.
(b) If goldfish can live in a fishbowl, then the water is aerated.   (c) If it rains, then Jane uses her umbrella.
(d) If Sally gives Morris a treat, then he ate all his food.
3. (a) Contrapositive: If the Yankees are not playing in Yankee Stadium, then they are not in New York City; Converse: If the Yankees are playing in Yankee Stadium, then they are in New York City.
(b) Contrapositive: If the earthquake is not considered major, then the Richter Scale does not indicate the quake is a 7; Converse: If the earthquake is considered major, then the Richter Scale indicates the quake is a 7.
(c) Contrapositive: If the coat is not warm, then it is not made of fur; Converse: If the coat is warm, then it is made of fur.

(d) Contrapositive: If Jane is not in Moscow, then she is not in Russia; Converse: If Jane is in Moscow, then she is in Russia.

4. (a) Two triangles are similar but their sides are unequal.   (b) For every real number x, $x^2 \neq 5$.

(c) There exists a positive integer n such that n is even and n^2 is not even.   (d) For every real number x, $x^2 + 4 \neq 0$.

5. (a) Tautology   (b) Tautology   (c) Not a tautology   (d) Not a tautology

6. (a)

p	q	r	$p \to (\sim q \vee r)$
T	T	T	T
T	T	F	F
T	F	T	T
T	F	F	T
F	T	T	T
F	T	F	T
F	F	T	T
F	F	F	T

(b)

p	q	r	$p \wedge (q \leftrightarrow (r \wedge p))$
T	T	T	T
T	T	F	F
T	F	T	F
T	F	F	T
F	T	T	F
F	T	F	F
F	F	T	F
F	F	F	F

7. (a) True   (b) False   **8.** (a) True   (b) False   **9.** (a) False   (b) True   **10.** (a) 17   (b) 100   (c) 100   (d) 100   **11.** (a) 50   (b) -25 (c) -15 (d) 10   **12.** (a) Cannot be determined   (b) TRUE   (c) TRUE   (d) Cannot be determined   (e) Cannot be determined   **13.** (a) Cannot be determined   (b) Cannot be determined   (c) TRUE   **14.** (a) TRUE   (b) FALSE   (c) TRUE   **15.** (a) Cannot be determined   (b) Cannot be determined   (c) TRUE

16. t = "Taxes go up."
s = "I sell the house."
m = "I move to India."

1. $t \to (s \wedge m)$	hyp.
2. $\sim m$	hyp.
3. $\sim s \vee \sim m$	addition (2)
4. $\sim (s \wedge m)$	DeMorgan (3)
5. $\sim t$	mod. tollens (1, 4)

17. m = " I study mathematics."
b = "I study business."
p = "I can write poetry."

1. $m \wedge b$	hyp.
2. $b \to (\sim p \vee \sim m)$	hyp.
3. b	subtraction (1)
4. $\sim p \vee \sim m$	mod. ponens (2, 3)
5. m	subtraction (1)
6. $\sim p$	disj. syllogism (4, 5)

18. d = "I shop for a dress."
h = "I wear high heels."
s = "I have a sore foot."

1. $d \to h$	hyp.
2. $s \to \sim h$	hyp.
3. d	hyp.
4. h	mod. ponens (1, 3)
5. $\sim s$	mod. tollens (2, 4)

19. a = "Asters grow in the garden."
d = "Dahlias grow in the garden."
s = "It is spring."

1. $a \vee d$	hyp.
2. $s \to \sim a$	hyp.
3. s	hyp.
4. $\sim a$	mod. ponens (2, 3)
5. d	disj. syllogism (1, 4)

20. t = "The professor gives a test."
h = "Nancy studies hard."
d = "Nancy has a date."
s = "Nancy takes a shower."
$H_1 = t \to h$
$H_2 = d \to s$
$H_3 = \sim t \to \sim s$
$H_4 = d$
$C = h$

1. $\sim h$	$\sim C$
2. $t \to h$	H_1
3. $\sim t$	mod. tollens (1, 2)
4. $\sim t \to \sim s$	H_3
5. $\sim s$	mod. ponens (3, 4)
6. $d \to s$	H_2
7. $\sim d$	$\sim H_4$; mod tollens (5, 6)

Chapter 12: Chapter Test

1.

p	q	$(p \wedge \sim q) \to q$
T	T	T
T	F	F
F	T	T
F	F	T

2. (a) Statement   (b) Not a Statement   (c) Statement   (d) Statement   (e) Not a Statement

3. If the coach does not buy Bob ice cream, then Bob did not hit a triple or a homerun.

4. Every integer is either even or greater than 8.   **5.** False; True

6. (a) Neither   (b) Tautology   (c) Contradiction

7. (a) True   (b) False   (c) True   (d) False   **8.** The argument is valid.

9. (a) Every English dictionary contains the word "internet".   (b) There is a student at the unversity who does not listen to jazz.   (c) There is a floor at which the elevator does not stop.   **10.** (a) $p \to q$ (b) $q \to p$ (c) $p \to q$
(d) $p \to q$ (e) $q \to p$ **11.** (a) -19 (b) 0   (c) 180   (d) 0   **12.** (a) False   (b) True

CHAPTER 13

Exercises 13.1

1. (a) G_1: no loops, parallel edges from c to d; G_2: loop at e, no parallel edges; $G3$: no loops or parallel edges

(b) G_1:

Vertex	a	b	c	d	e	f
Degree	1	2	3	3	1	0

G_2:

Vertex	a	b	c	d	e
Degree	4	4	4	4	6

G_3:

Vertex	u	v	w	x	y	z
Degree	2	2	2	2	2	2

(c) G_1: 4; G_2: 0; G_3: 0

(d) G_1: $1 + 2 + 3 + 3 + 1 + 0 = 10 = 2(5)$; G_2: $4 + 4 + 4 + 4 + 6 = 22 = 2(11)$; G_3: $2 + 2 + 2 + 2 + 2 + 2 = 12 = 2(6)$

3.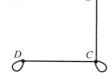

5. Drawing a graph of this situation would result in a graph with 13 vertices of degree 3. Since the number of vertices of odd degree must be even, this is impossible.

7. (a)   (b)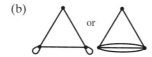

(c) Not possible since the number of vertices of odd degree must be even.   **9.** 10

11. (a) 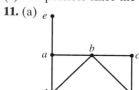   (b) 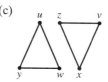   (c)

17. Not equivalent; G_1 has a vertex of degree 1, while G_2 does not.

19. Equivalent   **21.** Equivalent

23. Possible route: $A, k, m, j, n, m, z, y, n, o, p, q, r, p, y, x, r, s, t, l, u, t, x, w, z, A, B, w, u, v, B$; No   **25.**

Exercises 13.2

1. (a) 3   (b) 5   (c) 7   (d) 5   (e) 4   (f) 7   **3.** (a) 4, none   (b) 3, simple path   (c) 5, none
(d) 5, closed path, simple circuit   (e) 4, none   (f) 6, closed path, simple circuit
5. (a) $A\,B\,C\,D, A\,C\,D, A\,C\,F\,D, A\,C\,F\,E\,D$ (b) $C\,A\,B\,C, C\,F\,D\,C, C\,D\,E\,F\,C$; yes
7. (a)   **9.** No; Yes   **11.** (a)   **13.** (a) $v\,u\,w\,y\,u\,x\,y\,v$ (b) $v\,r\,u\,t\,y\,x\,z\,w\,s\,z\,t\,r\,s\,v$ **15.** Yes; $a\,c\,b\,e\,f\,d\,c\,f\,a$
17. Yes; $A\,B\,F\,G\,C\,D\,E\,B\,C\,A$ **19.** Yes; it must begin on D or E and end on the other.
21. b to d: $b\,c\,d$ or $b\,e\,d$, length $= 2$; d to g: $d\,e\,a\,f\,g$, length $= 4$; c to g: $c\,a\,f\,g$, length $= 3$

Exercises 13.3

1. (a) $S\,T\,Z\,X\,W\,V\,U\,Y\,R\,S$ (b) $b\,a\,h\,i\,g\,j\,f\,e\,d\,c\,b$ **3.** (a) No Euler or Hamiltonian circuits exist.   (b) Both Euler
and Hamiltonian circuits exist.   (c) No Euler circuits exist. Hamiltonian circuits exist.   **5.** No, G might contain loops or
be disconnected.   **7.** 23   **9.**

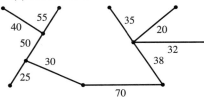

11. (a) Bipartite
(b) Not bipartite, 3 colors
(c) Not bipartite, 3 colors   **15.** 4

Exercises 13.4

1. (a) Neither   (b) Connected   (c) Both   **3.** (a)

Vertex	A	B	C	D	E	F
id	1	2	2	1	2	0
od	1	2	1	2	0	2

(b) id = the number of procedures called by that procedure; od = the number of procedures calling that procedure.
5. (a) $A\,B\,A$ (b) Acyclic   (c) Acyclic   **7.** (a) $p\,r\,s\,z\,y\,x\,z\,u\,v\,w\,p\,s\,w\,u\,p$ is an Euler circuit; no Euler path
(b) No Euler circuit or path   **9.** $A\,H\,G\,A\,F\,G\,E\,D\,C\,E\,B\,F\,C\,B\,A$ **11.** 25 days, $S\,A_1\,A_2\,A_3\,A_6\,A_7\,A_8\,A_{10}\,A_{11}\,E$.
13. Start $A\,C\,D\,E\,F$ End   **15.**   **17.**

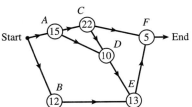
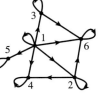
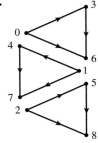

19. (a) 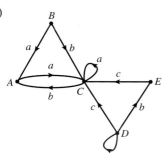 (b) Error Message (c) *C*

Exercises 13.5

1. (a) $\begin{bmatrix} 0 & 1 & 0 & 0 & 0 \\ 1 & 0 & 1 & 1 & 0 \\ 0 & 1 & 0 & 0 & 0 \\ 0 & 1 & 0 & 0 & 1 \\ 0 & 0 & 0 & 1 & 0 \end{bmatrix}$ (b) 1 (c) $\begin{bmatrix} 1 & 1 & 1 & 1 & 1 \\ 1 & 1 & 1 & 1 & 1 \\ 1 & 1 & 1 & 1 & 1 \\ 1 & 1 & 1 & 1 & 1 \\ 1 & 1 & 1 & 1 & 1 \end{bmatrix}$ **3.** (a) Not connected (b)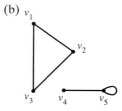

5. (a) $\begin{bmatrix} 0 & 1 & 1 & 0 & 0 \\ 1 & 0 & 1 & 0 & 0 \\ 1 & 1 & 0 & 1 & 0 \\ 0 & 0 & 1 & 0 & 0 \\ 0 & 0 & 0 & 0 & 1 \end{bmatrix}$ (b) 1 (c) $\begin{bmatrix} 1 & 1 & 1 & 1 & 0 \\ 1 & 1 & 1 & 1 & 0 \\ 1 & 1 & 1 & 1 & 0 \\ 1 & 1 & 1 & 1 & 0 \\ 0 & 0 & 0 & 0 & 1 \end{bmatrix}$ **7.** (a)
$$\begin{array}{c} \\ a \\ b \\ c \\ d \\ e \end{array}\begin{array}{ccccc} a & b & c & d & e \\ \begin{bmatrix} 0 & 1 & 1 & 0 & 0 \\ 1 & 0 & 1 & 0 & 0 \\ 1 & 1 & 0 & 1 & 0 \\ 0 & 0 & 1 & 0 & 1 \\ 0 & 0 & 0 & 1 & 0 \end{bmatrix} \end{array}$$
(b) 6

9. $v_1 \quad v_2 \quad v_3 \quad v_4$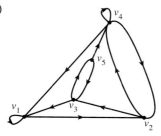

11. (a)
$$\begin{array}{c} \\ a \\ b \\ c \\ d \end{array}\begin{array}{cccc} a & b & c & d \\ \begin{bmatrix} 0 & 1 & 1 & 0 \\ 1 & 0 & 0 & 0 \\ 0 & 1 & 0 & 0 \\ 0 & 1 & 0 & 0 \end{bmatrix} \end{array}$$
(b) 2 (c) $a\,b\,a\,c\,b,\, a\,c\,b\,a\,b$ (d)
$$\begin{array}{c} \\ a \\ b \\ c \\ d \end{array}\begin{array}{cccc} a & b & c & d \\ \begin{bmatrix} 1 & 1 & 1 & 0 \\ 1 & 1 & 1 & 0 \\ 1 & 1 & 1 & 0 \\ 1 & 1 & 1 & 1 \end{bmatrix} \end{array}$$

(e) Connected, not strongly connected

13. (a)

Vertex	v_1	v_2	v_3	v_4	v_5
id	3	2	2	3	1
od	2	2	2	3	2

(c) 2 (d) $v_1\,v_2\,v_4\,v_4,\, v_1\,v_1\,v_2\,v_4$

(b)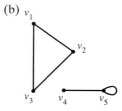

Exercises 13.6

1. 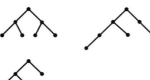 **3.**

5. (a) d, e, i, j, k, h (b) c, d, e, f, g, h (c) $x, 6, y$

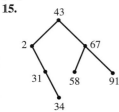

7. (a) a (b) b (c) $*$ **9.** Not possible, since a tree with 7 vertices must have 6 edges.   **11.** Not possible, a connected graph with 4 vertices and 3 edges must be a tree.   **13.** Not possible since a tree with 3 vertices must have 2 edges.

15.

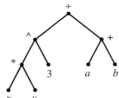

17. $[a \div (b + c)] - (b \wedge c)$ **19.**

21. 7 questions, 10 questions

Chapter 13: Supplementary Exercises

1. G_1:

Vertex	a	b	c	d
Degree	2	3	2	5

sum of degrees = 12; number of edges = 6

sum of degrees = 22; number of edges = 11

G_2:

Vertex	r	s	t	u	v	w	x
Degree	3	2	3	3	4	4	3

2. (a) G_1: abc; G_2: $uvwrst$ (b) G_1: $abcdba$; G_2: $trstvwrt$ (c) G_1: $dbcdd$; G_2: $rtvuwvxwr$

3. G_1: weight = 9 G_2: weight = 15

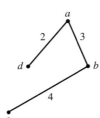

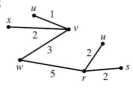

4. Neither graph has an Euler circuit since both have vertices of odd degree.

5. G_1:

Vertex	a	b	c	d	e	f	g	h
Degree	2	3	3	4	2	3	5	4

There are 4 vertices of odd degree.

G_2:

Vertex	a	b	c	d	e	f	g	h
Degree	2	4	2	4	4	2	4	4

There are 0 vertices of odd degree.

6. (a) G_1: $a\,h\,c\,d\,e$; G_2: $g\,f\,d\,e\,b$ (b) G_1: $f\,d\,c\,g\,d\,e\,f$; G_2: $b\,e\,h\,g\,e\,d\,c\,b$ (c) G_1: $a\,b\,g\,c\,h\,b\,a$; G_2: $a\,b\,h\,e\,b\,a$
(d) G_1: $a\,h\,g\,c\,h\,b\,a$; G_2: $a\,b\,h\,e\,g\,h\,a$

7. G_1: weight = 19 G_2: weight = 37

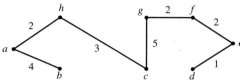
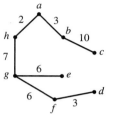

8. G_1 does not have an Euler circuit since it has vertices of odd degree; in G_2, $a\,b\,c\,d\,e\,b\,h\,e\,g\,d\,f\,g\,h\,a$ is an Euler circuit.

9. G_1:
$$A = \begin{bmatrix} 0 & 1 & 0 & 1 & 1 \\ 1 & 0 & 1 & 1 & 1 \\ 0 & 1 & 0 & 1 & 0 \\ 1 & 1 & 1 & 0 & 1 \\ 1 & 1 & 0 & 1 & 0 \end{bmatrix}$$

G_2:
$$A = \begin{bmatrix} 0 & 1 & 0 & 1 & 0 \\ 1 & 0 & 1 & 1 & 0 \\ 0 & 1 & 0 & 1 & 0 \\ 1 & 1 & 1 & 0 & 1 \\ 0 & 0 & 0 & 1 & 0 \end{bmatrix}$$

10. G_2 **11.**

G' is equivalent to G. Associate u to b, v to d, w to a, and x to c.

9 paths of length 3 from v_1 to v_4 in G_1

6 paths of length 3 from v_1 to v_4 in G_2

12. Path does not exist since rooms B, D, and H have only one doorway.   **13.** 3 colors   **14.** Start $A\ B\ D\ E\ F$ End

15.

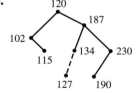

16. (a)

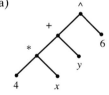

(b)

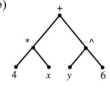

(c)

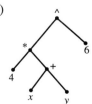

17. Start $A\ B\ D\ F\ G$ End   **18.** 3 cars   **19.** 3 colors

Chapter 13: Chapter Test

1. (a) $acdba$ (b) $bcdb$ (c)

2. No   **3.**

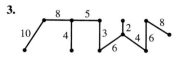

4. (a)

$$\begin{array}{c} & \begin{array}{cccc} a & b & c & d \end{array} \\ \begin{array}{c} a \\ b \\ c \\ d \end{array} & \begin{bmatrix} 0 & 1 & 1 & 0 \\ 1 & 0 & 1 & 1 \\ 1 & 1 & 0 & 1 \\ 0 & 1 & 1 & 0 \end{bmatrix} \end{array}$$

(b) 5   **5. (a)**

(b) No   **(c)** Yes; No   **6.** 3   **7.** Yes

8.

9. Start A C D G End

Index